LINCOLN THE PRESIDENT

SPRINGFIELD TO GETTYSBURG

THE HESLER PROFILE—1860

Soon after his nomination for the presidency Lincoln posed at Springfield for the Chicago photographer, Alexander Hesler. The date has been given as June 3, 1860. George B. Ayers, successor of Hesler, preserved this negative, contrary to the usual custom by which negatives were destroyed by acid removal of film coating on the glass, which was recoated for new work. Mr. Ayers moved in 1867 from Chicago to Buffalo and later to Philadelphia; his Chicago gallery was burned in the fire of 1871. It is a bit of good luck for Lincoln portraiture that the negative of this masterpiece has been preserved to our own time.

LINCOLN
THE PRESIDENT

SPRINGFIELD TO GETTYSBURG

VOLUME ONE

BY

J. G. Randall

ILLUSTRATED

DA CAPO PRESS • NEW YORK

*To Ruth, whose unfailing help and interest
illumined the labor of these pages.*

Library of Congress Cataloging in Publication Data

Randall, J. G. (James Garfield), 1881-1953.
    Lincoln the president / by J. G. Randall.
      p.   cm.
    Originally published: New York: Dodd, Mead & Co., 1946, 1952, 1955.
    Includes bibliographical references and index.
    Contents: v. 1. Springfield to Gettysburg—v. 2. Midstream to the last full measure.
    ISBN 0-306-80754-8 (v. 1: alk. paper).—ISBN 0-306-80755-6 (v. 2)
    1. Lincoln, Abraham, 1809-1865. 2. Presidents—United States—Biography. 3.
United States—Politics and government—1861-1865. 4. United States—History—Civil
War, 1861-1865. I. Title.
    E457.R2 1997
    973.7′ 092—dc20   96-36026
    [B]   CIP

First Da Capo Press edition 1997

This Da Capo Press paperback edition of volume one of *Lincoln the President* is an
unabridged republication of the edition first published in two volumes in New York
in 1946, supplemented with an introduction by Richard N. Current. It is reprinted
by arrangement with the author's estate.

Published by Da Capo Press, Inc.
A Subsidiary of Plenum Publishing Corporation
233 Spring Street, New York, N.Y. 10013

INTRODUCTION
TO THE
DA CAPO EDITION

WHEN THE FOUR volumes of J. G. Randall's *Lincoln the President* first appeared (1946, 1952, 1955), they received the enthusiastic acclaim of experts in the Lincoln field, who recognized Randall as the preeminent living authority. This work, they said, was "basic Lincoln literature." It was "the best portrayal of Lincoln and his difficult role as President." Indeed, it was "one of the most impressive works of historical scholarship ever written in America."

Randall had already established his reputation with *Constitutional Problems under Lincoln* (1926) and *The Civil War and Reconstruction* (1937). From 1920 to 1950 he also provided inspiration and guidance for a large number of historians who gained their doctorates from the University of Illinois at Urbana-Champaign. The most illustrious of his disciples is David Herbert Donald, prize-winning biographer of Lincoln, Herndon, and Sumner.

Conceiving of his Lincoln volumes as both history and biography, Randall provided a fairly broad coverage of wartime events as well as intimate pictures of life in the White House. Despite his title *Lincoln the President,* he included six chapters dealing with the pre-presidential years and an appendix appraising the Ann Rutledge romance. He deliberately excluded the assassination, avowing: "This biography knows only the living Lincoln."

Actually, the four volumes do not present continuous history or biography so much as they do a series of historiographical essays. Randall proposed to clear away existing misconceptions and thus make a "historical restoration" that would reveal the underlying truths about Lincoln and his times. This involved analyzing and synthesizing a vast quantity of both original and secondary sources and disagreeing with

vii

much that had been taken for granted in scholarly or in popular literature. Upon both the general reader and the Lincoln scholar, these essays had a refreshing, astringent effect.

So it was, for example, with Randall's treatment of William H. Herndon's stories of Lincoln's love for Ann Rutledge and difficulties with Mary Todd. Randall concluded that the supposed love affair with Ann was unproved in its essentials and disproved in its elaborations, and that Lincoln's later home life with Mary was pretty much that of a typical American family man.

Other conclusions were equally iconoclastic for the time. The Lincoln-Douglas debates revolved about insubstantial and purposely confused issues; the participants only *"seemed to differ."* Lincoln as President-elect did not block the path to sectional compromise in 1860–61, though he did bungle the delicate task of conciliating the upper South. He was innocent of the charge that he sent an expedition to Fort Sumter with the ulterior aim of maneuvering the Confederates into firing the first shot. He left foreign affairs largely to his secretary of state, William H. Seward, and was something less than the diplomat in carpet slippers that he had been depicted. Yielding to pressure, he let General George B. McClellan down and thus brought disaster upon the Army of the Potomac. Randall did not share the feeling of some of the older biographers that justice to Lincoln required the berating of McClellan or, for that matter, James Buchanan and Stephen A. Douglas.

Lincoln, according to Randall, was closer to the Rebels than to the Radicals, the extreme antislavery members of his own Republican party. His famous proclamation of January 1, 1863 failed to set the slaves definitely free. The assurance of freedom awaited the Thirteenth Amendment, which he helped to guide through Congress. "Of the stereotypes concerning Lincoln one of the most unhistorical is the stock picture of the Emancipator sitting in the White House and suddenly striking the shackles from millions of bondmen at a stroke of the presidential pen."

Slavery was not, however, the basic issue of the Civil War, as Randall viewed the matter. He assumed that the war was neither an "irrepressible conflict" nor a contest between right and wrong. Its "causes" were unreal, and there was right and wrong on both sides. The war resulted from the propaganda of politicians and agitators, North and South, particularly the abolitionists of the North.

This approach troubled some critics, even some who otherwise were favorable, at the time the volumes appeared. It was "doughface" history and "historical sentimentalism," they said. Slavery as a moral question was deeply involved, they insisted, and the issues of Union and freedom were not only real but fundamental.

Since that time, Lincoln scholars have questioned other judgments of Randall's besides his view that the Civil War was both undesirable and unnecessary, the work of a "blundering generation." Herndon has been rehabilitated to the extent that his view of the Lincoln marriage is now widely accepted, along with the Ann Rutledge story, at least in its essentials. According to some of the more recent scholarship, the Lincoln-Douglas debates revealed sharp differences between the participants in regard to human rights. Lincoln must have known that his Sumter expedition might provoke a warlike response. No Southerner at heart, he became increasingly a Radical Republican himself, and if he had lived he would probably have adopted a Radical policy in dealing with the postwar South.

These and other issues pertaining to *Lincoln the President* remain controversial. If Randall were writing in the 1990s, he would likely treat some of the topics differently, though not necessarily all of them. As the author of *The Civil War and Reconstruction*, he said of himself in 1937: "He has tried to avoid being unduly impressed by the mere newness of this or that historical contribution, and, while recognizing—indeed welcoming with keenest pleasure—the work of revisionists, he has at times suspected that some day the revisionists themselves may be revised." Randall's interpretations may be no less credible than some of the more recent ones, and in any case his views need to be considered if the controversies are to be fully understood.

But his volumes have much more in them than controversy. Quite apart from his stand on historical disputes, these books contain a full and accurate account of the events in which President Lincoln had a part, as well as a lively picture of the man himself and of the people with whom he was associated. Though *Lincoln the President* bears the marks of its time, it still has much to offer the reader interested in Lincoln and the Civil War period.

—RICHARD N. CURRENT
August 1996

PREFACE

THE vastness of Lincoln literature is a bit misleading. It requires a very small space to enumerate the authors who have produced significant biographies of Lincoln—i. e., works above the level of campaign lives or superficial treatments. Lincoln is an easy subject for one who merely writes "another book" about him. The field is one in which the public has been tolerant of uncritical writing. But Lincoln is an extremely difficult subject if the motive and design be that of careful, critical investigation off the beaten path. Though the literature is voluminous, and though the more thoughtful works will live through the years, no one conversant with these matters would think of supposing that the claims have all been staked out and the fields fully tilled. As for Lincoln's presidency the themes are so challenging, the source material so massive, the problems so complex, that reëxamination and rewriting have become a necessity in our time.

The treatment here offered is conceived both as biography and as history. It has been found impossible to present Lincoln's background and his crowded years of leadership except by integration with contemporary movements and thought currents. If history is attempted, the standards of historical craftsmanship must not be neglected. Statements must be tied to reality, and this not merely by way of something to quote or cite, but in terms of tested and competent evidence. There is nothing cryptic about this. The principle is simple; it is the fulfillment of the principle with imperfect and conflicting material that comes hard. The muse is strict and exacting. Without submitting to these requirements one can dabble in history, but it is a field where the tyro falls short and the amateur betrays himself. This is not said with the least assumption of professionalism. It is simply a recognition of realities within which the author has had to work.

If sources are diligently reëxamined, then by the same token the product may become "revisionist." Even in a simple matter it is not easy after the passage of years to recover the true picture. If the past situation was complicated, if many factors went into its making, if observers at the time lacked full understanding or differed as to what it meant, and especially if it has become controversial, then an uncommon effort is needed to disengage reality from the accumulated deposit which the years have brought.

What happens over and over is that a certain idea gets started in association with an event or figure. It is repeated by speakers and editors. It soon becomes a part of that superficial aggregation of concepts that goes under the heading "what everybody knows." It may take decades before a stock picture is even questioned as to its validity. Evidence is then unearthed, some of it being first discovered, or brought to light after having been forgotten or neglected. Discoloring is corrected, partisan misrepresentation—perhaps accepted unawares by the public—is exposed, predilections and presumptions stripped away. Historical insight cuts through with a new clarity. In this process the historian does not claim to arrive at perfection, but he does hope by fresh inquiry to come nearer to past reality.

This is called "revision," but that suggests mere change or rewriting; a much better word for it would be historical restoration. Where a building belonging to a past age has disappeared or fallen into ruin, there is the process of studying available traces and records, examining the period, and gradually building up a "restoration" to show the structure as it originally stood. With a like motive the historian seeks out original records, excavates, so to speak, clears away unhistorical debris, and endeavors, if he can, to restore events and essential situations of the past.

Certain accepted ideas of Lincoln and his period will probably be upset in the following pages. This does not mean that the account has been prepared in an iconoclastic spirit, nor does it imply any claim of finality. The task has been undertaken in some trepidation and in contemplation of the difficulty of attaining authentic truth. New conclusions come not from preconception, assuredly not from a wish to overthrow or destroy. The historian searches; he presents his findings; if he works validly he destroys nothing except misconception and unfounded tradition. It is only so that scholarship can be constructive. Where *clichés* have become fixed in the popular mind the historian's finding may occasion surprise or even dissatisfaction, but this cannot be avoided. If the critics pass the ammunition, that is one of the occupational hazards.

These chapters have not been made up from other biographies of Lincoln. The intent has been to take the basic material out of which history must be shaped (much of it in manuscripts never published and hitherto unused for this purpose), to discard the irrelevant or unhistorical, and to show the result. In treating McClellan the hope has been to give the reader some basis for forming his own judgment of a commander whose appraisal has not yet been cleared of the violent feeling of the time. So with other matters: the Ann Rutledge evidence has been sifted, Mrs. Lincoln restudied, the Lincoln-Douglas debates reanalyzed, wartime politics investigated, emancipation stripped of its crust of misconception, and so on.

Popular ideas of Lincoln are in large part traceable to that picturesque but provocative individual, William H. Herndon. One should give him credit for tireless searching, and for that intellectual questing which was almost pathetically revealed in his correspondence with Theodore Parker, but the Lincoln he has given us needs reconsideration. For long years his collection was closed to scholars generally. Only recently has general access been given to his impressive but unsatisfactory body of manuscripts, so that the presentation to the public of a full appraisal of Herndon may at the moment be regarded as unfinished business. Mr. David Donald, completing doctoral work at the University of Illinois, is doing a competent life of Herndon, and the author, who assigned him the subject, has benefited by seeing his chapters thus far prepared. Mr. Donald has found that, along with qualities that make this partner-biographer well worthy of study, he is sometimes unreliable even about the facts of his own life.

To take Herndon at face value is no longer permissible; we can now see his actual material. Mere citations to the Herndon-Weik Collection are by no means enough; the stuff of this collection is uneven and needs sifting. Beveridge used these manuscripts at a time when previous users included only Herndon, Weik, and Lamon (or Lamon's ghost writer), but in going over the papers at length the author cannot give as full acceptance to Herndon's material as Beveridge did. A body of sources, however, may not be all of a piece. Some of Herndon's statements have greater validity than others. He was Lincoln's partner for many years; he tried in his way to give the world both Lincoln's greatness and the everyday man; to use Lord Charnwood's apt phrase, his was "the task of substituting for Lincoln's aureole the battered tall hat, with valuable papers stuck in its lining, which he had long contemplated with reverent irritation." One can doubt his accumulated masses of reminiscence and still give a measure of credence to descriptions which arose from close daily association.

Herndon has profited by his well known statement that he loved the truth. But, as a court examines the competence of a witness, one must go back of this assertion to ask whether a man who thought he could grasp truth by intuition, who wrote of his "mud instinct" and "dog sagacity," who claimed he could "see to the gizzard" of a question, could recognize and adequately set forth the truth. Herndon was a self-made psychoanalyst long before that somewhat modern art became widely known. He prided himself on a kind of clairvoyance and a knack for mind reading. Information which he acquired by assiduous effort had to undergo Herndonian processing. It is not so much a matter of blaming him for the common human frailty of inaccuracy; it is enough to perceive it and bracket it with the Herndon record. One can follow a middle course, neither rejecting him out of hand nor accepting him in full, but assessing his uneven product and using it for what it is worth. His down-to-earth frankness, his pioneer tang and flavor, may be appreciated while one keeps a wholesome distrust for his excesses of rhetoric and his psychoanalytical conjecture.

In taking a subject as broad as that of the present work it has been found necessary at every point to condense, to select, and to leave out a great deal that the author has collected. Practically every paragraph could be elaborated from the material assembled; the purpose has been to keep the main story before the reader. By its title the book is concerned with the presidency; chapters for the period prior to 1860 are to be regarded as background; no treatment of Lincoln's early life is attempted. Chronologically speaking—though chronology is not all—the present study goes no farther than the latter part of 1863, the time of the Gettysburg address. A large mass of Lincoln manuscripts in the Library of Congress is to be opened in 1947, and it is the author's intention to publish a companion work (with a different subtitle) to deal with further aspects of Lincoln the President. If certain matters of the period are omitted here, the plan for that later work may in part offer the explanation. Life in Lincoln's day, the Lincolns in the White House, problems of government, the manner and technique of the war leader, cabinet dealings, relations with an uncoöperative Congress, further attacks and intrigues, new international episodes, military developments, plans and counter-plans for reconstruction, the dark summer of 1864, the presidential election of that troubled year, Grant's long delay and final triumph, Lincoln's planning for peace, his thought for the soldiers, his method of addressing the public, his second inaugural, his part in the ending of the war, the magnanimity which gave him serenity in the final phase despite war weariness, the statesmanship with which he looked ahead— these and other large matters are reserved for the later work.

For the present purpose the Gettysburg address, marking a climax in Lincoln's thought of America's larger role, offers a convenient terminus. To recover the Gettysburg Lincoln, to catch up with him, to put him in his full mold, belongs to the agenda of our times. There is a challenge for today in the study of his career as a proof of the meaning and opportunity of democracy. There is need for a fuller understanding of his grasp of liberal thought, his interest in the common man, his sense of human values, his sympathy for labor, his rising above partisanship, his concept of the statesman's task in its relation to order in society, and to peace and democracy in the world.

J. G. R.

Urbana, Illinois
September 8, 1945

ACKNOWLEDGMENTS

THE contribution of friends in the preparation of this book has created a sense of gratitude which cannot be adequately expressed. Where service has been very great, appreciation must nevertheless be briefly conveyed. From the inception of the book to the reading of the manuscript when at last it was ready for the publisher, the author has been encouraged and specifically assisted by Allan Nevins. Parts of the book, in that plastic stage in which corrections were yet possible, were read by Paul M. Angle, William E. Baringer, T. Harry Williams, Fred A. Shannon, and Raymond C. Werner. Profitable revision has resulted from their suggestions and corrections. On the first third of the book the comments of Harry E. Pratt, based on his unusual grasp of sources, have been of inestimable value.

Grateful recognition is due to Oliver R. Barrett for the use of his superb Lincoln collection; to Frederick H. Meserve for items from his unique array of Lincoln photographs; to F. Lauriston Bullard for illuminating suggestions from a rich background of specialized Lincoln learning; and to Jay Monaghan, author of *Diplomat in Carpet Slippers* and *Lincoln Bibliography,* for valuable and friendly service. For the stimulus of a great personality, for comparison of notes, and for access to his ample stores of material, the author acknowledges with gratitude and affection his indebtedness to Carl Sandburg.

So many demands have been made upon the Library of Congress that particular recognition must be given to that institution for its unexcelled resources and for the unfailing coöperation of its competent staff. St. George L. Sioussat has given courteous and scholarly help in the opening up of vast manuscript collections. To give a full statement of these collections for the subject of Lincoln would require a considerable book. Doors to these treasures have required unlocking; experts must be consulted. For this indispensable service the author owes a large debt of gratitude to T. P. Martin and C. P. Powell. For the library staff of the University of Illinois—especially for P. L. Windsor, Robert B. Downs, Willia K. Garver, Emma R. Jutton, Christopher U. Faye, Helen L. McIntyre, Mary L. Bull, and Nelle M. Signor—the writer has come to feel the regard and esteem that rises from scholarly and coöperative librarianship in all that pertains to the ordering, preserving, arranging, special binding, and servicing of manuscripts, photostats, microfilms, newspapers, and an appalling array of books. To the Illinois Historical Survey at the University of Illinois, and to its director, Theodore C. Pease, the author's obligation is heavy and his appreciation is sincerely given.

Generous assistance, including the appropriation of funds for research, has been regularly extended over a considerable period of years by the Graduate Research Board of the University of Illinois. Resources beyond the author's limitations have thus been brought to bear upon the project. The administering of this indispensable assistance, with personal attention to special needs and unfailing grasp of technical requirements, has been the contribution of R. D. Carmichael, Dean of the Graduate School. Others of the University of Illinois have given their help in the lending of manuscript items of the Lincoln period—Frederick Green supplied a letter showing the Commander in Chief in 1862; Sleeter Bull, from family papers, offered a soldier letter dealing with Lincoln.

The writer has turned to specialists, and he has not done so in vain. Paul M. Angle and Harry E. Pratt must be mentioned again here for competent advice and the clarifying of many points. Louis A. Warren, from his comprehensive understanding of the Lincoln field and his distinguished directorship of the Lincoln National Life Foundation, has been most helpful and generous. Assistance within the craft has also been ably supplied by Ernest E. East, Milo M. Quaife, William H. Townsend, Thomas I. Starr, and Stewart W. McClelland. On the subject of Lincoln and John Bright the author has enjoyed a helpful correspondence with Harold J. Laski of England. On the Sumter matter he has been introduced to a manuscript source by Vernon Munroe of New York City. James C. Malin of the University of Kansas gave valuable information on slavery; John H. Cramer of Cleveland Heights threw light on Lincoln's speaking in Ohio; P. G. Aucham·

paugh of the University of Nevada gave source material and illuminating comment on Pennsylvania politics; William H. Slade of Washington contributed Lincoln notes; Reinhard H. Luthin of Columbia University, in interview and correspondence, was ready with information on a variety of Lincoln topics. On other matters relating to Lincoln the writer has been assisted by Frank Freidel of the University of Maryland, Eugene M. Braderman, formerly on the staff of the University of Illinois, and Ollinger Crenshaw of Washington and Lee University. Years ago Miss Helen Nicolay generously contributed information concerning her father, John G. Nicolay; through the kindness of Tyler Dennett the author was given access to material on John Hay.

For help in the National Archives the author is indebted to R. D. W. Connor, Solon J. Buck, Philip M. Hamer, Edna Vosper, and Martin P. Claussen. The value of these vast collections, made accessible by up-to-date archival administration, cannot be overstated. Service of a like nature in Lincoln's own state has been given by Margaret C. Norton in charge of the superbly housed archives of Illinois at Springfield. For Lincoln material in these state archives the writer has enjoyed the able assistance of S. Ambrose Wetherbee.

The Illinois State Historical Library, under the directorship of Paul M. Angle and with the services of Jay Monaghan, Mildred Eversole Monaghan, Ernest E. East, and Margaret Flint, has offered constant coöperation. Its manuscript resources and its Lincoln originals have been of the greatest value. That vigorous and serviceable institution, the Abraham Lincoln Association, under a succession of secretaries who are also Lincoln authors (Paul M. Angle, Benjamin P. Thomas, Harry E. Pratt, William E. Baringer), has responded handsomely to numerous requests. Besides giving other assistance, Mr. Baringer read printer's proof throughout the book. The Association, under the presidency of Logan Hay and George W. Bunn, Jr., has put Lincoln students in debt by the usefulness and high standard of its *Bulletins*, its *Papers*, its frequent books, and its magazine, the *Abraham Lincoln Quarterly*. One is moved to admiration for its schedule of publications that contemplates for each year a significant Lincoln book, and that over and above the *Quarterly*.

Boston and Cambridge proved richly productive of Lincoln material. Not only manuscripts, but huge collections of them, have been consulted in the Massachusetts Historical Society—the papers of John A. Andrew, George Bancroft, Henry W. Bellows, Amos Lawrence, Edward Everett, and others. Since these men had contact with outstanding leaders including Lincoln, their correspondence offers a mine of information by way of direct source material. State archives under the gold dome on Beacon Street have been very useful; rare items were also found in the nearby Athenaeum. For the antislavery movement sources were found in abundance among the manuscripts of the Boston Public Library; extensive historical records, especially the voluminous Sumner papers, were made available in the Widener Library at Harvard. The Lincoln Group of Boston gave freely of their advice and counsel; as with similar groups over the country these choice spirits exemplify the manner in which the study and discussion of Lincoln brings men together on the stimulating plane of intellectual companionship.

Brown University, notable for Lincoln books, manuscripts, and photostats, was profitably visited; in the coöperation of the Librarian, Henry B. Van Hoesen, and of his staff, was found the helpfulness that comes of professional skill and readiness to serve. Miss Elizabeth Ring of Portland, Maine, gave assistance in research; in an area far distant Miss Norma Cuthbert of the Henry E. Huntington Library, San Marino, California, supplied the stuff of which history is written. In between these geographical extremes the author is indebted to R. N. Williams, 2d, of the Historical Society of Pennsylvania; Miss Margaret Pierson of the Indiana State Library; Torsten Petersson of Princeton University; Edward P. Alexander of the State Historical Society of Wisconsin; Miss Ethel L. Hutchins of the Public Library of Cincinnati; Harlow Lindley of the Ohio State Archeological and Historical Society; Sidney Goldmann of the New Jersey State Library; and the friendly staff of the Chicago Historical Society.

Grateful acknowledgment is due to D. C. Heath and Company for the use of two maps, and to the Department of Public Works and Buildings of the State of Illinois (Division of Parks and Memorials) for the loan of superb photograps of the Lincoln home today.

Young scholars of the author's circle have given stout assistance in library exploration, newspaper study, verification by checking with sources (no mean task), and many things that go with the function of research. For this service at his right hand the author, in sincere appreciation, wishes to thank Martin P. Claussen, Theodore L. Agnew, Jr., A. A. Dayton, J. Harvey Young, LeRoy H. Fischer, and David Donald. Much of the index making—a task calling for expertness combined with heavy labor—was done by the competent hand of Helen Hart Metz of Elmwood, Illinois. Valuable assistance in this respect was also given by graduate students at the University of Illinois—Paul G. Hubbard, Theodore Fisch, and Melvin J. Mateyka. Excellent typing was done by J. E. Cranston and Mrs. Milo D. Appleman.

In accepting all these services the author reasoned that his book should be as good as his friends could make it! For the defects and errors that may remain he must assume full responsibility.

In research labors, in advice on matters large and small, and in substantial literary collaboration, the partnership of the author's wife, Ruth Painter Randall, cannot be adequately acknowledged; in a true sense the book is also hers.

J. G. R.

CONTENTS

PART I

PART II

ILLUSTRATIONS AND MAPS

PART I

PART II

LINCOLN THE PRESIDENT
SPRINGFIELD TO GETTYSBURG

PART ONE

CHAPTER I

A MAN'S OUTLOOK

IN THE year of Our Lord 1860 the United States was at peace. In all that was sound and fundamental, in every instinct that was normal and sane, the people of America, and their genuine friends abroad, wanted that peace to endure. It is true that vicious forces were at work which would sweep beyond the point where reason could check them. An incredible and devastating war was to come; that war would become an absorbing preoccupation, greedily claiming energies that might have gone into natural pursuits; then, during and after the fighting those who survived would look back and discover in the "pre-war" age only elements of strife and seeds of sectional hate.

Yet to refer to the period as "pre-war" is only retrospection, however much it may be supported by massive historical studies that eternally point toward the Civil War as either the terminus or the point of departure of all discussion. Must an age be only ante- or post-? While a country is at peace are not the facts of peace worthy of note for their own sake?

I

Abraham Lincoln of Illinois thought that they were. He deplored strife and sought to dissociate himself from sectional hatred. Occupied with a considerable law practice, but recognized as an outstanding leader in Illinois and mentioned for the presidency, he made it his business in the period preceding his presidential nomination to emphasize the peacetime pursuits of his country and to recover for his own day some of the nation-building stimulus of the fathers. He was concerned with problems of slavery, and with such a handling of those

problems as would allay strife, as he hoped; but this was not all.
He turned his thoughts also to discoveries and inventions, to the
"iron horse," to "hot-water power" harnessed to help mankind, to the
"seventy or eighty thousand words" of the English language, to
influences that tend to "bring us together" and "make us better
acquainted," to the harvest-machine and the "steam plow," to the
problem of fifty bushels of wheat to the acre.

He made observations on the size of farms, disliking mammoth
ones. He gave thought to the farmer as a man, to the farmer's pride
in his work, to the laborer's enjoyment of the fruit of his labor, to
the relation of labor and capital. He disliked the "mud-sill" theory,
"that whoever is once a hired laborer, is fatally fixed in that condition
for life." He was concerned for the "prudent, penniless beginner,"
anxious that he should acquire a surplus and one day arrive at the
point where he could own his own land and tools. It was not only
untutored folk who must labor, he reflected; men with education must
work. The country could not sustain them in idleness; the laborer
should not be "a blind horse upon a tread-mill." These workings of
the mind do not make sense in terms of sectional strife; nevertheless
these were Lincoln's thoughts. He was like the majority of the
people of the nation. He was thinking of peace.[1]

He had been about considerably, this Lincoln, more than is usually
supposed. He knew Illinois, and chiefly the picturesque life of the
eighth judicial circuit which he had traveled for over twenty years.
He had journeyed rather widely in other states, from the eastern
seaboard to Kansas, from New Hampshire [2] to New Orleans. Men
of culture and training were his constant associates, but pioneers
came closer to the springs of his origin. The areas of his birth (Kentucky), his boyhood (Indiana), and his rising career (Illinois) had
been pioneer regions; he had moved west as pioneering itself moved
west. He had pondered the history of his people. He knew the law,
not from books only, but from life. He could draw a deed, collect a

---

[1] Up to this point Lincoln's statements are from his lecture on "Discoveries . . .
[etc.]," given in 1858–60, and his address before the Wisconsin state agricultural society at
Milwaukee, Sep. 30, 1859. *Complete Works of Abraham Lincoln,* ed. by John G. Nicolay
and John Hay (12 vols.), V, 99 ff., 236 ff. (hereafter cited as *Works*). This set is far from
complete and has textual inaccuracies. These, however, are of a minor and formal nature
(relating to punctuation, capitalization, the spelling out of abbreviated words, etc.); the
editing is not of a type to distort the meaning.

[2] Elwin L. Page, *Abraham Lincoln in New Hampshire.*

claim, argue an assumpsit; yet he could also advise a client to avoid litigation. He could put himself in his client's place. Law treatises and court reports, passing under the processes of his mind, had given him a respect for principles that must prevail because they are fundamental.[3]

He would tug at a problem and wrestle until he could make sense of it. Complicated though it was, he would not rest until he had mastered it. It is interesting to read what editors of his works call "fragments." In these bits of writing his concern was not mental gymnastics; it was clarification of some issue of his day, whether or not he was thinking of a particular speech or statement for publication. He would pose a question, then try to answer it, using processes of thought and speech to solve a thing, turn it around, see it whole, apply it to his times. In this manner as a boy, in early backwoods days, he had laid his own foundations in study. Self-education was his way; it had made him familiar with a few serviceable classics; what is more, it carried over into adult life. This was his liberal education.

His methods of thought and study had never proceeded in bookish fashion nor in the academic style. It was not sufficient that he know what a thing meant; it was not his to use unless it sounded right as he himself spoke it. When he could make it click in his own language, he felt that he had it; then he could impart it to others. Latin phrases or classical allusions, not uncommon in his day even on the frontier, did not appeal to him. They were like a frilled shirt, the kind of thing someone else might wear—Orville Browning or Ninian Edwards perhaps—but not himself. He did not use language to display his own learning, but to clinch a point. He had become adept at stump speaking, having learned to meet people by small groups or by shouting and jostling thousands and to divert and instruct them with ready anecdote and frontier oratory. His speeches had not only content; they had flavor.

He knew the ways of politicians, the manner in which things are arranged among leaders, the give and take of party maneuver. For politics he had a natural gift. He took to it avidly. As for ambition, the desire to rise and be influential, he had it in marked degree; at times it had become an almost pathetic craving. Yet he had met disappointment, and meeting it, had reasoned and tried to believe that

---

[3] For brief comment on Lincoln as a lawyer, see below, pp. 33-40.

it did not matter. Some of the accessories of ambition, such as self-conceit or low intrigue, he had somehow avoided. He could retaliate sharply, at times too sharply; yet he was learning, though perhaps slowly, to take a rebuff or feel an affront, but give no sign. He referred to himeslf as having come of "second families," [4] and spoke of his early life in terms of undistinguished poverty.

Mr. John L. Scripps of Chicago wrote to William H. Herndon of Lincoln's conscientiousness and sincerity in supplying data for what became the Scripps campaign biography of 1860. "The chief difficulty I had to encounter," wrote Scripps, "was to induce him to communicate the homely facts . . . of his early life. . . . 'Why Scripps' said he . . . 'it is a great piece of folly to attempt to make anything out of my early life. It can be all condensed into a simple sentence, and that sentence you will find in Gray's Elegy; "The short and simple annals of the poor." That's my life, and that's all you or any one else can make of it.' " [5]

His humility, however, did not end with self-depreciation, for he did not lack confidence; it was a quality of deferring to others, of working with men. It became more marked with him as the years passed. His character had defects and inadequacies; it had not reached its final phase. There were elements in the man yet undeveloped, indeed unsuspected.

II

Since the method and content of this volume require that space be reserved for the crowded years of Lincoln's leadership, there is no room for the details of his early life. That is a considerable subject in itself; the theme of the present book is the presidency. Lincoln's ancestral heritage, his birth, boyhood, young manhood, lowly family, hardscrabble surroundings, limited schooling and persistent self-education, his father's shifting from one unimproved farm to another,

---

[4] "My parents were both born in Virginia, of undistinguished families—second families, perhaps I should say." Brief autobiography sent to Jesse W. Fell, December 20, 1859. Lincoln's words in transmitting this short record are significant and characteristic: "Herewith is a little sketch, as you requested. There is not much of it, for the reason, I suppose, that there is not much of me. if anything be made out of it, I wish it to be modest, and not to go beyond the material." *Works*, V, 286.

[5] J. L. Scripps to Herndon, Chicago, Illinois, June 24, 1865, Herndon-Weik MSS. See also Paul M. Angle, ed., *Herndon's Life of Lincoln*, 1–2.

must be left to the reader's knowledge obtained elsewhere. The same must be said for Lincoln in tiny New Salem: his adventures and mis-adventures there as storekeeper, postmaster, mill manager and sur-veyor; his prowess in frontier sports; his rapid progress in making friends; his familiarity with debt and financial failure; his slowly widening opportunities; his early recognition among pioneer neigh-bors in the drawing of legal papers; his service in the Black Hawk War in which he was made captain by the men of his company. These matters, vivid and important as they are, are not treated here; it is too much to ask that one book contain everything about Lincoln.

From England to Massachusetts, to Pennsylvania, to Virginia, to Kentucky, to Indiana, to Illinois—such was the course of this branch of Lincolns over the generations. Contributions of three states were of abiding significance: Kentucky and Indiana influences remained with Abraham Lincoln as Illinois became his chosen home. He could not in later years identify the precise place of his birth though he knew the approximate location. It remained for later investigation to mark the site—the farm of the sinking spring near Hodgen's mill not far from Elizabethtown. The little that is known of the mother in that log-cabin birth but emphasizes the utter obscurity and limita-tions of her brief life, which was one with that of the American pioneer woman. Of that other Kentucky home to which the Lincolns moved when Abraham was two years old, he had more vivid memories: a cabin "on Knob Creek, on the road from Bardstown, Kentucky, to Nashville, Tennessee, at a point three or three and a half miles south or southwest of Atherton's Ferry, on the Rolling Fork." [1] That knobby region, richer in wild beauty than in fertility, took its place in Lin-coln's enduring impressions of little things in these earliest years: of pumpkin seeds planted on a hillslope and washed down by a dashing rain, of boys' adventures in and about the creek, of catching a fish and giving it to a passing soldier, of attending ABC schools kept by Riney and Hazel, of an old stone house—the Kirkpatrick place—where young people gathered for dances, of laboriously carrying water to the cabin and grist to the mill. It was here that the pithy informality of Lincoln's familiar conversation, with its wealth of anecdotes, began, but this did not exhaust Kentucky's contribution.

---

[1] Autobiography, *Works*, VI, 26. For the Lincolns' moving to the Knob Creek location in 1811, see Pratt, *Lincoln, 1809–1839*, 1.

Cultured Lexington, heart of the Blue Grass, center of gentlemanly living, being the birthplace of Mrs. Lincoln, was the scene of family visits by her husband. Lincoln kept up with Kentucky newspapers while in Illinois; indeed early Illinois itself was in considerable part a projection of Kentucky people and ideas into the West. The pioneers of New Salem were largely from Kentucky. All three of Lincoln's Springfield law partners were born in that state. His friend Joshua F. Speed was of Kentucky and his visits to Speed's Louisville home in 1841 was of more than ordinary personal importance. His developing political concepts followed the Clay pattern. The state of his childhood never ceased to hold a special place in his thought and feeling. Ties to Kentucky held strong and sure; they would later give the key to much of his presidential policy. Still later he was even to be suggested as one of the commonwealth's two sons to be honored in Statuary Hall in the Capitol at Washington.[2] Take it all in all, from his earliest breath to the public burdens of the fuller years, Kentucky was a part of Lincoln.[3]

III

It was in the woods and brush of southern Indiana that Lincoln spent fourteen basic years from the age of seven to his majority at twenty-one. Indiana too was part of him. If he had an appreciation of natural beauty, he did little to show it, but no visual impression of the lusty youth in the setting in which he moved would be complete without the picturesque features of the Indiana country: its thick-grown hills, its abundant game and fish, its wild fruit, its sassafras, pawpaw and dogwood, its heavier beech, maple, poplar and walnut, its tanagers and jays, its serene sky and friendly scene. Outwardly his life, in these teen-age years of sturdy growth, was one with that of his undistinguished father, Thomas Lincoln, and of that rugged individual and unforgettable country cousin, Dennis Hanks.[1] Inwardly there

---

[2] There were a number of suggestions that Lincoln and Jefferson Davis be chosen. The commission for the purpose chose Henry Clay and Ephraim McDowell. Frank L. McVey to author, Lexington, Ky., May 12, 1944.

[3] For a favorable account of Thomas and Nancy (Hanks) Lincoln, and for detailed study of Lincoln's birthplace and boyhood, with documentary support in court records, see Louis A. Warren, *Lincoln's Parentage and Childhood*. This book treats the Kentucky period.

[1] In the Herndon-Weik manuscripts one finds many pages of recollections touching

was something of Indiana that offered a stimulus to the poetic sense; there was a reaching out for the mastery of a few books, and there was trial of skill in tentative public speaking. Home ties, neighbors none too close, pioneering labors, early intellectual questing, were associated with the Indiana years. Much of all this was buoyant energy, though there was deep tragedy in the illness, death, and crude, remote burial of his pioneer mother.[2] Much of it also was raw pioneer life —packing through from Kentucky, rigging up a half faced camp in the brush, rearing a log cabin, squatting on land that was but slowly acquired by legal right, going to school "by littles" to Crawford, Sweeney, and Dorsey, spending long hours in that noble institution, Jones's village store at Gentryville, hearing an occasional preacher, never ceasing to wield the ax. Keeping soul and body together—an expression found in Lincoln's works as well as in the works of Dennis Hanks—was the pioneer's main preoccupation, but it is not to be forgotten that there was culture within the range of Lincoln's long legs and that the reading of well chosen classics was a basic factor in the determined self-education of the growing youth.

In this Indiana period the spell of the river, beckoning to unexplored worlds beyond the bend, was upon him. Floating on broad western currents all the way down to New Orleans by flatboat and traveling back by steamer, he found new experiences and gained wider contacts. Earning a few dollars by carrying passengers from the Indiana shore to passing steamers, the gawky youth was haled before the majestic presence of Squire Pate in the log house that served for home and court, charged with violating the laws of Kentucky by infringing upon ferrying rights. There was the dark threat of a heavy fine, but the squire settled the case of "Kentucky versus

---

Lincoln's life in the Indiana period by such pioneers as Mrs. Josiah Crawford, Nathaniel Grigsby, Charles Friend (a rather voluminous contributor), Dennis Friend Hanks (backwoodsy, amusing in spelling, unreliable on Hanks ancestry), Mrs. Allen Gentry (née Roby), and others by the names of Chapman, Romine, Wood, Turnham, Burba, Lamar, Pitcher, etc. Herndon also interviewed Mrs. Sarah Bush Johnston Lincoln, Abraham's stepmother. These recollections are the sources for much of what is known of Lincoln's Indiana life; unfortunately there is a lapse of forty or more years between the events and their recording. Herndon's account is based on this material, but the fullest history of the Indiana phase is in Beveridge, *Abraham Lincoln*, I, 38–99. Lincoln's autobiography, *Works*, VI, 24 ff., is, of course, indispensable.

[2] For an examination of milksickness, in which pioneer lore is skillfully combined with competent historical and medical investigation, see Philip D. Jordan, "The Death of Nancy Hanks Lincoln," *Ind. Mag. of Hist.*, XL, 103–110 (June 1944).

Abraham Lincoln" by enlightening interpretation of the statute and dismissal of the charge. It is the belief of W. H. Townsend that enduring impressions of the mystery and practical value of the law were thus engraved upon the mind of the eager youth.[3]

Thus passed these important Indiana years.[4] When Lincoln left the Hoosier state his physical stature had been reached; his thought was opening to national problems; his political maturity was far in the future, but he knew his mind as to the party of his choice. He was a Clay man in a Jacksonian family and a Democratic state. His politics came by independent reasoning, not by inheritance or inertia. He had known in Indiana a definite, not-to-be-repeated phase of western life. It was Indiana before the railroads. It had no dependence on factories though it needed local handcraftsmen, one of whom was Thomas Lincoln; its long journeys were by foot or horseback; its traffic by river craft, ox cart, or pioneer wagon; its farming resembled that of many centuries before; each community was a self-sufficing world. "Local self-dependence was well-nigh perfect. The town depended on the country and the country on the town, for nearly everything that was eaten or woven or otherwise consumed." [5] Men growing up in this setting learned much that was not in books. "Better still, each unlearned the prejudices, the bigotries, and the narrownesses in which he had been bred, and life in the West took on a . . . breadth of tolerance and sympathy, a generous humanity such as had never been known in any of the . . . provincial regions that furnished the materials of this composite population." [6] From now on Lincoln's character as a man and an American would include something of the Hoosier genius [7]—a mixture having its own distinct and friendly human ingredients, a product of migration and intermingling, a down-to-earth quality, a sense of humor, a self-dependence, yet a blending of customs, a western flavor of ideas and folkways.

---

[3] William H. Townsend, *Lincoln the Litigant*, 34–39.

[4] See "Indiana's Contribution to Abraham Lincoln," address by Louis A. Warren before Military Order of the Loyal Legion of the United States, Indianapolis, Sep. 28, 1944.

[5] George Cary Eggleston, *Recollections of a Varied Life*, 19.

[6] *Ibid.*, 27.

[7] *Ibid.*, 27. There were, of course, less admirable aspects of Indiana life and of the peopling of the West. "There is much in that story for Americans to be proud of, but there is also a seamy side to certain phases of the history of the Valley. . . . The splendid area . . . has been abused as well as used." William O. Lynch, in *Democracy in the Middle West, 1840–1940*, ed. by Jeannette P. Nichols and J. G. Randall, 39–40.

IV

In Lincoln's time Illinois was not all unbroken prairie, woods, wild life, and Indians.[1] He lived in the state from 1830 to 1861 and during that time the population of Illinois increased from 157,445 to 1,711,-951.[2] In 1860 Illinois was the fourth state in population in the Union, exceeded only by New York, Pennsylvania, and Ohio. Most of the states of the Union at that time had less than half the population of Illinois.[3] In no state in those three decades could one have better witnessed the stirrings of American growth from the breaking of virgin sod to the busy throb of great cities and modern industry. Nowhere else could one have had a better view of what all this meant in human migrations, surveyings, boom towns, fabulous increase of land values,[4] speculative fever, and the multifarious types of improvements and readjustments that a rising community exhibits.

Lincoln saw the world of civilized society starting from scratch and developing around him. He not only saw it; he was part of it. The man who was moved to lecture on discoveries and inventions, who thought of Young America moving on to material and moral conquests, had seen the burgeoning of a great society with his own eyes. In 1840 few towns of Illinois had more than two thousand people.[5] It is a curious fact that the largest Illinois settlement by far in the middle forties was the Mormon city of Nauvoo, beautifully situated on the broad Mississippi about a hundred miles northwest of Springfield. "Here, in the 1840's, when Chicago was a stripling village of less than 5,000, and Springfield . . . a muddy little town recently planted on the prairie, stood the largest city in Illinois, a community

---

[1] For an account of Illinois in this period, see T. C. Pease, *The Frontier State, 1818–1848*, and A. C. Cole, *The Era of the Civil War, 1848–1870* (*Centennial Hist. of Ill.*, vols. II, III). See also Florence Walton Taylor, "Culture in Illinois in Lincoln's Day," *Transactions*, Ill. State Hist. Soc., 1935, 125–137.

[2] In 1818, when Illinois entered the Union, its population was about 40,000, with only the far Southern portion settled. In its earlier decades the commonwealth had many of the features of a Southern state; in "Egypt" (southern Illinois) the people have always been unmistakably Southern in their manners and characteristics.

[3] By the census of 1860 only twelve states had more than half the Illinois population; twenty-one had less than half.

[4] Such was the "town lot" fever in Chicago that an acre near South Water Street had sold in 1830 for $1.55, while in 1834 lots in this area were selling for $3,500 each. Taylor, "Culture in Illinois," 130.

[5] Only four had over two thousand in 1840: Quincy, Chicago, Springfield, and Alton. The rise of Nauvoo to the stature of the largest city in Illinois came just after that.

of more than 20,000. Center of . . . Mormonism, Nauvoo possessed thousands of dwellings, and a great Temple into the construction of which had been poured a million dollars." [6]

Dickens might find an Illinois town crude with its hitching racks, its mud and slime, its music of pigs and frogs; [7] but Gustave Koerner, who lived in the region through which Dickens hastily passed, remembered an extraordinary social circle in historic Kaskaskia (the old capital) with its wealthy families, its "large and handsome Catholic seminary for ladies," and such gifted and forceful leaders as Nathaniel Pope, Pierre Menard, William Morrison, and Elias Kent Kane, "a descendant of a very well known family in New York, a relative of Chancellor Kent and of Judge Kane of Philadelphia and of the north-pole explorer, Elijah Kane." [8] Vandalia, capital in the days of Lincoln's earlier legislative service, had only eight hundred people, but in the season of the legislature it was a center of fashion and society. When Springfield became the capital,[9] it was no less gay with its "hops" and levees and its young ladies taking occasion to visit Springfield relatives during the legislative session, a custom by which Lincoln himself was not unaffected.

Adolescent Illinois had its quota of religious denominations, the Methodists, Baptists, and Presbyterians being specially active. It had its hopeful colleges.[10] Shurtleff College (later located at Alton) was organized in 1827; McKendree College was founded at Lebanon in 1828; Illinois College, a kind of New Haven in Illinois, began at Jacksonville in 1829; [11] Knox College at Galesburg was born in 1837 under the original name of Prairie College; Jubilee College was founded in a rural setting near Peoria two years later by the Right

---

[6] *Nauvoo Guide*, Federal Writers' Project of Illinois, Works Progress Administration (Chicago, 1939), 9.

[7] Charles Dickens, *American Notes for General Circulation* (1842), 67.

[8] Thomas J. McCormack, ed., *Memoirs of Gustave Koerner, 1809–1896*, I, 390–393. (The reference to the explorer, of course, is to Elisha Kent Kane of Pennsylvania.)

[9] The act making Springfield the capital was passed in 1837; the legislature first met there in December of 1839.

[10] In giving the dates when these colleges "began" (without writing a treatise on the subject) the author would caution the reader that beginning dates are not strictly comparable; there are distinctions between such words as established, founded, organized, chartered, and opened for first instruction. These distinctions are not elaborated above, and the purpose is not to deal with competitive claims among colleges. See Ernest G. Hildner, "Colleges and College Life in Illinois One Hundred Years Ago," *Papers in Illinois History*, 1942, 19–31.

[11] Charles H. Rammelkamp, *Illinois College: A Centennial History, 1829–1929*, 9–37.

EARLIEST KNOWN PORTRAIT

Daguerreotype said to have been made in Springfield in 1846, the year of Lincoln's election to Congress. The clothes are more carefully correct and the hair much smoother than was usual with Lincoln. The vigorous face, athletic form, and rugged hands give an impression of force and early strength.

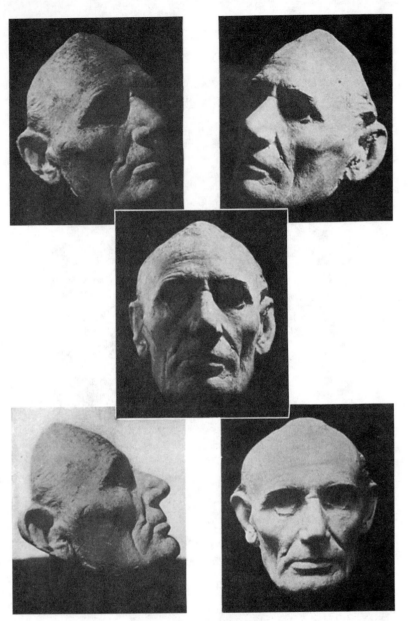

THE VOLK LIFE MASK

In late March and early April of 1860 Lincoln gave sittings to the sculptor Leonard W. Volk in his Chicago studio. Volk made a bust, and, which was more important, a plaster mold was placed over Lincoln's face and this remarkable life mask was the result. Lower right photograph from Meserve Collection through courtesy of Illinois State Historical Library. The other four (now first published) were made for the author by Ray R. Hamm of the University of Illinois. For the taking of the photographs this cast was courteously loaned by the owner, the Zeta Psi fraternity of Champaign, Illinois.

A MAN'S OUTLOOK 11

Reverend Philander Chase, pioneer bishop of the Episcopal Church.[12]
Rockford College began at Rockford in 1847. Other early colleges
in the state were McDonough College at Macomb, Blackburn at
Carlinville, Illinois Wesleyan at Bloomington, and Northwestern
University at Evanston. The state had also its Bible societies, its the-
ological seminaries, its public schools, inadequate to be sure, its state
superintendent of public instruction (from 1854), its girls' seminaries,
its laws for teachers' qualifications, its state medical society and
medical colleges, and its ubiquitous press, for there was a surprising
number of newspapers including not a few in the German language.
The commonwealth was not lacking in its lyceums,[13] theaters, library
associations,[14] dramatic reading societies, hippodromes, circuses, literary or musical festivals, and courses of public lectures. An example
of its intellectual activity was a solemn discussion of "Comparative
Capabilities of the Human Intellect in 'Different Sexes'" conducted
at the "Owl Club" of Ottawa in 1850.[15] Nor was the state backward
in its agricultural fairs, shooting matches, and balloon ascensions (as
early as 1859).

In the view of William H. Herndon, Lincoln's unique partner-
biographer, there was human excellence in Illinois in its primitive
pioneer aspects. The settlers in the great West, thought Herndon,
"were men of culture—so were the women—God bless 'em if culture
includes sharp observation—quick & broad experience and a manly
reason of or about men—commerce—laws—institutions—human
nature and the world & its affairs generally." Herndon had "never
seen such a people"; "for good horse sense . . . the old settlers [he
thought] were . . . equals, if not . . . superiors" of people in Massachusetts.[16]

---

[12] Lorene Martin, "Old Jubilee College and Its Founder, Bishop Chase," *Transactions,*
Ill. State Hist. Soc., 1934, 121–152.

[13] The Rockford *Register,* November 21, 1857, mentioned that the lyceum met at the
court house to discuss the "license question" with ladies and gentlemen in attendance.

[14] For these early cultural factors—libraries, lyceums, the "Chicago Polemical Society,"
the "Chicago Pythagorean Institute," and the like—see Gwladys Spencer, *The Chicago
Public Library: Origins and Backgrounds,* esp. chap. i. What is said of the high average
of Chicago's pioneers could be largely applied also to those areas of Illinois that Lincoln
knew best.

[15] Ottawa *Free Trader,* Feb. 9, 1850.

[16] Herndon to Joseph H. Barrett, Springfield, Illinois, July 27, 1887, MS., Mass. Hist.
Soc. Herndon was playing on the word *culture.* In the same letter he wrote: ". . . I said
of us western people . . . that they had no culture . . . you state that that expression

Men with whom Lincoln grew up in Illinois were largely Southern by birth and antecedents. Among his Southern-born associates one may mention John Todd Stuart, Stephen T. Logan, William H. Herndon, Orville H. Browning, David Davis, Ward H. Lamon, Stephen A. Hurlbut, Archibald Williams, Ninian W. Edwards, Usher F. Linder, Richard Yates, John J. Hardin, William Butler, Albert T. Bledsoe, W. L. D. Ewing, Josiah Lamborn, Jesse B. Thomas, and Orlando B. Ficklin. The first settlers of central and southern Illinois, said Herndon, "came from the limestone regions of Virginia—Kentucky—Tennessee &c and were men of giant strength— . . . mentally strong. They were . . . individualists. They had no education and no culture but good nature helped them. The strong *alone* . . . could get here and the strong *alone* could survive . . . ." Identifying himself with these men, Herndon wrote: ". . . the struggle for life in the wilderness—& the South gave us . . . mental force & forest life makes us sad—and thoughtful. I think that by nature we were a great people. We were rude and rough—had no polish nor culture. Each man and woman was himself or herself. . . . Lincoln was Lincoln—Grant Grant—Douglas was Douglas. Had Lincoln been a man of high culture—polish—of literary taste . . . he may have been a good country lawyer—that's all." [17] Just what Herndon meant by this will be for the reader to judge: perhaps he had in mind a quality of understanding derived from experience of life, a practical wisdom, a distinct originality in contrast to the conventional or imitative conduct that comes from academic polish or bookish training. As to his emphasis upon crudeness, he had already spoken of the settlers as people of "culture," then a few sentences later had said they had "no . . . culture." It was a matter of finding words to express shades of meaning; the meaning itself was not obscure.

V

The politicians' world in Illinois in the day of Lincoln's earlier career has been drawn from life in the vivid pages of Governor Thomas

in your section [Massachusetts] means a college education &c and not the culture that comes of observation experience—and reason."

17 Herndon to Truman H. Bartlett, Springfield, Ill., July 8, 1887, MS., Mass. Hist. Soc. For a comprehensive treatment of the people of early Illinois see T. C. Pease, *The Frontier State*, 1–32.

Ford. It was not an inspiring picture. Because of the want of true "issues" and the scramble for favor, as explained by Ford, an election became "one great fraud, in which honor, faith, and truth were . . . sacrificed, and politicians were debased below the . . . popular idea of that class of men." [1] Government might mean one thing to the people; its purpose in the minds of politicians was another matter. They had a "destiny to accomplish, not for the people, but for themselves." With the people caring little for matters of government, said Ford, the "politicians took advantage of this lethargic state of indifference . . . to advance their own projects, to get offices and special favors from the legislature, which were all they busied their heads about." [2] Politicians, he said, operated on the principle that "the people never blame any one for misleading them"; it was merely a matter of supporting or opposing measures because of their popularity or unpopularity at the time. A "public man," said the governor, "will scarcely ever be forgiven for being right when the people are wrong." That was why "so many" politicians were "ready to prostitute their better judgments to catch the popular breeze." [3] Whatever may have been the basis of parties in their early origin, Ford observed that "little big men, on both sides . . . feel the most thorough hatred for each other; their malice often supplying the place of principle and patriotism. They think they are devoted to a cause, when they only hate an opponent; and the more thoroughly they hate, the more . . . are they partisans." Party newspapers, he thought, promoted and perpetuated this unhealthy state of things. [4]

The convention system—i. e., the holding of conventions for party nominations—was an innovation in Illinois in the thirties which many defended because of its tendency to promote party concentration, but to Governor Ford it seemed "a most admirable contrivance to enable active leaders to govern without much responsibility to the people." [5] Digesting the arguments of the time, the governor said: ". . . it was urged, that the whole convention system was a fraud on the people; that it was a mere fungus growth engrafted upon the constitution; that conventions themselves were got up and packed by cunning, active, intriguing politicians, to suit the wishes of a few." [6] Referring to politicians' methods generally, Ford wrote: "The

---

[1] Thomas Ford, *History of Illinois*, 87. [2] *Ibid.*, 90. [3] *Ibid.*, 194. [4] *Ibid.*, 199.
[5] *Ibid.*, 207. [6] *Ibid.*, 205.

State [party] leaders . . . give the word to the little cliques . . . in each county; these . . . convey it to the little big men in each neighborhood, and they do the talking to the rank-and-file of the people. In this way principles and men are put up and put down with amazing celerity. And gentle reader . . . this is government! and if there is in point of fact any other sort, its existence cannot be proved by me, and yet I have been governor of the State for four years." [7]

The unlovely situation thus reflected in Governor Ford's pages is a necessary backdrop for a treatment of Lincoln as a developing leader. Lincoln himself spoke bitterly of "the spirit of party" taking "the lead in the councils of the State," of a party going beyond all expectations to "assume to itself the entire control of legislation," even invading the "sanctuary of the Constitution," and entering "with its unhallowed and hideous form into the . . . judiciary system." At the time Lincoln the Whig, with other Whig colleagues, was denouncing what the opposite party had done in the Illinois legislature by enacting a measure through which they obtained control of the state judiciary. With rising indignation not unlike that of Governor Ford but from a different angle, Lincoln in a statement signed by himself and other Whigs continued:

> . . . measures were adopted by the dominant party to take possession of the State, to fill all public offices with party men, and make every measure . . . operate in furtherance of their party views. The merits of men and measures . . . became the subject of discussion in caucus, instead of the halls of legislation, and decisions there made by a minority . . . have been . . . carried into effect by . . . party discipline, without any regard whatever to the rights of the people or the interests of the State.

> . . . the party in power, . . . wholly disregarding the rights, wishes, and interests of the people, has, for the unholy purpose of providing places for its partizans and supplying them with large salaries, disorganized that [the judiciary] department of the government. . . . Men professing respect for public opinion . . . have avowed . . . that the change . . . was intended to produce . . . results favorable to their party and party friends. The immutable principles of justice are to make way for party interests, and the bonds of social order are to be rent in twain, in order that a desperate faction may be sustained at the expense of the people.

[7] *Ibid.*, 274-275.

. . . The declarations of the party leaders . . . prove . . . that the object has been not reform, but . . . the predominance of party.[8]

Simultaneously with this Whig circular, Lincoln and his Whig colleagues in the legislature placed on the record of the lower house a signed protest on this same subject of party abuse apropos of the judiciary bill. They declared in part: "To the majority of a Legislature whose idol is party supremacy, we have addressed our reasons in vain. Announced as a party measure for party purposes, it has been strengthened by the startling admission [of such purpose], and it only remains for us to present to the people of the country, the causes of our opposition, ..."[9] It is amusing to note that Nicolay and Hay, in their huge biography, refer solemnly to Lincoln's having "uttered the voice of the conscience of the party."[10]

It was, of course, with parties and politicians that Lincoln had to work. That in so doing he kept his record clear is an achievement whose full value is not perceived until the Ford portrayal of the political merry-go-round in Illinois is read and appreciated. It cannot be denied that Lincoln was a party man; he had to be if he wanted a political career. He worked by and through party organization; he engaged in party maneuvers; it was as party candidate that he obtained elective office. But it is also worth noting that he saw the evils of party politics and that the worst party excesses never had his approval. In coming days of presidential leadership he was to speak of parties as existing on a low plane. "In . . . time of national peril" he "would have preferred to meet . . . upon a level one step higher than any party platform, because . . . from such more elevated position we could do better battle for the country we all love than . . . from those lower ones where . . . we . . . expend . . . our ingenuity and strength in finding fault with and aiming blows at each other."[11]

---

[8] "Circular from Whig Committee, February [8?], 1841: Appeal to the People of the State of Illinois," *Works*, I, 160–166. This paper was signed by Lincoln as one of a committee of six Whig members of the legislature.

[9] Protest against judiciary bill, Feb. 26, 1841, House *Journal*, 1840–41, 539–545. A small part of this protest, which was signed by thirty-five members including Lincoln, is included in his *Works* edited by Nicolay and Hay (I, 166–167), but the "extract" which they give is incomplete and textually inaccurate, as shown by a comparison with the *Journal*. The above-quoted passage is not given by Nicolay and Hay.

[10] John G. Nicolay and John Hay, *Abraham Lincoln: A History* (10 vols.), I, 167. This huge biography by Lincoln's secretaries is hereafter cited as Nicolay and Hay, *Lincoln*.

[11] *Works*, VIII, 310 (June 12, 1863).

VI

In the pioneer legislature of Illinois Lincoln had his earliest experience of public service on more than a local stage. Elected in 1834 at a time when earning the bare necessaries of life was a major problem,[1] he served continuously through four terms till 1841. That he was the leading man of his party at Vandalia and later at Springfield, was signified by his service as Whig floor leader and by caucus support as speaker of the lower house; his party being in the minority, he was not elected to this office. Making his mark in a body controlled by opponents, he was a man of influence beyond the average of legislators. He phrased petitions for friends to present and drafted bills for others to introduce. This part of his service would have remained almost hidden but for the recent discovery in the Illinois archives of papers recognizable as of Lincoln's handwriting but not otherwise identifiable.[2] Out of legislative sessions he used his time well in the study of law. "When the legislature met, the law-books were dropped, but were taken up again at the end of the session." [3]

Lincoln's one term in Congress (1847–49) fell in the period of the Mexican War and just before the 1850 crisis between North and South. His election as representative in 1846 showed strength especially in two respects: he became the only Whig in Congress from Illinois, and his victory at the polls was won over the redoubtable pioneer preacher, Peter Cartwright. Taking his seat after all the battles of the Mexican War had been fought, Lincoln voted and spoke to the effect that the war had been unnecessarily begun by President Polk,[4] but he was always careful in later years to add that he had supported

---

1 Autobiography, *Works*, VI, 32.

2 Harry E. Pratt, "Lincoln's Petitions for Pardon," *Illinois Bar Jour.*, Feb., 1942; S. Ambrose Wetherbee, "Lincoln Collection: Illinois State Archives," *Illinois Libraries*, Feb., 1943, 114–125.

3 Autobiography, *Works*, VI, 33.

4 Lincoln voted for the Ashmun amendment to a resolution of thanks to General Taylor (January 3, 1848); the amendment declared that the war was "unnecessarily and unconstitutionally begun by the President" (*Cong. Globe*, 30 Cong., 1 sess., pt. 1, 95). On January 12, 1848 Lincoln made a speech supporting his own "spot resolutions." By a series of questions he plainly implied that the spot on which American blood was shed as indicated in Polk's war message of May 11, 1846, was an isolated area never acquired by the United States and that Polk's statement justifying the war was "the sheerest deception." *Works*, I, 318–320; 327–345.

supply bills and measures favorable to officers, soldiers, and their families.

On the slavery question, while in Congress, Lincoln voted for the Wilmot proviso to prohibit slavery in national territory to be acquired from Mexico, and he worked out a formula of conservative legislation for the abolition of slavery in the District of Columbia.[5] According to Lincoln's proposal children born of slave mothers after 1850 were to be "free," but during minority were to be dependent upon their mothers' owners for support and education, being meanwhile treated as apprentices to such owners. Slaves then held in the District were to remain slaves, but owners, if they wished, could emancipate them at any time, receiving "full value" from the treasurer of the United States. Lincoln was thus applying the process of gradual emancipation. The board for the fixing of compensation was to consist of none other than the President of the United States, the secretary of state, and the secretary of the treasury. Fugitive slaves from the outside, finding their way into the District, were to be arrested and returned to owners. Finally a vote of free white male citizens over twenty-one years of age was to be taken in the District, and the act was to go into force only if a majority favored it. Here Lincoln applied the principle of a popular referendum on a congressional statute.

Thus the man who was later to become the emancipator was making an early tentative effort toward liberation. In doing so his approach was vastly different from that of radical abolitionists. It is true that he was seeking to deal with the question only on a very limited scale and at a time when slavery was strongly entrenched in the United States. He could hardly have gone farther in the existing Congress, but the significant point is that he recognized the realities. The phrasing of the bill—which if passed would have made Lincoln somewhat famous for a legislative measure even if fame had given no greater rewards—revealed the character and point of view of Lincoln the statesman: his conservatism, his patience in letting a process work itself out over the years, his lack of antagonism toward the South, his regard for the rights of slaveholders, his attention to legal details, and his valuing of popular and democratic processes.

---

[5] *Works*, II, 96–100. Lincoln presented his plan for abolition in the District and gave notice of intention to introduce it as a bill, but in the strict parliamentary sense it appears that this was never done. Beveridge, I, 482 n.

Lincoln fulfilled his duty in Congress, did committee service, watched out for Illinois interests in such a matter as land grants, and on party affairs showed himself an ardent hard-working Whig and supporter of General Taylor, candidate for President in 1848. His speech in the House on July 27, 1848, filling thirty pages of his *Works*, [6] was an example of rollicking and badgering campaign oratory, more suitable for the western stump than for the halls of a legislative body. Pertaining to no legislative proposal, it was a purely party speech, viewing Cass with alarm and pointing with pride to Taylor; it was a rather unconvincing defense of the candidate against the accusation of having no declared principles. The speech represents an exuberant, likable, joke-cracking Lincoln; it gives a clue to what he must have been when he let himself go on the hustings; but it does not give us the man at his best. Lincoln did not rise to his full stature when speaking merely the party language. Much the same can be said as to what we know of his campaign speeches in 1848 in New England, at Worcester, New Bedford, Boston, Lowell, Dorchester, Taunton, Chelsea, Cambridge, and Boston again, these being mostly unrecorded except in briefest summary. One of his tasks in these speeches was to show why men of Free Soil tendencies ought not to vote for the Free Soil candidate, but for Taylor. In this same campaign he spoke also in Maryland and canvassed "quite fully" and successfully his own district in Illinois.[7]

Lincoln's congressional term had given him little distinction, and there may have been somewhat of a feeling of futility in his mind as he returned to Springfield to resume the practice of law "with greater earnestness than ever before," [8] as if political leadership were no longer his main preoccupation. This futility may have increased as the nation met and temporarily averted a great crisis in 1850 without his help, and as General Winfield Scott led a declining Whig party to defeat in the campaign of 1852. In that year, by Lincoln's own words, he "did less than in previous presidential canvasses" owing to "the hopelessness of the cause in Illinois.[9] Lincoln's political frustration can be rather definitely dated. It belonged to the period 1849 to 1854. He saw his former partner Stephen T. Logan go down to defeat as candidate for Congress to succeed him; this could have been interpreted as an adverse verdict on Lincoln's record in his

---

own district, while the action of the national Whig party in nominating Scott could have been deemed a repudiation of President
Fillmore. That a Whig administration was in power (1849–1853)
was small consolation to Lincoln; [10] Illinois was of the opposite persuasion.

VII

If in seeking Lincoln's view of things one opens a window, that
window may be the concept of Young America versus Old Fogy, for
Lincoln himself used that approach. By Young America he did not
mean militant expansionism nor war-making "manifest destiny." [1]
Boastful patrioteering or flag-waving was not his thought. To know
what his thought was, one may read his essay or lecture on "Discoveries, Inventions, and Improvements," delivered in and around
Springfield on various occasions in 1858, 1859, and early 1860. It is a
bit of Lincoln's writing that has not received the analysis or attention
that it deserves. [2] In its flow of sentences it marks Lincoln as something of a stylist, but that is secondary. The main point is that in
lecturing on discoveries and inventions he was thinking of enlighten-
ment, of progress down the centuries, of the emancipation of the
mind, of men rising from the "dark ages." He stood in wonder of
human achievement, in admiration of "articulate sounds rattled off
from the tongue," of "phonetic writing," of "representing . . .
sounds by marks," and of printing, which he considered the "better
half" of writing. He thought the process was not ended. In considering
inventions, he considered even more the factor of inventiveness, the
"destined work of Adam's race to develop . . . hidden treasures."
Some of the mines had been overlooked. "There are more mines
above the earth's surface than below it," he said. "All nature—the

---

[10] Further humiliation came when Lincoln, seeking a crumb of patronage in the office
of commissioner of the general land office, was passed over and Justin Butterfield, a
Whig who had opposed Taylor, was chosen. Having made a real effort to obtain the appointment, and feeling that he had a claim upon the Taylor administration, Lincoln was
deeply mortified. *Works*, II, 114–115 (Apr. 25, 1849).

[1] The best possible evidence that Lincoln did not think of conquest or aggressive
expansion as the fit expression of Young America is found in his attitude toward the
Mexican War, above noted.

[2] See below, p. 44, for the manner in which Lincoln's lecture was received. It appears
in his *Works*, V, 99–113, under date of Feb. 22, 1859. Two versions of the lecture in
manuscript are in the collection of Oliver R. Barrett.

whole world, material, moral, and intellectual—is a mine . . . ."
Thus viewing Lincoln on the threshold of the presidency, one notes
how strife and sectionalism was not his main concern. Contemplating
the aspiration of his people, his mind was reaching out in terms of
normal progress and peaceable endeavor.

It had not been otherwise at the beginning of his political career.
Having read Lincoln's statements in the late 1850's, one can go back
to the thirties, when his thought was in its formative stage, its expression being already definitely Lincolnian in epigrammatic force.
In those days when Lincoln as a youth was living close to the frontier,
he had given some of his best pronouncements. He pointed to the
greatness of his country, which in his view was a matter of free institutions in a setting of law, order, and community will. Reverently
he referred to the edifice which the Fathers had bequeathed and of
which men of his generation were "legal inheritors." He spoke of
"that fair fabric which for the last half century has been the fondest
hope of the lovers of freedom throughout the world." He thought of
what the nineteenth century of the Christian era meant in "the great
journal of things happening under the sun." He found its meaning
in a political "system . . . conducing more essentially to the ends
of civil and religious liberty than any of which the history of former
times tells us."

The Fathers had possessed the land. They had upreared the edifice.
For his own generation the task, he thought, was to "transmit" the
heritage "unprofaned . . . , undecayed . . . and untorn by usurpation." It was a solemn duty, not a thing to prate about, and on this
theme young Lincoln uttered a stinging warning of "danger" and
"ill omen." If destruction was to come to the fair democracy of America, he believed that "we must ourselves be its author and finisher."
He was thinking of the rough and ready vigilantism of his day, of
men setting themselves up as bigger than the government, of mob
law, of lynching, of those who regard government as a bane and "make
a jubilee of the suspension of its operations." It is an entirely correct
interpretation to note that he was thinking of those arrogant, law-
defying influences which a century later were to go by the ugly name
of Fascism. His views on this point were unmistakably given. If one
doubts it, let him read Lincoln's address before the Young Men's
Lyceum of Springfield, January 27, 1838, as good a speech against

Fascism, or elements characteristic of Fascism, as was ever delivered.[3]

It would be by "suicide," he thought, if American destruction should come; by "disregard of law," by "wild and furious passions," by "savage mobs." Any supposition that by mob savagery he meant free men asserting their rights or aggrieved citizens seeking redress is belied by the context. That was not the problem he was discussing; those were not the elements causing the violence that distressed him. The days of the Revolution were over, he said. He was thinking of "dead men . . . dangling from . . . trees . . . in numbers almost sufficient to rival the native Spanish moss . . . of the forest." It was an ugly spectacle and he was not mincing words. He spoke of vicious men being "permitted to gather in bands of hundreds and thousands, and burn churches, ravage and rob provision-stores, throw printing-presses into rivers, shoot editors, and hang and burn . . . at pleasure and with impunity . . . ."

It is obvious that Lincoln in 1838 was giving a comment on his own time; if one thinks of the alleged purity of that early age it is a shock to realize the turbulent conditions that were causing so much concern to one who believed in democracy. It was Herndon's recollection that the occasion of this lyceum speech, whose "essence" was "obedience to and respect for law," was the "burning of a negro by a mob in St. Louis." [4] Lincoln, however, was dealing with a serious and widespread problem, not with one incident. Revolutionary agitation had degenerated into frontier vigilantism; this had further deteriorated into lawless violence. There had been bad men in Illinois—kidnappers, counterfeiters, horse thieves, desperadoes, and outlaws. Crime ranged widely; it was wholesale; law enforcement was local and ineffective. Courts being inadequate, a group known as "regulators," wishing to enforce order, had set up their extra-legal organization, with its irregular military force, conventions, trials, and executions in the name of the people. Development of this situation, however, had taken a downward trend till the result was a condition of private warfare—gang against gang—with the "regulators" pursu-

---

[3] *Works,* I, 35–50.

[4] Herndon to Weik, Springfield, Ill., Jan. 27, 1888, Herndon-Weik MSS. One thinks, of course, of the murder of Lovejoy at Alton in November, 1837. Though this particular incident is not specified, Lincoln's reference to throwing "printing presses into rivers" was an obvious allusion to the Lovejoy affair. For the dating of the Lyceum address, see below, p. 22. n. 6.

ing a course little better than the thieves. Finally the legislature and governor had to step in to tone up the courts and put down the regulators.[5]

Lincoln had his answer to this ill omen: ". . . let every man remember that to violate the law is to trample on the blood of his father, and to tear the charter of his own and his children's liberty." He continued: "Let reverence for the laws be breathed by every American mother to the lisping babe that prattles on her lap; let it be taught in schools, in seminaries, and in colleges; let it be written in primers, spelling-books, and in almanacs; let it be preached from the pulpit, proclaimed in legislative halls, and enforced in courts of justice. And, in short, let it become the political religion of the nation . . . ." Bad laws, he thought, should be repealed, but while on the books they should be "religiously observed." If there should be an unprovided case not covered by law, he would have people bear with it till "proper legal provisions be made . . . with the least possible delay."

The American experiment was successful, he proclaimed, but some man of ambition might rise to smash the edifice, some man to whom a seat in Congress or a presidential chair would not be enough. If such a person should spring up, some designing chief bigger than the law, someone of "the family of the lion, or the tribe of the eagle," the temple must be upheld by "pillars, hewn from the solid quarry of sober reason." "Reason, . . . unimpassioned reason—must furnish all the materials for our future support and defense." All this would have to be met by solidarity, not division. It would "require the people to be united with each other, attached to the government and laws, and generally intelligent . . . ." [6]

---

[5] Governor Thomas Ford, in his *History of Illinois* (written in the forties) 232 ff., dealt at length with the "mobocratic spirit" in Illinois, the very thing Lincoln was talking about. For criminal and terroristic gangs in Illinois see T. C. Pease, *The Frontier State, 1818–1848 (Centennial Hist. of Ill.*, vol. II), 427–429. The matter is also well treated in "The Regulator Movement in Illinois," by Alice Brumbaugh, master's dissertation (ms.), Univ. of Ill., 1927.

[6] Lincoln's address before the Young Men's Lyceum of Springfield, Illinois, January 27, 1838. This address appears in Lincoln's *Works*, I, 35–50, edited by Nicolay and Hay with the incorrect dating January 27, 1837. That 1838 is the correct date is shown by a number of facts presented by Beveridge (I, 230 n.), and by the present author's examination of the files of the *Sangamo Journal*, the newspaper in which the address was announced on January 27, 1838, and printed on February 3 of that year. In Herndon's letter to Weik, January 27, 1888 (Herndon-Weik MSS.), 1838 is given as the date. Lincoln was not in Springfield but in attendance at the legislature at Vandalia on Jan. 27, 1837. Pratt, *Lincoln, 1809–1839*, 65.

For that broad intelligence he favored popular education, and this in the earliest of his collected addresses, the first item in his *Complete Works*. Education, he said at the age of twenty-three, was "the most important subject which we as a people can be engaged in." Its value would be that "every man . . . may duly appreciate the value of our free institutions." These were his sentiments far back in the days when as an ungainly New Salem youth he was stepping out for political office for the first time in his life. He was addressing his neighbors in Sangamon County as a candidate for the state legislature and in doing so he was apologizing for having been "more presuming than becomes me," but already he felt it "a privilege and a duty to take that stand which . . . might tend most to the advancement of justice." [7]

VIII

Among the nation's founders it is clear that Jefferson offered more of a cue for interpreting Lincoln than Hamilton. In a halting way Lincoln favored a protective tariff.[1] Somewhat more confidently he favored a national bank. He believed in those measures that emphasized the functions of the Federal government, especially in the matter of expenditures within the states for public works ("internal improvements"). These, it is true, were Hamiltonian, though it should not be overlooked that in 1843 Lincoln was careful to quote Jefferson in support of a Federal tariff for the promotion of domestic manufactures.[2] When, however, one has enumerated a few matters of this nature, the similarity to Hamilton ends. On fundamental issues Lincoln's unlikeness to Hamilton and his resemblance to Jefferson are evident. Even in the matter of federalism Lincoln was closer to Jefferson than to Hamilton. Hamilton would have reduced the states to subordinate divisions and would have set up a life president and life senators, with state governors appointed by the national government. Lincoln could not support any such extreme program. He could, however, agree largely with Jefferson without surrendering his national policies, for Jefferson, though a prophet of state rights,

[7] Address to the People of Sangamon County, Mar. 9, 1832, *Works*, I, 1–9.
[1] Reinhard H. Luthin, "Abraham Lincoln and the Tariff," *Amer. Hist. Rev.*, XLIX, 609–629 (July, 1944).
[2] *Works*, I, 244 (Mar. 4, 1843).

actually did important things—e. g., in the Northwest Ordinance, the Louisiana Purchase, the Lewis and Clark Expedition, and the giving of advice looking to the Monroe Doctrine—which mightily promoted the success and prestige of the Federal government. It was in the bedrock of his beliefs that Lincoln was like Jefferson. The Declaration of Independence was his platform, his confession of faith. In those deeply sincere passages in which he expressed worshipful reverence for the Fathers, there was a Jeffersonian accent that was unmistakable. He favored human rights above property interests, repudiated (as noted above) the mudsill theory, spoke up for the farmer and the laborer, and withal showed trust in the people, which Hamilton assuredly did not. He favored the extension of popular education, a policy as prominent in Jefferson's urging and achievement as it was noticeably absent in Hamilton's.[3]

Lincoln frequently mentioned Jefferson, turning to him as to a basic authority. In the index to his writings, letters, and speeches, as edited by Nicolay and Hay, there are nineteen references to Jefferson while there are only two to Hamilton. References to Jefferson were on fundamental and far reaching matters; of the two meager citations of Hamilton, one was the briefest allusion to his support of the United States Bank, while the other was a passing mention of the New York leader as anti-slavery, which could have been said equally, indeed more emphatically, of Jefferson.[4] Lincoln was shocked to note the repudiation by a Virginia clergyman of Jefferson's doctrine of human equality. The repudiation, he thought, sounded "strangely in republican America." "The like was not heard," he said, "in the fresher days of the republic."[5] He found it painful in later troubled days to note that adversaries had "adopted . . . declarations of independence in which, unlike the good old one, penned by Jefferson, they

---

[3] Hamilton wrote of manufacturers employing large numbers of children "of a tender age," showing no concern for the obvious fact that such employment would interfere with their education. *Works* [etc.], *of Alexander Hamilton*, ed. by J. C. Hamilton, III, 208.

[4] In these references, found in the index of the Nicolay-Hay edition of Lincoln's *Works* (vol. 12), only citations to Lincoln's statements are noted; one omits accompanying matter such as Henry Watterson's brief reference to Hamilton in an address on Lincoln in 1895 (*Works*, III, v). If to Nicolay and Hay, one adds Tracy's *Uncollected Letters* and Angle's *New Letters and Papers*, the picture is much the same. Tracy gives four additional references to Jefferson (123–129, 161), and one to Hamilton (in connection with his support of national credit). Angle gives three new Lincoln references to Jefferson (134–135, 223, 251), but none to Hamilton.

[5] *Works*, II, 173–174 (July 16, 1852).

omit the words 'all men are created equal.' " [6] In 1854, the year of his stepping out for larger leadership in public affairs, he referred with admiration to Jefferson as "the author of the Declaration of Independence . . . a chief actor in the Revolution; . . . who was, is, and perhaps will continue to be, the most distinguished politician of our history . . . ." [7]

---

[6] *Ibid.*, VI, 320 (July 4, 1861).

[7] *Ibid.*, II, 193 (Oct. 16, 1854). Lincoln was using the word "politician" here in the sense of a man concerned with political affairs.

CHAPTER II

THUS STOOD LINCOLN

I

LINCOLN once penned a description of himself. With a characteristic quirk and amusing brevity the lines of that self portrait were as follows: "If any personal description of me is thought desirable, it may be said I am, in height, six feet four inches, nearly; lean in flesh, weighing on an average one hundred and eighty pounds; dark complexion, with coarse black hair and gray eyes. No other marks or brands recollected." [1] His friend H. C. Whitney of the law circuit, wrote: "He was six feet and four inches in height, his arms and legs were disproportionately long, his feet and hands were abnormally large, he was awkward in his gait and actions. His skin was a dark, sallow color, his features were coarse:—his expression kind and amiable:—his eyes were indicative of deep reflection, and, in times of repose, of deep sorrow as well. His head was high, but not large: his forehead was broad at the base, but retreated, indicating marked perceptive qualities, but not great reflective ones: and in this phrenology is sadly at fault. He wore a hat measuring seven and one-eighth. His ears were large; his hair, coarse, black and bushy, which stood out all over his head, with no appearance of ever having been combed." [2]

It was common to speak disparagingly of Lincoln's appearance, whether one was referring to his face, his figure, or his clothes. One observer wrote: ". . . his phiz *is* truly awful." [3] To another it seemed: ". . . he is the *homeliest* . . . and the *awkwardest* man in the

---

[1] Lincoln to J. W. Fell, Springfield, Ill., Dec. 20, 1859, *Works*, V, 288–289.

[2] H. C. Whitney, *Life on the Circuit with Lincoln*, Angle ed., 55.

[3] Journal of William L. Gross of Mt. Sterling, Ill., Oct. 19, 1858, MS., Ill. State Hist. Lib., printed in H. E. Pratt, *Concerning Mr. Lincoln*, 18–20.

Sucker State." [4] Edwin M. Stanton's description in 1858 was: "A long, lank creature from Illinois, wearing a dirty linen duster for a coat, on the back of which the perspiration had splotched wide stains that resembled a map of the continent." [5] The adjective "raw-boned" came to mind in characterizing him; it was said that he "might have passed for an ordinary farmer, so far as appearances were concerned." [6] His habiliments were country styled and careless, his tall hat innocent of nap, his carpet-bag delapidated, his outer garment "a short circular blue cloak, which he got in Washington in 1849, and kept for ten years." [7]

It is not easy to make up a composite of differing descriptions, and one should not give sole attention to comments by such an unfriendly and supercilious person as Stanton. In attire the quality that seemed to stand out was negligence of fashion rather than slovenliness. H. C. Whitney records that, though his clothes and shoes needed brushing, Lincoln was "scrupulously clean and close shaven." [8] In years of growing prominence his dress improved. "When he first ran for the legislature he . . . wore a blue jeans coat, claw hammer style, short in . . . sleeves, and . . . tail . . . homespun linen trousers, a straw hat and 'stogy' boots." "He commenced to dress better in the spring of 1858, and when he was absent from home on political tours usually did so: after he became President he had a servant who kept him considerably 'slicked up': but he frequently had to reason Lincoln into fashionable attire, by telling him his appearance was 'official.' " [9]

In passages which only William H. Herndon could write (and which are buried in manuscript collections) one gets flashes of Lincoln as pictorial as those of the camera, portraits which convey a setting and a sense of motion and sound as well as visual impressions of the man's face. Herndon's words are repetitious; he piles them high; yet there is a photographic quality in his record; he describes something he has seen. He seldom speaks of Lincoln's face or form alone; physical descriptions in the Herndonian manner usually blend with recordings of the man's mind, moods, and character. Often he goes into long paragraphs of psychoanalysis: [10] the reader is spared these

---

[4] Statement of J. H. Burnham, May 19, 1860, *Journal*, Ill. State Hist. Soc., XXVIII, 96 (Apr., 1935).
[5] Quoted in Whitney, *Life on the Circuit*, Angle ed., 48.
[6] *Ibid.*, 53.   [7] *Ibid.*, 55.   [8] *Ibid.*, 69.   [9] *Ibid.*, 55.
[10] For Herndon's irrepressible tendency toward psychoanalysis, see vol. II, appendix.

disquisitions, which are less significant than the pictorial passages. One of these, despite the repetition, is presented here as a kind of sample:

> Thus stood, walked—felt—thought, willed—acted and looked Abraham Lincoln: he was not a pretty man . . . , nor was he an ugly one: he was a homely man, careless of his looks; plain looking and plain acting: he had no aristocratic pomp—display or dignity so called. . . . Lincoln had . . . that inner quality which distinguishes one person from another, as much as to say "I am myself and not you." . . . Lincoln was easy of approach up to a certain limit and very democratic: he appeared simple in his carriage general behavior and bearing: . . . his sadness—gloom and melancholy dripped from him as he walked along. . . . Mr. Lincoln was sad and . . . humorous by turns. . . .
>
> Mr. Lincoln sometimes walked our streets cheerily, . . . perhaps joyously and then it was, on meeting a friend, he cried—How'dy, clasping one of his friends in both of his wide long big bony hands, giving his friend a good hearty soul welcome. On a winters morning he might be seen stalking and stilting it toward the market house, basket on his arm, his old grey shawl wrapped around his neck, his little Willie or Tad running along at his heels, asking a thousand little quick questions, which his father heard not . . . . When he thus met a friend on the road he said that something . . . put him in mind of a story which he heard in Indiana or Egypt or elsewhere and tell it he would and there was no alternative in his friend but to patiently stand and hear it
>
> . . . .
>
> . . . Mr. Lincoln's perceptions were slow, cold, precise and exact. Everything came to Lincoln . . . clean and clear cut, stript of all extraneous matter whatsoever. Everything came to him in its precise shape—gravity and color. . . . No lurking illusion—delusion—error, false in itself and clad for the moment in robes of splendor, woven by the imagination, ever passed unchallenged or undetected over the threshold of his mind, that divides vision from the relm [sic] and home of thought. Names to him were nothing and titles naught—assumptions always standing back abashed at his cold intellectual glare. . . . There was no . . . refraction there, in this man's brain: he was not impulsive fanciful or imaginative, but cold, calm, precise and exact: he threw his whole mental light around the object seen . . . . In his mental view he crushed the unreal, . . . the hollow and the sham: . . . he saw what no man could well dispute, but he failed to see what might be seen . . . by other men. . . . His own mind was his own and exclusive standard. . . .[11]

---

11 Herndon ms. fragment, "Lincoln Individually," undated, Herndon-Weik MSS.

THE MACOMB AMBROTYPE

The better of two ambrotypes taken at Macomb, Illinois, August 26, 1858, the day before the debate with Douglas at Freeport. Remarkable for striking facial contours, depth of personality, and sadness combined with confidence.

LINCOLN'S FULL FIGURE

It is stated by the L. C. Handy studios that this is a copy of an old original print discovered about 1931 in the effects of the sculptor, Henry Kirke Brown, who made a statue of Lincoln in Union Square, New York. Photographer not identified. Made probably in 1860. A recent addition to the known photographs of Lincoln, it has the number "Meserve no. 111."

Herndon reached out for rugged adjectives as he described his partner. He "was a great big—angular—strong man—limbs large and bony: he was tall and of a peculiar type." He "grew up like the forest oak, tough—solid—knotty—gnarly, standing out . . . against the storm, . . . defying the lightning." Herndon added: ". . . his mind was tough—solid—knotty—gnarly, more or less like his body: he was . . . a tall and big boned man and his speech was tall—strong . . . & enduring. The convolutions of his brain were long: they did not snap off quickly like a short thick mans brain: . . . when those convolution[s] . . . threw off an idea it *was* an *idea, ...*" In attempting to explain this to one of his numerous correspondents, Herndon wrote: "Please see Lincoln's strong—terse—knotty—gnarly and compact words—driven together as by a sledge hammer . . . ." "No other man on the continent," declared Herndon, "could have stood what Lincoln did in Washington: he had a frame of *iron*." [12]

One would not forget that face—the face of the Macomb ambrotype, the Volk life mask, the beardless Hesler profile. The bony structure, with strong planes and angles, gave the head a sculptural quality; hollows and creases showed ruggedness of character; the look of the eyes added a haunting sadness. The mouth, while heavy lipped and full of strength, was sensitive and expressive. If one takes a paper and conceals one side of the Macomb face at a time, there is an impression not easy to describe—not only the obvious fact of asymmetry which artists have noted, but different facets of the man's nature which that asymmetry suggests. No first glance would take in every aspect of this countenance. The Americanism of the man is revealed with an effect that is almost startling if one looks at the full standing form with scroll in hand, shown facing this page, and then tries to imagine that figure in court costume, with knee-breeches, close fitting stockings, and buckles. There was little of Europe here, as Lowell noted. The man's appearance was both unique and related to a well known American type, the type that might have been found among people close to the woods or mountains.

One factor of his appearance was not seen in photographs: the

---

[12] Herndon to Truman H. Bartlett, Greencastle, Ind., Aug. 7, 1887, MS., Mass. Hist. Soc. Again he wrote: ". . . his flesh was dark—wrinkled & folded: it looked dry & leathery—tough & everlasting: his eyes were small and grey—head small and forehead receding, ..." Herndon to Bartlett, June 24, 1887, *ibid.*

sparkle of the face in animation noted by those who described him from life, but too much a part of the face in action to be captured by the camera. "The moment Lincoln took his seat at the pho machine [wrote Herndon] & looked down the barrel of it he became sad— rather serious, as all business with him was serious, life included." [13] To Whitney it seemed: "His mobile face ranged . . . through a long gamut: it was rare that an artist could catch the expression, and Lincoln's face was of that kind that the expression was of greater consequence than the contour of the features." [14] When Lincoln was "moved by some great & good feeling—by some idea of Liberty or Justice or Right then [wrote Herndon] he seemed an inspired man." "It was just then that Lincoln's nature was beautiful and in complete harmony with the laws of the great Eternal. I have seen him in this inspired condition and thought that he was molded in the Spirits best mold." [15] Again Herndon wrote: ". . . he was odd—angular—homely but when those little gray eyes . . . were lighted up by the inward soul on fires of emotion, defending the liberty of man or proclaiming the truths of the Declaration of Independence . . . , then . . . all those apparently ugly or homely features sprang with organs of beuty [sic]—or sank . . . into the sea of . . . inspiration that on such occasions flooded up his manly face." [16] In somewhat the same sense Herndon wrote: "You will find the plains, mountains & outlines of Lincoln's head & face hard to catch: they are so subtle." [17] This aspect of singular attractiveness in Lincoln's countenance in moments of animation, something of the inner man shining through the weather-beaten countenance, was so clearly noted by various observers that it comes down to us with as much authenticity as the photographs themselves.

II

On the matter of Lincoln's popularity in Illinois the evidence is not all of a piece. "Lincoln was the favorite of everybody," wrote

---

13 Herndon to Bartlett, Feb. 27, 1891, *ibid.* At another time Herndon wrote that he would "give a good many dollars for a no one pho [number one photograph] of Lincoln," but added: ". . . there is none, as it appears to me." Herndon to Joseph H. Barrett, July 27, 1887, *ibid.*

14 Whitney, *Life on the Circuit,* 55.

15 Herndon to Bartlett, June 24, 1887, MS., Mass. Hist. Soc.

16 Herndon ms. fragment, "Lincoln Individually," undated, Herndon-Weik MSS.

17 Herndon to Barrett, July 27, 1887, MS., Mass. Hist. Soc.

Herndon,[1] and the manner in which people crowded round to hear his droll stories was proverbial. In the New Salem area in his earlier years he was popular for local reasons: he had been a wrestling champion,[2] and had favored improvements desired by the people of the region.[3] On the other hand, speaking of the attitude of Springfield, Herndon wrote: "Mr Lincoln was not appreciated in this city, nor was he at all times the most popular man among us. The cause of his unpopularity, or rather want of popularity here, arose out of two grounds—1st He did his own thinking and 2nd he had the courage of his convictions, and boldly and fearlessly expressed them." [4]

This comment by Herndon is seemingly corroborated by cold figures. Though for four terms (1834–1841) he was of the Sangamon County delegation in the state legislature, and despite his influence in procuring the removal of the capital to Springfield, the people of that county had a habit, on larger matters, of voting either against Lincoln when he was a candidate or against men of Lincoln's choice.[5] The strength of the Democratic party in the Springfield area was of course a factor in producing this result, which is not conclusive as to Lincoln's popularity. That in the troubled years of agitation and war he obtained as high a vote as he did in a section where the Republican party was unpopular, is significant, as also the fact that he sometimes carried his city of Springfield though not carrying the county of Sangamon.

That Lincoln should have referred to his own popularity is a matter of interest. In his autobiography (1860), after mentioning his service in the Black Hawk War, he wrote: "Returning from the

---

[1] Herndon to C. O. Poole, Jan. 5, 1886, Herndon-Weik MSS.

[2] Among other sources, an account of Lincoln's wrestling match with Jack Armstrong, said to be on a bet by Offutt, Lincoln's employer, that "Abe could throw down . . . any man in the county," is found in a long statement by R. B. Rutledge to Herndon, attested Oct. 22, 1866, Herndon-Weik MSS.

[3] Herndon to Lamon, Feb. 25, 1870, MS., Huntington Lib.

[4] Statement by Herndon, copied in letter, Alfred A. North to Truman H. Bartlett, July 1, 1887, MS., Mass. Hist. Soc.

[5] In 1856 Sangamon County showed large Democratic pluralities in the presidential and gubernatorial votes; in 1858 Springfield and Sangamon County gave majorities to candidates that favored Douglas over Lincoln; in 1860 Douglas carried Sangamon County for President; in 1862, when votes for a congressman involved the question of support for President Lincoln, "in both Springfield and Sangamon County the Democratic candidates were elected by sizable majorities"; in 1864, with Springfield almost tied (in Lincoln's favor) between Lincoln and McClellan, the county favored McClellan by a majority of several hundred. Angle, *"Here I Have Lived,"* 223, 234, 253, 274, 287.

campaign, and encouraged by his great popularity among his immediate neighbors, he . . . ran for the legislature, and was beaten [1832],—his own precinct, however, casting its votes 277 for and 7 against him—and that, too, while he was an avowed Clay man, . . . the precinct the autumn afterward giving a majority of 115 to General Jackson over Mr. Clay. This was the only time Abraham was ever beaten on a direct vote of the people." [6] When one recalls Lincoln's knack of exact statement together with his habit of understating his own achievements, this autobiographical comment gives us the best indication that his local popularity was both real and of importance to himself.

III

A sobriquet commonly has less value as biographical record than as an influence in shaping a man's superficial reputation. The idea that Lincoln was a kind of backwoods character is a misconception suggested in part by his sobriquet of "rail-splitter." It is true that Lincoln's origin was in a backwoods environment,[1] and it is interesting to note that his father's long life of over seventy years was lived almost entirely in remote backwoods settings, but Lincoln's early life had many windows into the larger world, and his rail splitting,[2] for which he neither apologized or bragged, was of much less significance than his cultural associations. Because of such factors as his marriage into an aristocratic Kentucky family and his first partnership (beginning in 1837) with the courtly and socially favored John Todd Stuart, his opponents as early as 1843 actually put him down as the candidate of pride, wealth, and family distinction.[3]

---

6 *Works*, VI, 31–32.

1 "It was a wild region [southern Indiana], with many bears and other wild animals still in the woods. There I grew up." Autobiographical sketch for Jesse W. Fell, Dec. 20, 1859, *Works*, V, 287.

2 In recalling his use of the ax Lincoln wrote as follows in his autobiography: "Abraham, though very young, was large of his age, and had an ax put into his hands at once; and from that till within his twenty-third year [1831–32] he was almost constantly handling that most useful instrument . . . ." *Works*, VI, 26.

3 "It would astonish . . . the older citizens to learn that I (a stranger, friendless, uneducated, penniless boy, working on a flatboat at ten dollars per month) have been put down here as the candidate of pride, wealth, and aristocratic family distinction. Yet

Nor is it adequate to refer to Lincoln as a country lawyer. In the forties and fifties he was one of the outstanding lawyers of Illinois at a time when Illinois was a populous and flourishing state, well supplied with able attorneys. Lincoln handled important cases and many of them, often practicing before the Illinois supreme court and in the Federal courts. He was admitted to practice before the Supreme Court of the United States and was counsel in Lewis *v.* Lewis [4] decided in 1849. This implied a considerable standing at the bar. Lincoln could even be referred to as a corporation lawyer, though far indeed from the type suggested by that term in its modern connotation; he successfully handled a highly important case for the Illinois Central Railroad, from which he collected a fee of five thousand dollars,[5] and was one of a group of lawyers retained by a combination of manufacturers who resisted the McCormick Harvester Company.

Yet the homespun quality pertaining to the country lawyer was not foreign to Lincoln. Most of his cases were prosaic enough and even boresome to review, but some were redolent of the country or picturesquely associated with common people, as his famous defense of Duff Armstrong or his recovery, on behalf of a widow of a Revolutionary soldier, of an excessive fee charged by a greedy pension agent. The Duff Armstrong case, memorable for the calendar incident and its association with the redoubtable Clary's Grove boys, gives no more concept of Lincoln the lawyer than many other cases which are unknown in the popular mind. Incidentally, the setting of this case has been distorted: though it occurred in 1858 it is usually thought of as belonging to a period more than twenty years earlier, a moving picture [6] having dramatized it in the younger setting.

Lincoln's prowess in the law has probably been overstated, yet there is ample evidence that his name as counsel carried prestige in a suit. Local attorneys would work up cases for Lincoln to argue when court days came round. In the case of Ward H. Lamon this extended to the forming of a partnership, the Danville attorney being proud

---

so . . . it was." Lincoln to "Martin M. Morris," Springfield, Ill., Mar. 26, 1843 (correct name Martin S. Morris), *Works*, I, 262. In referring to the Illinois legislature of 1838–39 Governor Ford dismissed many of the members with mere surnames, giving only the names of "prominent men" in full: "Abram Lincoln," at the age of thirty or less, was listed as one of the prominent men. Thomas Ford, *History of Illinois*, 194–195.

[4] 7 Howard 777.   [5] Pratt, *Personal Finances*, 48 ff.   [6] "Young Mr. Lincoln."

to advertise under the title "Lincoln & Lamon." [7] Little of Lincoln's practice was in criminal cases; the main substance of it was in civil suits. His proportionate share of criminal business was much less than the ratio which such cases bore to the total on the dockets of a typical court in his circuit. If it be asked how far he "won" his cases—though winning in the law is not such a clear-cut matter as is often supposed —it is Paul M. Angle's conclusion that he was much more successful in the higher courts than on the circuit; especially "in the Supreme Court of Illinois, both as to the extent of his business and the degree of success he enjoyed, Lincoln's record was outstanding." [8]

Though much of Lincoln's most important work was outside and apart from the famous eighth judicial circuit, it was inevitable that he should become bracketed with that circuit in popular memory. The practice of lawyers riding from one county seat to another was a picturesque feature of the times which Lincoln evidently enjoyed, for he "was the only lawyer who traveled over the entire circuit; he . . . made it a practice to attend every court, and to remain till the end." [9]

This circuit, which sprawled widely over central Illinois, is remembered for its combination of pioneer flavor with legal talent, but above all for the fact that Lincoln was a part of it. One passes over its agenda—crime, slander, riot, damages, promissory notes, divorce, the value of a saw mill, responsibility for loss of sheep by foot rot, or ownership of a litter of pigs. One remembers rather the off-duty aspects, the migratory life of the ponderous judge, David Davis, and his coterie of attorneys jogging over dirt roads,[10] sometimes stopping at farm houses, holding protracted night discussions of politics or

7 Lamon later became marshal of the District of Columbia with duties close to the President. He had pronounced ideas including bitter opposition to abolitionists. His life of Abraham Lincoln published in 1872 was based on material bought from William H. Herndon. It was written not by Lamon but by a ghost writer, Chauncey F. Black, son of Jeremiah S. Black, member of Buchanan's cabinet. See Albert V. House, Jr., "The Trials of a Ghost-Writer of Lincoln Biography," *Journal*, Ill. State Hist. Soc., XXXI, 262–296 (1938).

8 "Abraham Lincoln: Circuit Lawyer," Lincoln Centennial Assoc. *Papers*, 1928, 40.

9 Whitney, *Life on the Circuit*, 62. For an account of the eighth circuit of central Illinois with its various reorganizations, see Benjamin P. Thomas, "The Eighth Judicial Circuit," *Bulletin No. 40*, Abr. Lincoln Assoc., Sep. 1935.

10 "I saw him as he drove into town behind his own horse, which was an indifferent, raw-boned specimen, in his own blacksmith-made buggy—a most ordinary looking one" (Whitney, 53). It should of course be added that, in traveling the circuit, Lincoln used trains when they were available. Paul M. Angle, *Lincoln, 1854–1861 . . . .* 126.

philosophy, sleeping "two in a bed, and eight in a room," [11] enlivening the taverns with hilarious excitement, conducting "office" consultations, according to the weather, under a tree or "on the sunny side of a court house," [12] holding "orgmathorial court" [13] with mock solemnity, and, not the least of it, meeting the people of country and town, to whom the semi-annual "court week" was a shining period of shopping, entertainment, and political agitation.

It was natural and inevitable that the traveling lawyers should correlate their court practice with speech making. At Bloomington in September 1856, for example, finding himself on a case before the McLean circuit court (Bishop v. Illinois Central Railroad Co.), Lincoln addressed a Republican gathering in Major's Hall. It was reported that he spoke with "great eloquence and power. He showed up the position of the Fillmore party in fine style . . . ." [14] Another example was when Lincoln, while in Urbana on court duty, addressed a meeting at the court house on October 20 of the same year. [15] Lincoln's travel arrangements were known in advance and in July 1856, when his arrival in Chicago on legal business was anticipated, it was hoped that his arrangements would "permit him to meet the universal wish of the people of Chicago" by addressing them on political issues. A few days later Lincoln was reported having addressed an open-air Republican meeting at Dearborn Park. [16] Color and excitement were thus added to circuit duties. The lawyers were there—sometimes a choice assemblage of them. So were the crowds. The people demanded speeches and the lawyers needed no coaxing to satisfy them.

IV

The serious study of Lincoln as a lawyer has been covered elsewhere. [1] The law was his livelihood; it was the absorbing object of his

---

[11] Whitney, *Life on the Circuit*, 62.   [12] *Ibid.*

[13] In the *orgmathorial* court (it was a made-up word) the judge and his coterie, in proceedings said to be better than those of the Pickwick Club, amused and entertained themselves with great secrecy, dealt with breaches of decorum, and ranged at will over any topics they chose, including "metempsychosis" (*ibid.*, 67).

[14] Bloomington *Pantagraph*, Sep. 17, 1856, quoted in Angle, *Lincoln, 1854–1861*, 141.

[15] Angle, *Lincoln, 1854–1861*, 147.   [16] *Ibid.*, 133.

[1] Frederick Trevor Hill, *Lincoln The Lawyer*; John T. Richards, *Abraham Lincoln: The Lawyer-Statesman*; Albert A. Woldman, *Lawyer Lincoln*; Paul M. Angle, *One Hundred Years of Law*; Paul M. Angle, "Abraham Lincoln: Circuit Lawyer," in Lincoln Centennial Assoc. *Papers*, 1928, 19–41; Benjamin P. Thomas, "Lincoln's Earlier Practice

self-directed efforts as a young man arduously preparing for a career; it was his avenue of acquaintance; it was for long years his main interest. His practice embodied all phases of a lawyer's work, from jury eloquence to business documents, from office consultation to elaborate briefs and pleadings. One could write a considerable book to show the kaleidoscope of human problems, large and small, which passed before his eyes in his capacity as lawyer, and another book to exhibit, in Lincoln the lawyer, the essential qualities of Lincoln himself, his habits of thought and his character as a man. It was largely through the law that he acquired his knowledge of American institutions, of democratic traditions, of civil rights and duties.

It was also in the law that Lincoln exhibited one of his most characteristic traits, his knack of taking a complicated subject, going to the core of it, and coming through with a lucid statement of essentials. It was Herndon's observation that he was deficient in the knowledge of legal technicalities. He "knew nothing of the laws of evidence—of pleading or of practice, and did not care about them: he had a keen sense of justice and struck for that, throwing aside forms—methods and rules of all law. Lincoln look^d for justice through forms, pure as a ray of light flashes through a fog bank."

Herndon thought he knew in what respects Lincoln excelled as a lawyer and in what respects he fell short: ". . . if Mr. Lincoln had his time and thought that he was right, and could get the case swung to the jury, freed from technicalities he was a good lawyer, but if he did not have his time—did not think that he was right, and could not get his case swung to the jury, . . . then he was a very weak brother. In the Circuit Courts of the United States he was a good lawyer, because the practice of the Courts was liberal—moved slowly —freed from technicalities and gave Lincoln his own time to arrange his ideas and his plans for attack or defence. . . . But it was in the Supreme Court of the State of Illinois that he was truly a great lawyer, & no where else." Herndon believed this to be true because in the state supreme court Lincoln had time to prepare; everything

in the Federal Courts, 1839–1854," Abr. Lincoln Assoc. *Bulletin* (June, 1935). Benjamin P. Thomas, "The Eighth Judicial Circuit," *ibid.* (Sep. 1935); Paul M. Angle, "Lincoln and the United States Supreme Court," *ibid.* (May, 1937); Paul M. Angle, "Lincoln and the United States Supreme Court: A Postscript," *ibid.* (June, 1937); Harry E. Pratt, "The Genesis of Lincoln the Lawyer," *ibid.* (Sep. 1939); John M. Zane, "Lincoln, the Constitutional Lawyer," Abr. Lincoln Assoc. *Papers*, 1932.

that went before the court, the record of the case and briefs of counsel, was put in writing in advance. Sureness of slow reasoning rather than nimbleness or resourcefulness in inventing legal pitfalls, seems to have been Lincoln's forte. In this respect Lincoln compared himself to an old jack-knife that opens more clumsily and cuts more slowly than a "woman's little knife," but could "do more execution." [2]

There is both autobiographical detail and keen human wisdom in a Lincoln fragment, dated 1850, in which he set down his advice to lawyers. First of all he stressed diligence, attention to correspondence, leaving nothing for tomorrow which could be done today. He pointed out the importance of examining the books, noting authorities, giving close attention to the examination of titles and the drafting of decrees. Emphasizing extemporaneous speaking as "the lawyer's avenue to the public," he nevertheless warned against the "fatal error" of too much speech making, especially if relied upon as a substitute for "the drudgery of the law." He continued:

> Discourage litigation. Persuade your neighbors to compromise whenever you can. Point out to them how the nominal winner is often a real loser—in fees, expenses, and waste of time. As a peace-maker the lawyer has a superior opportunity of being a good man. There will still be business enough.
> Never stir up litigation. A worse man can scarcely be found than one who does this. Who can be more nearly a fiend than he who habitually overhauls the register of deeds in search of defects in titles, whereon to stir up strife, and put money in his pocket? A moral tone ought to be infused into the profession which should drive such men out of it.

> . . . .

> There is a vague popular belief that lawyers are necessarily dishonest. I say vague, because when we consider to what extent confidence and honors are reposed in and conferred upon lawyers by the people, it appears improbable that their impression of dishonesty is very distinct . . . . Yet the impression is common, almost universal. Let no young man choosing the law . . . for a moment yield to the popular belief—resolve to be honest at all events; and if in your own judgment you cannot be an honest lawyer, resolve to be honest without being a lawyer. Choose some other occupation, rather than one in the choosing of which you do, in advance, consent to be a knave.[3]

---

[2] Herndon ms. fragment, "Lincoln as Lawyer, Politician & Statesman," undated (written in the 1880's), Herndon-Weik MSS.

[3] *Works*, II, 140–143.

Toward those traits in a lawyer that smacked of chicanery, sharp practice, or anti-social attitudes Lincoln was indignant. In this he had both a high conviction of the ethics of his profession and a deep sense of personal integrity. Though not setting himself up as a "knight-errant of the law," as Beveridge has pointed out, he had been known to withdraw from a case during trial after being convinced that justice was not on the side of his client.[4] It was not in him, said his friend Gillespie, to "attempt to bolster up a false position." "He would abandon his case first." [5]

That Lincoln could be slighted by fellow counsel in a case to the point of stinging humiliation and chagrin, and yet take the snub in generous good spirit was shown in the McCormick reaper trial. For this and other reasons the case has "a national significance far broader than the immediate issues involved." [6] The McCormick Harvester Company was suing an Illinois manufacturer named Manny, together with eastern firms, for infringement of patent rights. It was a Federal case, first set for trial in Chicago, then shifted to Cincinnati. Lincoln was retained as counsel for the defendants (McCormick's rivals); others employed on the same side were George Harding of Philadelphia, Edwin M. Stanton of Pittsburgh, and (for assistance in preparation) Peter H. Watson of Washington, later assistant secretary of war and president of the Erie Railroad. Lincoln was impressed with the importance of the case, and made elaborate preparation, only to find himself excluded from active participation in the trial. Evidence was not put in his hands in advance, and it was Harding and Stanton who presented the argument. There are various versions of what passed between defense counsel. Lincoln's associates may simply have been watching their client's interests in a trial where a member of the Illinois bar proved not so indispensable as was expected, and where only two attorneys were needed in argument. Others have seen in the incident, not without cause, evidence of the disdain which smart eastern lawyers felt toward the gawky, unpolished, ill-dressed, and un-

---

4 The matter of Lincoln withdrawing from a case because of scruple is not emphasized by Beveridge, who associates his conduct with that of "most high-minded and honorable attorneys." The "dirty hands" incident (Lincoln leaving the court room during a trial and sending word to the judge that he had come to the tavern to clean his hands) is treated by Beveridge as non-typical; it is pointed out that as attorney Lincoln "did not try both sides." Beveridge, I, 546–547.

5 Statement of Joseph Gillespie, Jan. 31, 1866, Herndon-Weik MSS.

6 William T. Hutchinson, *Cyrus Hall McCormick: Seed-Time, 1809–1856*, 436.

prepossessing Lincoln—"that d—d long armed Ape" [7] as Stanton is said to have called him. Lincoln was deeply hurt and disappointed; yet he took the incident in good part. He yielded to superior talent, sat with rapt attention while the arguments were given, and accepted a lesson in the need for heavy study if he were to measure up to eastern lawyerly standards.[8] In appointing Stanton secretary of war in 1862 he rose magnanimously above personal resentment; as for Stanton, his manner toward his Chief was never to lose its overbearing tone.

Though careful to charge and collect what was due him,[9] Lincoln wanted no more. Not only would he not "consent to be a knave"; he would decline to accept unjustifiably high fees; if a case were questionable, he would refuse it. There was no unctuousness about such conduct; it was a matter of practicing what he preached. It is this that makes the more interesting those passages in which he extended advice. He had been through it himself; he warned that there was no royal road to success. In the midst of his campaign for the presidency he took the time to answer an inquirer who wanted to know "the best mode of obtaining a thorough knowledge of the law." He wrote:

. . . The mode is very simple, though laborious and tedious. It is only to get the books and read and study them carefully. Begin with Blackstone's "Commentaries," and after reading it carefully through, say twice, take up Chitty's "Pleadings," Greenleaf's "Evidence," and Story's "Equity," etc., in succession. Work, work, work, is the main thing.[10]

---

[7] Herndon to Weik, Jan. 6, 1887, Herndon-Weik MSS.

[8] Information on the McCormick reaper case is found in Hutchinson, *McCormick* (*Seed-Time*), 431–452 (fullest account of the business and legal aspects); Beveridge, I, 575–583 (a thorough analysis); Gilbert A. Tracy, ed., *Uncollected Letters*, 58–59, 61; W. M. Dickson, "Abraham Lincoln at Cincinnati," *Harper's*, LXIX, 62–66 (June, 1884); Harry E. Pratt, *Personal Finances of Abraham Lincoln*, 54–56. The side on which Lincoln was retained won the decision; his fee has been placed at $1,000 (Pratt, 56). Those versions of the episode that stem from Lincoln himself are remarkably free from resentment. For example, the account which Joseph Gillespie had from Lincoln's lips, while confirming that Lincoln had prepared carefully and expected to participate in conducting the suit, indicates also that Lincoln readily admitted greater mastery on the part of his younger associate. Gillespie to Herndon, Dec. 8, 1866, Herndon-Weik MSS. It has been said that it was Stanton's performance on this occasion that so impressed Lincoln that he made him secretary of war (statement of Ralph Emerson, based upon Lincoln's statement while President, Beveridge, I, 581).

[9] Lincoln made a comfortable income from the law, as was to be expected from a man of his prominence, ability, and industry. His earnings were adequate though moderate. He made a success of his chosen profession, but by no means did he grasp all the gains within his reach. Harry E. Pratt, *The Personal Finances of Abraham Lincoln*, 25–57.

[10] Letter to J. M. Brockman, Springfield, Sep. 25, 1860, *Works*, VI, 59. See also *ibid.*, XI, 114; *Ore. Hist. Soc. Quart.*, XXIII, 267 (1922).

On the basis of many years of partnership William H. Herndon made the following statement in which Lincoln the lawyer was blended with Lincoln the man:

... In 1843-4 [11] Mr Lincoln and I became partners in the law business in Springfield, but did business in all the surrounding counties. Our partnership was never legally dissolved till the night of his assassination. The good man the noble man, would take none of my fees made in the law business after his election to the Presidency. Mr Lincoln was a safe councilor, a good lawyer and an honest man in all the walks of life.

... Mr Lincoln was a cool, cautious, conservative, and long headed man. Mr Lincoln could be trusted by the people. They did trust him and they were never deceived. He was a pure man, a great man, and a patriot. In the practice of law he was simple honest, fair and broad minded. He was courteous to the bar, and to the court. He was open candid and square in his profession, never practicing on the sharp or low. Mr Lincoln met all questions fairly, squarely, . . . , making no concealments of his . . . intentions in any case. He took no snap judgments, nor used any tricks in his business . . . .

Mr Lincoln never deceived his brother in a law case. What he told you was the exact truth. . . . [12]

V

It is incorrect to regard Lincoln as versatile, or brilliantly accomplished in many fields. He was no Leonardo da Vinci, no universal genius; nor was he so variously gifted or widely read as, for instance, Thomas Jefferson,. His main interest was in politics, using that word both in its original and derived sense.[1] His studies focused on problems of government and of peaceful American development. It should of course be added that, over and above his main occupation as lawyer and political leader, Lincoln was an inventor, a surveyor, fond of geometry, something of a specialist in western river transportation (no mean subject), an athlete, a soldier (for a brief period,

[11] Surprisingly, Herndon was in error here as to the beginning of his partnership with Lincoln. The statement seems to imply that the year "1843-4" was the first year of their partnership; in Herndon's Lincoln (Angle ed., 210-211) the year 1843 is given. Though Lincoln writers have almost invariably followed Herndon on this point, the statement is incorrect. The Lincoln-Herndon partnership began late in 1844. Paul M. Angle, in Lincoln Centennial Assoc. Papers, 1927, 29-30.

[12] Statement by W. H. Herndon, Apr. 14, 1886, copied in letter, Alfred A. North to Truman H. Bartlett, July 1, 1887, MS.,.Mass. Hist. Soc.

[1] "Politics were his life . . . ." Herndon to C. O. Poole, Jan. 5, 1886, Herndon-Weik MSS.

including reënlistments, in the Black Hawk War, 1832), a lecturer (briefly),[2] a newspaper owner (again briefly),[3] and an orator. In the period before his career took shape he had been ferry boy, flatboatman, mill manager, small town clerk and merchant, day laborer at odd jobs, and postmaster. By his own statement he had "thought of learning the blacksmith trade." [4] He had been a part of his growing community wherever fortune had landed him, helping in community tasks while earning his livelihood. Later, in days of prominence, he referred to himself as a working man; [5] it was a satisfaction to him to identify himself with the ranks of labor. His range of activities, however, had not been so wide as to be remarkable. Farming was not his occupation at any time after he struck out for himself in 1831. Only on a limited scale, in New Salem days, was he ever a business man. He had neither a native nor a developed taste in art; country merrymaking was more to his liking than classical music; and, while growing up in picturesque regions, he showed little conscious appreciation of the beauties of nature.[6] Yet there was latent poetry in the man, there was fondness for Shakespeare, and there were times when he expressed himself in verse.

VI

As a speaker Lincoln ran the gamut from stumps in the woods through village platforms to juries, outdoor crowds, and cultured audiences. In the speaking to which he was accustomed there were no tables "to hit, beat and . . . bang"; the speaker's whole form was visible; he stood out "fully to public view." Lincoln did not like his speeches to smell of the study. In going over his debate with Douglas for publication he did not embellish, elaborate, or revise;

---

2 See below, pp. 43–44.

3 In collaboration with Theodore Canisius in 1859, Lincoln maintained ownership and control of the *Illinois Staats-Anzeiger*, published at Springfield, with a view to reaching German-American readers. Angle, *New Letters and Papers of Lincoln*, 204–205. Barton, *Life of Abraham Lincoln*, I, 416 ff.

4 *Works*, VI, 32.

5 "I am not ashamed to confess that . . . I was a hired laborer, mauling rails, at work on a flatboat—just what might happen to any poor man's son." Speech at New Haven, Conn., Mar. 6, 1860, *ibid.*, V, 361.

6 "I do not think that New Salem scenery . . . had much to do with Lincoln: he had no sense of the beautiful in the *physical* world but had in the *moral* world." Herndon to Bartlett, Aug. 22, 1887, MS., Mass. Hist. Soc.

he "only corrected his speeches—made them talk as he had talked on the stump." [1]

> . . . When he rose [wrote Herndon] to speak to the jury or to crowds of people he stood inclined forward—was awkward—angular—ungainly— odd . . . ; he was a diffident man, somewhat, and a sensative one, and both of these added to his oddity—awkwardness . . . as it seemed to me. Lincoln had confidence, full and complete confidence in himself, ... Lincoln's voice was, when he first began speaking, shrill—squeaking—piping—unpleasant: his general look—his form—his pose—the color of his flesh wrinkled and dry, his sensativeness & his momentary diffidence, everything seemed to be against him, but he soon recovered. I can see him now— in my mind distinct. On rising to address the jury or the crowd he . . . generally placed his hands behind him, the back part of his left hand resting in the palm of his right hand. As he proceeded and grew warmer he moved his hand to the front of his person, generally interlocking his fingers and running one thumb around the other. Sometimes his hands, for a short while, would hang by his side. In still growing warmer as he proceeded in his address he used his hands—especially and generally his right hand in his gestures: He used his head a great deal in speaking, throwing or jerking or moving it now here and now there—now in this position and now in that, in order to be more emphatic—to drive the idea home. Mr Lincoln never beat the air—never sawed space with his hands—never acted for stage effect—was cool—calm, earnest—sincere—truthful—fair—self possessed—not insulting—not dictatorial—was pleasing—good natured, had great strong naturalness of look, pose, and act—was clear in his ideas— simple in his words—strong, terse and demonstrative: [2] he spoke and acted to convince individuals and masses: he used . . . his right hand, sometimes shooting out that long bony forefinger of his to dot an idea or to enforce a thought, resting his thumb on his middle finger. Bear in mind that he did not gesticulate much and *yet* . . . every organ of his body was in motion and acted with ease—elegance and grace—so it all looked *to me*
>
> As Mr Lincoln proceeded further . . . , if time—place—subject and occasion admitted of it, he . . . gradually warmed up—his shrill— squeaking—piping voice became harmonious, melodious—musical, . . . with face . . . aglow: his form dilated—swelled out and he rose up a splendid form, erect straight and dignified: he stood square on his feet with both legs up and down, toe even with toe— . . . he did not put one foot before an other: he kept his feet parallel and close to and not far from each other. When Mr. Lincoln rose up to speak, he rose slowly—steadily— firmly: he never moved much about on the stand or platform when speak-

1 Herndon to Bartlett, July 11, 1887, MS., Mass. Hist. Soc.

2 In the word "demonstrative" here, Herndon seems to have had in mind the quality of one who demonstrates, the habit being informative or explanatory as to one's meaning.

ing, touching no desk—table—railing: he ran his eyes slowly over the crowd, giving them time to be at ease and to completely recover himself, ... He frequently took hold with his left hand, his left thumb erect, of the left lapel of his coat, keeping his right hand free to gesture in order to . . . clinch an idea. In his greatest inspiration he held both of his hand [sic] out above his head at an angle of about fifty degrees—hands open or clinched according to his feelings and his ideas. If he was moved in some indignant and half mad moment against slavery or wrong . . . and seemed to want to tear it down—trample it beneath his feet and to eternally crush it, then he would extend his arms out, at about the above . . . angle with clinched big, bony, strong hands on them—. If he was defending the right—if he was defending liberty—eulogizing the Declaration of Independence, then he extended out his arms—palms of his hands upward somewhat at about the above degree—angle, as if appealing to some superior power for assistance and support; or that he might embrace the spirit of that which he so dearly loved. It was at such moments that he seemed inspired, fresh from the hands of his creator. Lincoln's gray eyes would flash fire when speaking against slavery or spoke volumes of hope and love when speaking of Liberty—justice and the progress of mankind— [3]

VII

In days when lyceums were a prominent feature of intellectual life Lincoln took briefly to the lecture platform, but most of the contemporary comments on this phase are disparaging or even devastatingly unfavorable. The lecture that Lincoln fixed up for the purpose was the one on "Discoveries, Inventions, and Improvements" which has already been noted; [1] he delivered it in Springfield and other Illinois towns in 1858, 1859, and 1860. One of his hearers at Pontiac, Illinois, in January 1860 observed that Lincoln was a "Big Gun" in the political world, but that the "people . . . were disappointed" in the performance. [2] In Bloomington, about a year before his nomination for the presidency, Lincoln actually refused to give a scheduled lecture because on arriving to do so he found too scant a crowd. [3]

---

[3] Herndon to Bartlett, July 19, 1887, MS., Mass. Hist. Soc.

[1] See above pp. 19–20.

[2] "Gus" to Mary P. Christian, Pontiac, Ill., Jan. 28, 1860 (MS. owned by Jewell F. Stevens of Chicago), in Harry E. Pratt, *Concerning Mr. Lincoln*, 21–22. Later in the letter the writer reveals himself as a great admirer of Stephen A. Douglas. "Gus" has been identified as Augustus W. Cowan; see *Abr. Lincoln Quart.*, III, 150 (Sep., 1944).

[3] Writing from Bloomington, Illinois, to his father on May 19, 1860, J. H. Burnham recalled that "one year ago" Lincoln had been advertised to lecture at Bloomington

Herndon's explanation of Lincoln's venturing into the lecture field was that he felt hurt by his "failure" as inventor [4] and eulogist [5] and by his frustrated attempt to pick up the German and Latin languages "by some short cut," but, thought Herndon, he "had none of the elements of a lecturer." These efforts, said Herndon, before "the elite and cultured" were "utter failure and very disappointing: they went the way of his Clay eulogy." Though the lecturer "thought so much of one of these efforts" that he presented a copy as a friendly remembrance, Herndon reported that "Lincoln's friends were deeply and thoroughly mortified at all of these efforts." [6] Yet in its main content and in the pithy phrasing of some of its passages, the lecture when read today carries real significance. [7]

VIII

Lincoln's character was treated at great length by Joseph Gillespie of Edwardsville, Illinois, whose association with the Illinois leader went back to the time (1840–41) when they were fellow members of the state legislature. From this portrait we gather that he was "genial but not very sociable," "ambitious but not very aspiring," skillful in story telling yet thinking his debate with Douglas "too grave & serious"

"on *Invention,* . . . admittance 25 cts." He added: "I paid a quarter and went early . . . . It was a beautiful evening, and the lecture had been well advertised but . . . only about 40 persons were present, and old Abe would not speak to such a small crowd, and they paid us back our quarters at the door." *Journal,* Ill. State Hist. Soc., XXVIII, 95–97 (April, 1935).

[4] In 1849, with his continuing interest in river navigation, Lincoln patented a device for "buoying vessels over shoals" by means of adjustable air chambers. The patent, no. 6469, was dated May 22, 1849. Lincoln's model can be seen at the National Museum (Smithsonian Institution) in Washington; for illustration, see Tarbell, I, facing p. 226. The inventor's detailed specification, with mechanical drawing, has been supplied to the author by the U. S. Patent Office.

[5] At Springfield on July 6, 1852, Lincoln delivered a eulogy on Henry Clay. See *Works,* II, 155–177, where the address is misdated July 16.

[6] Herndon memorandum entitled "Lincoln's Ambition . . . [etc.]," (on pension office letter head, some time in the eighties), pp. 15–16, Herndon-Weik MSS. At another time Herndon wrote of Lincoln's lecture: "it was a failure—utter failure." Herndon to Lamon, Mar. 6, 1870, p. 8, MS., Huntington Lib.

[7] This is no more than the observation of the present writer; disparagement of this "effort" by Lincoln has been the stock comment. The lecture was uneven. Rather prosy throughout, it combined well written passages with an occasional banal or mistakenly humorous remark—e. g., a reference to Adam and Eve sharing in "the getting up of the apron," as showing that "the very first invention was a joint operation." *Works,* V, 106. Despite its unfavorable reception the lecture has meaning to one who would study the trends of Lincoln's thought on the eve of his nomination to the presidency.

for such levity. "He did not seek company but when he was in it he was the most entertaining person I ever knew." In "the discussion of great questions," said Gillespie, Lincoln thought "nothing adventious [*sic*] should be lugged in as a make weight. That was contrary to his notions of *fairness*." He was a man of comfortable means,[1] but did not reach out for easy gains in land speculation as did Judge Davis. His children "ran over him"; he was "powerless to resist their importunities." Gillespie had "seen him on several occasions display great heroism." He was sensitive where he thought he had fallen short, as when he "was pitted by the Whigs in 1840 to debate with Mr. Douglas."[2] Conscious of his failure and deeply distressed, he "begged to be permitted to try it again" and Gillespie had "never heard . . . such a triumphant vin[di]cation . . . ."

The importance of his homely origin in the molding of his outlook and in the shaping of his conversation is borne out by Gillespie's description. He was "never ashamed of the poverty and obscurity of his early life," was "master of . . . frontier life and woods craft," full of anecdote of "boyish days amongst his country playfellows," and had "the happiest faculty of turning . . . reminiscences to good account." "He never missed the nib of an anecdote. He always maintained . . . that the best stories originated with Country boys & in the rural districts. He had great faith in the strong sense of Country People and he gave them credit for greater inteligence [*sic*] than most men do. . . . Mr. Lincoln had more respect for & confidence in the masses than any statesman this Country has ever produced He told me in the spring of 1864 that the People were greatly ahead of the poloticians . . . . He prized the suggestions of . . . unsophistocated People more than what was called statecraft . . . ." Mr. Gillespie continued:

. . . Mr. Lincoln could hardly be considered a genius, a poet, or an inventor but he had the qualities of a reformer He endeavored to bring back things to the old landmarks but he never would have attempted to

---

[1] Treated with a wealth of detail in *The Personal Finances of Abraham Lincoln*, by Harry E. Pratt.

[2] It is of interest to think of Lincoln as debating against Douglas at so early a period, though this phase has received little attention. As to pitting him against Douglas "in 1840" the reference is to the preliminary campaign for 1840. The Whig state central committee arranged two weeks of debates in November and December of 1839, in which Lincoln and Douglas were antagonists. Harry E. Pratt, *Lincoln, 1840–1846*, xii.

invent and compose new systems He had boldness enough when he found the building rocked and going to decay to restore it to its original design but not to contrive a new & distinct edifice He believed that the framers of our government expected slavery to die out and adapted the system to that end but that their views were being frustrated by adventitious circumstances by which we were surrounded . . . . He contended that we were more indebted to our government than it was to us and that we were not entitled to greater credit for our liberality of sentiment on political questions than others equally liberal who were born and raised under less favorable auspices. . . .

Tracing further the Gillespie Lincoln, if we may so call it (for Gillespie's accounts were full and circumstantial), we find a man "contemplative rather than speculative," "fond of astronomy . . . and mechanical science," anxious "to trace out the source and development of language," [3] touched with "a slight tinge of fatalism," "a believer in destiny," one who put trust "more in Divine power than in human instrumentality." He "had a remarkably inquiring mind . . . [which] roamed over the whole field of knowledge . . . with special interest [in] those which were of a practical character . . . [with] a solid and indisputable basis." Being "undemonstrative," his salient traits were not perceived at first acquaintance; hence he was "sometimes misunderstood." He "would rather disoblige a friend than do an act of injustice to a political opponent." His never failing anecdotes were both humorous and illustrative; the application was perfect, yet entertainment was also the motive. Clearness and simplicity of statement he "cultivated with . . . assiduity." Logic appealed to him more than ornament; his forte was "an immense stock of common sense." "Mr. Lincoln was a great common man," "the representative of the unsophisticated People." [4]

Perhaps a man is never great to his valet. Herndon had at times served almost as Lincoln's caddie [5] (though such a statement conveys no idea of Lincoln's generous and partnerlike attitude towards him); yet in the close-up view, if we can trust his later accounts, the younger

---

[3] In his lecture on discoveries and inventions (above pp. 19–20) Lincoln paid a good deal of attention to language as a human invention.

[4] Gillespie to Herndon, Dec. 8, 1866, Herndon-Weik MSS. Gillespie's letters to Herndon in this period are carefully written accounts. They constitute thoughtful monographs on Lincoln's character by one who knew him well, writing not long after his death.

[5] Referring to a debate which Lincoln had in 1844 with John Calhoun on the tariff, Herndon wrote "I heard this discussion—'toated books' & 'hunted up authorities' for Lincoln, as I did in law." Herndon to Lamon, Mar. 6, 1870, p. 15. MS., Huntington Lib.

man saw always the soul and spirit of the older. Lincoln was Herndon's great enthusiasm. That he idolized and worshiped the man of "mystery" whom he "knew well," is beyond doubt. When writing on Lincoln he would burst into a tribute as if a spring of deep feeling were released. Emphasizing Lincoln's plainness and admitting his faults, he also repeatedly stressed what he thought his greatness. Whatever might have been Lincoln's changing aspects, Herndon saw him "through all situations, positions & conditions . . . one and the same—ever honest, & simple, & sincere . . . a primitive type of character . . . ." [6] He found him "incapable of falsehood—of base deception or of fraud"; [7] *"humble—tender—forbearing—liberal— . . . tolerant . . . ."* [8] "Lincoln," he said, "rose over so many disadvantages that he seems to me a hero . . . ." [9] "Mr. L's life is a sweet —clear—clean—manly noble life." [10] Lincoln was "a great man," [11] "truly a noble man." [12] Herndon considered him "Christ like" in his charity and liberality. [13]

IX

It would require deep understanding to depict Lincoln, thought Herndon. It could not be done with superficial strokes: "he was Lincoln and Lincoln alone, and none exactly like him." "Mr. Lincoln," he said, "thought too much and did too much for America and the world to be crammed into an epigram or shot off with a single rocket: he was too close to the touch of the divine everywhere and too near to the suggestions and whisperings of nature for such quick work, done with a flash." [1] He did not want Lincoln retouched by over-friendly art or too-refined portraiture. "Mr. Lincoln can stand un-staggeringly up beneath all *necessary* or other truths." [2]

---

[6] Herndon to Charles H. Hart, July 22, 1866, *ibid.*
[7] Herndon to Lamon, Mar. 6, 1870, p. 12, *ibid.*
[8] Though Herndon almost outdoes himself here in the piling up of adjectives, his choice of words is significant. Herndon to F. B. Carpenter, Dec. 11, 1866, Herndon-Weik MSS.
[9] Herndon to Lamon, Mar. 6, 1870, MS., Huntington Lib.
[10] Herndon to Hart, July 22, 1866, *ibid.*
[11] Herndon to Bartlett, June 24, 1887, MS., Mass. Hist. Soc.
[12] Herndon to Bartlett, July 8, 1887, *ibid.*
[13] Herndon to Hart, Dec. 28, 1866, MS., Huntington Lib.
[1] Herndon to C. O. Poole, Jan. 5, 1886, Herndon-Weik MSS.
[2] Herndon to Hart, Nov. 26, 1866, MS., Huntington Lib.

In Herndon's view his partner was always growing. "Lincoln," he said, "had not arrived, when he was assassinated, at the meredian of his intellectual power." [3] "Mr. Lincoln had not arrived at maturity in 1865 . . . ." [4] "He grandly rose up . . . and this is . . . why I say that Lincoln was not fully developed . . . he may have just entered the field of his . . . intellectual power . . . ." [5]

Such were his moods that he would sometimes pass by his friends unnoticed on the streets; to Herndon this did not matter, except that he "felt for him" in moments of suffering. [6] He was "sad and cheerful by turns—he was good natured generally, but it was terrible to see him mad"; [7] ". . . a gloomy man at one moment and a joyous man the next." [8] Herndon often repeated that he was unknown, "a big mysterious man," a puzzle to friends and neighbors, a "hidden man" who kept his secrets, a man of "deep prudences," a man to admire but "hard to get at." [9] Yet Lincoln's moods did not overwhelm or engulf him; they are rather to be regarded as among the elements blended in that composite which became his character. If he achieved serenity, he did not come by it easily. His philosophy, which gave steadiness to a sensitive, troubled nature, was chiefly a reliance on the working of elemental and eternal laws; his "patience sprang from his philosophy —his calm quiet waiting on the events of the times—his coolness . . . —his charity . . . and . . . want of malice." [10]

Viewed in retrospect the rise of Abraham Lincoln to influence and leadership was no inscrutable mystery. Given the conditions, the result was natural and logical. Politically, as will appear in later pages, the man was "available." He had distinctiveness—oddness perhaps, but without unfortunate eccentricities. He had no antagonisms, no attachment to special interests; yet he had character. He came from

---

[3] Herndon to Bartlett, June 24, 1887, MS., Mass. Hist. Soc.

[4] Herndon to Bartlett, Aug. 7, 1887, ibid.

[5] Herndon to "My Friend," (probably Truman H. Bartlett) Aug. 16, 1887, ibid.

[6] It is not feasible fully to present Herndon's analysis of Lincoln's sadness. In part the junior member of the firm attributed the man's suffering to domestic unhappiness, but, as this was somewhat of an obsession with Herndon, and as he confessed himself mystified, it is hard to know what degree of value to put upon this explanation as a matter of authentic biography. See below, chap. iii.

[7] Herndon to Bartlett, July 8, 1887, MS., Mass. Hist. Soc.

[8] Herndon to Bartlett, June 24, 1887, ibid.

[9] Quoted phrases are culled from manuscript letters written by Herndon: to Bartlett, Aug. 22, 1887; to Poole, Jan. 5, 1886; to Lamon, Mar. 6, 1870; to Hart, Dec. 28, 1866.

[10] Herndon to Weik, Feb. 25, 1887, Herndon-Weik MSS.

a large and "doubtful" state, from a broad section whose votes in 1860 were to be decisive of the outcome. He had a log-cabin origin, though this was less of an asset than has been usually supposed; he had also a peculiar reputation for honesty and a flair for appealing to what was fundamentally and basically American. If one takes a cue from Frederick Jackson Turner, Lincoln embodied the West when the West was the most characteristically American of the sections. From the great prairie environment [11] he had drawn his strength. In western campaigning he had developed aptness in assimilating the subject matter of politics and skill in the art of public appeal. His apprenticeship had been served, not chiefly in office (save as state legislator and briefly as congressman), but on the law circuit, the hustings, the political forum.

He was no stranger to the arts of rhetoric. No one could rightly call his speeches crude; on the contrary they sometimes rose to the height of literary mastery, though in familiar conversation and informal utterance he lapsed into colloquialisms. Not offending the scholar, his addresses seized the understanding of the man in the street. He had his own style, his special tang. In all his careful expression there was simplicity combined with distinction, an economy of competently chosen words, an easy flow of sentences, and a readiness in epigram which served well in the place of brilliant scintillation. Some of his statements have that unerring quality of hitting the target that stamps them as proverbs or aphorisms.

The tricks of the agitator or demagogue were foreign to Lincoln's nature. He avoided emotional harangues. This avoidance was total; his manner was not that of the rabble rouser, the passionate orator, the professional patrioteer. There was in Lincoln more of Euclid than of Demosthenes. He kept on a conservative keel, yet managed to infuse into his leadership enough stirring enthusiasm to rally the reformer and to make a campaign seem a crusade for a cause. Few leaders were less given to sentimentalism; few were more concerned with reason and mental testing. Though it cramped his soul to operate within the limitations of a party, and though as candidate he was to be everyone's game, he appreciated the meaning of statesmanship. He was

---

[11] Middle western intellectual life and culture are well treated in H. C. Hubbart, *The Older Middle West, 1840–1880;* see also *Democracy in the Middle West, 1840–1940,* ed. by Jeannette P. Nichols and J. G. Randall.

made of better stuff than that of politicians reaching out for the spoils of office. In later pages the devastating storm of sectional conflict usurps the theme, but no understanding of Lincoln in the days of his coming ordeal will be complete without envisaging the man he was and viewing his qualities against the quiet background of peace within which he had developed for fifty years.

CHAPTER III

THE HOUSE ON EIGHTH STREET

THE tangled story of Lincoln's courting of Mary Todd and the years of their married life are themes that call for more than common historical caution. In much of the writing concerning these matters regard for Lincoln often coexists with gross unfairness toward his wife. To do simple justice to that wife, and by honest inquiry to restore a kind of balance in the use of what evidence we have concerning this American home, is the plainest duty of a biographer.

I

Mary's story began amid genteel and well favored surroundings. Aristocratic background, ambition, conversational skill, and a vivid interest in politics, were attractively combined in the person of this Springfield belle.[1] Coming of a socially prominent and distinguished family of Lexington, Kentucky, she lived in the fine mansion of her brother-in-law, Ninian Wirt Edwards, son of Governor Ninian Edwards. That she and Lincoln should become acquainted was inevitable; it belonged to the natural course of events that she should know men of political prominence at the capital.[2] Douglas also was of

[1] On Mary Todd Lincoln one should read (in addition to the leading biographies of Lincoln) Katherine Helm, *The True Story of Mary, Wife of Lincoln;* W. A. Evans, *Mrs. Abraham Lincoln: A Study of Her Personality* . . . ; Gamaliel Bradford's well drawn portrait in *Wives;* William H. Townsend, *Lincoln and His Wife's Home Town;* and *Mary Lincoln: Wife and Widow,* by Carl Sandburg and Paul M. Angle. In the Sandburg-Angle volume one finds a sympathetic and readable account buttressed by numerous documents.

[2] "In our little coterie in Springfield, in the days of my girlhood, we had a society of gentlemen, who have since, been distinguished . . . in the political world. My great and glorious husband comes *first* . . . . Douglas, Trumbull, Baker, Hardin, Shields, such choice spirits, were the habitués, of our drawing room." Mary Todd Lincoln to Mrs. Gideon Welles, Dec. 6, 1865, Welles MSS.

her circle, though emphasis on his seeking her hand has probably been overdone.

Study of the Lincoln-Todd courtship is rendered difficult by inadequacy of contemporary evidence and by the unreliable nature of the account by Herndon. Herndon's amazing recital reads as follows:

The time fixed for the marriage was the first day in January, 1841. Careful preparations for the happy occasion were made at the Edwards mansion. The house underwent the customary renovation; the furniture was properly arranged, the rooms neatly decorated, the supper prepared, and the guests invited. The latter assembled on the evening in question, and awaited in expectant pleasure the interesting ceremony of marriage. The bride, bedecked in veil and silken gown, and nervously toying with the flowers in her hair, sat in the adjoining room. Nothing was lacking but the groom. For some strange reason he had been delayed. An hour passed, and the guests as well as the bride were becoming restless. But they were all doomed to disappointment. Another hour passed; messengers were sent out over town, and each returning with the same report, it became apparent that Lincoln, the principal in this little drama, had purposely failed to appear! The bride, in grief, disappeared to her room; the wedding supper was left untouched; the guests quietly and wonderingly withdrew; the lights in the Edwards mansion were blown out, and darkness settled over all for the night. What the feelings of a lady as sensitive, passionate, and proud as Miss Todd were we can only imagine—no one can ever describe them. By daybreak, after persistent search, Lincoln's friends found him. Restless, gloomy, miserable, desperate, he seemed an object of pity. His friends, Speed among the number, fearing a tragic termination, watched him closely in their rooms day and night. "Knives and razors, and every instrument that could be used for self-destruction were removed from his reach." [3]

The necessary point of departure is to go to Herndon's source. In 1840–41 he was not yet associated with Lincoln in the practice of law, and was not of the Edwards circle. He makes no claim to have been present on the alleged occasion he glibly described, but got his material, or rather an inadequate cue, many years later from Mrs. Ninian W. Edwards, Mary Todd's sister, who seems to have made three statements on the subject in two interviews with Herndon and one with Weik. In her first statement her words as recorded in Herndon's handwriting were: "Lincoln & Mary were engaged—Every thing was ready & prepared for the marriage—even to the supper &c—. Mr. L. failed to meet his engagement—Cause insanity."

---

[3] *Herndon's Life of Lincoln,* Angle ed., 169–170.

A number of years later, Mrs. Edwards made a second statement to Herndon, which also is available only in his handwriting. This time she referred to "the match" being "broken off," but said nothing of a non-appearing bridegroom on a wedding occasion.[4] Her statement to Weik appears as follows in Weik's diary of December 20, 1883: "Called on N. W. Edwards and wife. Asked about marriage Mary Todd to Lincoln—Mrs. E. said arrangements for wedding made—even cakes baked but Lincoln failed to appear. At this point Mr. Edwards interrupted—cautioned wife she was talking to newspaper man—she declined to say more—had said Mary greatly mortified by Mr. Lincoln's strange conduct. Later were reunited—finally married." [5]

There is also a vague record by Weik of recollections in later life by James H. Matheny, who, as Weik said, was one of Lincoln's "two best men." In this passage, which is poorly constructed as a historical treatment, it may be Weik rather than Matheny who states that the "marriage was originally set for a day in the winter of 1840–41, probably New Year's Day," but that Lincoln "failed to materialize at the appointed time." [6]

Such is Herndon's statement and such his evidence. All of it comes through indirectly; none was even approximately contemporary. Many who must have known whether such an event had occurred seem not to have been sought out or questioned. Mrs. Edwards's account came no nearer to the picturing of an actual wedding party than the statement that "Every thing was ready & prepared for the marriage—even to the supper &c—," and the later statement (attributed to her by Weik) that "arrangements for wedding [were] made—even cakes baked but Lincoln failed to appear." Her story stops short of Herndon's narrative in that she makes no mention of invitations issued, of guests assembled, of the bride "bedecked," of her grief, of the untouched wedding supper, of messengers sent out over town, of the guests' wondering departure after hours of waiting. These details are made up; they are fictional embellishments supplied for the Herndon-Weik biography.

---

[4] Mrs. Edwards's first statement, undated, was made before 1872; it appears in the Lamon biography published in that year, Lamon having acquired Herndon's material. Her second statement is dated Sept. 27, 1887, and then apparently changed to July 27. Herndon-Weik MSS. These statements attributed to Mrs. Edwards have a greater vagueness as to date than is common in the Herndon papers.

[5] Jesse W. Weik, *The Real Lincoln: A Portrait*, 63.

[6] *Ibid.*, 59–60. (Weik gives the misspelling "Matheney.")

It is obvious that Herndon did not assemble all the material he might easily have found, nor did he rightly use the material he had. In his papers there is a record of a statement by Ninian W. Edwards commenting on Lincoln's courtship with Mary Todd and telling how Lincoln loved Matilda Edwards [7] (of which, however, the alleged lover gave no hint directly or indirectly!), how the engagement with Miss Todd was broken in consequence, and how Mary released Lincoln, who "went crazy as a *loon*." [8] In this statement, however, there was a significant omission; there was no mention, not even the faintest suggestion, of a wedding occasion and an absent groom. Herndon also had a statement by Lincoln's friend James H. Matheny representing Lincoln as being greatly distressed at being "driven into the marriage" with Miss Todd, but giving no hint of his absence at the time of a planned wedding, this in spite of the fact that Matheny was the man described by Weik as one of Lincoln's "two best men." [9]

II

With so much pen swinging on so thin a basis, no competent historian will accept as authentic the Herndon-Weik story of the wedding party and the defaulting groom. Weik's passage on his conversation with Matheny [1] is vague as to what Matheny actually said. Mrs. Edwards's testimony, aside from the fact that it only partially upholds Herndon's narrative,[2] is insufficient; it exists in a kind of vacuum; it stands unsupported in the complete absence of contemporary proof. Mr. Angle has pointed out that recollections of the matter involve flat contradictions of Herndon's statements, and that no marriage

---

[7] Cousin of Ninian W. Edwards; later married William Strong of Alton. The infatuation of Lincoln for Miss Edwards is without serious historical support; see Sandburg and Angle, *Mary Lincoln,* 335–336.

[8] Statement of Ninian W. Edwards, Sep. 22, 1865, from Lamon copy in Huntington Lib.

[9] Statement of James H. Matheny, May 3, 1866, *ibid.*

[1] *The Real Lincoln,* 59–60.

[2] All of Mrs. Edwards's statements are indirect. None are contemporary. The time elapsed between the alleged event and the record is about a quarter of a century. Of three statements which she is said to have made, only two—her first to Herndon and the one mentioned in Weik's diary (see above)—give even partial support to Herndon's narrative. Where her statements seem to offer limp support to Herndon they are uncorroborated by her husband and flatly denied by Mary's other sisters. Finally, on the whole subject of her testimony one must consider how a broken engagement or release could, after the passage of years, have become somewhat confused in her own mind, so that her reminiscence might clumsily have suggested a wedding default.

license was issued, "which would hardly have been the case had he [Lincoln] changed his mind at the last moment." [3]

Some might make light of the failure to take out a marriage license, or construe it as consistent with Lincoln's default. Yet the tale of that default, in conjunction with the known lack of a license, suggests a most excessive degree either of deception or of mental derangement. To suppose that a wedding was planned with Lincoln not fully intending to go through with it, to assume that that is why he took out no license, and to believe that he nevertheless permitted wedding plans to go forward to the assembling of guests on the appointed night as Herndon asserts, is to put a severe strain on the reader's credulity, a strain which becomes disbelief in the lack of substantiating evidence.

The fact that no license was issued, as shown by the records of Sangamon County,[4] does not in itself refute the wedding-default story, but it harmonizes with the complete absence of any known facts whatever as of 1840–41 tending to suggest that a wedding was arranged. This, however, is not all; the matter has importance in another sense, for it happens that in one of Herndon's effusive literary flourishes—a kind of rough draft for this portion of his biography— we have the following: "The time came on for Mr Lincoln & Miss Todd to be married. The license for their marriage was issued by the Clerk of the County Court. . . . The hour was set—the room where the ceremony of marriage was to be performed was . . . richly and gorgeously draped. . . . The cultured—the wealthy—the brilliant were there, merry and happy . . . . Parson Dresser had, as supposed the license in his hands— The brides maid and the groomsman were dressed and anxious to perform their part. . . . [etc.]" [5] The chief point of this whole business is that Herndon was drawing on his imagination, depending on no source for his details, yet supplying those details with fabricated minuteness. This particular mention of the issuing of the license was not given in his book; we are dealing here with an earlier draft; but so far as the wedding default

---

[3] *Herndon's Life of Lincoln*, Angle ed., xliv.

[4] In the old marriage records of Sangamon County, which the writer has consulted, the issuing of licenses and the solemnizing of marriages are duly entered. In the period of Lincoln's alleged wedding default there was no license issued to him; the only license to Lincoln was at the time of his marriage to Mary Todd, November 4, 1842.

[5] Herndon ms. fragment, "Lincoln & Mary Todd." Herndon-Weik MSS.

is concerned the passage was of a piece with his published biography; this detail was dropped, but others, equally the product of invention, were kept. Herndon, lawyer that he was, made this statement concerning a non-existent license "issued by the Clerk of the County Court," in precisely the same sense in which he invented other aspects of the alleged scene. The falsity of his statement as to the license is of significance in judging his credibility.

Persons close to the Edwardses and to Lincoln had no recollection to support Herndon's narrative. Mrs. Elizabeth J. Grimsley, cousin of Mary Lincoln, remembered only an interruption in the courtship due to Lincoln's depression; Mrs. John Todd Stuart had "never heard" of the alleged absent groom till Herndon brought out his book; Mrs. Joshua F. Speed likewise had "never heard" of it; Mrs. B. S. Edwards, sister-in-law of Ninian W. Edwards, declared it a "fabrication." Mary's surviving sisters emphatically denied it.[6] One of these sisters, Mrs. William Wallace of Springfield, née Frances Todd, said: ". . . he did not break off one wedding," adding that she "would have known of it" if such an incident had occurred.[7] One should note also the statement by Mary Todd's niece, Katherine Helm: ". . . Emilie Todd (Mrs. Ben Hardin Helm), Mary Todd's sister, who at this writing [1928] is living and possessed of all her faculties, declares Herndon's story to be absolutely false . . . ."[8]

Then there is the question of Lincoln's presence in the Illinois legislature in this unhappy period. Though his attendance during January 1841 has been referred to as showing "negligence,"[9] he was present at least for a time on nineteen of the twenty-six days when sessions were held that month. Such presence, including a number of votes, does not bear out the theory of "insanity." His record in these weeks falls short of his habitual punctuality, but his illness in this month would account for nearly all his absence, which has been greatly exaggerated and misrepresented. On the day known as "the fatal first of January, 1841," he was recorded present.[10] On this point again, we have an instance of the unreliability of Herndon; he stated

---

6 Tarbell, *Life of Lincoln*, I, 176 ff.

7 "Lincoln's Marriage: Newspaper Interview with Mrs. Frances Wallace, Springfield, Illinois, September 2, 1895" (privately printed pamphlet, 1917).

8 Katherine Helm, *Mary, Wife of Lincoln*, 90.   9 Beveridge, I, 289.

10 As to Lincoln's attendance the author has been assisted by an excellent memorandum supplied by Miss Margaret C. Norton, archives division, Illinois State Library.

that "Lincoln did not attend it [the legislature] for some weeks"; [11]
this is a flat misstatement.

An excellent basis for doubting that a wedding had been planned
as Herndon states is that Mary Todd made no mention of it in a letter
she wrote in mid-December of 1840 to her close friend Mercy Levering,
later Mrs. James C. Conkling. In this letter Mary gave details of what
went on in her own affairs and in the Edwards circle, mentioned
Lincoln and Speed, chatted of matrimony in general, and gave reports of newly married friends in particular. She had not written
to "Merce" for a considerable time and was giving news from "the
hill," by which she meant the Edwards home.[12] Her letter is nicely
phrased. It is spicy and refreshingly natural. Miss Todd had an air
in such things.

III

From the man who has been called Lincoln's most intimate friend,
Joshua Fry Speed,[1] we have another account of the troubled courtship
which Herndon misused. Since history is a matter of evidence, and
evidence a matter of statements by those who knew, the quality of
Herndon's history at this point is best revealed by first giving the
Speed statement and then noting how Herndon twisted it. We have
Speed's statement in the Herndon-Weik manuscripts. It is undated; it
is in Herndon's handwriting, not Speed's; it obviously belongs to the
period after 1865 in which Herndon was collecting his material; it
has all the appearance of being Herndon's record of an interview with
Lincoln's friend; it is a hasty job, less legible than Herndon's usual
hand; it is disjointed and hard to make out. It reads as follows:

In 1840 Lincoln went into the southern part [?] of the state as election
canvasser debater speaker— Here first wrote his *Mary*—she darted after
him—wrote him—Lincoln—seeing an other girl—& finding he did not
love his wife [*sic*] wrote a letter saying he did not love her—.
[Here the manuscript has the following insertion] Speed saw the letter
to "Mary" written by Mr Lincoln. Speed tried to persuade Lincoln to burn
it up. Lincoln said— "Speed I always knew you were an obstinate man. If

---

[11] Herndon ms. fragment, "Lincoln & Mary Todd," p. 17, undated, Herndon-Weik MSS.
[12] Sandburg and Angle, *Mary Lincoln*, 174-178. This letter (the original), along with
many other treasures, is in the collection of Oliver R. Barrett of Chicago.
[1] Robert L. Kincaid, *Joshua Fry Speed: Lincoln's Most Intimate Friend.*

you won't deliver it I will get some one to do it. I shall not deliver it nor give it to you to be delivered: Words are forgotten—misunderstood— . . . but once put your words in writing and they stand as a living & eternal monument against you. If you think you have *will* & manhood enough to go and see her and speak to her what you say in that letter, you may do that. Lincoln did go and see her—did tell her &c—Speed said—Lincoln tell me what you said and did"—Lincoln told him—Speed said—The last thing is a bad lick, but it cannot now be helped—Lincoln kept his promises and did not go to see her for months—they got together somehow.

[Here the insertion ends; the statement continues:]—tell the conversation—between Lincoln & Speed—Went to see "Mary"—told her that he did not love her—she rose and said "the deceiver shall be deceived wo is me"; alluding to a young man she fooled—Lincoln drew he[r] down on his knee—kissed her—& parted—he going one way & she an other—Lincoln did love Miss Edwards—"Mary" saw it—told Lincoln the reason of his change of mind—heart & soul—released him—[At this point there is a marginal insertion which reads as follows:] Lincoln went crazy—had to remove razors from his room—take away all knives and other such dangerous things—&c—it was terrible—was during the special session of the Ills Legislature in 1840 [End of marginal insertion] Lincoln married her for honor—feeling his honor bound to her— [2]

Turning now from Herndon's basis (his own account of the Speed interview) to the Herndon-Weik biography, we find a result both subtly and palpably different from the record. The biography has it as follows:

. . . One evening Lincoln came into our store and called for his warm friend Speed. . . . Lincoln, drawing from his pocket a letter, asked Speed to read it. "The letter," relates Speed, "was addressed to Mary Todd, and in it he made a plain statement of his feelings, telling her that he had thought the matter over calmly and with great deliberation, and now felt that he did not love her sufficiently to warrant her in marrying him. This letter he desired me to deliver. Upon my declining to do so he threatened to intrust it to some other person's hand. I reminded him that the moment he placed the letter in Miss Todd's hand, she would have the advantage over him. 'Words are forgotten,' I said, 'misunderstood, unnoticed in a private conversation, but once put your words in writing and they stand a living and eternal monument against you.' Thereupon I threw the unfortunate letter in the fire. 'Now,' I continued, 'if you have the courage of manhood, go see Mary yourself; tell her, if you do not love her, the facts,

---

2 For a reproduction of this statement from the Herndon-Weik collection (a print from a microfilm) the author is indebted to the division of manuscripts of the Library of Congress.

and that you will not marry her. Be careful not to say too much, and then leave at your earliest opportunity.' Thus admonished, he buttoned his coat, and with a rather determined look started out to perform the serious duty for which I had just given him explicit directions."

. . . Speed was satisfied, from the length of Lincoln's stay, that his directions had not been followed.

"Well, old fellow, did you do as I told you and as you promised?" were Speed's first words.

"Yes, I did," responded Lincoln, thoughtfully, "and when I told Mary I did not love her, she burst into tears and almost springing from her chair and wringing her hands as if in agony, said something about the deceiver being himself deceived." Then he stopped.

"What else did you say?" inquired Speed, drawing the facts from him.

"To tell you the truth Speed, it was too much for me. I found the tears trickling down my own cheeks. I caught her in my arms and kissed her."

"And that's how you broke the engagement," sneered Speed. "You not only acted the fool, but your conduct was tantamount to a renewal of the engagement, and in decency you cannot back down now."

"Well," drawled Lincoln, "if I am in again, so be it. It's done, and I shall abide by it." [3]

Immediately following this, Herndon gives the famous above-quoted narrative of the wedding party and the absent Lincoln.[4] The reader may compare the Speed statement with the account given in the Herndon biography. The Speed account presents a severed engagement, a painful scene in which Lincoln tried to break the troth only to find himself drawing Mary to him and kissing her, after which Mary, seeing his perplexity, "released" him. The biography, on the contrary, treats the incident not as a release but as a ratification of the engagement; only so could it have been used as setting for the story of the wedding default. The biography's comment that things "went on smoothly as before" is not justified by Speed's statement. Above all, Speed made no mention of Lincoln's wedding default. This is very significant; if such default had occurred Speed would certainly have known of it. He had a long correspondence with Lincoln on matters of the heart in this period, he was of the Edwards circle, and Lincoln made an extended visit to his home (Louisville, Kentucky) in 1841.[5]

Mrs. Edwards also referred to Mary's release of Lincoln. Her words

---

[3] Herndon's *Life of Lincoln*, Angle ed., 168–169.   [4] Above, p. 52.

[5] Having lived some years in Springfield, where he kept a store, Speed moved to Louisville in 1841. Beveridge, I, 317.

come to us thus: "The world had it that Mr L backed out and this placed Mary in a peculiar situation & to set herself right and to free Mr Lincoln's mind she wrote a letter to Mr L stating that she would release him from his engagements. . . . Mrs L told Mr L that though she had released him . . . yet she . . . would hold the question an open one—that is that she had not changed her mind, but felt as always." [6] The date and sequence of this release as mentioned by Mrs. Edwards are a bit vague, so that a Herndonian might ask: Could not the release have been given after Lincoln had failed to appear at the wedding? This would sound better if there were any proof that such default ever occurred. In the absence of proof such a query suggests a debater begging the question; it implies assent to the thing which remains to be proved. Among other factors, Mary's lack of resentment, for which there is supporting evidence, is difficult to reconcile with the absent-groom story. The fancy touches which Herndon gratuitously added must be borne in mind in any discussion of the subject.

What, then, did happen in this troubled courtship? Taking all the evidence we have and sifting it carefully, one is led to the picture of a severed engagement—not a troth rudely broken, but an episode in which Lincoln's painful struggle with doubt and Mary's reluctant yet unresentful release were the main factors. The incomplete history of the case does not hold together without that release. Lincoln's deep and shattering depression, which may have approached the stage of collapse and prostration, is evident in his own letters of the period. Writing to John Todd Stuart, January 23, 1841, he referred to himself as "the most miserable man living," [7] and in his letter to Speed on March 27, 1842, he used the expression "the fatal 1st of January, 1841," [8] which evidently referred to an acute crisis in the disturbed courtship. [9]

A letter which Lincoln wrote on January 20, 1841, to John Todd Stuart concerning Dr. Anson G. Henry, his physician, also bears upon the matter. Lincoln said: "I have within the last few days, been making

---

[6] Mrs. Edwards's first statement to Herndon, undated, Herndon-Weik MSS.

[7] *Works*, I, 159.   [8] *Ibid.*, I, 214.

[9] In "The Fatal First of January, 1841," by Mary Leighton Miles, *Journal*, Ill. State Hist. Soc., XX, 13–48 (1927), emphasis is placed on the lack of evidence concerning a wedding party, the absence of proof that invitations were issued, and the like. Attention is given to Lincoln's doings and writings in the period as belying the charge of insanity, and to the inaccuracies of various biographies concerning Lincoln's visit to the Speed home in 1841.

a most discreditable exhibition of myself in the way of hypochondriasm[?] . . . ." He considered Henry "necessary" to his "existence," and sought Stuart's influence to have the physician appointed postmaster at Springfield; otherwise he would leave the city. Stuart was at that time congressman and Lincoln's law partner. Lincoln added that his heart was "very much set" upon this appointment; he concluded as follows: "Pardon me for not writing more, I have not sufficient composure to write a long letter." [10] All the evidence is that Lincoln's condition was that of severe mental distress with accompanying effects upon his health, that the interrupted courtship was the cause of it, and that he was making a conscious and deliberate effort toward restoration of normal life.

IV

The renewal of the engagement in 1842 was assisted by Mary's friend, Mrs. Simeon Francis, wife of a prominent Springfield editor, the reconciliation [1] being related to Lincoln's generously taking the blame for a partisan newspaper skit which Mary and her friend Julia Jayne had perpetrated at the expense of a prominent Democratic politician, James Shields.[2] Writing to Mrs. Gideon Welles in the year of Lincoln's death, Mary Todd Lincoln recalled the Lincoln-Shields incident, in which a duel was arranged and its consummation narrowly averted, and gave interesting details concerning her relation to Lincoln prior to their marriage. ". . . I committed his [Shields's]

---

[10] Harry E. Pratt, "Dr. Anson G. Henry, Lincoln's Physician and Friend," *Lincoln Herald*, XLV, nos. 3 and 4 (1943). This letter of January 20, 1841, is not in the Nicolay-Hay edition of the *Complete Works*. See Angle, *New Letters and Papers*, 8–9.

[1] According to Mrs. Edwards, "Doctr [Anson G.] Henry who admired and loved Mr. Lincoln had much to do in getting Mary and Lincoln together again." Second statement of Mrs. Edwards, Sep. 27 [corrected as July 27], 1887, Herndon-Weik MSS.

[2] In these pages the near-duel between Lincoln and Shields, and the "Rebecca" letters related thereto, are not treated. For an analysis see Roy P. Basler, "The Authorship of the 'Rebecca' Letters," *Abr. Lincoln Quart.*, II, 80–90 (June, 1942). The letters, which appeared in the *Sangamo Journal* in 1842, were abusive of Democrats in general and James Shields in particular. (A curious type of duel was arranged on Shields's challenge and Lincoln's acceptance, but by amicable arrangement it was averted.) It is Basler's conclusion that Lincoln did not write the first and third letters, but did write the second, in which Shields was subjected to "ridicule and contumely" (*ibid.*, 81). He concludes also that "Lincoln . . . had been responsible for the publication of the fourth, written by Mary Todd and Julia Jayne, and hence when Shields demanded to know the author . . . , Lincoln's name was properly given" (*ibid.*, 89). Basler's critical investigation is a check upon the account given by Beveridge (I, 337 ff.).

follies, to rhyme," she wrote, "and very silly verses they were, . . . offensive to the Genl." With her customary surplus of commas Mary proceeded: "A gentleman friend, carried them off, and . . . one day, I saw them, strangely enough, in the daily papers. Genl Shields called upon the Editor, and demanded the author. The Editor, requested *a day,* to reflect upon it. The latter called upon Mr Lincoln, to whom he knew I was engaged & explained to him, that he was certain, that I was the Author. Mr. L. then replied, Say to Shields, that 'I am responsible.['] Mr. L. thought no more of it, when about two weeks afterwards, . . . Shields . . . demanded   satisfaction . . . ." There is here a reference to the planned duel and the reconciliation of the men. Mary added: "The occasion, was so silly, that my husband, was always so ashamed of it, that . . . we . . . agreed—never to speak of it . . . . This occurred, six months, before we were married . . . . We were engaged & greatly attached to each other—Two years before we were married." [3] When the wedding came it was a quiet affair in the Edwards home. The date was November 4, 1842. It was a ring-and-book ceremony conducted by the Episcopal minister, Charles Dresser. On the ring which Lincoln gave to Mary were inscribed the words: "Love is eternal."

V

Mr. and Mrs. Abraham Lincoln started their married life at the Globe Tavern in Springfield where room and board could be had for four dollars a week. Later they lived for a time in a modest cottage; in 1844 they acquired their residence on Eighth Street. It was a comfortable and dignified house, unpretentious but not lacking in architectural taste. In 1856 it was enlarged by the addition of an upper story.[1]

The humble setting at the outset of their wedded life contrasted strongly with the spacious living to which Mary Todd had been accustomed. The contrast was similar to that between their early environments. Where she had memories of being driven to Madame Mentelle's fashionable school by a liveried coachman in the Todd carriage,[2] his recollections were of lonely trips through a pioneer's

---

[3] Mary Todd Lincoln to Mrs. Gideon Welles, Dec. 6, 1865, Welles MSS.
[1] Pratt, *Personal Finances,* 87–88.
[2] W. H. Townsend, *Lincoln and his Wife's Home Town,* 61, 63.

woods to fetch water to the cabin. Beauty of clothes and furnishings, parties and entertainments, pride of family and social prominence, were the things that mattered to her; to the young man of backwoods origin these things were never to matter much or penetrate deeply into his consciousness.

"She is the very creature of excitement . . . and never enjoys herself more than when in society and surrounded by a company of merry friends" wrote a member [3] of the social group of Springfield in which Mary Todd had had a lively part. Her early letters bear out this description; they are full of vivid interest in people and affairs, with frequent italics to show her intensity of feeling. They are lightened with playful humor as when she refers to the two children of a widower suitor of hers as "his two *sweet little objections.*" [4] The slow-tongued young lawyer, by Mrs. Edwards's statement, hung upon her sparkling conversation as if fascinated.[5]

Mary Lincoln had the virtues of her defects. Along with outbursts of temper and emotion there was enthusiasm for undertaking and achievement, interest in dress and fashion, contagious zest for the color of life. Her qualities were complementary to those of her husband. She was to be a stimulus to him, even if at times that stimulus was somewhat of an irritant. His friends unanimously testify to his sadness, his periods of absent thought when he saw nothing around him. To his reflective mind she added vivacity; to his indifferent abstraction she brought a wholesome preoccupation with the affairs of daily living. Dependence on each other was reciprocal; she needed his reasoned statements, his seeing both sides of a question where she saw only one—her own, his tolerance and patience; these needs were to grow as her congenital lack of self-control increased.

They had their congenialities. Both loved politics with absorbing interest; both were politically ambitious. His advancement was their mutual aim in life. Each had a sense of literary style. Emilie Todd Helm tells of Mary reading and reviewing books for her husband and of his great respect for her judgment.[6] Both loved theatrical entertainment and never missed anything of the kind if they could help

---

[3] Sandburg and Angle, *Mary Lincoln,* 172–173.

[4] *Ibid.,* 183.

[5] First statement of Mrs. Ninian Edwards, undated, Herndon-Weik MSS.

[6] Helm, *Mary, Wife of Lincoln,* 108.

it.[7] Both idolized their children. These things became welding influences.

In its Springfield phase the life of these contrasting personalities
lasted more than eighteen years. In ten years Mary Lincoln bore four
sons: Robert Todd Lincoln on August 1, 1843; Edward Baker Lincoln on March 10, 1846; William Wallace Lincoln on December 21,
1850; Thomas ("Tad") Lincoln on April 4, 1853. When elected to
the presidency Lincoln had three sons, Edward having died in 1850.[8]

Lincoln's doings have become more a matter of record than Mary's.
For her, life was a strenuous round of childbearing, tending babies,
feeding and clothing a household, sewing, struggling with servants,
watching constantly to keep a suitable establishment, carrying on
alone when her husband was away on the circuit—in short enduring
the strains of any wife and mother. Lincoln, too, when in town, was
busy with home tasks; a neighbor recalled that "he kept his own
horse—fed & curried it—fed and milked his own cow: he sawed his
own wood generally when at home." [9]

These years saw some triumphs for Lincoln, some disappointments. Major episodes were his election to Congress in 1846, his defeat
for the senate in 1855 and 1858, and the supreme climax of his nomination for the presidency and election to that office. The house on
Eighth Street mirrored these events. It witnessed family reunions on
the occasions of the master's return from circuit travel. The furniture
—ornate iron stove, cut-glass prisms of the candlesticks on the mantel,
lady's chair designed with due allowance for hoop skirts, heavy lace
curtains, whatnot, hassocks, sofa, mirror, oval-framed pictures—
each of these objects, satisfyingly Victorian and suitable, as *Leslie's*
said, to "a gentleman in comfortable circumstances," had for the
Lincolns its personal history and its family association.

VI

The question of the happiness or unhappiness of the Lincolns has
been as controversial as the matter of the defaulting bridegroom.

---

[7] *Ibid.*, 119.

[8] Willie died in the White House February 20, 1862; Tad died in Chicago on July 15,
1871; Robert alone lived to manhood. After a prominent career in public office and
business, followed by many years of retirement, he died on July 26, 1926, without surviving male issue; Lincoln's name was not perpetuated in offspring.

[9] Statement of James Gourley, undated, Herndon-Weik MSS.

Herndon fixed the popular conception of this marriage as a tragically unhappy one, and of Mary Lincoln as an intolerable shrew. His descriptions of her stormy tongue and temper, her lack of self control, and her violence when in a rage are familiar not only in his own pages, but in countless authors who have followed him. The story which he tells of Lincoln's asking a man, who had been abused by Mrs. Lincoln, if he could not endure for a few minutes what he, Lincoln, had endured for fifteen years, alone would fix the whole concept of a miserable marriage in the reader's mind.[1] In the uninhibited language of the Herndon manuscripts this story has much more detail and vividness than in the biography, and one can better judge the nature of the evidence. According to this account, Lincoln was reclining on the counter in "Edwards' store" telling one of his best stories, when the man—his name was Tiger—called him outside, told him of Mrs. Lincoln's abuse punctuated with blows of her broom, and demanded that her husband do something about it; Lincoln then sadly asked the above question.[2] There is no evidence that Herndon was present on the occasion, but such a tale would quickly go the rounds among men who lingered in the store, then went home and told their wives.

Other incidents from the manuscripts may be mentioned briefly. A passerby and a neighbor witnessed Lincoln one day being pursued in his own backyard by "a little low squatty woman with a butcher knife in her hand." Noticing that other people were approaching, Lincoln unceremoniously carried his infuriated wife back into the house, rising to the occasion in action and language! Such is the story. Herndon claims not to have witnessed this incident of home life; he had it second-hand from a neighbor of the Lincolns named White- hurst, whose account is given only through Herndon's memory; though he dated the occurrence about 1857, same period as the Tiger story, he wrote his version in 1886.[3]

Again in 1857 (this must have been a bad year) Mary is alleged to have asked her abstracted husband three times to mend the fire; then, wrote Herndon, she "blazed away at Lincoln with a stick of stove wood"; when he appeared next day his nose was "fixed up with court

---

[1] *Herndon's Life of Lincoln*, Angle ed., 347–348.
[2] Herndon to Weik, Jan., 1887, Herndon-Weik MSS.
[3] Herndon to Weik, Jan. 23, 1886, *ibid.*

plaster." This tale came from a servant girl; Herndon added: ". . . it is more probable that it is true than untrue. I believe it: it went around among the members of the bar as true." [4]

There is no doubt that Mary Lincoln had an ungovernable temper. That she suffered in later life from temporary insanity is a matter of court record, but that was after life had dealt crushing and devastating blows. Dr. W. A. Evans, whose account is based on historical material medically interpreted, finds in her no breakdown of intellect, but rather a kind of excess, amounting at times to abnormality, in emotional reactions.[5] Dr. Evans's account is by no means entirely unfavorable; he gives her "first suspiciously false note" as of January 1861 in the matter of purchases in New York.[6] Mrs. Lincoln's physician, Thomas W. Dresser, son of the minister who married the Lincolns, also referred to her abnormality as belonging chiefly to the tragically clouded period of her later life. He wrote: "She was bright and sparkling in conversation . . . . Her face was animated and pleasing; and to me she was always an interesting woman; and while the whole world was finding fault with her . . . , it was clear to me that the trouble was a cerebral disease." [7]

Mrs. Lincoln's personality must be reconstructed from incomplete sources, with constant allowance for unfriendly testimony. Even so, much of that record, to say the least, is creditable. Scattered incidents of bad temper, indirectly transmitted and interpreted by a roughhewn mind disposed toward an unfavorable judgment, do not constitute the whole story of the Lincoln marriage. Things that made for content and affectionate adjustment rarely found their way into the record, especially as gathered by Herndon. Friends did not set pen to paper in order to report the normal, everyday incidents of this home. It is remembered that she was quick tempered, caustic, and tactless of speech; touchy, proud, and willful. It is too often forgotten that she was endowed with natural kindness, that she bore herself with gaiety and grace, that there was sparkle in her face and speech, that she rose to the standards of a gentlewoman, that rearing and education fitted her for cultured society, and that she brought a full measure of affection and devotion to the countless unrecorded duties of wife and mother.

[4] *Ibid.*
[5] W. A. Evans, *Mrs. Abraham Lincoln: A Study of her Personality* . . . [etc.].
[6] *Ibid.,* 158.   [7] Thomas W. Dresser to Weik, Jan. 3, 1889, Herndon-Weik MSS.

In a lengthy account of Mrs. Lincoln angrily dismissing her servant, Sarah, Herndon said, after telling of the hiring of Sarah, "Everything went on well for sometime, Mrs L bragging on her Sarah all the while to her neighbors & visitors." [8] Evidently there were intervals of tranquillity in the household. To Weik, his literary collaborator, he wrote: "Lincoln, you know, was not a social man, and hence those little *incidents* in his office and around his hearth which you want so much are hard to gather and to get, for they are few and far between." [9] It is well to observe that "few and far between," to note that these stories were usually second hand, and to question how much Herndon knew at first hand about that hearth. He said, "This woman was to me a terror," [10] "She was a tigress," [11] and again "She hates me yet *I can* and *will do* her justice." [12] Writing freely to Weik he filled pages with comments of which the following is an example: "This domestic *hell* of Lincoln's life is not all on one side"; [13] ". . . sometimes he would rise and Cut up the very devil for a while—make thing[s] more lively and 'get.' " [14]

To "do . . . justice" is not always the same as being just; to love the truth, which Herndon did in his way, is not synonymous with knowing and understanding it. Herndon's testimony is refracted by his own emotions and mentality. He disliked and feared Mary Lincoln, perhaps the more because of his love for her husband, whom he represented as the victim of her temper. With his frontier, earthy type of mind, he "was firmly convinced that truth could be got at by intuition, and he never doubted his own clairvoyant capacity." [15]

To go further and explain in full the mutual dislike between Herndon and Mrs. Lincoln, and to give the documents, would require too much space. Her background was aristocratic, his quite the opposite. In attitudes, tastes, and standards they were miles apart. As a radical abolitionist and as a man whose drinking habits led to occasional sprees, he was not likely to be regarded by her as the most suitable partner for her husband. One can point to at least one friendly incident. When Herndon, in the earlier stages of assembling

---

[8] Herndon to Weik, Jan., 1887, *ibid.*   [9] Herndon to Weik, Feb. 24, 1887, *ibid.*
[10] Herndon to Weik, Jan. 9, 1886, *ibid.*   [11] Herndon to Weik, Jan. 8, 1886, *ibid.*
[12] Herndon to Charles H. Hart, Nov. 26, 1866, MS., Huntington Lib.
[13] Herndon to Weik, Jan. 9, 1886, Herndon-Weik MSS.
[14] Herndon to Weik, Jan. 8, 1886, *ibid.*
[15] *Herndon's Life of Lincoln*, Angle ed., editor's preface, xxxviii.

material for his biography, sought Mrs. Lincoln's help, she took the trouble in the period of her crushing bereavement to write him a gracious and cordial letter, promising an interview, referring to her husband's "truly affectionate regard" for his partner, and adding that those who idolized him were "very precious" to her and hers.[16] By January of 1874, however, there had been a definite break between them, brought on by Herndon's lecture on Lincoln's religion, in December of 1873, in which he quoted her in a manner which she resented. She indignantly and flatly denied statements which Herndon attributed to her; Herndon published a spirited refutation of her denial; from then on their relation was that of open warfare.[17] In interpreting Herndon's above quoted statements—calling her a "tigress" and noting how she hated him—it is not easy for the historian to know how much of this feeling harked back to the days when the Lincolns lived in Springfield and how much stemmed from the open break of 1873–74, but since this complete break occurred many years prior to the publication of Herndon's famous book, one must remember that when as a biographer he dealt with Lincoln's wife, Herndon was writing of a woman toward whom he had been for a number of years definitely unfriendly.[18]

The statement of James Gourley, Lincoln's back-door neighbor for many years, as preserved in manuscript by Herndon, sums up the situation in the Lincoln household: "Lincoln & his wife got along tolerably well, unless Mrs L got the devil in her: Lincoln . . . would pick up one of his children & walked off—would laugh at her—pay no earthly attention to her when in that wild furious condition." His further comment is a bit of testimony that any

---

16 In his biography (Angle ed., 412) Herndon prints this letter with some editing. He omits a sentence in which Mrs. Lincoln asked the meaning of a tactless passage which Herndon wrote in a letter to Robert Lincoln, saying that he wanted to "do justice" to Mrs. Lincoln "so that the world will understand things better." The letter is in the Herndon-Weik collection, being dated at Chicago, August 28, but without the year; the Herndon biography gives it as 1866, but a study of the evidence makes 1865 seem perhaps more likely. See *Illinois State Journal*, Jan. 15, 1874, p. 3, c. 3.

17 Herndon's lecture appeared in the *Illinois State Register*, December 13, 1873. As stated in the Springfield *Illinois State Journal* of December 19, 1873, p. 1, c. 1, Mrs. Lincoln denied the statement Herndon attributed to her and also denied having had the conversation with him. The same paper of January 15, 1874, p. 3, cc. 3–4, contained a wordy rejoinder by Herndon in which he referred to the "spasmodic madness of her denial."

18 In this matter the author has been aided by Mr. David H. Donald, graduate assistant at the University of Illinois.

human being might be content to hear: "Mrs & Mr Lincoln were good neighbors." [19]

Mary's sisters, Mrs. Frances Wallace, who lived in Springfield, and Mrs. Emilie Todd Helm, who had ample association with the Lincolns on family visits, both made statements after the Herndon life had been published. Their reaction to Herndon's use of backdoor gossip can easily be understood. Mrs. Wallace said: "I don't see why people should say Mr. Lincoln's home life was not happy, for I certainly never saw a thing there that would make me think either of them was unhappy. He was devoted to his home, and Mrs. Lincoln thought everything of him. She almost worshiped him. . . . Why, she was devoted to him and to her children. And he was certainly all to her that any husband could have been." [20]

"They understood each other thoroughly," wrote Mrs. Helm, "and Mr. Lincoln looked beyond the impulsive words and manner, and knew that his wife was devoted to him and to his interests. They lived in a quiet, unostentatious manner. She was very fond of reading, and interested herself greatly in her husband's political views and aspirations. She was fond of home, and made nearly all her own and her children's clothes. She was a cheerful woman, a delightful conversationalist, and well-informed on all the subjects of the day. The present writer saw Mr. and Mrs. Lincoln together for some part of every day for six months at one time, but saw nothing of the unhappiness which is so often referred to." [21]

This testimony has been simmered over the gentle fire of family affection and loyalty, and the historian would prefer it raw, so to speak, but it is logical to use the evidence of those who were closest to the Lincoln family life.

In *Mary, Wife of Lincoln,* by Katherine Helm, Mrs. Helm's daughter, Mrs. Lincoln appears as a devoted wife who was proud of her husband, watched carefully over his health, saw that he was warmly or suitably dressed, had faith in him, and opposed her gay moods to his dark ones.

Life-like pictures flash out from Mrs. Helm's account as quoted by

[19] Statement of James Gourley, undated, Herndon-Weik MSS.

[20] Pamphlet newspaper interview with Mrs. Frances Wallace, September 2, 1895, privately printed, 1917.

[21] Emily [Emilie] Todd Helm, "Mary Todd Lincoln," *McClure's Magazine,* XI, 479 (Sep., 1898).

her daughter: Mary calling Mr. Lincoln back to wrap his throat in
a muffler, patting his arm with a little air of coquetry, wearing her new
dress of "white silk with blue brocaded flowers scattered over it." In
the latter incident, Mr. Lincoln had come home from his office to find
her dressed in this creation of her own fashioning, and had been reminded he also must change his clothes to go to the Edwards's supper
party. With a smile, he said, "Fine feathers enough on you to make
fine birds of both of us," and added, "Those posies on your dress are
the color of your eyes." Mary said to her sister "You see, Emilie, I
am training my husband to see color. I do not think he knew pink
from blue when I married him." [22]

VII

Both Herndon and Mrs. Helm agree that the Lincolns idolized
their children and spoiled them. Herndon gives several accounts of
Lincoln's bringing one or more of the boys to the office on a Sunday
morning while Mrs. Lincoln was at church. They pulled the books
out of the shelves, scattered legal papers, spilled ink, smashed pens,
and generally tore up the office. Herndon wrote: "I have felt many
& many a time that I wanted to wring their little necks and yet out
of respect for Lincoln I kept my mouth shut. Lincoln did not notice
what his children was doing or had done." [1]

The junior partner returns to the subject in another letter; again
he "wanted to wring the necks of these brats and pitch them out
of the windows." [2] One wonders if Herndon went to the office on
Sunday mornings to salvage what he could from the wreckage. Perhaps his silent endurance can be explained by this statement: "He
[Lincoln] worshipped his children and *what* they worshipped[;]
he loved what they loved and hated what they hated . . . ." [3]

It was Herndon who preserved the familiar picture of Lincoln hauling his babies in a little wagon up and down the pavement in front
of his house. A child would fall out, and lie squalling while the abstracted father pulled the wagon on, unaware of what was happening.[4]

"It was the habit—custom of Mrs Lincoln [wrote Herndon] when

---

[22] Helm, *Mary, Wife of Lincoln*, 109.
[1] Herndon to Weik, Nov. 19, 1885. Herndon-Weik MSS.
[2] Herndon to Weik, Jan. 8, 1886, *ibid.*   [3] Herndon to Weik, Feb. 18, 1887, *ibid.*
[4] Herndon to Weik, Nov. 19, 1885, *ibid.*

any big man or woman visited her house to dress up and trot out Bob—Willie or Tad and get them to monkey around—talk—dance —speek—quote poetry &c &c. Then she would become enthusiastic & eloquent over the children much to the annoyance of the visitor . . . ." [5] Herndon adds that Lincoln would make some remark about the children being "rareripes" but quickly states that he was proud of his children and blind to their faults.[6]

All the basic fulfillment of parenthood was in this marriage. Looking back, Mrs. Lincoln could write in later years, in one of her tender and loving letters to her daughter-in-law, that most mothers "consider that in the outset in life—a nice home—loving husband and precious child are the happiest stages of life." [7] In another letter of affectionate reminiscence she expressed indignation at the suggestion that she had ever whipped a child. "In the first place," she wrote, "*they* never required it. A gentle, loving word, was all sufficient with them . . . ." [8]

Old accounts of stores in Springfield bring the house on Eighth Street into near focus. They show Mrs. Lincoln busy with her needle; they suggest old-fashioned thoroughness in home dosing; they bring to mind in dry record the things that were worn, eaten, and used in this residence. Among the Lincoln purchases one reads of "5 yds. Drilling," "13½ yds. Muslin," "16 lbs. Batting," "10½ yds. French Chintz per Lady," "16 yds. Plaid Silk," "36 yds. Buff Linen," "Castor Oil," "Calomel," "Box Pills," "Bottle Vermifuge," "Syrup Ipecac," "1 pair Boys Boots by A. Lincoln," "1 pair Boys Boots per Lady," "2 doz. Whalebones," large purchases of wall paper, "1 pair White Gloves per Robert," "2 pair Heavy Drawers," "6 doz. Pearl Buttons," "1 paper Horse Powder," "8 lb. Turkey @ .10," "4 doz. Eggs @ .10," "6 Doz. Eggs @ 8⅓," "1 Hooped Skirt per Lady," "2 Barlow Knives," "10 cords of Wood," and numerous entries of such items as candles, thread, sugar, coffee, blacking, buttons, and matches.[9]

Hospitality in the Lincoln home was somewhat limited by circumstances, but O. H. Browning records on February 5, 1857, that he had attended a "large & pleasant party at Lincolns" that night.[10] Writing to her sister Emilie on the sixteenth of the same month, Mrs.

[5] Herndon to Weik, Jan. 8, 1886, *ibid.*
[7] Sandburg and Angle, *Mary Lincoln*, 299.
[9] Pratt, *Personal Finances*, 145 ff.
[6] *Ibid.*
[8] *Ibid.*, 231.
[10] Browning, *Diary*, I, 274.

Lincoln tells of giving a party, presumably the one Browning mentions, to which five hundred people had been invited, though, owing
to a rain and the counter attraction of a bridal party in Jacksonville,
only three hundred came.[11] Mrs. Lincoln's pride and satisfaction in
this party are evident in her letter. Isaac N. Arnold spoke in nostalgic
reminiscence of the dinners and evening parties at the Lincoln home,
the excellence of Mrs. Lincoln's table, the "cordial and hearty
Western welcome" of "both host and hostess," "her genial manners,"
and his "wit and humor, anecdote, and unrivalled conversation."[12]

VIII

A direct source for the relationship between Abraham and Mary
Lincoln is found in a series of four letters which they wrote each
other in the spring and summer of 1848 while he was in Washington
in Congress and she was visiting the Todd family in Lexington. Not
written for publication, they are the unstudied messages between a
husband and wife who had been married for more than five years; to
examine them is to let the couple themselves come back and testify
as to their marriage.[1]

In the first of these missives he tells her that when she was with him
he thought she hindered him somewhat from attending to business,
but since she left and he had nothing but business it had grown
"exceedingly tasteless" to him. He adds "I hate to stay in this old room
by myself." He shares her delight over Eddie's treasured baby words,
and tells of shopping for little plaid stockings for his young son. Mrs.
Lincoln's inability to get along with people is hinted when he says
"All the house—or rather, all with whom you were on decided good
terms—send their love to you— The others say nothing—" The following paragraph was written by an affectionate and considerate husband: "And you are entirely free from headache? That is good—good
—considering it is the first spring you have been free from it since

11 Sandburg and Angle, *Mary Lincoln*, 198–199.
12 Isaac N. Arnold, "Reminiscences of the Illinois-Bar Forty Years Ago . . . ," read
before "The Bar Association of Illinois," Springfield, Jan. 7, 1881 (in miscellany pub. by
Fergus Printing Co., Chicago), 137–138. This testimony, of course, must be taken with the
reservation that applies to all sentimental reminiscence.
1 The four letters are in Sandburg and Angle, *Mary Lincoln*, 186–194. Originals are in
the collection of Oliver R. Barrett. For Lincoln's letter of April 16, 1848, see illustration
accompanying this chapter.

"HERE I HAVE LIVED"

In the upper view (during the campaign of 1860) Lincoln stands inside the fence with Willie and Tad. Lower view shows Lincoln front parlor sketched by special artist and published in *Leslie's Illustrated Newspaper,* March 9, 1861.

CONGRESSMAN LINCOLN
TO HIS WIFE

From his boarding-house room in Washington, A. Lincoln writes to "Dear Mary" who is at Lexington, Ky. He puts in a bit of teasing; the whole letter breathes playful affection. He admits lonesomeness, refers to Mary's letters, and mentions "Dear Eddy" whose baby words he quotes. There were two Lincoln boys in 1848. "Don't let the blessed fellows forget father," he writes.

Original owned by Oliver R. Barrett

THE LINCOLN HOME TODAY

These views of the Lincoln home in our own time may be compared with the home in Lincoln's day, shown on another page. Both photographs by courtesy of Division of Parks [etc.], Department of Public Works and Buildings, State of Illinois.

we were acquainted— I am afraid you will get so well, and fat, and young, as to be wanting to marry again— Tell Louisa I want her to watch you a little for me— Get weighed and write me how much you weigh—" Daily happenings that she would be interested in complete the letter. He asks what Bobby and Eddie thought of "the little letters father sent them," and adds "Don't let the blessed fellows forget father—" He signs it "Most affectionately."

Her letter written two or more weeks later deals with family news and events with much tender detail about the children. There are hints of coquetry in her lines as there is indulgent fondness in his. She expresses her longing for him: "How much, I wish instead of writing, we were together this evening, I feel very sad away from you." She reassures him: "Do not fear the children, have forgotten you, I was only jesting. Even E- eyes brighten at the mention of your name."

His next letter hints at Mrs. Lincoln's shortcomings and reveals his own wish for their reunion: "The leading matter in your letter is your wish to return to this side of the Mountains. Will you be a *good girl* in all things, if I consent? Then come along, and that as *soon* as possible. Having got the idea in my head, I shall be impatient till I see you."

These are the normal letters of a husband and wife who were adjusted, loved each other, and had common aims and interests. He does not hesitate to remind her of the results of her lack of self-control—that was nothing new to either one—but in his light way of touching on such things he suggests his adjustment to them.

All in all, the house on Eighth Street sheltered a typical American family where father and mother were united by love of their children, common interests, ties of affection, and the pattern of daily family life. To the extent that her tempestuousness was abnormal, the marriage was rendered difficult, but the husband had accustomed himself to this imperfection as husbands—and wives—have been adjusting themselves to imperfections from the beginning. In the larger picture each gave to the other full fidelity and devotion. Mrs. Lincoln, writing to a friend in later life, could say, "It was always, music in my ears, both before & after our marriage, when my husband, told me that I was the only one, he had ever thought of, or cared for." [2]

---

[2] Mary Todd Lincoln to Mrs. Gideon Welles, Dec. 6, 1865, Welles MSS.

In the first year of her bitter widowhood, referring to the last three weeks of Lincoln's life, she wrote: "Down the Potomac, he was almost boyish in his mirth & reminded me, of his original nature, what I had always remembered of him, in our own home—free from care, surrounded by those he loved so well & by *whom*, he was so idolized." [3]

It was the destiny of the Lincolns to live the latest years of their married life in the pitiless ordeal of war, personal sorrow, and fiercely ungenerous publicity. In an unfriendly White House these cruel forces were to beat upon an ailing woman in her forties whose lack of emotional balance unfitted her for the strain; in different manner they bore upon a harried President whose deepening sadness was a matter of general comment. [4] It was well for them that their earlier years had not been without their meed of daily happiness.

Something of all that those years of married life had meant and a consciousness that a certain phase of life had closed, might well have been in Lincoln's mind when he came to speak the moving words of his farewell to Springfield on February 11, 1861. He referred to events of deep personal meaning, the birth of his children and the loss of little Eddie. His words suggest that other domestic joys and griefs were in the unexpressed mental picture of those years. His utterance seemed tinged with premonitory homesickness for something past which, in retrospect, he found good. [5]

---

[3] Sandburg and Angle, *Mary Lincoln*, 242.

[4] The life of the Lincolns in Washington will be treated in a later companion work.

[5] In the present chapter on the Lincolns it has not been deemed necessary to include any account of Lincoln and Mary Owens, or Lincoln and Ann Rutledge. For a critical study of the Ann Rutledge story, and for some reference to Mary Owens, see vol. II, appendix.

CHAPTER IV

NORTH AND SOUTH

THAT America, devoted to peace and busy with the affairs of a growing nation, should have become a snarling arena of internal conflict, however voluminously explained, is a matter whose "causes" seem unconvincing. It happened; otherwise it would seem incredible. Psychological and social forces that engendered conflict, untoward incidents that aggravated it, have often been presented. They have become tiresome. In any recital of such forces it is important to remember that, by a different selection of subject matter, exactly the same period could be represented as one of progress, peaceable endeavor, hope-filled activity, and daily living. It is a question of trying to see a period as it was with all its crowded factors, instead of reading back from a later day and seeing only elements of discord. The ugly fate that showed itself in the sixties has caused the fifties to be read in terms of sectionalism and strife. It was as if the saner activities of the nation, the main purpose and essence of its life, had gone for nothing.

The menace of sectional bickering was not wholly grasped until its forces had passed the point where sanity and reason could check them. Its patterns were distortions. Its types of thought and propaganda were negations of essential truth. It is only fairly recently that some of its abnormal intensities have been duly exposed.[1] America was many things: "The Greater New England, The Ohio Valley, The Old Northwest, The Blue Grass regions, The Lower South, The Southwest, and The Prairies." Though the regions were many, there were, as Avery Craven has pointed out, four principal ones: "The North-

[1] These factors of strife are marshaled, interpreted, and effectively presented in *The Coming of the Civil War*, by Avery Craven (1942).

east, The Old South, The Northwest, and The Southwest." [2] Steady advance to subdue the wilderness, to master and occupy the vast national domain, had "meant modifications in economic life." In their pioneering, in going back to "first processes," [3] in facing compelling tasks of social order in new environments, the men of expanding America had not merely copied the old. The inland North was not a replica of New England; Texas was not another South Carolina.

Yet patterns of actual life were overlooked. A nation of many diverse areas and groups was oversimplified into a concept of two sections. Then a further trick was played: the two sections were pictured as hopelessly antagonistic. It was not merely North *and* South; it was North *against* South. Southerners might have cultural and financial dealings with the North and with Europe through the North. Men of Boston might be unaware that Virginians and Georgians should be deemed enemies or human opposites. No matter: let politicians and agitators work on them with pamphlets, tracts, and campaign speeches, let the stock phrases of sectionalism be repeated often enough, and there would come a wretched day when, "to the astonishment of the actors themselves," an explosion would be set off by an incident or occasion that was not validly disruptive but "comparatively trifling." [4]

Influences making for peace were of the quieter sort. They were not a matter of blare and noise. They attracted insufficient attention. Alarms tending toward war, on the other hand, were loud and vociferous. Their appeal was not to reason. Their menace was in a kind of emotional unbalance. Their language was that of name calling, shibboleths, epithets, tirades. Such mental currents bore within themselves the power to upset normal life and to precipitate a major conflict that no majority in any section would have deliberately willed. One of the most colossal of misconceptions is the theory that fundamental motives produce war. The glaring and obvious fact is the artificiality of war-making agitation.

I

It was not for any solid validity in itself that sectional antagonism became ominous. In a whipped-up crisis it is not enough to offset

---

[2] *Ibid.*, 5.   [3] *Ibid.*   [4] *Ibid.*, 3.

fanaticism with an equal amount of reason; somehow fanaticism seems to go farther. The decades prior to 1860 were years of notable achievement in western expansion, railroad development, growth of a brilliant merchant marine, education, science, discovery, invention, industrial advance, prairie agriculture, business organization, humanitarianism, literature, and intellectual life. The "cosmopolitan metropolis" that rose out of the Chicago mud on the shore of Lake Michigan and "gradually lifted itself by its own boot straps"[1] was an American fact. So was the series of Goodyear rubber patents, and the ambitious department store of A. T. Stewart of New York's Broadway. So also the Astor Library, the benefactions of George Peabody, the iron establishments of Pennsylvania, the oil drillings, the Morse telegraph, the Western Union Telegraph Company, the Cooper Institute, the *Atlantic Monthly*, the Saturday Club of New England's elite,[2] the western stage coach, the elevator, the balloon, the tireless struggles of Cyrus Field that would one day produce an Atlantic cable, the forward surge of steamer traffic on the Mississippi and the Great Lakes, the superb Yankee clipper, the new contact with the far orient, the spectacular era that was opening in California, the undaunted captains of the Gloucester fisheries, the many hopeful young colleges, the amazing quantity and energy of American newspapers, the Southern agricultural reforms, the rise of teeming commonwealths in newer parts of the South, the network of canals, the unceasing public works, and the masses of newly arrived immigrants.[3] All of this, and vastly more, was America. It somehow does not fit into the picture of an irrepressible conflict.

One could add that sectionalism was an American fact, but in this overworked field it is essential to avoid distortions. It has not yet been satisfactorily demonstrated that sectional tensions were greater than the possible elasticity of the Union; available resources of the Union were not put into full play while factors of sectional strife

---

[1] A. C. Cole, *The Irrepressible Conflict*, 21–22.

[2] Edward Waldo Emerson, *The Early Years of the Saturday Club, 1855–1870.*

[3] Anyone can conjure up his own picture of prewar America. To encompass the vast scene is impossible, yet some effort to see it whole is needful to correct sectional distortion. If in the above enumeration such things as the Goodyear patent and the Morse telegraph originated a considerable time before the war, they were part of the technical advance which one associates with that era, however backward it may seem by present standards. For comprehensive glimpses see Cole, *Irrepressible Conflict*, chaps. 1 and 2; Carl Sandburg, *Abraham Lincoln: The War Years*, I, 8 ff.

were greatly overplayed. Differences between North and South—e. g., industrial interests in one region and agricultural in another—were by no means inconsistent with a diversified and well rounded nation. Large Southern areas truly did not want to leave the Union. Particular grievances, when calmly considered, by no means amounted to serious injury of one section by another. Matters related to slavery offered no such injury, nor did the ante-bellum tariff, which existed by reason of Southern votes. Fear of future Republican action in the restriction of international trade did cause Southern apprehension, but it cannot be shown historically that the Union was broken for this reason. If sectionalism was a factor, so was integration. The very genius of the American federal system is multiplicity within unity. Southerners who ardently supported the Union would constitute a long and distinguished roster. Cohesive interests on these shores had as much valid popular basis as those tendencies that worked for division, subdivision, and Balkanization. If the question is raised whether the South was rightly entitled to its own type of integration, the answer is that in fact the movement for disunion was not promoted on an all-Southern level; coöperationists who wanted so grave a problem to be handled in that way were successfully opposed by the South-Carolina type of precipitate, uncoöperative, separate-state secession.

If one turns from sectional strife to regional values, there indeed is a subject worthy of study. The distinctive flavor of Southern culture was a priceless contribution to American civilization, if only the emphasis could have been centered on constructive contribution instead of upon truculent or ingrowing sectionalism. Statesmen who saw this were the ones who had a service to give. There was no need to blame the South for local attachment; such a sentiment was not only pardonable but wholesome. With all its variety and diversity the South was one in regional consciousness and cultural patterns. It had its plantation economy, its musical speech, its sense of orderly society, its emphasis upon human worth above riches, its chivalric honor, its habits and patterns of ancestral pride, hospitality, and *noblesse oblige*. The supreme beauty of Natchez mansions, the urbanity of Charleston, the unique flavor of Royal Street in New Orleans, were unrivaled elsewhere. The South, in its vocabulary, local settings and ways of life, rose above the commonplace and added richly to the American heritage. In popular literature, Northern audiences came long ago to accept this. In the longer run, in song and story, it is the South that has won the decision at Appomattox.

II

In studying the "prewar" years it is easier to note provocative episodes than to untangle conflicting threads of interest and causation. A sharp mid-century crisis had resulted from the Mexican War with its vast acquisition of new territory, and in 1850 it took all the states-manship of such men as Henry Clay, Stephen A. Douglas, and Daniel Webster to prevent a break. Robert Barnwell Rhett of South Carolina favored disunion then, but the convention of Southern delegates which convened at Nashville, though not representing all the South, offered a forum by which opinions were aired and consequences weighed. The advantages of secession were faced and studied co-operatively in contrast to its evils and in the light of concessions at Washington. In the outcome, secessionists did not carry the South. Never, in fact, was secession to carry "the South" in any all-over popular vote or general conference.

After voluminous debate there evolved the Compromise of 1850: this was a series of enactments by Congress intended to allay, per-chance to end, disruptive sectional strife. California came into the Union free; new territories (Utah and New Mexico) were organized without national statutory prohibition of slavery; ultimate slave or free status was to be determined by incoming states "as their con-stitution . . . [might] prescribe"; boundaries were adjusted between Texas and New Mexico; the slave trade (not slavery) was prohibited in the District of Columbia; and Federal processes for the recovery of fugitive slaves were made so drastic, one-sided, and destructive of civil rights (if Negroes had rights) that the law of 1850 was hard to square with the Constitution, or with elemental justice. Both sections had yielded something in this solution, which had not pleased anti-slavery elements. To speak of what each "side" gained or lost, how-ever, was misleading. It was a stupid fallacy to conceive that all the vast teeming interests of "the North" were bound up with one segment of the compromise, and those of "the South" with the other.

Despite the 1850 settlement, balance remained uneasy, and when in 1854 it became necessary to devise a form of territorial organization for the "Platte country"—the areas of Kansas, Nebraska, and the Dakotas—old phrases and shibboleths were tiresomely repeated and the nation was again stretched on the sectional rack with all the old tensions and a few more. With his leadership among Northern Democrats and his specialization in western problems, Senator Stephen A. Douglas pushed through the Kansas-Nebraska act which applied, as in the compromise measures of 1850, "the principle of non-intervention by Congress with slavery in the States and Territories." It was specifically stated that the intent of the act was "not to legislate slavery into any Territory or State, nor to exclude it therefrom." While they were territories, the people were, by this act, "perfectly free to . . . regulate their domestic institutions in their own way, subject . . . to the Constitution of the United States." When ready to become states, the territories were to be received into the Union with or without slavery, depending upon the provisions of their constitutions. The time-honored principle of local self-government was thus to control both the territorial phase and that of statehood.

The main purpose of Douglas's bill had not been to deal with the slavery question at all. It is strange how many historical readers have missed the patent fact that the law was framed for the broad regions designated as Kansas and Nebraska. In these areas slavery and the prospect of future slavery were of negligible importance. The reason for the bill was that people were moving into those regions. They needed a government. In the accepted American sense, when new lands were opened up in the West, that necessarily meant a territorial organization, a regime under national sovereignty and under congressional regulation, yet with representative government for its own affairs.

Many interests, including Douglas's own Chicago constituents and those who were promoting a transcontinental railroad, were urging that a territorial government be provided. Such a system in that area was long overdue and could not be endlessly deferred. That in reality was the problem, but by a perverse fate any territorial legislation in the fifties, though prompted by familiar American pioneer needs, would have to go far out of its rightful setting and take account of what was emotionally called "the issue of slavery." This did not follow because of any reason pertaining to the region itself, nor was it true that an over-all code covering every phase of domestic institutions had to be included in a law for the creation of a territory. Horse stealing, for example, was not mentioned when such a law was passed in Congress, yet the territorial government could deal with horse stealing and a hundred other matters not specified in the act of territorial organization. In 1854, however, slavery in the territories was a topic on which every politician had to make a speech, and that in spite of the fact that both major parties—the Whigs and the Democrats—had agreed to the pacifying legislation of 1850. Mental patterns were obscuring realities. In the noise and clamor of the day an unhampered examination of territorial needs for their own sake had become impossible.

Douglas had not created the slavery issue. He was never a sectional agitator. He was a responsible national leader with a task to perform, a member of the Senate charged with devising a program by which westerners could live under an American type of government. He had to come through with a bill, the kind of bill that would stand some chance of being enacted in the year 1854 by the particular members who then sat in Congress. By leaving the matter of slavery for the people of the territories to determine as they wished, he went as far in avoiding the emotionally disturbing aspects of the slavery question as it seemed possible to go. Even now it is difficult to see how any more reasonable bill could then have passed Senate and House and have been signed by the President, Franklin Pierce. Antislavery people, for instance, had no better chance in 1854 than that offered by the Douglas bill; it was in fact a very good chance.[1]

If the people of a territory wanted to, reasoned Douglas, they could keep slavery out. (That was before the Dred Scott decision by the Supreme Court, but even that decision was not to shake Douglas from his position in favor of local self-government for the territories.) If they had a Kansas need or a Nebraska use for slavery—a hundred-to-one chance—they could establish it by approved constitutional processes. It was not that they should have what Douglas should dictate, but what they should choose. It was "popular sovereignty." Douglas believed in it. It was the only formula that seemed to him possible or practicable at the time. It was utterly unjust to accuse Douglas of

---

[1] On Douglas and the Kansas-Nebraska bill, see George Fort Milton, *The Eve of Conflict: Stephen A. Douglas and the Needless War*, 96–154; Frank H. Hodder, "The Railroad Background of the Kansas-Nebraska Act," *Miss. Vall. Hist. Rev.*, XII, 3–22 (1925).

consigning a naturally free community to the demon of slavery. A few years later, when a constitutional trick for Kansas was devised which would have fixed slavery upon a people wishing its abolition, no one opposed that trick more strenuously, nor with more hazard in political prestige, than Douglas.

III

As it turned out, all the old troubles were stirred up after the passage of Douglas's bill. It is probable that they would have been equally stirred up by any alternative law on the subject. If sectional reactions were stimulated by a law intended to subordinate the slavery question and hold it in proper proportion, how much more would such re-actions have been stirred by a law to fasten slavery upon the territories, or to impose abolition. The latter might have been partially possible in 1820, though even then the matter was arbitrarily settled by latitude, not principle; but the Missouri Compromise, however consonant with the earlier concept of national housekeeping, was in 1854 beyond the sphere of practical politics. Times had changed. Many who were later to become good-and-true Republicans had re-fused to support the free-soil principle in the presidential election of 1848.

Times changed again, and men who had wanted slavery agitation muted in 1848, together with those who never wanted it muted, proceeded to use such agitation for a new party formed in 1854. The Republican party, whose story will not be attempted here, rose from early mass meetings (as at Jackson, Michigan, and Ripon, Wisonsin), spread rapidly in local movements, held its first national convention in 1854, and entered its first presidential campaign in 1856.[1] It evolved

---

[1] See William Starr Myers, *The Republican Party, a History* (1928); Francis Curtis, *The Republican Party . . . 1854–1904* (1904); Ruhl J. Bartlett, *John C. Frémont and the Republican Party* (Ohio State University *Studies,* Contributions in Hist. and Pol. Science, XIII); Andrew W. Crandall, *The Early History of the Republican Party, 1854–1856* (1930). Various attempts have been made to give a date and a locality for the "birth" of the party, but to speak in this sense of preliminary movements, local meetings, conventions, and the like, is misleading. Sherman W. Wakefield (*How Lincoln Became President,* 51, 69), refers to the meetings at Ripon, Wisconsin, Jackson, Michigan, and Springfield, Illinois, all in 1854, as occasions from which no permanent results followed. In the matter of unbroken continuity, he considers that what is known as the national Republican party "was born in Bloomington, Illinois, on May 29, 1856." Beveridge (II, 356) points out that on February 22, 1856 "the new party was organized on a national basis"

by a coalescence of various elements differing among themselves, including Democrats, Whigs, Free-Soilers, and Knownothings. Their original point of union was the "Wilmot proviso" doctrine that slavery must be excluded from national territory. In its founding there was enthusiasm, idealism, and withal the enlisting of thousands of men of high principle. Some, however, went into the new movement for lack of any other place to go in a day when old party patterns were dissolving. To promote a cause was the purpose of some; to have a party to belong to, was the motive of others; to make the party an end in itself and a vehicle for obtaining office was to become the interest of politicians.

The Republican party came upon the scene in an age of storm and stress. Kansas, intended as a normal American pioneer region, became so much a center of artificial agitation that Kansans were not allowed to live their own lives. "Bleeding Kansas" became a slogan. It suited distant outsiders to make it bleed. The real story of Kansas as a place to which people went to make homes has been obscured amid a welter of abolition agitation, artificially stimulated settlement, border-ruffian brawls, bogus legislatures, fraudulent constitutional devices, furious debates remote from Kansas itself, proslavery truculence, party conflict, and *opera bouffe* "wars." Kansas has been called a "state of mind." With equal truth it could be said that things un-Kansan constituted the national state of mind under which the birth-pangs of Kansas were endured. Had the territory been let alone, as was its sister Nebraska, a different story would have been told. The manner in which Kansas was used, abused, distorted, "investigated," and propagandized for partisan purposes is hard to realize. That a generation which could not settle Kansas without all this hysteria would soon find itself drawn into a maelstrom of civil war, is one of the few plausible things of the period.

While Kansas was thus playing, not its true part as a pioneer community, but a forced role as sectional troublemaker, many unsavory ingredients were being added to the witches' brew. Men were taking sides. A party that was entirely sectional was vigorously launched. Fire eaters, North and South—the Northern variety being as deadly

at Pittsburgh. In *Proceedings of the First Three Republican National Conventions*, 3–13, the formation of "the Republican Association of Washington," D. C. by a small group on June 19, 1855, is mentioned as the earliest organization of record, but the Pittsburgh meeting of February 1856 is treated as the national beginning.

as the Southern—were demonstrating how a small minority could become a great menace. Disturbance was engendered by men of honest intent. Humanitarian endeavor was taking a tack which involved abuse of the whole South, misrepresentation of slavery, and emphasis upon the slaveholder's brutality as if that were the typical Southern quality. To Southerners the word "Yankee" was becoming both a word of scorn and a label for all Northerners.

A new phraseology was coming into the language. Men spoke of "Beecher's Bibles," "doughfaces," "Black Republicans," "slaveocrats," "slave breeding," "a Southern platform," "a covenant with death [the Constitution]," "the Northern Democracy," "the Southern Democracy," "squatter sovereignty," "lawful property," "bogus delegates," "Northern men of Southern sentiments," [2] and of the day "when the Senate and the House shall swarm with Sumners and Lovejoys." [3] Words of hate, epithets that made it unrespectable to do otherwise than despise a whole class, or party, or area, phrases that burned and rankled (they cannot all be repeated here)—such was the jargon, not of most Americans perhaps, but of enough to create those mental images that rest on repetition and familiarity rather than on real content or rational thought. Such made-up images too often control the governance of men.

There was the tendency to associate slaveholding interests with expansion beyond the border. This would then be assailed both as a menacing wave of foreign conquest and as a program of slavery extension. Fuel for such assaults was supplied by adventuresome filibustering schemes, abortive though they were, in Cuba, Mexico's lower California, and Nicaraugua. Since these were not unlike earlier Texan episodes that entailed serious sectional troubles, men could not help asking themselves where it would all lead. Slavery in the world view was regarded as an anachronism, an abuse, a practice inharmonious with modern civilization; yet American ships were illicitly engaging in an international slave trade which was contrary to American law and in conflict with Britain's efforts to suppress the traffic by international coöperation. In such matters the United States had to speak internationally as a slave power, or as a nation that

---

[2] Said opprobriously of such men as Franklin Pierce of New Hampshire and James Buchanan of Pennsylvania as if it were a base thing for a Northern man to work with Southern fellows.

[3] D. L. Dumond, ed., *Southern Editorials on Secession*, 155.

recognized slavery, when other nations were treating it as an abomination and trying to stamp it out.

Sneers against the South as shiftless and unenlightened produced indignant reaction. Tempers of statesmen were on edge. They had been so for years. In December 1849 there had been bedlam in Congress when R. K. Meade of Virginia called William Duer of New York "a liar, sir." A duel was with difficulty averted, and, to quote the record, "Indescribable confusion followed—threats, violent gesticulations, calls to order, and demands for adjournment were mingled together." [4] The sergeant at arms raised high his mace, which people had thought a mere ornament or symbol, and somehow business was resumed without a knock-down fight, but a dangerous point had been reached if men could not debate, organize, and legislate without personal explosions. What would now be called pulp melodrama—*Uncle Tom's Cabin,* published (in book form) in 1852—became a sensation, reaching a sale of 300,000 copies the first year. Though its author, Harriet Beecher Stowe, had been able to see good in Southerners, the book functioned as an antislavery tract and a slogan of pious conflict.

Westerners were demanding liberal homestead legislation, which men of the South were resisting. A plan for establishing colleges to teach agriculture and the mechanical arts with Federal land-grant aid, originating in Illinois, met also the obstacle of Southern opposition. Economic rivalries between North and South were aired and fanned in the pages of *DeBow's Review*—an influential Southern publication—and in the proceedings of Southern commercial conventions. Northern and Southern groups were contending for control of a future transcontinental railway. Immigrants crowding in from Europe made for Northern destinations by the hundreds of thousands in the fifties; they were tending to produce in portions of the North a human type quite different from the native-grounded population of the South.

Questions pertaining to slavery, however, were the focal points of trouble and dissension. Paradoxically the matter of slavery was both enlarged and constricted. It was enlarged in agitation as if the very essence of all Southern life depended on the peculiar institution, and as if the slightest breath of criticism directed against human

---

[4] *Cong. Globe,* 31 Cong., 1 sess., 27; Craven, *The Coming of the Civil War,* 247.

bondage involved an attack upon vital Southern rights. At the same time, as will appear in later pages, the specific disputes that caused political wrangling did not touch large questions of slavery at all, being rather concerned with minor selected aspects such as western territorial status and recovery of fugitives. The broad question whether the fifteen slave states should keep their slaves was beyond controversy as a problem of American government within the Constitution; virtually no one in responsible political life was assailing this right. What should be done about an almost non-existent slave population in the West, or about a small trickle of runaway bondsmen, was magnified into an issue altogether out of scale with its importance.[5]

Pamphlets and books gave to slavery the aura of political, philosophical, social, economic, and religious sanction. Science, humanity, and fundamental instinct were marshaled in support of an institution which in fact was crumbling and declining in the presence of nineteenth century tendencies. In a made-up volume called *The Pro-Slavery Argument* these discussions became to many Southerners a kind of bible, to be set alongside the book entitled *Cotton Is King*, by David Christy, published in 1855. Scant hearing was given to realistic Southerners who saw the inadequacies of slavery and favored a more frank discussion of its merits and defects. The more Southern "institutions" were attacked, the more ardently were they defended. Arguments buttressing slavery were identified with basic Southern loyalty. Their hold in the press and in political discussion was dominant. Dissenting opinions were regarded as unorthodox and palpably false.

IV

No such widespread hearing or support was given in the North to antislavery screeds and tracts. Prewar abolitionist movements in the Northern states could claim among their followers only a tiny minority. Such leaders as Garrison and Lovejoy found in the North not only lack of support but scorn and persecution, and, in Lovejoy's case, fatal attack. That abolitionism existed at all was the serious thing;

---

[5] For the problem of fugitive slaves, see below, pp. 238–240. If there were slaveholders for whom the problem of the runaway may have been serious, this was especially true in the upper South or on the border, but in these sections secession *per se* (fundamental discontent with the Union) had small support.

it was exaggerated and advertised in the South out of all relation to its nationwide significance. As for William Lloyd Garrison, it could not be said that any sizable movement centered in this lone agitator. He offended the churches; he was mobbed in Boston; he lacked the support even of antislavery elements in New England; still less was he the guiding spirit of any antislavery crusade in the country. He was a free-lance journalist, tireless for the cause to which he devoted a burning and sincere loyalty, but utterly lacking in widespread influence.

Non-Garrisonian antislavery influences were already progressing toward national organization, and it was a fortuitous rather than a significant matter when Garrison, returning on a wave of reflected glory from England in 1833, prematurely organized at Philadelphia the American Anti-Slavery Society of which not himself, but Arthur Tappan, became the first president. In that year his *Liberator* had fewer than four hundred white subscribers. Never did its full subscription list exceed three thousand. As Gilbert H. Barnes has written, Garrison "had no qualifications for leadership. His one office in the society, secretary of foreign correspondence, was soon resigned; and so long as the national organization held together he was never asked to fill another. He was so little a leader that even in the New England Anti-Slavery Society his journal was endured as its official organ for but a brief, unhappy period." [1]

By 1839 the American Anti-Slavery Society was dwindling; in 1840 the national organization as it had existed in the thirties under the Tappans and other such leaders came to an end; it was felt by earnest antislavery men that decentralization was better and that a general society served no useful purpose. It was at this point that Garrison, deciding to capture the society as his own affair, packed its convention with his friends, carrying a boatload of citizens of Lynn, Massachusetts, to New York "at nominal cost, on the understanding that they would cast their votes at Garrison's direction" and using similar methods elsewhere.[2] It was this assembly of "delegates" that gave him the presidency of a now nominal organization from which the better element, such as the Tappans, had withdrawn.

Not Garrison's Northern supporters, but his Southern enemies, made him famous.[3] It was only at a distance that he was erroneously

---

[1] *The Antislavery Impulse*, 57–58.   [2] *Ibid.*, 169.   [3] *Ibid.*, 50.

supposed to embody a significant movement. His name cast "a vague and indefinite odium" over the abolition cause which "hampered its growth from the beginning."[4]

Those who did have influence with the small minority groups that conducted abolitionist movements were quite dissociated from Garrison. They included Arthur and Lewis Tappan of New York City, wealthy merchants, opponents of Garrison, philanthropists in many causes, pioneer organizers and financial supporters of the national society; Cassius M. Clay, whose neighbors of Lexington, Kentucky, expelled his *True American* from their cultured city; C. G. Finney, evangelist extraordinary, guiding spirit of the Oneida Community, and early leader of Oberlin College; Angelina and Sarah Grimké; and Angelina's husband, Theodore Dwight Weld, fellow worker in Finney's "holy band." It was Weld who became the chief promoter of abolitionism as an organized crusade. With burning zeal strangely combined with anonymity he marshaled speakers for popular meetings, conducted a lobby at Washington, and produced those pamphlets and tracts which purported to present slavery to the people, but in reality gave only selected instances of inhuman atrocity. If abolitionism is ground for canonization, Weld deserves sainthood more than Garrison.

The impact of the slavery issue upon American churches deserves a word. Long before war broke, secession had taken place among the Baptists and Methodists. In the Methodist church there was nothing resembling a violent attack of Northerners against Southern brethren; indeed there was an effort to smooth things over and to keep the family together. In 1844, however, the national governing body of the church, the general conference, mildly requested a Georgia bishop to desist from exercising episcopal duties while remaining a slaveholder; as a result, Southerners formed the Methodist Episcopal Church South and separation was complete. A Southern Baptist Convention was created in the same year with a similar motive.

It would be a serious mistake, however, to think of abolitionists as having captured the Northern churches. They fell very far short of doing that. While there was considerable antislavery sentiment among Northern Methodists, Baptists, and Quakers, as there might well be in an age of general humanitarian striving, such sentiment was not

---

[4] Barnes and Dumond, eds., *Weld-Grimké Letters,* I, viii.

always militant, and in general there existed in the ranks of organized religion in the North a considerable, perhaps a prevailing, attitude of abhorrence toward abolitionists as trouble makers, revolutionaries, and dangerous radicals. In the Presbyterian church in Northern states there was divided counsel, many of the socially influential of that sect being either proslavery or averse to agitation. Among Congregationalists there were a few bold abolitionists, but there were also "ardent defenders of the institution." [5] Such men as Finney and Weld, who burned with antislavery zeal, were very much like interlopers in the ecclesiastical field. They were evangelists, not church leaders. They went about exhorting; they made trouble within the churches in their drive for converts; they cared not if their preachings created dissension; they were not concerned with normal church activity; they were frowned upon by such a Congregational stalwart as Lyman Beecher.

In the South the power and prestige of organized religion was so completely enlisted in the cause of slavery that opposite church voices were negligible. Some of the most effective and emphatic writings in defense of slavery were penned by Southern ecclesiastics. This was in no sense surprising. It was but natural that Southern church leaders should be cut to the same pattern as Southerners generally; it was understandable that their guidance and interpretation should conform to the social order of which they and their flocks were a part. A Theodore Parker could contend for abolition in Boston in dissociation from other ministers who denounced him for his free thinking and iconoclasm; he could do this with no thought of being typical of the church. This was not easy even for Parker, whose friends organized a special church which became a social and religious forum; in the South such departure from orthodox and prevalent thought would have led to the most embarrassing and devastating consequences.[6]

Sentiment against slavery in this "ante-bellum" period was not all of a piece. There was a wide range of variation among men who

---

[5] Adelaide A. Lyons, "Religious Defense of Slavery in the North," *Historical Papers*, Trinity College Hist. Soc., Vol. 13, Durham, N. C., 1919, p. 8.

[6] For religion and slavery, with references, see Randall, *Civil War and Reconstruction*, 105–107; G. H. Barnes, *The Antislavery Impulse*, 64–78 (concerning the "rebels" [abolitionist students] at Lane Seminary); *Weld-Grimké Letters*, ed. by G. H. Barnes and D. L. Dumond; H. S. Commager, *Theodore Parker*.

deplored human bondage. Those who assumed to themselves a function of criminal violence and self-immolation to destroy slavery by murdering slaveholders were negligible. John Brown was not the prophet of anything that could be called a movement. Passing over Brown, one could begin the classification of antislavery men with William Lloyd Garrison as representing the extreme. His activity was that of agitator, not of responsible leader. He made no concessions, admitted no difficulties in the path of emancipation, and scorned any recognition of Southern feelings and interests. He and those who stood with him—Wendell Phillips, Thomas Wentworth Higginson, Gerrit Smith, Theodore Parker, and the like—were a small group; they were without serious political influence. It was a ticklish thing for anyone in political life in the North to be stamped with the abolitionist die. Less extreme was such a reformer as Horace Mann. He was vigorously antislavery, yet his quality was not that of a firebrand and the antislavery cause was not his main specialty. To bracket him with Garrison would be a mistake. Such a man as Joshua R. Giddings was a courageous and tireless advocate of antislavery causes in Congress, but his support was small, his cause was unpopular, and on one occasion, after presenting antislavery resolutions in the House of Representatives, he was "censured by his angry Whig colleagues, who refused him the right even to speak in his own defense.[7] Few indeed went so far as Giddings in futile congressional proceedings. James G. Birney was strong in the faith, but his emphasis was more upon free soil than upon the doings of the Anti-Slavery Society, from which he resigned in 1841. Running as the Liberty party's candidate for President in two elections, he polled only seven thousand votes in 1840, and while his support increased to sixty-five thousand votes in 1844, it constituted less than one-fortieth of the total.[8]

There were still other degrees and shades among those who did

[7] Barnes, The Antislavery Impulse, 187–188. On being censured, Giddings resigned, was reëlected by his Western Reserve constituency in Northern Ohio, resumed his antislavery attacks in the House, and escaped further formal censure, being from then on merely endured, but without appreciable influence. See also Robert P. Ludlum, "Joshua R. Giddings, Radical," Miss. Vall. Hist. Rev., XXIII, 49–60 (1936).

[8] Birney "believed slavery to be directly contrary to the fundamental principles upon which the nation was founded; and that Congress not only had the power, but should use it, to abolish slavery in the states," but he emphasized that this end was to be gained by constitutional methods, for he believed that "slavery was not only sinful . . . but incompatible with the Constitution." Dwight L. Dumond, ed., Letters of James Gillespie Birney, 1831–1857, I, xix, xxii.

not favor slavery. Charles Francis Adams went for free soil policies, not for abolitionist excess. The same was true of Salmon P. Chase. More moderate than Chase was Lincoln, who did not even support the Free-Soil candidate in 1848. Lincoln was a Whig of democratic impulses whose fundamental antislavery views were held within bounds and were not always carried over into the field of political measures. There were things regarded as proslavery—such as the fugitive-slave law—which Lincoln stood ready to tolerate because they were part of the existing system, and because in matters of practical government Lincoln did not think that a man ought to indulge all his moral or theoretical preferences.[9] In the mild group with Lincoln stood Orville H. Browning of Illinois. Kentucky-born, courtly and old-fashioned, conservative in all things, Browning was nevertheless antislavery in thought; he became a Republican, though he did not remain so for long. He was a man of considerable influence; he reached senatorial and cabinet rank in the North; yet in no valid sense was he ever anti-Southern. These are selected examples, but it is only in taking examples of living human beings of the time that correct concepts can be formed. The Yankee world was made up of many elements, but among its varied millions, haters of the South were far from typical. When degrees and groups are noted, Lincoln's place is found to be many miles away from that of radicals and firebrands.

V

Two violent events in May of 1856, both relating to slavery, were like a firebell in the night: the Potawatomie massacre in Kansas and the Sumner-Brooks affair in the United States Senate. At the time of corn planting in Kansas—they actually did plant corn there—Old John Brown of Osawatomie, a fugitive criminal and bloodthirsty fanatic, stepped out at night with several of his sons to do as foul a deed as the annals of that turbulent territory record. At a time when murders in Kansas had been few despite near-clashes of armed groups claiming militia or "posse" status, a party led by John Brown, Sr., attacked the homes of proslavery families on Potawatomie Creek and killed five men: William Sherman, Allen Wilkinson, and three men

---

[9] *Works*, X, 65 (April 4, 1864). For Lincoln's disinclination to disturb slavery in the states, see below, p. 297; vol. II, 127.

of the name of Doyle. For this crime the perpetrators were never properly prosecuted, though proslavery men took prompt revenge in what was called the "battle of Osawatomie" in which one of the Brown sons, Frederick, was killed.[1] Other events in Kansas loom large in the narrative of those times. Such were the so-called Wakarusa War and the sack of Lawrence: the "war" was a bloodless mustering of motley groups in and around Lawrence; the proslavery raid upon that town, though an outrage, amounted to little more than the destruction of various buildings, chiefly the free-state hotel. If the doings of John Brown had not occurred, violence upon human life would have been far less serious.

Kansas was peculiar. It was not viewed for what it was, but for what outside agitators pictured it to be. The concept of Kansas as a community of people "over head and ears—not in fighting—but in farming," to quote a contemporary newspaper, was "not . . . permitted to find lodgment in the public mind." [2] If stories of violence were played down by newspapers, it was when the perpetrators were their own party associates. The Republican press minimized the provocative deeds of such as Brown and James H. Lane, while always keeping up a high state of agitation in Kansan matters, giving particularly lurid accounts of proslavery "border ruffians." On the other hand, proslavery newspapers appealed for more Southern immigrants, denounced Lane, issued calls to arms, and did their part in fomenting what came to be called "civil war" within the territory. Squatter sovereignty became a turbulent thing not so much because of genuine conflicts of local interests, but because a minority of trouble makers, aided by outside agitators, made turbulence rather than reasonable pacification their business. In spite of all this, pacification went farther than one would realize when reading only partisan chronicles.

Occurring simultaneously with the Kansan trouble, the Sumner-Brooks affair produced a sensation throughout the nation. The senator from Massachusetts, in a speech on the floor of the Senate, May 19–20, 1856, had assailed slaveowners, denounced South Carolina, and indulged in personal abuse of an absent South Carolinian senator,

---

[1] Conditions in Kansas are elaborately treated and fully documented in James C. Malin, *John Brown and the Legend of Fifty-Six*, published in 1942. This rigidly critical book belongs in a category of its own; it is the first major study of John Brown by one who is primarily a historian.

[2] Malin, 109.

Andrew P. Butler. The speech had "abounded in such . . . terms as harlot, mistress, rape, pirate, tyrant, falsifier, assassin, thug, swindler, and criminal." [3] Coming at a time when sectional tension was bad enough in all conscience, this verbal assault was not offhand. It was a deliberate and studied insult to Butler. It was not typical of the North, and little harm would have come from ignoring it (supposing that were possible); but to the mind of Preston Brooks of South Carolina, relative of Butler and member of the House of Representatives, such a gross personal insult could not go unpunished. Confronting Sumner with all the self-control he could muster, Brooks stated that it was his duty to punish him. Then, wielding his cane, he rapped the senator with repeated blows upon the head, leaving the statesman "bloody and insensible." [4]

If, in studying this incident, one wishes an insight into Southern nuances and implications, he will find them developed by Charles S. Sydnor.[5] In the courtly Southerner's unwritten code of conduct personal matters were vital, but they were to be handled out of court. It was a man's own business to defend his honor or that of his family; to expect lawyers, judges, and juries to regulate an affair of honor was not the gentleman's way. Sumner being no gentleman in Brooks's view, the occasion did not call for a duel, but it did call for chastisement. Combat according to the *code duello* was not appropriate: a cowhide whip or other weapon of dishonor might have been chosen; a cane served as well, and the significance of its use would not be missed by Carolinian friends.

That was one side of the question; the other side was seen in the angry emotion of Sumner's friends who found a new theme for denunciation of Southern "brutality." The senator became a hero and the incident not only assisted the Republican party, but intensified all those elements of discord on both sides which moderates were pathetically hoping to repress.

VI

Such were some of the factors at work in the troubled fifties. There has been no effort to review them in detail. To do so would require

---

[3] Charles S. Sydnor, "The Southerner and the Laws," *Jour. of So. Hist.*, VI, 22 (Feb., 1940).
[4] *Ibid.*   [5] *Ibid.*, 3–23.

volumes. Lincoln knew of them as he studied documents, perused the newspapers, and read the controversial literature of the time. At times he seemed a passive observer. He was one of many. Moderate ideas, of the sort which he entertained, seemed unfortunately dormant, however deeply significant they might be. Lincoln was slow. In the early formation of the Republican party he was not out in front.[1] Something was happening to the country; people were using a new terminology; yet Lincoln still clung to the old. The Whig party had meant much to him. It hurt him that this historic party of the nation, a party of North and South which had never hoped to elect a President except with Southern support, was crumbling and passing into oblivion. In an elaborate speech on questions of the day at Peoria on October 16, 1854, a speech which occupies over seventy pages in his *Works,* he did not even mention the Republican party whose initial organization was by that time well launched.[2] Nor in this speech did he use the awkward early name for that party, which was "anti-Nebraska." With a disturbed glance at the changing times and a wistful desire for old alignments, Lincoln wrote as late as August 1855 to Joshua F. Speed:

> You enquire where I now stand— That is a disputed point— I think I am a whig; but others say there are no whigs, and that I am an abolitionist— When I was at Washington I voted for the Wilmot Proviso [for prohibition of slavery in national territory] as good as forty times, and I never heard of any one attempting to unwhig me for that— I now do no more than oppose the *extension* of slavery—
>
> I am not a Know-Nothing— That is certain— . . . As a nation, we began by declaring that '*all men are created equal*—' We now practically read it 'all men are created equal, *except negroes*' When the Know-Nothings get control, it will read 'all men are created equal, except negroes, *and foreigners, and Catholics.*' When it comes to this I shall prefer emigrating to some country where they make no pretense of loving liberty . . . ." [3]

Where did Lincoln stand? He did not favor those influences that were making for disruption. He was willing to rest upon the Com-

---

[1] When an effort was made in October 1854 to create at Springfield a Republican organization for Illinois, Lincoln neither joined nor encouraged the attempt. "A Republican State Central Committee was appointed, which included Abraham Lincoln, but he took no part in the convention [at Springfield] and refused to serve on the Committee." Wakefield, *How Lincoln Became President,* 50.

[2] *Works,* II, 190–262. For further comment on this speech, see below, p. 105.

[3] *Ibid.,* II, 286–287. (Though Nicolay and Hay's alterations, of punctuation etc., are unimportant, the text is given above as Lincoln wrote it.)

promise of 1850 with its concessions to the South. He was willing to let South Carolina continue to have the same number of representatives in Congress as Maine, though Maine had more than twice the number of white people.[4] He would go for Union-saving, but only when he believed that the means employed would actually save the Union.[5] Reorientation in the challenging fifties was difficult for him. He did not like being unwhigged. All this stirring of new factors sent him back to the contemplation of fundamentals. In this he was not overawed by phrases or labels. "Stand," he said, "with anybody that stands right. Stand with him while he is right, and part with him when he goes wrong. Stand with the Abolitionist in restoring the Missouri Compromise, and stand against him when he attempts to repeal the fugitive-slave law. In the latter case you stand with the Southern disunionist. What of that? You are still right. In both cases you are right. In both cases you expose the dangerous extremes. In both you stand on middle ground, and hold the ship level and steady. In both you are national, and nothing less than national. This is the good old Whig ground. To desert such ground because of any company, is to be less than a Whig—less than a man—less than an American." [6]

New party alignments being essential for all who had thought they were Whigs, and for others as well, Lincoln made his party affiliation definite, though still avoiding the name Republican, in the earlier months of 1856. The traditional account, accepted by a long line of Lincoln writers, is that Herndon maneuvered Lincoln into the party by a kind of trick, signing his partner's name to a published call for a meeting of Sangamon County men to choose delegates for the state convention to be held in Bloomington. There are, however, excellent reasons for doubting the Herndon version, especially insofar as it implies that Lincoln was not managing his own party alignment in this formative period.

On February 22, 1856, a group of Illinois editors of the "anti-Nebraska" persuasion gathered at Decatur.[7] Several interesting points

---

[4] *Ibid.*, II, 233–234.   [5] *Ibid.*, II, 236.   [6] *Ibid.*, II, 243.

[7] As to Lincoln's importance in these party beginnings in Illinois, we have a clue in a letter from Paul Selby (young Jacksonville editor who promoted the Decatur meeting of editors) to Richard Yates, dated at Springfield, February 14, 1856. Selby wrote: "I have had an interview with Mr. Lincoln to-day, ... He tells me he thinks he will try and have some business at Decatur at the time of the Convention. Can't you do the same. I think we all agree as to what is to be done . . . ." A postscript suggests concern that party strategy be not patterned in terms of "too much *ultraism*." Yates MSS.

about this gathering should be noted: it marked the "real beginning of the Republican party in Illinois"; [8] it was definitely preliminary to the state convention held at Bloomington in May; it summoned the clans for that very gathering; its business was party organization; it created a state central committee which included Herndon; and, significantly, all this was done with Lincoln present and in attendance, he being the one non-editor. [9] It is hard to believe that Herndon would have had the appointment to the central committee without Lincoln's consent. It was Herndon's business to organize the new movement in his own area, chiefly Sangamon County, and he was acting in this recognized capacity when on May 10 he issued a call for a convention of Sangamon County men. The county gathering met on May 24; the Bloomington state convention was to come on May 29. Such was the relation of Lincoln and Herndon that if the junior partner took action committing the senior partner, the latter probably knew and approved of it.

Herndon's garrulous correspondence in this period—e. g., with Theodore Parker and Lyman Trumbull—gives no contemporary corroboration of the later biography version so far as it implied that Lincoln was drawn into the new party by Herndon's bold stroke and by an unexpected use of his name. Lincoln was capable of speaking for himself; he was careful to make a correction if someone pledged him without authority; he had already participated in the Decatur convention of February; he had been concerned in planning the earlier movements of which both the local Sangamon gathering and the Bloomington convention were the logical results. Herndon may indeed have signed for his partner, but this was because of Lincoln's absence from Springfield; he probably knew Lincoln's wishes in the matter. Herndon himself stated that Lincoln promptly ratified the decision once the call was issued. In any case, on so important a matter as joining a party, Lincoln's motives and plans were

---

[8] Angle, *Lincoln, 1854–1861*, 112.

[9] At the time of the convention Lincoln gave a happily phrased after-dinner speech at the Cassell House in Decatur. Being toasted as the next candidate for the United States Senate, he opened with a story about a man being held up by a robber and giving his note for the money. "Mr. Lincoln then proceeded to address the assemblage for some half hour, in his usual masterly manner, frequently interrupted by the cheers of his hearers." *Illinois State Chronicle* (Decatur), Feb. 28, 1856, p. 1. cc. 6–7.

under his own hat.[10] He did not share all the opinions of those who were pushing the new party; he looked longingly back to Whig days before the new organization was launched; he particularly wished that the party should take a "conservative" (not strongly abolitionist) turn; this very concern, however, was because it was to be his party; from February 1856 it was from the inside that his influence was exerted.

Having become thus committed to the new party, Lincoln took a leading part in this Bloomington convention.[11] Staying at the mansion of the wealthy Judge David Davis (who was later to promote Lincoln's nomination as Republican candidate for President, and still later to withdraw from the party), Lincoln loomed as a leading figure among a small group of influential men whose prestige and conservatism were counted on to make the gathering "as respectable as possible." [12] Without the initial support of such men the new party could hardly have got very far in Illinois in 1856. The problem involved was revealed by Lincoln's concern lest the southern part of the state should be unrepresented—it turned out that a few delegates did appear from that area—and also by the attitude of John Todd Stuart, prominent Whig and first partner of Lincoln, who carefully avoided adherence to the new party.

Conservatives gave the party not only respectability; they supplied its platform, which was written by Orville H. Browning.[13] Hailing the "principles . . . of Washington, Jefferson and their great and good compatriots of the revolution" [14]—this ought to please everyone— the party declaration announced opposition to the existing administration, denounced the effort to force slavery upon Kansas, and favored

---

[10] For Herndon's version, see *Herndon's Life of Lincoln* (Angle ed.), 311–312. On this matter the author has been greatly assisted by a well-documented memorandum prepared by David H. Donald, graduate assistant at the University of Illinois, who is preparing a book on Herndon. Newspapers and manuscripts of the period were closely examined by Mr. Donald.

[11] This was known as "A State Convention of the Anti-Nebraska party of Illinois." The name "Republican" was avoided, being a term of reproach used by opponents, preceded by the word "Black." Soon after this, however, the term "Republican" was adopted in Illinois. Wakefield, *How Lincoln Became President*, 58–60, 68.

[12] George T. Brown, editor of the Quincy *Whig*, to Lyman Trumbull, May 12, 1856, Trumbull MSS.

[13] Browning, *Diary*, I, 237.

[14] These platitudinous verbalisms of the Republican state platform, written by Browning, are quoted in Beveridge, II, 370.

congressional prohibition of slavery in national territory. On one point the balancing act in the convention was truly amazing. Browning, according to his own statement, prepared "a resolution intended to reconcile both Know nothings and German's to act with us." [15] Finding discordant elements present and taking upon himself the framing of resolutions to harmonize them, he had procured a room, brought leading men of differing opinions together, and, after difficulty, obtained consent to his resolutions. Next day the resolutions he prepared, having been accepted in committee, were "unanimously adopted without change." [16] When one remembers how offensive to Germans and other foreign-born elements were the openly declared views of the Knownothings, this bit of reconciliation deserves a high place in the history of political straddling. At about this time Browning wrote: "We wish, if possible, to keep the party in this state under the control of moderate men, and conservative influences, and if we do so the future destiny of the state is in our own hands—victory will inevitably crown our exertions. On the contrary if rash and ultra counsels prevail all is lost." [17]

With conservatism so prominent in its making, but with feeling on slavery and sectionalism reaching a peak in that sensational month of May 1856, the occasion required something a bit unique in the matter of oratory. In addressing an eminently moderate convention, someone was needed who could make a vigorous and fighting speech. This need was notably supplied by Lincoln, who addressed this party gathering in which "all shades" of opinion had been neatly reconciled and brought it to its feet with cheers for his fervid eloquence. Beveridge has extravagantly called it "the greatest piece of oratory he ever produced." Then he added: ". . . Lincoln had to say things which, for the very same reason that he then spoke them extemporaneously, he never would put on paper for publication thereafter." [18]

This was the alleged "Lost Speech" concerning which a famous legend has arisen. Newspaper reporters, the story goes, were so thrilled by Lincoln's oratory that they gave up trying to take notes, Medill being in a kind of hypnotic trance.[19] But young H. C. Whitney, associate of Lincoln on the law circuit, was in attendance. He kept a

[15] Browning, *Diary*, I, 237.   [16] *Ibid.*, I, 238.
[17] Browning to Trumbull, May 19, 1856, Trumbull MSS.   [18] Beveridge, II, 372.
[19] Statement of Joseph Medill, quoted in Tarbell, *Life of Abraham Lincoln*, I, 295.

cool head, made notes, and many years later, when the lost speech had
become famous, he published in *McClure's Magazine* for September
1896 what purported to be a verbatim report of Lincoln's words. Miss
Tarbell accepted the Whitney reconstruction of the speech, incorporating copious extracts in her biography; Joseph Medill of the
Chicago *Tribune* endorsed its accuracy; Beveridge gave emphasis to
the Whitney version and quoted it at length.

By the canons of strict historical criticism, however, the Whitney
report stands discredited. As Paul M. Angle has pointed out, Whitney's
notes were sketchy. The speech is not included in Whitney's *Life on
the Circuit with Lincoln* published in 1892, which is strange if
Whitney had kept notes of the text; the report lacks Lincoln's "logical
precision"; some who heard it later declared that it "bore no relation"
to what Lincoln had said; and finally, a contemporary report of the
speech in the Alton *Courier* of June 5, 1856, shows "too great a
divergence in content to be easily reconciled." [20]

Considered as oratory, the speech was truly remarkable in its effect
upon the immediate audience. Yet it remains lost; [21] its content can
only be conjectured; its presentation by Whitney in an alleged verbatim report of an address which lasted an hour and a half, is unjustified; its inclusion in Lincoln's works edited by A. B. Lapsley
is an editorial error. The fame of the speech, of course, remains. Herndon said that on this occasion his partner was "seven feet" tall. [22]

Following the state convention at Bloomington the Republicans
held a ratification meeting at Springfield, in which Lincoln naturally
took part. It was a most curious affair according to Herndon's account.
Though all the usual efforts had been made to draw a crowd, the
courthouse being the place of assemblage, only three persons appeared,
said Herndon, one man in addition to Lincoln and himself. Lincoln
writers have usually followed Herndon in treating this incident, but
his statement, despite his presence on the occasion, is in error. The
Illinois State Journal (Republican) reported a large meeting, while
the *Illinois State Register,* whose Democratic editor was ready at all
times to belittle Republicans, admitted two hundred. [23] At this meeting (June 10), according to the *Journal,* "Lincoln took the stand

[20] Whitney, *Life on the Circuit with Lincoln,* Angle edition, intro., 24–25.
[21] Wakefield, *How Lincoln Became President,* 65.
[22] Herndon (Angle ed.), 313.
[23] See Paul M. Angle's editorial comment in *ibid.,* 315 n.

and pronounced the most logical and finished argument against the evils to be apprehended from the continued aggressions of the slave power, that it has ever been our good fortune to listen to." [24]

VII

In 1856 the Democrats nominated a man whose availability consisted in his having been outside of the country for a number of years. Douglas and Pierce being too close to the tempest of conflict to qualify as candidates, the choice fell upon James Buchanan of Pennsylvania. His career had been that of Federalist, Jacksonian senator, secretary of state under Polk, and diplomat in the capitals of Russia and Britain. His concepts and attitudes were those of Christian piety, orderly government, the rule of law, abhorrence of abolitionist agitation, alarm at the divisive tendencies of Republican policies, and a troubled sense of crisis as the tornado of discord was sweeping over the land. John C. Breckinridge of Kentucky was chosen for Vice President.

The American (Knownothing) party, promoting its prejudice against what were deemed non-American racial groups, nominated ex-President Millard Fillmore for President, and Andrew Jackson Donelson for Vice President.

As if to emphasize its obsoleteness and unimportance, the Whig party—or a pitiful remnant of it—met in Baltimore and went through the motions of a national convention. Instead of offering any candidate of their own in an age when most Whigs had gone into American or Republican ranks (though some preferred the Democratic party) they merely endorsed the candidates of the Knownothings. In the words of Edward Bates, who presided over its demise, this once powerful party "committed suicide, in 1856, and thereby left the nation without a *bodyguard*." [1]

In an era when Republicans were emphasizing Bleeding Kansas, other parties revealed a marked unwillingness to touch the sensitive question of slavery. The Whigs announced no principles but deplored the danger of sectionalism. Spokesmen of the American party made the enlightening statement that on the subject of slavery they stood "upon the principles . . . of the Constitution . . . , yielding noth-

---

[24] *Illinois State Journal*, June 11, 1856.

[1] Howard K. Beale, ed., *The Diary of Edward Bates (Annual Report*, Amer. Hist. Assoc., 1930), 390.

ing more and claiming nothing less." [2] The Democrats resisted all attempts at renewing the agitation concerning slavery and took their stand on "non-interference by Congress with slavery in state and territory, or in the District of Columbia." [3] The Republicans condemned slavery along with polygamy as twin relics of barbarism, and demanded that slavery be excluded from national territory.[4]

This declaration by the Republicans was a part of the platform adopted by their national convention of 1856 at Philadelphia. For presidential candidate the convention chose a man whose name was later to be associated with inefficiency, vindictive radicalism, and anti-Lincoln excess—John C. Frémont, "Pathfinder" and romantic hero. His surname bore, like an exotic flourish, the French accent mark. His merits for high civil office were largely negative; it was felt that he would not offend many people; it would have been difficult for his supporters to demonstrate that he possessed qualities requisite for a responsible leader and chief magistrate of the nation in the difficult fifties. More solid leaders, however, such as Seward, were not pushed forward with vigor; prospects for Republican success at the polls were not bright; it has been remarked that the party selected "a candidate whose defeat in November would not harm the party's future." [5]

For Vice President the Republicans presented William L. Dayton of New Jersey. His only serious rival was Abraham Lincoln, who received 110 votes for Vice President on informal ballot.[6] Orville

---

[2] This solemn statement was issued by the national council of the American party which met at Philadelphia on February 18, 1856. Bancroft, *Seward*, I, 417. The party convention which met at Philadelphia, February 22–25, 1856, did not adopt this resolution, noncommittal as it was, nor did it mention slavery. McKee, *National Conventions*, 101–102.

[3] McKee, *National Conventions*, 92. The quoted words were printed in full capitals.

[4] *Ibid.*, 98.   [5] Milton, *Eve of Conflict*, 230.

[6] H. C. Whitney tells of Lincoln, while attending court in Urbana (June 20, 1856), hearing a report of his receiving 110 votes for the vice-presidential nomination and passing it off with the remark that he thought it was "the other *great man* of the same name from Mass." This account, with additional details, appears in a MS. statement by Whitney, of which a copy was made for Ward H. Lamon. On the margin of the copy appears the comment: "This is not true L." Why Lamon doubted the statement is not known. (The Lamon MS. copy is in the Huntington Library.) Hertz (*Hidden Lincoln*, 390) gives the erroneous reading: "This is not true. H.", incorrectly implying that Herndon doubted the account. Soon after the time this news would have been received Lincoln is known to have been in Urbana, and it is quite possible that he was there as Whitney relates. Whitney, *Life on the Circuit*, Angle ed., 95–96; William B. Archer, in *Journal*, Ill. State Hist. Soc., XII, 273–275 (1919); *Bulletin No. 51*, Abr. Lincoln Assoc., March 1938, 3–5.

H. Browning of Illinois remarked laconically in his diary: "Heard to day of the nomination of Freemont by the Republican Convention at Philadelphia for President. He was not my first choice, but I am content. Would have preferred McLean . . . ." [7]

Lincoln had also preferred McLean (not a very exciting leader), yet he took an active part in the canvass of 1856, making over fifty speeches. [8] Fragments only of these speeches appear in his collected works. The campaign of that year is for the most part an unrecovered chapter in his life. At Galena he spoke vigorously for preservation of the Union, insisting that "All this talk about the dissolving of the Union is humbug." [9] At Kalamazoo [10] he stressed the preservation of a civilization in which "every man can make himself." [11] This type of civilization he considered doubtful of survival if the spread of slavery was not halted. And, as elsewhere, he strongly urged that the election of a Northern President should not be regarded as cause for disunion. He considered it "shameful" that so much was said of dissolution of the Union if Frémont and Dayton were elected. [12] As to Frémont being an "abolitionist," Lincoln answered "no such thing"; he added that he knew "of no word in the language that has been used so much as that one, 'abolitionist,' having no definition." [13]

When election came in November 1856 the popular vote stood: Buchanan 1,838,169; Frémont 1,341,264; Fillmore 874,534. Buchanan received 174 electoral votes Frémont 114, Fillmore 8. Fillmore had only the vote of Maryland; Buchanan carried the rest of the South and border, and in addition the states of Pennsylvania, California, Illinois, Indiana, and New Jersey; all the other commonwealths—including New York and constituting a startling number from the Southern viewpoint—went for the new Republican party. In commenting on the election Lincoln pointed out that voters for Buchanan were "in a minority of the whole people by about four hundred thousand votes" and that Buchanan's opponents were "divided between

---

[7] Browning, *Diary*, I, 241–242.   [8] *Works*, VI, 38.   [9] *Works*, II, 295 (Aug. 1, 1856).

[10] It is odd that one should speak of "the lost speech" of Lincoln. There are many lost speeches. After long remaining unknown, the speech at Kalamazoo on August 27, 1856, an ambitious extemporaneous effort before a huge crowd, was discovered a few years ago in the files of the Detroit *Daily Advertiser*. For the text of the speech stenographically reported, together with an account of its discovery and the circumstances of its delivery, see Thomas I. Starr, ed., *Lincoln's Kalamazoo Address against Extending Slavery*.

[11] *Ibid.*, 39.   [12] *Ibid.*, 40–41.   [13] *Ibid.*, 43.

Frémont and Fillmore." He hoped that factions then divided would "let bygones be bygones" and "come together for the future" on the basis of the "central idea" of the "equality of men." [14]

To the sectional disturbances of this overwrought decade the Supreme Court in 1857 made its own contribution. There had arisen the case of Dred Scott, a Missouri slave whose vicissitudes had carried him from slavery into territory made free by law of Congress, and back into slavery. Confused litigation in Missouri was followed by a misleading and fictitious transfer of ownership. Finally, via a Federal court in Missouri, the case found its tedious way into the Supreme Court of the United States.[15] From the impressive bench of that high tribunal nine justices gave nine opinions. Cutting through reams of legal verbosity the historian notes two main points, or doctrines, in the opinion as issued by Chief Justice Roger B. Taney. (1) A Negro, he held, can have no status as a citizen of the United States. (2) Congress has no constitutional power to exclude slavery from national territory; it has only "the power coupled with the duty of . . . protecting the owner in his rights." This meant that the law by which Congress had excluded slavery in the territories north of latitude 36° 30′ (the Missouri compromise of 1820), together with similar laws, was unconstitutional and void. Antislavery circles resounded with denunciations of Taney, of the opinion, and of the Court. Far from clarifying a point which many considered settled in the opposite sense, the decision intensified the unfortunate controversy. The Republicans, elated by the large popular support they had received in the election of 1856, were pleased to have an issue on which Douglas would be painfully embarrassed, and to which many good voters would honestly rally.

---

[14] *Works*, II, 308–312 (Dec. 10, 1856).
[15] Randall, *Civil War and Reconstruction*, 148–156.

CHAPTER V

LINCOLN AND DOUGLAS

I

THE year 1854 in Lincoln's life had marked a renewal of political activity.[1] After the close of his uneventful term in Congress in 1849 there had been a period of recession and passivity in which it appeared that Abraham Lincoln's story was to be that of a fameless Illinois lawyer, but in 1854 the Kansas-Nebraska question was changing the face of parties and offering a challenge to new leadership. It was plain that Lincoln's great opponent would be Douglas, with whom he had debated as long ago as the 1830's unless, as some feared and others hoped, Douglas would go over to the Republicans and become their leader.

In October 1854 the State Fair was in progress at Springfield, and the "gathering, devoted primarily to the interests of the farmer, became a rendezvous for state politicians," causing resentment as members of the Agricultural Society saw political leaders distracting the people's attention from their "Annual Jubilee and School of Life." [2]

---

[1] In 1854 Lincoln had been elected to the Illinois legislature but resigned his seat. His partner has stated that this was done because of his ambition to be chosen United States senator by that same legislature. Herndon (Angle ed.), 301. His senatorial ambition was real and intense, but when, after heavy strength in the initial balloting, his friends began to turn to Trumbull, Lincoln advised his "remaining friends" to support Trumbull, who was elected on the tenth ballot (February 8, 1855). This was not mere generosity to Trumbull. Lincoln had made a determined effort to obtain the senatorship and had promoted this effort to the point where all hope had ceased. Had he been chosen then, the famous senatorial canvass with Douglas in 1858 would not have occurred, and Lincoln's chance for the presidency might never have risen higher than Trumbull's. In a letter to E. B. Washburne, February 9, 1855 (*Works*, II, 274–277), Lincoln gave an account of the "agony" over the senatorship, from which one cannot but conclude that he wanted the office keenly. Other letters point to the same conclusion.

[2] Edwin Earle Sparks, ed., *The Lincoln-Douglas Debates of 1858* (Ill. Hist. Coll., III), 10–11.

This tendency of politicians to invade other than political domains was both a sign of the times and an American trait. It was a field day for political agitation, and both Lincoln and Douglas spoke at length before audiences in the hall of the House of Representatives.[8] Two weeks later at Peoria they met again, each making an extended address. Repeating the Springfield speech[4] of October 4, Lincoln was in his best campaigning form as he urged his countrymen to purify the republican robe, to wash it white, to readopt the Declaration of Independence, to turn slavery "back upon its existing legal rights," to save the Union, and in doing so to "make and to keep it forever worthy of the saving." This he urged in terms of "Fellow-countrymen, Americans, South as well as North," joining in "the great and good work."[5]

Between those October debates of 1854 and the great debate of 1858 Lincoln had continued his political activity, though busy with law practice, had been drawn somewhat tardily into the Republican party, had, as noted above, received 110 votes as vice-presidential nominee in 1856, and in that year had spoken many times for Frémont, whom he disliked.[6] Then on June 16, 1858, the Republican state convention at Springfield gave him its highest honor next to endorsement for the presidency by nominating him for United States senator. Having been the leading Whig of Illinois while yet in his thirties, he was now its leading Republican.

On the occasion of this nomination Lincoln delivered a carefully prepared speech which was not only to become one of his most famous; it was also to require frequent explanation and interpretation. "If we could first know *where* we are," he said, "and *whither* we are

---

[8] Douglas spoke on October 3. Next day Lincoln answered him, speaking for more than three hours. Douglas immediately followed with a rejoinder. At this point radical abolitionists, calling themselves "Republicans" (a word Lincoln was avoiding), arranged a meeting to form a Republican organization for Illinois. Lincoln deliberately avoided attending this meeting. Herndon (Angle ed.), 299; *Works*, III, 224.

[4] That this famous "Peoria speech" was a repetition of the Springfield speech of twelve days before has been pointed out by Beveridge (II, 268). Not to be outdone in city pride, Sherman D. Wakefield goes farther (*How Lincoln Became President*, 42–49, 165–173) and argues that the same speech was given still earlier, at Bloomington on September 12, 1854. He makes his case convincingly in parallel columns. See also Angle, *New Letters and Papers*, 133–137; E. E. East, "A Newly Discovered Speech of Lincoln," *Jour.*, Ill. State Hist. Soc., XXVIII, 65–77 (April, 1935).

[5] *Works*, II, 247–248 (Oct. 16, 1854).

[6] ". . . Frémont's strongest characteristics were those which Lincoln did not like or trust . . . ." Beveridge, II, 395.

tending, we could then . . . better judge *what* to do, and *how* to do it." Then he proceeded:

We are now far into the *fifth* year, since a policy was initiated, with the *avowed* object . . . of putting an end to slavery agitation,

Under . . . that policy, that agitation has not only, *not ceased,* but has *constantly augmented.*

In *my* opinion, it *will* not cease, until a *crisis* shall have been reached, and passed—

"A house divided against itself cannot stand."

I believe this government cannot endure; permanently half *slave* and half *free.*

I do not expect the Union to be *dissolved*—I dot [*sic*] expect the house to *fall*—but I *do* expect it will cease to be divided.

It will become *all* one thing, or *all* the other.

Either the *opponents* of slavery, will arrest the further spread of it, and place it where the public mind shall rest in the belief that it is in course of ultimate extinction; or its *advocates* will puch [*sic*] it forward, till it shall become alike lawful in *all* the States, *old* as well as *new—North* as well as *South.*[7]

The speech was an attack upon Douglas's "popular sovereignty," a doctrine which Lincoln proceeded to assail by history, ridicule, homely illustration, and rhetorical question. Citing the Kansas-Nebraska bill of Stephen Douglas, the Dred Scott decision of Roger Taney, and the endorsement of that decision by Franklin Pierce and James Buchanan (outgoing and incoming Presidents), he asserted that all the pieces fitted together in terms of a one-sided proslavery application of popular sovereignty till, as he said, "Under the Dred Scott decision 'squatter sovereignty' squatted out of existence, tumbled down like temporary scaffolding . . . —helped to carry an election, and then was kicked to the winds." [8]

Timbers had been turned out at different times by different work-men—Stephen, Franklin, Roger, and James; then behold, "we see these timbers joined together . . . , all the tenons and mortises exactly fitting, . . . in such a case we find it impossible not to believe that Stephen and Franklin and Roger and James all understood one another from the beginning . . . ." [9]

---

[7] *Illinois State Journal,* June 18, 1858. Because of Lincoln's reading of the proof, the *Journal's* version, with its italics, paragraphing, and somewhat eccentric punctuation, may be accepted as the best text; it reveals that Lincoln was weighing his words.

[8] *Works,* III, 6–7.   [9] *Ibid.,* III, 10.

Warming to his argument, Lincoln denounced what he called Douglas's "care not" policy regarding slavery, declared that slavery was being extended by putting "this and that together," observed that "another nice little niche" remained to be filled by a decision of the Supreme Court denying a state the power to exclude slavery, thus making slavery "alike lawful in all the States," and predicted the day when the people would "awake to the reality . . . that the Supreme Court has made Illinois a slave State," unless what he called the "present political dynasty" should be overthrown.[10] Then he took care to destroy the argument that Republicans should turn to Douglas as their leader, conceding that Douglas was "a great man," but adding, in a rather ill chosen phrase, that " 'a living dog is better than a dead lion.' "[11] He ended with the plea that if the Republicans should stand firm when their enemy was faltering, they would surely have the victory.

Unless biography is to be treated solely as fulsome eulogy, it becomes a duty to analyze this speech. Analyzing it, one finds in the first place that Lincoln had done the thing which fans a leader's fame without clarifying his position—that is, he had coined a quotable but debatable phrase. From now on, people might know next to nothing in true substance about Lincoln, yet know that he had used the words "house divided" and "half slave, half free." The difficulty about this was that Lincoln was in reality a conservative [12] when considered in contrast to those who were urging "radical" changes as to slavery; yet his slogan-like phrase was of the kind that an abolitionist, and a radical one at that, might have used. From 1858 Lincoln was in the position of Seward who was also a non-radical but whose phrases —"higher law" and "irrepressible conflict"—were so indissolubly as-

---

10 *Ibid.*, III, 12.   11 *Ibid.*, III, 13.

12 Basically Lincoln was a liberal; this becomes clear when one considers his attitude on matters of human dignity, civil liberty, justice, and fundamental problems of government. It has already been pointed out how Lincoln's thought went along with Jefferson's. On practical questions of dealing with slavery, however, Lincoln was the opposite of "radical" in a day when that word was coming to be applied to a policy of extreme measures toward the South—a policy which was radical only in the sense of being drastic and oppressive. Since the politicians who came to be called "radicals" were in truth reactionaries, as became evident in reconstruction days in economic as well as political matters, Lincoln's opposition to the radicals should be counted for liberalism. One cannot treat Lincoln at all in this period without recognizing two things which could only superficially be considered contradictory: his fundamental liberalism, and his marked preference for non-drastic measures in the realm of slavery and sectional adjustment.

sociated with his name that he could be superficially misrepresented as a radical. Lincoln's friends had urged him to omit this house-divided part of his speech, but Lincoln, in a moment of reliance on his own judgment of public policy—a reliance that was to reappear on occasion as President—concluded that his speech was the right doctrine and decided to stick to it.[13]

From the standpoint of correct representation of what was happening at the time, the speech was susceptible of criticism in at least two respects: (1) It implied a conspiracy or understanding between Douglas, Taney, Pierce, and Buchanan which (in the sense of a deliberate plot or agreement among these men) was quite fanciful and non-existent. (2) It assailed Douglas and his popular sovereignty as if in Douglas's mind the policy had never been intended otherwise than as promoting the proslavery cause in the territories. The battle royal that Douglas was waging with the Buchanan administration on that very point, with Douglas holding out against the Lecompton constitution in Kansas, ought to have been sufficient refutation of such a charge. Yet Lincoln had so phrased the case, with his homely illustration of the workmen and the timbers, that the accusation sounded most convincing.

The speech involved a certain shaping of interpretations for the speaker's purpose in a situation where another speaker could quite honestly have given an opposite interpretation. Lincoln was representing Douglas's break with Buchanan as if it amounted to nothing. One can hardly read the history of those times without realizing that it amounted to a great deal, and that Lincoln was denying to Douglas credit for resisting the very acts against Kansas which Lincoln himself was assailing.

There were yet other points open to question in this house-divided speech. Just what did Lincoln mean when he said that the Union would become all one or all the other? What Lincoln was in fact trying to do in this whole period was to put the damper on sectional conflict. Over and again that position was clearly stated. Yet people who knew nothing of that, or chose to ignore it, would quote this phrase and picture Lincoln as a man who would either insist on uniformity as to slavery or else divide the country—a man who would perhaps assent to disunion as many abolitionists were quite willing

---

[13] Herndon (Angle ed.), 326; Sparks, 23–24.

to do. Lincoln did not mean it that way. He thought of a peacefully continuing Union, as his very words in the whole passage implied; in this continuing Union he seemed to envisage a future day when uniformity as to slavery would exist, but he was not demanding disunion while it should not exist. Yet it was not the whole speech, nor even the connected passage, that was quoted; rather, it was only those few challenging words that kept recurring when Lincoln was mentioned. The fact that Lincoln was no firebrand and that he did not intend disunion nor any attack upon legitimate Southern rights, would be overlooked, especially by his opponents who would make it appear that he would oppose any type of Union-saving compromise.

At the time the speech went well. It added to Lincoln's fame, caused him to be in wide demand, and served as an opening salvo in the coming party contest in Illinois. It gave Lincoln's party an issue not only against Democrats generally but against Douglas at a time when otherwise men were thinking of the close similarity of Douglas to those Democrats who, like Trumbull, were now shifting to the new Republican party and being received with ready endorsement. One thing Lincoln could not endure was to have it thought that Douglas was Republican timber. Lincoln was concerned not only with promoting his party but with exerting large leadership within the party.

II

The coming legislature of Illinois would have the constitutional function of choosing a senator of the United States, and the extralegal obligation (or practical necessity) of restricting its choice to the two recognized party candidates. It looked like a close matter, and Lincoln was pushing hard. He was determined to follow on Douglas's trail, address audiences in the same places, and give a resounding reply to every one of his opponent's pronouncements. He was preparing carefully, assembling material, keeping a political notebook, writing letters, courting his friends in and out of the state, and watching the matter of alignment with the right groups. He would have pursued Douglas in any case had there been no special series of seven formal "joint debates." When Douglas's speaking engagements were announced, and when the Democratic senator was shifting emphasis away from Lincoln by assailing Trumbull, Lincoln seized the initiative, using Norman B. Judd of Chicago as intermediary, and formally challenged Douglas "to divide time, and address the same audiences the present canvass."[1] In a personal interview at Bement, Illinois, the agreement between the two senatorial candidates was duly sealed, and from then on the joint debates were the subject of main interest in the prairie state.

Considering that there were only seven such joint debates, the sizable state of Illinois was pretty well canvassed. The selection of places went by congressional districts, the Chicago area having already been the scene of a lively encounter between the candidates (July 9–10, 1858, at the Tremont House). The first two debates were in northern Illinois, at Ottawa on August 21 and Freeport August 27. Far down in "Egypt" the third debate was held at the picturesque Southern-like town of Jonesboro on September 15. The midway point was reached at Charleston in eastern Illinois on September 18. This was near the Thomas Lincoln home, in a region "prolific in Republicans."[2] Then in October the contest would draw to its close with debates at Galesburg on the seventh, at Quincy on the thirteenth, and lastly at Alton on the fifteenth. Election day, a time of excitement and some disorder, was to come on Tuesday, November 2.

People of the time thought of it as a "momentous" encounter.[3] Writing of the canvass while it proceeded, men noted that it was something new,[4] that both men were material from which Presidents might be made,[5] and that Illinois was "the battleground of the year."[6] A vigorous, some said "desperate," fight was expected.

Stump speaking was a powerful magnet in the Middle West, and huge crowds poured out. It is amusing to read the estimates of these crowds, varying according to partisan claims of the papers in which

---

1 *Works*, III, 189 (July 24, 1858).

2 New York *Evening Post*, Sep. 21, 1858, reprinted in Sparks, 319.

3 The word "momentous" as well as "desperate" was used by the Cincinnati *Commercial*, July 6, 1858. On July 13 the New York *Evening Post* declared: "Illinois is just now the theatre of the most momentous political contest, whether we consider the eminence of the contestants or the consequences which may result . . . , that has occured in this country in any state canvass since the defeat of Silas Wright [of New York] for Governor in 1846." These comments are quoted in Sparks, 31, 49. Perhaps the writer in the *Post* did not realize how soon men would scratch their heads in doubt as to why the Silas Wright campaign was so momentous, or even as to who Silas Wright was.

4 The New York *Herald* (July 27, 1858) referred to the canvass as "somewhat of an anomaly." Sparks, 46.

5 Sparks, 49.   6 *Ibid.*, 43.

they appeared. A Chicago crowd amounted to thirty thousand by one account, twelve thousand by another.[7] An open-air crowd at Charleston, drawn from adjacent counties in a strictly rural district, was estimated at from "twelve to fifteen thousand."[8] The canvass was more than a contest; it was a spectacle and a show, replete with all the devices and claptrap of rough-and-ready campaigning. It was clamorous and colorful, with bands, bells, artillery salvos, fluttering banners, fireworks, torchlight processions, placards, rockets, floats, decorations, shouts and cheers, boys hired for the congenial task of making a racket, and at Charleston a gayly bedecked wagon carrying thirty-two "pretty and intelligent ladies" representing the thirty-two states in the Union.[9] It was noted with pride that a Lincoln procession from Mattoon to Charleston was headed by the "Bowling Green Band" from Terre Haute.[10]

Speeches were long, but attention was good despite the difficulties of open-air acoustics and the discomfort of crowding masses. Rivalry was keen. Each side was eager to have the largest flag, the longest parade, the best and loudest music. The debates were stenographically —or, as they said, "phonographically"—reported, but each journalist colored his descriptions by his obvious preference for Douglas or for Lincoln. The wordy discourses were not all reason and light. There was twitting and banter, maneuvering for party advantage, and the shaping of appeals for local effect. Emphasis was upon the position that each party and each champion took on the "vexed question" of slavery in the territories. Lincoln made more effort to confine the discussion there than Douglas, who sought to broaden the controversy to cover the disruptive issue of social and political equality between the races and to associate Lincoln and the Republicans with all the stigmas that attached to abolitionists, whose popularity in large parts of Illinois was at zero level. Douglas was effective in ridiculing Lincoln's party, scoring its lack of a consistent name: up north they were Republicans or Abolitionists; at Springfield they avoided the name Republican, but referred to their meeting as "a Convention of all men opposed to the Democratic party"; in lower Egypt they advertised a "meeting of the Free Democracy" whereat Trumbull would speak. "Did you ever hear," said Douglas, "of this new party, called the 'Free Democracy'?" "What object have these Black Republicans in changing their name in

---

[7] *Ibid.*, 39.   [8] *Ibid.*, 312.   [9] *Ibid.*, 324.   [10] *Ibid.*, 267.

every county? . . . They have one name in the north, another in the center, and another in the south." [11]

In pointing to his long record in public life, Douglas made no apology. He defended his popular sovereignty—local self-determination—as right in principle and wise in practice. To his mind it was the only practical and typically American solution. He was in fact having trouble with the doctrine, as his article next year in *Harper's Monthly* [12] was to show, but there is no reason to doubt his sincerity in urging that he intended his doctrine to be understood and applied in good faith, and that he had never known "the Democratic party to violate any one of its principles, out of . . . expediency, that it did not pay the debt with sorrow." "There is no safety or success for our party," he said, "unless we always do right . . . ." [13] He conceived of the task and destiny of the Democratic party in terms of Union. The party must unite and stand together, he said, resisting men who thought only of sections. He reminded his hearers that both major parties, Whigs and Democrats, had united for Union in 1850 and had joined "in establishing the Compromise . . . and restoring tranquillity and good feeling." [14] Showing how Clay had worked for compromise in the mid-century crisis and how Lincoln had worked to throw Clay overboard, he declared: "Lincoln is the man, in connection with Seward, Chase, Giddings, and other Abolitionists, who got up that strife that I helped Clay to put down." [15]

He added that for himself, he stood in 1858 where he had stood in 1850, 1854, and 1856. Prior to 1854, said Douglas, the two leading parties were both national. "An Old Line Whig could proclaim his principles in Louisiana and Massachusetts alike." [16] But times had changed. Lincoln and his party had "set themselves up as wiser than . . . men who made this Government, which . . . [had] flourished for seventy years under . . . popular sovereignty . . . ." [17] On the practical question as to how slavery could be excluded from a territory if the people so desired, being pinned down on this point by Lincoln's famous question at Freeport, Douglas "emphatically" answered that it could be done by "local police regulations." Sensing at once that his

---

11 *Ibid.*, 299.

12 "The Dividing Line between Federal and Local Authority: Popular Sovereignty in the Territories," *Harper's Monthly*, XIX, 519–537 (Sep., 1859).

13 Sparks, 458.   14 *Ibid.*, 461.   15 *Ibid.*, 491.   16 *Ibid.*, 86.   17 *Ibid.*, 98.

STEPHEN A. DOUGLAS

Distinguished national leader, powerful antagonist, rival of Lincoln. Ably supported Lincoln and the Union in the crisis of 1860–61. The sobriquet "Little Giant," while appropriate for his prestige and influence, gave also a suggestion of physical power and impressiveness despite smallness of stature.

THE VOLK BRONZE

Bronze cast of life mask by Leonard W. Volk, photographed by Edward Steichen. Courtesy of Carl Sandburg, of Frederick H. Meserve, and of Oliver R. Barrett. (This copy of the photograph was loaned by Mr. Barrett.) The life mask, delight of sculptors, presents a challenge to photographers. A remarkable impression of the living face.

assertion conflicted with the Dred Scott decision, he added that the people of a territory would have "the right . . . to make a Slave Territory or a Free Territory . . . under the Nebraska bill" despite the attitude of the Supreme Court on the "abstract question." [18] If it be said that this involved a certain disregard of the Olympian finality and sanctity of the Court, an equal objection to the Court's infallibility was evident on Lincoln's side, such objection being counted a virtue. Douglas rode hard on Lincoln's house-divided declaration, declared that the "Black Republican" party had been abolitionized, and sought to make it appear that Lincoln and his partisans favored Negro equality.

On two points Douglas spoke with particular scorn and bitterness. (1) He resented the use of the ax against him by the Buchanan administration because he refused to allow his popular sovereignty to be distorted into a proslavery maneuver as at Lecompton. (2) He was equally indignant at the alliance of Illinois Republicans with Buchanan Democrats, both groups assailing him for agreeing with Lincoln in the Lecompton matter.[19] "A Democratic Administration," he said, "deems it consistent . . . to wield its power in this State in behalf of the Republican Abolition candidates in every county . . . ." [20] At another time he said: "What do you Republicans think of a political organization that will try to make an unholy combination with its professed foes to beat a man merely because he has done right? . . . You know that the axe . . . is suspended over every man in office in Illinois, and the terror of proscription is threatened every Democrat by the present Administration, unless he supports the Republican ticket . . . ." [21]

For each state its own laws, for each territory its own popular decision, was Douglas's principle. For the country, union and tolerance, defeat of the one party he deemed purely sectional, return to early principles. He would have each state allow or disallow slavery as it should choose; [22] he also thought that each state should choose whether to give or deny the vote to Negroes.[23] In the peroration of his first speech opening the joint debates, he grew eloquent on the

---

[18] *Ibid.*, 161–162.
[19] Phillip G. Auchampaugh, "The Buchanan-Douglas Feud," *Journal*, Ill. State Hist. Soc., XXV, 5–48 (1932).
[20] Sparks, 460.   [21] *Ibid.*, 337.
[22] This was also Lincoln's principle.   [23] Sparks, 97.

theme of a nation that had grown great, had crossed the Alleghenies, and had turned "the prairie into a garden" on the principles of the "fathers" who "intended that our institutions should differ," knowing "that the North and the South . . . [had] different climates, productions, and interests." What he opposed was "trying to array all the Northern States in one body against the South, to excite a sectional war between the Free States and the Slave States, in order that the one or the other may be driven to the wall." [24]

III

The amenities of debate were honored. There was some horseplay, but for the most part the etiquette though perhaps not altogether the purest ethics of forensic discussion was preserved. Verbal assaults were sharp and crushing, but unseemly personalities were usually avoided, and one witnessed the spectacle, as Douglas said, of a "large mass of people" made up of "various . . . parties" giving "kind and respectful attention" not only to friends, but to those with whom they disagreed.[1] At Springfield in July 1858, according to the New York *Herald,* whenever either Lincoln or Douglas referred to the other, it was "in the kindest, most courteous and dignified manner." [2] There was taunting, chafing, and derision; yet it stopped short of offensive insult. Douglas held Lincoln up as a man who had kept a "grocery" [3]—i. e., who sold liquor—which Lincoln denied,[4] who had made a kind of bargain to dissolve both the Democratic and Whig parties in order to erect an abolitionist party under the name Republican,[5] who proclaimed abolition doctrines,[6] and who "had to be carried from the platform" at Ottawa because of embarrassment at Douglas's questions.[7] When Lincoln stated that he would be sorry to have to vote on the admission of another slave state, Douglas said: "I trust the people of Illinois will not put him in a position [as senator] which he would be so sorry to occupy." [8]

Lincoln's manner toward Douglas was usually respectful and free

---

[24] *Ibid.,* 97–98.   [1] Sparks, 159.   [2] Sparks, 46–47.   [3] *Ibid.,* 91.
[4] *Ibid.,* 102.   [5] *Ibid.,* 88.   [6] *Ibid.,* 93.
[7] Lincoln had been borne off in the manner of a hero; Douglas admitted that he was merely playful in making it appear that he "had to be carried" because of embarrassment. *Ibid.,* 248, 250.
[8] *Ibid.,* 251.

from personal ill-feeling. Sometimes his banter took the form of ironic compliment, as when he blandly commended his opponent for "gradually improving" [9]—i. e., becoming more severe against the Buchanan administration. For this Lincoln claimed credit, flattering himself that Douglas had taken his advice. Lincoln, as he himself said, had used no "vulgarity or blackguardism." [10] Some months after the debates he was careful to point out that he felt "no unkindness . . . toward Judge Douglas." [11] As for Douglas, his attitude was indicated by a Cincinnati newspaper in which it was noted that while he was "able and bold," his relations with Lincoln were "friendly." [12]

In argument Lincoln drove in his strokes wherever he sensed a weakness in Douglas's position or an embarrassment because of matters for which, if all the truth were told, Douglas was not to blame. He severely scored Douglas's indifference as to slavery and riddled his popular sovereignty creed as either proslavery or unjustifiably noncommittal on a moral issue. He twitted Douglas for his inconsistency in once favoring the Missouri compromise and later opposing it.[13] On the Dred Scott decision Lincoln's position in debate was a bit like having it both ways: the decision was riddled, yet Douglas was rapped for taking a position not in accord with it. Asserting that in former years there had never been a man who said that the Declaration of Independence did not include Negroes in the term "all men," Lincoln said that Taney was the first man who said it and next to him was Douglas.[14]

He did not permit Douglas and his party to go unscathed with an assertion that the Dred Scott decision was merely a negative or hands-off declaration. He drove hard on the point that the decision was an affirmation of Federal power to protect slavery, and that, if Douglas's party was sustained in the elections, the result would be a

---

[9] *Ibid.*, 466. Feeling was in fact tense, but usually it was kept under control. Reports of the Ottawa debate, however, suggest that Lincoln lost his temper, making angry interruptions during Douglas's rejoinder (*ibid.*, 118).

[10] *Ibid.*, 182.   [11] *Works*, V, 116 (Mar. 1, 1859).

[12] Cincinnati *Commercial*, July 12, 1858, quoted in Sparks, 42. This was during the senatorial canvass, though prior to the formal joint debates. At Ottawa Douglas was careful to say that he meant "nothing personally disrespectful or unkind" to his opponent (*ibid.*, 91).

[13] Sparks, 466. Henry Clay, with whom Lincoln agreed in the early phases of his career, as well as other Whig leaders, could have been twitted for the same inconsistency.

[14] *Ibid.*, 470.

"new Dred Scott decision, deciding against the right of the people of the States to exclude slavery."[15] The Taney type of constitutional reasoning, argued Lincoln, would legalize slavery in all the states, in the sense that the right of property in slaves, according to that decision, was affirmed in the Constitution.[16]

In this phase of his argument there were two respects in which an opponent could have said with some reason that Lincoln was vulnerable. (1) He was using the familiar device of denouncing a thing because it *might* possibly lead to a predicted result, as in an earlier day opponents had denounced the Federal Constitution and argued against its ratification on the ground that the ten-mile-square Federal district *might* become a terrible arsenal of tyranny. Governmental power of whatever sort must be reasonably used; the chance that a power *might* be abused—e. g., the power of taxation or of raising an army—does not mean that government must never be trusted, under popular controls, to exercise the power. On this point Lincoln was carrying the Dred Scott decision beyond its setting. While he remained within that setting, he had better justification for assailing the decision. In strict logic, perhaps, he ought to have been content to denounce the decision for what it was, rather than to predict an imaginary new decision.

(2) It was by tendencies quite the opposite of those for which Douglas stood that a fundamental constitutional alteration was introduced in 1868 by which civil and property rights in the states were made subordinate to and controllable by the Federal Constitution. This was done not by a new Supreme Court decision, but by a constitutional amendment, the fourteenth. When Lincoln spoke in 1858, his declaration that the Taney property doctrine of 1857 *might* some day lead to a Federal imposition of slavery upon all the states, was something of a non-sequitur. Few constitutional lawyers would contend that the domain of the fifth amendment included the vastly broader field of the fourteenth. That a future Supreme Court would ever rule that the Federal government could impose slavery upon unwilling states was extremely unlikely. Such a doctrine would have been opposed where Northern states prohibited slavery and in the South because of state-rights principles. In such matters one must make allowance for campaign technique, in which Lincoln was skill-

---

[15] *Ibid.*, 359.   [16] *Ibid.*, 358 (Oct. 7, 1858, at Galesburg).

ful, without concluding that his every argument was unanswerable.

Not allowing Douglas an interpretation that would preserve his favorite doctrine, Lincoln showed popular sovereignty to be inconsistent with the Supreme Court's decision. Here he was on firmer ground. Douglas, of course, could not be blamed for the inconsistency. He believed in a doctrine which the Court had pretty well demolished. He was in a dilemma; it was not of his making, but it gave him no end of embarrassment. Lincoln was not the man to let him off or avoid making him squirm; this particular inconsistency was one of Lincoln's most telling points. The great difference was that it cost Lincoln nothing, and gained him much, to denounce the Court, since the winning of Southern support was not a prime object of the Republican party. Douglas had to consider all parts of the country. It would be fatal for him to offend the South. Rights all around, thought Douglas, were protected by what he called popular sovereignty. It injured no one.

Lincoln too had his embarrassment which Douglas did not hesitate to exploit. It was the stigma of abolitionism. He repudiated it with spirit, asserting at Alton that Douglas was trying to place him "in an extremely Abolition attitude" before an audience which had "strong sympathies southward." [17] On various occasions Lincoln explained his house-divided declaration. He went so far as to say (in the month before the first joint debate) that in his half-slave-half-free speech he did not say he "was in favor of anything"; he was making "a prediction only—it may have been a foolish one, perhaps." [18]

Was Lincoln regretting his famous slogan? Only to the extent that it was being used to make him appear as an abolitionist or a promoter of strife and war. In explaining it he brought out what he insisted was the "real issue" [19] of the whole contest: that slavery was wrong, that peace and harmony in the country prior to 1854 had been based on the belief that it was "in course of ultimate extinction," [20] that these were the sentiments of the fathers, and that he intended only to resist the "farther spread" of the institution, and to "place it where the founders . . . originally placed it." [21] This sentiment he repeated, with renewed declarations against slavery as a wrong, many times.

---

[17] Sparks, 468.
[19] Sparks, 482.
[21] *Ibid.*, III, 34 (July 10, 1858).

[18] *Works*, III, 31–32 (July 10, 1858).
[20] *Works*, III, 32 (July 10, 1858).

He did not hedge on his house-divided declaration in the sense in which he said it should be interpreted, but he did resent Douglas's effort to make it appear that he was stirring up sectional strife. He agreed that diversity of institutions according to state choice was desirable; "instead of being a thing to 'divide the house' . . . [he said] they tend to sustain it." [22] But he insisted that the territories—future homes of free men—be kept free, not only for the native born but for "Hans, and Baptiste, and Patrick, and all other men from all the world." [23] Reducing the matter to the simplest terms, he said: "The real issue in this controversy . . . is the sentiment . . . of one class that looks upon the institution of slavery as a wrong, and of another class that does not look upon it as a wrong." His party, he said, looked upon it "as being a moral, social, and political wrong." [24]

IV

Lincoln's electioneering in 1858 was not confined to the formal joint debates. Indeed, if one thinks of what was doing in Illinois in the summer and fall of 1858 rather than of particular things singled out for historical emphasis, the famous seven debates were a minor fraction of the whole story. The period of July to October 1858 was a time of intense activity. He traveled almost constantly. Cheering crowds met him, escorted him through the streets, greeted him with banners and brass bands, and everywhere insisted on hearing him speak. He did not disappoint them. Besides the seven formal debates he spoke in this period at Clinton, Beardstown, Havana, Bath, Peoria, Henry, Augusta, Amboy, Carlinville, Bloomington, Edwardsville, Greenville, Danville, Urbana, Pekin, Oquawka, Monmouth, Lincoln, Mount Sterling, Carthage, La Harpe, Macomb, Petersburg, and many other places. At the last-named town, so close to the familiar New Salem haunts, Lincoln's address before "a large and enthusiastic assembly" was referred to as his sixty-second speech of the 1858 campaign.[1] During all this time, in addition to the joint debates and numerous

---

[22] Sparks, 478.   [23] *Ibid.*, 481.   [24] *Ibid.*, 482.

[1] *Menard Index*, Nov. 4, 1858. After referring to Lincoln's clear logic, his alignment with the doctrines of the Fathers, and his dissipation of misrepresentations and slanders, the *Index* added: "As a whole, we have seldom heard a political speech so perfect in all the essentials of candor, force & completeness." (The date of the Petersburg speech was October 29.) See also Henry Villard, *Memoirs*, I, 96.

minor speeches, he conferred with party workers, struggled with his correspondence, took a hand in the party affairs of this or that district, arranged to have thousands of his speeches printed (not omitting German-language copies), and managed to attend several local Republican conventions as at Tremont on August 30.

The adventures of Lincoln in this senatorial campaign included dining with Douglas, riding a river packet to be met at the wharf by cheering adherents, witnessing a balloon ascension, attending barbecues, celebrating with German Turners and parading firemen, sitting at Macomb for the famous ambrotype, being carried on the shoulders of admirers, meeting men of his company in the Black Hawk War who greeted him on the platform of one of the towns, and recalling at the same town (Bath) that as a surveyor he had staked it out of a "wooded wilderness." At one place he rode in a conestoga wagon drawn by six white horses. A "constant stream of old friends" met him at Hillsboro. At Sullivan his supporters interrupted Douglas and a "brawl" was "narrowly averted." The weather was cruelly hot, and at Winchester it was remarked that "His horses were white with sweat and he and his friends were black with dust." Crowds were huge; much of the speaking was in the open air; and a typical speech would last for two hours. Add these labors to the weary journeyings and one can believe that there was truth in the opposition report that he looked "jaded."

This vigorous popular campaigning meant a strenuous effort for Lincoln, but it was an American show, an exciting recreation for many thousands, a series of reunions with friends, and a genuine demonstration of Lincoln's popularity in Illinois. His arduous trips, his readiness to meet everyone, the homely incidents of his wide ranging itinerary—all the informal and spontaneous aspects of his electioneering—meant as much as his many long hours of speaking. People expected all this. They seldom thought of sparing him. To Lincoln it all came naturally; this was one of the sources of his strength. Few political leaders have known the people by way of wide travel and close personal association as did Lincoln.[2] Some would make it appear that in 1858 Lincoln was after bigger stakes, that he was in reality

---

[2] Incidents here briefly sketched are treated in Angle, *Lincoln, 1854–1861*, especially pp. 235–253. Angle's pages give detailed references to sources and, of course, Lincoln's correspondence is largely found in his collected writings. (Other sources have been consulted by the writer.) Quoted phrases are from Angle.

campaigning for the presidency. For this supposition there seems to be no adequate basis so far as Lincoln's 1858 intentions were concerned. Nevertheless, the many popular incidents and associations of the canvass against Douglas, as well as the content of his speeches in that campaign with the publicity they received in the nation, were a significant part of his road to larger leadership.

On election day (November 2, 1858) Douglas was "triumphantly sustained" by the "invincible Democracy of Illinois." [3] Yet the *Illinois State Journal* pointed out that a fair apportionment of legislative seats according to population would have given Lincoln's friends forty-one members in the lower house and fourteen in the upper (majorities), as compared with the actual result, by which in the lower house the membership was forty to thirty-five in Douglas's favor, while in the upper house Lincoln had only eleven senators, the Douglas and Buchanan elements having fourteen.[4] It was claimed that Lincoln's friends who were elected, though a minority in the legislature, represented a larger population than Douglas's friends. On the other hand it was asserted by Lincoln's opponents that the apportionment was the same under which a legislature had been elected which chose Trumbull, a party associate of Lincoln, for the Senate, and that Governor Bissell, a Republican, had vetoed a new apportionment bill in the session of 1856–57.[5]

Lincoln felt his defeat keenly, but looked to the future, promised to "fight in the ranks," pledged support for Trumbull's reëlection, urged that the "fight must go on," and declared that the "cause of civil liberty must not be surrendered at the end of one or even one hundred defeats." [6] He took comfort in the thought that the "popular vote of the state" was with him. The "plain old Democracy" was on his side; the "silk-stocking Whiggery," the "nice exclusive sort," was against him.[7] He was glad he had made the race. It gave him "a hearing

[3] Quincy *Herald*, Nov. 4, 1858. See illustration in Sparks, facing p. 534.

[4] The actual choice of senator was made by joint ballot of the Illinois General Assembly on January 5, 1859, Douglas receiving 54 votes and Lincoln 46. *Journal of the House of Representatives* Jan. 5, 1859, p. 32; *Senate Journal*, p. 30. In certain accounts (Beveridge, II, 695–696; Wakefield, 93) it is erroneously stated that on this occasion Lincoln received only 41 votes.

[5] Sparks, 535. Bissell at first approved the bill, then recalled it, expunged his approval, and vetoed it. His action came so late in the session that there was no chance for the Democrats to pass it over his veto.

[6] *Works*, V, 94 (Nov. 19, 1858).   [7] *Ibid.*, V, 95 (Nov. 19, 1858).

on the great and durable question of the age." Even though he should
"now sink out of view, and . . . be forgotten," he had "made some
marks . . . for the cause of civil liberty." [8]

V

It is surprising how little attention has been given to the actual content of the debates. The canvass had been conducted in dead earnest,
yet it has always been easier to relate its picturesque features than to
analyze its substance. It was symptomatic of the times that the debaters were not concerned with a representative coverage of national
questions, but almost entirely with slavery, and with only a limited
and comparatively unimportant aspect of that subject. Public attention is seldom devoted to a balanced and fully rounded estimate of
public problems. It takes some selected issue and concentrates on
that. So do political parties, with the added factor that parties make
it appear that they are more opposite than they really are, that their
points of difference on an incomplete statement of issues are the
only things the people need to contemplate, and that party voting is
the infallible method of accomplishing large results. One may distinguish between a discussion that strives always for a solution of
governmental problems and a "canvass" in which the participants
engage in sparring for popular effect and party advantage. In the
main the joint debates between Lincoln and Douglas belong in the
latter category.

Swinging up and down and back and forth across Illinois, making
the welkin ring and setting the prairies on fire, Lincoln and Douglas
debated—what? That is the surprising thing. With all the problems
that might have been put before the people as proper matter for their
consideration in choosing a senator—choice of government servants,
immigration, the tariff, international policy, promotion of education,
westward extension of railroads, the opening of new lands for homesteads, protection against greedy exploitation of those lands (a problem to which Congress gave insufficient attention), encouragement
to settlers, and the bettering of agriculture, not to mention such social
problems as guarding against economic depression, improving the
condition of factory workers, and alleviating those agrarian grievances

---

[8] *Ibid.*

that were to plague the coming decades—with such issues facing the country, these two candidates for the Senate talked as if there were only one issue. Thus instead of a representative coverage of the problems of mid-century America, the debaters gave virtually all their attention to slavery in the territories. More specifically, they were concentrating on the question whether Federal prohibition of slavery in western territories, having been dropped after full discussion in 1850, should be revived as if it were the only means of dealing with the highly improbable chance that human bondage would ever take root in such a place as Kansas, Nebraska, or New Mexico. It is indeed a surprising thing to suppose that the negligible amount of human bondage in Kansas,[1] or the alleged inability of the people of that nascent state to decide the matter for themselves, constituted the only American question of sufficient importance to occupy nearly all the attention of senatorial candidates in one of the most famous forensic episodes of the century. Remembering that slavery in the large was not the subject of the debates, it may be said that if the highly unlikely inflow of slavery into Kansas was the main topic of national concern, the American people were more fortunate than they knew.

It was not that any frontal attack upon slavery in the states was involved. Lincoln was far from being an abolitionist, and nothing was more obvious in the controlling counsels of Lincoln's party in that period than the avoidance of any "ultra"—i. e., strongly abolitionist —tone. The "peculiar institution" was not being assailed by the Republican party in the commonwealths where it existed. Nor was it a case of one side demanding full civil and social equality for the Negro while the other side opposed such equality. Big and fundamental things about slavery and the Negro were not on the agenda of national parties. Each speaker could swell or mute the discussion on those fundamentals as he saw fit, and they were usually muted so far as commitments or constructive proposals were concerned. Despite all this, the intensity of the discussion baffled description. The people of Illinois were being worked up in party feeling by a discussion which contributed little to the practical solution even of such a matter as slaves in Kansas.

The debate was a spectacle, a drama, an exhibition, almost a sporting event. In addition it was a serious matter, but its dramatic quality

---

[1] For the tiny amount of slavery in Kansas see below, pp. 240–241.

could not be ignored, and that quality would perhaps have been lost if the speakers had not used the language of controversy. In other words, the Lincoln-Douglas canvass was not an effort to work out a formula of agreement. Had such an effort been made, it would have been found that these two leaders had much in common. On the broad problem of racial relations they did not fundamentally differ. Lincoln was not proposing any marked change in the depressed status of the Negro. "I am not . . . in favor of . . . the social and political equality of the white and black races," he declared.[2] Again he said: ". . . I am not in favor of negro citizenship." [3] It is not easy to put Lincoln's actual position in a word, for it did not fit any pat formula, certainly not that of the abolitionist. He cited Clay as showing that equality was abstract; you could not apply it.[4] The idea that he favored Negro suffrage or equality, he said, was a misrepresentation.[5] It was "untrue," a "fabrication." [6] As if to leave no doubt on that point he said: ". . . I did not at any time say I was in favor of negro suffrage; . . . I declared against it." [7]

This was not the whole of Lincoln's position on Negro rights. He denounced the principle that "all men" did not include the Negro.[8] He qualified his statements carefully. While holding that there was a "physical difference" which would "forever forbid the two races living together on terms of social and political equality," and while favoring the "superior position assigned to the white race," he did not believe that "the negro should be denied everything." [9] He did not favor "a tendency to dehumanize the negro, to take away from him the right of ever striving to be a man." [10] Matters of racial equality, intermarriage and the like, he dismissed as "false issues." [11] The equality he was interested in was not a matter of color or size but of inalienable rights.[12] He believed the Southern people entitled to a fugitive slave law. As to slavery in the states, not only did he recognize a lack of Federal power to overthrow it; he also disclaimed any "inclination" to "disturb" it.[13] He was not insisting that Missouri should emancipate its slaves. No such thing. Such a thought was a "perversion" of his meaning. His concern was for new societies, not old states.[14]

---

[2] Sparks, 267. [3] *Ibid.*, 303. [4] *Ibid.*, 471. [5] *Works*, V, 141 (Sep. 16, 1859).
[6] Sparks, 468. [7] *Works*, V, 145 (Sep. 16, 1859). [8] Sparks, 472–473. [9] *Ibid.*, 268.
[10] Sparks, 473. [11] *Ibid.*, 482. [12] *Ibid.*, 469. [13] *Works*, IV, 328–329.
[14] Sparks, 473.

As to slavery in Kansas, Lincoln wanted Kansas free by congressional prohibition; Douglas favored a program that would inevitably have made Kansas free both as a territory by popular sovereignty and as a state by constitutional processes. The attitude of the two men toward the Kansas policy of Buchanan was virtually identical, though on this point the Republicans were unwilling to give Douglas credit for agreeing with them—this in spite of the fact that some Republicans, but not Lincoln, even spoke of Douglas as a suitable leader for their own party.

Lincoln and Douglas were also alike in deploring sectionalism. Douglas wanted always to subordinate any issue that would split the people North and South. For that very reason he did not want to agitate the slavery question. Lincoln equally deplored disruptive tendencies, but he attributed the disunity to the discarding of the old concept that slavery was to remain of limited extent.

Statements flung about in the debates did not define the issue as a choice between a position taken by Lincoln and an opposite position taken by Douglas. This became evident when, early in the canvass, each candidate sought to impale his opponent upon spikes of formal interrogation. At Freeport Lincoln answered seven questions put to him by Douglas. In the first five his position differed not at all from his rival's. His answer to the seventh was noncommittal. Only on the sixth (prohibition of slavery in all the national territories) was there a difference between the two men.[15] Yet even on that point the difference was not vital in its practical effect upon the results. That is to say, in the territories that existed or might later be organized, Lincoln's demand of congressional prohibition for slavery would produce freedom, but so also would Douglas's principle of popular sovereignty honestly applied.

Conversely, Douglas's answers to Lincoln's questions at Freeport

---

[15] By negative answers to the first five questions Lincoln asserted that he (1) did not favor unconditional repeal of the fugitive slave act, (2) did not oppose the admission of any more slave states, (3) did not oppose the admission of a new state with such a constitution as the people might make, (4) did not "stand to-day pledged" to abolition in the District of Columbia, and (5) did not insist upon prohibition of the domestic slave trade. His principal difference with Douglas consisted of his belief (6) "in the *right* and *duty* of Congress to prohibit slavery in all the United States Territories." On the question whether he would oppose acquiring new territory without prior prohibition of slavery, (7) he answered that he "would or would not" oppose such acquisition according to his judgment as to whether it would aggravate the slavery question. Sparks, 149–150.

showed him taking either a free-state position or a non-committal attitude on those points on which Lincoln was also non-committal. Douglas's answers were as follows: (1) He would consider Kansas entitled to admission as a free state before reaching a set figure of population which Lincoln mentioned. (2) By police regulations he considered that slavery might be kept out of a territory. This was the famous question which has caused the others (on both sides) to be un-justly dwarfed. (3) Asked whether he would favor a decree of the Supreme Court that states could not exclude slavery, Douglas showed himself "amazed" at the question and clinched the matter in the free-state sense by saying that such a declaration "would be an act of moral treason that no man on the bench could ever descend to." (4) In the possible future acquisition of any new territories he would leave the people thereof free to make it slave or nonslave as they should prefer.[16]

VI

As to forensics the canvass can hardly be said to have exhibited the purest technique. In a genuine procedure of debate each speaker would have taken a position opposite to his opponent's, stuck to the question, shaped the argument as a progressive unfolding of the main issues, noted what was said by the opposite speaker, and, since the senatorship was at stake, would have shown the people how, on mat-ters likely to come before the Senate, he would have taken a stand contrary to that of his rival. For the debate to have had significance the contestants would also have been expected to enter upon the practical and substantial results of their contrary positions.

Instead of that in the case of Lincoln and Douglas, the two men *seemed to differ* while actually agreeing on many points, dragged red herrings over the trail, indulged in misrepresentations, hurled taunts, introduced extraneous matter, repeated the same statements from place to place with little regard by one debater for what the other had said, and seemed often more interested in casting reproach upon party opponents than in clarifying the issues. After laboring through the voluminous speeches, which few people ever do, any serious student of the subject should turn to the proceedings in Congress early in

---

[16] *Ibid.*, 159–165.

1861. If Lincoln had been elected senator, and if in that period he had voted as did the great majority of Republicans in Congress on bills organizing the territories of Colorado, Nevada, and Dakota, he would actually have been taking the Douglas position, for these territories were organized by Republican votes without prohibition of slavery. Or, if he had demanded prohibition of slavery in these territorial bills, thus seeking to enact into law what he had demanded in the debates, his position, as compared with men of his party in Congress, would have been very lonely indeed. This seems to suggest that, as events turned out, and as concerned the Republican party in a broader analysis, the "issue" of abolition in the territories was a talking point rather than a matter for governmental action, a campaign appeal rather than a guide for legislation.

The subject is bound up with the startling crisis of 1860–61 and will be dealt with later in that connection; [1] for the present purpose it is significant to note that Douglas was able, with pardonable self-justification but also with generous comments on the patriotism of his opponents, to show in 1861 that Lincoln's party had abandoned its basic principle—the principle which constituted the only point of difference in the debates of 1858 when the contestants were pinned down to specific governmental proposals as shown in the seven interrogatories above noted.

As to red herrings and such, there was little to choose between the contestants. Both were guilty. Douglas rang the changes on "Black Republicans," on Missouri abolishing slavery and sending a "hundred thousand emancipated slaves into Illinois, to become citizens and voters," on turning "this beautiful State into a free negro colony," [2] on Lincoln's fancied collusion with Trumbull, on his alleged lack of patriotism with reference to the Mexican War, and on his changeable doctrines, "jet-black" in the north, "a decent mulatto" in the center, and "almost white" in Egypt. [3] Lincoln countered with taunts as to Douglas's alleged support of a hypothetical future Supreme Court decision that would make slavery national, with accusations as to a conspiracy between Stephen, Roger, et al., and with charges of "fraud, . . . absolute forgery" traceable to Charles H. Lanphier, editor of the *Illinois State Register,* T. L. Harris, member of Congress, and Douglas. [4]

---

[1] See below, pp. 229–231.   [2] Sparks, 95.   [3] *Ibid.,* 300.   [4] *Ibid.,* 355.

It cannot be said that the debates as such, in any clarification of issues, loomed large in the solution of the "vexed question" with which the nation was bedeviled. By 1858 it was evident that slavery in Kansas had no chance. Indeed the decisive step on this matter was taken in the free-state sense on August 2, 1858, before the joint debates began. After that, as Professor W. O. Lynch has shown, "there was no remaining Federal territory where the conditions were so favorable to slavery." [5] The fight against the Lecompton proslavery constitution was won not by reason of any debate between Lincoln and Douglas, but by the logical workings of natural causes and by a specific contest in which, with "the aid of Republicans, he [Douglas] won the Lecompton fight." [6] In 1861 Kansas was admitted as a free state, but this was just as much in accordance with Douglas's principles as with Lincoln's. In no sense did it occur by any overruling of Douglas. It came about while Federal law concerning slavery in the territories remained *the same as in 1854*. Douglas "won" the debate, as they say; yet the free-state objective was not only successful in Kansas before war broke; it was successful with Douglas's free consent [7] and outspoken leadership. On the whole, any attempt to add luster to Lincoln's fame by belittling Douglas or by exaggerating the seriousness of differences between the two men, would be a perversion of history. In the sequel, when the severe national crisis came, Douglas "defended the Inaugural address of Mr. Lincoln against the assault of opposition senators," [8] and stood firmly with Lincoln in upholding the union.

On their merits, said Beveridge, the debates "deserve little notice." [9] The same general conclusion has been reached by George Fort Milton, who has written as follows: "Judged as debates, they do not measure up to their reputation. On neither side did the dialectic compare with that in the debates between Webster, Hayne and Calhoun." [10] Historically, aside from their content and merit, there were two main results of the debates, both of which were revealed in 1860: (1) Douglas's position at Freeport in answer to Lincoln's second question, gave Southern extremists a handle by which to produce a fateful schism

[5] *Dic. of Amer. Hist.*, IV, 309.   [6] *Ibid.*

[7] When in 1861 Kansas was admitted free while at the same time western territories were organized without prohibition of slavery, Douglas was in agreement with Republican congressional action in all the significant particulars.

[8] Blaine, *Twenty Years of Congress*, I, 287–288.   [9] Beveridge, II, 635.

[10] *Dic. of Amer. Hist.*, III, 278.

in the Democratic party. This Southern result followed not from any difference between Douglas and Lincoln but from what might be called the free-state aspect of Douglas's declaration. Douglas suffered, not from any dodge nor from Lincoln's adroitness in pinning him down to an embarrassing position, but rather by his own forthright courage in expounding an interpretation of popular sovereignty which would favor freedom where people wished it. (2) The debates so advertised Lincoln that he became a figure of national importance; without them his becoming the Republican presidential candidate in 1860 would have been far less likely. Lincoln achieved this result while taking an attitude on specific proposals that was antislavery only in the mildest and most cautious sense. He managed somehow to obtain both radical and moderate support. Dissociating himself from abolitionists without quite repelling them, he made a telling appeal to moderates of the North. With the help of circumstances, and by a kind of irony, he made Douglas pay dearly for a position which offended the South only as far as it favored freedom, which Lincoln also favored.

CHAPTER VI

THE POLITICAL SCENE IN 1860

I

AFTER the debates with Douglas it was remarked that Lincoln, like Byron, awoke and found himself famous. His office holding had been slight, his public career meager; yet he was now a political personage. Numerous invitations to speak had to be declined.[1] He had reached a point where every word he said had to be carefully weighed for its effect both upon his own fortunes and upon those of his party. His correspondence with well known leaders of the Republican party showed how his counsel was being sought in other states than his own. Typical examples were his exchanges of letters in 1859 with Schuyler Colfax and Henry J. Raymond. To each of these it was as if he had said: do nothing that will rock the Republican boat. The prospects of the party were now an important concern, and for this reason he warned Colfax that local Republican groups ought to make no declaration that could not safely be generalized as the position of the whole party. We should "look beyond our noses," said Lincoln, and "say nothing on points where it is probable we shall disagree." [2] Colfax's reply recognized the expediency, if also the difficulty, of this advice for a party made up of "men of all shades . . . of opinion." [3]

---

[1] Lincoln's speeches in 1859 cannot be fully noted, but special mention must be made of his address before the Wisconsin State Agricultural Society at Milwaukee, September 30, 1859 (*Works*, V, 236–256). It was a non-political address, and for that reason it is all the more interesting, as it shows his attention to agricultural matters, his attitude toward labor and the common man, and his broad philosophy of life. For an excellent account of Lincoln in Milwaukee see George William Bruce, ed., *History of Milwaukee City and County*, chap. xiv. Comments of Milwaukee papers which handled the speech do not suggest that Lincoln was then generally considered as a candidate for the presidency.

[2] *Works*, V, 132 (July 6, 1859).   [3] Nicolay and Hay, *Lincoln*, II, 180.

In these matters Lincoln was definitely conservative. He still looked back to Jefferson as the source of right principles, the more so as he accused Jefferson's party of defection from the standard of their founder, but for his own party and his own time he wanted no radicalism, no abolitionist excess, no striking of the wrong note. "The chief and real purpose of the Republican party," he said in one of his 1859 speeches, "is eminently conservative." [4] His was not, however, the reactionary type of conservatism. His praise of Jefferson, written in declining an invitation to attend a Jefferson's birthday celebration in Boston, was a reaffirmation of liberal faith in matters of fundamental right,[5] and on one subject concerning which many politicians were timid, he spoke out boldly—the matter of prejudice against foreigners. It may be counted as one of the main evidences of Lincoln's liberal mind that in an era of what was called "Americanism"—an age rife with laws, movements, propaganda, and pressure politics directed against Catholics and immigrants from Europe—Lincoln stood out as one of the none-too-numerous leaders of his party who labored for tolerance among races.

Asked whether he favored the constitutional amendment recently adopted by Massachusetts to curb aliens and delay their acquisition of political rights,[6] he answered clearly that he was opposed to it. To Theodore Canisius, German-American publisher at Springfield, he wrote: "Understanding the spirit of our institutions to aim at the elevation of men, I am opposed to whatever tends to degrade them. I have some little notoriety for commiserating the oppressed negro; and I should be strangely inconsistent if I could favor . . . curtailing the . . . rights of white men, even though born in different lands, and speaking different languages from myself." [7] In May 1859 Lincoln purchased control of the German newspaper which Canisius was publishing, the *Illinois Staats-Anzeiger*. By the contract the types, etc., were to "belong to Abraham Lincoln"; Canisius was to have full use of them, and if he conducted the paper according to agreement "until after the Presidential election of 1860" the "said press, types

---

[4] *Works*, V, 147–148 (Sep. 16, 1859).   [5] *Ibid.*, V, 124–127 (April 6, 1859).

[6] This constitutional provision, adopted by the voters of Massachusetts in 1859, was known as the "two year" amendment. It provided that no naturalized citizen of the United States could exercise the voting or office-holding right in Massachusetts until after a period of two years.

[7] *Works*, V, 130 (May 17, 1859).

&c" were to become Canisius's property. It was stipulated in the bond, however, that "said paper, in political sentiment, [was] not to depart from the . . . Republican platforms," nor "to print . . . any thing . . . designed to injure the Republican party." [8] It is clear that Lincoln was courting the German vote. This, however, was a matter of principle; he was not courting the nativist or intolerantly nationalist vote. He had the courage to repudiate those with whom he could not work because of principle. His policy was not that of the trimmer-politician who accepts all kinds of support, however diverse, and endeavors to repel no one.

In prominent speeches in 1859 at Columbus, Ohio, and Cincinnati, Lincoln carried forward the same type of political campaign as in the 1858 debate with Douglas. Indeed, these Ohio speeches were also a debate with Douglas who had previously spoken in the same cities. [9] The emphasis of these speeches was that in yielding to Douglas's popular sovereignty one yielded everything to the slave interests. Considering the savage fight waged against Douglas by Southern ultras, this might seem like strange doctrine. Over and over Lincoln stressed that to his own mind and to the Republican party slavery was wrong and should be checked in its further spread, while Douglas's view that it was neither right nor wrong, but a matter of indifference, would have the practical effect of making the institution national. On this point Lincoln wanted his party to stand foursquare. He took painful note of Republican embarrassment when its members in Congress failed to live up to this high principle. It hurt him sadly, for example, to reflect what the Republicans had recently done in the House of Representatives concerning what was known as the Crittenden-Montgomery bill. This was a measure providing that the proslavery Lecompton constitution be put to a vote in Kansas and that the state should be admitted as a slave commonwealth if the constitution were adopted. All the Republicans in Congress, said Lincoln, voted for the bill, whereupon Douglas claimed that they were "committed to his 'gur-reat pur-rinciple.' " For this, Republicans were accused of abandoning their own principles and were "embarrassed" in "trying to explain" that this was not so. [10]

---

[8] Angle, *New Letters and Papers*, 204–205.

[9] *Works*, V, 145, 190 (Sep. 16–17, 1859). Frank E. Stevens, *Life of Stephen A. Douglas* (*Journal*, Ill. State Hist. Soc., XVI, 1924), 607; Milton, *Eve of Conflict*, 399.

[10] *Works*, V, 278 (Dec. 1–5, 1859).

II

In this troubled year 1859 there were two factors which augmented, or reflected, the intensity of sectional feeling—the dissemination of a book by Hinton R. Helper, and the startling sensation created by John Brown's mad and criminal raid into Virginia. Helper was a North Carolinian writer of the non-planter class. Severely scoring the aristocracy of slaveholders and analyzing their potent influence, he presented with searing rhetoric the blighting effect of slavery upon the South itself. His book, *The Impending Crisis of the South: How to Meet It*, had been originally published in 1857; in 1859–60 it became a national sensation. A sum of money was subscribed for its extensive publication, and in 1860 it was widely disseminated in condensed form as a Republican campaign document. Endorsement of the book by leading men had been part of the drive for its use and politicians who had given this endorsement were made to suffer for it. An example was the supercautious John Sherman of Ohio, whose offhand endorsement of Helper, an uncharacteristic act accompanied by no conviction as to the merits of the book which he later confessed he had not read, served to prevent his election as speaker of the House of Representatives in 1859.[1] The fact that Lincoln had not given his endorsement to the book did not necessarily make him more conservative than certain men who had, but it enabled him to avoid the predicament of Sherman.

Having escaped punishment for his foul Kansas crime of '56, the abolitionist fanatic John Brown had concocted a scheme of bloody revolution against slaveholders, and for the furtherance of his violent enterprise had obtained the support of such men as Gerrit Smith of New York and Theodore Parker, S. G. Howe, T. W. Higginson, G. L. Stearns, and Franklin B. Sanborn of Massachusetts. These were high

---

[1] The New York *Tribune* assumed a special sponsorship of the Helper book, promoted its wide distribution, and solicited subscriptions for the purpose from Republicans in precisely the same spirit in which one would seek contributions to a party campaign. Many prominent Republicans did subscribe—including Schuyler Colfax, Anson Burlingame, Owen Lovejoy, Galusha Grow, Joshua R. Giddings, Justin S. Morrill, William Kellogg, E. B. Washburne, John Covode, F. P. Blair, Jr., John Jay, Lewis Tappan, Samuel May, and John Sherman—but not Lincoln. New York *Weekly Tribune*, Mar. 26, 1859. Seward, having endorsed Helper at an earlier time, found the subject so embarrassing that his endorsement was deleted in the edition of January 1860; see Luthin, *The First Lincoln Campaign*, 32.

minded men; they meant well; they were humanitarian reformers; Parker stood at the front among Boston ministers. Their willingness to sponsor or encourage Brown is hard to understand. The most serious misunderstanding would be to represent it as typically Bostonian or representative of the Bay State. When one remembers the powerful opposition encountered by abolitionists in Boston even in such a matter as rescuing a fugitive slave, one realizes that substance, influence, and government support in Massachusetts assuredly did not belong with Parker, Higginson, Stearns, and Sanborn in their encouragement of Brown. Much of the Brown legend, as has been shown by Professor James C. Malin,[2] is posthumous. As it has come down to us, the pro-Brown myth is a retrospective stereotype which grew up after Brown's execution and which is as far removed from historical truth, concerning Kansas and otherwise, as it is from sober rational thought.

The John Brown raid occurred in October 1859. From the Maryland side of the Potomac opposite Harpers Ferry, Virginia, on the night of October 16, the Brown party, approximately a score of desperate men including three of Brown's sons and led by the old man himself, assaulted the United States arsenal at Harpers Ferry. It was a forlorn and crack-brained affair and was easily suppressed by United States marines under Col. R. E. Lee with the assistance of Virginia militia. It embodied no serious movement in the North or anywhere else.[3] It was Brown's irrational idea, futile even for his wild purpose, and not even linked in its actual execution with the fantastic intention to form somewhere in the Virginia mountains a base for organizing and arming free blacks.

For this crime John Brown was executed at Charles Town, Virginia, on December 2, 1859. He had been tried in a local civil court at this small county seat; the indictment against him had listed three offenses, each of which carried the death penalty: traitorously making war and rebellion against Virginia, inciting slaves to insurrection, and murder.[4] In terms of popular passion, whipped-up hate, and intolerant social

---

[2] James C. Malin, *John Brown and the Legend of Fifty-Six.*

[3] Lee made light of the Brown affair. "It influenced his views of pending political questions not at all . . . ." He considered the plot an "attempt of a fanatic or madman" and let it go at that. "If he felt depression at the . . . appearance of . . . anti-Southern spirit in the North, he doubtless reflected that there were also extremists in his own section." Freeman, *Lee,* I, 403.

[4] John D. Lawson, ed., *American State Trials,* VI, 723 ff.; Villard, *John Brown,* 488.

psychology, the John Brown raid had an effect wholly out of balance with its intrinsic importance. The South was aroused, and odium for the crime was attached to the Republicans as if Brown's terrorist methods were the deliberate policy of their party. The affair was misrepresented by extremists as typical of "the North," this effect being heightened by a few radical abolitionists who joined in fatuous praise of Brown; thus on both sides the more extreme attitudes tended to overshadow the saner view of the nation's best minds. In genuine meaning the John Brown incident signified very little; it should have been passed off, as Lee thought; even as a disaster it was minor as compared with ocean wrecks in the same year; yet irrationally and as unfair sectional propaganda it was made into an ominous tragedy.

III

When all was said it was realized that Lincoln did not have much of a record in public life and that few men had any concept of his life story. Jesse W. Fell of Bloomington, Illinois, thinking at an early date of Lincoln as presidential timber, was not troubled by the lack of a record. "What the Republican party wants [he thought], to insure success in 1860, is a man of popular origin, of acknowledged ability, committed against slavery aggressions, who has no record to defend and no radicalism . . . to repel votes . . . ." [1] Fell did think, however, that more should be known of Lincoln's personal history, so at his request Lincoln prepared a very brief autobiography, submitting it to Fell on December 20, 1859, with the comment: "There is not much of it, for the reason, I suppose, that there is not much of me." [2] Fell took Lincoln's tiny self-sketch, made some additions, and sent them to Joseph J. Lewis of Westchester, Pennsylvania. Thus there appeared in the *Chester County Times,* Westchester, Pennsylvania, February 11, 1860, what W. E. Barton has called the first published life of Abraham Lincoln.[3] Lincoln's modest account covered less than six hundred words; the Westchester enlargement was more than six

---

[1] Wakefield, *How Lincoln Became President,* 96–97.

[2] *Works,* V, 286 (Dec. 29, 1859).

[3] W. E. Barton, "The Lincoln of the Biographers," *Transactions,* Ill. State Hist. Soc. 1929, 81. (At this point in the *Transactions* the Westchester article is printed in full.) See also Paul M. Angle, "Lincoln: Self-Biographer," *Abr. Lincoln Quart.,* I, 144–160 (Sep., 1940). Mr. Angle calls attention to Lincoln's tiny account of himself for the Dictionary of Congress compiled in 1858; it comprised but four printed lines.

times as long. Some of the statements were definitely pointed toward a Pennsylvania constituency, as for example the passage recommending Lincoln as "a consistent and earnest tariff man." In his sketch Lincoln had not mentioned the tariff. Lewis stated, contrary to fact, that "Mr. Lincoln was among the first to join in the formation of the Republican party." [4] In referring to the Lincoln-Douglas debates the Lewis article showed marked prejudice against Douglas, even berating him for supporting majority rule. The article had all the earmarks of a campaign biography, though belonging to the period of the prenomination canvass. It had a wide circulation "not only in Pennsylvania but in Illinois and throughout the country." The Chicago press reproduced it "almost entire, in response to the inquiry, then become general, 'Who is Abraham Lincoln?' " [5]

IV

As a continuance of his campaign of political speech making, but in a larger arena, Lincoln traveled to New York in February 1860 where, at the Cooper Institute, on the evening of the 27th he delivered one of his most significant speeches. There had been an earlier effort to have him speak in lyceum fashion at Plymouth Church, Brooklyn; after further consultation the place was shifted to New York, the purpose was changed to that of politics, and sponsorship of the address was assumed by the "Young Men's Central Republican Union of New York City," an organization which included such youths as William Cullen Bryant, aged sixty-five, and Horace Greeley, aged forty-nine. At the Cooper Institute Lincoln spoke as the contender against Douglas (the rising Democratic presidential possibility), and, in the immediate scene, as challenger against Seward. With Bryant presiding and Greeley present it was clearly an anti-Seward sponsorship under which he appeared. Greeley's *Tribune* gave special emphasis to the speech. It was almost as if it were the *Tribune's* party.[1]

---

[4] "The Lincoln of the Biographers," Barton, 83–84.

[5] Statement of Fell as quoted in Wakefield, 100. As noted earlier, Lincoln by this time had become measurably famous, but that did not mean familiarity with his career. The frequent question—Who is Abraham Lincoln?—exactly expressed both the growing interest in the man and the meagerness of knowledge concerning him.

[1] On February 27, 1860, the *Daily Tribune* (p. 4) urged one and all to come and hear Lincoln at the Cooper Institute that night, bringing non-Republican friends, and added: "It is not probable that Mr. Lincoln will be heard again in our City this year if

Lincoln's theme was a formulation of the principles on which the Republican party should face the electorate in 1860; but instead of attempting a full coverage of issues he spoke only of the slavery question. Federal slavery restriction, he urged, was consistent with the doctrines of the fathers. All that Republicans asked was to leave slavery where the fathers left it, as an evil to be tolerated but not extended.

His party, he urged, was not sectional. It would do no wrong to the South; it would deny the South no essential right. It was conservative, not revolutionary. It would stick to ways that were old and tried. It was the South, he said, that wanted a change, wishing to reject the old policy, though disagreeing among themselves as to any substitute. The John Brown raid, he insisted, was not of Republican instigation, nor was it traceable to Republican activity. Accusations to that effect were a slander. "Republican doctrines and declarations," he said, "are accompanied with a continual protest against any interference whatever with your slaves, or with you about your slaves. Surely, this does not encourage them to revolt." [2] The power of emancipation, Lincoln clearly recognized, was not in the Federal government. As for the "judgment and . . . feeling against slavery in this nation," [3] that was a thing that could not be destroyed; it was therefore better to keep it in the peaceful channel of the ballot box; to do otherwise would hardly lessen the number of John Browns. The threat that Southerners would not abide the election of a Republican President, that they would break up the Union in that event, blaming the crime upon the Republicans, he compared to the case of a highwayman terrorizing his victim.

In such passages there was indignation and biting sarcasm in Lincoln's speech. In its main emphasis, however, it was conciliatory toward the South. He advised his party associates to yield to Southerners wherever possible, to "do nothing through passion and ill temper," to try to determine what their demands involved, and make every effort to "satisfy them." [4] "Wrong as we think slavery is," he

---

ever. Let us improve the present opportunity." (The *Tribune* had been urging Douglas for Republican standard bearer. As nomination time approached, Greeley favored Bates.) On February 28 the *Tribune* printed the speech in full, giving it five full columns.

2 *Works*, V, 315–316 (Feb. 27, 1860).   3 *Ibid.*, V, 319.   4 *Ibid.*, V, 323–324.

urged, "we can yet afford to let it alone where it is . . . ." [5] He concluded: "Neither let us be slandered from our duty by false accusations against us, nor frightened from it by menaces of destruction to the government, nor of dungeons to ourselves. Let us have faith that right makes might, and in that faith let us to the end dare to do our duty as we understand it." [6]

Other speeches by Lincoln in this general period were in the same vein. Though not mere repetition, they struck the same note, emphasizing that slavery was wrong, but hoping for a cure, together with an abatement of factional strife and controversy. Besides the speeches mentioned in Ohio in 1859 he had spoken in that year at various places in Illinois, Wisconsin, Iowa, and Kansas. Now in February-March 1860 he made a New England tour, speaking in Providence, Concord, Manchester, Dover, Exeter (where his son Robert was a student), Hartford, New Haven, Meriden, Woonsocket, Norwich, and Bridgeport.[7] He arrived home in Springfield on March 14.

He was not merely a passive candidate, but was concerning himself actively with matters preliminary to the Republican national convention. Viewing his own chances for the presidential nomination at this stage, he reasoned that he was not the first choice of a great many, and that wise strategy was to give no offense, looking for second-choice support (for the presidency) if and when first choices should fail.[8] That he was now eager for the prize, which he considered not hopeless, is shown by his offering to furnish one hundred dollars to a Kansas supporter, expecting him to serve as delegate.[9]

V

The making of high policy by an aggregation of politician-delegates backed by ill-defined constituencies, uncertain as to credentials,

[5] *Ibid.*, V, 327.　　　　　　　　　　[6] *Ibid.*, V, 327–328.
[7] P. C. Eggleston, *Lincoln in New England.*　　[8] *Works*, VI, 7–8 (Mar. 24, 1860).
[9] In a letter to Mark W. Delahay, March 16, 1860, Lincoln made the offer of one hundred dollars to cover Delahay's trip to Chicago as Republican delegate. That Lincoln did not consider this unethical is shown by his statement to Delahay that he could not "enter the ring on the money basis," and that "in the main, the use of money is wrong," but that "for certain objects in a political contest, the use of some is both right and indispensable." Delahay was not a delegate, and the Kansas delegation was instructed for Seward; yet Lincoln advised his friend to come to Chicago anyhow, adding that he would keep his word about the expense money. *Works*, VI, 5–6. Pratt, *Personal Finances*, 106–107.

swayed by demagogues, pulled apart by factional caucuses, diverted from any unified course by clamoring minorities, deadlocked and stymied for desperate weeks, and finally breaking up into warring fragments—such was the story of the various Democratic conventions of 1860. The one man who seemed best able to lead the party to success if it remained united, and who on the same assumption seemed most likely to avert disunion if elected, was Stephen A. Douglas. When the Democrats themselves failed to unite for Douglas, failing also to unite on any common program or leader, it was almost as if they themselves had decreed disunion.

It was Congress and the President who were regularly authorized to legislate and govern; yet, by process none too regular, affairs had been turned over to the maneuverings and intrigues of parties, which had no constitutional existence. Parties controlled and exercised great public functions, yet they were so subject to manipulation that they served in a most unsatisfactory manner as public instruments.

It is not feasible to review the manner in which parties had fastened themselves upon the government. It is sufficient to note that, practically, there was no other available device by which the people were able to determine the most vital of their political affairs in the election of President and Congress. Not only was there no method by which the people could go ahead without parties to enact their will; neither was there much likelihood that they could compel a national party to perform adequately for the nation the task which its hands had seized. A convention was unpredictable, and in a time of artificial excitement the exertion of calm, reasoned, public opinion upon a convention was well nigh hopeless.

For the background of this party warfare among the Democrats one must read such a book as Laura A. White's study of R. B. Rhett, aggressive disunionist of South Carolina; for the intrigues of 1860 one may turn to George Fort Milton's *Eve of Conflict*. Rhett and his *Mercury* of Charleston worked for secession by a deliberate calculation of the cumulative measures, step by step, which were designed to produce that result. Rightly he has been called the "father of secession." Steps in the South toward preservation of the Union were countered by him with a boldness of purpose that was artfully combined with strategic skill. Working along the same line as Rhett was William L. Yancey of Alabama. Against the judgment of conservative

Southerners (numerous, distinguished, and as "Southern" as one could wish) Yancey, Rhett, and their colleagues built up among vigorous elements in the lower South a savage antagonism against Douglas for his popular sovereignty doctrine—the doctrine which, oddly enough, Lincoln characterized as yielding everything to the slave interests. It became evident, not only that Douglas was no spokesman for slave interests in any aggressive sense, but that a kind of secession against Douglas was the implacable purpose of a determined Southern element. If this element, failing to rule, should ruin the Democratic party, they were already prepared to take the next step—secession and the formation of a separate nation of the South. Some of their followers might not look that far ahead (as it turned out, it was just ahead); yet by being drawn into the earlier stages of the movement, they contributed to its main consequence.

The details being too elaborate and tiresome to repeat, it will be appropriate here to summarize what happened in Democratic councils. This may be done in terms of the five gatherings in April and June of 1860 which took the form of Democratic conventions, or meetings of Democratic convention delegates.

(1) When in April the national convention of the party, after canvasses in the states, met at Charleston, a long and bitter struggle ensued in which the Yanceyites seized upon the issue of slavery in the territories as a platform matter on which they staged a revolt, or bolt, from the convention. A majority of the convention favored a platform declaration that would reaffirm the Cincinnati platform of 1856 —i. e., non-intervention by Congress in the territories, with adherence to the Compromise of 1850; to this they added that on the whole question they would willingly abide by the decision of the Supreme Court of the United States. The Yanceyites, however, insisted on a platform declaration affirming the positive duty of Congress actually to establish and protect slavery in the territories. This would have meant that, even if the people of a territory were overwhelmingly opposed to slavery, Congress must forcibly maintain it in their midst and against their will. It would have been regarded by Douglas men as a slave code imposed upon territories. Douglas could not have well agreed to this doctrine; it would have been a repudiation of his whole position and a betrayal of both Northern and Southern supporters. By agreeing to abide by the action of the Supreme Court, however,

Douglas and his followers made as much of a concession as was decently possible; in this manner they even left the door open to the Yancey doctrine if the Court should endorse it.[1] Unwilling to accept compromise or consent to majority rule, Yancey headed a movement of bolters. With his Alabama delegation he left the convention hall; in this secession he was joined by certain other delegates of the lower South. By this defiant act the signal for disunion in the party of Jefferson, Calhoun, Benton, and Jackson, had been flashed.

There was now deadlock, Douglas men having a majority but not the two-thirds necessary to nominate. After protracted and anxious sessions they decided to adjourn, to meet in Baltimore in June. Meanwhile the appeal was made for the appointment of new delegates in those states where "vacancies" existed.

(2) Meeting in another hall in Charleston, and calling themselves the "Constitutional Democratic convention," the Yancey seceders decided to hold their own type of extreme Southern convention at Richmond in June. In this action the strings were not entirely pulled by Southerners. The maneuvers of Benjamin F. Butler of Massachusetts, the attitude of Caleb Cushing,[2] also of the Bay State, and the activities of the "Buchanan Ultras" with their plentiful use of Federal patronage to knife Douglas, served to strengthen the Southern extremists.

(3) The main adjourned convention met again in June in Baltimore. Here a curious thing happened. After revolting against the convention and withdrawing to form their own organization, the Yancey group, some of them, turned up at Baltimore and demanded that they be taken back into the fold. (This they did with no change of heart in

---

[1] If it be thought that the Court had already endorsed the Yancey doctrine, it should be remembered that the subject was not viewed in the same light even by Democrats. Douglas held the people of a territory to be empowered to prohibit slavery by unfriendly legislation despite the Dred Scott decision; on the other hand, the high court seemed by many to be in line with the extreme proslavery, or Yanceyite, view. When Douglas men at Charleston made the concession as to abiding by a future decision of the Court, they implied that if the Court should unequivocally uphold the Yancey view they would agree to it; but, at a time when both lawyers and laymen were puzzled by the Court's ponderous verbiage, they also implied that a further word from the Court would be needful.

[2] Caleb Cushing of Massachusetts, affiliated with the Buchanan wing of Northern Democrats, presided over the regular Democratic convention at Charleston and the main Democratic convention at Baltimore; in both these capacities he persistently gave rulings in the anti-Douglas sense. After the break at Baltimore he also presided over the convention of Southern bolters.

the matter of national or party unity; they were as determined as ever to insist upon the Yancey view as to slavery; nor were they ready to compromise with Northern delegates on this overemphasized point.) In the interval between April and June, however, a reaction against Yancey had developed, at least partially, in some of the lower Southern states, and organizations in these states, noting the Yancey revolt and obeying the injunction to fill vacancies, had sent delegates to Baltimore who were prepared to coöperate with the main convention. In Louisiana, for instance, there was a severe contest between Slidell, who was carrying his anti-Douglas attitude to the point of breaking up the Democratic party, and Pierre Soulé, who appeared at Baltimore as leader of a newly chosen Democratic delegation of Louisiana moderates. These moderates, supported by the *True Delta* of New Orleans, expressed the Union-saving sentiment of Louisiana, claiming that Slidell's seceders and bolters did not truly represent the state. There being similar cleavages in other states, one could see in this Louisiana situation an epitome of the angry struggle within the Democratic party in the South.

The pressure upon this Baltimore convention was so tremendous and its proceedings so difficult that at one point Douglas authorized the withdrawal of his name if that should become necessary to promote harmony. When votes in the convention went contrary to the Southern ultra faction, though some of the seceders (as from Mississippi, Texas, and Georgia) were readmitted to the roll, there occurred another bolt of Southern opponents of Douglas, animated by Yancey leadership but led this time by Russell of Virginia. Thus both at Charleston and at Baltimore the quarrels between pro-Douglas and anti-Douglas men had resulted in a bolt of the latter. In this phase there were intrastate quarrels, some of the delegates refusing to join this bolting movement. Having struggled with the problem of its membership, the Baltimore convention proceeded to the nomination of President and Vice President, choosing Stephen A. Douglas of Illinois and Benjamin Fitzpatrick of Alabama. On Fitzpatrick's declination, the Democratic national committee later chose Herschel V. Johnson, Georgia unionist, as Douglas's running mate.

(4) Up to this point, though numerical order is not the purpose, mention has been made of three convention meetings among the Democrats—the main convention at Charleston, the seceders at

Charleston, and the adjourned (reconstituted) convention at Baltimore. Another now occurred at Baltimore, whither Yancey had traveled with a considerable group of followers, instead of confining themselves to the Richmond gathering which the bolters themselves had promoted. By an amazing reach of authority, this Yancey group at Baltimore assumed the function of their own Richmond meeting as well as that of the main national convention. Adopting the Yancey platform, they nominated John C. Breckinridge of Kentucky for President of the United States and Joseph Lane of Oregon for Vice President. This Baltimore group was presided over by Caleb Cushing; one of its most prominent members was Benjamin F. Butler of Massachusetts. The country was now witnessing the spectacle of bogus party devices, easy to concoct, but difficult for the people to use as instruments in the management of public affairs. Yancey delivered a long speech to this Baltimore convention in the midst of which large numbers left the hall.

(5) The seceders had gathered at Richmond on June 11 [3] according to schedule, but had marked time while proceedings were in progress at Baltimore. Having waited, they found that they had virtually nothing to do. As if they constituted the Democratic party of the whole nation, they now made their nominations for President and Vice President of the United States; but since Yancey's group had already performed this function at Baltimore, the Richmond convention merely ratified the nominations of Breckinridge and Lane.

Douglas would now have to wage a campaign not only against Republicans, and against the Bell-Everett group (organized in May), but also against recent party associates whose enmity toward him was ugly and bitter. Had he been chosen President in such an atmosphere,

---

[3] If one wanted to spin out this analysis, he could speak of two conventions—or rather two convention sessions—at Richmond. The first met on June 11 and adjourned without transacting any significant business on June 12, most of the delegates (though not those of South Carolina) going to Baltimore. Reassembling at Richmond, with a very limited membership present, on June 21, the convention did nothing till June 26 when the Baltimore proceedings were over and a greater number of Southern delegates were in attendance. Then in a very brief and perfunctory session they ratified the nominations of Breckinridge and Lane. The numbering of these party gatherings is meant above only as a handy device. Since the Richmond convention marked time awaiting developments in the anti-Douglas convention at Baltimore, the latter has been called the fourth in these pages; the Richmond convention, which was the last of the Democratic conventions to act, has been called the fifth. Some might number them differently where conventions were running simultaneously, but numerical order is of little significance.

one can only wonder what the result would have been. It has already been noted that Douglas's ability to hold the country together was conditioned upon unity within his party. Would he as President have had the same type of secession to deal with that Lincoln had? Lincoln and Douglas had never in fact been so far apart as party exigencies had made them seem, and on the matter of the Union they thought alike. Soon the time would come when they would stand squarely together as they faced the sectional crisis.

VI

In early May, in between the Democratic gathering at Charleston and the Republican convention at Chicago, there met at Baltimore a group of conservatives whose main characteristic was "disgust at political trickery"[1] combined with deep patriotic concern for the endangered Union. If any body of men ever felt that they had a vitally important task to perform in other than partisan terms, it was these men; if any group saw clearly the coming effect of disruptive tendencies in 1860 and, seeing, hoped and endeavored to do something about it before it was too late, it was they. The tendency of most writers has been to speak lightly of them, while admitting their eminent respectability. The most vivid description of their convention, in an old church in the Maryland metropolis, is by the ubiquitous Murat Halstead who packed as much sarcasm into his account of their proceedings as his racy journalism could muster. Halstead wrote of the gathering as that of dignified venerables. On the fringes of the crowd, however, he found "plugs" and "Yahoos on a spree," while at a high spot in the proceedings he wrote of "Bedlam broken loose."[2]

These men carried forward the Whig and "American" tradition. Some of their proposed candidates were Crittenden of Kentucky, Houston of Texas, Bell of Tennessee, Everett of Massachusetts, and Botts of Virginia. Among those who figured in their convention were Washington Hunt of New York, W. G. Brownlow and Andrew Jackson Donelson of Tennessee, R. W. Thompson of Indiana, Alexander H. H. Stuart and Waitman T. Willey of Virginia, John Scott Harrison of Ohio, William L. Sharkey of Mississippi, Leverett Saltonstall of

---

[1] Halstead, *Caucuses of 1860*, 112.   [2] *Ibid.*, 110, 116.

Massachusetts, Leslie Combs of Kentucky, and John M. Morehead of North Carolina.

In a facetious speech as chairman Washington Hunt announced that he had prepared three platforms: one for the Democrats, "one for the 'irrepressible conflict' gentlemen," and one for "this Convention." For the "harmonious Democracy" he suggested two declarations: "one in favor of excluding slavery from the Territories . . . , and the other in favor of forcing it into them . . . ; both to be adopted unanimously . . . ."[3] For "the 'irrepressible conflict' philanthropists about to assemble at Chicago" he proposed the Connecticut blue laws amended to permit kissing one's wife on Sunday and burning "old witches." For his own convention he proposed: ". . . the Constitution . . . as it is, and the Union under it now and forever." That is "all we need," he said; if he were making a creed for Christians he would take "the Bible as it is, leaving all to construe it."[4]

In tune with the Hunt keynote the Constitutional Union convention adopted a refreshingly brief platform. Following a preamble in which "platforms . . . by . . . partisan conventions" were held to be misleading and disruptive, the sole resolution of the convention called for "no political principle other than the Constitution of the country, the union of the states, and the enforcement of the laws."[5]

Though on the first ballot Bell's vote did not greatly exceed that of Houston, he became on the second ballot the nominee of the convention, with the distinguished Everett as candidate for Vice President. With a Southerner and a slaveholder for standard bearer the appeal of the Constitutional Union party was chiefly to the upper South and border, to non-Republican areas in which Lincoln was impossible while both Douglas and Breckinridge were largely distrusted as being too factional.

This Bell group was to become an important anti-Douglas force, both in the process of party nomination and in the election. Feeling that they would have trouble carrying their own states for Douglas against a Southerner, those Democrats of the South who were not disposed toward a moderate course found additional reason, after Bell's nomination, to reject Douglas as standard bearer. According to James G. Blaine, they felt that it "would be poor recompense . . .

---

[3] *Ibid.*, 108.   [4] *Ibid.*
[5] Emerson D. Fite, *The Presidential Campaign of 1860*, 242–243.

to recover certain Northern States from the Republicans, if . . . an equal number of Southern States should be carried by Bell, and the destiny of the South be committed to a conservative party, which would abandon threats and cultivate harmony." [6] Later, when it came to the election, the really formidable opponent of Breckinridge in states of the South was not to be Douglas, but Bell. In that Douglas was a man of greater national leadership than Bell while his policy was moderation and sectional harmony, the followers of the Tennessean, by opposing Douglas, played into the hands of the ultras and helped to defeat their own cause of peace and union.

VII

In the prenomination situation in the Republican party there were five prominent contenders for chief place, and a somewhat indeterminate number of minor ones. The leading five were Seward of New York, Cameron of Pennsylvania, Chase of Ohio, Bates of Missouri, and Lincoln of Illinois. With all eyes on Chicago where the nominating convention of the party was to be held in mid-May, the hopeful candidates and their scheming managers marshaled their forces with the energy, maneuvering, and intrigue that is characteristic of preconvention politics. In this preliminary phase the man who stood out most conspicuously was Seward. His partisans took his coming success at Chicago for granted. He could point to a long record of public service as governor and senator, having been well known as a Whig during practically the whole lifetime of that party. Somewhat tardily, but in time, he had shifted to the new Republican party (this was in 1855); in 1860 it would not have been an overstatement to describe him as that party's most distinguished leader. It was a Republican necessity to "carry" New York with its heavy electoral strength, and those who knew were convinced that no one could do that better than Seward. In addition, he had in Thurlow Weed the shrewdest and most experienced of managers.[1] It was like a partnership—Seward, Weed and Company—and the sheer weight of party technique, clien-

---

[6] Blaine, *Twenty Years of Congress*, I, 163–164. Blaine adds: "Bell's nomination had, therefore, proved the final argument against the acceptance of Douglas by the Southern Democracy."

[1] For Weed's complex personality, his tendency to put the politician's interest first, his increasing big-business affiliation, and like matters, see Glyndon G. Van Deusen, "Thurlow Weed: A Character Study," *Amer. Hist. Rev.*, XLIX, 427–440 (Apr., 1944).

tele, and organization wielded by such a firm would have been hard to match.

Weed is an outstanding example of the type of American politician that operates in the field of party strategy, seeking not public office, but rather the patronage, power, spoils, and Warwick-like influence that comes of steering a party through the unseen intricacies of committee, caucus, and preliminary canvass, and down through the more visible processes of popular appeal and election. After election the processes again become somewhat invisible, being concerned with the rewards and perquisites of office. In all such matters Weed was regarded as a past master. The familiar term given to such a man is boss; Weed was Republican boss in New York, and he aspired to the same mysterious eminence for the nation. It was characteristic of his methods and of the time that he had his newspaper; for decades the famous Albany *Evening Journal* served as his medium, being usually more concerned with merchants and industrialists than with the common people, its interests in the latter being a matter of harvesting their votes.

These were elements of Seward's strength, but he had points of weakness. In 1850, when elder statesmen—Webster, Clay, Calhoun—were debating the great compromise, he had given his eleventh of March speech in which he opposed measures to appease the slave interests; on this occasion he had referred to "a higher law than the Constitution." In this same speech he had said: "The Constitution regulates our stewardship; the Constitution devotes the domain to union, to justice, to defence, to welfare, and to liberty." [2] This was entering the treacherous field of phrase-making; the better the phrase, the more tricky its effect in terms of practical politics.

Again, at Rochester on October 25, 1858, he had said: "Shall I tell you what this collision means? They who think that it is . . . the work of . . . fanatical agitators, and therefore ephemeral, mistake the case altogether. It is an irrepressible conflict between opposing and enduring forces, and it means that the United States must . . . become either entirely a slave-holding nation or entirely a free-labor nation." [3] Such phrases, with their judgment-day suggestion and their abolitionist flavor, did not suit the Republican party in its 1860 mood. There was an irony in it all, for in truth Seward in 1860 was the

---

2 Bancroft, *Seward*, I, 247.   3 *Ibid.*, I, 458–459.

opposite of radical. Weed was never the man to break a lance for abstract moral principles; both Weed and Seward had chosen the part of caution and moderation; between the sections they wanted nothing of irrepressible conflict; they wanted conciliation. It does not make sense that Seward should have suffered for these phrases or that he should have been represented as a stirrer of sectional trouble. His 1860 note was sounded on February 29 of that year in the United States Senate, and it was very far indeed from irrepressible conflict. For the time at hand and for the view ahead he believed that the Republican party must think little of metaphysical speculation and must hold itself within "the necessity of being practical in its care of the national health and life." Calling attention to the dominant strength of the Republican party in the North, and to the long standing attitude of Northern forbearance toward the South, he repudiated the charge that the party was sectional. In this he was not altogether convincing, but at least it could be said that in his view the party ought not to be sectional at the moment when it was about to enter upon the responsibility of office and of government. Instead of conflict, Seward urged a mutuality between North and South by which each might continue to cherish its own institutions, remembering that "All the world discusses all systems." With every thought of allaying sectional strife, he emphasized fraternity between all parts of the country and sought to make it appear that trouble was only imaginary. "There is not one disunionist . . . among us all," he declared. "We are . . . unconscious of any process of dissolution going on among us or around us." [4]

In addition to his undeserved and misleading reputation as a radical, Seward was otherwise vulnerable. His connection with Weed, useful as it was, savored too much of machine rule to suit progressive spirits. The very thoroughness and frankness of Weed's bossism produced dissension in New York. The name of Weed connoted tricky politics. In 1859–60 he had headed "a scheme to furnish, through the New York legislature, charters for city railroads, whose grantees were in turn to supply several hundred thousand dollars for the Republican campaign of 1860, in which Seward was expected to be the party candidate." [5] As a result of such methods there had arisen an influential anti-Seward faction of the Republican party in New York, headed by the

---

[4] *Ibid.*, I, 513–515.   [5] *Ibid.*, I, 524.

powerful Greeley, and graced by the adherence of the highminded W. C. Bryant. This lively faction stood squarely athwart the former governor's path.

In Pennsylvania Simon Cameron was not alone a Seward or a Weed; he was something like a combination of the two. He was both boss and candidate. After long years of service (if it could be called that) in the Democratic party, in which he had managed to antagonize many of its chief leaders, he had turned a full somersault, and the year 1860 found him in the United States Senate as a Republican. He was now over sixty, had amassed a fortune, had practiced on the profitable borderline of politics and business, had become an industrial magnate, and had managed to bring within his experienced grasp the complex range of party management. Regard for ideals or principles was less a factor with him than the use of his adopted party as a tool of large manufacturing interests. To get support in Pennsylvania, which had cast its vote for Buchanan in 1856 but which seemed a promising Republican state in 1860, meant appeasing Cameron; that in turn required support of a protective tariff. Such a tariff, for example, would coddle the iron business in which Cameron was personally interested. Nor were his other interests, such as banking and railroading, unlikely to color his political thought.

Cameron's men would come to Chicago with bargaining power. They would have to be reckoned with. Pennsylvania could not be ignored. The main prize, however, was not so likely to be within his reach. His name was associated with undertakings that did not imply the highest code of honor; his forte was party intrigue; few if any would think of calling him a statesman. That he had been a Democrat was not so serious as the obvious fact that mere expediency had caused him to shift his allegiance. Opposition to slavery had little if anything to do with this shift. He had traded on the confused party situation in Pennsylvania in the fifties. In this he had accepted Knownothing support and was therefore distrusted by the Germans. When in early summer, 1858, the New York *Herald* published a numerous list of Republican candidates (Bissell and Grow being included, but Lincoln omitted), Cameron was designated as "Democratic Know Nothing Republican Conservative." [6] Early in 1860 an effort to promote a

---

[6] New York *Herald*, June 28, 1858, p. 4, c. 3. The *Herald's* flair for picturesque journalism was illustrated in the labels attached to the various candidates. Some of

"Cameron and Lincoln" club (for Cameron as President with Lincoln as Vice President) made little progress; assuredly if it had achieved its object, the result would have been highly uncongenial to Lincoln. Within his own state Cameron had to contend with the determined opposition of the McClure-Curtin faction of the Republican party. This was one of the bitterest feuds of partisan history; it "continued as long as they [Cameron and Curtin] were in active political life." [7]

Salmon P. Chase of Ohio, puritan in politics, had done noble service in the antislavery cause, his activities in this capacity having been more pronounced than Lincoln's. After laboring in the Liberty party in 1840 and 1844, and in the Free Soil party in 1848, and after noting the futility of these third-party efforts, he had changed his strategy and had sought manfully to capture the Democratic party for the cause of antislavery, or to be more exact, the cause of slavery limitation. Failing in that, he had shifted, as inevitably he had to shift, to the Republican party, and as its leader had been elected governor of Ohio in 1855. In the course of his career he had incurred the opposition of old line Whigs, old line Democrats, and also Republicans of certain groups, as for example those who had little antislavery zeal and those who opposed nativism, for he had been embarrassed by the unsought support of Ohio Knownothings. Having been a free trader, he had shifted his economic position for political reasons and had come over to the cause of protection. In a letter to a member of the Ohio legislature, October 25, 1859, he had referred to international free trade as a policy which could not be realized and had indicated squarely that he would support legislation "to protect American industry." [8] His background was not Whig, nor would regular Democrats have called it Democratic. Entering the Republican party, he brought it little strength in terms of influential following. Moreover, he had little more than the prospect of complimentary support from Ohio. The faction of Benjamin F. Wade opposed him bitterly,[9] and

them were: "Anti-Know Nothing Democratic Free Soil and Free Trade Republican" (Frémont); "Know Nothing 'Free Wool' Republican" (Banks); "Other Republicans of the Kansas Tribe" (Chase, Hale, Wilson, Trumbull, Bissell, Grow). Douglas was bracketed with "Anti-Lecompton Anti Administration Democrats."

[7] A. K. McClure, *Abraham Lincoln and Men of War Times*, 149.

[8] Chase to Senator Stanley of the Ohio legislature, Columbus, October 25, 1859, Chicago *Press & Tribune*, Jan. 25, 1860, p. 3, c. 4.

[9] Wade was without appreciable strength. Greeley wrote as follows: ". . . I am not so sure about Wade. He is a good soul; but he has made some *awful* speeches—worse

he was to be denied full Ohio support even on the first ballot. Yet there was an upstanding quality in Chase. Toward this competitor Lincoln asked especially that "no ungenerous thing" be done. Chase, said Lincoln, "gave us his sympathy in 1858 when scarcely any other distinguished man did." [10]

Edward Bates, bearded patriarch of Missouri, was regarded as one of the outstanding Republican contenders; in 1860 he was sixty-seven years of age. In his unspectacular career a mild antislavery attitude had been superimposed upon a Southern planter tradition, but this attitude was held in bounds by an eminently respectable Whig conservatism. Bates's strength lay in the solidity of this conservatism and in the hope that his following in the border states and perhaps farther south might serve to avert secession if he should be elected. The movement to promote his candidacy was supposed to be of national proportions, being sustained by the impressive support of Horace Greeley as well as of the Blair clan. Being anti-Seward, yet finding no favorite son in New York to pit against Seward, being also something of a specialist on the great West, Greeley found no difficulty in going as far west as Missouri for his candidate. "My candidate for President in 1860 is Edward Bates of Missouri," he wrote in February of that year. He added: "As he is an old time Whig, and supported Fillmore . . . in 1856, I do not see how the Americans of that year can refuse to take him; and I, as a pretty advanced Republican, can risk a man who quietly, years ago, emancipated and provided for his own slaves." [11]

On the other hand, Bates's supposed or reputed favoring of nativist tendencies offended the Germans who were strong in the Middle West; he was a bit too much of a relic to suit the stirring times; his almost pathetic attachment to the Whigs seemed like harking back to a lost cause; and his practical chances were seriously reduced when Norman Judd, member of the Republican national committee, induced that committee to select Chicago as the place of meeting instead of Bates's home city, St. Louis.

---

than the 'irrepressible conflict.' " Greeley to Colfax, May 7, 1860, Greeley-Colfax MSS., New York Pub. Lib. For a characterization of Wade, see vol. II, 209–210.

[10] *Works*, VI, 8 (Mar. 24, 1860).

[11] Greeley to Hector Orr, Feb. 11, 1860, Greeley MSS., New York Pub. Lib.

VIII

In this brief survey of what we may call the big five, another glance at Lincoln, considered nominationwise, is desirable. When the convention met in Chicago, Lincoln's working support in Illinois had been fully implemented. The state Republican convention meeting at Decatur on May 9–10, 1860, had instructed its delegation for Lincoln for President.[1] In political parlance this marked him as more than a "favorite son," for many a favorite son has had little more than home-state support on early and indecisive ballots. Missouri Republicans were to put forth a considerable effort for Bates and New York men for Seward; but if one considers the others, Illinois was back of Lincoln to an extent that was not true of Pennsylvania toward Cameron or of Ohio toward Chase. Illinois men, with strategic concentration on control of the convention itself, worked for Lincoln. They labored not merely to give him initial support, but to make him President. They did this because of personal enthusiasm, or out of the zeal of conviction, or, as in the case of Browning, by reason of what was expected of them under the circumstances; but the point is, they did it. It is true that the degree of Illinois unanimity for Lincoln in the pre-convention phase is hard to estimate and has perhaps at times been exaggerated. Many of Trumbull's correspondents seemed to favor him—at least they wrote him so—and one may wonder what would have happened if Trumbull had made a determined fight for Illinois presidential support, which he did not do, favoring Judge McLean. Whatever may have been the previous possibilities of conflict or rivalry within Republicans of the state, support for Lincoln was strong and solid in the active and effective sense—i. e., in the work actually done from the opening of the convention and carrying through to the final ballot.

Lincoln had the conservatism which certain other candidates did

---

[1] Lincoln was present at this convention which is chiefly remembered for a backwoodsy incident. His country cousin, John Hanks, with a fellow pioneer, carried in two rails with a placard which said that they had been split by Lincoln; following this, amid rousing cheers, Lincoln spoke briefly, indicating that he had split rails in Macon County, of which Decatur was county seat, though not claiming that these particular rails were his. Angle, *Lincoln, 1854–1861*, 332. For further particulars on this homely incident, which "set a keynote for the campaign," see Helen Nicolay, in *Abr. Lincoln Quart.*, I, 129 (Sep., 1940).

not have, at least in reputation; to this he added an element not too common among conservatives—the vitalizing talent of arousing enthusiasm. Middle-of-the-road men could support him, but so also could ardent zealots. There were some, of course, who were all out for Lincoln. A correspondent of Lyman Trumbull wrote: "Of those *now* prominently before the people as Candidates for the Presidency, I think Lincoln is by far the strongest man for the race." [2] Others wrote in the same vein to Trumbull. "I believe we could elect either Seward or Chace [sic], but with Lincoln our success would be *much more certain* . . ." [3] " 'Old Abe,' " wrote another, "is the man for this region beyond a doubt, We can carry Illinois with him easy." [4] The very difficulty and uncertainty of Republican unity, not to mention the wish to win converts outside the fold, gave added logic to the Lincoln cause. Lincoln's chances were also enhanced by the feeling that a western man was needed in 1860; yet it should be such a western man as would find support in the East. [5] It was, therefore, of importance that Lincoln had made his appearance at the Cooper Institute at a significant moment in the prenomination canvass, that he had gone from there to various places in New England, and that in doing so he had made a favorable impression. In all these political situations there was an element of luck and chance. One of the chances to guard against was that the Lincoln movement would be sidetracked into the vice-presidency. Preferring Bates or Dayton as President, Greeley thought well of Lincoln for Vice President, though disliking the idea of two Whigs. [6] The idea of Lincoln for second place on the ticket was also put forth by an editor in Danville, Illinois. Carrying the name of Chase for President at his masthead, he wrote: "For Vice President the name of Hon. A. Lincoln . . . I have found to meet the hearty approbation of the leading Republicans of this County." [7]

Another chance to guard against was that the cause of compromise and harmony might overreach itself and go to such a limit as to choose

---

[2] S. York to Trumbull, Paris, Ill., April 20, 1860, Trumbull MSS.
[3] C. D. Hay to Trumbull, Newton, Ill., March 11, 1860, *ibid.,*
[4] J. R. Bulion to Trumbull, Marshall, Ill., April 9, 1860, *ibid.*
[5] "The 'Cinti Gazette' thinks the Republican candidate for Prest will be a western man." Lewis Dyer to Trumbull, Duquoin, Ill., Jan. 3, 1860, *ibid.* "My . . . opinion is that we must have a western, well known good & true Republican & from a free State . . . ." G. O. Pond to Trumbull, Griggsville, Ill., Dec. 28, 1859, *ibid.*
[6] Greeley to Colfax, Feb. 3, 1860. Greeley-Colfax MSS., New York Pub. Lib.
[7] G. Price Smith to S. P. Chase, Danville, Ill., Dec. 16, 1859, Trumbull MSS.

Judge McLean.[8] Joseph Medill of the Chicago *Tribune,* for example, feeling some doubt as to the nomination of Seward or Bates or Lincoln, thought it not unlikely that McLean would emerge as "the compromise candidate to harmonize . . . all segments of the opposition." [9]

Putting Lincoln's cards together, he had conservatism combined with zeal; he was a westerner not unacceptable to the East; his pre-Republican background had been Whig, which was an advantage for the presidential nomination, while a Democratic background might serve for the vice-presidency; he could enlist the Germans; he had prominence as a second choice; he stood forth as a challenger of Douglas; he was regarded as having thrown into the background those questions (except indeed that of the union) which divided the North and the South; [10] he was free from drawbacks, such as those which plagued Chase and Bates; he had the immense local advantage of the Chicago setting; he had the friendship of certain men even though they were pledged to Seward; [11] finally, he had the skillful support of political strategists working tirelessly for him at the tumultuous front of political action.

---

[8] McLean's frequent candidacy for the presidency though a member of the United States Supreme Court, and his support by some in 1860 though he was then seventy-five years old, are treated in Weisenburger, *The Life of John McLean: A Politician on the United States Supreme Court.*

[9] J. Medill to Trumbull, Chicago, April 16, 1860, Trumbull MSS.

[10] A. L. Kohlmeier in *Transactions,* Ill. State Hist. Soc., 1923, 161.

[11] In Kansas, for example, the delegates were for Seward but regarded Lincoln "as a highly acceptable and available candidate." T. Ewing, Jr., to A. Lincoln, Leavenworth, Kansas, May 6, 1860, T. Ewing MSS.

CHAPTER VII

DESTINY IN A WIGWAM

I

IN THE "vast tabernacle" [1] or "wigwam" erected for the purpose, the national convention of the Republican party assembled in Chicago for a three-day session, May 16–18, 1860. The off-duty activities of the delegates were convivial to say the least, perhaps in some cases disreputable; the make-up of the convention was ill defined; the assembly was disorderly; floor proceedings were hard to control. It was complained that delegates passed their tickets of admission over the railings and through the windows to friends not entitled to seats. So many spectators or guests were mixed in with the accredited delegations that the chairman had to ask each delegation to "purge itself." [2] There was an immense and restless crowd inside the hall, while outside the building surging thousands had to be entertained in the manner of stump speaking by orators selected from the convention.

It is an amazing exercise to read in cold print the proceedings of that gathering. There was haste, impatience, rudeness, uncertainty or inattention as to parliamentary situations, and a tendency of some to cry down a speaker they did not like. There were laughs and hisses, cheers and yawps, and moments that came close to the farcical. At one point the chair (George Ashmun of Massachusetts) was asked to inform the convention what motion was before it. [3] At another it was feared that the delegates would transact their business and pass their resolutions before they were "organized." [4] Far along in the third session (on the morning of the second day), when a vote by roll of

---

[1] *Proceedings of the First Three Republican National Conventions* . . . , pub. by Charles W. Johnson, Minneapolis, Minn. (1893). (Cited below as Johnson, *Proceedings.*) 91.

[2] *Ibid.,* 107, 146. [3] *Ibid.,* 92. [4] *Ibid.,* 93.

the states was called for, the chair knew of no rule by which that could be arrived at.[5] At the outset the convention got all tangled up because an invitation to an excursion on the lake seemed about to steal the show. After the acceptance of the invitation, followed immediately by the discovery of practical difficulties, a delegate from Missouri hoped that they would not "stultify" themselves by rescinding their acceptance.[6] So difficult did the momentous problem of the excursion seem, with the announcement that the Board of Trade had its fleet all ready for the purpose (though this would have interfered with the afternoon or evening session of the first day), that the convention's business seemed threatened with serious interruption. When at this stage a Rhode Islander suggested that "we are here on important business," the reporter recorded that there was so much confusion that the speaker's words could not be heard.[7] The matter was disposed of by deferring the excursion till after the convention was concluded. In this the delegates declined the gracious suggestion of the Board of Trade that their sessions could just as well be held on the decks of the ships. Another farcical touch occurred when a travel-weary delegate from California objected to the early hour for the next morning session; [8] still another when the convention, about to consider a night session on the first day, was informed that the hall was engaged that night for a Zouave drill.[9]

In the matter of fundamental organization two problems had to be threshed out by the convention—the question of admitting certain doubtful delegations, and that of determining what should constitute the majority necessary to nominate. Most doubtful of all was the admission of a bogus delegation from Texas,[10] but there was difficulty also as to groups offering themselves from Virginia, Kentucky, and Maryland, in which states it was charged that genuine Republican organizations did not exist. This topic brought heated and angry discussion, in which on the one hand it was feared that men might come in from the Southern states to demoralize the party,[11] while on the other hand it was answered that men from farther south had

---

[5] *Ibid.*, 123.   [6] *Ibid.*, 97.   [7] *Ibid.*, 100.   [8] *Ibid.*, 106.   [9] *Ibid.*, 96.

[10] Presenting themselves as the Texas delegation, six men were admitted to membership and their votes counted on various matters, including the nomination for President. Four of them supported Seward (these having been recruited in Michigan), while two supported Bates. *Ibid.*, 149; Reinhard H. Luthin, *First Lincoln Campaign*, 137.

[11] Johnson, *Proceedings*, 112.

been the ones who had really suffered for the cause.

When Wilmot of Pennsylvania contended that the convention was no mere mass gathering but a body of representatives with home constituencies, and that they "never had a Republican party in Maryland," Armour of Maryland dramatically insisted that having been mobbed and burned in effigy because of freedom, he had "dared more than he [Wilmot] has ever dared." "We are unpurchased, and unpurchaseable," he said. "And we tell Pennsylvania to put that in her pipe and smoke it." [12] As it turned out, these doubtful delegations (Texas, Virginia, Maryland, and Kentucky) were admitted; when it came to voting Virginia cast more ballots than Illinois.[13]

Related to the difficult matter of authorized delegates was the question whether a majority to nominate should be construed as a majority of the whole number of delegates when all states were represented, or merely a majority of delegates present. The rules committee favored the first-mentioned principle, but amid parliamentary confusion the majority-present rule, solidly favored by New York's seventy, was adopted.[14] When Mr. Goodrich of Minnesota wanted to say a word while this vote was being taken, there were hisses and cries of "Sit down." When the president said "Gentlemen do not forget yourselves. You must keep order," there were further cries of "Sit down," and renewed hisses.[15]

Though there were many confused moments in the convention, the ugliest snarl was over the resolutions, otherwise known as the platform. On the afternoon of the second day (Thursday) the platform was taken up and there was great applause for the tariff and homestead clauses. At this point Joshua Giddings of Ohio rose to speak, while Cartter of Ohio arrogantly and impatiently insisted on the previous question—that is, shutting off discussion. At this there was "Great confusion, and cries of 'Giddings' by the audience." [16]

---

[12] *Ibid.*, 113.   [13] *Ibid.*, 149. Virginia cast twenty-three votes, Illinois twenty-two.
[14] *Ibid.*, 129.   [15] *Ibid.*, 130.
[16] It is difficult to convey an idea of the snarl over Giddings's amendment. When the "previous question" was demanded, not only had copies of the resolutions not been distributed; no motion had even been put. It was supposed that the question was on acceptance of the platform in full, as read, but this was an assumption rather than a parliamentary fact. Immediately after the platform had been read, without even waiting for a motion that it be adopted, Cartter had moved to shut off all discussion. The matter is further complicated by the fact that in the official proceedings the platform, inserted at this point, is given not in the form in which it then stood, but as later amended and finally adopted. *Ibid.*, 130–135. Just before this (*ibid.*, 124 ff.)

There was now a full sized parliamentary tangle. Up to then the delegates had not seen copies of the printed resolutions, yet Cartter wanted them jammed through without debate. Further confusion was then "caused by the anxiety of the delegates and the crowd . . . to obtain copies of the platform, which . . . was being distributed." [17] Cartter used every parliamentary trick he could think of to prevent discussion, even questioning the vote after he had been voted down. The proceedings in dry print show a marked contrast between his rude bluntness and Giddings's courteous efforts to be heard. Amid great applause the previous question was voted down the second time, upon which Giddings grew eloquent on self-evident truths of the Declaration of Independence. He wanted the fundamental principles of human equality included in the platform; "when you leave out this truth you leave out the party," he said. He would amend the resolutions to this effect. Cartter referred sneeringly to "this amendment and the gas expended upon it." [18] Giddings's amendment to re-affirm the Declaration of Independence was submitted and voted down. "The old man quickly rose," wrote Murat Halstead, "and made his way slowly toward the door. A dozen delegates begged him not to go. But he considered everything lost, even honor. . . . The 'twin relics' [19] were not in the new creed. And now the Declaration of Independence had been voted down! He must go." [20]

The matter could not be dropped so easily, however, and the convention had to hear an eloquent appeal from Curtis of New York. Moving an amendment which was essentially the same as that of Giddings, he asked the convention "whether they are prepared to go . . . before the country as voting down the words of the Declaration of Independence." [21] The chair had ruled that Curtis's amendment, being equivalent to Giddings's, was out of order; after further explanation, and after a member stood ready to take an appeal to the floor,

---

there had been a sizable conflict as to the rules governing the membership of the convention, and the sense in which a majority vote should be construed.

[17] *Ibid.*, 134.

[18] *Ibid.*, 136.

[19] Polygamy and slavery, denounced as the "twin relics of barbarism" in the Republican platform of 1856. *Ibid.*, 43.

[20] Halstead, *Caucuses of 1860* . . . , 136. In this vivid book Halstead reported all the party conventions of 1860. It is far more colorful than the Johnson publication. For Giddings's lasting indignation concerning this Chicago episode, see vol. II, 209–210.

[21] Johnson, *Proceedings*, 141.

the chair changed his decision and the amendment was declared in order.[22] It was put to a vote and adopted; so the Declaration became a part of the Republican platform by a kind of general reference, though without any application in terms of racial equality. The voting down of Giddings, however, the gesture of dramatic departure on the part of that antislavery stalwart,[23] who felt that the party was deserting its whole cause, and a number of impatient remarks by various members who were irked because the Declaration was brought into the picture at all, were parts of this Chicago record.

II

Next morning, the third day (Friday), "Rev. M. Green, of Chicago" offered thanks that Providence had permitted the delegates to proceed "with such harmony and mutual respect," and, amid renewed admonitions from the chair that order be preserved and as much silence maintained "as possible," the convention got down to the business of nomination. To this end there had already been feverish and sleepless activity behind the scenes. A kind of grim, unremitting series of attacks upon the state delegations, together with caucuses within those delegations, had been occupying the real attention of the delegates. To this had been added pressure by paid shouters, and a self-constituted but influential mass "conference" of Germans at the Deutsches Haus.

It has been noted that there were five prominent candidates for the nomination, but by the time the convention actually proceeded to the balloting for candidates, the practical problem had been fairly well reduced to a choice between Seward and Lincoln. Seward's strength was found in certain "safe" states (New York, Maine, Michigan, Wisconsin, Minnesota, California, Massachusetts); his doubtful-state support had begun to slip. In the matter of convention strategy, these safe states, being taken for granted, were not the targets of the most concentrated attack. Courting their votes was not the main problem. One could write them off for Seward and the result would still remain open. Let Seward be stopped somewhere in the balloting, and the

---

[22] *Ibid.*

[23] Instead of a complete departure, Giddings seems to have lingered somewhere in the rear; when the Curtis amendment was carried he returned to his seat in the Ohio delegation. Baringer, *Lincoln's Rise to Power*, 262.

INSIDE THE WIGWAM

This drawing, showing the Republican delegates in session in the "Wigwam" hastily constructed for this purpose in Chicago, appeared in *Harper's Weekly*, May 19, 1860.

HOOP-SKIRT SPLENDOR

Mrs. Lincoln during the presidency, photographed by the famous Civil War photographer, Mathew B. Brady. The tilt of the nose suggests the vivacity so often spoken of by her friends.

candidate who was best able to recruit support from states considered
doubtful would come through with the prize. The word "doubtful"
in this immediate connotation is applied to states whose delegations
at Chicago were considered open or negotiable rather than irrevocably
committed. It was also true that these same states were doubtful in
another sense; they were likely to show a close contest between the
major parties at election time.

Though not neglecting any delegates open to persuasion, Lincoln
managers devoted particular attention to three important states—
Indiana, Pennsylvania, and New Jersey. Fortunately for Seward's
opponents, there was an interlocking of the situation as between the
Indiana and the Pennsylvania delegations because of teamwork between followers of Andrew G. Curtin of Pennsylvania and Henry S.
Lane of Indiana. Both the Curtin men and the Lane men were vigorously opposed to Seward; this was a fact of importance for Lincoln.
Curtin felt that he did not wish to go before the people of Pennsylvania as candidate for governor if Seward were to be the Republican
candidate for President.[1] By this he meant that a man with a more
conservative reputation than Seward was needed. Since Lane, seeking
election as governor of Indiana,[2] felt exactly the same way, being
equally unwilling to have his fortunes tied with Seward on the Indiana stage, Curtin and Lane worked gladly together at Chicago,
which signified that they worked against Seward.

They might have worked for Bates; thus it came about that in the
more advanced maneuvers the problem of the Lincoln men, assuming
that Seward could be stopped, was to stop Bates. Could this be done,
the rest was easy. In each of the doubtful state delegations—especially
those of Indiana, Pennsylvania, and New Jersey—the anti-Seward
movement could be trusted to take care of itself, despite the lavish
offering of money, with all of Weed's generalship, and with a thousand
Seward marchers behind a blaring Seward band. It was not so necessary for Lincoln men to stop Seward; other forces in the convention
were doing that. If, therefore, the Illinois group could put a damper
on the Bates movement, the tricks were theirs. Let it be noted here
that Seward, Lincoln, and Bates were the only men with a measurable

[1] Luthin, *First Lincoln Campaign*, 154.
[2] After being elected governor in 1860, with Oliver P. Morton as lieutenant governor,
Lane immediately allowed himself to be elected United States senator, resigning the
governorship which thus fell to Morton. All this was by previous understanding.

prospect of support beyond their own states. Outside of Pennsylvania Cameron sentiment was slight; outside of Ohio sentiment concerning Chase was for the most part colorless or definitely antagonistic.

This aspect of the situation—the importance that Lincoln men placed upon checking Bates—is well revealed in the record of Gustave Koerner, upstanding German-American of Belleville, Illinois. Knowing that the Indiana and Pennsylvania delegations were meeting jointly at the courthouse in Chicago on the important night of May 17 (the second day of the convention), Bates men "appeared . . . in force" at this meeting at which Frank Blair and others carried the ball for the Missouri statesman. Koerner and Orville H. Browning turned up at this Pennsylvania-Indiana caucus, and after the Bates guns had been fired they took the floor for Lincoln. Koerner argued that Bates could not even carry Missouri and that German-Americans could not honestly support this man "who in 1856 had presided over a Whig . . . Convention at Baltimore, which nominated Fillmore and Donelson, after they had been nominated by the Know Nothings." [3] Browning urged support for Lincoln on the basis of his strength among former Whigs, with a special eye to Whigs of Pennsylvania and Indiana. He also emphasized Lincoln's opposition to nativism and concluded with an "eloquent eulogy on Lincoln, which electrified the meeting." [4] That these men had done their work well was attested by Koerner's statement that a secret session was held after which it was learned that Indiana would go at once for Lincoln, while Pennsylvania would do so as a second choice. [5]

This Browning performance is the more remarkable when one remembers that in fact Browning's opinion of Lincoln's merits was never very high, and that his preference for President in 1860 was for Bates. Lincoln strategy did not work entirely through men who supported him as a matter of spontaneous conviction. One of the

---

[3] Koerner, *Memoirs*, II, 88.

[4] *Ibid.*, II, 89. It is amazing to turn from this account of Browning electrifying the Indiana and Pennsylvania delegations to his own colorless treatment in his diary. There is a leaf missing at the point where he might have mentioned this meeting. Then, with a change of handwriting, he put in a passage stating that Bates was his first choice, "but under instructions our whole delegation voted for Mr Lincoln." Having thus hinted that his support of Lincoln was reluctant or unwilling, he followed with a statement of the reasons which "influenced" him "to support Mr Bates," who "would probably have been nominated if the struggle had been prolonged." Browning, *Diary*, I, 407–408.

[5] Koerner, II, 89.

secrets of Lincoln's success was the manner in which men like Browning, not originally nor primarily for Lincoln, were enlisted in the drive to promote his nomination.

III

In the problem of why Lincoln was selected one must not omit the German-Americans, whose contribution to the Republican nomination has been elaborately studied and well treated by Professor F. I. Herriott.[1] The story narrows down about as follows: If Lincoln was to ride to victory, it would be largely because of the elimination of Seward and Bates, as already noted. Politically the Germans were a power in the land; many of them, some would say most of them, were a power in the Republican party. They were generally antislavery, but the issue of antislavery, as realized even by Greeley's New York *Tribune*, was not the factor to be greatly stressed by the Republican party in 1860. By overstressing that issue they would incur the danger of losing support in such states as Indiana, Pennsylvania, and New Jersey. Moreover, antislavery votes needed no coaxing; it could be confidently predicted that they would be predominantly Republican. Let the party misfire on other questions, however, and the issue might hang in doubt. Every vote-getting factor had to be weighed, particularly any factor that might involve the support of a specific mass of voters. One may leave aside for a moment the question whether the foreign-born vote was going to decide the election; in the nomination process the wooing of the foreign-born, notably the Germans, could in no case be ignored.

Remembering all this, three factors in 1860 should now be noted: (1) the indignant opposition of German-Americans to Knownothingism in general and the two-year amendment in particular; (2) the association of Bates's name, whether justly or not, with anti-foreign prejudice; (3) the complete satisfaction of the Germans toward the attitude of Lincoln, as shown in his Canisius letter and otherwise, as to friendliness toward men of foreign origin.[2] German-Americans

---

[1] F. I. Herriott, "The Conference in the Deutsches Haus, Chicago, May 14–15, 1860," *Transactions,* Ill. State Hist. Soc., 1928, 101–191.

[2] Among the slightly known Lincoln documents is a letter he wrote to a committee of Chicago Germans in 1858. Finding himself unable to accept their invitation to a July 4 celebration, he gave them a sentiment: *"Our German Fellow-Citizens:*—Ever true

would willingly have supported Seward, but they had to consider the possibility of Seward's defeat for the nomination, and in that case it looked in the earlier phases of the race as if Edward Bates of Missouri might be the man, since he was favored by the Blairs, by Greeley, by influential elements in Indiana, and by statements in certain newspapers—e. g., the Springfield (Massachusetts) *Republican,* which doubted the extent of Seward's support and predicted that non-Seward or anti-Seward elements would go for Bates.[3] Support Seward, was the program of the Germans; but by all possible means be ready to stop Bates in case Seward fails to make the grade. This became the more important as signs grew that Seward was slipping, that he was deemed "too radical," that his name was associated, unfairly of course, with the criminal violence of the John Brown raid, and that potent elements were working against him. Chase, Frémont, or McLean might possibly have satisfied the Germans, but none of these compared to Lincoln in all-round availability.[4]

In such a setting and background there had assembled at the Deutsches Haus in Chicago a conference of German-Americans, May 14–15, 1860. It was the work of ardent idealists; it had been prepared carefully in advance; it bore the determined quality of organized discontent; it assembled in response to a ringing "Call"; its membership was open to delegates from organized German Republican clubs in any city or state in the union. The strongest delegations were from Illinois, Wisconsin, Iowa, Missouri, Ohio, Michigan, and New York; in addition other states—e. g., Massachusetts, Connecticut, and Kansas—were represented.

The men of this convention made up a notable roster. Practically all had been born in Germany or Austria. Not many were from Prussia, or if so they had left for good and sufficient reason. Typical ones hailed from Saxony, Bavaria, Baden, or Frankfort-on-Main. The

---

to *Liberty,* the *Union,* and the *Constitution*—true to Liberty, not selfishly, but upon *principle*—not for special *classes* of men, but for *all* men . . . ." Lincoln to A. C. Hesing and others, Springfield, June 30, 1858, Chicago *Daily Press & Tribune,* July 7, 1858, p. 1, c. 4. Some would call this catering to the German vote. That Lincoln deliberately had votes in mind when he made such appeals is true and it would be idle to deny it, yet in issuing such a sentiment in a day when some were appealing for votes in the opposite (i. e., anti-foreign) sense, Lincoln did so in genuine conviction.

[3] Herriott, "Deutsches Haus," 114.

[4] Gustave Koerner to Lyman Trumbull, March 15, 1860, Trumbull MSS.

liberal spirit of the "Forty Eighters" was prominent among the delegates. The most distinguished member was Carl Schurz from Wisconsin. Others of importance, to pick out a few, were Reinhard Solger of Massachusetts, Johannes Gambs and Frederick Kapp from New York; Frederick Muench from Missouri; Frederick Hassaurek from Ohio; Hermann Kiefer from Michigan; Theodor Hielscher from Indiana (in attendance though not an accredited delegate); Bernhard Domschke and Carl Roeser of Wisconsin; and, from Illinois, a group that included notably, as participants in the discussion, Gustave Koerner of Belleville, George Schneider of Chicago, Jens Peter Stibolt of Peoria, and Frederick Hecker of St. Clair County near Belleville. Hecker has been described as "in many respects, the most interesting and picturesque character in the Conference." [5] His career included studies at Heidelberg, service in the parliament of Baden, agitation for "intense republicanism," daring participation in the revolutionary underground, membership in the Frankfort Parliament (hopefully devoted to the unification of Germany on liberal and democratic lines), flight to Switzerland, emigration to the United States, spirited ovations at New York and elsewhere as he moved across the country, success in cattle raising, and early activity as worker and speaker in the Republican party.

In a series of five brief but significant resolutions the assembled Germans put themselves squarely on record. They adhered to the Republican principles of 1856 "in a sense most hostile to slavery," strongly favored a homestead act, and urged immediate admission of Kansas without slavery. More especially they demanded full rights for all citizens regardless of descent, denounced the Massachusetts two-year admendment, and pledged support for any aspirant for the presidency who had "never . . . been identified with the spirit of the Massachusetts Amendment." [6] This resolution, or threat, "effectually ruined the chances of . . . Bates and Banks." [7] If, therefore, Seward failed of nomination, it would be unwise for the Republican convention to hazard German-American resentment by naming Bates. On the other hand, because of Lincoln's liberal and well known record toward the foreign born, his selection would not only be acceptable but would add real strength. In the narrowing list of available men this was a most significant factor.

---

[5] Herriott, "Deutsches Haus," 182.   [6] *Ibid.*, 189.   [7] *Ibid.*, 190.

IV

A trick of fate in the balloting for the presidential candidate—or a casual incident in the proceedings—deserves passing notice. At the end of the second day (Thursday), just following the unanimous adoption of the platform, the whole assembly was swept into "a transport of enthusiasm," with tremendous shouts and cheers, fluttering handkerchiefs and waving hats.[1] It was regarded as a Seward wave, and at this moment of high feeling a motion was made to proceed at once to the balloting for President, but it was then announced "that the tally-sheets had not been prepared, and that it would subject the clerks to great inconvenience to proceed to a ballot at that time." [2] Such is one report. According to another report the chair announced that the papers were "prepared," though "not yet at hand," and would be ready "in a few minutes." [3] This was one of those little things that belong to the essential story of that convention. There now came a motion to adjourn on which the unrecorded vote was light and uncertain, after which the chairman announced that the motion prevailed and the convention stood adjourned till the next day.

Seward men were displeased; they did not desire further canvassing that night nor did they wish delay. This does not mean, however, that they were disheartened. They still "abounded in confidence." [4] It is unprovable that Seward "would have been" nominated if the balloting had been taken at the fag end of the second day, but the incident of the tally-sheets is illustrative of a certain factor that one notes in the proceedings of this gathering. It was the factor of undeliberative, unpredictable, sometimes almost accidental, action. The next business at this point had been the presidential nomination; the tally-sheets were not ready; the motion to adjourn was given; the chair said that it prevailed; adjournment occurred, and that was that.

Anyone familiar with the informal or behind-the-scenes history of that convention knows that what was done Thursday night, which was considerable even after midnight, was not in Seward's favor. As Halstead tells it, he "saw Henry S. Lane at one o'clock, pale and haggard, with cane under his arm, walking as if for a wager, from

---

[1] Johnson, *Proceedings*, 142; Halstead, *Caucuses of 1860*, 139–140. Halstead wrote: "A herd of buffaloes or lions could not have made a more tremendous roaring."

[2] Halstead, *Caucuses*, 141.   [3] Johnson, *Proceedings*, 143.   [4] Halstead, *Caucuses*, 143.

one caucus-room to another, at the Tremont House." [5] Lincoln supporters were greatly assisted by workers whose strong motive for Republican success was combined with a distrust of Seward's vote-getting appeal. Seward men were not idle, of course, and the phrase went round that "Seward's friends 'would *spend oceans of money.*' " [6] But the New Yorker's non-availability was stressed and it was reported "that the Republican candidates for Governor in Indiana, Illinois and Pennsylvania would resign, if Seward were nominated." [7] Though it may have been only a rumor concocted and circulated for its obvious purpose, such talk is the stuff of which delegate decisions are made.

V

On the morning of the convention's third day, the delegates being asked to refrain from demonstration (!), it was announced that the next business was the selection of a candidate for President of the United States. Before this could be entered upon, however, there was discussion even at this stage concerning the proper voting strength of Maryland, and there were complaints that unauthorized outsiders were occupying the seats of members. With everyone "impatient to begin the work," there now followed the naming of candidates to be voted on for the nomination. Evarts nominated Seward and the applause was "enthusiastic," but "When Mr. Judd named Lincoln, the response was prodigious, rising and raging far beyond the Seward shriek." [1]

What followed was something that required rather the talents of a hog caller than those of party delegates. It was a tournament of noise, a colossal contest of yelling between the followers of Lincoln and Seward. Lincoln's nomination had inspired the Seward men to another prodigious effort which caused Murat Halstead to bethink himself of the lines:

> "As all the fiends from heaven that fell
> Had pealed the banner cry of hell."

The effect [continued Halstead] was startling.

Hundreds of persons stopped their ears in pain. The shouting was absolutely frantic, shrill and wild. No Camanches, no panthers ever struck

5 *Ibid.*, 142.   6 Ibid., 143.   7 *Ibid.*   1 *Ibid.*, 144.

a higher note, or gave screams with more infernal intensity. Looking from the stage over the vast amphitheatre, nothing was to be seen below but thousands of hats—a black, mighty swarm of hats—flying with the velocity of hornets over a mass of human heads, most of the mouths of which were open. Above, all around the galleries, hats and handkerchiefs were flying in the tempest together. The wonder of the thing was, that the Seward outside pressure should, so far from New York, be so powerful.

Now the Lincoln men had to try it again, and as Mr. Delano of Ohio, on behalf "of a portion of the delegation of that State," seconded the nomination of Lincoln, the uproar was beyond description. Imagine all the hogs ever slaughtered in Cincinnati giving their death squeals together, a score of big steam whistles going (steam at 160 lbs. per inch), and you conceive something of the same nature. I thought the Seward yell could not be surpassed; but the Lincoln boys were clearly ahead, and feeling their victory, as there was a lull in the storm, took deep breaths all round, and gave a concentrated shriek that was positively awful, and accompanied it with stamping that made every plank and pillar in the building quiver.[2]

There now came the tense moment of balloting for President. With the full support of New York, Michigan, Wisconsin, and California, and with considerable strength elsewhere, Seward came through on the first ballot with 173½ votes, easily the highest number; yet it was not a majority. Even at this early stage Lincoln was not only second; he stood far above any of Seward's other rivals. It was Lincoln 102, Cameron 50½ (of which 47½ came from Pennsylvania), Bates 48, Chase 49, Dayton 14, and McLean 12, with a negligible scattering of votes for Wade, John M. Read (of Pennsylvania), Collamer, Sumner, and Frémont. It was obvious now that the threat to Seward's success was formidable. The votes for three men—Lincoln, Cameron, and Bates—would be enough to outnumber Seward. Add those of Chase, and Lincoln would have more than the 233 necessary to a choice.

Under these circumstances the convention proceeded to the second ballot. The air was electric with impatience, taut nerves, and a kind of high strung ferocity.[3] The feature of the second ballot was the upswing for Lincoln. He picked up two votes from New Hampshire; then he gained the whole of Vermont's ten votes which had previously been cast for Collamer. Here was a significant turn of affairs; complimentary ballots cast at the outset for a minor favorite son were now

---

[2] *Ibid.*, 145.

[3] "The partisans of the various candidates were strung up to such a pitch of excitement as to render them incapable of patience, and the cries of 'Call the roll' were fairly hissed through their teeth." *Ibid.*, 147.

shifted to the support of an outstanding contender. At this the "New Yorkers started as if an Orsini bomb had exploded." [4] Then came the sensational action of Pennsylvania. Having given 47½ votes for Cameron on the first ballot to four for Lincoln, the state delegation on the second ballot gave one to Cameron and 48 for Lincoln. "Weed sickened as he perceived 'the change in the vote of Pennsylvania, startling the vast auditorium like a clap of thunder.' " [5]

In all Lincoln gained 79 votes on this second ballot. The tally now stood: Seward, 184½; Lincoln, 181; Bates, 35; Chase, 42½; Cameron, only 2; all others, 20 votes. There was "Great confusion while the ballot was being counted." [6]

With the third ballot the convention moved uproariously to its climax. As the roll of states was called, a "hundred pencils" [7] kept informal tally with attention riveted on the rising Lincoln vote. When Lincoln had come within a vote and one-half of the necessary majority, with a sense of fate and crisis stirring throughout the wigwam, Cartter of Ohio rose to announce "the change of four votes . . . from Mr. Chase to Mr. Lincoln." [8] "The deed was done," wrote Halstead. "There was a moment's silence. The nerves of the thousands, which through the hours of suspense had been subjected to terrible tension, relaxed, and as deep breaths of relief were taken, there was a noise in the wigwam like the rush of a great wind, in the van of a storm— and in another breath, the storm was there. There were thousands cheering with the energy of insanity." [9]

Having loosed the flood by his announcement of the change of four votes, Cartter now announced that Ohio's vote was unanimous for Lincoln. Thereupon one state after another announced that its entire delegation was for Lincoln, many of the states indicating a correction of their votes. "While these votes were being given," wrote Halstead, "the applause continued, and a photograph of Abe Lincoln which had hung in one of the side rooms was brought in, and held up before the surging and screaming masses." [10] When the third ballot was completed, it was announced that Lincoln had 364 of the 466 votes.[11]

---

[4] *Ibid.,* 147.

[5] Reinhard H. Luthin, in *Pa. Mag. of Hist. and Biog.,* Jan., 1943, 71, quoting T. W. Barnes, *Memoir of Thurlow Weed,* 264. Luthin adds: "Pennsylvania's action did more than any single thing to tip the scales in favor of Lincoln."

[6] Halstead, 147.   [7] *Ibid.,* 149.   [8] *Ibid.*

[9] *Ibid.*   [10] *Ibid.,* 150.   [11] Johnson, *Proceedings,* 155.

In an eloquent speech Evarts of New York moved that the nomination be made unanimous, but in the excitement of speeches on the motion, and amid the parliamentary irregularity which characterized the whole convention, it is impossible to find any evidence that the motion was ever put and carried. Reading the prosaic account by Charles W. Johnson, whose record was the official report of the party, one can only conclude that the motion was somehow lost in the proceedings; [12] in the vivid account by Halstead, however, it is stated, but with no parliamentary detail as to the passing of any particular motion, that "the nomination was made unanimous" after "a rather dull speech from Mr. Browning of Illinois." [13]

Balloting for Vice President was an unexciting anticlimax. If the "multitude" in the wigwam could have had its way, according to Halstead, Cassius M. Clay would have been nominated by acclamation; as it was he received 101½ votes on the first ballot to 194 for Hannibal Hamlin of Maine. On the next ballot, second thoughts taking effect, it was realized that Hamlin was geographically distant from Lincoln, that he was a friend of Seward, and that he had been once a Democrat. This ballot showed 357 for Hamlin, 86 for Clay, and 13 for John Hickman of Pennsylvania. More than half of the Clay vote came from the Virginia and Kentucky delegations. Lincoln's running mate, whom he had never met, had served as congressman, senator, and governor; he was dignified, handsome, and mildly popular; he was conservative while being sufficiently antislavery; he had done much to break down the Democratic party in his state; [14] taking it all together, in 1860 he filled a recognized party need.

VI

There were numerous factors that contributed to Lincoln's nomination, and not the least of them was the strategy of his managers. Judd had seen that united action by a few states—New Jersey, Indiana, Illinois, and Pennsylvania—would probably control the convention

---

[12] Johnson reports Evarts's speech with his motion for unanimity; several pages later, some speeches having intervened, he quotes Evarts as saying that his motion "has not yet been put"; he follows immediately with a speech by Browning (not particularly directed to the motion); then notes that the convention "then adjourned." On reassembling, it proceeded at once to the nomination of Vice President. *Ibid.*, 155, 159–160.

[13] Halstead, 151.   [14] Blaine, *Twenty Years of Congress*, I, 170.

and had worked for "a quiet combination" of these delegates.[1] The strategy was not to work for "delegates distinctly Lincoln," [2] for Illinois managers did not have their eye primarily on the first ballot. Rather they counted on Lincoln receiving enough second-choice votes on some later ballot to insure his success. There had been no movement of any significant force in the convention that could be called anti-Lincoln. This was one of the advantages of the fact that the Illinois leader, while enjoying prominence among the contenders, did not stand at the top in the pre-convention canvass. Leadership in the front ranks is a thing for which one may sometimes pay a high penalty in the American political scene.

The labors of David Davis were arduous and fruitful. Though in February Davis thought it likely that Bates or Seward would be chosen, he did probably more than any other man to crystallize the non-Seward elements behind Lincoln. "To Judge Davis," wrote Jesse W. Fell, "more than to any other man, . . . is the American people indebted for . . . the nomination . . . of Abraham Lincoln." [3] His work from headquarters at the Tremont House reached into every delegation whose vote was subject to persuasion. By midnight caucuses, ubiquitous pressure, and unauthorized bargains that were later to embarrass Lincoln, Davis skillfully promoted those behind-the-scenes maneuvers which usually do not find their way conspicuously into print but which have so telling an effect on the politician-like motives of party delegates.

In at least two instances the bargaining had gone to the point of proffering posts in Lincoln's cabinet. For the support of Indiana a promise was made for the appointment of Caleb B. Smith; for Pennsylvania a like promise was made "to place Simon Cameron at the President's council table." [4] "Make no contracts that will bind me," had been Lincoln's words,[5] but in playing for such high stakes this advice was disregarded. Lincoln did not like these maneuvers in his behalf.

---

[1] Judd to Trumbull, Chicago, April 2, 1860, Trumbull MSS. [2] *Ibid.*

[3] Letter of Jesse W. Fell, quoted in Chicago *Tribune,* June 27, 1886, p. 11, c. 2.

[4] Harry E. Pratt, "David Davis, 1815–1886," *Transactions,* Ill. State Hist. Soc., 1930, 167.

[5] Herndon relates that Lincoln penciled these words on the margin of a newspaper which was brought into the room where Davis and other managers were gathered in Chicago. Nevertheless, according to Herndon, deals were made on the theory that Lincoln was far from Chicago and could not appreciate the situation. *Herndon's Life of Lincoln,* Angle ed., 373–374. See also Baringer, *Lincoln's Rise to Power,* 214, 239.

Knowing his own caution in this respect, he would have liked to believe that the nomination had come to him unencumbered by conditions or pledges of favors to individuals or leaders. "It is . . . grateful to my feelings," he wrote, "that the responsible position assigned to me comes without conditions, save only such honorable ones as are fairly implied." [6] In some accounts it is made to appear that bargains did not exist and that Lincoln approached his task with a clean slate. [7] Yet Lincoln himself has been quoted as saying: "They have gambled me all around, bought and sold me a hundred times. I cannot begin to fill the pledges made in my name." [8] It is also true that Lincoln's own letters show how eager he was to win Indiana support at Chicago and how important was the influence exerted by David Davis and Jesse Dubois to that end. [9] All told, Lincoln was affected by commitments made by others. More than that, he was deeply embarrassed. The full effect of these convention maneuvers was to be regretfully felt by the new leader in his days as President Elect in connection with Cameron's forced entry into the cabinet.

Availability, or "a presumption of availability," [10] was the secret of the choice at Chicago. To the Seward men it was a grievous blow. They had been vociferously confident; they had in fact assumed success as a matter of course. With his customary economy of phrase Browning wrote that the New York delegation was "mortified and disappointed." [11] It was not only that the nomination of Lincoln struck the New Yorkers as a rude shock; it was also true that Seward, growing more conservative every day, was becoming the spearhead of a group that was constantly to be opposed to Republican radicals. In this dislike of radicalism, of course, Seward resembled Lincoln. James G. Blaine considered that the "great achievement at Chicago was the nomination of Mr. Lincoln without offending the supporters of Seward," [12] yet the tension in the Republican party was not between Lincoln and Seward. Beginning at the very outset of Lincoln's troubled

---

[6] Lincoln to Giddings, May 21, 1860, *Works*, VI, 13–14.

[7] T. W. Barnes, *Memoir of Thurlow Weed*, 330; Chicago *Press & Tribune*, May 19, 1860, p. 1, c. 1.

[8] O. J. Hollister, Life of Colfax, 147 n., quoted in Pratt, "David Davis, 1815–1886," 167.

[9] Tracy, *Uncollected Letters*, 145, 146–147. See also Baringer, *Lincoln's Rise to Power*, 215; White, *Trumbull*, 142.

[10] Halstead, 153.   [11] Browning, *Diary*, I, 408.

[12] Blaine, *Twenty Years of Congress*, I, 169.

administration, and from that time steadily forward, the Republican party, unified in appearance, was a thing of factions and severe internal pressures.

VII

In the making of the Republican platform the candidate had had no part. The convention's resolutions are best read in the light of the maneuverings and differences within the convention. In part the platform was a succession of noble phrases; in part it was a catch-all for a variety of vote-getting clauses; in part it was an appeal to special interests though the wording always pointed grandly to the general welfare; in part it was an indictment of the "present Democratic administration"; in general it identified the Republican party with all that was right in the nation and all that was fundamental in American institutions.

As already noted, the convention's action was unsatisfactory to staunch old Joshua Giddings in its hesitant and timid manner of dealing with the Declaration of Independence. In the wording finally adopted the platform declared "That the maintenance of the principles promulgated in the Declaration of Independence and embodied in the Federal Constitution, 'That all men are created equal; that they are endowed by their Creator with certain inalienable rights; that among these are life, liberty and the pursuit of happiness; that to secure these rights, governments are instituted among men, deriving their just powers from the consent of the governed' is essential to the preservation of our Republican institutions; and that the Federal Constitution, the Rights of the States, and the Union of the States must and shall be preserved." [1]

Certain principles of the Declaration, however, had not been "embodied" in the Constitution, and the Chicago resolutions did not, by any special mention of the Negro in the clause concerning the Declaration, unequivocally interpret human equality as covering that race even in the matter of political, much less social or economic, rights. Indeed it was only as an afterthought, after the ugly snarl in the convention which deeply offended Giddings, that the Declaration was recognized at all. As to slavery in general, the platform did not

---

[1] Johnson, *Proceedings*, 131.

characterize the institution as a moral wrong; [2] in that sense the party did not go so far as in 1856. Rather, the resolutions pointed emphatically to state rights—"especially the right of each state to order . . . its own domestic institutions according to its own judgment exclusively." This was contrary to the abolitionist demand that slavery, being wrong, must be abolished in the states where it existed. As to slavery in the territories—the over-agitated issue so importantly associated with the foundation of the Republican party—the platform denied as "heresy" the dogma that the Constitution carried slavery into the territories, declared that their normal condition was freedom, and denied the authority either of Congress or of a territorial legislature "to give legal existence to slavery in any territory of the United States."

The 1860 platform did not include the 1856 phrase that it was "the right and the imperative duty of Congress to prohibit" slavery (and polygamy) in the territories. The statement that neither Congress nor a territorial legislature could "give legal existence to slavery" was not so positive and unequivocal as the out-and-out statement that Congress was under the "imperative duty" to prohibit the institution. It could have been argued that the demand for such prohibition was implied in other clauses—i. e., the one denouncing the "new dogma" that the Constitution of itself carried slavery into the territories, and the clause declaring it "our duty" to uphold the constitutional guarantee against deprivation of life, liberty, or property —but since the explicit call for congressional prohibition had been made in the platform of 1856, its omission in 1860 was worthy of notice. The tendency of the party to recede from its 1856 position, stating that position less clearly and emphatically, is unmistakable in the record.

In a succession of miscellaneous "planks" the platform extolled the union, censured the opposite party for extravagance and subserviency to "a sectional interest," branded as a crime the reopening of the African slave trade, denounced popular sovereignty, proposed

---

[2] It is stated by Nicolay and Hay that in 1860 "the Republican party . . . held that slavery was a moral wrong . . . ." *Works*, VI, 12 n. If this refers to the official resolutions of the party it is an error; the platform of 1860 contained no denunciation of slavery itself on moral grounds, though it did denounce the reopening of the African slave trade. With this denunciation most Southerners, indeed Americans generally, agreed.

the immediate admission of Kansas under a free constitution, and commended a tariff policy that was ambiguously presented, but was supposed to favor protection. In addition it was declared that the Republican party favored a 'free homestead policy," opposed restrictions upon foreign immigrants, and, while urging "rigid economy," proposed Federal expenditures for "river and harbor improvements of a national character" and for a railroad to the Pacific Ocean.

VIII

Lincoln was fond of playing "fives" (handball) and it was the recollection of one of his neighbors—James Gourley—that he played the game on the day before his nomination, and "probably he played some on the morning—early." [1] That he was playing "a game of ball" when the dispatch was handed to him announcing his nomination has been emphatically denied by T. W. S. Kidd, court crier in Springfield.[2] The detail is unimportant except that in the personal feeling toward Lincoln one looks always for the close-up view and the personal touch. According to Kidd, he had been at the telegraph office awaiting dispatches, enduring the suspense until the balloting began at Chicago. Then he stepped into a store and was standing there when yell after yell was heard and a messenger ran to him with the news. People gathered quickly around him in great numbers, but, wanting to get out of the crowd, he remarked: "Well, there is a little woman who will be interested in this news . . . ," and started for home. Herndon, however, pictures him in a large arm chair in the office of the *Illinois State Journal* when the news came; he records also the remark about telling the little woman the news.[3]

In attempting to study Lincoln at close range, especially at climactic points in his life, one is impressed both with the importance given to small details by neighbors and the frequency with which recollections are fragmentary or contradictory. In addition to Gourley and Kidd there were various others who told of this exciting day in Springfield. We have the narrative of Clinton L. Conkling who explained that while the convention was in progress Lincoln remained in Spring-

[1] Interview with James Gourley recorded by Herndon (undated), Herndon-Weik MSS.
[2] *Journal*, Ill. State Hist. Soc., XV, 507–509 (Apr., 1922).
[3] "The news of his nomination found Lincoln at Springfield in the office of the *Journal*." Herndon (Angle ed.), 374.

field, going to his law office as usual, watching telegrams, and joining "in a game of hand ball, . . . favorite pastime of the professional men of the town." According to this account, Lincoln came into James C. Conkling's law office on the morning of May 18 (the day of the nomination), stretched himself on a settee, and chatted with James C., who had been in Chicago and had returned to Springfield. After Lincoln had left the office, according to this version, Clinton L. Conkling, having learned the big news, met him "on the west side of the Square" and was the first to tell him of his nomination, after which the nominee was surrounded by excited crowds.[4]

Gourley's reminiscence suggests the opposite of elation: "he was agitated—turned pale—troubled." Directly after the nomination, said Gourley, he went home from the *Journal* office.[5] If he hoped to retire to his own thoughts he was unsuccessful; at his house he was soon joined by friends in considerable number.

Next day, while the town of Springfield thrilled with demonstrations, music, fireworks, and festivity, the parlor in the house on Eighth Street became the scene of a restrained and solemn ceremony as the committee from the Chicago convention formally notified Lincoln of his nomination as President. Gustave Koerner, in describing the scene, mentioned that Lincoln "looked much moved, and rather sad, . . . feeling the heavy responsibility thrown upon him."[6] Carl Schurz, member of the committee, wrote:

---

[4] Clinton L. Conkling, "How Mr. Lincoln Received the News of His First Nomination," *Transactions*, Ill. State Hist. Soc., 1909, 63–66. In this article there are citations of further sources (66 n.), and photographic reproductions of "five original telegrams received by Mr. Lincoln on the day he was nominated." Weik (*Real Lincoln*, 263–267) repeats this Conkling account and adds details from other sources—e. g., as to Lincoln playing "fives."

[5] Gourley MS. interview, above quoted. Lincoln could have been told the news before the telegrams were given to him. He moved about that morning, and, as shown above, accounts differ as to just where he was when various phases of "getting the news" occurred. If one could piece together a complete narrative, which seems impossible now, the reminiscences, rightly interpreted, might be found to be supplementary rather than entirely contradictory. As to the handball detail there is really no contradiction between Gourley and Kidd.

[6] Koerner, II, 94. Koerner tells of Mrs. Lincoln's frustrated efforts in the matter of liquid hospitality. W. H. Townsend (*Lincoln and Liquor*, 100 ff.) adds further details, indicating that ice water was served at the Lincolns', whereas at the hotel (the Chenery House) the committee had everything except ice water. Townsend gives a photographic reproduction of a confidential letter of Lincoln to J. Mason Haight, June 11, 1860. "Having kept house sixteen years [wrote Lincoln], and having never held the 'cup' to the lips of my friends there, my judgment was that I should not, in my new position, change my habit in this respect."

Mr. Lincoln received us in the parlor of his modest frame house . . . . There the Republican candidate for the Presidency stood, tall and ungainly in his black suit of . . . new but ill-fitting clothes, his long tawny neck emerging gauntly from his turn-down collar, his melancholy eyes sunken deep in his haggard face. Most of the . . . committee had never seen him before, and gazed at him with surprised curiosity. He . . . did not present the appearance of a statesman . . . . Standing up with folded hands, he quietly . . . listened to the dignified . . . speech . . . by Mr. Ashmun, the president of the Convention, and then he responded with a few appropriate . . . and well-shaped sentences . . . . Then followed some informal talk . . . in which the hearty simplicity of Lincoln's nature shone out, and . . . the committee took its leave.[7]

Lincoln's response had been modest and brief, yet not colorless: he almost wished the "high honor" had fallen to another; he tendered "profoundest thanks"; he expressed himself as "painfully sensible of the great responsibility." By a literal reading it could almost be inferred that Lincoln was leaving open the question of his acceptance. He promised to read the platform and later to respond in writing "without . . . unnecessary . . . delay." [8]

This he did formally, again very briefly, on May 23, accepting the nomination, endorsing the platform, imploring Divine assistance, hailing the Constitution, and striking the note of "perpetual union, harmony, and prosperity." [9]

From among the millions of American citizens, delegates of a leading party had chosen one man. Upon him was now focused the hopes of party success, and beyond that the dread responsibility of chief magistracy. No longer for him the bustling county seat, the long rides on the circuit, the stir and challenge of western law practice. Abraham Lincoln was now candidate for President. He sat for his portrait to the photographer Alexander Hesler of Chicago. The camera caught him in perfect pose and expression; the Hesler profile is the finest of the Lincoln pictures. Without the beard, it has the sculptural ruggedness of the remarkable life mask by Leonard Volk. Lincoln now wrote out the basis for his campaign biography, producing an autobiography which was all fact and no flourish; yet for its priceless glimpses of

---

[7] *Reminiscences of Carl Schurz*, II, 187–188.

[8] *Works*, VI, 12–13 (May 19, 1860). This statement, giving thanks for the honor but promising a later response, did not include an acceptance of the nomination. Acceptance came four days later.

[9] *Ibid.*, VI, 14–15.

early life, its accuracy, and its unstudied revelations of character, it remains, now as in 1860, an indispensable source for any Lincoln biographer.

Soon the campaign "lives" appeared—the first trickles of a vast torrent of Lincolniana. With almost incredible promptness these books fell from the press.[10] Though priority in this field has been disputed, the "Wigwam Edition," published by Rudd and Carleton of New York, has been judged by a careful writer, Ernest J. Wessen, as the "first campaign life of Lincoln." Published on June 2, 1860, it was offered in paper wrappers at the price of twenty-five cents. The candidate's first name was spelled "Abram." No author's name appeared. The book was at once popular; 12,000 copies were sold within a week. Two days later came another paper-bound work by a journalist and popular writer, David V. G. Bartlett—price, twenty-five cents. Third place has been assigned to an anonymously written book brought out by Thayer and Eldridge of Boston and known to collectors by the publisher's name. It seems to have appeared about June 7, though "registered for copyright" on May 28, ten days after Lincoln's unforeseeable nomination. On June 11 there appeared a tiny 32mo volume edited and published by Reuben Vose of New York. Only a few pages were devoted to Lincoln's life; the rest consisted of Republican platforms (1856 and 1860), Lincoln's Cooper Union speech, and miscellaneous campaign material. The public was invited to apply to the publisher for other political publications, including, curiously enough, "5000 copies of the *Conservative*," which "contains the names of five hundred of the richest men in New-York." Other biographies followed in quick succession. With no effort to enumerate them all, nor to specify dates or order of appearance, mention may be made of a longer work by Thayer and Eldridge called the "Wide-awake Edition," a book by Joseph H. Barrett published at Cincinnati, a life by James Q. Howard, published by the Columbus firm that had first published the Lincoln-Douglas debates, and a joint biography of Lincoln and Hamlin, hastily written by W. D. Howells with the use of material assembled by this same Howard. In our own day the Abraham Lincoln Association has handsomely reproduced a

---

10 William E. Barton, in *Transactions*, Ill. State Hist. Soc., 1929, 87 ff. On this same subject one should not neglect Ernest J. Wessen, "Campaign Lives of Abraham Lincoln, 1860," *Papers in Ill. Hist.*, 1937, 188–220. See also Jay Monaghan, *Lincoln Bibliography, 1839–1939*. Wessen's account is more authoritative than Barton's.

special copy of this Howells biography in which a number of errors are corrected by penciled annotations in Lincoln's own hand.

Among the more substantial campaign biographies of 1860 was that by John L. Scripps, for whom Lincoln wrote the autobiography above mentioned. The Scripps book was closer to Lincoln and more truly a biography than any other of the campaign books. Yet none of the 1860 lives were particularly notable: they relied on "shears and pastebrush," [11] they bore the quality of padding, hasty writing, and party propaganda. It would have been better if the people had been given the superb Hesler profile along with Lincoln's autobiography undiluted and unadorned.[12]

---

[11] Barton, as cited in preceding note, 70.

[12] For fuller treatment of the subject matter of this chapter the reader is referred to the following important works: William Baringer, *Lincoln's Rise to Power* (1937); Reinhard H. Luthin, *The First Lincoln Campaign* (1944).

CHAPTER VIII

CAMPAIGN AND ELECTION OF 1860

I

FROM May to November, 1860, Lincoln must have seemed inaccessible to the country at large. The campaigning, all of it, was done by others while the Republican candidate remained quietly at Springfield. He had a flood of callers and his correspondence was heavy, yet his collected works contain only a moderate amount of writing for the period of the campaign. He made virtually no speeches, certainly none that could be called political declarations.[1] This avoidance of oratory, as also of talk and writing, was deliberate and was rationalized on the ground that "writing for the public" would "do no good." People, he thought, would not be persuaded, "though one rose from the dead." [2] When Trumbull delivered to Lincoln an invitation to speak in Detroit, the candidate declined, thinking it "would be departing from a line of policy he had adopted & which friends have commended." [3]

In his unadvertised manner Lincoln kept in touch with party strategy, noting the maneuvers of the three-fold opposition, showing concern as to the result in Maine, advising as to a speaking tour by Cassius M. Clay in Illinois, writing on politics to the past master politician, Weed, showing caution not to expose quarrels among friends in his party, discounting suggestions of intent to do him

---

[1] In his brief remarks at his home in Springfield on August 8, 1860, he was merely seeing the assemblage and being seen by them. Even such an appearance was rare. For the speech, if it could be called that, see *Works*, VI, 49–50, where it is given with the incorrect date of August 14. For an account of this Republican rally, see W. E. Baringer, in *Transactions*, Ill. State Hist. Soc., 1932, 253 ff.

[2] *Ibid.*, VI, 63–64 (Oct. 23, 1860).

[3] Lyman Trumbull to Zachariah Chandler, Springfield, Ill., Sep., 3, 1860. Chandler MSS.

violence, and taking care to deny campaign falsehoods.[4] With characteristic modesty he referred to the honor conferred upon him as "a tribute . . . to no man as a man" but as applicable to any "representative of the truth." [5]

In the excess of politics that swept the nation in this summer and fall, Republicans were exuberant and irrepressible. Their candidate's name inspired enthusiasm. Lincoln was a man that people could shout for, this being an early phase of his leadership. There was nothing tame or half-hearted about the canvass, nothing of the apathy that Lincoln himself had shown toward Scott. The American flair for political organization was impressively demonstrated, and with organization there went pageantry, merrymaking, feasting, shouting, singing, marching, and all those emotional outlets which have so large a part, yet make so little sense, in the political circus.

Things were not left to chance. There was a network of regular Republican committees, local, state, and national. Managers saw to it that Republican clubs were organized, not only down to the county, but to the township or precinct.[6] Long before the convention, plans had been laid for each county in Illinois to have its "guarantor" and "treasurer" for the party "assessment," [7] this phase being kept behind the scenes with the minimum of publicity. Correspondence was elaborately organized, with "corresponding secretaries" in the localities and voters' lists prepared for the mailing out of documents. These informal and unofficial lists were referred to as the *"registration of voters."* [8]

Marching groups or companies known as "Wide Awakes," with the importance of volunteer firemen and the exuberance of lodge brothers on parade, were formed throughout the North for pro-Lincoln campaigning. They functioned as party clubs, ready at all times with mottoes, torches, special uniforms, and exploding fireworks to demonstrate for the Union, for Lincoln, for free homesteads, free

---

[4] *Works*, VI, 44–55, *passim*.   [5] *Ibid.*, VI, 49–50 (Aug. 14, 1860).

[6] W. E. Baringer, "Campaign Technique in Illinois—1860," *Transactions*, Ill. State Hist. Soc., 1932, 203–281, esp. p. 248.

[7] The chairman and treasurer of the Illinois state central committee wrote as follows to Jesse W. Fell: "We need not tell you, that . . . we must have money. . . . In conclusion, we beg of you a prompt attention to the above, making, however, as little stir, and giving the matter as little publicity as may be compatible with the accomplishment of the objects designed." Quoted in *ibid.*, 205.

[8] *Ibid.*, 248.

labor, the Constitution, Plymouth Rock, Liberty throughout the world, American industry, river and harbor improvements, and, as catch-all for all this and more, the Republican party. Their music, pageantry, and army-like drill, being designed for spectacular show and sensational appeal, were unanswerable: it was theirs to shout, not argue; it was theirs also, at election time, to get out the vote. Some of the paraders, with the superiority of men on horseback, went by the name "Lincoln Rangers." In the wigwam-symbol the Republicans had their badge; in the *Railsplitter,* printed at Chicago, they had their special campaign sheet. Everywhere, as a matter of course, they had their newspapers. There were barbecues, rallies, processions, long wagon trips with farmers camping by the wayside, visits by delegations, and at Springfield a mammoth assemblage with a dozen speakers and several speaking stands. Led by carefully drilled glee clubs, people sang their party campaign songs, most of which have fortunately been forgotten. Their naïve rhythm and loud bluster usually had a pioneer flavor; the most famous of them, "Old Abe Lincoln came out of the wilderness," sang itself to the irresistible tune of "The Old Gray Mare." Another, belittling "Dug" as a plow "hoss" and rhyming him with "plug," was shouted to the melody of Stephen Foster's "Du da, du da day." [9]

II

If one turns from noise and show to the more serious aspects of the popular campaign, he finds a disturbing situation. The complex features of this momentous contest—the factions within historic parties (such as "Danites" [1] against Douglasites), the four contending parties of the troubled year 1860, the multiplicity of candidates, the talk of fusion across party lines, the simultaneous contests for presidential, congressional, gubernatorial, state executive, state legislative, and local tickets, the admixture of economic interests with moral questions, the contradictions among men supporting the same ticket —caused bewilderment whenever the campaign was thought of as an

---

9 *Ibid.,* 261, 264.

1 "The derisive term, 'Danite,' seems to have been taken from a despised Mormon group, and applied to the few Federal office-holders and pro-Southern Democrats who opposed Douglas in the elections of 1858 and 1860 in Illinois." H. P. James, *Lincoln's Own State in the Election of 1860* (abstract of doctoral thesis, Univ. of Ill., 1943), 7.

election instead of a spectacle or circus. The constant resort to mis-representation, charges and counter charges, smirching and counter smirching, the ominous sectional flare-up, the ugly rumors of armed resistance in case of Lincoln's election,[2] the realization of thoughtful men that violent forces were lurking behind the politicians' facade —all such factors made it seem that in 1860 politics was running amuck and that the recklessness and irresponsible fury characteristic of American campaigns might this time lead to disaster.

As people listened to political speeches or read party newspapers, they either made allowances for unreason and fantastic exaggeration or else they believed, in words attributed to an English observer at an earlier and less violent time, that, judging by American journals, "the different candidates for the presidency were the greatest rascals in America."[3] If they swallowed the statements of the politicians and the editors, they believed that the nation's institutions were being destroyed, that submission to the vilest domination would be their lot unless a particular candidate were elected, that a perpetual war of races was about to be let loose, that corruption unspeakable was abroad, and that the fireside, the family, the Constitution, and society itself were about to be utterly subverted.

Speakers were numerous and distinguished. Traveling by the more active campaigners called for Marathon-like endurance. Hardly anything else in American life produced the Barnum-like thrill and excitement of party canvasses. Showmanship and popular entertainment were larger factors than most leaders would have admitted. The buffoonery of Artemus Ward was enlisted for Lincoln; other soapbox sages supported their chosen candidates; the raising of flagpoles and the stringing of banners were given as much attention as logic and solemn discussion.

There were appeals to party regularity—to the motive of voting first, last, and always for a party all the way down the line; yet there was also the plea that a party shift was indicated, that the issues of the time transcended partisanship, that old parties were crumbling with new ones developing, and that the inertia of established voting habits

---

[2] A writer unknown to Lincoln wrote him that army officers at Fort Kearny had determined in case of Republican success "to take themselves, and the arms at that point, South, for the purpose of resistance to the government." *Works*, VI, 65 (Oct. 26, 1860).

[3] Quoted in Fite, *Presidential Campaign of 1860*, 219.

must be shaken off. Such appeals, however, were themselves partisan; what was asked for was not nonpartisanship, which had no outlet and no focus, but a change in party allegiance.

Breckinridge's campaign was mediocre, noncommittal, and comparatively inactive so far as the candidate himself was concerned. He had the support of powerful elements both North and South—of President Buchanan, of the emphatic New York *Herald,* and of Yancey, who invaded the North with his fiery rhetoric. While assailing Douglas plentifully, Breckinridge men used their heavy ammunition against Lincoln. They presented his party as Black Republicans who would "spurn the pretence of peace" and "have none of your conciliatory counsels." Since, as they asserted, "the South could not, ought not to, submit," [4] they stressed the acute peril which the country faced in the event of Lincoln's election, though predicting an entirely peaceable dissolution prior to inauguration which would give Lincoln and Hamlin "no South to reign over." [5] Even when admitting the existence of better and more moderate elements in the Republican party, they accused the party of monopolizing the territories for Northern benefit, playing second fiddle to Lovejoy, endorsing Helper, and approving the "bloody acts of John Brown." [6] The party was represented as promoting equality of the races and their movement was advertised as a threatened "revolution in our social organization." [7]

The dread word "socialism" was hurled into the arena of words as a devastating characterization of Republican policy. "Socialism in its worst form," it was said, "including . . . women's rights, the division of land, free love and the exaltation of the desires of the individual over the . . . family, and the forced equality of all men in phalansteries . . . are a part of the logical chain of ideas that flow from . . . the soul of black republicanism." [8]

As for Breckinridge arguments in full, they would be a composite of all that was said by Breckinridge men—by a South Carolinian editor who predicted the time when "the President shall . . . proscribe every man who dares to raise his voice in favor of the constitutional

---

4 Howard C. Perkins, ed., *Northern Editorials on Secession,* I, 32.

5 Dwight L. Dumond, ed., *Southern Editorials on Secession,* 180.

6 Perkins, *Northern Editorials,* I, 33, 37.   7 *Ibid.,* I, 36.

8 *Ibid.,* I, 36 (quoting N. Y. *Herald,* Sep. 19, 1860).

rights of the South," [9] by Wigfall of Texas who ridiculed "the twaddle about the fathers," [10] by Yancey of Alabama who insisted that the fathers intended the increase of slavery and denounced Lincoln and Seward for proposing "to take them away from us by infamous legislation," [11] by a sensational New York newspaper which declared that by Lincoln's election "all . . . opposed to him will be ground to powder." [12]

While thus delivering their full arsenal of denunciation against Lincoln, Breckinridge leaders found little better to say of Douglas, whom they accused of "catering for Republican success and sympathy" and giving "cordial support to the [future] administration of Abraham Lincoln." [13] Bell, Douglas, Lincoln—they were all utterly unsatisfactory to Breckinridge supporters. "In contrast to the three" an Ohio editor presented Mr. Breckinridge—"a Union-loving man, . . . a faithful supporter of the constitution as interpreted by the Supreme Court—a man of fine talents, . . . beloved and admired by those who know him best." [14]

III

Douglas swung about with great energy, visiting nearly every Northern state and some Southern ones, projecting his powerful voice over huge outdoor multitudes, overtaxing his strength, courageously appearing in centers of tense hostility, and bearing as best he could the canards of abuse that floated throughout the land, such as the rumors that he was a drunkard, had received the sacraments from the Pope, and was the tool of the Rothschilds. [1]

The Douglas line of argument was to stress the note of compromise and appeal to an earlier statesmanship of adjustment and moderation. There could, however, be angry indignation on the part of pro-Douglas editors and speakers. Toward Lincoln at one extreme and

---

[9] Dumond, *Southern Editorials*, 155.   [10] Quoted in Fite, *Campaign of 1860*, 162.
[11] *Ibid.*, 305.
[12] Perkins, *Northern Editorials*, I, 46 (quoting N. Y. *Herald*, Oct. 1, 1860).
[13] *Ibid.*, I, 41. (quoting Boston *Post*, Sep. 26, 1860). The accusation here was that Douglas, by favoring the maintenance of Federal authority *"in any contingency,"* meant that Republicans could do their worst and he would still support them.
[14] *Ibid.*, I, 60 (quoting the Columbus *Daily Capital City Fact*, Oct. 19, 1860).
[1] Milton, *Eve of Conflict*, 496.

Breckinridge at the other, both of whom they accused of defeating the cause of friendly adjustment, their language was severe and bitter. The Republicans, whom they identified with fanatical abolitionism, and the Breckinridge party, whom they denounced for seeking to impose slave codes upon the people of the territories, were equally assailed as promoters of disunion. Recognizing that fire-eaters were not all Southern and Cassandras of irrepressible conflict not all Northern, they hurled their epithets equally against "Northern negro-lovers and Southern nullifiers." [2] They did not fail to recognize that secessionist threats at the South were directed not only against Lincoln, but against Douglas as well. "As a dernier resort," declared the Peoria *Daily Democratic Union,* "the people of the South are made to believe that a dissolution of the Union, in case of the election of a northern man, will be an easy process . . . . This is an old trick . . . and must . . . result in humiliating defeat. The dissolution of this Union, . . . however much desired by . . . scoundrels . . . , is a moral, physical, and financial impossibility. A common language, a common religion, and the ties of consanguinity . . . forbid it. A common interest forbids it." [3]

Lincoln, it was argued, could not conduct a national administration on the basis of his 1858 principles. "When he shall have torn these States asunder," it was asked, "destroyed the internal trade of the country—and provoked a servile war, and flooded the whole North with fugitive blacks . . . —will he . . . have abolished slavery? Will he have made the negro the political equal of the white man? We can confidently answer, No!" What would be the result if Lincoln was elected? It would be "all anarchy and blood-shed where peace and prosperity reigned so long." The free states would force their abolition views "at the point of the bayonet." They would "subjugate the white men of the South." Revering the memory of John Brown, they would "follow his example and . . . revenge his death." [4]

The doctrine and policy of Douglas were forcefully developed by the senator himself at Raleigh, N. C., August 30, 1860.[5] Self government throughout the land, determination of local institutions by the people in every case, and, above all, adherence to the Union, were his points of emphasis. What he favored was the simple right of every

---

[2] Perkins, *Northern Editorials,* I, 51.   [3] *Ibid.,* I, 49.
[4] *Ibid.,* I, 53.   [5] Fite, *Campaign of 1860,* 276-300.

people to make its own laws. Two classes of politicians, he said, opposed this: the abolitionists on the one hand, and the interventionists or "Southern Secessionists" on the other. There would be no hope of electing Lincoln, he declared, except for the secessionists of the South.

On Lincoln's house-divided declaration the senator took bold issue. In a great and diverse country "there must necessarily be a corresponding variety of interests, requiring separate and different laws in each locality." This right, he said, "lies at the very foundation of our government." Uniformity in disregard of the wants and conditions of the people he considered neither possible nor desirable.

> The Revolutionary struggle [said Douglas] began in the defense of the right of the dependent colonies . . . to exercise . . . self-government as well as sovereign states. . . . George III . . . and his Tory friends . . . all denied the right of the people of these colonies to regulate their own domestic affairs. . . . Our fathers of the Revolution told the king that they did not get their rights from the king, but . . . from God Almighty. And the people of the territories will be likely to tell you that they do not get their rights from Congress, they get them from a purer source. (*Laughter.*) . . . There is no other argument used against squatter sovereignty, as they term it, that they have not copied from the Tories of the Revolution . . . . (*Applause.*) [6]

With telling effect he denounced the attitude of "the Secessionists of the South" toward the Cincinnati platform of 1856, which favored non-interference by Congress with slavery in the states and territories.

> At Charleston [he said] every friend I had from the Northwest offered to take the Cincinnati platform, word for word . . . . They [i. e., the anti-Douglas leaders] said it was not good Democracy. How came that platform to be adopted in 1856, if it was not sound? You know it was adopted at the suggestion of the Alabama legislature, on four propositions drawn by Mr. Yancey, and when introduced into the Cincinnati convention received the vote of every delegate from every state in the Union, free or slave. They proposed it and we of the North said it was fair and just, and we took it. It was adopted by a unanimous vote, and four years after you are told that a man is a traitor to the South who stands by the pledge we all made at Cincinnati. . . . I cannot change as rapidly as that. (*Applause.*) [7]

No topic in Douglas's speeches received stronger emphasis than his insistence upon recognition of whatever candidate was to be consti-

---

[6] *Ibid.*, 292–293.   [7] *Ibid.*, 293–294.

tutionally elected and his upstanding declaration that he would do all
in his power to uphold the laws and sustain the Union. The strongest
point he scored against Breckinridge was that disunionists were using
and supporting him. When he was speaking at Norfolk he was presented with two written questions from electors on the Breckinridge
ticket: would the Southern states be justified in seceding if Lincoln
was elected; and if so, would he advise resistance? He answered emphatically that it was the President's duty to enforce the laws of the
United States and that he would do all in his power to *"aid . . . in
maintaining the supremacy of the laws against all resistance . . . ,
come from whatever quarter it might."* "The mere inauguration of a
President," he said, "is not such a grievance as would justify revolution
or secession." [8] When at Raleigh a gentleman asked him to repeat
this declaration, he did so with great force, stating that if any man,
after the election of Lincoln or Breckinridge, should attempt to
violate the Constitution of the country, he would "hang him higher
than Haman, according to law." [9]

IV

Since there were many voices to speak for Lincoln, who was not
speaking for himself, the arguments for his party were somewhat
diverse. Sometimes the issue was presented as a high moral crusade,
but expediency often demanded that emphasis be shifted to other
matters, such as free homesteads, a tariff for protection, a railroad to
the Pacific, a glowing prospect of Republican prosperity, and the need
for a change of administration. To Democrats it was suggested that
parties come and go, that the time might come when existing parties
ought to be dissolved and new associations formed. The Republican
party was represented as embodying the vigorous spirit of the coming
age. "The spirit of radical democracy," it was said, "will always exist
and work in the country. That spirit has passed out of the old democracy into the new. To many the republican party looks radical, but it
cannot look more so than the old democratic party did twenty five
years ago when it had a life, a soul and a purpose. And the time was
when the old republican [Jeffersonian] party of 1800 was reproached

---

[8] Milton, *Eve of Conflict*, 492–493.

[9] Fite, *Campaign of 1860*, 294–296. Reported in a slightly different version in Milton,
493.

with the name 'democrat,' just as the modern republican party is with the term 'abolitionist!' " [1]

The Republican party was thus pictured as "radical" to those to whom the word connoted upstanding reform and democratic progress. In this sense the fact that the Democratic party was once called "Republican" was not overlooked. Sincere Democrats were in fact asked to embrace the party of the Chicago wigwam, to realize that their own party was dead, and to consider the new organization a kind of modern Democratic party.

On the other hand, and more importantly, the party of Lincoln was presented as eminently conservative. Sometimes the argument under this head involved a delicate balancing act. This was illustrated in the tiny campaign biography by Vose, wherein Lincoln was praised for "the conservative tendencies of his mind" and held up as a man under whom all factions and "every section" could unite, not excluding "Americans" (nativists); yet in another passage in the same book Lincoln was commended for having "left the ground that Mr. Clay occupied, of compromise and concession to slavery," and manfully taking "the stand of open opposition and unyielding resistance to all the . . . aggressions of the slave power." [2] It seemed to be the special concern of this writer to relieve the Republican party of the odium of being merely a prolongation of the Whig party; indeed it was amazing to note how large a part of this midget of a book was written in the anti-Clay sense. Yet in other publications Whig principles were approved, and Lincoln, rightly enough, was held up as a true Whig. Whatever might be the effort to dissociate Lincoln from the Clay tradition, which was strong among Whigs as late as 1850, it was also true that the Republican candidate was pictured as all things to all men—moderate, conservative, patriotic, a man of the people, honored lawyer, popular orator, industrious and intelligent, "a personification of the distinctive genius of our country and its institutions." [3] The tradition of Lincoln as America, as democracy, was thus beginning to take form at the very outset of his larger career.

[1] Perkins, *Northern Editorials*, I, 60–61 (quoting Hartford *Evening Press*, Oct. 25 and 26, 1860).

[2] Reuben Vose, *The Life and Speeches of Abraham Lincoln and Hannibal Hamlin*, v, xiii–xiv.

[3] *Ibid.*, ix. The writer continued: "Whatever is peculiar in the history and development of America, whatever is foremost in its civilization, . . . finds its best expression in the career of such men as Abraham Lincoln."

It was characteristic of the Republican campaign that practical politics were dominant. The idea of a moral crusade against slavery was muted, while emphasis was placed on such economic issues as free homesteads for western settlers and a tariff for protection of industry. The tariff question was complex [4] and the tariff "plank" in the Republican platform of 1860 was most cautiously worded. It *seemed* to favor a tariff primarily for protection, and was so understood by protectionists,[5] but the word "protection" was omitted, while references to "revenue for the . . . government" and "remunerating prices" to agriculture, together with the vaguely expansive verbiage of the whole paragraph, would enable others to interpret it quite differently.[6] Expediency dictated the tariff policy of the party at a time when "protectionist sentiment mounted to fever heat in Pennsylvania" while it was feared that the Republicans could not win the presidency without the electoral vote of that state.[7] There were, however, elements within the party that looked to freedom of international trade as the key to widely based economic welfare, particularly former Democrats who "resented their new party's tendencies toward protectionism." [8] As to Lincoln's own position, he favored "a moderate, carefully adjusted protective tariff," so long as it would not be "a perpetual subject of political strife, squabbles, changes, and uncertainties"; [9] yet he showed excessive caution in avoiding a public statement on the subject in 1859 and 1860.

That the cause of antislavery was not regarded by Republicans as sufficient for their 1860 appeal is abundantly shown in contemporary records. Greeley knew that the country was "not Anti-Slavery." [10] James G. Blaine showed that the tariff had a "controlling influence"

---

[4] For an elaborate treatment, see Reinhard H. Luthin, "Abraham Lincoln and the Tariff," *Amer. Hist. Rev.*, XLIX, 609–629 (July, 1944).

[5] The tariff paragraph was especially slanted toward Pennsylvania. When that part of the platform was read at Chicago, "Pennsylvania went into spasms of joy . . . , her whole delegation rising and swinging hats and canes." Halstead, *Caucuses*, 135.

[6] Though the twelfth paragraph of the Republican platform was supposed in Pennsylvania and elsewhere to favor protection, yet such was the juggling of words at Chicago that it could be given just the opposite interpretation. This is shown by a statement in the Pittsburgh *Post* of October 10, 1860, that "a tariff for protection" had been "formally abandoned in their Chicago platform." Quoted in Perkins, *Northern Editorials*, I, 51–52.

[7] Luthin, "Abraham Lincoln and the Tariff," 613–614.   [8] *Ibid.*, 624.

[9] *Works*, V, 256 (Oct. 11, 1859). For further statements concerning Lincoln, the Republicans, and the tariff, see below, pp. 280–281, 314–315.

[10] Luthin, "Abraham Lincoln and the Tariff," 615.

on the 1860 result.[11] Democrats, viewing the shift away from anti-slavery emphasis, were disturbed. One of them complained that in their speeches the Republicans were saying nothing of the Negro question, "but all is made to turn on the Tariff." [12] Along with the tariff were various questions of national finance, western expansion, rivers and harbors, and the like. As the Philadelphia *North American* remarked: "We have seen that slavery was not the dominating idea of the Presidential contest . . . ." [13]

V

In the raucous discord of party bickering the Bell-Everett plea was like a polite parlor conversation persisting in the midst of a riot. Why should we quarrel, they asked. Why all the sparks? Here is earth's paradise—here the kind uses of friendship with all the bright spots of national memory. We might have been a mighty and prosperous nation, a happy and contented people. In the days of the fathers we had our petty grievances but they did not rule us. We grew in harmony. The Constitution covered the nation as a blanket. We were National then. We were the people of one State. As a nation we were content, honest, flourishing. Why cannot we be so now? Love of country was once the universal theme. Now look at us—tangled in a maze, bewildered, angry with disputation, brothers no longer, pursuing a phantom, an *ignis fatuus* of demagogues. Surely we have a better destiny, a higher calling than that. From Maine to Georgia why can we not be united? Why not return to the happy days? [1]

Every one of the presidential candidates in 1860 was for the Union. To Bell and Everett the Union and the Constitution were the only issue. Douglas wanted no disunionist to vote for him.[2] In Lincoln's mind the Union was perpetual and fundamental, though he had to endure the distress of hearing Republicans accused of disunionism. "Many," he said, "charge upon us hostility to the Union"; then he added: "we claim that we are the only true Union men . . . ." [3] Even

---

[11] *Twenty Years of Congress,* I, 207.
[12] Luthin, "Abraham Lincoln and the Tariff," 621.   [13] *Ibid.,* 624.
[1] Cincinnati *Daily Times,* Sep. 22, 1860, reprinted in Perkins, *Northern Editorials,* I, 38–39. The author has condensed and slightly paraphrased this patriotic pro-Bell editorial.
[2] Milton, *Eve of Conflict,* 492.
[3] *Works,* V, 345–346 (speech at New Haven, Mar. 6, 1860).

Breckinridge took pro-Union ground; indeed his support in the North was largely based on the supposition that, of all the candidates, his election would be likeliest to avert disunion. This was the theme song of the New York *Herald,* while in Kentucky it was editorially asserted that the "charge of disloyalty to the Union against Mr. Breckinridge and his party is as groundless, as false and infamous a slander as ever emanated from a political pen." [4]

VI

Except for saner elements which seemed inadequately vocal, the campaign was waged in an emotional atmosphere of abnormal intensity. It was unreality made real—a conflict made inevitable by repeatedly and vociferously declaring it so. Social psychology of the time partook of the pathological. Examples could be adduced on both sides. In the North Carl Schurz spoke harshly of "slavery despotism," [1] while the language of Wendell Phillips in this period, discarding reason, became a kind of grandiloquent, self-righteous raving.[2] In the South, though restraining voices were not absent, the campaign was conducted amid luridly sensational accounts of violent plots against Southerners on the part of Yankee incendiaries, poisoners, and murderers in their midst. Especially in Texas there were charges of deep-laid schemes for "a gigantic servile uprising, when at a given signal the slaves would rise against their masters, burn towns and dwellings, and murder their owners and families." [3]

The stories grew. Monsters were said to be abroad in the South, concocting the vilest of crimes. There was to be systematic arson and treason. Negro cooks were to add strychnine and arsenic to their masters' diet. The South was said to be infested with hundreds of

---

[4] E. M. Coulter, *Civil War and Readjustment in Kentucky,* 22, quoting *Kentucky Statesman,* Aug. 28, 1860.

[1] Quoted in Fite, *Campaign of 1860,* 261.

[2] The trend of Phillips's oratory is illustrated by a speech at Brooklyn on November 1, 1859. Praising John Brown and approving insurrection, he poured out violent abuse against Virginia. Soldiers and civilians concerned in the apprehension of Brown were denounced as "only a mob fancying itself a government." "Virginia, the Commonwealth of Virginia!" cried Phillips. "She is only a chronic insurrection. . . . She is a pirate ship, and John Brown sails the sea a Lord High Admiral of the Almighty, with his commission to sink every pirate he meets on God's ocean . . . ." Wendell Phillips, *Speeches, Lectures, and Letters,* 272, 283.

[3] Ollinger Crenshaw, "The Psychological Background of the Election of 1860 in the South," *N. C. Hist. Rev.,* 260–279 (July 1942). For the quoted passage see pp. 263–264.

abolition agents. In night meetings Negroes were to be impressed with the blessings of freedom. Abolition scoundrels were reported as being hanged all over Texas. So it went on. Orators and Southern political leaders took it up. Yancey painted a horrible picture of Southern conditions if Lincoln were chosen. Senator Albert G. Brown of Mississippi, James L. Orr of South Carolina, and Henry A. Wise of Virginia, even John C. Breckinridge, made political capital of these senseless canards. Southern audiences or readers were stirred up by stories of "untiring fanatics," "abolition fiends," a "hellish" conspiracy, "poison [predicted] in the wells of Texas," slaves incited to murder and arson, "poison, knives & pistols, distributed among our slaves," and a "covert, dark, unholy, and fanatical, insidious" scheme cooked up by peddlers and teachers from the North.[4]

A few publications in the North, such as the intensely Republican Chicago *Democrat* edited and owned by John Wentworth, accepted these frightful Southern rumors, but wholesome skepticism was expressed by the more sober and moderate journals of the South. A Douglas journalist in Georgia referred to such gruesome accounts as "wholesale lies," [5] and Southerners were warned that stories of Negro insurrections were manufactured for political purposes; in Mississippi a newspaper supporting Bell declared that the reports had no basis,[6] while a Baltimore paper printed a statement from Texas showing that "the fires had not in a single case been connected with an abolitionist emissary." [7]

Reckless statements are to be found in almost any quadrennial election campaign in the United States. To the extent that they are appraised as party propaganda and discounted as such, they may perhaps not be particularly dangerous. There are always, however, some people who believe such violent and provocative literature; the real basis for worry was not that Northern-inspired violence was going to burn out and destroy the people of Texas or any other Southern state, but that the repetition of such wild stories would aggravate an already grave psychological malady in sectional relationships. The history of Lincoln's election is incomplete unless one recognizes the seriousness of a comment by a Southern observer shortly before that

---

[4] *Ibid., passim,* esp. pp. 261, 267–268.
[5] *Ibid.,* p. 266, quoting Augusta *Daily Constitutionalist,* Aug. 28, 1860.
[6] *Ibid.,* 267, quoting Raymond (Miss.) *Hinds County Gazette,* Nov. 7, 1860.
[7] *Ibid.,* 267, with citation to Baltimore *American,* Nov. 1, 1860.

election that "the minds of the people are aroused to a pitch of excitement probably unparalleled in the history of our country." [8]

VII

The campaign was not waged in all states with equal intensity. In the South, the Lincoln ticket being non-existent except for weak support in Kentucky and Virginia, voters usually had three choices, though in Texas only two, for in that state there was no Douglas ticket. Those three choices, of course, were Douglas, Breckinridge, or Bell; yet in practice it narrowed down still more, because the Douglas ticket had little chance of carrying any Southern state. Breckinridge captured the more strongly sectional vote, while the less sectional or pro-Union vote, which Douglas might have been expected under normal circumstances to have received, went chiefly to Bell, who was both Southern and pro-Union, while Douglas was only pro-Union. Bell had been a Whig, which meant something in the South; he was a conservative; he was the complete opposite of the disturbing agitator; he made harmony throughout the country the paramount issue. Teamed with the eminently moderate Everett, he could be relied upon to favor, as did Crittenden, a compromise that would safeguard "Southern rights" while averting disunion and war.

Only a few of the states of the South could have been called strongly pro-Breckinridge; these were South Carolina, Mississippi, Texas, and Florida. Other Southern or border states, it is true, would go for Breckinridge in the election, but only with heavy opposition —Alabama, Arkansas, Delaware, Georgia, Louisiana, Maryland, and North Carolina.

In the North there were certain states considered so safely Republican that the contest was not really in doubt: Maine, Michigan, Minnesota, and Vermont. In other predominantly Republican states the Democrats had sizable, though minor, strength: Connecticut, New Hampshire, and Wisconsin. In all the other Northern states the contest was keen, especially so in the populous yet doubtful states of Illinois, Indiana, Ohio, Pennsylvania, New Jersey, and New York. As the campaign proceeded there was a panicky alarm over the growing prospect of Lincoln's election, with all that it would probably

---

[8] *Ibid.*, 279, quoting Natchez *Daily Free Trader*, Nov. 2, 1860.

mean in national chaos, financial loss, and war. This effect was magnified by the circulation of threats—real ones—of disunion in case of Republican success.

Except in South Carolina, where presidential electors were still chosen by the legislature, popular ballots were cast for the electors. Their specific function—voting for President and Vice President—was constitutional, but their popular mandate as to casting their votes in the Electoral College was inescapable. It would not be a complete statement to say that that mandate came from party groups. Those groups set up the nominations, but the people had no other choices before them, so that the popular election was conditioned and limited by the party nominations, made in conventions of delegates. When, therefore, an election had been held and the people had expressed themselves, the electors' mandates were from the people. A vote for a ticket of electors was intended only as a vote for a nominated presidential candidate; electors had no other significance. In no other way could the voters over the land, in going to the polls, know that they were voting for Lincoln, for Douglas, or for any other declared candidate. When electors were chosen, it was clearly understood that they had no discretion; the rules of the game as actually practiced were the controlling fact. Even in South Carolina the electors were instructed, though by the legislature, not the people. Nowhere in the country were they considered free agents whose performance of a constitutional function was in their own hands. Deliberately the people of America, or politicians for them, had made the Electoral College a mere tool through which parties operated, and by which people voted for President.

VIII

With such complications and limitations the American people on Tuesday, November 6, 1860, cast their ballots in the most disturbing election the nation has ever known. Lincoln "carried" seventeen of the free states, all but one. In that one, New Jersey, the electoral strength was divided; four for Lincoln and three for Douglas.[1] Breckinridge carried the second largest number of states. Besides all the states of the lower South (South Carolina, Georgia, Alabama, Florida, Mis-

---

[1] See below, p. 196.

sissippi, Louisiana, and Texas), he captured the electoral vote of Arkansas, Delaware, Maryland, and North Carolina. John Bell and Edward Everett, with their stress on the Union, came through with a significantly large vote in the South, carrying the important states of Kentucky, Tennessee, and Virginia, and obtaining large minorities in Alabama, Arkansas, Georgia, Florida, Louisiana, Maryland, Mississippi, Missouri, and North Carolina.

In addition to the three in New Jersey, Douglas obtained only the nine electoral votes of Missouri. Thus the electoral count stood: Lincoln, 180; Breckinridge, 72; Bell, 39; Douglas, 12. Viewed thus, it looked like a Lincoln landslide.

Quite different from this showing for the Electoral College was the popular vote: Lincoln, 1,866,452; Douglas, 1,376,957; Breckinridge, 849,781; Bell, 588,879.[2] These figures have been analyzed up and down and across the country in search of their significance in terms of popular opinion and sectional attitudes in a day of momentous crisis. The most striking fact was the great discrepancy between the popular vote and the electoral vote, this discrepancy being truly amazing in the case of Douglas, whose electoral vote was less than one-third that of Bell, though his popular vote was far more than twice the Bell total. Or, taking Douglas and Lincoln, their relation in the popular vote was, roughly speaking, in the proportion of 180 to 130, while the electoral vote was 180 to 12.

Electoral totals did not make sense as indications of popular preference. Despite his tiny representation in the Electoral College, Douglas towered high above Bell and also above Breckinridge in the ballots over the country. Taking only the Douglas and Bell votes together, they outnumbered Lincoln by nearly 100,000; add that of Breckinridge, and Lincoln's opponents surpassed him in the popular voting by 949,000 in a total of less than five millions.

Thus Lincoln became a minority President. While this would have been true of any of the others, had he been elected, Lincoln's support was much more sectional than that of any rival. In the area that was later to be included in the Southern Confederacy Lincoln received not one ballot in the popular voting except in Virginia; even there most of his vote came from the panhandle, which was not to be a

---

[2] Edward Stanwood, *History of the Presidency from 1788 to 1897*, 297.

part of the Confederate South.[3] The popular vote for Breckinridge was much less sectional than Lincoln's; in the North, not counting the border states, he received over 278,000 votes.[4]

It is a curious fact that, of the four presidential candidates, only Bell carried his home county (Davidson County, Tennessee—county seat, Nashville). Douglas's home county (Cook County, Illinois, whose county seat was Chicago) went for Lincoln; [5] Breckinridge's (Fayette County, Kentucky—county seat, Lexington) for Bell; Lincoln's (Sangamon County, Illinois—county seat, Springfield) for Douglas.[6] That Lincoln failed of a majority, or even a plurality, in his home county was but an illustration of the intensity of the campaign, the perplexity of voters confronting grave issues, the high regard for Douglas, the strong Democratic tradition in Illinois, and the vigor of Douglas's important organ, the *Illinois State Register,* edited by the Little Giant's close friend, Charles H. Lanphier.

One comes now to a further complication in the election of 1860 —the matter of "fusion." This was a term applied to a device used in a few states—a departure from custom—by which it was expected that Douglas-Bell-Breckinridge forces would be consolidated for one "ticket" of presidential electors. This fusion idea encountered difficult obstacles: angry factional hostility between Breckinridge men and Douglas men, the necessity of party and interparty conferences, differences of view as to how fusion electors should be instructed, search for party advantage by each group, and suspicion by Douglas's

[3] Lincoln received a few votes in the border states: 3815 in Delaware; 1364 in Kentucky; 2294 in Maryland; 17,028 in Missouri; 1929 in Virginia. The Virginia votes were chiefly in what became the West Virginia (non-Confederate) area: more than half came from two Ohio River counties—Ohio and Hancock—both in the panhandle.

[4] To figure Breckinridge's vote in the North is a technical problem, involving a conjectural apportionment of "fusion" votes to particular candidates. If one follows Stanwood (p. 297), the Kentuckian's Northern vote, not counting border states, is in round numbers 278,000; if these figures are modified by Paullin and Wright's apportionment (*Atlas of the Historical Geography of the United States,* 99) it would be 279,000. Stanwood counts nothing for Breckinridge in New Jersey and New York while assigning him 178,871 in Pennsylvania; Paullin and Wright assign him 50,000 in New York, 30,000 in New Jersey, and 100,000 in Pennsylvania. There is little difference in the over-all result.

[5] In Cook County the popular vote was: Lincoln, 14,589; Douglas, 9,846; Bell, 107; Breckinridge, 87. "Record of Election Returns, 1850–62." Illinois State Archives, 253.

[6] There was a close vote in Sangamon County as follows: Lincoln, 3,556; Douglas, 3,598; Bell, 130; Breckinridge, 77. *Ibid.,* 254. In Springfield, however, Lincoln had a majority: 1395 votes to 1326 for Douglas. Angle, *"Here I Have Lived,"* 253.

followers that the device was chiefly a maneuver to favor the Breckinridge faction, whose bitter enmity to Douglas could not be easily forgotten. The device of fusion meant that coöperating party groups would join in naming a ticket of presidential electors whose voting instruction would be such as to suit the multiparty combination; the avowed object of such instruction would be to defeat Lincoln; fusion electors would, of course, be instructed, but the terms of their instruction would not come from any one party.

It is necessary to glance at the manner in which fusion operated in four states—New York, New Jersey, Rhode Island, and (partly) Pennsylvania.[7] The New Jersey situation was peculiar. A "fusion" ticket was put before the voters which represented a combination among the Bell, Breckinridge, and Douglas forces, three of the presidential electors on this ticket being earmarked for Douglas, two for Bell, and two for Breckinridge. In addition, as a minor affair there was a separate Douglas ticket in the field, and, as a very tiny affair, a separate Bell ticket. The three Douglas men on the fusion ticket received in round numbers 62,000 votes, whereas the Lincoln totals (which differed as to particular electors) ran in the neighborhood of 58,000. It seems obvious that if the Douglas supporters had gone down the line solidly for the fusion ticket, the whole of New Jersey's strength (seven electors) would have been carried against Lincoln and for fusion. The difference between full fusion success and the partial success which occurred was traceable to the unwillingness of several thousand Douglas men to vote for the four non-Douglas electors. The whole story of this election shows the confusion which faced the voters as well as the intense bitterness between the Douglas and the Breckinridge elements. The fact that Lincoln obtained four electors in the state and Douglas three—this being the only state in which the electoral vote was divided—indicated a chaotic condition in which party and factional lines were uncertain and shifting.[8]

---

[7] To a minor extent, which need not detain us, fusion was also tried in Connecticut and Texas. Paullin and Wright, *Atlas,* 99.

[8] Stanwood, 297; Paullin and Wright, *Atlas,* 99 (bottom of c. 1). New York *Herald,* Nov. 15, 1860, p. 4, c. 5, and the New York *Tribune,* Nov. 16, 1860, p. 5, cc. 3–4; C. M. Knapp, *New Jersey Politics during the Period of the Civil War and Reconstruction,* 34–37; W. S. Myers, "New Jersey Politics from the Revolution to the Civil War," *Americana,* XXXVII, 444–449; James M. Scovel to Stephen A. Douglas, Camden, N. J., Dec. 10, 1860, Douglas MSS. The Scovel letter reveals the intense personal devotion felt by Douglas's followers, their deep sense of the public issues involved, their

In Rhode Island the fusion movement meant that there was only one anti-Lincoln ticket; that ticket was defeated at the polls; Lincoln obtained the entire electoral vote of the state.

Special interest attaches to the fusion movements in New York and Pennsylvania. In New York, after a series of conferences among party leaders, a consolidated ticket of electors was placed before the people comprising the Breckinridge, Bell, and Douglas elements (eighteen electoral nominees adhering to Douglas, ten to Bell, and seven to Breckinridge),[9] instead of full separate tickets of thirty-five for each of these three men. Had the voters of New York chosen this fusion ticket, there was small prospect that Breckinridge, or Bell, or Douglas, would have had a majority in the whole Electoral College, but neither would Lincoln, for fusion would have prevented the Republican candidate from carrying New York, without whose thirty-five votes he would have lacked the 152 necessary for an electoral majority. This fact revealed the strategy of fusion. Its main object was, by a massing of otherwise scattered votes, to defeat Lincoln in the Electoral College; the next step—choice by the House of Representatives voting by states—was still to be worked out in detail, but among fusionists there was hope of anti-Lincoln victory there. The first battle of fusion men would have been won if they had carried only New York. This being so, the fact that Lincoln carried New York by a majority of 50,000 over the fusion ticket was a decisive factor in the result.

In Pennsylvania, where rivalry between Breckinridge and Douglas factions was exceedingly bitter, the common hostility of these two groups to Lincoln was strong enough so that their fusion was arranged by the Democratic state committee.[10] As it finally worked out, however, there was a Douglas ticket and a Bell ticket in Pennsylvania in addition to the "fusion" ticket, which was interpreted as chiefly a Breckinridge affair. The Bell group in the state was not a party to the fusion. Many Douglas followers accepted fusion, but some of them,

---

distrust of the Republicans, and their angry resentment toward the Breckinridge element in the Democratic party. For valuable information on this subject the author is indebted to Mr. Sidney Goldmann, State Librarian, New Jersey State Library.

[9] D. S. Alexander, *Political History of the State of New York*, 331. For fusion and its complications, see also S. D. Brummer, *Political History of New York State during the . . . Civil War*, chap. iii.

[10] On the complex Pennsylvania situation, which cannot be discussed in full, the author has been assisted by Mr. R. N. Williams, 2d. of the Historical Society of Pennsylvania.

led by John W. Forney, able Philadelphia editor, declined to fuse and supported a separate ticket of all-Douglas electors. The Buchanan (pro-Breckinridge) element was powerful in the state, and against their controlling voice in Democratic counsels the Douglas men had little chance. Breckinridge men in Pennsylvania, with great intensity of purpose, were out to beat Lincoln, though this did not involve all the anti-Union implications attributed to some of the Breckinridge men in the South.[11] It is significant of the die-hard Douglas element in Pennsylvania that its most prominent leader, Forney, took pleasure after the election in claiming that by supporting Douglas instead of going along with fusion he had done much to assist Lincoln's victory. This claim has little substantial validity if one considers the importance of the tariff issue in Pennsylvania and the large vote which Lincoln polled in that state (268,030) as compared with that of all his opponents (208,412). The significant point is not so much the solid basis for the Forney assertion as the fact that a sincere Douglas man could make such a claim with evident satisfaction. In the violent war years that followed, Forney, with his Washington *Chronicle* and Philadelphia *Press,* was to become a vigorous supporter of the Lincoln administration.

John Cabell Breckinridge, reputed to be the secession candidate despite assurances of his devotion to the Union, failed to carry the popular vote of the slave states. There were fifteen such states; he carried eleven, but in some he had mere pluralities, the majority of the voters being opposed to him. If one takes Stanwood's figures for the fourteen slave states in which popular votes were cast, it appears that Breckinridge votes numbered a bit over 571,000, while non-Breckinridge votes (for Bell, Douglas, and Lincoln) numbered a bit under 706,000. The story is different, however, for what was to become the Confederate South; Breckinridge commanded an over-all popular majority in that area. Taking the ten states of the future Confederacy in which popular votes were cast, and making a needed cal-

---

[11] William Bigler, prominent Democrat of Pennsylvania, wrote in this period to President Buchanan. Mentioning Southern "pronunciamentoes," he said that "the South will not be sustained in producing the election of Lincoln, and then making it cause of separation." Bigler to Buchanan, Aug. 13, 1860, MS., Hist. Soc. of Pa. (For calling his attention to this letter, and for informative comment on the Pennsylvania situation, the author is indebted to P. G. Auchampaugh of the University of Nevada, authority on Buchanan.)

culation as to Virginia,[12] the Breckinridge vote was 416,000 while the non-Breckinridge vote was 394,000. The Breckinridge advantage is greater when one conjecturally adds a figure to represent the popular vote that South Carolina might have cast. In all such calculations, however, in trying to determine whether the "secession candidate" [13] carried the South, one must not forget that Breckinridge's considerable number of Kentucky supporters (53,143) probably included many who voted for him in a pro-Union sense, since both Breckinridge himself and his advocates made pledges of Unionism, which was an important principle in Kentucky. In Virginia, where Breckinridge received 74,323 votes (53,703 in the portion that later adhered to the Confederacy), as well as in other states, the same principle must have had considerable application.

It can at least be said that if Southern secessionists had a candidate, it was Breckinridge; it could have been no other. What it amounted to was that the issue of Union or anti-Union was not clear-cut in his candidacy; on this question he was receiving opposite types of votes. The failure of secessionists to carry the whole South in the election of 1860 may therefore be stated thus: Even on the extreme assumption, which is obviously incorrect, that all those who voted for Breckinridge favored secession, disunion failed to carry "the South"; [14] much more did it fail to do so if one bears in mind the possible pro-Union interpretation of the Kentuckian's candidacy. While the trend of the Breckinridge ticket might be under question on this point of Union-

---

[12] Without any correction as to Virginia—i. e., including all the Virginia counties—the Breckinridge vote for these ten states was 436,000, the non-Breckinridge vote 419,000. Since, however, one is speaking of what was to become the "Confederate South," it is logical to subtract the votes of those forty-eight counties (Jefferson and Berkeley being not yet added) which were included in Lincoln's proclamation of April 1863 declaring the establishment of the state of West Virginia. In the figures given above, this calculation has been made, using Stanwood, 297, and *Tribune Almanac for 1861*, 50–51, in which some of the details of Lincoln's vote in Virginia are incomplete.

[13] The view that Breckinridge's candidacy had a secessionist tendency is a familiar part of the history of the time. Douglas said: "I do not believe that every Breckinridge man is a disunionist, but I do believe that every disunionist in America is a Breckinridge man." Frank E. Stevens, *Life of Stephen A. Douglas*, 623. When Douglas was speaking in Raleigh in August 1860 a gentleman in the audience referred to a Breckinridge elector as "an elector on the seceders' ticket." Fite, *Campaign of 1860*, 294. Such a statement came naturally to people's lips in 1860.

[14] The Southern border is of course included here; what is meant is that Breckinridge failed of a majority of the popular vote in the region south of the Mason-Dixon line.

ism, there could be no such doubt as to Douglas or Bell; their combined command of the popular mind south of the Mason and Dixon
line in 1860 is therefore a significant thing to remember.

IX

Since by a very wide margin Lincoln was a minority choice in the
popular voting, the question arises whether he could have been defeated by union among his opponents—i. e., by fusion tickets that
would actually have united these opponents in a great many of the
states instead of the ineffective "fusion" effort seen in only a few. The
supposition that comes naturally to mind is that such union would
certainly have defeated him, and superficial history has sometimes been
written in those terms, but on closer examination one finds the
curious fact that if all the opposing popular ballots had been cast for
anti-Lincoln tickets (by which is meant tickets for presidential electors set up by states), Lincoln would still have obtained a majority
in the Electoral College. The electoral vote would have been changed
only in a few non-populous states; the shift would not have affected
the whole election.[1] (One is speaking here of pro-Lincoln and anti-
Lincoln votes actually cast. As above noted, if fusionists had gained
enough votes, for instance, to have carried New York, Lincoln could
not have had a majority in the Electoral College.)

Lincoln's three opponents could have defeated him hands down if
popular votes could have been counted *in Federal totals*, disregarding
states, and if all the anti-Lincoln popular votes could then have been
united for one man in the Electoral College; but the existing system
did not permit such a procedure. A statement that it could have
happened under these conditions is intended only as an indication of
relative strength as between Lincoln and his opposition.

Lincoln's opponents made much of state rights, but in this par-

---

[1] The difference between what Lincoln carried in the Electoral College and what
he would have carried if fusion by states (within the existing electoral system) had
enabled all the votes cast against him to have been concentrated, consisted only of
California where fusion would have meant a Republican loss of four electoral votes,
Oregon with a loss of three, and New Jersey with a loss of four (since in that case all
seven of New Jersey's votes would have gone against the Republican ticket). Lincoln
would then have had eleven fewer electoral votes, but he would still have had a clear
majority in the Electoral College—i. e., 169 votes as compared to 134 for the opposition. Dumond, *Secession Movement*, 271; Nicolay and Hay, *Lincoln*, II, 295.

ticular the emphasis upon doing things by states, and by factions, worked against them. National election procedures, with consolidation of forces, would have helped them. The "general ticket" aspect should always be borne in mind. Electors in a commonwealth were not chosen by districts, nor apportioned to harmonize with ballots cast by the people. Each individual voter voted for a full slate which included all the state's electors. Except in New Jersey, only full slates, all alike, were chosen.

The fact that the winning ticket got *all the electoral strength*—all the legal voting power—of a state, though it might have only a slight superiority among the contenders, worked a pronounced inequality. Popular minorities in large doubtful states could not be thrown into a general total; they became wasted. In this Lincoln had an enormous advantage. He had practically no wasted votes. In ten states of the South he had not one popular vote; in three others (Kentucky, Virginia, and Maryland) his vote was small; in Missouri his wasted votes numbered only 17,028; in Delaware, only 3815; in New Jersey he actually obtained a majority of the presidential electors while receiving fewer votes than his opponents.

On the other hand, Douglas's wasted votes were tremendous. Taking his popular total, and counting out the vote of Missouri which he carried and of New Jersey which he partially carried, there were about 1,255,000 popular votes for Douglas that found no representation in the Electoral College.[2] It was, therefore, the peculiarity of the American system in the choice of President which gave Lincoln the election in spite of the fact that almost a million more voters cast ballots against him than for him.

Those whose views have not been firmly fixed in the anti-Douglas sense will find in the campaign and election of 1860 reason to note the unfriendly tricks of fate played upon the Little Giant. Since he was no trimmer, since people knew where he stood—for self-determination in the territories as well as in the states—he suffered woefully in a day when his own party was split in the North (between the Buchanan

---

[2] This calculation of Douglas's wasted support is based upon totals of popular votes as tabulated by Stanwood, 297. Douglas's vote should be figured somewhat differently if one follows Paullin and Wright, *Atlas,* 99. In that case one must add a considerable figure for Douglas for Pennsylvania, but this is much more than offset by what he must subtract from Stanwood's report of Douglas strength in New York and New Jersey.

and Douglas elements), while his hope of bridging the widening gap between North and South was crushed under the weight of sectional agitation. It was his unhappy destiny that in the South he was distrusted as pro-Northern, while in Northern Republican circles he was denounced as pro-Southern. Just what there was in his policy that in any way hurt the true interests of the Southern people, is hard to see now; while the Republican accusation that he was playing the game of slaveholders is entirely inconsistent with the furious opposition directed against him by Southern politicians at Charleston and Baltimore. That accusation is also contradictory to the well known fact that Greeley and others of the party thought favorably of Douglas as a possible Republican presidential candidate.

Douglas took into view the whole nation. It was neither his strategy nor his principle to appeal merely to one section. If his approach comprehended all sections, and if that fact worked against him, it was a sad commentary on the times; but it should not be taken as a disparagement of Douglas himself. Opposition to the foisting of slavery upon the people of Kansas against their will was a thing upon which Lincoln and Douglas agreed. In Lincoln it was counted a virtue; in Douglas it brought only grief. For Lincoln to take such a stand was to agree with his party in its campaign arguments to the extent that the party was emphasizing antislavery.[3] For Douglas to take the same position—against imposing slavery where the people did not want it —was to get little credit while incurring resentful opposition and proscription on the part of Democratic regulars. Douglas sacrificed more for the stand he took than any Republican, though opposition to the proslavery Lecompton constitution in Kansas was equally a Republican and a Douglas principle. The Republican party, searching in its early days for a name, was even for a time called the anti-Lecompton party. It would be easy in this troubled period to mention leaders whose tendency was sectional, but it would be hard to name any prominent statesman in either of the major parties— Democratic or Republican—who made a sturdier effort than did

---

[3] As to Lincoln developing such arguments, one is referring to the period from 1854 to February–March of 1860, not to the presidential campaign of 1860, in which Lincoln was silent while his party was giving much less emphasis to the antislavery issue. Lincoln's silence meant no retreat on his part, but it is fair to remember that Douglas kept repeating the same things throughout 1860 that he had been saying in previous years.

Douglas to discourage disruptive agitation and to build up those forces, widespread and sound though sadly inarticulate, that were tending to hold the nation together.

X

In retrospect there are several matters pertaining to Lincoln's election that appear a bit singular. All the emphasis in regular Republican efforts was upon the avoidance of what was called radicalism; perhaps it could better have been called excessive abolitionist agitation or unenlightened but self-righteous anti-Southernism. Yet in a few short years it was the radicals that captured the Republican party. In doing so, they assuredly went counter to Lincoln's wish. Again, Lincoln was anti-Knownothing and profited by it; yet Seward was anti-Knownothing and suffered by it. Lincoln gained by the fact that New Jersey support for Seward was lukewarm. One reason why it was lukewarm was that Seward was anti-Knownothing. Lincoln had the substantial support of those who were anti-Knownothing; yet when it came to voting, according to S. D. Brummer, there were "indications . . . that the greater part of those who supported Fillmore in 1856 voted for Lincoln in 1860."[1] Chase also was unpalatable to the nativists, as was Lincoln, yet no sheaves of political gain were garnered by the Ohioan because of this attitude.

Republicans in 1860 were appealing for the votes of Democrats. In doing so, as it turned out, they wanted it both ways: they cheerfully accepted Democratic support; then in later years they unfairly promoted the stereotyped charge that it was only the Republicans who had saved the country and that the Democrats had been anti-Union and disloyal amid war, which was the opposite of the truth. This latter charge, persisting for hate-filled postwar decades, was to be known as "waving the bloody shirt."

Parties give up something when they go out in pursuit of votes. Often, instead of taking a clear stand, they represent themselves as all things to all men. Their managers become vote brokers. They seek support in every quarter, then use the victory for party purposes. It is commonly the marginal, or border-line, appeal that sets the pattern of politician emphasis. Where in 1860 a state, a region, or a group

---

[1] *Political History of New York State during the* . . . *Civil War*, 96.

was known to be safely Republican, less attention was paid to it. Republican managers did not cater so actively to their known supporters—i. e., to groups that were likely to have pronounced Republican proclivities—as to those regarded as doubtful. They tried to win over men who distrusted or disliked them. The more they did this, the less clear-cut did their appeal become. Seeking the votes of doubters, they said things (or practiced silences) which caused their position to seem doubtful. If they made vote-seeking professions, the citizen might not sufficiently realize that professions are not all, and that an element that does not set the pattern openly at election time may exploit the results of the election and seize the reins when it comes to the business of government.

Questionable control of patronage and spoils was a factor whose true character in 1860 is not easy to analyze. Those among the Republicans who were most conspicuously associated with the deliberate use of partisan spoils were Seward and Cameron; their reputations in this respect worked against them and for Lincoln. Yet both Seward [2] and Cameron were brought into the cabinet; in the case of Cameron the Lincoln administration assumed a deadweight, an embarrassment, and, as to army contracts and the like, a taint of corruption.[3] In their 1860 platform the Republicans declared that the people "view with alarm the . . . extravagance which pervades . . . the Federal Government" as well as the "frauds and corruption at the Federal metropolis." [4] Their remedy was "an entire change of administration."

XI

One hears much of the perennial question: Who elected Lincoln? Answers are diverse: The great Northwest did it; New York did it; the "October states" did it, especially Pennsylvania.[1] The idea that

---

[2] It was not that Seward himself was responsible for such a reputation, but in practical politics the Seward movement was virtually identical with that of the boss, Thurlow Weed.

[3] See vol. II, 54–61.   [4] Johnson, *Proceedings*, 131–132.

[1] Though state elections usually coincided with the national presidential election, there were several states which held earlier elections for governor, etc. When Maine elected a Republican governor in September by a big majority, and when in October the Republicans elected governors in Pennsylvania and Indiana, while showing considerable gains in Ohio, these indications served to presage, perhaps partly to produce, Republican national success in November.

Carl Schurz made Lincoln President has had plausible support, being by no means denied by Schurz himself.[2] Southern secessionists, thought Douglas, were responsible. On a previous page the eccentricity of American election machinery, in its 1860 bearings, has been noted. It has also been argued that the foreign-born element, especially the Germans, elected Lincoln. Already the influence of German-Americans on the nomination at Chicago has been observed; in addition, it has been urged that they enabled Lincoln to carry doubtful states without which he could not have had an electoral majority. For the Northwest as a whole the case for the decisiveness of foreign-born influence has been presented by Donnal V. Smith.[3] For Illinois, populous and closely contested, the situation has been analyzed in similar terms by Jay Monaghan.[4] Yet this pattern of decisive German influence in the Republican sense has been significantly questioned. In a notably revisionist study, Joseph Schafer, whose Domesday Book for Wisconsin is a triumph of detailed historical scholarship, has carefully analyzed the familiar contention that the Germans turned the scale for Lincoln in 1860; he finds that no such conclusion is at all tenable, so far as Wisconsin is concerned.[5] It had been concluded by a former writer that there were 60,000 German voters in Wisconsin and that 40,000 of them voted for Lincoln. Since Lincoln's plurality over Douglas was 21,000, it had been concluded that the German vote was essential to this majority.[6]

By careful calculation, however, Schafer finds that the potential voting strength of Wisconsin Germans was something like 33,000, not 60,000; then he demolishes the facile assumption that two-thirds of

---

[2] Amer. Hist. Rev., XLVII, 52-53.

[3] Donnal V. Smith, "The Influence of the Foreign-Born of the Northwest in the Election of 1860," Miss. Vall. Hist. Rev., XIX, 192-204 (Sep., 1932).

[4] Jay Monaghan, "Did Abraham Lincoln Receive the Illinois German Vote?," Journal, Ill. State Hist. Soc., XXXV, 133-139 (June, 1942).

[5] Joseph Schafer, "Who Elected Lincoln," Amer. Hist. Rev., XLVII, 51-63 (Oct., 1941).

[6] Even taking this assumption at its face value, it could not mean that Wisconsin would have been carried for Douglas if the German vote had been omitted altogether. If one subtracts 40,000 from Lincoln's Wisconsin vote and 20,000 from that of Douglas— i. e., if one leaves out the Germans as allegedly measured—Lincoln would still have carried the state by a safe margin over Douglas. The only way this claim makes sense even in its own falsely exaggerated terms is to suppose that the imaginary 40,000 German voters-for-Lincoln had voted the other way. If this had happened—i. e., if there had been such a large German element and it had shifted—Douglas would have carried the state. The claim, however, presented by a writer named Hense-Jensen, is shown by Schafer to be "fantastic." Ibid., 57.

these German voters supported Lincoln.[7] Examining specific counties (there being, of course, no records in which voting totals are broken up in terms of racial groups), he found that those which showed a great preponderance of German family heads also showed a very strong predominance of Douglas votes, while Lincoln's majorities are found in counties whose population was simply part of the westward movement from older eastern portions of the United States. It was in "Yankee counties" in Wisconsin that Republican support was heavy, not in counties populated largely by foreign-born. Schafer notes that the same was true in New York. The New England element thus appears to have had a great effect in building up the Lincoln vote in the Northwest.[8] If one considers factors "without which" the result would not have happened, it must be remembered that various factors could qualify in that respect. It is much truer to say that the Yankees elected Lincoln than that the Germans did it.[9] German support for him, which in some states was large though it is difficult to measure, should of course be recognized. It should be properly credited and its significance correctly appraised, but it should not be overstated.

---

[7] Concerning the vote in Wisconsin Schafer writes: ". . . it is so certain that a large majority of Germans voted for Douglas as to make the Lincoln majority . . . a sure proof of the Germans' inability to alter the result. If all the Germans had voted for Douglas, Lincoln would, nevertheless, have won the state." *Ibid.*, 61.

[8] *Ibid.*, 56–57.

[9] Schafer concludes: ". . . it appears all but certain that the assignment of a dominant influence to the foreign born in the election of 1860 is 100 per cent wrong; . . . ." *Ibid.*, 63. This conclusion, based on close study for Wisconsin, is also supported, in Schafer's opinion, as to Indiana, Ohio, Michigan, and Iowa. In each of these states he finds Lincoln's majority greater than the probable total of German voters. As to Illinois, however, he concedes that the German vote may have made the difference between Lincoln's success and defeat.

CHAPTER IX

THE VEXED QUESTION

I

MANY and various were the threats, solutions, and panaceas that rose in answer to the question "what to do" as the result of Lincoln's election. Withdraw immediately and form a Southern government, declared the active secessionists. Meet Lincoln with a President of our own. Never live again with free-soil states.[1] Call a border-state convention, asked moderates of the Virginia-Kentucky area. Frankfort, Kentucky, was proposed as the place for such a gathering.[2] Call an official national convention broadly representative of the nation, was the wish of some of Buchanan's advisers. The President and also Lincoln favored the idea in principle. Call a peace conference of state representatives, said John Tyler and his associates of the Virginia legislature. Have nothing to do with such an Old Ladies Convention, said Republican radicals and Southern hotspurs; they are only tinkerers from the border states trying to save the Union. Accept disunion, said Mason of Virginia, though he would not have promoted it. When a state secedes, he said, let the President recognize the fact by proclamation and let Federal laws be suspended within the state.[3] Let the cotton states go in peace, said Horace Greeley. Secession may be revolutionary, but the right exists. "We hope never to live in a republic whereof one section is pinned to the residue by bayonets."[4]

---

[1] *Annual Report,* Am. Hist, Assoc., 1911, II, 529, 531.

[2] Edward McPherson, *Political History of the . . . Rebellion,* 6.

[3] *Ibid.,* 86.

[4] New York *Tribune,* Nov. 9, 1860. Perhaps the go-in-peace declaration was no more than an editorial flash. If it was a policy, it probably involved somewhat of hedging in the sense that its editorial sponsor never expected it to become a reality. It has even been contended that the hint of peaceable separation was a kind of trick, a

Have four unions by a rearrangement of the fragments of the United States, urged Winfield Scott, head of the army.[5] Let the slave states be trustees of the national territory south of 36° 30', was another suggestion, and let the free states be trustees of the territory north of that line. Admit New Mexico and Arizona as slave states, declared a border spokesman; after that, prohibit the acquisition of any additional territory by the United States.[6] Hold to the Union if compromise can be obtained, urged upper Southern and border-state leaders.[7] Promote compromise and meet this wish, was the policy of Buchanan, of Douglas, of the Douglas Democrats, and of such Republicans as Seward and Weed.

"Patriots ought to stand loyally and patiently in the Union," urged the Louisville *Daily Journal* (November 8, 1860). There are checks on Lincoln. He can do no harm. House, Senate, and Court will restrain him. These checks are insurmountable. Only a cabinet of temperate views will be confirmed. No "unconstitutional law adverse to slavery" can be enacted "since both branches [of the Congress] are Anti-Republican." Lincoln is at the mercy of his opponents. If he commits an aggression, impeach him. Above all, quell disunion; "curb Yancey and Rhett." [8]

Let Lincoln electors save the day, advised some of the Northern "doughfaces," by casting their votes for Breckinridge and Lane, thereby pacifying the fire-eaters.[9] Let Breckinridge go South, said some who labored to defeat him, and let him "use his influence as the man who, of all others, can do most to quiet the disaffected States." [10] It was assumed that Breckinridge, not yet a secessionist, would use that

---

forestalling of that type of compromise which was designed to save the Union without war. This comes close to saying that the go-in-peace proposal tended (as the event proved) to produce war, either because its advocates did not foresee consequences, or because they actually preferred war to the kind of bargains that meant concession to slavery. See David M. Potter, *Lincoln and His Party in the Secession Crisis*, 51–57. Dr. Potter writes (p. 57): "The fictitious go-in-peace alternative continued to obscure the situation until the occasion for compromise had passed and war remained as the only means by which the Union could be maintained."

[5] Scott even suggested boundaries and capitals for these new confederacies. C. W. Elliott, *Winfield Scott: The Soldier and the Man*, 676.

[6] McPherson, *Rebellion*, 74–75.

[7] In early February 1861 the Kentucky legislature passed resolutions calling for a national convention, at the same time protesting alike against Southern revolution and Federal coercion. *Ibid.*, 8.

[8] D. L. Dumond, *Southern Editorials on Secession*, 218–220.

[9] Chicago *Tribune*, Dec. 3, 1860, p. 1, c. 1.

[10] New York *Herald*, Nov. 17, 1860, p. 6, c. 1: Dumond, *Southern Editorials*, 255.

influence for the preservation of the Union. Let the people elect the President directly, declared a North Carolinian who at once added that this would require an adjustment or weighting to allow increased strength to Southern states because of non-voting slave population.[11] Choose the President by districts, advised Andrew Johnson; elect a President from the free states and a Vice President from the slave states, and *vice versa,* every four years; choose senators by popular vote; limit Supreme Court tenure to twelve years; *elect* [12] one-third of the Court every fourth year.[13] Have two Presidents, said R. M. T. Hunter of Virginia. Let each section elect its President, the chief of one section succeeding that of the other every fourth year. Barring the overriding of vetoes (with sectional safeguards) no law should be valid, he thought, unless signed by both Presidents. He would also readjust the Court, increase its membership, and add various elements of interstate retaliation not then allowed.[14] Secession, thought Hunter, ought to be adopted only if approved by a majority of the states *of the section concerned.*[15]

While these suggestions and proposals showed the serious dislocations produced by the election of a sectional President in a day of overwrought sectionalism, they showed also the wish of a vast majority of Americans North and South to preserve the Union. Far different were the steps taken by the secessionists. Working with the semblance of popular support these leaders carried one redoubt after another, beginning directly after the election when the South Carolina legislature passed its convention bill, until their movement swept seven states out of the Union a month in advance of Lincoln's inauguration. No incoming President had ever faced so difficult a situation. It should be added that no outgoing President was ever placed "in a more trying and responsible position" than Buchanan.[16] To understand the subject is not merely to recatalogue "facts" and incidents. It is to restudy a many-sided situation whose complex character still baffles

---

11 McPherson, *Rebellion,* 75.   12 Italics supplied.   13 McPherson, *Rebellion,* 73.

14 *Ibid.,* 86–88. Hunter's proposal was: "That each section shall elect a President, to be called the first and second President: the first to serve for four years as President, the next to succeed him at the end of four years . . . ." He proposed further "That no law should be valid which did not have the assent of both Presidents, or in the event of a veto by one of them, the assent of a majority of the Senators of the section from which he came."

15 Italics supplied.

16 James Buchanan, *Mr. Buchanan's Administration on the Eve of the Rebellion.* 109.

complete unraveling and still claims the attention of revisionist scholars. Published writings, reminiscences, biographies, newspapers, state studies, voluminous public documents, social and economic monographs must therefore be sought by the reader who would comprehend the factors that were moving in the whole wretched crisis.

It could hardly be said that Lincoln was the center of these moving factors. While the President Elect remained inconspicuously at Springfield, others were steering Republican policy; determination of events was but slightly in Lincoln's hands. The drama of the time was in truth a series of simultaneous dramas out of which few writers have produced a comprehensive picture. There was the drama of South Carolina rushing ahead with its little revolution, of other cotton states pausing in momentary doubt and then taking similar action, of Southern senators and congressmen acting with the same effect as their opponents (the Republicans) for the defeat of compromise efforts at the nation's capital. All this assisted those who had already turned their backs upon the very thought of compromise and were moving in the lower South for the launching of a rival government that would present Lincoln with a *fait accompli*. There was the episode of Buchanan's changing ministry, overdramatized as a "cabinet row" but in truth serious enough. It involved the resignations of Cobb, Floyd, Cass, and Thompson. After these men had withdrawn, the cabinet was strengthened by the appointment of firmer secretaries. As the new order in the lower South was boldly inaugurated there was striking contrast between those who took it as settled fact, not even open to argument, and those who continued to speak in familiar and established terms. Such a contrast was shown in the Buchanan administration's refusal to be stampeded by South Carolina into admitting the collapse of Federal authority. The same contrast appeared when Congress, whose main item on the agenda was conciliation, had to witness the spectacle of Southern solons rising in Senate and House to discharge parting oratorical shots. Through all this there was the homely drama at Springfield which is even yet viewed by Lincoln devotees as primarily a kind of success story of a local son who made good.

II

It is hard to convey an impression of the explosive effect of secession in the American scene. A complete reorientation was effected, with new shibboleths, thought patterns, phrases, loyalties, governments, and standards. In the lower South the bare events were as follows.

South Carolina passed its ordinance of secession on December 20. This was the first secession, the only one in 1860. On its own avowal the palmetto state was now a separate nation. Baffling governmental questions posed by this isolated status were never to be solved; the status was temporary and misleading. Completely separate existence was nominal. The Mississippi convention passed its ordinance of secession on January 9. In the electing of convention delegates the Mississippi vote was only sixty per cent of the presidential vote in 1860. The canvass for this purpose "did not command the active . . . interest of the voters of Mississippi"; the "time . . . for reflection . . . was exceedingly short"; "thousands stayed away from the polls because they were confused"; when the election was over the "Union forces felt that . . . they had been overwhelmed by the intemperate views of the Secessionists, and that the . . . country . . . was 'drifting into . . . anarchy . . . and ruin.'" [1]

Secessionists in Mississippi had the convention votes. Yet those who were actively promoting disunion showed no desire to have the question of secession submitted to the people. An amendment to this effect was submitted by Walter Brooke of Vicksburg but decisively defeated; the secessionists refused to submit to this popular test.[2] For this refusal the passing of the ordinance was denounced by the Natchez *Courier* as the work of a "dictatorial oligarchy." [3]

Florida's ordinance was passed on January 10, that of Alabama on January 11. In Georgia, where there was a keen contest and where the misleading argument of "better terms" out of the Union was effectively used,[4] the struggle was longer and the decision closer. On the main test of strength in the Georgia convention—a motion to substitute

---

[1] P. L. Rainwater, *Mississippi, Storm Center of Secession, 1856–1861*, 196–197.

[2] *Ibid.*, 211.   [3] Quoted in *ibid.*, 215.

[4] Unionists were enlisted in the secessionist cause, being assured that by a kind of temporary secession gesture they could get "better terms"—i. e., recognition of their "rights" in the Union—after which there could be a ready return to the old allegiance. For documentation, see Randall, *Civil War and Reconstruction*, 191.

coöperation among the Southern states in place of separate secession —the division was 133 for coöperation, 164 for secession. When an absent delegate later recorded his vote, it was 134 to 164; a change of sixteen votes would have defeated secession.[5] Finally the die was cast, January 19, by the passing of the ordinance. "I never felt so sad before," wrote Herschel V. Johnson.[6] It was his view that the election of Lincoln did not justify secession. Laboring actively against disunion, he believed that a fair canvass would have shown a majority of the Southern people against the policy of separation. The issue, he thought, was not fairly presented. Secessionists insisted "that it would be peaceable—that it would not bring war—that . . . the Yankees . . . would not fight—and that, at the worst it would be a short war . . . ."[7]

Two more states—Louisiana and Texas—completed the action of the lower South. The Louisiana convention voted secession on January 26, that of Texas on February 1. Secession in Texas was contrary to the loyalties of Sam Houston, its distinguished governor. On March 18, 1861, he was deposed.

Taking the journal of the Confederate provisional Congress and presenting its recital in condensed paraphrase, the legal birth of the Southern Confederacy was as follows. In the year of Our Lord one thousand eight hundred and sixty-one, in the Capital of Alabama, in the city of Montgomery, there assembled certain delegates from the several independent Southern States of North America, to wit: Alabama, Florida, Georgia, Louisiana, Mississippi, and South Carolina, the said delegates being assembled by virtue of divers ordinances adopted by conventions of the peoples of the independent states aforenamed. (Full texts of the secession ordinances appear in the record at this point.) A prayer to Almighty God was offered in behalf of the Congress of the States. Thirty-seven delegates presented their credentials and signed the roll (elaborate state papers giving credentials are here inserted in the journal). Howell Cobb of Georgia was chosen president of the Congress by acclamation, rules were adopted, and on February 7 a "Constitution for the Provisional Government of the Confederate States of North America" was presented. Stephens of Georgia moved that the word "North" be stricken out. It was agreed to.

---

[5] P. S. Flippin, *Herschel V. Johnson of Georgia*, 188–189.
[6] *Ibid.*, 192.   [7] *Ibid.*, 158, 170–171.

On February 8, fifth day of the Congress, the constitution was unanimously adopted. Next day, the vote being taken by states for President, the Hon. Jefferson Davis of Mississippi received all the votes cast, being six, and was thus unanimously elected President of the Provisional Government. With like unanimity the Hon. Alexander H. Stephens of Georgia received all six votes for Vice President.[8]

These fundamental measures were understood to be the solemn acts of sovereign Southern peoples, not directly but through chosen representatives. Only in Texas among the states of the lower South was the ordinance of secession submitted to popular vote, this being done after its adoption. It was argued, however, that the delegates who voted for secession had just been chosen with plenary powers by the people and that no later popular ratification was needed.

The Southern cause now had a new and exciting focus. In the initial stages it had all been accomplished with astonishing ease. The national government at Washington permitted this rival government to be set up without interference. The convention at Montgomery was not an all-Southern gathering. Of the fifteen slave states, only six were represented in the body that launched the Confederacy, created its constitution, and chose its high officials. In these early proceedings Texas was not represented, nor the states of the upper South, nor any of the states of the Southern border. The important state of Virginia had no part in the proceedings by which the Confederacy was set up. At Montgomery, of course, there was no debating of secession. No gathering of delegates from any grouping of Southern states for that purpose occurred in 1860–61, nothing comparable to the Nashville Convention of 1850. Withdrawal having already been decreed in the six states represented, the Montgomery Congress proceeded from there as an instrument for an independent Southern nation. By the time it met the secession movement had gained such momentum in separate-state terms that unionists such as Walter Brooke of Mississippi and Alexander H. Stephens of Georgia became supporters, one might say charter members, of the new Southern government.

Such men by the thousands might have willed a different result, but their states had acted, they had to share the fate of their people, the matter was considered beyond recall, and the spirit of state

---

[8] *Journal of the Congress of the Confederate States of America, 1861–1865* (Senate Document No. 234 [U. S.], 58 Cong., 2 sess.), I, 7–40 *passim*.

loyalty as well as the necessity of maintaining order was understood to require the support of all citizens of all groups. Constitutionally, in the Southern view, there was no doubt about the right of secession. Even unionists in the South, in that brief period when the matter was in process of decision, had not challenged the right, but rather the wisdom and desirability, of withdrawal from the United States.

With a stirring sense of revolution and military preparation in the air, but also with the manner of statesmen quietly altering their government in the midst of peace and in the exercise of well known American functions, Jefferson Davis was inaugurated provisional President of the Confederacy in the stately capitol at Montgomery on February 18, 1861. Lincoln, on his way to the seat of government, arrived that day in Albany, New York.

Davis and Lincoln were to stand at opposite extremes. Was there to be any middle ground? Practically, in terms of action open to American individuals and communities, there was not. Secession either had to be favored, at least admitted, or it had to be opposed. A state had to be either in or out of the union. Opposing a government, however, even a new "provisional" one, is no easy matter. Men of the time, knowing this, and realizing how quick was the pace from deliberation to irrevocable action, spoke of the casting of the die, the crossing of the Rubicon. No state of the South could balance itself somewhere in between the United States and the Confederate States. Even on the border that was impossible, as Kentucky was soon to discover.

When the consequences of secession unfolded, those who had been conspicuously in front as secessionist leaders—Rhett, Yancey, and the like—made very little contribution to the Southern Confederacy. Support for the Confederacy came rather in large part from men who had not favored secession, such as R. E. Lee and A. H. Stephens. According to Stephens's own statement directly after the war, his position in the Confederate government was retained after he "clearly saw that the great objects in view . . . in accepting it were not likely to be obtained even by the success of the Confederate Arms." [9] In the phase that followed Lincoln's election, when action was being hastily shaped in the lower South, Jefferson Davis had been "far from placing himself at the head of those who wished to precipitate . . .

---

[9] Alexander H. Stephens to President Andrew Johnson, Ft. Warren, June 8, 1865, Johnson MSS.

secession by separate state action." As matters were racing toward a climax in Mississippi, Davis "was opposed to such a program and was counselling delay and co-operation . . . ." [10]

III

Already the recital is both behind and ahead of the event. When a revolutionary thing happens on a vast scale with the tempo of impatient change, it may not be easy to view all its facets at once, or to see at a glance its background, incidents, exhibitionist phases, repercussions throughout the country, impact upon the established order, and consequences. Springfield was distant from Charleston, Washington from Montgomery; yet in reality the distance was deceptive. People and government were soon to find that they were all parts of the same interrelated American world. What South Carolina did was to have its effect in Virginia; December would show its results in April. The clarity of seeing consequences that were about to appear was given to some, but they were helpless to stem the current; the onrushing of events compelled on the part of millions a kind of horrified drifting. Debates in Congress, conventions in the farther South, popular explosions, proposals and remedies, conferences among leaders—all these, however opposite and conflicting, were parts of America in the tragic crisis of 1860–61. The action of South Carolina, taken with astonishing ease in its own setting, had brought reverberations everywhere. There were secessionist demonstrations at New Orleans, Mobile, Norfolk, Wilmington (Delaware), Baltimore, Petersburg, and even Washington. Elsewhere there were indignation meetings as at Pittsburgh where the threatened removal of artillery from the arsenal produced intense excitement.[1] By the end of December disunionists at Charleston were in possession of the post office, the Federal courts, the custom houses, and some of the forts (Castle Pinckney and Fort Moultrie) in the harbor. Taking their cue from this most truculent of the commonwealths, disunionists elsewhere, sometimes in advance of withdrawal by their states, took over Federal arsenals, forts, and custom houses. When on December 29 the resignation of Secre-

---

10 Rainwater, *Mississippi*, 162 n.; Jefferson Davis to Rhett, Nov. 10, 1860, in Dunbar Rowland, *Jefferson Davis Constitutionalist: His Papers* . . . [etc.], IV, 541–542.

1 Frank Moore, ed., *The Rebellion Record: A Diary of American Events, with Documents, Narratives,* . . . [etc.], (Diary), I, 6.

tary of War Floyd showed how deeply the crisis was cutting into the President's official family, people associated this action with Federal evacuation of Fort Moultrie and the removal of the garrison to Sumter.[2] By the middle of January such forts as Pulaski at Savannah, Fort Morgan at Mobile, and Fort Barrancas at Pensacola had been seized. Meanwhile Southern agents were abroad in the North purchasing munitions and other war material and having it shipped South. As these matters, or such as were not clandestine, were reported in the papers, the effect was registered in mass meetings, editorials, parades, and public resolutions. When Judah P. Benjamin of Louisiana declared in the Senate on the last day of 1860 that the South could never be subjugated, he was greeted with "disgraceful applause" and "screams" from the gallery and his admirers were overheard to say "That's the talk," "Now we will have war," "Abe Lincoln will never come here."[3] For every such event there was a pro-Union demonstration, as in the celebration held by the New England Society of New York which was addressed by Vice President Elect Hamlin and Senator Seward.[4]

To say that "the South" had acted to produce secession and form the Confederacy would be a doubtful generalization. Not only did the important states in the upper South and border have no part in the movement, as above noted; even in the deep South, which in population constituted a minority of the slaveholding section, every effort toward coöperation among the states in choosing between secession and union was avoided by secession leaders.[5] Had coöperation been likely to produce combined secession, Rhett and Company would have welcomed it; that it was expected to produce the opposite result

---

[2] It was also stated that Floyd's position in the cabinet had become untenable and that the Sumter garrisoning gave him a good excuse. It was even suggested that Buchanan eased the way by helping Floyd to resign in the best public light. *Ibid.*, I, 7–8; P. G. Auchampaugh, *James Buchanan and His Cabinet*, 97.

[3] New York *Times*, Jan. 1, 1861, p. 1, c. 1. It was not that Benjamin's manner was explosive. He spoke with calmness and deliberation. In his farewell speech, properly so called, delivered in the Senate on February 4, he even expressed affection for men of "other skies" with whom he was parting. *Cong. Globe*, 36 Cong., 2 sess., 212–217, 721–722; Robert D. Meade, *Judah P. Benjamin, Confederate Statesman*, 149, 152–153.

[4] Moore, *Rebellion Record* (Diary), I, 4.

[5] In the earlier sectional crisis of 1850–51 Rhett and other active secession leaders had been frustrated because coöperation among the Southern states had been the method. "Never did the Rhetts lose sight of the lesson . . . . In a struggle between separate state action and coöperation a second defeat was to be expected. This time there should be no such struggle." Laura A. White, *Robert Barnwell Rhett*, 172.

was admitted by Governor Gist of South Carolina who undemo-
cratically warned against an all-Southern gathering because he thought
"the Border and non-acting States would outvote us and thereby
defeat action." [6]

Though secessionists had laid their plans well in advance and were
ready to strike promptly after Lincoln's election (which they were
said to hope for, since it could be taken as a factor making for disunion), the actual election of Lincoln fell so far short of swinging
Southern sentiment against the Union that coöperative effort was
still considered undesirable as a method of promoting secession. At
a later stage commissioners were sent to other Southern states by
South Carolina, and these commonwealths, whose coöperation on
the main matter had been spurned, were now appealed to for secessionist support by a state that would otherwise have been left out
on a limb. While seeking pro-secession assistance the South Carolina
legislature on January 27, 1861, rejected Virginia's proposal for co-
operative action, declaring that they had "no desire or intention to
promote" the object Virginia had in view.[7]

There were evidences that secession as the answer to Lincoln's
election by no means commanded the preponderant support of the
Southern people. "Peaceful secession is a myth," declared the New
Orleans *Picayune*. "It is a mere phrase to conceal the sad train of
events that are inevitably to follow." [8] What is "the extent of the
wrongs . . . that so arouse the . . . passions . . . as to obliterate
. . . patriotism," asked the same editor. In answer he rejected the
plea that the election of the chief of a sectional party could justify
revolution.[9] How do "the Yanceyites propose to sustain the government they are engineering to impose upon us," inquired the New
Orleans *True Delta*.[10] Secession would mean "a baptism of blood,"
warned a Wilmington editor who sarcastically asked whether the
people of North Carolina wished "to be dragged into revolution and
anarchy . . . to please the State of South Carolina, who, by her in-
sufferable arrogance, . . . has been a constant source of annoyance
. . . to the whole country, North and South, for the last thirty
years?" [11]

"Stop and think," cautioned the *Daily Nashville Patriot*. Going out

---

[6] Dumond, *Secession Movement*, 137.   [7] McPherson, *Rebellion*, 2 n.
[8] Dumond, *Southern Editorials*, 200.   [9] *Ibid.*, 214.   [10] *Ibid.*, 214.   [11] *Ibid.*, 227–228.

of the Union "does not absolve the . . . citizen from the obligation to obey the laws of the Union . . . ." [12] To say that the people have no other recourse against oppression was "untrue," said the same editor; the government belonged to the people and they had the power to alter it in a peaceable manner. To try such peaceful redress, he said, was "our duty here in Tennessee." [13] "Let us meet in common council," urged the *Kentucky Statesman*. "Let us have a Southern convention, and let the slave States take counsel together as to the best mode of preserving their rights in the Union. . . . We see nothing else to save the Union than a Southern Convention; and we believe that will." [14]

There were some in the South who were not greatly outraged at the election of Lincoln. Many agreed that his election was not a just reason for disunion.[15] Large numbers of conservatives dreaded secession and preferred to await an "overt act" before undertaking it. The whole background of Lincoln's relation to the Republican party suggested that he himself would take the conservative side, and as for the fear that his party was abolitionized and would push him into radical measures (assuming there had been no secession and no war) the answer was that, if a further trial of preserving "Southern rights" within the Union were thought desirable, there was a convenient instrument for this purpose in the national Congress wherein the Republicans would not have had a majority in either house if the Southern states had retained their congressmen at Washington.[16] Thus even if measures hostile to the South had been attempted by the Republicans in opposition to Lincoln's well known wish for moderation as shown in his Cooper Union speech and elsewhere, such hostility could have been checked by the obvious device of a majority vote in Congress. As to the Lincoln threat being viewed as an attack upon

---

[12] *Ibid.*, 250–252.   [13] *Ibid.*, 252.   [14] *Ibid.*, 254–255.

[15] "A very large number of our citizens have joined in a call for a Mass Meeting . . . opposed to the secession movement . . . " A. Burwell to S. A. Douglas, Vicksburg, Miss., Nov. 16, 1860, Douglas MSS. A broadside is enclosed which carries sixty-six names, including Thomas S. Dabney, but it is stated that in addition to the printed names there were "many others." The appeal reads in part: "The Union men of Mississippi ought to meet together, not as partisans . . . but as citizens of the same country, bound to a common destiny."

[16] The Chicago *Tribune* (a Republican paper) referred at the opening of Congress in December 1860 to the "fact that the Democracy control both branches" of that body (Dec. 3, 1860, p. 2, c. 1). See also Dumond, *Secession Movement*, 130–144; Dumond, *Southern Editorials*, 209, 255; Randall, *Civil War and Reconstruction*, 231–232.

slavery, it is significant to note that even Yancey himself, with his diplomatic colleagues Rost and Mann, later declared that fear of emancipation was not the cause of secession for the simple reason that the party of Lincoln did not intend to impose emancipation upon the South.[17]

It is a significant thing to call the roll of those Southerners who opposed secession during the hectic crisis of 1860–61. Ignoring many minor names the list included H. S. Foote, W. C. Rives, John Minor Botts, John B. Baldwin, G. W. Summers, Alexander H. H. Stuart, Robert E. Lee, Jubal A. Early, Jonathan Worth, Andrew Jackson Hamilton, J. W. Throckmorton, Sam Houston, Herschel V. Johnson, Benjamin H. Hill, Alexander H. Stephens, Andrew Johnson, Winfield Scott, George H. Thomas, John J. Crittenden, George D. Prentice, Benjamin Fitzpatrick, William L. Sharkey, Benjamin F. Perry, John A. Gilmer, John Tyler, John C. Breckinridge, William Aiken, J. L. Petigru, Emerson Etheridge, Thomas S. Dabney, and James Moore Wayne. This group contained thoroughbred Southerners mindful of the rights of their section but unconvinced that disunion was a remedy made necessary by any denial of those rights.

"[S]hall the people of the South secede from the Union in consequence of the election of Mr. Lincoln?" asked Alexander H. Stephens. "I tell you . . . candidly . . . that I do not think that they ought. . . . Were we to make a point of resistance to the Government . . . on that account, the record would be . . . against us." [18] Stephens went further; he actually spoke favorably of Lincoln. "In point of merit as a man I have no doubt Lincoln is just as good, safe and sound a man as Mr. Buchanan, and would administer the Government . . . just as safely for the South . . . . I know the man well. He is not a bad man. . . . I consider slavery much more secure in the Union than out of it . . . ." [19]

Much of the whole struggle of secessionists versus moderates in the South was illustrated by the difference between the diminutive Stephens and his burly colleague Toombs. Stephens regretted that the South had forced the issue at Charleston in 1860.[20] He would have avoided the assault upon Douglas and would have kept the Democratic

---

[17] Owsley, *King Cotton Diplomacy*, 66–67.   [18] McPherson, *Rebellion*, 21.
[19] *Annual Report*, Am. Hist. Assoc., 1911, II, 487.
[20] U. B. Phillips, *Life of Robert Toombs*, 190.

party intact. In the election of 1860 he supported the Douglas ticket. After that he labored to avert secession by his state, though admitting the constitutional right. His was the language of adjustment, compromise, and union. In this respect Stephens resembled Gilmer of North Carolina who wrote during this crisis: "We have had so much talk from . . . politicians about Southern Rights, that many honest Southern[ers] . . . have got it into their heads that they are already by the North deprived of some great . . . right, and are in immediate danger of losing others of still more vital importance. The people are beginning to open their eyes. They need aid. If they can be armed with a little plain common sense . . . they will pursue . . . those who have been deceiving them . . . ." [21] Toombs, on the other hand, used the harsher tones of truculence and sectional antagonism. He scored the "Black Republicans," identified them with abolitionists, denounced "intervention . . . by squatters" (meaning popular sovereignty in the territories), and declared that he would resist Douglas to the bitter end, though in doing so he could see "nothing but disaster and defeat in the future." [22] To judge from his language one would have supposed that Toombs would as soon have seceded against Douglas as against Lincoln. Some of his fiercest invective was aimed at men of his own party, Northern Democrats whom, on one occasion, he called "a lot of rogues." [23]

IV

As Congress began its session in early December of 1860 President Buchanan addressed the body in a message which denounced secession, stressed a Union that rested on public opinion, and favored the adoption of "peaceful constitutional remedies." The message has been more often denounced than read. Such writers as Nicolay and Hay and J. F. Rhodes have set the pattern of traditional criticism of Buchanan. Emphasizing the President's "weakness," they have harped upon the contrasting example of Andrew Jackson, and this contrast has become part of the stock-in-trade of Lincoln biographers who unhistorically imply that Jackson's menace of force "solved" the nullification problem and that his sternness turned the trick in averting

---

[21] John A. Gilmer to S. A. Douglas, Greensboro, N. C., Mar. 8, 1861, Douglas MSS.
[22] *Annual Report*, Am. Hist. Assoc., 1911, II, 469, 477.   [23] *Ibid.*, 470.

a serious disaster threatened in his time by South Carolina. It is but a step from that to the denunciation of Buchanan for his avoidance of force. In view of the familiar assumption that a Jackson in the presidency in 1860 would have cleared up the whole situation, it is of interest to read contemporary comments by the sturdy New England ex-President John Quincy Adams who at the time of the nullification episode referred to Jackson's policy in terms of disgust, declaring that he was surrendering the Union "to the nullifiers of the South and the land-robbers of the West." [1]

In truth the nullification episode showed the success of compromisers, and it should not be forgotten that Calhoun of South Carolina as well as Clay of Kentucky and others, worked for compromise and union.[2] If one were so minded he could easily quote Jackson in the pro-Buchanan sense as when he declared in his "farewell address" (March 4, 1837) that the Union rested upon "the affections of the people" and was not to be maintained by the "exertion of the coercive powers confided to the General Government." [3] In the traditional criticism of Buchanan that has become a shopworn stereotype it is obvious that the critics place small value upon the avoidance of war and that the whole discussion is a matter of reading back after the fact of war to the supposition that no such avoidance was possible.

But Republican-minded critics were not alone in denouncing Buchanan. Jefferson Davis regarded his treatment of South Carolina as "perfidious" and furiously assailed him for not granting the demands of South Carolina's representatives who sought to negotiate with him.[4] "The President's message is condemned by the extremists from both North and South," declared a well known Republican paper, "while conservative members . . . approve . . . the general principles enunciated." [5]

In endless post-mortems Americans have been accustomed to view the Buchanan interval against a background of South Carolinian events, or cotton-state events. But the same interval can also be viewed from the background of the United States, of which Washington was still the capital. Buchanan did not lose this larger view. He believed

[1] C. F. Adams, ed., *Memoirs of J. Q. Adams*, VIII, 503.

[2] Randall, *Civil War and Reconstruction*, 32–33.

[3] Buchanan, *Mr. Buchanan's Administration*, 112; Richardson, *Messages . . . of the Presidents*, III, 297.

[4] Rowland, *Davis*, IV, 565.   [5] Chicago *Tribune*, Dec. 6, 1860, p. 4, c. 7.

that arbitration of the vexed issue rested with Congress. The message which is usually taken as the text for assailing him was delivered before any state had seceded and was presented to a Congress whose absorbing preoccupation was the avoidance of armed conflict. "The stake involved was no less than the peace and perpetuity of the Union." [6] Certainly in early December of 1860 the guarding of that stake was, in the eyes of moderates, a matter of adjustment. The issue could have been dramatized as a race between the precipitate action of the lower South and the peaceful policy that was being urged in the general latitude of Virginia, Kentucky, and Washington. That the secessionists of the cotton states controlled the event does not signify that theirs was the stronger position. It was a matter of playing the cards and of forcing the issue. As schemes to save the nation swarmed and multiplied it became necessary to create some device of parliamentary procedure to handle them; thus there arose the committee of thirteen in the Senate and a committee of thirty-three in the House, the latter being a special grand committee of one from each state. While these committees were delving into the problem of compromise, the President was hardly free to take measures that might have inaugurated war, nor to snatch the decision out of the hands of Congress.

The position of prominence belonged to the Senate committee, of whose distinguished membership much was expected. Including such men as Davis, Toombs, Seward, Douglas, Wade, Doolittle, Trumbull, Grimes, and Crittenden, the committee no· only represented the elite of the nation's statesmen; it seemingly contained a leaven of mediatory influence. Created simultaneously with South Carolina's secession, it held its first meeting on the day after that first fateful ordinance, but a week before this the anti-compromisers had, as the journalist would say, stolen the front pages. On December 13 a group of Southern members of the House of Representatives, having assembled in the rooms of Reuben Davis of Mississippi, issued a manifesto "To our Constituents" as they called it, which declared that all hope of relief in the Union was exhausted and that Southern safety could be found only in a Southern Confederacy, which could be ob-

---

[6] Buchanan, *Mr. Buchanan's Administration*, 113. See also Frank Wysor Klingberg, "James Buchanan and the Crisis of the Union," *Jour. of So. Hist.*, IX, 455-474 (Nov., 1943).

tained only by separate state secession.[7] It is only fair to add that Southerners defended this course on the ground that no reliance could be placed in compromise plans because of the attitude of the Republican party, but it is also true that the manifesto was deliberately used as a secessionist propaganda device at a time when the congressional search for compromise had hardly begun. It is further true that both the Northern radicals and Southern secessionists were vigorously opposed to compromise. What was back of the manifesto seems almost to have been a fear that compromise would be successful. An adjustment at Washington that would satisfy the upper South and the border was precisely the thing which disunionists of both extremes dreaded. Senator Toombs as early as November 14 wrote that he would sustain South Carolina in secession,[8] and on December 23 he issued his address to the people of Georgia in which he did his best to close the door, or declare the door closed, to compromise before adjustment plans could ever be launched. Charging that the Senate compromise committee was "controlled by Black Republicans, your enemies," he warned his people not to be "deceived" by peaceful efforts and concluded: "Secession by the fourth of March next should be thundered from the ballot-box by the unanimous voice of Georgia . . . ."[9] Equally uncompromising statements by Northern extremists could be cited.

Under these circumstances the task of the committee of thirteen, whose proceedings Lincoln constantly watched, became well nigh hopeless. Its utter failure was formally announced eleven days after its appointment. On December 31, an early day for such a failure, the committee reported its inability to agree upon any plan of adjustment. No other act of his public life, said Douglas, had caused him so much regret.[10] There have been times when the Senate has failed the country in an hour of need, or in a challenge to greatness; this was one of the times.

---

[7] Rhodes, *Hist. of U. S.*, III, 177–178: McPherson, *Rebellion*, 37.

[8] Phillips, *Toombs*, 203. On December 13 Toombs "sounded a different note," proposing delay until compromise amendments could be considered (*ibid.*, 203–204), but on that day the anti-compromise address "To Our Constituents" was made public with an indication (which may not have been correct) that Toombs, absent from Washington, would have signed. On December 23, as seen above, Toombs emphatically opposed further compromise efforts.

[9] *Annual Report*, Am. Hist. Assoc., 1911, II, 525.

[10] *Annual Cyclopaedia*, 1861, 175.

In the general futility that marked the mechanics of compromise the record of the House committee of thirty-three need not be given in detail. Ultimately it reported a series of proposals, a goodly number of which passed the House, but none of them became law or shaped the situation in the direction of sectional appeasement. The committee as appointed contained a majority of Republicans, including Adams of Massachusetts, Corwin of Ohio, Kellogg of Illinois (mouthpiece of Lincoln), and Morrill of Vermont. Prominent Democratic names were absent. The committee's report, delayed until January 14, contained a series of proposals, but none commanded a majority of its members. Concerning the work of this group Charles Francis Adams stated that the recusant states would accept no form of adjustment that did not involve the Federal obligation to protect and extend slavery.[11]

Two of the committee's proposals may be specially noted here. One was a resolution denouncing state laws that hindered the return of fugitive slaves and recommending the repeal of such laws. It passed the House by more than five to two (136–53).[12] The other was a curious "unamendable" amendment to the Constitution which read as follows: "No amendment shall be made to the Constitution which will authorize . . . Congress . . . to abolish or interfere, within any State, with the domestic institutions thereof, including that of persons held to labor or service by the laws of said State." [13] In the House this amendment was approved by a vote of 133 to 65, in the Senate by 24 to 12.[14] Its supporters thus barely mustered the necessary two-thirds, yet two-thirds was a heavy majority. To become effective it would have required ratification by three-fourths of the states. This never came about, but action concerning the amendment is significant because it registered the sentiment, even after the withdrawal of many Southerners, that Congress should never interfere with slavery in the states. One should also mention the earlier action of the House in adopting without a dissenting voice (161–0) the resolution of John Sherman of Ohio declaring that neither Congress nor the people of

---

11 McPherson, *Rebellion,* 57.
12 *Cong. Globe,* 36 Cong., 2 sess., 1263 (Feb. 27, 1861).
13 *Ibid.*
14 The vote was taken on February 28, 1861, in the House and on March 2 in the Senate. *Ibid.,* 1285, 1375.

the non-slaveholding states had the constitutional right to legislate upon or interfere with slavery in any of the states.[15]

Looming higher than all the committees was one man, the venerable John J. Crittenden of Kentucky, compromiser by nature, spokesman of the great border, political heir of Henry Clay, and fit representative of the nation's elder statesmen. It is easy to pick flaws in the specific proposals of this distinguished Kentuckian, but it is impossible to escape a sense of the patriotic earnestness of his efforts to stave off civil war. Harking back to previous compromises in the days of 1820 and 1850 which he personally remembered, Crittenden thought that Southern apprehension could be quieted by concessions concerning slavery in the territories and in interstate relationships. Extending the Missouri line (36° 30′) to the Pacific, he would, as it were, give the West a Mason and Dixon line, prohibiting slavery in the territories on the Northern side, and protecting (not merely permitting) slavery on the Southern side. He further proposed that Congress disclaim the power to abolish slavery in a state, that there be no abolition in the District of Columbia without the consent of Virginia and Maryland, and that full guarantees be given for the protection of Southern rights in escaping slaves. By amendments to prevent future amendments he would assure the South in the most solemn manner that a changed Constitution would never allow Federal abolition of slavery within the states, nor change the ratio by which three-fifths of a state's slaves were counted in the apportionment of congressional seats.[16]

Crittenden's proposal was furiously assailed by Republicans and its details sound unsatisfactory today, but the terms he offered were more of a restriction upon slavery than the existing policy of the Supreme Court. Moreover, before the session of Congress was ended the Republicans themselves, in specific territorial legislation, were to refrain from applying that Wilmot-proviso doctrine which constituted their chief basis of objection to the Kentuckian's formula of peace. Crittenden tried in vain to get his proposals adopted by the Senate committee of thirteen; later the Senate itself voted him down, 23 to 25.[17] That the proposals were solidly supported by the Democrats and

---

[15] *Ibid.*, 857 (Feb. 11, 1861).   [16] *Ibid.*, 36 Cong., 2 sess., 112–114.
[17] *Ibid.*, 409. The vote was on a motion to substitute a very different resolution for Crittenden's.

as solidly opposed by the Republicans was naturally emphasized at the South. On the other hand it has been urged that the failure was due to the refusal of six Southern senators to vote. It was charged that these senators did not want compromise.[18] There was truth in both these attributions of blame; intransigents on both sides, antislavery enthusiasts no less than ardent secessionists, opposed not only compromise "terms" but the very idea of any compromise whatever.

V

The Republicans of the time were not a close-knit party. Rather they were a mixture of differing groups. S. S. Cox declared that he did not know "where the head or the tail of the . . . party" was.[1] Among Republicans of Ohio, for example, Corwin had been an old-line Whig, Chase an antislavery Democrat, and Giddings a radical abolitionist. Between Sumner and Seward, or between Greeley and Weed, there was indeed a gulf fixed. Also there was a marked difference between Greeley's November attitude and his later belligerency. Perhaps it was the difference between Greeley couchant and Greeley rampant. The Republicans had no spearhead, no consistent spokesman, no fully recognized leader in those fateful weeks when Southerners were saying that all depended on the Republicans and that no settlement could even be considered unless it had the previous endorsement of the incoming administration. Such statements were used for propaganda purposes in the South where emphasis was placed upon the "Black Republicans" who, as was stated by Toombs, had treated compromise proposals with "derision or contempt." [2]

An analysis of the Republican attitude on compromise is therefore essential. When at the beginning of the congressional session it was proposed to create a compromise committee of thirty-three, the majority of the Republicans favored it; nevertheless all the thirty-eight votes in opposition were on the Republican side.[3] The committee was fully under Republican control, and it was futile as an instrument of compromise. Yet one cannot say that the committee favored no concessions. It was rather that its concessions did not avert the trouble,

[18] *Ibid.*, 37 Cong., 2 sess., 587–588.
[1] Samuel S. Cox, *Eight Years in Congress*, 78.
[2] McPherson, *Rebellion*, 37–38.
[3] *Annual Cyclopaedia*, 1861, 201; Dumond, *Secession Movement*, 156.

and if one seeks an explanation of why this was so he realizes how artificial difficulties had accumulated to make real obstacles out of shadow objections and how a problem that seems simple to a later generation was fraught at the time with sectional inhibitions till it was well nigh unsolvable. Even though they went a considerable distance, Republicans lacked that element which could make compromise take hold; on the other hand they could answer that the satisfying of the secessionists was an impossibility unless secession itself was to be admitted.

Nearly every generalization needs its qualifying corrective. In the midst of the sectional crisis there was noticed a "thinning of the ranks" among Republicans, which meant that a considerable number favored compromise.[4] Such men as Seward and Weed were willing to go far toward adjustment. In his influential Albany newspaper Weed came out with a formula of conciliation involving an effective fugitive slave law, repeal of the personal liberty laws, noninterference by Congress with slavery in the territories, and, if necessary, restoration of the Missouri line.[5] The last point involved a considerable retreat from the Chicago platform. The New York *Times* and the New York *Courier and Enquirer,* both Republican and pro-Seward, favored the Weed compromise.[6] On January 12, Seward, long the most prominent Republican in the country, made a notably conciliatory speech. He showed his entire willingness to satisfy the South concerning fugitive slaves and the unrestrained admission of future slave states.[7] Such Republicans as Grimes and Trumbull would not endorse the Crittenden compromise, though some Republicans would do so, yet they would make concessions. Grimes agreed to protection of slavery in the states, revision of the personal liberty laws, and the admission of slave states in the Southwest to offset the admission of Kansas free.[8] Trumbull would never agree to an open declaration making slavery perpetual, yet he disavowed any intention to interfere with Southern domestic institutions.[9] Cox of Ohio, ardent Democrat, was impressed with the extent of the things the Republicans would agree to, emphasizing that they

---

[4] David M. Potter, *Lincoln and His Party in the Secession Crisis,* 191.

[5] McPherson, 74. Greeley wrote: "Weed thinks he is saving the Union. I guess not." Greeley to Brockway, Dec. 8, 1860, Greeley MSS., Lib. of Cong.

[6] Rhodes, *Hist. of U. S.,* III, 156.　　[7] *Cong. Globe,* 36 Cong., 2 sess., 341–344.

[8] William Salter, *Life of James W. Grimes,* 137.　　[9] White, *Trumbull,* 132–133.

would have admitted New Mexico as a slave state. Controlling the patronage, he thought, they would "be content with the tricks" (jobs) and "allow us" the honors (concessions). Under "the lead of Bates, Raymond, Corwin, Ewing, Weed, ay, and Seward and Lincoln," they would "drown the Giddings crew" and would be "as harmless in office as most men are." [10]

By no means were the Republicans standing firm on any thorough antislavery principle. Many of them, especially urban dwellers, stood ready to support Weed.[11] The party in general supported the Adrian resolution "earnestly recommend[ing]" the repeal of the personal liberty laws, and this before any state had seceded.[12] They even agreed to the aforementioned constitutional amendment by which Federal action against slavery in the states should forever be prevented. It was common in these days for those Republicans who stood firm to express disgust or regret at the manner in which men of Lincoln's party were backing down. "It is sad," wrote Chase, "to think what is now yielded and by whom." [13] J. G. Blaine's account of Republican action on territorial legislation in the closing days of the Thirty-Sixth Congress should be carefully read in this connection. With Republican majorities in both houses of Congress (owing to the absence of Southerners) laws were passed organizing the territories of Colorado, Dakota, and Nevada without the prohibition of slavery. After seven years, declared Blaine, the Republicans abandoned the "cardinal principle" of their new-fledged party. Even Wade, Sumner, and Chandler joined in this action. It was not sufficient, said Blaine, to contend that there was no danger of slavery going into these territories: if the prohibition was proper for Oregon it was equally needful for Dakota; if for Kansas, then for Colorado and Nevada. References to the needlessness of the ter-

---

[10] Cox, *Eight Years*, 204, 206.

[11] "In our city & State some of their [the Republicans'] most prominent men are ready to follow the lead of Weed, and active agencies are at work to bring about a compromise." August Belmont to Herschel V. Johnson of Georgia, Dec. 30, 1860, Douglas MSS., Univ. of Chicago. As for the rural districts of New York the opposite opinion was reported. "Do not judge New York state by Mr Weed," wrote George E. Baker from Albany to Sumner. "He no longer speaks for her when he suggests a Compromise. . . . The rural districts repudiate the idea unanimously." Sumner MSS., Dec. 3, 1860.

[12] The Adrian resolution passed the House of Representatives on December 17, 1860, by a vote of 153 to 14. *Cong. Globe*, 36 Cong., 2 sess., 108.

[13] S. P. Chase to John A. Andrew, Jan. 26, 1861, Andrew MSS.

ritorial prohibition came strangely from Republican lips. They had
heaped abuse upon Webster and even more upon Douglas for
making the same point. Now they took action in Congress which
seemed to Blaine a triumph for Douglas.[14] And, to make the victory
complete and the futility of the territorial controversy crystal clear,
Southerners themselves conceded "that the demand they had so
loudly made for admission to the Territories was really worth nothing to the institution of slavery." The whole fuss and storm "related
to an imaginary negro in an impossible place." [15]

It has been noted above how Douglas was able in 1861 to taunt
the Republicans with abandonment of those principles on which
the Lincoln-Douglas debates had been waged in 1858.[16] That point
deserves further notice here. When the aforementioned acts organizing Colorado, Nevada, and Dakota were passed (February-March
1861), the prohibition or permission of slavery was not mentioned
in these statutes, which left the question of slavery in the territories exactly where it was in Douglas's Kansas-Nebraska act of
1854, so far as congressional legislation was concerned.[17] In the
Senate these bills were passed without division; this lack of challenge
and of recorded vote indicated Republican consent. In the House
the yeas and nays were recorded, and one may test the party attitude
by the vote on the Colorado bill, which Mr. Sickles desired to have
read "to see if the Wilmot proviso was in it"; he then pointed out
that "that principle is abandoned." [18] The bill was passed with 90
yeas and 44 nays; 86 Republicans favored it and only ten were opposed.[19] After the proceedings had been completed regarding the
three territorial bills, the only such measures pending at the time,
Douglas could not refrain from making his comment. "This very

---

[14] J. G. Blaine, *Twenty Years of Congress*, I, 269 ff. Blaine wrote (p. 271): "Every
prominent Republican senator who agreed in 1861 to abandon the principle of the Wilmot Proviso . . . had, in 1850, heaped reproach upon Mr. Webster for not insisting
upon the . . . principle . . . ." He added: "It was . . . a day of triumph for
Mr. Douglas. He was justified in his boast that, after all the bitter agitation which followed the . . . Kansas-Nebraska Bill, the Republicans adopted its principle . . . in
the first Territory which they had the power to organize."

[15] *Ibid.*, I, 272.   [16] See above, p. 126.

[17] Colorado was organized by act of February 28, 1861, Nevada and Dakota by acts
of March 2, 1861; except for such matters as boundaries and name, the acts were
identical. *U. S. Stat. at Large*, XII, 172, 209, 239.

[18] *Cong. Globe*, 36 Cong., 2 sess., 1003 (Feb. 18, 1861).

[19] *Ibid.*, 1005 (Feb. 18, 1861); McPherson, *Rebellion*, 90.

session," he said, "the Republican party, in both Houses of Congress, . . . have backed down from their platform and abandoned the doctrine of congressional prohibition. This very week three territorial bills have been passed . . . without the Wilmot proviso, and no man proposed to enact it; not even one man on the other side of the Chamber would rise and propose the Wilmot proviso. . . . They have abandoned the doctrine of the President elect . . . . He said . . . that he had voted for the Wilmot proviso forty-two times, ... Not one of his followers this year voted for it once. The Senator from New York, [Mr. Seward,] the embodiment of the party, . . . did not propose it. . . . Practically, the Chicago platform is abandoned; the Philadelphia platform is abandoned; the whole doctrine for which the Republican party contended as to the Territories is abandoned, surrendered, given up; non-interference is substituted in its place." [20] Again he said: "What you . . . said before the election was one thing. What you felt it your duty as patriots to do . . . after the election is a very different thing. After having secured . . . power, you . . . organized all the Territories that we have now got, on the principle of . . . popular sovereignty." [21]

Douglas was careful to commend the motives that prompted the action of his opponents in 1861 when their doctrine meant peril to the country. "For years," he said, "that party has aimed shafts at my breast . . . ." Then he showed that on attaining power they had come round to the Douglas program, and added: "I rejoice . . . to say that they acted like patriots . . . in abandoning the ground on which they had stood for years, and coming over to the Democratic doctrine . . . . I do not refer to this in any spirit of . . . crimination. . . . I refer to it as an evidence of patriotism . . . for which all Union-loving men will give them due credit." [22]

Having been led to believe that the territorial issue concerning slavery was the pivotal and vital issue of the age, that it was the basis of the Republican party or the intolerable challenge to Southern rights, Americans of the time were witnesses of a scene in Congress in which "Mr. Seward waived the anti-slavery guaranty on behalf of the Republicans" while James Stephens Green of Missouri moved

---

[20] Douglas in United States Senate, March 3, 1861, *Cong. Globe,* 36 Cong., 2 sess., 1391.
[21] *Ibid.,* 1503 (Mar. 25, 1861).   [22] *Ibid.,* 1460 (Mar. 15, 1861).

a corresponding waiver of pro-slavery guarantees "on behalf of the Breckinridge Democracy." [23] Republicans did not consistently adhere even to their own party ideology.[24] It seemed to an opponent that they were "like the man that drew the elephant in the raffle" and knew "not what to do with him . . . ." [25] To those who were firm in the antislavery faith it seemed that they were backsliders.[26] The truth was that their party was almost leaderless, that their leading men differed as to policy, and that their stickling at one or two points, though of little importance in itself, neutralized the effect of concessions offered, making it easy for opponents to overdramatize their position as the refusal of all compromise whatsoever.

For Union and peace the cards were wretchedly played. Such a valuable thing as the calling of a national convention was discarded. Secessionists were able by the bolder play of their hands to produce a result far beyond the cards they held. To change the figure, if politics be an art and mass emotions its medium, unionists were woefully unskillful in the technique by which the medium was handled.

VI

Lincoln's attitude on the vexed question was shaped in varying parts by Republican ideology, by his dislike of particular proposals, and by his none-too-perfect reading of popular sentiment. While controversy raged the thing most obvious to the public ear was Lincoln's silence. To write for publication, he said on October 23, "would do no good." "If I were to labor a month I could not express my conservative . . . intentions more clearly . . . than they are expressed . . . in my many speeches already in print and before the public." Any public statement, he thought, would be "useless." He could say nothing which he had not already said. To speak again

---

[23] Blaine, *Twenty Years of Congress*, I, 271.

[24] "I need not say how anxious I am that our friends . . . shall stand firm . . . . I am sorry to find so many cowards even among republicans." Joshua Giddings to Charles Sumner, Dec. 3, 1860, Sumner MSS.

[25] R. W. Massey to S. A. Douglas, Paola, Kan., Nov. 28, 1860, Douglas MSS.

[26] "There has been a great cave in by the Republicans in the [Pennsylvania] Senate. Today they voted virtually to extend slavery if the 'border states' demanded it." Thus wrote one of William Lloyd Garrison's correspondents who referred in the same letter to "Republican backsliders." E. W. Capron to W. L. Garrison, Harrisburg, Pa., Jan. 28, 1861, Garrison MSS. This note of disgust at Republican concessions runs all through the correspondence of Garrison, Sumner, and other antislavery men.

would give the opportunity for further garbling and misrepresentation. This he regarded as a situation to be prudently faced not "in a spirit of complaint or resentment" but as a guide to policy. He was not at liberty to shift his ground and he saw no reason for mere repetition. Indeed he thought a repetition "would do positive harm." "The secessionists *per se* . . . would clamor all the louder." While saying all this, however, he indicated that there should be no apprehension in the country that his course would be "other than conservative." [1]

When the Republicans planned a huge celebration of the election of Lincoln and Hamlin at Springfield on November 20, 1860, Lincoln was strongly urged to share the platform with such men as Trumbull, Yates, and Palmer, and to use the occasion to allay the growing distrust of his incoming administration. Such a meeting would have offered a sounding board for a repetition of his conservative views at an early stage in the crisis, and there were those who felt that a restraining and reassuring statement from him along conservative Union lines was a solemn public duty. Lincoln not only refused to make a speech at this Republican gathering but declined even to appear, confining himself to a few sentences of greeting to some Wide Awakes who stormed his home. Though joining in party rejoicing he counseled against "any hard feelings toward any citizen who . . . has differed with us." [2]

Not altogether, however, did he let the occasion pass without an expression of his views. He wrote out a passage to be incorporated into Trumbull's speech, so that the Illinois senator was actually using Lincoln's own words when he declared that all the states would have "as perfect liberty to choose and employ their own means of protecting property . . . within their . . . limits, as . . . under any administration." [3] Again he was using Lincoln's words when he declared that secessionists *per se* were "in hot haste to get out of the Union" because they could not continue to "maintain an apprehension among the Southern people that their homes and firesides [were] . . . to be endangered by the action of the Federal Government." [4]

---

[1] For statements quoted in this paragraph, see *Works*, VI, 63–71 (Oct. 23, to Nov. 16, 1860).

[2] *Ibid.*, VI, 72.   [3] White, *Trumbull*, 109.   [4] *Ibid.*, 110.

The flight of this trial balloon was not propitious. A week later Lincoln knew of no newspaper having made the Trumbull statement a basis for quieting anxiety, while the Boston *Courier,* correctly attributing Trumbull's remarks to Lincoln, used them as the text for denunciation of the President Elect for abandoning Republican ground. On the other hand the Washington *Constitution* held the speech up to the South as an open declaration of war against them.[5] All this served to confirm Lincoln in the view that nothing he could say could ease the troubled situation.

Even when expressing views of a sort to quiet the country in his correspondence with close friends, Lincoln insisted upon secrecy. One may take his published works from November to March, 1860–61, and find pithily worded, even eloquent expressions of good will, common sense, and restraint in letters that provokingly carried the heading "private," "confidential," "private and confidential," "strictly confidential," or for "your own eye only." It was in this manner that he wrote secretly to George D. Prentice, A. H. Stephens, John A. Gilmer, and Henry J. Raymond.[6] In the same period one may take the Trumbull manuscripts and note frequent inquiries as to why Trumbull, understood to be Lincoln's spokesman, did not speak out. Lincoln's words in correspondence were so conciliatory and reassuring that they seem to the present view precisely the kind of pronouncements which the emergency demanded from the President Elect. Why, then, did he let only a few favored friends have these salutary words from his pen while his public monosyllables were both colorless and rare? Possibly we have the explanation in a letter to George D. Prentice of Kentucky shortly before his election. His abstinence from speaking out, he wrote on October 29, 1860, was not punctilio. It was a conviction that speaking out would only "do harm." For the good men of the South, and he regarded "the majority of them as such," he would repeat his stand "seventy and seven times," but he had bad men to deal with, "both *North and* South;[7] men . . . eager for something new upon which to base new misrepresentations . . . ." These men were ready to accuse him of "timidity and cowardice" and "would seize upon almost any letter . . . [he] could write as being 'an awful coming down.' "[8]

[5] *Works,* VI, 74–75 (Nov. 28, 1860).
[6] *Ibid.,* VI, 66, 74, 79, 85 (Oct. 29 to Dec. 22, 1860).   [7] Italics supplied.
[8] *Works,* VI, 66–67.

This sounds very much as if Lincoln's silence was due, at least in large part, to a fear of men of his own party. It was they, not Southerners, who would convict him of cowardice. If he spoke it would be for conciliation, but this would be branded as timidity and a "coming down" from those elements of Republican ideology which after all represented only a minority of the people. Thus early did the force of Northern radicalism, which was to plague Lincoln's whole administration, make itself felt in the pre-war crisis. This tendency to call Lincoln timid was due less to any actual "coming down" than to the extremists' inherent dislike of compromise (let one go over the manuscripts and published sources of the time if he doubts this), and to the persistent attitude of rebel-baiting which was one of the foremost emotional factors of the time. Again and again it reveals itself in abolitionist denunciation of such men as Weed and Seward for their moderate views. Where radicals thought Lincoln leaned toward moderation they denounced Lincoln too. The words of William Lloyd Garrison in this connection were expressive of the extremist attitude, which sometimes went to the extent of favoring disunion. "Would to God," wrote Garrison, "that the people of the North, without distinction of party, could see that the time has come for a separation from the South . . . in obedience to the 'Higher Law'! Is it not self-evident that we are, and must be, with slave institutions in one section and free institutions in the other, two nations?" [9]

In spite of his studied reticence it is possible to reconstruct Lincoln's actual position touching the sectional crisis. He favored enforcement of the fugitive slave law. While he believed that such enforcement should be relieved of "vindictiveness," [10] he also thought that Northern personal liberty laws ought to be repealed to the extent of their conflict with the fugitive-slave clause of the Constitution.[11] It may fairly be said that he stood ready to make every reasonable concession to Southern sensibilities on this point. Suspected fugitives when caught, he thought ought to have a fair trial.[12] Unlike abolitionists Lincoln had favored a decision of the Ohio supreme court (1859) upholding the Federal courts in the enforce-

9 W. L. Garrison to Sumner, Feb. 26, 1861, Sumner MSS.
10 J. Dixon to Gideon Welles, Dec. 3, 1860, Welles MSS.
11 *Works*, VI, 81 (Dec. 15, 1860).   12 White, *Trumbull*, 112.

ment of the fugitive slave law. Writing on July 28, 1859, to Samuel Galloway, who called himself the first Ohioan to write to him suggesting his name for the presidency,[13] Lincoln had objected strenuously to the action of the Ohio Republicans in repudiating this decision and favoring a repeal of the fugitive-slave law. Hannibal Hamlin, who conferred personally with Lincoln in November 1860, stated that the new chief insisted that the law concerning fugitives must be executed in good faith and that no one who thought otherwise ought to enter his cabinet.[14]

On other points Lincoln's views showed a like conservatism. He had, as President Elect, no thought of recommending the abolition of slavery in the District of Columbia even on the safeguarding conditions outlined in previous declarations. Abolition of the slave trade among the states he did not contemplate. These were matters he cared little about [15] but he knew even if he were to recommend such abolition it was "quite clear Congress would not follow" him.[16] Nor did he care much about possible extension in New Mexico, "if further extension were hedged against." [17] Often he said he would do nothing to anger the people of the South, nothing to harass them.[18] "Rest fully assured," he wrote to Samuel Haycraft, "that the good people of the South . . . will find no cause to complain of me." [19] To Alexander H. Stephens he wrote: "Do the people of the South really entertain fears that a Republican administration would, directly or indirectly, interfere with the slaves, or with them about the slaves? If they do, I . . . assure you . . . that there is no cause for such fears. The South would be in no more danger in this respect than . . . in the days of Washington." [20] In particular he would not use the patronage against Southerners, would not discriminate against

---

13 Samuel Galloway to Andrew Johnson, April 21, 1865, Johnson MSS. For the letter to Galloway see *Works*, V, 136-138 (July 28, 1859).

14 After having consulted with Lincoln, Hamlin talked with James Dixon of Connecticut concerning the possibility of bringing Gideon Welles into the cabinet. The Vice President Elect "then said Mr. Lincoln & himself agreed that the fugitive slave laws must be executed in good faith— . . . that an agreement on that point was indispensable—that his cabinet could not act harmoniously unless they agreed with him . . . ." Lincoln had to be satisfied as to Welles's views on this matter, and in writing, before appointing him. Dixon to Welles, Washington, Dec. 3, 1860, Welles MSS.

15 *Works*, VI, 103-104 (Feb. 1, 1861).

16 *Ibid.*, VI, 80 (Dec. 15, 1860).　　17 *Ibid.*, VI, 104 (Feb. 1, 1861).

18 *Ibid.*, VI, 81 (Dec. 15, 1860).　　19 *Ibid.*, VI, 69-70 (Nov. 13, 1860).

20 *Ibid.*, VI, 85 (Dec. 22, 1860).

non-Republicans or slaveholders, and would not force carpetbag appointments upon an unwilling section. Not only did he make this clear in letters; [21] he told a New Orleans merchant who interviewed him just after his election that he would not send Northern men to fill Southern offices.[22]

This did not mean weakness in the matter of law enforcement. Lincoln is reported to have told Weed that "he did not quite like to hear Southern journals and . . . speakers insisting that there must be no 'coercion'; that while he had no disposition to coerce any-body, yet after he had taken an oath to execute the laws, he should not care to see them violated." [23] In similar vein he was quoted [24] as saying that he was opposed to "buying" the privilege of taking his rightful office.

On one point, slavery in the territories, which Republicans deemed "vital" (until they came to legislate upon it in 1861),[25] Lincoln repeatedly said that he would be unyielding. To Weed he wrote (for a convocation of governors) that he would be "in-flexible" on the territorial question. He explained why. Either "the Missouri line extended, or Douglas's and Eli Thayer's popular sovereignty," he said, "would lose us everything we gain by the election; . . . filibustering for all south of us and making slave States of it would follow . . . ." [26] On secession he said little before he became President, but said enough to let it be known that in his opinion "no State can in any way lawfully get out of the Union without the consent of the others." [27] The President and other Federal officers, he thought, ought "to run the machine as it is." To balance this he gave repeated assurances that he had no inten-tion of interfering with slavery as a state institution. He even stood ready to approve the contemplated constitutional amendment closing the door to any such future interference. "So far as we know," de-clared the Chicago *Tribune,* "all Republicans deny the power of Lincoln's or any other Administration to interfere with slavery in

---

[21] "As to the use of patronage in the slave States, where there are few or no Re-publicans, I do not expect to inquire for the politics of the appointee, or whether he does or [does] not own slaves. I intend in that matter to accommodate the people in the several localities . . . ." Lincoln to Gilmer, Dec. 15, 1860, *Works,* VI, 80–81.

[22] New York *Herald,* Nov. 9, 1860, p. 2, c. 5.

[23] *Autobiography of Thurlow Weed,* edited by his daughter, Harriet A. Weed, 606.

[24] McPherson, *Rebellion,* 67.   [25] See above, pp. 229 ff.

[26] *Works,* VI, 82 (Dec. 17, 1860).   [27] *Ibid.*

the States, to oppress . . . communities upon which the institution is saddled, or to use the Federal arm for destroying . . . property declared . . . such by the local law." [28] Referring to the charge that Lincoln was an abolitionist the same paper declared the accusation "so baseless that it ought never to have been credited for a moment," though it was "widely spread over the South" and was "the cause of much of the bad blood in that section." [29]

Aside from the maintenance of the government itself, the territorial matter was almost the only point on which Lincoln spoke the language of inflexibility. His statements to Hale, Weed, Seward, Kellogg, and Trumbull all carry the same note of conviction. If we surrender this, he said, "it is the end of us and of the government." [30] He would support no compromise which would permit the extension of the institution "on soil owned by the nation." Acquiring territory and then letting some local authority spread slavery over it, he thought, would "put us again on the highroad to a slave empire." He would watch compromise measures to avoid such a "trick." [31] On this matter Lincoln was less yielding than Weed and Seward, and this has led to the conclusion that among high placed Republicans it was Lincoln especially who blocked the road to adjustment. As if specifically to influence action in Congress Lincoln advised Kellogg and Washburne, Illinois congressmen, to entertain no compromise of any sort concerning slavery in the territories.[32]

VII

It is significant to note how far sectional agitation by politicians was concerned with two points—the fugitive slave question and slavery in the territories—and then, by analysis of the contemporary situation, to find how utterly inadequate each of these factors was as *casus belli* or ground for disunion. There is, of course, the broader explanation of the Southern movement on cultural lines, and volumes have been written on the economic background of the crisis.[1]

---

[28] Chicago *Tribune*, Nov. 24, 1860, p. 2, c. 1.
[29] *Ibid.*, Nov. 26, 1860, p. 2, cc. 1–2.
[30] *Works*, VI, 93 (Jan. 11, 1861).   [31] *Ibid.*, VI, 103 (Feb. 1, 1861).
[32] *Ibid.*, VI, 77–79 (Dec. 11 and Dec. 13, 1860).
[1] In Randall, *Civil War and Reconstruction*, especially 110 ff., the economic background is sketched. For bibliography, see *ibid.*, 887 ff.

The economy of a great nation, however, has many facets, and one does not exhaust economic truth by noting disruptive tendencies. Sections with diverse interests could logically have treated those interests as supplementing factors making for a well rounded nation. As for a Southern shift of economic control in banking, trade, cotton dealing, and the like, this was a business matter; if the ways of business had tended in that direction such a shift could have been accomplished within the Union. Economic interpreters ought not to be afraid of their own subject. It was economic factors which had placed New York where it stood in the financial and commercial life of the whole nation, as well as placing the South where it stood in agrarian specialization. The year of the beginning of secession, 1860, found a tariff law on the books which was not at all anti-Southern. As to the fear of an adverse law being passed in the new situation, historians have not pinned down enough evidence to show that this fear, nor any similar economic or cultural factor, actually moved a majority of Southern people to the point of demanding secession. If there was a group in the South who insisted upon secession for cultural motives, it was that group known at the time as secessionists *per se,* and all the evidence tends to show that this group was a minority. Even the men of this group, however, used slavery "grievances" to make their case, denouncing low-tariff Northern Democrats as well as Republicans, so that the stock complaints of the time cannot in any case be ignored if one is studying factors of agitation.

In this agitation the traditional "grievances" were used out of all proportion to their solid content. If "Nothing is more real than an emotional reaction," [2] it is also true that when emotions are whipped up the actual stuff of controversy may often be amazingly thin. Assuredly slavery in the territories, represented to be a cardinal factor in the formation of the Republican party, was a constant theme of intersectional bickering, and the same may be said of the fugitive slave issue. Remembering this, it is ironical to note how these "issues" were not only less of a stickling point than agitators represented them to be, but in practice utterly insignificant. If the Civil War was fought because of fugitive slaves or on account of slavery

---

[2] R. S. Henry, *The Story of Reconstruction,* 72.

in the West, the American people were miserably hoodwinked by the demon of strife. The census of 1860 numbered escaping slaves at 803, which was approximately one-fiftieth of one per cent of the total number of slaves in the country. By no means all of these eight hundred fugitives escaped to the North, but the number of free Negroes kidnapped in the North and brought South was considerable; thus the actual loss to the South was exceedingly small. The fugitive slave clause of the Constitution was implemented by a law that was so drastic as to be shockingly one-sided. Stephens of Georgia declared that the South had not made sufficient effort to negotiate with offending states concerning the rendition of fugitives.[3] The law of 1850 showed that Congress had gone a long distance to meet Southern objections. The Supreme Court was sustaining Federal law in this field. Some of the states had prohibited kidnapping and had sought otherwise to temper the fugitive-slave arrangements with a reasonable regard for civil rights, but even these laws were to be given up on Republican advice.[4] The personal liberty laws were a "remediable complaint" [5] and it was recognized by such a moderate Southerner as John A. Gilmer that no genuine grievance existed on this score. "With a perpetual guaranty against Congressional interference with slavery in the States," wrote Gilmer to Douglas, "and the Territory under . . . organization without the Wilmot proviso, . . . and . . . the free States repealing their personal liberty laws as rapidly as they can, what more does any reasonable Southern man expect or desire?" [6] S. S. Cox, ardent Democrat, was of opinion that prevailing sentiment in the House of Representatives was such as to encourage those who sought to cure sectional evils.[7] A considerable group of leading men of Massachusetts joined in a printed public declaration favoring repeal of their personal liberty laws, not under

---

[3] McPherson, *Rebellion*, 23.

[4] As one of many evidences on this point one may cite the following letter. "The only weak point in our position is the Personal Liberty bills which have never impeded the surrender of any fugitives yet, and probably never will, but which are used as justification of all kinds of wrong doing on the other side. And these would undoubtedly be repealed in every State, except perhaps Wisconsin, if some humane & proper modification of the Fugitive Law were made by Congress." Colfax to Yates, Dec. 10, 1860, MS., Chicago Hist. Soc.

[5] Rhodes, *Hist. of U. S.*, III, 147.

[6] John A. Gilmer to S. A. Douglas, Mar. 8, 1861, Douglas MSS.

[7] Cox, *Eight Years*, 196.

threat, as they said, but "under our own love of right . . . ." [8] Nor
did the Southerners have any valid complaint against Lincoln on
the fugitive matter. As has been seen he wanted less vindictiveness
in the system, but stood unequivocally for fulfillment of the Federal
obligation to promote the return of the fugitives. A number of
Northern governors had urged the repeal of the fugitive laws of
their states to which Southerners objected,[9] Banks of Massachusetts
even going so far as to call the law of his state "unnecessary to the
public service, . . . detrimental to the public peace, [and] . . . an
unexcusable public wrong." [10] Even if runaways had been numerous
it by no means appears that the number could have been decreased
by the erection of an independent slave nation in the South. At one
stroke this would have deprived the South of a powerful constitutional guarantee. Such a remedy for the fugitive grievance would
have been like moving Canada down to the Ohio. The main result
of Northern state and Federal action as to fugitives had been to
facilitate rather than hinder their recovery. Abolitionist rescues,
though sensational, were of less effect than the regular operation in
the North of legal processes favorable to slaveholders. Practically it
does not make sense to say that the South had to secede because
of fugitive slaves.

As to the territorial question it is well known that Kansas and
Nebraska had been written off for freedom by 1860 for the reason
that Southerners did not care to take slaves into those regions, and
that the prospect of slavery taking hold in New Mexico (then including Arizona) was negligible. Federal law permitted slavery in
Kansas, but since the census of 1860 showed only two slaves in that
territory,[11] which contained a population of over 100,000, it may be

---

[8] When one considers the Southern emphasis upon Northern personal liberty laws
as a grievance (these being state laws to obstruct the return of fugitive slaves as
required by Federal statute) it is important to note how these leading men of the Bay
State urged that by their own free will and as an act of right the people of that
commonwealth ought, in view of the excited condition of the country, to repeal this
legislation, after which recovery of fugitives would proceed according to Federal process.
The appeal was made by men "of different political parties" and the whole paper
breathes conciliation with the South. Among the signers were Lemuel Shaw, Benjamin
R. Curtis (former justice of the United States Supreme Court), Joel Parker, Joseph
Grinnell, George Ticknor, Jared Sparks, Levi Lincoln, Theophilus Parsons, and a
number of other prominent men. B. R. Curtis MSS., Lib. of Cong., no. 4319.

[9] Rhodes, *Hist. of U. S.*, III, 252–253.   [10] *Annual Cyclopaedia*, 1861, 576.

[11] For the census report of only two slaves in the territory of Kansas and fifteen
in the territory of Nebraska, see *U. S. Census, 1860*, Agriculture, 227, 246. When the

truly said that the colossal quarrel concerning slavery in Kansas had practically nothing to do with Kansas itself. Many Republicans said they would not yield on slavery in the territories; but, leaving aside the opportunity of the South to vote down the Republicans by staying in the Union, it is to be repeated that the Republicans themselves dropped the freedom principle as a matter of actual enactment in the Dakota, Colorado, and Nevada laws. Speaking on the eve of Lincoln's inauguration, Douglas asserted in the Senate that the South had, by the action of a Republican Congress, the full right to emigrate into all the territory of the United States, and showed that the Republicans had in fact abandoned their Chicago platform.[12] In the completed legal arrangements of 1860–61 slave interests were given a heavier, not a lighter, weighting than the broad nineteenth-century situation would naturally have provided. Southerners themselves said that sectional agitation had strengthened slavery. Some of them also said that no grievances pertaining to slavery existed which could form a valid basis for disunion.

VIII

Public leaders ought to be viewed against a background of public opinion, but opinion in the sectional crisis was of many colors. It followed no constant pattern; it was only in part vocal; its mouthpieces were often false; its gauges as they remain after eight decades are unsatisfactory. Selections could be made to "prove" the most diverse generalizations. There were Northern secessionists, there were Southern unionists, there were plain citizens pouring out petitions for adjustment, there were other citizens spurning any thought of compromise. There were manufacturers concerned only with such a matter as the tariff, there were business men alarmed at the economic

---

slavery struggle had waxed hot in the 1850's the number had not been notably large. A census taken by persons appointed by the governor of Kansas in February 1855 showed 192 slaves in a total population of 8601 (*House Rep. No. 200*, 34 Cong., 1 sess., p. 72). If this figure was correct, the slaves in 1855 numbered slightly above two per cent of the total. By 1860 the free-state element had gained control of the legislature, so that slaveholders left the territory or sold their slaves outside of Kansas. For some time after the Civil War Kansas remained anti-Negro in the sense that its people voted down Negro suffrage and maintained separate schools in many districts, including Lawrence, of New England Emigrant Aid Company notoriety. (In these matters the author has been assisted by Professor James C. Malin, University of Kansas.)

[12] *Cong. Globe*, 36 Cong., 2 sess., 1391 (Mar. 2, 1861).

depression that accompanied the crisis and pleading for reason and peace from the merchant's point of view. There were conservatives in the North who were ready to go as far as necessary to satisfy the South and avoid war.[1] There were army men, and others expecting to be called, looking anxiously on while politicians held not only their personal fate but the shaping and twisting of the cause for which they would have to fight. There were Lincoln men who repented of their votes when they viewed the consequences. And there were Democrats who declined to "thrust Republican wrongs down the throats of the South at the point of the bayonet."[2]

People were stirred by a crisis psychology. "These are times," wrote a New Englander, "to develope manhood. We have had none finer since 1776." "It is encouraging, and ennobling," he added, "to see true patriotism warm up—and the political conscience purge itself."[3] The literary perception of Edward Everett Hale did not miss the dramatic significance of the days through which he was living. A letter he wrote to Sumner the day after South Carolina's secession closed with the words: "Dec. 21, 1860—And of the Disunited States the first day."[4] The crisis, however, was not as painful to Hale as to others; he took secession calmly and thought "the Northwest . . . [would] take charge of the country and make us all keep the peace." In that sense he thought Abe Lincoln "a typical man."

Some were impressed by the head shaking, the "spinal paralysis" of the dominant party, and lamented the "doleful" uncertainty, the business stagnation.[5] At a moment when compromise seemed possible a grandson of William Ellery Channing wrote of the "demoralization of the Republican party" and declared that he felt "summoned to its obsequies." It was "an awful time for merchants," wrote a Bostonian. He saw more than half of them in his city facing ruin and he wished "every member of Congress from the North could keep

---

[1] In this crisis Henry Grinnell of New York City wrote earnestly to a friend insisting that if the South were to remain united with the North Lincoln would have to "renounce and denounce the issue on which he was elected." He added: ". . . if Mr. Crittenton's proposition was submitted to the people of New England it would be carried by a large majority.—People begin to believe that . . . a Slaveholder will be admitted into Heaven." Grinnell to Wm. Gooding, New York, Feb. 1, 1861. MS. (copy) loaned to the author by H. E. Pratt.

[2] S. S. Cox, *Eight Years in Congress*, 206.

[3] Joseph Sargent to Charles Sumner, Worcester, Mass., Dec. 30, 1860, Sumner MSS.

[4] Sumner MSS.   [5] Frank W. Ballard to Sumner, New York, Feb. 6, 1861, *ibid.*

silent." [6] Fearing loss of trade with the South and animated by general sympathy for Southerners, the mayor of New York City made the fantastic suggestion that the metropolis become a "free city," an independent city-state, "with but nominal duty on imports, . . . free from taxes, . . . [with] cheap goods nearly duty free . . . [enjoying] the whole and united support of the Southern States." [7] Again it was urged that the true policy of New York City was to "throw the weight of her influence in favor of a convention of the States." [8] To J. M. Forbes writing from Boston the question of the hour was the tariff. In contradiction to the demand for free trade he wanted "to increase the schedules generally." [9] While some deliberately intensified the quarrel and "feared" compromise, others were for avoiding the slavery question, as when a Philadelphia group cautioned those who addressed them to avoid the topic of slavery and antislavery.[10]

Sumner's correspondents often struck the note of heroics. Firmness was the word. Let there be no flinching. Meet the consequences of Lincoln's election. Compromise was "mean and degrading." The danger was not struggle and war, the senator was told; it was that some miserable compromise would be patched up. Let statesmen be steadfast; the Republican platform was law. It was better that the crisis had come. People should be glad of it. The cause of antislavery was reaching its triumph, its culmination. Friends in Great Britain were looking to us. Let them not be disappointed. Peace should not be preserved by selling out the liberties of the African race. If Seward and Adams bow to slavery, we are come upon evil times. If we are only to be saved by a Crittenden compromise, every dictate of patriotism demands that we perish.[11]

While these heroic demands were heard in some areas, pleas for peace, compromise, and union were no less numerous and their sources no less respectable. From Massachusetts came a petition of more than 22,000 citizens urging Congress to adopt the Crittenden compromise,[12]

---

[6] George G. Channing to Sumner, Brooklyn, Conn., Feb. 6, 1861; George Livermore to Charles Sumner, Boston, Dec. 12, 1860; *ibid.*

[7] McPherson, *Rebellion*, 43.   [8] New York *Herald*, Nov. 17, 1860, p. 4, c. 2.

[9] Forbes to Sumner, Boston, Feb. 2, 1861, Sumner MSS.

[10] W. H. Allen of the People's Literary Institute of Philadelphia, to Sumner, Dec. 17, 1860, *ibid.*

[11] For the material of this paragraph the basis is to be found in the Sumner MSS., vol. 47, items 22, 29, 33, 54, 58; vol. 49, items 4, 17, 22, 51.

[12] C. N. Feamster, *Calendar of the Papers of John Jordan Crittenden*, 248, 256.

and while Sumner claimed that many signed it in ignorance,[13] the Northern voice in favor of adjustment with the South was full and vigorous. Another mammoth petition earnestly demanding compromise came from Pennsylvania, signed by citizens who had voted for Lincoln and Hamlin and who "earnestly desire[d] a prompt adjustment of our National difficulties." [14]

It is a difficult problem to pass judgment on the failure of compromise efforts. Republican leaders have been charged with grave responsibility for this failure. Though they yielded some ground, it is contended that they did not yield enough, and that since theirs was the incoming executive administration, they were "at the center of the problem." [15] But it is to be remembered that the secessionists, who were equally at the center of the problem, did all they could to prevent compromise. In the critical months of the disunion crisis the Republican party was tending toward conservatism; antislavery radicals within the party were out of touch not only with its main emphasis, but also with its management. On close study it becomes evident that in this prewar period the Republican party was only in a very slight degree an antislavery party. On broad racial matters and on state rights Lincoln was closer to the attitude of Southerners than to that of extreme abolitionists. No one formula will serve in dealing with complex questions of sectional tensions, frenzied politics, and party propaganda; nor did it help the situation that bold stands were taken prematurely before even the chances of adjustment had been explored.

A leader clothed with public office cannot be a mere agitator. He must find solutions and in doing so must consider the claims of more than one class or section. Analysis of Lincoln's part in the crisis narrows down to the problem whether a greater emphasis on conciliation, seeing that conciliatory measures were favored by many Republicans, might not have defeated disunion efforts by keeping eight of the fifteen slave states in the Union. Many supposed that, had these eight been kept, a minority of Southern states could not permanently have main-

---

[13] Signers were much offended by the allegation that they signed in ignorance. *Ibid.*, 261.

[14] Papers of the House of Representatives (MSS., Library of Congress), boxes 161 and 162.

[15] D. M. Potter, *Lincoln and His Party in the Secession Crisis*, 60. On this subject of Republicans and compromise, see also pp. 155, 174, and *passim*.

tained their Confederacy. Looking ahead in mid-December, the Chicago *Tribune* declared that the seceding states would desire to return in a few years.[16] If such a thing was possible, then by not keeping the upper South Lincoln bore a heavy responsibility. Such a criticism, however, belongs not to the Rhett-Yancey-Toombs school of thought on one side nor to the Garrison-Phillips school on the other. It is faulty reasoning to assail Lincoln because he did not grant all that the secessionists wanted. He could hardly have been expected to please the Rhetts and Yanceys, nor could even a Southern President of the United States have pleased them. South Carolina was not asking redress nor seeking conciliation. Not the wiping out of causes of complaint, but the playing-up and exaggeration of "grievances" was the game of aggressive cotton-state leaders. Nor could Lincoln have been expected to please Garrison or Phillips at the North, both of whom welcomed disunion.

The criticism that does claim attention is the earnest complaint of the upper South and border, whose people wanted Union and peace as much as did Lincoln. What the people of this area desired was more the fact of compromise than the particular terms that would have nationalized slavery. They wanted adjustment, and they agreed with Lincoln in wanting to defeat the extremists who refused adjustment and wanted discord. In the November-to-March phase these Southern Union men were severely disappointed; in April, as will be seen later, their resentment and the dilemma of actual war was to carry four additional commonwealths all the way out of the Union. Republicans were unskillful in their courting of upper Southern states. They repudiated Sumner and the abolitionists without effectively dramatizing the fact or making the repudiation count in terms of accomplished results. Moderates to the contrary notwithstanding, Lincoln and his party continued to be advertised as Black Republicans and haters of the South.

---

[16] Chicago *Tribune*, Dec. 15, 1860, p. 1, c. 3. This comment was made before any state had seceded. It is one of many examples to show that secession was not taken with the gravity that it deserved. Yet to express apprehension as to dissolution might have been regarded as alarmist and as involving a certain truculence toward the South. Unionists, North and South, were making secession easier.

CHAPTER X

PRESIDENT ELECT

I

IN THE frenzied period between his election and his departure for Washington Lincoln remained continuously at Springfield except for brief visits to Chicago to confer with Hamlin and to Coles County where he visited his stepmother. The governor's office in the Illinois state house had been turned over to him and he kept regular hours there through November and December. As visitors poured in—statesmen, politicians, old friends, newspaper correspondents, office seekers, and casual callers—Lincoln met them with cordial informality. Those who saw him were favorably impressed by his witty conversation and unaffected friendliness, albeit they learned little to allay their concern as to the new leader's position and policy. Lincoln would appear quite early at the governor's office; beginning at ten he would hold a reception till noon, meeting all callers. "Altogether, probably no other President-elect was as approachable for everybody," was the comment of Henry Villard.[1] In the afternoon he was again at his office attending to correspondence with the help of secretaries and meeting men of importance by appointment. "In the evening old friends called at his home for the exchange of news and political views. At times . . . he would go to the telegraph or newspaper offices after supper, and stay there till late."[2]

His mail was "immense." Letters poured in from autograph collectors, place seekers (including some Southerners), anxious citizens, and politicians of many grades.[3] Republican politicians who had labored to defeat him now sought his confidence on the supposition

---

[1] Villard, *Memoirs*, I, 142.   [2] *Ibid.*
[3] New York *Herald*, Nov. 12, 1860, p. 1, c. 3; Nov. 16, p. 1, c. 6; Nov. 17, p. 7, c. 1.

that Lincoln had "forgotten their treachery" and would "accept them as his advisers." [4]

On the most devastating question of the day, the disintegration of the nation by the progress of secession, Lincoln maintained an attitude of such calmness that he was thought by some to be either unaware of the true situation or lacking in policy.[5] Readers of the Chicago *Tribune* were told that Mr. Lincoln "does not . . . believe that any of the States will . . . go off and organize a Confederacy" and further that "Abraham Lincoln and the Republican party will not interfere with the rights of the South." [6] He was reported to have expressed "doubts as to the practicability of holding the Slave States in the Union by main force, if they were all determined to break it up." [7] Up to the time of his departure for Washington, according to Villard, he "did not dream that his principal duty would be to raise great armies and fleets . . . for the suppression of . . . rebellion . . . ." [8] He found abolitionists a constant embarrassment, both because of their importunity and on account of the deliberate misrepresentation of himself as a *"confrere* of Garrison, Phillips, and Company." [9] When these abolitionists called on him it was with a sense of proprietorship and usually with the zeal of an exhorter. In a letter to Charles Sumner written at Springfield, Illinois, on December 3, 1860, Joshua Giddings wrote: "I . . . expect to meet him [Lincoln] today. I shall do what I can to strengthen his faith and nerve him to the business before him." [10]

That Lincoln, while commanding the respect of moderates, did not quite repel and offend antislavery radicals seems now something of a miracle. Perhaps the truth was that even though repelled they sought still to exert influence. The most common comment from abolitionists was an almost savage opposition to compromise. Jubilating over Lincoln's election as "a great . . . victory of Liberty over Slavery, of Freedom over Despotism," an Illinois radical declared: "I do pray . . . that he will make no compromises with the South on the slavery question." [11]

---

[4] *Ibid.*, Nov. 12, 1860, p. 1, c. 3.

[5] "This unusual silence derived not so much from native taciturnity, as from Lincoln's firm conviction that sectional antagonism fed upon discussion . . . , and . . . upon misconstruction of what he had said." Potter, *Lincoln and His Party*, 135.

[6] Nov. 17, 1860, p. 2, c. 1.   [7] Villard, *Memoirs*, I, 145.   [8] *Ibid.*, I, 146.

[9] Chicago *Tribune*, Nov. 26, 1860, p. 2, c. 1.   [10] Sumner MSS., vol. 47, no. 5.

[11] W. Kitchell to Lyman Trumbull, Trumbull MSS., Nov. 28, 1860.

Both Weed and Seward saw Lincoln in this pre-presidential period at Springfield, but their visits were in marked contrast. Seward's was not even a stop-over. Returning from Kansas, he passed through Springfield (October 1) and exchanged a few trivial words with Lincoln who turned up at the station to greet him.[12] He was in Springfield only as long as his train stood there. Concerning this incident a caustic journalist remarked that "the meeting . . . was conventional and formal, as if each was afraid of his own virtue in the presence of the other." [13] Weed paid two visits to Springfield in 1860. The first was on May 24 directly after the Chicago nomination which left the New York manager so disappointed "as to be unable to . . . talk on the subject." [14] This conversation lasted five hours. According to Weed's later account dressed up for public display, its main significance was that Weed admired Lincoln's good sense and left the interview prepared to work "with a will" for his election.[15] It was Gideon Welles's belief, however, that the full story did not appear in these reminiscences and that Weed was "intrusive to impertinence in presenting and pressing his claims." [16] Welles goes on to relate that Lincoln's Illinois friends were at special pains to make friends with the gentleman from New York, that they invited him to visit Springfield after the nomination, and that Weed "greedily availed himself of the courtesy" while postponing his visit until after the first rush from Chicago was over, reaching Springfield by a roundabout course involving a boat trip on the Mississippi. Lincoln made no commitments in the interview, and, contrary to the roseate picture in Weed's memoirs, Welles was of the opinion that the New York politician returned to Albany in "not a very complacent state of mind." [17] All the evidence leads to the supposition that in this period Weed expected, if nothing else, at least to be a kind of patronage dispenser and political manager for the new administration, as he had certainly expected to be in the event of Seward's election.

Weed's second visit to Lincoln, which was the object of a special trip from Albany, coincided with the secession of South Carolina (December 20, 1860). According to his memoirs, which again have the

---

12 P. M. Angle, *Lincoln, 1854–1861*, 353.

13 New York *Herald*, Nov. 12, 1860, p. 4, c. 4.

14 Thurlow Weed, *Autobiography*, 602–603; *Illinois State Register*, May 25, 1860.

15 Weed, *Autobiography*, 603.

16 Welles MS. (postwar recollections), Ill. State Hist. Lib., 12.   17 *Ibid.*, 15.

quality of public rationalization, Weed found Lincoln amusing, quaint, agreeable, and full of anecdotes. He stated specifically that Lincoln did not tell indelicate stories to his knowledge,[18] but Villard, who saw much of him, asserts precisely the contrary.[19] The substantive matters on which Weed and Lincoln conferred were chiefly two: compromise proposals to deal with the sectional crisis, and cabinet-making.[20]

The President Elect's visitors included many other notables: Giddings, Trumbull, Cameron (December 30), Chase (January 4), Bates, Amos Tuck, Francis P. Blair, Jr., Browning, Judd, William Kellogg, David Wilmot, George Opdyke, Hiram Barney, Judge Hogeboom, M. Romero (Mexican minister), and Horace Greeley. Sometimes Lincoln would call on such men at their hotels; at other times they would meet him in his home or state-house office.[21] While the new leader was secretive as to his plans the identity of his visitors could not be concealed, and journalists, as at present, spun out their stories accordingly. Rumors and guesses clustered round these interviews, and special emphasis was placed upon those visitors who came upon Lincoln's invitation, such as Chase and Bates. Some of the visitors wore homespun as in the case of an old man from Mississippi who was given an interview and expressed the wish that every Southerner could talk face to face with the President Elect.[22] "Offensively democratic exhibitions of free manners occur every once in a while," wrote the *Herald* reporter. "Churlish fellows will obtrude themselves with their hats on, lighted segars and . . . pantaloons tucked into their boots. Dropping into chairs, they will sit puffing away and trying to gorgonize the President with their silent stares, until their boorish curiosity is . . . satisfied." [23]

In the harassment and strain of a cruelly difficult position these visitors found a man who displayed little showmanship and lacked

---

[18] Weed, *Autobiography*, 605, 611–612.   [19] Villard, *Memoirs*, I, 143–144.

[20] "You know that Mr. Weed has been at Springfield. I can state positively, that, in the only two interviews he held with Mr. Lincoln, a third person was present at the request of Mr. L. That third person is here, & I think I can hardly be mistaken in saying that one of those interviews was . . . devoted to . . . the slavery question, . . . compromises, &c, . . . that the other was devoted to talking about men, offices, &c., . . . [and] that his [Weed's] line of remark drifted . . . towards Seward & Cameron." H. B. Stanton to S. P. Chase, Jan. 7, 1861, Chase MSS., Lib. of Cong.

[21] Angle, "*Here I Have Lived,*" 257.

[22] Angle, *Lincoln 1854–1861*, 366.   [23] New York *Herald*, Nov. 22, 1860, p. 3, c. 4.

dramatic exuberance but who kept an even keel and exhibited outward calm, often illuminated by flashes of prairie humor. Gloom and
sadness characterized his features as he "perceived . . . the danger of
the situation," but in spite of this, when in company, he was "as jovial
and . . . droll as usual." [24] "Of Mr. Lincoln the politician," wrote
an interviewer, "I say nothing; but Lincoln, the man, I was delighted
with." [25] Lincoln's reticence in this period was counted a virtue. "The
singularly small amount of self-revelation that he has given since his
nomination" was mentioned as "one of the best . . . indications." [26]
This democracy of manner stayed with Lincoln after he left Springfield and there was comment on the "perfect identity, in all his broad,
shrewd, western rusticity of style between President Lincoln and good
Neighbor Lincoln of Springfield aforetime." It was felt that his new
importance made "not the slightest impression on his nerves, proving
that the great office [was] not too much for him." [27] From *The Times*
in London came the comment that "Mr. Lincoln can do anything he
sets his mind to, partly from natural pliability, partly by an immense
power of fixing his attention on whatever is before him." [28]

Young Henry Villard, perhaps because he was employed by the
New York *Herald,* found the Illinois leader in many ways unsatisfactory. He disliked what he called his coarse "license" in telling stories
and confessed a feeling of "disgust" and "humiliation" toward a man
whom he was far from worshiping as hero. "I could not have persuaded myself [he wrote] that the man might possibly possess true
greatness." [29] Earlier he had been "no great admirer of the Republican
standard-bearer" though he had desired his election. This same observer wrote of Mrs. Lincoln as imprudently taking presents from
office seekers.[30] "She does not appear to realize [said the *Herald* writer]
that she has been elected to preside at the White House the next four
years." [31]

---

[24] Gustave Koerner, *Memoirs,* II, 116.
[25] Chicago *Tribune,* Dec. 17, 1860, p. 1, c. 2.
[26] New York *Sun* as quoted in *Weekly Illinois State Journal,* Feb. 27, 1861.
[27] *Ibid.*   [28] Quoted in Chicago *Tribune,* Dec. 19, 1860, p. 2, c. 5.
[29] Villard, *Memoirs,* I, 144.   [30] *Ibid.,* I, 138, 148.
[31] New York *Herald,* Nov. 16, 1860, p. 1, c. 6.

II

As Lincoln read the papers and viewed the national scene he witnessed an ominous succession of events. The January pace was so rapid that early February presented a picture startlingly different from that of late December. Sometimes a little thing contained the whole picture, as when a Charleston bookseller returned his package of *Harper's Weekly* because it contained a picture of the President Elect.[1] Some days later in the same city every Episcopal clergyman omitted the usual prayer for the President of the United States. As one fort after another fell into the hands of secessionist authorities, attention was centered upon "incidents" at Charleston where ominous rumblings followed the removal of the Federal garrison (December 26) from Fort Moultrie to Fort Sumter, and where a United States merchant vessel carrying military supplies and troops was fired upon with no formality of hostilities and without producing war (January 9). Shortly afterward Colonel Hayne of South Carolina called on the President of the United States and demanded (unsuccessfully) the "unconditional withdrawal" of the Sumter garrison.[2]

Whether such happenings were only "brag and bluster" as Edward Bates thought [3] or whether they meant the collapse of the nation he was called to lead, was a matter to give Lincoln pause. There were, it is true, other developments which seemed calculated to check secession and keep the road to compromise open. In the upper South Lincoln noted that the people voted against secession in Arkansas, Tennessee, and Missouri,[4] and that moderates were keeping the helm in Kentucky and Virginia. Through February the upper South and border were resisting the secession fever and efforts toward adjustment continued to be pushed at Washington where the Virginia-inspired Peace Convention, with Lincoln's friend Stephen T. Logan as an Illinois member, gave evidence that the desire for Union was not dead in the South. Those favorable to Union could also point to the stiffening of Buchanan and his cabinet as above noted, to Southern antisecession editorials, to the heartening attitude of Douglas, to popular Union demonstrations in the South, and to the refusal of the Mary-

---

[1] Chicago *Tribune*, Nov. 20, 1860, p. 1, c. 2.   [2] *Ibid.*, January 18, 1861, p. 4, c. 4.
[3] Bates, *Diary*, 157.   [4] Randall, *Civil War and Reconstruction*, 251, 253, 326.

land governor to receive a pro-secession commissioner from Mississippi.[5]

Throughout these days it was easy for Republicans to believe the
worst of Buchanan and it was even rumored in December that the
outgoing administration was using the whole power of the Federal
government to fill the South with arms and munitions.[6] It became
a stereotype of the period to attribute the blackest treachery in this
respect to the Southern secretary of war, John B. Floyd of Virginia,
but altogether aside from the alleged action of Floyd there was the
undeniable fact that Northern individuals and firms were contributing
in these anxious weeks to the military preparation of the South. Not
only were Jefferson Davis's emissaries successful in obtaining a great
variety of war supplies in Northern factories in this February-March
period, but even Kentucky, which never joined the Confederacy, was
busy arming itself in an anti-Lincoln sense. Simon B. Buckner, later
a Confederate general, wrote in March 1861 of a trip from Louisville
to New York via St. Louis "to attend to our arms." He told of "ship-
ments every week," indicating that he could be addressed in care
of General A. E. Burnside at the office of the Illinois Central Railroad Company, New York City.[7] If he looked westward Lincoln had
also to consider wild doings in Kansas where even Republicans found
it necessary to denounce "Free State men" who were invading Missouri
in as brutal a manner as any border ruffians.[8] This was the period of
James H. Lane and his "jayhawkers." Taking advantage of the turbulent conditions of the time, some of the free-state Kansans took their
own revenge upon Missourians for their hostility in border-ruffian
days. It was an ugly kind of irregular or private war, and it tended to
reflect discredit upon Lincoln's party by reason of the tendency to
associate the Republicans with everything that pertained to John-
Brownism and kindred tactics in Kansas and Missouri.[9]

The question of Southern military preparation thrust upon Lincoln
the trying problem of what announcements to make and what arrange-

[5] Moore, *Rebellion Record* (Diary), I, 3.

[6] Chicago *Tribune*, Dec. 29, 1860, p. 2, c. 1.

[7] Buckner to Magoffin, Mar. 8, 1861, MS., Ill. State Hist. Lib.

[8] Chicago *Tribune*, Nov. 26, 1860, p. 2, c. 1.

[9] For the jayhawkers see Hildegarde Rose Herklotz, "Jayhawkers in Missouri, 1858–
1863," *Mo. Hist. Rev.*, XVII and XVIII (1922–1923). For John Hay's reference to jayhawkers appearing among early volunteer fighters in Washington (April 18, 1861), see
Tyler Dennett, ed., *Lincoln and the Civil War in the Diaries and Letters of John Hay*, 1.

ments to promote for the maintenance of the government's authority. These questions were everywhere asked. Occasionally they were embarrassingly answered by a self-appointed Lincoln "spokesman." On the other hand it became a stock argument with a certain type of Southern editor to predict what Lincoln would do, as when the Richmond *Enquirer* pictured the day, soon to come, when Lincoln's "free-soil mirmidons" would be conveyed by Northern ships through Hampton Roads so that they could run off slaves, pillage the country, and insult the state of Virginia.

In this overwrought period even a gesture toward Federal military preparedness, if traced to Lincoln, would inevitably have been denounced and distorted by Southern extremists. Shortly after his election Lincoln received a statement of "views" from the head of the army, General Winfield Scott, which he answered with a noncommittal but respectful compliment to the "distinguished . . . military captain." [10] On November 20 he referred to "all American citizens" as "brothers of a common country." [11] On December 21, the day after South Carolina's secession, he indirectly sent his respects to General Scott with the confidential request to be "prepared . . . to either hold or retake the forts, as the case may require, at and after the inauguration." [12] In January he was similarly complimentary, cautious, and noncommittal in his correspondence with Scott, and on January 14 he wrote to General Wool with equal caution indicating that he had given "little attention to the military department of government" and saying that he would have to rely upon Scott and Wool for advice as to "how far the military force of the government may become necessary to the preservation of the Union, and more particularly how that force can best be directed to the object." [13] In all this he restrained himself from truculent declarations that would inflame Southern feeling while prudently leaving the way clear for a proper defense of Federal authority. The truth was that the manner of meeting the South Carolinian and later the lower Southern challenge was a problem of the utmost difficulty in which the processes to be chosen would have to be worked out after inauguration and after existing peace efforts had been allowed to develop.

---

10 *Works*, VI, 68 (Nov. 9, 1860).   11 *Ibid.*, VI, 72.
12 *Ibid.*, VI, 84–85.   13 *Ibid.*, VI, 92–93, 98.

III

Of the two trips which Lincoln made outside Springfield in the pre-presidential interval the first was political and the other intimately personal. On November 21, 1860, he took train at Springfield in the presence of a large crowd and proceeded to Chicago for a conference with Hannibal Hamlin. Mrs. Lincoln accompanied him and Senator Trumbull was also in the party. Lincoln was dodging ovations and avoiding speech-making for reasons already noted, and just before his departure he had disappointed Republican jollifiers by refusing to speak at their grand celebration. The train stopped at Lincoln and Bloomington; at each place Lincoln made a brief platform appearance, giving a sentence or two of greeting. Dealing only in generalities, these remarks were those of a leader who had decided to make no speeches but who could not refuse the courtesy of greeting friends and expressing appreciation. At Bloomington he stepped out on the platform of his car and thanked the people of "Old McLean" (County) for their part in placing him in his present position, declaring that the people will do well when they are well done by and that it was his intention to "do well by the people." Retiring into the car amid cheers he shook hands with acquaintances, while Trumbull added a few remarks, commending the people for supporting the "whole Republican ticket." [1]

At Chicago Lincoln discussed cabinet matters with Vice President Elect Hamlin, visited the Republican wigwam and other buildings, and held a reception which occupied the morning of November 23. He attended church in company with Isaac N. Arnold, spoke briefly at a mission Sabbath school, and spent an uneventful rainy day on the return to Springfield.[2] Real business had been transacted, for shortly after this Hamlin confidentially quoted Lincoln as saying that Gideon Welles's appointment to the cabinet was more probable than that of any other New Englander.[3] In this consultation Lincoln conferred upon Hamlin a unique distinction. In the case of no other

---

[1] Bloomington (Ill.) *Pantagraph*, Nov. 22, 1860, p. 3, c. 2.

[2] Typical reporters' accounts of Lincoln's Chicago trip are to be found in the Chicago *Tribune*, Chicago *Journal*, and New York *Herald*, November 22-27, 1860. For summaries see Angle, *Lincoln, 1854-1861*, 360-361; Charles E. Hamlin, *Life . . . of Hannibal Hamlin*, 366-375; Baringer, *A House Dividing*, 76-90.

[3] James Dixon to Welles, Dec. 3, 1860, Welles MSS.

statesman did he make a trip for the purpose of an interview while President Elect.

At the end of January Lincoln made an arduous two-day trip via Charleston, Illinois, to a remote spot in Coles County to see his aged stepmother, Sarah Bush Johnston Lincoln, widow of Thomas Lincoln. Besides the rail trip to Charleston there was a ten-mile rural drive which even then stopped short of the Thomas Lincoln cabin, for the more accessible frame house of a neighbor, with a convenient location on the highway, had been placed at Lincoln's disposal. Among the reminiscences pertaining to this occasion is that of James A. Connolly, a Charleston lawyer who stated that Lincoln missed the regular passenger train at Mattoon where a change of cars was necessary and arrived a number of hours later on a freight caboose. Those who met Lincoln at Charleston had a long wait. "Presently," said Connolly, "we saw a tall man . . . make his way through the long expanse of slush and ice beside the track . . . . [Q]uite a crowd of natives were gathered on the platform to see him. I confess I was not favorably impressed." In this bit of reminiscence we have glimpses of Lincoln dropping formality and addressing his old friend A. P. Dunbar as "Aleck," spinning out backwoods stories, delighting those who chatted with him, but disappointing some who merely glimpsed his "awkward, if not ungainly figure." [4] Herndon records that on this visit, besides seeing his stepmother, Lincoln met members of the Johnston and Hanks families, visited his father's grave, gave directions for a suitable stone marker, and made a brief public address at Charleston.[5] If fully recorded the episode would offer a picturesquely quaint and pathetic incident in Lincoln's personal life. There was drama in the homespun rusticity of the surroundings, the informality of the President Elect, the painful lowliness of relatives contrasted with the distinction of the illustrious son, and the genuine affection of Sarah Lincoln for the boy of whom she had seen little in thirty years. It was characteristic of Lincoln and of the time that the deep human interest of the visit was not played up in public print.

---

[4] Jesse W. Weik, *The Real Lincoln: A Portrait,* 294–297.
[5] Herndon (Angle ed.), 387–388.

IV

A necessary labor for every President Elect is the selection of a cabinet, and for many a chief this problem offers a bewildering and unpleasant eye-opener to the ambitions and tricks of politicians. In the case of Lincoln a please-all cabinet would have been an amazing thing. It would have recognized every section, comprised diverse elements of the winning though minority party, embraced opposites who refused to fraternize, allowed no place to an endorser of Helper's *Impending Crisis*,[1] included Democrats and Southerners along with New Englanders and abolitionists, contained no more than one from a state while pleasing quarreling factions within states, and, as a kind of afterthought, would have assigned to each post a man adapted by training and experience to its duties. To be "ideal" the cabinet would have to offend no politician, editor, or party worker, and lose no votes in coming elections. To do as much of this as possible within the limits of a seven-man ministry, to choose the manner of doing it so as to avoid premature leaks and embarrassing complaints, and after doing it to soothe the feelings of the disappointed, was an assignment that would have taxed Lincoln's utmost skill even if he had been as "consummate" a "politician" as some have supposed.

Two weeks after the election a writer in the New York *Herald* published his prediction of the new cabinet in which every one of the seven guesses was wrong. The following was the *Herald's* list: Secretary of State, John McLean of Ohio; Secretary of the Treasury, William L. Dayton of New Jersey; Postmaster General, Fitz-Henry Warren of Iowa; Secretary of War, Cassius M. Clay of Kentucky; Secretary of the Navy, Emerson Etheridge of Tennessee; Secretary of the Interior, Galusha A. Grow of Pennsylvania; Attorney General, Henry Winter Davis of Maryland.[2] Had Lincoln justified this prediction he would have been defended by a sufficiently belligerent minister of war, but he would have had a decrepit secretary of state, an inland secretary of the navy, and a ferocious hater of the South as attorney general. He would have had no one from New York nor New England, and nearly half his advisers would have come from south of the Mason and Dixon line.

---

[1] New York *Herald*, Nov. 17, 1860, p. 6, c. 6.   [2] *Ibid.*, Nov. 20, 1860, p. 1, c. 6.

That he was hounded almost to distraction by this cabinet problem was suggested by his own statement that he deferred the final selection as long as possible "to avoid being teased to insanity to make changes." [3] When asked for public statements on cabinet questions he would usually evade the issue, sometimes with a quirk about cabinet-making of the saw-and-hammer variety, sometimes with a solemn platitude. An example of the latter was a statement quoted by the Chicago *Tribune* as follows: "Gentlemen, in the formation of my Cabinet, I shall aim as nearly as possible at perfection. Any man whom I may appoint . . . must be, as far as possible, like Caesar's wife, pure and above suspicion, of unblemished reputation, and undoubted integrity." [4] The search for such paragons, however, was not easy, for, as he is reported to have said, "while the population of the country had immensely increased, really great men were scarcer than they used to be." [5]

It has been noted in a former chapter how Lincoln was not uninfluenced by agreements in the party convention of 1860 which have been construed as promises of cabinet appointments to Simon Cameron of Pennsylvania and Caleb B. Smith of Indiana. [6] In addition to these obligations, he had so profited by the friendliness of certain men that they may naturally have thought they had claims upon his favorable consideration. Among such were Gideon Welles of Connecticut, Montgomery Blair of Maryland, and Cassius Clay of Kentucky. Thus the bestowal of rewards for party service for which the successful candidate had reason to be personally grateful was a potent, though unwelcome, element in Lincoln's choice.

But these "conditions . . . fairly implied" [7] were only the beginning of Lincoln's worries. The very nature of his party, precarious, unrepresentative of the whole nation, never before victorious in a presidential election, presented complications. Already it was a party of factions, and these factions cut deep into practical Republican affairs in every important state. [8]

---

[3] This statement was in a letter to Seward, January 12, 1861. In the same letter Lincoln said he expected trouble "with every other Northern cabinet appointment," politely making an exception in the case of Seward himself. *Works*, VI, 94–95.

[4] Chicago *Tribune*, Feb. 7, 1861, p. 1, c. 2.   [5] Weed. *Autobiography*, 606.

[6] See above, pp. 169–170.   [7] Lincoln's own words; see above, p. 170.

[8] See vol. II, 222–223.

V

Nor were the factions merely intrastate. The severe antipathies between the Seward element and the Chase element, and between Seward and Welles, related precisely to those problems of broad national policy that were to become the peculiar harassment of the incoming administration. To all this was added the task of recognizing Southerners in a "black Republican" cabinet while keeping due regard for other sections, especially New England, whose claims were natural enough but whose chances of genuinely agreeing on a selection were slight. It was not merely a question of "a New England member" but *what* New England member, and so on throughout the country. Cabinet positions meant power. To politicians they meant plums. By many they were regarded as doors to patronage.[1] The question of a man's special fitness for a particular job in governmental administration was exceedingly difficult to work into the cabinet-making pattern; it was a subordinate factor in Lincoln's actual selection.

The New York situation, which was tied in with the national situation, was perhaps the point of departure, and it was one of the thorniest of Lincoln's problems. As Whig overlord and later as Republican "boss," Thurlow Weed had built up a powerful machine but had covered himself with discredit because of alleged "corruption at Albany during the last session of the legislature, in which many Republicans were implicated."[2] No account of the politics of this period would be complete without mention of "agents of vested wealth" (influential in both parties), the "lobby," "railroad and canal interests," and many a party manipulation behind the scenes.[3] Seward had benefited over the years by the support of Weed who has been called his Warwick.[4] The New York statesman's commanding position in the party, together with the almost pathetic grief of "Weed, Seward, & Co." at the May nomination, made it virtually imperative to choose him. Once that decision was faced, however, the incoming President

---

[1] ". . . Mr. [W. C.] Noyes expressed the opinion that Seward did not desire to go into the Cabinet unless he could control the patronage and thus serve his friends." White, *Trumbull*, 140.

[2] *Ibid.*, 140.

[3] P. G. Auchampaugh in A. C. Flick, ed., *History of the State of New York*, VII, 65.

[4] "While Seward sounded high idealism at Washington, Weed stoked the . . . fires at home." *Ibid.*

was confronted with two stubborn facts: the opposition of a high-minded New York element to such a choice, and the dislike of many Republicans outside New York to Seward himself [5] and even more to the prospect of Weed in "control" at Washington. For Weed was first and last a politician and thought in terms of control and intrigue. Those under his lead—"robbers" they were called by their critics—were said to hate Lincoln, while at the same time they planned to use him as a fulcrum for efforts at patronage control.[6] It was customary for such managers as Weed to draw upon the metropolitan police force and custom house of New York City (involving hundreds of appointments) for delegates to party conventions, the purpose being to keep such conventions in the hands of boss and machine. Weed was reported to be connected with "schemes of plunder" involving the national government,[7] and opposition to such tactics caused an indignant New York official to declare that "no human power . . . [could] make a majority of the electors of this state *bow* down to the corruption of the Weed dynasty."[8] From the same source we have a description of Weed's methods as embracing control of party primaries throughout the state, "assessments upon candidates and incumbents seeking and holding office," and the mustering of a "horde of political pensioners . . . which he has quartered upon our party" by which "every wish of the better portion" of the party had been "defeated."[9]

Friends of Seward were, as Gideon Welles saw them, "very officious in giving advice" and at the same time "vehemently opposed" to Mr. Chase,[10] who held as important a place in Lincoln's cabinet plans as did Seward. Their insistent advice to Lincoln covered much of the whole cabinet field. Besides opposing Chase they objected to Blair, sought to exclude Welles, and were ready with selections for the New England secretary.[11]

The effort of Weed to reach far beyond New York was certainly a factor with which Lincoln had to contend; it was thought that with Chase out and Seward in, the New York member would have "little

---

[5] Francis P. Blair, Sr. considered Seward a nightmare to the administration, and John A. Andrew shared this antipathy. Blair to Bigelow, Oct. 26, 1861, Blair MSS.; Andrew to Montgomery Blair, May 28, 1866, *ibid.*

[6] A. G. Tillinghast to S. P. Chase, June 18, 1862, Chase MSS., Lib. of Cong.

[7] John Jay to S. P. Chase, May 3, 1861, *ibid.*

[8] R. Campbell to S. P. Chase, Apr. 8, 1861, *ibid.*

[9] R. Campbell to S. P. Chase, Mar. 27, 1861, *ibid.*

[10] Welles MS. (postwar recollections), Ill. State Hist. Lib., 6.   [11] *Ibid.*, 10.

difficulty in shaping the policies of the Administration." [12] One of
Weed's intrigues was a kind of Seward-Cameron deal behind Lincoln's
back. Illinois friends of Lincoln, especially David Davis and Leonard
Swett, considering Weed a big man and realizing his bitterness at the
Chicago outcome, had joined with Weed and some gentlemen from
Pennsylvania in a meeting at Saratoga in the summer of 1860 at which
it was said to have been "arranged" that Seward should have the state
department and Cameron the treasury. [13]

Such maneuvers have their significance in the development of Lincoln's personality. There were efforts to get him, while President
Elect, to go to Auburn and confer with Seward in his home. Had he
gone it would have been a good deal like launching his administration with Seward and Weed in command. But, as Welles relates, Lincoln "knew too much of the proprieties of his position . . . to put
himself in the keeping of any man or men." [14] It was after Lincoln's
refusal to come to Auburn that Weed made his December visit to
Springfield with its disappointing results in terms of large control.
The difference between Lincoln going to Auburn and Weed coming
to Springfield was considerable. Under trying circumstances the new
and untried leader had made a real decision. He had taken on Seward,
though with more reluctance than is generally realized, [15] but, in the
matter of unofficial advisers, he had virtually refused to take on Weed.

VI

At the outset of his cabinet studies Lincoln had reached the decision
that Salmon P. Chase ought to be included. The appointment of the
Ohio leader would put into the cabinet an able administrator, a former
Democrat who was also a member of the "Old Liberty Guard" (i. e., a
leader of the Liberty party), an antislavery man untainted with abolitionist excess, and a rival for the nomination. Joshua Leavitt considered that the great danger of the Republican party was that it was
"alleged to be nothing but an elongation of the Whig party" with
the dismal prospect of sharing Whig fate. [1] That some of the cabinet
should have non-Whig antecedents was thus desirable. Chase went
to Springfield on Lincoln's invitation and Lincoln paid him the cour-

---

[12] *Ibid.*, 16.   [13] *Ibid.*, 15.   [14] *Ibid.*, 18.
[15] For a fuller discussion of this subject, see Baringer, *A House Dividing*, 87, 135 ff.
[1] Joshua Leavitt to S. P. Chase, Jan. 19, 1861, Chase MSS., Lib. of Cong.

tesy of calling at his hotel.[2] It was predicted by the *Herald* that Chase
would be offered the foreign office, but on January 7 Lincoln wrote
that in his opinion it was a *"necessity"* that Chase should take the
treasury.[3] Chase's own comments on the matter of a cabinet appointment were in his usual tone which was that of an unwilling recipient
of public office. Stating that Lincoln had talked over with him the question of the treasury appointment, Chase wrote to a friend: ". . . if
he . . . thinks I ought to take it (which I hope will not be the case)
I shall consider the offer with an anxious wish to do whatever may be
. . . best for the general interest." [4]

The Weed faction made a determined effort to eliminate Chase and
in particular they were anxious to exclude him from the treasury department which they wanted for Cameron. The most important factor, however, was that radicals were rallying to the Chase standard
and to their way of thinking the Weed opposition was a very good
reason for including him. The fact of having made the choice served
at the start as a salutary example of independence from Weed domination. Among those who took delight in the Chase appointment was
Horace Greeley who wrote that it took a desperate and intense fight
to achieve the appointment of "the ablest Republican living, who
(so Gen. Dix said) was almost indispensable to the treasury, . . ." [5] It
was not until shortly after Lincoln's inauguration that Chase's appointment was officially made and unanimously confirmed. In resigning
his senatorship Chase continued the role of reluctant acceptance, writing the governor of Ohio that he would have preferred to remain where
the people of his state had placed him.[6]

For the New England member various men were suggested. The
Weed element favored Charles Francis Adams, John A. Andrew,
N. P. Banks, Amos Tuck, or J. P. Hale, while objecting strongly to
Welles of Connecticut because they preferred not to see too much
recognition of the former Democratic element of the party.[7] Welles
attributed his success with Lincoln largely to the efforts of N. P. Banks,
Senator Dixon, and Preston King, who worked against the "Albany

2 Chase arrived in Springfield on January 4, 1861. Angle, *Lincoln, 1854–1861*, 366;
Schuckers, *Chase*, 201.

3 Lincoln's italics. Tracy, *Uncollected Letters*, 174.

4 Chase to G. W. Julian, Jan. 16, 1861, Giddings-Julian MSS.

5 Greeley to B. Brockway, Mar. 12, 1861, Greeley MSS., Lib. of Cong.

6 Schuckers, *Chase*, 207–208.

7 Welles MS. (postwar recollections), Ill. State Hist. Lib., 10.

clique" and the "intense partisanship" of Seward.[8] New England's importance in shipping made it appropriate to give the naval secretaryship to that region.

Welles believed that he had been the first in Lincoln's thoughts for this appointment, but George S. Boutwell reported otherwise. He records an interview with Lincoln about the time of his inauguration in which the President was said to have told him that had Banks remained in New England instead of moving to Chicago, "there would have been no second man thought of," that Banks's name "was in the first list that he ever made," but that removal from the state "put it out of his power to do what he should otherwise . . . have done without a suggestion from any one."[9] In this piece of cabinet making Lincoln gracefully allowed Hamlin to take a part, thus recognizing a species of "custom" that the Vice President, too likely to be a cipher, should have the chance of naming one cabinet member. Lincoln's conference with Hamlin in Chicago, the only one of its kind, was devoted to this subject. Before selecting Welles Lincoln made sure of his position on the fugitive-slave matter; in this he recognized that cabinet members ought to be in agreement with the President on matters of policy and that to the public his choice of advisers was sure to be regarded as a barometer of his future course as President.[10]

The choice of Edward Bates of Missouri caused little difficulty. In this bearded elder statesman it was recognized that the claims of regional recognition, presidential rivalry, individual worth, and personal agreeableness were united in one person. Bates was, perhaps, more similar to Lincoln in his general approach to public questions than any other member of the cabinet. Born in Virginia, he had carried into Missouri "many of the traditions of Virginia planterdom."[11] His Missouri career had been that of a conservative antislavery Whig whose legal aptitude had been particularly apparent. Though associated with the Republican party he was "never an orthodox Republican."[12] Like Lincoln he admired both Jefferson and Clay, pursued a moderate course, and regarded slavery as chiefly

8 *Ibid.*, 22. 24.

9 G. S. Boutwell to N. P. Banks, Boston, Mar. 8, 1861, Banks MSS.

10 See above, p. 235.

11 Howard K. Beale, ed., *Diary of Edward Bates, 1859–1866 (Annual Report,* Amer. Hist. Assoc., 1930), xi.

12 *Ibid.,* xii.

a state matter. Also like Lincoln he opposed slavery in the territories. On the crisis of the day he vigorously opposed secession and favored a strong policy for the suppression of any revolt against the government. He considered Southern politicians and newspapers "absolutely demented" and wrote caustic comments in his diary denouncing South Carolina for her "preposterous egotism" and her intention to "drag down into the pit . . . the *Cotton States* at least, if not all the *South.*" [13]

At first, though this was quite unusual, Lincoln offered to go to St. Louis to see Bates, but the latter felt it to be more fitting for him to come to Springfield, which he did on two occasions. On December 15 he had two long conversations with the new chief, with the result that Lincoln offered and Bates accepted a cabinet appointment, with a kind of understanding that it would probably be the attorney-generalship, though if a certain difficulty were out of the way, meaning Seward, it would have been the state department. [14] Being fully determined, even to the point of permitting public announcement, Lincoln arranged to have "a little editorial appear" in the *Missouri Democrat* saying that Bates would be offered a place in the cabinet. [15] Two weeks later, being summoned by telegraph, Bates turned up again at Springfield where he found himself in company with "General" Cameron in whose room he talked with Lincoln for two hours on the night of December 30, while on the next day he had two long conversations with the President Elect. In these conversations, of which we have only hints, Lincoln showed his "liberality," his friendliness toward the South, and withal his difficulties in the cabinet problem. [16] Until shortly before inauguration Lincoln withheld a definite statement as to the particular office Bates should fill; thus it came about that military men were pressing to have him made secretary of war. [17] By making him attorney general Lincoln chose a conservative legal adviser indisposed to push the enforcement of severe wartime laws. He thus gave a mild tone to those executive functions that have to do with the preparation and conduct of prosecutions in the courts.

---

[13] *Ibid.,* 162.   [14] *Ibid.,* 164–165.

[15] *Works,* VI, 83 (Dec. 18, 1860). The *Missouri Democrat,* published at St. Louis, was a Republican newspaper of the radical type.

[16] Bates, *Diary,* 170–171.

[17] F. P. Blair, Jr., to Montgomery Blair, Feb. 12, 1861, Blair MSS.

VII

Bates had shown a modest willingness to "relieve" the new President by withdrawing if that should seem desirable.[1] This was in vivid contrast to the greed of Cameron in ignoring an out-and-out request of Lincoln to withdraw from the picture. Most of the comments that have come down to us have been unfavorable to this Pennsylvania leader. Trumbull considered him "a trading, unscrupulous politician," a "manager" interested in "schemes," who had "not the confidence of our best men."[2] Welles stated that he had "no . . . devotion . . . to political principles of any kind" and did not command the full support of his own state.[3] He has been described as a politician interested chiefly in a "smooth-running party machine" for which object he used methods that were "often circuitous," building up a "patronage" that amounted to "political despotism."[4] For a time he had been a Democrat; later for "political" reasons he became a Republican, but it was remarked that he "had not . . . zealously espoused the . . . republican ticket."[5] Always he had been involved in factional politics; there was a Pennsylvania "cabal" both *pro* and *contra* Cameron.[6] His keenness in party dickering together with his espousal of a protective tariff served to explain his influence in Republican circles.[7]

By the Chicago "bargain" and the Saratoga arrangement Cameron was slated for the cabinet, but a remarkable series of developments ensued before the final selection. It was evident that Cameron was all mixed up with the Seward-Weed connection, so that if Lincoln made the appointment he would offend some of the best men of his party, who opposed both Cameron and Seward.[8] It was through David Davis, Lincoln's manager, that a cabinet post had been offered to Cameron,[9]

---

[1] "Seeing Mr. L[incoln]'s difficulties . . . I told him . . . I was ready to relieve him . . . and that if he could fill the places without me, it would be a relief rather than a disappointment. He answered promptly—'No . . . —that State [stake?] cant [sic] be pulled up.'" Bates, *Diary*, 172 (Dec. 31, 1860).

[2] White, *Trumbull*, 146.

[3] Welles MS. (postwar reminiscences), Ill. State Hist. Lib., 17.

[4] A. Howard Meneely, *The War Department, 1861*, 82–83. According to Blaine his field was that of a "party manager" in which he was an "indefatigable worker." Blaine, *Twenty Years*, I, 196.

[5] Welles MS. (above cited), 17.   [6] Villard, *Memoirs*, I, 147.

[7] For Lincoln's cautious treatment of the tariff question, see below, pp. 280–282.

[8] White, *Trumbull*, 146–147.   [9] *Ibid.*, 142.

but trouble was encountered with the new chief when it came to fulfillment of the promise. Lincoln was reluctant to have Cameron come to Springfield, but an invitation was arranged, says Horace White, through Davis and his *"Fidus Achates,"* Leonard Swett.[10] Cameron turned up inevitably in Springfield, Davis and Swett put on the pressure, and Lincoln with obvious reluctance sent the Pennsylvanian a brief note (December 31) promising him either the treasury or the war portfolio.[11] Willy-nilly, Lincoln was thus partly caught in the Chicago-Saratoga net.[12]

It became known that the appointment was promised and the knowledge produced a shock and a storm in Pennsylvania and elsewhere. From Washington H. B. Stanton, husband of Elizabeth Cady, wrote: "The strongest protests have gone from here, & from Pennsylvania, to Mr. Lincoln, against Mr. Cameron being called to the Treasury. Senators . . . have written most pointedly to that effect. So have Representatives, & others." [13] Lincoln was soon aware that the Cameron selection was anathema to such men as Trumbull, A. K. McClure, A. G. Curtin, W. C. Bryant, Preston King, Horace Greeley, Ebenezer Peck, Gustave Koerner, N. B. Judd, S. P. Chase, David Dudley Field, and Hiram Barney.[14] Accounts of Cameron's alleged corruption reappeared in the papers, and so great a stir was produced that it was thought necessary to keep Cameron from the treasury if the party was to be saved from ruin. In the correspondence of the time there was indignant denunciation of the "Cameron and Weed gang," while the choosing of the Pennsylvanian was referred to as an "error," a "calamity," and an occasion for "urgent protest." [15] "If Lincoln do appoint Cameron he gets a fight on his hands," wrote William H. Herndon, "and if he do not he gets a quarrel deep . . . & lasting. . . . Poor Lincoln. God help him." [16] At this time Lincoln is said to have told his old friend William Butler that the Cameron affair had given him

---

[10] *Ibid.,* 144.   [11] *Works,* VI, 90.

[12] Welles ". . . always understood that Mr. Lincoln became committed to this [Weed-Seward] scheme in a measure, though it was unlike him." Welles, *Diary,* II, 389–390.

[13] H. B. Stanton to S. P. Chase, Jan. 7, 1861, Chase MSS., Lib. of Cong.

[14] Harry E. Pratt, "Simon Cameron's Fight for a Place in Lincoln's Cabinet," in *Bulletin No. 49,* Abr. Lincoln Assoc., 6–7 (Sep., 1937); White, *Trumbull,* 147–148.

[15] White, *Trumbull,* 147–148; E. B. Washburne to S. P. Chase, Jan. 10, 1861, Chase MSS., Lib. of Cong.

[16] William H. Herndon to Trumbull, Jan. 27, 1861, Trumbull MSS.

"more trouble than anything . . . he had yet encountered." [17]

Lincoln was so impressed with the arousing of public conscience and with the quality and extent of the opposition to Cameron that he reconsidered his offer. On January 3 he wrote to Cameron that "things had developed" which would make it "impossible" to take him into the cabinet. An interview at Springfield with A. K. McClure of the anti-Cameron faction in Pennsylvania was one of the factors in this decision, but the "more potent matter" was outside Pennsylvania. Lincoln bluntly suggested that Cameron write him "declining the appointment," adding the further request that he do it "at once," signifying such intention by telegraph "instantly." [18] Shortly after this E. B. Washburne wrote to Chase that "Lincoln's administration is likely to escape a great calamity." Cameron, he said, "will *not* have a place in the cabinet, either by his declining the appointment, or by a withdrawal of it by Lincoln." [19] Washburne's statement of the case was precisely correct in terms of Lincoln's intentions and expectations in early January.

That any man could have ignored these expectations or have declined so pointed a request from a President Elect is difficult to comprehend, but Simon Cameron did just that. He neither wired nor wrote the declination that Lincoln demanded. Even had he done so, Lincoln still had the pro-Cameron men and the protectionists to consider. On January 12 Lincoln was visited by two of Cameron's emissaries, J. P. Sanderson and Edgar Cowan,[20] whose solicitations were buttressed by a telegram from members of the Pennsylvania legislature insisting that Cameron be included in the cabinet and Chase excluded. The next day Lincoln did a thing which showed how a marked regard for Cameron's feelings combined with a continuation of his sincere effort to resist the Cameron pressure. He wrote to Cameron expressing regret for what he had said on January 3, assuring him that he had intended "no offense," and suggesting, not definitely that he would give him a department, but that Cameron would be consulted if he should make a "cabinet appointment for Pennsylvania" before reaching Washington. Lincoln accompanied this with a letter pre-dated to

---

[17] White, *Trumbull*, 148. Ebenezer Peck is quoted as stating that the Chicago delegation in the Illinois legislature all worked to prevent Cameron's appointment, "believing him not to be a proper man for any place in the Cabinet." *Ibid.*, 147–148.

[18] *Works*, VI, 91–92; H. E. Pratt, "Simon Cameron's Fight," 6–7.

[19] Jan. 10, 1861, Chase MSS., Lib. of Cong.   [20] Pratt, "Simon Cameron's Fight," 8.

January 3 in which, in more tactful tones, he asked the Pennsylvanian to "relieve" him from "embarrassment" by allowing him to "recall the offer." [21]

At this point it was evident that Lincoln still hoped to keep Cameron out of the cabinet, but he had failed to get the declination which would have avoided embarrassment, while he had made friendly gestures toward the Cameron group.[22] It seemed, however, that as long as Cameron's ambitions were not met Lincoln was to have no peace. "Delegations of Cameronites from New York and Pennsylvania descended almost daily upon Lincoln in the last two weeks of January," [23] while David Davis at this time was said to be "quite huffy" because of the objections raised to Cameron.[24] There was further hauling and tugging, and Lincoln, still hesitating, told clamoring politicians in New York in February that he would have to take the responsibility,[25] which he did by making Cameron his secretary of war. As will appear later, this was but the beginning of further grief.

Lincoln particularly wanted a Southerner in his cabinet and it is not at all impossible that he might even have chosen a slaveholder. Of his own desire to appoint a Southerner there is clear evidence. On December 12, 1860, there appeared in the *Illinois State Journal* a cautious editorial supplied by Lincoln in which the new President's "supposed purpose . . . to call into his cabinet two or three Southern gentlemen from the parties opposed to him" was mentioned and queries were put as to whether any such "gentleman of character" would accept a place and whether such acceptance would involve "surrender" of political views or "open opposition" within the administration.[26] Among the Southerners mentioned for the cabinet were Winfield Scott, Robert E. Scott, John Minor Botts (all from Virginia), John A. Gilmer and William A. Graham of North Carolina, and from Tennessee such men as Emerson Etheridge, Andrew Johnson, John Bell, and T. A. R. Nelson. After conferring with Lincoln on the South's share in the cabinet, a Virginia Republican reported

---

[21] *Works*, VI, 96–97.
[22] Lincoln's hesitations, perplexities, and embarrassments on the Cameron matter are well treated in White, *Trumbull*, esp. 142–148, and Baringer, *A House Dividing*, 131–136, 166–174, 255, 288–291.
[23] Pratt, "Simon Cameron's Fight," 9.
[24] E. Peck to Trumbull, Feb. 2, 1861, Trumbull MSS.
[25] Pratt, "Simon Cameron's Fight," 10.   [26] *Works*, VI, 78.

that he seemed disinclined to appoint the more outspoken type of Southern Republican such as Cassius M. Clay or John C. Underwood, who represented a small Republican minority in their states, but was more favorably disposed toward a well respected moderate such as Gilmer.[27] In January Frank P. Blair, Jr. wrote to his brother Montgomery that Dr. Gitt of Virginia was at Springfield "on a special mission in behalf of C. M. Clay [of Kentucky] and Underwood of Virginia who it seems aspires to a seat in the Cabinet." [28]

To make the selection was not easy and on January 3 Lincoln wrote to Seward of his uncertainty whether he could "get any suitable men from the South, and [if so] who, and how many . . . ." [29] In this phase of Lincoln's search he indicated that if a man was "farther South" than another it would make him preferable, also that it would be better for a man to have "a living position in the South." [30] Lincoln definitely sought the inclusion of Gilmer of North Carolina, who, he hoped, would take a cabinet post "on a fair understanding." [31] While the Gilmer matter was pending Lincoln concluded that it was unwise to take "more than one who opposed us in the election" for fear of losing friends.[32] Gilmer as well as others, however, proved unavailable, cabinet posts meanwhile had to be filled, and, though ultimately three men from the region south of the Mason-Dixon line served him as ministers,[33] the out-and-out "Southerner" was lacking.

VIII

The appointment of Caleb B. Smith to the cabinet was a fulfillment of a Chicago bargain and a recognition of the importance of Indiana. Here again intrastate rivalries embarrassed Lincoln. Schuyler Colfax as well as Smith was pressing for the appointment, but Smith brought to bear a greater organized influence. Playing the office-seeking game, Smith asked George W. Julian to write Lincoln in his

---

[27] W. W. Gitt to W. P. Fessenden, Feb. 17, 1861, W. P. Fessenden MSS.

[28] Blair MSS. Underwood was a Virginia radical Republican who became a Federal judge, serving in war time and after. His views resembled those of Thaddeus Stevens. Lincoln had no intention of appointing such a man to his cabinet.

[29] Works, VI, 91.   [30] Ibid., VI, 94 (Jan. 12, 1861).

[31] Ibid.   [32] Ibid.

[33] Edward Bates of Missouri, Montgomery Blair of Maryland, and (later) James Speed of Kentucky.

behalf,[1] and Lincoln's friend Davis kept him reminded of the "pledge." By mid-January Colfax, having written unacknowledged letters to Lincoln, realized that "the game is up" and that Smith was preferred.[2] Lincoln seems to have had little enthusiasm for the Smith appointment which was deferred until a "late hour," [3] and the Indianian was placed only after Norman B. Judd of Chicago had been definitely excluded. This latter gentleman, a former Democrat, Chicago friend of Lincoln, and contender for the governorship, had the support of leading men such as Trumbull,[4] Grimes, Chandler, and Wade. Lincoln, however, hesitated to take any cabinet member from his own state,[5] and the choice of Judd would have offended the Seward-Weed-Cameron element as well as many influential Illinois Republicans. It appears that Mrs. Lincoln intervened against Judd, but this is not to say that petticoat influence was actually the factor that controlled Lincoln's decision.[6]

The name of Montgomery Blair of Maryland, a conservative emancipationist of Dred Scott fame,[7] had suggested itself to Lincoln at the outset of his cabinet studies,[8] yet it was not until shortly before the inauguration that Blair was actually determined upon. No one would have accused the Blairs of backwardness in office seeking, and Lincoln was kept steadily aware of the Marylander's availability.[9] Though the position of postmaster general has sometimes been considered a minor one, yet any cabinet place under Lincoln was im-

---

[1] Smith to Julian, Jan. 21, 1861, Giddings-Julian MSS. (Julian did not do as Smith asked. Baringer, *A House Dividing*, 179-180.)

[2] Colfax to Yates, Jan. 12, 1861, MS., Chicago Hist. Soc.

[3] Welles, *Diary*, II, 390.   [4] White, *Trumbull*, 150.

[5] "We . . . hope . . . Lincoln will not make such a mistake as to appoint Judd." O. H. Browning in his *Diary*, I, 448 (Jan. 13, 1861).

[6] Mrs. Lincoln wrote to David Davis urging him to advise Mr. Lincoln to make up his cabinet without Judd. Mary Lincoln to David Davis, Jan. 17, 1861, Davis MSS., cited in H. E. Pratt, "David Davis" (ms. dissertation, Univ. of Ill.), ch. vii, n. 27; Welles, *Diary*, II, 390. On January 24, 1861, F. P. Blair, Jr., just returned from Springfield, wrote his brother that Judd was not out of the question, that Lincoln wanted him and he wanted to be in (Blair MSS.).

[7] Blair had served as counsel for plaintiff when the Dred Scott case was tried in the Supreme Court, and had indeed done much to "make" this *cause célèbre*. He was "the only West Point graduate and the only one with any military experience in the Cabinet." William E. Smith, *The Francis Preston Blair Family in Politics*, II, 2.

[8] Welles MS. (postwar recollections), Ill. State Hist. Lib.

[9] Two letters of F. P. Blair, Jr. to Montgomery (January 24-25, 1861) refer to Frank's visit to Springfield to see Lincoln about cabinet matters, including, of course, the Blair claim (Blair MSS.).

portant, and this office, whether rightly or not, was referred to as involving "the casting vote of the new Cabinet." [10] Blair was much more conservative than Henry Winter Davis, a Maryland rival for cabinet place; thus the choice of Blair was an indication that Lincoln preferred to steer a middle course.

When the cabinet was made up it was found that Lincoln had representatives from populous states such as New York, Pennsylvania, and Ohio (though not from his own), that Massachusetts was unrepresented, that he had no Southerner as usually understood though he had two from the border region, and that diversity of political views rather than uniformity was the cabinet's most obvious characteristic. Writing in nautical figures a correspondent of Governor Andrew said that Lincoln's officers did not all look the same way: his "first officer (Seward) looks one way and rows the other, talks compromise and peace, but votes the Chicago platform . . ."; his second officer (Chase) "thinks the true way to sail a ship is to look and row in the same direction"; his third (Cameron) "gives no indication as to which direction he will be inclined to pull." This hopeful individual added that Captain Lincoln would summon them all into the after cabin and make known that he was master of the ship and that all his officers had to do was to "obey orders." [11]

No one consistent principle, unless that of opportunism, had been followed in the selection of the cabinet. Its members did not agree with Lincoln nor among themselves; they did not pull the same way. Only a study of the conflicting influences bearing upon Lincoln can explain how each appointment came about, and then the explanation becomes clear. The idea that the President was selecting a nonpartisan or "all parties" cabinet, though often put forward, is a misconception. Active Democrats such as Douglas, Reverdy Johnson, or Horatio Seymour were left out, and while some former Democrats were chosen, each and every member of the original cabinet had supported the Republican ticket in 1860. The differences between cabinet members were differences within the Republican party. Lin-

---

[10] Nicolay and Hay, *Lincoln*, III, 369. If one considers the other six members of the cabinet as three former Democrats and three former Whigs, then a preponderance of one or the other group would be involved in the appointment of postmaster general. The fact that, in appointing Blair, Lincoln actually chose four Democrats (by former affiliation) and only three Whigs, is treated below.

[11] L. B. Comins to J. A. Andrew, Mar. 6, 1861, Andrew MSS.

A JOB FOR THE NEW CABINET MAKER.

OLD ABE—"Oh, it's all well enough to say, that I must support the dignity of my high office by Force—but it's darned uncomfortable sitting—I can tell yer."

CARTOONS OF THE PRESIDENT ELECT

These cartoons are from Leslie's: "Old Abe" poised on bayonets is from the issue of March 2, 1861; the other from that of February 2, 1861.

Simon Cameron of Pennsylvania, Secretary of War

Salmon P. Chase of Ohio, Secretary of the Treasury

Edward Bates of Missouri, Attorney General

William H. Seward of New York, Secretary of State

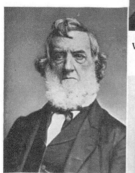

Gideon Welles of Connecticut, Secretary of the Navy

Caleb B. Smith of Indiana, Secretary of the Interior

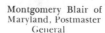

Montgomery Blair of Maryland, Postmaster General

ORIGINAL CABINET

Of these seven, only Seward and Welles remained throughout Lincoln's presidency. All are Brady photographs. Courtesy of the National Archives.

coln is said to have been reminded that he had appointed "four Democrats and only three Whigs" upon which he replied that he himself was an old-line Whig, making the parties even.[12]

Such statements are misinterpreted if they are understood to mean that Lincoln was taking party opponents as of 1860 as well as party supporters into his cabinet, or that he was creating a coalition of antagonistic parties. As noted above, Lincoln indicated his own doubts as to taking into the cabinet those who had opposed the Republican party in the elections.[13] What is often overlooked in comments on Lincoln's alleged all-parties cabinet is that former Whigs in the Republican party derived from a political organization that was dead in 1860, while the Democratic party was very much alive. This being the case, it is entirely misleading to speak of Lincoln appointing "Democrats" in 1861 in the sense of taking opponents into his official family. The four were only former Democrats; they were good Republicans who had drawn away from the Democratic party.

As constituted in 1861, Lincoln's cabinet was as follows: William H. Seward of New York, secretary of state; Salmon P. Chase of Ohio, secretary of the treasury; Simon Cameron of Pennsylvania, secretary of war; Gideon Welles of Connecticut, secretary of the navy; Edward Bates of Missouri, attorney general; Caleb B. Smith of Indiana, secretary of the interior; Montgomery Blair of Maryland, postmaster general. Of the seven secretaries only two (Seward and Welles) were still at their cabinet posts when Lincoln died in office. Cameron was appointed minister to Russia and was succeeded by Edwin M. Stanton of Pennsylvania on January 20, 1862. Chase resigned June 29, 1864, his place being filled by W. P. Fessenden of Maine until March 4, 1865, then by Hugh McCulloch of Indiana. Bates resigned in 1864 and was followed by another border-state man, James Speed of Kentucky. Blair resigned amid clamorous intraparty disputes in September 1864 and was succeeded by William Dennison of Ohio. Smith resigned in December 1862, accepting a position as Federal circuit judge under Lincoln's appointment. In January 1863 the department of the interior was placed under John P. Usher of Indiana; he served only until the end of Lincoln's first term and was followed in March

---

12 Nicolay and Hay, *Lincoln*, III, 369. Seward, Bates, and Smith were the former Whigs; Blair, Chase, Cameron, and Welles the former Democrats.

13 *Works*, VI, 94 (Jan. 12, 1861).

1865 by James Harlan of Iowa. This résumé omits the short service of Buchanan's ministers who held over for a few days after March 4, 1861, until Lincoln's men could be confirmed and assume control. Disregarding these cases there were thirteen men who served in Lincoln's cabinet. Yet there were only seven cabinet positions and six departments, the department of justice being a post-Lincoln establishment. Contenders for cabinet place who failed of selection were in a number of cases "cared for" by diplomatic or consular posts. Gustave Koerner went to Madrid, Dayton to France, C. F. Adams to London, Judd to Berlin, C. M. Clay to Russia. Had Cameron not been chosen to the cabinet it is likely that he would have received a rather choice foreign assignment.[14]

---

[14] The pre-presidential phase is ably treated by William E. Baringer in *A House Dividing: Lincoln as President Elect* (1945).

CHAPTER XI

LINCOLN TAKES HOLD

I

AS THE time for Lincoln's departure from Springfield on the long way to Washington approached, his last hours at home were occupied with official cares, social obligations, and homely incidents of a peculiarly western or Lincolnian flavor. A public reception was given at his home on the night of February 6, 1861; it was described as a large affair, made brilliant by beauty, fashion, and the political elite, with hundreds in attendance.[1] Vacating their home, "breaking up housekeeping," the Lincolns stayed a few days at the Chenery House. The chores of packing were partly performed by Lincoln himself; the personal trunks, tied with his own hands, bore his label: "Lincoln, Executive Mansion, Washington." On Sunday, February the tenth, his last day in Springfield, he turned up at the Lincoln-Herndon office for a talk with his partner and chatted easily of incidents in his early practice. On departing he asked that the old sign be permitted to hang so that clients might understand "that the election of a President makes no change in the firm of Lincoln and Herndon." [2] Next day there was enacted one of the most touching scenes of his life as he took his departure from Springfield, bound for untold anxieties in Washington. Friends had gathered despite the stormy weather and the early hour, and Lincoln, rising to a level that was rare among rear platform appearances, spoke his few words of parting; they were as perfectly fitted to the occasion as any of his more formal speeches:

My Friends [he said]: No one, not in my situation, can appreciate my feeling of sadness at this parting. To this place, and the kindness of these

---

[1] New York *Tribune,* Feb. 7, 1861.   [2] Herndon (Angle ed.), 390.

people, I owe everything. Here I have lived a quarter of a century, and have passed from a young to an old man. Here my children have been born, and one is buried. I now leave, not knowing when or whether ever I may return, with a task before me greater than that which rested upon Washington. Without the assistance of that Divine Being who ever attended him, I cannot succeed. With that assistance, I cannot fail. Trusting in Him who can go with me, and remain with you, and be everywhere for good, let us confidently hope that all will yet be well. To His care commending you, as I hope in your prayers you will commend me, I bid you an affectionate farewell.[3]

Synchronous with the beginnings of the Confederacy, the presidential journey came at a time of widespread apprehension for the new chief and for the government itself. Extra precautions were taken in dispatching the presidential train. The time card of the Great Western (Wabash) Railroad Company, printed under date of February 11, 1861, for the use of its employees, contained the following injunction: "It is very important that this train should pass over the road in safety . . . . Red is the signal for danger, but any signal apparently intended to indicate alarm . . . must be regarded, the train stopped, and the meaning of it ascertained. Carefulness is particularly enjoined." [4]

Of the President's traveling party some went all the way, some made only the trip from Springfield to Indianapolis, others joined the train en route for rides of varying length. To enumerate all that were in the party, with information as to where they got on and off, is quite unnecessary. Robert Lincoln was on the train as it left Springfield. Mrs. Lincoln, with the other two boys—William and Thomas —boarded it at Indianapolis. The party also included the private secretaries, John G. Nicolay and John Hay; Elmer E. Ellsworth, Lincoln's young friend who would soon fall at Alexandria; army officers (Col. E. V. Sumner, Major David Hunter, Capt. George W. Hazard, Capt. John Pope); relatives of the Lincolns (Dr. W. S. Wallace, Lockwood Todd); men of political prominence in Illinois (David Davis, Norman B. Judd, Orville H. Browning, Governor Richard Yates,

---

[3] *Works*, VI, 110–111. Henry Villard claims to have prevailed upon Lincoln to write down this speech and to have been the first to give it out for publication (*Memoirs*, I, 149). Nicolay and Hay (*Lincoln*, III, 291 n.) state that it was written down immediately after the train started (partly by Lincoln and partly by his private secretary at his dictation), and that it was first "correctly printed" in the *Century* for December 1887.

[4] Broadside, Ill. State Hist. Lib.

Ward H. Lamon); and others so slightly known that their presence seems wholly incidental. (In this latter group were such unknowns as J. M. Burgess, George S. Latham, and B. Forbes. For all that they mattered, they could have been there merely for the fun or the ride.) W. S. Wood, an eastern railway official, was present in a managerial capacity. The army officers, who took very seriously their duty of guarding the President without satisfying others on this point, were there by action of the war department. David Davis joined the party at Indianapolis, while Yates and Browning traveled only as far as Indianapolis. From Browning's pedestrian diary one gets the impression that he by no means regarded the journey as a notable episode. At first he declined, then later accepted, Lincoln's invitation to accompany him. At the end of the first stage he "determined to go no farther." "The trip to Indianapolis," he wrote, "has been very pleasant, but is just about as much of that sort of thing as I want." [5]

While Lincoln was en route there were numerous expressions of apprehension among his friends and threats among his enemies. The day after his departure his Springfield friend J. C. Conkling wrote Trumbull: "If he is inaugurated on the 4th March . . . I do hope the most . . . vigorous . . . policy will be adopted." [6] Some of the newspaper assurances that all would be well served only to register a feeling of insecurity, as when the Chicago *Tribune* unconvincingly declared that the "timid, who fear that a mob will prevent Mr. Lincoln's inauguration, do not stop to think that the inauguration ceremony . . . is an invention of the people," and added: "We have no doubt that he will be President of the United States and Commander-in-Chief of the Army and Navy, before he leaves Springfield." [7] It was feared that the spread of secession would extend to Virginia and Maryland, or at least one of these states, producing a direct threat of violence at the inauguration. "[I]f Virginia and Maryland *do not adopt measures to prevent Mr. Lincoln's inauguration at Washington,*" declared the Richmond *Enquirer,* "their discretion will be . . . a subject of ridicule . . . ." [8] "Beneath all this talk [declared the reassuring *Tribune*] . . . unquestionably lurks a scheme for the assas-

---

[5] Browning, *Diary,* I, 454-455.

[6] Conkling to Trumbull, Feb. 12, 1861, Trumbull MSS.

[7] Jan. 3, 1861. p. 1, c. 1. Legally, of course, Lincoln's term could not begin until March 4; he could perform no act as President before that.

[8] Quoted in Chicago *Tribune,* Jan. 4, 1861, p. 3, c. 3.

sination of Lincoln and Hamlin . . . ." [9] Not all the apprehended or imagined violence was directed against Lincoln. Greeley wrote from Springfield in February 1861: "I was engaged to arrive at St. Louis tonight, but do not, because my friends fear a mob." [10]

Much will be missed in recapturing the psychological setting of the inauguration if Lincoln's own calm is not remembered in contrast to the keen apprehension of danger to him and to the government on or about March 4. The substantial danger is hardly the main point. Even if this be dismissed as an exaggeration it is important to recognize that the feeling of danger was real and that it affected the most sober minded of the nation's leaders. Charles Francis Adams wrote in early January to the governor of his state: "It is beyond a doubt that the revolutionists have determined to take forcible possession of the Government at Washington before the fourth of March, and perhaps within thirty days." [11] "I am anxious . . . about the safety of the Capital," wrote Neal Dow a few days later. "The fear is, that Scott cannot collect force enough for its protection." [12] In this state of mind those who would rise up and save the country by unsolicited military help were an annoyance to the outgoing President and to General Scott. When Governor Andrew wrote to Scott offering help from Massachusetts the old general made it known that he was "much embarrassed" and was in a position where even an answer to Andrew's letter would be considered a "gross assumption" on his part. Further he thought that volunteers beyond the District would not be needed in the near future.[13] This was at the middle of January, but a few days later Sumner, having passed an hour and a half with Scott, reported that the general was "not without solicitude with regard to the capital." Sumner told of newly received information which confirmed the idea "of a wide-spread conspiracy." [14] The subject was the more annoying because of the inexactness and mystery that attached to it. Having conferred with the attorney general on January 27 "for a long time till after midnight," Sumner wrote to Andrew:

9 *Ibid.*, Feb. 13, 1861, p. 1, c. 1. Lincoln was en route as this was printed.

10 Greeley to L. U. Reavis, Feb. 6, 1861, Reavis MSS.

11 C. F. Adams to John A. Andrew, Washington, Jan. 4, 1861, Andrew MSS.

12 Neal Dow to John A. Andrew, Jan. 19, 1861, *ibid.*

13 Winfield Scott to Henry Wilson, Washington, Jan 15, 1861, *ibid.*

14 Sumner also wrote of Scott being unable to ride his horse, but being determined to ride in the inaugural procession in a carriage. Charles Sumner to John A. Andrew, Jan. 23, 1861, *ibid.*

"I know from him what I cannot communicate." Then he added: "Suffice it to say, he does not think it probable, hardly possible that we shall be here on the 4th of March. . . . General Scott is very anxious. It is feared that the Departments will be seized and occupied as forts." [15]

Trans-Mississippi fears matched or perhaps exceeded those of the Bay State. "What I fear," wrote S. T. Glover of St. Louis, "is the utter over throw of the government in all the slave states and a new government in successful operation before the 4th March." For his own locality he feared mobs, minute-men, and lynching.[16] Frank Blair the younger was much concerned about reënforcing the St. Louis arsenal, fearing that the enemies of the government would try to disarm the Northwest after arming themselves "by robbing the Southern arsenals." [17] A part of the "conspiracy," it was said, was "to withhold money from the Government, so as to place it at the mercy of the Seceders and their allies." [18] Provide against treachery was the burden of John Jay's advice from Katonah, New York. Keep Maryland open, he said. Watch out for the taking up of rails and the destroying of bridges. Let telegraph wires be guarded with religious care. "If we are to have war, let the Gov. shew not only moral but . . . military strength from the start." [19] In these matters he would have "no trusting to state honour" but would supply "a sufficient force . . . to crush on the instant the first effort at interference." He would "stand on the defensive," but he would restore the people's belief in the "sovereignty of gov[ernment]." [20]

In the deep South secessionist threats were both wildly exaggerated and exultant. A Mississippi man had written in December that his state would go out of the Union "with a perfect whoop," and would be followed "by all the Cotton States . . . , & if an army of 1.000.000 . . . do not take possession of Washington City before the 4th of March, I am very much mistaken." [21] J. M. Ashley wrote to Chase that Ohioans returning from Richmond declared in December that

15 Sumner to Andrew, Jan. 28, 1861, *ibid.*
16 Glover to Montgomery Blair, Jan. 18, 1861, Blair MSS.
17 Frank Blair, Jr., to M. Blair, Jan. 24, 1861, *ibid.*
18 Gustave Koerner to Lyman Trumbull, Feb. 19, 1861, Trumbull MSS.
19 John Jay to Charles Sumner, Feb. 8, 1861, Sumner MSS.
20 Jay to Sumner, Feb. 4, 1861, *ibid.*
21 J. W. Williams to S. A. Douglas, Holly Springs, Miss., Dec. 10, 1860, Douglas MSS.

the capital would be captured by Virginia and Maryland and Lincoln's inauguration "resisted by force" unless some compromise was worked out.[22] The "numerous stories of the intended assassination of Mr. Lincoln" that were "constantly promulgated" added to public apprehension while giving a text for partisan denunciation, for without any basis whatever these plots were attributed to the Democrats.[23]

If the alleged danger was a bluff, the government would err as well as aggravate the situation by taking it seriously. Cassius M. Clay wrote: "The South is weak and she knows it! She bullies again!" [24] It was felt that military assistance would have to be invited by the general government. Any marching of troops from Massachusetts in minute-man spirit would have been regarded as a "first move" toward "hostilities." [25]

In Lincoln's own mind the inauguration was "not the most dangerous point," for, said he, if the two houses of Congress refused to meet for the counting of the electoral votes on the legally fixed day (February 13), or if a quorum should fail, "where shall we be?" [26] Though the counting was only a legal formality, yet without it the President's title would have been faulty, and it was thought that his opponents would not scruple to interfere at this point by a parliamentary trick if they saw the chance. Whatever Buchanan's detractors might say about "imbecility" at Washington, the truth was that Federal authority was respected; people breathed more freely when on February 13 it was announced that the ceremony of counting the presidential votes had been uneventfully completed.[27] On the same day there met in Richmond a Virginia convention known to be predominantly unionist, and there was now less fear that this important state, whose efforts were still tied up with the Peace Convention, would secede before the fourth of March.

---

[22] Ashley to Chase, Washington, Dec. 18, 1860, Chase MSS., Lib. of Cong.

[23] Chicago *Tribune*, March 1, 1861, p. 2, c. 6, quoting Buffalo *Commercial Advertiser*.

[24] C. M. Clay to Andrew, Jan. 16, 1861, Andrew MSS.

[25] Sumner to Andrew, Jan. 17, 1861, *ibid.*   [26] *Works*, VI, 90–91 (Jan. 3, 1861).

[27] The full Congress being assembled in the House chamber, certificates of the electors were opened by the Vice President and the vote was counted and announced. Lincoln had 180 electoral votes in a total of 303. "Whereupon the Vice-President declared that Abraham Lincoln of Illinois, having received a majority of the whole number of electoral votes, is duly elected President of the United States . . . ." Senator Trumbull and Representatives Washburne and Burlingame were then appointed to notify Lincoln and Hamlin of their election. *Sen. Mis. Doc. No. 5*, 44 Cong., 2 sess. (1876), pp. 53–54. (This 1876 document gives a history of the counting of electoral votes.)

II

Never again was Lincoln to make so many speeches in so few days as on his presidential journey. If at times the speeches seem mediocre, the reasons are to be found in a continuance of the policy of silence, a prudent caution to avoid misrepresentation, a wish to make no mistake before taking further bearings, and a deferment of difficult public questions for appropriate and matured treatment in the coming inaugural. The point of his speeches en route was to show himself, acknowledge ovations, and satisfy the many who pressed forward to see and hear him. The crowds did not expect magic answers to questions of policy so much as they wanted to gaze upon the President Elect and hear his voice. Few leaders have met such a situation with better grace than Lincoln. The generalities were pardonable and there was as little triteness as could have been expected in this weary itinerary. Certainly the new leader could not treat fundamental national questions at each place where his train stopped. If the speeches are re-read with these conditions in view they will be found to contain pithy Lincolnian expressions and not to lack gracious elements of fitness to the local occasion. That they were not his most distinguished utterances is readily admitted.

Often Lincoln struck the note of self-depreciation. He referred to himself as an old man; once he had a passage read by "younger eyes"; at times he confessed that he had not the "voice" nor "strength" for longer speaking. He called himself "without mock modesty" the "humblest of all individuals that have ever been elevated to the presidency," [1] and declared that "without a name, perhaps without a reason why . . . [he] should have a name," there had fallen upon him "a task such as did not rest even upon the Father of his Country." [2] Repeatedly he showed his sense of the heavy responsibility that rested upon him; without cant he called upon the Supreme Being for help and invoked the undivided support of the people to sustain him. His thanks had a personal, genuine ring, yet he kept saying that honors and demonstrations were not for him; they were tributes to the cause he represented, to "the majesty of the nation," to the "perpetual liberty of the people of this country," to "something . . . more than

---

[1] *Works*, VI, 140 (Feb. 18, 1861).   [2] *Ibid.*, VI, 121 (Feb. 13, 1861).

any one man, . . . or ten thousand men," to "the elected representative of a free people." [3] With real eloquence he spoke from his pioneer heart of "civil and religious liberty for all time to come," of the fundamental processes of democracy, of the people rising in mass, of the business of preserving "the liberties of this people." In no other land, he said, could men come together as in America in the enjoyment of "free institutions." [4] Often he repeated that the demonstration was not for any political party. It would have been the same if Douglas or Bell or Breckinridge or "any citizen" had been "constitutionally elected." [5] "If Judge Douglas had been chosen President," he gracefully said at Cleveland, "and had this evening been passing through your city, the Republicans should have joined his supporters in welcoming him just as his friends have joined with mine to-night." [6] When "an election is past" a "free people . . . should be one people." [7] It was not often that he struck a false note, though perhaps he did at Indianapolis, where his sentences about coercion and state rights were of the sort to irk the Southerner, and where his metaphor of "free love" and of an "arrangement . . . maintained only on 'passional attraction'" hardly fitted his own Victorian age.[8]

Though more than vignettes, his speeches were fittingly brief. The longest and driest was at Pittsburgh where he rose painfully to the Republican duty of saying something about the tariff, "the specialty of Pennsylvania" which had been of more influence in obtaining the support of this area than slavery and antislavery. If a student searches the speech for economic wisdom or even for serious commitment on protection versus free trade, he will search in vain.[9] Plainly the tariff was not Lincoln's forte. He frankly confessed that he had no "thoroughly matured judgment" on the subject and was "not posted" on

---

[3] *Ibid.*, VI, esp. pp. 110, 111, 121, 129, 130. 143.

[4] *Ibid.*, VI, 141, 112, 116.   [5] *Ibid.*, VI, 115–116 (Feb. 12, 1861).

[6] *Ibid.*, VI, 131–132 (Feb. 15, 1861).   [7] *Ibid.*, VI, 139 (Feb. 18, 1861).

[8] Lincoln referred unfavorably to those who professed love for the Union, yet spoke of maintaining it as if that amounted to unjustifiable "coercion." Then he added: "In their view, the Union as a family relation would seem to be no regular marriage, but rather a sort of 'free-love' arrangement, to be maintained only on 'passional attraction.'" *Ibid.*, VI, 114 (Feb. 12, 1861). For the occasion of the Indianapolis speech, see below, pp. 284–285.

[9] "It proved him to be the veriest novice in economic matters, and strengthened my doubts as to his capacity for the high office he was to fill." Villard, *Memoirs*, I, 152. For the Pittsburgh speech, see *Works*, VI, 124–129 (Feb. 15, 1861).

the provisions of the Morrill bill then pending. Referring in homely fashion to the tariff as "housekeeping" and as "replenishing the meal-tub" (which would apply to a revenue producer, not to protection) he asked his secretary to read the platitudinous plank in the Republican platform, after which he admitted that there might be "differences in construing" its meaning and expressed the hope that every member of the next Congress would "post himself thoroughly" (as Lincoln said he had not done) "so as to contribute his part" to an adjustment that would "produce a sufficient revenue, and . . . be just and equal to all sections . . . and classes of the people," a phrase which could hardly describe a protective tariff. That the speech was taken as advocacy of protection at all was perhaps due to the fact that people were already used to generalities and verbalisms from politicians on this topic.

One of Simon Cameron's main interests had been to get a national administration that would favor protection, and he thought that Pennsylvania had "the power in her hands," by which he meant that the state's vote should be used for the benefit of manufacturing interests in the election of 1860.[10] When Cameron wrote to Lincoln (August 1, 1860) stating that he was gratified with "notes of speeches" (Lincoln speeches) which a "Mr. Lesley" had showed him, Lincoln replied with one of those cautious and embarrassed letters that a candidate not infrequently has to write. Briefly stating that "Yours of the 1st" was received, Lincoln wrote that David Davis would by that time have called upon Cameron and have shown him "the 'scraps' mentioned . . . by Mr Leslie." Then he added that "Nothing about these must get into the newspapers" and took care to mark the whole letter "Private." [11] Next month Lincoln sent G. Yoke Tams a letter that was both "Private and confidential" concerning an inquiry as to whether he favored a tariff of protection. Without specifically saying that he approved of protection he referred to the Republican platform, said he was not free "to publicly shift the position by adding or subtracting anything," for then the convention might "displace" him as their candidate, and remarked that his questioner would not wish him "to give private assurances to be seen by some and kept secret

---

[10] Cameron to W. D. Lewis, Dec. 14, 1859, Cameron MSS.

[11] Lincoln to Cameron (not in Nicolay and Hay, *Works*), Aug. 6, 1860, *ibid.*

from others." He enjoined "that this shall by no means be made public." [12] Neither publicly nor privately was Lincoln speaking his whole
mind on economic matters.[13] Once he did comment on the " 'respectable scoundrels' " who "got . . . up" the "financial depression" that
coincided with his election, hoping they would be "less greedy to do
the like again," but this letter he also marked private and confidential
in a headline at the top, repeating in the letter that it was "strictly
private" and that he had no "declaration for the public." [14]

III

The main burden of Lincoln's speeches en route was preservation
of the Union; to this theme he recurred continually. To the people
of the South he showed conciliation and recognition of local rights.
He referred to what would now be called the tyranny of words and
declared that there was "nothing going wrong," "nothing that really
hurts anybody." [1] As the context plainly indicates, this often misinterpreted statement showed no lack of anxiety and no callousness
toward the ugly crisis that was shaking the country. What Lincoln
meant and said was that in whipping up an unnecessary quarrel "men
wrangle by the month with no certainty that they mean the same thing,
while using the same word." [2] It was a matter not of essential invasion
of rights, but of misunderstanding and misrepresentation. The crisis
was "artificial." [3] It is strange that Lincoln was assailed [4] for this correct divination of the existing situation. It was almost as if he had
captured for his time the dispassionate and realistic interpretation of
a later age. The analysis given in a previous chapter [5] agrees with Lincoln's divination; on such matters as runaways and slavery in territories the fuss was about things that did not count. In such an emergency it behooved the people North and South to keep their temper,
get all the light possible, and wait till clouds could be dispelled. A
year previous to his election Lincoln had assured Kentuckians, as well
as all Southerners, that he meant no interference; now he said: "Fellow-

---

[12] Lincoln to Tams, Sep. 22, 1860, *Works*, VI, 58.
[13] Reinhard H. Luthin, "Abraham Lincoln and the Tariff," *Amer. Hist. Rev.*, XLIX,
609–629 (1944).
[14] Lincoln to Truman Smith, Nov. 10, 1860, *Works*, VI, 68–69.
[1] *Ibid.*, VI, 122 (Feb. 13, 1861).   [2] *Ibid.*, VI, 113 (Feb. 12, 1861).
[3] ". . . there is no crisis but an artificial one." *Ibid.*, VI, 125 (Feb. 15, 1861).
[4] Rhodes, *Hist. of the U. S.*, III, 303–304.   [5] Above, pp. 229 ff., 237 ff.

citizens of Kentucky!—friends!—brethren! may I call you in my new position? I see no occasion, and feel no inclination, to retract a word of this." [6]

At times his speeches on the journey were mere apologies for not speaking. This was true at Rochester, Syracuse, and Troy. At Syracuse he declined going upon the "handsome platform" prepared for him, passing it off with a cryptic and noncommittal reference presumably to the Chicago platform. At New York City, being introduced by one of his bitter opponents, Mayor Fernando Wood, he managed to capitalize the fact of party disagreement among those who welcomed him. Always he had a word for the occasion and the locality. At Albany he referred to "the great Empire State." At Cincinnati he addressed Germans with a note of sympathy for foreigners generally, saying that when people were "borne down by . . . shackles" he would not add to their burdens nor do aught to prevent their coming to the United States. On this occasion he hailed the working men as the "basis of all governments," voicing the hope that "every poor man . . . [might] have a home" and favoring measures to "give the greatest good to the greatest number." [7]

The impression made by these speeches was varied. At the Ohio capital it was thought by a friend of Chase that he had "impressed every one . . . favorably," but that he was making a "great *mistake* in making speeches all over the country." [8] The Indianapolis speech was given the twisted interpretation that the Republican party was only waiting the end of the existing administration to begin the war and that Lincoln's speech was really a signal for massacre and bloodshed.[9] Lincoln was accused of showing "ignorance" concerning the revolutionary happenings of the day and a lack of capacity to grapple with existing dangers.[10] It was remarked, however, that the Buffalo speech was totally different from preceding ones and that there was hope of Lincoln and Seward making history in the conservative sense. In this speech Lincoln had referred to the difficulties threatening the country, but he had done so most unprovocatively, stressing the note of calmness and predicting that when he should speak out on this subject

---

[6] *Works*, VI, 118 (Feb. 12, 1861).   [7] *Ibid.*, VI, 119–120 (Feb. 12, 1861).

[8] R. C. Parsons to S. P. Chase, Feb. 18, 1861, Chase MSS., Lib. of Cong.

[9] New York *Herald*, Feb. 13, 1861, p. 4, cc. 2–3; Feb. 14, p. 4, c. 4.

[10] *Ibid.*, Feb. 15, 1861, p. 4, c. 6. This was a reference to the statement that nothing was going wrong, that nothing was happening that hurt anyone.

he hoped "to say nothing inconsistent with the Constitution, the Union, the rights of all the States, of each State, and of each section of the country . . . ."

IV

Policy making was offering a fearsome challenge to the nation's new leader, but long hours of travel, ceremonial duties, parades, and numerous public appearances were claiming his time and strength. Not only was there an official welcome at each major scheduled visit; there were dozens of minor stops where Lincoln had to show himself on the platform, frequently with what the papers called "a few pleasant remarks." [1] To give an account of these appearances in detail would be pointless, though for thousands the seeing of the Rail Splitter with his son, the "Prince of Rails," was then and thereafter a high spot in their lives. A few selected instances must suffice to suggest the scenes that characterized this moving pageant.

When Lincoln's train stopped at Indianapolis at 5:00 p.m. on Monday, February 11, some blocks short of the union depot, it was greeted by a surging multitude headed by Governor Morton, together with public functionaries and "distinguished citizens," members of the legislature, committees from neighboring cities and states, and the ubiquitous firemen. Zouaves and militia, brass bands, streaming banners, the roar of saluting artillery, and the deafening cheers of the multitude signalized this first visit of a President Elect to the Hoosier capital.

At the very point of Lincoln's alighting from the train Governor Morton did the honors in a speech that was more than an address of welcome; it was a policy declaration and even an exhortation to the President Elect to stand firm for the Union and for the upholding of ballot-box decision. Replying to Morton, which he had to do without anticipation, Lincoln expressed hearty thanks for the "magnificent reception" and told the crowd that the salvation of the Union was in the "hearts of a people like yours." Preservation of the nation's liberties and of the Union, he said, rested "not with politicians, not

---

[1] For example. it was reported that on the first day "Crowds greeted the train at every station between Lafayette and Indianapolis, and at every place where it stopped Mr. Lincoln showed himself on the platform of the cars and spoke a few words to the people." Indianapolis *Daily Journal,* Feb. 12, 1861, p. 2, c. 2.

with Presidents, not with office-seekers, but with you." It was a well phrased brief speech, undistinguished but fitting in every way, though bearing the marks of impromptu utterance.[2]

Through dense crowds Lincoln passed through the streets, standing in his carriage and bowing to the people, till the procession ended at the Bates House, where a reception was held including members of the legislature, and where later Lincoln delivered to a large crowd a prepared address which constituted one of the major declarations of this itinerary. Deploring the prevailing confusion of words, he quoted Solomon's admonition as to "a time to keep silence"; then he gave a definite hint of coming policy—one of the few en route—in a rhetorical question which suggested that holding government property and collecting import duties could not properly be regarded as coercion or invasion.[3]

Because of this and other matters people were to hear a good deal of newspaper comment on this "Solomon speech." It is therefore interesting to note as a historical problem that Nicolay and Hay in their edition of Lincoln's *Works* give an erroneous statement as to the date, place, and occasion of this address, placing it on February 12 before the Indiana legislature,[4] whereas in fact it was given, perhaps contrary to plan, on the night of February 11 at the Bates House.[5] The matter is not of great importance in itself, yet it serves to show that correctness of detail was by no means always achieved by Lincoln's secretary-biographers who edited his *Works*.

From Indianapolis the President Elect traveled to Cincinnati to

---

[2] *Works*, VI 111–112.

[3] The end of this day (February 11) which began with the poignant farewell to his neighbors at Springfield was thus described in a newspaper of the time: ". . . the President's weariness induced him to retire [at the Bates House], although the rush to see and congratulate him continued unabated." Washington *Daily National Intelligencer*, Feb. 14, 1861, p. 3, c. 3.

[4] *Works*, VI, 112–115.

[5] Since the "Solomon speech" is reported in certain morning newspapers—e. g., the Chicago *Tribune*, New York *Tribune*, and New York *Times*—on February 12, and for other reasons, it appears that it was given to the crowd at the Bates House Monday night, February 11. In the hurried activities of Tuesday morning, February 12, no speech to the legislature occurred. This is confirmed by contemporary accounts, including the legislative journals. The above account of the Indianapolis visit is based on the Indianapolis *Daily Journal* and various other newspapers. The author has also been assisted by the diary of Calvin Fletcher, prominent Indianapolis citizen, and other material supplied by Margaret Pierson of the Indiana State Library. See also George S. Cottman, "Lincoln in Indianapolis," *Ind. Mag. of Hist.*, XXIV, 2–11 (Mar. 1928).

be greeted by another large reception (at the Burnet House) "where large crowds . . . called upon him." [6] At Buffalo ex-President Fillmore headed the delegation of citizens who greeted him; at Albany the honors were done by mayor, council, legislative committees, and Governor Morgan.[7] His speaking at New York City, already noted, was but an incident of his visit, which included meeting mayor and council, greeting citizens for long hours in parade and reception, conferring with politicians, receiving delegates at the Astor House with brief speeches, parrying insistent demands concerning his cabinet, and attending the opera at the Academy of Music. The long line through which his procession passed (February 19) "was densely crowded with spectators, almost equaling the turn-out to witness the pageant of the Prince of Wales." [8] The traveling Chief faced the public at close quarters, and some of the incidents en route were unpleasant. Crowds "almost crushed" Lincoln at Columbus; one of his party had to withdraw because of bodily injury. At the little town of Hudson near Cleveland, Ohio, he made an appearance to satisfy a large crowd, but he "was so hoarse that he was almost inaudible to people beyond the front row." [9] There was such "wearisome sameness" as the days wore on that one of the correspondents asked to be relieved of the "travelling show," detaching himself at New York.[10]

V

The last three days of Lincoln's journey, with their plots, rumors, and detective foils, would make a "thriller" if fully told; at least some attention must be given to this episode. Without an understanding of what went on, one might fail to appreciate the excitement of these pre-inauguration days and wrongly interpret a change of schedule which caused undeserved public censure.

Thursday, February 21.—The presidential party traveled from New York to Philadelphia with a scheduled stop at Trenton where Lincoln

[6] Washington *Daily National Intelligencer*, Feb. 14, p. 3, c. 3.

[7] *Ibid.*, Feb. 20, 1861, p. 3, c. 4.   [8] *Ibid.*, Feb. 21, 1861.

[9] John H. Cramer, "Lincoln in Ohio," *Ohio Archeol. and Hist. Quart.*, LIV, 167. In this article Mr. Cramer has given a fresh study of Lincoln's speech-making journey in Ohio, basing it on obscure and formerly unused newspaper articles. Concerning Lincoln's fatigue at Hudson, Mr. Cramer writes: "Thirty-seven speeches in five days was enough to tire any man."

[10] Villard, *Memoirs*, I, 152.

spent some hours, visiting the legislature of New Jersey and making speeches to the senate and house of representatives. He recalled his childhood reading of Washington's crossing of the Delaware, recognized again that he was addressing party opponents, and suggested amid prolonged cheers that for the preservation of "peace" it might be necessary "to put the foot down firmly."

The party traveled on to Philadelphia and put up at the Continental Hotel. In the evening Lincoln spoke at the mayor's reception. Meanwhile behind the scenes there had been close and anxious consultation between S. M. Felton, president of the Philadelphia, Wilmington and Baltimore Railway, Allan Pinkerton, head of a Chicago detective agency, and N. B. Judd, Lincoln's Chicago friend. The gist of it all was that Pinkerton's agents and spies reported a conspiracy to murder the President Elect as he passed through hostile Baltimore on February 23. Meeting secretly with Lincoln at the Continental, Pinkerton, Judd, and Felton explained the danger and urged him to cut remaining engagements and travel to Washington that night. At this point Judd alone of the presidential party knew of these consultations and suggestions as to change of plan. Lincoln cross-examined his interviewers and listened to their warning. Then, though facing possible assassination, he refused to abandon his Friday engagements at Philadelphia and Harrisburg.

About noon of this Thursday a page touched the arm of Frederick Seward as he sat in the Senate gallery at Washington. Soon he was informed by his father, Senator Seward, that General Scott had independent reports of the Baltimore plot and that Lincoln must be found and his arrangements changed. Colonel Charles P. Stone, a man of high reputation (which radicals were later to smear), had reported the plot to Scott, who had conveyed the information to Seward for transmittal to Lincoln. Traveling to Philadelphia, Frederick Seward managed with the help of Ward Lamon to see the President Elect alone, and Lincoln was given to know that "different persons . . . pursuing separate clues" [1] had concluded that the plot against his life was real. Judd states that he and Pinkerton devoted nearly the whole of that night, with railway and telegraph officials, to the task of arranging the difficult details of what was to follow.

---

[1] Frederick W. Seward, *Reminiscences*, 137.

Friday, February 22.—Lincoln's day began and ended at Philadelphia with a side trip to Harrisburg. In the early morning of this Washington's Birthday the new executive officiated in a scheduled flag-raising at Independence Hall, speaking to a group in the building and to a crowd outside. In this setting, where thought inevitably reverted to the Declaration of Independence, he offered the hope "that in due time the weights would be lifted from the shoulders of all men, and that all should have an equal chance." If the country could not be saved without giving up that principle, he added, "I was about to say I would rather be assassinated on this spot than surrender it." Speaking with "deep emotion" and giving rein to sentiment, he recalled the dangers and toils of Revolutionary soldiers, and stressed his belief that the Declaration was vital in 1861. There would be no giving up, he said; yet he particularly explained that his policy did not involve "bloodshed and war." [2]

Lincoln kept all his Friday engagements, traveling laboriously to Harrisburg, making two solid public speeches there, greeting a large crowd in a reception at the state house, and attending a hotel banquet given by Governor Curtin. At Harrisburg the men of the presidential party were informed by Judd of the suspected plot, and Lincoln was confronted with the problem of a night ride that would avoid the Baltimore danger. Unlike other cities and states Maryland and Baltimore had extended no official invitation to Lincoln and had arranged no speeches or receptions. The authorities had even failed to supply adequate police protection. Marshal George P. Kane described the plot rumors as a "political *canard,* receiving a . . . coloring of reality from the . . . expressions of a class of people who . . . are mostly to be found . . . in public bar-rooms." [3]

It had been publicly announced that about mid-day of Saturday the 23rd Lincoln would pass through Baltimore and that he would arrive at Washington that evening. To omit passing through the streets of an inhospitable city was a less serious matter than cutting the speaking engagements of Friday, and the President Elect, despite danger of ridicule and misunderstanding, reluctantly yielded to his advisers and consented to a secret night ride. With one companion,

---

[2] *Works,* VI, 156–158.
[3] *Annual Cyclopaedia,* 1861, 419. There is a tendency now to discredit rumors which, in this excited period, weighed heavily with Pinkerton.

THE UNFINISHED DOME

Capitol of a broken Union, a nation yet to be welded. The view at the left (from *Leslie's*) shows the East Front on the day of Lincoln's inauguration, March 4, 1861. The one at the right is a photograph of about May 1861, found in diary of M. C. Meigs, Library of Congress.

THE FLIGHT OF ABRAHAM.
(As Reported by a Modern Daily Paper.)

(1.) THE ALARM.

"On Thursday night, after he had retired, Mr. LINCOLN was aroused, and informed that a stranger desired to see him on a matter of life and death. * * * A conversation elicited the fact that an organized body of men had determined that Mr. LINCOLN should never leave the City of Baltimore alive. * * * Statesmen laid the plan, Bankers indorsed it, and Adventurers were to carry it into effect."

(2.) THE COUNCIL.

"Mr. LINCOLN did not want to yield, and his friends cried with indignation. But they insisted, and he left."

(3.) THE SPECIAL TRAIN.

"He wore a Scotch plaid Cap and a very long Military Cloak, so that he was entirely unrecognizable."

(4.) THE OLD COMPLAINT.

"Mr. LINCOLN, accompanied by Mr. SEWARD, paid his respects to President BUCHANAN, spending a few minutes in general conversation."

BELITTLING THE INCOMING PRESIDENT

These cartoons, about the time of Lincoln's inauguration, are typical of the widespread ridicule resulting from his secret night ride into Washington. *Upper Left:* Lincoln is aroused from bed. Organized enemies, he is informed, have determined that he shall never leave Baltimore alive. *Upper Right:* As his friends weep, Lincoln reluctantly yields to the demand that his itinerary be changed. *Lower Left:* Lincoln is unrecognizable in a Scotch plaid cap and a long military cloak. (This disguise was entirely imaginary, but was presented as news of the day.) *Lower Right:* Lincoln shivers with "a little attack of Ager" as he and Seward greet President Buchanan. An amusing trick of the artists of that day was always to exaggerate Buchanan's topknot. The four cartoons appeared in *Harper's Weekly,* Mar. 9, 1861, five days after Lincoln's inauguration.

Ward Lamon, he took a special train at Harrisburg with precautions to evade notice, entered the sleeper of a regular train at Philadelphia about eleven at night, and passed unnoticed through Baltimore in the early hours before daylight.

Saturday, February 23. Lincoln pulled into Washington at six a.m., and was met at the station by Congressman E. B. Washburne of Illinois. Though one finds conflicting claims as to this detail, Washburne stated that it was he who met Lincoln as he stepped off the train in company with Pinkerton and Lamon, that the four men entered a carriage and drove rapidly to the Willard Hotel, that they were shown into a receiving room, and that Seward then entered, "out of breath and . . . chagrined to think he had not been up in season to be at the depot on the arrival of the train." [4] The previous night ride had involved elaborate arrangements for cutting wires, intercepting messages, holding the night train at Philadelphia until a "package" was delivered (a Pinkertonian touch), preventing fire, putting guards at bridges and at a railway ferry, and creating the illusion that Lincoln had spent the night as planned at Harrisburg.[5]

The activities hinted at in this curtailed chronology must not be set down as mere nervousness. Events were soon to show that Maryland and Baltimore were capable of violence. Though some of the wildest rumors were canards (especially regarding a suspected *coup d'état* by which the "rebel" government would seize the capital), yet

---

[4] Statement by Washburne in Rice, *Reminiscences of Abraham Lincoln,* 37–39. Other statements, seemingly not so trustworthy, indicate that Seward and Washburne met Lincoln at the depot and were with him in the carriage as it arrived at Willard's. (Nicolay and Hay, *Lincoln,* III, 315; Chittenden, *Recollections of President Lincoln,* 65.) Pinkerton's postwar reminiscent writings were more popular than accurate. His *Spy of the Rebellion* (1883), p. 98, gives a faulty account with an incorrect illustration showing Lincoln leaving the depot escorted by Washburne *and* Seward. Pinkerton's MS., however, giving a contemporary record, states that "Washburne said . . . he was at the Depot . . . and that Gov. Seward was to have been at the Depot also, but that he (Washburne) did not see him." (The date is Feb. 23, 1861; Herndon-Lamon Collec., Huntington Lib., LN 2408, III: 305). In these matters the author gratefully acknowledges the assistance of Miss Norma Cuthbert of the Huntington Library.

[5] The following are among the references for the melodramatic episode of Lincoln's change of plan and secret ride: *Annual Cyclopaedia,* 1861, 416–419; Ward H. Lamon, *Life of Lincoln,* 511–526; Ward H. Lamon, *Recollections of Abraham Lincoln, 1847–1865,* ed. by Dorothy Lamon; Nicolay and Hay, *Lincoln,* III, 302–316; S. M. Felton, in William Schouler, *Mass. in the Civil War,* I, 59–65; *History . . . of the Passage of Abraham Lincoln from Harrisburg . . . to Washington . . .* (Republican print, undated); Charles W. Elliott, *Winfield Scott,* 693 ff.; Arthur Edwards, *Sketch of the Life of Norman B. Judd.* See also Chittenden, *Recollections,* and Rice, *Reminiscences.*

there was official information which could not be known to be so false as to be ignored. Secret service men of the Federal government were not then in the President Elect's party; had they been, Lincoln would have had even a poorer chance of resisting the demands for a change of schedule. The American method did not involve a pervasive national police, nor even an embryonic one; local police systems were uncoördinated, and it was, governmentally speaking, nobody's business in particular to see the President through in safety. Neither Lamon, Judd, Felton, nor Pinkerton had any governmental authority to act. Had President Buchanan detailed a military force to escort the President Elect, it would have added to the trouble besides being out of line with precedent. Had Lincoln been assassinated anywhere but in the District of Columbia, the national government would have been without authority even to punish the guilty party. Assurances of safety in Baltimore were unconvincing. George P. Kane, marshal of Baltimore, emphatically denied that there existed in his city any danger of mob action or of violence toward any public functionary, but his statement was dated January 16,[6] while Lincoln was to pass through on February 23. Kane himself was anti-Lincoln and feeling was at high pitch. Earlier in this narrative it has been shown that apprehension was real and widespread. The papers for many days had been full of serious talk of suspected violence. It was not as if Lincoln had evaded danger in the line of duty. He did not even have any ceremonial appointments in Baltimore; the passing through the streets was intended only as a necessary link in the itinerary. After he left Harrisburg his next duties were in Washington. He changed his plan not merely on the basis of Pinkerton's reports (Pinkerton having been brought into the picture on private arrangement by Felton and Judd) but on independent advice from the capital. In such matters a public chief is neither a free agent nor at liberty to take the public into his confidence.

What leaders have to suffer from, however, is not so much the essential situation as the manner in which it is publicly viewed. There were sorry consequences of Lincoln's night ride. He was reported going through Baltimore in a fictitious "Scotch plaid cap and . . . long military cloak," a fabricated description that has been traced to a journalist later imprisoned for forgery.[7] Cartoonists were particularly

---

[6] *Annual Cyclopaedia*, 1861. 419.   [7] Nicolay and Hay, *Lincoln*, III, 315

devilish in their caricatures of this imagined disguise. Opposition papers spread themselves on the subject and even Lincoln's friends were humiliated at the manner of his arrival in Washington.[8]

VI

The nine days between Lincoln's entry into the capital city and his inauguration were wearisome and difficult. On the day of his arrival he called upon President Buchanan and was introduced to members of the outgoing cabinet. With severe stress behind the scenes he had to make many public appearances. Congress, the mayor of Washington, hotel throngs, serenaders, members of the Supreme Court, and delegates to the Peace Conference had to be greeted, smiled upon, and in some cases addressed with an appropriate speech. Of more than common significance were the polite calls of his three 1860 rivals: John Bell, Stephen A. Douglas, and John C. Breckinridge. At Willard's the pressure was terrific, allowing "hardly . . . a chance to eat or sleep." Springfield, the harassed leader is reported to have said, was "bad enough . . . , but it was child's play compared with this tussle here." "I am fair game for everybody of that hungry lot." [1] The horde of office seekers [2] and the round of greetings and appearances allowed little time for public problems, yet his cabinet was not yet formally announced nor his inaugural address finally revised. To make things worse a major crisis in cabinet plans threatened at the very time of inauguration. Lincoln was informed that Seward could not serve in the same cabinet as Chase, and on March 2 Seward actually asked "leave to withdraw." [3] To lose Seward would mean seriously weakening the administration. The New York statesman and his friends were not of the sort to let the matter end there. Too radical a cabinet would not do; Lincoln found Seward indispensable. Yet it was not till the day after the inauguration that the matter was settled when Seward yielded to Lincoln's insistence that his eleventh-hour withdrawal be countermanded.[4] A matter of state was thus settled

---

[8] Rudolph Schleiden, minister resident of Bremen at Washington, reported on February 26 to his government that "like a thief in the night, the future President arrived here on the early morning of the 23d." R. H. Lutz, ed., in *Annual Report*, Amer. Hist. Assoc., 1915, 210.

[1] Villard, *Memoirs*, I, 156.   [2] For the rush of office seekers, see below, pp. 311–312.

[3] Nicolay and Hay, *Lincoln*, III, 370; Bancroft, *Seward*, II, 43–44.

[4] *Works*, VI, 185 (March 4, 1861); Nicolay and Hay, *Lincoln*, III, 371–372; Baringer, *A House Dividing*, 327–329.

by Lincoln and in Lincoln's favor.

That form of studiously favorable publicity which modern journalists turn on or off at will had been denied to Lincoln. In general it cannot be said that he had a "good press" at the threshold of office. Showmanship failed to make capital of his rugged origin, and there faced the country a strange man from Illinois who was dubbed a "Simple Susan," a "baboon," or a "gorilla." Writers of this period labeled Lincoln an "ape" (this being a favorite term in the South), a "demon," or an "Illinois beast." On one occasion it seemed to a Washington correspondent that his "attempt" at speaking was "crude, ignorant twaddle, without point or meaning." [5] There was the preposterous rumor that he had avoided a train because he feared a wreck and had then counseled his wife and sons to take it.[6] Publicity was unfortunately given to a trivial act of the traveling President Elect in kissing a little girl, described by Charnwood as the "dreadful young person" [7] who claimed credit for those ill-designed whiskers which now disfigured Lincoln's face. To Charles Francis Adams the younger it seemed that while Sumner "talked like a crazy man" and Seward "was laboring under a total misconception," the "absolutely unknown" Lincoln was "perambulating the country, kissing little girls and growing whiskers!" [8] An impertinent journalist linked the whiskers theme with the choice of a New York hotel: "Mr. Lincoln, having . . . brought his brilliant intellectual powers to bear upon the cultivation of luxuriant whiskers . . . , has now . . . concentrated his mental energies upon the question—what hotel he shall stop at in New York." [9] Though Lincoln's social *faux pas* have been exaggerated, there were men in the East who thought him lacking in polite ways and innocent of *savoir faire*. From this it was an easy step to consider him deficient in sagacity and qualities of statesmanship. This was one aspect of the matter that gave point to the criticisms apropos of the night ride to Washington. It was a lowering of a prestige that at best was none too high. " 'What brought him here so suddenly?' was

---

[5] Villard, *Memoirs*, I, 152. This was the tariff speech at Pittsburgh. The quoted statement was written later by Villard, but it presumably represents his contemporary attitude.

[6] Chicago *Tribune*, Feb 27, 1861, p. 2, c. 1.   [7] Charnwood, *Abraham Lincoln*, 204.

[8] C. F. Adams, *Autobiography*, 74–75, 79, 80, 82. This Adams was the son of the one who was soon to be minister to England.

[9] Albany *Atlas and Argus*, Feb. 15, 1861, p. 2, c. 4.

on everybody's tongue." [10] Yet some of the comments on the secret ride were favorable, recognizing that a calamity or at least an insult had been averted, that Lincoln had taken the advice of good counsellors, and that, even from the standpoint of Baltimore, the change was fortunate.[11]

VII

President Buchanan, Secretary of War Holt, and General Scott had paid heed to the possible danger of violence, and March 4, 1861, found Washington under unusual military protection, with guns commanding Pennsylvania Avenue, cross streets under guard, riflemen on housetops, new-drilled volunteers on parade, and "brawny young Republicans" on hand, "determined to see . . . [Lincoln] installed in office." [1] The militaristic touch had aroused the suspicions of the House of Representatives which had formally asked the reason for "so large a number of troops in this city." [2] In answer Secretary Holt referred to disorders in the South and to the belief of "multitudes" in a conspiracy to strike at the government, which belief he "fully shared." The general apprehension of a "raid upon the capital," and the open threat that Lincoln would never be inaugurated, he thought, could not be ignored.[3] Buchanan explained that, on March 1, there were only 653 "troops" in Washington exclusive of marines stationed at the navy yard, that these troops were there "to act as a *posse comitatus,* in strict subordination to civil authority," and that the existing condition of "high excitement," with rumors filling the air and threats freely expressed, was such that he "could not hesitate to adopt precautionary defensive measures." [4] Of course the protection of the government was not a mere matter of these 653 men. Contemporary accounts speak of a city full of troops, of "[t]housands of young men . . . well armed," [5] and especially of District of Columbia volunteers. These latter were organized by Colonel Charles P. Stone, charged with the defense of the capital, but they were not yet mustered into the Federal service and would not be Federal "troops" in the sense of

---

[10] Chicago *Tribune,* Feb. 26, 1861, p. 1, c. 2.
[11] *Ibid.,* Feb. 26–27, 1861.   [1] C. W. Elliott, *Winfield Scott,* 695.
[2] *Annual Cyclopaedia,* 1861, 750.   [3] *Ibid.,* 751.
[4] Richardson, *Messages . . . of the Presidents,* V, 669–670.
[5] G. Koerner, *Memoirs,* II, 117.

Buchanan's message. When thanked in Lincoln's behalf by Leonard Swett for his precautions, Stone replied that Lincoln should not be grateful to him, that he had opposed his election, and that his efforts were for "saving the Government." [6] Very much the same attitude toward Lincoln characterized the great majority of those who then held national office.[7]

Amid these military and quasi-military activities Lincoln performed the exacting duties of inauguration day. He entered President Buchanan's carriage at Willard's, and these diverse individuals rode side by side, in company with other "distinguished citizens," along the historic avenue.[8] Buchanan was described as grave and silent, Lincoln "calm and but little affected by the excitement around him." [9] For hours the human stream poured on toward the Capitol, the majority being Northerners according to the quaint remark of a reporter who noted the "lack of long haired [i. e., Southern] men in the crowd." [10] Part of the pageantry was a car decorated to symbolize the Union, the states and territories being represented by girls in white, the float being drawn by six white horses whose housing bore the word "Union." The parade was a Republican affair; marching delegations were politically sympathetic toward the incoming President. It was reported that Lincoln had to kiss the thirty-four states of the Union.[11] Arm in arm Lincoln and Buchanan entered the senate chamber where they faced crowded and brilliant galleries, while surging and heaving masses struggled in vain to view them. Here they attended a brief ceremony, Buchanan sighing "audibly, and frequently," Lincoln "impassive as an Indian martyr." [12]

On a temporary platform at the east front of the unfinished Capitol Lincoln faced an immense outdoor throng as he swore to "execute

---

[6] C. P. Stone, in *Battles and Leaders of the Civil War*, I, 22–23.

[7] It was reported that at the inauguration "nearly twenty of the . . . military companies of the District of Columbia were out, comprising . . . more than two thousand men under arms." Washington *Daily National Intelligencer*, Mar. 5, 1861, p. 3, c. 3.

[8] *Ibid.*

[9] New York *Herald*, Mar. 5, 1861, p. 1, c. 2. Buchanan wrote: "It is due to President Lincoln to state, that throughout his long progress in the same carriage with the late President, both on the way to the Capitol and the return from it, he was far from evincing the slightest apprehension of danger." Buchanan, *Mr. Buchanan's Administration*, 170.

[10] New York *Herald*, Mar. 5, 1861, p. 1, c. 2.

[11] Moore, *Rebellion Record* (Diary), I, 18.

[12] New York *Times*, Mar. 5, 1861, p. 1, c. 2.

THE INAUGURAL PROCESSION AT WASHINGTON PASSING THE GATE OF THE CAPITOL GROUNDS.—FROM A SKETCH BY OUR SPECIAL ARTIST.—[SEE PAGE 162.]

LINCOLN RIDES TO HIS INAUGURATION

Lincoln and Buchanan, on March 4, 1861, ride to the inaugural ceremony in an open carriage. Crowds are massed on the famous Avenue as soldiers guard rather ineffectively. (This is the west front of the Capitol.) The drawing appeared in *Harper's Weekly*, Mar. 16, 1861.

FIRST LADY

Taken early in the presidency. In an age of grandiloquence and excess in dress Mary Todd Lincoln had good taste and a sense of the appropriate, yet she passionately loved fine clothes and personal adornment.

the office of President of the United States, and . . . defend the Constitution . . . ," the oath being administered by Chief Justice Taney, whose court and whose opinion Lincoln had criticized. Near Lincoln on the platform were Buchanan, Breckinridge, and Douglas. In later accounts one finds of the dramatic story of how Senator Douglas held Lincoln's hat as he spoke his inaugural message, a fascinating and beautifully symbolic bit of Lincoln-Douglas biography for which a strictly contemporary source—i. e., an account written by a witness in March 1861—is difficult to find. None of the newspaper reports or other accounts written *at the time,* within the knowledge of the author, mentions the hat incident. A writer in the *Atlantic Monthly* in August 1861 described Douglas's sympathetic behavior at the inauguration without mentioning the hat.[13] The reference commonly given for the incident is "The Diary of a Public Man," published in 1879, but this diary, while rich in picturesque detail concerning Lincoln, has become a *cause célèbre* among historians and must be used with reservations. It purports to have been written in 1860–61 (December to early March), but as research on the subject now stands it is untraceable. Its authenticity is unproved, not to say doubtful.[14] (Those who accept the diary as authentic need look no further.) J. G. Holland referred to the hat incident, and his account has value, but his book did not appear until 1866.[15] Nicolay and Hay give only a passing reference to the holding of the hat, relegating it to a minor position in a footnote and offering it not as their own statement, but merely as part of a quotation from the post-war Holland account.[16] If they knew of the incident from direct observation or from contemporary statements, they give no sign of it. This is not to assert that the hat incident did not occur. The point is rather that a careful biographer looks for contemporary evidence, and where such evidence is lacking, or has not yet been found, it is his duty to say so. Henry Watterson reminiscently repeated the hat-holding story, reporting it as a witness, but his ac-

---

[13] *Atl. Mo.,* VIII, 212.

[14] "The Diary of a Public Man" appeared in four installments in the *North American Review* in 1879. For the hat incident see *ibid.,* CXXIX, 383. The present writer has commented briefly on the historical problem of the diary in *Amer. Hist. Rev.,* XLI, 277–279 (Jan. 1936). See also *The Diary of a Public Man . . . ,* Prefatory Notes by F. Lauriston Bullard, Foreword by Carl Sandburg, pub. by Abraham Lincoln Book Shop, 1945.

[15] J. G. Holland, *Life of Abraham Lincoln,* 278.

[16] Nicolay and Hay, *Lincoln,* III, 326 n.

count has by no means the value of a strictly contemporary record.[17]

Much more could be said of the vast crowds, of the incidents of inauguration day, of the hand-shaking, of the relief that came when no violence occurred, and of the President's ball that night. Lincoln's voice was described as "strong and clear," the cheers "loud and long." [18] "The opening sentence, 'Fellow-citizens of the United States,' was the signal for prolonged applause . . . . Again, when, after defining certain actions to be his duty, he said, 'And I shall perform it,' there was a spontaneous, and uproarious manifestation of approval, which continued for some moments." [19]

VIII

It is a mistake to suppose that prior to his inaugural Lincoln's attitude on resistance to secession, maintenance of the government, and like questions was altogether a cipher or an interrogation point. His policy had been one of caution and avoidance of public statement, but he had watched the situation, had kept in touch with Washington, and had at least made his position known to friends and counsellors. As noted in a previous chapter,[1] he had written in private letters that he would not persecute the South, would respect state rights, and would not push abolition measures. He had sought Southerners for his cabinet and had disclaimed any use of the patronage against the South. He had written to Weed that in his opinion "no State can . . . lawfully get out of the Union without the consent of the others," and that it would be his duty to "run the machine as it is." [2] He had cautioned General Scott to be ready to "hold or retake" the forts if necessary. He had protested against the interpretation that enforcement of the laws meant unjustifiable "coercion" or "invasion" [3] and had questioned the right of a "fiftieth part" of the nation to break up the whole.[4] He had been quoted as saying: ". . . I should regard concession in the face of menace as the destruction of the government

---

[17] *Marse Henry*, I, 78.

[18] Thurlow Weed, writing to Albany *Evening Journal*, Mar. 4, 1861, Weed's Book of Clippings, Division of Manuscripts, Lib. of Cong.

[19] New York *Times*, Mar. 5, 1861, p. 1, c. 3.

[1] Above, pp. 234–236.   [2] *Works*, VI, 82 (Dec. 17, 1860).

[3] *Ibid.*, VI, 113 (Feb. 12, 1861). For the "hold or retake" see *ibid.*, VI, 85 (letter to Washburne, Dec. 21, 1860).

[4] *Ibid.*, VI, 114 (Feb. 12, 1861).

itself . . . ." [5] He had said in February that there had been nothing (he meant no completed act of the Federal government against the South) "that really hurts anybody." [6] He had eloquently pledged allegiance, his life if need be, to free institutions, had praised the genius of American democracy, and had newly invoked the memories and principles of the Declaration of Independence. He had eschewed partisanship and uttered repeated expressions of friendliness toward the South and toward political opponents. If some were dissatisfied, he had nevertheless argued that "the defeated party . . . [were] not in favor of sinking the ship," but would "wait in the hope of . . . setting it right next time." He had summoned opponents to help pilot the ship, lest there "be no pilot ever needed for another voyage." [7] While avoiding a position from which he might later "be disposed . . . to shift," he had hinted that his known attitude would go far toward explaining his coming policy so far as the Union and the preservation of American civil liberties were concerned.[8] Though promising efforts toward a "peaceful settlement," [9] he had suggested that for this very object firmness might be needed. On vital and essential points he had expressed himself, yet his inaugural address came with real freshness and with the force of actual office-taking after important Washington consultations.

Proceeding without delay to the Southern fear that their security was endangered, Lincoln made it clear that he had no purpose "to interfere with . . . slavery in the States where it exists." [10] In doing this he underscored an attitude already announced, so as to make his pronouncement "the most conclusive . . . of which the case is susceptible." The peace and security of no section, he said, were endangered by the now incoming administration. Treating very guardedly the constitutional clause for the reclaiming of fugitive slaves, he declared that members of Congress must "keep good" their "unanimous oath" to support the Constitution, though he desired safeguards so that no free man would be surrendered as a slave. Applying historical perspective as against momentary or temporary agitations he referred to the "fifteen . . . distinguished citizens" who had

---

[5] Chicago *Tribune,* Feb. 5, 1861, p. 1, c. 1.   [6] *Works,* VI, 122 (Feb. 13, 1861).
[7] *Ibid.,* VI, 143, 154 (Feb. 19 and 21, 1861).   [8] *Ibid.,* VI, 147–148 (Feb. 19, 1861).
[9] *Ibid.,* VI, 153 (Feb. 21, 1861).
[10] *Works,* VI, 170. The quotations which follow are from *ibid.,* VI, 169–185, being the Nicolay-Hay edition of the inaugural address.

administered the executive branch in the seventy-two years since Washington's first inauguration. This sweep of time he contrasted with "the brief . . . four years" of the term on which he was entering. The "Union of these States," he said, "is perpetual." He dwelt in an extended passage on this theme, turning it over in its legal implications, declaring that the Union is "older than the Constitution" and concluding that the "Union is unbroken."

Lincoln did not dodge the problem of maintaining Federal authority in Southern areas where it was defied. His statement on this knotty subject had more in it than most writers have yet seen, though the address has been re-read and analyzed innumerable times. Just what did Lincoln say on this point, and how did he say it? These were his words:

I . . . consider that . . . the Union is unbroken; and to the extent of my ability I shall take care . . . that the laws of the Union be faithfully executed in all the States. Doing this I deem to be only a simple duty on my part; and I shall perform it so far as practicable, unless . . . the American people . . . shall withhold the . . . means, or . . . direct the contrary. I trust this will not be regarded as a menace, but only as the declared purpose of the Union that it will . . . defend and maintain itself.

In doing this there needs to be no bloodshed or violence; and there shall be none, unless it be forced upon the national authority. The power confided to me will be used to hold, occupy, and possess the property and places belonging to the government, and to collect the duties and imposts; but beyond what may be necessary for these objects, there will be no invasion, no using of force against or among the people anywhere.

Thus remembering his inescapable duty of seeing that the laws be faithfully executed, the new-sworn President nevertheless put in a modifying phrase or a conciliatory qualification at every possible point; this factor becomes especially impressive as one carefully re-reads the address with knowledge of the consultations back of it and the elaborate revisionary care devoted to its final wording. To miss this point is to fail to understand the inaugural. The very source of his authority, the Constitution of the United States, said Lincoln, expressly enjoined upon him the simple duty of enforcing the laws. This statement itself was conciliatory; it was intended to emphasize that his thought about the laws was in terms of his oath, of the American system, of the President's obligation to the people, of his own unavoidable need to be amenable to their mandate. Even at this point, however, he added the qualifying phrase; ". . . I shall perform it [the duty of seeing that the laws be observed] so far as practicable, unless my rightful masters, the American people, shall withhold the . . . means, or . . . direct the contrary. I trust this will not be regarded as a menace, but only as the declared purpose of the Union that it will constitutionally defend and maintain itself." With meticulous care he was emphasizing defense, omitting any suggestion of *re-possessing* strongholds that had fallen, avoiding the word "forts" (choosing rather the words "property and places belonging to the government"), and taking care repetitiously to give assurance that there need not be any violence, any trouble with the people in any locality. Then, having said this, Lincoln felt that an additional word, a further clarification, was needed. The unprovocative nature of his program is especially evident in his next statement:

Where hostility to the United States, in any interior locality, shall be so great and universal as to prevent competent resident citizens from holding the Federal offices, there will be no attempt to force obnoxious strangers among the people for that object. While the strict legal right may exist in the government to enforce the exercise of these offices, the attempt to do so would be so irritating . . . that I deem it better to forego for the time the use of such offices.

. . . So far as possible, the people everywhere shall have that sense of perfect security which is most favorable to calm thought and reflection. The course here indicated will be followed unless . . . events . . . shall show a modification . . . to be proper, and . . . my best discretion will be exercised according to circumstances actually existing, and with a view and a hope of a peaceful solution of the national troubles and the restoration of fraternal sympathies and affections.

The President was insisting on upholding governmental authority in principle, but as a practical matter this was not possible in certain troubled areas. This being so, the new leader actually went so far toward peace as to say that in regions where opposition was "great and universal" the performance of Federal functions would be suspended. The strict legal right existed, he said, but he deemed it better to "forego" that legal right for the time being. Government, as Lincoln saw, was more than a legal science; it was an art. Precise legality was not all. There must be due allowance for "discretion . . . according to circumstances actually existing." A bad situation must not be made worse by a wrong stroke from Washington. Confronted with a

choice of evils, the nation's chief thought it better to yield the exercise
of Federal authority than to do the thing which would be both irritating and fruitless of any favorable result. It was not a matter of
meeting defiance with force, but of changing the mood, forgiving a
certain truculence on the other side, having regard for an atmosphere
conducive to conciliation, and preserving "a view and a hope" of
peaceable adjustment.

In a scholarly study of the sectional crisis by David M. Potter this
passage of Lincoln's inaugural has been referred to as a formula and
a plan. Lincoln was doing more than uttering words. He was studying
solutions. The plan was to assert Federal authority with all cogency
and firmness and then, where such authority was angrily challenged,
to suspend its actual enforcement. Further "places and property" were
not to be yielded; yet Lincoln's policy, in practice, was shaped more
in terms of suspension than of enforcement. Where such enforcement
occurred it was to be non-truculent; it was to be off-shore; people in
the interior were not to be molested. The off-shore positions, of course,
were Pickens and Sumter. To surrender these was not promised,
but in matters pertaining to the customs, the national courts, the forts
and arsenals already seized, and the post offices, "obnoxious strangers"
(Federal officials) would not be forced upon the people. In such a
matter of daily life as the mails a qualifying phrase was used; the mails
would be continued "unless repelled." As to customs duties, if collected at all, this was to be done by an off-shore process; as it turned
out, even this effort was dropped, while collection at customs houses
was also avoided. Writing of this general subject, but with special
attention to the question of the forts, Dr. Potter remarks that "Lincoln's attitude toward this problem shows how completely he had
abandoned a policy of force." [11]

It is significant that Lincoln took this prominent occasion to deliver
a striking pronouncement concerning the Supreme Court. He by no
means admitted the authority of the Court to settle constitutional
questions and went much farther than most liberal legal commentators
in limiting the effect of the Court's decisions to the "particular case"
and to the "parties to a suit." Having said this much he proceeded:

11 David M. Potter, *Lincoln and His Party in the Secession Crisis*, 327. For the
wretchedly complicated questions of disunion, compromise, peaceable separation, and
rumblings of war that pertained to the crisis following Lincoln's election, Dr. Potter's
scholarly monograph offers a competent marshaling of material and a capable analysis.

At the same time, the candid citizen must confess that if the policy of the government, upon vital questions affecting the whole people, is to be irrevocably fixed by decisions of the Supreme Court, the instant they are made, in ordinary litigation between parties in personal actions, the people will have ceased to be their own rulers, having to that extent practically resigned their government into the hands of that eminent tribunal. Nor is there in this view any assault upon the court or the judges. It is a duty from which they may not shrink to decide cases properly brought before them, and it is no fault of theirs if others seek to turn their decisions to political purposes.

For grievances he recognized in general the peaceful processes of constitutional amendment, and in particular (though this was a hard concession) he indicated his consent to the pending amendment which would have made an "express and irrevocable" declaration "that the Federal Government shall never interfere" with slavery in the states.

In closing he begged for "patient confidence in the ultimate justice of the people" and asked "Is there any better or equal hope in the world?" To "dissatisfied fellow-countrymen" he said: "You can have no conflict without being yourselves the aggressors. You have no oath . . . to destroy the government, while I shall have the most solemn one to 'preserve, protect, and defend it.' " From reason and logic he turned in his last paragraph to sentiment and affection. "I am loath to close. We are not enemies, but friends. We must not be enemies. Though passion may have strained, it must not break our bonds of affection. The mystic chords of memory, stretching from every battlefield and patriot grave to every living heart and hearthstone all over this broad land, will yet swell the chorus of the Union when again touched, as surely they will be, by the better angels of our nature."

A significant chapter could be written on the composition of this inauguration speech. Privately printed in Springfield, it had undergone elaborate and careful revision en route and in Washington. The "original" soon became a patchwork of pastings, deletions, insertions, and printed residue; it was this patchwork which Lincoln held as he read, and a reproduction of it was given to the press. There had been in the earlier version a weak and embarrassed reference to the Chicago platform and an unenthusiastic promise to "follow" its "principles" while repeating none of its "aspersion[s] or epithet[s]." Deleting this limping passage on Seward's advice, Lincoln avoided anything like blanket approval of the Republican platform whose binding effect was already disputed among Republicans themselves, while the great popular majority of voters in 1860, being anti-Republican, had deprived the platform of all force as a "mandate." The clause in the platform which Lincoln did emphasize and endorse was that which recognized state rights in the American "balance of power" and promised noninterference with slavery in the states.

In one of his alterations Lincoln produced a passage which offered Federal assistance to the states ". . . as cheerfully to one section as to another." Where the earlier version had said the disruption of the Union had been ". . . on paper . . . effected" Lincoln made it read ". . . formidably attempted." A reference to the perpetuity of the Union was strengthened by a statement that the faith of all the states had been "expressly plighted." The word "revolutionary" was substituted for "treasonable" in a passage concerning Southern ordinances of secession. On the suggestion of his friend O. H. Browning, to whom he gave a copy of his printed draft while at Indianapolis, Lincoln made probably the most important change of all by deleting a statement that his power would be "used to reclaim the public property and places" already fallen, and confining himself to a pledge that he would "hold, occupy, and possess" the government property.

There were many other changes, an insertion assuring Southerners of reciprocal citizenship rights, an emphasizing of the pledge against aggressive use of force, and an underlining of his "hope of a peaceful solution." The passage referring to "destruction of our national fabric, with all its benefits, its memories, and its hopes" was an addition to the earlier printed version, as was also the notable passage deploring a situation by which vital policy could be "irrevocably fixed" by the Supreme Court. Finally, the peroration was a Lincolnian transmutation of a passage written by Seward. More high-flown than Lincoln's usual style, it nevertheless conveyed a sentiment so deeply moving that exalted rhetoric became its fitting medium.[12]

---

[12] Among the manuscripts in the Library of Congress is found the earlier printed version with secretarial reproductions of the many handwritten changes. This library also has a photostat of the letter of John Hay to Charles Eliot Norton (March 29, 1889) explaining how the address was revised. See also Nicolay and Hay, *Lincoln*, III, 327–343 (footnotes); Browning, *Diary*, I, 455 and n.

IX

Comment on the President's address ranged widely. There was reasoned praise, fulsome adulation, denunciation, ridicule, and caricature. Much of the comment was concerned with elements read into the address rather than with its explicit contents. For Americans of a later day it is interesting to note that Lincoln was not then regarded as a master of style and that the literary form of his speech received unfavorable comment. The Toronto *Leader* could not admire the "tawdry and corrupt schoolboy style" of the address, though giving "credit" for its "good sense" and abstention from threats of coercion.[1] J. C. Welling asked Sumner what he thought of the inaugural. "Is it a clear . . . and homogeneous paper, or is it, like the Cabinet, a little 'mixed,' as well in point of thought as of style?" He thought the style "exceedingly *plain,* not to say *hard-favored."* He was sure the concluding sentence was written either by Seward or Sumner. He thought Lincoln "would have done better if he had submitted the whole document to the revision of . . . [Sumner's] scholarly taste."[2] This very plainness, however, seemed a virtue to the Chicago *Tribune,* which admired the *"freshness* of Mr. Lincoln's utterances" and their "freedom from diplomatic vagueness and hackneyed political phrases."[3] Some of the comments were merely noncommittal. It seemed to a *Herald* writer that the address was received by Republicans with a lack of enthusiasm.[4] The Boston *Post* could not determine from the speech whether the new chief meant coercion or conciliation, and sagely remarked that time only could show whether the country's difficulties were to be adjusted or whether "rashness . . . [would] plunge it into the abyss of war."[5]

Part of the rejoicing over the inaugural was relief and pleasure over the fact of a successful inauguration. The Chicago *Tribune* referred to Monday, March 4th as "the day of deliverance."[6] Bells were rung and thirty-four guns fired at Wyandotte, Kansas, to express "general rejoicing" in the inauguration as an event.[7] In Hartford, Connecticut,

---

[1] Toronto (Canada) *Leader,* quoted in New York *Tribune,* Mar. 7, 1861, p. 7, c. 3.
[2] J. C. Welling to Charles Sumner, probably Mar. 5, 1861, Sumner MSS.
[3] Mar. 5, 1861, p. 1, c. 1.   [4] Villard, *Memoirs,* I, 158.
[5] As quoted in New York *Tribune,* Mar. 7, 1861, p. 7, c. 1.
[6] Mar. 4, 1861, p. 1, c. 1.   [7] New York *Times,* Mar. 6, 1861, p. 8, c. 2.

a national salute was fired on the afternoon of inauguration day.[8]
"I felt a hundred fold better and stronger the moment it [the in-
augural] was delivered," wrote one of Governor Andrew's friends.
Already, he said, the "public pulse" showed signs of "returning national health." "What an audience! . . . Every word was heard, &
the most perfect quiet & order prevailed—this is a great day." [9] "A
truer, or safer, or more patriotic policy it would be impossible . . .
to inaugurate," was the judgment of the Newark *Mercury*.[10] "The
whole civilized world [thought the Hartford *Courant*] will echo
Lincoln's Inaugural, and agree that it is fair to both sides, and worthy
of a patriot statesman." [11]

Some of the comment generalized as to the quality of the new leader.
A Plymouth paper saw reason to hope "that Abraham Lincoln will
prove a wise, prudent and fearless president, unbiased by the fanaticism
of his party, ..." [12] Praising the "ability, directness, candor and
purpose" of Lincoln's address, the New York *Tribune* found all doubt
removed "concerning his success as Chief-Magistrate." [13] To the New
York *Evening Post* it was evident that Lincoln was becoming "a great
favorite with all classes" and was winning "universal popularity." [14]
The sincerity and manliness of his address "extorted the praise even
of his enemies," [15] and "Republicans of all shades" were "delighted"
with the incoming leader.[16] An Illinois admirer thought the address
was "endorsed by all parties" and that nothing could have been added
or taken from it unless it might have been a sentence declaring that a
free people should have remunerative employment and that the government should protect the results of labor.[17]

Some of the praise was at a discount with Lincoln's conservative
supporters. Where the papers commending him were radical, praise
was an embarrassment. Such papers stressed Lincoln's firmness of purpose, his emphasis upon his oath to defend the government, his alleged
resemblance to General Jackson, and his determination to "hold"

8 *Ibid.*   9 I. Z. Goodrich to John A. Andrew, Mar. 4, 1861. Andrew MSS.
10 Newark (N. J.) *Mercury*, as quoted in New York *Tribune*, Mar. 6, 1861, p. 6, c. 5.
11 Quoted in New York *Tribune*, Mar. 7, 1861, p. 7, c. 1.
12 *Plymouth Rock* (Plymouth, Mass.), Mar. 7, 1861.
13 New York *Tribune*, Mar. 5, 1861, p. 5, c. 4.
14 Quoted in Chicago *Tribune*, Mar. 4, 1861, p. 1, c. 3.
15 *Ibid.*, Mar. 8, 1861, p. 2, c. 4.   16 *Ibid.*, Mar. 7, 1861, p. 1, c. 4.
17 W. H. Thomas to Lyman Trumbull, Mar. 12, 1861, Trumbull MSS.

the forts.[18] It is not true, however, that the radicals were completely satisfied, and the statement of the Chicago *Tribune* that the mere holding of the forts was "not enough" [19] suggested that if Lincoln were really to please such men he would be sure to offend multitudes of others. One of the most interesting comments, because it did not repeat the commonplace, was that of Elizur Wright of Boston, who admired the address as a "masterly piece of generalship." "I hardly know which most to admire [he wrote], the adroit . . . use of the rotten plank in the Chicago platform, or the sound argument which puts the supreme court back into its proper place." [20]

Adverse comments in the North served to underline the hazard of American presidents as of all leaders in democratic states—namely, running the gantlet of press criticism. That such criticism was expected, was even protected by the government itself as an indefeasible right, and was usually considered in relation to its source, was after all, perhaps, the most comforting factor in the situation. There was no suppression of such criticism. "The Inaugural, as a whole," declared the Baltimore *Sun*, "breathes the spirit of mischief. . . . It . . . intimates the design to exercise . . . authority to any extent of war and bloodshed, qualified only by the *withholding* of the requisite means . . . by the American people. . . . There is no Union spirit in the address, ..." [21] An Albany paper dealt out sarcastic paraphrase, thus: ". . . Mr. Lincoln declares: 'The minority have given me power, and I will use it . . . against the dissatisfied States; and the responsibility of civil war will rest upon the insurgents who resist.' " [22] Lincoln's policy of collecting the revenue and enforcing the laws in the South was held "impracticable, if not impossible" by the *Herald* and his position declared "pitiable." It was pointed out that no Federal court in the South would uphold him and that the only solution would be for Congress to give him despotic power.[23] The President, thought the

---

[18] Chicago *Tribune*, Mar. 5 to 11, passim.   [19] Apr. 11, 1861, p. 2, c. 1.

[20] Elizur Wright to S. P. Chase, Boston, Mar. 7, 1861, Chase MSS., Lib. of Cong. Wright appears to have objected to the Republican platform as not sufficiently abolitionist. Lincoln's use of the platform in his address had been to quote and stress the conciliatory passage renouncing interference with slavery ("domestic institutions") in the states.

[21] Quoted in New York *Tribune*, Mar. 7, 1861, p. 7, c. 1.

[22] Albany *Atlas and Argus*, as quoted in New York *Times*, Mar. 7, 1861, p. 4, c. 4.

[23] Editorial, New York *Herald*, Mar. 6, 1861, p. 4, cc. 2-3.

Herald, showed deliberate ignorance of the issue. Some of his words meant war, in others there was an attempt at mediation. His government was probably undecided. In particular he was assailed for attacking the Supreme Court.[24] The Chicago *Times* denounced the whole message as "a loose, disjointed, rambling affair" and concluded that the Union was "lost beyond hope." If the message was carried out, this paper expected civil war in thirty days.[25] To the New York *Staats Zeitung* it appeared that Lincoln had shown himself more the lawyer than the statesman, and that his success lay more with words than with accomplishments. Commenting on Lincoln's suggestion that nothing was to be lost by taking time, this German-American journal suggested that the Republican party had made poor use of its time by refusing compromise and cutting off the chances of reconciliation.[26] In the same spirit the St. Louis *Republican,* representing the Douglas Democrats, said: "We hoped for a more conservative and more conciliatory expression of sentiments." [27]

X

It was no surprise to find that the inaugural was unfavorably received in the South. As printed in New Orleans papers the address was, said the Chicago *Tribune,* "horribly botched" and its words so twisted as to give the opposite of the meaning intended.[1] A Savannah paper facetiously referred to the suggestion that people pray for Lincoln and remarked that he was "past praying for." [2] A Kentuckian, resenting the Republican refusal to compromise and the inaugural pledge to "collect revenue from . . . an independent Government," suggested capturing Lincoln and "showing him around the country as a curiosity." This same gentleman declared that he could raise ten thousand men in a week and have them "on the road to join Davis' forces the moment a blow is struck against him." [3] Charles J. Faulkner, a Virginia diplomat writing from the American legation at Paris, could

---

[24] Mar. 5, 1861, p. 4, cc. 2–3.
[25] As quoted in New York *Times,* Mar. 6, 1861, p. 8, cc. 1–2.
[26] As quoted in New York *Tribune,* Mar. 6, 1861, p. 6, c. 5.
[27] Reprinted in New York *Times,* Mar. 6, 1861, p. 8, c. 1.
[1] Chicago *Tribune,* Mar. 11, 1861, p. 2, c. 1.
[2] Savannah *Daily Morning News,* Mar. 5, 1861.
[3] B. Duncan, Louisville, Ky., to S. A. Douglas, Mar. 7, 1861, Douglas MSS. This Kentuckian ended with the impudent wish that Mrs. Douglas might be his wife.

see nothing in the inaugural calculated to tranquilize the South or to indicate whether the President meant peace or war.[4]

The denunciation of the inaugural as a call to arms was the commonest and most typical of the Southern comments. Dispatches from Montgomery brought the news that in the capital city of the new Confederacy war between North and South was now considered inevitable.[5] In North Carolina, where secession was yet resisted, the cry of the disunion leaders that the address was a "war message" was having its effect.[6] A Savannah journal predicted that Lincoln's program left little doubt that the volunteer military companies would have opportunity to serve the South.[7] At Nashville opinion was reported as unsettled, with an inclination toward the unfavorable. Jackson and Columbus, Mississippi, and Tuscumbia, Alabama, were reported as considering it a declaration of war, New Orleans condemned it, and Vicksburg dubbed it a "silly production."[8] In Richmond both the secessionist *Enquirer* and the conservative *Whig* deplored the address.[9] To the Richmond correspondent of the New York *Tribune* it seemed that in the latitude of Virginia the message was regarded as strengthening the hands of the secessionists, whereas this element had been but a few days previously a small minority.[10]

The Columbia *South Carolinian* caught up some hope (disunion hope) from the pledge to commit no aggressive act and felt assured that Lincoln would see the impracticability of exacting unjust tribute from the Confederate States.[11] The *Mercury* (Charleston) referred to Lincoln's "insolence" and "brutality," and declared that the United States had become "a mobocratic Empire." To this paper the policy of the South was now one of "war strategy."[12] While waiting for the inaugural, palmetto-state spokesmen had prepared their people for a

---

[4] C. J. Faulkner to W. H. Seward, U. S. Legation, Paris, April 5, 1861, MS., Ill. State Hist. Lib.

[5] New York *Herald*, Mar. 6, 1861, p. 4, c. 1.

[6] Q. Busbee to S. A. Douglas, Raleigh, N. C., Mar. 11, 1861, Douglas MSS.

[7] Savannah *Daily Morning News*, Mar. 5, 1861.

[5] New York *Herald*, Mar. 6, 1861, p. 4, c. 1.
Times.

[9] *Ibid.*

[10] "The Secessionists [in Virginia] now . . . say . . . 'We told you so.' . . . There is but little doubt *now* that henceforth the Secessionists, who a few days ago were but a small minority, will have things pretty much their own way." Statement of *Tribune* correspondent writing from Richmond, in New York *Tribune*, Mar. 9, 1861, p. 6, c. 2.

[11] Quoted in New York *Times*, Mar. 9, 1861, p. 1, c. 6.

[12] Charleston *Mercury*, Mar. 5, 1861.

Southern proclamation of a state of hostility between the cotton states and the North if the President promised a retention of the few remaining lower Southern forts.[13] Among some South Carolinians, however, there appeared to be a feeling of regret that the inaugural was not more bellicose, and that it contained so little "blood and thunder." This was reported as "annoying to the Rebels, who hoped to find in the address a provocation for extreme action." [14] In Georgia also it was reported that the lack of truculence in the President's address knocked the props from under the secessionists.[15]

Though, as the New York *Times* remarked, it would have been impossible for Lincoln to have delivered a message that would please the secessionists,[16] yet among Southerners who did not approve of secession the address did meet with some favor. After talking with Southern men a friend of Governor Andrew wrote that Lincoln's inaugural had broken the backbone of secession.[17] John Letcher, governor of Virginia, wrote that there was a sobering down, that conservatives intended to think calmly, and that they were turning their thoughts to a border-state conference.[18] An Alabama friend wrote Douglas that the inaugural was "not very warlike"; it was the papers, he said, that were "one and all making it out coercive in the extreme." [19] Jubal A. Early, speaking in the Virginia Convention, referred to Lincoln's intent to execute the laws as "a guarantee that he would perform his duty" and put the blame for the "perilous condition" of the country upon the states that had seceded "without having consulted our views." [20] John A. Gilmer, the North Carolinian whom Lincoln wished to bring into his cabinet, ably expressed the Southern unionist point of view. Mentioning the guarantee against interference with slavery in the states together with the other pledges of the President, and also the repealing by the Northern states of their personal liberty laws "as rapidly as they can," he asked: ". . . what

[13] Statement of *Tribune* correspondent at Charleston, Mar. 2, 1861, New York *Tribune*, Mar. 7, 1861, p. 6, c. 1.

[14] *Ibid.*, Mar. 9, 1861, p. 6, c. 1.

[15] Statement of *Tribune* correspondent at Savannah, in New York *Tribune*, Mar. 11, 1861, p. 6, c. 2.

[16] Mar. 7, 1861, p. 4, c. 2.

[17] L. B. Comins to John A. Andrew, Washington, Mar. 6, 1861, Andrew MSS.

[18] John Letcher to J. D. Davidson, Richmond, Mar. 9, 1861, Davidson MSS., McCormick Library, Chicago.

[19] Joseph C. Bradley to S. A. Douglas, Huntsville, Ala., Mar. 8, 1861, Douglas MSS.

[20] Quoted in B. B. Mumford, *Virginia's Attitude toward Slavery and Secession*, 266.

more does any reasonable Southern man expect or desire?" "Are not . . . these . . . cheering assurances enough to induce the whole South to wait for the sober second thought of the North?" [21] Unfortunately the mild and quieting comments just quoted from Letcher and Gilmer were conveyed in private correspondence, while the comments in Southern newspapers and in the published statements of politicians were usually of the truculent sort.

Neither South nor North had an adequate mirror of itself at the time, but it is significant that trouble-making comments traveled faster and attained far more publicity than moderate ones. Every clue to Lincoln's attitude confirms the conclusion that he spoke truth in saying he had no aggressive design whatever upon the South. Secessionists, as shown above, regretted the lack of blood and thunder in his address, thus admitting its unthreatening character, while moderates saw in it a basis upon which even Southerners could stand. It is interesting to note that Lincoln in Washington was more moderate than Lincoln in Springfield. Whether this was due to the influence of Seward or to a combination of various contacts and reflections en route and at Willard's, the fact remains that, aside from literary revision, the controlling motive in the extensive alteration of the inaugural in these days was that of friendliness, nonaggression, and adjustment with the South.

In short, if one would justly appraise Lincoln's first presidential state paper, this inaugural of 1861 deserves both to be read as delivered and to be set over against the alternative statements that Lincoln avoided or struck out in revision. Statements pledging maintenance of Federal authority were toned down and shorn of truculence, while promises of conciliation were emotionally underlined. Even in enforcing the laws Lincoln held himself subject to his "masters," the American people. Men who would destroy the Union were referred to as "persons in one section or another." Protection to the states was offered "as cheerfully to one section, as to another." The Republican platform was quoted not for anything the South might resent, but for the pledge of non-interference with slavery. The new chief would seek a "peaceful solution." He would stress "fraternal sympathies." As to military policy he showed special care in the choice

---

[21] Gilmer to Douglas, Mar. 8, 1861, Douglas MSS. Later in the letter he referred to "the sober second thought of a majority of those who voted for Lincoln."

of nouns and verbs. His statement was not that he would "recapture" the "forts," but that he would "hold, . . . and possess the property and places belonging to the government." Even this holding and possessing was qualified; it involved no need of bloodshed, no invasion, no use of force anywhere. This was decidedly not a promise to withdraw from Sumter, but it was a promise not to use Sumter for aggressive attack upon South Carolina. Maintenance of the Union was conceived as adjusting difficulties within the Union. Physically there could be no separation. Relations could be no more satisfactory after separation than before. One could not fight always. When fighting ceased the old questions were still to be faced. In the very words of Gilmer the President asked his countrymen to think calmly. The Union was not merely to be supported; it was to be cherished. Memories were bound up with it. In contrast to the remediable and trivial character of existing grievances, he warned of the gravity of "the destruction of our national fabric, with all its benefits, its memories, and its hopes." Could anyone hazard such a step "while the ills you fly from have no real existence?" Newspapers might denounce the "war message," but these were the concepts that the new President begged the nation to ponder.

CHAPTER XII

SUMTER

I

THE transition from the Buchanan to the Lincoln administration meant just one thing to politicians—offices and spoils. "The change from a long Democratic to a Republican régime involved a sweeping change of functionaries." [1] When a reporter noted that the new President was "about the busiest person in Washington" and that he was "working early and late," he indicated that most of this was due to office seekers. [2] Edwin M. Stanton wrote that the scramble for office was "terrific," as had been said at Willard's, and that Lincoln was reported to be "seeing no strangers alone." [3] It was also stated that Lincoln was doing the appointing himself, undertaking to handle "the whole patronage small and great leaving nothing to the Chiefs of Departments." [4] Joseph Medill of the Chicago *Tribune,* who was in Washington at this time, wrote of a "mob of candidates" and feared that they would "neutralize the strength of the Tribune folks with Mr. Lincoln." The case of the Chicago post office was typical of the hundreds of positions that Lincoln had to fill, for it was assumed that incumbents would be put out all over the country and that places would be made for Lincoln's friends. "To us the P. O. would be of great value," wrote Medill to Trumbull. "If Mr S. [John L. Scripps] had it the country Post Masters of the N. West would work to extend our circulation . . . . You observe that the office would be vastly more beneficial to us than to any individual . . . . The Republican people of Chicago expect . . . the 'Tribune'

---

[1] Nicolay and Hay, *Lincoln,* III, 443.
[2] Chicago *Tribune,* Mar. 14, 1861, p. 1, c. 2.
[3] E. M. Stanton to James Buchanan, Mar. 10, 1861, Buchanan MSS.
[4] Stanton to Buchanan, Mar. 16, 1861, *ibid.*

to have the P. O." [5] But Lincoln had not only to satisfy the *Tribune,* which considered the post office its proper quarry; he was expected to reward every element that helped him at Chicago, including, for example, a vigorous contingent of Germans.[6]

New York also had its *Tribune,* and its editor was no less interested in offices. On this subject Greeley felt deeply. "I tell you [he wrote] the chances are three to one against an honest man getting anything. The thieves hunt in gangs, and each helps all the rest. Three-quarters of the post-offices will go into the hands of the corruptionists." [7] So it went. In the eyes of party workers it was the local offices that counted, which meant rivalries, perplexities, and pressure from all over the country. This was the first phase of Lincoln's duty as executive; it made cruel demands on his time at the outset, and with an increasing number of offices to fill it remained an unending source of annoyance throughout his presidency.

The cabinet should have been an instrument to assist and sustain the President, but under Lincoln it was never that. It has been seen that his administration began with a cabinet crisis before the official council was installed,[8] and, had Lincoln known it, this might have been taken as a warning that his period of rule would be a series of minor cabinet crises, with now and then a major one. Confirmation of cabinet appointments by the Senate came with little difficulty on March 5, except for a few Southern votes cast against Bates and Blair. Senator Mason of Virginia opposed the confirmation of Blair on the ground that no Southern man ought to hold office under Mr. Lincoln.[9] When confirmation was announced it was remarked that Weed made no concealment of his chagrin, that Cameron took the event as a bitter pill, and that Greeley strode about with the air of a conqueror.[10] "Yes, we *did* [wrote Greeley], by desperate fighting, succeed

[5] Medill to Trumbull, Mar. 4, 1861 (marked "Private"), Trumbull MSS. Scripps was appointed; thus the *Tribune* got the post office.

[6] G. Koerner to Trumbull, Mar. 13, 1861, *ibid.*

[7] Greeley to B. Brockway of Watertown, N. Y., Mar. 12, 1861, Greeley MSS., Lib. of Cong.

[8] See above, p. 291.

[9] Senators Mason, Bragg, Clingman, and Mitchell (Southerners) voted against confirming Blair; Hunter, Wigfall, and others refused to vote. There was the same opposition in the case of Bates. New York *Tribune,* Mar. 6, 1861, p. 4, c. 6. This Southern attitude offers a significant commentary on Lincoln's problem so far as it related to intersectional compromise.

[10] New York *Herald,* Mar. 6, 1861, p. 1, c. 1.

in getting four honest . . . men into the cabinet—by a fight that you never saw equalled . . . . Gov. Chase, the ablest Republican living, . . . indispensable to the treasury, got it at last . . . . All the Kitchen Cabinet, including the Senate President, were dead against him . . . ." [11] Yet the satisfaction of Greeley, due to the choice of Chase, should not be understood to indicate that the cabinet was radical, or even particularly forward in its firmness for the Union. It was reported as a "common saying" in Washington that Lincoln's cabinet "did not contain three as absolute and strong defenders of the Union as Dix, Holt, and Stanton, who had just retired with Mr. Buchanan." [12] Under these circumstances the sterner type of Republicans looked to Chase to preserve the country "from dissolution," [13] while another type within the party looked to Seward to save it from wild radicalism. At the first meeting of the cabinet, which occurred on the night of March 6, it would appear that virtually nothing happened. At any rate Edward Bates recorded that the occasion was "formal and introductory only—in fact, uninteresting." [14]

In the first month or so the new administration was watched for indications of its direction or policy, and a surprising amount of the Northern comment was distrustful or unfavorable. Editors inevitably pronounced their pontifical judgments, and among these Bennett of the *Herald* was particularly caustic, declaring that the Lincoln government was interested only in spoils and in pursuing an antagonistic attitude toward the South.[15] Edwin M. Stanton reported to Buchanan: "Every day affords proof of the absence of any settled policy, or harmonious . . . action, in the administration. Seward, Bates, and Cameron, form one wing, Chase, Welles, Blair the opposite wing. Smith is on both sides, and Lincoln sometimes on one, sometimes on the other. There has been agreement on nothing." [16] Stanton noted a diminishing of loyalty to the government and thought the administration did not

---

[11] Greeley to B. Brockway of Watertown, N. Y., Mar. 12, 1861, Greeley MSS., Lib. of Cong.

[12] Blaine, *Twenty Years of Congress*, I, 285–286. "We have great faith in . . . our President but none in the majority of his Cabinet." W. B. Plato to Lyman Trumbull, Geneva, Ill., Mar. 29, 1861, Trumbull MSS.

[13] John Jay to S. P. Chase, Katonah, N. Y., Apr. 8, 1861, Chase MSS., Lib. of Cong. Similarly, an Ohio man wrote to Chase: "How deplorably has Mr. Seward mistaken the temper . . . of the Northern people. . . . We *Republicans* of Ohio look to you . . . to redeem us." W. D. Bickham of Columbus, Ohio, to Chase, Apr. 2, 1861, *ibid.*

[14] Bates, *Diary*, 177.   [15] New York *Herald*, Mar. 21, 1861, p. 4, c. 2.

[16] Stanton to Buchanan, Mar. 16, 1861, Buchanan MSS.

have the confidence of the people. "Seward," he said "rented a house 'while he should continue in the Cabinet,' " but five weeks after the inauguration he had not opened it, nor had his family come. They all acted as if "they meant to be ready 'to cut and run' [thought Stanton] at a minute's notice." Their tenure, he said, was "that of a Bedouin on the sands of the desert." Among the people Stanton observed "a strong feeling of distrust in . . . Lincoln personally, and of his Cabinet . . . ." [17]

Amid distrust of Seward, growls about Scott's "imbecility," [18] complaints of moneyed men, and disappointment at the adjournment of a Congress which had neither provided for defense nor promoted compromise, Stanton found a kind of grim comfort for Buchanan, whose administration he now considered vindicated. [19] As if other troubles were not enough, the new tariff bill (the partially protective Morrill act of February 20, 1861, favored by Republicans and passed after withdrawal of Southerners in Congress) was giving "great trouble"; [20] "The Republicans . . . [were] beginning to think that a monstrous blunder was made in the tariff Bill; and that it . . . [would] cut off the trade of New York, build up New Orleans, . . . and leave the government no revenue—they see before them the prospect of soon being without money, and without credit." [21] Pennsylvanians were reported "angry about the threatened repeal of the tariff" and saying that they voted for Lincoln with the "explicit understanding" that they would be satisfied on this point. [22] There was much to confirm the close connection between Pennsylvania Republicanism and the tariff. While the Morrill bill was pending, a Philadelphian had written Congressman John Sherman that a mere "loose aggregation" could be "knit together and crystalised into a genuine republican party" by the passage of the tariff bill; if not, he added, the state would relapse

---

[17] Stanton to Buchanan, April 11, 1861, *ibid.* Stanton wrote: ". . . no one speaks of Lincoln or any member of his Cabinet with respect or regard." *Ibid.*

[18] Stanton to Buchanan, Mar. 16, 1861, *ibid.*

[19] Stanton to Buchanan, Apr. 3, 1861, *ibid.* These letters of Stanton were written at Washington.

[20] *Ibid.* Stanton added: ". . . luckily it is a measure of their own." Stanton was thinking in anti-Republican and anti-Lincolnian terms.

[21] Stanton to Buchanan, Mar. 16, 1861, *ibid.*

[22] Chicago *Tribune,* Apr. 1, 1861, p. 4, c. 4. As an example of the opposite point of view, Joshua Leavitt wrote from New York to Chase, February 18, 1861: "I do hope we are not to be sacrificed to sordid Pa on the tariff," adding that duties were needed for revenue. Chase MSS., Lib. of Cong.

into the control of the "Bogus democracy." His advice was: "Save the Bill and you *make* a party in Penna." [23]

II

Cabinet troubles, post offices, and tariff worries might loom large in other administrations. For Lincoln the abnormality of the American situation left no time to settle down to a regular round of executive duties. At the very beginning there was thrust upon him an inescapable dilemma as to Charleston Harbor, where an early decision had to be made, but where any conceivable choice of conduct would be dangerous and bitterly distasteful. For it must be noted that the calamitous difficulty of the Sumter question, involving the most vexatious decision that Lincoln ever had to make, was inherent in the dilemma itself. It existed in the nature of the ugly factors of the problem as presented in March and April of 1861. Lincoln could not hope to avoid trouble; he could merely choose between alternatives of trouble. It was not merely a matter of inheriting Buchanan's dilemma, though it was partly that; under Lincoln an almost immediate decision had to be made, whereas Buchanan could deal in understandings, deferments, and status quo.

While conciliation seemed still possible and the avoidance of war supremely important, Buchanan had permitted Southern occupation of the great majority of the Federal forts, arsenals, navy yards, and custom houses within seceded areas. In this respect secessionists, instead of having a cause of complaint, achieved an easy success far beyond what might have been reasonably expected. Cards were placed in their hands. The list of the forts and places seized before Lincoln took hold is much too long to be given here, but any student of the period will find the list full of interest.[1] To mention but one aspect of this situation under Buchanan, the Federal military force then available was entirely inadequate to garrison the forts. To have attempted it would have exposed the weakness of the government and might thus have provoked war. Reënforcing the forts in December 1860, wrote Buchanan, "would have been little short of madness . . . with the small force at his [the President's] command. . . . Our army

[23] T. Webster to John Sherman, Philadelphia, Feb. 18, 1861, John Sherman MSS.
[1] As to Texas alone the list fills a closely printed page. *Offic. Rec.*, 1 ser., I, 502.

was still out of reach on the remote frontiers, and could not be with-drawn, during midwinter, in time for this military operation. . . . [T]he inhabitants on our . . . frontiers would have been . . . ex-posed to the . . . scalping knife of the Indians." [2]

This was the general situation, but in very few exceptional cases forts were still held. Lincoln himself referred to them as follows: "Within these States all the forts, arsenals, dockyards, custom-houses, and the like, . . . had been seized, and were held in open hostility to this government, excepting only Forts Pickens, Taylor, and Jeffer-son, on and near the Florida coast, and Fort Sumter, in Charleston Harbor . . . ." [3] Taylor and Jefferson were of no crisis value. Pickens was susceptible of adjustment. Sumter, on the other hand, was packed with psychological dynamite, being located in the proud port of the imperious little state that had led in secession, where coöperation of sister Southern states had been spurned and where restraint even by Confederate authorities was difficult and doubtful. Of the three forts in the harbor (Sumter, Moultrie, and Castle Pinckney), only Sumter remained in Federal hands; for on December 26, 1860, Robert Ander-son, commanding harbor forces, had evacuated Moultrie and moved his force to Sumter. This was after the United States had strengthened Moultrie [4] while Sumter was yet unfinished and some of its guns un-mounted. The forts were so placed, however, that Anderson thought Moultrie could be "very easily carried" if attacked,[5] while the more detached location of Sumter was considered less likely to invite attack.

Of the three men who had most to do with the removal from Moultrie, President Buchanan was a conciliatory and non-aggressive sympathizer with the South, Floyd was a Southern secretary of war at Washington, and Anderson, a Kentuckian, was above all anxious to avoid provocation and violence. South Carolina quickly seized Pinck-ney and Moultrie, and commissioners from that state demanded that the Federal authorities move back from Sumter to Moultrie, though on the latter fort the palmetto flag was then flying. Also they demanded complete evacuation of the harbor. Buchanan resisted these demands, and in early January he sent an unarmed merchant ship with men and munitions to strengthen the Sumter garrison. On January 9, 1861,

2 Buchanan, *Mr. Buchanan's Administration*, 169. See also Crawford, *Genesis of the Civil War*, 167–168.
3 *Works*, VI, 297–298 (July 4, 1861).   4 *Offic. Rec.*, 1 ser., I, 92.   5 *Ibid.*, 99.

this United States ship, the *Star of the West,* was fired upon by South Carolinian guns. Prior to that date South Carolina alone had seceded from the Union. This might have been considered the "first shot" of "the war," but the ship merely turned back and Buchanan preferred not to treat the incident as a provocation. From this point until Lincoln's inauguration the situation at Sumter continued with little change except that the Carolinians greatly strengthened their forces in the harbor, erecting sundry batteries in addition to the forts they had seized. Against these forces Sumter could hardly be said to have controlled the position. The main point, however, was that no Federal attack from Sumter was contemplated.

III

The Sumter pot of trouble had thus been filled before Lincoln took office and it contained the following elements: a complete impasse as to government status between Charleston-Montgomery and Washington, a trick of fate that threw the center of agitation in that part of the country that was psychologically most unstable, a trigger-like hazard that an incident might be magnified into a war, a surplus of unbending honor and legalistic logic, a shortage of statesmanship as a human art, a plethora of popular demonstrations that encouraged trouble makers and embarrassed conciliators, a time limit, and a change of administration that came at the most difficult stage of the developing quarrel. Another factor was an American democratic tradition in the direction of peaceable adjustment of internal quarrels combined with an inadequacy of standing force and a complete lack of trained reserves. This meant that the calling-out of troops would be provocative without being presently effective. As the imbroglio deepened there was a negotiation that proceeded in Washington which actually dealt with the Sumter question but which was considered irregular on one side though official on the other. There was also a looseness of official relations in the Lincoln administration which resulted in commitments—or seeming commitments—being made without regular authorization.

South Carolina first and the Confederacy later were making a demand that was logical enough to those who accepted the thesis that the Union was irrevocably dissolved and the new Southern nation already a foreign country. Lincoln had not thrown away the whole Union case by accepting this thesis; his inaugural indicated that he did not regard the government of the United States as merely that of the Northern people, but, as before, the government of the nation. The impasse was a clash of complete opposites; on the plane of governmental logic the Sumter question was the whole problem of status between the United States, an established government, and that of the Confederacy, struggling for recognition.

In the main neither side actually wanted war; yet vigorous American determination on both sides demanded opposite things. To the Confederacy and to South Carolina entire independence of the seceded area was a finality and the detaching of other areas an objective; to Lincoln the breaking of the Union was unthinkable. The deep South was not seeking any formula of settlement within the Union. In that area unilateral action had been taken; demands had been treated as accomplishments; *de facto* changes had been effected; full warrant was claimed for those changes; and leaders had proceeded from there as if the main question in dispute was already closed. While the upper South still thought of adjustment, it was far different with the cotton states; for them the die had been cast.

The eagerness of Charleston authorities presented difficulties at Montgomery. The Confederate Congress had resolved (February 12, 1861) to take "under its charge the questions . . . relating to the occupation of the forts, . . . [etc.]" within the seceded region,[1] but this was done over the protest of South Carolina, whose governor at once stated: ". . . it is due to us . . . to get possession of Sumter at a period not beyond the fourth [of March]."[2] He informed Montgomery that the "independence of the State [this was after South Carolina had joined in launching the Confederacy] carrie[d] necessarily with it the right to reduce Fort Sumter" and that soon "arrangements" would be completed "for its certain and speedy reduction." "The right to do so," he said, "has been considered the right of the State" and circumstances "remitted her to the necessity of employing force to obtain" that object. "Mr. Lincoln," said Governor Pickens, "can not do more . . . than Mr. Buchanan has done. . . . If war can be averted, it will be by making the capture of Fort Sumter a fact

[1] *Journal*, Confed. Cong., I, 47.
[2] *Ibid.*, 49.

accomplished during the . . . present [Buchanan] Administration . . . ." "Mr. Lincoln may not attack, because the cause of quarrel will have been . . . past." [3] It is of significance in recapitulating
Governor Pickens's position to note the following points: (1) he
treated the Sumter question as a problem for the state of South Carolina, rather than the Confederacy, to handle; (2) he predicted that
Lincoln would not attack; (3) he asserted that South Carolina would
be under the necessity of using force to take the fort; and (4) in the
averting of war he gave far too little regard to restraint on the part of
his own state.

It may be said that Governor Pickens had reason to believe that
Lincoln would not attack, and that, from the standpoint of the state
in its newly assumed status, acquisition of the fort under Buchanan
was desirable. It can even be said that it would have been easier for
Lincoln to have come into office with Sumter already fallen, as were
nearly all the forts in the seceded area, than to be faced with the
wretched problem of surrendering it under menace of civil war. Had
Sumter been peacefully taken under Buchanan, all the indications
are that Lincoln would not have attempted recapture. The tinder-
box element at Charleston would thus have been eliminated and more
time would have been allowed for cooling off, though one can only
guess how far such cooling off would have promoted adjustment in
terms of union. Tension at Charleston grew as March 4 approached,
and the newspapers, especially the *Mercury,* were full of rumors and
conjectures. While the supreme menace of a reënforcement of Sumter
was harped upon, there was constant emphasis upon the alleged danger that such reënforcement would be stealthily attempted.

On March 6, 1861, Joseph Holt, for a brief time secretary of war
under Lincoln (before Cameron took hold), met with Scott, Welles,
and other officials, and it was then revealed that Anderson could not
remain at Sumter more than six weeks longer because of insufficient
food.[4] Here entered the fateful time limit; on or about April 15 Anderson's garrison would have to be fed or the fort evacuated. On March
7 President Lincoln held an anxious conference in the White House
with various officials. While some urged reënforcement, it was pointed

---

[3] Governor Pickens to the President of the Confederate Provisional Congress, Feb.
13, 1861, *ibid.*, 56–58.

[4] Welles, *Diary*, I, 3–4.

out that successful resistance to attack would require a force of 20,000 at a time when the whole scattered army of the United States numbered less than 16,000. No decision was reached, but, as Welles recalled, Lincoln urged all to "forbear giving any cause of offense." [5] Knowing that he would either have to evacuate Sumter or feed the garrison, which could not be expected to rely upon the Charleston market for supplies, Lincoln on March 15 put the question of a provisioning expedition to his cabinet, requesting written opinions as to whether it was "wise to attempt" such an expedition.

Chase wrote a letter that looked both ways. He gave "an affirmative answer" to the question whether an expedition should be sent, but could not advise it if the attempt would "so inflame civil war as to involve . . . armies and the expenditure of millions . . . ." If, however, the attempt were accompanied by a statement of generous policy toward the disaffected states in harmony with the inaugural address, it seemed to Chase "highly improbable" that it would produce war. [6] Blair definitely favored the provisioning expedition and thought it "would completely demoralize the rebellion." All the others (Seward, Cameron, Welles, Smith, and Bates) emphatically counseled that the expedition would be unwise. General Scott agreed with his old Whig associate Seward, so that in mid-March Lincoln faced a situation where his army head and ministers of state, war, and navy, voted against the expedition, while his minister of finance had such doubts as to make his "affirmative" answer ineffectual. Only Blair of all the secretaries was clear-cut in advising retention of the fort, [7] but his advice hinged upon the illusion that Sumter could be "provisioned . . . with little risk."

This much appears in formal written opinions of cabinet members, all of which are readily accessible. When one gets behind the scenes via manuscript sources the near-unanimity for yielding the fort seems truly remarkable. On this matter the two "opposites," Seward and Chase, were very much alike. Seward favored conciliation, even "going in peace," and did not expect serious trouble. What is not so well known is that Chase also favored going in peace—i. e., letting the lower Southern states go their separate way. "It is true [wrote Chase

---

[5] *Ibid.*, I, 6.   [6] For these cabinet views, see Lincoln, *Works*, VI, 192–220.

[7] "[T]here was great opposition to any attempt at relieving Fort Sumter, and . . . Mr. Blair alone sustained the President in . . . refusing to yield . . . ." G. V. Fox, in *Offic. Rec.* (Nav.), 1 ser., IV, 247.

in 1862] that, prior to the attack on Fort Sumter, I shared a quite general opinion that . . . it would be better to allow the seven States . . . to try the experiment of a separate existence, rather than incur the evils of a bloody war . . . ." [8] On this point the elder Frank Blair wrote in 1864: "You know that while Chase was willing 'to let the South go in peace'— . . . not willing even to succor Fort Sumpter, . . . would have . . . consigned the blacks to eternal bondage & throw the Slave States out of the . . . Union that he might not have their votes to encounter, when looking to gratify his ambition by becoming President in the North, Montgomery withstood him at all points; . . . ." [9] Montgomery Blair stated that Chase openly advocated letting the South go at the time that Seward was advising the surrender of Sumter and Scott the surrender of both Pickens and Sumter. The postmaster general, holding out for firmness, nevertheless expected Sumter to be given up, and stated that he "had prepared . . . [his] resignation to be handed in in that event at the Cabinet meeting at which the President decided contrary to the opinions of all the other members . . . not to surrender that Fort." [10]

IV

Those aspects of the Sumter question that belong to the field of negotiation must now be examined. Three men (Martin J. Crawford, John Forsyth, and A. B. Roman) had been appointed in late February as commissioners from the Confederate States to the United States. Their credentials, instructions, and studiously correct diplomatic manner were all predicated on the assumption that Lincoln's Union policy had been completely defeated and that the Confederacy of the lower South was entirely and finally independent. The main subject of the commissioners' negotiation was Sumter; their instructions stated that it would be idle to talk of peaceful relations while the United States maintained a force obstructing entrance to one of the Confederacy's principal harbors. "Not even to avert war" would the Confederate government permit this; evacuation was a *sine qua*

---

[8] S. P. Chase to Elihu Burritt, Oct. 6, 1862, in Chase MSS., Hist. Soc. of Pa.

[9] F. P. Blair, Sr., to Simon Cameron, Silver Spring, Nov. 22, 1864, Cameron MSS. (Blair wrote this in urging his son's claims as against Chase's for appointment on the Supreme Court.)

[10] Rough draft of letter, M. Blair to President Johnson, Aug. 9, 1865, Blair MSS.

non; withdrawal of Federal troops from areas within the Confederacy was an indispensable condition.[1] To Robert Toombs, Confederate secretary of state, it seemed that the Washington government was "neither declaring war nor establishing peace," but he added that this afforded the Confederacy the advantages of both conditions and enabled them to provide for defense more expeditiously than otherwise. Hence, he said, "We . . . care little for Mr. Seward's calculations . . . ."[2] Confederates also felt that the "peace policy" of the war and state departments under Lincoln would be "beneficial to the Confederate States."[3]

On March 12 the three commissioners formally asked Seward to set a day for presenting their credentials to the President and stating the object of their mission. In this communication they referred to the Confederate States as "an independent nation, de facto and de jure, ..."[4] Seward avoided direct communication with the commissioners in order to avoid implied recognition of the Confederacy, but he managed to deal with them indirectly. He immediately wrote to Senator R. M. T. Hunter of Virginia (March 12) that he could not receive the gentlemen but had no "want of personal respect" for them.[5] Three days later he wrote a "memorandum" addressed to no specified person in which he indicated that he understood recent events in the South "very differently from the aspect in which they . . . [were] presented" by the commissioners, and pointed out that he could not "in any way admit that the so-called Confederate States constitute[d] a foreign Power . . . ."[6]

There now entered an element that was to cause endless controversy and misunderstanding—an episode of indirect and informal exchanges between the state department and the commissioners via intermediaries, especially John A. Campbell of Alabama, then a member of the Supreme Court of the United States. Campbell with his colleague Nelson talked earnestly with Seward and then reported to the commissioners the wish of Seward to preserve peace. The commissioners were given to understand in mid-March that Sumter would

---

[1] Confed. Gov't Instructions to Its Commissioners, Montgomery, Mar. 14, 1861, Pickett Papers (MSS., Lib. of Cong.).
[2] Secretary of State Robert Toombs to Confederate Commissioners, Apr. 2, 1861, *ibid.*
[3] Martin J. Crawford to Secretary Toombs, Mar. 6, 1861, *ibid.*
[4] Confederate Commissioners to Seward, Mar. 12, 1861, *ibid.*
[5] Bancroft, *Seward*, II, 112.   [6] McPherson, *Rebellion*, 108–109.

be evacuated in five days, and that Southern coöperation was desired
in order to allow time for evacuation to have its beneficial effect.[7]
There seems no reason for the claim that Campbell misrepresented
Seward. Lincoln's so-called "premier" evidently believed that he was
directing affairs, that the welfare of the country imperatively demanded avoidance of an outbreak at Sumter in order to prevent civil
war, and that, considering the intentions of Montgomery and Charleston, such avoidance required Federal evacuation. Nearly the whole
cabinet, as above indicated, agreed with Seward on this matter. When
the five days passed and Sumter was not surrendered "as . . . promised," the commissioners again sought out Campbell, who conferred
with Seward (March 21) and came back with the solemn assurance that
there was no want of good faith on the part of the United States government. It was stated that governments could not move with "bank
accuracy" and that delay was unavoidable without being serious.
Campbell then put in writing the assurance that the United States
government had no intention of hostile military action toward the
Confederacy. Again on March 22 it appears that Seward, in the
presence of Campbell and Nelson, gave a pledge that the vexatious
fort would be given up.[8] At the same time it was indicated that the
evacuation policy was exceedingly trying and was opposed by a powerful element in the North and the Republican party.[9]

There was yet another mediator, Baron de Stoeckl, the Russian
minister. On March 24 Commissioner Roman conversed in French
with Stoeckl, and his report confirmed the impression received from
Campbell that a policy of conciliation would prevail so far as Seward
was concerned. The Russian stated that Seward, whom he had just
seen, had an earnest desire to preserve peace and that there would
be no coercion of the South. No blockade, he said, was intended; the
Confederate authorities would be permitted to collect duties at their
custom houses. It was even reported by Stoeckl that Seward, while
hoping the seceded states would return to the Union, was nevertheless of the opinion that if they refused to do so, they should be suffered to depart in peace and that, if sufficient time were allowed, an
amicable separation could be arranged. To bring about this result
Seward was reported as willing to fight the ultras of his own party.

---

[7] Report of commissioners to Toombs, Mar. 22, 1861, Pickett Papers.
[8] *Ibid.*   [9] *Ibid.*

Stoeckl invited Roman to take a cup of tea with him on March 26 at which time Seward would drop in "by chance," Stoeckl would be compelled to go out, and the two men (Seward and Roman) would be left alone. Embarrassed, however, by the risk of newspaper publicity, Seward sent his regrets and the interview never took place.[10]

In terms of the later outcome these left-handed negotiations concerning Sumter were unfortunate. Though Lincoln himself made no promise to the commissioners that Sumter would be evacuated, they had the best reason to believe that it was the Lincoln administration which, through its secretary of state, had made a definite pledge of evacuation, for how otherwise could Seward's assurances have had any significance? In addition to the inherent difficulty of the Sumter question in all its complex relations there was thus the further difficulty of a new administration that had not found itself. The man who was directing "foreign" relations of the government was going to amazing lengths in assuming power on his own initiative, and President Lincoln had not brought administrative conduct within his control. In Southern eyes—and this included the upper as well as the lower South—the Lincoln administration began with a serious breach of faith. It is not pleasant to say this, but one is speaking here of the Southern view, and the evidence as to Seward's pledge and Southern understanding is incontrovertible. On this point the administration was not a unit nor a definite personality with one controlling will. In those March days when the Campbell interviews were proceeding, the President was feeling his way as to Sumter, but the secretary of state was assuming that the matter had been decided in the sense of his own desires.

In the vacillating period before Lincoln decided to attempt to hold Sumter there were various indications that the President himself was pondering the merits of evacuation. The importance of holding Virginia and the rest of the upper South in the Union was at stake and this required careful study. On February 4, with the Confederacy of the lower South already formed, the people of Virginia voted for the Union and against secession by electing a majority of unionists to the Richmond convention. This body was not authorized to act finally, but to consider whether secession should be adopted, subject to approval by vote in a general Virginia election. The convention as-

---

10 A. B. Roman to Secretary Toombs, Mar. 25, 1861, *ibid.*

sembled at Richmond on February 13. Had it been controlled by secessionists Lincoln might have found the vitally important state across the Potomac out of the Union by the time of his inauguration. For two months the non-secession delegates at Richmond held the state in the Union, thereby performing a service of great value to Lincoln and to the cause of peace. In the March phase of the Virginia convention it was reported that an ordinance of secession could not pass that body, and that if it could have passed, it would have been defeated overwhelmingly by the people.[11] Instead of rushing into secession in the manner of the lower South, the Richmond body devoted itself to a careful study of state and federal relations, exploring methods of compromise and avoiding any action that would hamper the conciliatory efforts of the Peace Convention then in session in Washington under Virginia's sponsorship.[12]

It was realized south of the Potomac, however, that one condition was indispensable to success of Virginia unionists—the preservation of peace between Washington and the lower South. George W. Summers, prominent Union sympathizer and delegate to the Virginia convention, wrote to a Washington friend that the anti-secession members were in a majority and would have no trouble in holding Virginia in the Union "if not disturbed from abroad," but, he added, it was "of the essence . . . that a pacific course be continued"; if a collision occurred anywhere they could not answer for the result. Under the impression that Sumter was being evacuated, he stated that this "acted like a charm" and "gave us great strength." [13] There was every reason to believe that Virginia could be held in the Union if an outbreak at Sumter was avoided, and Lincoln himself so far realized this as to arrange and hold an interview with one of the unionist delegates of the Virginia convention. First seeking a consultation with George W. Summers, whom the President would have found useful as a Virginia

---

11 New York *Times,* Mar. 14, 1861, p. 4, c. 1. "Until early April, nearly all of them [secessionists in the Virginia convention] realized that immediate separation was an impossibility, and that the submission of an ordinance to the people . . . would be unwise." Henry T. Shanks, *Secession Movement in Virginia, 1847–1861,* 188.

12 As an example, the Virginia convention voted (108 to 16) to thank Senator Crittenden for his "patriotic efforts" toward "honorable adjustment." *Journal of the . . . Convention of . . . Virginia,* 96 (Mar. 11, 1861).

13 George W. Summers to J. C. Welling, Richmond, Mar. 19, 1861, Blair MSS. Published in *Nation,* XXIX, 383–384 (1879). In a postscript Summers wrote: "What delays the removal of Major Anderson? Is there any truth in the suggestion that the thing is not to be done at all? This would ruin us."

Whig and former congressman, Lincoln accepted a substitute, John B. Baldwin, a like-minded Virginia unionist. The matter seemed almost to resolve itself into a kind of bargain—Sumter for Virginia, and Lincoln has been quoted as saying to Virginia "peace commissioners": "If you will guarantee to me the State of Virginia I shall remove the troops. A State for a fort is no bad business." [14] He might well have said four states for a fort, since the whole upper South was at stake in the Virginian sense.

Lincoln never left a statement of his consultation with Baldwin, and the somewhat labored and rationalized account by his secretaries, who show marked sarcasm toward Virginia unionism while disliking to admit that Lincoln might have yielded Sumter, is far from satisfactory.[15] Statements have been preserved, however, by Summers, Baldwin, John Minor Botts (a Virginia unionist in touch with Baldwin), and Allan B. Magruder, who served as messenger between Washington and Richmond.[16] Disregarding matters about which these accounts disagree, it appears that Lincoln, through Seward and Magruder, sought consultation with some responsible Virginia unionist, and that Summers, not wishing to leave Richmond, sent Baldwin. The conversation between Lincoln and Baldwin took place on April 4 [17] in a back room at the White House. It was secret and confidential; its main topic was Lincoln's urgent wish that the Virginia convention adjourn without passing an ordinance of secession. Baldwin stated that Lincoln received him "very cordially," that they conferred alone for an hour behind a locked door, that Lincoln feared Baldwin had come "too late," and that he asked why the Richmond convention did

[14] Lincoln is thus quoted by Schleiden, minister resident of Bremen (*Annual Report*, Am. Hist. Assoc., 1915, 211). Schleiden does not state that Lincoln said this to Baldwin specifically, and on this point Baldwin later wrote: "My . . . recollection . . . fails me if Mr. Lincoln used any such expression as that he 'would give a fort for a State any time' . . . ." Autograph statement by J. B. Baldwin, Staunton, Va., Aug. 26, 1869, from collection of Maj. Gen. S. W. Crawford, Catalogue no. 284, American Art Association sale, May 5–6, 1915. The Baldwin statement does not destroy the testimony of Schleiden, whose record is both impartial and close to the event. It seems to have been part of Baldwin's game to deny that a Virginia-Sumter bargain had ever been offered.

[15] Nicolay and Hay, *Lincoln*, III, 415–428.

[16] Baldwin's and Botts's accounts appeared as testimony before the committee on reconstruction in 1866. *House Report No. 30*, 39 Cong., 1 sess., pt. 2, 102–109, 114–123. Magruder's story appeared in the *Atl. Mo.*, XXXV, 438–445. Prior to publication Magruder wrote to J. S. Black (July 27, 1874) saying that Baldwin was his friend through A. H. H. Stuart and that he had Baldwin's full notes. J. S. Black MSS., vol. 62.

[17] *House Report No. 30*, 39 Cong., 1 sess., pt. 2, 102.

not adjourn. Did he mean sine die?, asked Baldwin. Yes, said Lincoln, sine die. To this Baldwin answered that unionists controlled the convention, that there was no need for adjournment, and that such a course would leave important matters unsettled, whereas the convention while in session could hold the state in the Union. According to Baldwin's recollection, Lincoln referred to the possibility of withdrawing from Sumter as a "military necessity," showing that such withdrawal seemed as late as April 4 to have been in the President's mind; the President strongly dissented when Baldwin predicted that the firing of a gun at Sumter would mean war and would lose the cause of Union and peace.

The main difference of evidence is on the question whether Lincoln made a "pledge" of evacuation in return for Virginia's avoidance of secession. Botts, trying to recall what Lincoln and Baldwin had told him, stated that Lincoln, anxious for peace and for keeping Virginia, made an offer to evacuate Sumter and take the chance of negotiating with the cotton states if the Union majority at Richmond would go home without passing an ordinance of secession.[18] According to Botts, Lincoln stated that Baldwin would not listen civilly to the suggestion. Baldwin, however, stated that no such pledge was made.[19] Much of Baldwin's report is made up of a kind of speech which he made to the President advising him what to do. He particularly suggested that Lincoln ought to withdraw from both Pickens and Sumter and call a national convention.

One reads of Lincoln's unsatisfactory contact with Virginia unionists with a sense of frustration. Had this contact been fully worked out at an earlier stage, the possibilities seemed highly significant, though Nicolay and Hay spurn the idea that it offered any satisfactory hope. The Baldwin interview came at a late stage in the Sumter muddle and it coincided with a conference of Northern governors at Washington whose chief object was to stiffen the President's position toward Sumter.[20] Also it came shortly after a memorable call of the older Francis P. Blair upon Lincoln. As related by W. E. Smith, Blair was told by the President (March 29) that he did not know whether he would withdraw Anderson, whereupon Blair sternly admonished the

---

18 *Ibid.*, 114–116. Botts stated that on April 7 he talked with Lincoln concerning the Baldwin interview and that later he talked of the matter with Baldwin (*ibid.*, 114).

19 *Ibid.*, 105.   20 *Atl. Mo.*, XXXV, 444.

President that withdrawal would be treason, and that by such a course the administration would forfeit public confidence.[21] Taking these and other stiffening influences into account at the time of the belated Virginia negotiations, one can understand how the harassed President was swung over to the policy of provisioning Sumter; what one finds hardest to reconcile with evidence is the supposition that all the while the President was planning a war-provoking maneuver.

One will miss the point of the Sumter imbroglio if he underestimates the merits or sponsorship of the evacuation policy. If it was a military and naval question, evacuation was favored by Secretary Cameron, General Scott and other leaders of the army, and (at first) by Welles of the navy; if diplomatic, it was favored by Seward; if broadly political, the advocates of withdrawal included Douglas, Andrew Johnson, Thurlow Weed, and scores of other prominent men; if sectional, the vast border and the important upper South were overwhelmingly in favor of withdrawal.[22] Some even of the extreme antislavery radicals were ready to consent to withdrawal on the assumption that union with slaveholders was wicked and that the North would not care to fight to maintain such an unhappy connection.

V

In his study of the Sumter situation Lincoln sought information on the spot, and for this purpose several investigators were sent. Gustavus V. Fox, able assistant secretary of the navy, had a plan for relieving Sumter by running the batteries with steamers at night; partly to ascertain the practicability of this plan, Lincoln consented to a visit which Fox made to Charleston in March, arriving on March 21. Fox met Governor Pickens, visited Sumter, and conferred with Anderson, finding repeated indications that South Carolinians expected evacuation. He found the garrison short of supplies, and "it was agreed that . . . [he] might report that the 15th of April at noon would be the period" beyond which the fort could not be held "unless supplies were furnished." [1] He studied conditions at Sumter without making any

---

[21] Smith, *Blair Family*, II, 9–10.

[22] John M. Harlan of Frankfort, Kentucky, wrote on March 11, 1861, to Joseph Holt that immediate Federal withdrawal from Pickens and Sumter would kill secession in Kentucky and the upper South, adding that the great worry in the border area was that the Lincoln government would attempt "coercion." Holt MSS.

[1] *Offic. Rec.* (Nav.), 1 ser., IV, 247.

arrangements with Anderson "for reenforcing or supplying the fort." Anderson seemed to doubt the success of a relief expedition, while Fox thought it would have a fair chance. On his return to Washington, Fox conferred frequently with the President and was called upon, in the presence of cabinet members, to answer military objections to his scheme.[2]

If it should turn out that a relieving expedition were to be sent, the advice of the chief naval authority who favored such an expedition would be indispensable, but other types of advice were also sought. Two other investigators, both Illinois men of Southern antecedents, had a more personal task, being expected to sound out Charlestonian sentiment. Stephen A. Hurlbut of Belvidere, Illinois, a former Charleston lawyer, visited his native city and conferred with J. L. Petigru, stout Charleston unionist, from whom he learned that attachment to the Union, "always feeble" in South Carolina, had been "extinguished and overridden." The visit of Ward Lamon of Bloomington, Illinois, was even more significant. Not only was he a close friend of Lincoln, but by birth and general temperament he had a special sympathy with the Southern point of view. No Southerner could have been more fervent in detesting abolitionists, nor, it is hoped, more profane in cursing them, than this Virginia-born westerner. In Lamon's recollections, however, edited by his daughter, it is recorded that the burly Illinoisan was insulted as the representative of the hated Lincoln and that the hostility of a crowd in a Charleston hotel was unpleasantly manifest.[3]

Arriving in Charleston on March 25, Lamon had interviews with the chief leaders, including Major Anderson, Governor Pickens, and General Beauregard. In the minds of each of these important men the President's "messenger" left the definite impression that Sumter would be evacuated. Though various sources could be cited, the whole story is contained in the following statement of Beauregard to Anderson: "Having been informed that Mr. Lamon, the authorized agent of the President of the United States, advised Governor Pickens, after his interview with you at Fort Sumter, that yourself and command would be transferred to another post in a few days, and under-

2 *Ibid.*

3 Ward H. Lamon, *Recollections of Abraham Lincoln, 1847–1865,* ed. by Dorothy Lamon, 76.

standing that you are under the impression that I intended . . . to require . . . a formal surrender . . . , I hasten to . . . inform you that our countries not being at war, . . . no such condition will be exacted of you, ..." [4] Anderson received from Lamon the same impression as did Beauregard, for he wrote on April 1 to General Lorenzo Thomas, adjutant general, that "since the return of Colonel Lamon to Washington" he had been "in daily expectation . . . of receiving orders to vacate this post . . . ." [5] Again he wrote: "The remarks made to me by Colonel Lamon, taken in connection with the tenor of newspaper articles, have induced me . . . to believe that orders would soon be issued for my abandoning this work." [6] Though Lamon's trip was an exploratory visit, it was considered more than that by some of the principals in the controversy, and it is likely that Lamon exceeded his authority. It appears that his part was badly played, but at the time the Colonel left Washington evacuation was in the air. Lincoln himself was studying its possibilities.

Amid all this tension there were three things that Lincoln did not do. (1) He did not order what would now be called mobilization, nor the remotest equivalent of it. The precautionary assembling of any force, however inadequate, for operations in the South was, in the existing military system, out of the question. The fact that military forces were not raised is, nevertheless, significant as showing not only the utter unpreparedness for war but also the unmilitaristic nature of Federal policy. The lack of peacetime armed strength was not an oversight or accident. In 1861 it was an American pattern of long standing—a pattern that called for law and order being upheld without a sizable army. In time of peace America has always, throughout its history, been unprepared for war. (2) Lincoln issued no public statements designed to inflame passion or whip up antagonism against the South. He did issue statements in the opposite sense. (3) He did not attempt to retake any of the occupied forts in the seceded portion of the South, though Union logic required this as much as secession logic required reduction or Federal abandonment of Sumter. Logic is not always wisdom.

Lincoln's attitude of mind during March gave the appearance of vacillation; rather it was that of prudent hesitation and cautious study

---

[4] *Offic. Rec.* 1 ser., I, 222 (Mar. 26, 1861).   [5] *Ibid.*, 230.   [6] *Ibid.*, 237; see also 294.

of the Sumter question. The President was working toward a decision which would partly depend on circumstances yet to develop. As his secretaries expressed it, he did not deem it prudent to order the expedition, nor did his "sense of duty permit him entirely to abandon it." [7] There is no proof that his March attitude involved any intention to send an expedition to Sumter in expectation and acceptance of war, or with the purpose of deliberately maneuvering the South into firing the first shot. Avoidance of trouble while in some way maintaining Federal authority was his chief concern. That Lincoln weighed and tested the possibility of evacuating Sumter is now clear, and in this connection the relation between Fort Pickens and Fort Sumter attracted his particular attention.

What emerged from the President's study of the question was a decision to arrange for two expeditions, but their purposes and orders were dissimilar. Properly deeming Pensacola a less emotional and explosive area than Charleston, Lincoln moved for an expedition with definite reënforcing orders to Pickens, while for Sumter he planned a tentative expedition to be "used, or not, according to circumstances." [8] One expedition was positive, the other provisional. The fundamental decision of the President was not that Sumter could not possibly be abandoned. Feeling that an abandonment of Sumter "under the [existing] circumstances" would be "ruinous" because it would "not be fully understood" and would be "construed as a part of a voluntary policy," Lincoln nevertheless felt that Pickens might be reënforced as "a clear indication of policy" and that (in his own words) this would "better enable the country to accept the evacuation of Fort Sumter as a military necessity." [9]

On March 12 [10] Lincoln's direct orders were sent to reënforce Pickens without an "if." [11] Maintaining Federal authority there, he would feel that evacuation of Sumter could better be endured. On this matter, as on about everything else in regard to "the forts," the President's plans went wrong. There had been a quasi-truce under

---

[7] Nicolay and Hay, *Lincoln*, III, 388.   [8] *Works*, VI, 302 (July 4, 1861).
[9] *Ibid.*, VI, 301 (July 4, 1861).
[10] Lincoln's order was issued through E. D. Townsend, assistant adjutant general, to Captain I. Vogdes, army officer on board the *Brooklyn*, then off Pensacola. *Offic. Rec.* (Nav.) 1 ser., IV, 90.
[11] No such orders were ever sent as to Sumter.

Buchanan which involved a Federal promise not to reënforce Pickens in return for a Florida promise not to attack.[12] The Lincoln administration had only "vague and uncertain rumors" concerning this "*quasi* armistice," [13] to which it was not a party, and did not consider it an official agreement of binding force after March 4; but Captain Vogdes, under Lincoln's orders to reënforce Pickens, was prevented from doing so by Captain Adams of the *Sabine*, to whom the troops had been transferred, Adams's reason being the truce, and what he considered insufficiency of orders for the undertaking.[14] Thus the informal truce arranged under Buchanan did tie Lincoln's hands, and the peremptory order to reënforce the Pickens garrison was not carried out. But Pickens and Sumter were related parts of Lincoln's policy concerning "the forts." The Sumter expedition was not a single item in the picture; it belonged to a combination of which the Florida situation was an essential part. Had Pickens been reënforced, we have Lincoln's own word for believing that his mind was ready to avoid using the tentative Sumter expedition, which did not sail till April 8–9, and which, unlike the Pickens plan, was made up at first without definite orders as to its use.

While matters were in this state (the reënforcing of Pickens having been ordered as a way of sugaring the possible evacuation of Sumter) Lincoln was advised by General Scott on March 28 that not only Sumter but Pickens also ought to be evacuated. When the President gave this information to his cabinet members at a state dinner that night, there was "blank amazement" in the group, followed by indignant denunciation on the part of Blair.[15] Next day the question of relieving Sumter was again put to the cabinet and again the answers were given in writing. Lincoln's secretarial biographers state that the former cabinet decision to evacuate was reversed,[16] but the record shows that only three of the seven secretaries (Chase, Welles, and Blair) were now unequivocally in favor of sending an expedition to Sumter.

---

12 Under Buchanan a kind of "agreement" had been entered into between the United States government and that of Florida (through Senator S. R. Mallory and Colonel William H. Chase, commanding Florida forces). As late as April 1 Captain H. A. Adams wrote to Secretary Welles: "This agreement binds us not to reenforce Fort Pickens unless it shall be attacked or threatened. It binds them not to attack it unless we should attempt to reenforce it." *Offic. Rec.* (Nav.), 1 ser., IV, 110.

13 *Works*, VI, 302 (July 4, 1861).   14 *Offic. Rec.* (Nav.), 1 ser., IV, 110.

15 Nicolay and Hay, *Lincoln*, III, 394–395; *Offic. Rec.*, 1 ser., I, 200–201.

16 Nicolay and Hay, *Lincoln*, III, 429–433.

Seward and Smith definitely opposed it, while Bates contributed the illuminating advice that Sumter ought to be either evacuated or relieved! [17] Cameron gave no written advice at all. It does not appear in any case that Lincoln's action depended upon cabinet advice, but the consultation of the cabinet marks the end of March as a kind of crisis in Lincoln's own mind on this fearfully vexing subject. Nicolay and Hay state that on the night of March 28 Lincoln's eyes did not close in sleep.[18]

VI

As the fateful month of April 1861 opened, two expeditions, both army undertakings with naval coöperation, were being prepared, but orders and purposes as to the expeditions differed. Colonel Harvey Brown was put in command of an expedition "to reenforce and hold Fort Pickens" and was to "proceed with the least possible delay to that place . . . ." [1] The Pickens reënforcement was thus not allowed to depend upon the earlier order to Vogdes from whom no word had come. Sumter plans and orders were in very different terms. Instead of an expedition to move at once with orders to reënforce, Lincoln's order was "that an expediton . . . be got ready to sail" by April 6.[2] In the case of each expedition there was not merely one order, but a series of orders, since military and naval coöperation involved a number of officers and vessels. In these collateral orders as of April 1 the Pickens expedition was directed to proceed and to act for the reenforcement of the fort, while the ships meant for Sumter were given no positive orders to reënforce nor even to sail, but were directed to be "in readiness for sea service." [3] On March 30 the assistant secretary of the navy, Gustavus V. Fox, was sent to New York "with verbal instructions to prepare for the voyage, but to make no binding engagements." [4] To put it briefly, one expedition was *sent;* the other was *prepared.* One was definitive, the other tentative.

Not until April 6 did the Lincoln administration learn that the Vogdes order to reënforce Pickens (the order of March 12 which Lincoln had considered vital in his plans) had not been carried out.[5] If

[17] *Works*, VI, 227–231 (Mar. 29, 1861).   [18] Nicolay and Hay, *Lincoln*, III, 395.
[1] *Offic. Rec.* (Nav.), 1 ser., IV, 107.   [2] *Ibid.*, 227.   [3] *Ibid.*, 228.   [4] *Ibid.*, 248.
[5] Nicolay and Hay, *Lincoln*, IV, 7.

one follows Lincoln's own reasoning it appears that this put a new face on the Sumter plans.[6] The point was that Lincoln was reluctant to evacuate Sumter unless Federal authority could somehow be upheld in terms of his inaugural address, which he thought might have been done by a reënforcement of Pickens; but the news of April 6 now made it impossible to achieve a reënforcement of the Florida fort in time to offset the Sumter situation, since the deadline for withdrawing or feeding the garrison was fast approaching. Part of the difficulty was that plans and orders had to be prepared some days in advance of the actual sailing of an expedition to proceed from New York with ships that were yet to be put into commission, which meant manning, fueling, stocking, equipping, and recalling officers on leave. Even if an expedition was tentative, elaborate preliminary preparations had to be made.

Fox stated that on April 4 the President "said that he had decided to let the expedition go." [7] At that time Fox told the President that by the time he should arrive in New York he would have only nine days to prepare, sail, and reach Charleston, so that if Lincoln ever intended to avoid a decision by default he would have to act very soon. After April 4, however, there would be a short interval of several days before the expedition would actually sail, so that up to April 6 by schedule, and longer as the event proved, Lincoln could still hold back the expedition by telegraph. But it was on April 6 that the President learned that the Vogdes order to reënforce Pickens had not been executed. The predicament at this point has been stated by Lincoln himself:

To now reinforce Fort Pickens before a crisis would be reached at Fort Sumter was impossible—rendered so by the near exhaustion of provisions in the latter-named fort. In precaution against such a conjuncture, the government had, a few days before, commenced preparing an expedition as well adapted as might be to relieve Fort Sumter, which expedition was intended to be ultimately used, or not, according to circumstances. The strongest anticipated case for using it was now presented, and it was resolved to send it forward.[8]

If the Sumter expedition had not been sent, could Lincoln have worried along with the sectional problem; rather, could he have

6 *Works*, VI, 300–304 (July 4, 1861).   7 *Offic. Rec.* (Nav.), 1 ser., IV, 248.
8 *Works*, VI, 302 (July 4, 1861)

solved it in the Union sense? Could ballots, in the face of the spirited Southern movement, seemingly so irrevocable, have given the answer, as the President himself suggested? It was this question which gave significance to Lincoln's careful consideration of contingencies before he acted—contingencies or circumstances under which Sumter might have been surrendered without loss of face. Not only did this difficult conjecture confront Lincoln; he was also confronted by fortuitous circumstance in the exhaustion of supplies at Sumter. Still another fortuitous circumstance arose in the unexpected non-compliance with his Pickens orders. Transition from hesitation to decision was thus partly a matter of what went on in Lincoln's mind, and partly a matter of events beyond his control.

April 6 would seem to have been the key-date of this transition. It is true, as above stated, that some of Lincoln's preparatory orders for the Sumter matter were issued on April 4, but more significant orders were issued on the sixth, after which the act of sailing was still delayed. It was on April 6 that news came to Washington of the Pickens disappointment, requiring, as Lincoln said, a recalculation as to Sumter policy. April 6 was the date of readiness for possible sailing as indicated in Lincoln's order of March 29 when tentative Sumter preparations began. It was the date when the instruction to Anderson, telling him that an expedition would go forward, was sent by Lincoln, though it was dated April 4. It was the date of Lincoln's instructions to Chew to notify Governor Pickens that a supply fleet would be sent. It was the date beyond which vacillation as to releasing the expedition would hardly be possible because of the low condition of Anderson's supplies. Even then, it was not the date of sailings, which occurred mostly on April 8 and 9. In acting as to Sumter, Lincoln's reluctance is illustrated by his waiting not merely till the last day, but till the eleventh hour.

The reënforcement of Pickens succeeded. It was not chiefly a matter of an expedition from New York; rather it resulted from orders issued through Captain J. L. Worden and delivered on April 12. In obedience to these orders a reënforcement was achieved at once (April 12); [9] it was followed by a further reënforcement which brought the force at Pickens up to 1100 men. The unprovocative strengthening of the fort was accomplished "without the firing of a gun, or the spilling of

---

[9] *Offic. Rec.* (Nav.), 1 ser., IV, 115; Nicolay and Hay, *Lincoln*, IV, 17.

one drop of blood." [10] This showed that such a thing could be peaceably done. At Pickens as well as Sumter Union efforts were nonaggressive. Colonel Harvey Brown, U. S. A., informed General Braxton Bragg, C. S. A., that he would hold himself on the defensive.[11]

The Sumter expedition, when at last it was released, had even yet no peremptory orders to reënforce. The primary object of the undertaking was to provision Sumter, merely to avoid withdrawal by delivering food to the garrison. If the authorities at Charleston had permitted the fort to be supplied, so read Welles's instructions, no further service was to have been required of the vessels. Only in case of attack by the other side was the expedition under orders to attempt to place additional troops in the garrison.[12] To underline the element of nonaggression Lincoln took from it any aspect of hostile surprise by sending his own messenger, R. S. Chew (a clerk in the state department), to Governor Pickens of South Carolina, notifying that official that an attempt would be made "to supply Fort Sumter with provisions only; and that, if such attempt . . . [were] not resisted, no effort to throw in men, arms, or ammunition . . . [would] be made without further notice, or in case of an attack upon the fort." [13] The date of the instructions to Chew, drafted by Lincoln and signed by the secretary of war, was April 6; the order was to deliver the written message by personal interview with Pickens; the interview took place on April 8.[14]

Provisioning was to be attempted only if Major Anderson's flag was flying over the fort, the major being authorized to capitulate if that should in his judgment be necessary. The authorization of capitulation to avoid bloodshed (the opposite of successful reënforcement) was yet another indication of a non-violent enterprise on the part of the President, whose attention, at the trying moment of sending the expedition, had been given not to the details of a possible military

[10] N. Y. *Tribune*, May 2, 1861, p. 8, c. 1; Moore, *Rebellion Record* (Docs.), I, 162–163. Throughout the Civil War the Union flag remained at Pickens.

[11] *Offic. Rec.* (Nav.), 1 ser., IV, 129, 138.

[12] "The primary object of the expedition is to provision Fort Sumter . . . . Should the authorities at Charleston permit the fort to be supplied, no further . . . service will be required . . . , and . . . [the ships] will return to New York and . . . Washington." Naval order to Captain Mercer, *ibid.*, 235. On the purpose of the expedition, see also *ibid.*, 232, 234; Lincoln *Works*, VI, 302 (July 4, 1861). "Gov. Pickens was formerly [*sic*] notified that . . . our only object was to supply our men with food." Caleb B. Smith to R. W. Thompson, Washington, Apr. 16, 1861, MS., Lincoln National Life Foundation, Fort Wayne, Ind.

[13] *Works*, VI, 241 (April 6, 1861).   [14] *Offic. Rec.*, 1 ser., I, 251.

operation by an utterly inadequate garrison, but to a set of plans and circumstances by which such an operation could be avoided, the fort being peaceably held on the basis of assurances communicated with great care and deliberation to Charleston. The thing expected of Anderson was to hold out if possible till food should arrive, to give as much resistance as military pride and judgment required, and if necessary to capitulate on honorable terms.[15]

VII

Among the extraordinary features of the Sumter episode was an amazing muddle in regard to one warship, the *Powhatan*. Secretary Welles, whose interest was in the naval aspects of the Sumter enterprise while Seward's thought was concentrated on the Pickens fleet, gave orders that the *Powhatan*, commanded by Captain Mercer, be made the flagship of the Sumter expedition. The President gave his approval to instructions to Mercer, signed by Welles, to that effect. In direct conflict, Seward *in the President's name* had ordered David D. Porter to take over the *Powhatan* and attach it to Seward's specialty, the Pickens expedition. The overworked President was giving more attention to the Charleston aspects of the expedition (making sure that it should not bear the aspect of menace or aggression) than to the New York details, and it came about that he signed the Seward order without realizing specifically what was involved. When the flat conflict of the Mercer and Porter orders became known, Welles and Seward made a night sortie upon Lincoln who ruled that the *Powhatan* must be restored to the Sumter expedition. When Seward objected, the President, as Welles stated, was "imperative," and ordered Seward to make the necessary change of orders. Seward then muddled the

---

[15] Both the instructions to Chew for the interview with Governor Pickens and those to Anderson were first drafted by Lincoln in his own hand, though issued as orders signed by Cameron. It was the duty of Captain Theodore Talbot to deliver the instructions to Anderson, but on reaching Charleston the captain was refused permission to make such delivery. Nicolay and Hay, who got behind the surface record by their use of the Lincoln papers (deposited in the Library of Congress but closed to investigators), have done a useful service by pointing out that certain of these documents were Lincoln's own autograph manuscripts. Such records in the President's hand offer mute testimony concerning Lincoln's close personal attention to those aspects of the Sumter expedition that promised avoidance of trouble by giving assurance of non-aggressive intent at Charleston. Nicolay and Hay, *Lincoln*, IV, 27–28, 34–35; *Works*, VI, 239–241 (April 4 and 6, 1861).

thing further by countermanding in his own name the former order issued in the President's name. The countermanding order instructed the bewildered Porter to turn the ship over to Mercer and to the Sumter expedition. The *Powhatan* had sailed before Seward's countermanding telegram arrived in New York, and it became necessary to send a swift steamer to overtake her. By great exertion the warship was reached, but Porter refused compliance with the amended order, claiming that it was too late and that the countermanding order was merely signed by a cabinet secretary while the earlier order giving him the *Powhatan* had been that of the President. Thus the President's instruction was disobeyed, Seward had his way, and the *Powhatan* remained detached from the Charleston-bound fleet.

The amazing nature of the administrative methods employed in this Pickens-Sumter imbroglio are revealed in the diary and manuscripts of Montgomery C. Meigs, then a captain in the regular army with engineering duties in Washington. It was Meigs whom Seward used, in a secret and underhand manner, to promote the Pickens expedition, which was in a peculiar sense Seward's own scheme. Working with Seward, Meigs on April 1 was busy all day making orders for the signature of the President. He related that he was being asked to assume command far beyond the level of his captain's rank, that Porter was "in despair" when he received the change of order above indicated, and that Meigs, taking his cue from Seward, deliberately sought to obstruct the plans of the secretary of the navy. "I took the ground," wrote Meigs, "that Capt. Mercer had been relieved by orders signed by [the] President, . . . that no man, secretary or other, had a right to take her [the *Powhatan*], and that the secretary could not do it as I was by the President made responsible and told not to let even the Secretary of the Navy know that this expedition was going on." [1] The full audacity of these statements by Meigs, prompted by Seward, can only be appreciated when one remembers what it means to have naval ships sent on an expedition without even the knowledge of the secretary of the navy, and also that "the ground" Meigs took was flatly contrary to orders peremptorily issued by President Lincoln.

The significance of this *Powhatan* muddle for a biographer of Lincoln is not alone the weakening of the Sumter expedition. The episode revealed looseness of administrative methods, meddling by

[1] *Amer. Hist. Rev.*, XXVI, 300–302.

Seward in army and navy affairs, and eagerness of that official to justify his sobriquet of "premier" by assuming functions belonging to the President. Yet it need not be concluded that Seward's motive in this affair was mere personal ambition or greed for power. He honestly believed that evacuation of Sumter was of supreme importance to the country. Up to the beginning of April there had been much in the attitude of cabinet and army officials to give a basis for expecting evacuation, while even the President had at least been contemplating it. Coupled with a conviction as to the wisdom or necessity of evacuation was the "premier's" belief in his own ability to bring it about. Behind the scenes in this critical April, Lincoln had to struggle with Seward's complacent assumption of control. Even after making decisions, the President could not always know that his authority would be respected.[2]

Lincoln's notification to Governor Pickens of the intention to provision Sumter caused anxious consultation and some delay at Montgomery, but on the tenth Beauregard, Confederate commander at Charleston, was instructed to demand evacuation of Fort Sumter, and if that was refused, to "reduce it." [3] The communication of President Lincoln to Governor Pickens, wrote S. W. Crawford, "precipitated the issue." [4] In other words, from the standpoint of Charleston and Montgomery, where Southern independent sovereignty was considered final and dissolution of the Union a *fait accompli,* the sending of an expedition, though only to feed the garrison, left no choice but force to resist what was deemed invasion. On the 11th Beauregard's demand for surrender was conveyed by three officers to Anderson, who made the formal written reply that the demand was one with which his sense of honor prevented compliance. He added orally and informally, however, that he would await the first shot and that in any case, if not attacked, he would soon be starved out.[5]

Again on April 11 Montgomery was consulted, and orders came

---

[2] Seward's April daring is treated in vol. II, 29–31. Narratives and sources for the *Powhatan* muddle are found in *Offic. Rec.,* 1 ser., I; *Offic. Rec.* (Nav.), 1 ser., IV, especially 229–240; Welles, *Diary,* I, 21–28; Bancroft, *Seward,* II, 139–149; Welles MSS.; Nicolay and Hay, *Lincoln,* IV, ch. 1; "General M. C. Meigs on the Conduct of the Civil War," *Amer. Hist. Rev.,* XXVI, 285–303 (1921); S. W. Crawford, *Genesis of the Civil War,* 409 ff.

[3] Order of L. P. Walker, Confederate secretary of war, April 10, 1861; in Crawford, *Genesis,* 421; *Offic. Rec.* 1 ser. I, 297.

[4] Crawford, *Genesis,* 422.   [5] *Ibid.,* 423–424.

to withhold bombardment if Anderson would promise not to attack and to evacuate by a definite date, otherwise to "reduce the fort"; [6] again a boat carried officers to Sumter (this being the night of April 11–12), and Anderson answered that he would evacuate Sumter by noon of the 15th and would not in the meantime fire upon Confederate forces unless attacked. He added, however, that evacuation was subject to the condition of receiving no "controlling instructions from . . . [his] Government or additional supplies." [7] Here was Anderson's conditional prediction of evacuation; here was his renewed offer not to attack. Could it have been taken as a basis for avoiding Confederate assault? The main responsibility in answering this question was with the Montgomery authorities, though in their decisions they could not ignore the position of the state of South Carolina and of Governor Pickens. Within the pattern of instructions from Montgomery the command at Charleston was that of Beauregard. Within this pattern also, certain last-minute matters were handled—perhaps "decided" is too strong a word—by the men who went on that night boat to Sumter. The function of these three Confederate messenger-aides (A. R. Chisolm, Stephen D. Lee, and James Chesnut, Jr.) was to visit Sumter, present to Anderson the Confederate demand for evacuation, and obtain his reply. Directly upon getting his reply, the purport of which has been noted, these aides (at 3:20 a. m., April 12) served notice on Anderson that Beauregard would "open the fire . . . on Fort Sumter" in one hour.[8] The notice of the aides was written at Fort Sumter and presented to Anderson without having been referred back to Charleston, but in this they considered that they were acting in conformity with their instructions from Beauregard who in turn was carrying out the will of the Montgomery authorities.

Among the slightly known documents of history is a manuscript journal by one of these aides, A. R. Chisolm.[9] He mentions various visits under flag of truce by Confederate officers to Sumter, characterized by military correctness and courtesy. When on the 11th the

---

[6] Order of Secretary Walker, April 11, 1861, *Offic. Rec.* 1 ser. I, 301. Confederate orders kept constantly emphasizing the condition that there be no attack upon Charleston from Sumter at a time when United States authorities had no intention of attacking.

[7] *Ibid.,* 1 ser., I, 14.   [8] *Ibid.*

[9] This Chisolm manuscript was unknown to the author until recently. For a copy he is indebted to Mr. Vernon Munroe of New York City.

aides presented a note "demanding the surrender of Fort Sumter,"
Major Anderson "showed a great deal of feeling and stated that if
we had not made the demand he would have been starved out in a
few days." On hearing Anderson's answer, Beauregard sent the men
back that same night; Anderson, wrote Chisolm, then told them that
"if his flag was fired on again he should . . . open on our Batteries." [10] Chisolm added that this answer was not "satisfactory," that
it was "discretionary" with the aides what to do next, and that "we
informed him that in one hour . . . our Batteries would open fire."
"The Major was very much affected and shoock [sic] us warmly by the
hand and said he hoped if we did not meet again in this world we
would in the better one." The Southern officers immediately proceeded to Fort Johnson and gave the firing order, which began with
the discharge of the signal mortar at 4:30. [11]

From a boat in the harbor the aides "saw the red ball scribe a semi-
circle and explode immediately over the Fort." [12] At the moment they
were on their way to report to Beauregard's headquarters.

Following the signal shot from Fort Johnson [13] there ensued a
general intense bombardment from various forts and batteries in
the harbor. For over thirty hours Anderson defended Sumter, by which
time great damage had been done; then (April 13) he submitted to
Beauregard's terms of evacuation, at which point Confederate officers
concerned themselves with generous assistance to Anderson and his
men. It is worth noting that Beauregard had been a pupil of Anderson in West Point days. [14] A poignant note in the whole Sumter in-

---

[10] This statement that if attacked he would fire back is mentioned by Chisolm as the
"unsatisfactory" part, though, as shown above, the major's reply contained other elements. Essentially, the unsatisfactory matters in Confederate eyes were Anderson's
refusal to surrender, and the knowledge that a relieving fleet was arriving. Chisolm
MS. (see preceding note).

[11] *Ibid.* It is of interest to note the reference to the "discretionary" authority of the
officers who issued the firing order on this fateful night. It is confirmed in the Chisolm
narrative that the aides themselves, without referring the matter to headquarters,
drew up the final reply to Anderson telling that firing would begin. This, he wrote,
was done "in about five minutes . . . Col. Chesnut dictating Capt. Lee writing and
I copying . . . ."

[12] *Ibid.*

[13] Crawford, *Genesis*, 427. The shell fired from Fort Johnson was a signal shot; the
traditional "first shot" was fired by the aged Edmund Ruffin of Virginia from a battery
on Morris Island. *Battles and Leaders of the Civil War*, I, 47.

[14] Anderson was an instructor of artillery at West Point from 1835 to 1837; Beauregard attended the Military Academy from 1834 to 1838. *Biographical Register . . . of
the U. S. Military Academy*, I, 277; *Register of the Officers and Cadets of the U. S.
Military Academy . . .* June, 1837, pp. 4, 9.

cident was the sense of brotherhood in military service and of honor among officers as between Northern and Southern army men thrust into antagonistic duties. On Sunday afternoon, April 14, the major marched out "with colors flying and drums beating, bringing away company and private property, and saluting . . . [his] flag with fifty guns." [15]

Though no use of Sumter for a Federal attack had been contemplated, the superiority of Confederate attacking power demonstrated that the Sumter menace had been overstated. The provisioning expedition had done nothing to assist Anderson. To have given such assistance would have been very difficult in view of the formidable Southern forces in Charleston Harbor. The little fleet was not equipped or designed as an adequate force to hold the one remaining Federal fort in the harbor against Southern attack. Landing of food was its main object; success in this object was, from the Lincoln standpoint, conditional upon the Southerners' taking the President's declaration of non-aggression at its face value. Even then, the problem of a broken Union was still to be solved. Thus Sumter was not in fact relieved, but in the act of sending the expedition Lincoln had made a decision; he had given up the Seward type of conciliation (if it was that) which was dependent upon voluntary Federal evacuation. [16]

VIII

There have been many post mortems on the Sumter affair, some anti-Lincoln, some otherwise. In the summer of 1861 there was an outburst against one James E. Harvey, recently appointed minister to Portugal, who was worried at Lisbon by attacks at home. Harvey was a Northern journalist with friendly connections at Charleston. His offending consisted in the fact that, while the Sumter situation was developing, he had telegraphed Charleston officials advising that Sumter would be evacuated. For example, on March 11 he wired A. G.

---

[15] Crawford, *Genesis*, 449.

[16] Fox's report of the Sumter expedition and of what preceded it is found in *Offic. Rec.* (Nav.), 1 ser., IV, 245–251. The lack of help from the relieving fleet is described on p. 249, where it is stated that S. C. Rowan, commander of the *Pawnee*, for instance, indicated "that his orders required him to remain 10 miles east of the light and await the *Powhatan*, and that he was not going in there to inaugurate civil war." For Rowan's orders from Welles (one of a series for the Sumter fleet), see *ibid.*, 235–236.

Magrath, former Federal judge, that Anderson would be withdrawn. After a series of such messages he wired on April 6 that supplies were being sent, supported by a naval force to be used if the landing of supplies were resisted. When in August Harvey was severely abused for this conduct, he wrote to Cameron explaining that his humble efforts to preserve peace had never been concealed and that Cameron himself had advised him of the necessity of evacuating Sumter. When informed that six members of the cabinet, including Cameron, had favored evacuation and that such a policy had been urged by Scott and other army officials, Harvey felt justified in assuming the withdrawal to be settled. His communication of this expectation to Petigru, Magrath, and others in Charleston was "with a view of preventing the attack on Fort Sumter . . . and the inauguration of Civil War." It is revealed in this letter that Cameron had resented Lincoln's hesitation "in failing to ratify the almost unanimous opinion of his cabinet," and attributed this attitude to Blair, who, according to Cameron as quoted by Harvey, "ought never to have been brought into the Cabinet . . . ." Harvey added that his aim was to save the border states and avert war, but that his patriotic efforts were tortured into the worst of crimes. One of the things clearly indicated in the Harvey episode was the fact that the Sumter expedition at the time of sailing was no secret. Lincoln himself had already notified the Southern authorities, and plans for the expedition had been noted in the Charleston papers.[1]

As early as August 1, 1861, a theory as to Lincoln's purpose was advanced which has become familiar in recent years. This was also from Lisbon, whence John L. O'Sullivan, New York Democratic politician and supporter of lost causes, wrote to Samuel J. Tilden concerning the "strange proceedings of the Administration about Fort Sumter." O'Sullivan was convinced that it was all an "adroit manouvre . . . to draw the fire of Beauregard's batteries and . . . precipitate the attack upon Sumpter [sic] . . . for . . . its expected effect upon the public feeling of the North." [2]

This same theory reappears in an independent and scholarly study of the subject by Professor C. W. Ramsdell, published in 1937. The

[1] Harvey to Cameron, Lisbon, Sept. 20, 1861, Cameron MSS.; N. Y. Times, Mar. 30, 1861, p. 4, c. 4; Cong. Globe, 37 Cong., 1 sess., p. 432–433 (Aug. 3, 1861); ibid., 40 Cong., 2 sess., 1308–1310, 1402–1403.

[2] J. L. O'Sullivan to S. J. Tilden, Lisbon, Aug. 1, 1861, Tilden MSS.

essence of Professor Ramsdell's thesis is a question postulated as a query that "must have" arisen in Lincoln's mind: "Could the Southerners be *induced* to attack Sumter, to assume the aggressive and thus put themselves in the wrong in the eyes of the North and of the world?" [3] In this episode Lincoln's course is compared to the alleged conduct of Bismarck in the Ems dispatch. Certain rationalizations of Lincoln's secretary-biographers (Nicolay and Hay) are produced in support of this thesis as to Lincoln's intent, as well as a fragmentary reminiscent remark attributed to Lincoln by his friend Browning. On July 3 Browning recorded in his diary that he had talked with Lincoln that night and that Lincoln spoke thus as to Sumter: "The plan [sending supplies] succeeded. They attacked Sumter—it fell, and thus, did more service than it otherwise could." [4]

If this remark by Lincoln nearly three months after the event was correctly quoted and if it meant a deliberate maneuver to cause the South to fire the first shot, it is, as to Lincoln's motive, unsupported by contemporary evidence of March and April, 1861. It is significant that when two expeditions were preparing, the one that was given orders to sail and act was directed to that fort at which Southern attack was *not expected* (Pickens), while the one made "ready" in a tentative sense was concerned with the fort where trouble was more likely. The purpose of the Sumter expedition when sent was merely to maintain the status quo as nearly as possible by giving food to the garrison. Only in case of Southern attack was there to be a forcible effort to land troops. The nature of the announcement of the expedition to Southern authorities should also be noted. Had the purpose been to trick the South into firing the first shot, a leakage of information as to a supposedly secret expedition with hints as to hostile intent would have served better. Instead of this there was an official notification with emphasis upon non-hostile intent and with a pledge not to reënforce unless attacked. It would be going very far indeed to imply that this emphasis was insincere. Lincoln's note to Governor Pickens did not read like the message of a leader trying to induce the other side to make an assault, nor did his actions and orders in April, taken in their

---

[3] C. W. Ramsdell, in *Jour. of So. Hist.*, III, 272 (Aug., 1937). For the whole article, an able review of the Sumter imbroglio, see *ibid.*, 259–288. The idea that Lincoln meant deliberately to maneuver the Southerners into firing the first shot also appears in Edgar Lee Masters, *Lincoln the Man*, 391.

[4] Browning, *Diary*, I, 476 (July 3, 1861).

setting and without reading meanings back into them, indicate any such intention.

If conjecture as to Lincoln's purpose is to be reduced to a hypothetical question, it might be worded thus: Could Lincoln, after pondering evacuation and reluctantly reaching the point of sending the expedition to Sumter, have determined to manage the expedition in such a way as to avoid hostile provocation? If it were desirable to advance any thesis as to intent, an affirmative answer to this question might become a pattern into which authentic evidence of March and April could be fitted more validly than into the provocation pattern. When Lincoln sent the Sumter expedition he was not putting the country on a basis of war expectancy. His cryptic remark to Browning, assuming it to be properly and fully recorded, is only part of a conversation in which the President is also quoted as saying that "all the troubles and anxieties of his life had not equalled" those which preceded the fall of Sumter, also that it was he himself who "proposed sending supplies, *without* [5] an attempt to reinforce [,] giving notice of the fact to Gov Pickins [*sic*] of S. C." [6] Sending food, avoiding reenforcement, giving notice—such was the nature of Lincoln's plan as revealed in that very Browning record which has been quoted against him! Lincoln is quoted as saying that the plan succeeded. What this meant, if he said it, is not clear, but at least the United States had not bunglingly thrown the switch.

Whether Lincoln showed supreme wisdom in sending the Sumter expedition against the judgment of important advisers need not be argued in these pages. In the upper South, as will be seen in the next chapter, the sequel of the Sumter outbreak was most unfortunate to the Union cause. It is more to the point to appreciate the difficulty of Lincoln's task, and to note that feeding the garrison was not considered by him to be incompatible with a continuation of peace. It is easier now to say that Lincoln misread the probable Charleston and Montgomery reaction than to have known for a certainty, before the event, that the President's efforts to avert a hostile reaction would fail. Nor can one find sufficient evidence to conclude that these efforts were insincere and that Lincoln was descending to a mere trick. One must distinguish between the intent of the President's Sumter move and its effect—or, more correctly, the effect of the firing upon the fort.

---

[5] Author's italics.   [6] Browning, *Diary,* I, 476.

On July 4, 1861, Lincoln addressed Congress with a message in which he indicated something very different from deliberate hostile provocation. It is true that public papers of Presidents do not always give the last word as to motives, and the question arises whether Lincoln's message may be interpreted as rationalization after the event, but the Browning conversation (even if correctly reported) could also be so interpreted. So far as the conversation conflicts with the message on the disputed question of Lincoln's purpose, the message has the better corroboration in the March-April record. The Baldwin interview on April 4, for example, reveals Lincoln as seeking to avoid, not provoke, violence. The whole March-April story—Lincoln's orders and instructions, his conversations with Baldwin and Botts, his delay in sending the expedition, his notification to South Carolina, his non-aggressiveness in the final phase, his adherence to inaugural declarations in which avoidance of bloodshed was emphatically stressed, his studious distinction between Pensacola and Charleston, and his denial that provisioning Sumter would mean war [7]—are facts which the doubtful remark to Browning is inadequate to refute.

Lincoln was talking in familiar terms, while Montgomery and Charleston were speaking a novel language of changed allegiance, consummated dissolution of the Union, and rival federal authority in the lower South, where states other than the seven seceded ones were regarded as foreign nations. At times the new terminology became almost ludicrously awkward, as when a resolution was passed in the Confederate Congress "to enforce the existing revenue laws against all foreign countries, except the State of Texas." [8] That Lincoln should avoid such terminology and speak in terms of Federal authority was the thing expected of the President of the United States. Taking a completely opposite view of authority, Charleston and Montgomery spoke in terms of a dissolved union before the country had time to rub its eyes. In the face of these opposite positions Lincoln had to

---

[7] Lincoln does not appear to have been among those who considered war inevitable. Magruder and Baldwin testify that he rejected the idea that a Sumter expedition meant war. *Atl. Mo.*, XXXV, 443; *House Report No. 30*, 39 Cong., 1 sess., pt. 2, 104. On March 12, 1861, the Confederate commissioners wrote to Secretary Toombs that a gentleman from Louisiana talked privately with Lincoln that day and was assured by the President that there would be no war and that he, the President, was determined to keep the peace. Pickett Papers.

[8] *Journal*, Confed. Cong., I, 60 (Feb. 16, 1861).

watch his step as to concessions. His exploration of the potentialities gave him little reason to expect that withdrawal would promote restoration of seceded areas. He had already made a big concession in avoiding a retaking of fallen forts to which he considered the United States had a clear right. To go farther and even avoid keeping the few remaining forts was a bitter alternative, made no easier by the nature of Southern threats. Considering the novelty of its governmental situation, South Carolina could more easily have endured the continued retention of Fort Sumter in Federal hands than Lincoln could endure its surrender. Surrender would have involved the greater change of status. In spite of all this Lincoln examined the policy of evacuation. By his own account he contemplated it if the quiet strengthening of Pickens could have been accomplished at the time he wished; there is fairly good evidence also that he thought of it as a kind of price for Virginia's definite rejection of secession.

Circumstances failed to develop any bargain as to Virginia. The expectation as to Pickens also failed, but knowledge of its failure did not come until the wretched Sumter situation would admit of no further delay. Then the President sent ships with food to Sumter, but even yet it was known that Lincoln would make no attack. Even in the Southern view, in which the United States by preserving existing attitudes was considered the "invader" from the first instant of secession, Lincoln was no more aggressive than his predecessor. Each day of mere retention of the fort was, to Governor Pickens, an act of offense. In respect to Sumter Lincoln went no farther than Buchanan, the man who has been so roundly denounced for weakness.[9] Orders for the April expedition were no more of a challenge than orders for the *Star of the West*. Even before the sending of that ship South Carolinian language against Buchanan had been sharp and severe. In a communication directed to Buchanan himself, in which diplomacy and respect for high office might have been expected to soften language, South Carolinian commissioners referred to the President's refusal to "re-

---

[9] Buchanan not only approved Lincoln's policy in connection with the Sumter bombardment, but identified it with his own. "They chose to commence civil war [he wrote] & Mr. Lincoln had no alternative but to defend the country against dismemberment. I certainly should have done the same thing had they begun the war in my time: & this they well knew . . . ." Buchanan to J. S. Black, Wheatland, Mar. 4, 1862, Black MSS.

store the status you had pledged your honor to maintain," and added: "You . . . hold by force what you have obtained through our misplaced confidence . . . ." [10]

Contemporary Southern criticism represented Lincoln as an aggressor. Scurrilous newspaper abuse may be omitted, but even Jefferson Davis made it appear that the Unionists had refused a mutual agreement not to fire on either side, that the aggressive Union purpose was to place the Southern "forces at Charleston between the simultaneous fire of the fleet and the fort," and that therefore there remained no alternative but to "direct that the fort should be at once reduced." [11]

It is but a commonplace now to say that each side accused the other not only of causing but also of touching off the war, and even yet the subject is frequently discussed in these controversial terms. In addition to the familiar line of censure there is one point of criticism that appears in an almost unknown document of the time which, as it takes a different Southern tack, deserves at least a glance. In the papers of Governor Pickens [12] are letters and memoranda, from a friend in Alabama, John W. Lapsley of Selma, in which veiled references are made to a "proclamation" and an "apology" by President Lincoln, both of which were referred to as documents which the President prepared for the purpose of announcing and explaining the abandonment of the Sumter garrison. A circumstantial account is given of how printed proof sheets of these documents were discovered in the White House and indirectly, through a brother-in-law of Mrs. Lincoln, turned over to "a friend" who turned them over to Pickens's correspondent. It is alleged that the documents indicate that Lincoln intended to abandon Sumter, to proclaim this officially, and, in a sort of manifesto or apology, to justify it to the people.

The subject is too involved for full discussion here, but one comment by Lapsley may be quoted, in which he refers to "one of the foulest and wickedest plots on record," i. e., a plot "to *cause the*

---

[10] Reply of S. C. commissioners to the President, Jan. 1, 1861, *Offic. Rec.*, 1 ser., I, 123–124.

[11] Message of President Davis to the Confederate Congress, April 29, 1861, *Journal*, Confed. Cong., I, 164.

[12] John W. Lapsley to Francis W. Pickens, June 4, 1861 and July 30, 1861; Lapsley to I. W. Hayne, June 25, 1861, MSS., Duke University.

destruction of a brave and faithful garrison . . . for the *sole purpose* of exciting their whole people to a pitch of phrenzy so as to command their treasures, for the support of the vast armies they expected . . . to rally under . . . the same phrenzy, to be precipitated upon the South." From the context it appears that these words refer to Lincoln's supposed plan to abandon Sumter which is referred to as if it meant withholding help and leaving the garrison to its fate. In other words, here is a severe Southern criticism of Lincoln (on the basis of inadequately explained "documents") for allegedly doing exactly the opposite of what he did. Instead of abandoning Sumter he attempted to provision and hold it. Had he abandoned it without such an attempt, the Lapsley assault suggests that this very abandonment would have been vigorously criticized at the South as an effort to cause a frenzy at the North, as a sacrifice of a brave garrison, and as a cause of war! Any suggestion that the withdrawal from Sumter would have been conciliatory is lacking in these documents.[13] Criticisms of this nature make it appear that anything Lincoln might have done would in some way have been attacked and misrepresented by enemies.

The sequel of the Sumter expedition, or rather of the bombardment, was so disastrous and ghastly that attacks upon Lincoln for his part in it were inevitable. It was in this light that the provocation theory, as old as 1861, originated. A careful restudy of elaborate sources, published and unpublished, for the purpose of this book, does not, in the opinion of the present writer, reveal evidence to show that Lincoln calculated in terms of a maneuver and provocation designed to produce war by a precipitated "first shot" on the other side. Still less is it tenable to assert that an unsuccessful effort to feed the garrison was *per se* the inaugurating of war; in any case the attack upon Sumter had something to do with the matter. That Lincoln, under severest pressure from Northern advisers demanding firmness, and under pledge to maintain Federal authority with no need of bloodshed, was drawn by untoward circumstances into a reluctant and non-aggressive provisioning of the Charleston fort, which he sought to control in such a way as to avoid provocation and to preserve the status quo as he

---

[13] Lapsley sought to have the documents published by way of a "canard" which would attribute them to a "Junius" writing at Washington. He wanted it all done with elaborate precautions to put inquirers on the wrong scent and to prevent tracing the documents to their actual source.

found it, seems the more valid conclusion.[14] That he did this after carefully testing the potentialities of evacuation, a policy which offered to his mind little in terms of Union advantage (though the upper South and border thought otherwise) seems also likely. When war came it turned out that he had kept the non-aggressive record of his government clear, which assuredly is not to his discredit; but to say that Lincoln meant that the first shot would be fired by the other side *if a first shot was fired,* is not to say that he maneuvered to have the shot fired. This distinction is fundamental.[15]

It may be fitting to close this chapter with the statement of a Virginian who had glimpses of some of the "secret history" of the time. Allan B. Magruder, concerned with the Lincoln-Baldwin interview above mentioned, disagreed with Lincoln's Sumter policy while honoring his peaceful motives. The satisfactory solution, in Magruder's view, was "withdrawal . . . from Fort Sumter and an earnest appeal to the country . . . to stand by the Union . . . and stay the mad career of secession." As to Lincoln's purpose he said: "It seems clear that Mr. Lincoln had fully resolved on the policy of peace, and did not mean to permit the war to be inaugurated, if it were possible . . . to avert that calamity. . . . All of the facts of the case go to fortify this conclusion." [16]

---

[14] In these paragraphs the subject is not discussed by way of controversy with any particular writer. Despite variance of conclusion, the author has high respect for the scholarly and unprejudiced survey by Professor Ramsdell. His study (above cited) is welcomed as a real contribution to the Lincoln and Sumter theme.

[15] The writer has attempted a rather full analysis of the problem of Lincoln and Fort Sumter in "When War Came in 1861," *Abr. Lincoln Quart.*, I, 3–42 (Mar. 1940). A strongly anti-Lincoln account of the whole subject (Sumter and Pickens) is to be found in John Shipley Tilley, *Lincoln Takes Command* (Chapel Hill, 1941).

[16] Allan B. Magruder, in *Atl. Mo.*, xxxv, 445 (1875).

CHAPTER XIII

EIGHTY DAYS

I

QUESTIONS of state for President Lincoln in the days and weeks after Sumter covered all the usual vexations of a new President displacing a rival party, magnified a thousandfold by the demands of unprecedented emergency. Merely to state the questions is something of a task. Must the Sumter incident become the appeal to arms? Had the gauntlet been thrown? Was the nation faced with the inescapable challenge that could not be ignored, the irrevocable closing of the door to compromise? Did it have to be war? Should troops be summoned?

On what ground should the summons be based, the putting down of insurrection, or war against a Southern nation? Should reliance be placed upon states—i. e., in practice upon state governors? If so, what states? Should the upper Southern states be expected to respond to a call from a President, a party, and a cause to which they did not adhere? What about Virginia, across the river from Washington? If Virginia should secede, what of the safety of the nation's capital, of the government itself? What of southern Illinois? What of Lincoln's native state, Kentucky? Would precipitate measures not drive wavering states out of the Union?

How far could the fighting spirit, whether in its ardent form or as a reluctant acceptance of war to preserve the nation, be counted on? Would sufficient men join up by choice? If not, the draft was, at the moment, beyond the sphere of practical measures. Not yet did conscription come within the implements available to an American president.

What if Maryland should resist, or balk at the passage of troops?

Was Washington thus to be cut off from the North? What of Baltimore hotheads? Should the President reason with the Maryland authorities, or should he command them? Should it be passive waiting, or action? If he acted, should he go so far as to imprison secessionists in the Maryland legislature? In the cause of liberty and the preservation of democracy, could Lincoln afford to lay himself open to the charge of dictatorship?

Should the actual raising of troops be left with the states, each governor being asked to furnish a stated number of regiments? Should the regiments be uniform? If so, on what pattern? Should it be a national army, or a hodge-podge of military units? How many troops should be called? What number from each state? Should the states bear the cost of raising, equipping, arming, paying, and transporting these regiments? If the governors balked at this, or even if they accepted it and pushed it with zeal, would this not shift too much national authority into the governors' hands and thus weaken the prestige of Washington? Since an army could not be organized overnight, could Washington keep pace with those states which became active and offered more troops than the circumlocution office knew what to do with?

War having been started, a strategic theory of the war would be imperative. The patriarchal attorney general, Edward Bates, even doubted whether war in fact ought to be waged at all. Bates proposed a plan that "would not necessarily lead to the shedding of a drop of blood," yet would be "very *coersive* [*sic*] and very promising of success." [1] Noting that Southerners were an "anomalous people," being agricultural yet unable to live on home products, he would bring them to terms by stopping the mails, closing Southern ports, guarding the Mississippi River, and enforcing a blockade that would offer the "easiest . . . and most humane method" of restraining them. [2] When a nation blunders into war, its leaders in the first phase are likely to promise painless measures, brief sacrifices, and easy victory. But this was not all: what it amounted to was that Bates even after Sumter could not stomach the idea that war was really upon the country.

If this painless theory of the war were not adopted, some military plan would have to be evolved, or rather improvised. The question of a blockade would arise in any case, and with it the danger that

---

[1] Bates, *Diary*, 184.   [2] *Ibid.*, 182–183.

foreign powers might differ with Washington as to international rights.[3] Should the Confederate States be regarded as a belligerent power, or should its acts of war be treated as piratical, traitorous, and insurrectionary? If the latter theory were chosen, would it be nominally maintained as a matter of status and legality, subject to Olympian revision by the Supreme Court, or would its dire effects upon human beings be envisioned and enforced? When Confederate privateers were captured, should officers and crews be hanged as pirates? What about traitors at home? Could officials of Lincoln's own government be trusted? Should government spies be at once set on foot to combat Confederate or pro-Confederate spies? Should disloyal or suspected employees be imprisoned or merely dismissed? Should arrests be arbitrary? If the slow processes of civil justice were followed, how could arrests be made in such number and with enough swiftness to sustain the government's vital activities?

But the President must not merely decide what action he ought to take; there is the further question what action he *can* take. There are laws, there are legal gaps, and there is Congress to be consulted if new laws are needed. Few American Presidents have got on well with Congress. For Lincoln the question arose, should Congress convene only by schedule? That would have postponed the next meeting to December 1861, by which time, it was devoutly hoped, the trouble would be over. A special session seemed indicated, but would such a session help or hinder a national uprising to meet the crisis? Would not too early a session force the issue in Kentucky to the detriment of the Union? When summoned, would Congress support the President and go forward with him, or would they check his further course while withholding retroactive approval of acts already accomplished?

What appointments should be made? How many major generals should New York have, and what men should be so honored? How could the President resist the pressure for appointments within his own state and among his friends? What of Benjamin F. Butler? How could he be used, yet ruin averted? (This problem, unlike some of the troops trickling in, was to stay with Lincoln "for the duration.") There was the case of General Scott, head of the meager army. He was seventy-five and could not mount a horse. Was he not too old,

---

[3] For a treatment of foreign affairs in the early stages of the Lincoln administration, see vol. II, 29–53.

too slow and cautious? But who should replace him, or make decisions for him? Would the army not require two heads, some kind of general in chief in the field, in addition to Scott at Washington? There were civil offices, both major and minor. What about the minister to London, to Paris, to scores of other places? And what about the postmastership at Salem, Massachusetts?

II

The firing at Sumter, whose evacuation Lincoln himself admitted to be a military necessity, was taken, whether necessarily or not, as the casting of the die, and Sunday, April 14, 1861, the time of Anderson's formal surrender, was a day of deep anxiety to Lincoln. The necessary papers were phrased on Sunday and on the next day the President issued a far reaching proclamation. There were Federal militia laws of long standing, especially an act passed under Washington (1795) under which provision was made for summoning the militia of the states into Federal service whenever the laws of the United States should be resisted by "combinations too powerful to be suppressed by the ordinary course of judicial proceedings." [1] As if with his finger on this old-time statute and in conscious imitation of similar action by Washington, Lincoln declared, not that states as such were in insurrection, but that "combinations too powerful [etc.]" existed in the states of the lower South, naming the states. In consequence, he called out the militia of the other states to the number of 75,000 "to suppress said combinations, and to cause the laws to be duly executed." For the "extraordinary occasion" he summoned Congress to meet in special session, not, as his reference to the emergency would seem to suggest, at an early date, but on July 4. [2]

This first appeal of Lincoln was greeted with a more vigorous response than some of the later calls. All over the North the air throbbed with mass meetings, rallies, cheers, resolutions, governors' proclamations, special legislative sessions, and parades with Revolutionary fife and drum. Rifle clubs and home guards were formed, arsenals seized, money subscribed, "traitors" arrested, cannon mounted, flags raised, pro-Confederate establishments attacked, companies drilled, camps formed, and the Almighty importuned to wipe the enemy from the face of the earth. So intense was the war excitement

---

[1] *U. S. Stat. at Large*, I, 424.   [2] *Works*, VI, 246–248.

at Boston, that, as it seemed to Edward Everett, the President might
have called out 500,000 men instead of 75,000, and the response would
have been equally prompt. Money, he thought, would be tendered as
readily as men.[3] There were those in Boston on this fateful week-end
who received the news "as a fortunate opening of a contest which . . .
[had] been deemed inevitable."[4] To the New York *Times* it seemed
that "a heavy burden of anxiety had been suddenly lifted" from the
public mind. The "one thing needful" had happened; it was " 'the
beginning of the end.' "[5] On the day of Lincoln's proclamation there
was but "one sentiment," thought the *Times,* and that was standing by
the government. "On every corner, . . . in every car, on board every
ferry-boat, in every hotel, in the vestibule of every church, could be
heard the remark: 'I am a Democrat . . . ; I voted against Lincoln,
but I will stand by . . . my country when assailed . . . .' "[6] In
Philadelphia there was equal excitement with keen demand for extras,
but there were also "large numbers who refuse[d] . . . to believe
that hostilities . . . [had] commenced."[7] Round the country the
effect was galvanic: "intense excitement" at Albany where large state
appropriations were at once suggested;[8] men with secession cockades
chased by crowds in Baltimore;[9] troops tendered at Providence,
Rhode Island, Columbus, Ohio, and elsewhere in advance of the
call; "profound sensation" in Chicago; bells tolled at Quincy, Illinois,
with Orville Browning refusing to believe the "story."[10]

In Washington, where pro-secession men still held office, there were
fights and knockdowns. The wildest agitation prevailed, with Union
men rejoicing that the issue was made at last. While General Patterson, in command of the troops that guarded the city, thought the
capital safe, many feared an immediate Confederate attack while it
was inadequately defended. Washington loomed as the great battleground upon which the Confederacy and Virginia would concentrate
a force of 100,000 men. Even though not holding the city, Southern
leaders were represented as determined that the Lincoln government
should be humiliated and driven out.[11]

---

[3] Edward Everett to J. J. Crittenden, April 18, 1861, Crittenden MSS.
[4] G. S. Boutwell to Charles Sumner, April 13, 1861, Sumner MSS.
[5] New York *Times,* April 13, 1861, p. 4, c. 3.   [6] *Ibid.,* April 15, 1861, p. 8, c. 2.
[7] *Ibid.,* April 15, 1861, p. 8, cc. 5–6.   [8] *Ibid.,* April 15, 1861, p. 8, c. 5.
[9] *Ibid.,* p. 8, c. 6.   [10] Browning, *Diary,* I, 462–463.
[11] New York *Herald,* April 19, 1861, p. 6, c. 4: April 25, 1861, p. 1, c. 1.

Yet not all latitudes and corners of the nation rose with equal fervor. In a typical town of southern Illinois the sheriff's feelings were "with the South" and many of the people showed a determination to prevent the formation of companies in the county.[12] From Marion in troubled Williamson County, Illinois, came confidential word to Governor Yates that disunion feeling was promoted by disappointed politicians, including "Logan, Cunningham, Hundley, Pulley and others." These men, Yates was told, had "assisted in getting up a company for the so called 'Southern Confederacy.' " [13] Sympathizers in the region accompanied the secession company to the Ohio River and saw them safely land on the Kentucky side at Paducah to "fite" under General Pillow.[14]

Attention was concentrated upon Virginia, recognized by both sides as a key state. For Virginians the problem had been to promote conciliation and avoid an outbreak. Had this been done, it was expected that they would have been content to remain in the Union in spite of Lincoln. The Union element in the state had been strong, but, as seen in a former chapter, Lincoln's negotiations with Virginia unionists had been neither prompt nor successful. Union sentiment was of the sober, thoughtful variety, but from the noise made it would have been easy to assume that secession and war were popular. Crowds in Richmond kept up a species of secession claque while the Virginia convention deliberated, and when the telegraph carried news of the surrender of Sumter a "wild shout went up and down the streets." [15] Even ten days previous to this a Massachusetts correspondent of Sumner, visiting Richmond, noted processions of secession men marching with bands of music and gaining in numbers with each beat of the drum. It would have been hard, said this writer, for one not on the spot to understand *"the agitation,* the insane excitement" of this city, which was attributed to "the vacillating, uncertain policy

12 "A Unionist" to Governor Yates, Nashville (Washington County), Illinois, April 22, 1861, Yates MSS.

13 Patrick H. Lang, Marion (Williamson County), Illinois, to Yates, May 28, 1861, Yates MSS. This letter is significant as one of the few extant bits of specific evidence to show the anti-Union attitude of John A. Logan in these early, uncertain days of the war.

14 Griffin Garland, Attila (Williamson County), Ill., to Governor Yates, May 29, 1861, Yates MSS.

15 New York *Times,* April 16, 1861, p. 8, c. 1.

of Mr Lincoln." [16] The cure suggested was the adoption by Lincoln
of a conciliatory policy toward the South.

On April 17 the Virginia ordinance of secession was passed (one of
the most fateful events in American history), and while at the time this
act was not understood to be legally binding until ratified by popular
vote in a special referendum set for May 23, all the measures of Virginia's government from April 17 on were in terms of adherence to
the Southern Confederacy. Indeed on May 16 James M. Mason, who
had been Virginia's senator at Washington, wrote an open letter urging that Virginia was already out of the Union and that a pro-Union
popular vote on the referendum would amount to betrayal and capture of thousands of soldiers from the lower South who had taken
their place on Virginia soil. [17]

The reluctant action of the Old Dominion set the pattern for post-
Sumter reaction throughout the upper South. By May 7 Arkansas
and Tennessee had followed Virginia out of the Union. In Arkansas,
by the familiar device of a "state convention," an "ordinance of secession" was passed on May 6. A different method was used in Tennessee,
where the people had decisively rejected the plan to call a convention,
at the same time registering their disapproval of secession by 91,803
to 24,749. [18] In direct contravention of this expressed will of the people,
the legislature (May 6) framed a declaration of independence and
ordinance of secession to be submitted to popular vote on June 8;
then, without waiting for this action, the pro-secessionist governor,
Isham G. Harris, appointed commissioners who negotiated and signed
a military league with the Confederacy, whereupon the compliant
legislature "ratified" this league and went so far as to offer Nashville
as the capital city for the Confederate States. [19] When it came to the
farce of voting on the ordinance of withdrawal (after withdrawal had
been made a fact by governor and legislature) "no speeches . . . in
favor of the Union were permitted" in large parts of the state. [20]

---

[16] Cornelia Walter Richards to Charles Sumner, Richmond, Virginia, April 3, 1861,
Sumner MSS.

[17] Open letter by James M. Mason, Winchester, Va., May 16, 1861, McPherson, *Rebellion*, 7.

[18] James Walter Fertig, *The Secession and Reconstruction of Tennessee*, 20. The
date of this election was February 9, 1861.

[19] James Welch Patton, *Unionism and Reconstruction in Tennessee, 1860–1869*, 17–19.

[20] *Offic. Rec.*, 1 ser., LII, pt. 1, 173.

Careful scholars have not regarded the popular vote of June 8 to ratify secession (108,399 to 47,223) as any genuine decision of the people of Tennessee to choose the road of disunion; [21] yet in judging of this subject the severe stresses of the post-Sumter period and the important role of West Tennessee, which was the section most similar to the dominant elements in the Old South, must be borne in mind. Tennessee did not secede till after war began. Its wish to adhere to the Union, however, was fruitless; that wish did not constitute leadership for the Union in the days of critical decision.

In North Carolina the ordinance of secession was passed without a dissenting vote, such was the prostrating effect of April events upon a state whose pre-Sumter attitude was that of resistance to secessionist pressure and preference for Union-preserving compromise.

It was evident that Lincoln's policy—inadequate conciliation, attempted provisioning of Sumter, calling out the militia of the states —had alienated the upper South; some would have said that this resulted not so much from Lincoln's deliberately chosen policy as from the action forced upon him by the course of events. However one might argue about causes, the effect was electric. At one stroke the Washington government lost four important and strategically located commonwealths whose preference for the historic relationship under the old roof had held them within the Union not only under Buchanan, but, if one may use the expression, under Seward—i. e., under the Seward-sponsored program of compromise, avoidance of outbreak, and repetition of the statesmanship of 1850.

In the election of 1860 these states had expressed their preference for the Union. When secession was in the making and the Confederacy forming, they had withheld support from a movement to dismember the nation. With eyes on the uncoercive attitude of Congress and the diplomacy of Seward, they had been led to expect that Lincoln would abandon Fort Sumter, which, they thought, could have been done without loss of face or surrender of principle.

It was not alone the expedition to Sumter and the "first shot" incident that plunged the upper South into secession. It was this, *plus* the appeal to the non-seceding states for troops to be used in "coercing"

---

[21] According to J. W. Fertig (p. 26) the people on June 8 were "no longer free to vote their sentiments." For the strong opposition to secession in East Tennessee, and the abortive effort to form a separate state, see vol. II, 14-15.

sister states. Objective historians are not agreed that Lincoln precipitated the war, but to the upper as well as the lower South it appeared that the President, having unnecessarily, as they thought, chosen a policy of force where conciliation would have worked, was the man upon whom war guilt rested.[22] In all this it was a further count against him in the eyes of the upper South that he had broken promises made through Judge Campbell to Southern negotiators that a Sumter outbreak would be averted. It is true that these negotiators had represented the seceded portion, not the upper South, and had been maneuvering wholly on the basis of a divided nation and an established Confederacy, while Virginians and their sympathizers hoped for union. It is also true, however, that upper Southern devotion to the Union was in terms of not having to fight against brethren of the lower South in order to maintain it. If it came to fighting, if North Carolinian troops would have to be used against South Carolinian neighbors, it was the parting of the ways so far as recognizing Mr. Lincoln was concerned. They might, indeed, detest the haste and precipitateness of South Carolina, and they might have little confidence in the prospect for Southern independence, but to them the day of choice was gone when Lincoln called for troops. Though their answer was in despair and gloom, it had to be an indignant negative.

Such a leader as Jonathan Worth epitomized the plight of the upper South. Worth was a high-minded moderate who had stoutly opposed secession in its earlier stages, but what Lincoln did in April was to Worth a thing for North Carolina to resent and resist. He was doing the unpardonable, seeking to stir up servile insurrection, to destroy the South, in a word to do the vile things which secessionists charged. If in so doing Lincoln had united the North, it was equally true, said Worth, that he had "certainly united North Carolina." [23]

This unity of sentiment in the states of the upper South was evident in the replies which their governors sent in response to Lincoln's requisitions for troops to put down "insurrection." The "militia . . . will not be furnished," wrote Governor Letcher of Virginia.

---

[22] What is stated here is that people in the upper South thought this. The writer by no means places war guilt upon Lincoln, as has been sufficiently indicated in the preceding chapter, but an honest account cannot ignore what the record amply shows— i. e., the resentful verdict of Virginia, North Carolina, *et al.*, that Lincoln had blundered, had precipitated war, and had betrayed Southern Union men.

[23] J. G. de R. Hamilton, *Correspondence of Jonathan Worth*, I, 150–151.

"Your object," continued Letcher, "is to subjugate the southern States . . . ." [24] Ellis of North Carolina professed to doubt the genuineness of the requisition, but stated that "if genuine" the levy of troops "for the purpose of subjugating the . . . South" was a "usurpation of power." [25] Replies from Arkansas and Tennessee were in like vein. The governor of Arkansas said the purpose was to "subjugate the Southern States" and went on to denounce Northern "mendacity and usurpation." [26] Harris of Tennessee sent a curt reply, briefest of all, stating that his state would "not furnish a single man for coercion, but fifty thousand . . . for defence . . . ." [27] Up to July 4, 1861, not one of the slave states except Delaware had supplied a regiment through regular state organization, though some privately recruited units from this area had been taken into the service. Union sentiment in that region, said Lincoln, "was nearly repressed and silenced." [28]

III

So little was the unwieldy American democracy shaped for war making in the hustling days of early recruitment that Lincoln's secretary of war was in a chronic state of being "overwhelmed" by the task of raising 75,000 three-months men among twenty-two million people. Over and over the secretary wrote that he was swamped by the throng offering their services. Often he said he could give no assurances that particular regiments would be accepted. Against the Southern charge that Lincoln planned all along to attack and subjugate them stands the patent fact of the lack of men, facilities, equipment, arms, or even military plans, suitable for so much as a mild policy of Federal defense. Congress, wrote Gideon Welles, "had been inexcusably neglectful" of preparedness, doing nothing itself and failing to confer extraordinary power upon the executive to meet the storm.[1]

It was a half-century prior to the formation of a general staff for the American army, and the unmilitary character of the Federal government in Lincoln's time is an amazing thing for a later day to con-

---

[24] McPherson, *Rebellion*, 114.   [25] *Ibid.*   [26] *Annual Cyclopaedia*, 1861, 23.
[27] Isham G. Harris to Simon Cameron, April 17, 1861, Misc. Papers, Dep. of State, MSS., Nat. Archives.
[28] *Works*, VI, 305 (July 4, 1861).
[1] Welles to Isaac Arnold, Nov. 27, 1872, photostat of MS., Chicago Hist. Soc.

template. Regulars constituted a mere 13,000 in April 1861, and
much of this tiny force was immobilized at various and sundry "posts."
What went on in late April, May, and June of 1861 was a disjointed
effort to improvise a fighting force with little help from Washington.
If fully told, which it cannot be here, the story would reveal spurts of
activity among governors, meetings and organizations of citizens tending their services, banks and individuals offering funds (as loans),
thousands of common men responding, and, through it all, cross
purpose, clumsy administration, and lack of program. Three factors
stand out as one makes a study of voluminous government sources:
(1) haphazard reliance upon private, impulsive, uncoördinated effort,
(2) state activity to the point where governors became little ministers
of national defense, and (3) repeated refusal of troops on the part of
Secretary Cameron. To select a few bits from Cameron's correspondence, he wrote that the "whole matter of organizing troops . . . [had]
been entrusted to the Governors of the Several States," [2] that it was
important for Connecticut "to reduce . . . the number [of soldiers],
and in no case to exceed it," that if more had been summoned the
excess should be discharged,[3] and that he was "obliged [in the case
of New York] to hold up . . . acceptance of any more." [4] To an
Illinois unit he wrote: ". . . it is impossible for this Department to
accept the services of your Company." [5]

After four months of war Governor Yates of Illinois confessed: "I
feel cramped when I am in vain begging from Washington for power
to do what so evidently ought to be done." [6] When volunteer commanders urged upon him the acceptance of their commands, the
President was under great pressure to satisfy them, but constant embarrassment resulted because all these matters belonged to the war
department and the President could do little or nothing about them,
either by seeking Cameron's coöperation or by going ahead without

[2] Cameron to J. D. Lawyer of Coxsackie, N. Y., May 28, 1861, Military Book, War
Office, No. 44, p. 189, War Dep. MSS., Nat. Archives. An examination of these archives
shows that in the early weeks of the war Cameron frequently confessed that he was
overwhelmed by the number offering their services. Often those seeking assurances from
him are referred to the governors of their states.

[3] Cameron to Governor W. A. Buckingham of Connecticut, May 16, 1861, ibid., vol.
44, p. 61.

[4] Cameron to Daniel S. Dickinson of Binghamton, N. Y. June 13, 1861, ibid., vol. 44,
p. 289.

[5] Cameron to George A. Richmond of Oconee, Ill., May 18, 1861, Yates MSS.

[6] Richard Yates to General John Pope (copy), Aug. 12, 1861, Yates MSS.

consulting him.[7] To Secretary Chase it seemed that the failures were due to the lack of "a strong young head." "Everything [he is reported to have said] goes in confused disorder. Gen. Scott gives an order, Mr. Cameron gives another. Half of both are executed, neutralizing each other." [8]

Against this backdrop it is painful to note the figure of a sorely harassed President pacing the White House floor, glancing toward the enemy on the Virginia side, hearing "feverish rumors about a meditated attack" upon Washington, and wondering whether the troops would ever come. Yet such is the picture etched by John Hay ten days after the fall of Sumter. "This has been a day of gloom and doubt," wrote Hay. On receiving soldiers from Massachuetts at the White House, Lincoln said, "I don't believe there is any North. The Seventh Regiment is a myth. R. Island is not known in our geography any longer. *You* are the only Northern realities." [9]

The picture becomes even more painful when one recalls the prodigious grief involved in getting this small trickle of soldiers through to Washington. The Massachusetts men left Boston on April 17, two days after Lincoln's call, and passed through New York and Philadelphia on the 18th. At Baltimore on the 19th a mob attacked them and a miserable street brawl resulted. Railroad cars bearing the troops had to shift between depots, the cars being drawn by horses on tracks through the streets of this highly wrought city. Though under orders to cause the minimum of annoyance, the troops had to leave the cars because of obstructions on the tracks, put there by angry citizens. Marching at double quick they were assailed with missiles and numerous pistol shots. Police, soldiers, and citizens were at once engaged in a hot battle; approximately nine citizens and four soldiers were killed, several dozen wounded. With better discipline some of the casualties among Baltimoreans might have been averted; according to their own colonel the men were "infuriated beyond control." [10] Under local police escort the troops reached their depot of departure. Arriving at Washington after their baptism of fire, they were quartered in the Senate chamber.

It would be difficult to exaggerate the startling effect of this behind-

---

[7] New York *Herald*, May 16, 1861, p. 1, c. 2.

[8] Tyler Dennett, ed., *Lincoln . . . in the Diaries . . . of John Hay*, 7. (Chase was so quoted by Hay.)

[9] *Ibid.*, 11.   [10] *Offic. Rec.*, 1 ser., II, 9.

the-lines conflict upon the country and especially within the capital. To Edwin M. Stanton it seemed that "no description could convey . . . the panic that prevailed . . . [in Washington] for several days after the Baltimore riot . . . ." This was increased, he said, "by reports of the trepidation of Lincoln that were circulated through the streets." He added the amazing statement that "Almost every family packed up their effects" and that women and children were sent away in great numbers. Provisions, he said, "advanced to famine prices." [11] River boats were seized for guard duty on the Potomac; buildings in Washington were barricaded; theaters were closed.[12] Through these anxious days an attack upon Washington, and a successful one at that, was feared by residents of the capital, indeed regarded as almost a certainty. Among Southerners in arms against Lincoln the "butchery" of Baltimore citizens was exaggerated and it was asserted on April 20 that Virginia authorities could put seven thousand men in Baltimore in twenty-four hours. In the opinion of a Southern railroad superintendent writing from Petersburg, Virginia, the hour of Southern opportunity had struck. "Lincoln," he wrote, "is in a trap. . . . An hour now is worth years of common fighting. One dash and Lincoln is taken, the country saved, and the leader who does it will be immortalized." [13]

Had the Confederates seized Washington, one cannot doubt that they would have found a great deal of sympathy. The capital was largely a Southern city, and even Baltimore violence met approval by some within its confines. The day after the Baltimore disturbance an anonymous letter was directed from Washington to Charles Sumner advising him never again "to come or stay in this city in *any* capacity; official or private." "To you and your coadjutors," said this writer, ". . . is this . . . people . . . indebted for the terrible events that are imminent." Asserting that the South could never be subjugated, he added: "Even the poor starved slaves . . . will join their *real* friends . . . in repelling the marauders, as they did on friday . . . at Baltimore." [14]

In an emergency loaded with a hundred pressing problems this Maryland situation demanded an amount of attention that was out of all reasonable proportion. Authorities of Maryland and Baltimore

---

[11] E. M. Stanton to James Buchanan, May 16, 1861, Buchanan MSS.
[12] Nicolay and Hay, *Lincoln*, IV, 140.   [13] *Offic. Rec.*, 1 ser., II, 771–772.
[14] Anonymous letter to Sumner, Washington, April 20, 1861, Sumner MSS.

took the ground that movement of army units through Baltimore was "impossible" and that the arrival of further men from the eastern and northern states must be prevented as an "absolute necessity." [15] So earnest a Unionist as Reverdy Johnson told Lincoln the day after the riot that an attempt to bring troops through Maryland to Washington would crush all Union feeling in the state.[16] Railroad bridges on the approaches to Baltimore were accordingly disabled by action of the city authorities, concurred in, said the mayor, by Governor Hicks.[17] In this they professed no disloyalty to the Federal government, yet the effect of their action was, for the moment at least, to let an obstructionist mob have its way in defiance of the United States.

In the first official reaction at Washington national necessity had to bow to Baltimore reality, and a temporary *modus vivendi* was quickly arranged by which troops from the North were shunted off by other routes to avoid Baltimore altogether. Scott and Lincoln agreed to this on the urgent demand of Mayor Brown, Governor Hicks, and prominent citizens. On the 21st a body of Pennsylvania troops was halted at Cockeysville, Maryland, fourteen miles north of Baltimore. A broken bridge would have stopped them in any case, but the men were actually ordered by Secretary Cameron to return to York, Pennsylvania, because the President desired "to gratify the mayor of Baltimore, who . . . [feared] that bloodshed would . . . result from the passage through that city . . . ." [18]

The peak of Lincoln's embarrassment on this Maryland question came on Sunday, April 21, when his cabinet met, not as usual at the White House, but at the navy department. It was a day of "feverish rumors" [19] when it seemed that the capital of the United States was caught in a vise between hostile Virginia and obstructionist Maryland. A series of important orders were prepared and were on the point of being telegraphed. Then came a further shock; insurrectionists at Baltimore had seized the telegraph office. For some days Washington was cut off from communication with New York by rail, mail, and telegraph.[20]

15 *Offic. Rec.*, 1 ser., II, 10.
16 *Works*, VII, 293 (July 26, 1862); Reverdy Johnson to S. P. Chase, May 8, 1861, Chase MSS., Lib. of Cong.
17 *Offic. Rec.*, 1 ser., II, 13.   18 *Ibid.*, 584.
19 Dennett, ed., *Lincoln . . . in the . . . Diaries of John Hay*, 6.
20 *Works*, VII, 191 (May 26, 1862).

Inevitably the President's momentary yielding, designed to prevent a bad situation from becoming worse, was made to look like trepidation. In a barrage of committees and delegations, Marylanders descended upon Washington with their complaints, demands, and oracular protestations of loyalty. On April 22 a committee representing the Y. M. C. A. of Baltimore pleaded with the President to pass no more troops through Baltimore or Maryland.[21] They might as well have asked him to give up the government or to remake the face of the earth. As his statements were reported in Baltimore, Lincoln said that he must have the troops and that they had to come through Maryland, since they could not crawl under the earth, nor fly over the state. Carolinians, he pointed out, were at the moment crossing Virginia to assail him. If he yielded, he said, "there would be no Washington . . . , no Jackson . . . , no spunk in that." [22]

Sentiment in Maryland was an uneasy mixture of genuine Union loyalty, outright secessionist sympathy, willingness to recognize the Southern right to secede while avoiding secession for Maryland, distaste and revulsion toward civil war (perhaps chiefly this), and partisan resentment toward Mr. Lincoln and all his works. Admission of Southern "rights" could be expressed on a lofty basis of peace and self determination. This was the tone of that influential paper, the Baltimore *Sun,* which declared on April 22: "Maryland has no quarrel with the North, . . . ; it is . . . not her fault, if she is to be thrust into an unusual conflict which she has no disposition to seek, ... [I]t is . . . with the people to use all their influence for the promotion of peace. Let us, therefore, . . . pending the crisis, demand only the peaceful recognition of Southern rights." Five days later the *Sun* declared that, under Lincoln, the government had "become a vast consolidated despotism."

Avoiding extreme measures, Lincoln's Maryland policy accomplished the two objects sought: assertion of authority, and temporary conciliation to avert further bloodshed inside the lines. Maryland officials and self-constituted delegations were patiently received and tactfully answered. A proposal of Governor Hicks that the President should send no more troops through Maryland and should request

---

21 New York *Herald,* April 25, 1861, p. 1, c. 4.
22 Baltimore *Sun,* April 23, 1861, p. 2, c. 1. Reported also with slight differences in Nicolay and Hay, *Lincoln,* IV, 139–140.

Lord Lyons to serve "as mediator between the contending parties in our country" was diplomatically answered by Seward in the President's name with the explanation that domestic issues could not be "referred . . . to the arbitrament of a European monarchy."[23] A highway was selected which traversed Maryland while avoiding populous cities.[24] Some of the troops were carried by water to Annapolis, thence by land to Washington. Firm measures were taken to reopen broken intercourse. Bridges were repaired. Baltimore cooled off; further riots were avoided. Secessionists went South; withdrawal of the state from the Union, which would have been a supreme menace to Lincoln, was prevented. Governor Hicks, treated with friendliness and understanding of his difficult position, became a factor for loyal Unionism, and succeeded in averting that state convention which was intended as the instrument of secession. In this clearing of the air hundreds of clerks in Washington resigned; higher officials also found this a convenient moment for deciding on which side they stood.[25]

When a Baltimore committee on May 5 went so far as to ask recognition of the independence of the Confederate States, Lincoln replied in strong terms, rebuking them for laying no straw in the way of those who would capture Washington, and asserting that the right of way through Maryland would be maintained "at all hazards."[26] By the 9th of May transit through Baltimore had been reopened and a contingent of Union troops traversed the city unmolested. Less than a month after the April riot a body of Baltimoreans tendered to the secretary of war a thousand volunteers over and above the Maryland quota.[27]

All this was accomplished in spite of the bombast and aggressiveness of General B. F. Butler, who commanded for a time at Annapolis, organized an "expedition against Baltimore," seized Relay House (May 6),[28] occupied Baltimore without authority but with a characteristic blending of flamboyance and maladroitness, issued a proclamation to its people,[29] and produced a series of added irritations in

[23] *Works*, VI, 252–254 (Apr. 22, 1861).   [24] *Ibid.*, 253.

[25] Nicolay and Hay, *Lincoln*, IV, 141.

[26] New York *Herald*, May 6, 1861, p. 1, c. 2; Nicolay and Hay, *Lincoln*, IV, 139–140.

[27] New York *Times*, April 16, 1861, p. 1, c. 1.

[28] In Maryland, about nine miles south of Baltimore on the road to Washington.

[29] On May 14, 1861, Winfield Scott sent the following dispatch to Butler: "Your hazardous occupation of Baltimore was . . . without my approbation. It is a Godsend that it was without conflict of arms." At 2:17 next morning came Scott's order to Butler: "Issue no more proclamations." *Offic. Rec.*, 1 ser., II. 28

sensitive Maryland till superseded by General Banks. Thus displaced, he was praised by Lincoln, who had transferred him to a scene of new vexations at Norfolk.

IV

Amid such imbroglios Lincoln's own preferences could make no claim upon his meager twenty-four hours a day. Executive planning, formulation of policies, phrasing of important papers, and like duties, were so interrupted by official and ceremonial activities as to become almost invisible. Meetings of the cabinet were long and tedious, the secretaries emerging with jaded faces. Once a whole cabinet session seems to have been devoted to General Butler. Again, as reported, the cabinet was "engaged all day in considering promotions and new appointments in the army," with every secretary presenting "a batch of names."[1] At times the President would call in army leaders to confer with the cabinet. Rumors of cabinet differences were in frequent circulation; these were unconvincingly denied in the newspapers "on the highest authority."[2] It is now known that these differences were real and stubborn, and one may doubt whether Lincoln's official family gave him as much assistance and relief as it gave annoyance and worriment.

It was not Lincoln's habit to dodge the time-consuming and often petty occasions of ceremonial duty. When the flag was hoisted over the new general post office building, it had to be Lincoln, flanked by the cabinet, who officiated.[3] Once in mid-May 1861 he was absent from the White House nearly all day, visiting Great Falls (not an easy trip), passing secessionist pickets on the Virginia side, and reconnoitering generally in the vicinity of Washington.[4] If, instead of studio poses, "spot pictures" had been made showing the President as he spent his time, they would have shown him riding up "the Avenue" in

---

[1] New York *Herald*, May 17, 1861, p. 1, c. 1.

[2] "The assertions that the Secretaries of State and of the Navy have differed . . . are without foundation. Equally untrue are the reports . . . that the Secretary of the Treasury differs . . . from the President or other members of the Cabinet. . . . The above is predicated on information from the highest authority." New York *Tribune*, May 6, 1861, p. 5, c. 1. That these differences were only too real is now so well known as to be a commonplace.

[3] New York *Herald*, May 23, 1861, p. 1, c. 2.

[4] *Ibid.*, May 20, 1861, p. 1, c. 1; p. 4, c. 2.

an open barouche with Seward amid manifestations of popular respect, making a tour of observation down the Potomac with Seward and Weed, receiving the First Michigan regiment, exposing himself within range of "rebel" fire, greeting the Kansas "Frontier Guard" in the East Room of the White House, attending the White House funeral of Colonel Ellsworth who fell at Alexandria, visiting the Seventy-first New York to whom he made a short speech, proceeding over Long Bridge in late afternoon with infantry escort to review Union regiments on the Virginia side, appearing at the Capitol to greet and chat with privates and officers, conducting a "grand review" of the "whole Rhode Island brigade," presenting a gold watch and chain to a British ship captain for saving an American crew, or conferring with important men. An example of the latter would be Evarts, Pierrepont, and Vanderpool of New York who were reported as having conveyed to him "the attitude of the North." [5]

Though the newspapers might not know the substance of these consultations, they did know the men with whom they were held or with whom the President appeared. Repeated contact with Seward did not fail to occasion comment. Count Gurowski, a gruff Polish nobleman whose prominence as a social lion contrasted strangely with his unimportant duties in the state department, wrote: ". . . Lincoln is under the tumb [sic] of Seward; to a degree allmost ridiculous, Seward brings him out to take airing as were he Lincoln's nurse . . . ." [6] When the Garibaldi Guard marched ceremoniously to the White House the President received them in company with General Scott and Secretary Seward.[7] This was proper enough in view of the circumstances, but the frequency of such occasions tended to give Seward a prominence beyond other secretaries and a position of influence that steadily weakened the Lincoln administration in radical eyes.

A paradox of American democracy appeared in the constant im-

---

[5] These minor incidents are recorded in the New York *Tribune* of May 1 and May 9, 1861, and the *Herald* of the following dates: April 30, May 1, May 14, June 11, June 14, June 25.

[6] Gurowski to Sumner, May 1, 1861, Sumner MSS. Gurowski's diary reveals the quality of this eccentric, picturesque, and violent personality. For a full, documented account, see LeRoy H. Fischer, "Adam Gurowski and the American Civil War: A Radical's Record," *Bulletin,* Polish Institute of Arts and Sciences in America, I, 476–488 (April, 1943).

[7] New York *Herald*, May 31, 1861, p. 1, c. 2.

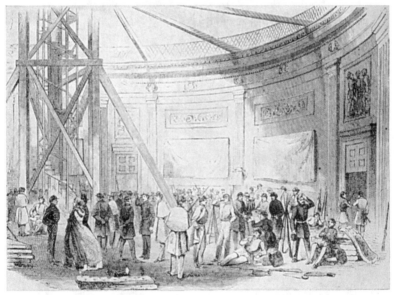

EARLY WARTIME SCENES

Dubuque gives a rousing demonstration as volunteers depart on a resplendent Mississippi River steamboat. Soldiers are given lodging under the unfinished dome in the Capitol at Washington. Both drawings appeared in *Harper's Weekly*, May 25, 1861.

LINCOLN IN VARYING POSES

All the pictures are by Brady except the lower right, which was taken by C. S. German in Springfield in February 1861. From the view by German one may visualize the President Elect at the time of his bidding farewell to Springfield. The upper left portrait, "Meserve No. 81," is one of a series of famous Brady profiles.

portance of two opposite factors in the social use of the Executive Mansion: it had to be democratically open to all, yet always a premium was placed upon exclusiveness when groups or individuals were recognized. It is hard to imagine Lincoln lending himself to a function that was not democratic, but news writers delighted in making these affairs seem exclusive. One read in the papers that officers of the regiments in and about Washington were disappointed that White House hospitalities had not been extended to them;[8] four days later the President gave a military reception for the officers. The public was told that this was a "brilliant affair," that the ladies present represented "the elite of Washington," and that "Mrs. Lincoln received with . . . elegance and dignity." The President was "in the best of spirits." Cadets newly graduated from West Point were in attendance, while among the "lions of the occasion" was Major Anderson, who was treated as a "special pet" of the President.[9] When it was a matter of full dress and furbelows the homespun President by no means dispensed with court etiquette. (The man of homespun background usually does not.) Presentations at levees were usually made by that swashbuckling Illinoisan, Colonel Ward Hill Lamon to the President and by some selected "dignitary" to Mrs. Lincoln.[10] The first public reception, held on April 8, 1861, proved at the same time huge and elegant. "The oldest frequenters of White House receptions declared they had never seen so many people pass through the House at any previous time, nor was it ever excelled in brilliancy."[11]

Though White House publicity was not of the "modern" sort, such publicity existed, being composed of close-up accounts of the President or explanatory statements of his policy. In late April it was conjectured that Lincoln would recognize the Confederacy. Later this was denied and it was asserted that the President was at one with the cabinet in vigorously prosecuting measures against the insurrectionary states.[12] A "gentleman, high in the confidence of the President" gave assurance that no truce, pacification or adjustment was intended until "rebellion" was crushed.[13] Southern papers, said the reporters, had no

[8] *Ibid.*, May 6, 1861, p. 1, c. 2.   [9] *Ibid.*, May 10, 1861, p. 1, c. 3.

[10] *Ibid.*, May 29, 1861, p. 1, c. 2.

[11] Virginia Kinnaird, "Mrs. Lincoln as a White House Hostess," *Papers in Ill. Hist.*, 1938, 69–70.

[12] New York *Herald*, April 25, 1861, p. 4, c. 4; April 30, 1861, p. 3, c. 4; May 16, 1861, p. 1, c. 2.

[13] New York *Tribune*, July 1, 1861, p. 5, c. 1.

basis for asserting that the correspondence of the Associated Press was directed by Lincoln.[14] Whatever the President did, or omitted to do, was "news," as when a Washington dispatch stated that pressure of duty required him to deny himself to visitors. Public business compelled him "inflexibly" to decline personal interviews, even members of Congress being refused admittance at the White House while the President's message was in preparation.[15] Journalists mentioned that the message was being prepared; having done so, some of them would make a prediction as to its content, with impressive guesses concerning the "next move" of the military forces.[16] A sizable article could be written on the hoaxes and canards that accompanied all this publicity. An example was the reported resignation of Gideon Welles from the secretaryship of the navy. This brought a letter from a citizen of Illinois who reminded Welles of the "great need for one honest man in the Cabinet" and urged him to remain as an "Argus over such aspirants to the Presidency as Mr. Cameron." [17]

Newspaper editors of the period seemed afflicted with a more or less chronic case of disgruntlement. It was reported that Greeley wanted the office of postmaster general, that Raymond spurned a consulship because he wanted the mission to Italy, that Webb aspired to be minister to England, and that even Bryant was grieved because he received no office.[18] As for Bennett, pungent wrath seemed to be his stock in trade. Whatever the cause or lack of cause, newspapers at an early stage joined in an almost concerted movement to force an overthrow or reconstruction of the cabinet. Pointing out that Lincoln was responsible to the people while the cabinet was moved by selfish motives, the *Herald* harped upon the theme of cabinet change and of "Something Wrong in High Quarters." This paper did not conceal its fear that the administration's "feeble" measures toward the "rebellion" would weaken the Union cause in European eyes.[19] Ridiculing the President's attention to office-seeking appeals, the *Times* queried:

---

14 New York *Herald*, May 21, 1861, p. 1, c. 2.

15 New York *Tribune*, June 1, 1861, p. 5, c. 2; June 20, 1861, p. 4, c. 6; New York *Herald*, June 22, 1861, p. 1, c. 2.

16 New York *Herald*, May 6, 1861, p. 1, c. 1; May 31, 1861, p. 1, c. 2.

17 George F. Wright to Gideon Welles, Springfield, Ill., July 4, 1861, Welles MSS. The final paragraphs of this letter were devoted to a request for a job in the navy department.

18 Editorial, New York *Herald*, May 9, 1861, p. 4, c. 4.

19 *Ibid.*, June 15, 1861, p. 4, c. 5; June 27, p. 1, c. 1.

"And if the old Whigs must not be forgotten, nor the Democrats slighted . . . , why not take equal care of Calvinists and Armenians [the writer meant Arminians]?"[20] "It is idle," said the *Times,* "to conceal the fact that the Administration thus far has not met public expectation"; a month after Lincoln's inauguration, things were no better than when Buchanan left Washington.[21] A few weeks later the *Times* discharged an editorial blast under the caption "Wanted —A Leader!" in which it characterized the administration's record as "one continued retreat" and as having "thus far only urged [waged] war upon itself." The spirited uprising of the North was described; then in contrast the *Times* put the question, "Where is the leader of this sublime passion?"[22] Everything in the editorial indicated that to the writer's mind Lincoln was not the man.

In distributing the spoils of victory Lincoln had to recognize those who had "made" him while not wholly ignoring men of the opposite party. He had to consider geographical distribution, claims of eminence, hazards of offending whole groups, and squabbles within Republican ranks. When one adds the factors of cabinet consultation, informal nomination by congressional delegations, senate confirmation, newspaper interference, and volunteer advice, it will be seen that only a sturdy or hard-skinned President could endure the strain. The inquisitive historian, rummaging among the manuscripts and documents of the time, will hardly escape the conclusion that the search and scramble for public favors, if not the party's chief preoccupation, constituted at least the most frequent theme running through the correspondence of statesmen. Half the letters sent out by the President in the first three weeks of May 1861 and included in his collected works dealt with matters of patronage.

Selections for military appointments in the volunteer units were in practice made by governors of the states at least as high as colonelcies; for brigadier- and major-generalships the states had a voice, and state delegations in Congress assumed the function of quasi-nomination to the President. Senator Browning of Illinois wrote of a night caucus of the Illinois delegation (of senators and representatives) in Senator Trumbull's room to "agree upon Brig: Genl[s] for our State."[23] If one takes only the state of Illinois and considers officers of the rank of

---

[20] New York *Times,* April 4, 1861, p. 4, cc. 3–4.
[22] *Ibid.,* Apr. 25, 1861, p. 4, c. 2.
[21] *Ibid.,* April 3, 1861, p. 4, c. 2.
[23] Browning, *Diary,* I, 487.

general, he finds that appointments for Civil War service included one lieutenant general (Grant), ten major generals, eighteen brevet major generals, 53 brigadier generals, and 120 brevet brigadier generals. Thus it will be seen that for one state the appointments to general rank exceeded two hundred.[24] Though recommendations were handed up to him, the President had to "make" each of these appointments.

It is only by laboring through masses of contemporary correspondence that one can glimpse the intrigues and personal jealousies back of these appointments. In the case of Pope a number of bigwigs in Illinois, including Yates, Dubois, Butler, Hatch, and Trumbull, were enlisted in a movement to obtain for him one of the early brigadier generalships, with "command of this State as a separate Military Dept." [25] When, for a time, Pope was passed over though McClernand received a brigadiership, he sent a hot letter of protest to Senator Trumbull in which Pennsylvania appointments were petulantly mentioned and Lincoln was accused of having "departed from his word" as to Pope, while the "personal and political friends of Mr. Cameron" had all been "cared for." His letter went so far as to refer to Lincoln's "failure to comply with his promise." [26]

Thus one might go on from department to department and state to state, taking into view postmasterships, collectorships, marshalships, surveyorships, consulships, diplomatic appointments, et cetera. With state claims, rivalries, and party demands crowding upon him, it was a bit of luck for the President if the public welfare crept into the picture. Under such stress and strain did Lincoln man his ship, sending Charles Francis Adams to England, Cassius M. Clay to St. Petersburg, John Lothrop Motley to Vienna (after Anson Burlingame had been rejected as *persona non grata* by the Austrian government because he favored Hungarian independence), William L. Dayton as minister to Paris, John Bigelow to the important Paris consulship, Thomas H. Dudley as consul to Liverpool, Thomas Corwin to Mexico, and George Perkins Marsh, erudite Vermont Whig, as the first United States minister to the Kingdom of Italy.

---

24 *Report of the Adj. Gen. of . . . Ill.* (revised, 1886), I, 170–173. (In 1866 Grant attained the title of general; his highest title during the war was that of lieutenant general.)

25 John Pope to Lyman Trumbull, June 16, 1861, Trumbull MSS.

26 *Ibid.*

V

By his emergency acts and his wide use of executive power in the months just following the outbreak of war, Lincoln set a pattern for his whole administration. It was the pattern of a President who did not as a rule depend upon, or work with, the Congress, but hewed out his own path, assumed executive power even when he questioned its legality, reached his own decisions (not without vacillation); and, on rare occasions, turned to Congress for *post facto* approval. Usually he did not even seek this ratification after the fact.

In the days of late April, May, and June of 1861, while human slaughter was deferred because neither side was in fighting fettle, Lincoln took purely executive steps of far-reaching importance. To his critics it seemed that he "started" the war; at least it was Lincoln who determined both the policy and the legal forms in which the challenge at Sumter was met. Accepting war as the consequence of the Sumter incident was the essential policy (some thought this unnecessary), while legal molds were chosen which gave the conflict, technically, the aspect of an intramural rather than an international affair. That is to say, the enemies whose challenge he met were regarded in theory, not as a foreign nation or a continuing, permanent government, but as rebellious or insurrectionary groups within the United States. In this light Lincoln's executive acts in April 1861 had at least five important aspects: (1) they inaugurated for the nation a state of war where there had been peace; (2) they set up a legal front in terms of theory and status; (3) they equally set the pattern for the President's own theory of executive measures with regard to Congress; (4) they launched a military policy (reliance upon "militia" and upon action by the states rather than upon national army expansion); (5) finally, these measures fixed the mold into which the government's policy was to be cast in its relations with foreign nations.

The proclamation of April 15 summoning the militia was followed by two proclamations (April 19 and April 27) setting on foot a blockade of Southern ports in pursuance both of United States law and of international law. An order of April 27 to General Scott repeated the declaration that the business in hand was "suppressing an insurrection" and authorized a regional suspension of the habeas corpus privilege, this power to be exercised either personally by the commanding general of the whole army (Scott) or by subordinate officers where resistance might occur.[1] This action applied to the military line between Philadelphia and Washington; later (May 10) the line was extended to New York, then Florida was subjected to the suspension, and the order was given to remove suspected persons from United States forts.[2] Deeming state authorities in Missouri unreliable, the President, through the adjutant general, directed that a close watch be kept upon their activities, and that any hostile movement be put down.[3] On May 3 Lincoln made an important supplementary call for troops, summoning 42,000 volunteers to serve for three years "unless sooner discharged" (instead of three months as indicated in April), and directing that additional regiments be added to the regular army.[4] This increase of the size of the regular army by executive action without even consulting Congress was most unusual. Those who remembered the American tradition for legislative control of the military machine, and the specific constitutional provisions for congressional authority in building and paying for the army, regarded this act as a very questionable proceeding. It is doubtful whether even Lincoln's supporters would have wished it to become a precedent for later administrations. It has not so become; in this respect Lincoln's assumption of power stands by itself. There was less question of the President's act when he required all army officers, except those who had entered the service after April 1, to renew their oaths of allegiance to the United States. This action was taken amid reports of disloyalty in the service and of "plenty of spies in the very midst of the federal troops." [5]

Other emergency acts fell equally into the category of independent executive measures. A series of such steps was taken on April 21, when the President had an urgent conference with his cabinet at the Navy Office. By unanimous agreement at this conference the President directed an armed revenue cutter to operate for the protection of inbound California treasure ships.[6] Other ships were purchased or chartered by presidential direction and armed for public defense with

---

[1] *Works*, VI, 258.   [2] *Ibid.*, VI, 271.
[3] *Ibid.*, VI, 288–289 (May 27, 1861).   [4] *Ibid.*, VI, 263–265.
[5] New York *Herald*, May 11, 1861, p. 1, c. 2; May 13, 1861, p. 1, c. 2.
[6] Lincoln himself reported this conference to Congress. *Works*, VII, 190 (May 26, 1862).

special attention to the water communications of Washington. New York notables were empowered to act for the government in forwarding troops and supplies during a temporary interruption of communication between Washington and New York. Men who were not Federal officials were thus given large governmental powers, while two million dollars from the Federal treasury was advanced to a kind of informal committee of three (John A. Dix, George Opdyke, and R. M. Blatchford) who spent the money without bond and without the constitutional prerequisite of congressional appropriation. Lincoln himself stated that the civil service contained so many disloyal persons that he had to go outside the field of officialdom and confide governmental duties to chosen citizens who were "known for . . . ability, loyalty, and patriotism." [7] The sequel to this episode, coming in 1862, was to be bound up with the President's necessity of getting rid of Cameron as secretary of war. In this sequel the President gave the war secretary a foreign assignment, the House of Representatives condemned him, the Senate gave evidence of formidable opposition to him, and the Supreme Court uttered a stern rebuke concerning his methods. Lincoln, however, showed a magnanimous willingness to take the blame upon himself. [8]

VI

Lincoln's relation to Douglas, which had begun in the eighteen-thirties at Vandalia and had increased in rivalry through the decades, now reached its final phase. In the last months of his life Douglas showed a patriotic disregard of partisanship which no American leader has surpassed. In the critical days when the nation faced dissolution, men had looked to him both for avoidance of war and for preservation of national integrity. ". . . I know the hopes of many patriot hearts are looking to you to save us if possible," wrote a Vir-

---

[7] *Ibid.*, VII, 192.

[8] The unfortunate complication here was that Lincoln's assumption of emergency powers at the outset of the war was later brought into the picture by the President himself as a way of shielding Cameron even after his forced withdrawal, and as a means of magnanimously transferring blame to the President's own shoulders. Yet in reality the questionable acts were not those associated with Lincoln's emergency executive measures as such—e. g., with the New York committee of three—but with Cameron's administrative looseness. This whole matter is reserved for later treatment. See vol. II, 59–60.

ginia leader.[1] "Your friends . . . throughout the Union look again to you in this hour of need," wrote a Louisianan.[2] "You are *the* Statesman of the time," wrote another Louisiana friend; "let us have . . . the greatest speech you ever made." [3] The large vote for Douglas, both in the North and the South, had been above all pro-Union. At both extremes it was the uncompromising radicals who had opposed him most keenly. His role was thus cast for him; it was the role of conciliation, and he played it with all his skill and force. Nor should it be supposed that because secession and war occurred, Douglas's efforts had gone for naught. "I have watched your course in the Senate during the final struggle," wrote an opponent on March 7, 1861, "and . . . I am satisfied that but for you, Mason and Dixon's line wo[ul]d now be the boundary of the Southern Confederacy. I have been your political opponent but feel it to be a sacred duty to thank you for your noble & patriotic course & to assure you that this universal sentiment pervades all classes of good men in the country." [4]

Constantly Douglas was consulted; always he spoke the language of loyalty to the United States. When certain senators in March 1861 assailed Lincoln's policy as expressed in his inaugural, Douglas spoke "boldly in defense of Mr. Lincoln." [5] This was one of the most significant efforts of Douglas's life. "While I expect to oppose the Administration upon all the political issues of the day," he said, "I trust I shall never hesitate to do justice to those who, by their devotion to the Constitution and the Union, . . . love their country more than their party." Noting that Lincoln's policy would be "peaceful and not aggressive," Douglas declared that he found "much cause . . . for encouragement" in the President's inaugural.[6] When challenged in debate by Mason of Virginia, he replied that he "must refer him . . . to those who have been intrusted by the American people according to the Constitution with the decision" as to national troubles.[7] Lincoln was represented as highly "elated" because Douglas had joined in defense of his administration; this was said to be the chief topic of

[1] John S. Carlile to Douglas, Clarksburg, Va., December 6, 1860, Douglas MSS.

[2] A. Lafargne to Douglas, Marksville, Parish of Avoyelles, La., December 9, 1860, *ibid.*

[3] Alfred Goodwill to Douglas, Minden, La., December 18, 1860, *ibid.*

[4] Britton A. Hill to Douglas, Washington, March 7, 1861, *ibid.*

[5] Blaine, *Twenty Years of Congress*, I, 288.

[6] *Cong. Globe*, 36 Cong., 2 sess., 1438 (March 6, 1861).

[7] *Ibid.*, 36 Cong., 2 sess., 1445.

his conversation with visitors to the White House.[8]

Shortly before the outbreak at Sumter Douglas met Gideon Welles on the street and had an earnest talk with him, making it clear that he was "for the Union and would stand by the Administration . . . regardless of party." The Little Giant was greatly saddened by events. "He had tried to rally the Democracy, but the party was broken up." He considered Buchanan feeble and incompetent, had no faith in Seward, and put his trust in a kind of vague hope that Lincoln would be independent of his "premier." [9] On Sunday, April 14, the day of the formal surrender at Sumter, Douglas had an interview with President Lincoln. There are various reports of this meeting. According to the account by George Ashmun, Douglas was requested by Ashmun to go at once to the President's and make an open declaration of a determination to sustain him.

"I well remember his first reply [wrote Ashmun]: 'Mr. Lincoln has dealt hardly with me, in removing some of my friends from office, and I don't know as he wants my advice or aid.' " On persuasion, however, Douglas called on Lincoln, finding the President alone and "most cordial in his welcome." Preparing the way for friendly conversation, Lincoln drew from a drawer and read the proclamation he meant to issue next day. Rising from his chair, Douglas spoke in great earnestness, saying that he concurred in "every word" of the proclamation, except that he would have called out 200,000 men instead of 75,000. Stepping to a map in the President's room he gave strategic suggestions for the coming contest. He found Lincoln "an earnest and gratified listener," and "no two men [thought Ashmun] . . . parted that night with a more cordial feeling of a united, friendly, and patriotic purpose than Mr. Lincoln and Mr. Douglas." [10]

A statement which Douglas prepared was given to the press and was read next day all over the North: "Mr. Douglas called on the President this evening and had an interesting conversation on the present condition of the country. The substance of the conversation was that while Mr D[ouglas] was . . . opposed to the administration on all its political issues, he was prepared to sustain the President in the exercise of all his constitutional functions to preserve the

---

[8] E. M. Stanton to James Buchanan, March 12, 1861, Buchanan MSS.
[9] Welles, *Diary*, I, 32–35.
[10] Washington *Daily Morning Chronicle*, October 26, 1864, p. 2, c. 5.

Union, . . . maintain the government, and defend the Federal capital. . . . He spoke of the present and future, without reference to the past." [11]

Realizing that his service could nowhere be better performed than in vigorous support of the Union in his own state, Douglas traveled back to Illinois, made contact with many friends there, urged firm support of the Lincoln government, and delivered a notable speech before a joint session of the Illinois legislature, together with "a great audience of citizens" at Springfield on April 25.[12] Speaking as one who had "omitted no opportunity, to secure a peaceful solution of all these troubles," Douglas denounced the "[h]ostile armies . . . marching upon the Federal Capitol" to promote a "war of aggression." Deriding the alleged cause of the conflict, he declared: "For the first time in the history of this Republic, there is no prohibitory act of Congress upon the institution of slavery, anywhere within the limits of the United States." Showing that no cause for rebellion could be found either in the territorial or the fugitive-slave question, he asked: "Can any man tell me of any one act of aggression . . . since the . . . election, that justifies this violent disruption of the . . . Union?" If Breckinridge had been elected, he said, and if Republicans had rebelled against him, "you would have found me tendering my . . . energies to . . . Breckinridge to put down the Republican rebels." "The first duty of an American citizen," he said, "is obedience to the constitution and laws of his country." Yet he favored no war upon the rights of the Southern states, no bloody triumph over his countrymen. Avoiding vengeance, he asked that the spirit of moderation and justice should prevail. Mindful of the world significance of the struggle, he urged that "whatever we may do must be the result of . . . the duty that we owe to ourselves, to our posterity and to the friends of . . . self-government throughout the world." [13]

The speaker of the Illinois lower house on this occasion records that Douglas spoke "with great earnestness, & power," and adds that never before was he "so impressed by the power of a man talking to

---

[11] *Ibid.*

[12] S. M. Cullom to I. N. Arnold, Springfield, March 19, 1883, Arnold MSS., Chicago Hist. Soc.

[13] *Speech of Senator Douglas, before the Legislature of Illinois, April 25, 1861* (contemporary pamphlet).

an audience." [14] Douglas made a similar speech on May 1, in Chicago, speaking at the National Hall, the old wigwam in which Lincoln had been nominated.[15]

Not all approved of Douglas's support of Lincoln; some denounced him as a traitor to his party [16] and as joining the hell hounds of Black Republicanism.[17] Such scurrilous attacks seem untypical; they are of interest chiefly as showing that it cost something for the Democratic leader to take the stand he did.

Shortly after his Chicago speech Douglas fell ill, borne down by financial embarrassments and the exhaustion of overwork. On June 3 he died, Adele, his wife, at his bedside. In token of popular mourning bells were rung, cannon boomed, business was suspended in Chicago, and public buildings were draped. The President denied himself to visitors,[18] and an army order was issued from the war department directing appropriate recognition of a "national calamity." [19]

---

[14] S. M. Cullom to Arnold, Springfield, Mar. 19, 1883, Arnold MSS., Chicago Hist. Soc.

[15] All the arrangements—the committee of welcome, procession, and the like—indicate that this was a big event in Chicago. The *Tribune* spoke of Douglas's magnificent ovation and warmly praised his speech "in which the necessity of sustaining the Government and the honor of the flag was eloquently enforced." It was added that Republicans and Democrats united to do him honor. Chicago *Tribune*, May 2, 1861.

[16] Referring to men who denounced the North as the aggressor, a pseudonymous writer stated that such men (in Southern Illinois) "voted for Douglas but when Douglas declared for the perpetuity of the Union they denounced him as a traitor to his party." "Leonidas," Fayette Co., Ill., to Richard Yates, Aug. 15, 1861, Yates MSS.

[17] T. N. Lawrence (of Golconda, Ill.) to S. Maynard, May 22, 1861, Yates MSS.

[18] New York *Herald*, June 8, 1861, p. 1, cc. 2–3.

[19] Major Donald B. Sanger, discussing the army order of June 4, 1861, directing that military ceremonies be held in honor of Douglas, tentatively suggests that this order may be traceable to Lincoln as author. For this conjecture (which Major Sanger properly presents as such) the present writer has found no confirmation. The slipshod wording of the order would suggest that Lincoln did not write or edit it. *Transactions*, Ill. State Hist. Soc., 1933, 67–79.

CHAPTER XIV

DEMOCRACY'S TESTING

WHEN Congress met on July 4, 1861, after eighty days of almost bloodless war, Lincoln faced a bitter mixture of frustration and grief. The coming months were to bring radical interference, military debacle, broken lines at home, and embroilment abroad. No one could tell how far the war would reach; yet there was no turning back; or, if one wanted to play upon words, there was nothing in sight except turning back—back from peace and normal relations to an unknowable future in which the only sure prospects were slaughter and destruction. For the addled sections to have recovered the pre-Sumter status would have been to go notably forward; this was psychologically impossible. July was vastly more distant from mid-April than the eighty days that intervened.

Lincoln had now reached a point of significant transition. He could go forward (if it was forward) only in terms of prosecuting the war in earnest; yet this presaged a storm of unpredictable hazards. The muddle had started as a little war, a mere sequel to the Sumter incident, the kind of trouble that short-service militia, and only a few at that, could "suppress." But when wars start they seldom give notice of the proportions they will assume or the course they will take. Rarely indeed can a war leader control a war. The month of July 1861 was to mark the transition from a short, little, unplanned war to a prolonged and vastly extended struggle in which organization and preparation would count heavily. Lincoln thought that the existing struggle was to prove whether democracy could survive not only on these shores but anywhere. No one felt more keenly the enormous values at hazard. If this nation broke into pieces, it was a serious question whether any nation based on popular rule could succeed. A major battle with the Confederacy was soon to be fought which would throw

this whole question into doubt. In addition, there was opposition brewing within the North, and within Lincoln's party ranks, which was to
throw into question the ability of a democracy to maintain its own
governmental lines. As if this were not enough, an international crisis
of terrible possibilities lay not far ahead.

I

The message which Lincoln presented to the called session of Congress stands as one of his most elaborate and carefully prepared papers.
It comprised a history of events, a report of stewardship, a constitutional argument, and an exalted commentary on fundamentals. In
these latter days of ghost writers and aides with a passion for anonymity it is worth recording that the message was Lincoln's own. For
weeks, as above indicated, reporters had been noting that the President
was denying himself to visitors while preparing his address; in style
and reasoning the address is unmistakably Lincolnian.

Though best studied in the distinguished original, the message must
be given here in brief paraphrase. Here, said the President, was the
situation faced by the present administration. Here was my duty; these
were my measures; here is what they mean in national survival and
broad human destiny; further things are now recommended which
rest with Congress. In March, he said, governmental functions were
suspended in seven states. Arsenals and forts had been seized, armed
forces assembled. An illegal organization "in the character of confederate States" had been set up. The Union was declared severed.
The problem was to prevent the consummation of disunion while
still preserving peace; the method proposed and inaugurally announced was to exhaust all peaceful measures before resorting to "any
stronger ones." The purpose was "only to hold" Federal property. No
disturbance of the Southern people in their rights was intended.
Pledges were given against such disturbance. In the waiting period of
March and early April the administration sought only to collect the
revenue, continue the mails, and to forbear "everything . . . without which it was believed possible to keep the government on foot." [1]

To hold Sumter, said Lincoln in retrospect, was militarily impossible. Twenty thousand troops were needed; they were not available.

---

[1] *Works*, VI, 299-300.

The military task was to remove the garrison. But that by itself, with no collateral measure to point up the government's policy of Federal maintenance, would have been ruinous. Friends of the Union would not have understood "the necessity under which it was . . . done." National destruction would have been consummated. "This could not be allowed." [2] What then? There was a peaceful way out. Starvation was not yet upon the garrison. Let Pickens be firmly yet peaceably held, and the country might accept the evacuation of Fort Sumter as a military necessity. A Pickens expedition was sent to accomplish this peace-promoting mission, but because of conflicting influences the troops were not landed. Till then, the Sumter expedition, tentatively prepared, had been withheld. It was now sent, but with full notice that no attack from Sumter was intended. There was no reason to mistake the government's purpose. The other side "well knew that the [Sumter] garrison . . . could by no possibility commit aggression upon them." The government was keeping the garrison there "not to assail them," but "to maintain visible possession, and thus to preserve the Union," trusting to "the ballot-box for final adjustment." They "assailed . . . the fort for precisely the reverse object—to . . . force it [the Union] to immediate dissolution." [3]

If America failed, thought Lincoln, in its experiment of free government—if it fell apart from some seemingly inherent defect—the loss would be tragic and world-wide. It was more than these United States that were at stake; the whole experiment of democracy as an example to the world was on trial. Thus early expressed, this concept was to be Lincoln's central idea of the significance of America's tragedy. Over and again the President was to return to the theme in his mental searching and in public address, notably at Gettysburg. [4]

Such was the President's approach. In developing his report to the nation Lincoln commented upon the anti-Union action of Virginia and the upper South, and recounted his own calls for troops and other emergency executive measures. Suspension of a few of the laws, he said, was necessary lest the government itself go to pieces and all the laws fail. In a vigorous passage the President denounced the attempt to make secession seem legal; such an attempt he considered only a

---

2 *Ibid.*, VI, 301.   3 *Ibid.*, VI, 303.
4 It is best to deal with this theme in connection with Gettysburg; see vol. II, 317 ff.

"sophism" to conceal what amounted to rebellion. The states, he said, "have their status in the Union, and they have no other legal status." Secession is "disintegration." "Whatever concerns the whole should be confided to the whole . . . ." [5]

"This," he said, "is essentially a people's contest. On the side of the Union it is a struggle . . . to elevate the condition of men—to lift artificial weights from all shoulders; . . . to afford all an unfettered start, and a fair chance in the race of life." [6] If free government succeeded in preventing dissolution of the nation, he argued, it would be "a great lesson of peace: . . . teaching all the folly of being the beginners of a war." Even as a private citizen, he said, the present Executive could not consent "that these institutions shall perish; much less could he, in betrayal of so vast . . . a trust as the free people have confided to him." [7]

According to later practice the message would have been delivered by the President in person before House and Senate in joint session. With this possibility of public delivery by the President in view, it is of interest to re-read the message. In its turning of epigrammatic phrases and its restrained yet exalted eloquence it was well adapted to such an occasion; it would have sounded the better for its noticeable lack of emotional denunciation.

At noon on July 3 the message was reviewed by the cabinet. That night, at about nine o'clock, Orville H. Browning of Illinois called at the White House. When told that Lincoln was busy, he turned to pay his respects to Mrs. Lincoln. The President "heard my voice [wrote Browning] and wished to see me. I went to his room, and as he had just finished his message, he said he wished to read it to me, and did so. . . . I remained . . . in conversation . . . when the reading was concluded." [8] Not the larger public, not the assembled Congress, the press, and galleries, but one lone senator, heard Lincoln's oral delivery. He also heard the President's off-the-record comments which accompanied and interpreted the message. In perfunctory manner the message was communicated to Congress as a formal public document one day after the convening. Thus undramatically presented, it attracted inadequate notice. For opening oratory the House

[5] *Works*, VI, 314–316.
[6] *Ibid.*, VI, 321.
[7] *Ibid.*, VI, 322, 324.
[8] Browning, *Diary*, I, 475–476.

had to listen to the "inaugural" of Galusha A. Grow, newly elected speaker. "It was a pretty thing," wrote Browning, "but on the Star spangled banner order." [9]

II

In terms of popular demand and press agitation the emphasis was upon intensified war effort. Up to July 1861 the clashes at arms had nowhere reached the point of a sizable engagement. They had been confined to rioting in Baltimore and in Missouri, minor though well advertised battles under McClellan in western Virginia, and small incidents elsewhere in Virginia, as at Harpers Ferry, Vienna, and Big Bethel. To the 75,000 asked for in April (instead of the 200,000 suggested by Douglas [1] or the 300,000 deemed necessary by Scott [2]) Lincoln had added a request for an additional 42,000 in May.[3] Now in July he asked for 400,000 men and 400 millions of money. He estimated that this number was "about one tenth of those of proper ages within the regions where, apparently, all are willing to engage." [4] At the same time he revealed the weakness of governmental organization by adding that one of the greatest perplexities was to avoid receiving troops faster than they could be provided for.

To the military historian the delay in active operations would occasion no surprise. New troops need drilling; major battles require elaborate preparation. In the American Civil War, however, those who had the least military understanding were loudest in their advice, and the radicals especially, men who were to become an increasing nuisance to Lincoln, were most insistent in demanding a quick movement "On to Richmond." As early as May 24 Sumner informed Governor Andrew of great pressure upon the administration for "active aggressive measures" and predicted a "collision soon." [5] In early June a member of Lincoln's cabinet wrote: "Matters are approaching a crisis & we will very probably soon have a fight." [6]

Urged on by an intense political demand, the Union army under

---

[9] *Ibid.*, 476.   [1] Above, p. 377.
[2] R. M. Johnston, *Bull Run: Its Strategy and Tactics*, 18. See also 68.
[3] Proclamation of May 3, 1861, *Works*, VI, 263–265.
[4] Message of July 4, 1861, *ibid.*, VI, 311.
[5] Sumner to Andrew, May 24, 1861, Andrew MSS.
[6] Caleb B. Smith to R. W. Thompson, June 10, 1861, MS., Lincoln Nat. Life Foundation, Ft. Wayne, Ind.

McDowell stepped daily closer to the hour of attack. To read of those anxious days is almost to watch the ticking of an irresponsible time bomb; the approaching crisis was less a matter of controlled preparation than of fate. Wagons had been drawn from the main arena, subsistence was interrupted, artillery horses and trains were delayed, men were sent forward "without having been together before in a brigade." [7] The Union troops were "unaccustomed to marching . . . and not used to carrying even the load of 'light marching order.' " [8] It is true that the Confederate troops were also raw, but they had the advantages of timely reënforcement, superior generalship, and, chiefly, the less hazardous task of defense as contrasted with difficult assault by exhausted men inadequately held together in battle command.

With miscalculation and unfulfilled plans the Moving Finger brought the army to the oppressive Sunday of July 21. Then a part of the Union force tardily crossed Bull Run (near Manassas, about twenty miles southwest of Washington) and struck the enemy under Beauregard and Johnston. That the moment of attack found the forces of these two important Confederate generals united, constituted one of the main points of Union miscalculation. Joseph E. Johnston had been in the Winchester–Harpers-Ferry region facing Robert Patterson, but had been permitted to slip away and join Beauregard at Manassas on July 20, the day before the battle; his operations on July 21 were an indispensable factor in Confederate victory.

The work of the Union army was not as badly done as has often been inferred. For a time some of the Confederates were driven back; indeed at an advanced stage of the battle it was supposed that "a complete [Union] victory had been won." [9] With all their lack of discipline, Union artillery and infantry had achieved an attack by which it seemed that the battle had been "virtually . . . lost" by the Confederates, and Richmond was shaken by "tales of a Confederate *débâcle*." [10] A difficult assault had been carried off well and the Confederates seemed broken after four hours of fighting. Beauregard's lines had been pushed back and in hot contest the Yankees had taken enemy positions and repulsed counter attacks until they thought the business was concluded.

---

[7] *Offic. Rec.*, 1 ser., II, 324.   [8] *Ibid.*
[9] Johnston, *Bull Run*, 195; *Offic. Rec.*, 1 ser., II, 320.
[10] D. S. Freeman, *R. E. Lee*, I, 537–538.

Then the tide turned. Retreating Southern troops were rallied, reserves and reënforcements were thrown in, weak spots were found in the over-extended Union lines. McDowell's men had been up since two o'clock in the morning, and it was now mid-afternoon. They had marched weary miles, had in some cases gone into battle without food, and had done a great deal of heavy and prolonged fighting. By the time the Confederates launched their final counter attack with strong reënforcements some of the Yankees were already out of ranks. They had done much, but not enough. They could not stand against "an enemy ably commanded, superior in numbers, who had but a short distance to march, and who acted on his own ground on the defensive . . . under cover," while the Union troops "were of necessity out on the open fields." [11]

Contrary to the general impression the conclusion of this battle was not a Confederate walk-over nor a complete Union rout. Some of the Federal brigades held firm, covering an orderly withdrawal, so that the lack of Confederate pursuit had a valid reason. The men under Louis Blenker and Israel B. Richardson, to mention examples, did not run. Confusion did not pervade the whole army. Yet the Union line had been broken; part of the army did become a disorganized mass; control over some of the troops was lost in a mêlée of spectators, soldiers, and congressmen; there was a certain amount of panic long after the main fighting was over; and the portion of the retreat that journalists noted at a considerable distance back of the lines, including stragglers who had not been in the fight, did take on the nature of a stampede.

The disorganized retreat to Washington is not to be denied; neither is it to be regarded as the most significant part of the story of that battle. It was, unfortunately, the phase which, alike in contemporary newspapers and in stereotyped history, has received most of the emphasis. According to R. M. Johnston, who has competently studied the whole campaign, it was "a mere incident of a not abnormal character." [12] Conditions productive of the stampede began, writes Johnston, even before the Union advance, when "the columns were kept standing long hours in the sun and the officers proved unable to prevent their men from going off into the woods after blackberries; . . . or even when Lincoln proclaimed that only the common soldier

11 *Offic. Rec.*, 1 ser., II, 322.   12 Johnston, *Bull Run*, 272.

could be trusted and his officer was a leader not entitled to confidence." [13]

The reference is to Lincoln's statement in his message of July 4 that "not one common soldier or common sailor is known to have deserted his flag." In contrast, said Lincoln, ". . . in this, the government's hour of trial, large numbers" of the officers in the army and navy "have resigned and proved false to the hand which had pampered them . . . ." [14] It was felt that those officers who stayed with the army and handled the difficult tasks of command under Scott and Mc-Dowell deserved better recognition, and these words of Lincoln had been denounced as the appeal of a demagogue who sought popular approval by putting the patriotism of privates above that of their officers.[15] In retrospect it does appear that Lincoln's pardonable censure of officers who left the service ought to have been accompanied with commensurate praise for those who remained. Though in the democratic Union army a private was as good as an officer, this principle was misapplied if it meant, as it did in July 1861 (not particularly because of Lincoln), that privates could disregard or disobey their officers.

In truth the outcome at Bull Run was an uncommanded retreat where, to withstand powerful Confederate counter attack, there should have been orderly withdrawal to a point, perhaps Centerville, where the army could re-form and stand formidably in a new position. In essence it was a lack of military cohesion among some of the troops of an army that, in the main, had fought well and had almost won the day. With all the Yankee panic and disorganization the Southern army failed to follow up its success. This brought Southern disapprobation upon Johnston who defended himself with the statement that all the military conditions known to him forbade an attempt upon Washington. The Confederate army, he said, "was more disorganized by victory than that of the United States by defeat." [16]

Yet in the North and abroad the Union rout was played up as evidence of Yankee cowardice, moblike inefficiency, and unmanly weakness. The most devastating rhetoric was that of William Howard Russell in the *Times* of London. In haughty and scornful passages, not unpleasing to Tory readers, Russell wrote of the "disgraceful con-

---

[13] *Ibid.*, 272–273.   [14] *Works*, VI, 321.
[15] Johnston, *Bull Run*, 70–71.   [16] *Battles and Leaders of the Civil War*, I, 252.

duct" of the Union troops. The retreat, he said, was a "cowardly rout
—a miserable, causeless panic." "Such scandalous behaviour . . . I
should have considered impossible" he added, though he admitted
that of his own knowledge he could only assert that the disorganization extended to "more than one regiment." It was not Sir William's
fault. In letters and conversation he had indicated the seriousness of
the task, "but in the state of [Union] arrogance . . . one might as
well have preached to the Pyramid of Cheops."

In a crescendo of devastating journalism Russell filled in the details. The complete Federal repulse was due to a "little skirmish at
Bull's Run." About forty casualties were magnified into fifteen hundred. General Scott was but "the mouthpiece of the more violent
civilians of the Government." A "Babel of tongues" revealed a mass
of Union men "in good spirits"; these were Pennsylvania troops
headed for home.[17] "Men literally screamed with rage and fright
when their way was blocked up. . . . Faces black and dusty, tongues
out in the heat, eyes staring—it was a most wonderful sight." [18] Warming to his theme, Russell emphasized the perfection of the Southern
troops (drawing upon notes prior to the battle); yet he revealed the
difficulty of the Union task as he expatiated upon the zigzag fortifica-
tion, angles, salients, abundance of food, perfection of communication, and admirable disposition of the Confederate forces.[19]

In a follow-up letter three days after the battle Russell generalized
as to the whole Union cause, for which he could see only the gloomiest
prospect. The Lincoln government would be beaten, he thought, if
they should "yield to the fanatics and fight battles against the advice
of their officers." [20] He questioned whether "the men and the money
[would] be forthcoming . . . to continue the war of aggression . . .
against the Seceded States." [21]

When, about a month after the battle, the *Times* account arrived
on these shores, Sir William's narrative was "received with execra-
tion" [22] and so great was the outcry against "Bull Run Russell" that
the correspondent's usefulness had virtually ended. Having fallen
ill, he recovered from "a state of powder and mint julep" [23] to find
himself threatened with tar and feathers and even assassination.[24]

---

[17] *The Times*, London, August 6, 1861, p. 7.   [18] *Ibid.*, p. 8, c. 1.
[19] *Ibid.*, p. 7, c. 5.   [20] *Ibid.*, Aug. 10, 1861, p. 9, c. 3.
[21] *Ibid.*   [22] John Black Atkins, *Life of Sir William Howard Russell*, II, 68.
[23] *Ibid.*, II, 67.   [24] *Ibid.*, II, 73.

Yet his biographer says that he "helped Englishmen to . . . see that the Federal cause was the cause of justice and truth." [25] In American comments on Russell's lurid description it was noted that he was not within musket shot of the enemy, that he was quietly eating his lunch at the moment of hottest fighting, and that he "only saw the rout." [26] Yet for admission of failure and dramatization of disaster one did not need to turn to the foreign press. One quotation, out of a vast literature of description, must suffice here. "Every account that comes [wrote John Russell Young], comes filled with disaster. . . . *We have sent into Virginia the best . . . of our grand army, we have fought the greatest battle ever fought on the continent, and we have been not only beaten, but our army has been routed, and many of its best regiments wholly demoralized.*" [27]

III

North of the Potomac the effect of Bull Run followed a complex pattern. The grave and reverend, as well as lesser folk, fell into a quagmire of despair. There was bickering against the government, doubt of Lincoln, and indignant demand for a scapegoat, but that was not all. In addition there was grim realization of the reality of war, with renewed determination to carry on. Even the latter sentiment, however, did not necessarily work in Lincoln's favor. In modern slang the Lincoln administration was "on the spot." "The truth is," wrote Lyman Trumbull, "there is a lack of . . . positive action & business talent in the cabinet. Lincoln though a most excellent & an honest man lacks these qualities." After several months it was on the Union side still a defensive war and Trumbull expressed the fear that "the men at the head of our affairs do not realize our condition and are not equal to the occasion." [1] Common themes of the time were distrust of commanders, lack of confidence in the cabinet, fear of imminent attack upon Washington (this continued for weeks), clamor for peace, and a determination to have no more trifling.[2] In this phase a kind of patronizing compliment to Lincoln, though many

---

[25] *Ibid.*, I, preface, vii.   [26] Moore, *Rebellion Record* (Doc.), II, 63.

[27] *Ibid.* (Doc.), II, 376.

[1] Lyman Trumbull to Judge Doolittle of Wisconsin, Lakeside, Conn., Aug. 31, 1861, MS., Ill. State Hist. Lib.

[2] New York *Herald*, July 27, 1861, p. 4, c. 4.

refused even this, would be balanced by denunciation of influences surrounding him. Lincoln, admitted the *Herald,* was "an honest . . . amiable man," but he should not trust "everything to his Cabinet, to his party and to Providence." [3] He should ferret out the ones responsible for the blunder at Bull Run and act at once. Next day the *Herald* put the blame upon the abolitionists and secondarily upon Lincoln for permitting abolition influence to defeat the Crittenden compromise.[4] When offering advice this paper could deliver a broadside of criticism, as when it stated that Lincoln's duty was to achieve a cabinet "superior to all Presidential cliques and intriguers, rising above all temptations for jobs and contracts, and spoils and plunder, renouncing all abolition vagaries, and discarding the delusion that the patience of the country will cover all delinquencies." [5] It was further asserted that Lincoln's first duty was to "cease to be the politician, and perform the duties of the statesman." [6]

To the President himself the news of Bull Run had come with a ruder shock because it had been preceded by a steady accumulation of convincing assurances. Lincoln spent this eventful Sunday at church, at the White House, and at the war department. While at the war building his interest was in the telegraph office where he "waited with deep anxiety for each succeeding despatch." [7] These despatches were encouraging, and Lincoln was led to believe "that Beauregard was being pushed back." [8] "At supper [wrote Browning] the news was that . . . our army had forced the batteries at Bulls run and driven the enemy back upon Manassas . . . ." [9] Feeling that the news of Union victory had been confirmed, the President went for his usual drive. By the time he returned, the telegraph had announced that McDowell was in full retreat, that the day was lost, and that it was a matter of saving Washington with the remnants of a broken army.[10] In factual manner Browning recorded the stunned bewilderment at Washington. It was thought that the fight was over with the Unionists "in possession of the field." Then, "in some unaccountable manner, our troops were seized with a panic, and fled. They were not pursued. . . . How it happened no body seems to know." [11]

---

[3] *Ibid.,* July 25, 1861, p. 4, c. 3. [4] *Ibid.,* July 26, 1861. p. 4, c. 3.
[5] *Ibid.,* Aug. 2, 1861, editorial, p. 4, c. 4. [6] *Ibid.,* Aug. 17, 1861, editorial, p. 4, c. 4.
[7] David H. Bates, *Lincoln in the Telegraph Office,* 88. [8] *Ibid.,* 91.
[9] Browning, *Diary,* I, 484. [10] *Offic. Rec.,* 1 ser., II, 747.
[11] Browning, *Diary,* I. 485

In all this painful frustration it was a kind of human necessity to put the blame somewhere, the blame of ordering "a battle before our troops were prepared for it." [12] General Scott's comment was given in a remarkable conversation with Lincoln, Cameron, and a group of Illinois men. In mock self-condemnation Scott called himself "the greatest coward in America" because he had fought this battle against his judgment. Lincoln is said to have remarked: "Your conversation seems to imply that I forced you to fight this battle," to which Scott replied that no President had been "kinder" to him than Lincoln. [13]

The problem of responsibility in the premises is more than a question of whether Lincoln "forced" the battle. A congressional opponent, W. A. Richardson of Illinois, though assailing the Republican administration, disclaimed any implication that Lincoln had compelled Scott to fight at this stage. Lincoln's friend Francis P. Blair, Jr., asserted that Lincoln, on learning that Johnston had joined Beauregard, suggested to Scott the propriety of waiting, but that Scott was determined to attack and disregarded the suggestion. [14] Lincoln's secretaries do not so easily relieve the President of at least partial responsibility, for they record that, at a council summoned by the President (June 29), the generals were of opinion that simultaneous victories could be won at Manassas and Winchester, that Scott preferred delay until autumn, and that "the President and the Cabinet, as political experts" intervened on the ground that the public could not brook delay. The secretaries assert flatly that "the Administration was responsible for the forward movement." [15] A good deal of this whole discussion was animated by a purpose to discredit Lincoln's cabinet and advisers. Lincoln was even complimented by some who were damning his administration. Yet the President and his cabinet seem to have been in no serious disagreement on this point.

At least two factors of a fortuitous nature had acted powerfully against the Union side in this battle: the failure of Patterson and the falling off of three-months volunteers. An essential link in the strategy of Scott and McDowell was General Robert Patterson, in command at Winchester. His task was to keep Johnston busy and prevent him from joining Beauregard at Manassas when McDowell's blow should fall.

[12] Remarks of Francis P. Blair in House of Representatives, August 1, 1861, *Cong. Globe*, 37 Cong., 1 sess., 388.

[13] Quoted in remarks of W. A. Richardson, July 24, 1861, *ibid.*, 246.

[14] August 1, 1861, *ibid.*, 387.   [15] Nicolay and Hay, *Lincoln*, IV, 360.

This he failed to do. Authorities are pretty well agreed that this failure made all the difference; [16] yet Union high command could not be blamed for this unforeseen factor. So also with the aggravating circumstance that the battle came just at the time when the service of three-months militia was expiring. According to McDowell's own words he could neither push on faster nor delay. "A large and the best part . . . of my forces [he said] were three-months' volunteers, whose terms . . . were about expiring, but who were sent forward as having long enough to serve for the purpose of the expedition." "In the next few days [he added], day by day I should have lost ten thousand of the best armed, drilled, officered, and disciplined troops in the Army. In other words, every day which added to the strength of the enemy made us weaker." [17] If the President was responsible for this amazing situation at the time of a major campaign, it was in introducing the three-months limitation in the first place, or in not correcting it before the moment of advance.

It was a case of a war leader suffering when unsuccessful, whatever the cause. Before the battle it seemed reasonable to hope that the Union campaign, not badly planned, might succeed. It was not so much Lincoln, or Scott, or the cabinet, or McDowell, but unforeseeable happenings, together with the unmilitary emphasis of the American democracy, that had produced a failure which to Browning seemed "unaccountable."

IV

More significant than post-mortem recrimination was the forward look which showed an unshaken government backed by a people that could close ranks, re-form lines, and push grimly on. If Lincoln was hurt and stunned, his resilience was equally manifest. The night after Bull Run he "did not go to his bed," [1] but began some pencil jottings which two days later (July 23) had been elaborated into "memoranda of military policy suggested by the Bull Run defeat." In brief his policy was: push the blockade, drill the forces at Fort Monroe and vicinity, hold Baltimore, strengthen "Patterson or Banks" (in the Winchester area), push forward in Missouri (this was Frémont's job),

---

[16] *Battles and Leaders of the Civil War*, I, 175, 230.
[17] *Offic. Rec.*, 1 ser., II, 325.   [1] Nicolay and Hay, *Lincoln*, IV, 355.

reorganize the main force in and near Washington, discharge those three-months men who declined longer service (a bitter lesson had been learned here), bring up new volunteers as fast as possible, seize and hold suitable points in Virginia, then advance with a coördinated movement on western fronts.[2]

For the new program a new commander was needed. Not that McDowell had served so badly; it was rather that this unfortunate commander bore the imprimatur of defeat and that conditions of army morale and popular feeling demanded a change. The name of George B. McClellan was in favor because of a minor but skillfully advertised campaign in western Virginia (June and July, 1861). In an address to his troops ("Soldiers of the Army of the West") he had dramatically acclaimed the achievements of his men; this address, whose publication was not neglected, was dated only five days before McDowell's defeat.[3] More than this, McClellan had real qualities. Training at West Point had been followed by regular army duty, Mexican War service, military surveys, observation in the Crimean War (perfectly reported and published by the United States government), and executive experience with the Illinois Central Railroad.

On July 27, 1861, McClellan formally assumed his duties in command of the Union army with headquarters at Washington.[4] No time had been lost in putting him there. His summons to Washington came the day after Bull Run (July 22);[5] the order assigning him to his new "department" was dated July 25.[6] This, the first important change in army command traceable to the fortunes of war, was less a presidential than a war-department affair; at any rate Lincoln's part in the business does not appear in the documents. Scott loyally accepted the new commander, though his biographer states that he was "slightly irritated . . . that McClellan had been invited to confer with the President and Cabinet on the afternoon of the 27th—a conference to which the General-in-Chief [Scott] had apparently not been summoned."[7]

Months of friction ensued between the General in Chief and the Young Napoleon, due in part to overlapping duties and in part to temperamental reasons on both sides. Meanwhile, for supporting the government he had served all his life, Scott was denounced by fellow

---

[2] *Works*, VI, 331–333. [3] *Offic. Rec.*, 1 ser., II, 236. [4] *Ibid.*, 766.
[5] *Ibid.*, 753. [6] *Ibid.*, 763. [7] Elliott, *Scott*, 733.

Virginians as a traitor and compared to Benedict Arnold.[8] The followers of "General Greeley" assailed him from a quite different quarter as an inefficient dotard.[9] The old warrior grew weaker and could no longer remain awake during working hours. Behind the scenes the President tried to ease matters between his top commanders. It was of no use; McClellan considered that Scott was in his way and was determined to "force the issue." [10] In cabinet meeting it was agreed (October 18) that Scott could "*command* no longer." [11] Here was a situation calling for presidential tact. Lincoln handled it with deferential respect to the distinguished septuagenarian, and with that added element of personal kindness to which the old general had already gratefully alluded. The President read in cabinet "a draft of a letter to Gen S.[cott] (delicately and handsomely written) importing that . . . [Scott] had expressed a wish to be retired, . . . that he would no longer object— That he would still . . . need his advice . . . and was disposed to deal generously by the Genl.'s military family." [12]

On October 31 Scott wrote asking formal retirement under existing law. In accepting his request (November 1) Lincoln paid him the compliment of a personal visit of himself and full cabinet to the general's headquarters. There was a "touching interview" at which the President made a "neat and feeling address." [13] The army order recognizing the retirement was drawn by Lincoln; it was "done chastely and in excellent taste." [14] In a published letter the President took note of the nation's sympathy for the retiring commander and its recognition of his "long and brilliant career." [15] McClellan was directed to "assume the command of the Army of the United States." This did not mean that he was accorded Scott's rank of Lieutenant General, yet he was appointed in his stead and Lincoln referred to him as "general-in-chief of the army." [16] In effect McClellan took the places of both Scott and McDowell. Stating that there was no difference of opinion as to the person to be appointed, Lincoln paid McClellan a handsome compliment in his annual message to Congress.[17]

[8] *Ibid.*, 725.   [9] *Ibid.*, 731–732.   [10] *McClellan's Own Story*, 170.
[11] Bates, *Diary*, 196.   [12] *Ibid.*, 196–197.   [13] *Ibid.*, 199.
[14] *Ibid.*   [15] *Works*, VII, 13–14 (Nov. 1, 1861).
[16] Annual message to Congress, Dec. 3, 1861, *Works*, VII, 55. (On November 1, 1861, Lincoln in a formal order directed that McClellan "assume command of the army of the United States." *Ibid.*, VII, 14.)
[17] *Ibid.*, VII, 55 (Dec. 3, 1861).

Thus did Winfield Scott lay down his duties after heavy overtime service. Writers have customarily emphasized his age, inadequacy, and pompous fussiness; yet this veteran, at the outset of the war, had embodied in his massive person a large share of such professional competence as belonged to the tiny army which Lincoln inherited. His biographer states that, except Scott and Wool, both over-age, "the Regular Army did not carry on its rolls a single officer who had directed, in peace or war, the evolutions of a brigade." [18] The unmilitary democracy that had stumbled into war had looked to the old general for organization and strategy far beyond the tools at his disposal. Experience of a half-century, reaching back to the days of Van Rensselaer's ineffective New York militia, when press and public were "howling for action," [19] had given him a low opinion of volunteers. Tiny as the professional army was, Scott felt that it ought to be the nucleus of the organization that would fight battles. On this point his advice was not followed. Instead of being expanded from a trained nucleus, the new army was a kind of emergency hodge-podge. As to high strategy, Scott's master plan—a broad, slow blockade and encirclement dubbed "Scott's anaconda" [20]—was likewise disregarded.

In a long lull of military operations McClellan concerned himself with replenishment and elaborate reconditioning of the force which, he knew, would face a task of major proportions in its campaign of 1862 against Richmond. This was a period when Washington saw much of the magnetic Young Napoleon who was "courted . . . as few men in our history have been." [21] His prolonged presence in Washington was a constant reminder that the war was at a standstill. Before he was on the march Lincoln was to undergo some of the most bothersome and menacing episodes of his administration.

---

[18] Elliott, *Scott*, 718.

[19] *Ibid.*, 54.

[20] *Ibid.*, 722–724.

[21] Nicolay and Hay, *Lincoln*, IV, 444.

LINCOLN THE PRESIDENT
SPRINGFIELD TO GETTYSBURG

PART TWO

THE GARDNER FULL FACE—1863

Taken by Alexander Gardner in Washington in November 1863, shortly
before the Gettysburg address.

CHAPTER XV

KENTUCKY TO THE RIGHT,
FRÉMONT TO THE LEFT

I

STUNNING defeat and shake-up in army command had not fallen as isolated blows. With these troubles there came to Lincoln in the wretched summer and autumn of 1861 a concerted onslaught of opposite and incurably antagonistic forces. A fateful dualism it was to be, and as time went on it showed increasing power to pester and harass. It was the dualism of Kentucky on the one side and Frémont on the other, of border-state moderation against crusading zeal, of opportunist realism against impatient reform, of limited objectives, with emphasis on the Union, *versus* an all-out abolitionist program of virulent anti-Southernism. On the one hand were moderate men who wished the South to be satisfied when the Union was remade, meantime sparing Southern civilians the worst horrors of war; on the other hand were unctuous rebel-haters to whom suffering on the part of slaveholders and "traitors" seemed a kind of Divine vengeance.

This pervasive dualism was a veritable *leitmotif* in the drama of Lincoln's presidency; in its constant recurrence in varying forms Lincoln found a problem hardly less serious than the war itself. Whether it was a question of emancipation, of the definition of war aims, of legislation against Southerners, of choosing army commanders, of the tenure of cabinet advisers, or, later, of reconstructing a shattered Union, Lincoln's eye was continually to meet this spectre of internal discord looming before him. He was never to hear the last of it, nor in the outcome was his leadership to be successful.

One side of this struggle was embodied in Lincoln's native state.

It could be literally said that for Kentucky the Civil War had no meaning. In sympathy the state was Southern; in culture it was akin to Virginia. In the election of 1860 and the prewar crisis its supreme representative was Crittenden and its preoccupation had been with conciliation, union, and avoidance of war. Kentucky had, of course, its vigorous concept of state loyalty, but that loyalty was in terms of national integrity; it did not require an anti-Washington focus. To be loyal to both state and Union was, after all, not so strange a thing, no more strange than a person's loyalty to brother and father, or a nation's loyalty to itself and to the compelling cause of international order. This concept was, in fact, the essence of that federalism which was the American nation's essential characteristic if there was an American nation. In its recognition of a comprehensive instead of a merely local allegiance, it was to be as essential to the Confederate States as to the United States. In the discussion of this theme it is a misnomer to speak of "divided loyalty." That concept would imply that state and nation were incompatible opposites or enemies, instead of complementary elements fitting together. Unionism in Kentucky, as envisaged by its most distinguished leaders, implied no coexistence of inconsistent or conflicting loyalties.

Unwilling to interpret Southernism in anti-Union terms themselves, Kentuckians resented the precipitateness of South Carolina. They considered the "antics . . . of the Yanceyites . . . damaging" to the Southern cause on the border.[1] It irked and disgusted many of them to observe the easy nonchalance with which the cotton states stirred up trouble "at a safe distance"; it was felt that Virginia, Maryland, Kentucky, and Missouri had no desire to "sacrifice themselves" for a separatist cause they cared not for.[2] Moreover, Kentuckians kept emphasizing a plan of their own—a "border state convention" (to include the upper South with the Southern border) by which it was hoped that the whole unwelcome crisis could be resolved by joint consultation among eight of the fifteen slave states. Such consultation, of course, was to be friendly to the Union while safeguarding Southern interests. As the pioneer state of the great West while equally a part of the South, Kentucky held itself to have as much right as any state

---

[1] Letter of Thomas T. Grant, probably to Montgomery Blair, St. Louis, Oct. 29, 1860, Blair MSS.
[2] *Ibid.*

to develop and present a program; its initiative was as rightful as that of South Carolina, especially since the Kentucky plan involved co-operative effort among the states concerned.

After the formation of the Confederacy and the inauguration of Lincoln the Union element in Kentucky had been able (as in Mary-land, Virginia, and the upper South) to stave off actual secession, which was vigorously sought by an active separatist faction. In sum, Kentucky, in general, had neither any motive to fight against the South nor any wish to break the Union, whose dissolution would sever commercial bonds and cut ties of blood kinship with thousands of fathers and brothers in nearby Northern commonwealths.

Policies become weaker when reduced to formulas; in this case the broad policy of the Union was whittled down to the formula of the Crittenden compromise. The failure of that compromise, marking the collapse and defeat of Kentucky's basic program, came as a heavy blow to border Southerners; this breakdown of constructive states-manship put ammunition into the hands of secessionists. Even so, there were enough good Kentuckians who felt that their contest was with Black Republicans rather than the United States to enable the legislature to scotch the secessionists' program and avoid calling the state convention which disunionists were promoting as the instrument of withdrawal.

This was the situation as of mid-April. Then came, with a cruel shock and a kind of dazed incredulity, the Sumter episode, unbe-lievable war, and the President's call for troops. Here began what E. M. Coulter calls a "maelstrom of events" in which "almost any re-action" might follow.[3] At this stage John M. Harlan, though Unionist in feeling, considered war inevitable unless Federal troops were with-drawn from the South; when war came he felt sure that the border states would join secessionist ranks.[4] Spirited agitation to promote Confederate influence was not lacking. By the familiar device of propaganda labels, Unionists were tagged as "Submissionists" and the Union policy was denounced as "suicidal madness" that would alienate Southern friends and isolate the state while "thirty millions of people . . . [were] engaged in bloody strife!"[5]

---

[3] E. M. Coulter, *Civil War and Readjustment in Kentucky*, 37.

[4] Harlan to Holt, March 11, 1861, Holt MSS. (cited in Coulter, 38).

[5] Louisville *Daily Courier*, April 18, 1861, in Dumond, *Southern Editorials on Seces-sion*, 494-495.

Governor Magoffin, who may be described as anti-Lincoln rather than fully pro-Confederate, answered the President's call for militia with the stinging comment that his state would "furnish no troops for the wicked purpose of subduing her sister Southern States." [6] Increasing secessionist activity in the state, however, caused him no less apprehension, and he acted to put a curb upon Confederate recruiting. [7] At this point Kentucky had not yet committed herself: ". . . there invoking peace, she stands" was for some months the post-Sumter as well as the pre-Sumter attitude of the state. [8]

II

With minds so conditioned, Kentuckians could not immediately adjust themselves to the violent reorientation forced by the outbreak of war. That outbreak left Kentucky with no place to go. It thickened the plot without offering a solution. Recruiting by both sides became active all over the state. Union and Confederate camps were quickly formed; families and communities were split; soldiers on opposite sides found themselves traveling on the same train. Unskillful Union agitation, particularly if couched in abolitionist terms, would hurt the Federal cause among its best friends. To offend the spirited pro-Confederate element would produce hot reaction. To force the issue prematurely might be the very factor that would precipitate secession.

Out of this confused situation there grew, as a natural if temporary *modus vivendi,* the famous Kentucky program of "neutrality." This soon became the state's declared policy, approved on May 16 by the lower house of the legislature, and on May 20 by Governor Magoffin's proclamation. "Thus was Kentucky . . . officially committed to a position which its people had been in the process of assuming since secession began." [1]

This neutral phase continued for some months, indeed through the summer of 1861, albeit individual Kentuckians were enlisting, and soldiers from the state fought on both sides at First Manassas. What this neutrality meant being interpreted, would require elaborate

---

[6] *Annual Cyclopaedia,* 1861, 396.   [7] Coulter, *Civil War* . . . *in Kentucky,* 49.

[8] "Kentucky," a poem by Forceythe Willson, in Moore, *Rebellion Record* (Poetry, etc.), II, 61.

[1] The quotation is from Coulter, 55; for references on Kentucky neutrality, see Randall, *Constitutional Problems Under Lincoln,* 407 n.

statement. Unable to conceive of war between the sections as other than a kind of nightmare, men of the border somehow hoped that a solution was yet possible in terms of peace and union. Meanwhile Kentucky would try not to enter the war, nor to let the war enter the state. The suspense and uneasiness of Kentucky were evidenced in an interview (June, 1861) between Simon Buckner of Kentucky, and George B. McClellan, Union general with headquarters at Cincinnati. Meeting informally and conversing without official guarantees, exchange of credentials, or agreements, these old friends talked over what would happen if Kentucky "should be invaded by the secession forces then collecting under Gen. Pillow . . . in Tennessee." The significance of this interview was seen in the ease of conference between the two military leaders (the one in the Union service, the other in Kentucky service as commandant of what were called "State Guards"), and in the earnest wish of Buckner to see that the neutrality of his state was respected; but the affair was formalized and magnified into a "Kentucky Concordat" or treaty, as represented to the public, the supposed terms being that Kentucky would respect Federal authority and keep Confederate troops out of the state, while no Union troops would be moved into the commonwealth.[2] The episode illustrates the extreme sensitiveness of Kentuckians at this time concerning "invasion" of their state by Federal troops. Such invasion might seriously have hurt the Union cause; yet Garret Davis noted another aspect of the situation when he wrote that a hundred Union companies were organizing over the state, that there was a great difference "between Union men armed and unarmed," and that thousands of Enfields or Sharps ought to be distributed where they would do the most good.[3]

Though there was constant fear that Kentucky could not be held for the Union, surprisingly few of the state's prominent leaders, in the spring and summer of '61, openly urged secession or adherence to the Confederacy. John C. Breckinridge, in this period, remained in the United States Senate and even after the Sumter crisis hoped for avoidance of general war. Just after Lincoln's call for troops Breckinridge urged that Kentucky call a Southern convention without delay, so

[2] G. B. McClellan, *McClellan's Own Story*, 48–49; W. S. Myers, *General George Brinton McClellan*, 177–182; New York *Times*, June 24, 1861, p. 4, cc. 2–3; *Offic. Rec.*, 1 ser., II, 674–675.

[3] *Offic. Rec.*, 1 ser., II, 678.

that Lincoln's special session of Congress would be confronted by fifteen opposing states. Thus alone, he thought, could general war be averted.[4] Vigorously assailing Lincoln's policy, Breckinridge nevertheless continued to profess lifetime attachment to the Union.[5] When, despite these protestations, he entered Confederate military service, his service was not yet terminated in the United States Senate; his equivocal membership in that body was ended by expulsion on December 4, 1861.[6]

Crittenden carried over his peacemaking attitude till it became a kind of wishful thinking after Sumter, advising that Kentucky take no part in the war but stand between the hostile sections as pacificator. Garret Davis and Guthrie worked untiringly for the Union. Magoffin wavered, being counted pro-Confederate, yet supporting neutrality and resenting Confederate interference. Young Henry Watterson, not then prominent, joined the Confederate army less from anti-Union conviction than from a wish to be associated with the Confederate set. Thomas E. Bramlette resisted the neutrality doctrine and took a commission with the Union army. Robert J. Breckinridge, staunch Unionist, opposed a secession convention, headed the "Unconditional Unionists," and became Lincoln's "chief counsellor" on Kentucky affairs. Other sturdy Kentuckians were strong Unionists, such as George D. Prentice, Benjamin H. Bristow, Joseph Holt, James F. Robinson, and the Speed brothers, James and Joshua F., these brothers being among the very few whose Unionism coexisted with genuine support of Lincoln. When Bell men joined with followers of Douglas to form the "Union State Central Committee,"[7] powerful support was offered by Prentice's paper, the influential Louisville *Journal*. Joseph Holt, recent secretary of war, addressed the citizens of Louisville in July, speaking unequivocally for the Union and denouncing secesion as a "great crime."[8]

---

[4] New York *Times*, April 18, 1861, p. 8, c. 4.

[5] Moore, *Rebellion Record* (Docs.), II, 305 ff.

[6] *Cong. Globe*, 37 Cong., 2 sess., 9. On October 1, 1861, the legislature of Kentucky had instructed both its senators (John C. Breckinridge and L. W. Powell) to resign on the ground that they did not represent the will of people of the state.

[7] Coulter, 28.

[8] Moore, *Rebellion Record* (Diary), II, 29–30; *ibid.* (Docs.), II, 297–303. For the reference to the "great crime," see p. 298.

III

The Kentucky situation offered a grave challenge to Lincoln's leadership. Had the presidency been held by a man of less shrewdness and tact, or less understanding of border-state sentiment, this pivotal state might have been lost and the Ohio River might have become the boundary between the embattled sections. What this would have meant, no one knew better than Lincoln. "I think to lose Kentucky is nearly . . . to lose the whole game," he wrote. "Kentucky gone, we cannot hold Missouri, nor, as I think, Maryland. These all against us, and the job on our hands is too large for us. We would as well consent to separation at once, including the surrender of this capital." [1]

Knowing what was at stake and realizing the consequences of a false step, Lincoln did not rush things in Kentucky. He waited, observed, kept in touch, and conferred with Kentucky leaders of different shades and degrees. He encouraged ardent Union men in the state but kept them within bounds. Listening to hostile protests, he answered them in a conciliatory spirit without selling his cause down the river. On those matters that required secrecy he left "no written records to accuse," [2] conducting his Kentucky affairs largely by word of mouth. His few papers on the subject are masterpieces of noncommittal statement couched in phrases of utmost candor and frankness. On one occasion—a minor one—a suave and imperturbable answer from the White House went hand-in-hand with a touch of prairie humor when John Hay, writing for the President, replied to a Kentucky state senator who had protested against the stationing of troops at Cairo. Lincoln's secretary said that the matter would have "due consideration," and added: "He [the President] directs me to say that . . . he would never have ordered the movement of troops complained of had he known that Cairo was in your senatorial district." [3]

Lincoln showed respect for the neutral attitude of Kentucky without tying his hands by any stultifying agreement. He assured Garret Davis that he would not "force" the state, and had no military movements then in mind that would require sending troops through Ken-

---

[1] *Works*, VI, 360 (Sep. 22, 1861).

[2] Coulter, 90.

[3] *Works*, VI, 266 (May 6, 1861). This letter, not signed by the President, is here given as having been written by John Hay. See also Dennett, *John Hay*, 37–38.

tucky. He promised not to molest Kentucky so long as she made no forceful demonstration against the United States, nor resisted Federal laws. In a comment that looked both ways he told Senator Davis that until the meeting of Congress he would make no attempt to retake the forts belonging to the United States "unless he should be constrained to depart from that purpose by the continued military operations of the seceded States." Lest his words be misunderstood to imply weakness or indecision he added that events had reached a point to test whether "the Constitution formed a Government . . . with strength . . . sufficient to uphold its own authority, and to enforce . . . the laws . . . ." That authority he intended to uphold "to the extent that he should be sustained by the people of the United States." [4]

Lincoln continued this waiting policy till after the June elections in Kentucky. Indeed the expectation of such elections (to the Federal Congress) had much to do in shaping Lincoln's post-Sumter statesmanship. It has been stated, for example, that his postponement of the special session of Congress until July was because of the pivotal importance of Kentucky and the hazard of having an untoward thing happen at these elections.[5] The whole border situation was complicated by the intrigues and electioneering that preceded this Kentucky vote.[6] When the election occurred the Unionism of Kentucky was decisively demonstrated. Of the ten congressional districts all except one chose a "Union" candidate, the total Union vote in the state being 92,460 as compared to a "state rights" vote of 37,700.[7] It is true that many Southern-rights men did not vote at all, and that Unionism itself was a flexible and complex affair, capable of an interpretation that meant only neutrality.[8] Even so, it was important for Lincoln to have those Union congressmen from Kentucky, though no one knew better than the President how largely pro-Union votes came from men who detested the Republican party and were ready to rise in

---

[4] Garret Davis to George D. Prentice (concerning an interview between Davis and Lincoln), *Cong. Globe*, 37 Cong., 2 sess., appendix, 82–83. For another Lincoln conversation with Kentucky leaders, see J. W. Forney, *Anecdotes of Public Men*, I, 264–265.

[5] Blaine, *Twenty Years of Congress*, I, 309.

[6] As showing the apprehension of Unionists concerning this Kentucky election, J. F. Speed wrote to Joseph Holt on June 18, 1861, with anti-secession bitterness: ". . . we are contending with a foe that pays no respect to the will of a majority unless that majority shall be with them . . . ." Holt MSS.

[7] *Annual Cyclopaedia*, 1861, 397.   [8] Coulter, 95.

revolt against the abolitionist radicalism and anti-Southernism which gave evidence of becoming ever more powerful at Washington.

IV

In the summer of 1861 the Kentucky situation took shape and crystallized. The border-state convention, frustrated by the progress of secession and the outbreak of war, met at Frankfort on May 27 with only Kentucky and Missouri represented. It declared Kentucky's loyalty to the Union; yet it was an affair of distressingly small effect when compared to the ambitious hopes of those who had looked to it as the key to the sectional crisis. Military units were forming on both sides, "Home Guards" being organized to uphold the Union cause in opposition to Buckner's "State Guards" which were disunionist in intent. The legislature, suspecting the governor of secessionism, deprived him of his constitutional authority as commander-in-chief of the state militia, placing the military force of the state in the hands of a special group of five men known as a "Military Board." [1] Arms flowed into the state and were somehow distributed among safe Union men, while conflict was meanwhile averted as if by a miracle. In this phase the hand of the Union government was "deftly kept hidden," though indignation was soon directed against Lincoln's alleged "atrocity" in "arming one class . . . by . . . clandestine agents." [2]

Arguing that Kentucky had no need of a military force, Governor Magoffin urged the removal of "the military force now organized and in camp within the State." [3] To this Lincoln replied that such force was small, that it consisted of Kentuckians camped near their homes, that he was acting in accordance with the wishes of "the Union loving people of Kentucky," that of his numerous Kentucky advisers no others had asked that the force be removed, and that he "must respectfully decline to so remove it." [4]

It soon became evident that neutrality for Kentucky, in the sense of isolation from the war or non-participation in it, was impossible. If for no other reason, this impossibility would have been due to the intense concern of individual Kentucky citizens for one side or the

---

[1] Coulter, 87.
[2] *Ibid.*, 90.
[3] *Annual Cyclopaedia*, 1861, 398.
[4] *Works*, VI, 349–350 (Aug. 24, 1861).

other. Though the majority wanted avoidance of war, opposite sympathies were inevitable once the war was started; the very wish to
avoid war meant aversion to secession on the one hand or to what was
called Federal coercion on the other. The war could not be exorcized
nor wished away; geography in its relation to military strategy or
intersectional communication could not be ignored. It was the fate
of Americans of the time to be drawn into the war; Kentuckians were
among these Americans.

For obvious military reasons Union forces occupied Cairo, Illinois,
and Belmont, Missouri. This was but part of a chain of circumstances
in which Confederates under Leonidas Polk took Columbus and Hickman, Federals under Grant seized Paducah, and at the other end of the
state Zollicoffer, Confederate general, moved in from Tennessee in
the area of Cumberland Gap, heralding his action with a resounding
proclamation to the people of Kentucky to resist subjugation by
"Northern hordes." [5] As war clouds thickened all around them and
in their midst, the people of Kentucky saw the fabric of neutrality
collapse; when this was evident the policy was officially abandoned by
a resolution of the legislature (September 12, 1861) passed over the
governor's veto.[6] Declaring that Kentucky's neutrality had been "wan-
tonly violated" by the "so-called Southern Confederate forces," this
resolution demanded that the "invaders" be expelled and that Federal
aid and protection be sought. Magoffin reluctantly acquiesced in this
policy, then patriotically resigned the governorship, which passed to
James F. Robinson,[7] a Conservative who favored the United States.
From this point, though a pro-Confederate phantom government
was erected, Kentucky remained uncomfortably in the Union.

Because the project of neutrality proved temporary, it would be
easy to condemn it in sweeping terms. It was, in fact, condemned by
both sides, which is significant, as well as praised or appealed to by
both sides. In the matter of joining one side or the other Kentucky's
choice was harder than that of other states; a temporary neutrality
or quasi-truce was needful for the early months of difficult adjustment. To avert the war would have been a high accomplishment; Kentucky could not continue to work for this end if she took sides. Averting war was, however, more of a Kentucky motive than retreating into

[5] *Annual Cyclopaedia*, 1861, 404.
[6] Moore. *Rebellion Record* (Docs.), III, 129; Coulter, 114.   [7] Coulter, 143.

a bomb-proof cellar of indifference after the conflict had started. In the weeks after mid-April 1861 the nation was psychologically inhibited from retracing its steps to the pre-secession status quo. Only if such a retracing had been possible could border neutrality have yielded any important result; there was in the policy an element that was essentially tentative, temporary, and provisional.

All told the policy contributed more good than otherwise to the Union cause; yet Lincoln condemned this "armed neutrality" as "disunion completed," and compared it to "the building of an impassable wall along the line of separation—and yet not quite an impassable one, for under the guise of neutrality it would tie the hands of Union men and freely pass supplies . . . to the insurrectionists, which it could not do as an open enemy. . . . It would do for the disunionists that which . . . they most desire . . . ." [8] Despite this rebuke, the attitude of impartiality and of marking time, besides being psychologically harmonious with the immediate postwar situation in the state, averted secession, kept the road open to conciliation, and averted civil war within the state in those heated days when fighting Kentuckians were rallying under opposing banners. It will not quite do to say that neutrality "broke down." It accomplished a number of definite results. Lincoln in general had no need to be disappointed in the ultimate course of his native state, which, as he reported to Congress in December 1861, was "decidedly, . . . unchangeably, ranged on the side of the Union." [9] His condemnation of border nonparticipation (in his July message) had occurred after Union benefits from that very policy had been reaped.[10]

V

Repercussions in northwestern Virginia did not follow the prevailing border pattern. Rather they fell, or were manipulated, into a unique formula not repeated elsewhere. Instead of statewide action stumbling through hesitation and indecision into a kind of reluctant

---

[8] *Works*, VI, 307 (July 4, 1861).   [9] *Ibid.*, VII, 53.

[10] In this specific historical account the intent is not to treat neutrality in general. The misguided isolationism of American neutrality from 1935 to 1939 is to be discussed in its own fearful setting. As to Kentucky, even if one regards its neutrality as understandable, it proved impossible. Kentucky's rightful contribution toward peace was frustrated. Denial of separatism and recognition of the imperative need of coöperation among states would have promoted such peaceful contribution.

Union allegiance, the program for the counties that became West Virginia was that of determined leaders in the Wheeling area who produced a fictitious adherence to the Union on the part of the whole state, and then, as if dissatisfied with their own fiction, created, perhaps unnecessarily, a detached commonwealth.[1] In Kentucky it was the pro-Confederate government that was a fabric of pretense; in Virginia the garb of fiction was worn by those who boldly asserted that the Old Dominion, none other than Virginia itself, adhered to the Union.

Since the story of Lincoln becomes too much clogged if one attempts to tell the complex history of the time, it will be possible only to glance at this development in the Kanawha region. Two diverse purposes were intertwined, the purpose of holding Virginia intact for the Union in defiance of the government at Richmond, and the further object of detaching the most Unionist part of the state by setting up a new political entity. The whole procedure is hardly intelligible unless one goes deep into historical backgrounds, intrastate sectionalism, geography, climate, topography, economic relations, and social diversities. When these are understood it will be seen that the mountain people of the Kanawha region had developed over the decades a marked diversity from the tidewater, middle, and piedmont areas. In contrast to dominant eastern forces, the westerners knew not the plantation economy, held few slaves or usually none at all, preferred evangelical sects to Episcopal forms, and dealt commercially with the area of the Ohio, having little converse with neighbors of the South. Wheeling was next door to Pittsburgh; the Panhandle was narrowly squeezed between Pennsylvania and Ohio; the Kanawha River was part of the Mississippi Valley.

Having no wish to secede from close neighbors and hotly resenting the action of the Richmond Convention, leaders in the western area, by a pattern that has been somewhat obscured in the older historical accounts,[2] moved with determination and vigor; once launched, the movement was about as easy to stop as an Appalachian torrent. Each

---

[1] On the theory that Virginia was adhering to the Union—in other words, that the Unionist efforts which erected a "restored state" were valid acts of the only legitimate Virginia government—the establishment of the new state, besides weakening the restored government, was logically unnecessary as a matter of federal relations.

[2] For a competent modern account see C. H. Ambler, *West Virginia, the Mountain State*.

step fitted into the whole comprehensive purpose. In mid-April, directly after the Sumter outbreak, preliminary organizational steps were taken; in May a mass convention of delegates at Wheeling prepared the road; in June a convention of doubtful authority, also at Wheeling, set up a reorganized government of Virginia on a Unionist pattern, at which point it could be asserted by the reorganizers that Virginia was a Union state; in August this same convention decreed that a new commonwealth by the name of "Kanawha" be formed, the name being later changed to West Virginia.

A few leaders arranged it so that forty-eight counties were included in the new state; ultimately, much against their will, two more, the counties of Jefferson and Berkeley in the Harpers Ferry area, were added. Half the area of the nascent commonwealth was unrepresented in the convention that gave it birth; in those parts that were "represented," some of the delegates bore the character of self-appointment or minority representation.

Other steps were taken as the months passed. A roster of state officials, with Francis Pierpoint [3] at the head as governor, was created for "restored [Unionist] Virginia"; Unionist senators for Virginia were chosen by the legislature at Wheeling; in due course a constitutional convention created an instrument of government for the new state of West Virginia. When completed, this constitution was ratified by a fragmentary vote of the people; then the "restored" legislature at Wheeling, in the alleged name of Virginia as a whole, gave the consent for the creation of the new state which the Constitution of the United States requires. Finally, by action of Congress, and reluctant consent on the part of President Lincoln,[4] West Virginia, in June of 1863, became one of the states in the American Union. Dispossessed by a government of its own creating, the restored government under Pierpoint stepped out of its true setting at Wheeling,

---

[3] This name is almost invariably given in historical accounts as "Pierpont," but contemporary usage, including the governor's own signature, was "Pierpoint."

[4] "Some conversation in Cabinet respecting the proposed new State of Western Virginia. The bill has not yet reached the President, who thinks the creation of this new State at this time of doubtful expediency." Welles, *Diary*, I, 191. Another indication of Lincoln's disapproval is found in a letter which Senator Willey wrote to Pierpoint, December 17, 1862, in which he said: "We have great fears that the President will veto the new State bill." Pierpoint Papers (MSS., Virginia State Archives). See also Browning, *Diary*, I, 596. Lincoln's recognition of the Pierpoint government, however, though never ostentatious, was generous and cordial.

moved to Alexandria where it abided under protection of Union arms, and, from that point until it was discarded by its friends in postwar years, maintained itself obscurely and precariously as the government of Virginia. From the wartime standpoint of Richmond, of course, both the new state and the Pierpoint government were pretending and illegal fabrications.

Efforts to promote the same type of separatist movement for the mountainous area of Eastern Tennessee, where Unionist sentiment was strong,[5] never proceeded beyond a preliminary and abortive stage. As noted above,[6] the people of all Tennessee, by referendum in February 1861 when the Confederacy was building, had emphatically rejected secession; in this rejection the eastern mountainous area had shown vigorous adherence to the Union. Since a mountainous region suggests a backwoodsy element, it must be added that some of the most cultured, conservative, and intellectually capable leaders of the state, such as Horace Maynard and Thomas A. R. Nelson, "regarded the secession movement with horror and disgust." [7] As in Virginia, though the points of the compass were reversed, intrastate sectionalism, compounded of many human and social factors, made the non-slaveholding area conscious of its distinctness from the rest of the state. Under the leadership of Nelson, who might have become the Pierpoint of East Tennessee, a convention was held at Knoxville in which pro-Union sentiments were vigorously expressed and the action of the governor and legislature in creating the military league with the Confederacy hotly denounced. This convention met on May 30, adjourned, and met again (at Greeneville, June 17), all without result so far as East-Tennesseean independence was concerned. Realizing that a stroke for such independence would be revolutionary, the leaders of the movement allowed their efforts to dwindle to an indignant declaration of grievances and a "memorial" to the legislature, praying that counties in the eastern area be permitted to form a

---

[5] In saying that Unionism was strong or prevalent, one should not imply that the opposite sentiment was negligible. Though a matter of minority opinion, pro-Confederate sentiment was stoutly supported in eastern Tennessee by such a leader as Landon C. Haynes. Sentiment for the Confederacy, or at least for not promoting revolution against the Confederacy, was an appreciable factor also in the counties that became West Virginia, though it has never been adequately measured. In southwestern Virginia such sentiment was stronger than in either the West-Virginia area or eastern Tennessee.

[6] See vol. I, 357.

[7] J. W. Patton, *Unionism and Reconstruction in Tennessee*, 22.

separate state. This harmless memorial died in committee, and with it perished the feeble but sincere efforts to hold East Tennessee for the Union.[8]

VI

It was in Missouri that the complex of border issues produced the greatest turbulence and confusion. As in Kentucky, there was spirited opposition between unionists and secessionists, but with a difference; in Missouri, unionists themselves were sharply divided between pro-slavery (or anti-abolitionist) conservatives and uncompromising anti-slavery radicals, this latter being a class almost unknown in Kentucky.[1] The Missouri governor, Claiborne F. Jackson (later deposed), tried to promote secession, and internecine war impended as military units formed on opposing sides, with many a neighborhood shaken by guerrilla warfare and civilian sniping.

Efforts toward a truce between opposing armed camps, though starting out with promise, broke down because of the impatience of such unionists as Nathaniel Lyon and Frank Blair, Jr. As a result the state endured the torments of civil war in dead earnest, as at Wilson's Creek (August 10, 1861) where "this little, rough-visaged, red-bearded, weather-beaten Connecticut captain," [2] Nathaniel Lyon, was killed, after having promoted Union victory. Early in 1862 (March 7–8) another Union victory was achieved at Pea Ridge in the northeast corner of Arkansas near the Missouri line. By decision of battle and by other factors (especially a notable state convention) Missouri was held for the Union, though a rival state government, a minor affair, functioned obscurely and claimed Missouri's adherence to the Confederacy.

In the early months part of the difficulty as to Missouri was the problem of government itself, for with Confederate and Union rivalry, ill-defined military authority, non-observance of orders, martial law, and conflicts within Union ranks between military officers and civil leaders, the mere maintenance of order, to say nothing of going forward for the Union cause, was a matter of doubt and risk.

---

[8] *Ibid.*, 22–25.

[1] In that state Cassius Clay was a *rara avis;* he was a voice crying, not in the wilderness, but in cultured Lexington, whose citizens took measures to suppress him.

[2] Col. Thomas L. Snead (C. S. A.), in *Battles and Leaders of the Civil War,* I, 273.

Intrigues behind the lines, charges and counter charges, tattle-tale visits to Lincoln, presidential politics, and clashes of personal ambition, caused Missouri to be a kind of constant headache at the White House.

Among other things there was the serious problem, not fully appreciated by army heads at Washington, of developing the promising military possibilities of the West—not merely victories such as those at Forts Henry and Donelson, but far reaching movements that might have pushed the river campaigns deep into the Confederacy, and have notably shortened the war.[3] Large strategy was thus added to other factors to make the Mississippi Valley and its St. Louis focus a challenge to the best thought of the administration.

VII

Into the turbulent Missouri mêlée Lincoln had thrust the colorful "Pathfinder" and former Republican candidate, John C. Frémont. The measure of his provocative character may be seen in the violent reactions it produced. By some he was superlatively praised, these being often the most bitter opponents of Lincoln; by others he was relentlessly denounced. His Missouri assignment became for Lincoln an embarrassment, a hornet's nest, and a grave hazard. It could almost be said that the sum of Lincoln's intramural vexations was focused in the Frémont muddle. Before he was removed from his post this political general had alienated border sentiment, seized functions that belonged to civilian chiefs at Washington, laid his administration open to charges of fraud and extravagance, challenged the President's leadership, divided those elements which Lincoln was seeking to weld together, and had precipitated one of those military-and-civil clashes which are always troublesome in a democracy. Whether or not such was his purpose, he had rallied to his own combative person that unctuous and impetuous abolitionism which flowed increasingly in anti-Lincoln channels.

The Frémont explosion came in the form of a sensational and unauthorized "proclamation" which that general issued from his headquarters at St. Louis on August 30, 1861. Asserting that he found it

---

[3] These military problems, and the part taken in them by a spirited woman, are treated in Marjorie Barstow Greenbie, *My Dear Lady: The Story of Anna Ella Carroll, the "Great Unrecognized Member of Lincoln's Cabinet."* See below, pp. 66–67.

necessary to "assume the administrative powers of the State," he ordered that all persons taken with arms in their hands within his lines would be "tried by court-martial" and shot if guilty. In addition, property of all persons who supported the enemy was declared confiscated and their slaves "hereby declared freemen." Instead of proceeding within existing law, this proclamation supplied "such deficiencies as the conditions of war demand"; persons in correspondence with the enemy or fomenting tumult, were warned of "sudden and severe punishment." [1]

In the matter of suppressing disturbances among the civilian population, admittedly bad in Missouri, President Lincoln claimed the right to fix the pattern of executive conduct. As to confiscation, Congress had already acted in a sense far different from that of Frémont's order, by providing that seizures be handled by Federal courts and be confined to such property as was used in aid of the rebellion.[2] As to emancipation, that assuredly was a matter of high policy in which the government at Washington had not only to make the major decision, but to choose the moment, the form, and the circumstances of public action. To allow undelegated authority in these delicate and important matters to be seized by generals in the field, and to permit such weighty affairs to be handled by military departments in limited areas instead of as a whole, would have amounted almost to an abandonment of orderly government.

On hearing of the proclamation Joshua F. Speed wrote Lincoln of his serious apprehensions as to its effect in Kentucky. Union men from all parts of the state, he said, shared his fears. In a few days he wrote again to Lincoln and others. To Holt he said that "we could stand several defeats like that at Bulls run, better than we can this proclamation if endorsed by the Administration." Then he added: "Do not allow us by the foolish act of a mi[li]tary popinjay to be driven from our present active loyalty." With almost evangelistic fervor he exclaimed: "And Oh how I desire that my most intimate friend Mr Lincoln—whom I shall ever regard as one of the best & purest men I have ever known, should be the instrument in the hands of God for the reconstruction of this great republic—." [3]

---

[1] *Offic. Rec.*, 1 ser., III, 466–467.
[2] Law of Aug. 6, 1861, *U. S. Statutes at Large*, XII, 319.
[3] J. F. Speed to Joseph Holt, Louisville, Sep. 7, 1861, Holt MSS.

At this juncture, which was the critical phase in Kentucky's transition from neutrality to Union adherence, Lincoln was finding abundant reason to steer cautiously as to all the points of the Frémont episode, yet in seeking to coördinate the radical commander with national policy the President avoided rebuke. Writing to the general "in a spirit of caution, and not of censure," he made two points clear: (1) no man should be shot without the President's consent, lest there be indefinite retaliation, man for man, in the whole broad war; (2) the general was asked to modify his proclamation to make it conform to existing law. While dealing with Frémont Lincoln was thinking of the border situation; he feared that Frémont's act would "perhaps ruin our rather fair prospect for Kentucky." [4]

Though mildly worded, this note from Lincoln amounted to an instruction from the President on the two points specified; yet on both points Frémont refused compliance. On the matter of inflicting the military death penalty, though regularly such a penalty was subject to presidential approval even without Lincoln's special admonition, Frémont replied: "As promptitude is . . . an advantage in war, I have . . . to ask that you will permit me to carry out *upon the spot* [author's italics] the provisions of the proclamation . . . ." [5] Concerning the other point (modifying his proclamation according to law) he declined to make the alteration of his own accord, and, as if to put the President in the wrong before Frémont sympathizers, asked "that you will openly direct me to make the correction." [6] Lincoln wrote: "Your answer . . . expresses the preference . . . that I should make an open order for the modification, which I very cheerfully do. It is therefore ordered that . . . said proclamation be so modified . . . as to conform to . . . the act of Congress . . . [etc.]." [7] It is not revealed in the unsatisfactory interchange between Lincoln and Frémont that the general ever properly bowed to the President's authority. After Lincoln's clear admonition touching the shooting of civilians condemned on military trial, Frémont instructed one of his colonels that the shooting clause in his proclamation would be "strictly enforced." [8]

Despite his popularity and wide prestige, Frémont soon came under

---

[4] *Works*, VI, 350–351 (Sep. 2, 1861).   [5] *Offic. Rec.*, 1 ser., III, 477–478.   [6] *Ibid.*
[7] *Works*, VI, 353 (Sep. 11, 1861).   [8] *Offic. Rec.*, 1 ser., III, 492.

a cloud of accusations. Pomp, official swank, employment of "foreigners" (non-Missourians), graft in government contracts, extravagance, and favoritism were among the charges against him. To this was added the charge of military incompetence, especially failure to strengthen Lyon, leading to that general's defeat.[9] With headquarters at the Brant mansion in St. Louis, rented by the government at $6000 per year,[10] he was so importantly busy with trifles and so surrounded by guards and orderlies that men with serious business became disgusted in trying to interview him.[11] It was said that he occupied "more time in recruiting a 'body guard' than in attending to the affairs of the country."[12] A confidant of Governor Yates wrote that, while accomplishing nothing with Frémont, he "found the City filled with contractors and jobbers, [with] a great flurry in the Quartermaster's Department, but on every side . . . insufficiency of supplies."[13] At times he would be "seized with a spasmodic rashness and . . . [send] some small force into places greatly exposed and from which it . . . [could] not easily be extricated."[14]

But there were worse accusations. An observer wrote that the situation at St. Louis was "terrible and the frauds . . . shocking."[15] One of his associate officers, McKinstry, was denounced as a "robber and a traitor," the Frémont ménage being described as a "horde of pirates,"[16] and again as a set of "California Vampires."[17] The general was accused of self importance and of a tendency to spread himself in the newspapers.[18] Lorenzo Thomas, adjutant general of the United States, reported questionable contracts, expensive barracks, inferior guns, ("20 out of 100 . . . would go off"), attention to Springfield when Price was marching toward Lexington, and, in general, unfitness for important command.[19]

In the sequel an elaborate official investigation was to reveal the

---

9 *Ibid.*, 545–546.   10 *Ibid.*, 543.

11 W. E. Smith, *Blair Family*, II, 69; F. P. Blair, Jr. to Montgomery Blair, Aug. 29, 1861, Blair MSS.

12 Same to same, undated, Blair MSS.

13 S. M. Wilson to Yates, Springfield, Ill., Sep. 30, 1861, Yates MSS.

14 F. P. Blair, Jr. to Montgomery Blair, undated (about August 1861), Blair MSS.

15 E. B. Washburne to S. P. Chase, Oct. 31, 1861 (typewritten copy filed among photostats of Trumbull MSS., Ill. Hist. Survey, Univ. of Ill.).

16 *Ibid.*   17 S. S. to F. A. Dick, St. Louis, Sep. 3, 1861, Blair MSS.

18 *Ibid.*   19 *Offic. Rec.*, 1 ser., III, 540–549.

sordid details. A contract was granted without competitive bidding to a California friend to build thirty-eight mortar boats at $8250 each, though an experienced builder stated that the cost would not exceed $4927. Another Californian, a special friend of Frémont with no knowledge of military engineering, was paid $191,000 to build forts at St. Louis, this being "about three times what they should have cost." [20] It was found that the forts were useless and the secretary of war ordered their construction stopped; nevertheless the lucrative work was pushed to completion. In purchasing tents, horses, mules, and all kinds of supplies, huge commissions were taken by middlemen for inferior products. "The most stupendous contracts [so read the official report], involving an almost unprecedented waste of public money, were given out by him [Frémont] in person to favorites, over the heads of the competent and honest officers appointed by law." [21]

Of the personal results of this Missouri muddle the most distressing was the feud between the Frémonts and the Blairs, whose previous close friendship and intimacy turned into enmity and hostile intrigue. At one stage in the imbroglio Lincoln sent Postmaster General Montgomery Blair "as a friend" to St. Louis,[22] with the Quartermaster General, M. C. Meigs,[23] whereupon Mrs. Frémont, daughter of the illustrious Thomas Hart Benton, traveled to Washington, interviewed the President, and proceeded to set him right in the matter of emancipation. As the plot thickened Frank Blair, Jr. loomed as rival of Frémont for Unionist leadership and military glory in Missouri. When the rivalry was carried forward in the newspapers an anti-Frémont editor was arrested; finally Frémont clapped Blair himself in jail for insubordination. In hot retaliation Blair drew up a convincing list of charges and specifications against the Pathfinder, stressing lack of help at Lexington, failure to suppress guerrillas, employment of incompetents, defiance of the President, and "conduct un-

---

[20] *House Exec. Doc. No. 94*, 37 Cong., 2 sess., pp. 17–18, 25–26. Undue emphasis in Frémont's defense has sometimes been placed upon the so-called investigation and report on his case by the congressional committee on the conduct of the war, but the Jacobin slant, gross unfairness, and radical prejudice of that committee are too well known for its judgments to carry much weight. See Williams, *Lincoln and the Radicals*, 278–279. Williams writes: "The inquisitors applied liberal daubs of whitewash to the episodes in his [Frémont's] career which shrieked of inefficiency, and commended lavishly . . . his . . . grasping the need for an emancipation proclamation before the president did" (*ibid.*, 279).

[21] *House Exec. Doc. No. 94*, 37 Cong., 2 sess., p. 34.

[22] *Works*, VI, 354 (Sep. 12, 1861).   [23] Nicolay and Hay, *Lincoln*, IV, 413.

becoming an officer and a gentleman." [24] Blair was soon released, but the Blair-Frémont feud continued unabated.

VIII

Agitation for and against Frémont was more than a matter of intrigue and ambition. It was a thunderous tempest that shook the country and seriously endangered the administration. To William Lloyd Garrison it seemed that if Lincoln was 6 feet 4 inches high, he was "only a dwarf in mind." [1] A Connecticut friend wrote to Welles after talking with gentlemen from Ohio, Indiana, Illinois, and Michigan: "They unanimously condemn the President's letter [2] [overruling Frémont] & as unanimously approve of Frémont's Proclamation." [3] Another correspondent of Welles wrote: "It is very easy for Mr Lincoln to make a record against the Pathfinder but another Benton will arise and set the ball in motion—to end in another expunging process. It is said that we must consult the border states . . . . Now with all due respect . . . , permit me to say *damn* the border states. . . . A thousand Lincolns and Sewards cannot stop the people from fighting slavery. . . . Perhaps it is thought that there are no more John Browns." [4] Gustave Koerner, prominent German-American of Illinois, disapproved of Lincoln's challenge to a man so popular as Frémont. Warning that the Blair faction was "determined to break down General Frémont," he admonished that the removal of the general would be "disastrous" and would almost "produce a Revolution . . . in our ranks." "The Blairs," he added, "are . . . implacable, and . . . [are supported] . . . by the quasi-Union-Neutrality, secession factions of the Country. Unless we counteract them by strong efforts they may succeed. . . . Frémont is no politician. . . . He is impetuous . . . ." [5]

[24] MS. in Blair papers, Library of Congress, undated. The charges were to be laid before the President. This manuscript is in a clerk's hand; it bears the name, not the autograph, of Frank P. Blair, Jr. On the Frémont-Blair imbroglio see also New York *Times*, Oct. 7, 1861, p. 1, cc. 4–6.

[1] W. L. Garrison to Oliver Johnson, Oct. 7, 1861, Garrison MSS.

[2] See above, p. 18.

[3] E. H. Owen to Gideon Welles, Hartford, Sep. 20, 1861, MS., Ill. State Hist. Lib.

[4] Gen. J. R. Hawley to Gideon Welles, New Haven, Sep. 17, 1861, MS., Ill. State Hist. Lib.

[5] Gustave Koerner to Yates, Hq., Western Department, St. Louis, Sep. 18, 1861, Yates MSS.

It was one of those overwrought moments in American democracy when people take sides emotionally and when everyone is a partisan on one side or the other. Even the conservative Browning of Illinois wrote a severe letter criticizing the President for taking issue with Frémont.[6] Concerning this epistle Lincoln wrote: ". . . coming from you, I confess it astonishes me"; this was the equivalent of saying that Browning was rightly a conservative and that, by his background and connections, he ought to have understood the border. With care and at some length Lincoln answered Browning, showing that Frémont's proclamation as to confiscation and emancipation was "purely political and not within the range of military law or necessity." These matters, said the President, "must be settled . . . by law-makers, and not by military proclamations. The proclamation . . . is simply 'dictatorship.' . . . But I cannot assume this reckless position, ..." Lincoln pointed out that the "Kentucky legislature would not budge till that proclamation was modified; . . . on the news of General Frémont having actually issued deeds of manumission, a whole company of our volunteers threw down their arms and disbanded." The President also showed the highly dangerous possibilities of letting Frémont "shoot men under the proclamation." [7] That Frémont was exploiting abolitionist impatience for his own political purposes in the anti-Lincoln sense was hinted, though not stated, in the President's letter; yet the very restraint associated with the President's office put him at a disadvantage in such a partisan agitation. The wide extent of Frémont's command must also be remembered. Such a matter as the seizure of Paducah and Columbus, for example, came under his jurisdiction. Grant, Pope, Sherman, McClernand, and others in the West, were under his orders. What went on in St. Louis was of broad importance.

Lincoln had shown great patience toward Frémont and had assured Mrs. Frémont that he was not animated by hostility toward the general.[8] He did not remove him because of the proclamation alone. That was serious enough, but the President had also to consider border-state resentment, the growing list of complaints against Frémont's regime, and the apparent impossibility of getting the general to right the situation himself. Lincoln took his time, considered both sides,

---

[6] Browning, *Diary*, I, 502 n. [7] *Works*, VI, 357–361 (Sep. 22, 1861).
[8] *Ibid.*, VI, 354 (Sep. 12, 1861).

or rather all sides, and finally removed the commander only when the Missouri situation had become virtually impossible. Before acting, Lincoln assembled and studied ample statements on the Frémont case, including a long report by General Thomas to the secretary of war.[9] Finally, on October 24, 1861, orders went out from Washington that David Hunter would "temporarily" relieve Frémont of the command of the Department of the West.[10] Even then, however, the delivery of this order was to be withheld if Frémont was engaged in battle, or "had fought and won a battle." On the same date Lincoln issued an order to Hunter as the new commander, with military instructions as to pursuing Price. Actual shift of command from Frémont to Hunter was effected on November 2, 1861. By that time Frémont had taken the field with his army; he was in southwestern Missouri advancing against Price. In a farewell to his men the deposed general expressed regret that he would not be there to lead them in the victory they were "about to win." [11]

IX

Various pleas in defense have been offered on Frémont's side. In his California career there had been the vindictive action of Stephen W. Kearny, leading to a severe court-martial decree, and there was the feeling that this episode exhibited an unfair attitude of West Point officers against army men who were not of the Academy. In the full and authoritative account by Allan Nevins it has been noted that "most historians have done less than justice to Frémont." [1] Nevins emphasizes the monumental difficulties of his command, when suddenly thrust into the newly created Western Department, "without organization, money, arms, or stores, without anything but raw recruits, . . . and compelled to deal with sedition at home as well as . . . enemies in the field." [2] "Beyond doubt," writes Nevins, "there was great waste and some corruption in St. Louis . . . ; but none of the corruption was Frémont's, and the waste was largely attributable to the War Department's own inefficiency." [3] Characteriz-

---

[9] See above, p. 19. [10] *Offic. Rec.*, 1 ser., III, 553. [11] *Ibid.*, 560.
[1] Allan Nevins, *Frémont, Pathmarker of the West*, 548. This one-volume work, published in 1939, supersedes the earlier two-volume work by Nevins. It is a most readable new study, with additional material, remodeled narrative, and fresh appraisal.
[2] *Ibid.*, 548. [3] *Ibid.*, 627.

ing Frémont's personality, Nevins observes "a disproportion between his ardent imagination, and his mediocre grasp of practical means to achieve the goal he so vividly saw . . . ." [4] As to the President's action, Nevins concludes: "Unquestionably, Lincoln did wisely in removing Frémont," but he adds: "Nevertheless, . . . observers in Missouri believed then and always that he had acted, not merely with high patriotism, but with sagacity and efficiency." [5]

It had taken Lincoln much longer to come to the point of displacing Frémont than to reach an estimate concerning the man's qualities. As early as September 9, 1861, he had written: "General Frémont . . . is losing the confidence of men near him, whose support any man in his position must have to be successful. His cardinal mistake is that he isolates himself and allows nobody to see him, . . . by which he does not know what is going on in the very matter he is dealing with." [6]

There were many who agreed with Washburne that the government had ample reason to check Frémont and his "horde of pirates." To many also it would have been distasteful for Frémont to have become the Zachary Taylor, or perhaps one should say the General Grant, of the war. All along the border and the lower Middle West resentment against Frémont was burning fiercely. More vociferous and vocal, however, was the torrent of applause for Frémont and abuse of the President for removing him. According to the New York *Independent* the "great mass of earnest, thinking men" sided with the general, while the "tricksters, the old fogies, . . . and the Secessionists" opposed him. [7] A Missouri admirer of Sumner wrote that the modification of Frémont's proclamation was "one of the many great errors of the President." [8] The same writer considered that the episode had made the general "much more dear to the people" and had "shaken confidence in the Government." [9] Denouncing the President's disposition "to kill off Fremont," a Michigan citizen wrote that Lincoln and his cabinet "have already or intend betraying the trust placed in their hands." [10] Sympathy for Frémont was lengthily voiced by a writer to the New York *Times*, who considered the general a vic-

---

4 *Ibid.*, 618.   5 *Ibid.*, 543.
6 Lincoln to General David Hunter, Sep. 9, 1861, *Works*, VI, 352.
7 *The Independent*, Sep. 26, 1861, p. 1, c. 6.
8 Thomas O'Reilly to Sumner, St. Louis, Oct. 27, 1861, Sumner MSS.
9 Same to same, Nov. 22, 1861, *ibid.*
10 T. P. Dunham to Sumner, Kalamazoo, Nov. 4, 1861, *ibid.*

tim of conspiracy, ramifying widely and extending to Washington, for the overthrow of "that energetic commander." He particularly stressed the fact that Frémont "possesses such a knowledge of the human character that he would not take into his confidence and give his plans to one who might betray them to the War Department, to go thence directly through the newspapers to the enemy." [11] When in late October, 1861, the Pennsylvania Anti-Slavery Society met at West Chester, Lincoln's treatment of Frémont was denounced and the President was compared to Pharaoh.[12] Such denunciation was an abolitionist *cliché*.

From this point the name of Frémont, along with that of Benjamin F. Butler, became a focus for radical attack upon the harassed President, while generals who were favored or kept in command by the President, McClellan especially, were by-words of radical denunciation. Though ill informed, such denunciation bore the fervid quality of righteous unction. It was the Anna E. Dickinsons, the Wendell Phillipses of the land who took up the pro-Frémont slogans. To them the whole war was viewed not only as a holy war against slavery but as a crusade against Southerners as wicked persons. For their inherent wickedness and for the centuries they had held the Negro in bondage these rebels of the South were to be punished. When Lincoln refused or omitted to do so, he was associated with "rebels," with the "traitorous" McClellan, with slave catchers. To such critics the President did nothing right. Even his handling of the *Trent* affair was denounced as weak bungling. Pulled at from right and left till he was nearly torn apart, the conservative Lincoln, President of the dis-United States, found among his own Republicans almost a greater vexation than among those of the opposite party, or even among enemies in arms.

X

Some concept of the difficulty of Lincoln's position can be had by noting the matters that pressed upon him at the turn of that year,

---

[11] Letter to Adjutant General Thomas from "An Impartial Reader," New York *Times*, Nov. 7, 1861, p. 2, c. 3–4.

[12] *National Anti-Slavery Standard*, Nov. 2, 1861, quoted in James Harvey Young, "Anna Elizabeth Dickinson and the Civil War" (ms. doctoral dissertation, Univ. of Ill., 1941), chap. 1. The same author has given a vivid account of this amazing girl orator and antislavery firebrand in *Miss. Vall. Hist. Rev.*, XXXI, 59–80 (June, 1944).

1861–62. Congress met and the Jacobins of Congress ominously whetted their blades. The affair of the *Trent,* with its appalling menace of war with Britain, was at the acute stage. English Tories and French aristocrats were persistently misunderstanding America and abusing its chief. An annual message to Congress, Lincoln's first, had to be prepared. Sinews of war had to be provided. A national military policy was yet to be devised. Troublesome aspects of the slavery question, including military emancipation, the use of Negro soldiers, and the treatment of fugitive slaves, could not much longer be evaded. Overdue appointments were awaiting the President's action, with three vacancies, for example, on the Supreme Court. Meanwhile, with a formidable enemy encamped near Washington, the secretary of war was about to be removed for good reason, while the head of the army (McClellan) was ill and could not be "disturbed with business." [1] "Since he had never delegated his powers," writes his biographer, "work at the headquarters of the army was paralyzed by his absence," while in the field a coördinating staff service was lacking.[2]

Not all these matters, nor the most serious of them, were treated in Lincoln's message of December 3, 1861. Comment on fundamentals was unsatisfactorily combined with miscellaneous departmental recommendations. What the President said about Haiti and Liberia, about the court of claims, patents, warfare against pirates, the land office, the international exhibition to be held at London, and the newly organized territories (Colorado, Dakota, and Nevada), can be passed over. On more critical matters he spoke confidently, though with no concealment of hard realities. Foreign nations, he thought, would not give the aid and comfort for which the enemies of the Union hoped. Even from the standpoint of commerce and self interest it seemed to him that governments abroad would prefer one strong nation on these shores rather than "the same nation broken in hostile fragments." Reviewing the war situation he found his chief encouragement on the border, where developments in Maryland, Kentucky, and Missouri were favorable to the Union side. Those three states, he said, while promising not a soldier at first, had sent no less than 40,000 men into the field for the Union, while in western Virginia the President was pleased to note that the winter found Union loving people masters of their own country. With footings ob-

---

[1] *Works,* VII, 70 (Jan. 1, 1862).   [2] Myers, *McClellan,* 228.

tained on the Southern coast the Union cause was advancing south-ward.

As to army command the President mentioned that McClellan was "in considerable degree" the choice of the country. This was faint praise, but even this much was hedged when the President added that one bad general was better than two good ones, and that if a ship is in a storm it may go down because "no single mind" is allowed to control. After ranging widely over many topics, Lincoln closed on the theme of popular government, the danger of despotism, and the superior claim of labor above capital. Predicting a nation of two hundred and fifty million souls within the lifetime of men then living, he reasoned that the "struggle of to-day is not altogether for to-day—it is for a vast future also." But this future was to be en-visaged in terms of "the popular principle, applied to government, through the machinery of the States and the Union . . . ."[3]

By the wonder of telegraphy the "7,578 words" of the message were received in New York in one hour and thirty-two minutes.[4] To the *Times* it seemed that the document showed "plain, clear common sense," being "written in the vigorous, compact and unostentatious style . . . characteristic of the President."[5] The *Herald* likewise considered it a "plain, concise, unpretending, business-like exposi-tion."[6] Not so William Lloyd Garrison. "What a wish-washy message from the President," he wrote. "It is . . . evident that he is a man of very small calibre, and had better be at his old business of splitting rails . . . . He has evidently not a drop of anti-slavery blood in his veins; . . . ."[7] "Not *one single manly, bold, dignified* position taken . . . but a . . . timid, timeserving, commonplace sort of an abor-tion of a message, cold enough . . . to *freeze* h-ll over," wrote a lesser abolitionist.[8] French journals read the message to imply that Lincoln considered war with Britain inevitable.[9] In Britain the na-tion's thought was so absorbed in the death of Prince Albert that the message received comparatively little attention, but the London *Herald* railed at Lincoln's "inexcusable" "*if not insulting, language*

[3] *Works*, VII, 28–60.   [4] New York *Times*, Dec. 4, 1861, p. 5, c. 1.
[5] *Ibid.*, Dec. 4, 1861, p. 4, cc. 2–3.   [6] New York *Herald*, Dec. 4, 1861, p. 6, c. 3.
[7] W. L. Garrison to Oliver Johnson, Boston, Dec. 6, 1861, Garrison MSS.
[8] S. York to Lyman Trumbull, Paris, Ill., Dec. 5, 1861, Trumbull MSS.
[9] Quotations from French newspapers as found in New York *Herald*, Jan. 3, 1862, p. 2, c. 5.

[which] *can only . . . apply to France and England,*" warning that
Lincoln must back down, else a war would follow which would an-
nihilate his country.[10] As if such pointless criticisms were not enough,
the President had to deal with advisers at home, even in his cabinet,
who doubted his ability to lead. On the last day of the year 1861 the
Attorney General wrote in his diary: "The Prest. is an excellent man,
. . . but he lacks *will* and *purpose,* and, I greatly fear he, has not *the
power to command.*" [11]

---

[10] Extracts from London *Herald* in New York *Herald,* Jan. 1, 1862, p. 2, c. 3. This
London paper was characterized by the New York *Herald* as the Derby organ of aristocrats and oligarchists (*ibid.*).
[11] Bates, *Diary,* 220.

CHAPTER XVI

A SEA OF TROUBLES

I

IN THE international domain it appears that few presidents have done less—i. e., performed fewer obvious presidential acts—than Lincoln. In comparison with Woodrow Wilson, or Theodore Roosevelt, or Franklin Roosevelt, Lincoln's activity in the realm of diplomacy was slight. Yet if one subtracts from American international dealings those touches that were peculiarly Lincoln's own, the difference becomes so significant that his contribution must be regarded as a sizable factor. Lincoln did not have much time to take his international soundings before the sailing became stormy and hazardous. Diplomacy was Seward's province. Lincoln was content that it should be so, but in the first phase of his administration and the early months of the war Lincoln showed not only sounder judgment than Seward, but, which is essential in an executive, the will to use that judgment, albeit without destroying Seward's usefulness.[1]

While painfully occupied with the Sumter crisis, Lincoln received from his foreign secretary a confidential paper which might well have served as sufficient reason for dismissing that official. Bluntly indicating that the administration was "without a policy," Seward proceeded to supply one. At home he would evacuate Sumter, but keep and defend the Gulf ports. Then he would demand explanations from Spain and France (on matters that had in no way reached, or approached, a

---

[1] For Lincoln's foreign problems one should consult Frank L. Owsley, *King Cotton Diplomacy* (closely devoted to the Confederate side); Ephraim Douglass Adams, *Great Britain and the American Civil War;* Jay Monaghan, *Diplomat in Carpet Slippers.* The work by Monaghan is a recent vivid treatment that emphasizes Lincoln. See also Martin P. Claussen, *The United States and Great Britain, 1861–1865: Peace Factors in International Relations* (abstract of thesis, Univ. of Ill., 1938); J. G. Randall, "Lincoln and John Bright," *Yale Rev.,* XXXIV, 292–304 (Dec., 1944).

crisis). He would demand these explanations categorically, at once! If the explanations were not satisfactory, he would convene Congress, and declare war! He would also seek an explanation from Great Britain and Russia, and would marshal on this side of the Atlantic a "vigorous . . . spirit of independence . . . against European intervention."

Whatever policy was adopted, it must be "somebody's business," said Seward, to direct it. Either the President must do it himself, "and be all the while active in it," or he must devolve it upon some cabinet member. Once a policy was determined, debate must end. Significantly the "premier" added: ". . . I neither seek to evade nor assume responsibility." [2]

Perhaps the kindest way to treat this amazing document, aside from noting its date (April 1), is to observe that its proposals never proceeded beyond the tentative stage, and that the history of Seward's diplomatic accomplishments could be written without even mentioning this fool's-day aberration. The secretary took no outward action in the terms of his "Thoughts for the President's Consideration." Foreign nations were not confronted with preposterous demands. Reason did not so rashly desert the state department. Next day and thereafter Seward was a reasonably normal person. If later he was to return (as on May 21) to his April illusion that European war had to result from the American situation and that such war would reunite the sections, the acute form of the illusion was definitely past.[3]

Before dismissing the subject, however, it is significant to note how Lincoln received this eccentric communication. In the first place, he protected his government, and his secretary too, by keeping the

---

[2] "Some Thoughts for the President's Consideration" [memorandum by Seward], April 1, 1861, Nicolay and Hay, *Lincoln*, III, 445–447. Evidently found among the President's papers after his death, this memorandum has been produced only by Nicolay and Hay. So far, their biography and their edition of Lincoln's works are the only traceable sources for the document. It is hardly to be supposed that they invented it or were misled by a forged document, and historians have accepted it as genuine. There is no corroboration, however, in the Seward papers.

[3] For a historical analysis of Seward's "Thoughts" see Frederic Bancroft, "Seward's Proposition of April 1, 1861 . . . ," 99 *Harper's Mo.*, 781–791 (1899). Bancroft shows how Seward, assuming in the winter of 1860–61 the function of saving the country, labored under strange illusions—e. g., that restoration of the Union would be promoted by a foreign war. The authenticity of the "Thoughts" is not questioned by Bancroft.

matter secret. His private secretaries, the sole agents in giving the document to the world, assert that "the affair never reached the knowledge of any other member of the Cabinet." [4] At the same time, without losing a day, the President sent a reply in which courteous patience was perfectly balanced by that firmness of which the pliable Lincoln was at times capable. He made it clear that the administration did have a foreign policy as displayed in circulars and instructions to ministers, and a domestic policy as announced in his own inaugural address. Then, with a dignity befitting the nation's elected chief who could not delegate final responsibility, Lincoln wrote: ". . . I remark that if this must be done [directing a policy], I must do it." [5] This carried no rebuke and had no apparent effect on the personal friendship of the two men; probably the matter was never "again alluded to by either Lincoln or Seward." [6] In a quiet episode of which the nation knew nothing the President had made it crystal clear that Seward was no "premier" and Lincoln no rubber stamp. What Lincoln may have thought about the matter was kept under his hat. Not a needless syllable was uttered. Nothing, probably, was said orally and face to face. Yet from that April day Lincoln was not only President but Chief; he was treated and recognized as such. Already, as in the Sumter affair, harm had been done by Seward's officious negotiation behind Lincoln's back. From this point there was less backstair diplomacy, while on vital matters there was on Lincoln's part at least a salutary minimum of attention to the wording of foreign despatches. Both in executive control and in international dealings the secret incident of the "Thoughts" had important consequences; to the biographer of Lincoln it has significance as a revelation of strength of personality combined with gentlemanly dealing.

II

As the foreign relations of Lincoln, Seward, and Company unfolded, they became enmeshed in a remarkable series of episodes, of which the most serious seemed to approach catastrophic proportions. At London Charles Francis Adams, Lincoln's chosen minister, represented the best of American statesmanship, while Lord John (later

---

[4] Nicolay and Hay, *Lincoln*, III, 449.   [5] *Ibid.*, III, 448–449.   [6] *Ibid.*, III, 449.

Earl) Russell, British foreign secretary, with whom Adams had to deal, was a reasonable man whose readiness to understand the United States was a factor of importance. Yet the upper class in England tended toward sympathy with the Southern cause, and Her Majesty's prime minister Palmerston had a veritable penchant for intervention in the affairs of distant nations. From what he saw and heard, Adams was led to feel that among aristocratic Englishmen there was a strong desire "to see the United States go to pieces." [1] Though British statesmen would seek to conceal the fact, Adams thought they distrusted the American Union as "an overbearing and powerful democracy." [2] As for the Tories, there is little doubt that they wanted the American national experiment to fail. This, in general, was the attitude of the London Clubs; much of the conversation that floated around in excusive circles would be in this vein. Such also was the tone of that influential but arrogant paper, the *Times* of London.

Lord Lyons, British minister at Washington, did not adequately take Lincoln's measure, nor Seward's either. During the campaign of 1860 he had referred to Lincoln as "a rough Farmer—who began life as a Farm Labourer—and got on by a talent for stump speaking." [3] He distrusted Lincoln and his party; yet he felt that loud Republican protests against England may have been partly to counteract the suspicions aroused by Anglo-American sympathy on the slavery question. [4] Cobden, later a conspicuous friend of the Union, prayed in March 1861 for a peaceful dissolution of the Union without bloodshed, though seeing no political leader who could have the "courage" to advocate it. Of the new President he wrote: "Lincoln whom I saw at Springfield, is a backwoodsman of good sturdy common sense, but . . . unequal to the occasion." [5] Of Seward he said: "He is a sort of Brummagen Palmerston always talking in a low cunning way to *Bunkum*." [6] Even Bright regarded Seward as "capricious." [7] Earl Rus-

---

[1] W. C. Ford, ed., *A Cycle of Adams Letters*, I, 220.

[2] C. F. Adams to Edward Everett, London, July 12, 1861, Everett MSS.

[3] Lyons to Russell (private), July 23, 1860, Russell Papers, G. D. 22/34, MSS., Public Record Office (London).

[4] *Ibid.*

[5] Cobden to Bright, Mar. 25, 1861, Cobden MSS. (Add. MSS. 43649), British Museum.

[6] Cobden to William Slagg, Dec. 19, 1861, typescript copy, Cobden MSS. (Add. MSS. 43677, pt. 2), British Museum.

[7] Bright to Cobden, Oct. 3, 1861, Bright MSS. (Add. MSS. 43383, pt. 8), British Museum.

sell so far misjudged Lincoln that he could think him capable of "getting up war cries to help his declining popularity." [8] Early in 1861 Russell could write: "President Lincoln looming in the distance is a still greater peril than President Buchanan." [9] At the time of the Sumter crisis he feared that Lincoln would use force, by which he would "clinch the separation, but injure trade . . . this year." [10]

Francis Lieber's observation was that all the foreign ministers in Washington with the exception of the Russian, inclined to the South. Coining the phrase "Le Pouvoir Dinatoire," he thought Southern members of Congress had "used the Dinatory Power much better than the Northern Congressmen." [11] Americans in England did little to help their cause. Adams wrote: "Even intelligent Americans are quoted here as talking about the right to dissolve the partnership just as if we were a mere trading firm." [12] From quite a different quarter Americans were causing British apprehension by advocating the acquisition of Mexican territory. Edward Bates feared that such schemes would alienate the sympathy of the British middle class, represented by Mr. Bright, whose attitude was friendly and who were able "to check even the ministers of the crown." [13]

The very existence of war and the necessity of carrying it on by war measures, involved international complications. Such a policy as the blockade of Southern ports, proclaimed by Lincoln on April 19 and April 27,[14] produced a crop of legalistic objections. President Jefferson Davis denounced it as a "mere paper blockade" which "could only have been published under the sudden influence of passion," [15] while abroad it raised at once the question of international legality. Under the recent Declaration of Paris of 1856, a blockade, to be binding, had to be effective, and there was doubt at the time whether such effectiveness existed. Though the United States was not a signatory of the Declaration of Paris, this matter of effectiveness was always

8 Russell to Lyons (private), Mar. 28, 1863 (copy), Russell Papers, G. D. 22/97, MSS., Public Record Office (London).

9 Russell to Lyons (private), Feb. 16, 1861 (copy), Russell Papers, G. D. 22/96, MSS., ibid.

10 Russell to Lyons, April 20, 1861, ibid.

11 Francis Lieber to S. B. Ruggles, May 24, 1861, Lieber MSS.

12 C. F. Adams to Edward Everett, London, July 26, 1861, Everett MSS.

13 Bates, Diary, 193 (Aug. 27, 1861).   14 Works, VI, 248–250, 256–257.

15 Message of President Davis to the Confederate Congress, April 29, 1861, Journal, Confed. Cong. (Sen. Doc. No. 234, 58 [U. S.] Cong., 2 sess.), I, 166.

considered in the international discussion of the subject. The double
nature of the war as a conflict between belligerents (each government
having recognition of belligerency) and at the same time an internal
problem of putting down insurrectionists conspiring (so it was said)
to overthrow their own government, was the cause of constant difficulty, and led to a situation where foreign statesmen, in referring
to the conflict, might use a different language than that of the Lincoln
administration.[16]

This difference of language came into view when the United
States government protested against the very idea of "neutrality"
abroad. In the Queen's proclamation (issued on May 13, 1861, "the
day Adams reached London, and before he had time to call at the
Foreign Office")[17] the British government cast the official mold in
which its main policy toward the American question was to be shaped.
Throughout the war it deemed itself a neutral between the United
States and the Confederate States. This ultimately was to disappoint
the latter much more than the former, besides setting the pattern for
substantial reparation to the Washington government in the course
of time; but when it was issued the British neutrality announcement,
quite natural considering the size and importance of the Southern
de facto government, was the theme of frequent complaint on the
part of Seward, to whom the proclamation seemed "designed to raise
the insurgents to the level of a belligerent state,"[18] while according
to the state department at Washington, the Confederate government
was a "pretended new State . . . existing in pronunciamento
only."[19] It is true that Lincoln himself, in his blockade order, had
virtually recognized the belligerent character of the Confederate
government, as did the courts of the United States.[20] It is also true
that in conducting semi-official communication with Southern agents
the British government was careful to explain that such communication did "not imply any acknowledgment of the confederates as
an independent state."[21] Remembering the non-application by the
United States of the piracy or traitor theory of Southern status (in

---

[16] Randall, *Constitutional Problems Under Lincoln*, ch. iii.

[17] Bancroft, *Seward*, II, 176.

[18] Seward to Adams, June 8, 1861, *Sen. Doc. No. 1*, 37 Cong., 2 sess., p. 101.

[19] *Works*, VI, 282 (May 21, 1861). Seward's statement.

[20] Randall, *Constitutional Problems Under Lincoln*, 72.

[21] Russell to C. F. Adams, Nov. 26, 1861, *House Exec. Doc. No. 1*, 37 Cong., 3 sess., p. 9.

other words, the non-prosecution of Southern individuals as insurgents), it is now realized that the attitude of the British government on this point did not differ vitally from that of Washington. The variance was intangible; it was a matter of status. Serious difference, on the other hand, did exist between London and Richmond; the Confederacy urged intervention as well as full international recognition, which neither Britain nor any other foreign country gave.

As a kind of initial keynote for Anglo-American wartime relations, the secretary of state, on May 21, 1861, directed to Adams a paper designated as "Despatch no. 10" which has also been called Seward's "bold remonstrance." This paper has special interest as one of the few examples of Lincoln's editing of his government's international correspondence. All that Lincoln did was to go over Seward's words, changing a phrase here and deleting one there, but by these touches he transformed a bellicose and threatening despatch that might well have caused serious offense into a restrained instruction intended for Minister Adams's confidential guidance. In Seward's draft there was the comment that British intercourse with Confederate commissioners, even though unofficial, was injurious to the United States; then came the drastic admonition that Adams "desist from all intercourse whatever, unofficial as well as official, with the British government, so long as it shall continue intercourse of either kind with the domestic enemies of this country."

The President examined the despatch. Seward had written: "The President is surprised and grieved that Mr. Dallas [minister to Great Britain preceding Mr. Adams] did not protest against the proposed unofficial intercourse between the British Government and the missionaries of the insurgents as well as against the demand for explanations made by the British government." Instead of the words "is surprised and grieved" Lincoln substituted "regrets." Then he deleted the whole reference to the British demand with the comment: "Leave out, because it does not appear that such explanations were demanded." Where Seward remarked that British intercourse with the Confederate commissioners "would be none the less wrongful to us for being called unofficial," Lincoln struck out the accusing word "wrongful" and substituted "hurtful." Identifying the possibility of British recognition with intervention, Seward had written: ". . . we from that hour shall cease to be friends and become once more, as we have twice before been forced to be, enemies of Great Britain." Drawing a line around this truculent passage, Lincoln wrote simply: "Leave out." "If Great Britain . . . shall . . . recognize them," wrote Seward, "and give them shelter . . . , the laws of nations afford an adequate . . . remedy and we shall avail ourselves of it." Lincoln closed the sentence with the word "remedy"; the threatening conclusion was omitted.[22]

But Lincoln's chief suggestion was at the end of the despatch which in the Seward draft contained two wordy paragraphs of admonition dwelling upon the danger of war, putting the blame upon the British, accusing Britain of provoking the revolution, and warning "that nation" not to "repeat the . . . error." At the beginning of this warlike passage Lincoln wrote: "Drop all from this line to the end, and . . . write, 'This paper is for your own guidance only, and not [to] be read or shown to any one.' "

Instead of issuing the despatch in every particular as emended by Lincoln, Seward, with a good deal less than the clear brevity of Lincoln's words, added an introductory statement that the paper was not to be read or shown to Russell, though its spirit was to be Adams's guide; then he retained the final passage which Lincoln had wisely directed him to delete.[23] In Seward's eyes the confidential nature of the paper made this deletion unnecessary. Yet all this bellicose and rhetorical language was out of place when addressed confidentially to Adams; it was meaningless unless intended for the British government. Seward's retention of the passage which Lincoln had asked him to drop seemed to indicate a fondness for the products of his own brain and a partial unwillingness to be governed by the President's leadership. This, fortunately, did not dissipate the importance of Lincoln's

---

[22] This study of Seward's despatch with Lincoln's handwritten emendations is based on a photostat copy among the manuscripts in the Library of Congress. J. C. Bancroft Davis, assistant secretary of state, found the document in the files of the state department in 1869, whereupon Secretary of State Hamilton Fish showed it to President Grant, who authorized the making of twenty photographic copies which were distributed to high officials. The negative was then destroyed. (The original is no longer in the archives of the state department.) In 1886, over the disapproval of Mr. Fish, the *North American Review* (CXLII, 410–411) published a reduced facsimile, taken from the photographic copy belonging to Benjamin H. Bristow of the Grant cabinet. For a printed reproduction of Seward's draft with Lincoln's changes, see *Works*, VI, 277–286.

[23] For Seward's emended despatch as sent to C. F. Adams, May 21, 1861, see *Sen. Exec. Doc. No. 1*, 37 Cong., 2 sess., pp. 87–90.

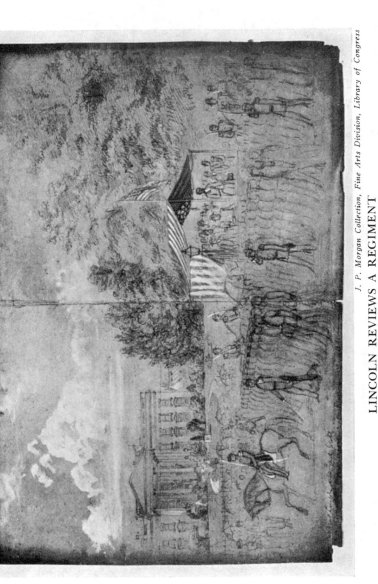

J. P. Morgan Collection, Fine Arts Division, Library of Congress

LINCOLN REVIEWS A REGIMENT

President Lincoln and General Scott review a three-years regiment on Pennsylvania Avenue in 1861. Large pencil sketch, intended as basis for a finished drawing. Under a flag covering Lincoln stands while the aged Scott sits. The marching ranks, the faint suggestion of spectators with women holding parasols, the sun glint on the swords, and the White House with its conservatory in the background under summer clouds, bring the scene to life without needless detail.

James M. Mason of Virginia, Confederate Envoy to Britain

John Slidell of Louisiana, Confederate Envoy to France

revision. That revision had its immediate and continuing effect. Lincoln's influence in this bit of diplomacy had been more than that of advice or suggestion; it had carried through to the actual shaping of international intercourse.

III

As the year 1861 drew to a close the stormy Atlantic resounded to the thunders of a fearful Anglo-American crisis when two diplomats of the Confederacy, en route to foreign posts, were seized by a naval officer of the United States. This exploit was performed by Captain Charles Wilkes of the warship *San Jacinto* who had stopped the British steamer *Trent* and had arrested James M. Mason on his way to Britain, and John Slidell accredited to France. The diplomats, with their secretaries, were triumphantly brought to the United States and held as state prisoners in Fort Warren, Boston Harbor. Though the Blairs at once denounced the act of Wilkes,[1] Welles expressed approval of his conduct,[2] and in the House of Representatives opposing factions joined in voting a "high sense" of the captain's "good conduct."[3] Edward Everett, formerly secretary of state and minister to Britain, joined with Caleb Cushing, former attorney general, in praising Wilkes,[4] whose action was loudly applauded in the Northern press. Though the seizure occurred on November 8, it was not until nearly three weeks later (November 27), that word of it reached England. The news found Charles Francis Adams absent in Yorkshire on a social visit. Notified of the event by telegram he returned to London, full of "anxiety for the fate" of his "unhappy country."[5]

There is no denying that a miserable war threat resulted from this sensational affair. It was, perhaps, a small incident; yet, as viewed abroad, it seemed an affront to the British flag, a violation of the law of nations, and a deliberate American effort to provoke war. This

[1] Smith, *Blair Family*, II, 194.

[2] ". . . I congratulate you on the great public service you have rendered in the capture of the rebel commissioners . . . . Your conduct . . has the emphatic approval of this Department." Secretary Welles to Captain Wilkes, Nov. 30, 1861, Moore, *Rebellion Record* (Docs.), III, 330.

[3] *Cong. Globe*, 37 Cong., 2 sess., 5.

[4] S. F. Bemis, ed., *American Secretaries of State*, VII, 63; Caleb Cushing to Fernando Wood, New York *Times*, Dec. 18, 1861, p. 6, cc. 3–5.

[5] Despatches nos. 80 and 81, C. F. Adams to Seward, London, Nov. 29, 1861, Dipl. Despatches (England, vol. 78), MSS., Dep. of State, Nat. Archives.

latter aspect was the serious factor. The incident was associated in British governmental minds with the conviction that Seward had been "acting with the desire of occasioning a war between the two countries . . . ." [6] From England it was privately reported that a foreign office employee had said at a dinner party that "it was the purpose of the Brittish [sic] government to have a war with us & that Lord Palmerston wanted to bring it on at once while we . . . [were] unprepared." [7] It "makes me sad," wrote one of Sumner's friends from Cardiff, "to see how many English presses are hot for war." [8] "This [the British] government expects—and I fear, welcomes war . . . [and] chooses its own time to strike . . . ," wrote Thurlow Weed from London. [9] "England is rampant," he wrote, "and France excited by the capture of Mason and Slidell. Everybody here expects war. An artificial . . . sentiment . . . has been . . . worked up against us. . . . London and Paris are full of noisy, adroit secessionists." [10]

The incident had brought into focus the main grievance against England—i. e., the reputed intention to interfere in the Civil War. The "first step toward interference in our domestic affairs," wrote John Jay, "will inaugurate war beyond all question." [11] Correspondence from London revealed such "bitterness and hostility" as to make it felt that Britain "must go to war." [12] Manchester was "intensely excited," with posters and "extra" papers dramatizing the crisis. [13] Journalists on both sides sensationally fanned the flames. The *Herald* of New York and the *Times* of London "seemed to be competing for a new high mark in jingo journalism." [14]

Speculation ranged widely as to probable developments in the expected war. Weed observed to Cameron that the Confederates wanted "us in war with England, that their ports may be opened and

---

[6] E. Twistleton to William Dwight (of Boston), London, Dec. 7, 1861, Sumner MSS.

[7] J. P. Usher to R. W. Thompson, Washington, Jan. 1, 1862, MS., Lincoln Nat. Life Foundation, Fort Wayne.

[8] Charles D. Cleveland to Sumner, Cardiff, Dec. 17, 1861, Sumner MSS.

[9] Thurlow Weed to Simon Cameron, London, Dec. 7, 1861, Cameron MSS.

[10] Weed to Cameron, Paris, Dec. 3, 1861, *ibid.*

[11] John Jay to Sumner, Nov. 8, 1861, Sumner MSS.

[12] Joseph Cooper to Sumner, London, Dec. 28, 1861, *ibid.*

[13] Henry W. Lord to Seward, Manchester, Nov. 27, 1861, Consular Letters (Manchester, vol. I), MSS., Dept. of State, Nat. Archives.

[14] Martin Paul Claussen, *The United States and Great Britain, 1861–1865: Peace Factors in International Relations* (abstract of doctoral dissertation, University of Illinois, 1938), 1.

ours closed." [15] Another of Cameron's informants wrote glibly from Paris that the United States had no escape from a war with England and that the British fleet was all set for an attack in three grand divisions: (1) to open Southern ports; (2) to attack ports of New Hampshire and Maine (these to be held as "indemnity"); (3) to enter the Chesapeake, seize Baltimore and Annapolis, combine with Southern military forces, capture Washington, and destroy the Federal army. [16]

That so many people placed so low a value upon international good will while every element of misunderstanding was absurdly inflated, seems at this distance almost incredible. Tenseness of feeling destroyed the pleasure of social intercourse. Soon after the *Trent* affair an Englishman friendly to the United States found himself at a large dinner party "disagreeably prominent as the only advocate of the North against numberless taunts." [17] When, during this crisis, a distinguished English geologist, Sir Charles Lyell, pleaded the cause of the American union among his countrymen, the more effectively because he and Lady Lyell had enjoyed warm friendship with certain planters of the South, "the contumely became so fierce, that for a while they [Sir Charles and his lady] kept aloof from society, as it was too much for a lady's strength to bear it." [18]

IV

When it came to formulating Britain's policy in the *Trent* case, Palmerston at first took a threatening attitude, and governmental steps were taken that bore the appearance of preparations for possible war. Eight thousand troops were sent to Canada; [1] in Confederate correspondence this force was represented as "10,000 picked troops" together with "immense war material." [2] Warships were fitted out, officers were ordered to be in readiness for embarkation, and orders were issued forbidding the export of saltpetre, gunpowder, and munitions. [3] Seward was informed by the American consul in Manchester

[15] Thurlow Weed to Simon Cameron, London, Dec. 7, 1861, Cameron MSS.

[16] M. Balch to Simon Cameron, Paris, Dec. 11, 1861, *ibid.*

[17] Francis W. Newman to Epes Sargent, London, Feb. 22, 1865, MS., Boston Public Lib.

[18] Same to same, London, April 26, 1865, *ibid.*

[1] Theodore Martin, *Life of . . . the Prince Consort*, V, 419 n.

[2] W. L. Yancey to R. M. T. Hunter, London, Dec. 31, 1861, *Offic. Rec.* (Nav.), 2 ser., III, 313.

[3] C. F. Adams to W. H. Seward, London, Dec. 6, 1861, Despatch No. 84, Dipl. Despatches (England, vol. 78), MSS., Dept. of State, Nat. Archives.

that military and naval preparations were "going on with the greatest energy" and that the "whole nation" seemed to be "completely aroused." [4] War feeling was high in Quebec and a military board in that city was active in preparing the provinces for an expected contest with the United States.[5] In these circumstances, while diplomacy moved slowly, rumor spread like an epidemic, and it was reported in London that at the time of the American tour of the Prince of Wales "Mr. Seward . . . [had told] the Duke of Newcastle he was likely to occupy a high office; that when he did so it would become his duty to insult England, and he should insult her accordingly." [6]

Yet on the other side there were factors of a conciliatory nature; these indeed deserve more study than threats and alarms. The Queen, remembering American kindness to her son, made appeals to her ministers for peace as she signed proclamations.[7] The feeling of high excitement, the intensity of which has not been exaggerated, belonged to the period of two or three weeks following the reception of the news in England. As days passed British sentiment improved and arbitration came to be spoken of favorably. Leading British liberals, notably Bright and Cobden, spoke courageously of peace—for it took courage—even while military preparations were in progress and war feeling was up. When Americans began to think it over, it was realized that Slidell and Mason would be "a million times less mischievous" in London than in Fort Warren,[8] and that a policy of caution was indicated by all the rules of prudence. The strength of the Confederate wish for war between the United States and England was in itself sufficient evidence that this was a thing for Lincoln to avoid. Above all, thoughtful people began to realize the supreme folly of a needless war with so formidable a naval power as Britain when the government was desperately engaged with the domestic enemy, and when the occasion of such a war would have put the United States in the equivocal position of opposing its own traditional policy of supporting neutral rights at sea. It was reported from Boston, for example, that the "almost universal opinion . . . among intelligent men" was that this country must not have war with England, that

[4] Henry W. Lord to W. H. Seward, Manchester, Dec. 5, 1861, Consular Letters (Manchester, vol. I), MSS., Dep. of State, Nat. Archives.

[5] New York *Times*, Jan. 1, 1862, p. 5, c. 1.

[6] Benson J. Lossing, *Pictorial History of the Civil War*, II, 162.

[7] Weed to Cameron, Dec. 7, 1861, Cameron MSS.   [8] *Ibid.*

the envoys should be given up even though it be in response to peremptory demand, and that mortified pride was nothing compared to "a divided empire and a devastating war." [9]

This feeling became stronger when the legal aspects of the controversy were studied. While Wilkes had the belligerent right to search the *Trent* and take it into port for adjudication (on such a matter as carrying contraband), his summary procedure in the arrest of the envoys at sea and their forcible removal from the deck of the British steamer amounted to arbitrary disregard of legal usage and essential rights. On the other hand, a graceful yielding by the United States, while accomplishing everything in the avoidance of war, would involve no loss of "face" or sacrifice of prestige, since Wilkes's act was entirely unauthorized by his government. American concession could even be reasonably construed as gaining a point on England, because the Washington government would be disavowing such an act as it had traditionally complained of in "impressment" days. This would be putting England in the wrong, yet magnanimously yielding for the sake of peace—[10] something like eating one's cake and having it too! As a writer in a Washington newspaper expressed it, the United States was "as much estopped from defending the act of Capt[ain] Wilkes as Great Britain from complaining of it." [11]

V

In steering his country through this imbroglio, Lincoln gave his chief thought to avoiding the folly of having, as he said, "two wars on his hands at a time." [1] Benson J. Lossing, the historian, who participated in an interview with the President on the subject, quoted him as saying: "I fear the traitors will prove to be white elephants. . . . If Great Britain . . . demands their release, we must give them up . . . and thus forever bind her over to keep the peace in relation to neutrals, and so acknowledge that she has been wrong for sixty years." [2] Opinion in the cabinet was conflicting and not particularly

[9] Horatio Woodman to Charles Sumner, Boston, Dec. 20, 1861, Sumner MSS.

[10] Charles D. Cleveland to Charles Sumner, Cardiff, Dec. 17, 1861, *ibid.*

[11] Washington *National Intelligencer*, Dec. 9, 1861.

[1] Lincoln was so quoted in a letter from R. M. Mason to Amos Lawrence, Jan. 14, 1861 [1862], Amos Lawrence MSS.

[2] Lossing, *Pictorial Hist. of the Civ. War*, II, 156–157.

helpful. Seward, as reported by Welles, "at first approved" Wilkes's act,[3] while, as already noted, Welles commended the captain in a letter of congratulation. (Later both Seward and Welles came around to the position that Wilkes's method of procedure was incorrect.) The attorney general misread the situation, thinking Wilkes's seizure of the men lawful and apprehending no danger from Britain.[4] More than a month after the incident Lincoln passed a remark to Browning that indicated he was not worried; [5] this, however, was before information had been received of the official British attitude. The rash view of Browning himself was that the seizure was fully justified and that this country intended "at all hazards, to hold on to the prisoners" even though the result might be "a general upheaving of the nations." [6]

It should be remembered that it was not until about six weeks after the *Trent* incident that the official statement of the British government's position reached Washington; following that, it would be another three weeks before the American reply would be known in England. Cyrus Field's patient attempts to lay the Atlantic cable had failed prior to the Civil War and were not to achieve success until 1866. It is mere speculation to say what would have been the result in the crisis of the *Trent* affair if the cable had been in operation in 1861. The reasonable guess would seem to be that man's inventiveness would have been a menace in this case and that instantaneous communication between England and the United States would have been unfortunate. As it was, public feeling had time to cool down, sober opinion had a chance to mature, and the uses of diplomacy were allowed their opportunity. In this case diplomacy, in the sense of a sincere communication between governments for the purpose of arriving at a settlement, was genuine; it was not a mere façade or screen behind which, as in recent times, warmaking forces were ruthlessly operating. What Russell said to Lyons, or Seward to Russell, really counted; governments were speaking to governments through officially constituted spokesmen. A consultation as to the wording of an Anglo-American despatch was a matter of vital importance. What-

---

[3] Welles, *Diary*, I, 299.
[4] "While the fact gives . . . general satisfaction, . . . timid persons are alarmed, lest Great Britain should take offense . . . . There is no danger on that score. . . . Not only was it lawful to seise the men, but, I think, the ship itself was subject to confiscation," Bates, *Diary*, 202 (Nov. 16, 1861).
[5] Browning, *Diary*, I, 513-514.   [6] *Ibid.*, 514 n.

ever influence went into the shaping of such a despatch was pregnant with historic consequences. Under these circumstances, at a time when Palmerston and his cabinet seemed to be heading toward a breach with Washington, it was a matter of no small importance that the Queen and the Prince Consort took a hand at diplomacy.

Royal personages are supposed in Britain to be glorified figureheads, but this episode offered an important exception. On November 30 it had been decided at a meeting of the British cabinet that immediate reparation be demanded and a virtual ultimatum delivered.[7] A despatch to that effect (Russell to Lyons) was prepared and laid before the Prince Consort in his capacity as confidential adviser and private secretary to the Queen. It was the last official document submitted to the Prince, who was ill, "very wretched," and could eat no breakfast.[8] It was his last illness; he died on December 14. In this matter Albert's thoughts were those of Victoria; their combined deliberations appear in a memorandum of December 1, dated at Windsor Castle, written by Albert and only slightly modified by the Queen, in which it was suggested that Her Majesty would have liked to see the expression of a hope that the American captain had not acted under instructions, and that Her Majesty's government were unwilling to believe that the United States would do otherwise than spontaneously offer redress.

Whereas the tone of the contemplated British note had been that of peremptory demand, of putting the United States in the wrong, and of forcing a breach of relations if reparation and apology were not forthcoming,.the modified note which Russell sent to Lyons, while firm enough in safeguarding the British position, was cast in far more conciliatory language. As sent, the despatch was "remodelled upon the lines indicated by the Prince, its language being little more than his own cast into official form." [9] It is the belief of the Prince's biographer that the peaceful decision of the United States government would hardly have occurred "but for the temperate and conciliatory tone in which, thanks to the Prince, the views of the [British] Government had been conveyed." [10] Her Majesty's government in the modified despatch took the attitude of believing the best of the United States, of recalling the friendly relations that had long subsisted between the countries, and of assuming that Wilkes's "aggression" had

---

[7] Spencer Walpole, *Life of Lord John Russell*, II, 346.
[8] Martin, *Prince Consort*, V, 421.   [9] *Ibid.*, V, 423.   [10] *Ibid.*, V, 425.

not been committed in compliance with his government's orders. The captain's affront, of course, could not be passed over without being set right, but it was believed that the United States government was fully aware of this and would not unnecessarily force a discussion on "a question of so grave a character, and with regard to which the whole British Nation would be sure to entertain such unanimity of feeling." Accordingly, the British expectation was that Washington, of its own accord, would give satisfaction by releasing the four gentlemen (the envoys with their secretaries) and would offer a suitable apology.[11]

VI

It was not alone on the British side that governmental restraint was apparent. When Lincoln submitted his first regular annual message to Congress on December 3, 1861, he made no mention of the *Trent* case, though the imbroglio was on everyone's tongue. The management of foreign affairs and the framing of diplomatic intercourse being so peculiarly executive in character, there is little evidence that the participation of Congress in this task of international adjustment would have been helpful. Heroically to take a stand, or to deliver a resounding stump speech in the form of a legislative resolution, was hardly calculated to improve the situation. On innocuous and collateral aspects, however, Lincoln did submit to Congress some of the correspondence. The Austrian authorities, for example, had expressed deep concern in the matter, and Seward had assured the imperial-royal government that the United States was incapable of disturbing the peace of the world and would in no sense fail as an advocate of the broadest liberality in matters of international law.[1] When the Prussian government complained, the secretary of state, mentioning in a typical bit of diplomatic patter that that government was eminently distinguished by a generous ambition to ameliorate the condition of mankind, produced evidence to show that, if the peace was to be broken, the fault would not lie in anything the United States had done.[2] On the same subject there were communications with France, whose government took the incident very seriously, with Russia, whose emperor expressed sentiments of warm friendship,

---

11 *Ibid.*, V, 423.   1 *Sen. Exec. Doc. No. 14, 37* Cong., 2 sess.   2 *Ibid.*, no. 18.

and with the King of Italy. The President formally submitted all these communications to the nation's legislature. What it amounted to was that if Congress wished to debate the Russian, Austrian, or Siamese aspects of the *Trent* affair, this was agreeable to Lincoln! [3]

In his anxiety to preserve American dignity while promoting reasonable adjustment, the President turned his thoughts to arbitration. Employing a characteristic technique which appeared on various other occasions, he carefully sketched a despatch on the subject; then the despatch was never sent. In this document, a kind of experimental draft of a possible letter from Seward to Lyons,[4] Lincoln showed considerable wariness as to yielding any American point, but stated that Wilkes had acted "without orders from or expectation of the government." Specifying matters regarding the existing conflict which he wished to "bring into view," Lincoln then proceeded to suggest that the United States would "go to such friendly arbitration as is usual among nations," and would abide by the award; or, in lieu of this, he proposed "reparation" by the United States, provided such reparation should become the law for future analogous cases.[5] This was about the time that matters were coming to a head, the British position having been communicated to Lord Lyons, and Lincoln now "feared trouble." He showed Browning his proposed letter. The matter was talked over fully and "both agreed that the question was easily susceptible of a peaceful solution . . . and . . . that it was a proper case for arbitration." [6]

Pacific influences now came into play. Seward, as early as November 27, had sent word to Adams that Wilkes had acted without instructions.[7] This cost Washington nothing and proved a very considerable factor. Charles Sumner, chairman of the Senate committee on foreign relations, even before the *Trent* affair, was in correspondence with two outstanding British liberals, Bright and Cobden. As the correspondence continued these British leaders stressed not only the need of peaceful adjustment, but also the necessity of America's release of the envoys, since no other solution would be adequate. At one point Bright wrote: "I need not tell you . . . that Nations *drift*

---

[3] *Ibid.*, nos. 8, 22, 30; *Works*, VII, 75, 86, 107–108, 111.

[4] Browning, *Diary*, I, 517.

[5] "Draft of a Despatch proposing Arbitration in the 'Trent' Affair—not used or sent," *Works*, VII, 63–65. Tentatively dated December 10 (?), 1861.

[6] Browning, *Diary*, I, 516 (Dec. 21, 1861).   [7] Bancroft, *Seward*, II, 233.

into wars . . . often thro' the want of a resolute hand at some moment early in the quarrel. So now, a courageous stroke, not of arms,
but of moral action, may save you and us." [8] Sumner showed these
letters to Lincoln; then he wrote Bright that the President was "pacific
in disposition, with a natural slowness," adding, "Yesterday he said
to me, 'There will be no war unless England is bent upon having
one.' " [9] Sumner also quoted Lincoln as saying: "I never see Lord
Lyons. If it were proper I should like to talk with him, that he might
hear from my lips how much I desire peace. If we could talk together
he would believe me." [10]

In Paris, three leading Americans—Thurlow Weed, John Bigelow,
and Winfield Scott—made their contribution toward pacification.
(Weed was an informal emissary of Seward; Bigelow was consul at
Paris; Scott was simply a distinguished American abroad.) Weed wrote
letters to his right bower Seward advising that Wilkes's act be not
approved. Bigelow drafted a public letter to be signed by Scott; then
Weed induced Scott to sign it as his own. This letter, to which the
high prestige of Scott's name was attached, emphasized American
friendship toward Britain and gave the assurance that, with understandings that "could emancipate the commerce of the world," the
United States would willingly give up the envoys.[11] Weed also played
his part by conferring in person with Earl Russell and by contributing
a letter which appeared prominently in the *Times* of London, and
was republished in Paris, Liverpool, Manchester, Dublin, and St.
Petersburg. The main point of the letter was the emphatic assurance
that Seward's "badinage" had no significance and that both the secretary and the American people had the earnest wish to maintain friendly
relations with Britain.[12] While speaking thus to the British nation
Weed did not fail in his letters to Seward to report the seriousness of
the Wilkes incident as viewed from London; the same report was
given to Seward by Adams and Bigelow.

British leaders had contemplated an ultimatum to the United

8 Bright to Sumner, Rochdale, Dec. 5, 1861, *Proceedings,* Mass. Hist. Soc., XLV, 151.
9 E. L. Pierce, *Memoir and Letters of Charles Sumner,* IV, 57.
10 *Ibid.,* IV, 61.
11 John Bigelow, *Retrospections of An Active Life,* I, 387-390.
12 Thurlow Weed Barnes, *Memoir of Thurlow Weed* (Harriet A. Weed, ed., *Life of Thurlow Weed* . . . . vol. II), 354 ff.

States—i. e., a demand, with a time limit, that the men be released.—
This was to have been followed, in case of non-compliance, by withdrawal of the British legation from Washington. The next step would
probably have been war. Since in some historical accounts it is erroneously stated that an "ultimatum" was *actually delivered* to the
American government, it is necessary carefully to review the situation to see precisely what happened. On November 29, two days after
England received news of the incident, the cabinet having held a
meeting, Palmerston sent the Queen a note proposing that a release of the envoys be demanded, and that, on refusal, Lyons should
leave Washington; along with this was a proposed despatch to Lyons
to the same effect. This is the document which, as noted above, was
modified and softened by the Prince and Queen. Russell's despatch
to Lyons as actually sent (November 30) expressed the hope that the
United States would of its own accord offer the needed redress—i. e.,
release of the men, with a suitable apology. All this was in a note which
Lyons might show to Seward, and it contained no suggestion of an
ultimatum, merely the statement that, if Seward did not offer the
release, it should be proposed to him. The whole despatch was carefully worded to avoid any injury to American sensibilities. The factor
that has caused some writers to think in terms of a British ultimatum
came not in the despatch intended for Seward's perusal, but in a
private note of Russell to Lyons, in which the Earl indicated that
Lyons should consent to a delay of no more than seven days after the
release demand was submitted; if at the end of that time such release
had not been agreed to, Lyons was *confidentially* instructed to leave
Washington with his whole legation. Having written the despatch
and the private note, Russell thought the matter over yet again. Then
he sent a second private note to Lyons on the same day, suggesting
that in his first interview with Seward Lyons should not take the
despatch with him but should prepare his mind for it, and allow him
to arrange a settlement with the President and cabinet. Next time
he was to bring the despatch and read it to Seward fully, but with
not a word as to *delivering* any "ultimatum." If at this second interview Seward should ask what would be the consequence of non-
compliance, Lyons was instructed to say that he wished to leave Seward
and the President free to take their own course, and to add that he

desired to abstain from anything like menace. It was also stated that the British cabinet would be "rather easy about the apology." [13]

This diplomatic maneuver can hardly be regarded as an ultimatum in the accepted sense of that word. An ultimatum involves a situation in which all the elements—demand, time limit, and threat as to what would happen on non-compliance—are communicated to the threatened government; such a process of governmental communication did not take place in the *Trent* case. Russell's first private note did suggest a rather menacing possibility; the saving features lay in the second private note and in the mildness and unthreatening character of the open despatch. In spite of all this the seven-day limit (even though not paraded publicly), and the suggestion to Lyons to leave Washington, were serious matters; to remember them is to point up the gravity of Lincoln's problem.[14]

Informed of the British position by Lyons, Seward sparred for a few days' time, realizing the while that settlement was rather urgent but giving no thought to a fact that must have constantly bothered Lyons—namely, that by December 30 the seven days would have expired. In preparation for the final decision, papers had been tentatively drafted for alternative courses. Lincoln, as above noted, had drawn up his paper suggesting arbitration or conditional release, while Seward had drafted a letter to Lyons [15] announcing simple release. Under these circumstances Lincoln's cabinet met on Christmas Day "impressed with the magnitude of the subject" and aware that upon their decision "depended . . . probably the existance [*sic*], of the nation." [16] Despite the reference to the "white elephant" already quoted, it appears that at the time of the assembling of the cabinet not even Lincoln was fully convinced of the necessity of release; "no one except [Montgomery] Blair and Seward seems to have favored a full compliance with the British demand." [17] Yet the Blair patriarch was blaming Seward for international troubles; at the time of this cabinet

---

[13] Walpole, *Lord John Russell*, II, 346–347.

[14] The purpose of British diplomacy has thus been described: ". . . publicly to browbeat and menace the United States by a . . . threat of war, . . . privately to pave the way for getting out of the difficulty without a resort to arms." Thomas L. Harris, *The Trent Affair*, 172. (A more friendly view would be that while diplomacy worked toward peace, a certain boldness in asserting national rights would, in the days of acute difficulty, give harmless outlet to the more belligerent sentiment at home. This dualism existed on both sides of the Atlantic.)

[15] Bates, *Diary*, 216.   [16] *Ibid*.   [17] Bancroft, *Seward*, II, 235.

meeting Francis P. Blair, Sr., wrote to ex-President Van Buren that he did not care if "Billy Bowlegs" (Seward) were delivered up along with the envoys to appease British pride, Seward being held in lieu of an apology! [18]

This Christmas cabinet meeting may be regarded as one of those occasions when genuine deliberation on matters of high policy brought results. Though not a member of the cabinet, Sumner was invited in; the ponderous senator's reading of friendly letters "just rec'd" from Bright and Cobden was a unique feature of this consultation. It was realized that internal politics in Britain was a factor of importance, that if Palmerston's government did not obtain satisfaction from the United States the opposition might "force a ministerial crisis." The cabinet also realized that the United States could not hope for success "in a super added war with England." The hard facts in the case were realistically canvassed, and though all, "even the President," were reluctant to acknowledge "obvious truths," "all yielded to the necessity," and unanimously accepted Seward's letter to Lyons, "after some verbal . . . amendments." [19]

Thus was the important decision reached. The solution—yielding to the British wish—seems in retrospect so simple that one can easily miss the fatefulness of this moment in history, for this solution came exceedingly hard. Chase, who in cabinet meeting advised "surrender of the rebels," qualified the advice with anti-British remarks, and noted in his diary that his consent to Seward's solution was "gall and wormwood" to him. [20] That it was also wormwood to Bates is shown by his hope that three months later the case might be different "if we do half our duty." [21]

Lincoln's paper proposing arbitration, being less conciliatory than immediate release, seems not to have been presented at this cabinet meeting. That night the President told Browning at a White House dinner that the cabinet "had agreed not to divulge what had occurred, but that there would be no war with England." [22] Seward's letter went to Lyons; the envoys were released; the incident was closed. From that point one heard little of Mason and Slidell.

Speaking to full galleries with most of the foreign envoys present,

---

[18] Smith, *Blair Family*, II, 194. [19] Bates, *Diary*, 214–216.
[20] Diary and Letter Book of S. P. Chase (MS., Lib. of Cong.), Dec. 25, 1861.
[21] Bates, *Diary*, 215. [22] Browning, *Diary*, I, 518.

Sumner reviewed the whole question in the Senate,[23] and his conciliatory speech brought a flood of congratulatory comment. Chase
thought it "admirable," [24] and Lincoln's secretary asked for a copy
so the President could read it.[25] The Sumner manuscripts for this
period contain numerous compliments on the senator's effort.[26] In
Paris it produced an "excellent effect," wrote Bigelow, and "still
better in England." [27] Even the adverse comment of the *Times* in
London seemed to Henry Adams a measure of the excellence of the
senator's effort.[28] To the unemotional Adamses in London the relief
amounted to a complete change of atmosphere. Early in 1862 Charles
Francis Adams wrote of a "complete lull" in London, noting that
the *Trent* affair had done much good by dispelling the notion that
"we were intending to pick a quarrel." [29]

Though Lincoln's part in the episode was not publicized, it was
of decisive importance. It is now possible to see the President's contribution in his restraint, his avoidance of any outward expression
of truculence, his early softening of the state department's attitude
toward Britain, his deference toward Seward and Sumner, his withholding of his own paper prepared for the occasion, his readiness to
arbitrate, his golden silence in addressing Congress, his shrewdness
in recognizing that war must be averted, and his clear perception that
a point could be clinched for America's true position at the same time
that full satisfaction was given to a friendly country. This is not to
say that Lincoln was entirely conversant with international dealings,
nor that he was finding the solution through his own efforts. His
deference to others who were finding the solution and his acceptance
of other men's contributions were deliberate. Where he deemed it
necessary he would sometimes overrule his own cabinet; his part in

[23] *Cong. Globe*, 37 Cong., 2 sess., 241–245 (Jan. 9, 1862).

[24] "Went to the Capitol and heard Mr. Sumner's speech. . . . [It was] admirable.
. . . Most of the foreign Ministers were present, and full galleries." Diary and Letter
Book of S. P. Chase (MS., Lib. of Cong.), Jan. 9, 1862.

[25] "The President would like to read your speech on the Trent question." J. G. Nicolay to Charles Sumner (undated but headed "Sunday Morning"), Sumner MSS., 56:19.

[26] Among those who wrote with glowing praise of Sumner's speech on the *Trent*
affair were C. P. Huntington, Jan. 20, 1862; H. W. Torrey, Jan. 21; J. W. Hanson, Jan.
22; Orestes A. Brownson, Jan. 30. Sumner MSS.

[27] John Bigelow to Charles Sumner, Paris, Jan. 30, 1862, *ibid.*

[28] ". . . I was . . . pleased to see that the *Times* lost its temper in criticising you.
It is a significant fact . . . ." Henry Adams to Charles Sumner, London, Jan. 30,
1862, *ibid.*

[29] C. F. Adams to Edward Everett, London, Feb. 21, 1862, Everett MSS.

the making of executive decisions was not often usurped. In this light, the peaceful outcome of the cabinet meeting of December 25, 1861, over which he presided, must be regarded as a matter of executive purpose and of presidential method.

It is beyond the scope of this book to exhibit the factors that worked effectively for peace between Britain and America: essential harmony of related peoples; antislavery sentiment in Britain; sympathy between laborers in the two lands; liberal opinion in England, exemplified by Bright, rising in response to enlightened sentiment on American shores; reasonableness on the part of men in official position; and finally, the realization that peace and economic interest go hand in hand. The economic factor has sometimes been misinterpreted and the importance of cotton overstated. Essentially it was realized in Britain that war with the United States, besides being otherwise unthinkable, would be economically disastrous by breaking down trade, overthrowing the countless advantages that go with world stability, closing profitable markets, inducing reprisals in shipping, and inflicting industrial and material injuries vastly greater than the supposed issues leading to war.[30]

VII

The tone of moderation and restraint which appeared in the *Trent* affair was carried over into later phases of Anglo-American relations during the Lincoln presidency.[1] The subject of these relations is not to be adequately understood by mentioning only a part of them or by overemphasizing those elements on both sides of the ocean that were pushing their governments toward a more truculent course. In America there were those who served their own short-sighted ends by

---

[30] Claussen, *United States and Britain, 1861–1865*. The shutting off of American wheat has been given more emphasis by other writers than by Claussen, who shows that little attention was given to the matter in the diplomatic correspondence of the time and that the American West supplied no controlling share of the whole British wheat consumption. See also Randall, *Civil War and Reconstruction*, 653 n.

[1] Further international phases—e. g., the blockade, the fitting out of warships, the peaceable adjustment in the matter of the Laird rams, the severe resentment of the Confederacy toward Britain from late 1863 to the end of the war, the preponderant influence of Union sympathizers in Britain, the distinguished service of John Bright, the notable friendliness of Russia toward the United States, and the difficulty with France concerning Napoleon III's intervention in Mexico—are reserved for treatment in a later companion work.

misrepresenting and denouncing Britain. Within England there were groups who looked with disdain upon the United States. The point to be remembered, however, is that in neither country did these trouble-making groups set the pattern of official action or determine the direction of international dealing. It is true that class-conscious aristocrats of British society wanted the United States adventure to fail and for that reason favored the Confederacy. On the other hand liberals in England, and with them the masses of the people, favored the American union even if, with Bright, they might regret the "folly" of the tariff in contrast to the Confederacy's gesture toward free trade, and in spite of the economic dislocation and real human distress produced by the Union blockade.

Whatever may have been these varying attitudes, it was the great English nation, rather than the few, who had their way. Britain's connection with Washington was not only unbroken; it grew notably more friendly in the latter half of the war. It is very important that this fact be understood, the more so since misconceptions in this field of history are all too common. It has even been mistakenly said that Britain "intervened" for the Confederacy. Such ignorant statements have appeared in American newspapers. This is the exact opposite of the truth. It is true that there were tensions; there were disputes; on two or three occasions there came what were called crises. It is precisely in such situations that the friendship of nations is tested. Peace does not depend upon the lack of dispute or difference. It depends upon the basic common sense of statesmen and the fundamental harmony of peoples when faced with disputes and confronted with international problems.

Summarizing the British attitude throughout the war in briefest terms, the Confederacy failed in its hope of a warlike outcome over the *Trent* affair; it failed in its strenuous drive for recognition as a nation of full standing; its hopes were dashed in the matter of mediation and intervention; its objectives were unrealized as to the breaking of the blockade. Even in the matter of furnishing warships to the Confederacy the British gave no help after the year 1862. The pattern of Britain's controlling policy in this field was set not by the case of the *Alabama* and a few sister ships in which help was extended (and reparation given after the war), but in the significant cases of the *Alexandra* and the Laird rams in 1863, in which the ardent efforts of the Richmond government to obtain the further delivery of British-built ships were entirely frustrated.

The British government refused to receive Confederate diplomats, and in other respects the Confederacy was so disappointed with the action of the English authorities that there occurred in the latter part of 1863 a complete breach between Richmond and London, if one can speak of a breach between governments that never had regular relations, nor anything approaching it. In September of 1863 the Southern diplomat, Mason, withdrew from London on the instruction of his own government, and in the same year British consuls, whose status was irregular, were expelled from cities within the Confederacy by the government of Jefferson Davis. This was but the natural result of repeated negative decisions by the British ministry on those fundamental matters—mediation, recognition, and actual support in the war—on which Confederate hopes were based and on which the diplomacy of Confederate agents was pivoted. Thus it was not Washington, but Richmond, that broke with England, and that in 1863, the middle year of the war.

There is another point on which a word should be said. The people of the South, with their leaders and warriors, commanded the admiration of many English minds. That admiration has become a long-standing tradition, but it needs to be rightly viewed. Where friendliness to the South was motivated by willingness to see the United States fail as a nation and as a democratic experiment, it became only a vexatious and complicating, but not a controlling, wartime factor. This, however, leaves much to be said; for in the long run, and in its healthier aspects, British interest in the South has somehow managed to transcend or by-pass the political implications of the American controversy. If Britons admired Lee and Jackson, that did not mean that they turned against Lincoln. Governmentally, their regular relations and their unbroken amity was with the United States. In the sense of ultimate American reunion that amity has embraced both North and South. One is by no means overlooking Southerners as Americans when he emphasizes British friendship for that government which preceded and survived the American struggle.

CHAPTER XVII

EXIT CAMERON

I

SIMON CAMERON, who had maneuvered his way into the cabinet against Lincoln's clearly expressed wish, was the first to leave it. While military effort was yet in its early stages the secretary of war was under a fire of criticism. Inefficiency in war administration, failure to provide for the new volunteers (many of whom were without tents), and unreadiness to accept recruits offered by the states, might have been passed over as curable faults traceable to the unpreparedness of the nation and the habit of putting politicians into cabinet posts without training for their duties. More serious than this, however, was the saturnalia of fraud and extravagance which characterized the business dealings of the war department. The report of the investigating committee on this subject is a stinging comment on the greed of profiteers and the shocking laxness of government officials. In 1109 pages of testimony one may read the disgusting details. Rejected and worthless Austrian muskets, twenty-five thouand of them, were purchased at $6.50 each only to be stored in an arsenal. But while buying arms discarded by European nations, the government condemned a lot of Hall carbines, sold them at a nominal price, bought them back at fifteen dollars each, sold them to a private firm at $3.50, and bought them again at $22 each! In a factual statement the committee referred to a "corrupt system of brokerage," "prostitution of public confidence to purposes of individual aggrandizement," "remarkable combinations . . . to rob the treasury," treatment of an act of Congress as "almost a dead letter," "contracts . . . universally injurious to the government," articles purchased as army supplies which bore no relation to regulations—in a word favoritism, corruption, waste, colossal graft, and baneful inefficiency.[1]

Having endured Cameron till endurance was no longer possible, Lincoln let it be known to close friends that a change was contemplated, suggesting indirectly that the secretaryship of war be given back to Holt.[2] "Cameron ought to be turned out forthwith for incompetency, to say nothing of the rumors of jobbing . . . ," wrote Lyman Trumbull in the summer of '61.[3]

But how could Cameron be eased down—i. e., induced to resign without loss of face? This was not simple in the case of a man who had boldly pushed his way into the President's official family when plainly told to stay out. Lincoln did not wish actually to dismiss Cameron. Removal of the politician-secretary would have seemed too drastic. Yet Cameron was so great a liability to the administration and so serious a drawback to the public service that a new secretary was necessary. Finding that Cassius M. Clay was tired of court routine at St. Petersburg and ambitious to serve his country in a military capacity commensurate with his importance,[4] Lincoln satisfied Clay by a generalship and thus eased the jolt for Cameron, who took the diplomatic post in Russia as a graceful way of withdrawing.

There was, however, more to the story, which illustrates the difficulty of constructing historical accounts on the basis of statesmen's letters. On January 11, 1862, Lincoln wrote a curt letter to Cameron indicating that he could gratify the latter's "desire for a change of position" and informing him that he was about to nominate him as minister to Russia. The situation was not so simple as this, however, for at this point Cameron had not actually resigned; his vague verbal comment that his resignation was at Lincoln's disposal did not mean that under the circumstances of January 1862 he was actually sub-

---

[1] *House Report No. 2*, 37 Cong., 2 sess., passim. (For specific statements quoted above, see pp. 34, 40, 53, 54.)

[2] R. W. Bush to Holt, Nov. 23, 1861, cited in A. Howard Meneely, *The War Department, 1861*, 365.

[3] Trumbull to Doolittle, Aug. 31, 1861, MS., Ill. St. Hist. Lib.

[4] "I asked him [Lincoln] if it was true that Cash M Clay was to be made a Major General—he said it was—I protested very earnestly against it— . . . asking . . . that we should not be troubled with him, remarking . . . that he was now in great hopes that the rebelion [sic] would be pretty much ended before he would get here." J. F. Speed to Joseph Holt, Feb. 4, 1862, Holt MSS. For Lincoln's mention of Clay's desire for military appointment, see *Works*, VII, 80 (Jan. 11, 1862). For Clay's brief acceptance of high command, his insistence on abolition of slavery as a condition of his service, his return to Russia in 1863 to remain till 1869, and his later dissatisfaction with the Republican party, see *Dic. of Amer. Biog.*, IV, 170.

mitting an unsolicited resignation. A. K. McClure relates that Lincoln's short letter was handed to Cameron by Chase and that he (McClure), in company with T. A. Scott, assistant secretary of war, conferred that night with Cameron, who, far from accepting this solution without question, "exhibited an extraordinary degree of emotion." According to McClure, Cameron "was affected even to tears, and wept bitterly over . . . [the] personal affront from Lincoln," [5] saying that it "meant personal as well as political destruction, and was an irretrievable wrong committed . . . by the President." [6]

Because of Cameron's agitation it was arranged as an afterthought that the secretary should write a letter of resignation predated to January 11, whereupon Lincoln wrote a similarly predated letter to Cameron expressing, as he had not done originally, "affectionate esteem" and confidence in the secretary's "ability, patriotism, and fidelity to public trust," and referring to the "not less important" services the Pennsylvanian could render in his new St. Petersburg location.[7] Considering that it took a bit of forcing to get Cameron out of the cabinet, one reads the public correspondence with a realization that it tactfully concealed the true situation. When this true situation is recalled, some of the newspaper comments of the time have an odd sound. The *Herald,* for instance, informed its readers that "General Cameron" [8] had accepted the secretaryship "with great reluctance" (!), had preferred the Senate, had always been ready to retire, and now, "having accomplished so much," could "well afford to lay aside his exhausting labors." [9]

For a striking example of Cameron's manner of coöperating with his chief one may go back to the previous month. Seizing advantage of radical displeasure with Lincoln, he had taken a step which seriously embarrassed the President while it gave Cameron some weeks of publicity and ill-won glory in antislavery circles. Without consulting the President, Cameron had included in his annual report of December 1861 a long passage advocating the employment of slaves as soldiers. In language sweet to vindictive ears the secretary gave less emphasis to the merits of the Negroes than to the punishment of "rebellious traitors" who had forfeited their rights.[10] Secretarial re-

---

[5] A. K. McClure, *Abraham Lincoln and Men of War-Times,* 165.
[6] *Ibid.,* 164.   [7] *Works,* VII, 79–82.
[8] The misleading military title was a matter of informal courtesy.
[9] New York *Herald.* Jan. 14, 1862, p. 5, c. 1.   [10] McPherson, *Rebellion,* 249.

ports were customarily assembled in the President's office and transmitted through him to Congress by assimilation with his own annual
message. What to do as to slaves and Negro troops was the President's
problem. It was an important and central matter of policy, yet of his
own initiative Cameron had his report "printed, and, without being
submitted to his [Lincoln's] inspection, mailed to the postmasters of
the chief cities to be handed to the press as soon as the telegraph should
announce . . . the reading of the message . . . in Congress." [11]

When Lincoln found what had been done behind his back he
caused advance copies of the Cameron report to be recalled by telegraph, a new edition being issued which omitted the questionable
passage. Lincoln was shocked, was "greatly grieved," and considered
the episode a "severe strain" upon his trust in his colleague's
"fidelity"; [12] yet the incident did not break their friendly relations. He
continued to extend kind treatment to a secretary who did not re-
ciprocate; yet in the "suppression" of the original report there was a
touch of presidential censorship which worked to Lincoln's detriment
because the passage was not in fact withheld from the public, but
appeared simultaneously with the expurgated version, so that the
attempted suppression was pointed up and emphasized. Persons who
did not ordinarily read a secretary's report began to make compari-
sons, and a Connecticut friend of Cameron wrote that he preferred the
"Simon pure" article printed in the *Tribune* to the "*bogus* report"
in the *World*.[13] Bishop Simpson, a power among Methodists, wrote:
"We are tired of the dilatory policy of the President," and added: "I
approve fully of your Report before it was *amended* by the Pres^t." [14]
Publishing the report in its original form, E. L. Baker of the *Illinois
State Journal*, wrote that Cameron was "*very strong in Illinois*," [15]
while from Pottsville, Pennsylvania, came the comment that the
President's message was "tame," and that the "overwhelming majority" favored Cameron's "great document." [16] "You have touched
the national heart," wrote a Pittsburgh friend. "Your Report . . .
is universally approved and you now occupy a position a head & shoul-

---

[11] Nicolay and Hay, *Lincoln*, V, 125. [12] McClure, *Men of War-Times*, 162–163.
[13] D. Wellman, Jr., to Cameron, Watertown, Conn., Dec. 10, 1861, Cameron MSS.
[14] M. Simpson to Cameron, Evanston, Ill., Dec. 9, 1861, *ibid.*
[15] E. L. Baker to Cameron, Office of the *Illinois State Journal*, Springfield, Dec. 10,
1861, *ibid.*
[16] Wm. L. Helfenstein to Cameron, Pottsville, Pa., Dec. 9, 1861, *ibid.*

ders above the President & all the Cabinet beside." [17]

Despite Lincoln's avoidance of any sharp dealing, when the secretary's resignation became known in January there were many who put Cameron in the persecuted role of a man who was sacrificed for loyally serving the antislavery cause. Adulation of Cameron and denunciation of the President became once more the theme of abolitionist critics. One man wrote: "I am astonished to learn that you have been removed from the cabinet because you advocated the use of all the means within our reach to put down this outrageous rebellion. . . . I am . . . sad . . . to see the course Lincoln is pursuing." [18] Another supposed "that the policy of the border states . . . [had] triumphed in the councils of the President, and that the emancipationists . . . [had] to go under." [19] And another: "Yr resignation, when understood is not only approved by yr friends, but excites their admiration. . . . But I must confess yr resignation gives me some fears for the future of the country." [20] Even Cameron's supporters, however, if only between the lines, betrayed their realization that charges of corruption had something to do with his departure from the cabinet. In a letter of friendly sympathy Governor Morton of Indiana remarked: "It is a leading feature in the policy of the opponents of the war to charge corruption against every man engaged in its prosecution . . . ." [21]

Two branches of the United States government, the Supreme Court and the House of Representatives, put on record a denunciation of the practices that prevailed under Cameron. In a case at law involving the activity of a lobby "agent" (to the tune of $75,000 for no other "service" than the use of influence to place a contract) Justice Field on behalf of the Court wrote:

"All contracts for supplies should be made with those, and with those only, who will execute them most faithfully, and at the least expense to the Government. Considerations as to the most efficient and economical mode of meeting the public wants should alone control . . . the action of every department of the Government. No other consideration can lawfully enter into the transaction, so far as the Government is concerned.

17 Sam'l A. Purviance to Cameron, "Confidential," Pittsburgh, Dec. 6, 1861, *ibid.*

18 N. P. Sawyer to Cameron, Pittsburgh, Jan. 14, 1862, *ibid.*

19 Wm. S. Garvin to Cameron, Jan. 16, 1862, *ibid.*

20 Wm. L. Helfenstein to Cameron, Willards [Hotel], Jan. 13, 1862, *ibid.*

21 O. P. Morton to Cameron, Indianapolis, Jan. 13, 1862, *ibid.*

Such is the rule of public policy; and whatever tends to introduce any other elements into the transaction, is against public policy. That agreements, like the one under consideration, have this tendency, is manifest. They tend to introduce personal solicitation, and personal influence, as elements in the procurement of contracts; and thus directly lead to inefficiency in the public service, and to unnecessary expenditures of the public funds." [22]

In the same sense the House of Representatives, after an elaborate investigation, passed the following resolution:

"*Resolved*, That Simon Cameron, late Secretary of War, by investing Alexander Cummings with the control of large sums of the public money, and authority to purchase military supplies, without restriction, without requiring . . . any guarantee for the faithful performance of his duties . . . , and by involving the Government in a vast number of contracts with persons not legitimately engaged in the business pertaining to . . . such contracts, . . . has adopted a policy highly injurious to the public service, and deserves the censure of the House.[23]

With characteristic willingness to shield a colleague and bear the blame for subordinates, President Lincoln replied at length to this resolution. He was unwilling to "leave the censure . . . to rest . . . chiefly upon Mr. Cameron." He added: "It is due to Mr. Cameron to say that, although he fully approved the proceedings, they were not moved nor suggested by himself, and that not only the President but all the other heads of departments were at least equally responsible . . . for whatever error, wrong, or fault was committed in the premises." [24]

In this communication Lincoln reviewed the war crisis and the earlier methods of dealing with it. Stressing the sharpness of the emergency and the "condition of a siege" at the capital, he showed that, with Congress not in session, it was for the President to choose whether to let the government fall into ruin or avail himself of broad powers. After summoning advisers he had decided to take a number of quick steps to promote the public defense.[25] Intrusting distinguished citizens with important duties in the forwarding of supplies and troops, he

---

[22] The Court continued "Agreements for compensation contingent upon success, suggest the use of sinister and corrupt means for the accomplishment of the end desired. The law meets the suggestion of evil, and strikes down the contract from its inception." Tool Company *vs.* Norris, 69 U. S. 45, 54–55.

[23] *Cong. Globe*, 37 Cong., 2 sess., 1888, April 30, 1862.

[24] *Works*, VII, 193–194 (May 26, 1862).   [25] See vol. I, 374–375.

had directed that Governor Morgan of New York and Alexander Cummings be authorized by Secretary Cameron "to make all necessary arrangements for the transportation of troops and munitions . . . in aid . . . of the army . . . until communication should be completely reëstablished between . . . Washington and New York." Finding government departments shot through with disloyal personnel, he had directed that public money be used "without security" by selected non-official individuals. Confessing that these measures were "without authority of law," Lincoln defended them as his own and as necessary to save the government from overthrow.

Implicit in this relationship was the honorable obligation to avoid abuse of so unusual a trust imposed by so high an official. Nevertheless an admission that things went wrong was suggested in the last sentence of this message, in which Lincoln took for himself equal responsibility for "such error" or "wrong" as might have been committed. Lincoln did not say that censure by the House was unjustified, but that it should not be aimed exclusively at Mr. Cameron. The financial transactions themselves, as they worked out, were not defended, nor did the President attempt to give the detailed history of these transactions. That Cummings obtained his profitable opportunity only because he was a crony of Cameron was part of this history.

The Senate also was deeply moved by the charges against Cameron, and there was formidable opposition to his confirmation as minister to Russia. Protracted debate on this subject in executive session ended inconclusively in adjournment. According to the *Herald* the "objections . . . were chiefly on the ground of alleged mismanagement of the War Department, and favoritism in the appointment of military officers and the award of contracts . . . ." It was not expected that confirmation would be withheld, "but the array against the nomination . . . deprive[d] the confirmation of any complimentary complexion, and amount[ed] to a censure of the conduct of the War Department." [26] In this connection it must be remembered that Cameron had been recently a member of the Senate, that readiness to confirm a fellow senator was traditional, and that in spite of this several leading senators of Cameron's own party voted against the appointment (Trumbull, Grimes, Harlan, Hale, Wilkinson, and Foster). John Sherman was reported as speaking against the confirmation, then

---

[26] New York *Herald,* Jan. 17, 1862, p. 1, c. 1.

voting for it.[27] Trumbull's opposition to the appointment was expressed in "a very bitter speech." [28]

II

For the vital post of successor to Cameron, Lincoln chose Edwin M. Stanton of Pennsylvania, thus making his first cabinet appointment of an 1860 Democrat.[1] Originating in Ohio and shifting to Pittsburgh, Stanton had developed as a prominent lawyer, while in politics he was known as an antislavery Democrat. Coming at a late hour into the Buchanan cabinet when its stiffening was signalized by cabinet reorganization, his presence in that body was interpreted as giving solidity to a wavering administration. His fright on the eve of civil war and his ill words concerning Lincoln were not generally known, nor could one foresee that he would ultimately prove a worse headache than Cameron. Emphasis at the moment was upon his intellect, competence, and efficiency; J. F. Speed wrote of order and precision instead of "that loose shackeling way of doing business in the war office." [2]

The appointment of Stanton seemed to many a strange proceeding. Welles noted that no member of the cabinet "was aware of his selection until after it was determined upon, except Mr. Seward," [3] while Bates stated that the act took him by surprise, since no hint of it had been given in cabinet meeting, nor had the President or any cabinet member mentioned it to him.[4] Lincoln's act was indeed so unexpected as to appear sudden; Stanton himself, according to his own statement, had not spoken to Lincoln "from the 4th of March, 1861, until the day he handed me my commission." [5] Though at the time the emphasis was upon the expectation that Stanton would prove an efficient contrast to Cameron, the sequel was to show that the new secretary "loved antagonism, and there was hardly a period during

---

[27] *Ibid.*, Jan. 18, 1862, p. 1, c. 4.   [28] Browning, *Diary*, I, 524.

[1] See vol. I, 270–271.

[2] J. F. Speed to Joseph Holt, Washington, Feb. 4, 1862, Holt MSS.

[3] Welles adds that after the matter had been decided it was made to appear that Cameron had had a hand in choosing his successor. Since Chase was "sensitive in matters where Seward was operating," the treasury head, according to Welles, "was called in and consulted on a predetermined question." Welles, *Diary*, I, 58–59.

[4] Bates, *Diary*, 226.

[5] Stanton to Buchanan, May 18, 1862, quoted in McClure, *Men of War-Times*, 174.

his . . . service as War Minister in which he was not . . . in positive antagonism with the President." A. K. McClure, who made this
comment, added: "In his antagonisms he was, as a rule, offensively
despotic, and often pressed them upon Lincoln to the very utmost
point of Lincoln's forbearance . . . ." [6]

Soon after the Cameron-Stanton shift there were rumors of other
cabinet changes. It was whispered that Chase would withdraw and
resume his place in the Senate,[7] and there were more persistent reports that Welles would step out and be replaced by his able assistant,
Gustavus Fox, or, as some of the gossip would have it, by General
Banks.[8] Part of the rumor as to Welles was that he would become
minister to Spain.[9] Editorializing on this subject, the *Herald* remarked that Welles's successor, "if picked up in the streets at a venture, . . . [could not] possibly be worse." [10] Commenting in general
on the President's cabinet early in 1862, Ebenezer Peck of Illinois
made the displaced Cameron out to be a "nether millstone," Welles
"worse than a granny," Smith "busy about his salary only," and
Seward "eagerly looking for the succession." [11]

III

Immediately upon assuming his unexpected office Stanton had an
interview at his own request (January 20, 1862) with a new fangled
congressional organization known as the committee on the conduct of
the war.[1] Whatever else this visit did, it made pro-Stanton copy in
the newspapers, which did not omit to report the "magnetic influence" of the new secretary, his "honesty," his "regard to public
economy," and his purpose to reduce the rebellion "with all possible
despatch." [2] The story of this committee, and the grief it gave to Lincoln and to competent army leaders, is one of the most vexing phases
of Civil War history. The movement for such a committee began with

---

[6] McClure, 171.   [7] New York *Herald*, Jan. 15, 1862, p. 1, c. 4.
[8] *Ibid.*, Feb. 2, 1862, p. 5, c. 1; April 25, 1862, p. 4, c. 5; April 26, 1862, p. 10, c. 4.
[9] *Ibid.*, April 25, 1862, p. 1, c. 3.   [10] April 25, 1862, p. 4, c. 5.
[11] Peck to Trumbull, Chicago, Feb. 15, 1862, Trumbull MSS.
[1] ". . . all the members present, and [the committee] had a conference of several
hours' duration with honorable Edwin M. Stanton, Secretary of War, at his request."
Journal of the Committee, Jan. 20, 1862, Report, Committee on the Conduct of the
War, *Sen. Rep. No. 108*, 37 Cong., 3 sess., I, 75.
[2] New York *Herald*, Jan. 23, 1862, p. 8, c. 2.

Roscoe Conkling's resolution of December 2, 1861, calling for the investigation of the disasters at Bull Run and Ball's Bluff. The latter affair was a small engagement (October 21, 1861) on the Potomac not far above Washington, in which Union forces had been sharply defeated and cut to pieces. Bad though it was, the affair was exaggerated, the more so because of the death of Colonel (Senator) Edward D. Baker, a man of the radical type, whose error on the battlefield was largely responsible for the unfortunate outcome, but whose sacrifice called for a living scapegoat.

This Baker was Lincoln's close friend, indeed the namesake of one of his sons. Born in London, he had won political and legal success in Illinois, fought against Mexico, shifted to the Far West, and risen to the position of senator from Oregon. On the outbreak of the war he had defended the Union cause with fiery oratory in New York, and had then spectacularly entered the military service, in command of the "California regiment" which he had raised. Performing the "anomalous duty of commanding his regiment and representing Oregon in the Senate," [3] Baker had appeared in uniform on the floor of the Senate on August first and had theatrically denounced a pro-Confederate speech by Breckinridge of Kentucky. According to Blaine, in the history of the Senate "no more thrilling speech was ever delivered." [4]

Stirred by the death of a popular hero (who had rashly exposed himself and his brigade), and maddened by the inactivity of McClellan's main army, the "Jacobins" (or radicals) of Congress in December 1861 were in a mood to get action and punish those guilty of mistakes. Debate and proposals arising from Conkling's resolution led to the creation of a standing "joint committee on the conduct of the war," which consisted of three senators (B. F. Wade of Ohio, Zachariah Chandler of Michigan, and Andrew Johnson of Tennessee) and four representatives (D. W. Gooch of Massachusetts, George W. Julian of Indiana, John Covode of Pennsylvania, and Moses F. Odell of New York). Wade and Chandler, Republicans who vindictively hated the South and viewed the war as an opportunity for party gain, were its leading spirits. By the bold ruthlessness of its leaders, by the partisan vote which created it, and by the star-chamber quality of its proceedings, the character of the committee can be gauged. In the name of

---

[3] Blaine, *Twenty Years of Congress*, I, 344.   [4] *Ibid.*, 345.

promoting military efficiency, injecting energy into the service, exposing mistakes, and "obtaining information" for the President, this impressively busy organization conducted elaborate inquisitions, took generals and war officials away from their proper duties, stirred the country with misplaced publicity, ruined the reputations of able generals while building up their own military pets, worried Lincoln, bandied unproved charges of treason, and created dissension and distrust within the lines. Not a member had had military experience,[5] yet the committee assumed a finality of military judgment commensurate with their marked intolerance toward men of West Point.

The chief targets of the committee were McClellan (he above all), Charles P. Stone, and Fitz-John Porter; their pets were Frémont, Burnside, Pope, and McDowell. By a preposterous inquisition which never got round to substantiation of specific charges, Charles P. Stone was blamed for Ball's Bluff, pilloried before popular opinion, arrested, imprisoned without trial (for 189 days in flagrant violation of law as to the discipline of officers), and subjected to such out-of-court persecution and defamation that he resigned the army in whose service his usefulness had been broken, and took a commission under the Khedive of Egypt.

When army officers spoke a language which the committee did not like, Wade and Chandler would hold back senate confirmation of an advanced commission.[6] With political motives constantly in view, they not only persecuted Democratic generals, but "became the spearhead of the radical drive against the [Lincoln] administration."[7] Though the full activity of this aggressive group is hard to visualize, the persistent energy of their "investigations" must be constantly remembered in any study of the military campaigns of the Army of the Potomac.[8]

---

[5] This was true of the committee as originally constituted. W. W. Pierson, in *Amer. Hist. Rev.*, XXIII, 558.

[6] T. Harry Williams, *Lincoln and the Radicals*, 74, citing: New York *Tribune*, Dec. 24, 1862; *ibid.*, Jan. 26, 1863; Col. W. B. Hazen to John Sherman, Dec. 10, 1862 (John Sherman MSS.); Detroit *Free Press*, April 7, 1863.

[7] T. Harry Williams, *Lincoln and the Radicals*, 64.

[8] Though not ignoring other sectors, they concentrated chiefly upon the Army of the Potomac, finding in that army "all that is necessary" for their investigation. Report, Com. on Conduct of the War, *Sen. Rep. No. 108*, 37 Cong., 3 sess., I, 4. The committee is treated by W. W. Pierson in *Amer. Hist. Rev.*, XXIII, 550–576: its work is more elaborately told by T. Harry Williams in the account above cited; for a brief summary, see J. G. Randall, *Civil War and Reconstruction*, 367–370.

CHAPTER XVIII

BEHIND McCLELLAN'S LINES

I

AFTER slight activity in 1861, the year 1862 was to witness for the Union army "stupendous . . . operations . . . on a theatre . . . almost the size of a continent." [1] Democracy's makeshift, the army was an aggregation of units indifferently commanded, inadequately equipped, and shot through with unmilitary procedures, distrust, disrespect for officers, and desertion. It was a slowly evolving volunteer army to which the drafts of 1862 (minor affairs) made slight contribution. Titles in the volunteer service were much higher for comparable training and experience than in the regular army, against which there seemed to be a kind of prejudice among men in authority. Those who had left the regular army, gone into civilian pursuits, and entered the volunteer service for the emergency, fared much better as to promotion and rank than those who continued their regular-army status. In the absence of a general staff the central control of the army was amorphous, changeable, and difficult to define.

Before large operations opened, or even the armies began to move, in the East, shining advances had been made in the West. General command in this area centered at St. Louis under Frémont till his removal in November 1861, then under Halleck. It was not the headquarters men, however, but commanders in the field, who achieved results. These results, in which gunboat flotillas coöperated with land forces, included the early occupation of river positions on the Ohio and upper Mississippi, the signal victory of Grant and Foote in the

---

[1] *Annual Cyclopaedia*, 1862, 25. Bull Run, of course, offers an outstanding exception to the statement as to slight activity in 1861.

capture of Forts Henry and Donelson on the Tennessee and Cumberland Rivers, Confederate retreat following the heaviest battle of the whole war in the West at Pittsburg Landing (Shiloh), the capture of Island Number Ten and New Madrid, and seizure of New Orleans in May 1862. These were major events, giving great prominence to such generals as Halleck (though this was hardly deserved), Pope, "Unconditional Surrender" Grant, and Sherman, and to such naval leaders as Foote, Farragut, and Porter. After Donelson had capitulated (February 16, 1862), soon after the surrender of Fort Henry (February 6), the *Times* remarked that the "monster" was in the "death struggle," [2] while Edward Bates considered that "the heart of the rebellion" had been broken.[3]

To give the story of these western military matters, assigning credit in exactly the right degree to leaders and participants—e. g., to say just how much was the contribution of Halleck, Frémont, Grant, Foote, Charles F. Smith, et cetera—is as impossible here as to discuss Confederate blame for the surrender of Donelson. Smith himself, with his "superb physique" [4] and perfect soldierly bearing whether on review or in battle, would deserve considerable attention. Nor can space be given to the obscure claims presented for Anna E. Carroll of Maryland. This able and energetic woman, overlooked and almost completely forgotten, has been credited in a remarkable recent biography with service of great significance. It is claimed (with an impressive show of documents) that she knew in advance of secession plots, worked on Governor Hicks and other leaders to save Maryland, and helped to prevent the secession of that crucially important state. Finding fatal flaws in the military plans of Halleck and Frémont, and envisaging the importance of the western rivers, she is said to have done much to invent and develop that land-and-water strategy which yielded such shining results in Union success, and which might well have yielded much larger results if her full program had been followed. For advising Lincoln, and preparing a paper on the war powers which helped the President's case when he was threatened with congressional assault upon his authority, she has even been called (perhaps with exaggeration) "the great unrecognized member of Lincoln's cabinet." It has been argued that she saw through the incompetence

---

[2] New York *Times*, Feb. 17, 1862, p. 4, c. 4.   [3] Bates, *Diary*, 248.
[4] *Battles and Leaders of the Civil War*, I, 405 (portrait, 411).

of some of the highest generals, and that that may be the reason why the facts concerning her record seem for years to have been suppressed.[5]

To these Union advances in the West the navy was able, in eastern coastal operations, to add the famous ironclad duel in Hampton Roads [6] and the capture of such Atlantic positions as Norfolk, Virginia, Port Royal (approach to Beaufort, S. C.), and Fort Pulaski (approach to Savannah, Georgia). The city of Savannah, however, as well as Mobile, Charleston, and Wilmington, remained in possession of their Southern defenders. Coincident with the inland river campaigns was the amphibious operation at Roanoke Island on the North Carolina coast (February-March, 1862). Under the joint command of General Burnside and Admiral Goldsborough this campaign resulted in the capture of Confederate positions on the Island and at Newbern, a bitter setback as viewed from Richmond. These naval developments had the sharper effect in the South because until the *Monitor* swung into action Southerners had been led to expect great things of their naval forces, especially when the *Virginia*, in sending Union warships to the bottom, had produced a first class scare in Washington. Even the calmness of Lincoln was broken at this time. "The President . . . was so excited," noted Gideon Welles, "that he could not deliberate or be satisfied with the opinions of nonprofessional men, but ordered his carriage and drove to the navy yard to . . . consult with Admiral Dahlgren and other naval officers, who might be there." [7] The "most frightened" of all on that "gloomy day," [8] however, according to Welles, was Stanton. "He was . . . almost frantic, and . . . I saw well the estimation in which he held me with my unmoved and unexcited manner and conversation." [9] With sage prophecy Welles pointed out that the *Merrimack* "could not come to Washington and go to New York at the same time," and he had "no apprehension of her visiting either." [10] Despite Stanton's "sneering inquiry" concern-

---

[5] Marjorie Barstow Greenbie, *My Dear Lady: The Story of Anna Ella Carroll, the "Great Unrecognized Member of Lincoln's Cabinet."* Appended to Mrs. Greenbie's biography are reprints of slightly known documents of the United States government in which after the war her services were belatedly revealed.

[6] In which the *Monitor* met the Confederate ironclad *Virginia* (formerly the *Merrimack*), checking the destructive career of that much feared vessel, and giving infinite relief to Washington. The date was March 9, 1862.

[7] Welles, *Diary*, I, 62.

[8] March 9, 1862, before news had been received of the retirement of the *Virginia* after its duel with the *Monitor*.

[9] Welles, *Diary*, I, 62.   [10] *Ibid.*, I, 63.

ing the *Monitor*,[11] authorities at Washington and the people generally were mightily relieved when the ironclad argument was settled in Lincoln's favor.

II

For certain writers the military career of George B. McClellan has become a fixed stereotype. It is assumed that if one is pro-Lincoln, he must be anti-McClellan, though the most bitter of McClellan's foes were also opponents of Lincoln. According to his detractors McClellan remained for many months uselessly inactive with a magnificent army, suffered delusions and infatuation as to enemy superiority, snubbed the President, treated the congressional war committee with contempt, evaded questions as to his intentions, exhausted Lincoln's patience, made erroneous plans, missed golden opportunities, demanded needless reënforcements, was a victim (or accomplice) of his secret service, clamored loud and long when troops were denied him, blamed the government with the intention to destroy his army, allowed himself to be surprised by enemy maneuvers, permitted subordinates to endure heavy fighting without sending them reënforcements, instructed the President concerning political duties, and in the Seven Days failed to take Richmond when all he had to do was to brush aside Confederate defense under Johnston, then under Lee and Jackson! It was even charged that he was a colossal traitor, that he did not mean to whip the enemy, and that he planned (some say he "considered") a military *coup d'état* by which Congress would be ousted, Lincoln removed, and himself made dictator. Perhaps the best indication that this traitor charge is fantastically false is the admission by Nicolay and Hay that it is "totally unjust." [1] One must remember that Hay's purpose to tear down McClellan was self-confessed. In a letter to Nicolay he said: ". . . we ought to write . . . like two everlasting angels—who . . . tell the truth about everything and don't care a twang of their harps about one side or the other"; then he showed how he meant this only as a kind of pose when he added in the same letter, speaking of McClellan: "It is of the utmost moment that we should *seem* fair to him, while we are destroying him." [2]

---

11 *Ibid.*   1 Nicolay and Hay, *Lincoln*, V, 169.
2 Hay's italics. Quoted in Tyler Dennett, *John Hay: From Poetry to Politics*, 139.

In attempting a fair appraisal of McClellan the following points should be noted: (1) Competent military writers speak favorably of his leadership. He is most bitterly assailed, not by those who have gone afresh into the elaborate sources to restudy his campaigns, but by those who repeat or perpetuate a party bias. (2) Even critics of McClellan give him credit for whipping an inefficient army into military shape. (3) McClellan's hold on the esteem and affection of his men was unmistakable; perhaps no tradition has been stronger among surviving veterans than approval of McClellan. (4) No one can measure the effect of non-coöperation in Washington in such matters as withholding McDowell's corps and Blenker's division, but the fact of such non-coöperation is a matter of record. (5) McClellan operated against the Confederacy at its military peak. (6) Only an amateur could suppose that the head of a reorganized and untried army was unwise in demanding full preparation and a heavy force when taking the offensive against Richmond. (7) The worst that Lee accomplished against him was to administer a momentary setback at Gaines's Mill; never did the Union army under McClellan suffer a major defeat.

(8) McClellan was going strong when recalled from the Peninsula; his campaign was in mid-progress; it had not spent itself. To picture McClellan as defeated in July 1862 was a misrepresentation due less to conditions at the front than to unmilitary factors behind his lines. (9) At an hour of agonizing peril McClellan saved Washington and the Union cause in the checking of Lee's invasion at Antietam; in its effect on both international and domestic policy this achievement was of untold importance. (10) It was when the Army of the Potomac was turned over to McClellan's successors that the Union cause suffered its worst military disasters. (11) Nothing worth while in the East was done on the Northern side in 1862 except under McClellan; yet 1862 was the turning point favorably for the Union in the matter of foreign intervention, a factor always closely linked with military events. Had McClellan collapsed at Antietam as Pope had done at Second Bull Run, it is hard to see how the Lincoln government and the Union cause could possibly have survived, to say nothing of launching an ambitious emancipation policy, which occurred directly after Antietam.

(12) Comparison of McClellan and Grant to the former's discredit is misleading. Had Grant been the target of furious partisan intrigue

that McClellan was, it is doubtful how far he could have gone. If one must compare generals it should be noted that, despite terrific butchery as at Cold Harbor, Grant's progress in 1864 was no more successful in a comparable period than McClellan's in 1862. If McClellan failed to "take Richmond" in '62, so did Grant in '64. Even with vastly better support and a better army, Grant's slowness and the seemingly fruitless butchery of his troops in 1864 was a bitter thing, so that August of that presidential year was an exceedingly dark period for the Lincoln administration. Had the main army of the East been *withdrawn from its position against the earnest protest of its commander* in midsummer of 1864 as McClellan's was for no better cause in midsummer of 1862, Grant would have gone down in history as a failure. McClellan in '62 had no Sherman or Sheridan in the East, but Lee did have Jackson. Finally, when at long last Grant succeeded in 1865, the Confederacy was a much weaker affair than in 1862. These things are by no means said as a disparagement of Grant, but any comparison of Grant and McClellan requires that one consider the inequality in conditions behind their lines and in the enemy strength that faced them. It requires one to remember that McClellan's slowness in getting results was certainly no greater than Grant's. Had McClellan at Antietam been merely another Pope, Grant might never have had his opportunity.

It was McClellan's destiny to take command of a demoralized and formless army, work it into shape, direct the Union effort as general-in-chief for a period, lead a difficult operation against the South's finest commanders, see his plan wrecked not by enemy action but by interference at home, suffer displacement at the height of a great campaign, step down not because of defeat but because of hostile intrigue, step back when disaster befell his first successor, direct a desperate yet successful defense when Lee struck north via Maryland, prepare another advance (his second offensive and third major campaign in a year), and, at the moment of forward movement, fall a victim to a relentless political pressure which Lincoln could not resist. A restudy of the manner in which the harassed general comported himself under these intolerable circumstances will give little evidence of self-promoting acumen nor ability to play "the game," but will assuredly reopen the case as to the condemnation of McClellan.

Assuming command at Washington (July 27, 1861) after the disaster of Bull Run, McClellan found what Stanton called a condition of "irretrievable misfortune . . . national disgrace . . . ruin . . . and national bankruptcy as the result of Lincoln's 'running the machine' for five months." [3] Approaches to Washington were virtually undefended, and, to quote the contemptuous Stanton again, it seemed "inevitable" that Washington would be captured and that Jeff Davis would turn out "the whole [Lincoln] concern." [4] What McClellan found "could not properly be called an army," [5] but a defeated, undisciplined, largely unarmed, ill supplied, demoralized, and even mutinous [6] mass. In succeeding months he instituted strict discipline (despite the "deficiency of instructed officers" and the utter lack of officers familiar with even the sight of a large army), reorganized and rearranged the troops, built fortifications, guarded the fordable Potomac, organized a staff,[7] constructed military telegraph lines, and, in sum, transformed the Army of the Potomac into a trained fighting machine ready to face a powerful foe. Passing "long days in the saddle and . . . nights in the office," [8] he by no means wasted his time, as critics have asserted. He knew thoroughly the Washington area [9] and visited every camp; [10] in another general such a knowledge of his army would have been counted a virtue. Having started with what was "not worthy to be called an army," he considered that it "would have been madness to renew the attempt until a complete change was made." [11]

In personality and the power to command respect McClellan was not wanting. After a three-hours conference with him H. W. Bellows wrote of a "well-knit, perfectly balanced form" that bent and swayed "as a panther," of an "eye, small but calm, direct and powerful," of "complexion deepened by exposure," of a man whose talk was "to the point," who was "not afraid of responsibility," and about whom there was "an indescribable *air of success*" and "something of the 'man of destiny.' " " *'How to do it'* [wrote Bellows] is stamped on his whole

[3] Stanton to Buchanan, Washington, July 26, 1861, quoted in *McClellan's Own Story*, 67 n.

[4] *Ibid.* Stanton added: ". . . what can he [McClellan] accomplish? Will not Scott's jealousy, cabinet intrigues, and Republican interference thwart him at every step?" [5] *Ibid.*, 68.   [6] For mutiny, see *ibid.*, 86.

[7] Col. R. B. Marcy was at its head (*ibid.*, 112). In his life of Lee (II, 237) Douglas Freeman pays high tribute to the "excellence" of McClellan's staff.

[8] *McClellan's Own Story*, 69.   [9] *Ibid.*, 141.   [10] *Ibid.*   [11] *Ibid.*, 71-72.

person." [12] To some, however, he seemed an egotist, and the diary of John Hay contains an amazing statement by which it appears that he went so far as to snub the President and secretary of state. According to this account Lincoln called at McClellan's house with Seward and Hay; finding the general not at home they all waited; McClellan came in and went upstairs without greeting his guests; when a servant "once more" reported their presence there came the cool answer that the general had gone to bed! The President, wrote Hay, seemed not to have noticed "this unparalleled insolence of epaulettes" and remarked that "it was better at this time not to be making points of etiquette & personal dignity." [13] To explain such incredible behavior in a manner favorable to McClellan seems impossible if the incident was fully and correctly reported by Hay. Though McClellan's home letters reveal an overwhelming strain of work in this period,[14] one balks at attempting an explanation and ends by wondering what refreshments were served "at the wedding of Col. Wheaton at General Buell's" which McClellan attended that night.[15] It would be helpful if one had a fuller record, or at least a confirmation, of the incident, which Hay himself referred to as the "first indication" he had "yet seen" [16] of this sort of thing. Only two nights before, Hay recorded a presidential visit to McClellan's house in which the "Tycoon [Lincoln] and the General were both very jolly." [17]

In general, McClellan's bearing toward Lincoln, while not comparable in deference to that of Lee toward Davis, was proper and respectful; nevertheless he did not relish conferences with the President, nor put a high value upon his ability. On one occasion he wrote to his wife of being "interrupted" by Lincoln and Seward; [18] at another time he mentioned a call by this pair before breakfast; [19] apropos of the *Trent* affair he deplored the weakness and unfitness of those who controlled the destinies of the nation; [20] a few days later he thought that the President was honest and meant well; [21] yet again, when "thoroughly tired out" and under heavy pressure and blame

---

12 H. W. Bellows to his wife, Willard's Hotel, Sep. 12, 1861, Bellows MSS.

13 Diary of John Hay, Nov. 13, 1861, in Tyler Dennett, *Lincoln* . . . *in the Diaries* . . . *of John Hay,* 34-35.

14 At 1:30 a. m., November 2, McClellan wrote: "I have been at work . . . since I arose yesterday morning—nearly eighteen hours." *McClellan's Own Story,* 173.

15 Dennett, *Lincoln* . . . *in the Diaries* . . . *of John Hay,* 34.

16 *Ibid.,* 35.   17 *Ibid.,* 34.   18 *McClellan's Own Story,* 170.

19 *Ibid.,* 174.   20 *Ibid.,* 175.   21 *Ibid.,* 176.

at a time when he was preparing a "very important" letter to Cameron, he confessed avoiding his home and concealing himself "at Stanton's to dodge all enemies in shape of 'browsing' Presidents, etc." [22] (It should be noted that McClellan was consulting Stanton at a time of the latter's scornful hostility to the Lincoln administration.)

Back in July 1861 McClellan had written:

I find myself in a new and strange position here—Presdt., Cabinet, Genl. Scott and all deferring to me—by some strange . . . magic I seem to have become *the* power of the land. I almost think that were I to win some small success now I could become Dictator or anything else that might please me—but nothing of that kind would please me,—*therefore* I *wont* be dictator. Admirable self denial! . . .

. . . .

. . . All tell me that I am held responsible for the fate of the nation, and that all its resources shall be placed at my disposal. It is an immense task that I have on my hands, but I believe I can accomplish it. . . . Oh! how sincerely I pray to God that I may be endowed with the wisdom and courage necessary to accomplish the work. Who would have thought, when we were married, that I should so soon be called upon to save my country? [23]

Such statements as these have been used by anti-McClellan writers to confirm the impression of arrogance and egotism. McClellan wrote these words, however, in confidential letters to his wife. They were a kind of unstudied release, not to be taken too seriously. They were written just after the new commander had assumed his duties at Washington in the wake of Bull Run. What the general wrote to Mrs. McClellan did no harm at the time. The letters are racy and quotable and have been used against him, but this resulted from their being printed after the war in *McClellan's Own Story*. At the age of thirty-six McClellan was at the head of the Union armies; it was not unnatural for a young man so placed to write to his wife of the immense task resting upon him. To be confident of his own ability was a lesser fault, if it was a fault, than to be uncertain and insecure in a time of crisis. McClellan had a monumental task to perform. Unlike certain other generals, his was not the confidence of rashness.

---

[22] *Ibid.*   [23] Myers, *McClellan*, 212–214.

III

Lincoln's comment that one bad general was better than two good ones was a canny aphorism rather than an effective guiding principle. Certainly in 1862 it could be said that neither in the field nor at the capital was there any coördinating and directing mind. In the period while McClellan was still general in chief the attorney general advised Lincoln to "act out the powers of his place, to command the commanders," and become "in fact, what he is in law, the *Chief Commander*." Bates thought this idea entirely feasible, since the President's "aids" could keep "his military . . . books and papers" and do his bidding. If he (Bates) were President he would know what to do with officers who were restive under a superior. As for Lincoln, he thought that a change for the better would occur "if he will only trust his own good judgment more, and defer less, to . . . subordinates." [1]

Whether the advice of "General Bates" was to be taken or not, the turn of the year found the North impatient for action. Summer, autumn, and early winter had passed and McClellan had not moved. End the war in a hurry, or else! This seemed to be the thought of loyal citizens generally as they tired of military parades, noted the mounting expense, watched the enemy grow, heard rumors of a revolution in the Northwest, and witnessed a constant slipping in the administration's hold upon popular confidence. As one of Trumbull's correspondents expressed it: "The people say if we can whip them let it be done at once if we cannot we want to know it now and save ourselves from bankruptcy if we cannot the nation from disunion." [2]

This unrest was evident in the applause given to Greeley on January 3, 1862, when in Washington he declared that national misfortune had been due to reluctance to meet the antagonist. [3] As the elected leader in a democracy the President naturally did not escape the effect of this widespread impatience and disapproval.

A kind of crisis in military affairs (one of many) came in December and January, 1861-62, when McClellan lay ill of typhoid fever for about three weeks. O. H. Browning records that at this time he had a

---

[1] Bates, *Diary*, 223–224. [2] P. P. Enos to Trumbull, Jan. 7, 1862, Trumbull MSS.
[3] New York *Herald*, Jan. 4, 1862, p. 3, c. 3.

long talk with the President about the war. "He told me [wrote Browning] he was thinking of taking the field himself, and suggested several plans of operation." [4] McClellan's enemies took advantage of the situation, represented that army matters were at a standstill, and intrigued for his downfall. McClellan himself maintained that his intellect was not dulled, that his strong constitution enabled him to continue to transact business daily, and that each of "the chiefs of the staff departments" knew the condition of affairs and could deal, through him, with the President and secretary of war, so that no change in the machinery of army control was needed. [5] Nevertheless there began at this point a series of steps that tended progressively to create those elements of political interference which led at length to McClellan's ruin. Thinking that the sick general ought not to be "disturbed with business," [6] the President, with none of McClellan's confidence, took up the military part of his task with grim intensity. He gave close attention to western operations, advised Halleck to attack Columbus from up-river, concerned himself with affairs in eastern Tennessee where he noted that "our friends" were "being hanged and driven to despair," admonished Buell that "Delay is ruining us," and instructed that general to "name as early a day as you safely can" for a southward thrust. [7] It was at about this time that he took Halleck's *Science of War* out of the Library of Congress, and his secretaries relate that he "read a large number of strategical works," held long military conferences, and "pored over the reports from . . . the field of war." [8] On the tenth of January the President conferred with General Montgomery C. Meigs in the general's office. In "great distress," according to Meigs's account, the President said: "General, what shall I do? The people are impatient; Chase has no money . . . ; the General of the Army has typhoid fever. The bottom is out of the tub. What shall I do?" Meigs suggested a council of military chiefs. Accounts differ at this point. Meigs stated that a council of several generals and cabinet officials met on January 12, and that the President adjourned it till next day so that McClellan could attend. [9] McClellan stated that the conclave was called without his knowledge, that he mustered enough strength to be driven to the

[4] Browning, *Diary*, I, 523 (Jan. 12, 1862).   [5] *McClellan's Own Story*, 155–156.
[6] *Works*, VII, 70 (Jan. 1, 1862).   [7] *Ibid.*, VII, 71–74.
[8] Nicolay and Hay, *Lincoln*, V, 155.
[9] Montgomery C. Meigs, in *Amer. Hist. Rev.*, XXVI, 292.

White House, and that his unexpected appearance had "the effect of a shell in a powder-magazine." [10] Next day another conference was held, with McClellan present.[11] It was a strained and difficult meeting, at which Chase, according to McClellan's account, showed great anger because the "original and real purpose" was " 'to dispose of the military goods and chattels' of the sick man," and Chase could not bear the "sudden frustration of his schemes." [12] The meeting proceeded with a good deal of desultory whispering; then Chase, with "uncalled-for irritation" of manner, challenged McClellan to present his military program in detail. McClellan declined to reveal his plans in answer to Chase; when the same request came from the President, the general declined to submit his plans to that assembly, some of whom were "incapable of keeping a secret," unless the President would give the order in writing and assume the responsibility. On this note the council was declared adjourned by the President.[13] In the sullenness of McClellan's behavior one can see not only the caution of a field marshal who did not wish his intentions to become the property of everybody including the enemy, but also the resentment of a man who felt that the whole meeting was intended as a plot to destroy him.

In his impatience to get action Lincoln now took a step which almost suggested that he considered himself a general in chief or head of staff. On January 27, 1862, he issued "President's General War Order No. 1," which suggested that there were more to follow, in which he ordered a general forward movement of the land and naval forces to be launched on February 22, with details as to particular armies that were to move on that day. Secretaries, subordinates, the general in chief, and all other commanders were to be held severally to "strict and full responsibilities" for the "prompt execution of this order." [14]

---

[10] *McClellan's Own Story*, 156.

[11] Those present were the President, Generals McClellan, McDowell, Franklin, and Meigs, and Secretaries Seward, Chase, and Blair. Cameron, secretary of war, seems not to have been present.

[12] *McClellan's Own Story*, 157. McClellan thought that Chase wished to put his friend McDowell into the chief military command.

[13] It was not that McClellan refused to reveal his plans to the President, nor other chosen officials; he strongly distrusted the existing meeting, suspected insincere motives, and did not want his coming movements "spread over Washington." *Ibid.*, 158.

[14] *Works*, VII, 89–90. The order was peculiarly the President's own; it was not prepared in the war department and merely signed by the President. It is stated by Nicolay and Hay (*Lincoln*, V, 160) that the President wrote the order "without con-

Two things may be said of this presidential paper: (1) It was no mere advice or admonition; it was a peremptory order from the constitutional commander in chief of the army and navy. If it was not an order to be obeyed by all, high and low, its title was a misnomer and its wording a misfit. (2) In terms of actual fact the order got nowhere; nothing happened that bore any resemblance to fulfillment of the President's command.

As a sort of expansion of his "President's General War Order No. 1" Lincoln issued four days later his "President's Special War Order No. 1" directing that on or before February 22 an expedition should move out for the seizure of a railroad point "southwestward of . . . Manassas Junction." [15] The nation's chief was getting down to particulars. One cannot say that military commands in the American army have never been debated; at any rate McClellan was given "permission" [16] to debate this one, and it was never carried out. The President's order got no farther than a proposal. Execution was not required, yet the order was never formally revoked.[17]

In the giving of these orders it was as if Lincoln, though ineffectively, were performing as "Chief Commander" in the manner of Bates's suggestion. The more significant fact was that he was under pressure from all sides, and particularly under political and popular pressure, to send the troops forward. In the sense of military commands his orders were not taken seriously, nor has American army practice proceeded on the theory that the President functions as supreme field marshal. The fundamental meaning of the constitutional provision making the President "Commander in Chief of the Army and Navy" is to be found in the Anglo-Saxon concept that the military power shall be subject to the civil. It is for this reason that the highest civil official is given the power to determine, broadly, the national purpose and occasion for which the troops are used. That he should actually command an army or direct a fleet is not contemplated. Lincoln's giving of these war orders must be considered exceptional,

---

sultation with any one, and read it to the Cabinet, not for their sanction, but for their information."

[15] *Works*, VII, 91.

[16] "I asked his excellency whether . . . I could be permitted to submit . . . my objections to his plan and my reasons for preferring my own. Permission was accorded . . . ." *McClellan's Own Story*, 228–229.

[17] *Ibid.* 237.

rather than in line with established procedure. Nicolay and Hay state that they were issued when the President was "at the end of his patience." [18]

It is in this sense—i. e., in terms of troubled emergency, perplexing anxiety, and exceptional proposals—that one must read the above-noted remark of Lincoln to Browning as to the possibility of taking the field himself. To do that was not his function, nor is there reason to suppose, as some have superficially done, that such taking of the field would have promoted a better central war direction or strategic success, though it would have thrown the President more fully into the very midst of military controversy than he already was. To those who realize what the presidency involves, with all its civil responsibilities and its challenge of national leadership, the plan of the President becoming a great political general in actual command of the main army will be dismissed as beyond serious consideration. As for Lincoln, he was at his military best when he deferred to and supported able commanders, whom it was his duty to appoint, not when he overruled or displaced them.

Mention should be made of one other occasion on which Lincoln seemingly assumed the function of actual military-naval command. Early in May of 1862, though business was pressing in Washington, Lincoln made a somewhat curious visit to Fort Monroe, taking Secretary of the Treasury Chase and Secretary of War Stanton with him, and there is evidence that on this occasion he not only conferred with naval and military commanders but also took a hand in the actual direction of operations. Chase referred to "a brilliant week's campaign of the Prest." as if the President had been in command, and attributed the Union capture of Norfolk to Lincoln's direction of the movements involved.[19] A Massachusetts gentleman, James D. Green of Cambridge, left an account of this episode on the basis of information which Senator Sumner gave him: "The President [wrote Mr. Green], with his Secretaries, immediately put himself at the head of the troops then under the command of Gen. Macl, & at once proceeded to the capture of Norfolk, which was in no condition to defend itself, & of no importance in a military point of view; but, on the contrary, being sur-

---

[18] *Lincoln,* V, 159.
[19] Salmon P. Chase to his daughter "Nettie," May 11, 1862, Diary and Letter-book of S. P. Chase (MS., Lib. of Cong.).

rendered, its garrison forthwith marched up to aid in the defence of Richmond. The President next dispatched three Gun Boats up the James River, ..."

Historians of this period will recognize at once that Chase and Stanton were the most violently anti-McClellan of the cabinet members, and Mr. Green saw in this episode an effort on the part of the President, by the sending of gunboats up the James, to "anticipate McClellan in the capture of Richmond." He quotes Sumner as saying that Lincoln and his cabinet, just before this, had unanimously decided to remove McClellan from the command of the army (which Mr. Green considered "madness"), but that on receiving news of the evacuation of Yorktown they decided to "let the matter stand for the present." As for the astounding suggestion of removing McClellan just as he had come in front of the enemy, the thought occurred to this Cambridge gentleman, though "it seemed too atrocious to be admitted," that opposition to McClellan was motivated by "a *political object*—the interest of a *political party*"; McClellan was to be sacrificed, and perhaps also his army, because "the politicians in control of the Government had an ulterior object in view, more important in their estimation than the restoration of the Union, viz. that, let what would come, *the war should not cease till slavery was abolished.*"

Though Mr. Green in his perplexity (after talking with Sumner) questioned this astonishing theory, he considered it confirmed when he soon heard of Lincoln going with Chase and Stanton to Fort Monroe where the President took charge of operations, as he was led to believe, in the anti-McClellan sense.[20] This whole affair of Lincoln's presence at the front at the time of the capture of Norfolk is a bit hard to unravel in all its aspects, but confirming evidence does sustain the impression of the President serving as actual commander, expressing strong disapproval of what was being done under General Wool's

---

[20] James D. Green to Nahum Capen, Cambridge, Mass., Aug. 10, 1871, MS. copy in possession of Professor Frederick Green, Urbana, Ill. This letter, available through the kindness of Professor Green, is a remarkable document (see copy in Mass. Hist. Soc.). The substance of the letter, which loses somewhat of its force by not being strictly contemporary, is Mr. Green's recollection of an interview with Sumner, May 6, 1862, and his subsequent interpretation of events, especially in connection with the Lincoln-Chase-Stanton visit to Fort Monroe and the politically minded interference by the Washington government in the whole Peninsular campaign. Men in Washington, thought Green, did not want McClellan to capture Richmond, thereby becoming a popular idol and the next President.

direction, questioning subordinate officers, vehemently throwing his tall hat on the floor, and dictating military orders.[21]

IV

To give in detail all, or a major part, of the cross purpose behind the lines in the military planning for 1862 is quite impossible. There was basic difference as to the main strategic pattern and as to the fundamental organization and command of the army. McClellan had his plan, but Lincoln disapproved of it.[1] McClellan would move the army down the Chesapeake, up the Rappahannock to Urbanna, Virginia, thence across land to a railroad terminus (West Point) below Richmond on the York River; from there he would move to assault the Confederate capital. This may be designated as McClellan's "Urbanna plan." In contrast to this roundabout approach by water, Lincoln favored a direct land movement.

At this time the Union force was across the Potomac from Washington, at Alexandria; the Confederate force, under Joseph E. Johnston, was near by at Manassas. Lee, restless for action, was pinned down to staff duty in Richmond. As a military leader he had yet to be discovered. With logical modification McClellan's Urbanna plan developed into his Peninsular Campaign. This involved water transportation down the Potomac and Chesapeake to the Peninsula between the York and James Rivers, allowing from that point what McClellan considered a feasible and comparatively short advance against Richmond by the line of the James.

While McClellan pursued these plans in close consultation with Lincoln, there had developed a bitterly hostile and relentless intrigue behind the general's back. Perpetrators of this intrigue set traps to influence Lincoln with whom they sought private interviews, circulated falsehoods against McClellan, used the war committee to

---

[21] *Battles and Leaders of the Civil War*, II, 151–152.

[1] On June 18, 1862, O. H. Browning recorded a conversation with Lincoln on matters of strategy. He wrote: "During the conversation the President stated . . that his opinion always had been that the great fight should have been at Manasses . . . —that McClellan was opposed to fighting at Manassas, and he, the President, then called a Council of twelve generals, . . . and that eight of them decided against him, and four concurred with him, ... The majority being so great . . . he yielded, but subsequent events had satisfied him he was right." Browning, *Diary*, I, 552.

THE
EASTERN FRONT

Scale of Miles

0   10   20   30   40   50

BATTLE AREAS
OF THE
CIVIL WAR

Scale of Miles

0   50 100   200   300

From The Civil War and Reconstruction, *by courtesy of D. C. Heath & Co.*

defame the general, misrepresented his illness,[2] fomented jealousies among officers,[3] and plotted the commander's downfall. To replace him they favored Frémont, Pope, McDowell, or Banks. While shrieking "Onward to Richmond," these meddlers were accused by a newspaper correspondent of having defeated McClellan's projects to strike the enemy, while with their determination to know all of McClellan's secrets they were "aiding and assisting the rebels." [4] With entire confidence in their top general, according to this reporter, soldiers of the Army of the Potomac thought it "a pity that the Greeleys, Gurleys,[5] Chandlers, Wilkinsons, Garrisons and Lovejoys . . . [could not] be compelled either to close mouths which are perpetually vomiting forth slander and falsehood, or else be drafted . . . and made to wade through . . . thigh deep mud . . . ." [6]

There was evidence to indicate that McClellan's foes did not scruple to use that vilest of partisan tricks, the whispering campaign. A meeting of the Young Men's Republican Association of New York, according to the *Herald,* marked out a scheme to circulate rumors against McClellan and Mrs. Lincoln with the design of forcing McClellan to resign. It was further reported that private meetings were held in Wall Street, and that the campaign included an "editorial barrage," circulation of anti-McClellan literature among soldiers, and a hue and cry in religious publications.[7]

The motives of this conspiracy against the nation's chief commander were a mixture of partisanship, ambition, and honest abolitionism. Though far from pro-slavery, McClellan favored conducting the war on Congress's own platform of July 22, 1861, in which the nation's

[2] *McClellan's Own Story,* 155.

[3] Writing in this period to McClellan, Halleck mentioned a caucus of the abolition group in Congress which considered the question of high army ranks for their favorites, adding: "You . . . see the attempts of the abolition press to create jealousies between us." Halleck to McClellan ("Private"), Feb. 24, 1862, McClellan MSS.

[4] New York *Herald,* Jan. 14, 1862, p. 8, c. 1.

[5] John A. Gurley, Representative from Ohio, on January 29, 1862, had denounced the administration's inactive war policy, saying that the army had long been ready and the soldiers burning with a desire to strike at the traitors. He deplored the fact that the country had looked in vain for a commander in chief with enough enterprise to lead the forces to victory. Significantly he insinuated: "Did a general stand in the way to hold in check more than half a million of men? take him out of the way . . . ." *Ibid.,* Jan. 30, 1862, p. 8, c. 2. Next day, sarcastically denouncing the " 'On to Richmond' Orator," the *Herald* referred to Representative Gurley as "an 'onward' man before . . . Bull run, and . . . the same individual who ran twenty-seven miles without hat, coat or boots from that battle . . . ." *Ibid.,* Jan. 31, 1862, p. 5, c. 1.

[6] *Ibid.,* Feb. 1, 1862, p. 1, c. 2. [7] *Ibid.,* Feb. 19, 1862, p. 5, c. 3.

war aim was officially declared to be not the eradication of slavery in the South against the will of the states, but preservation of the Union on the prewar constitutional basis.[8] He thought of Southerners as human beings, recognized the existence of diverse elements in a composite country, deplored the tendency to associate the abolition cause with vindictive radicalism, and, above all, looked forward to a genuine return of the Southern people, after military defeat, to a satisfactory instead of a hateful Union.[9]

There was much to support McClellan's belief that the radical clique were determined to ruin him,[10] first by forcing a premature and unsuccessful movement, and afterwards by withholding the means necessary to success. "The success of McClellan in 1862," wrote W. C. Prime (an early biographer), "would have been doubly fatal to the politicians. The old Union would have been restored and the general would command the political situation. . . . His popularity must be destroyed. . . . Above all, he must not be allowed to win a decisive victory. Neither a quick ending of the war nor a victorious campaign by McClellan would enure to party success." [11] To probe the minds of men is no easy historical task. It is sufficient to say that the deeds of McClellan's detractors were entirely in line with the motives just outlined.

One of the methods of this radical intrigue—which, if feasible, would have gone to the extent of congressional action to dismiss Mc-Clellan—was a plan to "reorganize" the Army of the Potomac. Known as the "army corps" plan, and impressively clothed with French phrases and references to continental practice, this was in truth a scheme to take away McClellan's authority as general in chief and put the army under several corps commanders who would take orders from the secretary of war. The plan was the subject of long conferences between Lincoln and radical leaders,[12] and was embodied in an order

---

[8] See below, pp. 127–128. [9] *McClellan's Own Story*, 35.
[10] *Ibid.*, 150. [11] *Ibid.*, 8.
[12] ". . . the committee [on the conduct of the war] waited upon the President . . . , February 25. They made known . . . that . . . dividing the great army of the Potomac into *corps d'armée* had impressed the committee . . . [as] essential . . . . The President observed that he had never considered the organization . . . into army corps so essential as the committee seemed to represent it to be; still he had long been in favor of such an organization. . . . The committee left without any conclusion having been reached . . . ." Journal of the Committee on the Conduct of the War, February 26, 1862, in their Report (*Sen. Rep. No. 108*, 37 Cong., 3 sess.), I, 86–87.

by Lincoln under date of March 8, 1862.[13] It was done over McClellan's head, without consulting him, and against his judgment.[14]

The main significance of the order was a matter of personnel; of the five corps commanders named (McDowell, Sumner, Heintzelman, Keyes, and Banks), only Keyes had agreed with McClellan on fundamental strategy and supported him in councils of war.[15] Officers close to McClellan, in whom he had highest confidence, such as W. B. Franklin, Andrew Porter, and Fitz-John Porter, were conspicuous by their absence in this order of reorganization. The order was a demotion for McClellan. He was now head of the Army of the Potomac and commander of the "Department of the Potomac," but was relieved of authority over other departments. The most serious aspect of the reorganization business was not that McClellan, about to take the field, was no longer general in chief. It was that the control of the army was inadequate, timid, and bungling, and that political influences were successfully at work to hamper, worry, and destroy the man who yet remained head of the main army, and upon whom the Lincoln government depended for victory and even for survival. Until March McClellan had planned as to all the eastern sectors, seeking to make them a unified front. For this he needed coördination of the divisions and "departments." But now the "President's Special War Order No. 3" (March 11, 1862),[16] relieved him of general command and required the various commanders to report "severally and directly" to the secretary of war at a time when that inexperienced official was not only unable to initiate and conduct strategic plans,[17] but was rapidly becoming a tool of the anti-McClellan cabal. Such an order was nothing less than a vote of no confidence in a commanding general about to launch upon his first major campaign.

V

Before the army moved there were yet other instances of groping and experimentation. One of the most curious and futile was the

---

[13] *Works*, VII, 116–117. The President was again consciously functioning as commander in chief. This order was designated as "President's General War Order No. 2."
[14] *McClellan's Own Story*, 222.   [15] Myers, *McClellan*, 256–257.
[16] *Works*, VII, 129–130.
[17] Stanton's peevish inadequacy and indecision appear in the Hitchcock episode which follows immediately.

Hitchcock episode. Ethan Allen Hitchcock was a Vermont soldier of long and varied record. He had instructed at West Point, served in the Seminole and Mexican Wars, held command on various western assignments, traveled widely, and made himself known as a man of experience, religious feeling, and learning. In tastes and aptitudes, however, he was "a scholar rather than a warrior," [1] and in 1862 he reached the age of sixty-four, having long before (1855) resigned from the army, which he seems to have entered because, being the grandson of Ethan Allen, it was expected of him. One can but imagine the feelings of this old soldier in March 1862 as he hastened to Washington on telegraphic summons, suffered a hemorrhage on the way and another on arrival, lay in bed while the secretary of war told him that he and Lincoln needed his services, and was soon after asked if he would take McClellan's place in command of the Army of the Potomac! According to Hitchcock's diary Lincoln received him civilly, mentioned how he was urged to remove "the traitor McClellan," stated that as President he was "the depository of the power of the government and had no military knowledge," and expressed the wish to have the benefit of the veteran's experience. After leaving the President, Hitchcock was in a mist as to what would come of it all. In his diary he wrote: "I want no command. I want no department. . . . I am uncomfortable. I am almost afraid that Secretary Stanton hardly knows what he wants, himself." [2] Declining the "high station" proffered, he accepted an ill-defined staff appointment as adviser to Stanton and Lincoln,[3] rendering such service as he was capable of, though in this capacity he was popularly held responsible for the very movements which he disapproved.[4]

In a scene of petulance and impatience (April 26, 1862) Stanton complained to Hitchcock that he had no one around him to give military opinions. " 'It is very extraordinary that I can find no military man to give opinions. *You* give me no opinions!' he added. The . . . subject . . . was the position of General Banks. Now I had given him a very definite opinion on that very point two or three days

---

[1] W. A. Croffut, ed., *Fifty Years in Camp and Field: Diary of Major-General Ethan Allen Hitchcock, U. S. A.,* 437.

[2] *Ibid.,* 439.

[3] His signature in this period was: "E. A. Hitchcock, Maj. Gen. Vol. on duty in the War Dept." Memorandum, April 19, 1862, Hitchcock MSS.

[4] Croffut, 443.

before . . . ." Thus reads the Hitchcock diary,[5] which proceeds to record an extraordinary interview several days later when Hitchcock's resignation reached Stanton's hands. What bothered Stanton on this occasion to the point of humiliating lamentation and supplication was the thought that he would be ruined by the general's resignation, upon which Hitchcock destroyed the paper.[6] "His idea that my resignation would destroy him [wrote Hitchcock] was not from the loss of my supposed services, but because he knows his reputation for acting on impulse and . . . that my withdrawal would be construed to his disadvantage."

Finding himself in a "painful situation" without ability to perform his duties and denied even the boon of resignation, Hitchcock continued to struggle with his anomalous position until he was so weak that he could scarcely reach his room from the lower story of his hotel. With a twinge of conscience all too rare among men of the time he wrote: "I feel my presence here as no other than a tax on the Treasury, without being able to render any adequate service." [7] When he made recommendations to Lincoln and Stanton they were "ignored," so that he "insisted" on resigning rather than remaining "in a false position." [8] Though thrice offered, his resignation was not permitted. With collapse of health, relief came by leave of absence from May to November 1862; when he was again called for duty after recuperation, it was as commissioner of prisoners, "and for the next three years this was his principal duty, though intermitted with that of counsellor at headquarters [in the war department], and assignments to courts-martial . . . ." [9] Though this Hitchcock episode has been all but forgotten, it offers an amazing revelation of the uncertainty and futility of war administration under Stanton. The whole trend of Hitchcock's advice had been in opposition to McClellan's plans; in this situation neither Hitchcock nor McClellan, nor any general, was given a free

[5] *Ibid.*, 442.

[6] Hitchcock's diary records that he burned the letter of resignation in Stanton's presence (*ibid.*, 442). His own copy, preserved in his papers, bears the penciled endorsement: "This was presented—but recalled at the earnest request of Mr. Stanton." In his letter to the secretary he frankly stated that he had tried his strength and found it wanting. Hitchcock to Stanton, Washington, April 28, 1862, Hitchcock MSS.

[7] Hitchcock to Stanton ("Private"), Washington, May 13, 1862, *ibid.* In his diary of May 21 Hitchcock wrote: "I told him [Stanton] . . . that I am positively ashamed to be in receipt of the pay and emoluments of a major-general and render no adequate service . . . ." Croffut, 443.

[8] Croffut, 443.   [9] *Ibid.*, 445.

hand and undivided support.

As a part of the whole confused situation, an equally curious assignment had been given to the secretary of the treasury. To relieve an overburdened war department in 1861, problems of organization had been put into Chase's hands. This applied to such matters as the three-battalion organization for a regiment, the numbering of regiments, the three-year term for volunteers, and the like. Fortunately, for the working out of these details, Chase had the assistance of competent officers—Lorenzo Thomas, Irwin McDowell, and W. B. Franklin—but this was not all; beyond the tasks assigned to him, Chase showed a degree of activity in military matters that was quite surprising in a secretary of the treasury. Indeed much of his correspondence in 1861–62 reads like that of a secretary of war. To an Ohio friend he wrote: ". . . I have urged the sending of an adequate force up the James River to coöperate with the gunboats." [10] Writing to his friend McDowell he mentioned that he had tried unsuccessfully to get Lincoln to direct a forward movement by that general; then he counseled: "If I were you I would move forward with all the forces I could . . . ." Realizing the ineffectiveness of central army direction, and anxious to build up McDowell's reputation in the public mind, he added: "Only *act* on your judgment; do not wait for directions from Washington . . . do your own thinking, moving and fighting—and when you accomplish anything report it . . . . You know I believe in reports—by Generals." [11] It is unnecessary to add that Chase's persistent zeal was directed toward the destruction of McClellan, with whose radical opponents the secretary was in close touch.

[10] Chase to M. Halstead, May 24, 1862, copy in Chase MSS., Hist. Soc. of Pa.
[11] Chase to McDowell, June 6, 1862, copy in *ibid.*

CHAPTER XIX

McCLELLAN'S DEMOTION ASSISTS LEE

I

SUCCESS for McClellan in his complicated undertaking against a powerful and brilliant defense required coöperation of the navy, availability of an adequate force, unity of command, and generous support at Washington. To say that these elements were lacking would be an understatement; back of the lines there was active obstruction and opposition to McClellan's campaign from its hampered start to its abrupt termination in mid-course. In contrast to the coöperation of Lee and Jackson which gave superiority of striking force to Confederate arms, the Union situation involved divided effort, political interference, and uncertainty of plan.

McClellan wanted more men.[1] Those who assail him for such a request may, if they wish, base their opinion upon the sage advice of the War Committee that "fighting, and *only* fighting" could end the rebellion [2] (what could be more simple!) or upon the expansive boast that if General Pope had been given McClellan's force and opportunity, nothing could have prevented him from marching promptly to New Orleans.[3] If, instead of this, one prefers the critical approach,

---

[1] In the voluminous literature that has grown up in criticism of McClellan there constantly recurs the stereotyped comment that he always overestimated the strength of the enemy and made excessive requests for a heavy force of his own. With this in view it is interesting to read the statement of Gideon Welles under date of August 31, 1862: "Halleck walked over with me from the War Department as far as my house, . . . ; [he] says that we overrate our own strength and underestimate the Rebels' . . . . This has been the talk of McClellan, which none of us have believed." Welles, *Diary*, I. 99.

[2] Report, Committee on the Conduct of the War (*Sen. Rep. No. 108*, Part I, 37 Cong., 3 sess.), p. 66.

[3] Pope's statement was in the form of brief assent to a leading question by Senator Chandler. *Ibid.*, 282. For another example in which Pope permitted bold words in criticism of McClellan to be put into his mouth, see below, pp. 99–100.

he may perceive hard realities not evident to a Zach Chandler or a Ben Wade. Lee was one of those realities. So was the Confederate army. McClellan had crack troops to oppose. The condition of the Union cause when he took charge after Bull Run was pitiful. McDowell and Scott had failed. To repeat that failure would have been to lay Washington open to enemy occupation.[4] Transition of the army from a small-scale unmilitary aggregation to a colossal yet manageable organism was McClellan's achievement. That transition had to be accomplished amid the hazards of war and the interference of politicians. He had to "create a real army and its material out of nothing." [5] There was justification for his statement that not a day of his preparation in camps of instruction had been wasted.[6]

Once he had his army, McClellan's task was not to move out and take an enemy position or win a battle; it was *to force a military decision in the whole war.* It was not a sporting proposition of showing what he could do on equal terms. It was a matter of overwhelming the enemy with a heavy force in his own country, destroying his fighting power, making it impossible for him to strike again, and thus forcing an end to the struggle. Whether McClellan could have done this no one can say with absolute certainty. At least he saw what was to be done; only a simple-minded person would have expected him to do it without a huge army under unified command. Instead of such unity the broad Virginia front was under six generals: Frémont, Banks, McDowell, Wool, Burnside, and McClellan.[7]

Abandoning his Urbanna-West-Point scheme, McClellan launched his Peninsular campaign with Fort Monroe as a base. Beginning in March, the sailing of his troops carried over into the first days of April. Before he embarked, the enemy had abandoned its position at Manassas, leaving wooden guns which became the theme of anti-McClellan sneers, though by their withdrawal the Confederates showed their recognition both of McClellan's striking power and of the importance of concentration near Richmond. Step by step as he proceeded, McClellan found the area of his authority restricted and his available force reduced. Contrary to previous understanding, his base at Fort Monroe was removed from his control; it was ordered by

---

[4] *McClellan's Own Story,* 74.   [5] *Ibid.,* 72.   [6] *Ibid.,* 98.
[7] Statement of E. D. Keyes in McClellan, *Report on the . . . Army of the Potomac* (1864), 168.

the President that troops were not to be detached from the Fort without General Wool's sanction.[8] Naval coöperation, necessary for control of the York and James Rivers, failed him; then a whole division— an important one—under General Blenker was detached from his command.[9] Though done with the promise that such a thing would not be repeated, this was immediately followed by a severe blow in the withholding of the First Army Corps under McDowell. Taken together, these dispositions meant a loss of nearly 60,000 men by McClellan's estimate, or more than a third of his force at the outset of a major campaign.[10] This blow "frustrated" McClellan's plans when he was "too deeply committed to withdraw" and forced the adoption of a less effective plan. He called it a "fatal error." [11]

After three and a half weeks of siege McClellan took Yorktown on May 4, 1862. Protecting Johnston's main force, Longstreet checked McClellan at Williamsburg (May 5), following which the Union fleet was stopped at Drewry's Bluff, so that McClellan lacked the flotilla support that had proved so essential in the West. With about 85,000 troops "for duty," [12] McClellan advanced to meet an enemy of approximately equal strength concentrating for a powerful stand in front of Richmond. The logical Union approach to Richmond was by the James, and it was so that McClellan intended it, planning that McDowell's force should join him by the best route—i. e., by water through Hampton Roads. Interference in Washington, however, put McDowell in independent command, kept his force back, and then tardily ordered it to join McClellan *by land,* a much more difficult matter.[13] It never did join him and was never effective in the campaign,

---

8 *Ibid.,* 156.   9 *Ibid.,* 160.   10 *Ibid.*   11 *Ibid.,* 161.

12 In letters to Washington McClellan stated on April 7 that his entire force for duty amounted to only 85,000, and on May 10 that he did not think he could bring more than 70,000 men upon the field of battle. *Report on the . . . Army of the Potomac,* 162, 191. Before Washington, in March, his command had embraced about 200,000. On the eve of Mechanicsville Lee hoped, with Jackson, to open battle "with about 85,500 soldiers of all arms" (Freeman, *Lee,* II, 116).

13 Illustrating the bad effect of the effort to manage things from Washington, McClellan wrote to Stanton showing how unsatisfactory was the secretary's plan for an overland march by which McDowell would join the main army on the Peninsula. Mentioning the destruction of railroad bridges and the delay (four weeks) before this could be remedied, all this at a time when the enemy was giving every indication of a fight McClellan pointed out the slowness of wagon transportation and the hazard of extending his own right to meet McDowell. The latter, he said, ought to be sent by water transports. McClellan to Stanton (autograph draft, signed), June 12, 1862. McClellan MSS.

but the effort to hook up with McDowell caused McClellan to expose his right, straddle and bridge the Chickahominy, operate in swampy country in a wet season, incur unnecessary delay and loss, and give battle under the difficult conditions of the Seven Days. A water movement of McDowell's force to join the main army on the James seemed to McClellan to offer better results; it was part of the considered and coördinated plan of the man who was in responsible command of the Army of the Potomac. Knowing this, political heads at Washington killed the plan, but they substituted nothing better.

II

Possible junction of McDowell and others with McClellan was deeply dreaded by Confederate leaders, and in Stonewall Jackson they found the answer. In the month between May 8 and June 9,[1] while McClellan was challenging Johnston and Lee on the Peninsula, Jackson was shifting, feinting, and striking in the Valley of the Shenandoah with the dash and mystifying cunning for which he has become famous. All the scattered and puzzled Union forces north of the Rappahannock—those of Frémont and Banks west of the Blue Ridge and of McDowell east of that barrier—were Jackson's game; part of them he engaged, managing to have superior force when he struck; others he baffled and neutralized. Near McDowell, [West] Virginia, he defeated units of Frémont's command under Milroy and Schenck; this engagement occurred on May 8. Disappearing, fooling Frémont, and keeping Union forces separated, Jackson next turned his attention to Banks, striking him at Front Royal (left defenseless by Stanton's bungling), racing him to Winchester, fighting him there, and sending his force in precipitate flight across the Potomac (May 23–25).

In this period none of the maneuvers directed from Washington contributed to the timely reënforcement of Banks or the effective concentration of any Union force to meet Jackson when and where his blows fell. With far more than enough men to have disposed of Jackson, Federal leaders were now in a kind of panic for the safety

---

[1] Prior to his famous May-June campaign Jackson's Valley operations had included the sharp battle of Kernstown near Winchester (March 23, 1862). Shields attacked him successfully while he was demonstrating against Winchester with a view to preventing Union concentration under McClellan; in the sense that he did prevent such a concentration, even this lost battle was no failure.

of Washington as reports came in that the enemy was about to descend upon the capital, this being the opposite of what Jackson was doing. As newsboys were shrieking "Washington in Danger" on the morrow of Banks's defeat, a badly worried government was intensifying the panic by measures taken to relieve it. The President took military possession of the railroads of the United States. The secretary of war summoned Northern governors to send all the militia and volunteer force they could muster. To create counter excitement, secessionists at Baltimore made a demonstration of rejoicing at Banks's defeat.[2]

Lincoln at this time, with his uninspired war minister, was taking a good deal to himself in the maneuvering and shifting of men, but his remote control did not work; the men did not shift as ordered. Frémont had been ordered to move toward Harrisonburg to put himself in Jackson's rear; instead of that he turned up at Moorfield. The usefulness of Frémont was to be assessed in terms of intercepting Jackson and relieving Banks; what happened was that Jackson swept Banks out of the Valley and eluded Frémont's pursuit. This bit of business may be a detail, but it is worth while to take a closer look at the records. When Banks was being hard pressed, Lincoln sent the following to Frémont:

> The exposed condition of General Banks makes his immediate relief a point of paramount importance. You are therefore directed by the President to move against Jackson at Harrisonburg . . . . This movement must be made immediately. You will acknowledge the receipt of this order, and specify the hour it is received by you.[3]

This was signed "A. Lincoln" and dated "War Department, May 24, 1862. 4 P. M." It was nothing if not a presidential order for the immediate movement of troops to a specified place for a stated purpose. That night at 7:15, having received Frémont's telegram of compliance, Lincoln wired:

> Many thanks for the promptness with which you have answered that you will execute the order. Much—perhaps all—depends upon the celerity with which you can execute it. Put the utmost speed into it. Do not lose a minute.[4]

To show what a jolt Lincoln received in his effort at remote control, he wired to Frémont on May 27: "I see that you are at Moorefield. You

---

[2] Moore, *Rebellion Record* (Diary), V, 17.   [3] *Works*, VII, 179 (May 24, 1862).
[4] *Ibid.*

were expressly ordered to march to Harrisonburg. What does this mean?" [5] One could show by the records how that refrain "What does this mean?" ran through the war despatches from Washington in these days. Lincoln wanted to know whether or not the enemy were "north of Banks, moving on Winchester." For all he knew Banks might be "actually captured." He desired from Banks "more detailed information . . . respecting the force and position of the enemy" pressing upon him. He queried one of the lesser officers: "Are the [enemy] forces still moving through the gap at Front Royal and between you and there?" When Jackson was heading southward up the Valley Lincoln was fearing a general and concerted Confederate movement in large force northward, such as would menace Washington. He wanted to know what had happened to men sent to Harpers Ferry, and wondered if any of them had been cut off. He thought Banks's retreat was "probably" a "total rout." He feared Jackson was about to cross the Potomac. All the while he was puzzled as to why Mc-Dowell and Frémont did not get action in Jackson's rear. He was anxious to learn what Geary's scouts under Banks's command were doing. They found no enemy "this side of the Blue Ridge," but had they been to the Blue Ridge looking for them? Four days after Jackson's defeat of Banks he was uncertain "whether any considerable force of the enemy—Jackson or any one else— . . . [was] moving on to Harper's Ferry or vicinity." He wondered whether the enemy in force was "in or about Martinsburg, Charlestown, and Winchester, or any or all of them . . . ." "Where is your force?" he wired Frémont on May 30. "It ought this minute to be near Strasburg." That morning he had a despatch from Frémont, not telling where he was, but representing Jackson's force "at 30,000 to 60,000." (This was absurd; not more than about 15,000 or 16,000 would have been a fair guess.) Next day, referring to a rumor of more forces having entered the Valley, Lincoln commented: "This . . . may or may not be true." On June 3 he wired McDowell: "Anxious to know whether Shields can head or flank Jackson. Please tell about where Shields and Jackson . . . are at the time this reaches you." [6]

Much of this fog of war was inevitable; the remarkable thing was

5 *Ibid.*, VII, 195.

6 These bits are from Lincoln's telegrams in the confused days of Jackson's Valley maneuvers. *Works*, VII, 178–211, *passim.*

that in the Valley campaign the hampering obscurity of the fog worked almost entirely for the detriment of the Union side. With a small mobile force Jackson was keeping much larger Union forces jumping, wondering, pursuing, and backing. After Banks's defeat a force under Shields was shifted from the east side to the west side of the Blue Ridge to coöperate with Frémont and destroy Jackson, but Stonewall's God again "blessed his army" as he prevented the junction of these Union generals, and, in two more of his famous Valley battles (Cross Keys and Port Republic, June 8–9, 1862) defeated them separately.

So great was the Washington scare produced by Jackson's scant force that Lincoln even suggested to McClellan that he "give up the job" on the Peninsula and come back to defend Washington on the erroneous supposition that there was a "general and concerted" movement of the enemy against the Northern capital.[7] This spasm of alarm, known as the "great scare,"[8] was short lived, but it weakened Lincoln's faith, never strong, in the Peninsular Campaign, while it confirmed his determination to hold back McDowell's forces.[9] When Union consternation was at the keenest Jackson was making a well calculated feint, not an attack, against Harpers Ferry and then withdrawing up the Valley. In a brilliant month he had marched 245 miles, won four "desperate battles,"[10] and prevented Union forces several times his size from threatening Richmond. He had thwarted that Union concentration under McClellan which, since the Confederates feared it, must have been the reasonable line of Federal strategy. Then, when it was erroneously supposed that Lee would reënforce him, Jackson reënforced Lee and took part in the major campaign to save Richmond.

Stonewall was supporting Lee at the time that McDowell, to mention one among an array of generals, was supposed to be supporting McClellan, but in the manner of this support there was a marked difference. In Jackson's shifting about he accomplished much by the very shifting, but above all he did strike effectively in widely separate

---

[7] "I think the movement [of Jackson] is a general and concerted one, . . . not . . . a . . . defense of Richmond. I think the time is near when you must either attack Richmond or give up the job and come to the defense of Washington." *Ibid.*, VII, 183 (May 25, 1862). Confederate leaders were hoping that authorities in Washington would interpret Jackson's movement in precisely this manner.

[8] Rhodes, *Hist. of the U. S.*, IV, 19.　　[9] *Works*, VII, 186–188 (May 25, 1862).

[10] *Battles and Leaders of the Civil War*, II, 297.

areas. On the other hand McDowell, one of three [11] corps commanders each of whom had a force much larger than Jackson's, did precisely the opposite. When Confederates were tensely anxious lest he march toward Richmond, he marched away from it.[12] He was poised uncertainly between two sectors without striking in either, and the manner of his poising and shifting was not such as to baffle or immobilize the enemy, but to relieve their fears.

III

It was Stanton's constant anxiety, and also Lincoln's, that Union forces even larger than McClellan's own be held back, north of the Rappahannock and in the Blue Ridge area, to "cover" the capital. On the other hand it was McClellan's contention that the Confederates would have to concentrate near Richmond and that the heavier his own attack the more likely such concentration would be. Any serious Southern effort to seize Washington, he judged, was out of the reckoning so long as the main Union army was not disposed of. In short, McClellan believed that offense constituted defense, that Washington was being defended on the Peninsula. Taking the whole situation in retrospect it is almost as if Lee and Jackson exercised a magic control over official minds at Washington. Union performance as hampered by these official minds was in precisely the terms which Lee and Jackson desired and foresaw.

On this point it is pertinent to note the well considered judgment of a Confederate officer: "McClellan had planned and organized a masterly movement to capture, hold, and occupy the Valley and the Piedmont region; and if his subordinates had been equal to the task, and there had been no interference from Washington, it is probable the Confederate army would have been driven out of Virginia and Richmond captured by midsummer, 1862." [1] After summarizing his own plans for holding the Valley and Piedmont areas (in the general region of Washington, Winchester, Warrenton, and Manassas), by which Jackson would have been held back and Washington "covered by a strong force well entrenched," McClellan wrote: "If these

---

[11] Frémont, Banks, and McDowell.   [12] Freeman, *Lee*, II, 66.
[1] Statement of General John D. Imboden, C. S. A., in *Battles and Leaders of the Civil War*, II, 283.

measures had been carried into effect Jackson's subsequent advance down the Shenandoah would have been impracticable; but, unfortunately, as soon as I started for the Peninsula this region was withdrawn from my command, and my instructions were wholly disregarded." [2]

It was not as though McClellan had neglected the Valley, nor the approaches to Washington. The main differences between his plans and those of the political leaders at Washington were on two points: (1) McClellan would send much the heavier force into the Peninsula, retaining smaller, yet adequate forces in the Winchester-Strasburg-Warrenton-Manassas region; (2) he would coördinate all fronts, planning that Banks's movement against Jackson in the Valley should coincide with his own against Richmond. He would not waste large bodies of troops by having them merely held back and scattered; he would plan movements to include the action of Banks and Frémont as well as himself and McDowell. Emphasis is upon the word *plan*. His Peninsular campaign constituted part of the plan, his disposition of Banks a complementary part. Always regarding his advance upon Richmond as the main business,[3] McClellan made arrangements for the more immediate defense of Washington without getting into a state of nerves about it. In the knowledge that Washington defenses were strong, his plan for dealing with Jackson was to throw that general "well back, and then to assume such a position as to . . . prevent his return"; this he thought could be done with a force of 25,000 or 30,000.[4] Rightly he regarded Jackson's move as "merely a feint." On that basis he wrote: ". . . if McDowell had joined me on the James the enemy would have drawn in every available man from every quarter to make head against me. A little of the nerve at Washington which the Romans displayed during the campaign against Hannibal would have settled the fate of Richmond in very few weeks." [5]

---

[2] *McClellan's Own Story*, 240.

[3] "I think that the time has arrived to bring all the troops in Eastern Virginia into perfect cooperation. I expect to fight another and very severe battle before reaching Richmond. . . . All the troops on the Rappahannock, & if possible those on the Shenandoah should take part in the approaching battle. We ought immediately to concentrate everything . . . . All minor considerations should be thrown to one side & all our . . means directed towards the defeat of Johnston's army in front of Richmond." Rough signed draft of telegram, McClellan to Stanton, May 8, 1862, McClellan MSS.

[4] McClellan, *Report*, 137–138.   [5] *McClellan's Own Story*, 346.

IV

McClellan's first grapple (May 31-June 1) with Johnston's main force was at Seven Pines (Fair Oaks), several miles east of Richmond. The Union army was at a disadvantage on account of rains, high water on the Chickahominy, and dispersion of forces. Throwing a heavy force against exposed parts of McClellan's position, Johnston struck at the moment when McDowell, in obedience to orders from Washington, was marching the wrong way. Resisting stoutly, McClellan repulsed Johnston, whose severe wounding at this "desperate hour" [1] put Robert E. Lee in command of the main Confederate army. Twenty-five days passed, during which Jackson completed his Valley operations and headed toward Richmond. Then Lee fought his first battle (June 26), which was a Confederate failure.[2] Finding McClellan's forces scattered and divided by the Chickahominy, Lee attacked north of that river at Mechanicsville, hoping to turn McClellan's right, push down the Chickahominy, and threaten his base at White House on the Pamunkey. By preventing this, McClellan saved his army, deprived Lee of the element of surprise, and, after severe fighting, forced his enemy to retire.

Immediately came the second major battle of the Seven Days at Gaines's Mill, where Lee won a costly victory without dangerously shaking McClellan's army. Something of the proportions and intensity of this encounter is suggested by McClellan's comment just after it was fought that he believed it would "prove to be the most desperate battle of the war." [3]

In the face of a pursuing and attacking enemy, confident, powerful, and ably led, McClellan now accomplished the daring and difficult feat of changing his base from White House on the Pamunkey to Harrison's on the James. This involved moving "enormous trains and heavy artillery" [4] over swampy terrain, under such pressure that "there was not a night in which the men did not march almost continually, nor a day on which there was not a fight." [5] By this successful maneuver, which showed his ability to make quick decisions in field command, McClellan deflected Lee's next effort, kept his own forces

---

[1] Freeman, *Lee*, II, 72.   [2] *Ibid.*, II, 135.   [3] *McClellan's Own Story*, 424.
[4] *Battles and Leaders of the Civil War*, II, 376.   [5] *Ibid.*, II, 382.

intact, got away with slight loss of equipment,[6] and kept the cards for the next play. The armchair strategist could say that McClellan "should have" struck at Richmond, from which Lee had been drawn away, instead of withdrawing to a point fifteen miles below Richmond on the James. But the opposing army was the main objective. If McClellan had broken into Richmond, Lee might have crashed into his rear, severed his communications, nullified his chance for naval support, and isolated his army. Under such circumstances, even if "taken," Richmond might have been, not a Union triumph, but a death trap. In this connection anti-McClellan comment even goes to the point of stressing the lack of troops "in Richmond" as if McClellan had merely to march in and "take" the place. There were few troops there for the sufficient reason that Lee was managing his army by placing it where necessary for operation against his foe, watching for an opportunity to get on his flank or behind his lines.

The final phase of the bloody Seven Days was a matter of sharp rearguard fighting at White Oak Swamp and Savage's Station (June 29), then two more major battles, Frayser's Farm (Glendale) and Malvern Hill. At this point Jackson's coöperation with Lee was disappointing, and Frayser's Farm stands as "one of the great lost opportunities"[7] for the Confederates, in that they did not destroy McClellan's army while in the vulnerable process of hasty withdrawal. It was on the note of Confederate failure that the Seven Days ended when, at the terrific engagement of Malvern Hill (July 1, 1862), a series of Confederate assaults was stopped by McClellan's solidly placed army. In the sense that he had not yet "taken" Richmond, McClellan was alleged to have "failed." On the other hand, Lee had not won his objectives; McClellan had "escaped the destruction Lee had planned for him."[8] Union arms came through the Peninsular campaign well. With his army powerfully poised and well based at Harrison's Landing, McClellan was ready to continue the argument, while Lee, having lost 20,000 of the 85,000 he had at the beginning of the campaign,[9] concerned himself during the weeks after Malvern Hill with the recuperation and reënforcement of his troops.[10]

---

[6] *Ibid.*   [7] Freeman, *Lee*, II, 199.   [8] *Ibid.*, II, 219.   [9] *Ibid.*, II, 230.   [10] *Ibid.*, II, 256.

V

A period of confusion, perplexity, and political intrigue followed the Seven Days. The President's confidence in McClellan was slipping, he was looking elsewhere for captains, and the enemies of McClellan were taking advantage of the alleged "failure" of the Peninsular campaign to ruin that general and radically alter the whole strategic picture. On other than military fronts the President was hard pressed. A long session of Congress was drawing to a close, with radicals driving ahead with compelling force for laws that Lincoln did not want. The problem of emancipation was at a critical stage; coming weeks would see important developments in that explosive field. Foreign intervention was now a dread danger; never was this hazard more serious than in the summer and fall of '62. Should the military situation in the East show delay or defeat, a turn for the worse in international relations could be surely predicted. The campaign was about to begin for the election of a new Congress, and victories were keenly awaited for their effect on vote-getting prospects. Many Republicans, and these the most influential, were at odds with Lincoln in his basic political ideas of conducting the war. To placate these men, at least in part, might be a party necessity, however much it might be a national disadvantage. The war was in an early stage; the military leaders that were to see it through were yet to emerge; failures in military experimentation were yet to be made. Civil strife was not merely a matter of warring states. The North itself was badly divided; in presiding over a distraught nation Lincoln had to feel his way. Except for the briefest intervals he could not get away from Washington, and the atmosphere of the capital in the summer of '62 was not of the healthiest.

On the very day of Mechanicsville (June 26, 1862) Lincoln had taken a step which revealed a kind of discounting of McClellan's battles with Lee together with a persistent emphasis upon the Valley even after Jackson had left it, and upon covering Washington when it was not threatened. On that day John Pope, known for easy triumphs on the Mississippi and for favorable attention by Wade's officious war committee, was made commander of the "Army of Virginia," to be distinguished from the Army of the Potomac under McClellan.[1] Under

---

[1] *Offic. Rec.*, 1 ser., XII, pt. 2, 20

Pope were the scattered forces of Frémont, Banks, and McDowell, together with minor units near Alexandria and in the intrenchments that guarded Washington. This was as if the administration was giving notice that it would not reënforce McClellan when the main business of the Peninsular campaign was well under way. Pope was anti-McClellan. He was a strong dissenter to McClellan's fundamental plans, and was expected to get results from opposite methods. That McClellan should be discredited was now a well formulated policy at Washington. Yet the new commander (Pope) was so uncomfortable and so full of "grave forebodings" that he asked at once to be relieved from command of the Army of Virginia and returned to the West.[2] On assuming command (July 14) Pope issued an address, as follows:

To the Officers and Soldiers of the Army of Virginia:
By special assignment of the President of the United States I have assumed the command of this army. I have spent two weeks in learning your whereabouts . . . and your wants . . . .
. . . I have come . . . from the West, where we have always seen the backs of our enemies; from an army whose business it has been to seek the adversary and to beat him when he was found; whose policy has been attack and not defense. . . . I presume that I have been called here to pursue the same system and to lead you against the enemy. It is my purpose to do so, and that speedily. . . . I hear constantly of "taking strong positions and holding them," of "lines of retreat," and of "bases of supplies." Let us discard such ideas. . . . Let us study the probable lines of retreat of our opponents, and leave our own to take care of themselves. Let us look before us, and not behind. Success and glory are in the advance, disaster and shame lurk in the rear. . . .[3]

Armchair pertness and amateur strategy [4] are implicit in this whole document as it casts slurs at "bases of supplies" and glibly promises to "lead . . . against the enemy" as if such a movement were a glorious parade. In army eyes on both sides this bragging was a matter of jest and ridicule. "I regret [wrote Fitz John Porter] . . . that Gen Pope

---

[2] "I . . . took the field in Virginia with grave forebodings of the result . . . ." Statement of Pope, *Offic. Rec.*, 1 ser., XII, pt. 2, 22.
[3] *Offic. Rec.*, 1 ser., XII, pt. 3, 473–474.
[4] That these were not the most grievous of Pope's defects was indicated in an amazing series of severe military orders at the time of taking his new command, in which he threatened destruction of homes, taking of supplies from enemy civilians without compensation, arrest of male non-combatants within his lines, expulsion of those refusing the Union oath, imposition of the death penalty for minor offenses, et cetera. See Freeman, *Lee*, II, 263–264.

has not improved since his youth and has now written himself down what the military world has long known, an ass. His address to his troops will make him ridiculous in the eyes of military men . . . , and will reflect no credit on Mr Lincoln who has just promoted him. If the theory he proclaims is practised you may look for disaster." [5] Confederate gibes against Pope were in much the same tone, various of his supposed expressions being Southern army jokes, as for instance that his headquarters were in the saddle and that he did not care for his rear.[6] Between the lines Pope's boastful address was a denunciation of McClellan and was so intended. According to General Jacob D. Cox the address was dictated by Stanton;[7] indeed, according to Gideon Welles, the whole episode of introducing Pope to high command in the East was "an intrigue of Stanton's and Chase's to get rid of McClellan."[8] Coming from Pope, when one remembers his trepidation and his wish to resign before he ever started moving, the loudly heralded words of this address are grimly amusing.

VI

In a quandary as to what to do after Malvern Hill, but under painful pressure for a change, Lincoln made a visit to Harrison's Landing (arriving on July 8) to see McClellan and view the army. Conferring at headquarters with McClellan and other generals, the President asked a series of questions as to the whereabouts of the enemy, the size of the army, and sanitary conditions in camp. The set questions, asked of one officer after another, suggest a lawyer who seeks in cross examination to produce a predetermined conclusion. More especially, Lincoln asked: "If it were desired to get the army away from here, could it be safely effected?" [1]

---

[5] Pencil copy of a letter from Fitz John Porter to Hon. J. C. G. Kennedy, dated Westover Landing, James River, July 17, 1862. In the same letter Porter also wrote: "I have heard that Gen McClellan has lost favor at Washington; a report which I hope is unfounded and that Gen Halleck is to be called to Washington as General-in-Chief." McClellan MSS.

[6] Statement of Gen. James Longstreet, C. S. A., in *Battles and Leaders of the Civil War*, II, 513.

[7] Jacob D. Cox, *Military Reminiscences of the Civil War*, I, 222.

[8] Welles, *Diary*, I, 108. Welles added: "A part of this intrigue has been the withdrawal of McClellan and the Army of the Potomac from before Richmond and turning it into the Army of Washington under Pope."

[1] "Memorandum of questions and answers . . . at Harrison's Landing," July 9, 1862, *Works*, VII, 262–266.

On this last point, Lincoln's chief question at the moment, only Keyes and Franklin would agree to a removal. McClellan opposed it. Sumner said "we give up the cause if we do it." Heintzelman said "it would be ruinous to the country." Porter said "Move the army and ruin the country." [2] All the circumstances of this interrogation of high officers indicate that Lincoln was personally taking a hand in strategic decisions, and was seeking to justify a contemplated withdrawal of the army from before Richmond. The note of retreat offers a strange contrast to Pope's bombastic address which came at nearly the same date.

The occasion of Lincoln's visit was used by McClellan to hand the President a document known as the "Harrison Bar Letter" in which he stated his ideas of broad policy in the conduct of the war. With great earnestness the general advised that the Union cause was the cause of free institutions and self government, and must never be abandoned. He would have the President consider war aims "covering the whole ground of our national trouble." The conflict had "assumed the character of war"; as such it should be conducted on the "highest principles," not with a view to "subjugation." It should not be a war upon populations, but upon armed forces. Instead of confiscating property (on which a bill was soon to be presented for the President's signature), executing persons for political reasons, reducing states to the territorial organization, and forcibly abolishing slavery, he would confine military action to the military sphere, avoiding all trespass upon the persons and property of the Southern people. Military government, he thought, should not be abused nor carried over into the regulation of domestic relations. He would appropriate slave labor where necessary but would compensate the owner. This might even require manumission for a whole state as in Missouri, "Western Virginia" and Maryland (on this aspect McClellan was not

---

[2] *Ibid.* In their biography of Lincoln (V, 453) Nicolay and Hay give a quite inadequate account of the President's visit to McClellan's army and his questioning of the generals. They briefly slur over the preponderant opinion of the generals which was strongly opposed to what became the next step from Washington—removal of the army from before Richmond. Furthermore, by putting all the stress on officer opinion concerning the slight extent to which the enemy was threatening McClellan, they give the wrong impression. If the enemy did not plan to attack at that time, that was evidence of McClellan's strength in his existing position, but the whole twisted context in Nicolay and Hay suggests that because the enemy was not planning to attack, therefore the army ought to be removed far to the rear and its commander reduced to a minor role.

a stickler for slavery interests), but any exploitation of the war to promote radical and vindictive views would, he feared, cause disintegration of the armies. With a sense of being on the brink of eternity, McClellan protested that this advice was given with love of country and with sincerity toward the President. "I am willing," he said, "to serve you in such position as you may assign me, and I will do so as faithfully as ever subordinate served superior."[3]

It is amazing how much abuse has been lavished upon McClellan apropos of this letter. Nicolay and Hay, writing (it is now known) with the studied purpose of tearing down McClellan while seeming to be fair to him,[4] treat the letter with stinging sarcasm. They refer to it as "mutinous," which it certainly was not, and mention the general's preference for the Democratic party as if to imply that partisanship offered the motive for the letter. As a kind of *post facto* comment they assert that the letter marked "the beginning of General McClellan's . . . political career."[5]

As for partisanship one can find that abundantly manifest in McClellan's contemporary opponents and historical critics. Rightly to judge the letter itself one must consider its occasion, content, and method. The occasion was one in which the President had to choose whether or not he would go along with the radicals in their drive for a vindictive war; the content was politico-military and was pertinent to problems at hand; the unpublicized method was that of a confidential communication for the President's consideration. It is even debatable whether McClellan was going outside his proper military sphere in this quiet personal advice to the President. In this connection two points should be remembered: (1) It was well known that many officers and men, keen to fight for the Union, would find their ardor seriously diminished if they felt that the war was directed by radicals bent upon punishing the Southern people. McClellan was properly concerned with the morale of his army. In this sense what was called political was of obvious military importance. (2) Instead of playing up the tendency of his soldiers to discuss politics in such a way as to sow disaffection against the administration, McClellan used his influence to discourage it, even though he might personally agree with the dissenters.[6] Remembering this, what better way was

---

[3] *McClellan's Own Story*, 487–489.   [4] See above, p. 68.
[5] Nicolay and Hay, *Lincoln*, V, 449–451.   [6] Cox, *Military Reminiscences*, I, 360–362.

there for him to convey this dissent to the President than by the respectful Harrison Bar letter? McClellan wanted the President to avoid the excesses of the radicals who were not merely interested in suppressing slavery but were out for punitive measures against the South. Such measures, he felt, were extraneous to the nation's military purpose and were calculated both to weaken the Northern war effort and to give the Southern people valid cause for resisting reunion. If in July 1862 "political" factors were linked with the military situation, which was painfully true, the radicals were as much to blame for it as McClellan.

By a strange error Nicolay and Hay refer to the language and tone of the letter as that of a "manifesto." [7] In truth it was a confidential document handed to the President; even the general's close friends did not see it until after McClellan's final removal from command.[8] To concede that the leading Union general, at a hard moment, may have failed in tact or political aptness is reasonable enough. The remarkable thing is that a purely confidential letter of advice handed in person to the President, addressing him with respect for his authority on topics of prime importance and timeliness, should have become the basis of the violent abuse which writers on Lincoln have traditionally emitted. It leads one to wonder why it is that a Lincoln writer may so obviously lack the Lincoln spirit. The letter was not a blast from a defiant Frémont nor a gaucherie from a blustering Butler. What was least likely was that the quiet handing of such a letter to the President in person could have promoted McClellan's fortunes in the "political" sense. If McClellan had intended his advice on the war as a means of promoting his political ambitions in opposition to the President, which critics broadly imply, he would hardly have handled the matter so inconspicuously as a communication for Lincoln's own personal attention. As for Lincoln, he read the letter in McClellan's presence as the general gave it to him; in doing so he showed no indignation and made no comment.[9]

There were, of course, things which McClellan did not say to Lin-

---

[7] Nicolay and Hay, *Lincoln*, V, 451.

[8] ". . . no one of McClellan's most intimate personal friends . . . knew . . . of this letter until rumors about it came from members of Mr. Lincoln's cabinet. None of them saw it until after the general was finally removed from command." Editorial note by W. C. Prime, *McClellan's Own Story*, 489–490.

[9] *Ibid.*, 487.

coln's face. These he said to his wife, or otherwise in private correspondence. Such correspondence is very revealing, and it shows that McClellan, while honestly serving the administration, had no faith in it. As for Stanton, he hated to think that humanity could sink so low. Referring to his political enemies, he feared they had "done all that cowardice and folly can do to ruin our poor country." Feeling so, as he told his wife, he had given the President the Harrison Bar letter to clear his conscience.[10]

So fully was McClellan convinced of the purpose of his foes to overthrow him that he wrote his friend Aspinwall, New York business leader, asking for assistance in obtaining some kind of employment in New York against the day when he might be forced to leave the army. He was receiving no reënforcements and he felt that the game was to deprive him of the means of moving and then cut off his head for not doing so, to weaken his command and then hold him responsible for results. He was weary of it; if he could no longer be of service he would rather resign his commission.[11]

VII

Lincoln returned to Washington where Chase, Stanton, and the radicals were intensifying their anti-McClellan drive. Then he attempted another bit of military experimentation on July 11 by ordering Halleck "to command the whole land forces of the United States," making him general in chief.[1] In his painful search for commanders other than McClellan it appears that Lincoln sought wisdom from that feeble old veteran, Winfield Scott. "The President [wrote Gideon Welles], without consulting any one, went about this time on a hasty visit to West Point, where he had a brief interview with General Scott, and immediately returned. A few days thereafter General Halleck was . . . ordered to Washington . . . as General-in-Chief, ..."[2] Another ineffective complication was now added to a confused military situation. Matters drifted till Halleck assumed com-

---

10 *Ibid.*, 449.

11 McClellan to Aspinwall, July 19, 1862, McClellan MSS., quoted in Myers, *McClellan*, 314.

1 *Works*, VII, 266–267.

2 Welles, *Diary*, I, 108–109; see also Charles W. Elliott, *Winfield Scott*, 755.

mand, which he did on July 23. They drifted further while the new general in chief visited Harrison's Landing. Then, having denied reënforcements to the Peninsular forces, Halleck on August 3 ordered McClellan to remove his whole army from before Richmond to Aquia Creek, south of Bull Run and close to Washington.[3] With military operations at a pause it was consistent with the existing situation and with unwritten practices in the American army to regard such an order as subject to consideration between brother officers. At any rate, McClellan could not let it pass without earnest protest. Withdrawal, said he, would be "disastrous in the extreme"; it would be a "fatal blow." His army was well placed twenty-five miles from Richmond, with conditions of transportation and supply in his favor. To move would demoralize the army, discourage the Northern people, and adversely affect the attitude of foreign powers. "Here," he said, "in front of this army is the heart of the rebellion. . . . It matters not what partial reverses we may meet with elsewhere; here is the true defense of Washington. It is here on the bank of the James River that the fate of the Union should be decided." "Clear in my convictions of right," he concluded, "actuated solely by love of my country, . . . I do now what I never did in my life before, I entreat that this order may be rescinded. If my counsel does not prevail I will with a sad heart obey your orders . . . whatever the result may be, and may God grant that I am mistaken . . . . I shall at least have the internal satisfaction that I have written . . . frankly, and have sought . . . to avert disaster from my country."[4]

Chapters could be written on this withdrawal of McClellan's army when that general, hampered though he was by orders from Washington, was planning a new advance against Lee. Two years were to follow before another such opportunity was to be presented, when Grant was to move in the same manner intended by McClellan. "All the lives [thought W. C. Prime] and all the agonies of the country which were expended in regaining that same position two years afterwards were wasted for the only purpose of getting rid of McClellan."[5] Leslie Combs considered that "nothing but Military madness or folly could have induced the withdrawing." "It was . . . fatal." What high officials, queried Combs, could have advised it? Then he added:

---

[3] *Offic. Rec.*, 1 ser., XII, pt. 2, 5.   [4] *Ibid.*, 8–9.   [5] *McClellan's Own Story*, 12.

"I presume one of them was . . . Stanton, whose administration of his high office has proved him to be an ass—if not a knave . . . ." [6]

The order for withdrawal was not rescinded and McClellan obeyed, getting "the army away from here," as Lincoln expressed it, and setting up new headquarters at that "wretched place," [7] Aquia Creek (August 24). There were now two main Union armies in Virginia—the Army of Virginia under Pope, and the Army of the Potomac under McClellan. In the strict sense the army was well nigh headless. Over all, not to mention Providence (on whose support Stonewall Jackson claimed priority), stood Henry W. Halleck. Behind the lines, with more power than wisdom, was the arrogant and intriguing Stanton, none too sure of his own place. [8] Mediating as best he could between conflicting factions, [9] with imperfect controls in his hands, was the buffeted Lincoln.

Pope was expected to stand on the defensive, holding the line of the Rappahannock until there could be a general Union concentration behind that river. Such concentration effected, it was expected that "Halleck, the General-in-Chief, was to take the field in command of the combined armies." [10] This, however, was a mere vague understanding; it was so indefinite that McClellan, retaining command of the Army of the Potomac, understood that he was to "direct . . . all the forces in Virginia, as soon as they should be united." [11] Still further vagueness was added when Pope received "information . . . of a secret character, afterwards suppressed" that a campaign was to be launched "without waiting for a union of all the forces, and under

---

[6] General Leslie Combs to McClellan, Dec. 4, 1862, McClellan MSS.

[7] *McClellan's Own Story*, 528. (Lincoln's reference to the desire "to get the army away from here" is found in his memorandum of questions and answers, July 9, 1862, cited above.)

[8] In midsummer of 1862 there were reports that Stanton was to be replaced by Banks. One of Banks's admirers wrote him: ". . . New England is looking to the change in the War Dept. & to you as the riseing man, all concede McClellans lack of capacity . . & Stantons inability to fill so responsible a post . . . ." He added: "You . . . are the . . . riseing man . . . on whom we must rely as the successor of Lincoln. The War Dept. is the step to it. A successful administration of that Dept puts you in the White House." John Fitch to N. P. Banks, July 7, 1862, Banks MSS.

[9] "The meddlers have tried to raise an issue between McLellan [sic] and Stanton. The President has overruled them firmly." John Ely to R. W. Thompson, New York, Aug. 8, 1862, MS., Lincoln National Life Foundation, Fort Wayne.

[10] *Offic. Rec.*, 1 ser., XII, pt. 2, 515. See also *Battles and Leaders of the Civil War*, II, 542 and n.

[11] *Offic. Rec.*, 1 ser., XII, pt. 2, 515.

some commander other than either of those before named." [12] For practical purposes McClellan was out of the picture. There was little point to recent dispositions except in the anti-McClellan sense, yet it was not until August 30 that he knew he had been deprived "of the command of all his troops then between the Potomac and the Rappahannock," remaining only in nominal command of the Army of the Potomac.[13] As revealing looseness in army management it is instructive to note McClellan's remarks in writing to his wife on the uncertainty of his own status, this on the eve of an important major battle. In this critical stage he had learned "nothing whatever of the state of affairs," did not see how he could "remain in the service if placed under Pope," could "hardly think that Halleck would permit" such a "disgrace," was without word from Washington as to where he stood, and was waiting "for something to turn up." "I presume [he wrote] they are discussing me now, to see whether they can get along without me." [14] These things he wrote on August 24. On August 29 he wrote: "I have a terrible task . . . . No means . . . , no authority, ... I find the soldiers all clinging to me; yet I am not permitted to go to the post of danger! . . . I have just telegraphed . . . to the President and Halleck what I think ought to be done. I expect merely a contemptuous silence. . . . I am heart-sick . . . . I see the evening paper states that I have been placed in command of all the troops in Virginia. This is not so. I have no command at present— . . . I have none of the Army of the Potomac with me, and have merely 'turned in' on my own account to straighten out whatever I catch hold of. . . . I have seen neither the President nor the secretary since I arrived here; [15] have been only once to Washington, and hope to see very little of the place. I abominate it terribly." [16]

---

[12] *Ibid.* This meant some commander other than McClellan or Pope. The reference was probably to Burnside.
[13] *Ibid.* See also *McClellan's Own Story*, 520.   [14] *McClellan's Own Story*, 528.
[15] The letter appears to have been written at his camp near Washington.
[16] *McClellan's Own Story*, 530–531.

CHAPTER XX

THE BREAKING OF McCLELLAN

I

EVENTS now moved with appalling swiftness to crisis and disaster. In a complicated campaign, whose details the reader may seek elsewhere, Pope and his subordinates got tangled up with Lee and Jackson. Operating separately from Lee, Jackson sped north through Thoroughfare Gap, struck Pope's rear, destroying supplies and communications, then shifted to a point where in two days of furious fighting (August 29 and 30) he acted powerfully with Lee to administer to Pope a smashing defeat on the unpropitious battleground of Bull Run.

To read the Union documents on Second Bull Run is to contemplate one of the saddest chapters of the war. "A terrific contest with great slaughter . . . , our men behaving with firmness and gallantry." The "enemy's dead and wounded were at least double our own." "The action raged furiously all day." "My cavalry was utterly broken down." "Our men, much worn down by . . . continuous fighting . . . and very short of provisions." "Kettle Run," "Manassas," "Centreville." "Hooker," "Sigel," "Reynolds," "Heintzelman," "Kearny," "Banks," "King," "McDowell," "Reno." "An unfortunate oversight." "I do not hesitate to say that if . . . Porter [1]

---

[1] Charged with disobedience of orders and failure to push forward his forces in cooperation with Pope in the campaign of Second Manassas, General Fitz John Porter, on court-martial trial, was cashiered and forever disqualified from holding office. In a long standing controversy, famous in American military history, Porter had strong support, uncertainty in high command being one of the factors in the case. Convicted in 1863, Porter was vindicated in 1886 when Congress passed a special act restoring him to army rank. With McClellan, Porter was one of the chief targets of the radicals; his court martial was regular, but in addition he was subjected to prejudiced "trial" by the committee on the conduct of the war. Accusations against Porter are given in *Offic.*

had attacked . . . we should have crushed Jackson before . . . Lee could have reached him." Night "must see us behind Bull Run." Confronting "a powerful enemy with greatly inferior forces." "All hope of being able to maintain my position . . . vanished." "The troops . . . I cannot say too much for them." "I am, . . . respectfully, your obedient servant." [2]

Such were the strokes and phrases of Pope's report. Only a part of the Army of the Potomac, as of Pope's own command, had been used. Superb fighting on the part of the men had gone for naught because of poor generalship. The idea had been to "save" Washington,[3] but Lee had been drawn north when McClellan's withdrawal relieved the pressure on Richmond,[4] had won a ringing victory, and confidently decided that his next move was to invade Maryland. The peninsular front, which occupied Lee at what McClellan called the "heart of the rebellion," had been stupidly given up. McClellan's contention that Washington was being defended on the Peninsula had now been impressively verified. Pope's grave forebodings had been fulfilled. His beaten army, in disorder and low morale, withdrew "within the defenses of Washington." [5] To look back at this point and quote the bombastic words put into his mouth on assuming eastern command, would be an excess of irony.

So complete and obvious was Pope's failure that he was relieved of command of the Army of Virginia and returned to the West. An incidental result of his brief occupation of a high military pinnacle had been the retirement of Frémont. This general, whose advancement to highest command had been sought by some of the anti-McClellan radicals, was to have become a corps commander in Pope's army. Feeling that he could not serve in that capacity, he was relieved of command at his own request.[6] This "faux pas," as the Herald ex-

---

Rec., 1 ser., XII, pt. 2, 507–511. For his defense by an army board that made a full investigation after the war, see *ibid.*, 513 ff.

[2] *Offic. Rec.*, 1 ser., XII, pt. 2, 12–17 (especially 15–17).

[3] On August 29 McClellan wrote to his wife: "There was a terrible scare in Washington last night. A rumor got out that Lee was advancing rapidly on the Chain bridge with 150,000 men. And such a stampede!" *McClellan's Own Story*, 530–531.

[4] ". . . Lee did not move northward from Richmond with his army until assured that the Army of the Potomac was actually on the way to Fort Monroe, . . . so long as the Army of the Potomac was on the James, Washington and Maryland would have been entirely safe . . . ." *Ibid.*, 482.

[5] *Offic. Rec.*, 1 ser., XII, pt. 2, 8.

[6] Cox, *Military Reminiscences*, I, 202, 222. With Frémont's retirement his useless "Mountain Department" ceased to exist.

pressed it,[7] ended his military career. If in this gesture he was essaying the martyr's role, hoping to gain popular support over the President's head, he failed as completely as in other factious and disrupting efforts.

The Union cause had now reached a sorry pass. Pope wrote to Halleck: "You have hardly an idea of the demoralization among officers of high rank . . . , arising . . . from personal feeling in relation to changes of commander-in-chief and others. . . . When there is no heart in their leaders, . . . much cannot be expected from the men." [8] Feelings had been hurt, jealousies were running high, Pope was held in contempt, confidence in prevailing army direction was upset, Philip Kearny was dead, men were exhausted and broken in spirit, organization was badly impaired. Halleck was "utterly tired out." [9] The army, said Welles, had "no head." [10] Annoyance was caused by a "drunken rabble who came out as nurses by permission of the War Dept." [11] To McClellan's eyes there was a "total absence of brains" in army control from Washington.[12] Roads toward the capital were clogged with an "innumerable herd of stragglers,—mingled with an endless stream of wagons and ambulances, urged on by uncontrollable teamsters,—which presently poured into Washington, overflowed it, took possession . . . , and held high orgie." Such was the description by an eye-witnessing officer, who continued: "Disorder reigned unchecked and confusion was everywhere. The clerks in the departments . . . were now hastily formed into companies and battalions for defense; the Government ordered . . . arms and . . . money . . . to be shipped to New York, and the banks followed the example; a gun-boat, with steam up, lay in the river off the White House, as if to announce . . . the impending flight of the Administration." [13]

Even the President doubted that the capital city could be saved.[14] In this grave emergency, despite the radicals, Lincoln turned to

---

[7] New York *Herald*, June 29, 1862, p. 4, c. 6.

[8] Sep. 1, 1862, 8:50 a. m., at Centreville. *Offic. Rec.*, 1 ser., XII, pt. 2, 83.

[9] Halleck so described his condition in a telegram to McClellan, Aug. 31, 1862, 10:07 p. m., McClellan MSS.

[10] Welles, *Diary*, I, 107.

[11] H. Haupt to Gen. R. B. Marcy, Aug. 31, 1862, McClellan MSS.

[12] That McClellan used this language in writing "frankly" to Halleck, Aug. 31, 1862, is itself significant. *Ibid.*

[13] Richard B. Irwin, in *Battles and Leaders of the Civil War*, II, 541–542.

[14] *McClellan's Own Story*, 535.

McClellan, but the manner of calling him once more to highest field command was casual and somewhat grudging. On September 1, two days after Pope's defeat, Halleck personally asked McClellan to command the defenses of Washington, that and no more. Halleck's misreading of the situation was shown on this occasion when he specifically limited McClellan's authority to the works and garrisons guarding the capital, giving him no commission to step into Pope's shoes. This gave McClellan "no control over the active army." [15] In the inadequacy of Halleck the decision fell to Lincoln himself. An officer of Halleck's staff (J. C. Kelton) was sent to investigate the condition of Pope's army. "Next morning [wrote McClellan] while I was at breakfast, . . . the President and Gen. Halleck came to my house. The President informed me that Col. Kelton had returned and represented the condition of affairs as much worse than I had stated . . . ; that there were 30,000 stragglers on the roads; that the army was entirely defeated and falling back to Washington in confusion. He [Lincoln] then said that he regarded Washington as lost, and asked me if I would, . . . as a favor to him, resume command and do the best that could be done. . . . I at once said I would accept . . . . Both the President and Halleck again asserted that it was impossible to save the city, and I repeated my firm conviction that I could and would save it. They then left, the President verbally placing me in entire command of the city and of the troops falling back upon it . . . ." [16]

II

It was thus upon the President's informal and verbal request that McClellan assumed command at this desperate hour. The only published order in the premises was that of Halleck dated September 2, putting him in command "of the fortifications of Washington and of all the troops for the defence of the capital." [1] It took courage and

[15] *Ibid.*, 542.   [16] *Ibid.*, 535.

[1] *Offic. Rec.*, 1 ser., XII, pt. 3, 807. On September 2, 1862, Chase wrote as follows in his diary: ". . . the fact was stated . . . [in cabinet meeting] that McClellan had been placed in command of the forces to defend the Capital—or rather, to use the President's own words, he 'had set him to putting these troops into the fortifications about Washington,' . . . . I remarked that this could be done equally well by the Engineer who constructed the Forts . . . . The Secretary of War said that no one was now responsible for the defense of the Capital . . . ." *Annual Report*, Amer. Hist. Assoc., 1902, II, 64.

decision for Lincoln to act as he did. There were persistent efforts by McClellan's foes to make it appear that his refusal of coöperation had caused Pope's defeat, whereas in fact McClellan had chafed at the restraints which had held him detached from the main operation. At a time when the anti-McClellan drive had produced an appalling condition and threatened to make it worse, Lincoln quietly appealed to McClellan to step in and take over command.

This act was Lincoln's own. It was taken in opposition to his military advisers and his cabinet. The day it was done a meeting of the cabinet was held. The historian would give a good deal for an adequate report of that meeting; from the fragments we have, given by Chase and Welles, it is evident that Chase and Stanton vigorously took issue with Lincoln in his determination to restore McClellan. According to Chase there was considerable discussion as to the responsibility for the order, Stanton disclaiming responsibility for himself and Halleck, and Lincoln thinking that Halleck was as answerable as before. Chase used the occasion for a severe denunciation of McClellan, remarking upon his "series of failures," "omission to urge troops forward" to support Pope, and unworthiness of trust. The secretary of the treasury "could not but feel that giving the command to him was equivalent to giving Washington to the rebels." [2] Others in the cabinet, except Blair, agreed with Chase.

At this point one finds a cryptic statement in Chase's diary (September 2, 1862). As edited by Warden the diary reads: "The President said it distressed him exceedingly to find himself differing on such a point from the Secretary of War and the Secretary of the Treasury; that he would gladly resign his place; but he could not see who could do the work wanted as well as McClellan. I named Hooker, or Sumner, or Burnside, either of whom could do the work better." [3] Did Lincoln on this occasion express a wish to be relieved of the presidency? The words "resign his place" are not as clear as one could wish. They are so read by Warden, who prints this portion of the diary, and this is the reading which Carl Sandburg adopts.[4] In the

---

[2] *Ibid.*, 65.

[3] This is the version as given by R. B. Warden, in *Private Life and Public Services of Salmon Portland Chase*, 459–460. In the ms. diary the sentence concludes: ". . . either of whom, I thought, would be better." Warden's editing is careless.

[4] Carl Sandburg, *Abraham Lincoln: The War Years*, I, 543–544. Sandburg, of course, had basis for this reading by following Warden. It is a tricky point.

Manuscript in Library of Congress

DESPONDENCY IN WASHINGTON: A PAGE FROM THE WELLES DIARY

After Pope's defeat at Second Bull Run the Union prospect seemed very low. At the moment of McClellan being ordered by Lincoln to "take command of the forces in Washington" (in reality to command the Army of the Potomac at a time of acute crisis) Welles records a cabinet meeting. Stanton was "trembling with excitement," the President "greatly distressed." At the top of the page Welles is writing of the conviction that Pope is a failure. This manuscript differs from the printed edition of the diary. The date is September 2, 1862.

The Small Politicians in Congress CACKLING at GENERAL McCLELLAN.

GREAT NEWS.
FIRST CITIZEN. "So the *Army of the Potomac* has crossed the Rappahannock again!"
SECOND CITIZEN. "Ah! indeed! which way?"

ONE OF THE EFFECTS OF THE WAR.
ARMY CONTRACTOR'S WIFE. "And say, Young Man, put me up a Diamond Necklace, and a couple of Gold Watches *along of them other things!*"

WARTIME CARTOONS

The upper cartoon appeared in *Harper's Weekly*, Jan. 25, 1862, not long after the formation of the arrogant congressional "Committee on the Conduct of the War." The other two appeared in the same magazine, Feb. 7, 1863, when Burnside's failure on the Rappahannock, and the ill-gotten wealth of army contractors, were current topics.

best published text of the diary, however, the reading is "resign his plan." [5] When one consults the manuscript he finds a passage written in a clerk's hand, not Chase's, in which the doubtful word looks like "place," but the better reading seems to be "plan" considering this clerk's peculiar *n's*.[6] Since in any case the diary is not a verbatim recording, Lincoln's actual words are in doubt, but of his deep distress and his determination to reinstate McClellan despite almost unanimous cabinet opposition, there is no question.

Reading Welles's diary, one has further details. Those who had favored Pope were "disappointed" with his performance. Blair, who had known him intimately, called him "a braggart and a liar." Before the President came into the room Stanton, "trembling with excitement," announced that McClellan had been given command. Then Lincoln came in, confirmed the statement, and said that he was responsible, though he added that Halleck had agreed to it. "Much was said [wrote Welles]. There was a more disturbed and desponding feeling than I have ever witnessed in council; the President was greatly distressed. There was a general conversation as regarded the infirmities of McClellan, but it was claimed, by Blair and the President, he had beyond any officer the confidence of the army. . . . These, the President said, were General Halleck's views, as well as his own, and some who were dissatisfied . . . and had thought H. was the man for General-in-Chief, felt that there was nothing to do but to acquiesce, yet Chase . . . emphatically stated . . . that it would prove a national calamity." [7]

It was with such lack of war-department and cabinet support that McClellan led the army while Lee, shifting his forces from before Washington, launched upon the invasion of Maryland, threatening Baltimore, Philadelphia, and the capital. Conditions at Washington were pitiful. "The War Department [wrote Gideon Welles] is bewildered, knows . . . little, does nothing, proposes nothing." [8] Some days passed before Lee crossed the Potomac; at this moment there

---

[5] *Annual Report,* Amer. Hist. Assoc., 1902, II, 65.

[6] The ms. diary is available in the Library of Congress, and the author has a photostat of it before him as he writes. No record for this date in Chase's own hand has been found. The clerk's doubtful script seems the closest we can come to the original.

[7] Welles, *Diary,* I, 104–105. Welles also treats the subject in his *Lincoln and Seward,* 194 ff.

[8] Welles, *Diary,* I, 111.

was no telling whether the northward push was not a mere feint and Washington the immediate object of attack. As the Confederate columns advanced, McClellan interposed his army between Washington and the enemy, the timid Halleck meanwhile nagging him with querulous complaints that he was too precipitate and too neglectful of guarding the seat of government.

The pros and cons of the fearful Antietam campaign cannot be reviewed here, much less settled. Was McClellan too cautious? Did he err in not striking when Lee's forces were scattered? Was he to be censured for not immediately throwing all his troops into the front line? Was the lack of earlier and more effective assaults due to himself or to Burnside? Was he too timid in not pressing and striking his stunned foe immediately after the battle? Such questions may be left to the military writers. Sequences can at least be noted. In the passes of South Mountain (September 14) McClellan fought so effectively with Lee, and his forces were so disposed, that after the battle the Confederate commander contemplated immediate retreat into Virginia, this before Antietam was ever fought.[9] The battle along Antietam Creek, September 17, 1862, was up to that time the heaviest and bloodiest engagement of the Civil War; McClellan called it "the most severe ever fought on this continent." [10]

Lee was in a tight place. McClellan's maneuvering before and after South Mountain made it a desperate question whether the Southerner would be able to rush his scattered troops into concentration soon enough and in sufficient force to stop the Union assault. It was an aggressive McClellan with plenty of fight in him that the Confederates were facing. Maryland, whatever its sentimental attachment to the South, had not risen in practical response to Lee's proffer of "liberation." North of the Potomac the Confederates were in Union territory. Lee was the invader; yet at that moment, in a doubtful struggle,

---

[9] "Lee looked . . . at the facts: the day [of South Mountain] had been bad; the morrow might be worse. . . . The Army of Northern Virginia . . . must seek the friendly soil on the south side of the river, ... So reasoned Lee. . . . Then Longstreet and D. H. Hill arrived . . . . Hood came also. Their opinion was unanimously in concurrence with . . . Lee . . . : The army must retreat. It could not hold South Mountain the next day." Freeman, *Lee*, II, 372–373. (Further developments—e. g., Confederate capture of Harpers Ferry, and the expectation of reënforcement by Jackson—caused Lee almost immediately to reconsider, delay his retreat, and make a stand at Sharpsburg.)

[10] *McClellan's Own Story*, 613.

he was standing on the defensive against McClellan's attack. Since, however, McClellan was defending Washington, which Lee was threatening, the terms defense and offense seem almost interchangeable. As matters stood on September 17, Lee would not have attacked. It was indeed a question whether he could save his army from destruction. That he did save it despite Federal strength, stands as one of his biggest achievements, and authorities still dispute the issue as to which side was the victor in the tremendous battle that raged for fourteen hours and involved casualties of over twenty-three thousand.[11] When the "terrific" yet "superb" [12] fighting was over McClellan had not destroyed Lee's army. He had, however, turned the hopeful Confederate invasion into a complete failure; on September 20 Lee was back on the Southern side of the Potomac. The stereotyped statement that each side failed to accomplish its objective suggests an unrelieved checkmate. Yet the campaign was more than that; the advantages of South Mountain and Antietam were more on the Union than on the Confederate side. Union morale had been lifted from the morass into which it was plunged by Pope's disaster. The Confederate army's ambitious thrust into Union territory had been parried; its "dreams of 'invading Pennsylvania' dissipated." [13] Lincoln was provided with a favorable military situation without which the emancipation proclamation [14] would have fallen flat. "The efficacy of the President's proclamation," wrote the elder Frank Blair to McClellan, ". . . depends on the power that is to enforce it. You and the army you lead are relied on to make this measure fruitful of good results." [15] British observers, convinced until then that overthrow of the Union was inevitable, now harbored doubts as to the wisdom of intervention for, or even recognition of, the Confederacy. McClellan's objectives—defense of Washington, Baltimore, and Pennsylvania, driving the enemy out of Maryland—were accomplished. Tough fighting qualities in the Union army had been impressively demonstrated. Lee's men and generals had also fought superbly, but Confederate weaknesses had been exposed in the excessive number of Southern stragglers and in

---

[11] Union losses (killed, wounded, captured, and missing), 12,410; Confederate, 11,172. Union dead, 2108, Confederate, 1512. Total losses on both sides: 23,582. *Battles and Leaders of the Civil War*, II, 603.

[12] *McClellan's Own Story*, 612.   [13] *McClellan's Own Story*, 613.

[14] See below, p. 159.

[15] F. P. Blair, Sr., to McClellan, Silver Spring, Sep. 30, 1862, McClellan MSS.

the failure to rally Maryland's support.

Less than his just meed of commendation was given by Lincoln to McClellan, yet the President considered South Mountain and Antietam significant victories. Of the first he said: ". . . General McClellan has gained a great victory over the great rebel army in Maryland. . . ."[16] Concerning the two engagements he remarked in brief reply to a serenade: "On the fourteenth and seventeenth . . . there have been battles bravely, skilfully, and successfully fought. . . . I only ask you . . . to give three hearty cheers for all . . . who fought those successful battles."[17] McClellan may be pardoned for "some little pride" (when writing in confidence to his wife) in having taken over a "beaten and demoralized army" and used it to defeat Lee and save the North.[18]

III

After Antietam the credit bestowed upon McClellan was in no proportion to the savage denunciation that would have descended had he failed to drive Lee back. Disparaging the service he had performed, the radical cabal against him was continuing its incessant attack, supported by McClellan's implacable cabinet enemies—Stanton and Chase. Against terrific pressure Lincoln had held an open mind toward McClellan while doubting the main pattern of his strategy, but the case that was being built up against the general was getting ever stronger than Lincoln's wavering favor. War weariness was an increasing psychological factor in the North as battle after battle brought frightful casualties with nothing settled. The North had not yet adjusted itself to the concept of a long, serious war with heavy sacrifices. People were impressed by facile assertions that Lee could have been easily crushed once for all; the failure of McClellan to pursue was made a more prominent thing than his checking of an invasion. There was no adequate appreciation of what was gained by McClellan's caution in face of Lee's formidable power;[1] and just

---

[16] *Works*, VIII, 34 (Sep. 15, 1862).   [17] *Ibid.*, VIII, 44 (Sep. 24, 1862).
[18] *McClellan's Own Story*, 613.

[1] ". . . Lee was still confident that he could resist successfully a Federal attack and he waited expectantly." Freeman, *Lee*, II, 405. ". . . I should have had a narrow view of the condition of the country had I been willing to hazard another battle . . . ." McClellan, in *McClellan's Own Story*, 618.

at this juncture it came to Lincoln's ears that a talkative officer, Major John J. Key, had expressed the view that Lee's army was not bagged after Sharpsburg because that "was not the game." Both sides were to be kept in the field till exhausted; fraternal relations were then to be restored with slavery saved; that was the "only way the Union could be preserved." [2] Fearing that this was "staff talk" and that it was indispensable to make a signal example of Key, Lincoln dismissed him from the service, though sending him a personal letter which contained more sympathy than rebuke.[3] On October 1 the President visited the army, viewing the camps, going over the battlefields, and holding "many and long consultations alone" with McClellan.[4] When the general explained his reasons for delay and for preparation before the next round, Lincoln said repeatedly that he was "entirely satisfied." "The President was very kind personally [wrote McClellan]; told me he was convinced I was the best general in the country, etc., etc." [5] "He told me that he regarded me as the only general in the service capable of organizing and commanding a large army, and that he would stand by me." [6]

Lincoln's main purpose in visiting the army was to get McClellan to move.[7] Returning to Washington, he made another of those efforts at presidential direction of the army which never quite amounted to positive command of operations. Through Halleck (October 6) he instructed McClellan to "cross the Potomac and give battle to the enemy, or drive him south." [8] Nothing happened. October days passed and McClellan lingered. Then Lincoln sent him a long, earnest letter.

---

2 *Works*, VIII, 47.

3 *Ibid.*, VIII, 48–49 (Nov. 24, 1862). See also Dennett, ed., *Lincoln* . . . *in the Diaries* . . . *of John Hay*, 219.

4 *McClellan's Own Story*, 627. Lincoln spent the night at Harpers Ferry, which had fallen to the Confederates just before Antietam, but was once more in Union hands.

5 *Ibid.*, 655. This was McClellan's statement in a letter to his wife, to whom he wrote with unstudied frankness of himself and others. For Lincoln's repeated expression of entire satisfaction with McClellan, see *ibid.*, 627–628.

6 *Ibid.*, 627. Such a view of McClellan on Lincoln's part is amply confirmed by sources independent of that general; see Welles, *Diary*, I, 105; Chase's diary as quoted above, p. 112. The quintessence of Lincoln's judgment of McClellan seems to be contained in the following statement by O. H. Browning: "He [the President] again repeated to me what he had previously said about McClellan, that he could better organize, provide for and discipline an army, and handle it with more ability in a fight than any general we had, but that he was too slow." Browning, *Diary*, I, 591 (Dec. 2, 1862). See also *ibid.*, I, 525, 537–538, 552, 619.

7 Dennett, *Lincoln* . . . *in the Diaries* . . . *of John Hay*, 218.

8 *Works*, VIII, 53.

"Are you not over-cautious [he wrote] when you assume that you cannot do what the enemy is constantly doing? . . . Change positions with the enemy, and think you not he would break your communication with Richmond within the next twenty-four hours? . . . If he should . . . move toward Richmond, I would press closely to him, fight him if a favorable opportunity should present, and at least try to beat him to Richmond on the inside track. . . . If we cannot beat the enemy where he now is, we never can, he again being within the intrenchments of Richmond." [9]

It is easy to read this well written letter of Lincoln's, a long epistle whose substance is only briefly suggested here, and assume that it put McClellan completely in the wrong. To do so would be to forget that McClellan, in field command, knew what was needed in reconditioning and concentrating his army, that he already realized the need for checking and striking Lee, that the "true approach" [10] via the Peninsula had been barred by opposition in Washington, and that watchful delay when Lee was in no position to strike was less dangerous than ill-planned engagements which were the forte of McClellan's successors. It was not as if the general needed all this admonition. He had previously written to his wife (September 25) indicating a purpose to watch the Potomac and to attack Lee if he remained near Washington, or, if he retired toward Richmond, to follow and strike him.[11] With old regiments reduced to skeletons and new regiments in need of instruction, with a deficiency of officers and want of horses, McClellan would not then have maneuvered to bring on a battle unless necessary to protect Washington; yet all the evidence shows that he was actively building a stronger and larger force and was waiting to choose his moment for an effective blow when it should fall.[12] This, of course, was a matter of painful rebuilding. One can never estimate the full dimensions of the setback to McClellan's plans and to Union success produced by the incredible removal of his army in August 1862 from its strong position on the James River near Richmond.

Eager for an immediate knockout victory, Lincoln waited further, meanwhile reading a despatch in which McClellan, in an ill-chosen passage, referred to sore-tongued and fatigued horses. Then Lincoln

---

[9] *Ibid.*, VIII, 57–60 (Oct. 13, 1862).   [10] *McClellan's Own Story*, 642.
[11] *Ibid.*, 615.   [12] *Offic. Rec.*, 1 ser., XIX, pt. 1, 70–71.

burst out: "Will you pardon me for asking what the horses of your army have done since the battle of Antietam that fatigues anything?" [13] A few days later [14] the President admitted "something of impatience" in his despatch and assured McClellan of his deep regret if he had done him any injustice. Self control was becoming difficult. With momentous decisions in the balance nerves were frayed, tempers were rising, and trivial misunderstandings were in danger of producing ominous results.

Beginning on October 26 McClellan did cross the Potomac; a few ·days later his army was "massed near Warrenton, ready to act in any required direction, perfectly in hand, and in admirable condition and spirits." [15] He was now planning and expecting another battle. He was confident and ready. Then came the abrupt final blow against him. On November 7 General Buckingham [16] came by special train from Washington and turned up at Burnside's camp. Suspecting the purpose of this visit, McClellan kept his own counsel. Late at night, sitting alone in his tent writing to his wife, he heard a rap on his tent pole. Burnside and Buckingham then entered bearing an order "By direction of the President" relieving him of command of the Army of the Potomac and putting Burnside in his place.[17] There was immense resentment among soldiers and officers, so intense that many were in favor of McClellan's "refusing to obey the order, and of marching upon Washington to take possession of the government." [18] It was to quiet this restless feeling, and in compliance with Burnside's request, that McClellan remained with the army until November 10; then, with feelings beyond description and with "thousands of brave men . . . shedding tears like children," [19] he uncomplainingly turned his command over to Burnside and took his departure not only from the Army of the Potomac, but from active military service. Anger at his removal, felt keenly among raw recruits who had become

---

13 *Works*, VIII, 67 (Oct. 24 [25?], 1862).   14 *Ibid.*, VIII, 69 (Oct. 27, 1862).
15 *McClellan's Own Story*, 648.
16 Brigadier General C. P. Buckingham, "confidential assistant adjutant-general to the Secretary of War." *Battles and Leaders of the Civil War*, III, 104.
17 In Lincoln's order that McClellan be relieved and that Burnside take the command, he included the statement that Halleck was authorized to issue an order to that effect; on the basis of this several war department orders were issued, all these under date of November 5, 1862. It was not until November 7, however, that these orders went into effect. *Offic. Rec.*, 1 ser., XIX, pt. 2, 545 ff.
18 *McClellan's Own Story*, 652.   19 *Ibid.*

veterans in his ranks, would have deepened into more bitter anguish of heart if these men had foreseen the sequel.

IV

The unhorsing of McClellan, with its disheartening of the Union army and its heightening of Confederate chances, was the result of a complex situation in which politician interference, congressional meddling, radical intrigue, amateurism, personal jealousy, McClellan's inattention to matters of tact, and a calculated campaign of misrepresentation were among the controlling factors. So far as the removal was Lincoln's responsibility it was an act of a buffeted President in whose mind there were enough doubts of McClellan's usefulness to give weight to heavy and unremitting attacks of a sort which any President would have found it hard to resist. Lincoln sometimes made mistakes, and it may be seriously questioned whether he had in military matters that unerring sureness of control which some of his eulogists claim. In McClellan's behalf it may be said that at least four serious errors were committed by authorities in Washington: (1) withholding McDowell's corps as well as other troops, and in a word giving less than its proper attention to the campaign against Richmond, while keeping forces ineffectively immobilized elsewhere; (2) relieving the pressure on Lee and inviting Union disaster by ordering withdrawal from the Peninsula; [1] (3) taking the army out of McClellan's hands and intrusting it to Pope, thus incurring defeat at Second Manassas; (4) finally removing McClellan when he was set with a reconditioned army for advance against Lee in November 1862, and substituting the incompetent Burnside.

Two cabinet men, Chase and Stanton, played important parts in McClellan's undoing. Wearing "two faces," [2] Stanton had professed friendship to McClellan, while intriguing to destroy him. In a long letter to Rev. H. Dyer, Stanton represented himself as the "sincere and devoted friend" of McClellan and justified his course toward him. [3] On July 5, 1862, Stanton wrote to the general: "Be assured you shall have the support of this department . . . ." [4] Three days later Mc-

---

[1] "The recall of the army from the vicinity of Richmond I thought wrong, ... But in this Stanton had a purpose . . . ." Welles, *Diary*, I, 113.

[2] Chase, *Diary* (*Annual Report*, Amer. Hist. Assoc., 1902, pt. II), 105.

[3] May 18, 1862, Stanton MSS., no. 51407-13.   [4] *McClellan's Own Story*, 475-476.

SOME OF LINCOLN'S MILITARY PROBLEMS

Upper left: Maj. Gen. John Pope

Upper right: Maj. Gen. John C.
    Frémont

Center: Lt. Gen. Winfield Scott
    (General-in-Chief)

Lower left: Maj. Gen. Ambrose E.
    Burnside

Lower middle: Maj. Gen. Henry W.
    Halleck (General-in-Chief)

Lower right: Maj. Gen. Joseph
    Hooker

UNION GENERALS
Upper row: George H. Thomas, Irvin McDowell, U. S. Grant.
Lower row: William T. Sherman, William S. Rosecrans, George G. Meade.

Clellan, smarting under the withholding of troops in his time of dire need, wrote a bluntly candid letter to Stanton mentioning the secretary's "deeply offensive" acts and "bitter personal prejudice" toward him, but accepting the assurance of friendship.[5] Despite his professions there is abundant evidence that Stanton talked McClellan down, intrigued against him, and actively sought his removal.[6]

With more of forthright honesty, Chase worked as persistently to the same end. He and Stanton concocted a paper denouncing McClellan and demanding his removal.[7] With this as a round robin, bearing, as they hoped, the signature of cabinet members, they proposed to put the matter up to Lincoln in such a way as to make it extremely difficult for him to refuse to act. When Chase circulated the paper it was signed by himself and Stanton, and also by Smith and Bates. Blair disapproved of it, while Welles thought the whole procedure underhand, factious, and disrespectful toward the President. Seward, who blithely dodged such controversies, was conveniently out of town. The plan was dropped and the paper not presented.

When little groups would meet there would be secret confabulations about McClellan. On the night of Pope's defeat (August 31) Caleb Smith, Stanton, and Welles had such a chat at the war department. Stanton held forth at great length recounting the whole history of McClellan, with emphasis upon his delay, the enemy's wooden guns, et cetera, all of which led up to a renewal of the demand that Welles join in the move to "get rid of him." [8] Welles expressed dislike of this "manner of proceeding" as being discourteous to the President. Then, as he records, "Stanton said, with some excitement, he knew of no particular obligations he was under to the President, who had called him to a difficult position and imposed upon him labors . . . which no man could carry, and which were greatly increased by fastening upon him a commander who was constantly striving to embarrass him in his administration of the Department. He could not and would not submit to a continuance of this state of things." [9] On further reflection Welles was yet more confirmed in his view that this method of

---

[5] McClellan MSS.. July 8, 1862.

[6] Welles, *Diary*, I, 97, 104, 118–119; Browning, *Diary*, I, 538–539. In the interest of condensation further material on this matter in the writer's possession is omitted.

[7] For Welles's account of this intrigue by Chase and Stanton to force McClellan's removal, see his *Diary*, I, 93 ff. (Aug. 31, 1862).

[8] Welles, *Diary*, I, 95 ff.   [9] *Ibid.*, 98.

"conspiring" to control the President was "offensive." Stanton he characterized as "mad . . . and determined to destroy McClellan," and Chase as "credulous, and sometimes the victim of intrigue." [10] Chase's design, said Welles, was "to tell the President that the Administration must be broken up, or McC. dismissed." [11]

Mere removal was not the only object. Denouncing McClellan as a traitor, these men wanted to "disgrace" him.[12] So sorely was McClellan tried by Stanton's interference that, unwisely but with much truth, he wrote to him after Gaines's Mill: ". . . a few thousand more men would have changed this battle from a defeat to a victory. . . . If I save this army now, I tell you plainly that I owe no thanks to you or to any other persons in Washington. You have done your best to sacrifice this army." [13]

V

In the diary of John Hay under date of September 25, 1864, there occurs a remarkable passage concerning McClellan. Talking with Hay, Lincoln is said to have mentioned a "story" told him by J. Gregory Smith, governor of Vermont and brother of General William Farrar ("Baldy") Smith. According to this story the Democratic politician Fernando Wood, visiting McClellan's camp on the Peninsula, had urged him to become presidential candidate against Lincoln. McClellan, so the tale continued, had written a letter of acceptance, "Baldy" had protested that it looked "like treason," and McClellan had destroyed the letter in "Baldy's" presence. In this letter he had advocated such a method of conducting the war as would assure the people of the South that their rights were not endangered. Again, so the story went, after Antietam McClellan told "Baldy" that the same men had renewed the proposition, and that he had this time acceded, whereupon Smith at once applied for transference from McClellan's army.

It is to be noted that this story was used by Thurlow Weed to ruin McClellan in the presidential campaign of 1864.[1] The tale is very indirect; it comes from General Smith to Governor Smith, then to Lincoln, and through John Hay to the reader. Whatever may have

---

[10] *Ibid.*, 101.   [11] *Ibid.*, 102.   [12] *Ibid.*   [13] *McClellan's Own Story*, 425.
[1] Dennett, *Lincoln . . . in the Diaries . . . of John Hay*, 217-218.

passed between Fernando Wood and the general, there was nothing in McClellan's actual conduct which showed anything like treachery against the Union or any deep-laid intrigue against Lincoln. What McClellan did as a candidate for the presidency, duly chosen by one of America's historic parties, was done nearly two years after his dismissal from command; it constitutes a separate and an honorable story. According to the very terms of "Baldy" Smith's narrative as indirectly transmitted, it was McClellan himself who told Smith whatever he knew about the whole episode. If McClellan had been plotting anything dark and disreputable after Antietam he would hardly have revealed it to the New England conscience of William Farrar Smith. In its implications of dishonorable intrigue on McClellan's part, the story, which Lincoln repeated to Hay without vouching for its authenticity, lacks that element of directness and corroboration which the realistic historian demands. So far as it bears upon Democratic efforts to use McClellan and upon the general's preference for a war that would not unduly invade the private rights of the Southern people, it offers nothing startling.

When the drive against McClellan was at its keenest in early September Lincoln resisted it, saying with emphasis: "I must have McClellan to reorganize the army and bring it out of chaos," adding "McClellan has the army with him." [2] Two months later he dismissed him. In trying to answer why he did so one is impressed with a growing impatience on Lincoln's part in the post-Antietam phase. After Antietam, said Lincoln in reminiscent mood in 1864, he had tried repeatedly to induce McClellan to move. There were nineteen days of delay before he began to cross the Potomac, nine further days before he crossed, then still further halting on what Lincoln called "pretexts." "I began to fear [said Lincoln as quoted by John Hay] he was playing false—that he did not want to hurt the enemy. I saw how he could intercept the enemy on the way to Richmond. I determined to make that the test. If he let them get away I would remove him. He did so & I relieved him.[3] Looking back from this reminiscence to the event, it will be remembered that there were in the spring and summer of 1862 furious accusations as to McClellan's alleged disloyalty, that the fabrication and spreading of such rumors was the deliberate business

[2] Welles, *Diary*, I, 113.
[3] Dennett, *Lincoln . . . in the Diaries . . . of John Hay*, 218–219.

of the war committee, that many weeks of such attacks had caused no Lincoln-McClellan break, and that some of the radicals considered it treasonable to advocate even so much as the preservation of Southern rights, which Congress was under pledge to recognize. While the smirching and whispering campaign against McClellan had raged in the spring of 1862 Lincoln had been unmoved by it,[4] though on one occasion, as O. H. Browning records, Stanton gave the President a long account of rumors which made it appear that McClellan, as an alleged member of the Knights of the Golden Circle, would "do nothing against the rebels" inconsistent with his obligations to that order.[5] McClellan's post-Antietam delay is explainable on military grounds, and it is somewhat curious to find Lincoln making army "delay" the basis for a suspicion that the general was "playing false," and then appointing Burnside, whose slowness had been recently demonstrated at Antietam and who waited five more weeks before making his disastrous and unsuccessful stroke. Taking this whole muddling period of 1862, the delay had resulted from what had been done at Washington over McClellan's head.

Knowing that Lincoln had thus referred to "playing false," Nicolay and Hay, bitter as they were against McClellan, took no stock in the accusation of treachery.[6] Against that charge, whatever may have been his defects otherwise, McClellan stands acquitted. Though his full vindication cannot be given in these pages, his record stands up in other respects. On the one hand, his soldiers adored and trusted him; on the other hand his opponents considered him a formidable antagonist. To give evidence that the soldiers wanted McClellan and followed him gladly would be to select from an abundant store of source material. General Cox, whose reminiscences contain many a severe criticism of McClellan, reports that in the pre-Antietam phase, when he was restored to command, the cheers of the soldiers "were given with wild delight." [7] In the anxious days before Gettysburg a soldier

---

[4] "I asked him [Lincoln] if he still had confidence in McClellands fidelity. He assured me he had, and that he had never had any reason to doubt it." Browning, *Diary*, I, 537.

[5] *Ibid.*, I, 538. According to Browning, Stanton told Lincoln he did not believe these imputations of disloyalty, but after they had parted from the President he told Browning virtually the opposite. For the hollowness of the charges of treason against McClellan (*apropos* of the K. G. C. and otherwise) and for their being disbelieved even by the commander's more intelligent critics—e. g., Bates—see *ibid.*, I, 538–539 n. See also Bates, *Diary*, 423 (Oct. 28, 1864).

[6] See above, p. 68.   [7] Cox, *Military Reminiscences*, I, 245.

in the Army of the Potomac wrote: "You . . . ask whom do they want to lead them? I answer the universal clamor is give us McClellan. . . . There is not a day but that you hear cheers for 'Little Mac' in the various camps in this command . . . ." [8] Friends of Senator Browning, having visited the army in January 1863, reported "that the soldiers are unanimous . . . for the return of Genl McClellan, believing that he is the only man competent for the command." [9] For a foe's appraisal one can point to a quoted statement in 1863 by a daughter of General Lee that "Genl. McClellan was the only Genl. Father dreaded." [10] Lee's biographer leaves no doubt on this subject. He writes:

"Who was the ablest Federal general he had opposed? He [Lee] did not hesitate . . . for the answer. 'McClellan, by all odds,' he said emphatically." [11]

---

[8] J. R. Blinn to R. W. Thompson, Thoroughfare Gap, Va., Army of the Potomac, June 24, 1863, MS., Lincoln National Life Foundation, Fort Wayne, Ind.

[9] Browning, *Diary*, I, 621. See also *ibid.*, I, 601, 619, for strong expressions of soldier confidence in McClellan.

[10] Quoted in a letter to McClellan signed "A Friend," Washington, Mar. 28, 1863, McClellan MSS. (no. 18141).

[11] Freeman, *Lee*, IV, 475.

CHAPTER XXI

A BLUEPRINT FOR FREEDOM

I

WHEN Lincoln said that he claimed not to have controlled events and confessed that events had controlled him,[1] his words might have fitted many episodes and policies of his presidency, but at the moment he was referring to the problem of the Negro slave. Lincoln never claimed that his emancipation proclamation was a matter of long-view planning, nor that it was a carefully calculated program, nor even that it was motivated by a moral judgment against slavery. Lincoln did in fact have a major plan of liberation, but it was not that of the proclamation, nor was it ever put into effect. Lincoln also had a strong moral judgment against slavery. Such a judgment was bred in the bone, for he said "I am naturally antislavery. If slavery is not wrong, nothing is wrong. I cannot remember when I did not so think and feel . . . ." Moral judgments of a leader, however, may be one thing, and his authorizations in office quite a different thing. John Quincy Adams, though antislavery in sentiment, had to bargain and argue for slave interests while secretary of state of the United States. It is sometimes forgotten that Lincoln was elected and inaugurated President of a slaveholding nation in 1861, and that, to use his own words, he did not understand "that the Presidency conferred . . . an unrestricted right to act officially upon . . . [his] judgment and feeling." It was his view that in civil administration his oath forbade him "to practically indulge . . . [his] abstract judgment on the moral question of slavery." [2]

Nor was slavery considered the main issue when trouble broke and disunion loomed. At the outset of Lincoln's administration the New

---

[1] *Works*, X, 68 (April 4, 1864).   [2] *Ibid.*, X, 65 (April 4, 1864).

York *Times* remarked: "The question which we have to meet *is precisely what it would be if there were not a negro slave on American soil.*" [3] Though the slavery question could not be so blithely muted, the statement of the *Times* correctly interpreted the attitude of the United States government when it was written (April 6, 1861); it also squared with a policy that persisted long after the abrupt shift from war to peace might have brought reorientation and discovery of new powers.

True to the platform of his party and to his previous declarations, Lincoln disclaimed in his first inaugural address (March 4, 1861) any "purpose, directly or indirectly, to interfere with the institution of slavery in the States where it exists." The lack of such official purpose was not all; he further declared that he had "no lawful right . . . and . . . no inclination to do so." [4] This was not a recanting of his "moral judgment" against slavery; it was a matter of using presidential authority. In making the declaration emphatic he sought to strip the slavery issue of its nuisance value, or rather of its explosive menace; he meant to assure the people of the South that their "property, peace, and security" were not "in any wise endangered by the now incoming administration."

Lincoln's next statement, addressed to the slaveholding section, was an assurance not merely of avoiding interference with the institutions of the dissatisfied states, but of extending "protection . . . consistently with the Constitution and the laws . . . as cheerfully to one section as to another." [5] Lincoln was no abolitionist President. According to an interpretation from which neither he nor the United States government ever swerved, he was from March 1861 the constitutional President of the whole country: deep South, upper South, border, and North. Nor did he consider himself merely President of the Republican party. As he faced the multitudes that honored or curiously viewed him on his way to Washington, he was well aware that the same honors would have been given to Douglas, or Bell, or Breckinridge, had one of these men been "constitutionally elected President of the United States."

The war came, Bull Run was fought and lost, and Congress echoed

---

[3] New York *Times*, editorial, April 6, 1861, p. 4, c. 2.

[4] *Works*, VI, 170. This passage was quoted from an earlier speech.

[5] Lincoln was choosing his words with meticulous care in this inaugural; he did not say "to one section as to *the* other." *Ibid.*, VI, 171.

Lincoln's disclaimer. On July 22, 1861, the House of Representatives resolved:

> That the . . . war has been forced . . . by the disunionists of the southern States, now in arms against the . . . Government . . . ; that . . . Congress, banishing . . . passion or resentment, will recollect only its duty to the whole country; that this war is not waged . . . for . . . conquest or subjugation, or purpose of overthrowing or interfering with the . . . established institutions of those States, but to . . . maintain . . . the Constitution, and to preserve the Union with all the . . . rights of the . . . States unimpaired; and that as soon as these objects are accomplished the war ought to cease.[6]

On July 25 the Senate passed a similar but more ably worded resolution sponsored by the senator from Tennessee, Andrew Johnson. In the House there were only two negative votes, in the Senate only five; seldom in the whole period of Lincoln could one find such an approach to unanimity.[7] Yet the unanimity was misleading. The vote was complex in that the resolution was a kind of catch-all. It was so worded as to contain, among other elements, an indictment of war guilt directed against the South (phrased as a statement of fact), a declaration for maintaining the old Union, and a renunciation of any purpose to subjugate the Southern states or interfere with their domestic institutions. It was essentially a moderate declaration of war aims. Radical extremists objected in debate because they felt that "traitors" ought to be subdued; at the opposite extreme such a man as Breckinridge objected because he thought that the purpose was in fact subjugation, and because he could not accept the imputation of Southern war guilt. A significant interpretation of what Congress was doing was given by Senator Willey of "Western Virginia"[8]

---

[6] *Cong. Globe*, 37 Cong., 1 sess., 222.

[7] The House voted twice on the resolution. There was a vote of 121 to 2 on the earlier part (approximately the first third), and a vote of 117 to 2 on the remainder (*ibid.*, 223). In the Senate the vote was 30 to 5 (*ibid.*, 265). The two who voted nay in the House, Henry C. Burnett of Kentucky and John W. Reid of Missouri, were both expelled in December 1861. The five who voted nay in the Senate were Lazarus W. Powell and John C. Breckinridge of Kentucky, Trusten Polk and Waldo P. Johnson of Missouri, and Lyman Trumbull of Illinois. Polk, Johnson, and Breckinridge were later expelled. The votes of certain prominent men are conspicuous by their absence—e. g., those of Thaddeus Stevens in the House and Charles Sumner in the Senate. It is safe to say that both these men dissented from the resolution. The affirmative votes of Senators Wade of Ohio and Chandler of Michigan seem hardly sincere except as to fastening war guilt upon the South.

[8] "Mr. Willey, of Western Virginia, stated [in the Senate] the views of the people of

who favored the resolution in order to quiet the fears of his own people that they would have to pass under the yoke, and who warned that if the war were directed against local institutions, "every loyal arm on the soil of the Old Dominion . . . [would] be . . . paralyzed." [9] On this point Senator Hale of New Hampshire assured him that the government had no more constitutional right to strike at slavery in the South than to deal with Russian serfs or English laborers.[10]

These disclaimers by President and Congress marked a stage in a rapidly shifting drama. It will not do to say that the President's disclaimer was insincere; [11] his inaugural assurance to the South was not an announcement of what might happen in case of a long civil war which he wished to avert. When ultimately Lincoln acted in the matter of slavery it was under circumstances vastly different from those of March 1861 and his action was not directed against areas adhering to the Union. As for Congress, there were indications that its members in July of 1861 were taking panicky counsel of their fears on the morrow of defeat; the resolution of that month was not reaffirmed when the question was reopened and put to vote in December 1861.[12]

II

The truth was that affairs could not remain static; the very fact of war was creating complications, posing slavery questions that could not be evaded, forcing piecemeal action, and presenting hard dilemmas. Slavery was, in Cleveland's famous words, a condition, not a theory. A resolution in Congress was one

---

the Old Dominion . . . ." (*Annual Cyclopaedia*, 1861, 242). In 1861 there was inexactness in referring to the governmental situation in Virginia (see above, pp. 11–14). The "reorganized" legislature at Wheeling, purporting to act as the legislature for all Virginia, had, in a special session of July 1861, chosen Waitman T. Willey and John S. Carlile as United States senators from Virginia (at a time when West Virginia had not yet been formed), to take the places of James M. Mason and R. M. T. Hunter, adherents of the Confederacy, whose seats had been declared vacant. *Journal of the House of Delegates of Virginia* (extra session commencing July 1, 1861, Wheeling), 32; *Journal of the Senate* (same session), 24. Thus, in Wheeling and Washington parlance Mr. Willey was United States senator from Virginia.

[9] *Cong. Globe*, 37 Cong., 1 sess., 259.   [10] *Ibid.*, 260.   [11] See below, p. 163.
[12] On December 4, 1861, the House refused to reaffirm the resolution by a vote of 65 to 71. *Cong. Globe*, 37 Cong., 2 sess., 15.

thing, a group of fugitive slaves fleeing enemy service quite another. The generalized question of emancipation might be deferred, but Negroes crowding into Union camps, though uninvited, could hardly be regarded as non-existent. A government conducting war with a slaveholding power over a vast and loosely held line could expect incidents aplenty involving fugitive slaves, and it was in this connection that some of the earliest issues concerning Negroes had to be met. In May 1861 General B. F. Butler, commanding at Fort Monroe, took a step in a small matter which opened up a wide problem when he detained three slaves who had appeared on his picket line. Acting on information that Negroes in the neighborhood were "employed in the erection of batteries and other works by the rebels," [1] Butler not only refused to return them but used their services, keeping an account of their labor and cost of maintenance for future settlement. As for the fugitive slave act, he treated that as applying only among states of the American Union, which would exclude Virginia by her own definition,[2] though he was ready to restore the Negroes if their owner would take oath to obey the laws of the United States.

As the number of such fugitives increased by hundreds, with whole families seeking protection, Butler dealt with the matter as a military problem, keeping and employing the slaves because of their enforced hostile service against the United States, and holding the women and children for "humanitarian" reasons.[3] His action was approved by the war department with the reservation that it was not to extend to interference with slavery as a state institution.[4] As with everything that Butler did, the incident acquired a sententious publicity, and "contraband" [5] was lifted from the code of war to become a slang term applying to Negroes.

If these Negroes, whose seizure was assumed to be roughly analogous to the taking of contraband property, had not acquired a new status, it could at least be said that their unsought appearance within Union army lines tended to push forward the complex question of war policy toward slavery. Refusing the return of so-called property that had been put to military use by the enemy, authorities had to decide whether these persons were in truth being held as property, or, in

---

[1] B. F. Butler, *Private and Official Correspondence of B. F. Butler*, I, 106.

[2] *Ibid.*, I, 107.   [3] *Ibid.*, I, 112–113.   [4] *Ibid.*, I, 119.

[5] For the use of the word "contraband" see Moore, *Rebellion Record* (Docs.), II, 437; Randall, *Constitutional Problems Under Lincoln*, 354–356.

Butler's words, as men, women, and children, "free, manumitted, . . . never to be reclaimed." [6]

It was only slowly that a general policy on this matter was worked out. In the earlier stages some generals acted as Butler did, while others, such as Williams at Baton Rouge and Halleck in Missouri,[7] refused to permit fugitive slaves to enter army camps or join a marching force. In some cases, to implement the exclusion order, fugitives were restored to their masters.[8] When, because of this, there arose the abolitionist outcry that the army was being employed as slave catchers, the subject became the theme of spirited debate in Congress. Exclusion of Negroes from Union lines was defended as a matter of withholding information from the enemy, and the return of those who escaped from slavery and entered such lines was held to be necessary in order to make exclusion effective. In reply it was remarked that generals arresting slaves and delivering them back to their masters ought to be stripped of their epaulets. Denunciation shifted from commanders to the President when it was charged that exclusion of refugees with the penalty of arrest and return to slavery was the policy of the Lincoln administration. At this point Kellogg of Illinois, speaking as one conversant with the purposes of the administration, denied the accusation and was stoutly joined in the denial by Owen Lovejoy, also of Lincoln's state.[9]

To remove what was regarded as the slave-catching stigma, Congress prohibited the use of the armed forces for the restoration of escaping slaves (March 13, 1862).[10] This was followed by a law (July 17, 1862) which was definitely a measure of emancipation; it declared that slaves whose owners were hostile to the United States, finding their way within Union lines, were free.[11] Only to a loyal owner could slaves be returned. Much later in the war the fugitive slave acts (the old measure of 1793 and the drastic law of 1850) were repealed.[12]

It was not so much that policy was shaping events. Events were shaping policy. The force of circumstances and the position of armies were having their emancipating effect. "We have entered Virginia," wrote Seward, "and already five thousand slaves, emancipated simply

---

[6] Moore, *Rebellion Record* (Docs.), II, 438.   [7] *Annual Cyclopaedia*, 1862, 754.
[8] *Ibid.*, 754–755.   [9] The debate is condensed in *ibid.*, 279 ff.
[10] *U. S. Stat. at Large*, XII, 354.   [11] *Ibid.*, XII, 591.
[12] *Ibid.*, act of June 28, 1864, XIII, 211.

by the appearance of our forces, are upon the hands of the Federal government there. We have landed upon the coast of South Carolina, and already nine thousand . . . hang upon our camps. Although the war has not been waged against slavery, yet the army acts . . . as an emancipating crusade. To proclaim the crusade is unnecessary, ..." [13] The New York *Herald* remarked that military and legislative action touching slavery had been "controlled by circumstances," [14] while the London *News* declared: "It has been understood . . . that this negro question was to be left *an open question . . . in order that events might decide* where rulars [*sic*] could not agree." [15]

III

On many a day in the long session of 1861–62 the grave and reverend in House and Senate directed their verbal fireworks as well as their laborious committee deliberations to this or that aspect of slavery. Under the head of confiscation, for instance, two emancipatory acts were passed. Under the first measure (the mild confiscation act of August 6, 1861) [1] slaves put to military or naval use against the United States were declared forfeit by a legalistic phrasing which did not declare them free. In the sweeping confiscation act of 1862 (July 17) the lawmakers went much farther; on the broad principle of punishing traitors and rebels, Congress enacted that slaves of traitors should be "declared and made free," and that rebel-owned [2] slaves were to be "forever free of their servitude, and not again held as slaves." [3]

There were other bits of emancipating legislation by Congress. If an enemy-owned slave rendered military service to the United States, he and his family (if they were enemy-owned) were declared free. [4] After national conscription had been adopted, drafted slaves as well

---

13 Seward to Charles Francis Adams, Feb. 17, 1862, MSS., Dept. of State (Great Britain: Instructions, vol. 18, no. 187), Nat. Archives.

14 Jan. 24, 1862, p. 1, c. 1.

15 London *News*, Dec. 21, 1861, as copied in New York *Herald*, Jan. 4, 1862, p. 2, c. 2.

1 *U. S. Stat. at Large*, XII, 319.

2 Legally there seemed to be a distinction between traitors and those who engaged in or aided rebellion. Mere residence in what was called "rebel" territory, however, made one a "rebel." The subject is heavily encrusted with legalistic pronouncements, though in practical execution such legislation meant little. Randall, *Constitutional Problems Under Lincoln*, 358; *The Civil War and Reconstruction*, 482 and n.

3 *U. S. Stat. at Large*, XII, 589–592.   4 Militia Act of July 17, 1862, *ibid.*, XII, 599.

as colored volunteers were declared free, with compensation to loyal owners.[5]

Out-and-out emancipation by Congress, with no *if's* and *and's* about confiscation or enemy ownership or territorial restrictions, was urged by such men as Ashley [6] and Bingham of the House of Representatives, both from Ohio. "Pass your laws liberating the 4,000,000 slaves held by the rebels," said Bingham, ". . . and let the oppressed go free . . . . Do you say this is fanaticism? Do you say God was a fanatic when He commanded it, . . . ?" [7] If this were done, Steele of New York predicted that "this war would become one of extermination and death all over the country," [8] while Wadsworth of Kentucky declared that from the enactment of emancipation "the lines of the rebellion would advance; . . . its original pretense would be justified as truth." "Millions . . . now faithful," added Wadsworth, ". . . with one heart would join the foe. That instant . . . loyal men . . . from the free States . . . who have not gone into the war . . . to accomplish the Africanization of our society, will disband." [9]

Though support was not forthcoming for universal emancipation, Congress did abolish the institution in the District of Columbia and in the territories. In the debate on the District bill Senator Hale of New Hampshire deplored the fact that emancipation was rarely discussed as a measure of fundamental right or Christian humanity, but only in terms of the price of sugar or some such matter. Not confining itself, however, to economics, the discursive debate rambled among such topics as Haiti, Santo Domingo, Liberia, the torrid zone, the Caucasian race, the poet's dream, the Creator's design, the case of the *Antelope*,[10] the Chicago platform, the Constitution, the Supreme Court, habeas corpus, trial by jury, freedom of conscience, due proc-

[5] *Ibid.*, act of Feb. 24, 1864, XIII, 11.

[6] "The defeat of Mr. Ashley's Universal Emancipation bill to-day, under the cloak of providing provisional governments for the Territory recovered from the rebels, was a salutary lesson to the radicals. . . . This vote [to lay the bill on the table] was a . . . Bull Run . . . to the ultra faction, and has tamed them down considerably." New York *Herald*, March 13, 1862, p. 1, c. 1.

[7] *Cong. Globe*, 37 Cong., 2 sess., 348.   [8] *Ibid.*, 404.   [9] *Ibid.*, 355–356.

[10] In the case of the *Antelope* (1825) Chief Justice Marshall held that a foreign slave-trading ship, captured by an American warship in time of peace, should be restored. Legality of the capture was construed as depending upon the law of the country to which the vessel belonged. J. B. Moore, *Digest of International Law*, II, 917–918.

ess, liberty of the press, the nation's pledged word, the purpose of the war, social life at the capital, idolatry, cannibalism, and the dignity of the State of Maryland.[11] Through the oratorical maze Congress somehow focused upon the difficult problem, not only of *whether* to abolish, but *how* to abolish slavery in the capital. Of necessity the President's influence was important. There was doubt whether Lincoln would sign the District bill;[12] he was reported as opposing such a measure unless certain conditions were met. He wanted Maryland's consent, and insisted upon compensation to slaveholders and also upon adequate provision for removal and colonization of liberated blacks.[13] Radicals were accused of rushing the bill through so as to put the President in the uncomfortable dilemma of vetoing it or "signing it in direct opposition to all his hitherto expressed views on the subject."[14] Finally the bill was passed, incorporating Lincoln's provisions for colonization and compensation,[15] and the President signed it after holding it two days. Cross currents beating upon the harassed President were perfectly reflected in the conflicting reactions to his approval of this controversial bill. On the one hand the New York *Herald* found his signature disappointing to conservative men in Congress and depressing in its effect upon border-state feeling.[16] On the other hand Sumner "regretted that the Prest held the Bill back for two days—making himself as I told him, for the time being, the largest slaveholder in the country."[17] The *Herald,* having seriously doubted the expediency of the bill, looked on the matter in a different light when Lincoln appointed commissioners to administer the act, seeing in the appointments an honest intention to "deal fairly" with slaveowners.[18]

Some of those slaveholders, however, with their noisy supporters, were making it difficult for anyone in office to deal favorably with them. This was most evident in the capital city itself where there occurred in 1862 an amazing *opera bouffe* war between conflicting

---

[11] The debate is condensed in *Annual Cyclopaedia,* 1862, 333–344.

[12] New York *Herald,* April 15, 1862, p. 10, c. 3.

[13] *Ibid.,* April 6, 1862, p. 4, c. 6.   [14] *Ibid.*

[15] "I am gratified that the two principles of compensation and colonization are both recognized and practically applied in the act." Lincoln in message to Congress, April 16, 1862. *Works,* VII, 146–147.

[16] New York *Herald,* April 17, 1862, p. 10, c. 1.

[17] Sumner to Andrew, Senate Chamber, April 22, 1862, Andrew MSS., 16:41; see also Sumner, *Works,* VI, 393.

[18] New York *Herald,* April 17, 1862, p. 10, c. 1.

authorities. The combination of martial law, inefficient local government, and unsettled procedures offered the setting for this melodrama; its cast included Maryland slaveholders of doubtful loyalty, a pro-slavery circuit court in the District, a swashbuckler of a Federal marshal (Ward H. Lamon) whose hatred of abolitionists coexisted with a much-advertised intimacy with Lincoln, bands of rowdies seeking deviltry for its own sake, and on the other side a vigorous antislavery general, James S. Wadsworth, in command of United States troops as military governor of the District. It was a degrading spectacle, unworthy of a controlled democracy. Slaves pouring from Maryland into the District constituted a daily annoyance, and the laws on the subject were not clear. Slaveowners claimed that the fugitive slave law of 1850 applied to the District, but this was stoutly denied, and the question was so unsettled that Governor Bradford of Maryland wrote to Attorney General Bates to know where the law officers of the government stood. The governor wanted to know whether it was true that the United States government had forbidden the execution of warrants for the arrest of these alleged escaping slaves, not omitting to state that slaveowners and politicians were excited about it.[19] As for the Attorney General, he could give little satisfaction; he was himself struggling through a maze of puzzles concerning wartime legal aspects of the fugitive slave question.[20]

Appealing to the fugitive-slave law for the seizure and arrest of Negroes, many of whom were in fact free men kidnapped by rowdies, Marshal Lamon, with the support of the police and the circuit court, filled the jails of Washington with these unfortunates. At one point in the shifting drama Wadsworth's soldiers arrested the jailer, released the marshal's dark prisoners, and even seized some of his force as kidnappers. There followed spirited work on Lamon's part, as when his merry men turned out at two in the morning and regained the jail. When, late in 1862, Wadsworth was transferred from the military governorship of the District to the Army of the Potomac under Burnside, the issue was still unsettled. It disappeared only with the repeal of the fugitive-slave laws in 1864 and the progress of emancipation.[21]

[19] A. W. Bradford to Edward Bates, May 9, 1862, MSS., Attorney General's Office, Nat. Archives.

[20] Bates, *Diary*, 209–211.

[21] On this Wadsworth-Lamon imbroglio see Henry Greenleaf Pearson, *James S. Wadsworth of Geneseo*, 130–140.

Two months after having provided emancipation in the District, Congress abolished slavery in territories of the United States then existing or thereafter to be formed or acquired.[22] In this instance, as in the District case, Congress passed and Lincoln signed a bill which, by ruling law according to Supreme Court interpretation, was unconstitutional. This fact, as well as the legal extinction of that explosive territorial situation which had produced such prodigious prewar agitation, was allowed to pass over with little comment. Compensation to slaveholders was not included in the territorial bill, though there seems no logical reason why it should have been omitted there while applied in the District. Owing to the fewness of slaves the expense would have been negligible. To administer compensation in the District an evaluating commission was set up, the sum of one million dollars being appropriated with the proviso that the total sum paid out should not add up to more than $300 per slave.[23]

In this period several important steps looking toward Negro freedom were taken by the Lincoln government in the diplomatic field. Administrations prior to Lincoln's had avoided recognition of the Negro republics of Haiti and Liberia, but Lincoln was "unable to discern" any good reason why this recognition should be withheld.[24] Relations were established with the sanction of Congress, and negotiations were promptly instituted for treaties with these countries, with consequent commercial advantages.[25] Heretofore the United States had given unsatisfactory support to enlightened efforts of Great Britain to set up an international program for suppressing the slave trade. Certain limited steps had been taken at Washington in the 1840's toward the eradication of a practice which civilized nations were treating as piracy, but ships illegally flying the American flag, as well as American vessels, continued to engage in the hateful traffic.[26] It was therefore an important step when, in May 1862, a treaty was completed between the United States and England by which the two nations agreed to coöperate in an effective manner for suppressing the trade.[27] Though importation of slaves into the United States had been punishable by death under national law since 1820, the first

---

[22] Act of June 19, 1862, *U. S. Stat. at Large*, XII, 432.

[23] In 1860 census takers found 3185 slaves and 1229 slaveholders in the District of Columbia. *U. S. Census*, 1860, Agriculture, p. 246.

[24] *Works*, VII, 33 (Dec. 3, 1861). [25] *Ibid.*, VIII, 98 (Dec. 1, 1862).

[26] Randall, *Civil War and Reconstruction*, 44–46. [27] *Ibid.*, 481.

enforcement of the law came in February 1862 when Nathaniel Gordon, captain of a slave ship, was executed in New York, having been denied presidential clemency. These details indicated that in its outlook on international problems the United States government was no longer conducting itself in the manner of a slave power.

IV

Viewing the increasing difficulties that emerged as liberating incidents inevitably arose out of the war, Lincoln seriously weighed the process of colonization. The idea was not new to him. While debating with Douglas he had shown an interest in Negro emigration, and in his first annual message to Congress (December 1861) he had advised that slaves presumably freed by the confiscation act of that year be colonized in some genial clime. If any of the states should adopt emancipation measures, Lincoln thought that their ex-slaves might be accepted by the United States in lieu of taxes—a rather curious idea—and that they might be included in a general colonizing scheme. He would also extend the process to those of the free colored who might desire a foreign home.[1]

With such preliminaries colonization came to be treated as an active policy, and Congress appropriated $100,000 for the purpose in the District emancipation act. This was later raised to a total of $600,000,[2] and in the second confiscation act the President was "authorized" to make arrangements for colonizing Negroes freed (on paper) by that enactment, again on a voluntary basis. This action by Congress may have been taken to assist in obtaining Lincoln's signature to a measure which he strongly disliked.

A curious scene in the White House in this period, and one which seems almost to have been forgotten, was a conference between the President and a committee of intelligent colored men who came by Lincoln's special request to confer regarding the departure of members of their race to Central America.[3] To one who thinks of the

---

[1] For these several suggestions see *Works*, VII, 49–50.

[2] By act of April 16, 1862 (the emancipation act for the District, *U. S. Stat. at Large*, XII, 378) Congress appropriated $100,000 for colonization. An additional $500,000 was appropriated by act of July 16, 1862 (*ibid.*, XII, 582).

[3] "The conference of the President, held last evening, at the Executive Mansion with . . . colored men in reference to . . . colonization . . . , is a noted . . . event. . . . He desires to see them . . . take their proper position as citizens in a separate

Emancipator in terms of abolitionist stereotypes the words of his remarkable address to this group, preserved in his published works,[4]
will come as something of a surprise. In this address Lincoln's thesis
was utterly different from the concepts of those to whom sudden and
complete abolition presented no obstacles in terms of post-liberation
adjustment. To Lincoln such adjustment, as well as the presence of
large numbers of Negroes long free, offered very serious difficulties,
and his words could have given little encouragement to his colored
auditors.

Whites and Negroes, he told them, are of different races. Your race,
he said, suffer greatly, and we of the white race suffer from your
presence. It affords a reason why we should be separated. Even "when
you cease to be slaves, you are yet far removed from being . . .
on an equality with the white race. . . . [O]n this broad continent
not a single man of your race is made the equal of a single man of
ours. . . . I cannot alter it if I would. It is a fact . . . ." "But for
your race among us [said Lincoln] there could not be war, although
many men engaged on either side do not care for you one way or the
other. . . . It is better for us both . . . to be separated."

Continuing his unflattering advice, Lincoln told his dark friends
that there was an "unwillingness" on the part of whites to allow the
free colored to remain. He therefore appealed to intelligent free
colored men, as he could not appeal to the systematically oppressed, to
make sacrifices and endure hardships, as whites had done, for the sake
of a future day. Fearing that Liberia was too remote, he highly recommended an area in Central America, mentioning its natural advantages, its nearness to the United States, its "very rich coal-mines,"
and its excellent ports on two great oceans. He was referring to
Chiriqui on the Panamanian isthmus; already Northern capitalists
were inquiring into the profits of a colonization scheme in that area.
Referring to the fact that men of the colored race had been "talked to"
concerning a speculation by gentlemen who had an "interest" in the
project, the President explained that "everybody you trade with
makes something," and that he would see to it that they would not be
wronged. As to success of the venture he wasn't sure. Having justified

---

Republic, and enjoy rights and privileges which the President tells them, they can
never receive in this country," Cincinnati *Daily Gazette*, August 20, 1862, p. 1, c. 1.

   [4] *Works*, VIII, 1–9 (August 14, 1862).

the profit interest on the part of capitalists, Lincoln urged the Negro delegation to rally to the support of the project "not . . . for the present time, but . . . for the good of mankind . . . ." On this theme he burst into poetry:

> From age to age descends the lay
> To millions yet to be,
> Till far its echoes roll away
> Into eternity.

V

In favoring colonization Lincoln was promoting a scheme and a point of view violently opposed by nearly all abolitionists,[1] including notably Senator Sumner. Radical antislavery men were unready to admit that Negroes needed to be separated from whites, nor did they trouble themselves with practical consequences of emancipation. Garrison strongly opposed colonization. On the other hand there were Southerners who favored it, some of them paying from their own pockets to promote private emigration enterprises. This was not the only instance in which Lincoln was nearer to the Southern than to the average abolitionist viewpoint in regard to the Negro race.

Lincoln's efforts toward colonization would make a long story and a dismal one. He asked his cabinet for written advice, sought treaties with foreign nations,[2] and gave detailed attention to the two areas upon which actual efforts of the time were focusing. One of these was the Chiriqui location near Panama, a part of New Grenada (Colombia); the other was a Haitian island known as *Isle a'Vache*. Both ventures were abortive. The Chiriqui project was dropped when samples of the coal deposits failed in scientific tests. This disappointment of promising hopes [3] made it seem the more desirable to proceed

---

[1] There were a few exceptions. Governor Andrew favored colonization and Senator S. C. Pomeroy of Kansas became officially associated with the abortive attempt to establish a Negro colony in Central America. Cincinnati *Daily Gazette*, March 16, 1864, p. 3, c. 5; Browning, *Diary*, I, 577.

[2] Countries in the Western Hemisphere did not take avidly to these schemes. Diplomats from various Central and South American states remonstrated with Seward, urging that foreign colonies of this nature were not desired. Cincinnati *Daily Gazette*, August 29, 1862, p. 3, c. 3. For a rather lengthy comment on these treaties by the Attorney General, see Bates, *Diary*, 262–264.

[3] "The Chiriqui colonization scheme was discussed in a cabinet meeting today. . . . [I]t was . . . decided to abandon the whole scheme, ... It is understood, however,

with the Haitian experiment, and in an unguarded moment Lincoln became a party to a scheme promoted by one Bernard Kock, an alleged "business man" whom Edward Bates denounced as "an errant humbug" and "a charlatan adventurer." [4] In spite of Bates's denunciation, Lincoln and his secretary of the interior signed a contract with this Kock by which, at fifty dollars a head, five thousand Negroes were to be colonized. With government backing and predictions of colossal profits, Kock enlisted the financial support of certain New York capitalists, and the ill-fated Haitian venture was launched.

Over four hundred hapless Negroes were transported to the island at government expense, but the whole scheme, which, even if successful, could have been no more than "a tub to the whale," [5] collapsed from inadequate planning, want of essentials, poor housing, smallpox, unemployment, cupidity, Haitian opposition, and the strutting unpopularity of Kock. Midway in the venture Lincoln saw to it that the contract with Kock was canceled. When, on March 20, 1864, the government-chartered *Marcia C. Day* docked near Washington carrying back 368 of these colonists, about a hundred less than were sent, the Washington *Chronicle* reported the great joy of the returning survivors, while remarking upon "the folly of attempting to depopulate the country of its valuable labor." [6]

For Lincoln the idea died hard. This was partly because he considered it an important part of a comprehensive plan of emancipation, and it is interesting to note that Governor John A. Andrew of Massachusetts agreed with him. In February 1861 Andrew wrote: "If our . . . government would establish . . . a colony for the emancipated col'd people, . . . I think it wd. prove a blessing in a thousand ways, . . . would . . . help to . . . create a hereafter for the oppressed race, & would remove the prejudices of many . . . who now refuse to tolerate . . . liberty for the slaves. . . . I wish we might take some pains to prove that we are friends & not enemies to all classes of Southern society. A very strong anti-slavery man myself, I yet

---

that the President does not desire to have the matter abandoned . . . ." Cincinnati *Daily Gazette*, Aug. 30, 1862, p. 3, c. 3.

[4] Bates, *Diary*, 268.

[5] "As a tub to the whale, it may do to provide for voluntary colonization. But if Emancipation waits on colonization, that means eternal slavery . . . ." Alphonso Taft to S. P. Chase, Cincinnati, Ohio, Aug. 26, 1862, Chase MSS., Lib. of Cong.

[6] Washington *Chronicle*, Mar. 21, 1864. p. 2, c. 1. See also New York *Herald*, Mar. 22, 1864, p. 1, c. 2.

am conscious of only kind & fraternal feelings to our Southern people . . . ." [7]

Though colonization failed utterly as a solution,[8] so utterly that it is difficult to think of it as a serious undertaking, the motives of Lincoln in favoring it are worth remembering. These motives were much the same as those expressed by Governor Andrew. They did not, however, embrace the catch argument, as Lincoln called it, that the presence of the free colored would "injure and displace . . . white laborers." "Emancipation," he thought, "even without deportation, would probably enhance the wages of white labor, and very surely would not reduce them." Ex-slaves would do no more than their old proportion of the work to be done, and probably less. Having made his own rationalization to deal with the catch argument, Lincoln retained in December 1862 his strong interest in colonization, associating gradual emancipation with "deportation" and referring to a temporary adjustment after emancipation while awaiting the time when, for the colored people, "new homes . . . [could] be found . . . in congenial climes and with people of their own blood and race." [9]

VI

Where Lincoln gave thought to large-scale national planning in the matter of liberating the slaves, such thought was not embraced within the bounds of the emancipation proclamation. Speaking relatively and with a view to the President's main concept for solving the problem, it is correct to regard the proclamation as of minor importance. The famous edict was to Lincoln a war measure of limited scope, of doubtful legality, and of inadequate effect. In his reaching out for an adequate solution the President developed an elaborate blueprint for freedom in terms of gradual emancipation by voluntary action of

[7] John A. Andrew to Montgomery Blair, Feb. 23, 1861, Blair MSS.

[8] For these abortive colonization efforts, see W. L. Fleming, "Deportation and Colonization: An Attempted Solution of the Race Problem," in *Studies in Southern History . . . Inscribed to William Archibald Dunning*, 3–30; N. A. N. Cleven, "Some Plans for Colonizing Liberated Negro Slaves in Hispanic America," in *Journal of Negro History*, XI, 35–49. For the disappointing Liberian experiment, see E. L. Fox, *The American Colonization Society, 1817–1840* (*Johns Hopkins Univ. Studies . . .* [etc.], series 37, no. 3).

[9] Lincoln's views as here condensed are found in his annual message to Congress, Dec. 1, 1862, *Works*, VIII, 126–128.

the slave states with Federal coöperation in two matters: foreign colonization of emancipated Negroes (already treated),[1] and compensation to slaveowners.

This blueprint was envisaged not merely with reference to the war, though its integration with a broad war policy was a vital factor; beyond the war the President's solution was projected into a peace-minded future with a view to the ultimate, statesmanlike elimination of an institution in which, as Lincoln felt, North and South had a common responsibility and a community of interest. Though the plan failed, a familiarity with it becomes necessary to an understanding of wartime currents and especially of Lincoln's manner of tackling a large problem. As one studies the President's pathetically earnest efforts to promote this "proposition," one is impressed with his conservatism, his sense of fair dealing, his lack of vindictiveness, his attention to legal adjustments, his respect for self-determination in government, his early vision of state-and-federal coöperation,[2] and his coördination of a domestic reform with the nation's paramount purpose to restore the Union and then to preserve it. The proposition is also significant as perhaps the major instance in which Lincoln tried manfully to enlist the support of Congress. On no other matter did he so far extend his presidential leadership in attempted legislation. The only other project of the period that compares with it is that of reconstruction, but in that case Lincoln did not rely upon congressional enactment of a presidentially sponsored measure.

Announced in a special message to Congress on March 6, 1862, and fully elaborated in his message of December 1 of that year, Lincoln's plan was unfolded as part of a grand concept of a large and growing people, a nation of untouched resources whose future, he hoped, would not be frustrated "by any political folly or mistake." [3]

---

[1] Correct sequences and relations cannot always be preserved as one topic after another is taken up. If it were possible to treat two topics simultaneously, the project for colonization ought to be studied step by step with that of voluntary compensated emancipation. Lincoln showed a tenderness for colonization largely because he held it to be part of his main comprehensive scheme of liberation.

[2] At the time such coöperation for peaceful projects was virtually an unused resource; its development, reaching the proportions of a new and enlarged federalism, remained for a distant future. Voluntary action by states in non-war enterprises, involving immense expenditures by the national government, is now such a commonplace that it takes something of an effort to realize the path-breaking nature of this kind of suggestion in Civil War days.

[3] *Works*, VIII, 113.

A long-term policy was envisaged, to be completed "at any time or times" before 1900.[4] Thirty-seven years did not seem too high a maximum for the consummation of such a reform. Though a broad solution was projected, the President was immediately concerned with initiatory steps. Emancipation was to be gradual. Both races were to be spared the "evils of sudden derangement."[5] No Federal claim of the right to impose emancipation upon a state was involved. Abolition was to be voluntary; "absolute control" of the matter by the states was recognized;[6] "perfectly free choice" was to govern their action.

Compensation was to be made to slaveholders, for, as Lincoln said, "the liberation of slaves is the destruction of property."[7] The Federal government was to bear the cost of such compensation but not to administer it. The states would emancipate with compensation; the Federal government would reimburse them "by installments" as abolition proceeded. This it would do by interest-bearing bonds. Freedmen were to be transported at Federal expense to new homes in some foreign land. In this connection the President used the strong word "deportation," though he intended no compulsion; only those freedmen who desired it would be colonized.[8]

Such in brief was Lincoln's emancipation plan. He proposed it first as a congressional resolution expressive of general approval of the whole concept, then as a bill which he himself drafted for applying the plan in Delaware,[9] later in more elaborate form as a constitutional amendment. Reactions at home and abroad reflected conflicting opinions on the merits of the project. To the *Herald* it appeared that no plan yet devised was "so simple, so just, so profound";[10] the President had taken "a sensible and conservative view."[11] The *Delaware State Journal* considered the proposal "one of the most important

---

[4] *Ibid.*, VIII, 116.   [5] *Ibid.*, VIII, 118–119.   [6] *Ibid.*, VII, 114.

[7] *Ibid.*, VIII, 119. Lincoln qualified this statement as to property by the words "In a certain sense."

[8] *Ibid.*, VIII, 128.

[9] There have come down to us two drafts of a bill prepared by Lincoln for compensated abolishment to be enacted by the State of Delaware; this was an experiment in state lawmaking by presidential sponsorship. The period of these Lincoln drafts was November 1861 (Paul M. Angle, *New Letters and Papers of Lincoln,* 285–286; Nicolay and Hay, *Works,* VII, 21–23). Support in Delaware was lacking and the project was dropped. See H. Clay Reed, "Lincoln's Compensated Emancipation Plan and Its Relation to Delaware," *Delaware Notes,* seventh series (Univ. of Del., 1931), 27–78.

[10] New York *Herald,* editorial, Mar. 8, 1862, p. 6, c. 3.

[11] *Ibid.*, Mar. 7, 1862, p. 4, c. 4.

[executive] documents . . . since the foundation of the Republic." [12]
It seemed to the New York *Post* that the plan would bring its author
"honorable fame" and "praise wherever civilized men dwell." [13]
Though predicting that it would be "distorted and misconstrued by
. . . politicians," the Chicago *Journal* regarded the plan as "in the
highest degree sound." [14] If the slave states did it voluntarily, the
Alton (Illinois) *Telegraph* felt that "the great majority of the people
in the free States" would aid them. [15] A good deal of popular support
for Lincoln's solution was suggested by the comment that many who
privately denounced the plan were publicly supporting it. "Very
soon [it was added] they . . . [would be] joining in the praises of
General McClellan sounded by the . . . masses of the loyal people."
Abolitionists, it was pointed out, would be trying to "make a merit
of necessity" by joining in support of Lincoln's scheme. [16]

Yet these very abolitionists, many of them, were denying that the
President was on their side. "I am afraid," wrote William Lloyd Garrison, "the President's message will prove 'a decoy duck' or 'a red
herring,' so as to postpone that decisive action by Congress which
we are so desirous of seeing." [17] A supporter of Frémont's Missouri
policy thought it strange "that the President should ignore the sentiments of 18 millions [18] of men who elected him . . . and adopt the
principles of the pro-slavery Union men & the 'West Point' aristocracy." [19] Expressing a middle-of-the-road sentiment, the New York
Times doubted that the scheme would work, but rejoiced that the
President had placed himself on the side of freedom. [20]

These varying comments show that Lincoln's program was one
of those compromise schemes that are distasteful to widely diverse
elements. Border-state moderates did not rise to it; on the other hand
radical abolitionists were usually indignant at it, though some of
them gave it reluctant support. "The Message," declared the *Herald*,
"has taken all parties by surprise. A majority of the Senators and Repre-

---

[12] Issue of Mar. 11, 1862, as quoted in H. Clay Reed, as above cited, 47.

[13] As quoted in *Illinois State Journal* (weekly edition), Mar. 19, 1862, p. 1, c. 2.

[14] *Ibid.*, p. 2, c. 6.   [15] *Ibid.*   [16] New York *Herald*, March 21, 1862, p. 5, c. 1.

[17] Garrison to Oliver Johnson, Mar. 18, 1862, Garrison MSS.

[18] Actually, the popular vote for Lincoln in 1860 was only 1,866,000 in a total of
more than four and a half million. The pro-Frémont writer was indulging in a tenfold
exaggeration.

[19] W. M'Caulley to Charles Sumner, Wilmington, Del., Mar. 3, 1862, Sumner MSS.

[20] Mar. 7, 1862, editorial, p. 4, c. 3; Mar. 8, 1862, editorial, p. 4, c. 3.

sentatives are unprepared to express themselves upon it. All are afraid of it, and all are afraid to oppose it. The radicals look blank . . . . The conservatives . . . are anxious to sustain the policy . . . but they fear that they may be entrapped . . . from their chosen position." [21] To the London *Post* the message indicated Union despair in victory by arms; skeptical as to how it could be carried out, the *Post* ridiculed the plan as puerile and vain, the last resort of a government headed for ruin.[22] *The Times* of London considered it important, not for likelihood of acceptance, but as a bid toward ending the war; if raised, the bid might lead to something acceptable.[23]

VII

One can hardly find any subject on which Lincoln argued and pleaded more earnestly than on this. Sumner, who saw him frequently as he studied slavery matters, bore witness that "the invitation to Emancipation in the States" was "peculiarly his own" and that in furthering it his "whole soul was occupied." "In familiar intercourse with him," added Sumner, "I remember nothing more touching than the earnestness and completeness with which he embraced this idea." [1] Addressing border-state representatives at the White House Lincoln told them that they had more power for good than any other equal number in Congress. Let the border states adopt gradual emancipation and the war would be substantially ended. "Let the States . . . in rebellion see . . . that in no event will the [border] states . . . ever join their . . . confederacy, and they cannot much longer maintain the contest." The incidents of the war, said the President, could not be avoided. Slavery was doomed by "mere friction and abrasion." How much better to obtain compensation for a dying institution than to wait till both the institution and the power of compensation were forever sunk in the war. As President, he explained, he was constantly pressed for decisive measures of emancipation. It was an increasing pressure from an element whose support he could

---

[21] New York *Herald*, Mar. 8, 1862, p. 3, c. 5.
[22] Editorial, London *Post*, Mar. 21, 1862, in New York *Herald*, April 6, 1862, p. 8, c. 2.
[23] Editorial, *The Times*, London, in New York *Herald*, April 1, 1862, p. 3, c. 4.
[1] Charles Sumner to ——, June 5, 1862, Sumner, *Works*, VII, 117. This letter appeared in the Boston *Journal*, with editorial comment, June 13, 1862. See also McPherson, *Rebellion*, 233.

not afford to lose. With all the persuasion that he could muster he urged that border-state leaders take the patriotic view.

Before leaving the capital [he pleaded], . . . discuss it among yourselves. You are patriots and statesmen, and as such I pray you consider this proposition, and . . . commend it to . . . your States and people. As you would perpetuate popular government for the best people in the world, I beseech you that you do in no wise omit this. Our common country is in great peril, demanding the loftiest views and boldest action to bring it speedy relief. Once relieved, its form of government is saved to the world, its beloved history and cherished memories are vindicated, and its happy future fully assured and rendered inconceivably grand. To you, more than to any others, the privilege is given to assure that happiness and swell that grandeur, and to link your own names therewith forever.[2]

This fervid eloquence, contrasting as it did with Lincoln's habitual economy of crisply effective words, betokened unusual emotional earnestness. Returning to the subject at a later time the President addressed himself to some of its more practical aspects. He showed that the plan was a "compromise";[3] as such it took account of the slave interest within the Union. To those who considered the cost a conclusive objection, Lincoln explained that the scheme would in fact be "economical"; it would save money by shortening the war. He was proposing a long-time fiscal plan in a rapidly growing nation, giving bonds in future years as emancipation unfolded. Thus there would be the "great advantage of a policy by which we shall not have to pay, until we number a hundred millions, what by a different policy we would have to pay now, when we number but thirty-one millions." Each dollar for emancipation would be easier to pay than for the war, and it would "cost no blood, no precious life."[4] Far from the financial burden being fatal to the enterprise, Lincoln calculated that compensation at $400 each for all the slaves of Delaware could be paid and the total would amount to only one-half-day's cost of the war. Eighty-seven days' cost would pay for all the slaves in Delaware, Maryland, the District, Kentucky, and Missouri at the same price.[5]

---

[2] *Works*, VII, 270–274 (July 12, 1862).

[3] "This would be compromise; but it would be compromise among the friends, and not with the enemies of the Union." *Ibid.*, VIII, 118 (Dec. 1, 1862).

[4] *Ibid.*, VIII, 125 (Dec. 1, 1862).

[5] For the border area Lincoln calculated that the total emancipated cost at 173 millions of dollars ($400 per slave); the cost of eighty-seven days of war at two millions a day would be 174 millions. Lincoln to Henry J. Raymond, Mar. 9, 1862 (*ibid.*, VII, 119); Lincoln to Senator James A. McDougall, Mar. 14, 1862 (*ibid.*, VII, 132–134).

That the North should bear a heavy share of the money cost Lincoln considered entirely equitable. For the introduction of slavery he thought that the Northern people were as responsible as the Southern; considering the Northern use of cotton and sugar and "the profits of dealing in them," they were as responsible for its continuance.[6] Some might regard this as a considerable concession by a leader opposed to slavery, yet the statement is in entire harmony with Lincoln's main attitude toward the slave issue throughout his public career. He always spoke in measured tones and with wholesome respect for slaveholding friends. His was never the vocabulary of vituperative abolitionists intemperately denouncing Southerners and seeking their punishment. When Lincoln spoke of slavery, he treated it as a problem for statesmen to deal with, not as a theme for heaping blame upon Southern masters or putting a stigma upon the Southern people.

Lincoln's pleadings and his carefully figured schemes were of no avail. Border-state response was not forthcoming. There were objections to the cost as the President anticipated, questions of constitutionality, doubts as to procedure. Above all, there was indecision, and, as the *Herald* thought, the same dread of responsibility that had paralyzed the efforts of border-state men in Congress "when civil war first began to darken the horizon." It was a paralysis which emasculated their influence when they might have been leaders.[7]

It was not that the action of Congress was clear-cut in opposing Lincoln's plan; it was rather a matter of leaderless incompetence. The curious thing is that the plan was approved in principle, yet it came to nothing in practice. (Compensated emancipation was applied in the District, but this measure was separate from Lincoln's broad scheme for slave states.) The record of Congress was neither one thing nor the other; there was no consistent pattern. On April 10, 1862, Congress resolved that "the United States ought" to give pecuniary aid to any state that would adopt gradual emancipation.[8] A few days later it adopted the emancipation measure for the District (already treated)[9] which constituted the only bit of completed legislation in which actual compensation in a specified part of the country was provided. Proposals to apply the scheme in Missouri seemed early in 1863 to promise legislative success, and sizable sums were provided in

---

[6] *Ibid.*, VIII, 120 (Dec. 1, 1862).   [7] New York *Herald*, July 15, 1862, p. 5, c. 1.
[8] *Cong. Globe*, 37 Cong., 2 sess., appendix, p. 420.   [9] Above, pp. 133–134.

bills passed by the houses of Congress severally (ten million dollars in the House, twenty million in the Senate). When, however, the hectic short session ended in March 1863, the project had fallen down, despite majority votes of approval, because of the failure to pass the same bill through the two houses.[10] In this project for freedom Lincoln knew where he was going. As for Congress, the project went down by default. The war went on, and as its deadly toll increased Lincoln's attention was directed to other measures; yet late in the war his thought reverted in wistful contemplation to his "earnest and successive appeals to the border States to favor compensated emancipation." [11] As the war entered its last phase and terms of peace were under discussion Lincoln once more repeated his advocacy of a fair indemnity to Southern slaveowners, his willingness to be taxed for the purpose, and his belief that the people of the North were as responsible for the institution as those of the South.[12]

VIII

Slavery policy unfolded by changing phases, and by the middle of '62, with congressional action mounting and slave incidents multiplying, Lincoln was in the stage when anti-slavery pressure on the one side and border-state unresponsiveness on the other were driving him to a bold use of presidential power. Conservative as he was, and ready to put other questions above slavery, he was finding that on the complex issue of bondage he could not be neutral. Measures against slavery were being taken, and he had either to permit or repudiate them. Repudiation had been tried. Having overruled Frémont's emancipatory proclamation and suppressed Cameron's self-advertising pronouncement in 1861,[1] Lincoln had felt compelled in May 1862 to take similar action in overruling another order of military liberation which had attracted wide publicity. General David Hunter, with headquarters at Port Royal, South Carolina, had proclaimed that, as slavery and martial law were incompatible, persons held as slaves in the "Military Department of the South" (Georgia, Florida, and South

---

[10] Randall, *Constitutional Problems Under Lincoln*, 366.

[11] *Works*, X, 67 (letter to A. G. Hodges, April 4, 1864).

[12] Lincoln spoke in these terms at the Hampton Roads Conference, February 1865. Alexander H. Stephens, *A Constitutional View of the . . . War Between the States*, II, 617.

[1] Above, pp. 56–58.

Carolina) were "declared forever free." [2] When this sensational order was issued Lincoln's slavery policy had not matured, his emphasis being upon the proposal for compensated emancipation. Naturally, he felt that if executive power were used on a great national problem, that power ought to be wielded by the President. In a crisp endorsement he wrote: "No commanding general shall do such a thing upon my responsibility without consulting me." [3]

In these circumstances there was nothing for Lincoln to do but repudiate and revoke Hunter's unauthorized order, and this he promptly did. Declaring the general's proclamation of freedom "altogether void," the President made it known that such questions belonged to him as commander in chief and were not to be handled by generals in the field as if they were matters of "police regulations in armies and camps." He did not let the occasion slip, however, without reverting to the solemn resolution of Congress relating to compensated emancipation. For the slave states he had a special word:

> . . . To the people of those States I now earnestly appeal. . . . You cannot . . . be blind to the signs of the times. I beg of you a calm . . . consideration . . . , far above personal and partizan politics. This proposal makes common cause . . . , casting no reproaches upon any. It acts not the Pharisee. The change . . . would come gently as the dews of heaven, not rending or wrecking anything. Will you not embrace it? . . . May the vast future not have to lament that you have neglected it.[4]

Lincoln did not enjoy taking this action against Hunter, nor had he gained much by it. Hunter, "an honest man," he said, was a "friend" with whom he agreed "in the general wish that all men everywhere could be free." In revoking the order the President had given "dissatisfaction, if not offense, to many" whose support could not be spared.[5] Not only was the repudiating proclamation an embarrassment; it had the further defect of being inconclusive. Nothing was settled. The pressure was increasing. Conservatives who agreed with the President as to the Hunter affair [6] might include some whose praise

---

[2] *Offic. Rec.*, 1 ser., XIV, 341.   [3] *Works*, VII, 167 (May 17, 1862).

[4] These earnest words were part of a presidential proclamation, May 19, 1862 (*ibid.*, VII, 172–173).

[5] *Ibid.*, VII, 272–273 (July 12, 1862).

[6] Among anti-abolitionists the President's squelching of Hunter's order was highly approved. Thus the New York *Herald* (editorial, May 20, 1862, p. 6, c. 3) rejoiced that the country had this conservative at the helm, adhering to rights under the Constitution rather than listening to radicals.

was of doubtful value; this would only increase the attacks of radicals who had no compunctions about causing him continual embarrassment.

On July 17, 1862, a none-too-helpful Congress brought a long and wordy session to a close, having passed a number of piecemeal laws, and one seemingly comprehensive one,[7] concerning slavery. Lincoln was indeed being pushed by the "signs of the times" and the pressure of events. He was buffeted by opposite forces. His own words show his dilemma. "As an anti-slavery man," he later wrote, "I have a motive to desire emancipation which pro-slavery men do not have . . . ." [8] As a check to this motive there was the whole border-state complex, with slavery entrenched as a legal institution within the Union, and on this very point there were Lincoln's repeated assurances that border-state sentiment and pro-slavery loyalty were to be respected. As long as he remained in the White House, he had told Representative Crisfield, "Maryland had nothing to fear . . . for her institutions or her interests." [9] As between the conflicting tendencies beating upon him, the President's assurances had been for the most part given to slaveholding interests. He was under no out-and-out pledge to abolish slavery, yet he was being uncomfortably forced to choose between the downright protection of slavery and some use of executive war power against the institution which he referred to as the "lever" of the Union's foes.[10] No one could accuse him of indulging his moral judgment or personal feeling. He was being assailed for exactly the opposite reason, as when he overruled Frémont and Hunter. He distrusted the radicals and disliked the pressure of the Greeley faction. He tried a long-range, statesmanlike solution on the basis of friendly recognition of slaveholding interests, and obtained no more than nominal support. His thoughts had been focused upon peaceful schemes of compensated abolition, with wishful eyes turned toward Central or South America. Yet these were not the measures fated to succeed. The day was fast approaching when blunt weapons of war would have to be used against human slavery by a leader whose legal sense and concepts of fairness preferred more considerate instruments.

---

[7] The treason act of July 17, 1862, also known as the second confiscation act. The seeming comprehensiveness of the slave clauses of the act contrasted strikingly with the utterly negligible effect of these clauses in actual practice.

[8] *Works*, IX, 57 (Aug. 5, 1863).   [9] *Ibid.*, VII, 125 (March 10, 1862).

[10] *Ibid.*, VII, 270–271 (July 12, 1862).

CHAPTER XXII

PRESIDENTIAL EMANCIPATION

I

THE painful and crowded summer of 1862 found Lincoln's slavery policy in a state of transition. As one gets the "feel" of the times through contemporary records one senses a rising demand that the President do something decisive for freedom, not through Lincoln's conservative plan, but as a dramatic wartime stroke. Abolitionists, of course, had been demanding this right along. Reporting a meeting in October 1861, an abolitionist leader mentioned that Gerrit Smith had "a grand hearing," that he was "really magnificent," and that the audience "gave Fremont three rousing cheers." [1] A similar response came when Frederick Douglass, distinguished Negro orator, addressed a large crowd in February 1862 at Cooper Institute. [2]

It was felt that the cancer had to be cauterized, and that Republicans could not sustain a wavering President. [3] Antislavery souls could not understand Lincoln's policy. They saw none of the complications that Lincoln saw; they saw only a clear-cut issue of right and wrong, with no shadings. They wanted the death of slavery, had voted for it (they thought), and were fighting for it; yet to their outraged eyes here was a President of their own choosing actually trying to preserve the institution. "A more ridiculous farce was never played," wrote one of them, than permitting slaveholders to keep their human property on taking oath of loyalty. Let the administration continue thus, and the Republican party would be forever broken and Lincoln the "most unpopular man in the nation." [4] "It strikes me," wrote an anxious

---

[1] Oliver Johnson to J. M. McKim, Oct. 31, 1861, MS., Boston Pub. Lib.
[2] New York *Times*, Feb. 13, 1862, p. 4, c. 2.
[3] W. Kitchell to Trumbull, Hillsboro, Ill., Dec. 10, 1861, Trumbull MSS.
[4] John Russell to Trumbull, Bluffdale, Greene Co., Ill., Dec. 17, 1861, *ibid.*

patriot, "that now is the time to emancipate the slaves . . . and that it is either emancipation *now* or . . . St. Domingo hereafter." [5] To end the war a blow had to be struck at the vital spot of the rebellion. When this was done, pious believers were sure that God would take the Union side.[6] To such persons it seemed that Trumbull had the right idea when he brought in his bill for the confiscation of rebel property.

To Salmon Chase's embattled view it was folly to think of winning the war while upholding or permitting slavery. "The government," he thought, could not succeed "in the attempt to put down this rebellion with the left hand while supporting slavery with the right hand." [7] When at the end of the Seven Days the "war cloud" loomed "blacker than ever," he felt that the way "to draw the lightning" was to "make . . . emancipation the conducting rod." [8] To an Ohioan writing to Chase it seemed that if the President saved slavery in the struggle, not only would he fail after all to save the Union, but he would "be ruined & forever disgraced." And, he added, "We all have too much invested in Mr Lincoln to wish to make him out a failure." [9] As to method, Chase would "declare free all Slaves of . . . [seceded] States and invite them to organize for the suppression of rebellion and the establishment of order." The border states, he thought, ought to be left free to choose whether to keep or abolish slavery.[10] Thus he would make forcible abolition a penalty for rebellion. Nor was Chase the man to keep these views to himself. In midsummer of '62, in cabinet meeting, he expressed the conviction just stated "for the tenth or twentieth time." [11]

Sumner wished to go farther than Chase. In an evening drive with the President in May 1861 he urged a blow for emancipation when the moment should come. Again, directly after first Bull Run, when Congress was proclaiming the opposite view, Sumner called on the President, repeating that he must strike at slavery and that the moment

[5] Bradford R. Wood to C. M. Clay, Copenhagen, Nov. 28, 1861, MS., Ill. St. Hist. Lib.
[6] D. T. Linegar to Trumbull, Cairo, Ill., Dec. 7, 1861, Trumbull MSS.
[7] Cyrus Pitt Grosvenor to S. P. Chase, London, July 28, 1862, Chase MSS., Lib. of Cong. (In this letter Grosvenor approvingly quoted the above words of Chase.)
[8] Chase to H. Barney, Washington, July 2, 1862, Chase MSS., Hist. Soc. of Pa.
[9] Alphonso Taft to Chase, Cincinnati, Ohio, Aug. 26, 1862, Chase MSS., Lib. of Cong.
[10] Typed copy of a long letter by Chase to an unspecified correspondent, Aug. 9, 1862, *ibid.*
[11] Diary of Chase, Aug. 3, 1862, as quoted in Warden, *Chase*, 445.

had come.[12] In December 1861 Sumner wrote: "He [Lincoln] tells me that I am ahead of him only a month or six weeks." [13] Interviewing Lincoln on July 4, 1862, Sumner told the President that he not only needed more men at the North, he needed them "at the South, in the rear of the Rebels." He needed the slaves. All he had to do was to say the word; by choosing July 4 as the day on which to say it he could outdo the Continental Congress in making the day sacred and historic.[14] According to Sumner's narrative of the interview Lincoln replied: " 'I would do it [issue an edict of emancipation] if I were not afraid that half the officers would fling down their arms and three more States would rise.' " [15] Yet Sumner was capable of more patience toward the President than other abolitionists. Criticism directed against him was "hasty," thought the Senator, who wrote: "Could you —as has been my privilege often—have seen the President, while considering . . . [these] great questions . . . , even your zeal would be satisfied . . . ." [16]

Though Sumner expected fulfillment of his heart's desire it must not be supposed that abolitionists were the President's most welcome callers. "Be sure that Lincoln is at heart with Slavery," growled Gurowski. "He considers that *emancipation is a job which will smother the free States. Such are his precise words.*" [17] When Wendell Phillips turned up at Washington early in '62 his presence "roused up proslavery spite and malice in every direction"; as for Garrison, he wrote in March of that year that he had not been invited to come to the capital.[18] At Cincinnati in March 1862 popular resentment against Phillips had been expressed with groans, hisses, and flying eggs.[19]

II

Lincoln's ending of delay and arrival at a decision are best told in the President's own words. "It had got to be midsummer, 1862," he

[12] Sumner, *Works*, VI, 31.　　　[13] *Ibid.*, VI, 152.
[14] Speech at Faneuil Hall, Oct. 6, 1862, *ibid.*, VII, 215.
[15] Sumner to Bright, Boston, Aug. 5, 1862, Pierce, *Sumner*, IV, 83.
[16] Letter of Charles Sumner to unnamed correspondent, Senate Chamber, June 5, 1862, Sumner, *Works*, VII, 116–117.
[17] Gurowski to John A. Andrew, Washington, May 7, 1862, Andrew MSS., vol. 14, no. 32.
[18] W. L. Garrison to Oliver Johnson, Boston, March 30, 1862, MS., Boston Pub. Lib.
[19] Moore, *Rebellion Record* (Diary), IV, 67–68. The date was March 24, 1862. The meeting broke up in a fight.

said. "Things had gone . . . from bad to worse, until I felt that we had reached the end of our rope on the plan . . . we had been pursuing; that we . . . must change our tactics, or lose the game. I now determined upon the adoption of the emancipation policy; and without consultation with, or the knowledge of, the Cabinet, I prepared the original draft of the proclamation, and, after much anxious thought, called a Cabinet meeting upon the subject." [1]

On July 13, on a long carriage ride with Welles and Seward, Lincoln had informally broached the matter of a proclamation, that being "he said, the first occasion when he had mentioned the subject to any one." [2] "He dwelt earnestly [wrote Welles] on the gravity, importance, and delicacy of the movement, said he had given it much thought and had about come to the conclusion that it was a military necessity . . . for the salvation of the Union, ..." Welles emphasized that this "was a new departure for the President, for until this time, . . . whenever . . . emancipation . . . had been . . . alluded to, he had been prompt and emphatic in denouncing any interference by the General Government with the subject." [3]

Gloom rested heavily upon the Union cause. The Seven Days had passed, Southern defense had been strong before Richmond, the storm raged bitterly for McClellan's removal, a shake-up in military command and in operations was imminent, and, as to slaves, already "thousands . . . were in attendance upon the [enemy's] armies." [4] It was in this atmosphere of depression and frustration that Lincoln worked out alone the basic problem and the wording of his historic proclamation. His friend Eckert of the military telegraph service recalled that Lincoln wrote the first draft of the edict in the cipher room of the war department telegraph office. He began it, said Eckert, shortly after the Seven Days (this would put it about the beginning of July 1862). He would write a line or two on long foolscap sheets, study a while, look out of the window, and now and then stop to pass a remark with the operators. This continued for "several weeks," the sheets being locked up at the telegraph office and taken out "nearly every day" by Lincoln for careful composition and revision of every sentence. The President, added Eckert, told him that he had been

---

[1] *Works*, X, 1–2 (Feb. 6, 1864).
[3] *Ibid.*

[2] Welles, *Diary*, I, 70–71.
[4] *Ibid.*, I, 71.

able thus "to work . . . more quietly and . . . better than at the White House, where he was frequently interrupted." [5]

It was on July 22, 1862, that Lincoln broached the subject of his proclamation to the Cabinet. In his undramatic diary Chase gives incidental mention of the President's proposal to proclaim "the emancipation of all slaves within States remaining in insurrection on the first of January, 1863." This proposed proclamation, said Chase, was based on the confiscation bill (which had a clause concerning the freeing of slaves as a penalty for rebellion); yet as a kind of collateral approach to the slave problem it contained a renewed recommendation for compensation to slaveowners within the pattern of Lincoln's proposal for gradual abolition by state action.[6]

It is clear that Lincoln had made up his mind as to the proclamation; of his Cabinet he asked incidental rather than primary advice. His own statement, given in 1864 to F. B. Carpenter, the artist, was: "I said to the cabinet that I had resolved upon this step, and had not called them together to ask their advice, but to lay the subject-matter of a proclamation before them, suggestions as to which would be in order after they had heard it read." [7] Chase gave the proposal "entire support" chiefly because he considered it "much better than inaction on the subject." [8] Cabinet secretaries gave their suggestions, most of which had been anticipated,[9] but Seward came out with a bit of counsel that gave pause to the President. He doubted the expediency of a proclamation issued at a time of depression in the public mind, dreading the effect of such a step following so closely upon recent reverses. The government, he thought, would seem to be "stretching forth its hands to Ethiopia, instead of Ethiopia stretching forth her hands to the government." It "would be considered a last *shriek* on the retreat." The secretary approved the measure, but he said: ". . . I suggest, sir, that you postpone its issue until you can give it to the country

---

[5] Statement of Major Thomas T. Eckert of the war department telegraph staff, quoted in Bates, *Lincoln in the Telegraph Office*, 138–141.

[6] Diary of S. P. Chase, (*Annual Report*, Am. Hist. Assoc., 1902, II), 48.

[7] Statement of Lincoln to the artist F. B. Carpenter, Feb. 6, 1864, *Works*, X, 1–3. In his *Inner Life of Abraham Lincoln: Six Months at the White House* (20 ff.), Carpenter records these words of Lincoln. By including the passage in his *Works* the President's secretaries accept it as Lincoln's own account. Carpenter's enormous painting to represent the proclamation has hung for many years in the House wing of the Capitol at Washington.

[8] Diary of S. P. Chase (*Annual Report*, Amer. Hist. Assoc., 1902, II), 49 (July 22, 1862).

[9] *Works*, X, 2.

supported by military success . . . ." The "wisdom" of this view struck Lincoln "with very great force." "The result was," said Lincoln to the artist, "that I put the draft of the proclamation aside, as you do your sketch for a picture, waiting for a victory." [10]

Lincoln and those near him had a secret to keep the next two months; in keeping it the President was under the embarrassing necessity of seeming to be noncommittal or even hostile toward a policy upon which he was in fact determined. It is amusing to note the manner in which, with the draft proclamation in his desk drawer,[11] Lincoln gave out laborious and unsatisfactory answers on the subject of slavery while enduring severe taunts against his alleged proslavery attitude. It was in this period, for example, that he advocated separation of the races and colonization in a foreign country.[12] His embarrassment was increased in the anxious days of September when a delegation of Christian leaders descended upon him carrying a petition for national emancipation which had been adopted at a public meeting at Bryan Hall in Chicago. The President received these men courteously and listened "with fixed attention" while the memorial was read. Then he gave reply "in an earnest and . . . solemn manner, as one impressed with the weight of the theme, yet at times making a characteristically shrewd remark with a pleasant air" (such was the clumsy report of the delegation). [13]

The main tone of the President's answer was negative and disappointing. "What good would a proclamation of emancipation from me do, . . . ?" he asked. "I do not want to issue a document that the whole world will see must . . . be inoperative, like the Pope's bull against the comet." In the "rebel States" such a proclamation could no more be enforced, said Lincoln, than the recent ineffective law offering freedom to slaves coming within Union lines. And suppose they did throw themselves upon us in large numbers, what should we do with them? How could we "feed and care for such a multitude"? Much more the President gave them, impressively piling up doubts concerning the wisdom and feasibility of a liberating edict. Conceding that slavery was the *"sine qua non"* of the "rebellion," that emanci-

---

[10] *Ibid.*, X, 2–3.

[11] For this draft proclamation, dated July 22, 1862, see *ibid.*, VII, 289–290.

[12] Above, pp. 137–139.

[13] Report of the Christian delegation's interview with Lincoln, signed by W. W. Patton and John Dempster, Chicago, Sep. 21, 1862, MS., Chicago Hist. Soc.

pation would help the cause in Europe, and that it would weaken the enemy by drawing off their laborers, Lincoln would have the visiting committee consider the difficulties of freeing helpless thousands, the danger of their reënslavement, the impotence of the government to do anything about it if they were reënslaved, and the danger that arms put into Negro hands would be seized by the enemy. Especially he emphasized the importance of fifty thousand Union bayonets from the border slave states; if in consequence of a proclamation they should go over to the enemy, it would be a very serious matter.[14] He went on thus for "an hour of earnest and frank discussion." [15] Then, with the meeting about to break up, Lincoln remarked, as if giving a broad hint on a matter that could not go into the record: "Do not misunderstand me, ... I have not decided against a proclamation of liberty to the slaves, but hold the matter under advisement; and I can assure you that the subject is on my mind, by day and night, more than any other." He trusted that in freely canvassing their views, he had not injured his visitors' feelings.[16]

III

Among the commonest gibes against the President was the assertion that he had no policy. In a roundabout manner such a taunt came to him from New Orleans through the wealthy Democratic leader, August Belmont. Lincoln must take a decisive course, said this writer. Trying to please everybody would satisfy nobody. Let the North declare officially for restoration of the Union as it was. This complaint, with a motive opposite to that of the religious brethren from Chicago, drew from Lincoln the suggestion that if the objector would but read the President's speeches he would find "the substance of the very declaration he desires." [1] In a similar setting Lincoln

<hr>

[14] *Works*, VIII, 30 ff. (Sep. 13, 1862).   [15] Patton and Dempster MS. (see note 13).

[16] *Ibid.* Lincoln's reply appears in his *Works*, VIII, 28-33, and in the Patton and Dempster manuscript above cited. The statement as published in the *Works* reads like a state paper and seems more formalized than the President's actual utterance in the interview. One can only imagine Lincoln's feelings as he heard the delegation urge a proclamation which he had decided to issue, but against which he felt it necessary to give convincing objections. Late in the war, in a letter that seems a bit amusing, Governor Yates of Illinois wrote to Patton and Dempster (July 2, 1864) that their Bryan Hall meeting "must have had great influence upon the President" (MS., Chicago Hist. Soc.).

[1] *Works*, VII, 299 (July 31, 1862).

wrote as to slavery that what was "done and omitted" was on military necessity, and that he was holding antislavery pressure "within bounds." [2]

With his mind full of anti-abolitionist complaints of a lack of policy, Lincoln now became the target for an editorial blast from the opposite direction. From Greeley's resounding sanctum there came the reproachful admonition that "attempts to put down the Rebellion and at the same time uphold its . . . cause . . . [were] preposterous and futile." In an editorial "Prayer of Twenty Millions" the *Tribune* pundit informed the President that an "immense majority of the Loyal Millions" of his countrymen required of him a frank execution of the laws in the antislavery sense.[3] With bland equanimity for Greeley's fervor and with balanced, noncommittal phrases for his heated rhetoric, Lincoln replied in the famous "paramount object" letter which showed, among other things, that he was not swayed by abolitionist outcries. Calm down, and get off your dictatorial horse, would be an offhand paraphrase of his opening sentences. "I have just read yours of the 19th," wrote Lincoln to Greeley. ". . . If there be in it any inferences . . . falsely drawn, I do not . . . argue against them. If there be perceptible in it an impatient and dictatorial tone, I waive it in deference to an old friend . . . ." Having thus set the pitch for his even-toned reply, Lincoln wrote:

My paramount object in this struggle is to save the Union, and is not either to save or to destroy slavery. If I could save the Union without freeing any slave, I would do it; and if I could save it by freeing all the slaves, I would do it; and if I could save it by freeing some and leaving others alone, I would also do that. What I do about slavery and the colored race, I do because I believe it helps to save the Union; and what I forbear, I forbear because I do not believe it would help to save the Union. . . .

I have here stated my purpose according to my view of official duty; and I intend no modification of my oft-expressed personal wish that all men everywhere could be free.[4]

Antislavery folk did not like the calculated restraint of this famous letter. They wanted no such even balance between action and forbearance. They wanted a crusade. One of them sarcastically wrote: "From his policy hitherto, we must infer, that the way he applies it is,

---

[2] *Ibid.*, VII, 295 (July 28, 1862).   [3] New York *Tribune*, Aug. 20, 1862, p. 4, cc. 2–4.
[4] *Works*, VIII, 15–16 (Aug. 22, 1862).

CUTTING HIS OLD ASSOCIATES.
Man or Cows. "Ugh! Get out. I ain't one ob you no more. I'se a Man, I is!"

DIFFERENT ANGLES OF EMANCIPATION

The "Great Union and Emancipation Meeting Held at Exeter Hall, London," was one of a numerous series of demonstrations all over England in which popular enthusiasm was expressed for emancipation, for Lincoln, and for the cause of the American Union. (*Harper's Weekly*, Mar. 14, 1863.) The humorous cartoon of the "Man of Color" appeared in the same magazine, Jan. 17, 1863.

GEORGE B. McCLELLAN

to *save the Union with Slavery, if he can do it at whatever sacrifice of life & treasure.* If that is found impossible . . . [his policy is] *to save the Union without slavery,* unless it should be . . . too late. This is like the duel in which the terms . . . as prescribed by the challenged party were, that they should have but one sword between them, & that he should use it five minutes, & afterward the challenger should have it five minutes." [5]

Such complaints, many of them, Lincoln had to endure while all the time he was awaiting the appropriate public opportunity for launching the proclamation on which he had determined. To supply this much-to-be-desired opportunity rested with McClellan and his men. Major Union victories were not so frequent in '62; if McClellan had not checked Lee at Antietam, Lincoln's proclamation, withheld in hope of Federal triumph, would have been indefinitely delayed. From the day (July 22, 1862) when Lincoln put the famous paper aside on Seward's suggestion that it be not a shriek on the retreat, no important triumph for the United States came, except for Antietam, until July 1863. One appreciates the timeliness of this achievement by the much abused McClellan when one tries to speculate just where Lincoln and emancipation would have stood had the story of McClellan in Maryland been of a piece with that of Pope, Burnside, or Hooker.

It was in this very period of waiting for a victory that there came the word of Pope's disaster at Second Bull Run. "Things looked darker than ever." [6] McClellan was grudgingly reinstated. Further anxious days passed. On Wednesday, September 17, Antietam was fought. Lincoln, according to his own account, was then staying at the Soldiers' Home outside Washington. Here, determining to wait no longer, he finished the "second draft of the preliminary proclamation"; coming in on Saturday, he summoned his Cabinet for Monday. [7]

If contrary to custom there had been an observer at the President's cabinet meeting at the White House beginning at noon of Monday, September 22, 1862, he would have seen all the members in attendance. An important announcement was to come, but it was preceded by a trivial thing, frozen into recorded history as trivial things some-

---

[5] Alphonso Taft to S. P. Chase, Cincinnati, Ohio, Aug. 26, 1862, Chase MSS., Lib. of Cong.

[6] *Works,* X, 3 (Feb. 6, 1864).   [7] *Ibid.*

times are, the better to enable posterity to visualize the human aspects of a significant historic moment. Ready to enter upon the agenda, the Cabinet secretaries, whose formalized visages have been preserved on Carpenter's mammoth canvas, had first to give attention to something that was the antithesis of formal; Lincoln had an Artemus Ward book, sent him by the humorist, and he proposed "to read a chapter which he thought very funny." The "High handed Outrage at Utica" was the selected passage. Lincoln read it "and seemed to enjoy it very much." We are told that the "Heads" also enjoyed it, though Stanton, and (as the context shows) Chase, who recorded the trivial event, were exceptions. One can only picture them sitting with dour faces while the President sought to enliven a serious occasion with the leaven of humor.[8]

Assuming a "graver tone," the President made a statement. He had thought a great deal about the relation of the war to slavery. Ever since the former meeting when he had read an order on the subject, it had occupied his mind; now had arrived "the time for acting." He had determined, as soon as the enemy had been driven out of Maryland, to "issue a Proclamation of Emancipation." He had made the promise to himself and to his Maker; now he proposed to fulfill that promise. On the main matter he was not seeking counsel, his mind was made up; as to the expressions he used, or as to minor matters, he would be glad to have suggestions. He had one other observation to make. It pertained to himself as leader. He said:

. . . I know very well that many others might . . . do better than I can; and if I were satisfied that the public confidence was more fully possessed by any one of them than by me, and knew of any Constitutional way in which he could be put in my place, he should have it. I would gladly yield it to him. But though I believe that I have not so much of the confidence of the people as I had some time since, I do not know that . . . any other person has more; and, however this may be, there is no way in which I can have any other man put where I am. I am here. I must do the best I can, and bear the responsibility of taking the course which I feel I ought to take.[9]

Evidence is lacking on which to follow all the implications of this idea of Lincoln's that he would gladly yield his office to another if that procedure were possible and were demonstrably in the public

---

[8] Diary of S. P. Chase (Annual Report, Am. Hist. Assoc., 1902, II), 87. [9] Ibid., 88.

interest. It is clear that the whole subject of his relation to his high office, and the nature of his own personal responsibility to make and enforce a decision, had been traversed in his deliberations on the emancipation question. If these deliberations had given him humility, and a sense of association with Divine purpose (which was more than once indicated),[10] they had also given executive confidence. In reaching his important decision there is ample reason to believe that Lincoln had not only endured anxious hours, but had undergone a significant inner experience from which he emerged with quiet serenity.

The President read the proclamation through with running comments. In the Cabinet discussion that followed Chase agreed to take the document as written, though he would have charted a somewhat different course; Seward wanted it definitely stated that the government would maintain the freedom proclaimed; only Blair offered a substantial criticism. This was not an objection to emancipation *per se;* the party-minded secretary, whose position in the postal portfolio was peculiarly associated with "politics," was thinking of the coming elections; he feared the effect of the proclamation in the border area, and stated his apprehensions "at some length." [11]

IV

Lincoln's proclamation of emancipation is more often admired than read. Since there were two proclamations one hundred days apart, the first being monitory, one must read them both for a full understanding. In addition, one must read thousands of Lincoln's less formal words giving his own commentaries on the theme, to say nothing of elaborate contemporary statements and reminiscences by many who had a part in the historic act, or who, as in the case of the artist Carpenter, were in a position to hear and record Lincoln's asides and parentheses.

The preliminary proclamation of September 22, 1862, whose slow

---

[10] ". . . I made the promise to myself, and . . . to my Maker" (*ibid.*); ". . . it is my earnest desire to know the will of Providence in this matter." *Works*, VIII, 29 (Sep. 13, 1862).

[11] Diary of S. P. Chase (*Annual Report*, Amer. Hist. Assoc., 1902, II), 89. Blair seems at this time to have repeated the apprehensions which he had expressed in the meeting of July 22, to which Lincoln referred in the following words: "Mr. Blair, after he came in, deprecated the policy on the ground that it would cost the administration the fall elections." *Works*, X, 2 (statement to F. B. Carpenter, Feb. 6, 1864).

composition extended over anxious weeks, opened with a declaration that reunion (not abolition) was the object of the war. At the outset Lincoln designated himself as the "commander-in-chief of the army and navy," using a phrase which was not customary in presidential proclamations and which did not appear in the call for troops in April 1861. Thus Lincoln began his document with a military wording and a non-abolitionist flavor. Continuing, the President promised to renew his recommendation that Congress pass a "practical measure" (something beyond the paper declaration of April 10, 1862) tendering financial aid to such Union states as might adopt gradual abolition of slavery. In close association with this program, the "effort" toward foreign colonization of Negroes would, he said, be continued.

Then came the core of the proclamation: on the first day of 1863 "all persons held as slaves" in areas "in rebellion against the United States" were to be "then, thenceforward, and forever free." The Federal executive and the armed forces were to "recognize and maintain" this freedom, and not to "repress such persons . . . in . . . efforts . . . for their actual freedom." (A critic could cavil at this. He could note the President's announcement of a declared or constructive liberation that fell short of "actual freedom." Also, this declaration was open to violent objection as an encouragement of servile insurrection,[1] that hideous nightmare of Southern racial dread.) Particular states or areas in which the proclamation was to apply were to be designated "on the first day of January aforesaid." Congressional representation at Washington, by men chosen at an election wherein a majority of qualified voters participated,[2] would relieve a state from the liberation edict. Stay in the Union and you may keep your slaves, though you will be urged to free them on a voluntary, coöperative basis, was the meaning.

Measures of Congress were then quoted prohibiting the armed forces from returning fugitive slaves to their masters, denying such return in any case except to loyal owners, and liberating all slaves "of persons . . . hereafter . . . engaged in rebellion against the government of the United States."[3] Closing his edict on a note of friend-

---

[1] See below, pp. 195–197, where it is shown that such objection was unfounded.

[2] Next year (December 1863) Lincoln adopted the idea of ten per cent of the voters as a loyal nucleus for the reconstruction of state governments.

[3] This was section 9 of the second confiscation act of July 17, 1862, *U. S. Stat. at Large*, XII, 591.

liness to slaveholders rather than adherence to any abolitionist program, Lincoln promised that, on restoration of the Union, he would recommend that loyal citizens "be compensated for all losses by acts of the United States, including the loss of slaves." (Rather a sweeping promise of reparations to be paid by the victor.)

Turning to Lincoln's numerous comments on the subject one may acquire some sense of the motives and circumstances that prompted the act, as well as the patience with which the President answered his critics and reviewed the whole project in its relation to the war, to reunion, and to the future of American society. Despite his antislavery sentiment he had done no official act, he said, on the basis of abstract judgment on the moral wrong of slavery.[4] He had begun his administration with a pledge not to interfere with slavery within the states; the general government, he felt, had no lawful power so to interfere.[5] Some might have reasoned that such a pledge should not tie the future to the past. Lincoln took a different line; he had struggled nearly a year and a half to get along without touching the institution; when finally he "conditionally determined to touch it" he "gave a hundred days' fair notice . . . to all the States and people, within which . . . they could have turned it wholly aside by . . . becoming good citizens of the United States."[6] Lincoln by no means considered that he had violated a pledge or repudiated a disclaimer. The disclaimer was made within the pattern of the government of the United States to apply to adherents of the United States. It was made in time of peace and as an inducement for continuance of peace. It presupposed that non-interference was conditioned on loyalty. It did not amount to a prediction of future war policy toward areas that should have become enemies of the United States. When proclaiming conditional future emancipation in his September edict, Lincoln adhered to his disclaimer by announcing no interference except in the case of areas "in rebellion." Later, in a retrospective passage written in 1864, he reverted to his announcement to Greeley that the Union was paramount. Then he added: "All this I said in the utmost sincerity; and I am . . . true to the whole of it . . . . When I afterward proclaimed emancipation, and employed colored soldiers, I only followed the declaration . . . that 'I shall do more whenever . . . doing more will

---

[4] *Works*, IX, 57; X, 65–66.   [5] *Ibid.*, VI, 170; VII, 114; IX, 245–246.
[6] *Ibid.*, VIII, 182 (Jan. 8, 1863).

help the cause.' " [7]

Over and again Lincoln repeated that the Union, not abolition, was his main concern. When George Bancroft wrote him that civil war was the divine instrument to root out slavery, Lincoln, withholding agreement with this sentiment, suggested "caution." [8] "I have . . . thought it proper," he said, "to keep the . . . Union prominent as the primary object of the contest"; [9] yet constantly he felt that the necessity for unshackling and arming the blacks would come unless averted by the more normal and peaceable measures of compensated emancipation.[10]

By that earnestly advocated measure he would have eradicated slavery in conservative terms after the manner of the moderate liberal he was; by doing so he hoped in orderly manner to remove the main cause of the war,[11] and to deprive the disaffected leaders of all hope of winning over the more northern slave states.[12] So to deprive them, he thought, would substantially end the rebellion. When Congress nominally approved his conservative project, he could not think of it otherwise than as "an authentic, definite, and solemn proposal." "So much good . . . [had never] been done," he thought, as "in the providence of God" the border states could do by implementing the proposal.[13] Gradual emancipation he thought better than immediate; if temporary Federal protection for slaveholders' rights were needed in a transitional period, he was ready to brave abolitionist wrath by giving it.[14] He would not thwart efforts in the slave states to work out problems of emancipation.[15] Where slaves were returned to a loyal owner, Lincoln would withhold the full punishment permitted by law.[16] If a system of apprenticeships would ease the transition away

[7] Ibid., X, 194 (Aug., 17, 1864).   [8] Ibid., VII, 20–21 (Nov. 18, 1861).

[9] Ibid., VII, 51 (Dec. 3, 1861); ". . . what is done and omitted about slaves is done and omitted on . . . military necessity" (ibid., VII, 295, July 28, 1862).

[10] Ibid., X, 67 (April 4, 1864).   [11] Ibid., XI, 45 (Mar. 4, 1864).

[12] Ibid., VII, 113 (Mar. 6, 1862).   [13] Ibid., VII, 172–173 (May 19, 1862).

[14] Ibid., VIII, 329 (June 22, 1863).   [15] Ibid., VIII, 330.

[16] The reference here is to Lincoln's comment on the case of a man sentenced to five years at hard labor in the penitentiary for returning a slave to a loyal owner. Lincoln pointed out that the man was guilty under the law; he added, however, that what he did had been "perfectly lawful only a short while before," that the public mind had not fully accepted the change which made it unlawful, that the offense was not of frequent occurrence, and that the severe punishment indicated was "not at all necessary." Ibid., X, 47 (Mar. 18, 1864).

from slavery, he would favor such a scheme.[17] He wanted "some practical system by which the two races could gradually live themselves out of the old relation . . . , and both come out . . . prepared for the new." [18] With this in view, he wanted due attention given to "the element of 'contract,' " to a probationary period, and to the education of young blacks.[19]

When Lincoln justified his long-delayed emancipation as an act of military necessity, he meant it as a kind of high political instrument which the President himself had to wield for military success; he did not favor emancipation by generals on their own authority.[20] He referred to this necessity sometimes to explain his delay (for he would not use the instrument till it was indispensable), sometimes to repel criticism by those who opposed abolition, sometimes to relieve himself of the charge of performing a dictatorial act.[21] He was striking at a constitutionally protected institution; this he justified on the ground that the restriction applied to "ordinary civil administration," that "a limb must be amputated to save a life," that "measures otherwise unconstitutional" might become lawful in a dire emergency, and that he had been "driven to the alternative of either surrendering the Union, and with it the Constitution, or of laying strong hand upon the colored element." [22]

Thus his executive oath to preserve the Constitution was constantly in his mind; when he did unusual things he stressed his function as military chief. The Constitution, he thought, "invests its commander-in-chief with the law of war in time of war." "Civilized belligerents," he added, "do all in their power to help themselves or hurt the enemy, except . . . things regarded as barbarous or cruel." [23] It was only as a matter of promoting Union success in the war that Lincoln cared to justify his course; the imputation that he most resented was that he was willfully seizing arbitrary power. He put the matter in a nut-

---

[17] *Ibid.*, VIII, 182 (Jan. 8, 1863); Dennett, *Lincoln . . . in the Diaries . . . of John Hay*, 73.

[18] *Works*, IX, 56 (Aug. 5, 1863).   [19] *Ibid.*, IX, 56–57.

[20] *Ibid.*, VI, 351, 358–359; VII, 171–172.   [21] *Ibid.*, VII, 113–114; IX, 245–246.

[22] *Ibid.*, X, 65–67 (April 4, 1864).

[23] *Ibid.*, IX, 98 (Aug. 26, 1863). This identifying of the military aspect with the constitutional is shown in Lincoln's statement: "The . . . proclamation has no constitutional or legal justification, except as a military measure." (*ibid.*, IX, 108–109, Sep. 2, 1863).

shell when, in the final edict, he characterized his measure not as a dictator's stroke, but as "a fit and necessary war measure." [24]

V

Taking a chronological liberty, we step forward a hundred days to January 1, 1863. It was then that the President promulgated the definitive edict without which the September document would have been useless. Curiously enough, there were doubts whether Lincoln would actually issue the January proclamation. In his annual message to Congress under date of December 1, 1862, he had indeed discussed emancipation elaborately, but not in terms of sweeping liberation by presidential act. Rather he treated it as a matter of compensated emancipation to be embodied in articles amendatory to the Constitution and implemented by uncoerced compliance on the part of such states as wished to adopt it. Furthermore, he presented it as a grave issue on which a program was yet to be framed, by no means as a problem already neatly solved by the President. More than two months after the preliminary proclamation had been issued, the Executive in addressing Congress was thus emphasizing a very different scheme of liberation. He did not say that proceedings under the proclamation would be stayed because of the "recommendation" of this more permanent solution, but its "timely adoption," he said, by bringing restoration, would stay both the war and presidential emancipation.[1] Thus even as late as December 1862 Lincoln was hinting that, under an assumed set of circumstances, forcible liberation by the executive might not actually go into effect. Though he meant this only in the sense of the warning proclamation as issued, and only toward areas that might return to allegiance (a dim prospect), it was possible to read, or misread, the December message as almost a relegation of the emancipation proclamation to a position of secondary importance.

Was it possible that the effective decree would not be issued at the New Year? There were friends of the edict who doubted it and opponents who wanted to avert it. Lincoln's Illinois adviser, Orville H. Browning, suggested to Judge Thomas of Massachusetts that the judge ought to try at the last minute to reason the President out of his an-

---

nounced policy. ". . . I said to Judge Thomas [wrote Browning] that I thought he ought to go to the President and have a full, frank conversation with him in regard to the threatened proclamation of emancipation—that . . . it was fraught with evil, and evil only and would do much injury; and that . . . he might possibly induce him to withhold, or at least to modify it . . . . He informed me . . . that he had taken my advice, and had the talk [with Lincoln] but that it would avail nothing. The President was fatally bent upon his course, saying that if he should refuse to issue his proclamation there would be a rebellion in the north . . . . There is no hope. The proclamation will come . . . ." [2]

Misgivings of a different sort troubled those who differed with Browning and his doubting Thomas. A supporter of emancipation wrote to Sumner: "We feel no reliance that he [Lincoln] will [carry out the proclamation in full] while we see him guided by the baleful councils of Seward & the Border State men." [3] To J. M. Forbes the prospect seemed dubious. "The first of January is near at hand," he wrote, "and we see no signs of any measures for carrying into effect the Proclamation . . . . Before next April we ought to have 100,000 blacks under arms, ... Everything ought to be prepared on the 1st of January to *begin the war* in earnest." [4] To Sumner such doubts seemed unfounded. "The President is occupied on the Proclamation," he wrote on Christmas Day 1862. "He will stand firm. He said to me that it was hard to drive him from a position which he had once taken." [5] Soon afterward he wrote: "The President says he would not stop the Proclamation if he could, and he could not if he would. . . . Hallelujah!" [6]

With a lawyer-like "Whereas" and a resounding "Now, therefore,' the proclamation came on January 1. By virtue of military power in time of actual armed rebellion, so the document read,

> . . . I, Abraham Lincoln . . . do, . . . in accordance with my pur-
> pose . . publicly proclaimed for . . . 100 days . . . , order and des-
> ignate as . . . in rebellion, . . . the following . . . . [The designation

---

[2] Browning, *Diary*, I, 606–607 (Dec. 31, 1862).

[3] G. F. Williams to Charles Sumner, Boston, Dec. 19, 1862, Sumner MSS.

[4] J. M. Forbes to Sumner, Boston, Dec. 18, 1862, *ibid.*

[5] Sumner to George Livermore, Washington, Dec. 25, 1862, *Proceedings*, Mass. Hist. Soc., XLIV, 596.

[6] Same to same, Washington, Dec. 28, 1862, *ibid.*

here given omitted the state of Tennessee altogether and made important territorial exceptions as to Virginia and Louisiana; otherwise it comprised the commonwealths of the Confederate States of America.]

And . . . I do order and declare that all persons held as slaves within said . . . States [etc.] . . . are, and henceforward shall be, free; and that the Executive Government . . . will recognize and maintain the freedom of said persons.

And I hereby enjoin upon the people so declared . . . free to abstain from all violence, unless in necessary self-defense; and I recommend . . . that . . . they labor faithfully for reasonable wages.

And I . . . declare . . . that such persons . . . will be received into the armed service of the United States . . . .

And upon this act, sincerely believed to be an act of justice, warranted by the Constitution upon military necessity, I invoke the considerate judgment of mankind and the gracious favor of Almighty God.

Rarely has a President signed so famous a document as this, but in the execution of the deed there was no fanfare. In disregard of the President's right hand the customary New Year's reception had been held, on which occasion, as often, the White House was open to any and all. Not till after three hours of wearisome handshaking did Lincoln sign the proclamation. According to Sumner the President "found that his hand trembled so that he held the pen with difficulty." [7]

It was at almost the last minute that the final touches had been placed on the document. On December 31, 1862, the proclamation had been discussed in special Cabinet meeting. There had been a few suggestions of emendations—e. g., Seward's suggestion that freedmen be enjoined, not merely appealed to, to avoid tumult.[8] The "felicitous closing sentence" [9] with its invocation of Divine favor, was the product of Chase's prompting and Lincoln's revision. To Chase's words "an act of justice, warranted by the constitution," Lincoln significantly added "upon military necessity." [10] It was Sumner's recollection,

---

[7] Charles Sumner to George Livermore, Senate Chamber, Jan. 9, 1863, *Proceedings*, Mass. Hist. Soc., XLIV, 597. For information on the pen itself, claimed by the Massachusetts Historical Society through the Livermore family, see *ibid.*, XLIV, 595–604. A conflicting claim as to the pen appeared in the catalogue of the Kolb Collection (auctioned by W. D. Morley of Philadelphia), item 204, where it is stated that the pen had been given by Sumner to James Wormley, colored, owner of the Wormley Hotel in Washington.

[8] Welles, *Diary*, I, 210.   [9] *Ibid.*

[10] For Chase's letter to the President, December 31, 1862, giving lengthy suggestions for revision of the final proclamation and enclosing a full draft as Chase would have worded it, see Warden, *Chase*, 513–515.

however, that the first suggestion for this passage had come from himself.[11]

Men of the time were not without a sense of the historic importance of the document. The learned George Livermore of Cambridge, Massachusetts, in whose essay on slavery [12] Lincoln had shown an interest,[13] had arranged that Sumner should procure a gold pen for the signing at Livermore's expense; the pen was then to become Livermore's valued treasure.[14]

VI

Repercussions from the proclamation were as complex as were social and political groups within and without the lines. The edict was jubilantly hailed; it was roundly cursed; it was exaggerated and twisted as to meaning both by supporters and opponents. "God bless President Lincoln. He may yet be the Moses to deliver the oppressed," [1] was the typical comment of Northern abolitionists. "All . . . trials . . . are swallowed up in the great deep joy of this emancipation." [2] By its dating on January 1, the edict captured the note of New Year bells ringing in an era of freedom.[3] "The . . . proclamation," wrote a Massachusetts Coolidge, "touches the key note of public expectation, and is universally acceptable to the people. For the good sense of the people . . . teaches them that this war cannot, & *ought not* to end until Slavery . . . is removed." [4] "President Lincoln has . . . hurled against rebellion the bolt which he has so long held suspended," declared Lincoln's home paper, the *Illinois State Journal,* which added: ". . . those who refuse to support the Government . . . are traitors and should be so treated . . . ." [5] Theodore Til-

[11] "The last sentence was actually framed by Chase, although I believe that I first suggested it both to him and to the President." Sumner to Livermore, Jan. 9, 1863, *Proceedings,* Mass. Hist. Soc., XLIV, 597.

[12] George Livermore, "An Historical Research Respecting the Opinions of the Founders . . . on Negroes as Slaves, as Citizens, and as Soldiers," read before the Massachusetts Historical Society, August 14, 1862. *Proceedings,* 1862–1863, 86–248.

[13] Livermore to Sumner, Dec. 29, 1862, Sumner MSS.

[14] *Ibid.*

[1] Joseph Emery to S. P. Chase, Cincinnati, O., Sept. 29, 1862, Chase MSS., Lib. of Cong.

[2] Rev. Charles E. Hodges to W. L. Garrison, Jan. 2, 1863, MS., Boston Pub. Lib.

[3] In the diary of John Wingate Thornton the first entry for 1863 reads: "The new year gloriously ushered in by Prest. Lincoln's proclamation of freedom" (Jan. 6, 1863). MS., Boston Athenaeum.

[4] B. Coolidge to Charles Sumner, Lawrence, Mass., Sumner MSS., vol. 57 (misdated).

[5] *Illinois State Journal* (weekly ed.), Oct. 1, 1862, p. 2, c. 4.

ton of the New York *Independent,* ardent abolitionist and reformer, avowed himself to be "in a bewilderment of joy"; the spirit of the edict he said, "is . . . so racing up and down and through my blood that I am half crazy with enthusiasm"; a friend, he said, had been down on his knees in prayer and praise.[6]

Where antislavery enthusiasm was joined, as it often was, with unstudied *naïveté,* the tendency to burst into emotional ecstasy took a tone of exaggerated burbling that may be illustrated by the following example: "*The Proclamation,* too! Isn't it glorious? . . . *Now* I am impatient to see our idolized *Fremont* . . . , Carrying that glorious Proclamation in his hand—bring Liberty . . . to thousands of oppressed ones." [7] To the Cincinnati *Gazette* it seemed that the proclamation would be received in the loyal states with a "perfect furor of acclamation," restoring old friends and uniting the "main portion" of the people.[8] From Concord, Massachusetts, E. R. Hoar congratulated Sumner, finding the military aspects of the measure even more important than the philanthropic, and concluding: "How this can do us any thing but good I cannot see." [9] Another of Sumner's friends was "overjoyed" that the President had created a "land of freedom" as he reflected that this "glorious result" was a compensation for all that had been suffered.[10]

Just after the proclamation was issued the President was serenaded; then the crowd rushed to Chase's residence, called loudly for the Secretary, and greeted him with resounding cheers as he appeared on the balcony. Referring amid cries of approval to the "great act of the President," Chase ventured the assertion that it was the "dawn of a new era." [11] Bostonians attended a carefully planned public assemblage to listen to stately and spirited oratory. The big meeting was held at noon on October 6, 1862, at Faneuil Hall. City and ward committees perfected the arrangements; Boston's best was represented in numerous vice-presidents and secretaries for the occasion; as for the speaker, he was none other than Charles Sumner, then seeking reëlection for

---

6 Theodore Tilton to W. L. Garrison, Sept. 24, 1862, Garrison MSS.

7 Lillie T. Atkinson to Anna E. Dickinson, Jan. 4, 1863, Anna E. Dickinson MSS.

8 Cincinnati *Daily Gazette,* Sept. 25, 1862, p. 3, c. 3.

9 E. R. Hoar to Sumner, Concord, Dec. 29, 1862, Sumner MSS.

10 T. Gilbert to Sumner, Boston, Sept. 23, 1862, *ibid.*

11 Cincinnati *Daily Gazette,* Sept. 26, 1862, p. 3, c. 4.

a third term in the United States Senate.[12] Waving hats and fluttering handkerchiefs greeted the senator as he stepped upon the platform; the demonstration was said to have been unsurpassed since Webster had been greeted in the same historic hall. The orator began with ancient Athens, took note of the Mohammedans in Africa and Spain, paid vote-getting respects to embattled sons of Erin, and touched every throbbing New England chord as he voiced his impressive support of the policy of the Lincoln administration, for which he claimed sponsorship and credit.[13] In its double character as an electioneering occasion and a ratification of the proclamation, the meeting boosted Sumner while conferring a kind of reflected glory upon the President.

Even among abolitionists, however, enthusiasm for the proclamation was somewhat dampened by doubts and dissatisfaction. Neither Lincoln's preliminary nor his final edict met their wishes. To Oliver Johnson, friend of William Lloyd Garrison, the President's decree was "not all that justice requires, nor all that we would wish." [14] The proclamation, croaked Gurowski, was issued "without a fixed, broad, positive plan what to do & at once with the emancipated." [15] Some who accepted the Emancipator's act at even more than face value nevertheless withheld praise from Lincoln himself; among such the tendency was to give "thanks for the Proclamation of Emancipation coming from a reluctant govt. trembling beneath the retributions of justice." [16] Wendell Phillips, out for blood and bursting with horrendous rhetoric as he denounced "bedeviled Southerners," thought it "childish" for the President "to hide himself in the White House and launch a proclamation at us on a first of January." As shipways are oiled before a vessel is launched, he would have preferred to see preparations made "for the reception of three million bondmen into the civil state." [17] Admitting that the proclamation was "a great step onward," Lydia Maria Child wrote that it excited "no glow of enthusi-

---

12 Sumner was renominated for the Senate by the Republican state convention of Massachusetts on September 10, 1862, and overwhelmingly reëlected by the legislature on January 15, 1863. Public discussion of the emancipation was intimately associated with his campaign for this post. Sumner, *Works*, VII, 240, 245.

13 For the ratification meeting and the Sumner speech see *ibid.*, VII, 194–236.

14 Oliver Johnson to Garrison, Sept. 25, 1862, Garrison MSS.

15 Gurowski to John A. Andrew, Washington, Oct. 27, 1862, Andrew MSS.

16 Mary Grew to W. L. Garrison, Philadelphia, Oct. 2, 1862, Garrison MSS.

17 Phillips, *Speeches, Lectures, and Letters*, 547.

asm"; she could not "get rid of misgivings" as to what might occur before the edict went "into effect." [18] Despite his above-noted exuberance, Tilton had to take a fling at the defects of the proclamation, with "its . . . imperfect statesmanship, . . . its . . . delay of . . . operation, . . . [and] its rheumatic and stiff-jointed English." [19]

Though a number of antislavery reformers took credit for the edict, and though the fame of Garrison was advanced by its issuance, there was a tendency to award the palm to Chase, as when a New York lawyer noted that the government was on his (Chase's) "platform" and that the President had "adopted" the secretary's views.[20] By his own statement, Chase preferred a more vigorous act, but, said he: "As the President did not concur . . . , I was willing, and indeed very glad, to accept the Proclamation as the next best mode of dealing with the subject." [21] Associating a prolongation of the war with the freeing of the slaves, Chase saw in all this the judgment of Providence upon the North "for having so long shared the guilt of slavery." [22] In Garrison's mixed feelings on the proclamation one can see both the joy and the dissatisfaction of abolitionist reformers. In a letter to his daughter about the time he received the news, Garrison wrote: "The President's Proclamation is certainly matter for great rejoicing, as far as it goes . . . , but it leaves slavery, as a system . . . , still to exist in all the so-called loyal Slave States . . . . What . . . is still needed, is a proclamation distinctly announcing the total abolition of slavery." [23] After the final proclamation the Boston agitator wrote with his old bitterness toward the Lincoln government: "The policy of the Administration is singularly paradoxical and self-defeating. Think of . . . Fremont, Butler, Sigel and Phelps laid upon the shelf, to propitiate the 'copperhead' element . . . !" Reflecting upon the weakness of abolitionism, Garrison could only lament: "How vulgar and brutal, and yet how fearfully prevalent, is . . . colorphobia at the North." [24]

[18] Lydia Maria Child to Sumner, Wayland, Mass., Oct. 3, 1862, Sumner MSS.
[19] Theodore Tilton to W. L. Garrison, Sept. 24, 1862, Garrison MSS.
[20] John Livingston to S. P. Chase, New York, Oct. 1, 1862, Chase MSS., Lib. of Cong.
[21] Chase to N. B. Buford, Oct. 11, 1862 (copy), Chase MSS., Hist. Soc. of Pa.
[22] S. P. Chase to Elihu Burritt, Oct. 6, 1862 (copy), ibid.
[23] W. L. Garrison to Fanny Garrison, Boston, Sept. 25, 1862, Garrison MSS.
[24] Garrison to "Dear Friend May" (probably Samuel J. May), Boston, April 6, 1863, ibid.

VII

Lincoln was never in fact hostile, as were the Jacobins, to the Southern people; yet the Richmond *Whig* treated his measure of emancipation as "a dash of the pen to destroy four thousand millions of our property." [1] In this stinging comment one finds the epitome of Southern interpretation. The Richmond *Examiner* stigmatized the act as the "most startling political crime . . . in American history." [2] Referring to the savagery and "darkest excesses" of the Negro in the Nat Turner insurrection (which, as the paper omitted to state, was altogether exceptional for the United States), the Richmond *Enquirer* asserted: "This is the sort of work Lincoln desires to see." [3] To the embittered E. A. Pollard the proclamation seemed "the permanent triumph of fanaticism under a false pretense." [4] To President Jefferson Davis it offered "but one of three . . . consequences—the extermination of the slaves, the exile of the whole white population from the Confederacy, or absolute and total separation of these States from the United States." [5] The bogey of slave insurrection, which had intense emotional value, was the chief motif of Southern criticism, but the economic factor was not neglected, as when a Louisianian, urging that agriculture could not exist without slaves, lamented that the proclamation would effect "the ruin of the State." [6]

With almost equal vehemence the proclamation was denounced at the North, both by Lincoln's opponents and by some of his more moderate friends. The subject was entangled with the heated campaign for the state and congressional elections of 1862, as in New York where General James S. Wadsworth, Republican candidate for governor, stood firmly for the President's policy, while Wadsworth's opponents, supporting Seymour, denounced emancipation

---

[1] Richmond *Whig*, Oct. 1, 1862, quoted in Moore, *Rebellion Record* (Diary), V, 89. The reference to "four thousand millions" (of dollars) was an exaggeration. (The readiness of Lincoln to give compensation for emancipated slaves in the South is well known.)

[2] Jan. 7, 1863, *ibid.* (Diary), VI, 32.

[3] Richmond *Enquirer*, Oct. 1, 1862, quoted in Cincinnati *Daily Gazette*, Oct. 8, 1862, p. 1, c. 4.

[4] E. A. Pollard, *The Lost Cause*, 360.

[5] Message of President Davis, Jan. 12, 1863, *Journal*, Confederate Congress (Jan. 14), III, 14.

[6] Letter from unnamed correspondent to Lincoln, New Orleans, Sept. 29, 1863, MS., N. Y. Hist. Soc.

as the butchery of women and children.[7] The September edict, it must be remembered, had synchronized with another presidential proclamation suspending the habeas corpus privilege and legitimizing arbitrary arrests; often the two executive acts were linked in the same denunciation. The case of Browning, whose wish to avert the edict has been noted, serves as an illustration of misgivings among Northern conservatives. To Browning it seemed that the "useless and . . . mischievous" proclamations served only "to unite and exasperate . . . the South, and divide and distract us in the North." [8] Thomas Ewing thought these proclamations "had ruined the Republican party in Ohio," [9] while another doubter feared that in his brief service as pilot Lincoln might "drive the ship of state on the shoals of *proclamations,* or the snags of *'Habeas Corpus.'* " [10] Senator W. P. Fessenden of Maine expressed surprise that the proclamation was ever issued. It was, he thought, "very unfortunately worded, and was, at best, but *brutem* [sic] *fulmen.*" [11]

Northern criticism of Lincoln's decree appeared in the vigorous pamphlet literature of the day. In a brochure that appeared in New York in 1863 it was asserted that "freed negroes of the North were a standing monument to the folly of Abolitionism," and that the "idea of working for pay never entered in black nature." After exhibiting deplorable conditions resulting from emancipation in the West Indies, the author concluded: "Practically the link is broken—the blacks are pushed off the plank, and we of the North, who are not in office [a fling at the Lincoln government], are rolling in the dirt." [12]

---

[7] Pearson, *Wadsworth,* 156.   [8] Browning, *Diary,* I, 609 (Jan. 2, 1863).

[9] *Ibid.,* I, 592 (Dec. 5, 1862).

[10] Hugh Campbell to Joseph Holt, St. Louis, Nov. 15, 1862. In an earlier letter (Sept. 26, 1862) Mr. Campbell, a merchant at St. Louis of Irish birth and Southern connections, had written to Holt: "Stop him! Hold him!—is all I can say by way of advice to you, as the friend of the President. Beg him to write no more letters to newspapers, and never to publish a proclamation. . . . His proclamations have paralized [sic] our armies . . . . We must retrocede—but let us do so . . . with dignity." On July 24, 1862 Campbell had written to Holt: "The *rump* Congress has ruined the country. The President has yielded to . . . the most destructive party [the radical Republicans] that the country has ever known, and we now find ourselves fighting for emancipation & confiscation." Holt MSS.

[11] Browning, *Diary,* I, 587–588 (Nov. 28, 1862).

[12] *Emancipation and Its Results,* Papers from the Society for the Diffusion of Political Knowledge, No. 6, (N.Y., 1863), 5, 15, 30. The president of this society was S. F. B. Morse; the copy used by the author bears the inscription of a gentleman (Shepard Devereux Gilbert) who lived in Beaufort District, S. C. Here was a bit of Northern propaganda which found an appreciative reception in the South.

In Kentucky there was excitement, dissatisfaction among army men, demand for a change of dynasty, conservative wrath, and genuine alarm as to Lincoln's course even among his friends. One of these friends, the clear-headed George D. Prentice who had predicted in his Louisville *Journal* that sectional war would spell the doom of slavery, and who had sought to dissuade the South from what he deemed the madness of secession, still considered slavery doomed, but preferred that it be destroyed "by the . . . inevitable operations of the war [rather] than by emancipation proclamations and Congressional legislation." [13] Another patriotic Kentuckian wrote: "There are vast numbers . . . who feel that there are two wars against the integrity of the Government, one by Secessionism and the other by Abolitionism." He thought abolitionism had to be prostrated; that done, the rebellion might be settled. [14] When it was suggested that Emerson Etheridge, Tennessee Unionist, be named for a Federal judgeship, he declared he could not accept it, for, said he, ". . . since his Proclamation of the 22d of Sept. last, and his treachery to the Union men of the South, any Southern man would be disgraced to accept any appointment under the President unless in . . . military service . . . ." He added that on the restoration of peace he wished to live in Tennessee, which he "could not do wearing his [Lincoln's] official livery." [15]

From an unexpected quarter came vigorous opposition in the outspoken criticism of Benjamin R. Curtis of Massachusetts, former member of the Supreme Court of the United States. Curtis's public and forensic utterances had not justified the antislavery approval that had greeted his famous dissenting opinion in the Dred Scott case. [16] In a pamphlet whose effect was regretted by friends of the proclamation, [17] Curtis argued against "subserviency to a man." Deploring

---

[13] George D. Prentice to John Hancock, Louisville, Ky., Feb. 25, 1864, MS., Ill. State Hist. Lib.

[14] Charles G. Wintersmith to Horatio Seymour, Elizabethtown, Ky., Feb. 23, 1863, *ibid.*

[15] Emerson Etheridge to R. W. Thompson, Washington, D.C., Mar. 23, 1863, MS., Lincoln National Life Foundation, Ft. Wayne, Ind.

[16] For Curtis's attitude, which by no means presented a clear-cut antislavery record, see F. H. Hodder, in *Miss. Vall. Hist. Rev.*, XVI, 3–22 (June, 1929).

[17] Having written a pamphlet in Lincoln's defense, G. P. Lowrey, a New York lawyer, wrote to S. P. Chase (December 1, 1862): "I wished . . . to undo . . . the bad effect of Judge Curtis' pamphlet on the popular mind, ..." Chase MSS., Lib. of Cong.

that "every citizen" was placed "under the direct military command and control of the President" (here he referred to arbitrary arrests), he assailed the proclamation of emancipation as a misuse of executive power.[18] Such a denunciation by Curtis, with its impressiveness of legal phrasing, leads one to wonder what would have been his role had he remained a member of the United States Supreme Court in a day when the very legality of the President's wartime acts was tested by that Court and approved (in the *Prize Cases*) [19] by a five-to-four decision. Every statement such as that of Curtis came as an increment to the vast body of less dignified opposition typified by Bennett's mordant *Herald,* to whose editorial mind the January proclamation, besides being "practically a dead letter," was "unwise and ill-timed, impracticable, and outside of the constitution." [20]

VIII

Reception of the proclamation in England varied according to economic or social patterns. Sophisticated and aristocratic elements were unfavorable and sarcastic, while popular mass meetings were jubilantly enthusiastic, being usually linked with demonstrations for workingmen's rights and with liberal agitation at home. To Earl Russell the edict appeared to be "of a very strange nature," for, said he: "It professes to emancipate all slaves in places where the United States' authorities cannot . . . now make emancipation a reality, but . . . not . . . where . . . emancipation, if decreed, might have been carried into effect." Pointing out that "friends of abolition" expected "total and impartial freedom for the slave," Russell stated that the proclamation made slavery "at once legal and illegal," and that it lacked altogether any "declaration of a principle adverse to

---

[18] Benjamin R. Curtis, *Executive Power* (29 pp., Boston, 1862).

[19] When the President's proclamation of a blockade at the beginning of the conflict (in the absence of a congressional declaration of war) was challenged in the *Prize Cases,* decided in 1863 (67 U. S. 635), the majority of the Court (five members) decided in favor of the legality of Lincoln's acts, but four, including the Chief Justice, dissented. Of those who sustained the President, three (Swayne, Miller, and Davis) were Lincoln's appointees, while another of the five (Wayne of Georgia) came from the deep South. Had Wayne decided differently, as he might well have been expected to do, this vitally important case would have gone against the President. In such a close situation the presence of Curtis on the Court might have made a great difference. Randall, *Constitutional Problems Under Lincoln,* 51–59.

[20] New York *Herald,* Jan. 3, 1863 (editorial), p. 4, cc. 2–3.

slavery." [1] In a memorandum intended for his cabinet Russell wrote: "There is surely a total want of consistency in this measure [the proclamation of September 22]. . . . If it were a measure of Emancipation it should be extended to all the States of the Union . . . ." He added: ". . . emancipation . . . is not granted to the claims of humanity but inflicted as a punishment . . . . Mr. Lincoln openly professed his indifference as to the . . . fate of the four millions of blacks who inhabit the Republic. He declared that if their freedom would help to restore the Union, he was willing they should be free; if their continued slavery would tend to that end he was willing they should remain slaves." [2]

In a "leader" the *Times* of London referred to the preliminary proclamation as the President's "last card," adding that if anything could induce the South to continue the war to the "last extremity," it was this decree. While not pretending to attack slavery, declared the *Times,* the decree launched the threat of servile insurrection as a means of war against certain states.[3] The "harmlessness of the proclamation," said the pro-Confederate Manchester *Guardian,* did "not excuse its utter want of principle." [4] Agreeing as to the ineffectiveness of Lincoln's act, Francis W. Newman wrote from London in 1864: ". . . what is one to make of his [Lincoln's] . . . speeches, & his . . . shilly shallying about slave property, . . . ?" [5]

These complaints were overwhelmingly offset, at least as to numbers, by spontaneous demonstrations in a series of remarkable meetings in British cities at the turn of the year, 1862–63. Held at York, Bolton, Halifax, Sheffield, Birmingham, Leicester, Preston, Coventry, Manchester, and at the Great Exeter Hall in London, these meetings issued declarations which, for Englishmen, had both international and domestic significance. In the National Archives at Washington one finds the original "Address of the Inhabitants of Birmingham to

---

[1] Earl Russell to Lord Lyons, Jan. 17, 1863, *Annual Cyclopaedia,* 1863, 834.

[2] "Original draft of Memorandum respecting interposition in American contest," Oct. 13, 1862. (Such "interposition," of course, did not materialize.) The above quotations were taken by the author from the memorandum, which was confidentially circulated in the British Cabinet. For brief references to the document, see E. D. Adams, *Great Britain and the American Civil War,* II, 49, 101–102; Spencer Walpole, *Life of Lord John Russell,* II, 351.

[3] *The Times,* Oct. 6, 1862, p. 6, cc. 2–3; Oct. 7, 1862, p. 8, cc. 2–4.

[4] Manchester *Guardian,* Oct. 7, 1862.

[5] Francis W. Newman to Epes Sargent, London, Sept. 10, 1864, MS., Boston Pub. Lib.

His Excellency Abraham Lincoln, President of the United States of America." This gigantic document is an unbroken scroll, an amazingly long roll of paper carrying at least ten thousand signatures, headed by that of Charles Sturge, Mayor, and including such names as Burgoyne, Wallington, Pownall, Wilkes, Butler, Heseldine, Lambert, Morgan, Cadwalader, Smallwood, Derrington, Bowden, Bates, Royston, Pollock, Heath, Harris, Thompson, and Partridge. These Birmingham friends conveyed to Lincoln their "deep and heartfelt sympathy" and assured him of the "good wishes of all Men who love liberty." [6]

Home of the "Manchester school" and seat of economic liberalism associated with Cobden and Bright, the city of Manchester was a center for agitation in favor of labor rights as well as for free trade and other reforms; as such it was the target of Tory scorn.[7] This must be borne in mind in reading of the notable meeting at the Free Trade Hall in Manchester on the night of December 31, 1862. Called by a committee of laborers to enable the working classes to express their sympathy with the United States and their endorsement of the President's emancipation proclamation, the meeting opened about seven o'clock and lasted till nearly eleven. The mayor presided, John Stuart Mill sent a letter, speeches in the liberal tone were delivered, and a glowing "Address to President Lincoln by the Citizens of Manchester, England" was issued. Honoring the President for his acts for human liberation, and striking the chord of common "blood and language," the citizens ventured to "implore" the President "not to faint" in his "providential mission," and hailed the "mighty task" of reorganizing "the industry not only of four millions of the colored race, but of five millions of whites." [8]

In reply Lincoln sent his famous letter *To the Working-Men of Manchester*. Referring to the "integrity of the . . . Republic" as

---

[6] MS., Dep. of State, Nat. Archives.

[7] The opponents of the Cobden and Bright school, wrote Henry W. Lord, United States consul at Manchester, "under the leadership of the *Times* now point with derision to . . . 'a nation in the pangs of dissolution, from the . . . very agencies sought to be introduced into England.'" Lord to Seward, Manchester, Aug. 20, 1862, MSS., Dept. of State (Consular Letters, Manchester, vol. 1), Nat. Archives.

[8] The text of the address is given in Moore, *Rebellion Record* (Docs.), VI, 344–345. Meetings in Manchester and elsewhere are described as "assemblies of the largest dimensions" evincing "absolute unanimity and enthusiasm" in the *Morning Star*, London, Jan. 2, 1863. The author has consulted numerous documents on the subject among the MSS. of the U. S. Department of State in the National Archives (Consular Letters, Manchester, vol. 1; Diplomatic Despatches, Britain, vol. 81).

the "key" to all his measures, the President pointed out that he could not always "enlarge or restrict the scope of moral results" a1 'sing from public policies. Though he considered that the duty of "self-preservation" rested solely with the American people, he warmly welcomed foreign favor, and found it pleasant to acknowledge the demonstration at Manchester of a desire "that a spirit of amity and peace toward this country may prevail in the councils of your Queen, . . . respected and esteemed . . . by the kindred nation . . . on this side of the Atlantic." He continued:

> I . . . deeply deplore the sufferings which the working-men at Manchester, and in all Europe, are called to endure in this crisis. It has been . . . represented that the attempt to overthrow this government, . . . built upon . . . human rights, and to substitute . . . one which should rest . . . on . . . human slavery, was likely to obtain the favor of Europe. Through the action of our disloyal citizens, the working-men of Europe have been subjected to severe trials, for the purpose of forcing their sanction to that attempt. Under the circumstances, I cannot but regard your decisive utterances . . . as an instance of sublime Christian heroism . . . not . . . surpassed . . . in any country. . . . I do not doubt that . . . [these] sentiments . . . will be sustained by your great nation; and . . . I have no hesitation in assuring you they will excite . . . reciprocal feelings of friendship among the American people. I hail this interchange . . . as an augury that . . . the peace and friendship which now exist between the two nations will be, as it shall be my desire to make them, perpetual.[9]

In a similar though briefer address to the working-men of London (February 2, 1863) Lincoln gave eloquent thanks for their "exalted and humane sentiments," which he interpreted as manifestations in support of "free institutions throughout the world." He asked them to accept his best wishes for their individual welfare, "and for the welfare and happiness of the whole British people." [10]

British popular demonstrations and the President's graceful response constituted a pleasing chapter in Anglo-American relations. Charles Francis Adams wrote of "signs of extensive reaction in the popular feeling toward the United States" as shown in many meetings and addresses to the President.[11] "The President's proclamation," thought Adams, "has had a great effect here, if not in America. It has

---

9 *Works*, VIII, 194–197 (Jan. 19, 1863).

10 *Ibid.*, VIII, 211–212.

11 C. F. Adams to Edward Everett, London, Jan. 23, 1863, Everett MSS.

rallied all the sympathies of the working classes, and has produced meetings the like of which, I am told, have not been seen since the days of reform and the corn laws." [12] Nor was reaction less favorable on the continent of Europe. It was reported that France was "unanimously for emancipation," [13] while in Spain the "entire press, the Clerical and reactionary not excluded, was loudly in our favor." [14] In general the foreign outlook was so influenced by emancipation as to be deeply disappointing to the architects of Confederate international policy. Judah Benjamin was soon to concede that spades were trumps. [15]

---

[12] Adams to Everett, London, Feb. 27, 1863, *ibid.* "The . . . proclamation has had a remarkable effect here. It has consolidated the popular sentiment friendly to us, which had before lain dormant, whilst it has equally developed the alienation of the higher classes. The meeting at Exeter Hall [London] was a phenomenon which surprised even those who understood it." Adams to Everett, London, Feb. 13, 1863, *ibid.* Such crowds had sought entrance at the Exeter Hall meeting (January 29) that a second and third meeting were held to accommodate the overflow.

[13] John Bigelow to Seward, Oct. 10, 1862, Bancroft, *Seward,* II, 340.

[14] Gustave Koerner to I. Baker, Belleville, Ill., Feb. 5, 1868, MS., Ill. State Hist. Lib. Koerner was United States minister to Spain, 1862–1865.

[15] Owsley, *King Cotton Diplomacy,* 552.

CHAPTER XXIII

A LIMPING FREEDOM

NOT only was Lincoln's emancipation of limited scope; where applied, it was beset with difficulty and delay. Indeed it was but a limping freedom that was launched by virtue of the war power, to be followed by political disappointment and by that Union military defeat which came after McClellan's removal. To manage the transition from a stabilized order of society into an untried system could never be easy. To attempt it on a colossal scale involving millions of human beings would be a major problem at its best, but the attempt was made at its worst, for the new regime was proclaimed during war, was imposed by military force, and was promoted in the absence of that governmental and civilian planning which such an ambitious social, economic, and agricultural program rightly demanded. In its initial stages the new dispensation was haphazard, casual, utopian in some of its aspects, and unable to proceed under its own social and economic power.

As a measure to be some day imposed upon an enemy not yet conquered, the dispensation of freedom lacked immediateness and partook of the nature of a paper pronouncement. In the North many did not favor it, but among those that did, it was greeted with rhetorical burbling; to the lowly blacks in the South it was only in part the theme of kingdom-come shoutings, for even within their bewildered ranks there were deep-seated Southern loyalties, as there were prejudices against Yankees. To suppose that the sense of being part of a definite Southern way of life existed only in white skins is to harbor an erroneous assumption. As the act of a far-away government at war with the South, the edict of emancipation was denied that home coöperation and that local support which so extensive and so intimate a program required. In the absence of that voluntary effort which Lincoln desired as he unsuccessfully sought peaceable liberation in the midst of war, there was little reason to hope for everyday friendly assistance and wise guidance being extended to millions of dependents who were soon to realize that erstwhile owners had been protecting guardians as well as taskmasters, and that incoming employers might have as much of an eye to money-getting as to Negro welfare. As a questionable assumption of executive power the proclamation was bound in legal shallows. Launched as a punishment for rebellion, it lacked even that moral denunciation of slavery for which friends of freedom earnestly, though often abstractly, yearned. Programs to deal with hard facts of Southern economy were of less concern to sentimental abolitionists than sonorous pronouncements; the satisfaction of such persons came from reading into the proclamation a moral quality which its hard-headed critics failed to see. Justified by Lincoln as a measure of war, the edict had the disadvantage of close association with the military arm and with that "martial law" by which John Quincy Adams had declared that liberation could some day be imposed.[1] Coming at a stage when the government at Washington was on crutches (in the period of the election of 1862, of Fredericksburg, and of Lincoln's cabinet crisis)[2] it was open to criticism as a kind of last resort. Such were the conditions under which the embattled sections labored in the early phases of Lincoln's regime of emancipation. Before glancing at the realities of that regime, attention must be given to the policy of organizing Negroes for service in the Union army.

I

The question of Negro troops was among the unsought but inevitable problems laid upon Lincoln's doorstep. Just as general recruiting was largely by haphazard popular effort, so the raising of colored soldiers arose spontaneously as a matter of civilian agitation and as a concomitant of emancipation. First results were unpromising, as in the abortive efforts of General David Hunter, whose premature organization of a black regiment (the first South Carolina) in April 1862 proved a bad beginning and an unkindness to ill-treated

---

[1] Randall, *Constitutional Problems Under Lincoln*, 343–347, 374–376. Ex-President Adams argued thus while a member of Congress.

[2] See below, pp. 242–249.

Negroes.[1] Champions of the colored man persisted, however, until they formed under Colonel Thomas Wentworth Higginson the "first slave regiment mustered into the service of the United States during the . . . civil war." [2] Though an invitation to command "a regiment of Kalmuck Tartars" would have been no more unexpected,[3] Higginson trained and led his colored force, whose minor service in an area near Charleston seemed almost a flaunting of Negro fighters in the faces of proud Carolinians. In his vivid account of his experience with these "perpetual children," the colonel emphasized the blackness of his men, with hardly a mulatto among them, their innocence of vandalism, and their fine military qualities.[4] The youthful Robert Gould Shaw, commanding "the first colored regiment of the North to go to the war," [5] lost his life when leading his colored troops as they assaulted Battery Wagner in the harbor of Charleston (July 18, 1863); the artistry of St. Gaudens has given him sculptural immortality on Boston Common. Another commander who ardently favored the recruitment of Negro troops was J. W. Phelps, in command near New Orleans. Out of these efforts there grew a quarrel between Phelps and B. F. Butler, culminating in Phelps's resignation.[6] Following this, Butler himself organized several colored regiments, comparing their complexion to that of "the late Mr. Webster." [7] It was asserted that one of these regiments had been in Confederate service.[8] Some of the advocates of Negro troops proposed Frémont as organizer and chief commander.[9] Urged by an impressive memorial on the subject, Lincoln gave consent, but in a lengthy letter the inactive general

---

[1] "The trouble is in the legacy of . . . distrust bequeathed by the abortive regiment of General Hunter,—into which they [the Negroes] were driven like cattle, kept for several months in camp, and then turned off without a shilling, by order of the War Department." T. W. Higginson, *Army Life in a Black Regiment*, 15. See also Fred A. Shannon, in *Jour. of Negro Hist.*, XI, 563–583 (Oct., 1926).

[2] Higginson, 1.　　　　[3] *Ibid.*, 2.　　　　[4] *Ibid.*, 10, 29, 127–128.

[5] J. F. Rhodes, *Hist. of the United States*, IV, 332.

[6] Nicolay and Hay, *Lincoln*, VI, 447 ff.　　　　[7] *Ibid.*, 450.

[8] "By accepting a regiment which had . . . been in Confederate service, he [Butler] left no room for complaint . . . ." George S. Denison to S. P. Chase, New Orleans, Sep. 9, 1862, Chase MSS., Lib. of Cong. Mentioning that Southern authorities were quietly arming the Negroes, a friend of Chase wrote: "Their plea is, 'Lincoln offers you freedom but with colonization. We will give it you & you stay here.'" B. Rush Plumbley to S. P. Chase, Philadelphia, Pa., Sep. 30, 1862, *ibid.*

[9] "I learned from the President . . . that he was about to offer to the General the command of the Negro Army . . . . I hope Fremont may accept it, and beat all the white troops . . . , and thereby acquire glory." Letter by Thaddeus Stevens, Lancaster, [Pa.], June 9, 1863, Thaddeus Stevens MSS., no. 52749.

dissociated himself from the enterprise.[10]

In the recruitment of these Negro units, which were always commanded by white officers, much of the activity was outside of, or in opposition to, the war department. From the first the strongest impulse for the whole movement had come from Massachusetts, and when Secretary Stanton authorized Governor John A. Andrew to organize volunteer units to include "persons of African descent," the task "cut out for Andrew [was] a piece of work after his own heart." [11] Under Andrew's leadership the work was done by a committee of private citizens headed by the wealthy George L. Stearns, who had done so much to encourage John Brown. Among other distinguished names on the committee were Amos A. Lawrence (prominent capitalist), LeBaron Russell, William I. Bowditch, and John M. Forbes. One of the tasks of the committee was to promote the recruiting of colored men; another was to raise a large sum of money by private subscription to defray recruiting expenses beyond those which could be borne by the government.[12] It was in this manner that the men for Robert Gould Shaw's famous Fifty-Fourth Massachusetts were found. A curious feature of the whole scheme was that Negro recruiting for Massachusetts was conducted mainly in other states, with complications that can readily be imagined.[13] Enough Boston Negroes could be brought together to form a company, and a few more might be found in New Bedford. "Elsewhere in the State the negro population, small and scattering, could not possibly supply eight hundred able-bodied men." [14] On the morning of May 28, 1863, however, these difficulties were forgotten as the colored regiment marched down Beacon Street and paraded on the Common, while public officials including Governor Andrew gave dignity to the grand review.[15]

---

[10] Nicolay and Hay, *Lincoln*, VI, 457–459.

[11] H. G. Pearson, *Life of John A. Andrew*, II, 73.

[12] On this point the author has consulted the papers of Amos Lawrence (vol. 25), MSS., Mass. Hist. Soc. See also Pearson, *Andrew*, II, 81 ff.

[13] Pearson, *Andrew*, II, 82 ff.

[14] Pearson, *Andrew*, II, 81. (The total number of free Negroes of all ages and sexes in Massachusetts was reported as 9602 in 1860.)

[15] Pearson, *Andrew*, II, 88. Andrew complained to Lincoln that a hundred Negroes in Alexandria, Virginia, eager to go to Massachusetts and enlist, were hindered by Stanton's orders, whereupon the President is reported to have ordered: *"Let them go!* A. Lincoln." There seems to have been a prodigious gubernatorial ado over this rather absurd incident. *Ibid.,* II, 93.

II

The use of colored soldiers produced a crop of legal complications.[1] The attorney general of Massachusetts concluded that he could not legally refuse to enroll black men,[2] while the attorney general of the United States declared that native-born colored persons were citizens of the United States despite the contrary dictum of the Supreme Court in the Dred Scott case.[3] Though urged to insert the word "white" in the conscription law of 1863, thereby eliminating colored conscripts, Congress refused to do so,[4] and in the law as passed all able-bodied male citizens were made liable to service.

As to other legal matters, slave-soldiers, with their families, became free as above noted;[5] compensation up to $300 was provided for their owners;[6] persons of color in the District of Columbia were given the same legal standing as whites;[7] colored soldiers, late in the war, were declared entitled to the same uniform, clothing, arms, rations, medical attendance, pay, and emoluments as "other soldiers";[8] where a slave of a loyal master should be drafted (this was long after the emancipation proclamation), the slave becoming free, the hundred-dollar bounty was to be paid to the master.[9]

There were numerous emphatic protests against the raising and employment of Negro soldiers.[10] Governor Andrew of Massachusetts, enthusiast for Negro recruitment, must have been rudely shocked when a friend in the sea island area of South Carolina informed him of army brokers' scandals by which the raising of colored fighters had

---

1 Legal matters concerning the use of Negro troops are treated at length in William Whiting, *War Powers Under the Constitution of the United States* (Boston, 1871), 478–511. Written first as wartime pamphlets, this volume is by the solicitor of the war department.

2 New York *Herald*, Aug. 19, 1862, p. 4, c. 5. On the other hand the circuit court sitting in Montgomery county, Illinois, ruled that Negroes were not citizens; this obscure decision revealed how much anti-Negro law there was in Lincoln's own state in 1862. The court pointed out that Negroes were forbidden to migrate into and settle in the state; they were further denied the right to vote, hold office, do jury service, or testify where whites were parties. *Annual Cyclopaedia*, 1862, 752–753.

3 *Ibid.*, 752. The Cincinnati *Gazette* (Dec. 27, 1862, p. 3, c. 3) deemed this "the ablest, as it is the most important, legal paper drawn up by him since he assumed . . . office."

4 *Annual Cyclopaedia*, 1863, 289.   5 Above, p. 132; *U. S. Stat. at Large*, XII, 599.

6 *Ibid.*, XIII, 11.   7 *Ibid.*, XII, 407.   8 *Ibid.*, XIII, 129.

9 *Ibid.*, XIII, 11 (act of Feb. 24, 1864).

10 For a debate in Congress in which the use of colored troops was severely denounced, see *Annual Cyclopaedia*, 1863, 289.

become a "disgrace to all concerned." The governor was told that the "poor negroes" were "hunted like wild beasts," that very few able ones were found, that there was money in it, and that "outrageous frauds" had been practiced.[11] It was feared that the border would be offended,[12] that a "war of races" would result, and that "white men . . . [would] not rally to . . . the Union if . . . mixed . . . with negro battalions."[13] There was "prejudice in the [Union] army against the military employment of the blacks," and there was trouble in the war department with the result that payment of colored troops was held up.[14] Unwillingness among white officers to recognize colored men as soldiers raised serious questions of army discipline, and it was found advisable to avoid the mixture of the races in a given army unit.[15]

In addition to Northern white prejudice, serious aspects of the question were encountered in the angry resentment of Southerners, the bitter policy of retaliation pursued by the Confederacy, and the embarrassment attendant upon the Northern demand for counter retaliation. Lincoln's answer to that demand was two-fold: he issued on July 30, 1863, a seemingly severe order directing that penalties be inflicted in retaliation for the killing of Union soldiers "in violation of the laws of war"; next April, when precisely this kind of retaliation was demanded of him in a specific instance (the so-called Fort Pillow "massacre"),[16] he gave out a restrained and cautious statement explaining his avoidance of retribution in practice. That retribution, which would have been the execution of captured Confederate sol-

---

[11] Pearson, *Andrew*, II, 144–145; Andrew MSS., vol. 28, no. 70. This was in connection with the recruiting of Negroes in South Carolina, with credit to the quota of Massachusetts. The New York *Semi-Weekly Tribune* (Jan. 1, 1864, p. 1, c. 1), referred to frauds perpetrated by sharpers upon colored men entering the Union army.

[12] For the ferment in Kentucky over the bill to make slaves liable to military service on the same basis as whites, see New York *Times*, Mar. 17, 1864, p. 4, cc. 3–4.

[13] J. S. Gallagher to R. W. Thompson, Washington, D. C., Aug. 4, 1862, MSS., Lincoln National Life Foundation, Ft. Wayne, Ind.

[14] S. P. Chase to Maj. Gen. O. M. Mitchel, Washington, D. C., Oct. 4, 1862 (copy), Chase MSS., Hist. Soc. of Pa.

[15] Boston *Daily Advertiser*, Feb. 25, 1863.

[16] This affair occurred on April 12, 1864, when Confederate soldiers killed hundreds of Negroes in a garrison at Fort Pillow, Tennessee. In accusations that shook the North with indignation an investigating committee charged that about three hundred Negro soldiers were deliberately massacred in cold blood; the Confederate statement was that the men were killed in warfare, not slaughtered after surrender. In spite of strenuous urgings Lincoln saw to it that there was no retaliation by the Union government. Randall, *Civil War and Reconstruction*, 506–507.

diers, was not in fact applied. The key to the July 30 order was Lincoln's reference to "the usages and customs of war, as carried on by civilized powers," and his insistence on the "duty of every government to give protection to its citizens of whatever . . . color . . . , and especially to those . . . organized as soldiers." [17] In his Fort Pillow statement he referred to the fact that the colored soldier, being used, must have protection, but he also made a clear-cut distinction between "stating the principle" and "practically applying it." On the matter of practical application he said: "To take the life of one of their prisoners on the assumption that they murder ours, . . . might be too serious, . . . [too] cruel, a mistake." [18] A study of all the factors in this complicated subject, and not merely the harsher words of the retaliatory order, leads to the conclusion that Lincoln's purpose was not retaliation. On the contrary, his aim was to avert trouble and to restrain enemy action in dealing with a sensitive and vexing problem. In a word he intended to avoid unjustifiable severity on the part of his own government without forgoing protection to Negro soldiers who had been put into uniform by the law of the land.

In keeping with his habit of facing the realities of a subject and viewing all its sides, Lincoln proceeded circumspectly in handling the problem of Negro troops. At the first broaching of his emancipation decree to his Cabinet he had shown himself "unwilling to adopt" a measure for "arming slaves" which Chase "warmly" advocated.[19] Even after Congress had authorized the President to "employ" Negroes for the war purpose,[20] Lincoln "felt constrained to postpone a systematic organization of negro troops for active campaigns." [21] "The President's great difficulty," wrote Sumner, "is as to arming the blacks. He invites them as laborers, but . . . holds back from the last step to which everything . . . tends." [22] Though as a practical issue the movement for raising colored soldiers had gone far by September 1862, having been discussed in the Cabinet, the subject was omitted

[17] *Works*, IX, 48–49.

[18] Address at Sanitary Fair in Baltimore, Apr. 18, 1864, *ibid.*, X, 78–80.

[19] Diary of S. P. Chase (*Annual Report*, Am. Hist. Assoc., 1902, II), 48. Chase reported Lincoln as thinking in July 1862 that using Negroes as soldiers would be "productive of more evil than good" (*ibid.*, 49).

[20] Section 11 of the second confiscation act of July 17, 1862, *U. S. Stat. at Large*, XII, 592.

[21] Nicolay and Hay, *Lincoln*, VI, 441.   [22] Pierce, *Sumner*, IV, 84.

in the emancipation proclamation of September 22. When it was briefly mentioned in the January proclamation, the cautious reference to "forts, positions, stations, and other places" seemed to suggest a limited army use of Negroes. By March 1863, however, the President was speaking emphatically in favor of promoting a Negro military force. Advising Governor Andrew Johnson of Tennessee to raise such a force, he said: "The colored population is the great available and yet unavailed force for restoring the Union." [23] In the summer of 1864 he remarked to Governor Randall of Wisconsin: "Abandon all the posts now garrisoned by black men . . . and we would be compelled to abandon the war in three weeks." [24] Generalizing as to Lincoln's treatment of the whole matter, his secretaries, after noting with favor the tangible results, point out that he would have wrecked his administration if he had rushed to adopt the policy when enthusiasts first urged it, but that by restraint and delay and by playing the card at the opportune moment, he made it both a "military overweight . . . to crush . . . rebellion" and a "lever to effect emancipation." [25]

As the months passed people of the North became accustomed to the concept of Negro troops; in March 1864 a colored regiment was given a genuine ovation in New York City. In the words of the *Times:* "A thousand men, with black skins, and . . . with the uniforms and arms of the United States . . . , marched . . . through the most aristocratic . . . streets, received a grand ovation . . . , and then moved down Broadway to the steamer which bears them to their destination—all amid the . . . cheers, . . . plaudits, . . . waving handkerchiefs, . . . showering bouquets, and other approving manifestations of a hundred thousand of the most loyal of our people." [26] Dark-skinned warriors were used in a number of operations; many gave their lives to the cause; in time even the bitter New York *Herald* reported a "change . . . in . . . opinion" concerning colored fighters. Captured guns, declared the *Herald*, "spoke in eloquent terms of the bravery of the colored troops." [27] Covering only the late phases of the war, a writer in 1865 stated that in "battles be-

---

[23] *Works*, VIII, 233 (Mar. 26, 1863).   [24] *Ibid.*, X, 190 (Aug. [15?], 1864).
[25] Nicolay and Hay, *Lincoln*, VI, 469.
[26] New York *Times*, Mar. 6, 1864, p. 8, c. 1. This was in striking contrast to anti-Negro riots in New York City the previous July.
[27] New York *Herald*, June 27, 1864, p. 1, c. 4.

fore Nashville, the capture of Fort Fisher, the final operations around Richmond, and numerous minor engagements, [colored troops] sustained their previous well-earned reputation for bravery and soldierly qualities." [28] Their numbers were impressive; the war department's postwar summary showed colored troops to the total of 186,000 in Union service.[29]

III

Of the stereotypes concerning Lincoln one of the most unhistorical is the stock picture of the Emancipator sitting in the White House and suddenly striking the shackles from millions of bondmen at a stroke of the presidential pen. The fact is that Lincoln issued his proclamation and nothing happened in the immediate or prompt freeing of slaves by virtue thereof. The September proclamation was only a warning and a prediction, while the January proclamation had the curious feature of making declarations which applied only to areas where Lincoln's arm could not reach. With occupied portions of Louisiana and Virginia, as well as the whole state of Tennessee, excepted, the only regions to which the proclamation extended were those in which the Confederacy was still in control. The measure did not touch slavery in Kentucky, Maryland, Delaware, or Missouri, these being slave states adhering to the Union. Though such a situation was most unlikely, any other slave state could have avoided its emancipatory effect by return to Union allegiance.

Writing six days after the September proclamation, Lincoln confessed that the situation was "not very satisfactory," and that his expectations for the edict were "not as sanguine as . . . those of some friends." [1] What the government was doing, according to Seward, was to emancipate slaves where it could not reach them and to hold them in bondage where it could have set them free.[2] Horace White considered it doubtful whether the edict "freed anybody anywhere." [3]

---

[28] *Annual Cyclopaedia*, 1865, 32.

[29] *Offic. Rec.*, 3 ser., V, 661–662. Many of these were recruited or drafted within the states of the Confederacy—e. g., 17,869 from Mississippi, and 24,052 from Louisiana. Massachusetts was credited with 3,966, of whom probably no more than one fourth came from the state itself.

[1] *Works*, VIII, 49–50 (Sep. 28, 1862).

[2] Donn Piatt, *Memories of the Men Who Saved the Union*, 150.

[3] Horace White, *Life of Lyman Trumbull*, 222.

"The efficacy of the proclamation," declared a contemporary writer, "was probably very imperfectly manifested during 1863. On the one hand, it did not appear to make free any slave by its own operation during the year. . . . On the other hand it tended to awaken . . . sympathy among the slaves for the Union cause, which held out . . . the promise of certain freedom by its success . . . ." [4] "No wonder the Proclamation of January 1st has produced so little effect at the South," wrote William Lloyd Garrison in April 1863.[5] Abolitionist work, thought Garrison, was yet unfinished. "If slavery were really abolished," he declared, "I should care very little about continuance of the Liberator . . . ." [6]

In 1864 an earnest antislavery group headed by Robert Dale Owen, known as the American Freedmen's Inquiry Commission, submitted a voluminous report which treated emancipation as a task unachieved. Created by order of the war department to study methods that might contribute to the protection and improvement of freedmen, the commission doubted whether its object could be accomplished under existing conditions, and raised the question "whether the protecting freedom of these people is reliably founded," and whether it could endure, unless emancipation became "universal throughout the Union." [7] As to the proclamation of 1863, the commissioners declared: "It cannot free a single slave." [8]

Something more was needed than a proclamation; how much more only a detailed study could reveal. Directly after the preliminary edict General O. M. Mitchel wrote of the "mighty work which now lies before us." [9] Men of the time had yet to determine how to make emancipation legally effective, how to integrate Federal liberation with state laws, how to set freedmen to work at wages, how to give them training, education, and perchance some land of their own, how to instruct ignorant thousands as to their new status, how to avoid social disorder, how to mitigate the handicap of unequal opportunity, and how to deal with the problem of civil and political rights for the submerged race. Problems of the freedman had to be solved on the

---

[4] *Annual Cyclopaedia*, 1863, 835.

[5] W. L. Garrison to "Dear Friend May" (probably Samuel J. May), Boston, April 6, 1863, Garrison MSS.

[6] Garrison to Oliver Johnson, Boston, Dec. 14, 1862, *ibid.*

[7] *Offic. Rec.*, 3 ser., IV, 290.   [8] *Ibid.*, 361.

[9] Having been in western service, Gen. O. M. Mitchel was at Hilton Head, S. C. when this letter was written (Sep. 28, 1862), Chase MSS., Lib. of Cong.

basis of hard facts, not of doctrinaire opinions. Among these facts were the ineradicable instinct for racial separateness, the slight desire of Southern Negroes to go North, the vulnerability of the dark race to exploitation, the sterility of paper freedom if unaccompanied by economic security, and the risk that "under the guise of guardianship, slavery, in a modified form, . . . [might] be practically restored." [10]

As the problem presented itself under Lincoln it posed the almost unsolvable puzzle of trying to promote liberation in some states, and those the more Southern, while keeping slavery in others. As to the seceded area, slavery was declared abolished in Alabama and Mississippi, for example, but not in neighboring Tennessee. Even within the Union itself, where the border states differed considerably as to future policy, the institution appeared to have a greater life-expectancy in some states than in others. The proclamation of emancipation did not apply to either Missouri or Kentucky; in Missouri, however, emancipation was well under way as a matter of state polity in 1863, while conservation of slavery was still the persistent purpose in Kentucky. Such a situation offered a chance for gain that was not likely to be overlooked in that profiteering age. Since slavery was to be still active even after the January proclamation, and since the value of slaves in Missouri depended chiefly upon the prospect of selling them in Kentucky at several hundred dollars a head, there existed "a system of kidnapping constantly practiced . . . by slave traders—a kidnapping of both fugitive slaves and . . . emancipated *contrabands*—freed by the Proclamation." It was reported that this occurred "almost daily, & the villains evade[d] punishment by . . . laws which exclude[d] negro evidence & by the sympathisers who . . . [held] offices . . . ." [11]

In the records of the time one finds, even among friends of the proclamation, extensive doubts as to its law-worthiness. "In thinking of the future," wrote George Bancroft, "I feel unwilling to rely on the President's proclamation for the termination of slavery . . . ." [12] When in 1864 Lincoln sought to inaugurate loyal state governments in the South on the basis of individual oath-taking, Secretary Chase suspected that many in Louisiana might take the oath who were not

---

[10] *Offic. Rec.*, 3 ser., IV, 381.

[11] Lucien Eaton to Richard Yates, Oct. 16, 1863, Reavis MSS., Chicago Hist. Soc.

[12] George Bancroft to Gen. Robert C. Schenck, New York, Nov. 18, 1863, Bancroft MSS., Mass. Hist. Soc.

loyal at heart; such persons, he thought, might consider the oath merely conditional—e. g., "binding in case the emancipation clauses of the Proclamation" should not be "annulled by the Supreme Court or modified or abrogated by Congress." [13] There was the possibility that Lincoln's successor might "repudiate, and declare null and void the proclamation . . . emancipating slaves, and all acts and doings under it." [14] A learned legal writer who upheld its validity regarded the proclamation as a "mere command, which . . . could work no change . . . until executed by the hand of war . . . ." [15] Though he considered slavery a "rotten" and disappearing institution, Gideon Welles doubted the "ultimate effect" of the proclamation as to the "exact status of the slaves and the slave-owners"; for solution of the problem he looked to the courts and to legislation by Congress and by the states. He expressed a general questioning in which he did not share as he said: "I do not trouble myself about the Emancipation Proclamation, which disturbs so many." [16]

If there had been no other factor, such questioning would have arisen from many declarations by Lincoln himself as to the limits of emancipatory power on the part of the Federal government. Lincoln was frank in admitting legal doubts concerning the proclamation which he had once compared to "the Pope's bull against the comet." [17] No one saw more clearly the need of a constitutional amendment to clear up the subject. "I think it is valid in law," wrote the President in July 1863, "and will be so held by the courts"; yet in the same letter he voiced a preference for "gradual emancipation" as "better" for both races.[18] Next year, when a petition of youngsters besought him to "free all slave children," he confessed that he had not "the power to grant all they ask[ed]." [19]

The proof of legal effectiveness is in specific cases, but there is a dearth of material as to the application of the emancipation proclamation by legal process in the liberation of particular individuals. As late as July 1863 a Missouri sheriff was "arresting slaves of rebels

13 S. P. Chase to Col. Frank E. Howe, Feb. 20, 1864, Chase MSS., Lib. of Cong.

14 Hiram Ketchum to Horatio Seymour, New York City, Jan. 27, 1863, MS., Ill. State Hist. Lib. (Ketchum advocated such repudiation to the man who in 1868 became the Democratic candidate for President.)

15 J. I. C. Hare, *American Constitutional Law* (1st ed., Boston, 1889), 946.

16 Welles, *Diary*, I, 415, 429–430.   17 *Works*, VIII, 30 (Sep. 13, 1862).

18 *Ibid.*, IX, 52 (July 31, 1863).

19 Letter to Mrs. Horace Mann, April 5, 1864, *ibid.*, X, 68–69.

inside . . . [Union] lines, and returning them in great numbers." [20] Contrarywise, a magistrate at St. Louis, using a trivial case as text for an ambitious decision, passed favorably upon the legality and constitutionality of the emancipation proclamation. One Williams, a Negro convicted of grand larceny in the criminal court of the city, was a slave who had escaped from Arkansas, to which the emancipation proclamation applied. Holding that the proclamation was valid, the judge ruled that the offender was punishable by imprisonment in the penitentiary, this being the penalty for grand larceny committed by a free person, instead of by lashes on the bare back, as in the case of a slave. This obscure decision upholding the constitutional validity of the proclamation became the target of a sarcastic editorial in the New York *World,* in which the "St. Louis functionary" was represented as "conscious that his position was untenable, yet desirous to stand well with the administration at Washington." As a legal basis the judge had cited an inapplicable passage from Vattel, as well as hasty remarks by John Quincy Adams which were in opposition to the official position which Adams had taken when conducting American diplomatic affairs.[21] The unimportance and uniqueness of the case serve only to emphasize the scarcity of contemporary judicial action giving effect to the proclamation.

Imperfections in the self-sufficiency of the proclamation were revealed in suggestions put forth for implementing it. A distinguished New Englander suggested an emancipation bureau.[22] William Whiting, solicitor of the war department, suggested the creation of a separate executive department of emancipation whose head should have a place in the President's Cabinet.[23] Another inventive citizen, noting the vague ideas of the Negroes concerning the boon that had come to them, and wishing to get hold of their minds, proposed some "token" that would make liberation seem real. He suggested a cheap pewter medal bearing the words "Free Negro, January 1, 1863," with

---

[20] *Ibid.,* IX, 40 (July 21, 1863).

[21] New York *World,* Feb. 6, 1863, p. 4, c. 3 (editorial).

[22] In a letter to Secretary Chase (Nov. 19, 1862) S. G. Howe advocated such a bureau because of the need "for the possible political birth of millions on the first January," arguing that it would have "potent moral effect South as well as North." Chase MSS., Lib. of Cong. Howe later became a member, with Robert Dale Owen and J. McKaye, of the organization known as the American Freedmen's Inquiry Commission, forerunner of the Freedmen's Bureau. See above, p. 190.

[23] Whiting, *War Powers Under the Constitution,* 466.

a quotation from Scripture. Such a medal, he thought, ought to be about the size of a quarter dollar, so that it could be concealed if necessary. The words *"omne ignotum pro mirifico"* he considered appropriate; if its owner could not read, so much the better. Every man possessing such a medal would believe himself free by law and would be encouraged to seek practical realization of that freedom. For the difficult and tricky work of distributing such medals, he would employ picked contrabands who knew the by-paths through woods and swamps better than the whites.[24]

There were various proposals that Congress should add its legal sanction to the proclamation. On February 9, 1863, Charles Sumner presented a mammoth petition of a hundred thousand men and women praying that Congress pass "an act emancipating all persons of African descent held to involuntary service or labor in the United States." [25] George Bancroft, who knew history and statecraft, asked: "Could not Congress enact, that henceforward every one born in our common country should be born free?" [26] For putting the proclamation "into more complete and immediate execution" Representative Isaac Arnold of Illinois presented a bill prohibiting the reënslavement of freedmen; [27] in 1864, when the Wade-Davis reconstruction bill was taking shape, Sumner moved an amendment in the Senate providing that the proclamation "is hereby . . . enacted as a statute of the United States," the senator being unwilling that emancipation be "left to float on a presidential proclamation." [28] None of these proposals was enacted. Congress refused to pass the ones mentioned, and when in 1864 it did provide in the Wade-Davis bill for the emancipation of slaves and their posterity in the seceded states, the measure fell before Lincoln's veto.[29]

---

[24] B. C. Tilghman to W. M. Tilghman, Camp near Falmouth, Va., Dec. 27, 1862, Stanton MSS.

[25] The petition, examined by the author, was promoted by the Loyal National Woman's League, Susan B. Anthony, Secretary. Papers of the House of Representatives, 37 Cong. (Misc., Box 6), MSS., Lib. of Cong.

[26] George Bancroft to Gen. Robert C. Schenck, N. Y., Nov. 18, 1863, Bancroft MSS., Mass. Hist. Soc.

[27] *Cong. Globe*, 38 Cong., 1 sess., 20 (Dec. 14, 1863).

[28] Senator Saulsbury of Delaware was quick to use Sumner's suggestion as a confession by Lincoln's friends that his proclamation was without validity. *Ibid.*, 3460. See also Randall, *Constitutional Problems Under Lincoln*, 383.

[29] In explaining this veto, Lincoln stated that he was unprepared "to declare a constitutional competency in Congress to abolish slavery in States," thus denying to Congress a power which he had exercised as President. *Works*, X, 153 (July 8, 1864).

IV

The story of how freedom actually came to Negroes in camp, home, or plantation is one of the imperfectly understood chapters of the Lincoln administration. It is not merely a matter of groups, classes, and categories, of legal declarations and governmental pronouncements. It is a question of dark-skinned human beings in person, millions of them. To tell the story would be to locate these human beings where they were, which was for the most part beyond the reach of the proclamation, to know their feelings, their long-standing loyalties, and their faithful records in servitude. It is a truism that to do this they must be viewed in association with their white folk; on that matter the two facts that stand out most clearly are the dependence of Negroes upon their masters for sustenance and all that goes with everyday living, and their prideful habit of identifying themselves with their white families. It was only in association with a white household that a slave had any social status. Within that pattern of service he had importance; at least he had a place (as a slave, to be sure) in the social order. He had a more secure social status than the free Negro of the South. This is not to argue that slavery was justifiable; it is merely to note the fact that the Southern slave was part of an all-enveloping system of society. He could not suddenly jump out of his skin or transport himself to a new order of existence. This was the more impossible since freedom was proclaimed not by his own protectors and rulers but by an alien and an enemy. To say this is to speak in the Southern sense, but that is precisely the point; one cannot understand the subject at all unless he treats these people in terms of the locale and the regime in which they lived, not in a hypothetical setting imagined by a distant abolitionist.

The first fact to note is the absence of servile insurrections. To stir up such insurrections was no part of Lincoln's purpose; Southern accusations of such a purpose were in the nature of propaganda, though doubtless to a large extent such was the Southern belief. Lincoln was not the man to promote uncivilized methods of warfare. Though in the September proclamation the President predicted, perhaps unfortunately, that the Federal executive would not repress Negroes in efforts "for their actual freedom," he meant no sanction of domestic violence, having in mind rather the fact that if freedom was proclaimed it must, under proper procedures and only so, be substantively recognized. His disapproval of slave insurrections had been expressed in his Cooper Union address of February 1860, where he emphatically disclaimed Republican responsibility for such uprisings.[1] In the January proclamation the matter was left in no doubt; the President enjoined those declared free to abstain from violence and to "labor faithfully for wages."

It is true that Lincoln spoke of "arming the blacks," and approved the raising of Negro troops, which at the South was accounted the equivalent of stirring up insurrection. No soldier, however, is supposed to strike except within the pattern of army command. If it was legitimate to use Negroes as soldiers under army discipline, their service in that capacity was no more inhuman or uncivilized than that of the white men. If one is dealing with the whole wretched subject of war itself, the matter is more than a question of Negro troops; one hardly touches fundamentals when he supposes that whites may go into authorized armies but Negroes may not. As to guerrilla warfare and all those hidden irregular activities that accompanied the war, including much that was criminal, it was the whites that were chiefly at fault.

Colored servants in the South did not feel themselves called upon to rise against their masters; the absence of such uprising is one of the attested facts of the period.[2] The "devotion and faithfulness" of Southern Negroes in war time has been mentioned as "one of the beautiful aspects of slavery." Though slaves, except those deep in the interior, had "every opportunity to desert to the Federals, . . . desertions were infrequent until near the close of the war." "On the whole," writes W. L. Fleming, "the behavior of the slaves during the war . . . was most excellent."[3] Confederate authorities had naturally made use of slaves as "teamsters, cooks, nurses, and . . .

---

[1] *Works*, V, 315 ff. In this passage Lincoln showed how insubstantial was the actual danger of slave insurrection and how unfounded was the "elastic fancy" by which it was imagined that the Republican party was engaged in promoting Negro uprisings.

[2] The famous diarist of the Confederate war department wrote on July 3, 1864: ". . . there has been no instance of an attempt on the part of the slaves to rise in insurrection." J. B. Jones, *A Rebel War Clerk's Diary* (Phila., 1866), II, 244. See also Randall, *Civil War and Reconstruction*, 496.

[3] Walter L. Fleming, *Civil War and Reconstruction in Alabama*, 210, 212.

laborers." [4] Soldiers of the South did not care to dig trenches, cook, or split wood. As body servants of Confederate officers many a Southern slave performed a war service in which he was faithful unto death; in after years those who survived showed a truly Southern pride in recalling their records in "Virginny" or "Ilun 10." [5] If some of the Negroes hailed "Linkum's" freedom as the sound of Gabriel's trumpet or an occasion for a barbecue, others, especially in the deep South, thought of a Yankee as a thing with horns.[6] They were more inclined to save "massa's" property from Yankee plunder than to perpetrate an insurrection for which they lacked both the impulse and the organization. "To the last day of bondage the great majority were true against all temptations. With their white people they wept for the Confederate slain, were sad at defeat, and rejoiced in [Southern] victory." [7]

How did that last day of bondage and first day of freedom come? Not as a rule with fanfare nor with much of drama; certainly not by any universal pattern. Even among Higginson's dark soldiers the celebration of the proclamation was more like a solemn religious service than a dramatic event.[8] In Florida, where raiding for the recruitment of Higginson's and Saxton's men was active, a Federal recruiting agent might offer the first uninviting contact with the new regime. In occupied parts of Louisiana conditions of free labor were first experienced by ex-slaves on "abandoned" plantations administered by Union authorities, not under the emancipation proclamation but under a law of Congress known as the captured and abandoned property act. In displacement of their Southern owners, these estates were operated by "loyal" lessees, put there by the United States treasury department. Negroes in such a situation, unused to conditions of free labor, had little concept of a contract and were likely to suppose that they were under no obligation to remain at one place any longer than they pleased. Hands were easily seduced from one plantation to another by promises of higher wages, which in the existing scarcity of laborers was a serious annoyance; furthermore, they claimed the right to plant cotton or anything else on their respective patches regardless of the overseer's requirements. Unfaith-

---

[4] *Ibid.*, 205.　　　　[5] *Ibid.*, 207.　　　　[6] *Ibid.*, 211.　　　　[7] *Ibid.*, 212.
[8] Higginson, *Army Life in a Black Regiment*, 40–41.

fulness to contract, however, was not alone the fault of laborers; lessees fell down in the matter of rations, clothing, and care of the wives and children of plantation workers. Discontent led to mutiny; military force was in some cases necessary to settle difficulties between emancipated workers and their bosses. Such military intervention might produce an order to the overseer to conform to what the Negroes were used to—i. e., to issue rations to all hands whether working or not —after which the crop would look after itself, for the Negroes would have little incentive to work.[9]

To refugee Negroes who flocked by the thousands to Union camps or joined the Federal line of march, first contacts with freedom came under distressing circumstances. Forsaking tradition, "garbed in rags," bleeding, urged by terror or "blind hope," "often nearly naked," they stumbled forward in a planless exodus, with "no Moses to lead it." [10] Such, at least, is the description of Chaplain (and Brigadier General) John Eaton, who under Grant assumed the difficult initial work of dealing with "these hordes" by forming Negro camps, caring for the sick, and striving amid tragedy and travail to bring order, systematic labor, and relief to masses of helpless blacks. Union commanders in general had this problem thrust upon them; the usual policy was to urge the colored people to stay "where they were," as Sherman said, "not to load us down with useless mouths, which would eat up the food needed for our fighting-men." [11] In Virginia and North Carolina B. F. Butler organized an elaborate system of Negro rehabilitation as a phase of army control. Perhaps the best known episode of this sort is that of General Rufus Saxton, Higginson's chief, who, with headquarters at Beaufort, South Carolina, promoted the tasks of organizing colored soldiers and giving relief to thousands of refugees, setting up courts, superintending property interests, initiating agricultural efforts, directing labor contract systems, protecting his wards from fraud, and seeking to develop in

---

[9] Records of these transactions are among the papers of the treasury department, being for many years in charge of the "miscellaneous division," but now in the National Archives. They consist of plantation lists, accounts of inspection, treasury agents' reports, inventories of estates, records of the "plantation bureau" at New Orleans, et cetera. A doctoral dissertation (in manuscript) by the author, "The Confiscation of Property during the Civil War" (Univ. of Chicago, 1911), and an article based thereon (*Am. Hist. Rev.* XIX, 65–79) have been drawn upon for the above account.

[10] John Eaton, *Grant, Lincoln and the Freedmen*, 2.

[11] *Memoirs of General William T. Sherman*, II, 181.

them "habits of carefulness and prudence." [12]

Guardianship, however, had to be exercised with discretion and restraint. Exploitation of the blacks, sometimes by their new bosses, sometimes by Union army pickets who returned them to former masters and pocketed the reward,[13] was distressingly prevalent. One reads with disgust the statement of a government report: "To cheat a negro by a private citizen or by a public officer is too much of a pastime. To plunder him of all he has seems little of a crime, because he has so little. To . . . starve his family, while he fights to maintain a government which supports the plunderers, is the . . . business of too many who wear the nation's livery." [14] Lurking evils of freedom were suggested in a Union general's special order in 1863 near Vicksburg referring to injurious results of Negroes coming under Union protection and advising prospective wards of Uncle Sam to remain on their plantations.[15] Mistreatment was the easier because wages were an indeterminant entity; they might be monthly but were more likely to be yearly; often compensation was on a crude share-crop basis. Incoming bosses were less likely than former masters to care for "non-productive" members of Negro families. According to a competent observer, Negroes preferred a Southern to a Northern employer. Even at his best, the Northerner was energetic, economical, and determined to exact a full day's labor, while the Southerner, "accustomed to the ways of slaves from his youth up," was "languidly and good-naturedly indifferent." Left to his own choice, the freedman preferred to "return to the service of the southerner." [16]

As the Union armies proceeded to occupy one area after another in their Southern march, military contact with the population enabled more and more slaves to find freedom in the shadow of the army and thus to taste the results, not always very exciting, of Lincoln's proclamation. For the vast majority of Southern slaves, however, liberation came with defeat of the Confederacy, the close of the war, and Union occupation of the South. Such occupation in its earlier phases was not as harsh as it might have been (the worst excesses began with about the

---

[12] *Offic. Rec.*, 3 ser., IV., 1022 ff.   [13] *Sen. Exec. Doc. No. 53*, 38 Cong., 1 sess., 12.
[14] *Sen. Exec. Doc. No. 28*, 38 Cong., 2 sess., 20.

[15] Special Order No. 45, Vicksburg, Miss., Aug. 18, 1863, *Offic. Rec.*, 3 ser., III., 686–687. See also *ibid.*, 917–918, in which it is emphasized that camps for freed Negroes were to be considered simply as places of temporary refuge.

[16] Report of Benjamin C. Truman, April 9, 1866, *Sen. Exec. Doc. No. 43*, 39 Cong., 1 sess., 10–11.

year 1868); harsh or not, the new regime made no revolutionary difference in the daily lives of ex-slaves. The governmental pattern as it applied generally was illustrated in the order of General John M. Schofield directly after Appomattox in North Carolina, in which he declared that former slaves were free by virtue of Lincoln's proclamation, but advised that freedmen remain with former masters working for wages, and that they avoid congregating about towns or camps. They were told that they would not be supported in idleness.[17] In a typical Southern home the domestic pattern was that described as follows by W. L. Fleming: "For several weeks before the master came home from the army the negroes knew that, as a result of the war, they were free. They, however, worked on, somewhat restless, . . . until he arrived and called them up and informed them that they were free. This was the usual way in which the negro was informed of his freedom. The great majority of the blacks . . . waited to hear from their masters the confirmation of . . . freedom. And the first thing the returning slaveholder did was to assemble his negroes and make known to them their condition with its privileges and responsibilities."[18]

In an elaborately documented study Mr. Bell Irvin Wiley has given us a composite picture of the emerging freeman.[19] With the coming of the Yankees, as Mr. Wiley shows, there were two opposite kinds of refugee movements: a flow of slaves toward Union camps, and, to counteract this, an effort of Southern masters to move their slaves toward the interior, in which there was some Confederate compulsion. Since a longing for freedom was a general motive among Southern Negroes,[20] the emancipation proclamation was commonly hailed with elation. The cause of this, however, was the shining lure of liberty rather than defection toward masters. There were those who felt the lure and yet refused when freedom knocked at the door. The high record of loyalty among Southern Negroes to their masters is in the main confirmed by Mr. Wiley, though he finds it impossible to accept all the familiar encomiums on the subject. He emphasizes the slightness of any tendency toward insurrection, the nonviolent nature of

---

[17] John M. Schofield, *Forty-Six Years in the Army*, 368.
[18] Fleming, *Civil War and Reconstruction in Alabama*, 270.
[19] Bell Irvin Wiley, *Southern Negroes, 1861–1865.*
[20] *Ibid.*, 19–21. Mr. Wiley writes: ". . . many of them, had they known what freedom entailed, would have recoiled from it" (p. 19).

the dark race, and the fact that a Negro seldom betrays a trust.[21] He finds more disorder (falling short of insurrection) than Southern writers usually admit, but emphasizes that such disorder was more common in invaded areas than in the interior.[22] Though he finds that by 1865 it was recognized in the South that slavery was a "dying institution," he shows the dissatisfaction felt by such a man as Robert Barnwell Rhett because of the provision in the Confederate constitution that permitted the admission of new states. Rhett had no wish to admit the people of the Northwest who were "fundamentally unsound on the question of slavery." [23] Noting conditions of hardship that came with liberation, Mr. Wiley finds enthusiasm and elation giving way to disillusion; when war ended in 1865 it was obvious that "the fight for real freedom had just begun." [24]

V

There remained, of course, the inspirational aspect and slogan value of Lincoln's proclamation. There were overtones of the edict which a literal examination of its words would not reveal. In the popular mind the document was dramatized as the opening of a new phase of the war. From the moment of its issuance the conflict took on, in the emotional sense, a new meaning. It "made emancipation the policy of the Administration," wrote a contemporary writer, "and encouraged the friends of that great cause to make every exertion to secure its speedy accomplishment." [1] Beginning with January 1863 the conflict was both a war for the Union and a crusade against slavery. Legalistic arguments might refute this, but factors other than the legal word were coming into play. Gaps in the antislavery front were now more easily closed, as in the border states where the proclamation gave impetus to the movement for state laws to sweep away the institution of slavery as it remained within Union lines. One step led to another. The doctrine of "contraband" had come first; then preparatory acts of Congress; then the preliminary proclamation; in due course the definitive proclamation with its reverberations over the civilized world; then Negro troops; later on, state laws to stop the chinks; finally, by a movement well launched while Lincoln was yet

---

21 *Ibid.*, 65.   22 *Ibid.*, 66, 83–84.   23 *Ibid.*, 164.   24 *Ibid.*, 344.
1 *Annual Cyclopaedia*, 1863, 835.

President, the "king's cure all" of a constitutional amendment prohibiting slavery. All this except the slow enactment of the amendment had come to pass by the end of the war.[2] It was a cumulative process in which the President's edict was the central element, but to which many factors, not the least being popular opinion and world approval, made a contribution.

In the minds of many earnest people at the North emancipation was a greater stimulus and a loftier challenge than even the preservation of the Union. If it were to be a Union with slavery, many considered it not worth fighting for, or at best an inadequate goal. That the hand of war was working its liberating effect in part outside the pattern of governmental intent was to many minds a source of strength. This movement for human liberation seemed a bigger thing than Lincoln, a mightier force than that of constituted rulers. A sense of destiny and of providential intervention gave to the movement a spiritual element of evangelistic fervor which can in no wise be left out of the account. With the uplifting sense that God was taking a hand in human affairs there came an increment of power to meet the new challenge. War aims now had to be recast. The Crittenden resolution of July 1861 was outmoded. The Union was not to be reconstructed except on the basis of abolition of slavery in the Southern states. "The problem . . . to be solved was . . . the re-appearance of the slave-holding . . . States in the Union, with the shackles of their slaves knocked off, with their bondmen and women and children sent forth as free." [3] If this seemed to require a fuller subjugation than otherwise, if it tended to prolong the war, it offered a higher challenge than statesmen of the time realized, for with greater control there would need to be greater generosity if a sorry postwar bitterness were to be avoided.

Men of the time were quick to adopt the view that the emancipation

---

[2] The constitutional amendment abolishing slavery, not treated in the present volume, was introduced by Senator Trumbull in February 1864. On December 18, 1865, Secretary Seward proclaimed that its ratification by state legislatures had been completed and that it was from that date a part of the Constitution. By that time emancipation had been loyally accepted in the South. Ratification of the amendment by eight of the seceded states was counted in estimating the three-fourths necessary for adoption. Congress subsequently refused to recognize the validity of "Johnson's reorganized states," which had thus participated in amending the United States Constitution, but this non-recognition was not construed as invalidating the amendment.

[3] *Annual Cyclopaedia*, 1863, 836.

proclamation was the "crowning act" of Lincoln's administration.[4] Lincoln himself caught the spirit and remarked to John Hay that he considered this problem "the greatest question ever presented to practical statesmanship." Hay added: "While the rest are grinding their . . . organs for their own glorification the old man is working with the strength of a giant . . . to do this great work." [5]

For a down-trodden and submerged race the Negroes made a worthy and honorable war record. Some of them in their daily associations came close to the Lincolns, such as Elizabeth Keckley, modiste to the First Lady, or William Slade, messenger to the President; their stories have recently been recovered.[6] Some of them, otherwise forgotten, have come down to us in the rhetorical pages of Thomas Wentworth Higginson,[7] who did not fail to record the picturesque and the comical among these capering brothers while noting the "minor-key pathos" of their responsive natures. In guffawing antics they added a welcome touch of comedy to the army scene. In their tugging and chorusing gangs heavy labor became a pastime; in drill their rhythm and love of swank made for snap and style; when off duty their whirling and frolicking made camp a delight; in grim action, where many paid the supreme sacrifice, they proved themselves real soldiers. Deep in the South the great majority not only avoided insurrection but gave their all in faithful service to mistress and master.

---

[4] Seward was reported to have protested against such a concept, saying that "the formation of the Republican Party destroyed slavery," and that the bigger work of Lincoln's government was preserving the Union and thereby saving popular government for the world. Thus wrote John Hay in his diary, June 24, 1864. Dennett, ed., *Lincoln . . . in the . . . Diaries of John Hay*, 197.

[5] Diary of John Hay, July 31, 1863, *ibid.*, 73.

[6] John E. Washington, *They Knew Lincoln*. Dr. Washington conveys the broad race memories of his people and their folk thoughts of the Emancipator as he recovers the stories of those few who knew and served the Lincolns, whom they devotedly loved.

[7] *Army Life in a Black Regiment.*

CHAPTER XXIV

POLITICS AS USUAL

THAT Lincoln had a war to fight, a country to save, and, as he believed, a contribution to make to the abiding cause of free government in the world, is but a partial statement of his task. He had to endure inefficiency, factional bickering, and some of the sorriest "politics" that this party-ridden country has ever witnessed. Ideologically Lincoln was an ardent democrat, an enthusiast for popular rule, an enemy of tyranny; yet he was always wary of revolutionary or too drastic methods. Working for human progress in conservative terms, he was essentially a moderate liberal. Cautious reform, stability combined with enlightened change, was his ideal. As President he was less of an intense party man than he had been in earlier days. The muting of politics for the higher unity of a nation struggling for survival was his aim, but this aim was not achieved by the American people in Civil War times; they did not even achieve unity within either of the major parties. Petty men kept grinding their little axes; Congress made life miserable for the President; politicians jostled for favor and prominence; rocking-chair strategists won battles on paper; editors emitted streams of advice or denunciation. If in some respects the war effort brought exaltation, party politics remained on its regular uninspired plane.

I

It would be pleasant, if true, to record that Lincoln's voice was the dominant note, or that he rode the storm to his own destined port. the disturbing fact was the growing dominance of that group of hard driving Radicals whom Hay dubbed "Jacobins," and who have also been designated as "vindictives." A more unlovely knot of politicians would be hard to find. Self important, humorless, itching for power, and scornful of ethical scruple, they sold their wares at their own valuation and paraded behind a front of crusading zeal.[1] Unmerciful in their pressure upon Lincoln, they used the stratagems of patronage, party trickery, and propaganda to impose their pattern upon all phases of war effort. With a technique of intimidation that moderates found hard to resist, they made it their business to take over problems of army command, conduct of campaigns, composition of the Cabinet, formulation of war aims, and reconstruction of a shattered nation in proscriptive and punitive terms. Their assaults upon McClellan have already been seen; they actually dreaded Union success if achieved under McClellan's leadership. If a general did not wear their livery, especially if he were a Democrat, they set out to destroy him by inquisitorial investigations and unfair publicity; if commanders spoke their glib language, they were petted or promoted, though the outcome might be defeat of Union arms. With all their emphasis upon action and efficiency they were capable of obstructing the effective prosecution of the war, or even of deliberately protracting it in order to promote their political purposes.[2]

The reason usually mentioned to explain this—i. e., the determination that the war must become the lever for dislodging slavery—was only part of a complex bill of goods which involved sectional supremacy, social revolution, capitalistic exploitation, and such a program of future party ascendancy as would make the Radicals the controlling element in the whole country. A Yankee colonel in the South stated the case in exaggerated form. "Do we fight them to avenge . . . insult, . . . ?" he asked. "No! The thing we seek is *permanent* dominion; & what instance is there of a permanent dominion without changing, revolutionizing, absorbing, the institutions, life, and manners of the conquered peoples? . . . They think we mean to take their *Slaves.* Bah! We must take their *ports,* their *mines,* their *water powers,* the *very soil* they plough, and develop them by the hands of our *artisan* armies. . . . We are to be a regenerating, colonizing

---

[1] In T. Harry Williams, *Lincoln and the Radicals,* one finds a competent and readable account of this influential group.

[2] "They believed that if the struggle continued long enough, public opinion would force the government to resort to emancipation and the arming of the slaves. Hence they favored a policy that would prolong the war until they . . . [could] force the radical program upon the reluctant Lincoln." *Ibid.,* 12–13.

power, or we are to be whipped. Schoolmasters, with howitzers, must instruct our Southern brethren that they are a set of d—d fools in everything, that relates to . . . modern civilization. . . . *This army must not come back.* Settlement, migration must put the seal on battle, or we gain nothing." [3] In terms that would have shocked the majority of his fellow-soldiers, this sizzling colonel declared: "Vindicating the majesty of an insulted Government, by extirpating all *rebels,* & fumigating their nests with the brimstone of unmitigated Hell, I conceive to be the holy purpose of our further efforts. I hope I shall . . . do something . . . in 'The Great Fumigation,' before the sulphur gives out." [4]

This extirpator and fumigator was too drastic to be typical; certainly his tone was altogether exceptional in the army. Nevertheless the increasing amount of such clamor outside the army is a recognized factor of the war which explains Lincoln's wholesome dislike of the "ultra" element. "We are growing more radical . . . every day," wrote a friend of Trumbull. "The people are ripe for extreme measures." [5] "We have been too angelic to rebels both north and south," wrote another, "& I think we have got to be more severe with them." [6] Having visited St. Louis, Theodore Tilton was dissatisfied with western men, finding them "not sufficiently actuated by *moral* convictions to make them safe . . . leaders in a good cause." [7] In a lengthy diatribe Jonathan B. Turner of Illinois College at Jacksonville deplored too much forgiveness and wanted the divine power of the sword exerted upon offenders. "Mr. Lincoln," wrote Turner, "seems to imagine that he is a sort of half way clergyman . . . . Mr. Lincoln has nothing whatever, as commander of the army & navy to do with the N.T. [New Testament]; He never ought to read it . . . . Let him turn to the O.T." Referring to a coming "traitor conclave" in Louisville, Kentucky, Turner wanted the President "to surround . . . and take every dog of them, . . . and either *hang them on the spot,* or imprison them till the war is over." He mentioned that loyal men wanted him to write either to Trumbull or the President. "But as

---

[3] Lt. Col. Sargent to Gov. John A. Andrew, Annapolis, Jan. 14, 1862, Andrew MSS.

[4] Sargent to Andrew (again), Camp Williams, Beaufort, S. C., Mar. 3, 1862, *ibid.*

[5] P. P. Enos to Lyman Trumbull, Springfield, Ill., July 14, 1862, Trumbull MSS.

[6] T. J. Moore to Lyman Trumbull, Stanfield, Ill., May 26, 1862, *ibid.*

[7] Theodore Tilton to Horace Greeley, Chicago, Jan. 6, 1865, Greeley MSS., New York Pub. Lib.

I have been thorning the President about McClellan, Fits John Porter . . . & other cursed West Point fools & traitors, ever since I was in Washington in September, I dont like to write him . . , now." [8]

While some of the above-quoted expressions of radical doctrine are vitriolic to excess, one can hardly give a mere record of their position that is not emphatic and extreme. In that restrained and factual year-book, the *American Annual Cyclopaedia,* one finds the following characterization: "Their bitter and unsparing denunciation of all Northern citizens who stood aloof . . . from . . . strictly anti-slavery views . . . [gave] another turn to the screws under which the President was writhing." [9]

II

Foremost among the Radicals in the House was Thaddeus Stevens, whose dour countenance, protruding lower lip, limping clubfoot, and sarcastic invective made him the perfect type of vindictive ugliness. Though chairman of the ways and means committee he paid compara-tively little attention to finance; it was as leader of Republicans in the lower house that his overbearing power was exerted. Proscriptive measures against Southerners were a veritable obsession with him. With a blunt forthrightness that had in it a certain terrible honesty he blurted out his searing passages, scorning to find excuse for them either in ethics or the Constitution. It was natural for him to join in the Radical sport of "thorning" Mr. Lincoln. "Mr. Thaddeus Ste-vens," wrote a Boston journalist, "has never been sparing of his insinuations against the administration, for which he is nominally the leader in the House of Representatives," adding: "he has attacked it openly, with the vehemence, and . . . ferocity, which is apt to characterize his action in moments of deep excitement." [1] The quality of his stinging tongue can be judged from one of his personal flings at an opponent: "Mr. Speaker, it will not be expected of me to notice the thing which has crawled into this House and adheres to one of the seats by its own slime." [2]

---

[8] The contents of this bristling epistle have only been faintly suggested here. Jonathan B. Turner to Lyman Trumbull, Jacksonville, Ill., Feb. 1, 1863, Trumbull MSS.

[9] *Annual Cyclopaedia,* 1862, 792.

[1] Boston *Daily Advertiser,* Feb. 26, 1863.

[2] Quoted in Thomas Frederick Woodley, *Great Leveler: The Life of Thaddeus Ste-vens,* 10.

In the Senate Charles Sumner had impressiveness and prominence rather than practical leadership. Tall and massive, with distinguished head rising from stuffy cravat, complete with side whiskers and Latin phrases, he moved with a pompous superiority which told the world that he expected to be admired. To him the war was not the battlefield nor the garrison; it was the Senate Chamber. Its supreme product was the *Congressional Globe* in which his grandiloquent speeches were embalmed. There were those who spoke highly of him. Emerson referred to his "singularly pure character," [3] but Emerson also praised John Brown with equal extravagance. A greater tribute was that of L. Q. C. Lamar whose address in the Senate after Sumner's death in 1874 served double duty as an official encomium and a handsome gesture of postwar friendship from the South to the North. It was said that the general upper class of Boston regarded Sumner "as a renegade and a menace." [4] This might be far from a condemnation, but contemporary statements from men who personally knew the man (as Lamar did not) were often unfavorable. Hugh McCulloch considered him prejudiced, "open to flattery" and "too lofty to descend to persons." [5] Carlyle's verdict was: "the most completely nothin' of a mon that ever crossed my threshold,—naught . . . in him or of him but wind and vanity." [6] The confidential estimate of senatorial colleagues was recorded by Browning who mentioned a train ride in which the Bay State solon was the topic of conversation which he had with Foote, Fessenden, and Collamer, who concurred "in characterizing him as cowardly, mean, malignant, . . . hypocritical, . . . cringing and toadyish to every thing, and every body that had the odor of aristocracy." [7] Sumner's learning tended toward pedantry; his constitutional reasoning was clumsy and bookish; his opposition to slavery—the main emphasis of his life—left him cold to "appeals by needy colored people." [8] It was a day, however, when senators were expected to spread themselves, and the Websterian prominence of the man makes it impossible to dismiss him with a deprecation. It is significant of Lincoln's shrewdness that he not only treated the humorless statesman with respect, but got on well with him and gained much in the process.

---

[3] Emerson, *Miscellanies (Complete Works,* XI), 234.
[4] Carl Sandburg, *Abraham Lincoln: The War Years,* I, 100.
[5] Hugh McCulloch, *Men and Measures of Half A Century,* 234.
[6] M. A. DeWolfe Howe, ed., *Letters of Charles Eliot Norton,* I, 422.
[7] Browning, *Diary,* I, 588   [8] McCulloch. *Men and Measures,* 234.

VINDICTIVES

Upper left: Senator Zachariah Chandler of Mich., member of Com. on Conduct of the War.

Upper right: Senator Benjamin F. Wade of Ohio, member of Com. on Conduct of the War; involved in anti-Lincoln intrigue.

Center: Edwin M. Stanton of Pa., Sec. of War beginning in Jan. 1862. Scornful of Lincoln in 1861; opponent of McClellan; unfriendly toward Lincoln-Johnson plan of reconstruction.

Lower left: Thaddeus Stevens of Pa., Republican leader in House of Representatives. Antithesis of Lincoln in personality and policy.

Lower right: Benjamin F. Butler of Mass., political general. Favored anti-Douglas faction of Southern Democrats in 1860; commander in Baltimore, Norfolk, New Orleans, etc.; brought disrepute to the Union cause.

Brady photographs, National Archives

COURT, SENATE, AND PRESS

Upper left: Roger B. Taney of Maryland, Chief Justice of the United States. His opinions were opposed to Lincoln's policies.

Upper right: Orville H. Browning of Illinois, Senator to fill Douglas's unexpired term, 1861–63.

Lower left: Horace Greeley, Editor of New York *Tribune.*

Lower right: Charles Sumner, Senator from Massachusetts.

It may be said of Sumner that his anti-Southern radicalism did not often, as in the case of Wade and Chandler, take an anti-Lincoln turn, nor did he descend to partyism of the coarser kind. In 1872, for example, he withheld support from Grant. Nor can one forget the vast importance of Sumner's relation to John Bright, and the specific focusing of this historic Bright-Sumner friendship in terms of Anglo-American amity, especially with reference to the *Trent* affair. Much might have been done with Sumner if his contact had been less with books and more with life.

Between Sumner and Henry Wilson, his colleague from Massachusetts, there was little to choose. Lacking Sumner's ornate façade, Wilson was like him as to basic policies. Count Gurowski, though himself a radical, could not abide either of them. "Oh what an infernal nu[i]sance," he wrote, "are your Wilsons or Sumners, without brains the one, without a heart the other." [9] Two westerners, Bluff Ben Wade of Ohio and Zachariah Chandler of Michigan, were at the very front of the radical movement; they were alike in their insolence, coarseness of method, and vulgarity. Referring to a day when both these seigniors had spoken, the *Herald* declared: "Ben. Wade, the stupid old pug dog, and silly Chandler, the cowardly and impertinent puppy, of the abolition faction of traitors, distinguished themselves in the . . . Senate . . . ." [10] That Wade was anti-Lincoln was well known. Giddings of Ohio attributed his ill will to bad humor because of defeat for the presidential nomination in 1860. Wade, said Giddings, "denounced the President as a *failure* from the moment of his election and began to lay his plans for his own advancement. . . . The truth is that . . . the congress has been the theatre for making Presidents and not to carry on the war. . . . Wade proclaimed that no party could succeed on *moral principle*. That if we intended ever to elect a President we must cease to avow immutable truth as the basis of our party and get every man to vote with [us] who objected to the democracy [i. e. the Democratic party]. He was a candidate for nomination at Chicago, and his friends were anxious to strike from our [Republican] platform all allusion to principle. They were acting as he dictated. By . . . wireworking . . . I was kept from the Committee on platforms . . . and the Committee reported a plat-

---

[9] Gurowski to Gov. Andrew, Feb. 1, 1864, Andrew MSS.
[10] New York *Herald*, July 18, 1862, editorial, p. 4, c. 3.

form . . . without reference to any doctrine or moral or political principal [*sic*]. . . . [T]hen and there the party was disbanded and our *principles abandoned* . . . ." [11] At another time Giddings wrote to Julian of Indiana: "The probability is that Wade will be blown up with the explosion he has kindled. He ought to be, for he has demoralized the party which you and I had spent our political lives in building. It was by the influence of that party that he was elected to the Senate; but having ascended to that chamber he kicked away the ladder to prevent other republicans from ascending it." [12]

Zach Chandler, "that Xantippe in pants," [13] was as firmly set against Lincoln and as ruthless in politics as Wade. Mustering a powerful publicity campaign and carrying "the Republican organization in his breeches' pockets," [14] Chandler sought power and domination by pressure, intimidation, spoils, wealth, and the blunter instruments of politics. Welles found him "steeped & steamed in whisky . . . coarse, vulgar, and reckless." [15]

In Lyman Trumbull of Illinois the radicals had a senatorial leader of finer fiber who nevertheless served their purpose on many wartime occasions. His authorship and sponsorship of the bill for the confiscation of Southern property was the most prominent of his activities in the earlier half of the war. A stickler for the Constitution "rightly interpreted," more regardful of civil rights than most Jacobins, he was a caustic and able critic of the Lincoln administration. His competence on the Senate floor made him a formidable antagonist.

Revolving around these major stars of the Jacobinical world were satellites, secondary bodies, and briefly flaming meteors whose main function was voting and whose place among the political constellations was a matter of party conformity. To enumerate them would be

---

[11] Joshua R. Giddings to G. W. Julian, Montreal, Jan. 28, 1862, Giddings-Julian MSS., marked "Private." This indignant letter is full of disillusionment as to party politics.

[12] Giddings to Julian, Montreal, Jan. 18, 1863, *ibid.*

[13] The characterization is that of Senator Graham N. Fitch of Indiana. *Cong. Globe,* 36 Cong., 1 sess., 2403.

[14] Wilmer C. Harris, *Public Life of Zachariah Chandler, 1851–1875,* 66. Dr. Harris states (65–66): "Mr. Chandler's agents had been busy in . . . caucuses and . . . conventions. . . . By 1862 Mr. Chandler owned the Republican organization [in Michigan] . . . . His power was due in part to . . . patronage and to a judicious use of money, ..."

[15] MS. Diary of Gideon Welles, Dec. 5, 1866, quoted in Howard K. Beale, *The Critical Year,* 14.

to give a catalogue of the unknown, but one should not overlook such men of the lower house as Lovejoy of Illinois, Colfax and Julian of Indiana, Ashley and Bingham of Ohio, Roscoe Conkling of New York, Henry Winter Davis of Maryland (after 1863), and Covode of Pennsylvania. In the Senate, in addition to those mentioned, the radical ranks were filled out with John Sherman of Ohio, Henry S. Lane of Indiana, James H. Lane of Kansas, and Pomeroy of Kansas.

III

Of the Democrats it may be said that in general they failed to perceive the distinction between genuine service by an opposition party in a democracy and exploitation of the nation's misfortune for party advantage. Yet this was not all. Much of their criticism was directed against leaders who were foes not only of the Democrats but also of Lincoln. Where their darts were directed against Lincoln this was often on points concerning which the administration was vulnerable, as in the matter of arbitrary arrests. No one generalization covers all the Democrats of the period; they were of varying shades and hues. Between the solid Reverdy Johnson of Maryland and the sensational Vallandigham of Ohio there were as great a gulf as between Lincoln and Ben Wade.

Democrats had a longer history than the Republicans. Theirs was the party of tradition and ancient strength. Seldom indeed had it been a party of opposition. As the year 1860 had opened the Democratic party had had what seemed a promising chance to continue as a national organization uniting North and South. The loss, or throwing away, of that opportunity had signified the removal of the only important party that was national in scope. It was not mere claptrap for them to hope for their restoration as a reëstablishment of stability and unity in the nation. It was logical for those who thought in terms of the old Union and who noted the utter sectionalism of the Republican movement, to place their stakes on the time-honored party of Jefferson, Jackson, Calhoun, and Douglas. On the wide border, which reached far up into Ohio, Indiana, and Illinois, the Democrats were the only promising party. In the free West theirs was the tradition of that "progressive western democracy" of which H. C. Hubbart has written.[1] This was the term attached to a vigorous group which formed in the buoyant forties, championed Jeffersonian liberty and the rights of man, opposed soulless capitalism, took up for the farmer, and carried high the banner of free institutions. Much of their wartime feeling against the Republicans is explainable on the ground of deep disappointment that the war had to interrupt their hopes of reform. It was due also to sympathy with Southern brothers, and resentment against Lincoln's party for, as they thought, causing the war. If the South was ever to be won back, they naturally considered themselves better fitted to do the winning and holding than the party of Wade and Chandler.

Meeting at their state capital in January 1862 the Democrats of Indiana resolved that only Democrats could preserve the Union, that the war was the result of the formation of a sectional party with consequent Southern reaction, and that Republicans in Congress were to blame for the failure of peace proposals. With a sarcastic quip at the affair of Mason and Slidell, the convention declared that the war could have been avoided if the controlling party's desire for peace with the South had been equal to its leniency toward England in the *Trent* case.[2] In their public address the Democratic state convention of Wisconsin denounced abolition in the District and assailed the presidential policy of arbitrary arrests and of suppression of newspapers.[3] These examples serve to give the tone of Democratic declarations.

Unionism was no monopoly of the Republicans. The "war Democrats" were for greater solidarity in support of the existing war administration than the "peace Democrats," but even the latter looked ultimately to an integrated United States rather than a dismembered nation. This quality of Unionism, however, should not be understood as an adjournment of politics. Being out, and wanting to get in, and also being honestly convinced that their party could best promote peace and welfare in the country, the Democrats found no lack of honest reasons for opposing the Lincoln administration. In the convention at Indianapolis above mentioned (January 1862) there was manifest "a determination amongst the leading Democrats . . . of Ind & Illinois to crush the present administration and with it the

---

[1] H. C. Hubbart, " 'Pro-Southern' Influences in the Free West, 1840–1865," *Miss. Vall. Hist. Rev.*, XX, 45–62. See also H. C. Hubbart, *The Older Middle West, 1840–1880.*

[2] New York *Herald*, Jan. 10, 1862, p. 8, c. 2.   [3] *Ibid.*, Sep. 10, 1862, p. 4, c. 1.

republican party . . . ." At this meeting Joseph Holt of Kentucky was "privately agreed upon as the next President." [4]

Democratic declarations often gave a pronounced proslavery impression. The party was assuredly critical of abolitionist agitation and of various antislavery measures including the emancipation proclamation. It was nevertheless true that by the summer of 1862 prominent Democrats were prepared to admit that slavery "must go down if necessary to save the union." [5] Both parties were sick of the political nuisance of slavery. Young Democrats in New York wished to sidestep the Negro question; in inviting Samuel J. Tilden to join them in a meeting they declared themselves "opposed to the further agitation of the Negro question and in favor of the prosecution of the War for the restoration of the Union as it was and the . . . Constitution as it is . . . ." [6] In a "largely attended" state convention the Democrats of New Hampshire were "firm and uncompromising in favor of sustaining the Union and constitution." [7] An address to the nation issued by combined Democrats of various states (May 8, 1862) invited all men without distinction of party "who are for the constitution as it is, and the Union as it was" to unite with them in preserving both these principles. This, they agreed, was the "great issue." [8]

Gloom and defeat, of which there was plenty, tended to help the Democrats and embarrass the Republicans. That Lincoln's opponents should fail to capitalize this gloom was too much to expect. In state convention at Columbus, Ohio, in August 1861 some (not all) of the Democratic delegates "were rejoicing at the defeat at Bull Run, and were ready to make political capital out of the mismanagement of the War Department." [9] This did not mean, however, that the convention was anything but overwhelmingly pro-Union. The prevailing sentiment was not rejoicing at defeat, but indignation at corruption and mismanagement combined with a strong and optimistic purpose to appeal to Union-minded Southerners to return to the fold. It would be a mistake to regard as typical the few, if any, Democrats who would

[4] E. T. Bainbridge (prominent Democrat) to Joseph Holt, Louisville, Ky., Jan. 20, 1862, Holt MSS.

[5] H. S. Bundy to S. P. Chase, Reid's Mills, Ohio, Aug. 1, 1862, Chase MSS., Lib. of Cong.

[6] C. F. Averill, Chairman, to Samuel J. Tilden, New York, June 21, 1862, Tilden MSS.

[7] News item from Concord, N. H., New York *Herald*, Jan. 10, 1862, p. 3, c. 1.

[8] *Ibid.*, May 9, 1862, p. 5, c. 3.

[9] G. H. Porter, *Ohio Politics during the Civil War Period*, 83.

actually have sold their country short. The men who perhaps went farthest in capitalizing Union defeat, for which they were largely responsible, were the anti-Lincoln radicals in the Republican party.

Of the Democrats in the House the most prominent were Pendleton of Ohio, Vallandigham of Ohio (he being more extreme than the Democratic norm), S. S. Cox of Ohio, Corning of New York, Crittenden and Grider of Kentucky, W. J. Allen of Illinois (beginning with 1863), and Voorhees of Indiana. Among the Democratic senators were Bayard and Saulsbury of Delaware, Pearce and Hicks of Maryland, Davis and Powell of Kentucky, McDougall of California, and, from 1863, Richardson of Illinois and Hendricks of Indiana. Taking the last-mentioned leader, a man above the Civil War average, it is safe to say that, though a Democrat, he was closer to Lincoln's genuine views than were the Jacobins.

There are certain persisting misconceptions regarding the "War Democrats" as contrasted with the "peace Democrats" of the period. There is the concept that, while a very large element of the Democratic party as such supported the Lincoln administration, those who did not do so formed a separate party group (of "peace" or anti-Lincoln Democrats) distinct from the main Democratic party. The only way to become clear on the matter is to study it by states; to do so here would be too long a story, but some examples may be briefly noted. In Ohio, for the state and congressional elections of 1862, the contest was between the Union party and the Democratic party. The Union party was the Republican party (for the moment held together by the conservative element) and a small minority of the Democrats. The Democratic party in that election was the regular organization which carried on a vigorous anti-Lincoln campaign. The Democrats won the election.[10] In Indiana, as J. A. Woodburn has pointed out, there were three Democratic groups: war Democrats, constitutional Union Democrats, and "anti-war" Democrats. The war Democrats came into such "close harmony, if not identification, with the Republicans" that they may be "eliminated as a part of the Democratic opposition."[11] The constitutional union Democrats comprised the

---

[10] *Ibid.*, 100–109.

[11] James A. Woodburn, "Party Politics in Indiana during the Civil War," *Annual Report*, Am. Hist. Assoc., 1902, I, 231. See also Winfred A. Harbison, "Lincoln and Indiana Republicans, 1861–1862," *Ind. Mag. of Hist.*, XXXIII, 301.

main bulk of the party and held it together. They were strong for the union and civil rights, but took a firm stand against the administration. They favored compromise with the South, opposed the abolitionists, whom they blamed (with the Republicans) for the war, and referred to the Republican appeal for all-party support as the "no-party dodge." "In their eyes this 'no-party party' . . . was merely . . . [a] pretense of the Republicans by which they hoped to take to themselves the spoils of office and perpetuate their own power." [12]

As for the third group, the minor faction of anti-war Democrats, they worked within the main Democratic party, but with far less importance than the regular or constitutional union element. The so-called Copperhead faction, in other words, "did not determine the official utterances and leadership of the party." As to the "great body of the party," writes Woodburn, "We have no sufficient reason to doubt . . . their loyalty to the Union or . . . to . . . the Constitution, ..." [13] In a brief treatment of an elaborate situation these points as to Ohio and Indiana give the general pattern. There were still two main parties. The Republicans, seeking to make the nation's cause a party possession, added some Democrats to their own group by using the name "Union" party; despite this the main bulk of the Democrats remained in their own organization, keeping it as an opposition party, but claiming withal as much loyalty, pro-Unionism, and determination to prosecute the war, as the Republicans. Indeed they claimed that they could do better in administering the government and restoring the Union. Their opposition was not directed against the Union cause, but against the abolitionists, the Republicans, and the existing administration.

The use of the name Union party by the Republicans implied that the moderate element was in command, and this was emphasized by the fact that radicals found it hard to go along with the movement. The fact is, however, that the dominant party as a whole might gain by the "union" feature, giving an impression of conservative control, and yet the Democrats who joined them might have insufficient guarantee that "radicalism," by which is meant intolerant excess, would not in time prevail. In order to get votes there was the tendency to give the Republican party a conservative coloration at election time. The radicals would support the party anyhow because they had no-

---

[12] Woodburn, "Party Politics in Indiana," 242.   [13] *Ibid.*, 232.

where else to go; they hoped that after election theirs would be the controlling party voice. In Ohio, for instance, it was by the influence of conservative Republicans that some Democrats went into the Union party with the Republicans in 1862; this, however, did not prevent the reëlection of the super-radical Wade to the United States Senate. If one thing was clear above others in the Ohio election of 1862 it was that the people of that state had declared themselves against all that Wade and his policies involved. Not only had both the state and congressional elections gone Democratic; it was also true that the Republican party, with its "Union" appeal, was professing moderation. It is unnecessary to note the factors that brought about Wade's reëlection by the Ohio legislature in January 1863; it is sufficient to note that genuine popular choice did not determine the selection of a man who, by reason of his position in the Senate, was to come within an inch of succeeding to the presidency in 1868.[14]

IV

Conservatives of the time found their great point of difference with the radicals on the basic purpose of the war. With Lincoln, they wanted the South to be spared the horrors of a conflict directed against civilian homes and to be genuinely satisfied when the Union should be remade. They did not want Union victory to be understood as subjugation. They stood at the opposite pole from the Jacobins, to whom suffering on the part of wicked slaveholders was a much relished expression of divine vengeance, and to whom continuing domination over the South offered the indispensable weapon of power politics. For the Union the conservatives had burning zeal, but they felt, as a sturdy Bostonian put it, that "the best fighting material in the New England ranks . . . [was] inspired not by *negrophilism,* . . . but by the spirit of the political grandfathers." [1] It was not that they were friendly to slavery; one of them urged making "short shrift of slavery"

---

[14] Being president pro tempore of the Senate, Wade would have become President if Andrew Johnson had been removed on impeachment charges in 1868. With this personal interest at stake, Wade himself voted for Johnson's conviction, which failed by only one vote.

[1] Elizur Wright to Abraham Lincoln, Boston, May 23, 1862, photostat of MS., Lib. of Cong.

for the very reason that "Jacobins . . . would be unhorsed but for this hobby." [2] Sympathizing with border Unionists and even with men of the upper South, these conservatives opposed proscriptive schemes, objected to confiscation, and preferred to avoid a war of legislation against individuals. They were ready to treat the South fairly, and were mindful of equitable and constitutional procedures. If they differed markedly with Lincoln on any point it was in the matter of civil rights, for they did not favor arbitrary arrests. Among the conservative, nonvindictive Republicans may be found some of the ablest men of the Senate: Edgar Cowan of Pennsylvania, Orville H. Browning of Illinois, James W. Grimes and James Harlan of Iowa, Jacob Collamer of Vermont, John B. Henderson of Missouri, and that "enthusiastic Jeffersonian Republican," [3] James R. Doolittle of Wisconsin.

In the House such men as Owen Lovejoy and Isaac Arnold of Illinois and A. G. Riddle of Ohio, though definitely on the Stevens side because of opposition to slavery, were innocent of the anti-Lincoln tone that was so common among radicals. They even rose to the support of Lincoln when attacked; in this they were exceptional. Francis P. Blair, Jr. of Missouri was another Republican in the House who supported the President, but his combativeness, factional tendency, desire for military distinction, and readiness to attack persons with whom Lincoln had to deal—e. g., Chase—made him a somewhat doubtful champion.

Being of the cultured, milder variety, conservatives in Congress had less boldness and dominant force than the radicals; they differed from them also in the possession of scruples and the lack of fighting organization. This situation worried men who had the welfare of the Lincoln administration at heart. Joshua Fry Speed of Kentucky, old friend of Lincoln, was "persuaded" that there was "mischief brewing." A "large and powerful party of . . . ultra men," he wrote, was "being formed to make war upon the President and upon his conservative policy." He feared that while the "other party" was

---

[2] F. P. Blair, Sr., to Montgomery Blair, Silver Spring, Md., Dec. 28, 1863, Blair MSS.

[3] James L. Sellers, "James R. Doolittle," reprinted from *Wis. Mag. of Hist.*, (vols. XVII and XVIII), p. 18 of reprint. (Henderson was a Republican, though a former Democrat; in 1868 he was to become one of the seven Republicans who voted not to convict President Johnson on impeachment charges.)

"rapidly organizing, coaxing & driving," Lincoln's friends were drifting with no concert of action.[4]

Noticing and regretting the superiority of the radicals over conservatives in the matter of organization, Speed wanted the situation
corrected: he wanted the few Southern men in Congress, the Northern
Democrats, and the conservative Republicans to form a union under
some competent leader. If necessary Speed thought the President
ought to "go before the country on the next congressional election
[of 1862] upon the issue," but he preferred it should not go that far;
conservatives ought "to beat them at every point from the picket
skirmish to the grand charge," in "parliamentary movements as in
the field." He continued: "We need a cool, active young man—one
capable of forming combinations—and our friends should be willing
to give the leadership to some conservative republican . . . . I have
talked to all of our Ky delegation on the subject. They all agree with
me—but they don't go to work." [5]

This statement by Speed touched a fundamental matter in the party
situation under Lincoln. The unnatural development by which the
radicals constituted an increasingly influential portion of a party that
also included Lincoln and the moderates was a matter of tactics, drive,
and organization. Suspicious of vengeful reform, and wary of disruptive tendencies, milder Republicans would seem to have been
more at home with the Democrats than with the Jacobins; the most
distinguished of the Democratic leaders, Douglas, had supported Lincoln on the war issue. The true party alignment, if there had to be
parties, would have been moderate liberals on one side (non-vindictive
Republicans together with the main body of the Democrats), and
on the other side Republican Jacobins mustering under such a
leader as Stevens or Wade. This would have left the more bitter
Democrats of the Fernando Wood or Vallandigham school with no
place to go except in a hopeless group to themselves, which is where
they might well have been left. The Northeast would thus have had
less directing influence, big business would have had smaller opportunity in the exploitive sense, and the party associated with Lincoln
would have had larger influence in his own section, the Middle West.
Such a group would have been antislavery in the constructive, not
punitive, sense.

---

[4] J. F. Speed to Joseph Holt, Washington, D.C., Dec. 8, 1861, Holt MSS.   [5] *Ibid.*

Such a consolidation of political forces was actually discussed and attempted. After the adjournment of the House of Representatives on May 9, 1862, there was read from the clerk's desk a call for "a meeting of the conservative members of Congress in this hall to-morrow, Saturday, May 10, at two o'clock, P. M." Conservatives from all states were invited to attend and "counsel . . . as to the best means to defeat the schemes of the abolitionists and secessionists." [6] The purpose, according to the *Herald,* was "to rally the democratic [this probably meant democratically minded] party" by inviting the cooperation of those who "go for the constitution as it is, and the Union as it was" in the congressional campaign.[7] The meeting was held at the scheduled time with the venerable Crittenden in the chair and forty-three members from both houses of Congress in attendance. Agreeing that they were not forming a political party, they announced that they were trying to get their views before the people; for this purpose a committee of one member from each state was designated to promote the good work. The possible result, as stated by the *Herald,* was "an organization of the conservative majority in the House for a systematic resistance to the radical revolutionary measures of the abolition disunionists . . . ." [8] The group was reported as containing twenty-seven Unionists, thirteen Democrats, and two Republicans.[9] As a similar sign of the times it was reported that a "new political party" was forming in New Hampshire, to be "composed of the conservative elements of both the old democratic and republican organizations, or rather of the honest supporters of the administration of Mr. Lincoln." [10] Connecticut was doing likewise; there was held at Hartford on January 8, 1862, a convention "participated in by Union democrats and republicans, representing each county in the State." [11]

Here there appears at first glance an effort to offer moderate and tolerant men a *modus vivendi* of coöperation for national, constructive measures. For one reason and another, however, the movement collapsed. Lack of leadership was an important element, but perhaps the chief reason was the ingrained tendency of American party men toward politics as usual. When another of the congressional group meetings was held on June 28, 1862, only thirty-five members attended; not

---

6 New York *Herald,* May 10, 1862, p. 6, c. 5.
8 *Ibid.,* May 11, 1862, p. 4, cc. 5–6.
10 *Ibid.,* Feb. 2, 1862, p. 4, c. 2.

7 *Ibid.,* May 7, 1862, p. 7, c. 1.
9 *Ibid.,* May 14, 1862, p. 6, c. 2.
11 *Ibid.,* Jan. 9, 1862, p. 1, c. 5.

all the border-state men were there, and there were no Republicans by that name. It was feared that the movement would have forced some of the conservative Republicans, the more party-minded ones, back into the arms of the radicals because of their strong influence in the party. Resolutions passed at this meeting of June 28 expressed belief in war for the Union only, conservatism as to property and slaves, observance of the Constitution, and adherence to the Crittenden resolution of July 22, 1861.[12]

Throughout this discussion of conservatism there was a frequent recurrence of two themes: that radicals were intent on seizing power, and that, as Lincoln belonged among the conservatives, the danger of such a seizure was a real challenge to his leadership. A Cabinet member wrote to the President: "I am apprehensive that you do not realize the truth of your own words ´. . . to the effect that the Radicals are planning a new war to maintain themselves in power." [13] The New York *Herald* in the summer and fall of 1862 harped continually on the contrast between Lincoln's conservatism and radical excess, lauding the President to the skies whenever he took a step to check the radicals. Apropos of his veto message on the confiscation bill the *Herald* declared that the President had "immortalized himself"; he had performed the "crowning act of his career." [14] "The President," declared the *Herald*, "is sustained in this [moderate] policy by Secretary Seward and the conservative members of the Cabinet, by most of the generals and by the great mass of the people." [15] Mentioning radicalism as "the only danger . . . we have now to fear," the *Herald* said: ". . . in President Lincoln we have found the man who has thus far been able to grapple it successfully," then added: "The time has come . . . when the conservative Union men of Congress and the country should rally . . . to his support . . . ." [16]

Lincoln's moderation versus radical fury—such was the recurring theme. David Davis, Illinois friend of Lincoln, destined for the Supreme Court, wrote: "The abolitionists not only intend to ostracise

---

12 *Ibid.*, June 29, 1862, p. 5, c. 2.

13 Rough draft of letter, Montgomery Blair to Lincoln, undated, probably 1862 or 1863, Blair MSS.

14 New York *Herald*, July 18, 1862, editorial, p. 4, c. 4. As it turned out, however, Lincoln did not veto the confiscation bill. See below, pp. 228–229.

15 *Ibid.*, June 16, 1862, editorial, p. 4, c. 3.

16 *Ibid.*, June 17, 1862, editorial, p. 6, c. 3.

every Southern man, but all in the free States, who do not think with them." "[I]f he [Lincoln] preserves his conservatism inflexibly [added Davis] & makes himself the breakwater agt the radicalism that is rampant—then his fame will be undying . . . & his deeds of omission & commission will be buried out of sight." [17]

V

One is struck with the lack of significance (in terms of public service) attaching to parties in Lincoln's day of power. It was in the narrow and uninspired sense that parties functioned—i. e., as organizations or machines owned and operated by politicians for winning elections and seizing or retaining government offices, not as groupings of citizens for civic-minded betterment. It was in the party sense that Republican and Democratic organizations carried on. This suited the politicians; in their view the party sense was dominant. There was little regrouping according to principle; existing party models were perpetuated as instruments for gaining political power. Had parties been made over for the emergency each group would have been composed of like-minded men. Instead of that, each of the major parties was made up of diverse elements, in keeping with the practice of party managers whose object is not to create a clear-cut division for deciding a public issue, but rather to garner the votes of all kinds of citizens, whether they agree or not.

Thus it cannot be said that one of the two major parties stood for a particular thing, and that the other party stood for the opposite thing. A friend of Lincoln said that "there would be as much propriety in saying that Mr. Lincoln was an anti-war Republican as [that] Samuel J. Tilden was an anti-war Democrat." [1] The course of John A. Dix illustrates the flexibility of party principle together with the persistence of party solidarity; he was urged as Democratic candidate for governor, but his name was also presented to the Republican Union convention in New York for the same office.[2] Neither party chose him, however, preferring more regular party men: Seymour for the Demo-

---

[17] David Davis to Joseph Holt, Bloomington, Ill., Mar. 27, 1862, Holt MSS.

[1] Statement of J. D. Caton, quoted in A. C. Flick, *Samuel Jones Tilden: A Study in Political Sagacity*, 138.

[2] *Ibid.*, 135, 136.

crats, Wadsworth for the Republicans.

Divisions as to sentiment were more evident among factions within a given party than between one major party and another. The Democrats had factions which did not break up the party; they had their Vallandighams on the one hand and their Belmonts or Tildens on the other. As to the Republican party there were factions all the way through. In Indiana Schuyler Colfax was a rival of Caleb Smith; Henry S. Lane, "resenting the charge of Abolitionism," [3] was an Indiana Republican of a very different type than George W. Julian. Rivalry was exceedingly keen in Ohio between Wade and Chase; neither faction was friendly toward Lincoln. Touching on one of the rising young Republicans in Ohio, John Hay referred to Whitelaw Reid as "outrageously unfair to the President and . . . servilely devoted to Mr. Chase." [4] In New York it was the Greeley faction versus the Weed-Seward group; in Pennsylvania it was the McClure-Curtin element versus the Cameron clan. Delahay of Kansas had no use for Pomeroy of Kansas. The Howard group in Michigan went down as the Chandler group in Michigan went up. In Massachusetts the outgoing Republican governor, N. P. Banks, spoke a different language in 1861 than the incoming Republican governor, John A. Andrew.[5] In Missouri the Bates following was vastly different from the pro-Frémont element, and so keen was the agitation on the part of Republican antislavery Germans that, as a conservative Republican said at the time, there was "no freedom of discussion" in Missouri; it did no good to refer anything to popular vote.[6] "These . . . Radicals," he wrote, "are of the class that in any well ordered state would either be hanged or sent to the penitentiary." No one can rival them, he added, "unless he is willing, as Aubrey said in the time of Charles I 'to risk a term in Purgatory.' " To enter this rivalry, he asserted, one would have "to burn, rob, lay waste . . . , pillage for gain, and

---

[3] Woodburn, "Party Politics in Indiana," 227–228.

[4] Diary of John Hay, Dec. 13, 1863 (Dennett, *Lincoln . . . in the Diaries . . . of John Hay*, 138). That Reid was the Washington correspondent of the Cincinnati *Gazette* and also of the western Associated Press, made his anti-Lincoln animus the more dangerous.

[5] Pearson, *Andrew*, I, 137. Banks's conservative valedictory was challenged two days later by Andrew's anti-slavery inaugural. Andrew considered Banks's performance "execrable"; Andrew's biographer characterized it as "distinctly outside the proprieties" (*ibid.*).

[6] Thomas T. Gantt to Montgomery Blair, April 25, 1863, Blair MSS.

murder . . . ." [7] All this is merely a suggestion of what some Republicans thought of other Republicans in Missouri. In Illinois there was Trumbull who thwarted Lincoln, and there was Browning who voted against confiscation while Illinois radicals voted for it. In the nation at large it was the moderate element against the Jacobins; in each community it was Republican Smith versus Republican Jones.

This meant that the trend in public questions would be determined, not so much by straightforward and untrammeled expressions of opinion in popular balloting, but by a process of jostling and maneuvering among rival and antagonistic groups. It was not that a party as such had a clear-cut policy reducible to yes-and-no voting at election time; the shaping of affairs was more a reflection of the skill, one might almost say the effrontery, of politicians in playing their vote-getting tricks. Over and above the question as to which party won an election was the important issue as to which element would dominate the party. It is remarkable how seldom this turned out to be the Lincoln element.

Republican factionalism meant that the President might lose, no matter which "party" won an election to Congress. Americans had parties and believed in them, yet their political tradition was a bit fogged as to the party role, if any, that a President ought to play. If parties had statesmanlike, not merely politicianlike, significance, if (for example) Republican success had great public importance, it is hard to see the harm in a Republican President taking the lead in a party appeal. To deny the propriety of such a presidential role is to suppose that a President ought to be "above" parties—in other words, that parties are something other than clean and genuine public instruments. The result was that Republican leadership slipped into coarser hands than Lincoln's; even where his party had success his moderate purposes were often frustrated. An editor of the time wrote thus: ". . . it is our great desire to sustain the President, and we deplore the opportunity he has let go by, to sustain himself. . . .

---

[7] Gantt to Montgomery Blair (again), May 12, 1863, *ibid.* Going from state to state the account of these disagreements among Republicans could be greatly extended. In Maine W. P. Fessenden thought poorly of Hannibal Hamlin (letter to J. Washburn, Jr., Nov. 18, 1864, W. P. Fessenden MSS.). In Illinois David Davis was distrustful of Trumbull and his followers. Considering the Chicago *Tribune* friendly to Trumbull, Davis was of the opinion that this newspaper was doing "infinite harm" to the Lincoln cause. (Davis to Simon Cameron, Oct. 13, 1861, Cameron MSS.).

[We] regard the fact of his being . . . isolated from his party, as the greatest danger of the State. . . . Supported by a great branch of the American people, . . . the President remains an object of power and respect, but Tylerized and alienated, he becomes merely Abraham Lincoln, who cannot be supported . . . merely because he is filled with good intentions. If he lose the support of his own party, he cannot . . . guide the Nation through these stormy times." [8]

In the temper of the time there was hardly an episode not colored by "politics." A move to remake the constitution of Illinois, for example, was used by the Democrats for party advantage. Using a partisan constitutional convention for the purpose, the Democratic managers framed (and nearly established) a new constitution for Illinois which contained provisions excluding Negroes from settling in the state and denying them the vote and the right to hold office. The "anti-administration complexion of the convention" was unmistakable. [9]

On the Republican side one of the party stratagems was the expulsion from the Senate of Jesse Bright of Indiana in February of 1862 on the excessive charge of disloyalty against the United States. Accused of having written a letter to Jefferson Davis recommending a man interested in firearms, the senator replied that the letter had been written in March 1861 when, like many others, he did not expect war, and that it was a mere device for getting rid of a man who had become a nuisance. It was as a party measure that Bright was expelled. The judiciary committee had found the basis for expulsion insufficient. Had the man been guilty of treason he should have been judicially prosecuted as well as expelled. No such prosecution took place. One misses in the political contests of that era those informing elements that are designed to enlighten the people as they exercise their sovereign rights of democratic suffrage. In Michigan, for instance, where political results were manipulated by Chandler, the campaign

---

8 *Wilkes's Spirit of the Times*, Sep. 13, 1862, p. 25, c. 1. This editorial continued in the pro-Hooker and pro-Burnside sense. The above passage is quoted for itself rather than for approval of the tone and policy of this rather racy sheet, owned and edited by George Wilkes, whose political editorials served a purpose not unlike that of later-day columnists.

9 Jasper W. Cross, Jr., *Divided Loyalties in Southern Illinois during the Civil War* (abstract of doctoral thesis, Univ. of Ill., 1942), 7. Dr. Cross points out that the anti-Negro sections received a good majority in the whole popular vote, but "the body of the constitution (on whose passage the addition of the anti-Negro sections was contingent) was rejected."

of 1862 was far from "educative." "Ridicule and abuse were greatly relied upon by both sides." [10]

Contemplating the futility of existing instruments in the political field, David Davis of Illinois wrote in October 1861: "Parties are dead. The Republican party . . . accomplished the object of its being, and it cannot exist as a party organization any more. No matter what may be the result of this contest [the war], when it is over, other organizations must arise . . . ." [11] On the same day J. M. Palmer wrote to Trumbull as one Republican to another: "I think . . . like you that parties are dead in Illinois . . . ." [12]

VI

Radical-conservative jousts of the period were evident on many a weary day in the long congressional session of 1861–62. It was typical of this session that it began with a refusal of the House to reaffirm its former moderate (anti-radical) statement of war aims, and ended with enactment of the radical confiscation act. A glance at these two developments, both unfavorable to Lincoln, will suggest something of the reason why the President welcomed every recess of Congress. It was on December 4, 1861, that a vote came in the House of Representatives on the important resolution of William S. Holman (Democrat of Indiana) to reaffirm the conservative Crittenden resolution that the war was being waged for the Union with "rights of the . . . States unimpaired," and not for conquest or subjugation. In a maneuver which has been characterized as "a direct repudiation of Lincoln's message and . . . concept" [1] the House voted, 71 to 65, to lay the reaffirming resolution on the table. All the votes against reaffirming, except one, were Republican. The rear guard of conservatism in the dominant party, however, was shown by the fact that twenty-six Republicans voted with thirty-nine Democrats in favor of the reaffirmation—i. e., against laying the Holman resolution on the table. [2]

---

[10] Harris, *Zachariah Chandler*, 66.

[11] David Davis to Cameron, Lincoln, Ill., Oct. 13, 1861, Cameron MSS.

[12] J. M. Palmer to Lyman Trumbull, Camp near Tipton, Mo., Oct. 13, 1861, Trumbull MSS.

[1] Williams, *Lincoln and the Radicals*, 60.

[2] *Cong. Globe*, 37 Cong., 2 sess., 15; McPherson, *Rebellion*, 287. As usual in McPherson, Republicans appear in roman type, Democrats in italic.

A similar situation was revealed in the proceedings on the radical bill for the confiscation of Southern property. Sponsored by Senator Trumbull and presented in December 1861, the bill wended its stormy and devious way through House and Senate, coming up repeatedly for spirited and voluminous debate and finally achieving passage on the last day of the session, July 17, 1862. To steer the measure through Congress was something of a trick. Not only was it difficult to get a bill on which a majority would agree; it took parliamentary maneuvering to weed out extraneous matter and to insert features that might avert a presidential veto. After months of complicated debate, during which Trumbull frequently urged that deliberation cease and a decision be reached, the Senate voted (May 6, 1862) to refer the matter to a select committee of nine to shape a measure for further consideration. Meanwhile the House had built up its own bill presented by Eliot of Massachusetts; it was passed on May 26, by a vote of 82 to 68.[3] An analysis of this vote throws considerable light on the political situation. All but two[4] of the voting Democrats opposed the bill. No such solidarity appeared in the majority party, for twenty Republicans or Unionists voted nay. Of the 82 who voted for the bill, 78 were Republicans representing constituencies north of the Ohio. The Senate substituted its own measure, prepared by the committee of nine, for the House bill, and for a time there was deadlock, neither house receding. In the closing week, a conference committee reported a measure which was mainly that of the lower house. Finally the bill as thus shaped drew a vote of 82 to 42,[5] the notable shrinking in the negative vote probably signifying that moderate Republicans had ceased to struggle. In the Senate the bill drew 27 yeas and 12 nays.[6] All but three of the affirmative votes were Republican. In both houses the proceedings showed that confiscation was a Republican measure, but with a goodly number of Republicans dissenting.

Declarations for vindictive seizure of property were blunt and crude. "Rebels" had no constitutional rights, so the argument ran; "if their whole country must be . . . made a desert . . . to save this

---

[3] *Cong. Globe*, 37 Cong., 2 sess., 2361.

[4] The two Democrats who voted for the confiscation bill were William G. Brown, from the unionist portion of Virginia, and John W. Noell, Union Democrat of Missouri. They were highly exceptional; most border men were solidly against the bill.

[5] *Cong. Globe*, 37 Cong., 2 sess., 3267.   [6] *Ibid.*, 3276.

POLITICS AS USUAL 227

union . . . , so let it be." [7] Wholesale confiscations had taken place in England and by American states in the Revolution; Northern confiscation was a necessary retaliation against Confederate sequestration; Southerners in rebellion should pay the cost of the war; penalties should be imposed upon traitors, and so on. Opposite arguments were presented by Browning, Henderson, Collamer, and others. Conciliation toward erring brothers, they said, was better than stripping millions of their property; partisanship should be sunk "in one universal . . . service by every Union man to the cause of the country." [8] The measure, said its opponents, was in effect a bill of attainder; it violated the fifth amendment as well as the constitutional prohibition against forfeiture beyond the offender's life; lawmakers should not take counsel of their resentments; punitive measures would only aggravate a confusion already bad enough; the path of confiscation was not the road to peace. Conservatives in the confiscation debate talked in the Lincolnian sense; radicals, on the other hand, assaulted the President. An example was the outburst of Representative John Hickman of Pennsylvania, who denounced the "refusal on the part of the President . . . to discharge . . . a plain duty . . . ." Referring to the President's tendency to "shirk," he spoke of Congress being forced into discord and disagreement because of the Chief's "lack of . . . traits of character necessary to the discharge of grave responsibilities." [9]

Emerging from the legislative hopper the confiscation bill decreed judicial forfeiture of all the property of specified classes of "rebels." Several of its clauses related to slaves and have been considered in another connection.[10] The inclusion of antislavery provisions drew more votes than straight confiscation would have done; many, in fact, regarded it as an antislavery bill. It was known that Lincoln opposed confiscation, as had McClellan, also that men of Lincoln's party in Congress had deliberately ridden roughshod over his expressed wishes. It was further known that the President found Congress an embarrass-

---

[7] Though this statement was made by Thaddeus Stevens in support of the confiscation bill of 1861, it expressed his view also as to the much stronger measure of 1862. *Ibid.*, 37 Cong., 1 sess., 414–415.

[8] Statement of Garret Davis of Kentucky, a Democrat proud of his loyalty. *Ibid.*, 37 Cong., 2 sess., 1757.

[9] *Cong. Globe*, 37 Cong., 2 sess., 1801 (April 23, 1862).

[10] See above, p. 132.

ment and did not desire the prolongation of its session.[11] The bill had supposedly been made more palatable to the presidential mind by unnecessarily declaring that the pardoning power applied to confiscation and by including an appropriation for colonization of Negroes, which Lincoln favored. Nevertheless the President's veto was considered likely and radicals were wondering whether they could muster two-thirds to override it.

With courage in opposing legislators of his own party and with lawyerlike comprehension of constitutional questions, Lincoln did prepare a veto message expressing his disapproval of the bill. It is one of his ablest state papers. Some sections he could approve, since loyal men, he understood, were not touched, civil trials were provided, and "especially" since offenders were "within the . . . pardoning power." As to the slave provisions he raised no objections, though he noted a defect as to determining "whether a particular . . . slave does or does not fall within the classes defined." As was natural with an executive, the President's mind went forward to the problem of enforcement, on which he significantly remarked that there ought to be a "power of remission" and that the "severest justice may not always be the best policy." What the President chiefly objected to was that the bill declared "forfeiture extending beyond the lives of the guilty parties"; this, he thought, violated a plain clause of the Constitution. Also, as in admiralty cases, the bill permitted forfeiture by proceedings *in rem* (against the property) "without a conviction of the supposed criminal, or a personal hearing given him in any proceeding." [12]

Had Lincoln so far challenged the radicals as to veto their pet measure? Not quite. In the knowledge that the veto message was in preparation, an "explanatory joint resolution" was rushed through both houses which declared that the bill should not be construed to apply to acts prior to its passage, nor "to work a forfeiture of the real estate of the offender beyond his natural life." Though this did not touch the President's objection concerning the lack of a personal hearing in court, he approved the bill and joint resolution as substantially one. Curiously, however, and perhaps irregularly, he did something further; though signing the bill, he sent to Congress the

----

[11] New York *Herald*, July 13, 1862, p. 4, c. 6.
[12] *Works*, VII, 280 ff. (July 17, 1862).

executive veto message to become part of the record. It was read in both houses "amid the sneers and laughter of the abolitionists." [13]

VII

Lincoln had his technique in meeting the radical challenge, which was in all conscience a serious threat to his leadership. He avoided an open break or explosion, but did what he could to prevent the vindictives from seizing the reins. When it was evident that Cameron had been converted to radicalism for political reasons, Lincoln removed him, yet kept him on the reservation, so to speak, by an appointment to Russia. He overruled Hunter's emancipating order, but combined the incident with a warning to those who were obstructing the President's moderate solution of the slavery problem. In answering Greeley he suggested that preservation of the Union was paramount to abolitionism. He exposed and partly corrected the injustice of the confiscation bill; then he signed it, but submitted a veto message as a check to the radicals. He seized an interval when Congress was not in session to issue his emancipation proclamation, stealing the radicals' own thunder at a point where they could not but agree with him. He showed enough antislavery zeal to work along with Sumner and Chase, while holding the Negro sufficiently in the background to mollify Seward. At times he yielded to radicals on military matters, though his regret in doing so sometimes reached the point of acute pain.[1] In recalling McClellan after Pope's defeat, however, he stood up to the radicals, and the general justified his confidence at Antietam. Visiting committees unexpectedly found themselves taking Lincoln's cue. He would politely listen to them, thank them for their advice, tell them an amusing anecdote to ease the termination of the interview, bow them out, and then follow his own judgment.

When he had a conference of indignant governors on his hands in 1862, he turned an embarrassing situation entirely to his own advantage. Under the lead of Governor Curtin of Pennsylvania such a conference had been called to meet at Altoona in September 1862.

---

[13] New York *Herald*, July 18, 1862, p. 1, c. 1.

[1] In withdrawing Blenker's division from McClellan's force and sending it to Frémont, Lincoln wrote to McClellan: ". . . I did so with great pain, understanding that you would wish it otherwise. If you could know the full pressure of the case, . . . [etc.]" *Works*, VII, 138 (March 21, 1862).

In the sequel the evidence as to the original purpose of the gathering was obscured and conflicting statements have been made; this was partly because of a change of outlook between the calling and the holding of the conference, and partly because some of the participants had a purpose which they did not wish publicly to avow. It was just after Pope's defeat, when the Union cause looked very dark, that the call was issued; when the conference was held (September 24) the situation had been radically changed by Antietam and the emancipation proclamation.

The conference as planned had a double basis: desire for action against slavery, and distrust of the President because of military defeat. It was felt that the President should become both more radical and more efficient. This was illogical, since radicalism produced military inefficiency, but consistency was no part of the movement. Whatever the inner purpose of the conclave, the talk that floated about at the time associated it with some kind of a drive against the President, at least a move to admonish him or tell him his duty, at most an effort to supplant him. "The governors may declare," wrote Count Gurowski, "that the country is in danger, . . . that if he Lincoln sees not the . . . danger, the people & the governors see it, . . . that it is the duty of the governors to save the country's cause in spite of the faults & the predilections of the president . . . ." [2] It was suggested that the purpose of the state executives was "to dictate a policy for the president"; an adviser of Governor Yates thought that "such a course . . . would be fatal" as it would give "unnatural authority" to inferiors.[3] The conferring governors were understood to be anti-McClellan; it was cynically stated that their hope was "to extort from the President, by fair means or foul, . . . submission to their dictation as to . . . generals," and that they were working "to have McClellan removed and Fremont installed in his place." [4] To the Washington correspondent of the *Herald* it seemed that "a vast conspiracy has been set on foot by the radicals . . . to depose the present administration, and place Frémont at the head of a provisional gov-

---

[2] Gurowski to Governor Andrew, Aug. 2, 1862, Andrew MSS. (This may have been associated with an earlier gubernatorial combination to promote a new call for troops, but it also fits the Altoona incident.)

[3] L. U. Reavis to Governor Richard Yates, Beardstown, Ill., Sep. 19, 1862, MS., Chicago Hist. Soc.

[4] New York *Herald*, Sep. 27, 1862 (editorial), p. 4, c. 4.

ernment; in other words, to make him military dictator." It was reported on the authority of prominent politicians that one of the features of the conspiracy was the proposed meeting of Northern governors whose purpose was "to request President Lincoln to resign, to enable them to carry out their scheme." [5]

What the state executives would have done if events had not stolen their thunder is a question. What is certain is that two days after the conference, when some of the governors met Lincoln personally at Washington (September 26), the President held the trumps. By that time he had clipped the gubernatorial wings by publicly associating himself with their effort, giving it his own emphasis, and the governors found themselves with nothing to do but to endorse the President's policy, which they did in a laudatory public statement.[6] Lincoln smilingly thanked the visiting magistrates for their support and indicated that no fact had so thoroughly confirmed to him the justice of the emancipation proclamation as the approval of the executives of the loyal states. On some aspects he would not answer them specifically at the time, he said, but he would give these matters his most favorable consideration, carrying them out "so far as possible."

After the formal proceedings there followed an informal interview of some length, but the historian can give no detailed report of it. According to the *Tribune* a "phonographic [stenographic] reporter" belonging to that paper appeared in the anteroom at the White House while the Cabinet was in session upstairs, the ante-room being alive with "the Governors in waiting." When the Cabinet departed, the reporter requested Lincoln's permission to attend the conference; the request was granted by the President and he entered with the rest. Curtin of Pennsylvania, however, protested at the presence of the news writer and stated that according to his understanding the interview was not public, whereupon the *Tribune* man mentioned Lincoln's permission and Lincoln himself added (as reported) that "he was . . . willing to have the results of the interview go . . . to the people if the Governors did not object." Yates and others, however, rejoined "that the interview was . . . strictly confidential," and the reporter retired.[7] This incident suggests that the governors meant to have it out with Lincoln on matters of disagreement or complaint,

[5] *Ibid.*, Sep. 17, 1862, p. 4, c. 5.   [6] *Annual Cyclopaedia*, 1862, 793–794.
[7] New York *Tribune*, Sep. 29, 1862, p. 3, cc. 1–2.

but that the President was entirely confident of his ability to command the situation, and even to use the occasion for his own purpose. According to one account the governors found the President doing the talking, then ushering them out before their complaints had been presented.[8] The public statements that issued from the White House interview were favorable to the President; it was in that sense that the Altoona incident took its place in history.

VIII

In the fall of 1862 the American electorate performed the solemn duty of choosing representatives in Congress to hold until 1865. Orators, agitators, and editors belabored the people with catchwords and arguments. Military deadlock, new calls for troops, compulsory military service (in a mild form), emancipation, arbitrary arrests, internal blockade, negrophilism, abolitionism—such elements on the Republican side were denounced by the Democrats who advocated the Union, the Constitution, suppression of corruption, respect for civil rights, readiness to deal with Southern unionists, and sane reconstruction. People were asked whether they wanted their communities Africanized and whether the Petition of Right and Magna Charta were forgotten. Editors spoke out and were arrested; then their friends raised the issue of freedom of the press. Examples were Dennis Mahoney of Iowa and Edson B. Olds of Ohio; especially in Ohio, where Olds was not the only victim, the effect on popular feeling was acutely felt.

When Republicans met in secret congressional caucus on July 12, 1862, they became involved in a protracted discussion that revealed differences within the ranks on current issues. In a meeting that lasted till nearly midnight they rejected an address that had been carefully prepared by a committee and contented themselves with a colorless resolution which in resounding rhetoric asked all loyal men to stand by the Union and to support the prosecution of the war. It was remarked by the *Herald* that points of Republican policy were not particularized in any way; radicals had been "shrieking against the President, and demanding some more specific annunciation of policy"; there had evidently been "trouble in their

---

8 Williams, *Lincoln and the Radicals*, 185–186.

camp," with "irreconcilable divisions" throughout the party; as a result they had found it "easier to demand a policy than to adopt one." [1]

Naturally the problem of supporting the administration was an issue in the congressional campaign, and on that issue the Republicans suffered, not an overthrow, but a setback of such seriousness that "Mr. Lincoln was . . . very uneasy." [2] The former Congress may be usefully compared with the new one in connection with the election for speaker. In the case of the old Congress, the Thirty-Seventh, 111 out of 159 votes had been cast for Republican candidates for Speaker (71 for Galusha A. Grow and 40 for Frank P. Blair, Jr.) In the Thirty-Eighth Congress Schuyler Colfax received a vote for speaker which James G. Blaine mentioned as "the distinctive Republican strength," but it amounted to only 101 out of a total of 182.[3] From nearly 70 per cent of the speakership vote, the Republicans thus slipped to 55 per cent. Casting up party totals of membership in the lower house one finds the following result: In the Thirty-Seventh Congress there were 106 Republicans, 42 Democrats, and 26 Unionists, nearly all the "Unionists" being from the border states; in the Thirty-Eighth Congress there were 102 Republicans and Unionists, 9 border-state men, and 75 Democrats. The Senate did not change much. The old Senate had 35 Republicans and Unionists out of a total of 48 (subtracting vacancies and omitting seceded states); the new one had 36 Republicans and Unconditional Unionists out of a total of 50.[4]

Five important states which had given their full electoral vote to Lincoln in 1860 now chose Democratic majorities for Congress: New York, Pennsylvania, Ohio, Indiana, and Illinois. In Indiana Lincoln "received the equivalent of a vote of want of confidence." [5] New Jersey, which had given Lincoln four of its seven electoral votes in 1860, went Democratic; Wisconsin, a Lincoln state in 1860, chose an evenly divided delegation. Prominent Republicans of the preceding Congress did not return; among these were Roscoe Conkling and

---

1 New York *Herald*, July 13, 1862, p. 4, c. 6.

2 A. G. Riddle, *Recollections of War Times*, 249.

3 Blaine, *Twenty Years of Congress*, I, 324, 497.

4 New York *Tribune Almanac*, 1862, pp. 17–18; 1864, p. 24.

5 W. A. Harbison, "Lincoln and Indiana Republicans, 1861–1862," *Ind. Mag. of Hist.*, XXXIII, 301. A Republican majority of 10,000 in 1860 in Indiana was "replaced by a Democratic majority of approximately the same size" (*ibid.*).

E. G. Spaulding of New York, John A. Bingham of Ohio, and the Republican speaker, Galusha A. Grow of Pennsylvania. It was a serious "political re-action," wrote James G. Blaine; there were "radical changes," and "the narrow escape of the Administration from total defeat" was evident when the roll was called.[6]

One of the features of the congressional election was the failure of Lincoln's own state to sustain him, for there was no doubt that the President was on trial in the balloting for Congress. Of the fourteen congressmen returned from Illinois, five were Republicans and nine Democrats. What made the defeat particularly poignant for the President was that in his home district his old friend and first law partner, John Todd Stuart, being the Democratic nominee, was chosen to Congress in opposition to another friend, Leonard Swett. As a Whig, Stuart had been a party associate of Lincoln in the old days; now he had carried on an active campaign against his former partner's presidential policies, while Swett, carrying the Republican banner, had announced himself as champion of the President. Swett's defeat showed that, with Lincoln's administration as the unmistakable issue, the President's home district gave a verdict of thumbs down.[7]

On the western map the party division showed Lincoln's opponents in command in southern and central Illinois, southern Indiana, some of northern Indiana, and most of Ohio. H. C. Hubbart, in a close analysis, treats the election under the title "The Free West Repudiates Abraham Lincoln, 1862."[8] Though in Ohio Vallandigham went down in this election, a southern Illinois equivalent in the person of W. J. Allen was chosen to represent "Egypt." Of Southern antecedents, this one-time partner of John A. Logan was a vigorous critic of Lincoln's policies; he opposed the emancipation proclamation, arbitrary arrests, use of Negro troops, and conscription. Men of Southern Illinois, he said, were fighting to bring the South back into the Union, not to free the Negroes.[9] The Republican governors of Illinois and Indiana found themselves greatly embarrassed by the election of

---

[6] Blaine, *Twenty Years of Congress*, I, 498.

[7] Harry E. Pratt, "The Repudiation of Lincoln's War Policy in 1862 . . . ," *Journal*, Ill. State Hist. Soc., XXIV, 129–140.

[8] Hubbart, *Older Middle West*, chap. xi.

[9] These matters, with many other divisive factors in Illinois, are ably treated in Jasper W. Cross, Jr., "Divided Loyalties in Southern Illinois during the Civil War" (ms. doctoral dissertation, Univ. of Ill., 1942).

Democratic legislatures in 1862; deadlock resulted in each case between the executive and the lawmaking branch. Yates solved it by
proroguing his legislature, Morton by a kind of budgetary miracle
which enabled him to finance the state's war effort (with support from
Washington and from friendly banks) without a regular appropriation. When William A. Richardson, elect of the "copperhead" legislature of Illinois, succeeded Orville Browning in the Senate of the
United States in 1863, the President had to face a bitter opponent in
the place of a former part-time supporter.

Agreeing with the *Herald* that the Republican party was "defeated"
because it had changed the war into an abolition crusade,[10] Browning
wrote in his diary: "Badly beaten by the Democrats. Just what was to
be expected from the insane ravings of the Chicago Tribune, Quincy
Whig, [etc.] . . . ." Considering that Browning had been a prominent Republican, his attitude is especially significant. Convinced
that Lincoln had gone over to the radicals, and displeased with
emancipation, arrests, and confiscations, he went about "denouncing
leading Republicans as traitors and enemies to the country," and
entirely omitted to endorse the President's policy in a public speech
on the eve of the election.[11]

Browning was virtually a man without a party. Not only had he
lost confidence in Lincoln; he was also out of tune with anti-Lincoln
trends which were growing in intensity. His disappointment with
Lincoln, whom he considered "fatally bent upon his course," [12] was
that he had not successfully resisted these trends. From late 1862 to
his death in 1881 he was to withhold support from Republican candidates.[13] Browning's case was that of a disillusioned friend of the Lincoln
administration giving way to a bitter opponent. Facing home with a
sense of utter frustration, he wrote: ". . . I feel that I can do no
good here— The counsels of myself and those who sympathize with
me are no longer heeded. I am despondent, and have but little hope
left for the Republic." [14]

It was a common Republican assertion that absence of soldiers from
the polls determined the result; this implied that Democrats were at

---

10 Nov. 8, 1862, editorial, p. 4, c. 3.
11 Quincy (Ill.) *Whig*, Nov. 10, 1862, quoted in Browning, *Diary*, I, 582 n.
12 Browning, *Diary*, I, 607 (Dec. 31, 1862).   13 *Ibid.*, II, xxi.
14 *Ibid.*, I, 621 (Jan. 30, 1863).

home voting while Republicans were at the front.[15] In general, state laws of the time did not give soldiers the privilege of absent voting,[16] and it was assumed that the lack of their votes explained Democratic success, especially in such states as Ohio, Indiana, and Illinois. Various writers have shown the assumption to be unfounded. George H. Porter writes that "the facts . . . do not support this charge"; J. F. Rhodes finds that this factor had "little to do with the result."[17] There is no historical basis for the partisan assertion that Democrats lagged behind Republicans in military service for the Union. Records do not exist to show the party affiliations of individual volunteers, but one can take election figures by counties in Illinois and compare them with county statistics in the state adjutant-general's reports giving the number of volunteers and also the number properly liable to military service. Calculations based on such records show that the ratio of volunteers to the total of men subject to military duty was in fact higher in Democratic than in Republican counties.[18] Though the soldier-vote argument brought Republicans the comfort of wishful thinking, there were enough other factors to determine the result— imprisonments, factional disputes within the Republican party, corruption, the draft, taxes, and dissatisfaction with radicalism. Most potent of all was "failure of the army to accomplish decisive results." [19]

The President had not actively participated in the drive for congressional votes. Where it was a contest between Republicans seeking nomination, he was especially careful to avoid interference. Yet his name and his policies could not be dissociated from the campaign; indeed it is characteristic of congressional contests in the United States that they have as much to do with executive as with lawmaking

---

[15] Blaine, *Twenty Years of Congress*, I, 443.

[16] In Iowa, Wisconsin, and Pennsylvania voting in the field by the soldiers was permitted in 1862, soldier preferences being heavily weighted on the Republican side. In Illinois, soldiers were not allowed to vote in the general election of 1862, but on the proposed new state constitution their votes were taken by commissioners who, under the provisions of the proposed constitution, visited camps, barracks, hospitals, etc., for that purpose. The soldier vote was unfavorable to the constitution by 10,151 to 1,687, this being deemed a Republican victory. For Illinois, information has been obtained from Margaret C. Norton, Archivist, Illinois State Library; see also Benton, *Voting in the Field*, 51, 66, 203, 253.

[17] George H. Porter, *Ohio Politics During the Civil War Period*, 109; J. F. Rhodes, *Hist. of the U. S.*, IV, 166.

[18] In this connection the author has used elaborate notes and calculations prepared by one of his students, Mr. A. R. Hoeflin of Peoria, Illinois.

[19] Harbison, "Lincoln and Indiana Republicans," 302.

matters. The voting in 1862 was as much for or against Lincoln's administration as it was a judgment upon congressmen for their purely legislative records. Had the election gone against the President's party in an absolute, instead of a relative, sense, the further course of his administration would have been seriously hampered. In the actual sequel the Democrats took a bolder tone in assailing some of the more vulnerable measures of the government, but the Republicans retained control of the House and Senate, and with the crude force of Stevens's domination, which tended to scare any dissenting Republican out of his skin,[20] they were able to pass their measures. More often than not, these were non-Lincoln or anti-Lincoln measures.

To one of its Ohio members who left a frank record, service in the wartime Congress was "irksome" and distasteful. Noting with relief that he had at least escaped personal injury, he considered congressional service a kind of dissipation. A retiring congressman, he said, loathes the word "Honorable" affixed to his name, this being his only emolument, "save personal and political animosities and alienated friends." The Capitol, "its passage-ways and odors," had grown "offensive." This Republican had found Cox, Pendleton, and Vallandigham among his "assured friends." "Indeed," he added, "I have always found disinterested friends among the Democrats, and have observed among politicians that the warmest personal ties are usually across party lines." [21]

---

[20] Referring to Stevens's "iron will and relentless mastery," A. K. McClure tells how he received a protest from a Republican congressman against a particular measure, then ordered the member to vote for it or be branded as a coward. The quaking legislator complied. Had he refused obedience, the "Commoner" would have ruined him. *Abraham Lincoln and Men of War-Times,* 280–281.

[21] A. G. Riddle, *Recollections of War Times,* 225–227.

CHAPTER XXV

GENERALS, SECRETARIES, AND "SOME SENATORS"

AT the turn of the year 1862–1863 Lincoln was approaching the mid-point of his administration. As President in a democracy he occupied an office of great power, but it was a power that had to be exercised with deference. He could govern, but only if his governing voice was not too bluntly audible. There were those who wanted to take the power of government out of his hands. Men of such intent were not confined to the opposite party whose increased strength had just been demonstrated at the polls; in his own party were men of extreme views who were determined to seize dominant influence out of all proportion to the number of their popular supporters. Moderates were making so little fuss that their influence was in danger of being dissipated; radicals were intensifying the tempo of their drive. News from the military fronts was to tell of disaster and disappointment before it took a turn for the better. Disaster could be politically exploited, and if a steady hand were not at the helm, confusion and worse disaster might be the direct result. There were forces of morale which made it possible that defeat might produce a tightening of the belt and a courage for renewed effort, but these forces had to be brought into play; they had to have a focus. Without that focus, defeat could mean defeatism and divided counsel. To produce a concentration which could overcome the evident tendencies toward dissipation, to prevent disruptive elements from playing havoc with the machinery of government and with the military management, and to do it with the tact of a moderator instead of the scowl of a dictator, was Lincoln's task.

I

The poorly based hope of victory which came with Burnside's displacement of McClellan was dashed to pieces on the line of the Rappahannock in mid-December 1862. Under conditions that were due precisely to poor generalship the army which had repelled Lee at Antietam obeyed the death order of its commander in a bravely hopeless encounter at Fredericksburg on December 13. Courage the men had in abundance, but every factor of battle planning, of terrain and position, was unfavorable to Union triumph. Massed with artillery support on Mayre's Heights behind the city of Fredericksburg or crowded within the protection of the "sunken road" just ahead, Lee's troops stood unshaken as repeated charges were launched against them, only to be broken in sickening slaughter. Having "persisted in crossing the river after all hope of a surprise had faded away," and having been restrained by supporting generals from repetition of suicidal assaults, Burnside could only recross to the north side of the river, where the best hope for the army under its "dazed . . . and grief-stricken" commander was a period of inaction.[1]

In reporting the "truthful and terrible panorama of that bloody day" a New Hampshire colonel wrote of "brave legions . . . struggling against the terrible combination of the enemy's artillery and infantry, whose unremitting fire shook the earth," of crowded Union hospitals that had "no note of triumph," of the enemy's "unyielding resistance," of "direct and enfilading batteries," of "death-dealing artillery," of "one startling crash, . . . one simultaneous sheet of fire and flame." "The arrangement of the enemy's guns," wrote this officer, "was such that they could pour their concentrated and incessant fire upon any point occupied by our assailing troops . . . ."[2] "It was impossible the result should be otherwise," wrote an observing journalist, "as the converging fire of the enemy was plainly crushing. . . . [T]heir bellowing batteries . . . and the swarm of sharpshooters, secure . . . behind a stone wall, and in a sunken road, like that Victor Hugo finds on the field of Waterloo, were too much for

---

[1] *Battles and Leaders of the Civil War*, III, 133, 138.

[2] Moore, *Rebellion Record* (Docs.), VI, 84–85. Realistic and rhetorically vivid accounts of the battle by a number of minor officers appear in this volume, pp. 80 ff.

the naked valor of our infantry." [3]

This maddening defeat was the second major disaster on the Virginia front in 1862. Both unhappy events had resulted from factors emanating from Washington, the most alarming of which was radical interference. For twenty months the war had been raging. Not only was it beginning to seem interminable; its toll of dead and mutilated men and of treasure seemed a useless sacrifice under existing leadership. People in the North were still loyal, but their loyalty to functionaries at Washington was being sorely tried. Credit slumped; gold took a leap; government censorship, never effective, was tightened; indignation meetings were planned; radicals "searched frantically for some device which would lift from their party the onus of Fredericksburg." [4]

McClellan's reinstatement was urged; [5] scapegoats were demanded; European repercussions were feared; citizens generally were losing confidence in those who guided and commanded. Civil morale was one with military elan and force. If the existing army went down, some doubted whether it would be replaced.[6] The army is melting away, it was said; "we cannot get another, except by using the blacks." [7] The people were not yet conditioned for a long and desperate war. While they were thinking of past and present contributions and puzzled to know why they were not of greater avail, the government was demanding additional sacrifices. Suppose those further burdens and losses were endured, what assurance was there that they would not again be wasted?

It was upon Lincoln that much of the popular wrath descended. Ironically the most wrathful were the radicals, who did not scruple to abuse Lincoln for unhappy results which they themselves had produced. "May the Lord hold to rigid account the fool that is set over us," wrote an abolitionist who had begun to think that Higginson's black troops were the country's "only real hope." He continued: "What suicide the Administration is guilty of! What a weak pattern of

---

[3] *Ibid.*, VI, 100.   [4] Williams, *Lincoln and the Radicals*, 201–202.

[5] Bates, *Diary*, 270.

[6] ". . . I find that the South is more united . . . than we . . . . What then. Shall we stop fighting. . . . We must go on . . . . But the armies now in the field must do the work. . . . [T]his army destroyed, cannot be replaced—at least [it] wont be." Willard Warner to S. P. Chase, Columbus, Ohio, Nov. 27, 1862, Chase MSS., Lib. of Cong.

[7] Grant Goodrich to Trumbull, Chicago, Jan. 31, 1862, Trumbull MSS.

Old Pharaoh! What a goose!" [8] "My opinion of Mr. Lincoln," wrote a friend of Sumner, "is that nothing can be done with him . . . . He would damp the ardor of the bravest . . . & neutralize the efforts of the ablest . . . . He is wrong-headed, . . . the petty politician not the statesman, & . . . ill-deserving the *sobriquet* of Honest. I am out of all patience with him." [9] "I am losing confidence in the *executive* capacity of Mr. Lincoln's administration," wrote a perplexed New Englander. "I see plainly that doubt and discouragement are spreading among the people . . . ." This downcast citizen feared a demand for termination of the war with the Union objective unattained, not because of incapacity or unwillingness of the people to fight and crush the enemy, but because of "a fixed belief that the managers . . . at Washington are incompetent . . . ." [10]

II

Dissatisfaction now focused on the question of secretarial change. If only the President could have a reorganized ministry, perhaps something could be done. "Reorganization" of the cabinet was the talk; this being interpreted meant getting rid of Seward. A Pennsylvanian who foregathered with Stevens, Pomeroy, and other radicals accused Seward of doubling the proportions of the rebellion, promoting party opposition to the administration, inviting "insult" from abroad, and being bullied by Palmerston and Russell. Deploring Seward's ascendancy to the cabinet, he denounced the nation's secretary of state as "a thorough, ingrained, moral and physical coward." [1] This was not one man's opinion. It was the Jacobin theme.

Thus again were anti-Lincoln radicals using a time of national disaster to promote factional attacks, and that too directly after an election in which the Republican appeal had been made in "Union" or conservative terms, and in which distrust of Jacobin influence had produced Democratic popular gains. If Seward were dropped, radicals felt that Montgomery Blair and possibly Bates should go down with

8 James Sloan Gibbons to W. L. Garrison, N. Y., Dec. 3, 1862, MS., Boston Pub. Lib. This was written before Fredericksburg; after that defeat the feeling was yet more intense.

9 O. A. Brownson to Charles Sumner, Dec. 26, 1862, Sumner MSS.

10 John D. Baldwin to Sumner, *Daily Spy* Office, Worcester, Mass., Dec. 30, 1862, *ibid.*

1 Amasa McCoy to Joseph Holt, Harrisburg, Pa., Dec. 14, 1862, Holt MSS. McCoy was circulating a petition, asking a change of cabinet.

him. Smith, as revealed by Welles, was tired of the cabinet and ready to serve his country in the pleasanter life-office of judge. [2] Various men were mentioned as suitable cabinet members. On the conservative side there were suggestions of Thomas Ewing of Ohio, who had served in the cabinets of Harrison, Taylor, and Fillmore; of Banks, who had been associated with the Democratic, American, and Republican parties; or of James Guthrie of Kentucky, who had been in the Pierce cabinet. Preston King of New York was also suggested.[3] It was from the radicals, however, that suggestions flowed most freely: their favorites were such men as Sumner, Holt, Fessenden (in Seward's place), Grow (to be moved from the speakership), Henry Winter Davis, and B. F. Butler. Architects of military ruin were demanding that theirs be the controlling voice. Demands for cabinet reorganization came with greatest emphasis from those who had vociferously demanded the overthrow of McClellan, whose demotion on two occasions had been followed by two major defeats.

While rumors spread and people wondered what was afoot, the Republican senators assumed a kind of informal cabinet-making function. On December 16 and 17 they held lengthy caucus deliberations, debating, complaining, almost adopting a resolution denouncing Seward by name, and finally coming through with a decision to call upon the President for a "re-organization" of the cabinet. In these senatorial wranglings the air was thick with denunciations of Lincoln and Seward. Wilkinson of Minnesota assailed the President and his secretary of state; Grimes spoke in the same sense; Fessenden alluded to the "back stairs & malign influence which controlled the President"; Wade outdid all of them, declaring that the Senate should go in a body and demand Seward's dismissal. What Wade wanted was a Lieutenant General "with absolute and despotic powers." He would never be satisfied "until there was a Republican at the head of our armies." [4] "Many speeches were made," wrote Browning, some of

---

[2] Welles, *Diary*, I, 193.   [3] Browning, *Diary*, I, 601, 603.

[4] *Ibid.*, I, 597. The military judgment of Wade, so coarse in his opposition to Lincoln and so dominant in the partisan proceedings of the congressional committee on the conduct of the war, may be measured by the generals he sought to destroy and by those he favored. Besides McClellan, he vigorously opposed Grant, Meade, and Sherman; he favored Frémont, Pope, Burnside, Hooker, and Butler. See T. Harry Williams, *Lincoln and the Radicals* (index under Wade). On the question of Frémont he "scathingly assailed" Lincoln, declaring that only a man sprung from "poor white trash" (by which he meant the President) could have acted as he did. *Ibid.*, 40–41, 108.

them "denouncing the President and expressing a willingness to vote for a resolution asking him to resign." [5]

Hearing of these doings, Seward and his son Frederick, assistant secretary of state, presented their resignations to Lincoln and packed their private papers for departure from Washington.[6] This raised the question of other resignations. Some thought the whole cabinet should resign.[7] Stanton became alarmed. Fearing that Seward's resignation might be a signal for a general reorganization in which he might be left out, he tried to induce Seward to return, several "weak-kneed Senators" (in the words of the Cincinnati *Gazette*) working to the same end.[8] This only added to the complication; Stanton's conduct proved one of the difficulties of the whole movement.

In great distress the President questioned his friend Browning about the caucus. What did these men want? he asked. Browning could only reply that they were "exceedingly violent towards the administration." The Browning diary continues: "Said he [Lincoln] 'They wish to get rid of me, and I am sometimes half disposed to gratify them.' I replied Some of them do wish to get rid of you, but the fortunes of the Country are bound up with your fortunes, . . . stand firmly at your post . . . . Said he 'We are now on the brink of destruction. . . . I can hardly see a ray of hope.' . . . He then added 'the Committee [of Republican senators] is to be up to see me at 7 O'clock. Since I heard last night of the proceedings of the caucus I have been more distressed than by any event of my life.' " [9]

Bates and others attested Lincoln's acute distress.[10] An old friend who saw the President described him as "perplexed to death nearly," adding: "It certainly is enough to make a man crazy." [11] So "haggard and care-worn" did the President appear to another friend that he was reluctant to spread the story.[12]

---

[5] Browning, *Diary*, I, 598–599.

[6] The resignations were personally presented to the President by Senator Preston King of New York on the night of the 17th. Bates, *Diary*, 269; Cincinnati *Daily Gazette*, Dec. 22, 1862, p. 1.

[7] Such was the view of Reverdy Johnson, who said "we would go [to] the Devil unless a new cabinet was formed." Browning, *Diary*, I, 601.

[8] Cincinnati *Gazette*, Dec. 22, 1862, p. 1.   [9] Browning, *Diary*, I, 600–601.

[10] Bates, *Diary*, 269.

[11] S. Noble to E. B. Washburne, Washington, Dec. 25, 1862, Washburne MSS.

[12] "[Joshua F.] Speed tells me that the President looked haggard and care-worn beyond what he expected . . . . I have mentioned it to no one except to you and one other personal friend. I wish he could show a . . . cheerful look, and let the world

Lincoln's upright and puritanical secretary of the treasury bore a peculiar relation to the whole embarrassing movement. This is not to say that Chase pulled all the strings himself, nor that one should believe in full the bald statement of Tom Ewing in conversation with Browning that "Chase was at the bottom of all the mischief, and was setting the radicals on to assail Seward." [13] That Chase was the main instigator of an underhand intrigue seems hardly likely. It was rather that the radicals themselves wanted to exalt Chase, that a cabinet of the "ultra" type was in contemplation, and that Chase had given unfavorable accounts of the President and his cabinet in conversation with disaffected senators. While gunning for Seward, these men intended that Chase should come through with increased influence. This was the point and purpose of the reorganization. Chase was the type of man who, with entire sincerity, could have lent support to the senatorial onslaught.

The distrust of Seward on the part of radicals and antislavery men was deep and profound. Sensing that he had more influence over the President than any other secretary, they knew that this influence was a moderate factor at the time when they wanted extreme measures. They even found occasion to complain bitterly of some of the secretary's diplomatic despatches. A great objection was raised, for example, to a published note from Seward to Charles Francis Adams (July 5, 1862) criticizing vehement opponents of slavery for helping to precipitate servile war by demanding universal emancipation as a way of saving the Union. The comment may have been unfortunate and it would presumably not have been made, much less published, if submitted to Lincoln. Nevertheless it was but an expression of opinion to Adams and it would probably have done no harm except for the antislavery dither made over it.[14]

III

Lincoln was presented with no mere tempest in a teapot. He was face to face with a challenge to his position and leadership, but this

---

see that disaster cannot make him quail. There are many . . . expressing doubts of his ability and I grieve over the feeling that such an idea . . . should take possession of the Union men." T. S. Bell to Joseph Holt, Dec. 22, 1862, Holt MSS.

[13] Browning, *Diary*, I, 602.

[14] Bancroft, *Seward*, II, 365; Pierce, *Sumner*, IV, 110; Nicolay and Hay, *Lincoln*, VI, 263–264.

was not all. He was at a crisis which involved the success of the government and the fate of the nation. Even if, in response to selfless prompting, he should step out, what of the country and of the cause he was serving? The President's unhappy state of mind was not merely personal. Already the question of his own leadership had been canvassed in his mind. He had pondered dispassionately whether he ought to yield to another, supposing that were constitutionally possible,[1] and had decided that such action was not indicated as the solution of the nation's difficulties. Yet he must stay in office as a real and not a merely nominal leader. If senators could push him around, his effectiveness would be seriously weakened, with the possibility of further disaster to the Union cause. He could not forget that in the minds of conservative men it was the radicals who had been responsible for the unhappy outcome of Fredericksburg.[2] The men who were using the caucus of Republican senators as their instrument were, as Browning said, the President's "bitterest enemies"; they were "doing all in their power to break him down." They were the "ultra, radical, unreasoning men who raised the insane cry of on to Richmond in July 1861, and have kept up a war on our generals ever since—who forced thro the confiscation bills, and extorted from the President the proclamations and lost him the confidence of the country . . . ." Fearing that popular indignation would fall upon their heads, thought Browning, they were "intent upon giving it another direction." [3]

The art of governing was put to the test. For a leader to fail in skill and finesse at such a time might be productive of irreparable injury. It would take careful steering to prevent division at home, with consequent comfort to the enemy. If the President was to come out of the episode without an impairment of his own leadership and a cracking of the governmental structure, a high degree of tact was indicated. "There should be harmony," Browning told his colleagues, "and unity of . . . action between all the departments of government . . . ." The plan of the complaining senators, he thought, "would be war between Congress and the President, and the knowledge of this antagonism would injure our cause greatly in the Country. It would produce strife here, and strife among the peo-

---

[1] *Diary of S. P. Chase*, Sep. 22, 1862, *Annual Report*, Am. Hist. Assoc., 1902, II, 88.
[2] Bancroft, *Seward*, II, 364.   [3] Browning, *Diary*, I, 598 (Dec. 16, 1862).

ple . . . ." [4] Lincoln had to keep the machine running. Soon he would have to prepare a new military advance, probably with a new commander. At such a time he could not permit senatorial interference nor allow a "party or faction" to "dictate to the President in regard to his Cabinet." [5] Yet it was equally imperative that the assertion of presidential leadership be not too abrupt. Willingness to talk things over must be shown, yet nothing vital could be yielded. The President must see to the outcome, yet the issue must not be in terms of explosion or unseemly combat.

Lincoln's technique, or diplomacy if that is the word, rose to the occasion. It was arranged that a committee of the senators should call on the President on the evening of Thursday, December 18, and state their demands. Patiently the nation's Executive listened while senators presented the case against Seward—his lukewarmness and responsibility for failure. "To use the P[r]est's quaint language, while they believed in the Prest's honesty, they seemed to think that when he had in him any good purposes, Mr. S.[eward] contrived *to suck them out of him unperceived*." [6]

Lincoln arranged that the senatorial committee (nine men selected to represent the Republican caucus) should meet him again on the evening of Friday, December 19. That morning, beginning at 10:30, he had a long and earnest session of his cabinet. Enjoining secrecy, he reported the resignation of the two Sewards and the conference with the senators. The President stated how "shocked and grieved" he was to hear the senators' objections to Seward, knowing as he did how there had never been any disagreements in the cabinet "though there had been differences," and how their confidence and zeal had "sustained and consoled" him. [7]

Having given the cue for the cabinet's attitude—coöperation with the President and among themselves—Lincoln made an adroit move which disarmed the critics and doubters. He contrived it so that when the senatorial committee of nine [8] came again they found themselves

4 *Ibid.*, I, 597–598. 5 Welles, *Diary*, I, 199.
6 Bates, *Diary*, 269. 7 Welles, *Diary*, I, 195.
8 The committee of nine Republican senators consisted of Collamer of Vermont as spokesman, Wade of Ohio, Fessenden of Maine, Harris of New York, Grimes of Iowa, Sumner of Massachusetts, Trumbull of Illinois, Howard of Michigan, and Pomeroy of Kansas. The committee had an obvious majority of radicals. Wade seems not to have attended the conferences at the White House.

confronted by the whole cabinet except Seward. One effect of this was that Chase, who had talked with some of the senators in the anti-Seward sense, found himself in a situation in which he could not do otherwise than confirm the President's statement of essential harmony in the cabinet. The mere confronting of the legislators with the cabinet, in a meeting of which Lincoln was moderator, gave the President a notable advantage. It was one thing for senators to use strong language in a caucus; it was quite another to do it face to face with President and cabinet. When questioned directly by the President, only four of the solons stuck to their guns in insisting upon Seward's removal.[9]

As with the senators, so with the secretaries. For any cabinet member to associate himself with a senatorial drive against a colleague would put him clearly in the wrong. "This Cabinet," said Stanton, "is like yonder window. Suppose you allow it to be understood that passers-by might knock out one pane of glass—just one at a time— how long do you think any panes would be left in it?"[10] At length the meeting of President, cabinet, and senators broke up "in a milder spirit" than when it met.[11] The senators had shot their bolt, yet no explosion had occurred.

Thus ended Friday. Next day Washington buzzed with rumors that the whole cabinet had resigned and the President was in receipt of a number of new slates.[12] Holding another cabinet meeting, Lincoln found himself in possession of another resignation. What happened is best told in the language of Gideon Welles: "Chase said he had been painfully affected by the meeting last evening, . . . and . . . informed the President he had prepared his resignation . . . . 'Where is it?' said the President quickly, his eye lighting up in a moment. 'I brought it with me,' said Chase, ... 'Let me have it,' said the President, reaching his long arm and fingers toward C., who held on, . . . reluctant to part with the letter, . . . Something further he wished to say, but the President . . . did not perceive it, but took and hastily opened the letter. 'This,' said he, . . . 'cuts the

[9] Collamer, spokesman of the senators, expressed the view that there should be more general consultation of secretaries and President. Fessenden "felt . . . more than he cared to say"; Grimes, Sumner, Trumbull, and Pomeroy urged Seward's withdrawal. Harris wanted Seward to remain. (Wade did not attend.) Welles, *Diary*, I, 196–198.
[10] Bancroft, *Seward*, II, 367.   [11] Bates, *Diary*, 270.   [12] *Ibid.*

Gordian knot.' . . . 'I see my way clear.' " [13] In his prairie phrase, Lincoln could ride; "I have got a pumpkin in each end of my bag," he said.[14]

Having maneuvered the situation to precisely the point which he desired, and having arranged it so that both secretaries stayed in town, Lincoln now addressed to Seward and Chase identical notes mentioning their resignations and adding that the public interest would not admit of their acceptance. He therefore requested each to resume his duties.[15] Seward promptly complied; Chase, not forgetting the President's gratified look at the cabinet meeting, asked leave to "sleep on it." On the same day that his resignation was presented (Saturday, December 20) he wrote out a letter asking that the resignation be accepted and advancing the view that both he and Seward could serve better as private citizens. He gave the matter further thought over a painful Sunday; then on Monday, December 22, he sent the President two letters. Enclosing the Saturday letter, he stated that he had changed his mind and would resume his post.[16]

It was a fortunate week-end for Lincoln. He had kept the game in his hands and had adjusted a menacing crisis; moreover, he had so managed the incident that neither secretary was humiliated in the public eye. As on other occasions Lincoln sustained himself by a selfless attitude. In taking on his own shoulders the blame that had descended upon secretaries, he had warded off a threat to presidential as well as secretarial prestige. If he could not gain positive coöperation from senators, he could serve a high purpose by avoiding open hostility with them. As the committee of the caucus returned to Capitol Hill and the secretaries to their offices, both groups and both factions bore less of disruptive force on Monday than on Friday. Looking back over recent proceedings they could not fail to realize that the steering had been Lincoln's and that the quiet outcome had been of his determining. Lincoln's inmost thoughts of the affair can only be guessed. Though his severe mental suffering is well attested, he had not fallen prey to distress of mind. He had retained his equipoise and even his power to joke. If one may lift a phrase from a Gilbert and Sullivan lyric, he may have longed for an upper house that

---

> Did nothing in particular,
> And did it very well.

There were some conditions that the President could control, but there were others he simply had to live with. He had to work with senators. He could not make over the Senate, but he could study the best method of approaching its members. With luck, and with attention to the human art of government, he might turn a senatorial upheaval into a triumph of presidential prestige. Whatever happened, he could not afford an open break. In addition to all his other complications, he had to deal with what he once called the objections of "some Senators." [17] In using the phrase the President was referring to a minor matter, the Senate's rejection of a lesser general; yet in Lincoln's mind the expression could easily have had a larger meaning. To give the sum of Lincoln's difficulties with "some Senators" would indeed be a large order.

---

[17] *Works*, VIII, 233 (Mar. 25, 1863).

CHAPTER XXVI

EXIT BURNSIDE

I

THE army was Lincoln's main anxiety. Morale after Fredericksburg was low and desertions numerous. The men were "disheartened and almost sulky." [1] The President is said to have remarked that a marching Union army "dwindled . . . like a shovelfull of fleas pitched from one place to another." [2] Having been in a ferment on the subject of cabinet change, the North was now demanding such a shuffle of commanders as would "give more vigor to our armies." [3] Prominent generals—McClellan, Porter, Stone, Buell, McDowell, Frémont, and others—were without commands. In some cases this was fortunate; in others it was a wasted resource and a cause of resentment. With radicals insisting on greater legislative control of army movements, with urgent demands that conservative men should force the administration "to a change of measures and men," [4] with army affairs in a tangle and a conscription act in the making, the civilian mind was deep in the gloom of defeat while the soldier mind was in a state of "savage" dissatisfaction that "tended strongly to mutiny." [5]

This unhealthful state in the army was due to a combination of factors: delay in pay, jealousy among generals, prejudiced proceedings of military courts and of the congressional war committee, "politicians

[1] *Battles and Leaders of the Civil War*, III, 154.

[2] Random notes in 1863 of John Hay, Dennett, *Lincoln . . . in the Diaries . . . of John Hay*, 53.

[3] Lyman Trumbull to Norman G. Flagg, Washington, Jan. 21, 1863, MS., Ill. State Hist. Lib.

[4] August Belmont to S. J. Tilden, Jan. 27, 1863, Tilden MSS.

[5] Isaac M. Brown to R. W. Thompson, Burnside Barracks, Indianapolis, Feb. 8, 1863, MS., Lincoln National Life Foundation, Ft. Wayne. Nicolay (*Short Life of Abraham Lincoln*, 365) also speaks of a "spirit akin to mutiny" in the army.

seeking to influence military movements in favor of their own partisan and selfish schemes," [6] legislative patronage in military appointments,[7] and, most of all, a pervading sense of hopelessness under existing command. To mention the three men who had the highest military functions at the time, Lincoln had Burnside, he had Stanton, and he had Halleck. Stanton was as unstable as he was arrogant and stubborn. Some of his decisions were reversed by himself, often from "mere caprice"; "there . . . was none with whom men found it more difficult to deal." [8] "The extent to which Lincoln interposed his tact and patience between Stanton and generals of the army, . . . preventing injustice and insuring . . . continuity, is a commonplace of history." [9] At times it appeared that the President and his minister of war were at loggerheads; at other times it seemed that Lincoln knew Stanton to be "unprincipled" but felt he had to retain him to get the country's business done.[10] The best of men found it impossible to get along with the secretary. Henry W. Bellows, promoting the fine work of the sanitary commission, sought secretarial coöperation in vain.[11] Welles referred to Stanton as "unreliable" and impatient toward Lincoln; [12] Bates described him as "brusque—not to say uncivil." [13]

Lincoln would give an order and Stanton would undo it.[14] The secretary had allied himself with radicals, had withheld coöperation from McClellan, and had been one of the chief agents in the ruin of that general. Defeats of 1862 were largely of his making.

---

[6] "Extracts from the Journal of Henry J. Raymond," ed. by his son, *Scribner's Monthly*, XIX, 703 (1880).

[7] Cox, *Military Reminiscences*, I, 433.   [8] Pearson, *Andrew*, II, 95.   [9] *Ibid.*

[10] Draft of letter by Montgomery Blair to unnamed correspondent, undated (probably summer of 1865), box marked "Various," Blair MSS. (Internal evidence shows this to have been written after Lincoln's death.)

[11] ". . . I believe the Secy of War allows himself to speak of our Commission with contempt, ..." Henry W. Bellows to S. P. Chase, N. Y., Nov. 25, 1862, Chase MSS., Lib. of Cong. In the Bellows MSS. there is ample evidence of disappointment with Stanton on the part of Bellows.

[12] Welles, *Diary*, I, 98; II, 293.

[13] Bates, *Diary*, 280.

[14] When the vice-regent of the Mount Vernon Association asked that a vessel be allowed to run from Washington to Mount Vernon, Lincoln approved it, but Stanton did not "deem it expedient." Letter from vice-regent to Lincoln, Feb. 26, 1864, MS., N. Y. Hist. Soc. When J. P. Usher tried to get something done (on a matter not fully stated), he wrote a friend: ". . . the President made the order & . . . it is withheld in the War Department." J. P. Usher to R. W. Thompson, Mar. 31, 1864, MS., Lincoln National Life Foundation, Ft. Wayne.

Halleck's task was no easy berth. Condemnation should be tempered by a realization of his difficulties, yet it was the prevailing view of contemporaries that his performance after taking up his duties in Washington was unsatisfactory. Bates wrote of his "bad judgment," his "cunning and evasive" manner; he summed it up by referring to "that poor thing—*Halleck*," and again to the "improvidence (not to say imbecility) of . . . Stanton and Halleck." [15] One of the keenest of military observers, General Jacob D. Cox, a man of measured words, referred to the general in chief as "unequal to his responsibility" and as "in no true sense a commander of the armies." [16] In the opinion of Nicolay and Hay, as a nominal general in chief "his genius fell short of the high duties of that great station." [17]

The count against Burnside is simply that of failure. He was a man of courage, of fine military bearing, of "single-hearted honesty and unselfishness." [18] As a defeated general, however, he could not have been expected to retain the confidence of his men and officers; this was the less possible in view of his post-Fredericksburg attitude and intentions. Having determined upon a move across the Rappahannock in the face of almost unanimous opposition by his generals, Burnside created a further difficulty for a buffeted President by putting the responsibility for a decision on Lincoln's shoulders; this he did by a letter stating his purpose, with an offer to resign if his plan should not be approved.

The plan of Burnside seemed to smack of reckless blundering, and under these circumstances the President turned for advice to "Old Brains" (Halleck); yet in the very act of doing so he revealed his lack of faith in that general. "If in such a difficulty . . . you do not help," wrote Lincoln, "you fail me precisely in the point for which I sought your assistance." He wanted the general in chief to go over the ground, gather all the elements for forming a judgment, and then come through with an approval or disapproval. "Your military skill," he said, "is useless to me if you do not do this." [19]

This was written on January 1, 1863, the day of Lincoln's definitive proclamation of emancipation and of a protracted public reception. It was a crowded day, one incident of which was a painful conference

[15] Bates, *Diary*, 304, 389, 398.   [16] Cox, *Military Reminiscences*, I, 257; II, 2.
[17] Nicolay and Hay, *Lincoln*, V, 357.   [18] Cox, *Military Reminiscences*, I, 390.
[19] *Works*, VIII, 165.

with Burnside, as a result of which that commander submitted his resignation. On receiving Lincoln's New Year's Day letter through Stanton, Halleck promptly wrote out his resignation.[20] At a time of hazard and anxiety the President was thus presented with the resignations of the general in chief and of the commander of the principal army. The immediate difficulty as to the resignations was patched up. Halleck's was at once withdrawn on the President agreeing to withdraw his January first letter.[21] Burnside also for the time remained. The case of each was that of an offer of resignation rather than a definite withdrawal.

The President still had his generals, but what of the army's plans? Against the objections of competent officers, Burnside's project of the crossing of the Rappahannock was approved by Halleck, and (with a note of caution) by Lincoln. Its result was the "mud march" of the Army of the Potomac which failed so completely in its hopeless floundering that it became a by-word in military tradition.[22]

As if the mud episode were not enough, Burnside now took another step which made it utterly impossible to retain him. On January 23 he prepared an order dishonorably dismissing an impressive list of generals, including Joseph Hooker, W. T. H. Brooks, John Newton, John Cochrane, W. B. Franklin, and William Farrar Smith. This sensational order declared that Hooker was "dismissed the service of the United States as a man unfit [etc.]"; he had been "guilty," said the order, of making criticisms, creating distrust, producing incorrect impressions, and "habitually speaking in disparaging terms of other officers." Newton and Cochrane were declared dismissed "for going to the President . . . with criticisms . . . of their commanding officer." [23] These orders, being published in the newspapers, added to the existing demoralization, but they never went into effect; Lincoln saw to that. Burnside had unintentionally made Lincoln's task of decision easier. He had made his own incapacity for command so unmistakable that his removal was no longer open to question. There

---

[20] *Ibid.*, VIII, 165–166.   [21] *Ibid.*, VIII, 166, n. 1.

[22] In late January 1863 several grand divisions of the Army of the Potomac were caught south of the Rappahannock by rains which made the roads impassable; stuck in the mud, the dejected army had to abandon the whole enterprise. It was Burnside's hopeless attempt to redeem himself. *Battles and Leaders of the Civil War*, III, 118–119, 239 n.

[23] *Ibid.*, III, 216 n.

was nothing to do but relieve the luckless general of his command of the Army of the Potomac. This the President did on January 26, 1863, giving that post to Joseph Hooker.

What went on behind the lines as this bit of business took place would make a sorry story: officers leaving the field for Washington where they poured criticisms in the ears of the President; congressional inquisitors plotting which generals to besmirch and which to whitewash; journalists becoming the depositaries of information that should have remained confidential. When matters were at the sharpest crisis Burnside, with Raymond of the *Times,* had darted back in a sensational night ride from army headquarters at Falmouth to Washington (January 24–25). Both of them saw Lincoln: Burnside handed the President his bold order, tendering his resignation if the order should not be approved; the announcement hit Lincoln like "a clap of thunder." Having delivered the bolt, the general sped back to the army; obviously he was thinking more of disciplining certain generals, especially Hooker, than of accepting the alternative of resignation. Raymond sought out Chase, poured into his ears the "whole story," then drew Lincoln aside at a White House reception and told him of Burnside's difficulties with Hooker and other subordinates.[24] If Burnside's purpose, with Raymond's support, was to force the issue, they succeeded, but not in the sense intended. It was directly after these intrigues and conferences that Hooker's displacement of Burnside was announced.

The new commander was not the choice of Stanton and Halleck. Rosecrans, operating effectively in the West, would have suited them.[25] Those who like to ponder the "ifs" of history may speculate as to how far and how high Rosecrans "might have" gone if appointed. Would he have been another failure, or would his have been the triumph and postwar fame that came to Grant? Lincoln's appointment of Hooker, which was his own decision, showed how little value he placed upon the counsel of his high military advisers. As it turned out, the President had picked another failure, but that could not be

---

[24] "Extracts from the Journal of Henry J. Raymond," *Scribner's Monthly,* XIX, 704–705 (1880). See also Williams, *Lincoln and the Radicals,* 266.

[25] "Both Stanton and Halleck were dissatisfied with the choice. They had set their hearts upon General Rosecrans." Statement by the editors (Nicolay and Hay), in *Works,* VIII, 206.

known in advance. In January 1863 Hooker had a fightng reputation; he exuded confidence; he had been with the Army of the Potomac through hard campaigns and battles; he had the experience and prestige of a corps commander. On the other hand were factors that made the appointment doubtful: he had been part of the intrigue against Burnside, had "talked blatantly to the reporters about the new regime that would prevail if Joe Hooker were in command," [26] had violently denounced McClellan, and, perhaps worst of all, had played the game of the radicals—e. g., in his testimony before the war committee—so that the "bosses of the Jacobin machine were delighted" [27] with his appointment.

That the President was uncertain as to Hooker at the moment of appointing him is revealed in an admonishing letter which he wrote to the new chieftain. It is one of the most remarkable of Lincoln's epistles, being of the kind that he sometimes wrote and did not send; this time he sent it. "General," he wrote, "I have placed you at the head of the Army of the Potomac. . . . I have done this upon what appear to me . . . sufficient reasons. And yet . . . ." Then the President explained that he was "not quite satisfied" with the general, that he considered him ambitious, and that in thwarting Burnside he had done "a great wrong to the country." He continued:

I have heard . . . of your . . . saying that both the Army and the Government needed a Dictator. Of course it was not *for* this, but in spite of it, that I have given you the command. . . . What I now ask of you is military success, and I will risk the dictatorship. . . . I much fear that the spirit which you have aided to infuse into the Army, of criticising their Commander, and withholding confidence from him, will now turn upon you. I shall assist you . . . to put it down. Neither you, nor Napoleon, if he were alive . . . , could get any good out of an army, while such a spirit prevails in it. And now, beware of rashness. Beware of rashness, but with energy, and sleepless vigilance, go forward, and give us victories.[28]

There have been various commentaries on this letter, including the conjecture that Lincoln paced the floor after writing it before

---

[26] Williams, *Lincoln and the Radicals*, 265.

[27] *Ibid.*, 266.

[28] In *Works*, VIII, 206–207, this letter appears with numerous errors of punctuation, capitalization and the like. Quotations here have been checked with the superb Caxton Club facsimile mentioned in the following note.

adding his signature.[29] For an understanding of the epistle one must remember the buzz and intrigue that had been going on for weeks in military circles, the recent conferences Lincoln had held with various generals, the realization of low morale in the army, the President's pathetic sense of the urgency of victory, and his troubled misgiving as to whether he had chosen the man who could deliver it. To attach any particular significance to Lincoln's comment on dictatorship as applying to himself, would be an error.

II

It is no part of the purpose of this book to include the elaborate and complex history of military operations. George Bancroft refers to "six hundred and twenty-five battles and severe skirmishes" fought in the Civil War.[1] Everyone has heard of Bull Run and Gettysburg; the action at Carnifex Ferry, West Virginia, has been forgotten, except by the families of those killed and wounded. The same may be said of literally hundreds of incidents such as the action at Big Creek Gap, Tennessee, the skirmish on the Purdy Road (near Adamsville, Tennessee), or the affair at Cave City, Kentucky. A man killed at Wartrace, Tennessee, was as much of a casualty as those who fell at Antietam; such incidents, however minor they were, loomed large to thousands of participants. Though the impossibility of a complete account is obvious, the military literature of the conflict is stupendous. The merely statistical aspect is formidable, and a writer learns to think twice before he mentions the number of troops under a general's command at a given time, the number available for duty, the active and reserve forces, the number engaged in a particular combat, and the losses in killed, wounded, captured, and missing.

If one takes the period of April 1863 he finds the doubtful struggle at its midway phase with honors approximately even, except that the naval advantage was with the Union. Both sides had seen political interference with armies; in each case there had been a plummeting of

---

29 William E. Barton, *Abraham Lincoln and the Hooker Letter*, address before the Pennell Club, Philadelphia; Paul M. Angle, *Abraham Lincoln's Letter to Major General Joseph Hooker . . . a Facsimile . . . with Explanatory Text* (printed by Caxton Club, Chicago, 1942).

1 Memorial address, joint session of the houses of Congress, Feb. 12, 1866, reprinted in *Works* [of Lincoln], VIII, xxxvii.

some reputations and a soaring of others. In high placed commanders the Confederacy had the edge in the fine adjustment of Lee and Jackson to their specific tasks. Over-all factors in the war were the indecisiveness of leading campaigns, the rapid shifting of battle areas, the inexperience of troops and officers, the frequent turnover of army command, and the ineffectiveness of centralized direction. Gallantry, courage, and individual fighting power was shown on both sides; nevertheless it was plain that Americans were not a military people. Whatever may have been the talk of irrepressible conflict, the element of preparation was utterly lacking in the North and only somewhat less so in the South. To look squarely at a situation which is seldom correctly stated, the United States prior to 1861 had not seen its destiny in terms of an intensive program of militarization to deal with an internal war to destroy the Union. Preparedness for dissolution would have been an absurdity; on the other hand, preparedness that would have given a distinct advantage to a Union-preserving North was hardly conceivable in the anxious fifties when Presidents were of Southern sympathies and secretaries of war were Southerners. The lack of a compact nation had been illustrated in the unchallenged resignation and withdrawal of Southern officers trained at West Point. It had been for the service of the United States that they had been trained, but the army of the United States made no point of holding them.

Then as always the statesmanlike way to deal with war was to prevent its breaking out by promoting reason in the adjustment of disputes and by keeping predominant military power in the hands of those who meant to keep the peace; the power being there, it would not have had to be used. In this high purpose statesmanship had failed. Divisive forces and irrational movements had been allowed to rise; they had been so little restrained that a war was now raging to tear the nation apart. For Americans North and South to be slaughtering each other was unthinkable; yet here the fratricidal conflict was and it had to be fought to the death. It could not be stopped halfway. If there was not victory for the Union, the result was disunion. Once war had been allowed to develop, compromise was not in the cards. If for no other reason, men would continue to fight in order not to be beaten; they would be fighting because there was a war; it was no longer a matter of war aims according to the original calculation. Men might consider the war senseless; yet there seemed no way of terminating it short of a military decision. Solutions that had been easy in 1860 appeared now as a wistful mirage; a backward look at that far-off year could only bring remorse; it could not restore a lost peace. Many a time history has revealed that a war cannot be controlled nor its uses appropriated in terms of the intentions of rulers. The American war had changed its character. It was a monster let loose, not an instrument to be applied for a predetermined object.

On the eastern front the year 1861 had witnessed near panic in the brief isolation of Washington, minor campaigns in western Virginia, one major campaign with its indecisive Union defeat at Manassas close to Washington, and Confederate failure to press the advantage at the moment of Union demoralization. With a change of commanders on each side the year 1862 had seen the ambitious Peninsular campaign, the placing of a Federal army in a position of great striking power near Richmond, the Valley diversion, the indecisive Seven Days between Lee and McClellan, the amazing cross purpose between Washington and the army, and the releasing of Lee's forces by the foolish removal of McClellan from the Peninsula. Having been pinned down by McClellan to the close defense of Richmond, the army of Lee was invited to shift north and threaten Washington; it was then able to inflict a smashing defeat on McClellan's successor (Pope). In a time of great desperation on the Union side McClellan was grudgingly reinstated and was able to save Washington by the defensive victory of Antietam. Lee's first offensive was thus stopped. Weeks passed and McClellan was finally dropped. Burnside was put in and the heartbreaking defeat of Fredericksburg showed how a superb fighting force could be wasted by faulty generalship. After further floundering Burnside gave way to Hooker. Facing the Northern foe on the line of the Rappahannock, Lee's army was not only a mighty obstacle on the path to Richmond; it was a reminder that Washington was in danger, that the Confederacy was still potent for offense, and that Hooker's "finest army on the planet" had grim business ahead.

Meanwhile in the West the war had been waged first in Union territory—Kentucky and Missouri; then it shifted south as important river positions were taken by the Federals. This inland river war, favorable to the North, yet disappointing when compared with its large possibilities, was one of the main aspects of the struggle. Transports and gunboats assisted the Union armies; the South was made to regret its naval inferiority. Activity, however, was spasmodic; battles were not followed up; the checking of an army in one sector meant that it would turn up in another. Results of river operations were seen in the capture of Fort Henry on the Tennessee and the more significant capitulation of Fort Donelson on the Cumberland (February 1862). This "unconditional surrender" episode was Grant's first big victory; to make it possible the coöperation of Foote's naval force had been an indispensable element. Consolidating the results of Donelson, Union forces soon occupied Nashville, Tennessee, and Columbus, Kentucky. Southern armies were being pushed back to internal lines of defense. Further land-and-water operations at New Madrid and Island Number Ten produced another formal Confederate surrender, produced also the exaltation of Pope and his transfer to the East.

On April 6–7, 1862, occurred the main western military event of the year in the battle of Shiloh, another incident in the river war. In this fierce but uncoördinated battle the combined forces of Beauregard and Albert Sidney Johnston were able to deliver a surprise attack upon Grant's unready army before it could be joined by Buell. On the first day the Federals were driven back in confusion. With the arrival of Buell on the second day, however, the tide was turned and the Confederates were pushed back to Corinth, Mississippi. The river war now shifted to the lower Mississippi as the shining prize of New Orleans, largest city and greatest port of the South, fell into Union hands following a great naval battle (April 1862) under Farragut and Porter. B. F. Butler stepped in and the hated Federal occupation of the proud city and much of Louisiana began. Butler's rule continued for seven and a half months, bringing such odium to the Union cause that Lincoln removed him in December 1862. On the upper Mississippi Forts Pillow and Randolph were evacuated by the Confederates. Memphis was taken after a naval battle (June 6, 1862), but the efforts of Farragut and Porter against the next big prize, Vicksburg, were unavailing. This well defended Southern city could be passed, but another year was required before it fell, and then only after repeated failures and as a result of an elaborate and arduous campaign.

These advances had been the work of Halleck, or, more accurately, the work under Halleck. In the earlier phases of his western command, by contrast with the chaos, futile effort, and corruption under Frémont, Halleck had made a good impression. With headquarters at St. Louis, he, or the commanders and forces under him (Pope, Foote, Grant, Sherman, Buell, etc.), had shown real achievement. This, however, was while Halleck was in desk command at St. Louis. When he took the field after Shiloh his performance was so slow and cautious that, as Sherman remarked, an army carrying a hundred thousand bayonets moved (if it could be called moving) toward Corinth "with pick and shovel." [2] Crawling at a snail's pace, and encountering little opposition, the army "fortified almost every camp at night"; its advance was "provokingly slow." [3] The twenty-three miles from Pittsburg Landing to Corinth, with negligible fighting, took over a month, the whole of May 1862 being occupied in this enterprise. Misreading the capacities of his generals, Halleck had reorganized his command, leaving Grant "without any apparent authority." Uncomplaining as he was, Grant felt keenly the "indignity, if not insult, heaped upon him." [4] Such had been the complaints against him directly after his victory at Donelson that his arrest had been authorized by McClellan on the basis of advices from Halleck; fortunately the arrest was not effected. [5] The fact that it could have been seriously planned showed how little the controlling military minds in March 1862 appreciated the qualities of the man who was later to emerge as the North's chief army hero. Pope's army, fresh from its accomplishments at New Madrid and Island Number Ten, had been brought on river transports to the Shiloh-Corinth area; yet the combined Union forces did not come to grips with Beauregard. They merely occupied the empty prize of Corinth after Beauregard evacuated it. Meanwhile Halleck had disappointed Lincoln's wish that something be done in eastern Tennessee and withheld coöperation from Farragut at Vicksburg; he had chosen virtually to "go into summer quarters." [6]

In his report to Washington Halleck had managed to cause his

---

[2] *Offic. Rec.*, I ser., XVII, pt. 2, 83. Sherman to Halleck, July 8, 1862.

[3] Sherman, *Memoirs* (1875 ed.), I, 251.   [4] *Ibid.*, I, 250.

[5] The complaints were that Grant had neglected his duty, had resumed his "bad habits," and had gone off to Nashville, leaving his troops, without authority. His arrest, which was not carried out, was authorized for the sake of military discipline. Halleck had written: "It is hard to censure a successful general . . . , but I think he richly deserves it." McClellan authorized the general's arrest on what seemed adequate basis; later the matter was explained and adjusted satisfactorily. *Offic. Rec.*, 1 ser., VII, 679–680, 682–684.

[6] Nicolay and Hay, *Lincoln*, V, 350.

occupation of Corinth to appear as a supreme achievement. In a statement that was almost entirely hearsay and boasting he quoted Pope as claiming the capture of 10,000 prisoners and deserters, and referred to a farmer's statement that Beauregard had become "frantic, and told his men to save themselves the best they could." [7] From Halleck's report, published in various newspapers, one may turn to Beauregard's statement that the Confederate evacuation of Corinth was a "complete surprise" by which the foe was "utterly foiled," that Union reports were "inaccurate, reckless, and unworthy," and that Halleck's dispatch of June 4 (the one about the farmer and the ten thousand captives) was "disgracefully untrue." [8] The Federal general's statement was said to have contained "as many lies as lines." [9] When confronted with this refutation Halleck made no reaffirmation of his expansive statements. Instead, he weakly stated that he was "not responsible for the truth" of the statements he communicated, that the report of prisoners was taken from Pope, and that any error was Pope's responsibility.[10] One could find a far better basis for complaint concerning Halleck's performance from April to July of 1862 than concerning McClellan's. Yet McClellan was demoted and ordered to withdraw his whole army from its position before Richmond, while Halleck was called to Washington and lifted to the surprising eminence of general in chief.

When Halleck stepped out of the western picture, so did Beauregard; the argument was now between their successors—Buell and Bragg. (Later it would be between Grant and Pemberton; still later, between Grant and Bragg.) Buell's task was to shift his force to eastern Tennessee and take Chattanooga and Knoxville. His movement (through northern Alabama) was painfully slow and all his calculations for an offensive on his own part were upset by harassing Confederate raids and by the Southern enemy seizing the initiative and launching an ambitious invasion of Kentucky by two armies under Bragg and Kirby Smith. This was no mere diversion. It was a serious effort to occupy, "liberate," and hold Kentucky, whose people were expected to join in a pro-Confederate uprising. The political motive of the invasion was not permitted to wait upon the military; rather, for a time the political factor took precedence as Bragg diverted a

[7] *Offic. Rec.*, 1 ser., X, pt. 1, 669.   [8] *Ibid.*, 764–765.   [9] *Ibid.*, 671.   [10] *Ibid.*

considerable force of men to conduct a ceremony at Frankfort where Richard Hawes, with questionable legal right, was inaugurated as secessionist governor of Kentucky. The popular uprising did not materialize; [11] Hawes's day was brief; he was soon in flight from the state; the episode of the inauguration had but enabled the Union forces to occupy Louisville and make other defensive dispositions. Finally, Bragg's Kentucky thrust ended in the battle of Perryville (October 8, 1862). This hard fought struggle was indecisive in that it was an incomplete testing of strength. Since it resulted in the abandonment of the Confederate invasion, however, the advantage was with the Federal side, as Bragg withdrew to Nashville and Buell to eastern Tennessee, soon to give way to Rosecrans.

While this Confederate offensive in Kentucky had been in progress, there had been waged an important campaign between Rosecrans and two Confederate generals (Price and Van Dorn) who had been shifted from trans-Mississippi operations to the area of Corinth. By the battles of Iuka and Corinth (September 19 and October 3–4, 1862) western Tennessee had been kept clear of Confederate forces and the coöperation of Price and Van Dorn with Bragg had been prevented. The Southern way of putting it, however, was that Rosecrans had been hindered from joining Buell.

The success of Rosecrans had synchronized with what was regarded as the failure of Buell. That general had not mastered eastern Tennessee; he had not anticipated Bragg's invasion of Kentucky; after checking the invasion he had not pressed the retiring enemy. For political reasons he was a target of the Jacobins and a suspect of their war committee. He had also incurred the wrath of midwestern governors (Morton, Yates, and Tod) whose troops from Indiana, Illinois, and Ohio were under his command. He was a Democrat and it was customary for Republicans to associate him with McClellan. The result of it all was that on October 30, 1862, a few days before McClellan's dismissal, Buell was removed from command of the Army of the Ohio whose organization and fighting power he had done so much to develop. His command, involving the Department of the Cumberland,

---

11 It had been Bragg's hope that the people of Kentucky would "rise in mass to assert their independence," but he was "distressed to add" that there was "little or no disposition" to make any such effort. Report of General Bragg, Oct. 12, 1862, *ibid.*, 1 ser., XVI, pt. 1, 1088.

was turned over to Rosecrans.[12] Months passed; then at the turn of the year (1862–1863) Bragg and Rosecrans clashed in bloody but indecisive combat at Murfreesboro (Stone's River). As the battle ended Bragg retired from the field. For a long time, however, he blocked the Federals from the next objective of Rosecrans, which was Chattanooga.

Heading the Army of the Tennessee, and commanding the important area of western Tennessee and northern Mississippi, was Ulysses S. Grant.[13] He and Sherman, with the loyal coöperation of Porter and the jealous interference of McClernand, were to be occupied for months with bravely conceived and hard-fought failures in the earlier stages of their complex efforts against Vicksburg. At the mid-point in the war (April 1863) this river stronghold was a center of stout Southern resistance, a point of Confederate contact with the trans-Mississippi, a challenge to Union strategy, and a test of strength between powerful antagonists.

III

There were, of course, many other factors in the vast war at this midway point. Political allegiance was rather well stabilized. The Confederacy still had eleven states as in June of '61. Their efforts to add Kentucky and Missouri had failed, though they still kept up a paper claim to these commonwealths. West Virginia had its full birth as one of the United States in 1863.[1] Whether or not the South wanted to add the Northwest, which was debatable with them, that great area was holding fast to the Union, though not without irritation; it was sending its hundreds of thousands to the front while also producing those huge quantities of grain that meant so much in the feeding of

---

[12] Buell was not only removed from his western command but was subjected to a harrowing trial by a military commission which reported no charges against the general but severely condemned his operations. In testimony before the commission and in various writings Buell put up a strong defense, remarking upon the "irregularities" of its proceedings and the "spirit" of its members. *Offic. Rec.*, 1 ser., XVI, pt. 1, 65. For the opinion of the commission, see *ibid.*, 8 ff.

[13] It had been under Grant that the operations of Rosecrans against Price and Van Dorn were conducted. Grant's command had been comparable with that of Buell, but in a different area. He had sought a greater coördination of western command than had been put into effect.

[1] See above, p. 13.

the Federal armies. Social and economic dislocations at the North were being endured, adjustments being made. There were mighty loans, all-inclusive taxes, a new national banking system, and a flood of paper money. There was great economic expansion, not all of which was healthful, in the extension of railroads, the opening up of new lands, and the manifold activities of wartime manufacturing. Social controls were feeble; unsocial practices rampant. Greed, profiteering, cheating, and fraud were prevalent. On the other hand there were enlightened humanitarian enterprises afoot in the work of the sanitary commission, the mustering of brave nurses, and sundry measures of relief and stimulus intended to keep life going on the home front. In spite of this, perhaps the greatest lack at home was national social and economic planning. This was to be evident in the small gains made by labor during the war and in the coming aftermath of panic, greed, and depression. Local and voluntary effort and state activity were not adequate to the problems at hand.

In the naval war the superior achievement was on the Union side, though there had been disappointments to offset this advantage. Welles and Fox, secretary and able assistant secretary of the navy, had virtually produced a navy *de novo*, having increased Lincoln's war-ships tenfold, from forty-two in March 1861 to 427 in December 1862. The gigantic blockade of Southern coasts was ineffective if judged by Confederate reports and measured only by those swift specialized vessels of limited tonnage that slipped through as blockade runners (often with more of a selfish than civic-minded motive), but it was powerful if seen in terms of larger ocean-going vessels that did not even try to enter Southern ports. Perhaps the best proof of the potency of the blockade was the fact that none of the Confederacy's few cruisers enjoyed access to Southern harbors. As Welles reported in December 1862, "in no previous war had the ports of an enemy's country been so effectually closed by a naval force." [2]

In both inland and coastal operations the influence of sea power upon history was being confirmed; a youthful officer, Alfred T. Mahan, was even then gaining in combat service under the Union flag the experience that would later enable him to master the history of modern sea power and marshal it in those epoch-making studies that

---

[2] Report of the Sec. of the Navy. Dec. 1, 1862, *House Exec. Doc. No. 1*, 37 Cong., 3 sess., vol. III, p. 3. See also Randall, *Civil War and Reconstruction*, 575.

were to become so potent a factor in world politics.[3] In March 1862 had occurred that battle of the ironclads in Hampton Roads which put a brake upon the brief threat of Southern floating power while it also marked the transition from old methods of wooden sailing ships to steam-driven, iron-plated craft. By April 1863 the Union navy had seized important coastal positions. Hampton Roads (commanded by Norfolk), Roanoke Island (conquered by Admiral Goldsborough and General Burnside, February-March 1862), the sea-island area of Beaufort, and Port Royal, South Carolina (Du Pont's achievement, November 1861), Fort Pulaski (guarding Savannah), and New Orleans. The ocean gateways of Virginia, Georgia, Florida, and Louisiana, were in Union possession. Not so Charleston, which was to resist a series of determined assaults upon its land and sea defenses. In April 1863 Du Pont conducted an ambitious effort with a fleet of monitors and an army force under Hunter, against the proud Carolinian city. The result was a failure which produced the greater psychological shock at the North because ironclads were considered an invincible innovation that would insure unbroken Northern superiority. These operations, as those of April 1861, found Beauregard in command of forces centering in Charleston. This general, mistreated by the Confederate President, was as popular there as his immediate predecessor, Pemberton, had been unpopular. There were other failures.[4] The Union navy had been checked on the James. It had not yet mastered the Mississippi. Maritime commerce of the United States was still a prey to the roving *Alabama*. Wilmington, Mobile, and Galveston remained in Confederate hands.

IV

With military and naval fortunes at the focus of his thought, Lincoln was made to realize the complications of remote control from Washington and the hazards of interference by civil officials, not to

---

[3] Alfred T. Mahan, *The Influence of Sea Power Upon History, 1660–1783* (1890). *The Influence of Sea Power upon the French Revolution and Empire, 1793–1812* (2 vols., 1892).

[4] Another army-navy failure on the Union side occurred in August 1863 when Admiral Dahlgren and General Gillmore bombarded the city (this was suspended after Confederate protest) and reduced Fort Sumter to ruins without winning the coveted prize. It was not until near the very end of the war (February 1865) that Charleston was evacuated by its defenders and put under Federal occupation.

say politicians, in the operations of his warriors. In general terms, or at times in considerable detail, he would make known his wish for a particular operation; he would even plead with his generals to bring it about, only to meet with frustration or to see enacted the very result he wished to avoid. In the pre-Shiloh phase he wanted Halleck to prevent the junction of A. S. Johnston with Beauregard. They were permitted to join. He strongly desired, almost as a kind of specialty, that eastern Tennessee, because of its Unionist sympathies, should be occupied and possessed. He urged that efforts be made against Chattanooga; [1] he wanted to know how the expedition for that purpose was progressing; [2] he studied closely the almost unsolvable problem of sending western troops east, yet launching successful offensives in the West. He kept asking Halleck for reënforcements to be sent to Virginia [3] (this at a time when reënforcements for Halleck himself were being urged),[4] yet insisted that the movement against Chattanooga and eastern Tennessee must not be interfered with,[5] and "must not on any account be given up." [6] "To take and hold the railroad . . . in East Tennessee," he considered "fully as important as the taking and holding of Richmond." [7] Noting in mid-October 1862 that Buell's "main object"—i. e., capture of eastern Tennessee—was unattained, the President, through Halleck, wanted to know why the Union army could not do as the Confederate—"live as he lives, and fight as he fights." [8] This implied that in Lincoln's thought the people of that mountain region would be as ready to avoid harassment of the Union as of the Confederate army. The activities of guerrilla bands and of bold Confederate raiders in Tennessee and Kentucky were a matter of concern to the President, who advised that vigorous counter measures be taken.[9]

[1] *Works*, VII, 214 (June 8, 1862). [2] *Ibid.*, VII, 228 (June 18, 1862).
[3] *Ibid.*, VII, 238, 255, 260, 261. [4] *Ibid.*, VII, 179–180 (May 24, 1862).
[5] *Ibid.*, VII, 238 (June 28, 1862). [6] *Ibid.*, VII, 247 (June 30, 1862).
[7] *Ibid.*, VII, 248 (June 30, 1862). [8] *Ibid.*, VIII, 63–64.

[9] Not only guerrilla bands, but also the most famous of Confederate raiders, N. B. Forrest and J. H. Morgan, were highly active in 1862 in Tennessee and Kentucky. (*Battles and Leaders*, III, 3, 28, 37, 451; Comte de Paris, *Civil War in America*, II, 365; John A. Wyeth, *Life of General Nathan Bedford Forrest*; Robert Selph Henry, *"First with the Most" Forrest*; *Offic. Rec.*, 1 ser., XVI, pt. 1, 731–784, 815–819, 871–882.) The frequency and daring of such raids bothered Lincoln. In no other way, he said, did the enemy give "so much trouble at so little expense." He wanted counter-raids organized and suggested getting up a corps for the purpose. Yet he wanted this done "without any or many additional troops." *Works*, VIII, 215–216 (Feb. 17, 1863).

The President's hopes for eastern Tennessee, however, were again and again deferred. After the time of his strong urging upon Halleck in the spring of 1862 it was to take a year and a half before that area was brought under Federal mastery. In Halleck's slow conduct before Corinth Lincoln found equal disappointment. Halleck was doing next to nothing, yet asking for more men. Patiently and with only an oblique hint of his dissatisfaction, Lincoln wrote the general that he was doing the best he could, that commanders all along the line wanted more men, and that lines were being thinned with heavy loss. The men who were needed, he said, were not at hand. Then, with the gentlest possible hint that the general had better bestir himself, Lincoln closed the letter: "My dear general, I feel justified to rely very much on you. I believe you and the brave officers and men with you can and will get the victory . . . ." [10]

Lincoln had constantly to contend with the fog of war, the imperfect state of military intelligence, and the hazardous difficulty of operational direction at a distance. It is seldom indeed that one finds the imperative mood in his communications to generals, but the interrogation point was typical. On September 8, 1862, with Bragg's invasion of Kentucky in full swing, he asked Buell how he could be certain that Bragg, with his command, was not at that time in the Valley of Virginia. [11] Four days later he asked General Boyle at Louisville: "Where is the enemy which you dread in Louisville? How near to you? What is General Gilbert's opinion? With all . . . respect for you, I must think General [Horatio G.] Wright's military opinion is the better. . . . Where do you understand Buell to be, and what is he doing?" In the same letter Lincoln showed his concept of remote control. Referring to the same General Wright, in command in Kentucky, he said: ". . . for us here to control him there . . . would be a babel of confusion which would be utterly ruinous." [12]

No part of Lincoln's military task was more vital than the making of appointments, and at no time was this function more difficult than in the summer and fall of 1862, when also the questions of foreign policy and of emancipation were at their most acute stage. The transfer and elevation of Halleck and Pope, the removal of Buell, and the assigning of important new commands to Rosecrans, Grant, and Schofield—all these western matters had to be studied, argued over,

---

10 *Ibid.*, VII, 180 (May 24, 1862).   11 *Ibid.*, VIII, 22.   12 *Ibid.*, VIII, 26-27.

and decided under pressure in the very period when the affairs of the Army of the Potomac and the problem of McClellan were at the stage of greatest anxiety. He even had to write to an aggrieved colonel explaining that he could not "conjecture what junior of yours you suppose I contemplate promoting over you." [13] To another disgruntled officer he wrote that he had "too many family controversies" already on his hands "to voluntarily . . . take up another." [14] The feelings of Rosecrans had to be soothed by the President's assurance that the general had "not a single enemy" in Washington.[15] When Fitz John Porter was convicted in the military trial above mentioned,[16] it was Lincoln's painful duty to issue the order that he be "cashiered and dismissed from the service . . . , and forever disqualified from holding any office of trust or profit under the . . . United States." [17] This matter of military appointment rested heavily upon Lincoln's shoulders. Taking it along with many other military aspects, it shows that the President's task as Commander in Chief was not merely nominal. Every time an appointment, change of rank, or shift of command was made, the President had to study alternatives; he had to deal with military men as persons, as fallible and sensitive human beings; he had to consider not only this or that army or campaign involving perhaps the fate of the nation, but the traditions and attachments of men in the service, the often unknowable capabilities of leaders, the delays of reorientation when a new command was assumed, the numerous pressures and interferences behind his back, and the sometimes difficult questions of senatorial confirmation or congressional attack. Of all the many duties that weighed upon Lincoln in the crowded war years, the function of Commander in Chief of the army and navy was the most serious as well as the most harassing and burdensome.

---

[13] *Ibid.*, VIII, 72 (Nov. 5, 1862).   [14] *Ibid.*, VIII, 201 (Jan. 22, 1863).

[15] *Ibid.*, VIII, 226 (Mar. 17, 1863).   [16] See above, p. 108 n.

[17] *Works*, VIII, 199 (Jan. 21, 1863).

CHAPTER XXVII

WAR AT ITS PEAK

I

"ELATED and depressed. Cheered and chagrined. Exultant and desponding. The rebels were between two fires. Hooker had them just where he wanted them. They could not retreat. They would be annihilated. The Rebellion was nearly at an end. Such was the talk—the feeling. All is now changed. The army is back in its camp. The victory that was to be is not." [1] Such were the opening lines of the Boston *Journal* account of Hooker's frustrated effort at Chancellorsville in May 1863. Men thought that Hooker could not fail: his numbers were greatly superior (about 130,000 to Lee's 60,000); his army was in fine condition; his strategy seemed faultless; his manner exuded confidence; his fighting reputation promised successful attack.

Holding Lee's threatening line by a powerful demonstration under Sedgwick near Fredericksburg (making the Confederates think this was the main operation), the Union commander would push a strong force across the upper Rappahannock and the Rapidan, pass by forced marches around Lee's left, and deliver a crushing attack on his rear. So confident was Hooker of his scheme that he sent off all his cavalry on the wide flanking movement (under Stoneman), leaving his right in the air, with insufficient reserves and no protecting terrain. He conceived of the coming battle in his own terms; the idea that his right would be assaulted had not entered his mind. Not fully aware of the Federal trap, but boldly resolving to take risks against a superior enemy, Lee had divided his forces, already small because of the detachment of Longstreet to a distant venture against Suffolk. For

---

[1] Moore, *Rebellion Record* (Docs.), VI, 593.

the operation against Hooker Lee's army was in three parts: Early disputed Sedgwick in the Fredericksburg area; Lee took care of the center near Chancellorsville; Jackson was to deal with the enemy's right. The main feature of the battle, whose details must be omitted, was a terrific surprise blow by Jackson who swung a heavy force into action against Howard's men of the Eleventh Corps on the Union right, catching them off guard at supper (May 3, 1863), and driving them into hasty retreat. Superior Confederate numbers were brought to bear upon the sector selected for attack, despite over-all superiority on the Union side.

The bold audacity of Jackson's maneuver brought Southern triumph at Lee's zenith; it was not, however, as crushing a stroke as Lee had hoped, and the Confederates paid heavily for their victory by the disaster of Jackson's death. Hooker had been stunned by a minor injury and when the fighting was over he did not know that a general engagement had been fought. It was as if he had been bluffing. Not only had he sent his cavalry on the unsuccessful flanking movement; he had deliberately withdrawn his forces on the main line of the two armies, and had left huge portions, by far the major part, of his army out of the conflict altogether. Nevertheless, the action had not reached the proportions of a Union disaster; it was rather a maddening setback at a moment when fate seemed to offer conspicuous success.

In painful deferment of his hopes Lincoln had watched Hooker's operations while also keenly interested in western developments. His watching was none too hopeful. Two weeks before the battle he feared Stoneman's flanking expedition was too slow and was "another failure already." [2] Those who thought only of Baltimore, or of Pennsylvania, or of General Schurz, asked him to weaken Hooker for a supposed benefit elsewhere, but he saw that this was precisely what the enemy wanted.[3] On the day of the main fighting in the Chancellorsville battle the obscurity of the operation as viewed from Washington was shown by Lincoln's questions: "Where is General Hooker? Where is Sedgwick? Where is Stoneman?" [4] When the battle was over and it was learned that Hooker had failed—this on top of so many failures—and had withdrawn behind the Rappahannock, Lincoln, according to his secretaries, "was for a moment in despair." [5] Reacting

---

[2] *Works*, VIII, 249 (April 15, 1863). [3] *Ibid.*, VIII, 244, 261.
[4] *Ibid.*, VIII, 262 (May 3, 1863). [5] *Ibid.*, VIII, 263 n.

promptly, however, he conferred with Halleck, visited Hooker's headquarters, and urged another "early movement," pointing out that it
would "help to supersede the bad moral effect of the recent one." [6]
In its immediate sequel the Chancellorsville chapter of accidents had
no such depressing effect as that at Fredericksburg. Realizing that
Hooker's main purpose had been frustrated, the President and his
chiefs took satisfaction in Stoneman's damaging of Lee's communications [7] and in the fact that no disorganizing blow had been dealt to
the structure and effectiveness of the Union army, whose power for
further fighting, considered relatively to that of the enemy, had not
diminished.

II

The peak of the furious war was now at hand. With a tempered and
confident army Lee struck north in the most ambitious undertaking
of the whole Southern effort. Invasion of the Yankee realm held out
high prospects to Confederate eyes. How far Lee could seriously expect his northward thrust to cause a depletion of Grant's strength before Vicksburg is a question, but he could reasonably hope that a
successful Confederate invasion might bring a decisive turn of the tide
against the cause of Lincoln and of the United States. Hooker might
be caught at a disadvantage as the terms of service of thousands of his
men were about to expire. Confederate needs of supply and food might
be satisfied. Virginia might be given a welcome respite. Dissension
and defeatism might be fomented behind Union lines. Perhaps Baltimore, Philadelphia, or Washington could be captured. If these things
were done, foreign powers might recognize the Confederacy; this
would be a major blow to the Union.

At any rate, to remain at Fredericksburg waiting for Hooker to
strike south, was of no use. Even failure in an offensive move, with
successful withdrawal, might have defensive importance. The summer was going to witness heavy fighting in any case, and if the
enemy's country could be invaded, his devices and strategic plans
could be disrupted and a good deal of time consumed before another
Virginia campaign could be launched. Above all, in the Southern view
the main consideration was that never again could the Confederate

---

[6] *Ibid.*, VIII, 265 (May 7, 1863).   [7] Moore, *Rebellion Record* (Diary), VI, 72.

chieftain hope for a better chance than in the post-Chancellorsville phase. If ever the cause of secession was to gain the victory, a fighting offensive was a necessity. Added to all this was Lee's low opinion of the Army of the Potomac under the kind of generals that had led it since the displacement of McClellan.

Pushing north in three great army corps under Longstreet, Ewell, and A. P. Hill, Lee was paralleled by Hooker's grand army, whose obvious business was to cover Washington and seek the advantage of favorable position when the foe should strike. On June 27 Hooker was near Frederick, Maryland, when a flare-up of antagonism between himself and Halleck occasioned his removal from command of the Army of the Potomac. Doubts as to support by authorities at the capital had been troubling the Union commander for some days; in a request for more definite orders he added the comment: ". . . outside of the Army of the Potomac I don't know whether I am standing on my head or feet." [1] Correctly enough, Hooker had requested the abandonment of Maryland Heights (at Harpers Ferry), where he said that the garrison of ten thousand was "of no earthly account," [2] so that these troops could be added to his army. Halleck, with the old obsession for guarding Washington by a scattering and immobilizing of Union forces, replied that he could not approve the abandonment.[3] Hooker then impatiently requested that he be unburdened of his command.[4]

A strategic difference and a clash of feeling between his general in chief and commander in the field were thus laid upon Lincoln's doorstep at a time when a false move would bring disaster. A momentous decision was called for and Lincoln made it. With what seemed like breathtaking promptness he accepted Hooker's resignation and appointed George Gordon Meade as commander of the Army of the Potomac.

This important bit of executive business requires explaining. It is not to be naïvely supposed that Hooker's asking to be relieved offered a sufficient reason for a change of command at so hazardous a moment. To swap horses while crossing a river was contrary to Lincoln's famous aphorism.[5] As for Hooker, his maneuvering of the army

---

[1] *Offic. Rec.*, 1 ser., XXVII, pt. 1, 56.   [2] *Ibid.*, 60 (see also p. 58).
[3] *Ibid.*, 59.   [4] *Ibid.*, 60.
[5] It was later, in the presidential campaign of 1864, that the aphorism was uttered.

as a foil for Lee had caused his stock to rise and it is altogether likely that he expected to be retained, his gesture of resignation being intended to bring a showdown with Halleck. According to an inside story of the episode as given by Charles F. Benjamin of the war department, the removal of Hooker and the appointment of Meade had been ordained weeks before it occurred. Just after Chancellorsville, according to this account, when Lincoln, taking Halleck with him, had hastened to the front in disgust at Hooker's retirement behind the Rappahannock, an investigation on the spot had virtually sealed the decision so far as Hooker was concerned. On return to Washington Lincoln and Halleck had agreed that Chancellorsville was "inexcusable," and that "Hooker must not be intrusted with the conduct of another battle." [6] Having checked Hooker on more than one occasion, Lincoln had come to be watchful of mistakes in his strategy. When in early June it seemed that the general might cross to the south of the Rappahannock on finding Lee to the north of that stream, Lincoln picturesquely advised against "being entangled upon the river, like an ox jumped half over a fence and liable to be torn by dogs front and rear without a fair chance to gore one way or kick the other." [7]

The advance decision to dismiss Hooker may help to explain the rising tension between that general and Halleck, a tension which led Lincoln to write to Hooker an admonition which applied equally to both men: "If you and he [Halleck] would use the same frankness to one another, and to me, that I use to both of you, there would be no difficulty. I . . . must have the . . . skill of both, and yet these suspicions tend to deprive me of both." [8] When Hooker questioned Halleck's right to control him, Lincoln, exercising the supreme power of commander in chief, again took Halleck's side as he peremptorily wired to Hooker: "I shall direct him [Halleck] to give you orders, and you to obey them." [9] These "family quarrels" [10] should probably be regarded as an unholy nuisance and annoyance to Lincoln, of the sort

---

Speaking to a delegation of the Union League just after his renomination, Lincoln attributed his selection not so much to his own merit as to the view that "it is not best to swap horses while crossing the river." *Works*, X, 123 (June 9, 1864).

[6] Charles F. Benjamin, in *Battles and Leaders of the Civil War*, III, 241.

[7] Lincoln offered the advice gently, as a mere suggestion. *Works*, VIII, 291–292 (June 5, 1863).

[8] *Ibid.*, VIII, 321 (June 16, 1863).   [9] *Ibid.*, VIII, 323 (June 16, 1863).

[10] *Ibid.*, 320 n.

that he had often to endure, rather than as the full cause of Hooker's dismissal.

A complicating factor in the episode was the attitude of Chase and his friends. As they were known to be partisans of Hooker, a "temporizing" policy had to be followed to avoid rupture with the "Treasury faction." [11] Matters were allowed to drift as weeks passed, Stanton being meanwhile determined to push the dismissal of Hooker. The drifting went so far, with Hooker growing stronger, that, according to Mr. Benjamin, "severe measures had to be resorted to in order to wring from him . . . [a] tender of resignation . . . ." [12]

Final details of the transfer of command seem nothing less than melodramatic. Meade had been slated for appointment when Hooker's sought-for resignation finally came, but impending battle was then so close that Stanton was alarmed lest "by accident or design" the transfer could not be effected. Never in the war was the Army of the Potomac at a more critical point: the North invaded, Philadelphians shaken by the rumor that Harrisburg was being bombarded, the railroad broken between Baltimore and Harrisburg, business suspended, gold taking a tell-tale leap, militia and thirty-day men mustering in haste, farmers aghast at the loss of harvests and stock, men and women of the North trembling [13] as they read their newspapers or peered at bulletins. In a proclamation that suggested the crack of doom Governor Curtin of Pennsylvania asked for sixty thousand men; appealing to "the patriotism and pride of every Marylander," Governor Bradford asked for ten thousand. [14] All the fighting potentialities of the Army of the Potomac were undimmed; yet there was danger that these potentialities might again be thrown away. [15]

As fateful moments passed there was a conference at the war department, Lincoln participating, and the transfer of command was agreed upon. [16] General James A. Hardie was ordered to start for the

---

[11] Charles F. Benjamin, in *Battles and Leaders of the Civil War*, III, 241. Mr. Benjamin explains (p. 240) that Hooker's influence had been enlisted in the movement to make Chase President.

[12] *Ibid.*, 241.   [13] Rhodes, *Hist. of the U. S.*, IV, 279.

[14] *Offic. Rec.*, 1 ser. XXVII, pt. 3, 169–170, 347–348.

[15] Ten days before Hooker's removal an observer in Washington had written: "Hooker does not know Lee's position. Halleck does not know what Schenck, or Hooker is doing or where Hooker is, ... We are adrift . . . ." Richard H. Rush to McClellan, Washington, June 18, 1863, McClellan MSS.

[16] Details are given by Charles F. Benjamin, in *Battles and Leaders*, III, 239–243.

front. As the personal representative of Lincoln, he was directed to deliver carefully prepared and authenticated duplicate orders to Hooker and Meade, with a previous personal word to Meade. Risking capture by Stuart's raiders and obstruction by whiskey-filled Union soldiers, Hardie reached Meade's tent at night and roused him from sleep. Feeling that the command ought to go to Reynolds, Meade could not be induced to accept until it was made clear that he had no choice and that, by orders from Washington, "it should be done immediately." There was a meeting next day (June 28) between Meade and Hooker, made painful by "Hooker's chagrin and Meade's overstrung nerves." [17] The transfer was effected. Meade then made a friendly explanation to Reynolds and was handsomely assured of the latter's support. Hooker took his leave; after a period of inactivity he was to have heavy duties, and perform them well, in the Chattanooga area.[18] To the scholarly Meade, unobtrusive officer that he was, the startlingly sudden promotion gave less of ambitious thrill than of "just diffidence" [19] as he rose to the soldier's challenge and obeyed the imperative order from Washington. Accepting extraordinary prerogatives conferred by the President, he prepared to fulfill a responsibility unexcelled, unless by Washington, in previous American history.[20]

For some days the talk, or hope, of a change of Union commanders had been floating about. The demand rose high for the recall of McClellan; it came with force and determination from many quarters —from the *National Intelligencer*,[21] from the New York board of councilmen, from the common council of Philadelphia, from A. K.

---

[17] *Ibid.*, 243.

[18] Neither defeat at Chancellorsville nor the humiliation of being displaced by Meade before Gettysburg served to spoil the spirit or blunt the fighting qualities of Joseph Hooker. For a careful study of his personality and career see Walter H. Hebert, *Fighting Joe Hooker* (1944).

[19] "By direction of the President of the United States, I hereby assume command of the Army of the Potomac. As a soldier, in obeying this order—an order totally unexpected and unsolicited—I have no promises or pledges to make. . . . It is with just diffidence that I relieve in the command of this army an eminent and accomplished soldier, whose name must ever appear conspicuous in the history of its achievements . . . ." Meade's General Order No. 67, June 28, 1863, *Offic. Rec.*, 1 ser., XXVII. pt. 3, 374.

[20] "Meade has . . . proved an excellent general, the only one . . . who has ever fought the army of the Potomac well. He seems the right man in the right place. Hooker was worse than a failure. Had he remained in command he would have lost the army & the capital." H. W. Halleck to Grant, July 11, 1863, MS., Ill. State Hist. Lib.

[21] Washington *National Intelligencer* (tri-weekly edition), June 18, 1863, editorial, p. 3, c. 1.

McClure (friend of Curtin and of Lincoln), from an audience addressed by Curtin, and from Governor Joel Parker of New Jersey.[22] Men of both parties joined in this earnest move, which expressed "a serious and powerful sentiment at the North."[23] Edward Everett had vigorously urged Lincoln to put McClellan back in command and had pleaded with the general, despite the interference of Halleck and Stanton, to accept.[24] It was indeed rumored that McClellan had been appointed general in chief of the army. The effect of the rumor, so the *Herald* reported, was "astonishing," as shown by a decline in gold and a "general revival of public confidence." Happening to be in New York City at the time, having come over from his home in New Jersey, McClellan was greeted by a "spontaneous ovation" which the *Herald* considered "unmistakable evidences of the extreme popularity of the General."[25] There was also a counter rumor, or fabricated whisper, that certain Democratic leaders in New York were planning to raise a force which, with McClellan at the head, would march upon Washington, and effect a *coup d'état* by which the Lincoln administration would be expelled.[26] From time to time similar reports had circulated concerning McClellan. A sensational account could be made up by putting these stories together, but they have no place except in the category of partisan falsification. It is a relief to note that men who were active against McClellan did not always traffic in this sort of slander. Referring, for instance, to an infamous tale concerning an alleged treasonable interview between McClellan and Lee before Antietam, Carl Schurz characterized such talk as "mere headquarters bluster."[27] Concerning the same canard a friend of McClellan wrote to him: "These are sad times when men can be brought to perjure themselves."[28] As for putting McClellan again at the head of the Army of the Potomac in the crisis of Lee's Pennsylvania invasion, it is clear that patriotic appeals to this end were made to Lincoln but that the old political prejudice against McClellan made such action impossible. Lincoln said virtually as much when he

[22] Rhodes, *Hist. of the U. S.*, IV, 277–278. [23] *Ibid.*, IV, 277.

[24] ". . . I . . . urge[d] upon him [Lincoln] the expediency of replacing you in command of the army. . . . Notwithstanding the disgusts you have received . . . I hope . . . you will not hold back." Edward Everett to McClellan, Boston, June 18, 1863, McClellan MSS.

[25] New York *Herald*, July 1, 1863, p. 6, c. 5.

[26] Edward Everett to McClellan, Boston, July 25, 1863, McClellan MSS.

[27] Myers, *McClellan*, 374–375. [28] *Ibid.*, 375.

telegraphed as follows in reply to an appeal by Governor Parker: ". . . no one out of my position can know so well as if he were in it, the difficulties and involvments of replacing General McClellan in command, and this aside from any imputations upon him." [29]

III

One seldom reads of the Civil War in terms of blood and filth, writhing men, spilled brains, and mutilated flesh. Even the terms "sick," "wounded," and "dead" are so generalized as to be almost abstract. Realities are so revolting that writers prefer to tell of flanking movements, of position and assault, of retreat or advance, of batteries opening up handsomely, of divisions doing this or brigades doing that. The very word "war" is a euphemism for "human slaughterhouse." Murder in drama usually occurs offstage. In historical accounts, especially military narratives, the war is offstage in the sense that its hideousness and stench do not appear.

So it is with the shambles at Gettysburg. Richard Brooke Garnett of Virginia, brigadier general under Pickett, went into battle ill but upstanding. He came out of it dead. His "cool and handsome bearing . . . devoid of excitement" won the admiration of his men. He was shot from his horse at the mouth of Union cannon. Armistead, another of Pickett's brigadiers, fell with Garnett. Kemper, commanding yet another of Pickett's brigades, received a serious wound. Where fighting was closest there seemed almost a suicidal rivalry "to plant the Southern banner on the walls of the enemy." [1]

When figured by regiments the losses under Pickett were appalling. Of the Eighth Virginia, under Col. E. Hunton, fifty-four were reported killed or wounded. It was an understatement; nearly all of Hunton's men were slain, wounded, or captured. Other losses among Virginia regiments included 87 of the Eighteenth Virginia, 77 of the Twenty-Eighth, 62 of the Fifty-Sixth, 67 of the Third, 81 of the Ninth, 108 of the Fourteenth. [2] The toll of field officers was enormous. "Regiments that went in with colonels came out commanded by

[29] Telegram to Governor Joel Parker of New Jersey, *Works*, IX, 13–14 (June 30, 1863).

[1] Report of Maj. Charles S. Peyton, commanding Garnett's brigade, Pickett's division, July 9, 1863, *Offic. Rec.*, 1 ser., XXVII, pt. 2, 386–387.

[2] Jesse Bowman Young, *The Battle of Gettysburg*, 426–427.

lieutenants." [3] The Twenty-Sixth North Carolina went in with over eight hundred; only 216 came out unhurt.[4] Heth's division of A. P. Hill's corps totaled about fifteen hundred effective men after the slaughter; it had numbered eight thousand.[5] Other Southern regimental losses, picked at random, were as follows: Of the Second South Carolina, 154 were lost at Gettysburg; of the Thirteenth Mississippi, 165; of the Seventeenth Mississippi, 200; of the Thirty-Eighth Virginia, 170; of the Fifth Texas, 109; of the Eleventh Georgia, 194; of the Forty-Eighth Alabama, 102.[6] In Garnett's brigade under Pickett it was officially reported that "the identity of every regiment . . . [was] entirely lost, and every regimental commander killed or wounded." [7] This brigade lost 941, Armistead's 1191, Kemper's 731, Pickett's division as a whole, 2888.[8] Captain Michael P. Spessard of the Twenty-Eighth Virginia was in Pickett's charge. "His son fell," so the report read, "mortally wounded, at his side; he stopped but for a moment to look on his dying son, gave him his canteen of water, . . . pressed on . . . to the wall . . . and fought the enemy with his sword in their own trenches . . . ." [9] Of the First Texas it was reported: " . . . many were killed and wounded, some losing their heads, and others so horribly mutilated and mangled that their identity could scarcely be established; but . . . all the men continued . . . unflinchingly to maintain their position." [10] Private W. J. Barbee of this regiment, "mounted a rock . . . , and there, exposed to a raking . . . fire from artillery and musketry, stood until he had fired twenty-five shots, when he received a Minie ball . . . in the right thigh, and fell." [11] The report of General Henry L. Benning, commanding a Georgia brigade, mentioned two of his colonels, William T. Harris and John A. Jones, killed on the second day—Jones by a fragment of shell which "passed through his brain," Harris by a ball that "passed through his heart, killing him instantly." [12]

On the Union side the roll of deeds and men was no less heroic. One Pennsylvania regiment, the One Hundred Fiftieth, known as

---

[3] *Offic. Rec.*, 1 ser., XXVII, pt. 2, 644.

[4] *Ibid.*, 645.   [5] *Ibid.*   [6] *Ibid.*, 338–339, 396.   [7] *Ibid.*, 387.

[8] *Ibid.*, 339.   [9] *Ibid.*, 387.   [10] *Ibid.*, 409.   [11] *Ibid.*, 410.

[12] *Ibid.*, 415. These losses are more impressive when compared with pre-battle strength. For example, for the brigade of General Alfred Iverson, C. S. A., it was reported that "out of the 1,470 officers and men present, June 30th, . . . there were but 400 left after the battle . . . ." Young, *Battle of Gettysburg*, 437.

"Second Bucktails," lost 264 men. The report read: "They all fought as if each man felt that upon his own arm hung the fate of . . . the nation." [13] Of the One Hundred Forty-Third Pennsylvania the losses were 253 out of 465; [14] the Twenty-Eighth Massachusetts lost one hundred.[15] General John Gibbon reported that his division "went into action about 3,800 strong; lost in killed and wounded over 1,600, and captured more prisoners than it had men on the ground at the end of the conflict." His "fearful" loss in killed and wounded was reported as especially high among field officers.[16]

IV

With no attempt to "cover" the battle of Gettysburg in these pages, it may be convenient to jot down some of the features of the three-day horror.

First Day, July 1, 1863. Lee's scattered forces, some of which had gone deep into Pennsylvania, were being cautiously concentrated at Cashtown, about nine miles west of Gettysburg, when Pettigrew's brigade of Heth's division (under A. P. Hill), moving toward Gettysburg in quest of shoes and other necessaries, "found a large force of cavalry near the town, supported by an infantry force." Getting no farther than the "suburbs of Gettysburg" (a rather amusing expression for a town that had 2390 inhabitants in 1860), Pettigrew returned to Cashtown and reported his observation (June 30); [1] the "enemy had now been felt, and found to be in heavy force in and around Gettysburg." [2] The Union cavalry was that of Buford; it was part of Meade's advance wing under Reynolds. Neither Lee nor Meade had planned that this should be the scene of combat, but their converging forces had met, and each commander now decided that Gettysburg was the place to fight it out. In making this decision while the choice to withdraw was still open, Lee was vigorously opposed by Longstreet, who advised him to swing around Meade's left and select a place to fight between him and Washington, with Meade making the attack. The battle of July 1 was a sharp preliminary fight which raged outside Gettysburg and through its streets as forces under Hill and Ewell met

---

13 *Ibid.*, 389.   14 *Ibid.*   15 *Ibid.*, 391.
16 *Offic. Rec.*, 1 ser., XXVII, pt. 1, 418.   1 *Offic. Rec.*, 1 ser., XXVII, pt. 2, 637.
2 *Ibid.*, 638.

those under Reynolds. Fierce attacks by numerically superior Confederates drove the Federals into retreat, but before the day closed a Union line of defense formed on Cemetery Hill, south of the town. There, with artillery support and reënforcements, they stood firm. The Confederates did not push their initial advantage to the point of dislodging the foe from that important position. Meade having not yet arrived, the Unionists at Gettysburg had been led by Reynolds, who was killed that day, then by Howard and later by Hancock; they had fought an excellent delaying action; there are those who say that the seemingly minor incidents of the first day determined the whole result.

A general battle had been precipitated not in terms of Confederate initiative, but of casual encounter. With tens of thousands streaming in on both sides a major engagement was on. Lee knew that he could not always control conditions and incidents; he also knew that a battle was inescapable. At the time it seemed reasonably promising of Confederate success. In the backward view it is evident that the attacking side was at a disadvantage. Conditions favored the defense if key positions could be quickly taken and held. Meade was growing constantly stronger; a few hours' delay meant everything to the Union cause.

Second Day, July 2. The morning was quiet. Action was delayed till past mid-afternoon. Then the Union left was badly threatened in a long and desperately fierce encounter, in the Peach Orchard and Devil's Den, between Longstreet and Sickles, the latter having detached himself in a rash forward movement instead of holding Little Round Top, key point in that part of the line. Sickles's move tended to expose and endanger the whole Union left; perhaps his ambitious thrust was in the hope of winning special prominence and glory; it became later the subject of a rankling dispute between himself and Meade. The wounding or killing of generals was one of the features of this battle; Sickles received a leg injury which necessitated amputation; in the controversy that followed there was a tendency for censure to be silenced in consideration of this costly sacrifice.

Longstreet's men in the powerful drive of their forward movement had all but taken Little Round Top, whose capture would have unhinged Meade's line. Fortunately for the Federals, however, General Warren hurried artillery and infantry into position just in time to repulse the on-rushing Confederates and keep both Round Tops in Union hands. On the Union right Edward Johnson's men of Ewell's corps made an attack upon Culp's Hill, east of Cemetery Hill, which was briefly successful. The hill was captured only to be released next day. Cemetery Hill was sufficiently well defended to withstand Early's strokes and with this vain assault the day ended. In a council of corps commanders that night Meade decided to strengthen and hold the Union line against Lee's attack next day.

Lee was disappointed. Confederate timing had gone wrong. Longstreet had been counted on to deal a crushing blow upon the Union left while Ewell struck the right and Hill took care of the center. These blows were expected to be delivered in advance of Meade's concentration. For success of the scheme, speed and coördination were essential and both were lacking. Longstreet was not only non-coöperative and "disgruntled"; he was so sincerely distrustful of Lee's strategy that he seemed determined to force his own plan "to be adopted in spite of Lee," while Lee's temperament was such that he did not sternly assert himself. It has been said by Lee's biographer that "on July 2 the Army of Northern Virginia was without a commander." [3]

Third Day, July 3. Though Pickett's charge in the afternoon was the chief event of the final day at Gettysburg, the morning's business on Meade's right was an essential factor. The basis for this phase of Union victory had been laid in the night hours by Geary's action in slipping Federal troops and artillery into inside positions along the Baltimore turnpike and on the rocky ground of Culp's Hill, then held by Johnson; all this was done "with the utmost silence and secrecy . . . within a few rods of the enemy's lines." [4] This part of the battle began at dawn (3:30) with a Union assault and raged with a series of shifting charges and countercharges for seven hours. It ended after terrible slaughter, with Federal recapture of Culp's Hill; and Meade's army occupied a hooklike position (a fishhook or reversed question mark), holding firmly on the Round Tops at the south, stretching for about two miles along Cemetery Ridge, and curving at the north on the now formidable positions of Cemetery Hill and Culp's Hill. Opposite stood Lee on Seminary Ridge; not

---

[3] Freeman, *Lee*, III, 149–150.　　　[4] *Offic. Rec.*, 1 ser., XXVII, pt. 1, 828.

quite a mile of open country separated the armies. From Confederate batteries there came at one o'clock a terrific and prolonged cannonade concentrated against the Union center; "the experience of the terrible grandeur of that rain of missiles and that chaos of strange and terror-spreading sounds, unexampled, perhaps, in history, . . . can never be forgotten by those who survived it." For almost two hours the artillery raged without shaking the Union position. The withstanding of that terrible test, with horses, men and carriages "piled together" and with limbers or caisson wheels shot off and replaced under fire,[5] was one of the chapters of bravery that contributed to Federal success.

Lee's supreme effort followed.[6] Against powerfully placed infantry and massed batteries there came in perfect order the "fearfully ir-resistible" [7] advance of the Confederates' best regiments. With colors carried high and a "precision and steadiness that extorted . . . ad-miration" [8] from their opponents they came on unhindered while tense moments passed as Union fire was withheld. The ensuing ordeal is beyond description. As the Confederates came within close range a deadly and destructive fire was opened upon them, mowing down thousands and throwing regiments into disorder. This, however, did not stop all of them; about a hundred penetrated to the low stone wall that marked the crest of the Union position, some even crossing the Union breastworks in an intensity of close and deadly combat which forced, momentarily, a partial Union retirement. For brief moments the battle seemed almost to waver, some of the Union bat-teries being nearly exhausted of ammunition, but soon it was over. Meade's line (Hancock's corps) had held; the magnificent Southern charge was utterly shattered and broken. Bloody Angle, apex of the assault, was too strongly covered for the utmost that an Armistead or a Garnett could do.[9]

---

[5] *Ibid.*, 437.

[6] This supreme Southern effort goes by the name of Pickett's charge, but of the forty-seven regiments in the attack, totaling about fifteen thousand men, less than a third (fifteen regiments) were those of Pickett. The brigades were those of Mayo, Davis, Marshall, Fry, Lane, Lowrance, Garnett, Kemper, Armistead, and Wilcox; the divisions were Pickett's, Heth's, Pender's (commanded by Trimble), and Anderson's. Hill's corps furnished more troops than did Longstreet's, which included Pickett's command.

[7] *Offic. Rec.*, 1 ser., XXVII, pt. 1, 439.   [8] *Ibid.*, 373.

[9] Longstreet's distrust of this assault is shown in his report: "The order for this attack, which I could not favor . . . , would have been revoked had I felt that I had that privilege." *Offic. Rec.*, 1 ser., XXVII, pt. 2, 360. See also Freeman, *Lee*, III, 121.

GENERAL ROBERT E. LEE

JEFFERSON DAVIS
President of the Confederate States of America

Only a desperate few had pierced the Union wall. Discharges from Meade's artillery [10] and infantry had broken up the main waves of Confederate advance on the plain between the armies. As for Pickett's men, who had been under terrific fire, the account of General Alexander, Confederate artillery commander, was that they "never halted, but opened fire at close range, swarmed over the fences and among the enemy's guns—were swallowed up in smoke, and that was the last of them." [11]

One of the reasons for Lee's failure was the uselessness of Stuart's cavalry. Having lost contact with the main army when Lee needed him most for intelligence, Stuart failed completely when counted on to strike Meade's rear simultaneously with blows on his front. On July 3, in a portion of the battle that has received small attention, Stuart's men, especially those commanded by Fitz Lee and Wade Hampton, made a dashing cavalry charge in approved style with sabers drawn, but Union cavalry under Gregg and Custer drove them back and defeated them at every point. In judging the nature of Stuart's failure, it is to be noted that his success in Meade's rear "would have been productive of the most serious consequences"; [12] also that most of the other mistakes on the Southern side resulted from the "injudicious use of the Confederate horse during the . . . campaign." [13]

Where there was all this superb sacrifice there was also bravery tempered with prudence, courage that stopped short of self-immolation. Some of the attackers in the confused hand-to-hand fighting, according to a Union report, "threw down their arms and were

---

[10] It was claimed, however, that Federal artillery had not done enough. Among the controverted points at Gettysburg (which cannot be treated here) was the statement of General Henry J. Hunt, able chief of artillery for the Army of the Potomac, that if his instructions had been followed on the third day, he did "not believe that Pickett's division would have reached our line." *Battles and Leaders of the Civil War*, III, 375. Correctly judging that the Confederate cannonade was preparatory to an infantry assault on the Union center, Hunt instructed Meade's artillery commanders to withhold fire for fifteen or twenty minutes, then to concentrate it accurately on those enemy batteries that were doing the greatest damage. (Many of them were doing virtually no damage at all, merely sweeping open ground in the Union rear.) As it turned out, the weight of Confederate assault fell at a point where Union projectiles had been exhausted during the preliminary cannonade, and the possible effectiveness of Federal artillery was partly lost. See also *ibid.*, III, 385–387.

[11] *Ibid.*, III, 365–366. [12] *Offic. Rec.*, 1 ser., XXVII, pt. 1, 956.
[13] Freeman, *Lee*, III, 148.

taken prisoners of war, while the remainder broke and fled in great disorder." [14] Incidentally, in the shifting battle, retirement by one side or the other was essential where fighting organization was preserved; at times on each side the choice was between withdrawal and utter loss of fighting power. "With but two exceptions" wrote a Confederate colonel, "each and every man of the regiment proved himself a hero." [15] Another wrote: "Both officers and men, with scarcely an exception, did their duty . . . unflinchingly." [16] Censurable conduct sometimes found its way into reports. A Union colonel, reporting the capture of twenty battle-flags in "a space of 100 yards square," added: "Several colors were stolen or taken with violence by officers of high rank from brave soldiers who had . . . honestly captured them . . . , and were probably turned in as taken by commands which were not within 100 yards of the point of attack." [17] There were men "making to the rear as fast as possible"; [18] as in other battles men were posted behind the line to shoot stragglers.

To speak only of men enduring the fire at Gettysburg is to understate the fierceness of the battle. Longstreet, reporting on what is usually called Pickett's charge, referred to "wavering columns." Then, having indicated how some of his troops "advanced to the charge, . . . entered the enemy's lines, . . . and gained his works," he added: "About the same moment, the troops that had before hesitated, broke their ranks and fell back in great disorder, many more falling under the enemy's fire in retiring than while they were attacking." [19] The number of prisoners taken is another indication of how sharply the battle raged. The division commanded by General Alexander Hays claimed the capture of more than fifteen battle flags, not less than 1500 prisoners, and "2,500 stand of arms, besides an estimate of 1,000 left upon the ground for want of time to collect them." [20] Where there were willing prisoners, they became so usually by reason of the unmistakable decision of battle against them. In the close and confused fighting at Culp's Hill on July 3 General Geary re-

---

[14] *Offic. Rec.*, 1 ser., XXVII, pt. 1, 440. "Many of the enemy . . . crawled . . . under the sheet of fire, and, coming up to our lines, surrendered themselves prisoners." *Ibid.*, 450.

[15] *Ibid.*, pt. 2, 410.

[16] *Ibid.*, 572. Another statement read: "The whole regiment behaved admirably, with one or two exceptions." *Ibid.*, pt. 1, 286.

[17] *Ibid.*, pt. 1, 440.   [18] *Ibid.*, 439.   [19] *Ibid.*, pt. 2, 360.   [20] *Ibid.*, pt. 1, 454.

ported large numbers begging to be captured; they had advanced, he said, "until met by our terrible fire, and then, throwing down their arms, rushed in with white flags, handkerchiefs, and even pieces of paper, in preference to meeting again that fire which was certain destruction." [21] This is but another way of saying that at Gettysburg there were artillery and infantry volleys which men could not withstand. As to the main generalization, reports of soldier conduct agree in emphasizing the superb performance of the troops. Over and over the officers reported in substance: "Where all behaved so nobly, individual distinction cannot with propriety be made." [22] In Peach Orchard or Devil's Den, at the stone wall or "clump of trees," each side met the fiery test with unstinted valor. It is this valor of both sides, rather than the unedifying spectacle of Americans killing Americans with furious intensity of purpose, that constitutes the chief tradition of Gettysburg.

V

Pickett's remnants staggered back and Confederate lines quickly formed to repulse a counter stroke, but it did not come. Meade's men had taken terrific punishment. Lee's army was to escape from the campaign. Despite that escape the Confederacy had passed what has been traditionally called its "high tide." From that hour it was to be a receding flood, and writers are expected to expatiate upon Gettysburg as *the* turning point of the whole war.

Such expatiating may be left to others; it will not be reproduced in these pages. One could argue that in the larger view the turning of the tide in September 1862, with McClellan in command, had been even more significant, particularly as to emancipation and as to policy abroad. One does no injustice to the importance of Gettysburg to say that in the phase which preceded Antietam the Confederacy stood at a high point in solid prospects which not even the Gettysburg phase could quite equal. The struggle, of course, was a continually shifting affair. Decisiveness in the whole war is hard to focus in any one battle or campaign, but in the uncertainty of military control at Washington the possibility of Union recovery in the event of Lee's offensive victory at Antietam was so low, and the situation abroad so

---

[21] *Ibid.*, pt. 1, 830.   [22] *Ibid.*, pt. 2, 406.

critical, that September of 1862 was at least as decisive as July of 1863. The averting of disaster at Antietam permitted the momentum of 1863–4–5 in both the East and West to develop. This was true despite those setbacks at Fredericksburg and Chancellorsville which prevented the Federals from exploiting the advantages that were reasonably to have been expected under more effective leadership than that of Burnside and Hooker.

This is a point which many writers have missed. Turning points are favorite themes and traditional viewpoints have great power of survival. It is hardly correct to speak of only one turning point in the war and that at Gettysburg. If a national cause escapes disaster more than once, each escape is as important as the whole cause. In that sense Gettysburg was of supreme importance, while in intensity of fighting it marked the peak of the struggle in the East. To speak of it as *the* turning point is unnecessary. It is to be remembered that the Confederacy never followed up a military victory with anything important in the political sense. Such a following up was certainly as much of a possibility in the event of a Confederate triumph at Antietam (before Grant had done much in the West) as at Gettysburg. If in each episode such a chance existed—if the cause, having been saved before, had to be saved again—that is enough tribute to the men of Cemetery Hill and the Round Tops.

As Confederates viewed the peaks and valleys of their effort, Gettysburg offered a devastating contrast to Chancellorsville. "Yesterday," wrote a Confederate general after Lee's defeat, "we rode on the pinnacle of success; to-day absolute ruin seems to be our portion. The Confederacy totters to its destruction." [1]

The fourth of July 1863 was a day of rare Union triumph as Grant at Vicksburg received the surrender of Pemberton's army of thirty thousand. This shining achievement was the culmination of a boldly conceived campaign that showed Grant at his best, yet the achievement was as much a matter of grim struggle as of brilliant execution; it came only after repeated failures to approach Vicksburg directly from the North, or to divert the Mississippi River, causing that stream to by-pass the famous city. Fighting the mighty river was no good; the day would come when the "Father of Waters" would go "unvexed

---

[1] Diary of General Josiah Gorgas, Chief of Ordnance, C. S. A., July 28, 1863, Gorgas MSS.

to the sea," but for heartbreaking months it refused to be enlisted on the Union side. The Yazoo approach had been no better; its creeks and bayous, bluffs and forested hills seemed made for Confederate defense.

Bitter frustration stopped Grant's early efforts, then he tried a new tack. He cut loose from his base, crossed his army to the Louisiana side, pushed it through a tangle of swamps and bayous to a point far south of Vicksburg, joined the fleet under Foote, who had daringly run the Confederate batteries, recrossed the Mississippi, and launched upon an almost faultless series of operations that sealed the doom of Pemberton as early as May 19, from which time Vicksburg was under tightly held Federal siege. The ending of that siege with Confederate surrender, coming dramatically on July 4 and coinciding with Meade's victory over Lee, gave Lincoln's cause the uplift in morale and the advantage in international standing which only military victory could bring.

To speak of the destructive effect of Gettysburg upon the Confederate cause is to refer to a long and slow process. Though checked, the military power that challenged the Union was still formidable. Great as was that Fourth of July, Lincoln had expected more.[2] Vicksburg had surrendered. As he wrote Halleck, if Meade could have effected the destruction of Lee's army the war would have been over. Instead of this, Lee got away keeping his army intact; the chance was lost. There had been almost incessant rains. Days passed while the Confederate host, with prisoners and wounded, was "compelled to await at Williamsport the subsiding of the river and the construction of boats." In this vulnerable position Lee expected attack; his position was "becoming daily more embarrassing."[3] The attack did not come; on July 13–14 he crossed the Potomac by pontoon bridge and ford. It seemed that Meade had wasted the ten days following Gettysburg. He had failed to pursue, and the possible stakes had not been won. A seemingly entrapped enemy had eluded its fate.

In his report Meade said in effect that he was preparing to attack, but the enemy got away.[4] One of Meade's difficulties was indecision,

---

[2] In response to a serenade on July 7, 1863, Lincoln said: "These are trying occasions, not only in success, but for the want of success." *Works*, IX, 21.

[3] *Offic. Rec.*, 1 ser., XXVII, pt. 2, 309.

[4] "The 13th [of July] was occupied in reconnaissances of the enemy's position and preparations for attack, but, on advancing on the morning of the 14th, it was ascer-

to which was added that fatal weakness, a council of generals. He submitted the question of an attack to his corps commanders; five out of six voted no; later there was reconnaissance with preparations for possible attack; it was too late; on advancing his army, he found the enemy lines evacuated.[5]

To Lincoln it had seemed that Meade had held Lee in his grasp. He was "close upon him"; the river was "so swollen as to prevent his crossing," wrote Lincoln on July 11. At that point the President was "more than satisfied," [6] but that was on the expectation that Meade would strike. Yet Lincoln had not actually ordered Meade to attack,[7] and now the chance was gone. The President had naturally been elated by hopes of putting an end to the war; the dashing of these hopes plunged him into deep distress. His thoughts may be read in a "draft of a letter" to Meade under date of July 14. This being the day of Lee's southward crossing, Halleck had informed the general that "the escape of Lee's army without another battle has created great dissatisfaction in the mind of the President"; he referred to the army as "not . . . sufficiently active." [8] Meade, conscious only of duty done, considered the censure "so undeserved" that he respectfully asked "to be immediately relieved from the command of this army." [9] Lincoln began his letter with a reference to Meade's request, dealing with the "supposed censure" by giving assurance of his gratitude for the general's "magnificent success . . . at Gettysburg." Then he frankly explained his distress of mind at "the magnitude of the misfortune involved in Lee's escape." "He was within your easy grasp, and to have closed upon him would . . . have ended the war. As it is, the war will be prolonged indefinitely. . . . I do not expect . . . you can now effect much. Your golden opportunity is gone, and I am distressed immeasurably because of it."

Lincoln generously explained that he wrote only because Meade had heard of his dissatisfaction, and that he "thought it best to kindly tell . . . why." Had the words of the Chief Executive reached Meade, no amount of kindness could have disguised the rebuke; the President's truest kindness in the whole matter was his withholding

---

tained he had retired the night previous by a bridge at Falling Waters and the ford at Williamsport." Report of General Meade, *ibid.*, pt. 1, 118.

[5] *Ibid.*, 91–92.   [6] *Works*, IX, 25.   [7] *Ibid.*, IX, 28 n.

[8] Halleck to Meade, July 14, 1863, *Offic. Rec.*, 1 ser., XXVII, pt. 1, 92.

[9] Meade's resignation came in a communication to Halleck, July 14, 1863. *Ibid.*, 93.

of the letter. It was a "draft"; that was all. The pain that Meade would undoubtedly have felt if he had received such a letter from the President was not inflicted. Lincoln's own endorsement on the envelope read: "To General Meade; never sent or signed." [10] Next year, when sharp criticism of Meade appeared over the cloaking signature "Historicus" in the *Herald*,[11] and when it was thought that Sickles inspired if he did not write the stinging articles directed against the man who was still in command of the Army of the Potomac, Meade wanted a court of inquiry, but Lincoln discouraged the idea. Again Lincoln spoke in kindly terms: "The country knows that . . . you have done grand service; . . . it is much better for you to be engaged in trying to do more than to be diverted . . . by a court of inquiry." [12]

No such generosity characterized the Republican radicals of the congressional war committee. Pouncing upon Meade with the prejudiced fury that marked their "investigations," they "screamed taunts," [13] disseminated whispers, and created a publicity pattern of their own to rob the commander at Gettysburg of all credit. The radical version was that the success at Gettysburg was the achievement of the corps commanders and that Meade should have only blame for his "criminal vacillation" [14] in failing to pursue. When in February-March 1864 Wade and Chandler, of the war committee, demanded of Lincoln that he remove Meade, whom radicals disliked for politicians' reasons, and put Hooker in his place, Lincoln showed yet another favor to the harassed general by refusing the demand,[15] well knowing that his refusal would intensify the radical assault upon his administration in election year.

VI

The midway point in the war was reached before measures to raise an army became commensurate with the magnitude of the struggle. Not till March 1863, with Hooker poised for a desperate struggle with Lee and Grant for a duel with Pemberton, did Congress pass the first

---

[10] "Draft of Letter to General G. G. Meade," July 14, 1863, "never sent or signed." *Works*, IX, 28–30.

[11] For the bitter controversy between Meade and Sickles apropos of the "Historicus" contribution to the *Herald*, see *Offic. Rec.*, 1 ser., XXVII, pt. 1, 127 ff. See also *Battles and Leaders of the Civil War*, III, 413–419.

[12] *Offic. Rec.*, 1 ser., XXVII, pt. 1, 139.   [13] Williams, *Lincoln and the Radicals*, 304.

[14] *Ibid.*, 303.   [15] *Ibid.*, 337–341, 361–363.

strictly national conscription law for the United States. This warborn statute introduced a radical modification into the American military system. In January 1861 the United States army had consisted of 16,402 officers and men.[1] When war broke at Sumter Lincoln had summoned 75,000 three-months "militia" of the states (April 15, 1861). On May 3 he had called for forty regiments of volunteers for three years as well as for eight regular regiments and 18,000 seamen. After the shock of the Bull Run defeat Congress passed a series of acts authorizing the President to accept volunteers in such numbers as he should deem necessary, not to exceed one million; the service was to be for not less than six months nor more than three years. In the spring of 1862 there were 637,126 men in the service, according to the report of the provost marshal general.[2] There was a general impression that enough men had been raised, and on April 3, 1862, there came an amazing order of Secretary Stanton that recruitment be stopped. The whole elaborate service for raising men was discontinued, "the property at the rendezvous sold, and the offices closed throughout the country." [3]

In a short time, however, the mood changed and with it government policy, so that the recruiting service was resumed (June 6, 1862) and a series of far-reaching efforts was made toward the raising of new forces. A realistic study of the situation showed that, while the number of men drawn into the service might seem an impressive total, the effective strength of the army for combat duty was a far different matter. As the months passed that strength was depleted by many factors: time required for training, absenteeism, desertion, battle casualties, disease, military service far from the front, and a system of hospitals by which governors saw to it that many a man was brought back "first to his State and then to his home." [4] Along with this diminishing of the army there came a new realization of the military task which confronted the Union government in the summer of 1862 in the crushing of a formidable and determined Confederacy. On July 1 an impressive group of Union governors—eighteen of them from Maine to Missouri and from Michigan to Tennessee—insisting that the "decisive moment" was at hand to "crush the rebellion," presented a

---

[1] *Offic. Rec.*, 3 ser., V, 605.   [2] *Ibid.*, 608.   [3] *Ibid.*

[4] Emory Upton, *Military Policy of the United States*, 439.

Both illustrations by courtesy of Massachusetts Historical Society

RECRUITING POSTERS

At the left, the stakes being a nation's life, the odds favor Lincoln's "W. M." (White Mare), UNION, whose pedigree includes Independence, Wisdom, Patriotism, etc., over Davis's "Blk G." (Black Gelding). CONFEDERACY, sired by Treason, "he by Belzebub out of Nullification." The final note in this poster is an advertisement for Searle, whose facilities for printing are "unsurpassed."

At the right Captain Nims's "famous and gallant HORSE BATTERY" is featured, with "HIGHEST BOUNTIES PAID For Recruits in this favorite branch of the service."

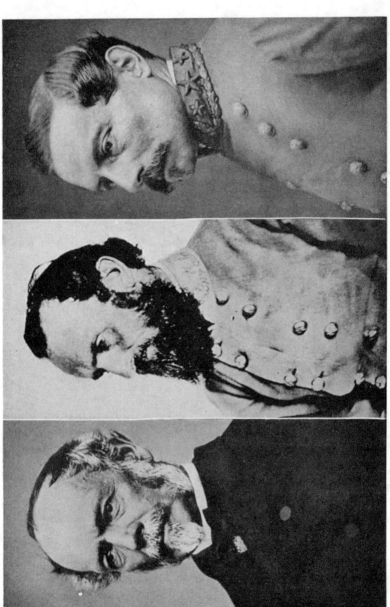

CONFEDERATE GENERALS

Joseph E. Johnston; Thomas J. ("Stonewall") Jackson; (P.) G. T. Beauregard.

paper urging the President to issue a new call for men. By this they meant that the governors were taking the initiative and that state agencies were to be used in the raising of volunteers. They meant also to organize a needless and inefficient number of new military units, with many new commissions, allowing the depletion of veteran regiments to continue. Their system also included other ineffective procedures.

In response to this appeal of the governors Lincoln issued a call for 300,000 men (volunteers for three years) on July 2, 1862.[5] He hoped that they would be "enrolled without delay, so as to bring this unnecessary and injurious civil war to a speedy and satisfactory conclusion." [6] The nation's law makers now added their contribution, tinkering with the machinery at a time when the war had produced small results in Union victory. Falling back on the system of short-term militia, Congress passed a militia act (July 17, 1862) by which the President was given a qualified power of conscription for Federal militia service through state machinery. Having been under the urging of governors, the President was now given a mandate by Congress, and on August 4 he ordered a draft of 300,000 militia for nine months' service—this on the heels of his July 2 call for 300,000 volunteers.[7] With many technicalities and complications as to shares and credits, this draft of 1862, though demanded by the general government and launched by orders of the President, was conducted by state authorities. Even in the midst of gigantic conflict the unmilitary American democracy was slow to go on a genuine war basis. The latter part of 1862, in this respect, was chiefly significant for the half measures and failures which, according to the provost marshal general, demonstrated "the necessity for a radical change in the method of raising troops." "The old agencies," he reported, "for filling the ranks proved more and more ineffective." Adoption of a drastic system, however, was dreaded, and it was not until after "a protracted, searching, and animated discussion" that the conscription act of March 3, 1863, was passed. "It was the first law enacted by Congress by which the Gov-

---

[5] *Offic. Rec.*, 3 ser., IV, 1264–1265. Under this call 421,465 men were reported furnished.

[6] *Works*, VII, 250.

[7] *Offic. Rec.*, 3 ser., V, 609. Under this call of August 4, 1862, for nine-months militia 87,588 men were reported furnished (*ibid.*, 3 ser., IV, 1265).

ernment of the United States appealed directly to the Nation to create large armies without the intervention of the authorities of the several States." [8]

Under this ill-devised statute a Federal provost marshal general's bureau was set up and a vast national network of enrolling officials was spread over the country. Though in the long run its results were small, this elaborate machinery reached into every locality and into every home that included able-bodied men of military age. The thankless and dangerous business of these officials was to list the men liable to service, examine state "credits," equalize the burden by a process that resembled higher mathematics, determine exemptions, conduct the draft, make arrangements in the matter of substitutes and commutation money, and bear up as best they could against secret societies, newspapers, and politicians in the use of local pressure, intimidation, questions of legality, evasion, open violence, and every "imaginable artifice . . . to deceive and defeat the enrolling officers." [9]

The moment of adoption of national conscription was one of depression. As the provost marshal general reported, there was "general apathy" as to volunteering, recruiting had "subsided," and desertion had so "greatly increased" as to become a "formidable and widespread evil." [10] Defeats and setbacks were fresh in the public mind. Operations against Vicksburg had been frustrated; Stone's River had left Rosecrans inactive for months; Charleston had withstood Federal assaults; the gloom of Fredericksburg still lingered; in the same blood-soaked vicinity Lee was soon to win another triumph. Conscription was a "novelty." It was contrary to American tradition. "The people had become more accustomed to the enjoyment of privileges than to the fulfillment of duties under the General Government, and . . . beheld the prospect of compulsory service in the Army with an unreasonable dread." [11]

The mere manning of the administrative machine was highly elaborate, with the appointment of officials for each district and subdistrict. It required special care to see that dishonest persons were not appointed and that competent and patriotic men were put in charge of districts containing hostile elements. Beginning in late May 1863, the provost marshal general's bureau proceeded with its work

---

[8] *Ibid.*, 3 ser., V, 611.   [9] *Ibid.*, 618–619.   [10] *Ibid.*, 612.   [11] *Ibid.*, 611.

throughout the rest of the war. They found opposition "in almost every house, if not to the act itself, at least to its application to . . . particular persons." [12]

VII

It is not intended to indicate here the frauds, abuses, and fundamental defects of the conscription system. Exemption from military service was permitted to any who provided a substitute or contributed $300 commutation money. The number who escaped by the money provision exceeded 86,000.[1] Many localities, according to the bureau's report, entirely cleared themselves "by raising money and advancing it to the persons drafted." The report adds: "This appeared to be the favorite method adopted by disloyal sections to prevent the re-enforcement of the armies . . . ." [2]

Along with the abuses of conscription as then applied there existed in Lincoln's day a wretched system of bounties whose purpose seemed not primarily to get men to go all the way in performing soldier duty, but rather to stimulate "enlistments"—i. e., to fill quotas, build up credits, and avoid or diminish the drafting of men. Local communities would often pay bounties in full at the time of enlistment, and this method of cash payment, as well as the whole mercenary principle, produced a medley of vicious effects and inequalities that can hardly be realized.[3] Exploitation by bounty brokers and substitute brokers added an odious element to the system, which opened the door to that degraded individual, the "bounty jumper." This was the man who enlisted, collected bounties, deserted, reënlisted under a change of name, collected more bounties, and repeated the process until a final desertion left him free and enriched, or until caught. How far bounties encouraged fraudulent enlistment is hard to say, but the provost marshal general made the statement that by reason of the bounty system "profligate and corrupt men amassed fortunes from the money raised for . . . bounties to soldiers," and that veterans "who had enlisted early . . . , without expectation of bounty, had good cause to murmur when late in the war unworthy recruits came

---

[12] *Ibid.*, 618.   [1] *Offic. Rec.*, 3 ser., V, 720.   [2] *Ibid.*, 718.
[3] Ably treated in F. A. Shannon, *The Organization and Administration of the Union Army 1861-1865*, II, 57 ff.

among them rich with bounty for one year's enlistment." The official report demonstrated that the whole bounty system was an expensive way of obtaining inferior soldiers.[4]

The provost marshal general's bureau calculated the number of Union desertions as 201,397,[5] the ratio of desertions to enlistment credits being 62 per thousand in the loyal states generally, reaching as high as 117 in some areas.[6] Men deserted for a variety of reasons. Sometimes the desertions, arising from an inadequate concept of military discipline, were technical; they were committed with no thought of abandoning the cause. Certain military practices produced disgust, as when election of unsuitable officers by men under their command caused intolerable dissatisfaction among an "often highly intelligent minority." [7] Other factors were false stories as to harsh conditions in the service, dread of becoming prisoners, the effect of physical exactions upon the less vigorous, and the urgency of home obligations. When such obligations coincided with inactivity at the front, a man might feel that his family needed him more than did the army.

Some of the opposition to conscription was due to "politics," some of it was no better than vulgar mob psychology; yet much of it was due to a genuine hatred of compulsion, resentment against the rich (supposed to be favored by the prevailing system), and dissatisfaction at what was believed to be unfair or partisan discrimination in the administration of the law. There was violence in Lincoln's own state; there was an "insurrection" in Holmes County, Ohio; there were disturbances in Wisconsin, Indiana, Kentucky, and Pennsylvania; there was rioting at Troy, Albany, and Newark; there was a flare-up of border violence in Missouri.[8] These, however, paled into insignificance beside the furious riot which raged in New York City from July 13 to July 16, 1863. As a center of busy industry and a port of entry for numerous immigrants, New York had more than the normal per-

---

[4] *Offic. Rec.*, 3 ser., V, 675.   [5] *Ibid.*, 677.

[6] *Ibid.*, 668. The figuring of percentages is complicated by the fact that there were more enlistments than troops and more desertions than individual deserters. With something like two million in Union army service (W. F. Fox, *Regimental Losses in the American Civil War*, 527), those who deserted constituted about ten per cent. Conscription fell short of making up the loss by desertion. See Ella Lonn, *Desertion during the Civil War*.

[7] *Offic. Rec.*, 3 ser., V, 678. Election of officers was abandoned later in the war.

[8] Randall, *Civil War and Reconstruction*, 412–413.

centage of adult males. It thus came about that an entirely just draft, proportioned to the total of men properly subject to military duty, would take more men from Manhattan, in proportion to population, than from rural areas; it was easy for agitators to represent this as deliberate discrimination. The fear that freed Negroes might come North and compete for poor white men's jobs was also a factor. Rational explanation, however, breaks down. The demons of party feeling, race hatred, and class prejudice were whipped up in one vast orgy of murder and destruction, precipitated at the moment when officers had come to the drawing of names from the wheel. Half-crazed rioters stormed through the city, overpowering police with rifles seized from an armory, pillaging, burning buildings, slaying hundreds of Negroes, assailing the *Tribune* establishment, destroying property, burning a colored orphan asylum, and fighting bloody battles on sidewalks and barricaded streets. Estimates of the number killed vary from three hundred to twelve hundred; F. A. Shannon considers five hundred the minimum.[9] Property to the value of some millions was destroyed. Finally, with the help of police, naval forces, militia, a company from West Point, and a detachment of Federal troops rushed north from the Gettysburg campaign, the rioters were suppressed and order restored. Next month the draft was quietly resumed and no resistance offered.[10]

Apropos of conscription there had arisen a controversy between the President of the United States and Horatio Seymour, Democratic Governor of New York. In the pages of Nicolay and Hay, the governor is made to appear in a very bad light. By their account, he denounced enrollment, demanded that Federal authorities submit to state control, asked to have the draft suspended, showed sympathy for the rioters, accused draft officials of frauds, directed "insulting charges" against Lincoln, and showed himself a partisan in his hostility to the execution of the law.[11] He and his friends, say Nicolay and Hay, made the proceedings of the government "the object of special and vehement attack." [12]

On the other hand it is shown by Alexander J. Wall [13] that Seymour stood firmly for the Union and the Constitution, sustained Lincoln

---

[9] Shannon, *Union Army*, II, 213. For other estimates see Wall, *Horatio Seymour*, 39.
[10] Nicolay and Hay, *Lincoln*, VII, 37.   [11] *Ibid.*, VII, 32 ff.
[12] *Ibid.*, 39.   [13] Wall, *Horatio Seymour*, 20 ff.

in essential war measures, and was all in all a loyal Democrat. He believed, however, that the South had rights, distrusted an abolitionist war, was vexed at the Republican party's claim to a "patent right for all the patriotism," [14] favored adherence to constitutional methods, considered conscription unconstitutional as well as unnecessary, and felt confident that recruitment, which he actively promoted in New York, would accomplish the purpose. He was not the politician type. The people of New York had elected him knowing his views, thereby rejecting Wadsworth who upheld Lincoln, and he felt that acquiescence in certain of the doubtful measures of the administration would be a kind of desertion from his party's and his people's standard. His opposition to Lincoln was genuine; it was not that of the demagogue; yet in the controversy between them Lincoln came through with the better showing. Perhaps it should be added that the nature of the contest gave Lincoln the advantage. To oppose conscription in time of gigantic and desperate war, and to do it with an unavoidable suspicion of party motive, is no easy task. When Lincoln wrote a frank and conciliatory letter asking coöperation, the governor sent a cold and guarded reply,[15] but it cannot be said that he showed actual noncoöperation with the Washington government in the more vital matters. Lincoln's approach was to treat the situation as if no difference or controversy existed, or at least to relegate disputes to the background. He addressed the governor with respect, spoke generously in conference with the governor's brother,[16] showed readiness for reasonable adjustment, and in the outcome was successful in upholding the draft law.

One does not need to single out Seymour, except for the prominence of his position. There were many Union men of both parties who opposed conscription in general and the odious Civil War brand of it in particular. Even Horace Greeley wrote that drafting was "an anomaly in a free State"; it oppressed the masses, he thought, and it would have to be "reformed out of our systems of political economy." [17] There were grave doubts of the constitutionality of the law of 1863, and so long as the Supreme Court of the United States remained silent on the issue, the legal question, after the manner of Americans with

---

[14] *Ibid.*, 30.
[15] Due to pressure of work, according to Seymour's biographer. *Ibid.*, 29.
[16] *Ibid.*, 29–31.   [17] Greeley to Stanton, June 12, 1863, Stanton MSS.

a law they distrusted, was considered open. The Supreme Court never passed on the constitutionality of the 1863 act, though a half-century later it unanimously upheld that of 1917, and Lincoln felt that the advantage of the Court's silence should not all be on one side. "I do not object," he said, "to abide a decision of the . . . Supreme Court, . . . but I cannot consent to lose the time while it is being obtained." He thought it impossible to match an enemy that used every able-bodied man "if we first waste time to reëxperiment with the volunteer system already . . . inadequate, and then more time to obtain a court decision as to whether a law [for conscription] is constitutional . . . ." [18]

VIII

Though the Supreme Court was silent on the validity of the conscription law, it is noteworthy that two high officials of the Federal government, the President and the Chief Justice, prepared undelivered opinions on this subject—the President upholding, and the Chief Justice emphatically denying the constitutionality of the statute. Taney's paper on the subject survived as a manuscript in his handwriting.[1] Though an undelivered opinion, it reads exactly as if it were a pronouncement from the bench in a specific case involving the validity of the draft law. It appears to have been prepared at the Chief Justice's leisure for future use if such a specific case should arise. Elaborately marshaling judicial and historical citations, the high justice comes through with the conclusion "that this [conscription] Act . . . is unconstitutional and void—and confers no lawful authority on the persons appointed to execute it." The reasoning starts with a restrictive interpretation of the whole American federal system, with emphasis on reserved powers of the states and limited powers of the nation; the argument then proceeds to the assertion that the power of Congress to raise armies does not confer authority to cause the militia of the states to be "of no practical value"; even more, it

---

[18] Lincoln to Seymour, Aug. 7, 1863, *Works*, IX, 60–61.

[1] That the Chief Justice prepared an opinion on conscription seems but slightly known. A copy of Taney's manuscript, made from the unpublished original for the use of George Bancroft, is in the New York Public Library. See Phillip G. Auchampaugh, "A Great Justice on State and Federal Power. Being the Thoughts of Chief Justice Taney on the Federal Conscription Act," *Tyler's Quarterly Historical and Genealogical Magazine*, XVIII, 72–87 (Oct., 1936).

is asserted that the law in question is invalid because it "enables the general government to disorganize at its pleasure the government of the States,—by taking forcibly . . . the . . . officers necessary to the execution of its law." [2]

Lincoln's opinion on the subject was left among his papers, but never issued or published during his lifetime. It is an opinion which cuts through to fundamentals and deals with the ethical justice as well as the legality of universal service. Getting down to bedrock, the President canvassed the elements of democracy, the dominance of patriotism over party strife, the need for doing things we dislike, the survival of republican institutions, and the integrity of the country. The legal objection he considered utterly flimsy. Congress had power under the Constitution to raise armies; that was the whole of it. Congress "must prescribe the mode, or relinquish the power." The country had gone as far as it could, thought Lincoln, with volunteering, yet more men were needed or it would lose all that already had been poured out. The cause required armies. Armies required men. "We have ceased to obtain them voluntarily, and to obtain them involuntarily is the draft . . . ."

To those who denied the need for conscription Lincoln appealed with the request that they prove their case by increased volunteering. He referred to the law itself apologetically, admitting that "it may not be exactly such as any one man out of Congress, or even in Congress, would have made it." As to its application he compared it to a tax law, which becomes "a dead letter" if no one pays until it becomes certain that all will pay equally, also to congressional apportionment, in which entire equality of population among the districts, required by the Constitution, is impossible in practice. He allowed that "errors will occur" in the draft and argued that the best the government could hope for was "an approach to exactness."

In a somewhat labored passage the President justified the clauses pertaining to substitution and to commutation money. Without the three-hundred-dollar clause he thought that rich men only, being able to pay a thousand dollars or so for a substitute, could escape the draft. In other words, the favoring of the more wealthy was due to substitution, to which, he said, the people did not object. Once substitution

---

[2] For quoted passages, see *ibid.*, 80, 83, 87. In Taney's paper "general government" appears in lower case while the words "State" or "States" are capitalized.

was permitted, the money provision was an advantage to men of moderate means, because it prevented the price of substitutes from going above three hundred dollars. If a man could not pay that much he could not escape, but he could come "as near escaping as . . . if the money provision were not in the law." "The inequality . . . pertains in greater degree to . . . substitution . . . , and is really . . . lessened by the money provision."

Conscription, wrote the President, was not new. It had been "practised in all ages." It was known to the framers who worded the Constitution so as to make it possible. "Shall we shrink," he said, "from the necessary means to maintain our free government, . . . ? Are we degenerate? Has the manhood of our race run out?" Early in the paper he had said with some sarcasm: "We are prone . . . to find false arguments . . . for opposing . . . disagreeable things." In his concluding passage he put his foot down: ". . . I feel bound to tell you it is my purpose to see the draft law faithfully executed." [3]

In this paper one finds Lincoln's rationalization of the draft in essence and his excuses for it in particular. It was an able document, worded and constructed in Lincoln's characteristic style. Why, then, did he never issue it? One can only speculate on the answer. If the President had used his usual publicity technique, the communication would probably have been addressed to some person or group. What person or group? That was something of a poser. There were passages in the document which made it appear that the Executive was exhorting those who were not doing their part. The paper would have been a plea for an unpopular law. It would have been depressing in its admission of the failure of recruiting. Its justification of the money clause, which was repealed in 1864 (less than a year after it was passed), would hardly have made pleasant reading. Some of its phrases, though understandable in the sense intended, were of a sort which the President's opponents might have twisted and used against him.

In any case the chief objection to the existing system, applicable both to substitution and to the commutation feature, was the matching of a money payment against the sacrifice of human life. There was, in this unissued paper, too much attention to what the citizen would have to do to "escape" the draft. Even Lincoln's reasoning would

---

[3] "Opinion on the Draft, never issued or published by the President" (Aug., 1863), *Works*, IX, 74–83.

hardly have convinced those who felt that the system as set up in 1863 did work for the benefit of the rich by putting a price on exemption, and fixing that price well above the ability of the average American laborer to pay. Millions of Americans were getting, for a year's average, less than a dollar a day. To poor men, the sum of $300, supposing it to have been laboriously saved, was a huge amount.

Taking it all in all, it was fortunate that this presidential defense of the conscription law of 1863 was never issued by Lincoln. To justify the concept and constitutional right of compulsory national service was one thing; to plead for the unsatisfactory law of 1863 was quite another. The vulnerability of Lincoln's argument, and the chance of its being misread, were doubtless canvassed in his own mind. The preparing of the paper and the decision not to issue it illustrated two things: Lincoln had the intellectual grasp and ability in debate which enabled him to argue a case well; he also had the restraint to withhold a product of his own thought. His caution in not presenting the paper to the public, thus avoiding a presidential misstep, is an interesting factor in the leadership of a rough-hewn man who seldom erred in his reading of popular sentiment.

For a basis on which to judge the matter one may turn to selective service as framed and administered during the World War. Universal service under Wilson was planned by the war department in advance, not left to Congress after the emergency had arisen. It was promptly enacted at the outset of the war. No stigma attached to the conscript; the whole emphasis was on the honor of national selection. Self-registration was wisely used; volunteer unpaid service by local officials made for economy; there were no bounties nor substitutes, and no provision as to commutation money; industrial deferments were provided. The Supreme Court unanimously upheld the law; opposition was never a widespread menace. In all administrative respects the system under Wilson was far superior to that of Civil War times, and in the total result its effectiveness was shown in the raising of two thirds of the nation's forces. Indeed the selective system was regarded by the war department not only as adequate for raising of all the troops, but as preferable to volunteering.[4]

---

[4] "It is not certain . . . that the country . . . understood the imperative necessity of eliminating indiscriminate volunteering. . . . To carry selection to its logical . . . end, there could be no deviation from the rule that each registrant must await his'

At every essential point the conscription system of Civil War days presents to the historical student an unfavorable contrast to that of the Wilson administration. The law providing compulsory service came not at the outset, but midway in the struggle. Its adoption was a confession of failure; its very premise was the breakdown or inadequacy of volunteering, whereas the law of Wilson's day was based on the considered judgment that governmental selection was the most fitting and effective method of raising a huge army. Under Lincoln there was insufficient planning. Men in Congress, not military experts, wrote the statute. The drafted man was under a stigma; it was a stigma that hurt the pride both of the drafted man and of the community or state from which he came. A costly and elaborate system blanketed the country; enrolling officers laboriously made the lists instead of the men offering themselves for registration. Details of administration were lamentably designed, as shown by the abuses of substitution, bounties, and commutation. The constitutionality of the statute was vigorously assailed under Lincoln without being upheld by the Supreme Court, the Chief Justice, in fact, being under the strong conviction that the law was invalid. Serious disturbances, with hundreds of casualties, were encountered. Finally, when the results were cast up it was seen that about 46,000 conscripts and 118,000 substitutes were dragged into service for an army of about two million.[5]

For these defects Lincoln was not responsible, but an unconscionable amount of his time was occupied with patient adjustments and answers to complaining governors who in some cases seemed more concerned with minor inequalities, some of them imagined, than with the broad needs of the service. When the governor of Vermont complained of an unjust quota, Lincoln mentioned "keeping . . . faith" with New Hampshire, which had furnished a larger surplus and explained that it was "impossible to concede what Vermont asks without coming out short."[6] When Seymour of New York asked a suspension (postponement) of the draft, Lincoln adjusted the matter in terms of reënrollment. On the main matter of his executive duty he wrote to Seymour: "My purpose is to be . . . just and constitutional,

time and perform his military obligation only when his call, in orderly process, came to him." *Second Report of the Provost Marshal General* (1918), 6–7.

[5] Randall, *Civil War and Reconstruction*, 411.   [6] *Works*, XI, 6–8 (Feb. 8, 1865).

and yet practical, in performing the important duty with which I am charged, of maintaining the unity and the free principles of our common country." [7]

---

[7] *Ibid.*, IX, 61 (Aug. 7, 1863).

CHAPTER XXVIII

THESE HONORED DEAD

ON an autumn day in '63 Lincoln reached a high moment in his life as he stood at tragic Gettysburg to deliver a simple tribute to the nation's dead. If this formerly peaceful Pennsylvania town brings to mind Reynolds, Pickett, Armistead and Garnett, if it connotes Lee's frustration and Meade's triumph, even more does it suggest Lincoln's timeless words. By these words Gettysburg becomes more than a scene of carnage, for above the waste and slaughter rises the challenge of a society founded and maintained in enduring terms of democracy, order, and sanity. Without Lincoln's ideal, Bloody Angle and Cemetery Hill produce only a shudder of horror. In the bewildering excess of monuments at Gettysburg the one most appealing is the undying flame of aspiration—the perpetual light that points, albeit from a battlefield, to peace.

I

So famous is this dedicatory vignette and so inexhaustible the popular interest in Lincoln's smallest act that writers have probed every corner of the episode.[1] In the voluminous literature covering Lincoln's address one finds less appreciation of its larger world significance than minute inspection of its most trivial detail. What did the President wear? How did his white gauntlets look with otherwise black attire? Did he ride his horse awkwardly or well? What kind of chair was provided for the nation's Chief on the platform? Not a chair of

[1] For a fresh and competent study see F. Lauriston Bullard, *"A Few Appropriate Remarks": Lincoln's Gettysburg Address* (1944). Where others have adorned the tale with excessive verbiage Bullard gives the essential points in compact form; where less careful writers have been misled he offers an important contribution in strict matters of historical evidence.

state, according to a contemporary report, but "an old, dingy, un-cushioned settee" which he shared with others.[2] What about his ges-tures? None, we are told, except a sweep of the hand at the words "these honored dead." [3] Did Lincoln smile? Only once, was one man's memory; that was when telling a story to a group that included Curtin and Seward.[4] How many times did he use the word "that" in the address? William E. Barton gives the answer: thirteen times! [5] How did he adjust his spectacles and hold his manuscript, how was his "Kentucky idiom" manifest, how did he pronounce his vowels? We have that too.[6] Were the words "under God" extemporaneously inter-jected? Competent investigators conclude that they were. When he spoke of government of, by, and for the people, did he stress the *of, by,* and *for,* or did he put the accent on the *people?* Barton would "like to think" [7] that he did the latter. How would the address read if rewritten in the manner of Theodore Roosevelt, or of Woodrow Wilson? Barton is "quite certain" that these men "would have said" so-and-so. Not only the big, solemn things, but the little things are presented to us. We are given the picture of Lincoln holding proof-sheets of Everett's address as he sat to Gardner for what has come to be known as the Gettysburg portrait.[8] We are told who were in the President's party, how he was entertained, who were on the platform, who took notes, how the crowd felt (there are variant accounts here), what sources he drew from, what the papers said, what copies were made by Lincoln, and even, in the words of Barton, "what he wished he had said." [9]

There has been much speculation as to where and how Lincoln prepared the address. Did he jot it down while on the railway journey to Gettysburg? It is clear to scholars that this tradition has no founda-tion, but the story persists. It has gathered further details: a pencil

[2] Cincinnati *Daily Gazette,* Nov. 23, 1863.

[3] Interview (May 25, 1929) by the author with W. H. Tipton, lifelong resident of Gettysburg, who heard the address.

[4] *Ibid.*

[5] William E. Barton, *Lincoln at Gettysburg: What He Intended to Say; What He Said; What He Was Reported to Have Said; What He Wished He Had Said,* 147.

[6] As to the Kentucky idiom, see *ibid.,* 92.   [7] *Ibid.,* 83.

[8] In Barton's frontispiece the Gardner portrait is given with the erroneous statement that it was made in Gettysburg on November 11, 1863. It was made in Washington, as Barton correctly states on p. 54. The source for the Gardner portrait incident is Noah Brooks, *Washington in Lincoln's Time,* 285–286.

[9] Barton, *Lincoln at Gettysburg,* chap. xv.

was borrowed from Andrew Carnegie; the hasty jottings were put down on a yellow or brown envelope (some say a pasteboard), which reposed in the President's tall hat after the manner of his earlier technique as postmaster.[10] To unfounded tradition has been added obvious error; in an article giving "new facts" about the occasion it is stated that while Lincoln was in Gettysburg he received word "that his little son, Willie, who was very ill, had passed the crisis," a statement which overlooks the fact that Willie died in February 1862.[11] One could multiply such samples, but there is no need to go further into the unprofitable realm of Lincoln-at-Gettysburg apocrypha.

The first impulse toward the Gettysburg occasion was the imperative demand of decency and health. Where twenty thousand wounded had shocked Henry W. Bellows of the Sanitary Commission with their "unspeakable" suffering, the battleground presented a "fearful" spectacle.[12] The exposure of horse carcasses and soldiers' bodies,[13] hastily interred and soon uncovered by heavy rains, produced a press-

---

[10] This point has been covered by various writers, including J. G. Nicolay who rode with Lincoln (see *Century Magazine*, XLVII, 601 [1894]). In *Zions Herald*, CXVI, 1351 ff. (1938), F. Lauriston Bullard ably treats the sources of the legend, which he attributes to misstatements by J. G. Holland, Isaac N. Arnold, William O. Stoddard, Ben: Perley Poore, and others; he finds the "evidence . . . conclusive that the President did not prepare the speech on the train, that he did not borrow . . . paper from . . . Seward nor a pencil from Andrew Carnegie (p. 1351)." On other details of the preparation of the address Bullard finds Governor Curtin's recollections "curiously unreliable" (p. 1352). See also Charles Moore, *Lincoln's Gettysburg Address and Second Inaugural*. Moore states (p. 14) that the evidence is "conclusive" against the story that Lincoln wrote the address on the back of an envelope or sheet of brown paper borrowed from Seward.

[11] This is in a newspaper article giving the recollections of W. H. Tipton of Gettysburg, Pittsburgh *Sun-Telegraph*, Feb. 12, 1929, p. 3. It does not appear that Tipton himself made the mistake. The error was a matter of the identity of the "sick boy" mentioned by Lincoln (letter to Everett, Nov. 20, 1863, *Works*, IX, 211). It was Tad who was ill.

[12] H. W. Bellows to his wife, undated (evidently shortly after the battle), Bellows MSS. In referring to twenty thousand wounded, Bellows considerably understated the case. T. L. Livermore (*Numbers and Losses in the Civil War* . . . , 102–103) gives 14,529 as the number of wounded on the Union side, 18,735 on the Confederate side. Freeman (III, 154) gives the aggregate of all casualties in the Gettysburg campaign as 23,371 for the Confederates; 28,129 for the Federals.

[13] "In traversing the battlefield, the feelings were shocked . . . at the sights that presented themselves at every step. The remains of our brave soldiers . . . in many instances were but partially covered with earth, and . . . in some instances were left wholly unburied. Other sights, too shocking to be described, were . . . seen. These appearances presented themselves promiscuously over the fields of arable land . . . which would . . . be farmed over in a short time." *Address of Hon. Edward Everett* . . . [etc.] (Boston, 1864), 8.

ing problem of sanitation, while at the same time the need for a fitting burial of fallen heroes, together with the motive of state pride, led to the acquisition by the state of Pennsylvania of a seventeen-acre plot on Cemetery Hill. Though from the outset the term "national cemetery" was used, the movement was at first a coöperative project of a number of states with Pennsylvania in the lead. It was not until 1872 that the ground was ceded to the United States government, not till many years later that the whole battle area became a great national park.

Arrangements were in the hands of David Wills of Gettysburg, who acted as Governor Curtin's special agent and later as head of a select committee for the purpose. For the ceremony of dedication it was intended that the chief honors should be done by a distinguished orator and a great poet. Edward Everett, orator extraordinary, ex-president of Harvard, "master of elegance," [14] "Apollo in Politics," [15] full of days and public honors at seventy, consented to be the speaker of the day, but a poet was sought in vain. In the absence of a poet laureate, who might have been expected to grow lyrical by official command, unsuccessful approaches were made to Bryant, Longfellow, and other bards of the time.[16] The failure was symbolic. Nobly conceived poetry was and remained lacking during the Civil War; the verse that did appear in enormous reams and bushels was unmitigated drivel.[17] A noteworthy exception, which came just after the war, was Lowell's ode recited at Harvard College on July 21, 1865, in commemoration of the sons of Harvard who had given their lives in the war. The most famous part of the ode, the sixth stanza devoted to Lincoln,

---

[14] Everett was thus characterized by Emerson, who spoke also of his "radiant beauty of person . . . ; sculptured lips; . . . perfect utterance," and "florid, quaint, affluent fancy." Paul Revere Frothingham, *Edward Everett: Orator and Statesman,* 63–64. Emerson was a fervent admirer, almost worshiper, of Everett.

[15] *Ibid.,* chap. v.

[16] Benjamin Brown French, commissioner of public buildings at Washington, assisting in arrangements for the dedication, had sought to obtain an original ode for the occasion by a distinguished poet, and had appealed to Longfellow, Bryant, Whittier, and George H. Boker. Unsuccessful in these efforts, French himself wrote a dirge or hymn which was sung "in good style" after Everett's oration by "a delegation from the Union Musical Association of Baltimore." Charles Moore, *Lincoln's Gettysburg Address and Second Inaugural,* 12; Cincinnati *Daily Gazette,* Nov. 23, 1863.

[17] In the twelve volumes of *The Rebellion Record: A Diary of American Events, with Documents, Narratives, Illustrative Incidents, Poetry, Etc.,* ed. by Frank Moore, one may find these forgotten lyrical atrocities embalmed. Their only significance is to illustrate the low state of the muse when devoted to contemporary war themes.

"was not recited, but was written immediately afterward." [18] Lowell and Whitman were among the very few of Lincoln's time who could do justice to him in verse. As for a grandly conceived major poem on the theme of the war, that did not come until the appearance of Stephen Vincent Benét's *John Brown's Body* in 1928. It was in the same period that Sandburg's great interpretation of Lincoln, lacking none of the magic of poetry, took the form and substance of biography.

A poet and an orator had been the committee's first thought; the invitation to Lincoln came as a secondary matter. Plans were well advanced in August; Everett was invited on September 23; yet Wills's letter of invitation to the President came on November 2. By that time the date of the dedication, November 19, had been fixed to suit Everett, who asked more time for preparation than was at first allowed. It is not recorded that the President's convenience was consulted in setting the date. Lincoln gave ready acceptance; it was an occasion in which he plainly wanted a part.

II

In ancient Athens appropriate public attention was given to obsequies for those who died in battle. Famed Ceramicus held the remains of men who had fallen.[1] With their appreciation of the fine arts, one of which was oratory, Athenians would not be satisfied unless a master of speech was selected to deliver a panegyric; the elaborate care he would take in its preparation was considered comparable in the Greek mind with that of a sculptor. To have a great thing to say required that it be said well; to achieve great expression was to add to the world's indestructible treasure. The arrangements for the dedication at Gettysburg, especially the choice of Everett, a Webster of his day, gave advance notice of the dignity of the event.

The President and his party arrived by slow train from Washington on the evening of Wednesday, November 18, 1863, and the President was the overnight guest in the home of Mr. Wills on the central square or "diamond" of the town. That night Lincoln appeared in response to a serenade and made a few undistinguished remarks, mentioning

---

[18] Horace E. Scudder, *James Russell Lowell: A Biography*, II, 70.

[1] Soldier funerals among the Athenians are described, with details obviously taken from Thucydides, in the early paragraphs of Everett's oration.

that in his position it was important not to "say any foolish things."
"If you can help it," said an impertinent voice in the audience!

This was not the only indication that some among the Gettysburg
crowds failed to appreciate their President. Addressing a "large and
clamorous" group John W. Forney, newspaper publisher and secretary of the Senate, upbraided his serenaders for inadequate cheers to
Lincoln. To that "great man," he said, "you owe your name as American citizens." "He went on," according to the diary of John Hay,
"blackguarding the crowd for their apathy" and "went back to the
eulogy of the President, that great, wonderful mysterious inexplicable
man who holds in his single hands the reins of the republic; who keeps
his own counsels; who does his own purpose in his own way, no
matter what temporizing minister in his Cabinet sets himself up in
opposition . . . ." [2]

Throngs filled the town that night; next morning thousands more
poured in, many of them traveling in covered wagons of the Conestoga
variety. The unfinished work of re-interring the dead by wholesale at
$1.59 per body had been temporarily suspended and coffins were much
in evidence, while souvenir hunters roamed the battlefield to view the
scene of death and pick up a dismal relic—a bullet, button, or fragment
of uniform.

Smart young John Hay wrote of the night and the day of the ceremony with sophisticated sarcasm, recording various pranks and drinking parties, and indicating withal a restlessness as to what to do with
himself. "[Wayne] MacVeagh," he wrote, "young Stanton, & I foraged
around for awhile—walked out to the college, got a chafing dish of
oysters then some supper and finally loafing around to the Court
House where Lamon was holding a meeting of marshals, we found
Forney and went around to his place, Mr. Fahnestock's, and drank a
little whiskey with him. He had been drinking a good deal during the
day & was getting . . . ugly and dangerous." [3]

Though many of the arrangements had been stupidly handled, the
ceremony itself was elaborate and imposing. A procession, marshaled
by Ward H. Lamon, moved in what Hay called "an orphanly sort
of way" [4] to the cemetery, the homely President riding horseback.

---

[2] Diary of John Hay, Nov. 20, 1863 (Dennett, *Lincoln . . . in the . . . Diaries of
John Hay*, 121).

[3] *Ibid.*, 119.   [4] *Ibid.*, 121.

The prepared order of procession included high military officers, the President and Cabinet secretaries, judges of the Supreme Court, the "orator of the day" (Everett), governors, commissioners, the Vice President, the Speaker, "bearers with flags of the States," members of Congress, a Gettysburg local committee, officials of the Sanitary Commission, religious committees, the telegraph corps, representatives of the Adams Express Company—and so on through the hospital corps, Knights Templars, and masons, to the press, loyal leagues, fire companies, and citizens of Pennsylvania, "citizens of other States" and of the territories.[5] During the march minute guns were fired which suggested to a reporter the "roar of battle, reverberating from the hills and mountains."[6]

There was a dirge followed by a prayer, the audience standing uncovered. Old Hundred was played by the band, then the "venerable orator" Everett rose and stood a moment in silence, regarding the battlefield and the distant beauty of the South Mountain range.[7] By the standards of that day Everett delivered a great speech, though for an audience unprovided with seats after a restless night and long travel, it was much too long. "Standing beneath this serene sky," the "Alleghenies dimly towering" before him, the orator raised his "poor voice to break the eloquent silence of God and Nature." He reviewed the funeral customs of ancient Athens, referred to Marathon, paid tribute to the dead, discussed the purpose of the war, and gave a closely documented summary of the three-day battle. Avoiding any flings at the common people of the South, he minced no words in denouncing the "foul revolt" as a crime. The heart of the people, North and South, he said, was for the Union. Some of his best phrases were devoted to "bonds that unite us as one people— . . . community of origin, language, belief, and law, . . . common . . . interests; . . . common·pride . . . ." Elements of union, he said, were "of perennial . . . energy, . . . causes of alienation . . . imaginary, fictitious, and transient."[8]

Everett had not spared himself. He had avoided "sentimental or patriotic commonplaces."[9] He had delivered a learned and volumi-

---

[5] Cincinnati *Daily Gazette*, Nov. 23, 1863.   [6] *Ibid.*   [7] *Ibid.*

[8] Everett's address is reprinted in Barton, *Lincoln at Gettysburg*, 211 ff.

[9] "The occasion is . . . not to be dismissed with a few sentimental or patriotic commonplaces." Everett to David Wills, Boston, Sep. 26, 1863. *Address of Hon. Edward Everett at . . . Gettysburg . . .* [etc.] (Boston, 1864), 17. Commenting on the signifi-

nous address, had piled it high with historical and classical allusions, had omitted no effort to dignify the occasion. In contrast to all this stateliness and elaboration the impression of Lincoln's simple speech was that of almost shocking brevity. For the immediate occasion—posterity was a different matter—it was as if the highest official of the republic was playing second fiddle. The President's thought and manner were less conditioned by the immediate occasion than by the timeless aspect of his dedicatory duty, that quality being the greater because achieved in spite of tragic realities and official vexations. Mindful that the war was still raging and that armies were massed for doubtful combat in Tennessee, facing the unsightly work of reburial, immersed in hateful details of politics, surrounded in office by those who distrusted him, pressed, buffeted, roundly assailed, yet remembering that he stood in the presence of the dead, Lincoln looked beyond battles, politicians, and hatred to enduring verities. As revised by himself in the form that has become standard,[10] these were his words:

Four score and seven years ago our fathers brought forth on this continent, a new nation, conceived in Liberty, and dedicated to the proposition that all men are created equal.

Now we are engaged in a great civil war, testing whether that nation, or any nation so conceived and so dedicated, can long endure. We are met on a great battle-field of that war. We have come to dedicate a portion of that field, as a final resting place for those who here gave their lives that that nation might live. It is altogether fitting and proper that we should do this.

But, in a larger sense, we can not dedicate—we can not consecrate—we can not hallow—this ground. The brave men, living and dead, who struggled here, have consecrated it, far above our poor power to add or detract. The world will little note, nor long remember what we say here, but it can never forget what they did here. It is for us the living, rather, to be dedicated here to the unfinished work which they who fought here have thus far so nobly advanced. It is rather for us to be here dedicated to the great task remaining before us—that from these honored dead we take

cance of Everett's oration, Paul Revere Frothingham wrote: "Posterity has forgotten . . . that Everett . . . was the first to sound the note of reconciliation and eventual harmony between North and South" (Frothingham, *Everett*, 454). Whether he was "the first" need not be argued; the essential point is the importance which Everett placed on this factor.

[10] The text as here given is that of Lincoln's final and most careful autograph revision, known as the "Bliss copy" made for the Sanitary Fair at Baltimore in 1864, and used in a volume known as "Autograph Leaves of Our Country's Authors."

increased devotion to that cause for which they gave the last full measure of devotion—that we here highly resolve that these dead shall not have died in vain—that this nation, under God, shall have a new birth of freedom—and that government of the people, by the people, for the people, shall not perish from the earth.

III

It is not easy to recover the manner of Lincoln's speaking, nor the reaction of the immediate audience. According to John Russell Young, reporter for the Philadelphia *Press*, the perfection of Everett was "like a bit of Greek sculpture—beautiful, but cold as ice." It was "resonant, clear, splendid rhetoric." In contrast, he said, Lincoln spoke "in his high tenor voice, without the least attempt for effect." "Very few," wrote Young, "heard what Mr. Lincoln said, and it is a curious thing that his remarkable words should have made no particular impression at the time." He added that spectators were more interested in the efforts of a photographer to get a picture of the President while speaking (in which he unfortunately failed) than in the address.[1] Others, however, reported greater appreciation by Lincoln's auditors. The "right thing in the right place, and a perfect thing in every respect," was the description by the Cincinnati *Gazette's* correspondent, who reported long continued applause as the President concluded.[2] Mr. French, who was of the President's party, noted that the address was received with "a tumultuous outpouring of exultation." [3]

Some of the slighting remarks concerning the President's address were similar to the insulting voice at the President's serenade; some of the unawareness was traceable to the fact that humans cannot always be expected to hail a classic at birth. It is not true, however, as often stated, that the speech was unappreciated by contemporaries. On the day after the dedication Everett wrote thanking Lincoln for his kindness to him at Gettysburg, including thoughtfulness for his daughter's accommodation on the platform "and much kindness otherwise." "I should be glad," said Everett, "if I could flatter myself that I came as near to the central idea of the occasion in two hours as you

---

[1] John Russell Young, in *Frank Leslie's Illustrated Newspaper*, April 10, 1886, 119.
[2] Cincinnati *Daily Gazette*, Nov. 23, 1863.
[3] Diary of Benjamin B. French, MS., Lib. of Cong., quoted in Charles Moore, *Lincoln's Gettysburg Address and Second Inaugural*, 22.

did in two minutes." [4] Lincoln replied: "In our respective parts yesterday, you could not have been excused to make a short address, nor I a long one. . . . The point made against the theory of the general government being only an agency, whose principals are the States, . . . is one of the best arguments for the national supremacy." [5]

With equal promptness Longfellow pronounced the speech "admirable." This also was on the day after its delivery, while on the second morning "the *Springfield Republican* declared it 'a perfect gem' and that evening the *Providence Journal* described it as 'beautiful . . . touching . . . inspiring . . . thrilling.' " [6]

Column writers were few in those days, but a near approach to later columnists was George William Curtis, whose little essays on the world in general appeared in *Harper's Weekly* as the comments of "The Lounger." It is of interest to note what Curtis said of Lincoln at Gettysburg. "The few words of the President," he wrote, "were from the heart to the heart. They can not be read . . . without kindling emotion. . . . It was as simple and felicitous and earnest a word as was ever spoken." [7]

In Lincoln's own day the address became famous; this is shown by the demand for its text in Lincoln's hand. It is to this demand that we owe the President's careful attention to the final form of the address, which he rewrote several times and which has therefore come down to posterity as Lincoln wished it. This is not to imply that Lincoln changed his speech substantially, nor that he had failed to give careful thought to the text before delivery. For such an address to have been hastily prepared, or for the President to have trusted to the moment, would have been altogether contrary to Lincoln's habit. There were

---

[4] Nicolay and Hay, *Lincoln*, VIII, 203. In a letter to Mrs. Hamilton Fish, Mar. 18, 1864, Everett referred to "President Lincoln's singularly appropriate & much admired dedicatory remarks." Everett MSS.

[5] *Ibid.* Everett had argued that the authority established under the Constitution was the "Government of the United States" established by "the People of the United States." Noting that state officers were required to take oath to support the national government, he added: ". . . I never heard . . . of sovereigns being bound by oath to be faithful to their agency." Barton, *Lincoln at Gettysburg*, 241.

[6] F. Lauriston Bullard, in *Zions Herald*, Nov. 16, 1938, 1353.

[7] "The Lounger," *Harper's Weekly*, Dec. 5, 1863. George William Curtis was the "Lounger" (Frank L. Mott, *A History of American Magazines: 1850–1865*, II, 474). In 1859 he wrote: "I make my Lounger a sort of lay pulpit . . . ." (Edward Cary, *George William Curtis*, 120.) Curtis was also the "Easy Chair" of *Harper's Magazine*; as such he has been called the "American Addison" (William M. Payne, *Leading American Essayists*, 351).

BOSTON DAILY ADVERTISER.

NO. 12,079.   VOL. 102.—NO. 126.   BOSTON   FAMILY MORNING, NOVEMBER 20, 1863.   THREE CENTS.

The Consecration at Gettysburg.

Dedicatory Address by the President.

GETTYSBURG, Pa., Nov. 19.—The ceremonies attending the dedication of the National Cemetery commenced this afternoon by a grand military and civic display, under command of Major-General Couch.

The line of march was taken up at 10 o'clock, and the procession marched through the principal streets to the Cemetery, where the military formed in line and saluted the President. At a quarter past 11 the head of the procession arrived at the main stand. The President and members of the Cabinet, together with the chief military and civic dignitaries took position on the stand.

The President seated himself between Mr. Seward and Mr. Everett, after a reception with the respect and perfect silence during the solemnity of the occasion, every man in the immense gathering uncovering on his appearance.

The military then formed in line extending around the stand, the area between the stand and the military being occupied by civilians, comprising about 150,000 people, and including men, women and children. The attendance was quite large.

The military escort comprised one squadron of cavalry and two batteries of artillery and a regiment of infantry, which constituted the regular funeral escort of honor for the highest officer in the service.

After the performance of a funeral dirge by the band, an eloquent prayer was delivered by Rev. Mr. Stockton.

Mr. Everett then delivered his oration, which was listened to with marked attention.

The President then delivered the following dedicatory speech:—

"Four score and seven years ago our fathers brought forth upon this continent a new nation, conceived in liberty and dedicated to the proposition that all men are created equal. [Applause.] Now we are engaged in a great civil war, testing whether that nation, or any nation so conceived and so dedicated, can long endure. We are met on a great battle-field of that war; we are met to dedicate a portion of it as a final resting place of those who have given their lives that that nation might live. It is altogether fitting and proper that we should do this, but in a larger sense we cannot dedicate, we cannot consecrate, we cannot hallow, this ground. The brave men living and dead who struggled here have consecrated it far above our power to add or detract. [Applause.] The world will note nor long remember what we say here, but it can never forbid what they did here. [Applause.] It is for us, the living, rather, to be dedicated here to the unfinished work that they have thus so far nobly carried on. [Applause.] It is rather for us to be here dedicated to the great task remaining before us, that from these honored dead we take increased devotion to that cause for which they here gave the last full measure of devotion that we here highly resolve that the dead shall not have died in vain; [applause] that the nation shall, under God, have a new birth of freedom, and that government of the people by the people and for the people shall not perish from the earth." [Long continued applause.]

Three cheers were here given for the President and the Governors of the States.

After the delivery of this address, the dirge and the benediction closed the exercises, and the immense assemblage departed about 2 o'clock.

BEST NEWSPAPER REPORT OF LINCOLN'S WORDS AT GETTYSBURG

Charles Hale, of the Boston *Daily Advertiser*, heard the address and made this report, being well fitted by family and training to do so. He was a grandnephew of Nathan Hale, brother of Edward Everett Hale, relative of Edward Everett, and student at Harvard. He was to have a considerable career in journalism, diplomacy, and public office. Though not free from typographical error, this text cannot be far from the words as uttered by Lincoln.

times when the President appeared in response to crowds and frankly did not try to make a speech. His remarks on such occasions were conversational and intentionally casual, but no public man was more cautious of the public word, written or spoken, than Lincoln. He had more than two weeks in which to prepare for Gettysburg, and the well known correspondent Noah Brooks states that some days before the dedication Lincoln told him in Washington that the speech was short, and that it was "written, 'but not finished.' " [8]

That the President prepared the address carefully may be regarded as certain, and from a study of the evidence, including five autograph copies in Lincoln's hand which have survived to our own day, it is possible to reconstruct the development of the address as it evolved in successive versions. What is known as the "first draft," on official stationery of the Executive Mansion, is accepted as having been written (at least the first page of it) in Washington. The second page, consisting of ten lines, together with a substitution for words deleted on the first page, were written in pencil. In the two drafts that preceded the occasion one can see the turning of the literary lathe, the search for the effective phrase. Instead of the words "It is rather for us, the living, to stand here," the words " . . . to be dedicated here" were substituted. While in the Wills house on the morning of the day of dedication, Nicolay being with him,[9] the President probably worked over his first draft, then made the "second draft" which has survived in his handwriting, and which "is almost certainly that which Lincoln held in his hand when he delivered the Address." [10] It is a slight revision of the first draft.

The third stage in the evolution of the text of the address came a few days after the President's return from Gettysburg when he responded to a request from Mr. Wills, who desired the original manuscript for an official report of the proceedings which he was preparing. The President, as reported by Nicolay, directed his secre-

---

[8] Noah Brooks, *Washington in Lincoln's Time*, 286.

[9] Though he was with Lincoln in the Wills house on the morning of November 19, Nicolay seems to have been unaware that the President wrote the second draft on this occasion; the private secretary assumed that the President was merely doing over the latter part of the first draft. Nicolay's account appears in *Century Magazine*, XLVII, 596–608 (1894), esp. pp. 596, 601, but see Charles Moore, 16.

[10] Typed label accompanying the second draft of the Gettysburg address, MS., Lib. of Cong. (The Library of Congress has the originals of both the first and second drafts, being the gifts of the children of John Hay, 1916.)

taries to make copies of the Associated Press report; using this together with his original draft and his recollection "of the form in
which he delivered it," Lincoln made "a careful and deliberate revision." [11] Just what form this revision took is a bit uncertain. Nicolay
refers to it as "a new autograph copy," [12] but no such copy has survived and it is more likely that what Wills received was a version
made under the President's supervision,[13] with secretarial help, while
the President was sick. Though the original of this Wills copy has not
survived, it is worth noting that as printed [14] it includes the words
"under God" in the passage: "this nation, under God, shall have a
new birth of freedom." The speech as prepared had not included these
words, but the newspaper reports as well as all of Lincoln's later
revisions, contain them; they were added by Lincoln as he spoke.

At the time of the address it was, of course, reprinted in the newspapers. Those papers that used the Associated Press report had an
imperfect version; the report that is accepted as perhaps the nearest
to an actual recording of the words which Lincoln uttered is that
published on Friday morning, November 20, 1863, in the Boston
Daily Advertiser. This version is reproduced herewith as an illustration, and the reader may be interested in its minor differences from
the standard text as printed above.

Leaving aside the newspaper reports and returning to the evolution
of the oration in successive versions, we may note that a third autograph copy by Lincoln was made at the request of Edward Everett,
who "presented it, together with the manuscript of his own address,
. . . to Mrs. Hamilton Fish, . . . president of the . . . committee
of . . . ladies having charge at the fair in aid of the sanitary commission . . . in New York in March, 1864, to be disposed of for the
benefit of our soldiers . . . ." [15] It was bought by an uncle of Senator
Henry W. Keyes of New Hampshire and remained for many years a
possession of the Keyes family. In 1944 this Everett-Keyes copy, having
been purchased from a private owner by hundreds of thousands of

---

11 Nicolay, as above cited in *Century Magazine*, 604–605.   12 *Ibid.*

13 Barton, *Lincoln at Gettysburg*, 103–104. Barton is of the opinion that Wills never
owned an autograph of the address. See also William H. Lambert, in *Pa. Mag. of
Hist. and Biog.*, XXXIII, 401 (1909).

14 It appeared in the official Gettysburg volume published by the state of Pennsylvania in 1863. Barton, *Lincoln at Gettysburg*, 104–105.

15 *Sen. Doc. No. 236*, 66 Cong., 2 sess. (1920).

small contributions from Illinois school children, was presented to the State of Illinois. Its place of deposit is the Illinois State Historical Library at Springfield.

A fourth autograph version was made by Lincoln at the request of George Bancroft. It was intended for sale at the Sanitary Fair at Baltimore in 1864, and for reproduction in a volume known as *Autograph Leaves of the Country's Authors*. Since it proved unavailable for this purpose by reason of being written on both sides of the paper, Bancroft was allowed to keep it, and Lincoln made yet another autograph, known as the "Bliss copy." This final version was done by Lincoln "with great care"; it was used both at the Baltimore Fair and in *Autograph Leaves,* edited by Colonel Alexander Bliss. Because it is in all probability the last copy written by Lincoln, and because of the obvious care devoted to it, it has become the standard form of the address.

In recapitulation, it may be noted that Lincoln made five autograph copies of his famous address which have come down to us: (1) the first draft, written probably in Washington, and perhaps partly revised at Gettysburg; (2) the second draft, written probably in the Wills house at Gettysburg and held by the President as he spoke; (3) the Everett-Keyes-Illinois copy, made at Everett's request and sold at the Sanitary Fair in New York in 1864; (4) the Bancroft copy, meant for the Baltimore Fair, but not used for that purpose; (5) the standard and definitive "Bliss copy," written carefully by Lincoln in 1864, sent to the Baltimore Fair, and reproduced in *Autograph Leaves of Our Country's Authors*. In addition, Lincoln directed and supervised the making of the version sent to Wills soon after the occasion, which was prepared with secretarial help and was probably not in the President's handwriting.

IV

In the Declaration of Independence Jefferson's authorship was no less important because he used concepts and phrases which were part of the currency of political thought. Similarly, it takes nothing from Lincoln's fame to find previous utterances which invite comparison with the famous reference to "government of the people, by the people, for the people." In a work published in London in 1794,

Thomas Cooper, formerly of Manchester, in advising Englishmen to come to America, wrote: "The [American] government is the government *of* the people, and *for* the people." [1] In 1798 Virginians of Westmoreland County sent an address to President Adams concerning the trouble with France, in which the following sentence occurred: "The Declaration that our People are hostile to a Government made by themselves, for themselves and conducted by themselves is an Insult . . . ." [2] Similar statements were made by Webster [3] and Marshall, [4] while Lamartine, paraphrasing Robespierre, wrote of a representative sovereignty "concentrated in an election as extensive as the people themselves, and acting by the people, and for the people . . . ." [5] Bibliographical search has also unearthed expressions of a like character by James Douglas in Edinburgh in 1830 [6] and by Matthew Fontaine Maury in a government report in 1851. [7] The most famous instance, however, and the one most often linked with Lincoln's phrase, is that of Theodore Parker, abolitionist preacher, who in 1850 used these words: "This [American] idea, demands . . . a democracy, that is, a government of all the people, by all the people, for all the people . . . ." [8]

---

[1] *Some Information respecting America, collected by Thomas Cooper, late of Manchester* (London, 1794), 53.

[2] In reply President Adams wrote: "The declaration that our People are hostile to a Government, made by themselves, for themselves, and conducted by themselves, if it were true, would be a demonstration that the people despise and hate themselves . . . ." *Proceedings of the American Antiquarian Society,* IX, 323, 326 (1894).

[3] "It is, Sir, the people's Constitution, the people's government, made for the people, made by the people, and answerable to the people." Webster's second reply to Hayne, Jan. 26, 1830, *Works of Daniel Webster* (Boston, 1851), III, 321.

[4] "The government of the Union . . . is . . . a government of the people. . . . Its powers are granted by them, and are to be exercised directly on them, and for their benefit." Chief Justice Marshall, in McCulloch *vs.* Maryland, 4 Wheaton 404–405.

[5] Lamartine, Alphonse de, *History of the Girondists* (Bohn ed., London, 1850), III, 104.

[6] Douglas referred to "a government where all power is from the people, and in the people, and for the people." James Douglas, *The Advancement of Society in Knowledge and Religion* (Edinburgh, 1830), 3rd. ed., 70. Quoted in *Century,* XLVII, 607 (1894).

[7] "Unlike Europe, . . . there are no disaffected people in this country for a foe to tamper with. The Government is by the people, for the people, and with the people. It is the people." M. F. Maury, in report on fortifications, *House Exec. Doc. No. 5,* 32 Cong., 1 sess., p. 190 (1851).

[8] Theodore Parker, *Speeches, Addresses, and Occasional Sermons* (Boston, 1852), II, 176. For the general subject of utterances parallel to Lincoln's, see J. G. Nicolay, in *Century Magazine,* XLVII, 606–608 (1894); Samuel A. Green, in *Proceedings,* Mass. Hist. Soc., 2 ser., XV, 92–94 (1901). The matter is treated also in Henry Steele Commager, *Theodore Parker.*

Courtesy of Ill. State Hist. Libr.

EVERETT-KEYES-ILLINOIS MANUSCRIPT

At the request of Edward Everett, Lincoln wrote this copy of the Gettysburg address. It was for a fair given for the benefit of the Sanitary Commission in New York in 1864. For many years it was in the family of Senator Henry W. Keyes of New Hampshire. In 1944, on purchase by Illinois school children from a private owner, it was presented to the State of Illinois, being deposited in the Illinois State Historical Library.

NOT ENTIRELY A FAILURE

On the day after the Gettysburg address Lincoln wrote his appreciation of Everett's oration, with a happily phrased comment on "our respective parts." It was Everett who wrote "The President of the United States" at the top, with date of receipt.

To point out that Lincoln had read Webster and Marshall is superfluous, nor is there much doubt that he was familiar with the saying of Parker, who had been a correspondent of William H. Herndon. That he consciously copied from any of these is less evident. As to the more obscure passages, they belong in the voluminous category of literary coincidence, dealing as they do with a concept whose universality among democratic minds constituted its main significance. Like Jefferson, Lincoln had the knack of taking an idea that was part of the heritage of the race and immortalizing it by pithy and unforgettable utterance. In the array of quotations here presented, it will be noted that the similarity of Lincoln's words to those of predecessors, while close, is not complete.[9] Whatever his sources, it was Lincoln who gave the phrase its setting, its precise form, and its dominant place in American tradition.

V

More noteworthy than literary parallels is the significance of the Gettysburg address as a tying together of Lincoln's fundamental concepts touching the basic theme of the American experiment. If one seeks passages for comparison, they are best to be found in Lincoln's own writings.

In the emotional release that had come with victory after so much delay, the President, on July 7, 1863, responded to a serenade at the Executive Mansion. Already Gettysburg to him meant dominant values: human liberty, democracy, aims of the Fathers, the Declaration, the cause of free government in the world. Frankly the President did not attempt a speech—he was always wary of impromptu utterance—yet in his casual remarks one can find the germ of the Gettysburg address that was to follow in November. The nation's birth "eighty-odd years since" was the point of departure. At one end of Lincoln's thought was Philadelphia in 1776; at the other, Gettysburg in 1863. From this it was a natural development to note the elemental importance of a nation founded on the "self-evident truth" of human equality, "the first time in the history of the world" that a nation had so founded itself by its own representatives. Coming to the present year and month, the President noted in victories just achieved "a

---

[9] Samuel A. Green, (see preceding note), 92.

glorious theme, and the occasion for a speech" which he was "not pre-pared" to make in a manner "worthy of the occasion." He briefly paid tribute to all who had "fought in the cause of the Union and liberties of their country"; then, mentioning no names lest he might wrong those unmentioned, he made his bow and called for music.[1] It was but a brief appearance before a celebrating crowd, yet the theme, and the clear call for a speech worthy of the theme, were not forgotten.

In his first inaugural Lincoln had expressed his central idea as to what the country was about in maintaining the republic against internal disruption. "A majority held in restraint by constitutional checks . . . and . . . changing easily with deliberate changes of popular opinions," he had said, "is the only true sovereign of a free people. Whoever rejects it does, of necessity, fly to anarchy or to despotism."[2] In the same address he had asked: "Why should there not be a patient confidence in the ultimate justice of the people? Is there any better or equal hope in the world?"[3] In his annual message to Congress of December 1, 1862, he spoke again of America's larger responsibility. Hoping his nation would choose the course which "the world will forever applaud," he warned: "We shall nobly save or meanly lose the last, best hope of earth."[4]

Shortly after the opening of the war Lincoln had said to Hay: "For my part, I consider [that] the central idea pervading this struggle is the necessity that is upon us, of proving that popular government is not an absurdity. We must settle this question now, whether in a free government the minority have the right to break up the government whenever they choose. If we fail it will go far to prove the incapability of the people to govern themselves."[5] When thus thinking aloud to his young secretary the President had been much occupied with composing his message to the special session of Congress of July 4, 1861, in which the following significant words, so like the theme of Gettysburg were used:

And this issue embraces more than the fate of these United States. It presents to the whole family of man the question whether a constitutional

---

[1] Response to a serenade, July 7, 1863, *Works*, IX, 20–21.
[2] *Works*, VI, 179.   [3] *Ibid.*, VI, 183.   [4] *Ibid.*, VIII, 131.
[5] Diary of John Hay, May 7, 1861, Dennett, *Lincoln . . . in the Diaries . . . of John Hay*, 19–20.

republic or democracy—a government of the people by the same people—
can or cannot maintain its . . . integrity against its domestic foes. It
presents the question whether discontented individuals . . . can . . .
break up their government, and thus practically put an end to free government upon the earth. It forces us to ask: "Is there, in all republics, this
inherent and fatal weakness?" "Must a government, of necessity, be too
strong for the liberties of its . . . people, or too weak to maintain its own
existence?"

· · · · · · · · · · ·

This is essentially a people's contest. On the side of the Union it is a
struggle for maintaining in the world that form and substance of government whose leading object is to elevate the condition of men—to lift artificial weights from all shoulders; to clear the paths of laudable pursuit for
all; to afford all an unfettered start, and a fair chance in the race of life.

· · · · · · · · · ·

Our popular government has often been called an experiment. Two
points in it our people have already settled—the successful establishing
and the successful administering of it. One still remains—its successful
maintenance against a formidable internal attempt to overthrow it. It is
now for them to demonstrate to the world that . . . ballots are the rightful and peaceful successors of bullets . . . . Such will be a great lesson of
peace: teaching men that what they cannot take by an election, neither
can they take it by a war; teaching all the folly of being the beginners of
a war.[6]

Where words were so simple it took something of genius to make
them so meaningful. As Everett himself generously recognized, Lincoln said more in two minutes than the orator of the day in as many
hours. Rarely indeed is Everett quoted for his own sake. Had Lincoln
not participated, Everett's stately periods would have gone into oblivion, while Lincoln's phrases are the stuff of literature. Innocent
of the cant of the patrioteer, they nevertheless touched the chord of
elemental loyalty. It is for such utterance, and for the man he was,
that Lincoln has become synonymous with fundamental Americanism.

Both in form and substance the address at Gettysburg was completely Lincolnian. Oratorically it had those elements that made Lincoln at his best a master of words. Fitness to the situation was the
first element; the occasion made the speech. This was true, however,

---

[6] For quoted portions, see *Works*, VI, 304, 321, 322.

not in terms of exigent pressures or superficial demands of the moment, but rather with regard to the occasion as viewed in perspective. The second element, also typically Lincolnian, was a matter of the choice of words: thoughts that touched heights of exalted feeling were conveyed in language at once unpretentious and stirringly effective. Utter simplicity and restraint were somehow suffused with inspired dignity. It is as significant to note what was omitted as what was included in a speech whose brevity made every syllable valuable. There was not a breath of hatred, not a hint of vindictiveness, not a trace of vengeful judgment. Sensing the greater opportunity of the hour, Lincoln used the Gettysburg occasion for two purposes: in unforgettable phrases he paid tribute to those who had fallen; not failing in that, he coupled the deepest and most dominant sentiments of his people with the political idea that was central in his own mind: the wider world significance of democracy's testing, the enduring importance of success in the American democratic experiment as proving that government by the people is no failure. Standing at a cemetery, which men of classical turn were lugubriously calling a "necropolis," he did not confine his thoughts to the dead. Rather he showed that it is only by constructive deeds of living men that the sacrifice of the dead can have value.

SIFTING THE ANN RUTLEDGE
EVIDENCE

This appendix includes an account of how the Lincoln-Rutledge story arose, an evaluation of the evidence, citations to guide the questioning student, and, especially, emphasis upon the need for historical criticism in dealing with a theme which has been almost usurped by fiction writers.

FROM the Lincolns in Springfield and Washington to Ann Rutledge is something of a digression. If one is treating only the things whose reality and significance for Lincoln are matters of solid proof, the too familiar story of Lincoln and Ann may be omitted altogether. To present the subject as one of the earlier chapters in a book on *Lincoln the President* would seem inappropriate. It would be out of key with the main emphasis. Yet popular writing has created a stock picture, and the true state of the evidence requires attention. For this reason the subject is included (in the subordinate status of an appendix), not for any intrinsic importance at all, but because historical criticism finds here a challenge and a needful task.

From uncertain and conflicting memories of a courtship in picturesque New Salem the story has amazingly grown until the romantic linking of Abraham and Ann has become universal. In drama it has usurped the spotlight. Perhaps the majority of those who think of Lincoln not only believe that Ann Rutledge was the only woman he ever loved; they go on from there to the fictional assumption that an unambitious and lazy lad became a student of law and a man of note only because of Ann, that her death left him crushed in spirit, that her memory remained his inspiration through life, that his tenderest emotions were always thereafter in retrospect, and that real love for the woman he married was non-existent.

I

For the historian the problem is that of tracing the account to its sources, finding the evidence, noting how far the testimony holds together, and rejecting those elements that are but the froth and chaff of unchecked imagination. One may trace the popularizing—indeed the exaggerated exploitation—of the tradition to Herndon; it was he who gave it wide publicity, filled in the gaps, added his irrepressible contribution of psychoanalysis, and set the pattern which has become familiar to millions. Back of Herndon, to be sure, there were vague memories reaching to far-off New Salem days which in some manner tended to connect the name of Lincoln with that of Ann Rutledge.

An early mention of the story in print—a very obscure mention—was in an article written by John Hill and published in the *Menard Axis* of Petersburg, Illinois, February 15, 1862. Under the title "A Romance of Reality" the author, son of Sam Hill of New Salem, strung out an unflattering account of an awkward youth, a store clerk, a soldier who reached the field of action after the war was over, keeper of a stallion, day laborer, infidel writer, surveyor, hog drover, and love-sick swain. The reader was then informed that this was none other than Abraham Lincoln, President of the United States. On the theme of the love-sick swain there was a passage telling how this youth had met an angelic lady, could think of naught but her, found his feeling reciprocated, and awaited the day when the twain would be one flesh. The lovely beauty died; melancholy fell upon the lad; friends noted his strange conduct; they kept him under guard to prevent suicide. That, in summary, was the story. Ann's name was not mentioned, but the identity was plain enough. This obscure mention of the matter was long buried, though contained in the Herndon collection; only recently has it been brought to light.[1]

Hill was not the best witness of New Salem days, he was addressing an anti-Lincoln audience, he was riding a theme, his memories were indirect (through his father), his account was pubished long after the supposed event, and there were flaws in his narrative.[2] His passage

---

[1] Jay Monaghan, "New Light on the Lincoln-Rutledge Romance," *Abr. Lincoln Quart.*, III, 138–145 (Sep. 1944).

[2] Hill was opposed to Lincoln in 1862 and his account is strangely belittling. He disparages Lincoln's service in the Black Hawk War, emphasizes his uncouthness and

has been summarized above because in the literature of the subject it has a certain priority in that it is pre-Herndonian.

From November 16, 1866, however, the subject was peculiarly Herndon's. On that date he delivered in Springfield a lengthy, lush, and sentimental lecture under the title "Abraham Lincoln. Miss Ann Rutledge. New Salem. Pioneering and *the* Poem." With fruity periods and lavishly bestowed adjectives he told the world that "Abraham Lincoln loved Miss Ann Rutledge with all his soul, mind and strength," that she "loved him as dearly," that they "seemed made in heaven for each other," that Ann was "honestly engaged" to two men at the same time, that she sickened under the conflict of emotion and duty and died, that Lincoln's heart was buried with her, that reason left him, that he was racked in heart and body, that he lost his logical faculty, speaking incoherently and wildly (Herndon supplied Lincoln's imagined words at great length), that he rose up a man once more after visiting "Bolin" Green, that from then he was radically changed (for the better), but that he committed the poem "Immortality" to memory and was ever thereafter influenced by the solemn contemplation of these deep thoughts.[3]

Paul M. Angle published an excellent study of this subject in 1927, but did not use the Herndon manuscripts, which were not then available to the historical profession. Concerning the familiar romance Angle concluded that "it is entirely traditional." He added: "No reliable contemporary record has ever been discovered. Instead, there are numerous reminiscences, put in writing at the request of Hern-

---

failure, makes him appear utterly unimportant, and gives an unfavorable twist to the lad's service in the little store by mentioning that an "opposition liquor shop" attracted the custom. In writing to Herndon several years after the article appeared, Hill admitted his error as to the stallion, and confessed that at the time of Lincoln's youth he "knew no more as to who he was than . . . of the inhabitants of the Fegee Islands." He mentioned James Short as one who could give more information than "any or all the men in the county"; it was Short who reported that he knew of no engagement or tender passages between Lincoln and Ann during the latter's life. For Short's statement see below, p. 330; John Hill's letters are in the Herndon-Weik MSS., June 6 and June 27, 1865.

[3] Brief summary of the last two columns of Herndon's lecture. It was given at Springfield on Friday, November 16, 1866, and was privately printed as a broadside on a large sheet, newspaper style. The original broadside is rare; the author has used a copy in the Illinois State Historical Library. The lecture was published in book form by H. E. Barker (Springfield, 1910). As for the poem, Herndon associated Lincoln's fondness for the lines "Oh, Why Should the Spirit of Mortal Be Proud?" with the tragedy of Ann Rutledge.

don, who, once given the lead, followed it tirelessly." [4]

This fits the case. Herndon did have something of a "lead" in none too reliable recollections. A careful study of the Herndon manuscripts reveals what those recollections were and confirms Angle's conclusion that all the material was non-contemporary—i. e., none of it belonged in or near the eighteen-thirties. In his lecture, Herndon invites all who doubt his story to come to his office and look over his records; now after nearly eight decades the author is happy to accept the invitation for this inspection.

As Herndon's papers reveal, old settlers, or in some cases their children, told of a friend of Lincoln's, a beautiful girl named Ann Rutledge, who had been engaged to one John McNamar and had died. Her lover was using the name McNeil; while building his fortunes in the West he did not want to be traced by his family. He had left New Salem, spending some years with his people in New York (sometimes misstated as Ohio); he had returned shortly after Ann's death. There was the tradition that Lincoln was greatly saddened by the girl's death; this, and the engagement to McNamar, are the factors that stand out most clearly in the mosaic of New Salem reminiscence.

The subject appealed to all the sentimentalizing and psychoanalyzing impulses of Herndon's nature. [5] He talked to survivors of those days or if he could not reach them he had them interviewed by proxy or got their statements by correspondence. He labored with an assiduity that gave importance to his very questions. The resulting mass of confused and contradictory evidence, found in his voluminous manuscripts, serves as the chief basis for the famous tradition so far as it had basis; the lecture and Herndon biography added the glowing details.

The vagueness of reminiscence given after many years is familiar to all careful historical students: if, in the haste of general reading, this matter is disregarded, the essence of the subject is overlooked.

---

[4] Paul M. Angle, "Lincoln's First Love?" *Bulletin No. 9*, Lincoln Centennial Assoc., Dec. 1, 1927, p. 5.

[5] "I being somewhat of a psychologist . . . ." Herndon to Ward H. Lamon, Springfield, Mar. 6, 1870, MS., Huntington Lib. It is impossible to evaluate Herndon without keeping in mind the vagaries of his amateur psychoanalysis. It amounted to an obsession. He even thought of himself as a kind of mind reader. He wrote: "You know my love of reading men—mind—moods—characteristics &c. . . . I love the science of the mind quite over all studies . . . ." Herndon to Weik, Feb. 21, 1891, Herndon-Weik MSS.

Huge tomes could be written to show the doubtfulness of long-delayed memories. Out of thousands of examples that could be cited, one may take the admitted case of Salmon P. Chase; it is exactly pertinent to the kind of problem we are handling. Chase had supplied from memory certain biographical details to J. T. Trowbridge, who in 1864 published a life of the Ohio statesman entitled *The Ferry Boy and the Financier*. After the book appeared Chase wrote to Trowbridge: "You have . . . thrown a great deal of attraction about . . . dry facts. Indeed, from information or fancy, you have collected some facts which are quite out of my recollection." Again he wrote: "It is strange to me how dim every thing is in that distant time. I see just one little part of things—glimpses of transactions—the (reality-totality?) hid behind clouds with little fissures revealing a part of an affair or person, and that little with mist clinging round and obscuring it. I dare not vouch for the entire authenticity even of what I seem to remember best." [6]

The historian must use reminiscence, but he must do so critically. Even close-up evidence is fallible. When it comes through the mists of many years some of it may be true, but a careful writer will check it with known facts. Contradictory reminiscences leave doubt as to what is to be believed; unsupported memories are in themselves insufficient as proof; statements induced under suggestion, or psychological stimulus, as were some of the stories about Lincoln and Ann, call especially for careful appraisal. If reminiscences are gathered, but only part of them used, that again is a problem. It is not so much a matter of taking Chase, a cultured man who confessed fallibility as to past events, and arguing that simple country people ought to be trusted even less; it is rather that proneness to uncertain recollection is a common human trait. The matter is brought to notice here because readers often overlook it, not being always aware of the basis for statements as to past incidents, while it is the very essence of historical study to find, sift, question, and evaluate sources of information. When faulty memories are admitted the resulting product becomes something other than history; it is no longer to be presented as a genuine record.

---

[6] Robert B. Warden, *Private Life and Public Services of Salmon Portland Chase*, 589, 56.

II

Looking into what Herndon collected, we find varying responses to his inquiries; the whole constituted a product he could not well digest. A Miss Berry and a Miss Short were mentioned mistakenly and a Miss Owens quite definitely as objects of Lincoln's attentions during Ann's lifetime.[1] Samuel Hill and William Berry were added to the list of Ann's suitors.[2] As above noted, it was generally agreed that the girl was betrothed to McNamar, and that Lincoln was plunged into gloom after her death. Mentor Graham, New Salem schoolmaster, briefly supported the tradition of the Lincoln-Rutledge engagement. In an interview with Herndon he is reported to have said: "Lincoln and she was engaged—Lincoln told me so—she intimated to me the same: He Lincoln told me that he felt like committing suicide often, but I told him God higher purpose . . . [etc.]."[3] These words were scribbled by Herndon; over his own signature Graham referred even more briefly to a "momentary derangement" in Lincoln caused in part by "the death of one whom he dearly and sincerely love[d]."[4]

Mrs. Lizzie Bell, daughter of Mentor Graham, furnished none too reliable glimpses of a quilting party where Ann kept her eye on Mr. Hill, while Lincoln flirted with another girl, with the result that "Lincoln & Ann had a fly up, but on her death bed she sent for Lincoln & all things were reconciled." Incidentally, Herndon's note on the page containing this reminiscence described both Mentor Graham and his daughter as "cranky—flighty—at times nearly non copus mentis—but good & honest."[5] In evaluating their contributions one should remember this comment. One should also remember that, by Mrs. Bell's own statement, she was a child at the time and did not know these things of her own knowledge.[6]

Though one does not wish to bear down too severely upon the schoolmaster, whose educational influence on Lincoln has probably

[1] G. U. Miles to Herndon, Mar. 23, 1866, Herndon-Weik MSS. (Concerning Miss Owens, see below, pp. 336–337.)

[2] R. B. Rutledge to Herndon, Nov. 21, 1866, *ibid.*

[3] Herndon's memo. of statement by Mentor Graham, Apr. 2, 1866, *ibid.*

[4] Mentor Graham to Herndon, May 29, 1865, *ibid.*

[5] Herndon's memo. of statement by Lizzie Bell, undated, *ibid.*   [6] *Ibid.*

been exaggerated,[7] one should note the following statement written by Graham to Herndon in 1865: ". . . I saw him [Lincoln] frequently when a lad about 12 years of age though was not personally acquainted with him this was at his residence at his place of birth in the winter of 1819 & 20 I went to school in the County of Hardin Ky . . . , during my attendance . . . I often past by old Mr. Lincoln's house & often saw his son Abraham out about the premises . . . ."[8] In this, of course, Graham was badly mistaken as to what he claimed to have remembered. The Lincolns moved from the birthplace location when Abraham was two years old (1811); they left Kentucky for Indiana when he was seven (1816). That the schoolmaster was at fault or confused (at least as to dates) in this case does not necessarily overthrow his New Salem recollections; but, taken in connection with Herndon's comment made in the period when he was interviewing Graham and his daughter, they do suggest the need for wholesome doubt. At any rate Graham's contributions on the Lincoln-Rutledge romance were meager, especially so in what he himself wrote. His account was more concerned with Lincoln's life in the New Salem period and with his own function in teaching the future President.

One of Herndon's principal witnesses—a lengthier one than Graham—was R. B. Rutledge, Ann's younger brother who was seventeen the year she died. After recounting Ann's engagement to John McNamar and the latter's long absence, Rutledge (in a statement attested by John Jones) declared:

In the mean time Mr Lincoln paid his addresses to Ann, . . . and those resulted in an engagement to marry, conditional to an honorable release from the contract with McNamar. There is no kind of doubt as to the existence of this engagement. David Rutledge [a brother long since dead] urged Ann to consummate it, but she refused until such time as she could see McNamar—inform him of the change in her feelings, and seek an honorable release. Mr Lincoln lived in the village, McNamar did not return and in August 1835 Ann sickened and died. The effect upon Mr Lincoln's mind was terrible; he became plunged in despair, and many of

---

[7] Kunigunde Duncan and D. F. Nickols, *Mentor Graham, The Man Who Taught Lincoln.* This book, rich in flavor and atmosphere, has been characterized as "neither sound biography nor reliable history" (*Abr. Lincoln Quart.,* III, 211). Graham's own considerable claims as to having taught Lincoln grammar and surveying are seen in his letter to Herndon, May 29, 1865, Herndon-Weik MSS.

[8] Mentor Graham to Herndon, July 15, 1865, Herndon-Weik MSS.

his friends feared that reason would desert her throne. His extraordinary emotions were regarded as strong evidence of the existence of the tenderest relations between himself and the deceased.[9]

At another time Rutledge wrote:

> . . . the facts are Wm Berry first courted Ann and was rejected, afterwards Saml Hill, then John McNamar, which resulted in an engagement to marry at some future time, he McNamar left the Country on business, was gaun some years, in the meantime and during McNamars absence, Mr Lincoln Courted Ann and engaged to marry her, on the completion of the sudy of law. In this I am caroborated by James Mc [McGrady] Rutledge a cousin about her age & who was in her confidence, he say in a letter to me just received, "Ann told me once in coming from a Camp Meeting on Rock creek, that engagements made too far a hed sometimes failed, that one had failed, (meaning her engagement with McNamar) and gave me to understand, that as soon as certain studies were completed she and Lincoln would be married. . . . "[10]

Here is one person reporting what another person had written him concerning what that person recollected he had inferred from something that Ann had casually said to him more than thirty-one years before! Anxious though he was to please, Rutledge could not accept Herndon's emphasis upon Ann's pining away because of conflicting emotions in her maiden heart. He courteously but firmly disagreed and reminded Herndon that Ann died of brain fever.[11]

There are inconsistencies and contradictions in Rutledge's assertions, and in reading his labored statements one can sympathetically understand his difficulty in reconstructing a picture of what happened. A writer of today ought not to put a higher value on his recollections than he himself did. He confessed uncertainty on points of Herndon's questioning and spoke of comparing notes with others.[12] In part this

---

[9] R. B. Rutledge to Herndon (in neat clerklike handwriting, not Rutledge's), attested by John Jones, Wintersett, Iowa, Oct. 22, 1866, *ibid.* This same Jones refers to himself as an "eye-witness to the events" and adds: "As to the relation . . . between Mr Lincoln and Ann Rutledge, I have every reason to believe that it was of the tenderest character, as I know of my own knowledge that he made regular visits to her. . . . It was generally understood that Mr Lincoln and Ann Rutledge were engaged to be married." (Though an "eye-witness," Jones was qualifying his statements by such phrases as "I have every reason to believe," and "It was generally understood." Other testimony shows that it was by no means generally understood.)

[10] R. B. Rutledge (own handwriting) to Herndon, Nov. 21, 1866, Herndon-Weik MSS.

[11] R. B. Rutledge to Herndon, Nov. 18, 1866, *ibid.* What the pioneers called brain fever has been identified as typhoid.

[12] R. B. Rutledge to "Herendon," Burlington, Ia., Oct. 30, 1866, *ibid.*

consultation may have been intended to supplement his own knowledge, which he did not claim to be complete in itself. In the law of evidence, however, it is insisted that testimony ought to come straight. If witnesses arrange their recollections so as to make them agree, or if they seek to build them up where they admit uncertainty, the result lacks the validity of statements obtained from witnesses separately and unretouched. One must give full credit to the sincerity of R. B.'s effort to deliver the truth and some investigators might not consider that his product was rendered less valuable by this consultation. It is not an easy problem. Rutledge was not always able to make his words convey his idea as to the engagement between Lincoln and Ann. At one point he said it was "conditional"—i. e., dependent upon release from McNamar; elsewhere he stated that it was "not conditional . . . but absolute." [13] On Lincoln's mental suffering Rutledge wrote: "I cannot answer this question from personal knowledge, but from what I have learned from others at the time, you [Herndon] are substantially correct." [14] In contrast to this the attested statement had said: "The effect upon Mr Lincoln's mind was terrible; . . . [etc.]" [15] In R. B. Rutledge's letters there were cases in which he told his questioner that he (Herndon) was in error; yet he confessed liking Herndon's lecture, which, incidentally, had not been confined to Ann Rutledge, but had included a glowing description of the timber, bottoms, bluffs, meadows, hills, flowers, lichen, moss, rolling brook, wild fruit, birds, animals, fish, and more especially the early settlers of New Salem and the surrounding region.

The nature of Rutledge's recollections, however, is best indicated by a qualifying statement at the outset of his attested account:

I trust largely to your courtesy as a gentleman, to your honesty and integrity as a historian, and to your skill in writing for the public, to enlarge

---

[13] Rutledge's mention of the conditional engagement (in his statement attested Oct. 22, 1866) has already been noted. In his letter to Herndon in his own hand, Nov. 18, 1866, Rutledge said: ". . . during his [McNamar's] prolonged absence Mr Lincoln courted Ann, resulting in a second engagement, not conditional as my language would seem to indicate but absolute, She however in the conversation . . . between her & David urged the propriety of seeing McNamar, inform him of the change in her feelings & seek an honorable releas, before consumating the engagement with Mr L. by Marriage." (He doubts the word "conditional"; yet after all his explanation leaves the impression that Ann's marrying of Lincoln was not to be thought of except in terms of a release from her acknowledged and betrothed lover.) Herndon-Weik MSS.

[14] R. B. Rutledge to Herndon, Nov. 21, 1866, *ibid.*   [15] Quoted above, pp. 327–328.

wherever my statements seem obscure, and to condense and remove whatever seems superfluous. . . . Many of my statements are made from memory with the aid of association of events; and should you discover that
the date, location and circumstances, of the events here named should be
contradictory to those named from other sources, I beg of you to consider
well the testimony in each case, and make up your history from those
statements, which may appear to you best fitted to remove all doubt as
to their correctness.[16]

Rutledge did his sincere best, but what we have in his testimony is
dim and misty with the years; he became doubly indirect where he
quoted James McGrady Rutledge and others; [17] and his record is
qualified by his prefatory caution to Herndon as to how to use it. Yet
if one adopts the familiar Ann Rutledge tale, this is a sample of the
type of material he must accept.

III

The testimony of James Short, a close and true friend of Lincoln
and of the Rutledges, deserves consideration if one has to deal with
far-off rememberings. He lived in the Sand Ridge area near the farm
where Ann spent the last few years of her life. (This farm was about
seven miles north of New Salem.) There is a matter-of-fact quality un-
tinged by sentiment in his statement. He said:

Mr L. boarded with the parents of Miss Ann Rutledge, from the time he
went to New Salem up to 1833. In 1833 her mother moved to the Sandridge
& kept house for me, until I got married. Miss R. staid at N. S. for a few
months after her mother left, keeping house for her father & brothers,
& boarding Mr L. She then came over to her mother. After my marriage,
the Rutledges lived about half a mile from me. Mr L. came over to see me
& them every day or two.[1] I did not know of any engagement or tender
passages between Mr L and Miss R at the time. But after her death, which
happened in 34 or 35, he seemed to be so much affected and grieved so
hardly that I then supposed there must have been . . . something of the
kind.[2]

---

[16] R. B. Rutledge to Herndon, attested Oct. 22, 1866, Herndon-Weik MSS.

[17] It will be noted above that he quoted a letter from James McGrady Rutledge
"just received" (in 1866), which is different from reaching back into his own untouched
memories.

[1] Lincoln's surveying and various odd jobs took him all over the country around New
Salem and he often stayed all night at the Short home.

[2] James Short to Herndon, July 7, 1865, Herndon-Weik MSS. Lincoln had a very high
opinion of Jim Short. On March 26, 1843, he wrote: ". . . I know him to be as honorable a man as there is in the world." *Works*, I, 265.

That Lincoln was deeply saddened by Ann's death was generally reported by these witnesses, several of whom retrospectively inferred, as did James Short, that if he grieved so much, he "must have been" in love with her.

John McNamar, Ann's fiancé who was in the East at the time of the alleged Lincoln-Rutledge courtship, wrote in 1866: "I never heard and [i. e., any] person say that Mr Lincon addressed Miss Ann Rutledge in terms of courtship neither her own family nor my acquaintance otherwise." [3] McNamar knew the Rutledges well not only because of his engagement to Ann but because he had bought half of the Rutledge farm, this being referred to as a "family arrangement." [4] If Lincoln did court Ann to the point of betrothal, and McNamar who was known to be engaged to her was not told of this fact when he returned to New Salem, human nature in country towns has radically changed! McNamar was respected by his neighbors and his word was trusted.[5] He said that two prominent men, personal friends of his, told him Lincoln "was Grieved very much" at Ann's death.[6] Bowling Green was said to have feared that the young man's grief might impair his mind; he took him to the Green home for a week or two and "succeeded in cheering him Lincoln up . . . ." [7] But Mrs. Green thought Ann loved McNamar as much as Lincoln, though the former had been absent so long, and one of Ann's aunts said she thought Ann would have married McNamar if she had lived.[8] Again Mrs. Green, sometimes called Mrs. "Bolen" Green, was quoted as saying that Miss Owens visited the New Salem region "for about a year next preceding the death of Miss Rutledge" and that "Lincoln went to see her frequently during that time She living handy to

---

[3] McNamar to G. U. Miles, May 5, 1866, Herndon-Weik MSS.

[4] Beveridge, I, 148; Thomas, *Lincoln's New Salem*, 81.

[5] "His [John McNamar's] conduct was strictly hightoned, honest and moral, and his object, whatever any may think of the deception . . . in changing his name, entirely praiseworthy." R. B. Rutledge to Herndon, attested Oct. 22, 1866, Herndon-Weik MSS. For unfriendly comment on McNamar, see Barton, I, 221-222.

[6] John McNamar to G. U. Miles, May 5, 1866, Herndon-Weik MSS. Miles sent this letter to Herndon, for whom it had been obtained.

[7] G. U. Miles to Herndon, March 23, 1866, *ibid.*

[8] *Ibid.* This aunt was Mrs. William Rutledge. Miles wrote: "Mrs Wm Rutledge who resides in Petersburg [1866] and did reside in the neighbourhood at the time of the Said courtship and who is . . . acquainted with the parties & all the circumstances . . . thinks that Ann if she had lived would have married McNamer or rather . . . liked him a little the best though McNamer had been absent in Ohio for Near two years at the time of her death though they corrosponded by letter."

Salem." [9] James Short denied that Lincoln refused to eat after Ann's death [10] and John Hill said that he bore up very well until, some days afterwards, a heavy rain fell which unnerved him.[11]

Various other witnesses contributed fragments of reminiscence. W. G. Greene, an intimate friend of Lincoln in New Salem days, agreed that Lincoln and Ann were engaged, and that his friends feared he would commit suicide after her death. Caleb Carman stated that Lincoln loved Ann but said he did not know "mutch" about it, as he was not in New Salem at the time. A cousin of W. H. Herndon, J. R. Herndon, referred to Miss Rutledge and said he had "know dout he [Lincoln] would have married iff she had of lived." L. M. Greene asserted they were engaged; William McNeeley presented hearsay evidence that Lincoln was "insane" after Ann's death; Henry McHenry described Lincoln's depression and desire for solitude, but added that some thought it was due to an increased application to his law studies. George Spears approved of Herndon's lecture, but remarked with refreshing candor that while he had lived through the time and events mentioned, he could not remember about them. Jasper Rutledge, relative of Ann born after her death and brother of James McGrady Rutledge, gave the traditional family version. He added the detail that McNamar's real name was revealed by his signing of some deeds (he had been using the name McNeil) and that Ann was suspicious of a man with two names. According to his account, correspondence between Ann and McNamar gradually ceased and Ann and Lincoln became engaged. Mrs. Sam Hill endorsed the main points of the Rutledge tradition, but gave it as her "honest opinion" that Ann would have married McNamar if he had returned before her death. Henry Hohhiner (?) expressed his "opinion" that Lincoln and Ann were engaged, while Jason Duncan thought Lincoln refrained from courting Ann because of her engagement to McNamar.[12]

---

[9] *Ibid.* In a postscript Miles wrote: ". . . in 1835 when Miss Rutledge died & when Lincoln was going to see Miss Owens this was Sangamo County—Menard being formed at the Session of 1838 & 9."

[10] Caleb Carman to Herndon, Nov. 30, 1866, *ibid.*

[11] John Hill to Herndon, June 6, 1865, *ibid.*

[12] For this paragraph the references, given in the order mentioned, are: W. G. Greene to Herndon, May 30, 1865; Caleb Carman to Herndon, Nov. 30, 1866; J. R. Herndon to Herndon, July 3, 1865; L. M. Greene to Herndon, July 30, 1865; William McNeely to

So the testimony runs—some *pro*, some *con*, some inconclusive, all of it long delayed reminiscence, much of it second- or third-hand, part of it consisting of inference or supposition as to what "must have been" true. The old settlers were contradictory among themselves. One of them wrote concerning an alleged bit of early Lincoln reminiscence: "If that old Lady . . . who says, Lincoln made a crop for her husband some time in 1831–32 or 33, was not a *woman*, I would say she *lied* like *hell* . . . ." [13]

One must now consider the statement of Isaac Cogdal regarding an interview he said he had with President Elect Lincoln in Springfield some time between November 1860 and February 1861. Cogdal was a farmer and former brick mason who studied law late in life, being admitted to the bar in 1860.[14] He lived in the Rock Creek precinct and had known Lincoln when they were both young men, being some three years younger than Lincoln. According to Cogdal's story as it comes to us, Lincoln asked him to come to his office in the State House and talk over old times and acquaintances of New Salem days. The manuscript record runs as follows:

Abe is it true that you fell in love with & courted Ann Rutledge said Cogdall. Lincoln said, "it is true—true indeed I did. I have loved the name of Rutlege to this day. I have kept my mind on their movements ever since & love them dearly"—said L [Just before this is the statement that Lincoln had asked Cogdal where the Rutledges were, an inconsistency not explained.] Ab—Is it true—said Cogdall, that you ran a little wild about the matter: I did really—I ran off the track: it was my first. I loved the woman dearly & sacredly: she was a handsome girl—would have made a good loving wife—was natural & quite intellectual, though not highly Educated—I did honestly—& truly love the girl & think often—often of her now.[15]

Herndon, Nov. 12, 1866; Henry McHenry to Herndon, Jan. 8, 1866; George Spears to Herndon, Nov. 21, 1866; Herndon's memorandum of statement by Jasper Rutledge, Mar. 9, 1887; Herndon's undated memorandum of statement by Mrs. Sam Hill; Herndon's undated memorandum of statement by Henry Hohhiner [?]; Jason Duncan to Herndon, undated. Herndon-Weik MSS.

[13] W. G. Greene to Herndon, June 11, 1865, *ibid.*

[14] *History of Menard and Mason Counties, Illinois* (pub. by O. L. Baskin & Co., 1879), 749.

[15] Statement of "Isaac Cogdall," undated, Herndon-Weik MSS. In the manuscripts Herndon's spelling of the name seems to be "Cogdall" though it could be read "Cogdale." In the Herndon biography (Angle ed., 389) it appears as "Cogsdale." As shown by legal papers, newspapers, and letters by the man himself, the name was Isaac Cogdal.

The most obvious thing about this effusive statement is its unLincolnian quality. The record is Herndon's memorandum of an interview with Cogdal, who was presumably reconstructing from memory what Lincoln had said to him some years before. Words ascribed to Lincoln have been refracted by passing through two minds, and have been exposed to the possible embellishment of both Cogdal and Herndon. It has been suggested that Lincoln's friends did not usually address him as "Abe" [16] but in this record of jottings "Abe" and especially "Ab" may have been abbreviations, for Herndon troubled himself very little about periods. "Jas" without a period is used for James in the same manuscript. On the other hand, Lincoln is quoted as having addressed Cogdal as "Ike," and Cogdal may have called him "Abe" when they were young men. Lincoln was a man of deep reserve about personal matters. As President Elect he guarded his speech with the utmost care. His lack of reticence here seems as unnatural as the language attributed to him.

B. F. Irwin mentioned hearing the story of the Cogdal interview. Irwin, who stated in an August letter that Ann died and Lincoln took it very hard, wrote in September that his informants differed as to Miss Rutledge's death. He followed this with a statement which illustrates how twisted some of these recollections could become: "Cogdal says she [Ann] was living in Iowa in 1860 as Lincoln told him and Lincoln did say in 1860 that he . . . loved her still . . . ." The same letter mentioned that Ann was unfavorably impressed with Lincoln, who was poor and awkward, while McNamar and other suitors had much more to offer.[17]

Cogdal's story comes to us with such indirectness in the telling as to becloud with doubt what was actually said. Lincoln was not a man to express himself so effusively to friends. "Lincoln never told Speed nor Gallespie nor Judge Matheny—nor myself of this courtship— death and unsanity" wrote Herndon. He added: ". . . he was the most reticent & mostly secretive man that ever existed: he never

---

[16] Sometimes they used the contraction affectionately in the third person, but they usually referred to him simply as Lincoln. Henry C. Whitney stated that Lincoln gave no license for being called "Abe"; Horace White confirms this and refers to "pretended conversations . . . where his interlocutors addressed him as Abe this or Abe that" as "imaginary." Roy E. Appleman, ed., *Abraham Lincoln From His Own Words and Contemporary Accounts* (National Park Service Source Book Series, no. 2), 9.

[17] B. F. Irwin to Herndon, Aug. 27, 1866; B. F. Irwin to Herndon, Sep. 22, 1866. Herndon-Weik MSS.

opened his whole soul to any man: he never touched the history or quality of his own nature in the presence of his friends." [18] That Herndon's lecture with its tale of Lincoln and Ann was news to Speed is known by his own statement.[19] In the face of such reticence the Cogdal record seems artificial and made to order. It was given out after Lincoln's death; it presents him in an unlikely role; it puts in his mouth uncharacteristic sayings.

There is, to the writer's knowledge, no thoroughly verified utterance by Lincoln, written or oral, in which Ann Rutledge is even mentioned, though one does find Lincoln's own statements concerning women whom he knew in this period—namely, Sarah Rickard [20] and Mary Owens.

IV

The effect of Ann's death on Lincoln seems to have been exaggerated by local gossip. Mrs. E. Abell, at whose cabin Lincoln was staying at the time of Ann's death, wrote in detail about his deep grief over the event, but added "the community said he was crazy he was not crazy but he was very disponding a long time." It is worthy of note that while she had first-hand knowledge of Lincoln's grief, she said she could tell little about the courtship.[1] Less than a month after Ann's death a close friend of Lincoln, Mathew S. Marsh, wrote his brother a letter containing a newsy paragraph devoted to Lincoln, which fails to mention any sorrow or abnormal condition of his at this time.[2] The letter establishes the fact that Lincoln was attending to his postmaster duties as usual,[3] and there is a record of a survey which Lincoln

---

[18] Herndon's MS. entitled "Miss Rutledge & Lincoln," 188—, *ibid.*

[19] J. F. Speed to Herndon, Nov. 30, 1866, *ibid.*

[20] For Lincoln's reference to Sarah Rickard, see Kincaid, *Joshua Fry Speed*, 47. Beveridge (I, 317) definitely states that Lincoln asked Sarah to marry him, but that she declined. Weik (*Real Lincoln*, 66–68) emphasizes Lincoln's attentions to Sarah; he also affirms that Lincoln proposed to her. (His material was the same as that used by Beveridge.) Sandburg and Angle, however, though pointing out that "Lincoln and Sarah went places together" (*Mary Lincoln*, 54) leave the impression that Sarah's interest was in Speed, whose departure left her disconsolate.

[1] Mrs. E. [Elizabeth] Abell to Herndon, Feb. 15, 1867, Herndon-Weik MSS. This lady, at whose cabin Lincoln was staying when Ann died, was Mrs. Bennett Abell, sister of Mary Owens.

[2] The original of the Marsh letter is in the collection of Oliver R. Barrett.

[3] Paul M. Angle, "Lincoln's First Love?" *Bulletin No. 9*, Lincoln Centennial Assoc., p. 7 (Dec. 1, 1927).

made, dated September 24, 1835, in his usual handwriting which shows that he was carrying on his surveying work.[4] This was at a time when, according to Herndon's embroidered account, Lincoln was a mental wreck. "He slept not," said Herndon, "he ate not, joyed not . . . until his body became emaciated and weak, and gave way. His mind wandered from its throne. In his imagination he muttered words to her he loved. His mind, his reason . . . walked out of itself along the uncolumned air, and kissed and embraced the shadows and illusions of the heated brain." [5] (A choice example, this, of Herndon's combination of soaring psychoanalysis with glowing language.)

By the statement of her brother, Ann Rutledge died on August 25, 1835.[6] The fall of 1836 found Lincoln absorbed in a prolonged courtship of Mary Owens. She had visited New Salem three years before —when Ann was living—and even then (i. e., in 1833), by his own statement, Lincoln considered her a desirable matrimonial partner.[7]

How did Herndon regard the known fact of Lincoln's courting of Mary Owens? He did not believe that Lincoln's profession of love for the lady could be taken otherwise than seriously. He thought "the letters expressed his honest feelings and his deepest convictions and that they were written sincerely—truthfully and honestly." Lincoln, he said, "was in love [with Miss Owens]—deeply in love." [8] Herndon had written effusively of the Ann Rutledge romance; now he spoke of Lincoln being thoroughly in love with Miss Owens; again he had it that Lincoln, in the period of his courtship of Miss Todd, "saw & loved an other woman—Miss Edwards and . . . desired to break away from Miss Todd & to join Miss Edwards." [9] In telling of Lin-

[4] *Bulletin No. 12*, Lincoln Centennial Assoc. (Sep. 1, 1928), 8.

[5] Broadside of Herndon lecture, Nov. 16, 1866, column 7, near bottom.

[6] R. B. Rutledge to Herndon, attested Oct. 22, 1866, Herndon-Weik MSS.

[7] "I had seen the said sister [Mary Owens] some three years before [i. e., before 1836], . . . and saw no good objection to plodding life through hand in hand with her." Lincoln to Mrs. O. H. Browning, April 1, 1838, *Works*, I, 88. In these words Lincoln admitted having a tender feeling for Miss Owens at a period two years before Ann's death. It has been noted how Mary Owens's sister, Mrs. Abell, knew little of Lincoln's attentions to Ann, though he was staying at the Abell cabin at the time of Ann's death. As to his courting of Miss Owens she had more to say. Lincoln, she wrote, told her sister he would rather have her "than any woman living." Mrs. Abell to Herndon, Jan. 13, 1867, Herndon-Weik MSS.

[8] Herndon's ms. fragment, "Lincoln's Courtship with Miss Owens," undated, Herndon-Weik MSS.

[9] Herndon to Lamon, Feb. 25, 1870, MS., Huntington Lib. One is dealing here with Herndon's comments—perhaps somewhat tentative—at a time long before he and Weik put their biography into shape.

coln's affections being given to Miss Edwards (this without adequate foundation), he mentioned the incident as "Miss Edwards flitting a cross the path"—this flitting made Lincoln "crazy *the second time*." [10] Taking all that Herndon said, one gets the impression that he almost considered his hero weak-minded in the matter of women. As for Herndon's collaborator, he states specifically that Lincoln proposed marriage to at least four women: Ann Rutledge, Mary Owens, Sarah Rickard, and (of course) Mary Todd.[11]

In striking contrast to the Rutledge romance, there is ample documentation for the Owens courtship. We have several letters which Lincoln wrote her in which he discussed the question of her marrying him, and a complete account of the whole affair, including Miss Owens's refusal of his marriage proposal, which Lincoln wrote to his friend Mrs. O. H. Browning.[12] In 1866 Mary Owens herself (Mrs. Vineyard) wrote: "From his own showing . . . his heart and hand were at my disposal, ..." [13] This statement, indeed the full record on this point, fails to harmonize with the popular concept that Lincoln's whole life was influenced by his love for Ann.

Herndon treasured the Ann Rutledge story. Referring to Nicolay and Hay's articles in the *Century* he wondered if they were going to "suppress" the tale. He called it "the finest story in Lincoln's life." [14] It is the stuff of which poetry and song are bodied forth—young love, the picturesque life of a vanished pioneer town, the tragic death of a

---

[10] *Ibid.*   [11] Weik, *Real Lincoln*, 56, 66–67.

[12] Lincoln gave a long and chatty account of his courtship of Miss Owens in a letter to Mrs. Orville H. Browning, April 1, 1838. (*Works*, I, 87–92.) Some have stressed the April fool date and have discounted this letter as having been written in a joking spirit. Lincoln, however, is quoted as having said that it had "too much truth for print" (*ibid.*, 87 n.), and his own letters to Miss Owens (*ibid.*, 52–54, 55–57) indicate an intention to marry her if that should be her wish, combined with a rather excessive amount of plain speaking to make sure it was her wish. If Herndon took the courtship with Miss Owens seriously there was good reason for it; the fact of Lincoln's offer of marriage was confirmed by the lady herself in later life. In a letter to Isaac N. Arnold, November 25, 1872 (MS., Chicago Hist. Soc.), O. H. Browning tells of how he and Lincoln were at Vandalia in 1836–38, how the Brownings boarded at the same house with Lincoln, how Lincoln was very fond of Mrs. Browning's society, and how the above-mentioned April letter was received after they left Vandalia in 1838. For a long time they thought it was one of Lincoln's funny stories; later, wrote Browning, it was learned that Lincoln was writing "a true account of an incident in actual life."

[13] In the same letter she wrote: ". . . I thought Mr. Lincoln was deficient in those little links which make up the great chain of womans happiness . . . ." Mrs. Vineyard to Herndon, May 23, 1866, Herndon-Weik MSS.

[14] Herndon to Weik, Dec. 5, 1886, *ibid.*

beautiful young woman, the beating of rain and storm upon a new made grave, the age-long questioning concerning human mortality.

But there is repeated mention in the manuscripts of Herndon's worried doubts on the subject. The fact of Ann's engagement to McNamar seems greatly to have bothered him. Writing to Weik when the biography was in proof, he said: "Again the more I think of the Ann Rutledge story the more do I think that the girl had two engagements— i e that she was engaged to two men at one and the same. . . . I shall change my opinion of events & things on the coming of new facts and on more mature reflection in all cases—and so excuse me for 'sorter' wabbling around." [15] Herndon's account, which was to establish the story indelibly in the public mind, was already in printer's proof; yet here he is confessing that he is " 'sorter' wabbling around" in regard to the engagement of Lincoln and Ann.[16]

In the collection of Oliver R. Barrett in Chicago there is a stone (turtle shaped, about ten inches long) whose inscription records that A. Lincoln and Ann Rutledge "were betrothed here July 4 1833." (The carving is clear enough. The "J" in July is ignorantly reversed.) The pedigree of the stone, as often in such cases, is incomplete. One can get statements as to its having been found in New Salem, also as to its carving resembling that of an ax handle bearing Lincoln's name; back of that, information is lacking.[17] There are various counts against this stone if considered as a genuine record cut by Lincoln. Herndon, prominent advocate of the romance, said definitely that Ann stood firm in her feeling toward McNamar "up to 1834" and that Lincoln proposed to her in 1835. He said that "Soon after this . . . engagement Ann was taken sick . . . ," [18] this being her final illness. It has already been noted that she died in 1835. Without presuming to give a date to a matter that is alleged but not verified, it may be noted that those who would build up a case for the Lincoln-Rutledge

[15] Herndon to Weik, Jan. 11, 1889, *ibid.*

[16] He added, however, that he did not want the text of the book changed in its treatment of this theme. *Ibid.* At this point it is appropriate to note Weik's view that the story of Ann Rutledge was peculiarly due to Herndon's preservation. Her "melancholy history," wrote Weik, "but for the indefatigable and exhaustive researches of Mr. Herndon, would probably never have been preserved." *Real Lincoln,* 66.

[17] The writer has examined the stone through the courtesy of Mr. Barrett. The subject is discussed in *Bulletin No. 12,* Lincoln Centennial Assoc., 6–8 (Sep. 1, 1828). In this article it is stated that the stone was found at New Salem in 1900 and that the ax handle was dug up on the site of the Lincoln-Berry store in 1878.

[18] Herndon's MS. entitled "Miss Rutledge & Lincoln," 188—, Herndon-Weik MSS.

engagement will rely upon various recollections and upon the analysis of Herndon who believed such an engagement to have existed; they will therefore have great difficulty in arguing for the betrothal on so early a date as July 4, 1833. They will be confronted with Lincoln's own written statement that in 1833 he did not object to "plodding life through hand in hand" with Mary Owens. They will also have to remember that, where the Lincoln-Rutledge engagement was spoken of, it was related to a considerably prolonged absence of McNamar; in July 1833 Ann's lover had not been absent that long. (In a letter to George U. Miles, May 5, 1866, McNamar wrote that he left New Salem "in 32 or 33." The words "or 33" were then crossed out.) Another point to remember is that in 1833 (well on in his twenty-fifth year) Lincoln certainly knew how to form his letters; he would not have carved a reversed "J". To put the criticism of the stone in the very mildest form, too little is known of it to establish its authenticity. It is not known by whom or when it was made.

Space is lacking in which to show how other biographers have dealt with the Ann Rutledge theme. Many of them do little more than repeat Herndon. Beveridge bases his full account on Herndon's material and presents Lincoln's engagement to Ann largely along the line suggested by R. B. Rutledge, as above quoted. Yet he admits that Lincoln's courting of Ann was "misty" and states that "No positive [i. e., unconditional] and definite engagement resulted." [19] W. E. Barton accepts the tradition. "Abraham Lincoln and Ann truly loved each other," he writes.[20] Yet Barton adds on a later page: "We know very little about the Ann Rutledge incident. If Lincoln wrote any letters to Ann they were not preserved. If there is any other documentary proof of their love-affair, it is unknown. We know that much that has been told about it is unreliable." [21]

V

To recapitulate: In its origin the Ann Rutledge story rests on wavering memories recorded many years after the event. No proved contemporary evidence is known to exist. Herndon did not invent the romance. He loved the truth and sought it eagerly. Whether he always found it is another matter, but if he did we know that it had to

[19] Beveridge, I, 149.   [20] Barton, *Life of Abraham Lincoln*, I, 214.   [21] *Ibid.*, I, 225.

undergo his inevitable psychoanalysis before it emerged. He did elaborate the story, publicize it, and cast it into the mold which it has retained in popular thought. From the doubtful beginning of distant memory there has evolved a full-grown tradition; in the now classic form which the tradition has taken the main handiwork is that of Herndon. Few indeed were familiar with the episode prior to Herndon's sensational lecture of 1866, which came a considerable time after Lincoln's death. Other biographers, in presenting the story, have followed the Herndon line; but the reader will recognize that the quoting of many repetitions of Herndon and Weik adds nothing in terms of historical contribution.[1] Reminiscences gathered long after the event were not all in favor of the romance; they were contradictory and vague.[2] The two elements on which there is agreement are Ann's engagement to McNamar and Lincoln's grief at her death. Concerning the first of these elements it may be noted that in the popular conception of the Rutledge story, John McNamar is the forgotten man; yet it is worth while to note a passage that brings poignantly to light the feeling of the one who, after all, was Ann's acknowledged and accepted lover. ". . . I cut the Initials of Miss Ann Rutledge on a b[o]ard at the head of her grave 30 years ago,"[3] wrote McNamar to Herndon in 1866. It was McNamar, not Lincoln, who marked Ann's grave. As to Lincoln's grief it has been seen that his alleged derangement of mind is without adequate substantiation; in the "uncolumned air" of Herndon's lecture it is nothing more than fiction.

Whether Lincoln was in love with Ann, or grieved over the untimely death of one who was both a lovable young woman and a dear friend; whether his grief was due to a romantic attachment or to a

---

[1] Such repetitious "evidence" is found in Percival Graham Rennick, *Abraham Lincoln and Ann Rutledge: An Old Salem Romance* (1932).

[2] It is only by a study of Herndon's manuscripts that one can realize the uncertainty of his material. G. U. Miles, Herndon's father-in-law in Petersburg, Illinois, deputed to interview various persons concerning Lincoln and Ann, replied: ". . . the references you gave me knew little or nothing of what you wanted to know." Miles to Herndon, Mar. 23, 1866, Herndon-Weik MSS.

[3] McNamar to Herndon, Dec. 1, 1866, *ibid.* By way of further reference to the strangely neglected subject of McNamar's love for Ann, it is of interest to quote the following description in his handwriting: "Miss Ann was a gentle Amiable Maiden without any of the airs of your city Belles but winsome and comly withal a blond in complection with golden hair, 'cherry red lips & a bonny Blue Eye.'" McNamar to G. U. Miles, May 5, 1866, *ibid.*

temperament subject to gloom and deeply sensitive to the tragedy of death; whether Ann loved him or was friendly to but unimpressed by one who called himself a "friendless, uneducated, penniless boy"; [4] whether there was an engagement between them or it was Ann's intention to marry McNamar when he returned, are matters open to question. Ann's feeling and intent are left in considerable doubt by contradictions in regard to an engagement between them, by the opinion of some that she was unimpressed with him and would have married McNamar if she had lived, and by the unanimous testimony that she was engaged to McNamar.

Whatever may have been the true situation as to Lincoln and Ann, that situation seems now well nigh unrecoverable. As to a romantic attachment, it has not been *dis*proved. It is more correct to characterize it as *un*proved; as such it has been a famous subject of conjecture. It is a memory which lacks support in any statement recorded in Ann's lifetime. Since it is thus traditional and not reliably established as to its nature and significance, it does not belong in a recital of those Lincoln episodes which one presents as unquestioned reality.

As a historical puzzle or an exercise in the evaluation of reminiscence the Lincoln-Rutledge story is a choice subject; but its substance is far from clear while its fringe is to be discarded from the record of established history. By that fringe we mean the elaboration, the trimmings and embroidery, the fictional sentimentalizing, the invented poeticisms, and the amazing aura of apocryphal material that have surrounded the whole overgrown tale.

The present treatment has been concerned only with essential results in the telling, though masses of documents have gone into the investigation.[5] To spin out the analysis into an extended account

---

[4] Lincoln thus described himself in terms of the recollections of "the older citizens"; he had just referred to "old friends of Menard." Letter to Morris, Mar. 26, 1843, *Works*, I, 262.

[5] Not all of these documents are in the Herndon-Weik Collection. Some of the delayed reminiscence by those who had lived in the 1830's was as late as 1922. In that year Mr. George P. Hambrecht of Madison, Wisconsin, received a letter from Sarah Rutledge Saunders, written (March 18) by James Rutledge Saunders, her son, from Lompoc, California; this Mrs. Saunders was Ann's sister. Concerning Ann's last illness she said: "Finally my Brother David who was attending school at Jacksonville, Ill. and Lincoln were sent for. I can see them as they each came, and when Lincoln went into the sick room where Sister Ann lay, the others retired. A few minutes later Lincoln came from the room with bowed head and seemed to me, at the time, to be crying. Soon After this Ann died and was followed by my Father." She wrote also of seeing Lincoln

would, in the writer's view, not change the conclusion, though a full
exhibiting of the subject would require a reproduction of numerous
letters and jottings, an amassing of details about each witness with a
studious examination of each bit of testimony, and withal a portrayal
of the vanished background of New Salem.

Assuredly the effect of the episode upon Lincoln's later life has been
greatly exaggerated—or rather, fabricated. Nor should one lightly
overlook the shabby manner in which the image of Ann has tended
to obscure the years of Lincoln's love and devotion for Mary, his
wife, and to belittle her love and devotion for him. There is no need
to comment on the expansive popular embellishment of the story—
in novels, dramas, radio scripts and the like—nor to remind the
reader of the voluminous flow of literary invention which has out-
Herndoned Herndon in our own day.[6] Evaluation of the evidence,
which one seldom finds anywhere but which has been attempted in
the preceding pages, is the only answer to the inquiry as to where the
pedestrian course of history ends and the limitless soaring of fiction
begins.

"at our table and fire side." Well over ninety and very feeble, Mrs. Saunders confessed:
"I am sorry to have so little recollection of the time . . . , being a mere child of six
or seven." As to Lincoln and Ann in the final illness she added: "These are so dimly
seen that I cannot speak of them with that degree of assurance that I would like." In
this letter Ann's sister made no assertion that Lincoln and Ann were engaged. For a
loan of the letter the author is indebted to the Abraham Lincoln Book Shop of Chicago.

[6] Popular interest has stimulated the hand of forgery. For the "Minor Collection"
hoax, whose day of deception was fortunately brief, one may consult the files of the
Atlantic Monthly from December through April, 1928-29. See especially Paul M.
Angle, "The Minor Collection: A Criticism," *ibid.*, vol. 143, 516-525 (Apr., 1929).

BIBLIOGRAPHY

BIBLIOGRAPHICAL NOTE

The bibliography here given is designed as a rather full coverage of significant titles on Lincoln. It is, however, definitely selective. No item is included without a reason; thousands have been purposely omitted. The present list stands somewhere between *A Shelf of Lincoln Books* by Paul M. Angle (an expansion of his "Basic Lincolniana") and the elaborate volumes entitled *Lincoln Bibliography, 1839–1939,* by Jay Monaghan. In the latter work one finds not only the fullest of all Lincoln bibliographies (arranged by years), but an excellent introduction by Mr. Monaghan which traces the beginning, growth, and mature elaboration of Lincoln bibliography with attention to technical matters, variants, pitfalls and frauds, collectors' activities, dealers' adventures, location of rare items, conferences and friendships among Lincoln devotees, and the like. It has been announced that the publisher of this bibliography, the Illinois State Historical Library, intends to issue supplements at ten-year intervals.

No student of Lincoln needs to be told that the list here attempted is far from "complete." There has been no wish to make it complete, for that would require the inclusion of thousands of trivial or valueless items. The following pages, however, do give a very large number of titles not included in Monaghan's work, since that work was purposely designed to exclude magazine articles (unless reprinted with new paging), all books and pamphlets since 1939, and many contributions to the Lincoln theme that do not have the name of Lincoln in the title. The present list includes these classes so far as they come within the selective design. There has been no intention to limit the selection by any definition of "Lincolniana"; such a limitation sets up a generalized formula (on which Lincoln devotees have had many an amiable argument), while the only principle of inclusion herein has been the significance of each item for some aspect of Lincoln study. In making this explanation the author by no means claims that his selection is without fault. He fears that a number of omissions, and perhaps some inclusions, will be considered unjustified. For such defects he can only plead fallibility and ask indulgence. The list will be considered by many over-long; yet it gives only an imperfect idea of the vast flood and sweep of Lincoln literature.

For all titles the present list gives the author, compiler or editor, title, publisher, date and place of publication, and name of periodical where appropriate. In addition, the number of pages is given except for works that run to more than one volume. This is to enable the reader at a glance to distinguish between a short pamphlet and an item of book length. No effort is made to list all the varying editions of a given work. The plan usually followed has been to indicate either the first edition or one which may be taken as typical or most significant. (One of the exceptions to this rule is in the case of Herndon, whose varying editions have been briefly noted.)

The present volumes emphasize the presidency and carry the story no farther than the time of the Gettysburg address, but the bibliography is intended to serve for the whole Lincoln subject. Titles are included on topics which the author has not treated. Such a matter as the assassination, for example, has no place in the author's text, but books, articles, and reports on the assassination have been listed.

It is difficult for any bibliography to have every desirable feature. This list, for example, is not arranged by categories, classes, or topics. The method has been to throw all the titles into one continuous alphabetical arrangement, using surnames of authors, compilers, or editors as key-words. The obvious convenience of such an over-all alphabetization has been the controlling factor; to overload the pages with a topical guide has not seemed practicable. (The index, of course, guides to particular topics; annotations throughout the book carry references on the topics treated.)

Though titles are not arranged by topic or type, it may be useful to note where some of them fit into the whole pattern of Lincoln studies. This is in part attempted, with realization of inadequacy, in the following paragraphs. For this rough classification, which is not meant to be complete, only authors' names (key-words) are given; the items appear in their alphabetical places.

Bibliographies of the Lincoln subject have been prepared by P. M. Angle, W. E. Barton, Richard Booker, Andrew Boyd, Daniel Fish, C. H. Hart, J. B. Oakleaf, G. T. Ritchie, J. W. Starr, Jr., E. J. Wessen, and, as above noted, Jay Monaghan.

For Lincoln's writings, speeches, and letters, there is no one complete collection: one must use the editions by Nicolay and Hay, and by Lapsley; then he must supplement these by Angle, the Brown University volume, Hertz, Tracy, Sparks (for the debates with Douglas), and the appendix of Miss Tarbell's second volume. These are the basic titles as to writings. Selections of Lincoln's works are a different matter. There have been many of them; one of the handiest is that edited by Philip Van Doren Stern. Often the lists put out by autograph dealers are useful for Lincoln originals. Forgeries of Lincoln writings have been exposed by Worthington C. Ford, Paul M. Angle (as to the "Minor Collection"), Milo M. Quaife, and F. W. Taussig (for Lincoln and the tariff).

For reminiscences one uses such writers as D. H. Bates, John Bigelow,

Noah Brooks, F. B. Carpenter, L. E. Chittenden, W. H. Crook, C. A. Dana, G. M. Dodge, J. M. Forbes, J. W. Forney, J. R. Gilmore, Horace Greeley, Elizabeth Todd Grimsley, W. H. Herndon, O. O. Howard, Gustave Koerner, Ward H. Lamon, U. F. Linder, A. K. McClure, Hugh McCulloch, Helen Nicolay, J. M. Palmer, Donn Piatt, David D. Porter, H. B. Rankin, A. T. Rice, A. G. Riddle, Carl Schurz, F. W. Seward, John Sherman, W. T. Sherman, Goldwin Smith, J. F. Speed, A. H. Stephens, W. O. Stoddard, Henry Villard, William H. Ward, Thurlow Weed, Gideon Welles, Horace White, and H. C. Whitney. (The list could be greatly extended by mention of autobiographies, speeches, and the like in which scattered recollections of Lincoln are included. It was a prolific age for this type of writing.)

Far better than reminiscences are contemporary statements. To have a full collection of descriptions or comments written *at the time* by those who saw or heard Lincoln would be an impressive and useful thing; it is one of the Lincoln projects, of which there are a number, still to be developed. Awaiting such a collection, one takes real delight in the attractive volume titled *Concerning Mr. Lincoln,* by H. E. Pratt. More books of this type would be welcome. It should be added, however, that anything like a full gathering of strictly contemporary comments on Lincoln would seem, in many of its parts, a voluminous anthology of abuse, and that largely by men of his own party. (A sampling of such unfavorable appraisals has been attempted by the present author in "The Unpopular Mr. Lincoln.")

In noting that there has been a tremendous volume of Lincoln literature, it should be realized that only a small portion of the writing has taken the form of comprehensive full-length biography, while some of the life stories are superfluous or negligible in that they contribute nothing. Significant biographies are fewer than is commonly supposed; their authors may be listed in a very small space. Campaign lives in 1860 and 1864 (e. g., by Barrett, Bartlett, Howard, Howells, Raymond, Scripps, Vose, etc.) were superficial and defective; one can turn to the monograph by Ernest J. Wessen for a competent treatment of them. Leaving them aside, one may list the significant biographers almost in a nutshell as follows.

(1) Before Nicolay and Hay: Isaac N. Arnold, Herndon and Weik, J. G. Holland, and Ward H. Lamon (ghost writer, Chauncey F. Black).

(2) From 1890, including that year, to 1920: Francis F. Browne, Lord Charnwood, W. E. Curtis, J. T. Morse, Jr., J. G. Nicolay and John Hay, E. P. Oberholtzer, Alonzo Rothschild, W. O. Stoddard, and Ida M. Tarbell.

(3) Since 1920: W. E. Barton, Albert J. Beveridge, Edgar Lee Masters, N. W. Stephenson, J. W. Weik, and (putting him last for emphasis) Carl Sandburg. (Emanuel Hertz has written much on Lincoln, but none of his writing took the form of a comprehensive biography.)

The important diaries that contain considerable source material on Lincoln are those of Edward Bates, Salmon P. Chase, Orville H. Browning, John Hay, W. H. Russell, and Gideon Welles. There are many others, but these are the leading ones. "The Diary of a Public Man" is a special problem (see Public Man, below).

For Lincoln day-by-day one uses the excellent volumes by P. M. Angle, H. E. Pratt, and Benjamin P. Thomas.

Lincoln's ancestry has been presented by W. E. Barton, F. L. Bullard, J. Winston Coleman, Jr., Caroline Hanks Hitchcock (unreliable), J. H. Lea and J. R. Hutchinson, Marion D. Learned, Waldo Lincoln, Louis Richards, Ida M. Tarbell, and L. A. Warren. (Waldo Lincoln is outstanding for the Lincoln family.)

For early life, besides biographers already mentioned, there are special authors: Edwin Davis, Bess V. Ehrmann, J. E. Iglehart, J. Edward Murr, Frank E. Stevens, Benjamin P. Thomas, and Louis A. Warren. (See also H. E. Pratt's day-by-day account for the early years.) Leading biographers have treated the Ann Rutledge subject, Herndon and Weik making it a specialty; others who have dealt with this theme are Angle, Monaghan, and Rennick.

Place studies of Lincoln have been produced by the following authors: for Bloomington, Illinois, H. E. Pratt, Sherman D. Wakefield; for California, Milton H. Shutes; for Chicago and vicinity, W. E. Barton, J. S. Currey, B. B. Gernon; for Cincinnati, J. M. Dickson; for Indiana, Bess V. Ehrmann, J. E. Iglehart, J. E. Murr, G. S. Cottman; for Iowa, F. I. Herriott; for Kansas, F. W. Brinkerhoff (and see "Lincoln in Kansas"); for Lexington, Kentucky, W. H. Townsend; for the "Lincoln country," Rexford Newcomb; for Macon County, Illinois, Edwin Davis; for Milwaukee, W. G. Bruce; for Minnesota, S. J. Buck; for Missouri, W. B. Stevens; for New England, F. L. Bullard, P. C. Eggleston; for New Hampshire, Elwin L. Page; for Ohio, J. H. Cramer, D. J. Ryan; for Peoria, Illinois, E. E. East, B. D. Bryner; for Springfield, Illinois, Paul M. Angle; for New Salem, Benjamin P. Thomas.

On Lincoln the lawyer one may read P. M. Angle, F. T. Hill, J. M. Palmer, H. E. Pratt, J. T. Richards, Benjamin P. Thomas, W. H. Townsend, A. A. Woldman, and J. M. Zane.

For Mrs. Lincoln the leading writers are Gamaliel Bradford, W. A. Evans, Katherine Helm, Elizabeth Keckley (assisted by James Redpath), Virginia Kinnaird, Mary L. Miles, H. E. Pratt and E. E. East, C. C. Ritze, Carl Sandburg and P. M. Angle, and W. H. Townsend.

Matters of politics are treated by W. E. Baringer, S. D. Brummer, A. C. Cole, E. M. Coulter, S. S. Cox, Avery Craven, H. M. Dudley, E. D. Fite, Horace Greeley, Murat Halstead, W. A. Harbison, F. I. Herriott, H. P. James, G. W. Julian, R. H. Luthin, W. S. Myers, Louis Pelzer, G. H. Porter, P. Orman Ray, D. C. Seitz, J. L. Sellers, Donnal V. Smith, T. E. Strevey, Charles R. Wilson, Henry Wilson, O. O. Winther, and James A. Woodburn.

Works on causes of the Civil War, the crisis of 1860 and '61, and the Sumter tragedy have been produced by Henry Adams, J. B. Baldwin, L. E.

Chittenden, J. A. Campbell, S. W. Crawford, Avery Craven, D. L. Dumond, G. F. Milton, D. M. Potter, C. W. Ramsdell, J. G. Randall, J. F. Rhodes, G. W. Summers, J. S. Tilley, and Gideon Welles. The manner in which "causes" of the war have been marshaled and interpreted by various writers has been analyzed by Howard K. Beale in a manuscript which the author has been privileged to read. It has not yet been published, but for scholarly coverage of this broad field and for compression of elaborate material within brief form, nothing compares to it.

International matters are discussed in works by E. A. Adamov, E. D. Adams, C. F. Adams, Frederic Bancroft, S. F. Bemis, John Bright, F. L. Bullard, L. M. Case, M. P. Claussen, Tyler Dennett, W. C. Ford, H. Nelson Gay, F. A. Golder, F. L. Owsley, L. M. Sears, C. C. Tansill, Benjamin P. Thomas, and, for the diplomat in carpet slippers, Jay Monaghan.

On problems of the Lincoln administration the reader may consult the following: for the New Almaden scandal, Leonard Ascher, Milton H. Shutes; for conscription and army administration, Fred A. Shannon (for Taney's opinion, P. G. Auchampaugh); for statehood of Nevada and for courts of the District of Columbia, F. L. Bullard; for the patronage, J. D. Carter, H. J. Carman and R. H. Luthin, C. R. Fish; for clemency, J. T. Dorris; for disloyalty (fifth column, etc.), W. A. Dunning, Wood Gray, G. F. Milton; for emancipation, John Eaton, F. T. Hill, W. R. Livermore, Charles H. Wesley; for peace making, E. C. Kirkland; for the war department, A. H. Meneely; for constitutional problems, J. G. Randall; for state and federal relations, W. B. Weeden; for Lincoln and the radicals, T. Harry Williams.

The subject of Lincoln and the South has been treated by J. M. Botts, A. C. Cole, Avery Craven, J. G. de R. Hamilton, C. H. McCarthy, J. G. Randall, E. G. Scott, and (for the border) E. C. Smith.

Special studies on Lincoln are numerous and no attempt will be made to list the authors at this point. A few examples may be noted: for Lincoln at Gettysburg, W. E. Barton, F. L. Bullard, C. E. Carr, Robert Fortenbaugh, S. L. Green, W. H. Lambert, H. E. Luhrs, Charles Moore; for the offer to Garibaldi of a commission as major general in the Union army in 1861, C. F. Adams, H. N. Gay, Carey Shaw, Jr., C. C. Tansill; for the contribution of the Germans in politics, Andreas Dorpalen, F. I. Herriott, Jay Monaghan, Joseph Schafer, Donnal V. Smith; for Lincoln and agriculture, Earle D. Ross; for the Bixby letter (awaiting a forthcoming work by F. L. Bullard and Edward C. Stone), W. E. Barton, Kendall Banning, Edith H. Madigan; for civil liberty, A. C. Cole; for medical matters, M. H. Shutes; for personal finances, H. E. Pratt; for Lincoln and the Jews, Isaac Markens, Emanuel Hertz; for the Lincoln legend, R. P. Basler, C. B. Coleman, Lloyd Lewis, T. V. Smith; for literary style, Daniel K. Dodge, L. E. Robinson, Benjamin P. Thomas; for *Punch*, W. S. Walsh; for religion, W. E. Barton, F. B. Carpenter, A. V. House, Jr., D. C. McMurtrie, John W. Starr, Jr. (and see "Abraham Lincoln's Religion: His Own Statement"); for the railroads,

John W. Starr, Jr.; for the tariff, R. H. Luthin, Thomas M. Pitkin, F. W. Taussig; for Walt Whitman, W. E. Barton.

For Washington in Lincoln's time one may read Henry Adams, George Borrett, Noah Brooks, Wilhelmus B. Bryan, A. C. Clark, W. A. Croffut, John Hay, Margaret Leech, "Ben: Perley Poore" (who for reasons best known to himself often used this peculiar form for his name), and G. A. Townsend ("Gath").

For the assassination and related myths the main writers are S. B. Arnold, Finis L. Bates, G. S. Bryan, Grace Julian Clarke, W. H. Crook, D. M. DeWitt, Otto Eisenschiml, W. J. Ferguson, A. K. McClure, Nettie Mudd, Allan Pinkerton, Benn Pitman, B. P. Poore, Moorfield Storey, C. S. Taft, James Tanner, and Francis Wilson.

Under a special heading below some of the main manuscript collections are listed and at that point a brief word is given concerning archives. No such listing will be attempted for the great masses of published government documents belonging to the Lincoln period. Debates in Congress are impressively embalmed in the *Congressional Globe*. They are given also in shorter summary in Appleton's *American Annual Cyclopaedia*, these volumes constituting handy and useful yearbooks full of information. Many topics of the time are treated in the congressional documents (voluminous serial issues known as *House Executive Documents, House Miscellaneous Documents, House Reports,* and their counterparts for the Senate); the guide to all this impressive material is B. P. Poore's *Descriptive Catalogue of Government Publications, 1774–1881.* These government issues are often very useful, but the guide by Poore gives a key to their contents, and any listing of the particular documents would be impracticable here.

The same may be said as to newspapers. They are indispensable if used with critical care, but they are too numerous to be listed. Useful guides are to be found in *A Check List of Newspapers in the Library of Congress* (1901); *Checklist of Newspapers . . . in the New York Public Library* (1915); *A List of Newspapers in the Yale University Library* (1916); and Frank W. Scott, *Newspapers and Periodicals of Illinois, 1814–1879* (Ill. Hist. Coll., vol. VI). One should consult also Winifred Gregory, ed., *American Newspapers, 1821–1936: A Union List of Files Available in the United States and Canada* (1937). Newspaper opinion for the secession crisis has been conveniently presented in Dwight L. Dumond, *Southern Editorials on Secession* and Howard C. Perkins, *Northern Editorials on Secession.* Besides reproducing a full and representative selection of editorials, these books offer a working guide to the journals of the time. There are, of course, histories of particular newspapers, such as that of Elmer Davis for the New York *Times,* Allan Nevins for the New York *Evening Post,* Ralph R. Fahrney for Greeley and the New York *Tribune,* and Tracy E. Strevey for the Chicago *Tribune.* The author has treated some of the problems of newspapers during Lincoln's presidency in the *American Historical Review,* XXIII, 303–323.

Without any listing of the magazines of Lincoln's day it must be noted that the *Railsplitter,* published at Chicago, was a campaign organ for the Republicans in 1860, and that *Harper's Weekly* and *Frank Leslie's Illustrated Newspaper* contained a wealth of excellent pictorial material for the period, together with many articles dealing with contemporary events. Such magazines extended themselves in presenting the work of special artists who went nearly everywhere for their pictures. Some of the unpublished originals of these interesting drawings, often better than the printed ones, are in the Library of Congress and the New York Public Library. For photographs the contemporary work of Brady was outstanding; the foremost collector of Lincoln photographs is Frederick H. Meserve. Magazines and periodical publications in our own day devoted to Lincoln have not been at a loss for material to fill their pages. The best known are the *Lincoln Herald, Lincoln Lore,* and, above all, the handsome *Abraham Lincoln Quarterly.*

MANUSCRIPT COLLECTIONS

Besides enumerating bodies of unpublished papers in alphabetical array, the purpose of this list is to indicate where the manuscripts are located. (Where more than one substantial collection exists for the papers of a particular man—e. g., Salmon P. Chase—footnote references give the library location; otherwise, and usually, the footnote reads: "Andrew MSS.," "Sumner MSS.," etc.) It is by no means claimed that the following list is "complete" for Lincoln information. It does not include all the collections which the author has examined, nor does it give detached or scattered manuscript items, for which footnotes must suffice for those cited. Manuscript material in the Library of Congress is indicated in considerable detail in the *Handbook of Manuscripts in the Library of Congress* (1918) and in subsequent reports and supplements issued by the Library.

Robert Anderson MSS., Lib. of Cong., Washington.
John A. Andrew MSS., Mass. Hist. Soc., Boston.
Isaac N. Arnold MSS., Chicago Hist. Soc.
Nathaniel P. Banks MSS., Essex Institute, Salem, Mass.
Truman H. Bartlett MSS., Mass. Hist. Soc.
Henry W. Bellows MSS., Mass. Hist. Soc.
Jeremiah S. Black MSS., Lib. of Cong.
Blair MSS., Lib of Cong. Papers of F. P. Blair, Sr., F. P. Blair, Jr., and Montgomery Blair. Known as Gist-Blair MSS.
John Bright MSS., British Museum, London.
James Buchanan MSS., Hist. Soc. of Pa., Philadelphia.
Benjamin F. Butler MSS., Lib. of Cong.
Simon Cameron MSS., Lib. of Cong.
Zachariah Chandler MSS., Lib. of Cong.
Salmon P. Chase MSS., Hist. Soc. of Pa.

Salmon P. Chase MSS., Lib. of Cong. Includes papers, letter books, and diaries.

Richard Cobden MSS., British Museum.

John J. Crittenden MSS., Lib. of Cong.

Benjamin R. Curtis MSS., Lib. of Cong.

Anna E. Dickinson MSS., Lib. of Cong.

Stephen A. Douglas MSS., Univ. of Chicago.

Edward Everett MSS., Mass. Hist. Soc.

Thomas Ewing MSS., Lib. of Cong.

William P. Fessenden MSS., Lib. of Cong.

Benjamin B. French MSS., Lib. of Cong.

William Lloyd Garrison MSS., Boston Pub. Lib.

Giddings-Julian MSS., Lib. of Cong.

Horace Greeley MSS., Lib. of Cong.

Horace Greeley MSS., New York Pub. Lib. Includes numerous letters from Greeley to Schuyler Colfax.

Count Adam de Gurowski MSS., Lib. of Cong.

Charles H. Hart MSS., Henry E. Huntington Lib., San Marino, Calif.

Herndon-Parker MSS., Univ. of Iowa, Iowa City. A series of 68 letters between Herndon and Theodore Parker during the 1850's giving an inside picture of the Lincoln & Herndon office, together with details on Illinois politics. Many of these letters are published, with some editorial errors, in Newton, *Lincoln and Herndon.*

Herndon-Weik Collection, Lib. of Cong. Voluminous body of papers collected by W. H. Herndon. Includes numerous reminiscences of Lincoln, records of interviews, letters to Herndon from a wide range of persons, hundreds of letters of Herndon to Weik (his literary collaborator), field notes, scrapbook of political material, fragments by Herndon intended as drafts of particular passages to be rewritten for the biography, etc. Lincoln autographs are included, as well as a number of Lincoln's own papers and hundreds of legal documents pertaining to the Lincoln-Herndon law practice. The collection has been used by Herndon and Weik, and by Beveridge. It is, however, so voluminous and so uneven in quality, that it deserves far more critical appraisal than it has ever received. It is both indispensable and unsatisfactory; it is altogether unique. The University of Illinois has the collection in the form of photostats, microfilms, and prints from microfilms. For the most part the many items in the collection are unpublished. In *The Hidden Lincoln* by Emanuel Hertz one finds a minor portion of the papers poorly selected and unskillfully edited. (Many letters from Herndon are to be found in the collected manuscripts of Truman H. Bartlett, Charles H. Hart, Ward H. Lamon, Charles Sumner, Lyman Trumbull, and Jesse W. Weik. See also Herndon-Parker MSS.)

Ethan Allen Hitchcock MSS., Lib. of Cong.

Joseph Holt MSS., Lib. of Cong.

House of Representatives, Papers of, Lib. of Cong. Voluminous masses of material, being chiefly the papers of committees of the House. In the National Archives are similar papers for the Senate.

Andrew Johnson MSS., Lib. of Cong.

Ward Hill Lamon MSS., Henry E. Huntington Lib.

Amos Lawrence MSS., Mass. Hist. Soc.

Francis Lieber MSS., Henry E. Huntington Lib.

Francis Lieber MSS., Lib. of Cong. Includes 200 letters of Lieber to his intimate friend, Samuel B. Ruggles of New York.

Lincoln Collections. Among the most valuable Lincoln collections—rich in manuscripts, rare books, and unique material—are those of the Abraham Lincoln Association, Springfield, Ill.; Allegheny College, Meadville, Pa. (the Ida M. Tarbell collection); Oliver R. Barrett, Chicago, Ill. (of great importance); Brown University, Providence, R. I.; Chicago Historical Society; the William L. Clements Library, University of Michigan, Ann Arbor, Mich. (the Greenly collection); the Henry E. Huntington Library, San Marino, Calif.; Illinois State Historical Library, Springfield, Ill. (including the collection of Henry Horner and a great deal besides—rich in Lincoln originals); Illinois State Library, division of archives, Springfield, Ill. (Lincoln MSS., rather recently found, are included here); Indiana University, Bloomington, Ind. (the J. B. Oakleaf collection); the Library of Congress, Washington, D. C.; Lincoln Memorial University, Harrogate, Tenn.; the Lincoln National Life Foundation, Fort Wayne, Ind.; Frederick H. Meserve, New York, N. Y. (photographs); the J. P. Morgan Library, New York City; University of Chicago, Chicago, Ill. (the William E. Barton collection); University of Illinois, Urbana, Ill. (rich in photostats); Western Reserve Historical Society, Cleveland, Ohio; Yale University, New Haven, Conn. (the Stuart W. Jackson collection). For excellent descriptions of the leading Lincoln collections of the country see *Abr. Lincoln Quar.*, March 1940-March 1943, *passim*.

Lincoln Papers, Lib. of Cong. A great mass of Lincoln papers, given to the Library of Congress by Robert Todd Lincoln, has been in the Library since 1919. By the donor's restriction they will not be open to investigators until July 26, 1947—i. e., twenty-one years after Robert Lincoln's death. Apart from this closed collection, the Library of Congress contains a considerable number of Lincoln MSS. (autograph letters, facsimiles, photostats, public documents, etc.) to which the author has had access. See also Herndon-Weik Collection.

Hugh McCulloch MSS., Lib. of Cong.

Hugh McCulloch MSS., Lincoln National Life Foundation, Fort Wayne, Ind.

George B. McClellan MSS., Lib. of Cong.

John A. McClernand MSS., Ill. State Hist. Lib., Springfield.

John McLean MSS., Lib. of Cong.

Edward McPherson MSS., Lib. of Cong.

Montgomery C. Meigs MSS., Lib. of Cong.

Justin S. Morrill MSS., Lib. of Cong.

National Archives. Enormous masses of official records of the U. S. government are preserved, housed, and serviced in the superb National Archives Building at Washington. Significant material is to be found in the records of the departments of war, navy, state, and treasury, in the papers of the attorney general, and in those of many other agencies. For guides, see C. H. Van Tyne and W. G. Leland, *Guide to the Archives of the United States* . . . ; House Document 1443, 62d Congress, 3d session; *Guide to the Material in the National Archives* (Washington, Govt. Ptg. Off. 1940).

Nicolay-Hay Collection, Ill. State Hist. Lib. Correspondence of John G. Nicolay and John Hay in connection with the writing and publication of their ten-volume *Lincoln*.

John T. Pickett Papers, Lib. of Cong. Masses of official diplomatic papers of the Confederate States of America. Instructions, correspondence, and miscellaneous archives of the department of state of the Confederacy.

Francis Pierpoint MSS., Virginia State Archives, Richmond.

L. U. Reavis MSS., Chicago Hist. Soc.

Lord Russell Papers, Public Records Office, London.

John M. Schofield MSS., Lib. of Cong.

Carl Schurz MSS., Lib. of Cong.

John Sherman MSS., Lib. of Cong.

William T. Sherman MSS., Lib. of Cong.

Edwin M. Stanton MSS., Lib. of Cong.

State Department. See National Archives.

Thaddeus Stevens MSS., Lib. of Cong.

Charles Sumner MSS., Widener Library, Harvard Univ., Cambridge, Mass.

R. W. Thompson MSS., Lincoln National Life Foundation.

Samuel J. Tilden MSS., New York Pub. Lib.

Lyman Trumbull MSS., Lib. of Cong.

Benjamin F. Wade MSS., Lib. of Cong.

War Department. See National Archives.

Elihu B. Washburne MSS., Lib. of Cong.

Thurlow Weed MSS., Lib. of Cong.

Thurlow Weed MSS., Univ. of Rochester.

Jesse W. Weik MSS., Ill. State Hist. Lib.

Gideon Welles MS. (postwar recollections), Ill. State Hist. Lib.

Gideon Welles MSS., Lib. of Cong. Includes MS. of the famous Welles diary (whose published version does not fully represent the original), besides elaborate correspondence, scrapbooks, clippings, articles by Welles, etc.

Henry Wilson MSS., Lib. of Cong.
Richard Yates MSS., Ill. State Hist. Lib.

BOOKS, PAMPHLETS, AND ARTICLES [1]

Abraham Lincoln Association, *Bulletin* nos. 1–58 (1923–1939). Known formerly as Lincoln Centennial Association; earlier numbers (prior to 1929) bear this name.

Abraham Lincoln Association, *Papers Delivered Before the Members.* 1929–1939. Issued as *Lincoln Centennial Association Papers, 1924–1928.* See concluding issue, 1939, for index of the set.

The Abraham Lincoln Quarterly. Published in March, June, September, and December, by the Abraham Lincoln Association, Springfield, Ill. First issue appeared in March 1940.

"Abraham Lincoln to Henry W. Hoffman." 27 *Md. Hist. Mag.* 42 (1932). Transcript of a letter dated Oct. 10, 1864, regarding a new Maryland constitution.

"Abraham Lincoln's Religion: His Own Statement." 2 *A. L. Q.* 1–3 (1942). Writing on August 11, 1846, Lincoln denies charge of infidelity.

Adamov, E. A., ed., "Documents Relating to Russian Policy during the American Civil War." 2 *Jour. Mod. Hist.* 603–611 (1930).

———, "Russia and the United States at the Time of the Civil War." 2 *Jour. Mod. Hist.* 586–602 (1930).

Adams, Charles Francis (1807–1886), *An Address on the Life, Character and Services of William Henry Seward.* Albany: Weed, Parsons, and Co., 1873. 77 pp.

Adams, Charles Francis (1835–1915), *Charles Francis Adams, 1835–1915: An Autobiography* . . . . Boston: Houghton Mifflin, 1916. 224 pp.

———, "Lincoln's Offer to Garibaldi." 7 *Mag. of Hist.* 159–165 (1908).

———, "President Lincoln's Offer of a Military Command to Garibaldi in 1861." 1 *Mass. H. S. P.* (3 ser.) 319–325 (1908).

———, *Richard Henry Dana: A Biography.* Boston: Houghton Mifflin, 1890. 2 vols.

---

[1] Most of the abbreviations used for compactness of citation will be obvious as to meaning, but the following explanations may be noted: A. H. R. (*American Historical Review*); A. L. A. Bull. (*Bulletin of the Abraham Lincoln Association*); A. L. Q. (*Abraham Lincoln Quarterly*); Ann Rep. A. H. A. (*Annual Report, American Historical Association*); Atl. Mo. (*Atlantic Monthly*); Ind. Mag. Hist. (*Indiana Magazine of History*); J. H. U. Stud. (*Johns Hopkins University Studies in History and Political Science*); Jour. Ill. S. H. S. (*Journal of the Illinois State Historical Society*); M. V. H. R. (*Mississippi Valley Historical Review*); Mass. H. S. P. (*Proceedings of the Massachusetts Historical Society*); Proc. M. V. H. A. (*Proceedings of the Mississippi Valley Historical Association*); S. A. Q. (*South Atlantic Quarterly*); Trans. Ill. S. H. S. (*Transactions of the Illinois State Historical Society*); Wis. M. H. (*Wisconsin Magazine of History*). Where standard abbreviations are used a key is hardly needed—e. g., Assoc. (Association), Biog. (Biography), Lib. (Library), So. (South), Soc. (Society), and recognized forms for states of the American Union.

Adams, Ephraim Douglass, *Great Britain and the American Civil War.* New York: Longmans, 1925. 2 vols.

Adams, Henry, "The Great Secession Winter of 1860–61." 43 *Mass. H. S. P.* 660–687 (1910). See also pp. 655–660. Written by Henry Adams at the time; he was then secretary to his father, Charles Francis Adams, a representative from Massachusetts. For many years the paper was over-looked and lost. Its publication after almost a half-century was arranged by Henry's brother, Charles Francis Adams. Of illuminating interest concerning the crisis of 1860–61.

Aldrich, Charles, "At Lincoln's First Inaugural." 8 *Ann. Iowa* (3 ser.) 43–50 (1907).

Allen, James Sidney, "Abraham Lincoln in 1848." 31 *National Mag.* 523–525 (1910).

Ambler, Charles H., ed., *Correspondence of Robert M. T. Hunter, 1826–1876 (Ann. Rep. A. H. A.* 1916, II). Washington: Govt. Ptg. Off., 1918. 383 pp.

———, *Francis H. Pierpont: Union War Governor of Virginia and Father of West Virginia.* Chapel Hill: Univ. of N. C. Press, 1937. 483 pp.

———, *West Virginia, the Mountain State.* New York: Prentice-Hall, Inc., 1940. 660 pp.

Ander, O. Fritiof, "Swedish-American Newspapers and the Republican Party, 1855–1875." 2 *Augustana Hist. Soc. Pub.* 64–79 (1932).

[Anderson Auction Co.]. *Library of the Late Major William H. Lambert of Philadelphia. Part I, Lincolniana. First Section to be Sold January 14, 15, and 16, 1914 . . . On Public Exhibition from January 5th at the Anderson Galleries, Metropolitan Art Association, Madison Avenue at Fortieth Street, New York.* 123 pp. Lincoln items also to be found in catalogues of numerous other auctions of the Anderson Galleries.

Angle, Paul M., "Abraham Lincoln: Circuit Lawyer." *Lincoln Cent. Assoc. Papers* 19–41 (1928).

[———, *A Shelf of Lincoln Books.* To be published by Abr. Lincoln Assoc., Springfield, Ill.]

———, "Basic Lincolniana." *A. L. A. Bull.,* nos. 43, 3–9, and 44, 3–9 (1936).

———, *"Here I Have Lived": A History of Lincoln's Springfield, 1821–1865.* Springfield, Ill.: Abr. Lincoln Assoc., 1935. 313 pp.

———, *Lincoln, 1854–1861: Being the Day-by-Day Activities of Abraham Lincoln from January 1, 1854 to March 4, 1861.* Springfield, Ill.: Abr. Lincoln Assoc., 1933. 400 pp. Companion volumes by Benjamin P. Thomas and Harry E. Pratt (see below) cover other periods; the day-by-day record thus covers 1809–1861.

———, "Lincoln and the United States Supreme Court." *A. L. A. Bull.,* no. 47, 1–9 (May 1937). See also no. 47 (supplement), 1–3 (June 1937).

———, "Lincoln Defended Railroad." 17 *Ill. Cent. Mag.* 40–43 (1929).

———, "Lincoln: Self-Biographer." 1 *A. L. Q.* 144–160 (1940).

————, "Lincoln's First Love?" *Lincoln Cent. Assoc. Bull.*, no. 9, 1–8 (Dec. 1927).

————, "The Minor Collection: A Criticism." 143 *Atl. Mo.* 516–525 (1929).

————, ed., *New Letters and Papers of Lincoln.* Boston: Houghton Mifflin, 1930. 387 pp. Significant additions to Lincoln's collected writings.

————, *One Hundred Years of Law: An Account of the Law Office which John T. Stuart Founded in Springfield, Illinois, a Century Ago.* Springfield, Ill.: Brown, Hay and Stephens, 1928. 53 pp.

————, ed., "The Record of a Friendship: A Series of Letters from Lincoln to Henry E. Dummer." 31 *Jour. Ill. S. H. S.* 125–137 (1938).

————. See also Herndon, William H.; Sandburg, Carl.

Appleman, Roy E., ed., *Abraham Lincoln, from His Own Words and Contemporary Accounts* (National Park Service *Source Book Series*, no. 2). Washington: U. S. Dept. of Interior, 1942. 55 pp.

[Appleton's] *American Annual Cyclopaedia and Register of Important Events.* New York: Appleton. Vol. I covers the year 1861.

Armstrong, Ida D., "The Lincolns of Spencer County." 18 *Proc. S. Ind. Hist. Soc.* 54–62 (1923).

Arnold, Isaac N., "The Baltimore Plot to Assassinate Abraham Lincoln." 37 *Harper's Mo.* 123–128 (1868).

————, *The History of Abraham Lincoln, and the Overthrow of Slavery.* Chicago: Clarke & Co., 1866. 736 pp.

————, *The Life of Abraham Lincoln.* Chicago: Jansen, McClurg & Co., 1885. 462 pp.

————, "Reminiscences of the Illinois Bar Forty Years Ago . . . ." 14 *Fergus Hist. Ser.* 53–164 (1881).

Arnold, Samuel Bland, *Defence and Prison Experiences of a Lincoln Conspirator.* Hattiesburg, Miss.: Book Farm, 1943. 133 pp. Arnold admits complicity in the plot to abduct, but not to assassinate, Lincoln. Denounces Stanton's methods.

Ascher, Leonard, "Lincoln's Administration and the New Almaden Scandal." 5 *Pac. Hist. Rev.* 38–51 (1936). Reviews the case of U. S. *v.* Andres Castillero.

Atkins, John B., *The Life of Sir William Howard Russell* . . . . London: J. Murray, 1911. 2 vols.

Auchampaugh, Phillip G., "The Buchanan-Douglas Feud." 25 *Jour. Ill. S. H. S.* 5–48 (1932).

————, "A Great Justice on State and Federal Power. Being the Thoughts of Chief Justice Taney on the Federal Conscription Act." 18 *Tyler's Quar. Hist. and Geneal. Mag.* 72–87 (1936). Unpublished and undelivered opinion of Taney holding Federal conscription act unconstitutional.

————, *James Buchanan and his Cabinet on the Eve of Secession.* Lancaster, Pa., 1926. 224 pp.

————, "James Buchanan, the Court and the Dred Scott Case." 9 *Tenn.*

Hist. Mag. 231–240 (1926).

Bache, Richard Meade, *Life of General George Gordon Meade, Commander of the Army of the Potomac.* Philadelphia: H. T. Coates & Co., 1897. 596 pp.

Bailey, Louis J., "Caleb Blood Smith." 29 *Ind. Mag. Hist.* 213–239 (1933).

Baker, George E., ed., *The Life of William H. Seward with Selections from his Works.* New York: Redfield, 1855. 410 pp.

Baldwin, John B. *Interview between President Lincoln and Col. John B. Baldwin, April 4th, 1861.* Staunton, Va.: "Spectator" job office, 1866. 28 pp.

Ballard, Colin R., *The Military Genius of Abraham Lincoln.* London: Humphrey Milford, 1926. 246 pp.

Baltz, John D., *Honorable Edward D. Baker . . . .* Lancaster, Pa., 1888. 248 pp.

Bancroft, Frederic, "Gideon Welles and his Diary." 93 *Nation* 598–601 (1911).

———, *The Life of William H. Seward.* New York: Harpers, 1900. 2 vols.

———, "Seward's Proposition of April 1, 1861 for a Foreign War and a Dictatorship." 99 *Harper's Mo.* 781–791 (1899).

Bancroft, George, *Memorial Address on the Life and Character of Abraham Lincoln, delivered, at the request of both Houses of the Congress of America, before them, . . . on the 12th of February, 1866.* Washington: Govt. Ptg. Off., 1866. 69 pp.

Banning, Kendall, "The Case of Lydia Bixby." 54 *Bookman* 516–520 (1922).

Baringer, William E., "Campaign Technique in Illinois—1860." 39 *Trans. Ill. S. H. S., 1932,* 203–281.

———, *A House Dividing: Lincoln as President Elect.* Springfield, Ill.: Abr. Lincoln Assoc., 1945. 356 pp.

———, *Lincoln's Rise to Power.* Boston: Little, Brown, 1937. 373 pp.

Barnes, Gilbert H., *The Antislavery Impulse, 1830–1844.* New York: Appleton-Century, 1933. 298 pp.

———, and Dumond, Dwight L., eds., *Letters of Theodore Dwight Weld, Angelina Grimké Weld and Sarah Grimké, 1822–1844.* New York: Appleton-Century, 1934. 2 vols.

Barrett, Joseph H., *Life of Abraham Lincoln, . . . with a Condensed View of his Most Important Speeches . . . .* Cincinnati: Moore, Wilstach, Keys & Co., 1860. 216 pp.

———, *Life of Abraham Lincoln . . . .* Cincinnati: Moore, Wilstach & Baldwin, 1864. 518 pp. The 1860 book modified, considerably amplified, and brought up to date. There were other editions—e. g., a vol. of 842 pages in 1865 and a 2 vol. work in 1904.

Barrett, Oliver R., *Lincoln's Last Speech in Springfield in the Campaign of 1858.* Chicago: Univ. of Chicago Press, 1925. 22 pp. Lincoln's speech of October 30, 1858, handsomely reprinted with introduction, contemporary newspaper account, and letter of an eye-witness.

Bartlett, David Vandewater Golden, *The Life and Public Services of Hon. Abraham Lincoln*. New York: H. Dayton, 1860. 354 pp. Given by Ernest J. Wessen (see below) as the second of the campaign lives.

Bartlett, John R., *The Literature of the Rebellion: A Catalogue of the Books and Pamphlets Relating to the Civil War in the United States* . . . . Boston: Draper and Halliday, 1866. 477 pp.

Bartlett, Ruhl J., *John C. Frémont and the Republican Party (Ohio State Univ. Studies: Contributions in Hist. and Pol. Sci.,* no. 13). Columbus: Ohio State Univ. Press, 1930. 146 pp.

Barton, William E., *Abraham Lincoln and the Hooker Letter* . . . . New York: Bowling Green Press, 1928. 29 pp.

———, *Abraham Lincoln and Walt Whitman*. Indianapolis: Bobbs-Merrill, 1928. 277 pp.

———, *Abraham Lincoln of Illinois*. Chicago: Union League Club, 1921. 20 pp.

———, *A Beautiful Blunder: The True Story of Lincoln's Letter to Mrs. Lydia A. Bixby*. Indianapolis: Bobbs-Merrill, 1926. 135 pp.

———, *The Influence of Chicago upon Abraham Lincoln* . . . . Chicago: Univ. of Chicago Press, 1923. 54 pp.

———, *The Life of Abraham Lincoln*. Indianapolis: Bobbs-Merrill, 1925. 2 vols.

———, *Lincoln at Gettysburg: What He Intended to Say; What He Said; What He Was Reported to Have Said; What He Wished He Had Said*. Indianapolis: Bobbs-Merrill, 1930. 263 pp.

———, "The Lincoln of the Biographers." 36 *Trans. Ill. S. H. S., 1929,* 58–116.

———, *The Lineage of Lincoln*. Indianapolis: Bobbs-Merrill, 1929. 419 pp.

———, *The Paternity of Abraham Lincoln* . . . . New York: George H. Doran Co., 1920. 414 pp.

———, *President Lincoln*. Indianapolis: Bobbs-Merrill, 1933. 2 vols., paged as one.

———, *The Soul of Abraham Lincoln*. New York: George H. Doran Co., 1920. 407 pp.

Basler, Roy P., "As One Southerner to Another: Concerning Lincoln and the Declaration of Independence." 42 *S. A. Q.* 45–53 (1943).

———, "The Authorship of the 'Rebecca' Letters." 2 *A. L. Q.* 80–90 (1942).

———, *The Lincoln Legend: A Study in Changing Conceptions*. Boston: Houghton Mifflin, 1935. 335 pp.

Bateman, Newton, *Abraham Lincoln: An Address*. Galesburg, Ill.: Cadmus Press, 1899. 46 pp.

Bates, David H., *Lincoln in the Telegraph Office* . . . . New York: Century, 1907. 432 pp.

———, *Lincoln Stories Told by Him in the Military Office in the War Department during the Civil War* . . . . New York: W. E. Rudge, 1926. 64 pp.

Bates, Edward. See Beale, Howard K.

Bates, Finis L., *The Escape and Suicide of John Wilkes Booth or the First True Account of Lincoln's Assassination* . . . . Boston: Geo. M. Smith & Co., 1907. 309 pp. Presents as sober fact the discredited story that Booth lived many years after the assassination; gives the false impression that an embalmed corpse, exhibited for profit, was that of the assassin.

Bayne, Julia Taft, *Tad Lincoln's Father*. Boston: Little, Brown, 1931. 206 pp.

Beale, Howard K., *The Critical Year: A Study of Andrew Johnson and Reconstruction*. New York: Harcourt, Brace, 1930. 454 pp.

——, ed., *The Diary of Edward Bates, 1859–1866 (Ann. Rep. A. H. A. 1930, IV)*. Washington: Govt. Ptg. Off., 1933. 685 pp.

——, "Is the Printed Diary of Gideon Welles Reliable?" 30 *A. H. R.* 547–552 (1925).

Bemis, Samuel F., ed., *American Secretaries of State*. New York: Knopf, 1927–1929. 10 vols.

Beveridge, Albert J., *Abraham Lincoln, 1809–1858*. Boston: Houghton Mifflin, 1928. 2 vols. A distinguished work of standard thoroughness.

Bigelow, John, *Retrospections of an Active Life*. New York: Baker & Taylor Co., 1909–1913. 5 vols.

Binns, Henry R., *Abraham Lincoln*. London: J. M. Dent & Co., 1907. 379 pp.

Blaine, James G., *Twenty Years of Congress: From Lincoln to Garfield*. Norwich, Conn.: Henry Bill Publishing Co., 1884–1886. 2 vols.

Blegen, Theodore C., ed., "Campaigning with Seward in 1860." 8 *Minn. Hist.* 150–171 (1927).

——, *Lincoln in World Perspective* (A Lincoln's Day address delivered at Carleton College, Feb. 12, 1943). 12 pp.

Bonham, Milledge L., Jr. "New York and the Election of 1860." 15 *N. Y. Hist.* 124–143 (1934).

Booker, Richard, *Abraham Lincoln in Periodical Literature, 1860–1940*. Chicago: Fawley-Brost Company, Inc., 1941. 66 pp. An incomplete bibliography of magazine articles on Lincoln.

Borrett, George, "An Englishman in Washington in 1864." 38 *Mag. of Hist.* 5–15 (1929). Extra no. 149.

Botts, John Minor, *Union or Disunion. The Union Cannot and Shall Not be Dissolved. Mr. Lincoln not an Abolitionist*. 23 pp. (Speech at Holcombe Hall in Lynchburg, Va., Oct. 18 [1860?]).

Boutwell, George S., *Speeches and Papers Relating to the Rebellion and the Overthrow of Slavery*. Boston: Little, Brown, 1867. 628 pp.

Boyd, Andrew, *A Memorial Lincoln Bibliography* . . . . Albany: Andrew Boyd, 1870. 175 pp. Part I includes material published in Hart's *Bibliographia Lincolniana*.

Bradford, Gamaliel, *Union Portraits*. Boston: Houghton Mifflin, 1916. 330 pp.

——, "The Wife of Abraham Lincoln." 151 *Harper's Mo.* 489–498 (1925).

——, *Wives.* New York: Harpers, 1925. 298 pp. Done in Bradford's interesting style of character analysis.

Brady, Matthew B. *Brady's National Photographic Collection of War Views, and Portraits of Representative Men.* New York: C. A. Alvord, 1869. 139 pp.

Brigham, Johnson, *James Harlan.* Iowa City: State Hist. Soc. of Iowa, 1913. 398 pp.

Bright, John. "Letters of John Bright, 1861–1862." 45 *Mass. H. S. P.* 148–159 (1912).

——. *Speeches . . . on the American Question.* Boston: Little, Brown, 1865. 278 pp.

Brinkerhoff, Fred W., "The Kansas Tour of Lincoln the Candidate." 13 *Kans. Hist. Quar.* 294–307 (1945).

Brogan, Denis W., *Abraham Lincoln.* London: Duckworth, 1935. 143 pp.

Brooks, Noah, *Abraham Lincoln and the Downfall of American Slavery.* New York: Putnam, 1896. 471 pp.

——, "Lincoln Reminiscences." 9 *Mag. of Hist.* 107–108 (1909).

——, "Personal Recollections of Abraham Lincoln." 31 *Harper's Mo.* 222–230 (1865).

——, "Personal Reminiscences of Lincoln." 15 *Scribner's Mo.* 673–681 (1878).

——, "Two War-Time Conventions." 27 *Century* (new ser.) 723–736 (1895).

——, *Washington in Lincoln's Time.* New York: Century, 1895. 328 pp. As Washington correspondent for the Sacramento *Daily Union* in war time, under the name "Castine," Brooks covered life at the capital in Lincoln's day.

Brown University. *Lincoln Letters Hitherto Unpublished in the Library of Brown University and Other Providence Libraries (McLellan Lincoln Collection Publication* I). Providence, R. I.: University Library, 1927. 72 pp.

Browne, Francis F., *The Everyday Life of Abraham Lincoln . . . .* New York: N. D. Thompson Publishing Co., 1886. 747 pp.

Browne, Robert H., *Abraham Lincoln and the Men of His Time.* Cincinnati: Jennings & Pye, 1901. 2 vols.

Browning, Orville H., *Diary.* See Pease and Randall, eds.

Bruce, William George, ed., *History of Milwaukee City and County.* Chicago-Milwaukee: S. J. Clarke, 1922. 3 vols.

Brummer, Sidney, D., *Political History of the State of New York during the Period of the Civil War (Col. U. Stud.,* XXXIX, No. 2). New York: Columbia Univ. Press, 1911. 451 pp.

Bryan, George S., *The Great American Myth.* New York: Carrick & Evans, 1940. 436 pp. Deals competently with the assassination. Stands high as a treatment of this difficult subject.

Bryan, Wilhelmus Bogart, *A History of the National Capital* . . . . New York: Macmillan, 1914–1916. 2 vols.

Bryner, B. D., *Abraham Lincoln in Peoria, Illinois*. Peoria: E. J. Jacob, 1924. 127 pp.

Buchanan, James, *Mr. Buchanan's Administration on the Eve of the Rebellion*. New York: Appleton, 1866. 296 pp.

Buck, Solon J., "Lincoln and Minnesota." 6 *Minn. Hist.* 355–361 (1925).

Buel, Clarence C., and Johnson, Robert U., eds., *Battles and Leaders of the Civil War*. New York: Century, 1887–1888. 4 vols.

Bullard, F. Lauriston, "Abraham Lincoln and Henry Adams: A Contrast in Education." 1 *A. L. Q.* 227–272 (1941).

———, "Abraham Lincoln and the Statehood of Nevada." 26 *Am. Bar Assoc. Jour.* 210–213, 313–317 (1940).

———, *"A Few Appropriate Remarks": Lincoln's Gettysburg Address*. Harrogate, Tenn., Lincoln Mem. Univ. (250 signed copies), 1944. 77 pp.

———, "Lincoln and the Courts of the District of Columbia." 24 *Am. Bar Assoc. Jour.* 117–120 (1938).

———, "Lincoln Pardons Conspirator on Plea of an English Statesman." 25 *Am. Bar Assoc. Jour.* 215–220 (1939). Deals with Lincoln's pardon of Alfred Rubery at the request of John Bright.

———, "Lincoln's 'Conquest' of New England." 2 *A. L. Q.* 49–79 (1942).

———, "The New England Ancestry of Abraham Lincoln." 39 *New Eng. Mag.* (new ser.) 685–691 (1909).

———, *The Other Lincoln* (Baccalaureate address delivered at Lincoln Memorial University, Harrogate, Tenn., June 1, 1941). 31 pp.

———, *Tad and His Father*. Boston: Little, Brown, 1915. 102 pp.

———, "When Lincoln Visited Mount Vernon." 2 *A. L. Q.* 281–283 (1943).

———. See Public Man, Diary of.

Burrage, Henry S., *Gettysburg and Lincoln: The Battle, the Cemetery, and the National Park*. New York: Putnam, 1906. 224 pp.

Butler, Benjamin F., *Autobiography and Personal Reminiscences* . . . : *Butler's Book*. Boston: A. M. Thayer & Co., 1892. 1154 pp.

———. *Private and Official Correspondence of General Benjamin F. Butler during the Period of the Civil War*, ed. by Jessie A. Marshall. Norwich, Mass.: Plimpton Press, 1917. 5 vols.

Cale, Edgar B., "Editorial Sentiment in Pennsylvania in the Campaign of 1860." 4 *Pa. Hist.* 219–234 (1937).

Campbell, John Archibald. *The Administration and the Confederate States . . . a Correspondence Between Hon. John A. Campbell . . . and Hon. Wm. H. Seward, All of Which Was Laid Before the Provisional Congress on Saturday by President Davis*. 1861. 7 pp. Campbell was an informal mediator for peace in 1861.

———, "Hampton Roads Conference." 1 *Trans. So. Hist. Soc.* 187–190 (1874)

————, "Memoranda of the Conversations at the Conference in Hampton Roads." 1 *Trans. So. Hist. Soc.* 190–194 (1874). These *Transactions* were published in the *Southern Magazine,* to be bound separately. This and the preceding item are in the Huntington Library, to whose courtesy the author is indebted.

————. "Papers of Hon. John A. Campbell—1861–1865." 4 *So. Hist. Soc. Papers* (new ser.) 3–81 (1917).

————, *Recollections of the Evacuation of Richmond, April 2d, 1865.* Baltimore: J. Murphy & Co., 1880. 27 pp.

————, *Reminiscences and Documents Relating to the Civil War during the Year 1865.* Baltimore: J. Murphy & Co., 1887. 68 pp.

Carman, Harry J., and Luthin, Reinhard H., *Lincoln and the Patronage.* New York: Columbia Univ. Press, 1943. 375 pp.

————, and ————, "Some Aspects of the Know-Nothing Movement Reconsidered." 39 *S. A. Q.* 213–234 (1940).

Carpenter, Francis B., *The Inner Life of Abraham Lincoln: Six Months at the White House.* Boston: Houghton Mifflin, 1883. 359 pp. Published in 1866 as *Six Months at the White House with Abraham Lincoln: The Story of a Picture.*

Carr, Clark E., *Lincoln at Gettysburg: An Address.* Chicago: A. C. McClurg & Co., 1906. 92 pp.

————, "Why Lincoln was not Renominated by Acclamation." 54 *Century* (new ser.) 503–506 (1907).

Carr, Julian S., "The Hampton Roads Conference." 25 *Confed. Vet.* 57–66 (1917).

Carter, John Denton, "Abraham Lincoln and the California Patronage." 48 *A. H. R.* 495–506 (1943).

Case, Lynn M., comp., *French Opinion on the United States and Mexico, 1860–1867* . . . . New York: Appleton-Century, 1936. 452 pp.

Catalogue of Articles Owned and Used by Abraham Lincoln. Now Owned by the Lincoln Memorial Collection of Chicago. Chicago: Lincoln Memorial Collection, 1887. 16 pp.

Cavanagh, Helen Marie, "Antislavery Sentiment and Politics in the Northwest, 1844–1860." Doctoral dissertation (MS.), Univ. of Chicago, 1938. 215 pp.

Caverno, Rev. Charles, "A Day with Lincoln." 22 *Mag. of Hist.* 94–99 (1916). Reminiscence of Lincoln's visit to Milwaukee in 1859.

Chambrun, Marquis de. See Pineton, Charles A.

Charnwood, Lord, *Abraham Lincoln.* London: Constable & Co., Ltd., 1916. 479 pp.

Chase, Salmon P. *Diary and Correspondence of Salmon P. Chase (Ann. Rep. A. H. A.* 1902, II). Washington: Govt. Ptg. Off., 1903. 527 pp.

Chittenden, Lucius E., *Lincoln and the Sleeping Sentinel: The True Story.* New York: Harpers, 1909. 53 pp.

————, *Personal Reminiscences, 1840–1890* . . . . New York: Richmond,

Croscup & Co., 1893. 434 pp.

———, *Recollections of President Lincoln and His Administration.* New York: Harpers, 1891. 470 pp.

———, *A Report of the Debates and Proceedings . . . of the Conference Convention . . . held at Washington, D. C., in February, A. D. 1861.* New York: Appleton, 1864. 626 pp. Peace Convention called by Virginia legislature. Twenty-one states were represented, but not the seven seceded states. Presided over by ex-President Tyler. Unsuccessful in its effort toward peaceable adjustment and union.

Clark, Allen C., *Abraham Lincoln in the National Capital.* Washington: W. F. Roberts Co., 1925. 179 pp.

———, *Abraham Lincoln, the Merciful President: The Pardon of the Sleeping Sentinel.* Washington: W. F. Roberts Co., 1927. 41 pp.

Clarke, Grace Julian, *George W. Julian (Ind. Hist. Coll.,* XI). Indianapolis: Ind. Hist. Com., 1923. 456 pp.

———, ed., "George W. Julian's Journal—The Assassination of Lincoln." 11 *Ind. Mag. Hist.* 324–337 (1915).

Claussen, Martin P., *The United States and Great Britain, 1861–1865: Peace Factors in International Relations* (abstract of doctoral thesis, Univ. of Ill., 1938). Urbana, Ill., 1938. 12 pp.

Clay, Cassius M., *The Life of Cassius Marcellus Clay . . . .* Cincinnati: J. F. Brennan & Co., 1886. Title page indicates two volumes, but only one appeared. 600 pp.

———. "The 1860 Presidential Campaign: Cassius M. Clay to Cephas Brainerd." 1 *Moorsfield Antiquarian* 104–110 (1937).

Cleven, N. A. N., "Some Plans for Colonizing Liberated Negro Slaves in Hispanic America." 9 *Jour. Negro Hist.* 35–49 (1926).

Codding, Ichabod, *A Republican Manual for the Campaign. Facts for the People: The Whole Argument in one Book.* Princeton, Ill.: "Republican" Book and Job Printing Office, 1860. 96 pp. Gives Republican doctrine in abolitionist terms. Exceedingly scarce. Believed by Ernest J. Wessen to have been suppressed or withdrawn on advice of Republican friends.

Coffin, C. C., "Lincoln's Visit to Richmond April 4, 1865." 1 *Moorsfield Antiquarian* 27–29 (1937). Letter by Coffin to Thomas Nast, July 19, 1866.

Cole, Arthur C., "Abraham Lincoln and the South." *Lincoln Cent. Assoc. Papers* 47–78 (1928).

———, *The Era of the Civil War (Centennial Hist. of Ill.,* III). Springfield, Ill.: Ill. Centennial Com., 1919. 499 pp.

———, *The Irrepressible Conflict, 1850–1865 (A History of American Life,* VII). New York: Macmillan, 1934. 468 pp.

———, "Lincoln and the American Tradition of Civil Liberty." 19 *Jour. Ill. S. H. S.* 102–114 (1926).

———, "Lincoln and the Presidential Election of 1864." 23 *Trans. Ill. S. H. S., 1917,* 130–138.

———, "Lincoln's Election an Immediate Menace to Slavery in the States?" 36 *A. H. R.* 740–767 (1931). Part of a debate; see also Hamilton, J. G. de R.

———, *Lincoln's "House Divided" Speech; Did it Reflect a Doctrine of Class Struggle?* Chicago: Univ. of Chicago Press, 1923. 36 pp.

———, "President Lincoln and His War-time Critics." 9 *Hist. Outlook* 245–249 (1918).

———, "President Lincoln and the Illinois Radical Republicans." 4 *M. V. H. R.* 417–436 (1918).

Coleman, Christopher B., "The Lincoln Legend." 29 *Ind. Mag. Hist.* 277–286 (1933).

Coleman, J. Winston, Jr., "A Preacher and a Shrine: Rev. Jesse Head and the Lincoln Marriage Temple." 46 *Lincoln Herald* 2–9 (Dec. 1944). Deals with the marriage of Lincoln's parents and with the memorial structure at Harrodsburg, Ky., which houses the cabin where the ceremony was performed by Rev. Jesse Head, June 12, 1806.

———, "Lincoln and 'Old Buster.'" 46 *Lincoln Herald* 5–11 (Feb. 1944). Treats Lincoln's relationship with Judge George Robertson of Lexington, Ky., to whom Lincoln in 1855 wrote a letter foreshadowing his house-divided declaration.

Colfax, Schuyler, *Life and Principles of Abraham Lincoln.* Philadelphia: J. B. Rodgers, 1865. 29 pp.

Collier, T. Maxwell, "William H. Seward in the Campaign of 1860, with Special Reference to Michigan." 19 *Mich. Hist. Mag.* 91–106 (1935).

Conger, Arthur L., "President Lincoln as War Statesman." 64 *Proc. Wis. Hist. Soc.* 106–140 (1916).

———, *The Rise of U. S. Grant.* New York: Century, 1931. 390 pp.

Conkling, Clinton L., "How Mr. Lincoln Received the News of his First Nomination." 14 *Trans. Ill. S. H. S., 1909,* 63–66.

Conlin, Sister Francis L., "The Democratic Party in Pennsylvania from 1856 to 1865." 47 *Records of Am. Catholic Hist. Soc. of Philadelphia* 132–183 (1936).

Connor, Henry G., *John Archibald Campbell, Associate Justice of the United States Supreme Court, 1853–1861.* Boston: Houghton Mifflin, 1920. 310 pp. Bears upon Campbell's efforts toward peace in 1861 and upon his conference with Lincoln in Richmond in April 1865.

Cooper, H. H., "The Lincoln-Thornton Debate of 1856 at Shelbyville, Illinois." 10 *Jour. Ill. S. H. S.* 101–122 (1917).

Cottman, George S., "Lincoln in Indianapolis." 24 *Ind. Mag. Hist.* 1–14 (1928).

Coulter, E. Merton, *Civil War and Readjustment in Kentucky.* Chapel Hill: Univ. of N. C. Press, 1926. 468 pp.

Cox, Jacob D., *Military Reminiscences of the Civil War*. New York: Scribners, 1900. 2 vols.

Cox, Samuel S., *Eight Years in Congress, from 1857 to 1865. Memoir and Speeches*. New York: Appleton, 1865. 442 pp.

———, *Three Decades of Federal Legislation, 1855 to 1885* . . . . Providence, R. I.: J. A. & R. A. Reid, 1885. 726 pp.

Cramer, John H., "Lincoln in Ohio." 54 *Ohio Arch. and Hist. Quar.* 149–168 (1945).

Crandall, Andrew W., *The Early History of the Republican Party, 1854–1856*. Boston: R. G. Badger, 1930. 313 pp.

Craven, Avery, *The Coming of the Civil War*. New York: Scribners, 1942. 491 pp. The author does not accept glib explanations of an "inevitable" war, nor does he follow "orthodox" treatments.

———, ed., *Essays in Honor of William E. Dodd* . . . . Chicago: Univ. of Chicago Press, 1935. 362 pp.

———, "Southern Attitudes toward Abraham Lincoln." *Papers in Ill. Hist., 1942*, 1–18.

Crawford, Samuel W., *The Genesis of the Civil War: The Story of Sumter, 1860–1861*. New York: C. L. Webster & Co., 1887. 486 pp.

Crenshaw, Ollinger, "The Knights of the Golden Circle: The Career of George Bickley." 47 *A. H. R.* 23–50 (1941).

———, "The Psychological Background of the Election of 1860 in the South." 19 *N. C. Hist. Rev.* 260–279 (1942).

Croffut, W. A., ed., *Fifty Years in Camp and Field, Diary of Major-General Ethan Allen Hitchcock, U. S. A.* New York: Putnam, 1909. 514 pp.

———, "Lincoln's Washington." 145 *Atl. Mo.* 55–65 (1930). From the journal of William A. Croffut.

Crook, William H., "Lincoln as I Knew Him." 115 *Harper's Mo.* 41–48 (1907).

———, "Lincoln's Last Day." 115 *Harper's Mo.* 519–530 (1907).

———. *Through Five Administrations: Reminiscences of Colonel William H. Crook, Body-guard to President Lincoln* (edited by Margarita Spalding Gerry). New York: Harpers, 1910. 279 pp.

Cross, Jasper W., *Divided Loyalties in Southern Illinois during the Civil War* (abstract of doctoral thesis, Univ. of Ill., 1942). Urbana, Ill., 1942. 12 pp.

Cunningham, Joseph O., *Some Recollections of Abraham Lincoln* (delivered before the Firelands Pioneer Association at Norwalk, Ohio, July 4, 1907). Norwalk, Ohio: American Publishing Co., 1909. 20 pp.

Currey, Josiah Seymour, "Abraham Lincoln's Early Visits to Chicago." 12 *Jour. Ill. S. H. S.* 412–416 (1919).

———, *Abraham Lincoln's Visit to Evanston in 1860*. Evanston, Ill.: City National Bank, 1914. 16 pp.

Curtis, Francis, *The Republican Party* . . . *1854–1904*. New York: Putnam, 1904. 2 vols.

Curtis, George T., *Life of James Buchanan* . . . . New York: Harpers, 1883. 2 vols.

Curtis, George W., "The Lounger." 7 *Harper's Weekly* 771 (1863).

Curtis, William E., *The True Abraham Lincoln*. Philadelphia: Lippincott, 1903. 409 pp.

Dana, Charles A., *Lincoln and His Cabinet* (Lecture before New Haven Colony Historical Society, March 10, 1896). Cleveland: De Vinne Press, 1896. 70 pp.

————, *Recollections of the Civil War* . . . . New York: Appleton, 1898. 296 pp.

————, "Reminiscences of Men and Events of the Civil War." Under this title portions of Dana's story appeared in *McClure's*, vols. 10 and 11 (1898).

Davis, Charles G., "March of Captain Abraham Lincoln's Company in the Black Hawk War." 31 *Trans. Ill. S. H. S. 1924*, 25–27.

Davis, Edwin, "Lincoln and Macon County, 1830–1831." 25 *Jour. Ill. S. H. S.* 63–107 (1932).

Davis, J. M., "Origin of the Lincoln Rail." 40 *Century* (new ser.) 271–275 (1900).

Davis, Stanton L., *Pennsylvania Politics, 1860–1863*. Cleveland: Bookstore, Western Reserve Univ., 1935. 344 pp.

Dawes, Anna Laurens, *Charles Sumner*. New York: Dodd, Mead, 1892. 330 pp.

Dennett, Tyler, *John Hay: From Poetry to Politics*. New York: Dodd, Mead, 1933. 476 pp.

————, ed., *Lincoln and the Civil War in the Diaries and Letters of John Hay*. New York: Dodd, Mead, 1939. 348 pp.

————, "Seward's Far Eastern Policy." 28 *A. H. R.* 45–62 (1922).

DeWitt, David M., *The Assassination of Abraham Lincoln and its Expiation*. New York: Macmillan, 1909. 302 pp.

————, *The Judicial Murder of Mary E. Surratt*. Baltimore: John Murphy & Co., 1895. 259 pp.

Dickson, W. M., "Abraham Lincoln at Cincinnati." 69 *Harper's Mo.* 62–66 (1884). Deals with Lincoln and the McCormick case.

Dodd, William E., "The Fight for the Northwest, 1860," 16 *A. H. R.* 774–788 (1911).

————, *Lincoln or Lee* . . . . New York: Century, 1928. 177 pp.

————, "Lincoln's Last Struggle." 92 *Century* (new ser.) 46–61 (1927).

————, "The Rise of Abraham Lincoln." 91 *Century* (new ser.), 569–584 (1927).

Dodge, Daniel K., *Abraham Lincoln, Master of Words*. New York: Appleton, 1924. 178 pp.

————, *Abraham Lincoln: The Evolution of his Literary Style* (*U. of Ill. Stud.*, I, no. 1). Urbana, Ill.: Univ. of Ill. Press, 1900. 58 pp.

Dodge, Grenville M., *Personal Recollections of President Abraham*

Lincoln, General Ulysses S. Grant and General William T. Sherman. Council Bluffs: Monarch Printing Co., 1914. 237 pp.

————, "What I Saw of Lincoln." 13 *Appleton's Booklover's Mag.* 134–140 (1909).

Donald, David, "Billy, You're Too Rampant." *A. L. Q.*, Dec. 1945. Treats Lincoln and Herndon in the period 1859–1860.

Dorpalen, Andreas, "The German Element and the Issues of the Civil War." 29 *M. V. H. R.* 55–76 (1942).

Dorris, Jonathan Truman, *Pardon and Amnesty during the Civil War and Reconstruction* (abstract of doctoral thesis, Univ. of Ill., 1929). Urbana, Ill., 1929. 23 pp.

[————, "Pardon and Amnesty during the Civil War and Reconstruction." Not yet published, but the author had the privilege of seeing parts of the book in manuscript.]

————, "President Lincoln's Clemency." 20 *Jour. Ill. S. H. S.* 547–568 (1928).

Douglas, Stephen A., "The Dividing Line between Federal and Local Authority: Popular Sovereignty in the Territories." 19 *Harper's Mo.* 519–537 (1859).

————, *Speech . . . before the Legislature of Illinois, April 25, 1861 . . . .* 1861. 8 pp.

Douglass, Frederick. *The Life and Times of Frederick Douglass Written by Himself.* Hartford: Park Publishing Co., 1881. 516 pp. Other editions in 1882, 1892, 1893, and 1941.

Drell, M. B., ed., "Letters by Richard Smith of the Cincinnati Gazette." 26 *M. V. H. R.* 535–554 (1940).

Dudley, Harold M., "The Election of 1864." 18 *M. V. H. R.* 500–518 (1932).

Dumond, Dwight L., *Antislavery Origins of the Civil War in the United States.* Ann Arbor: Univ. of Mich. Press, 1939. 143 pp.

————, "Issues Involved in the Movement for Conciliation, 1860–61." 16 *Papers of Mich. Academy of Science* 453–466 (1932).

————, ed., *Letters of James Gillespie Birney, 1831–1857.* New York: Appleton-Century, 1938. 2 vols.

————, *The Secession Movement, 1860–1861.* New York: Macmillan, 1931. 294 pp.

————, ed., *Southern Editorials on Secession.* New York: Century, 1931. 529 pp.

————. See also Barnes, G. H.

Duncan, Kunigunde, and Nickols, D. F., *Mentor Graham: The Man Who Taught Lincoln.* Chicago: Univ. of Chicago Press, 1944. 274 pp.

Dunning, William A., "Disloyalty in Two Wars." 24 *A. H. R.* 625–630 (1919).

Dyer, Frederick H., *A Compendium of the War of the Rebellion . . . .* Des Moines: Dyer Publishing Co., 1908. 1796 pp.

East, Ernest E., *Abraham Lincoln Sees Peoria: An Historical and Pictorial*

Record of Seventeen Visits from 1832 to 1858. Peoria: Record Publishing Co., 1939. 37 pp.

————, ed., "A Newly Discovered Speech of Lincoln." 28 *Jour. Ill. S. H. S.* 65–77 (1935).

————. See also Pratt, H. E.

Eaton, John, *Grant, Lincoln and the Freedmen* . . . . New York: Longmans, Green, 1907. 331 pp.

Edwards, Arthur, *Sketch of the Life of Norman B. Judd.* Chicago: Horton & Leonard, 1878. 20 pp.

Eggleston, Percy C., *Lincoln in New England.* New York: Stewart, Warren and Co., 1922. 36 pp.

Ehrmann, Bess V., *The Missing Chapter in the Life of Abraham Lincoln.* Chicago: W. M. Hill, 1938. 150 pp. Deals with Lincoln in Spencer Co., Ind., 1816–1830, 1844.

Eisenschiml, Otto, *The Case of A. L.—, Aged 56.* Chicago: Abr. Lincoln Book Shop, 1943. 55 pp.

————, *In the Shadow of Lincoln's Death.* New York: W. Funk, Inc., 1940. 415 pp.

————, *Why Was Lincoln Murdered?* Boston: Little, Brown, 1937. 503 pp.

Elliott, Charles W., *Winfield Scott: The Soldier and the Man.* New York: Macmillan, 1937. 817 pp.

Emerson, Ralph. *Mr. and Mrs. Ralph Emerson's Personal Recollections of Abraham Lincoln.* Rockford, Ill.: Wilson Brothers Co., 1909. 18 pp.

Emerson, Ralph Waldo, "Abraham Lincoln: Oration . . . at Concord, N. H." 85 *Littell's Living Age* 282–284 (1865). Delivered April 19, 1865. (*Littell's* contains considerable material on Lincoln.)

————, *Complete Works.* Boston: Houghton Mifflin, 1884. 11 vols.

"English Opinion on the Inaugural." 85 *Littell's Living Age* 86–88 (1865). Reprints from English newspapers.

Evans, William A., *Mrs. Abraham Lincoln: A Study of Her Personality and Her Influence on Lincoln.* New York: Knopf, 1932. 364 pp.

Everett, Edward. *Address of Hon. Edward Everett, at the Consecration of the National Cemetery at Gettysburg* . . . . Boston: Little, Brown, 1864. 87 pp.

Ewing, Thomas, "Lincoln and the General Land Office." 25 *Jour. Ill. S. H. S.* 139–153 (1932).

————, "Some Thoughts on Lincoln's Presidency." 26 *Jour. Ill. S. H. S.* 60–69 (1933).

Fahrney, Ralph R., *Horace Greeley and the Tribune in the Civil War.* Cedar Rapids, Iowa: Torch Press, 1936. 229 pp.

Feamster, C. N., ed., *Calendar of the Papers of John Jordan Crittenden.* Washington: Govt. Ptg. Off., 1913. 335 pp.

Ferguson, W. J., *I Saw Booth Shoot Lincoln.* Boston: Houghton Mifflin, 1930. 63 pp. Reminiscence by a well known actor who was call boy on the fatal night.

Fertig, James W., *The Secession and Reconstruction of Tennessee* . . . . Chicago, 1898. 108 pp.

Fessenden, Francis, *Life and Public Services of William Pitt Fessenden* . . . . Boston: Houghton Mifflin, 1907. 2 vols.

Field, Henry M., *Life of David Dudley Field*. New York: Scribners, 1898. 361 pp.

Fischer, LeRoy H., *Adam Gurowski and the Civil War: A Radical's Record* (abstract of doctoral thesis, Univ. of Ill., 1943). Urbana, Ill., 1943. 18 pp. Virtually the same material is reprinted in *Bulletin of the Polish Institute of Arts and Sciences in America*, I, 476–488 (1943).

Fish, Carl R., "Lincoln and Catholicism." 29 *A. H. R.* 723–724 (1924).

———, "Lincoln and the Patronage." 8 *A. H. R.* 53–69 (1902).

Fish, Daniel, *Lincoln Bibliography: A List of Books and Pamphlets Relating to Abraham Lincoln*. New York: Francis D. Tandy Co., 1906. In Nicolay and Hay, *Complete Works of Abraham Lincoln*, XI, 137–380. Voluminous and none too selective. Familiar tool for collectors, with numbered titles. Omits magazine articles.

Fite, Emerson D., *The Presidential Campaign of 1860*. New York: Macmillan, 1911. 356 pp.

Fleming, Walter L., *Civil War and Reconstruction in Alabama*. New York: Columbia Univ. Press, 1905. 815 pp.

Flick, Alexander C., ed., *History of the State of New York*. New York: Columbia Univ. Press, 1933–1937. 10 vols.

———, and Lobrana, Gustav S., *Samuel Jones Tilden: A Study in Political Sagacity*. New York: Dodd, Mead, 1939. 597 pp.

Flower, Frank A., *Edwin McMasters Stanton, The Autocrat of Rebellion, Emancipation, and Reconstruction* . . . . New York: W. W. Wilson, 1905. 425 pp.

Forbes, John Murray. *Letters and Recollections of John Murray Forbes*, ed. by Sarah F. Hughes. Boston: Houghton Mifflin, 1899. 2 vols.

Ford, Thomas, *A History of Illinois* . . . . Chicago: S. C. Griggs & Co., 1854. 447 pp.

Ford, Worthington C., ed., *A Cycle of Adams Letters, 1861–1865*. Boston: Houghton Mifflin, 1920. 2 vols.

———, "Forged Lincoln Letters." 61 *Mass. H. S. P.* 183–195 (1927–28).

———, ed., *Letters of Henry Adams*. Boston: Houghton Mifflin, 1930–38. 2 vols.

Forney, John W., *Anecdotes of Public Men*. New York: Harpers, 1873–1881. 2 vols.

Fortenbaugh, Robert, "Abraham Lincoln at Gettysburg, November 18 and 19, 1863." 5 *Pa. Hist.* 223–244 (1938).

Foulke, William D., *Life of Oliver P. Morton, Including His Important Speeches*. Indianapolis-Kansas City: Bowen-Merrill Co., 1899. 2 vols.

Freeman, Douglas S., *R. E. Lee, A Biography*. New York: Scribners, 1934–1935. 4 vols.

Freidel, Frank Burt, "Francis Lieber, Charles Sumner, and Slavery." 9 *Jour. So. Hist.* 75–93 (1943).

———, "The Life of Francis Lieber." Doctor's dissertation (ms.), Univ. of Wis., 1941. 692 pp. Includes a chronological list of Lieber's writings.

———, "The Loyal Publication Society: A Pro-Union Propaganda Agency." 26 *M. V. H. R.* 359–376 (1939).

French, Benjamin B., *Address Delivered at the Dedication of the Statue of Abraham Lincoln, Erected in Front of the City Hall, Washington, D. C. . . . .* Washington: McGill and Witherow, 1868. 16 pp.

Fry, William H., *Republican "Campaign" Text-Book for 1860.* New York: A. B. Burdick, 1860. 108 pp.

"Gath." See Townsend, G. A.

Gay, H. Nelson, "Lincoln's Offer of a Command to Garibaldi. Light on a Disputed Point of History." 53 *Century* (new ser.) 63–74 (1907).

Gernon, Blaine B., *Lincoln in the Political Circus . . . .* Chicago: Black Cat Press, 1936. 258 pp.

———, "Lincoln's Visits to Chicago." 1 *Chicago Hist. Soc. Bull.* 33–41 (1935).

———, *The Lincolns in Chicago.* Chicago, 1934, 64 pp.

Gilmore, James R., *Personal Recollections of Abraham Lincoln and the Civil War.* Boston: L. C. Page and Co., 1898. 338 pp.

Golder, Frank A., "The American Civil War through the Eyes of a Russian Diplomat." 26 *A. H. R.* 454–463 (1921).

———, "The Russian Fleet and the Civil War." 20 *A. H. R.* 810–812 (1915).

Gorham, George C., *Life and Public Services of Edwin M. Stanton.* Boston: Houghton Mifflin, 1899. 2 vols.

Grant, Ulysses S., *Personal Memoirs of U. S. Grant.* New York: Charles L. Webster & Co., 1885. 2 vols.

Gray, Wood, *The Hidden Civil War: The Story of the Copperheads.* New York: Viking Press, 1942. 314 pp.

———, *The Peace Movement in the Old Northwest, 1860–1865: A Study in Defeatism.* Chicago, 1935. 18 pp.

Greeley, Horace, *The American Conflict . . . .* Hartford: O. D. Case & Co., 1864–1866. 2 vols.

———, and Cleveland, John F., comps., *A Political Text-book for 1860: Comprising a Brief View of Presidential Nominations and Elections . . . .* New York: Tribune Association, 1860. 254 pp.

———, *Recollections of a Busy Life . . . .* New York: J. B. Ford & Co., 1868. 624 pp.

Green, Samuel L., "President Lincoln's Speech at Gettysburg." 15 *Mass. H. S. P.* (2 ser.) 92–94 (1901-1902).

Greenbie, Mrs. Marjorie Latta (Barstow), *Lincoln's Daughters of Mercy.* New York: Putnam, 1944. 211 pp.

———, *My Dear Lady: The Story of Anna Ella Carroll, the "Great Un-*

recognized Member of Lincoln's Cabinet." New York: McGraw-Hill Book Co., 1940. 316 pp.

[Greer, Col. Allen J., U. S. Army, Ret., "Abraham Lincoln, Commander in Chief, United States Army." 394 pp. Prepared as a master's thesis, University of California, Los Angeles, 1938. Enlarged for publication. Used by author in MS.]

Griffith, Albert H., "Lincoln Literature, Lincoln Collections, and Lincoln Collectors." 15 *Wis. Mag. Hist.* 148–167 (1931).

Grimsley, Elizabeth Todd, "Six Months in the White House." 19 *Jour. Ill. S. H. S.* 43–73 (Oct. 1926).

Gurowski, Adam, *Diary* . . . . Boston: Lee and Shepard, 1862–1866. 3 vols. For a study of Gurowski see Fischer, LeRoy H.

Hale, Edward Everett, "Memories of a Hundred Years." 72 *Outlook* 78–91 (1902). Conversation with Sumner about Lincoln and emancipation.

Hale, Edward E., Jr., *William H. Seward.* Philadelphia: G. W. Jacobs & Co., 1910. 388 pp.

Hall, Wilmer L., "Lincoln's Interview with John B. Baldwin." 13 *S. A. Q.* 260–269 (1914).

Halstead, Murat, *Caucuses of 1860: A History of the National Conventions of the Current Presidential Campaigns* . . . . Columbus: Follett, Foster and Co., 1860. 232 pp.

Hamilton, J. G. de Roulhac, "Lincoln and the South." 17 *Sewanee Rev.* 129–138 (1909).

———, "Lincoln's Election an Immediate Menace to Slavery in the States?" 37 *A. H. R.* 700–711 (1932). See also Cole, A. C.

———, "The Many-Sired Lincoln." 5 *Am. Mercury* 129–135 (1925).

Hamlin, Charles E., *The Life and Times of Hannibal Hamlin.* Cambridge: Riverside Press, 1899. 627 pp.

Harbison, Winfred A., "The Elections of 1862 as a Vote of Want of Confidence in President Lincoln." 14 *Papers of Mich. Academy of Science* 499–513 (1931).

———, "Indiana Republicans and the Re-election of President Lincoln." 34 *Ind. Mag. Hist.* 42–64 (1938).

———, "Lincoln and Indiana Republicans, 1861–1862." 33 *Ind. Mag. Hist.* 277–303 (1937).

———, "The Opposition to President Lincoln within the Republican Party." Doctoral dissertation (MS.), Univ. of Ill., 1930. 354 pp.

———, "President Lincoln and the Faribault Fire-Eater." 20 *Minn. Hist.* 269–286 (1939).

———, "Zachariah Chandler's Part in the Reëlection of Abraham Lincoln." 22 *M. V. H. R.* 267–276 (1935).

Hare, J. I. C., *American Constitutional Law.* Boston: Little, Brown, 1889. 2 vols.

Harrington, Fred H., ed., "A Peace Mission of 1863." 46 *A. H. R.* 76–86 (1940).

Harris, Thomas L., *The Trent Affair* . . . . Indianapolis: Bowen-Merrill

Co., 1896. 288 pp.

Harris, Wilmer C., *Public Life of Zachariah Chandler, 1851–1875.* Lansing: Mich. Hist. Comm., 1917. 152 pp.

Hart, Albert B., *Salmon P. Chase.* Boston: Houghton Mifflin, 1899. 465 pp.

Hart, Charles Henry, *Bibliographia Lincolniana: An Account of the Publications Occasioned by the Death of Abraham Lincoln* . . . . Albany: Joel Munsell, 1870. 86 pp. Part I of Boyd's *A Memorial Lincoln Bibliography* . . . . Hart corresponded with Herndon, planning to contribute the bibliography for Herndon's life, but he published independently. Systematic Lincoln bibliography may be said to have begun with him.

——, *A Biographical Sketch of His Excellency Abraham Lincoln, Late President of the United States.* Albany: Joel Munsell, 1870. 21 pp.

Hay, John, "Life in the White House in the Time of Lincoln." 19 *Century* (new ser.) 33–37 (1890).

——, "Abraham Lincoln." *Appleton's Cyc. of Amer. Biog.*, III, 715–727 (1887).

——. For the diary of John Hay see Dennett, Tyler, ed.

——. See also Nicolay, John G.

Hay, Logan, "Lincoln in 1841 and 1842." 2 *A. L. Q.* 114–126 (1942).

——, "Lincoln One Hundred Years Ago." 1 *A. L. Q.* 82–93 (1940).

Hebert, Walter H., *Fighting Joe Hooker.* Indianapolis: Bobbs-Merrill, 1944. 366 pp.

Helm, Emily [Emilie] Todd, "Mary Todd Lincoln . . . ." 11 *McClure's* 476–480 (1898).

Helm, Katherine, *True Story of Mary, Wife of Lincoln* . . . . New York: Harpers, 1928. 309 pp. By the daughter of Emilie Todd Helm, half-sister of Mrs. Lincoln.

Helper, Hinton R., *The Impending Crisis of the South: How to Meet It.* New York: A. B. Burdick, 1860. 438 pp.

Henderson, William O., *The Lancashire Cotton Famine, 1861–1865.* Manchester, Eng.: Manchester Univ. Press, 1934. 178 pp.

Henry, Robert S., *The Story of Reconstruction.* Indianapolis: Bobbs-Merrill, 1938. 633 pp.

Herndon, William Henry, *Abraham Lincoln. Miss Ann Rutledge. New Salem. Pioneering and the Poem.* This lecture, delivered at Springfield, Nov. 16, 1866, was privately printed as a huge broadside, newspaper style. It was published in book form in 1910 by H. E. Barker, Springfield. The lecture is less significant for Ann Rutledge and Lincoln than for its flavorful account of Illinois settlers in general and of the New Salem region in particular. Pub'd also by Trovillion Private Press, Herrin, Ill., in eds. de luxe (1945), intro. by Harry Rosecrans Burke.

——, "Analysis of the Character of Abraham Lincoln: A Lecture." 1 *A. L. Q.*, 343–383 (Sep. 1941), and 403–441 (Dec. 1941). Two separate lectures with the same title. Delivered in Springfield Dec. 12, 1865, and Dec. 26, 1865. The original Herndon manuscripts for these lectures are in the Henry E. Huntington Library.

————, "Facts Illustrative of Mr. Lincoln's Patriotism and Statesmanship." 3 *A. L. Q.* 178–203 (Dec. 1944). Third of a series of three lectures delivered by Herndon at Springfield in the winter of 1865–1866. Printed from MS. in the Huntington Lib. Delivered on January 23, 1866; reported in Springfield newspapers January 24.

————, and Weik, Jesse W., *Herndon's Lincoln: The True Story of a Great Life* . . . . Chicago: Belford, Clarke & Co., 1889. 3 vols. This is the original edition, now very rare, of the Herndon biography. There was also a London issue in 1889 and a Chicago re-issue without alterations in 1890. In 1892 a new edition, under the title *Abraham Lincoln: The True Story of a Great Life* . . . was published in two volumes by Appleton; a few references to Lincoln's alleged illegitimacy and the "Chronicles of Reuben" episode, found in the original edition, were expurgated, and new matter by Horace White added. Other issues of this edition appeared in 1893, 1896, 1908, 1913, 1916, 1920, 1928, and 1930. In 1921, under the title *Herndon's Lincoln* . . . , another three-volume edition was published by the Herndon's Lincoln Publishing Co., Springfield, Ill.

————, and ————, *Herndon's Life of Lincoln: The History and Personal Recollections of Abraham Lincoln* . . . *with an Introduction and Notes by Paul M. Angle.* New York: A. & C. Boni, 1930. 511 pp. Handy one-volume edition. Especially useful because of Angle's critical notes and introduction. Published also by World Publishing Co., Cleveland, Ohio (1942, reprint in 1943).

————. See also McMurtrie.

"Herndon's Lincoln: A Study." 140 *Publishers' Weekly* 2019–2021 (Nov. 29, 1941).

Herriott, Frank I., "Abraham Lincoln and his Clients." 9 *Ann. Iowa* (3 ser.) 389–391 (1910). A letter of Lincoln to L. M. Hays, Oct. 27, 1852.

————, "The Conference in the Deutsches Haus, Chicago, May 14–15, 1860." 35 *Trans. Ill. S. H. S., 1928,* 101–191.

————, *Iowa and Abraham Lincoln, Being Some Account of the Presidential Discussion and Party Preliminaries in Iowa 1856–1860.* Des Moines, 1911. 189 pp. Reprinted with additions from *Annals of Iowa.*

————, "Memories of the Chicago Convention of 1860." 12 *Ann. Iowa* (3 ser.) 446–466 (1920).

————, *The Premises and Significance of Abraham Lincoln's Letter to Theodore Canisius.* Chicago, 1915. 74 pp.

Hertz, Emanuel, *Abraham Lincoln: A New Portrait.* New York: Horace Liveright, Inc., 1931. 2 vols. Vol. II consists of letters and documents, many of which had already been published by Nicolay and Hay, Tracy, Angle, etc.

————, ed., *Abraham Lincoln, the Tribute of the Synagogue*. New York: Bloch Pub. Co., 1927. 682 pp.

————, ed., *The Hidden Lincoln, From the Letters and Papers of William H. Herndon*. New York: Viking Press, 1938. 461 pp. A sampling of material chiefly from the Herndon-Weik MSS., though other collections are tapped. Full of errors and poorly edited. Far from complete.

————. (*Note*. There are many items on Lincoln by Hertz—pamphlets, magazine and newspaper articles, speeches, etc. They are fully listed in the new comprehensive bibliography by Monaghan.)

Hesseltine, William B., *Ulysses S. Grant, Politician*. New York: Dodd, Mead, 1935. 480 pp.

Higginson, Thomas Wentworth, *Army Life in a Black Regiment*. Boston: Fields, Osgood & Co., 1870. 296 pp.

Hill, Frederick T., *Lincoln, Emancipator of the Nation* . . . . New York: Appleton, 1928. 284 pp.

————, *Lincoln the Lawyer*. New York: Century, 1906. 332 pp.

Hitchcock, Caroline Hanks, *Nancy Hanks: The Story of Abraham Lincoln's Mother*. New York: Doubleday & McClure, 1899. 105 pp. Deals unreliably with Hanks ancestry.

Hodder, Frank H., "Some Phases of the Dred Scott Case." 16 *M. V. H. R.* 3–22 (1929).

Hofstadter, Richard, "The Tariff Issue on the Eve of the Civil War." 44 *A. H. R.* 50–55 (1938).

Holland, Josiah G., *The Life of Abraham Lincoln*. Springfield, Mass.: Gurdon Bill, 1866. 544 pp. Pub. also in 1887 by Dodd, Mead. A popular biography which for its early date has considerable merit and fullness.

Holmes, Fred L., *Abraham Lincoln Traveled This Way* . . . . Boston: L. C. Page & Co., 1930. 350 pp. Tourist's account of Lincoln shrines. Inaccurate.

Hooker, Joseph. *Abraham Lincoln's Letter to Major General Hooker dated January 26, 1863*, ed. by Paul M. Angle. Chicago: Caxton Club, 1942. Printed text by Angle gives historical account of the famous Hooker letter, owned by Alfred W. Stern of Chicago. Accompanied by superb reproduction of the letter.

House, Albert V., Jr., "The Genesis of the Lincoln Religious Controversy." 36 *Proc. of the Middle States Assoc. of Hist. and Soc. Sci. Teachers* 44–54 (1938).

————, "The Trials of a Ghost-Writer of Lincoln Biography." 31 *Jour. Ill. S. H. S.* 262–296 (1938). Treats Chauncey F. Black as writer of the Lamon biography.

Howard, James Quay, *The Life of Abraham Lincoln: With Extracts from His Speeches*. Columbus: Follett, Foster and Co., 1860. 102 pp. Published at nearly the same time as the campaign life by Howells, for whom the young author collected material. Rare.

Howard, Oliver O., "Personal Recollections of Abraham Lincoln." 53 *Century* (new ser.) 873–877 (1908).

Howe, M. A. DeWolfe, ed., *Letters of Charles Eliot Norton* . . . . Boston: Houghton Mifflin, 1913. 2 vols.

Howells, William D., *Lives and Speeches of Abraham Lincoln and Hannibal Hamlin.* Columbus: Follett, Foster & Co., 1860. 170 pp. Lincoln repudiated the claim that this was an "authorized" biography. A copy owned by S. C. Parks, read by Lincoln, and corrected by him in pencil, was reproduced by the Abraham Lincoln Association in 1938. An item of unique interest.

Hubbart, Henry C., *The Older Middle West, 1840–1880* . . . . New York: Appleton-Century, 1936. 305 pp.

————, " 'Pro-Southern' Influences in the Free West, 1840–1865." 20 *M. V. H. R.* 45–62 (1933).   [(1931).

Hubbell, Jay B., "Lincoln's First Inaugural Address." 36 *A. H. R.* 550–552

Hutton, Graham, "Lincoln Through British Eyes." 3 *A. L. Q.* 63–92 (1944).

Iglehart, John E., "The Environment of Abraham Lincoln in Indiana . . . ." 8 *Pub. Ind. Hist. Soc.* 147–182 (1925).

James, D. D., "Lincoln-Douglas Debate—Charleston." 8 *Jour. Ill. S. H. S.* 569–571 (1916).

James, Harold Preston, *Lincoln's Own State in the Election of 1860* (abstract of a doctoral thesis, Univ. of Ill., 1943). Urbana, Ill., 1943. 21 pp.

Jayne, William, *Personal Reminiscences of the Martyred President Abraham Lincoln.* Chicago: Grand Army Hall and Memorial Assoc., 1908. 58 pp.

Johnson, Allen, *Stephen A. Douglas: A Study in American Politics.* New York: Macmillan, 1908. 503 pp.

Johnson, Charles W., *Proceedings.* See Republican Convention.

Johnson, Reverdy, *An Argument to Establish the Illegality of Military Commissions in the United States* . . . . Washington: John Murphy & Co., 1865. 31 pp.

Johnston, Robert M., *Bull Run: Its Strategy and Tactics.* Boston: Houghton Mifflin, 1913. 293 pp.

Jones, John B., *A Rebel War Clerk's Diary at the Confederate States Capital.* Philadelphia: Lippincott, 1866. 2 vols.

Jones, John Paul, Jr., "Abraham Lincoln and the Newspaper Press during the Civil War." 35 *Americana* 459–472 (1941).

Jones, Mildred E., "Lincoln's Representative Recruit." 1 *A. L. Q.* 179–191 (1940). First appeared in Easton (Pa.), *Express* Feb. 12, 1940.

Jordan, Donaldson, and Pratt, Edwin J., *Europe and the American Civil War.* Boston: Houghton Mifflin, 1931. 299 pp.

Jordan, Philip D., "The Death of Nancy Hanks Lincoln." 40 *Ind. Mag. Hist.* 103–110 (1944).

Julian, George W., "The First Republican National Convention." 4 *A. H. R.* 313–322 (1899).

———, *Political Recollections, 1840 to 1872*. Chicago: Jansen, McClurg & Co., 1884. 384 pp.

———. *Select Speeches of Hon. George W. Julian* . . . . Cincinnati: Gazette Steam Book and Job Printing Establishment, 1867. 68 pp.

Kaiser, P. H., "Lincoln at Fort Stevens." 31 *National Mag.* 525–526 (1910).

Keckley, Elizabeth, *Behind the Scenes*. New York: G. W. Carleton & Co., 1868. 371 pp. Ghost-written for Mrs. Lincoln's slave-born friend and modiste. Hard to assess as evidence but full of intimate material on Mrs. Lincoln.

Kelley, William D., *Lincoln and Stanton: A Study of the War Administration of 1861 and 1862* . . . . New York: Putnam, 1885. 88 pp. Controversial. Anti-McClellan.

Kendall, Amos, *Letters, Exposing the Mismanagement of Public Affairs by Abraham Lincoln, and the Political Combinations to Secure His Reelection*. Washington: Continental Union Office, 1864. 46 pp.

Kidd, T. W. S., "How Abraham Lincoln Received the News of His Nomination for President." 15 *Jour. Ill. S. H. S.* 507–509 (1922).

Kincaid, Robert L., *Joshua Fry Speed: Lincoln's Most Intimate Friend*. Harrogate, Tenn.: Lincoln Memorial Univ., 1943. 70 pp.

Kinnaird, Virginia, "Mrs. Lincoln as a White House Hostess." *Papers in Ill. Hist., 1938*, 64–87.

Kirkland, Edward C., *The Peacemakers of 1864*. New York: Macmillan, 1927. 279 pp.

Koerner, Gustave. See McCormack, T. J.

Kuhn, Madison, "Economic Issues and the Rise of the Republican Party in the Northwest." Doctoral dissertation (MS.), Univ. of Chicago, 1940. 179 pp.

Lambert, William H., "The Gettysburg Address, When Written, How Received, Its True Form." 33 *Pa. Mag. Hist. and Biog.* 385–408 (1909).

———, ed., "A Lincoln Correspondence." 55 *Century* (new ser.) 617–626 (1909). Twenty-two letters published here for the first time.

———, ed., "Unpublished Letters of Abraham Lincoln." 27 *Pa. Mag. Hist. and Biog.* 60–62 (1903).

Lamon, Ward H., *The Life of Abraham Lincoln from His Birth to His Inauguration as President*. Boston: James R. Osgood and Co., 1872. 547 pp. Ghost-written by Chauncey F. Black (see article by Albert V. House). Based on material obtained from Herndon. Unfavorably received by the public. Projected second volume never appeared.

———, *Recollections of Abraham Lincoln, 1847–1865*, ed. by Dorothy Lamon. Chicago: A. C. McClurg and Co., 1895. 276 pp.

Landon, Fred, "Canadian Opinion of Abraham Lincoln." 2 *Dalhousie Rev.* 329–334 (1922).

Lansden, John M., "Abraham Lincoln, Judge David Davis and Judge Edward Bates." 7 *Jour. Ill. S. H. S.* 56–58 (April 1914). A personal reminiscence.

Lapsley, Arthur Brooks, ed., *The Writings of Abraham Lincoln* . . . *With an Introduction by Theodore Roosevelt, together with the Essay on Lincoln by Carl Schurz* . . . . New York: Putnam, 1905. 8 vols.

Lea, J. Henry, and Hutchinson, J. R., *The Ancestry of Abraham Lincoln.* Boston: Houghton Mifflin, 1909. 212 pp. Of value as to the English Lincolns, but very faulty where reliance is placed on Mrs. Hitchcock.

Leale, Charles A., "Lincoln's Last Hours." 53 *Harper's Weekly* 7–10, 27 (Feb. 13, 1909).

Learned, Marion D., *Abraham Lincoln: An American Migration.* Philadelphia: William J. Campbell, 1909. 149 pp. Carefully traces Lincoln migrations; confirms English, not German, ancestry.

Leech, Margaret, *Reveille in Washington, 1860–1865.* New York: Harpers, 1941. 483 pp.

Lester, C. Edwards, *The Life and Public Services of Charles Sumner.* New York: United States Publishing Co., 1874. 506 pp.

"A Letter from Lincoln When in Congress." 19 *Century* (new ser.) 156–157 (1890). Letter to Josephus Hewett, Feb. 13, 1848.

Lewis, Lloyd, *Myths After Lincoln.* New York: Harcourt, Brace, 1929. 422 pp.

Lincoln, Waldo, *History of the Lincoln Family: An Account of the Descendants of Samuel Lincoln of Hingham, Massachusetts, 1637–1920.* Worcester, Mass.: Commonwealth Press, 1923. 718 pp. Competent and elaborate genealogy on the Lincoln side; the best for this purpose.

"Lincoln and the Bridge Case." 3 *Palimpsest* 142–154 (1922). Lincoln's argument in the case of the *Effie Afton,* wrecked against the Rock Island bridge.

Lincoln and the New York Herald: Unpublished Letters of Abraham Lincoln from the Collection of Judd Stewart. Plainfield, N. J., 1907. 15 pp. Lincoln's letters to George G. Fogg, in facsimile.

"Lincoln in Kansas." 7 *Trans. Kans. Hist. Soc.* 536–552 (1901–1902).

Lincoln Centennial Association. See Abraham Lincoln Association.

Lincoln Herald. "A Quarterly Magazine devoted to the interests of Lincoln Memorial University and the promotion of Lincoln Ideals in the education of American Youth." Published at Harrogate, Tenn., Feb. 1938 to date. Continuation of *Mountain Herald.*

The Lincoln Kinsman. See Warren, Louis A.

Lincoln Lore. See Warren, Louis A.

"Lincoln's First Campaign for the Presidency." *A. L. A. Bull.* no. 28, 8–9 (1932).

"Lincoln's Nomination to Congress, 1846." 1 *A. H. R.* 313–314 (1896).

Linder, Usher F., *Reminiscences of the Early Bench and Bar of Illinois.* Chicago: Chicago Legal News Co., 1879. 406 pp.

Livermore, W. R., "The Emancipation Pen." 44 *Mass. H. S. P.* 595–599 (1911).

Lorant, Stefan, *Lincoln: His Life in Photographs*. New York: Duell, Sloan & Pearce, 1941. 160 pp.

Lossing, Benson J., *Pictorial History of the Civil War* . . . . Philadelphia: G. W. Childs, 1866–1874. 3 vols.

Ludwig, Emil, *Lincoln*. Boston: Little, Brown, 1930. 505 pp.

Luhrs, Henry E., *Lincoln at the Wills Home and the Gettysburg Address* . . . . Shippensburg, Pa.: Lincoln Publishers, 1938. 20 pp.

Luthin, Reinhard H., "Abraham Lincoln and the Massachusetts Whigs in 1848." 14 *New Eng. Quar.* 619–632 (1941).

———, "Abraham Lincoln and the Tariff." 49 *A. H. R.* 609–629 (1944).

———, *The First Lincoln Campaign*. Cambridge: Harvard Univ. Press, 1944. 328 pp. Most thorough treatment of campaign of 1860.

———, "Indiana and Lincoln's Rise to the Presidency." 38 *Ind. Mag. Hist.* 385–405 (1942).

———, "Organizing the Republican Party in the 'Border-Slave' Regions: Edward Bates's Presidential Candidacy in 1860." 38 *Mo. Hist. Rev.* 138–161 (1944).

———, "Pennsylvania and Lincoln's Rise to the Presidency." 67 *Pa. Mag. Hist. and Biog.* 61–82 (1943).

———, "Salmon P. Chase's Political Career Before the Civil War." 29 *M. V. H. R.* 517–540 (1943).

———. See also Carman, Harry J.

Lutz, Ralph H., "Rudolph Schleiden and the Visit to Richmond, April 25, 1861." *Ann. Rep. A. H. A.*, 1915, 209–216.

Lyman, Theodore. *Meade's Headquarters, 1863–65; The Letters of Theodore Lyman,* ed. by George R. Agassiz. Boston: Atlantic Monthly Press, 1922. 371 pp.

McBride, Robert W., *Personal Recollections of Abraham Lincoln, by a Member of His Bodyguard* . . . . Indianapolis: Bobbs-Merrill, 1926. 78 pp.

McCarthy, Charles H., *Lincoln's Plan of Reconstruction*. New York: McClure, Phillips & Co., 1901. 531 pp.

McCartney, Clarence E., *Lincoln and His Cabinet*. New York: Scribners, 1931. 366 pp.   [226 pp.

———, *Lincoln and His Generals*. Philadelphia: Dorrance and Co., 1925.

McClellan, George B. *McClellan's Own Story* . . . . New York: C. L. Webster & Co., 1887. 678 pp.

———, *Report on the Organization and Campaigns of the Army of the Potomac* . . . . New York: Sheldon & Co., 1864. 480 pp.

McClure, Alexander K., *Abraham Lincoln and Men of War-Times*. Philadelphia: Times Publishing Co., 1892. 462 pp. Sketches of Lincoln himself and of his relation to Hamlin, Chase, Cameron, Stanton, Curtin, Stevens, Greeley, and others. 4th ed., 1892, has 496 pp.

———, "The Night at Harrisburg. A Reminiscence of Lincoln's Journey to Washington in 1861." 5 *McClure's* 91–96 (1895).

McCormack, Thomas J., ed., *Memoirs of Gustave Koerner, 1809–1896.* Cedar Rapids: Torch Press, 1909. 2 vols.

McCormick, R. C., "Abraham Lincoln's Visit to New York in 1860." 85 *Littell's Living Age* 327–332 (1865). Reprinted from N. Y. *Evening Post;* personal recollections.

McCulloch, Hugh, *Men and Measures of Half a Century* . . . . New York: Scribners, 1888. 542 pp.

McKee, Thomas Hudson, *The National Conventions and Platforms of All Political Parties, 1789 to 1900.* Baltimore: Friedenwald Co., 1900. 370 pp.

McLaughlin, Andrew C., "Lincoln, the Constitution, and Democracy." *Abr. Lincoln Assoc. Papers,* 1936, 25–59. Also in 47 *Internat. Jour. Ethics* 1–24 (1936).

McMaster, John B., *History of the People of the United States During Lincoln's Administration.* New York: Appleton, 1927. 693 pp.

McMurtrie, Douglas C., ed., *Lincoln's Religion: The Text of Addresses Delivered by William H. Herndon and Rev. James A. Reed and a Letter by C. F. B.* Chicago: Black Cat Press, 1936. 98 pp. Includes the Herndon lecture, "Lincoln's Religion," published as broadside supplement to the *Illinois State Register,* Dec. 13, 1873.

McMurtry, Robert Gerald, *Ben Hardin Helm* . . . . Chicago: privately printed for Civil War Round Table, 1943. 72 pp. Devoted equally to General Helm, C.S.A., and his wife, Emilie Todd Helm, half-sister of Mrs. Lincoln.

——, "Lincoln Knew Shakespeare." 31 *Ind. Mag. Hist.* 265–277 (1935).

McPherson, Edward, *The Political History of the United States . . . During the Great Rebellion* . . . . Washington: Philp & Solomons, 1864. 440 pp. Other editions in 1865, 1871, and 1882.

Madigan, Edith H., "Lincoln's Famous Letter to Mrs. Bixby." 4 *Am. Book Collector* 98–101 (1933).

Madigan, Thomas F. *A Catalogue of Lincolniana with an Essay on Lincoln Autographs by . . . William E. Barton.* Thomas F. Madigan, N.Y. 88 pp. Detailed descriptive catalogue of 211 autograph items by or concerning Lincoln. Useful for printed text and facsimiles of Lincoln originals. Other Madigan catalogues should also be consulted.

The Magazine of History with Notes and Queries. Slightly known material on a variety of subjects. Entire issues bear the title, "Rare Lincolniana."

Magruder, Allan B., "A Piece of Secret History: President Lincoln and the Virginia Convention of 1861." 35 *Atl. Mo.* 438–445 (1875).

Malin, James C., *John Brown and the Legend of Fifty-Six.* Philadelphia: American Philosophical Society, 1942. 794 pp. Deals critically with Brown's Kansas career.

Markens, Isaac, *Abraham Lincoln and the Jews.* New York, 1909. 60 pp.

————, *President Lincoln and the Case of John Y. Beall.* New York, 1911. 11 pp. Also in 6 *Americana* 425–435 (1911).

Marraro, Howard R., "Italy and Lincoln." 3 *A. L. Q.* 3–16 (1944).

Marshall, John A., *American Bastile: A History of the Illegal Arrests and Imprisonment of American Citizens during the Late War.* Philadelphia: T. W. Hartley, 1869. 728 pp. Reprinted in 1870 and with additions in 1883.

Masters, Edgar Lee, *Lincoln the Man.* New York: Dodd, Mead, 1931. 520 pp. One of the few unfavorable biographies of Lincoln.

Meade, George G. *Life and Letters of George Gordon Meade,* by his son, George Meade. New York: Scribners, 1913. 2 vols.

————. See Lyman, Theodore.

Meigs, Montgomery C. "General M. C. Meigs on the Conduct of the Civil War." 26 *A. H. R.* 285–303 (1921).

Meneely, A. Howard, ed., "Three Manuscripts of Gideon Welles." 31 *A. H. R.* 484–494 (1926).

————, *The War Department, 1861: A Study in Mobilization and Administration (Col. Univ. Stud.,* no. 300). New York: Columbia Univ. Press, 1928. 400 pp. Critical monograph on the war department under Cameron.

Meserve, Frederick H., *Lincolniana: Historical Portraits and Views Printed Directly from Original Negatives* . . . . New York, 1915. 104 pp. Hundreds of photographs, of which 108 are of Lincoln.

————, *The Photographs of Abraham Lincoln.* New York, 1911. 110 pp. One hundred actual photographs.

————, and Sandburg, Carl, *The Photographs of Abraham Lincoln.* New York: Harcourt, Brace, 1944. 30 pp. of text (pictorial pp. unnumbered). All the known photographs of Lincoln, with numerous other subjects. Rich in colorful text as well as in pictures.

Miles, Mary L., " 'The Fatal First of January, 1841.' " 20 *Jour. Ill. S. H. S.* 13–48 (1927).

Miller, Paul I., "Lincoln and the Governorship of Oregon." 23 *M. V. H. R.* 391–394 (1936).

Milton, George Fort, *Abraham Lincoln and the Fifth Column.* New York: Vanguard Press, 1942. 364 pp.

————, *The Eve of Conflict: Stephen A. Douglas and the Needless War.* Boston: Houghton Mifflin, 1934. 608 pp.

Minor, Charles L. C., *The Real Lincoln* . . . . Richmond: Everett Waddey Co., 1904. 230 pp. Statements unfavorable to Lincoln are an authentic part of the literature of his time. The overwhelming mass of them has never been collected. A selection appears here. An edition in 1901 had 66 pp.

Minor, Wilma F., "Lincoln the Lover." 142. *Atl. Mo.* 838–856 (1928) and 143 *ibid.* 1–14, 215–225 (1929). Worthless forged material purporting to be original documents on Lincoln and Ann Rutledge.

"Misdated Lincoln Letters and Speeches." *A. L. A. Bull.*, no. 24, 7–9 (1931).

Monaghan, Jay, *Diplomat in Carpet Slippers: Abraham Lincoln Deals with Foreign Affairs.* Indianapolis: Bobbs-Merrill, 1945. 505 pp.

———, comp., *Lincoln Bibliography, 1839–1939* (Ill. State Hist. Lib. *Collections*, XXXI, XXXII). Springfield, Ill.: Illinois State Historical Library, 1945. 2 vols. Foreword by J. G. Randall. For books the most complete of all Lincoln bibliographies. Omits magazine articles. Excludes general histories and such sources as the diaries of Welles, Browning, Bates, Chase, etc. Gives evaluating comments. Titles are numbered (to 3958 items) and arranged by years.

———, "New Light on the Lincoln-Rutledge Romance." 3 *A. L. Q.* 138–145 (1944). Reprints article by John Hill in *Menard Axis*, Petersburg, Ill., Feb. 15, 1862.

"Monthly Record of Current Events: United States." 21 *Harper's Mo.* 258–259 (1860). Republican Convention at Chicago and Lincoln's nomination.

"Monthly Record of Current Events: United States." 22 *Harper's Mo.* 690 (1861). Lincoln's journey to Washington and inaugural.

"Monthly Record of Current Events: United States." 29 *Harper's Mo.* 401–402 (1864). The Baltimore Convention of 1864.

Moore, Charles, *Lincoln's Gettysburg Address and Second Inaugural.* Boston: Houghton Mifflin, 1927. 70 pp.

Moore, Frank, ed., *The Rebellion Record: A Diary of American Events, with Documents, Narratives, Illustrative Incidents, Poetry, etc.* New York: Putnam, 1861–1869; D. Van Nostrand, 1864–1868. 11 vols. and a supplement. Vols. 7–11 published by D. Van Nostrand. Each volume has separate paging for "Diary," "Documents," etc. Vast storehouse of source material, with anti-Southern editorial slant.

"More Light on Lincoln and Ann Rutledge." *Lincoln Centennial Assoc. Bull.*, no. 12, 6–8 (Sep. 1, 1928).

Morse, John T., Jr., *Abraham Lincoln.* Boston: Houghton Mifflin, 1893. 2 vols. Other editions in 1896, 1898, and 1924.

———, ed., *Diary of Gideon Welles, Secretary of the Navy under Lincoln and Johnson.* Boston: Houghton Mifflin, 1911. 3 vols. Unique view from inside Lincoln's cabinet. Packed with information and caustic comment. For critique, see Beale, H. K.

Mudd, Nettie, ed., *The Life of Dr. Samuel A. Mudd* . . . . New York: Neale Publishing Co., 1906. 326 pp.

Murr, J. Edward, "Lincoln in Indiana." 13 *Ind. Mag. Hist.* 307–348 (1917).

Myer, Walter E., "The Presidential Campaign of 1860 in Illinois." Master's thesis (ms.), Univ. of Chicago, 1913. 63 pp.

Myers, Gustavus A., "Abraham Lincoln in Richmond." 41 *Va. Mag. Hist.* 318–322 (1933). "Memoranda" of Lincoln's interview with J. A. Campbell after the fall of Richmond, at which Mr. Myers was present.

Myers, William Starr, "New Jersey Politics from the Revolution to the Civil War." 37 *Americana* 395–449 (1943).

——, *The Republican Party, a History*. New York: Century, 1928. 487 pp.

——, *A Study in Personality: General George Brinton McClellan*. New York: Appleton-Century, 1934. 520 pp.

Nevins, Allan, *Frémont, the West's Greatest Adventurer* . . . . New York: Harpers, 1928. 2 vols.

——, *Frémont, Pathmarker of the West*. New York: Appleton-Century, 1939. 649 pp. Supersedes the earlier 2-vol. biography by Nevins. A new study with additional material, remodeled narrative, and fresh appraisal.

Newcomb, Rexford, *In the Lincoln Country: Journeys to the Lincoln Shrines of Kentucky, Indiana, Illinois and Other States*. Philadelphia: Lippincott, 1928. 191 pp.

Newton, Joseph Fort, *Lincoln and Herndon*. Cedar Rapids: Torch Press, 1910. 367 pp. See above, p. 350, Herndon-Parker MSS.

Nichols, Roy Franklin, "Some Problems of the First Republican Presidential Campaign." 28 *A. H. R.* 492–496 (1923).

Nicolay, Helen, "A Candidate in His Home Town." 1 *A. L. Q.* 127–143 (1940).

——, "Characteristic Anecdotes of Lincoln; from Unpublished Notes of His Private Secretary, John G. Nicolay." 62 *Century* (new ser.) 697–703 (1912).

——, "The Education of an Historian." 3 *A. L. Q.* 107–137 (1944).

——, *Personal Traits of Abraham Lincoln*. New York: Century, 1912. 387 pp. Based on J. G. Nicolay's material.

Nicolay, John G., *Abraham Lincoln*. Boston: Little, Brown, 1882. 21 pp. Written originally for *Encyclopaedia Britannica*, 9th ed.

——, and Hay, John, *Abraham Lincoln: A History*. New York: Century, 1890. 10 vols. By Lincoln's secretaries. Has the merits and defects of an official biography. Authorized by Robert Lincoln. Only biography yet published with use of the great mass of Lincoln papers. Elaborate and useful, but marred by party bias. Voluminous in political and military history.

——, and ——, eds., *Complete Works of Abraham Lincoln*. New York: Francis D. Tandy Co., 1905. 12 vols. (Cited as *Works*.) Usable set; fairly reliable, but not always accurate nor perfectly edited. In 1894 Nicolay and Hay edited a two volume collection under the title *Abraham Lincoln: Complete Works* . . . (New York: Century).

——, "Lincoln's Gettysburg Address." 25 *Century* (new ser.) 596–608 (1894).

——, *A Short Life of Abraham Lincoln* . . . . New York: Century, 1902. 578 pp. Condensation of the 10-vol. life by Nicolay and Hay.

"The Nomination of Lincoln." 4 *Harper's Weekly* 338 (1860).

Oakleaf, Joseph B., *Lincoln Bibliography: A List of Books and Pamphlets Relating to Abraham Lincoln.* Cedar Rapids: Torch Press, 1925. 424 pp.

Oberholtzer, Ellis P., *Abraham Lincoln (American Crisis Biographies).* Philadelphia: George W. Jacobs & Co., 1904. 389 pp.

Offic. Rec. See *War of the Rebellion: . . . Official Records . . .* [etc.].

Oldroyd, Osborn H., comp. and ed., *The Lincoln Memorial: Album-Immortelles . . . .* New York: G. W. Carleton & Co., 1883. 571 pp. Tributes to Lincoln from an impressive array of distinguished contributors, collected and edited in a spirit of pious hero worship. (The autograph originals, in the collection of Oliver R. Barrett, Chicago, are more interesting than the book.)

The Oldroyd Lincoln Memorial Collection, Located in the House in Which Lincoln Died. Washington, 1903. 11 pp. Typical of pamphlets issued at various times, giving contents of the collection and urging its purchase by Congress.

Orme, William W. "Civil War Letters of Brigadier General William Ward Orme—1862–1866." 23 *Jour. Ill. S. H. S.* 246–315 (1930).

Owsley, Frank L., *King Cotton Diplomacy: Foreign Relations of the Confederate States of America.* Chicago: Univ. of Chicago Press, 1931. 617 pp.

Page, Elwin L., *Abraham Lincoln in New Hampshire.* Boston: Houghton Mifflin, 1929. 165 pp.

Palmer, George T., *A Conscientious Turncoat: The Story of John M. Palmer, 1817–1900.* New Haven: Yale Univ. Press, 1941. 297 pp.

Palmer, John McAuley (1817–1900), *The Bench and Bar of Illinois. Historical and Reminiscent.* Chicago: Lewis Publishing Co., 1899. 2 vols.

———. *Personal Recollections of John M. Palmer: The Story of an Earnest Life.* Cincinnati: R. Clarke Co., 1901. 631 pp.

Palmer, John McAuley (1870—), *Washington, Lincoln, Wilson: Three War Statesmen.* New York: Doubleday, Doran, 1930. 417 pp.

Pargellis, Stanley, "Lincoln's Political Philosophy." 3 *A. L. Q.* 275–290 (1945).

Paris, Louis Philippe Albert d'Orleans, Comte de, *History of the Civil War in America,* tr. by L. F. Tasistro; ed. by Henry Coppee. Philadelphia: Porter & Coates, 1875–1888. 4 vols.

Parker, Theodore, *Speeches, Addresses, and Occasional Sermons.* Boston: W. Crosby and H. P. Nichols, 1852. 2 vols.

Parton, James, *General Butler at New Orleans . . . .* New York: Mason Brothers, 1863. 649 pp. Other editions in 1864 ff.; 17th edition in 1892.

Patton, James W., *Unionism and Reconstruction in Tennessee, 1860–1869.* Chapel Hill: Univ. of N. C. Press, 1934. 267 pp.

Paullin, Charles O., "Abraham Lincoln in Congress, 1847–1849." 14 *Jour. Ill. S. H. S.* 85–89 (1921).

————, ."Hawthorne and Lincoln." 4 *Americana* 889–895 (1909).

————, "President Lincoln and the Navy." 14 *A. H. R.* 284–303 (1909).

Peace Convention, See Chittenden, L. E.

Pearson, Henry Greenleaf, *James S. Wadsworth of Geneseo, Brevet Major-General of United States Volunteers.* New York: Scribners, 1913. 321 pp.

————, *Life of John A. Andrew, Governor of Massachusetts, 1861–1865.* Boston: Houghton Mifflin, 1904. 2 vols.

————, "Lincoln's Method of Ending the Civil War." 59 *Mass. H. S. P.* 238–250 (1926). Reprinted in 1 *Tenn. Hist. Mag.* (2 ser.) 49–61 (1930).

Pease, T. C., *The Diary of Orville H. Browning, a New Source for Lincoln's Presidency* (lecture before the Chicago Hist. Soc., Mar. 29, 1923). Chicago: Univ. of Chicago Press, 1924. 36 pp. Also in *Chicago Hist. Soc. Bull.*, April 1924.

————, *The Frontier State, 1818–1848 (Centennial Hist. of Ill., II).* Chicago: A. C. McClurg and Co., 1919. 475 pp.

————, and Randall, J. G., eds., *The Diary of Orville Hickman Browning* (Ill. State Hist. Lib. *Collections,* XX, XXII). Springfield: Illinois State Historical Library, 1925–1933. 2 vols.

Peckham, Howard H., ed., "James Tanner's Account of Lincoln's Death." 2 *A. L. Q.* 176–183 (1942).

Pelzer, Louis, "The Disintegration and Organization of Political Parties in Iowa, 1852–1860." 5 *Proc. M. V. H. A.* 158–166 (1911–1912).

————, "The History of Political Parties in Iowa from 1857 to 1860." 7 *Iowa Jour. of Hist. and Pol.* 179–229 (1909).

Phillips, Ulrich B., ed., *The Correspondence of Robert Toombs, Alexander H. Stephens and Howell Cobb (Ann. Rep. A. H. A.,* 1911, II). Washington: Govt. Ptg. Off., 1913. 759 pp.

————, *The Life of Robert Toombs.* New York: Macmillan, 1913. 281 pp.

Phillips, Wendell, *Speeches, Lectures, and Letters.* Boston: Walker, Wise, and Co., 1864. 562 pp.

Piatt, Donn, *Memories of the Men Who Saved the Union.* New York: Belford, Clarke & Co., 1887. 302 pp.

Pierce, Edward L., *Memoir and Letters of Charles Sumner.* London: Sampson Low, Marston, Searle & Rivington, 1878–1893. 4 vols.

Pierson, William W., Jr., "The Committee on the Conduct of the Civil War." 23 *A. H. R.* 550–576 (1918).

Pineton, Charles A. (the Marquis of Chambrun), "Personal Recollections of Mr. Lincoln." 13 *Scribner's Mag.* 26–38 (1893). The author was a guest of Lincoln on the *River Queen* at City Point and accompanied him to Petersburg.

Pinkerton, Allan, "Unpublished Story of the First Attempt on the Life of Abraham Lincoln." 75 *Am. Mag.* 17–22 (Feb. 1913).

Pitkin, Thomas M., "Western Republicans and the Tariff in 1860." 27 *M. V. H. R.* 400–420 (1940).

Pitman, Benn, *The Assassination of President Lincoln and the Trial of the Conspirators* . . . . Cincinnati: Moore, Wilstach & Baldwin, 1865. 421 pp. Abridged and unreliable report by stenographic expert. Shows official editing. A better report is that by Benjamin ("Ben:") Perley Poore.

Political Debates between Hon. Abraham Lincoln and Hon. Stephen A. Douglas, in the Celebrated Campaign of 1858, in Illinois . . . . Columbus: Follett, Foster and Co., 1860. 268 pp.

Pollard, Edward A., *The Lost Cause* . . . . New York: E. B. Treat & Co., 1867. 752 pp. The Richmond author is bitter against both Lincoln and Jefferson Davis.

Pomeroy, Earl S., "Lincoln, the Thirteenth Amendment, and the Admission of Nevada." 12 *Pac. Hist. Rev.* 362–368 (1943).

Poore, Ben: Perley, comp., *The Great Conspiracy Trial for the Murder of the President.* Boston: J. E. Tilton and Co., 1865–1866. 3 vols. Fuller and more satisfactory than the Pitman report.

——, *The Life and Public Services of Ambrose E. Burnside* . . . . Providence: J. A. & R. A. Reid, 1882. 448 pp.

——, *Perley's Reminiscences of Sixty Years in the National Metropolis* . . . . Philadelphia: Hubbard Brothers, 1886. 2 vols. "Perley" was a pen name of this journalist, columnist, compiler, and author.

Porter, David D., *Incidents and Anecdotes of the Civil War.* New York: Appleton, 1885. 357 pp.

——. *Memoir of Commodore David Porter, of the United States Navy.* Albany: J. Munsell, 1875. 427 pp.

——, *The Naval History of the Civil War.* New York: Sherman Pub. Co., 1886. 843 pp.

Porter, George Henry, *Ohio Politics during the Civil War Period (Col. U. Stud.* XL, no. 2). New York: Columbia Univ. Press, 1911. 255 pp.

Porter, Horace, "Lincoln and Grant." 8 *Century* (new ser.) 939–947 (1885).

Potter, David M., "Horace Greeley and Peaceable Secession." 7 *Jour. So. Hist.* 145–159 (1941).

——, *Lincoln and His Party in the Secession Crisis (Yale Hist. Pub.,* XIII). New Haven: Yale Univ. Press, 1942. 408 pp. A thorough and scholarly treatment of this difficult crisis.

Potts, W. J., "Abraham Lincoln, and Lincoln Records in Pennsylvania." 3 *N. Y. Geneal. and Biog. Record* 69–71 (1872).

Pratt, Harry E., "Abraham Lincoln in Bloomington, Illinois." 29 *Jour. Ill. S. H. S.* 42–69 (1936).

——, "Albert Taylor Bledsoe: Critic of Lincoln." *Trans. Ill. S. H. S., 1934,* 153–183.

——, ed., *Concerning Mr. Lincoln: In which Abraham Lincoln is Pictured as he Appeared to Letter Writers of his Time.* Springfield, Ill.: Abr. Lincoln Assoc., 1944. 145 pp.

——, "David Davis, 1815–1886." Doctor's dissertation (ms.), Univ. of Ill., 1930. 179 pp.

——, *David Davis, 1815–1886* (abstract of preceding item, 1930). Springfield, Ill.: Journal Printing Co., 1931. 29 pp. Virtually the same material appeared in *Trans. Ill. S. H. S., 1930*, 157–183.

——, "Dr. Anson G. Henry, Lincoln's Physician and Friend." 45 *Lincoln Herald* 3–17, 31–40 (1943).

——, "The Genesis of Lincoln the Lawyer." *A. L. A. Bull.*, no. 57 (Sep. 1939), pp. 3–10.

——, *Lincoln, 1809–1839: Being the Day-by-Day Activities of Abraham Lincoln from February 12, 1809 to December 31, 1839.* Springfield, Ill.: Abr. Lincoln Assoc., 1941. 256 pp.

——, *Lincoln, 1840–1846: Being the Day-by-Day Activities of Abraham Lincoln, from January 1, 1840 to December 31, 1846.* Springfield, Ill.: Abr. Lincoln Assoc., 1939. 391 pp.

——, "Lincoln Pilots the Talisman." 2 *A. L. Q.* 319–329 (1943).

——, "Lincoln's [Illinois] Supreme Court Cases." 32 *Ill. Bar Jour.* 23–35 (Sep. 1943).

——, "Lincoln's Petitions for Pardon." 30 *Ill. Bar. Jour.* 235–240, 261–262 (Feb. 1942). Reveals Lincoln autographs previously unknown.

——, and East, Ernest E., "Mrs. Lincoln Refurbishes the White House." 47 *Lincoln Herald* 3–12 (Feb. 1945).

——, *The Personal Finances of Abraham Lincoln.* Springfield, Ill.: Abr. Lincoln Assoc., 1943. 198 pp.

——, "The Repudiation of Lincoln's War Policy in 1862—Stuart-Swett Congressional Campaign." 24 *Jour. Ill. S. H. S.* 129–140 (1931).

——, "Simon Cameron's Fight for a Place in Lincoln's Cabinet." *A. L. A. Bull.*, no. 49, 3–11 (1937).

——, "When Lincoln Failed to Draw a Crowd." 28 *Jour. Ill. S. H. S.* 95–97 (April 1935).

"Propaganda in History: the Lincoln Myth." 1 *Tyler's Quar. Hist. and Geneal. Mag.* 223–230 (1920).

The Pro-Slavery Argument . . . Containing the Several Essays . . . of Chancellor Harper, Governor Hammond, Dr. Simms, and Professor Dew. Charleston: Walker, Richards & Co., 1852. 490 pp.

Public Man. "The Diary of a Public Man: Unpublished Passages of the Secret History of the American Civil War." 129 *No. Am. Rev.* 125–140, 259–273, 375–388, 484–496 (1879). For the difficult question of the authenticity of this "diary" see 41 *A. H. R.* 277–279. A handsome edition, the first in book form, with foreword by Carl Sandburg and introduction by F. Lauriston Bullard, was issued by the Abraham Lincoln Book Shop, Chicago, in 1945 (117 pp.).

Putnam, George H., *Abraham Lincoln: The People's Leader in the Struggle for National Existence.* New York: Putnam, 1909. 292 pp.

——, "The Speech That Won the East for Lincoln." 130 *Outlook* 220–223 (1922).

Quaife, Milo M., "The Atlantic Lincoln Discovery." 15 *M. V. H. R.* 578–584 (1929).

Ramsdell, Charles W., "Lincoln and Fort Sumter." 3 *Jour. So. Hist.* 259–288 (1937). For comment, see 1 *A. L. Q.* 3–42 (1940).

Randall, J. G., "Abraham Lincoln." *Dic. of Amer. Biog.*, XI, 242–259 (1933).

——, "Civil and Military Relationships under Lincoln." 69 *Pa. Mag. of Hist. and Biog.* 199–206 (1945).

——, *The Civil War and Reconstruction.* Boston: D. C. Heath and Co., 1937. 959 pp.

——, "The Civil War Restudied." 6 *Jour. So. Hist.* 439–457 (1940).

——, *Constitutional Problems Under Lincoln.* New York: Appleton, 1926. 580 pp.

——, "Has the Lincoln Theme Been Exhausted?" 41 *A. H. R.* 270–294 (1936).

——, "Lincoln and John Bright." 34 *Yale Rev.* 292–304 (Winter, 1945).

[——, "Lincoln and the South." To be published by the Louisiana State University Press. The Walter Lynwood Fleming Lectures, Louisiana State University, 1945.]

——, "Lincoln in the Rôle of Dictator." 28 *S. A. Q.* 236–252 (1929).

——, "Lincoln's Peace and Wilson's." 42 *S. A. Q.* 225–242 (1943).

——, "Lincoln's Task and Wilson's." 29 *S. A. Q.* 349–368 (1930).

——, "The 'Rule of Law' under the Lincoln Administration." 17 *Hist. Outlook* 272–278 (1926).

——, "The Unpopular Mr. Lincoln." 2 *A. L. Q.* 255–283 (1943).

——, "When War Came in 1861." 1 *A. L. Q.* 3–42 (1940). Deals with Sumter episode.

Rankin, Henry B., *Intimate Character Sketches of Abraham Lincoln.* Philadelphia: Lippincott, 1924. 344 pp.

——, *Personal Recollections of Abraham Lincoln.* New York: Putnam, 1916. 412 pp.

Raum, Green B., *History of Illinois Republicanism,* .... Chicago: Rollins Pub. Co., 1900. 815 pp.

Ray, P. Orman, *The Convention that Nominated Lincoln* .... Chicago: Univ. of Chicago Press, 1916. 38 pp.

Raymond, Henry J. "Extracts from the Journal of Henry J. Raymond," ed. by his son. 19 *Scribner's Mo.* 57–61, 419–424, 703–710 (1879–1880).

——, *History of the Administration of President Lincoln* .... New York: Derby & Miller, 1864. 496 pp.

——, *The Life and Public Services of Abraham Lincoln* ... *together with His State Papers* .... New York: Derby and Miller, 1865. 808 pp. Expanded edition of preceding item. Includes "Anecdotes and Reminiscences" by F. B. Carpenter.

"Recollections of Lincoln: Three Letters of Intimate Friends." *A. L. A. Bull.*, no. 25, 3–9 (1931).

Reed, H. Clay, "Lincoln's Compensated Emancipation Plan and its Relation to Delaware." *Delaware Notes,* 7 ser. 27–78 (Univ. of Del., 1931).

Rennick, Percival Graham, *Abraham Lincoln and Ann Rutledge: An Old Salem Romance*. Peoria, Ill.: E. J. Jacob, 1932. 103 pp.

Republican Convention. *National Convention. 3d, Baltimore, 1864. Presidential Election, 1864. Proceedings of the National Union Convention Held in Baltimore, Md., June 7th and 8th, 1864. Reported by D. F. Murphy*. New York: Baker & Godwin, 1864. 94 pp.

———. *Press & Tribune Documents for 1860. No. 3. Proceedings of the National Republican Convention, Held at Chicago, May 16th, 17th, & 18th, 1860*. Albany: Weed, Parsons and Co., 1860. 44 pp.

———. *Proceedings of the First Three Republican National Conventions of 1856, 1860 and 1864* . . . . Minneapolis: Pub. by Charles W. Johnson, 1893. 264 pp. Cited as Johnson, *Proceedings*.

Rhodes, James Ford, *History of the United States from the Compromise of 1850* . . . [to 1877]. New York: Macmillan, 1896–1919. 7 vols.

———, "Lincoln in Some Phases of the Civil War." 24 *Harvard Graduates Mag.* 1–19 (1915).

Rice, Allen T., "A Famous Diplomatic Dispatch." 142 *No. Am. Rev.* 402–410 (1886).

———, ed., *Reminiscences of Abraham Lincoln by Distinguished Men of His Time*. New York: No. Amer. Rev. Pub. Co., 1886. 656 pp.

Richards, John T., *Abraham Lincoln, the Lawyer-Statesman*. Boston: Houghton Mifflin, 1916. 260 pp.

Richards, Louis, "The Berks County Ancestry of Abraham Lincoln." 2 *Berks County Hist. Soc. Trans.* 369–377 (1910).

Riddle, Albert G., *Recollections of War Times: Reminiscences of Men and Events in Washington, 1860–1865*. New York: Putnam, 1895. 380 pp.

Risdon, F. Ray, ed., *Assassination and Death of Abraham Lincoln: A Contemporaneous Account of a National Tragedy as Published in the Daily Morning Chronicle, Washington, D. C.* Gardena, Calif.: Spanish American Institute Press, 1925. 17 pp.

Ritchie, George T., *A List of Lincolniana in the Library of Congress*. Washington: Govt. Ptg. Off., 1903. 75 pp. Enlarged ed. in 1906.

Ritze, C. C., "In Defense of Mrs. Lincoln." 30 *Jour. Ill. S. H. S.* 5–69 (1937).

Robinson, Luther Emerson, *Abraham Lincoln as a Man of Letters*. Chicago: Reilly and Britton Co., 1918. 342 pp.

Rockwood, George I., *Cheever, Lincoln, and the Causes of the Civil War*. Worcester, Mass.: Davis Press, 1936. 83 pp.

Roll, Charles, "Indiana's Part in the Nomination of Lincoln for President in 1860." 25 *Ind. Mag. Hist.* 1–13 (1929).

Ross, Earle D., "Lincoln and Agriculture." 3 *Agr. Hist.* 51–66 (1929).

Ross, Harvey Lee, *The Early Pioneers and Pioneer Events of the State of Illinois* . . . . Chicago: Eastman Brothers, 1899. 199 pp.

Rothschild, Alonzo, *Lincoln, Master of Men: A Study in Character*. Boston: Houghton Mifflin, 1906. 531 pp.

Russell, William Howard, *My Diary North and South*. Boston: T. O. H. P.

Burnham, 1863. 602 pp. See also Sears, Louis M.

Rutledge, Archibald, "Abraham Lincoln Fights the Battle of Fort Sumter." 34 *S. A. Q.* 368–383.

Ryan, Daniel J., "Lincoln and Ohio." 32 *Ohio Arch. and Hist. Quar.* 7–281 (1923).

Salter, William, *Life of James W. Grimes* . . . . New York: Appleton, 1876. 398 pp.

Sandburg, Carl, *Abraham Lincoln: The Prairie Years.* New York: Harcourt, Brace, 1926. 2 vols.

———, *Abraham Lincoln: The War Years.* New York: Harcourt, Brace, 1939. 4 vols. Together with the *Prairie Years* this is the fullest of all Lincoln biographies. A voluminous Civil War omnibus; a glowing portrait gallery; a monumental task impressively performed. Combines realistic detail with human appreciation. A vivid panorama of America in Lincoln's day. In the final volume the threnody of Lincoln's death and burial is handled with deeply moving eloquence.

———, "Lincoln's Genius of Places." *Abr. Lincoln Assoc. Papers*, 19–34 (1931).

———, and Angle, Paul M., *Mary Lincoln, Wife and Widow.* New York: Harcourt, Brace, 1932. 357 pp. Another ed. in 1935.

———, *Storm over the Land.* New York: Harcourt, Brace, 1942. 440 pp.

———. See also Meserve, Frederick H.

Schafer, Joseph, "Who Elected Lincoln?" 47 *A. H. R.* 51–63 (1941).

Schneider, George, "Lincoln and the Anti-Know-Nothing Resolutions." 3 *Trans. McLean Co. Hist. Soc.* 87–90 (1900).

Schofield, John M., *Forty-Six Years in the Army.* New York: Century, 1897. 577 pp.

Schouler, William, *History of Massachusetts in the Civil War.* Boston: Dutton, 1868–1871. 2 vols.

Schuckers, Jacob W., *Life and Public Services of Salmon Portland Chase* . . . . New York: Appleton, 1874. 669 pp.

Schurz, Carl, *Abraham Lincoln.* Boston: Houghton Mifflin, 1919. 129 pp.

———, *Abraham Lincoln: An Essay.* Boston: Houghton Mifflin, 1891. 117 pp.

———, "Reminiscences of a Long Life." 28 *McClure's* 250–264 (1907). Describes the Lincoln-Douglas debate at Quincy, Ill.

———. *The Reminiscences of Carl Schurz.* New York: McClure Co., 1907–1908. 3 vols.

———. *Speeches, Correspondence, and Political Papers of Carl Schurz,* ed. by Frederic Bancroft. New York: Putnam, 1913. 6 vols.

Scott, Eben G., *Reconstruction during the Civil War in the United States of America.* Boston: Houghton Mifflin, 1895. 432 pp.

Scovel, James M., "Recollections of Seward and Lincoln." 51 *Lippincott's* 237–242 (1893).

Scoville, Samuel, Jr., "When Lincoln and Beecher Met." 116 *Independent* 180–182 (1926).

Scripps, John L., *Life of Abraham Lincoln*. Chicago: Press & Tribune Co., 1860. 32 pp. Campaign biography extensively published as a pamphlet. Based on Lincoln's autobiography. Handsome memorial reprint issued in 1900 (Fish no. 843). Annotated ed. by M. L. Houser (Peoria: E. J. Jacob, 1931, 72 pp.).

Sears, Louis M., ed., "The London *Times'* American Correspondent in 1861: Unpublished Letters of William H. Russell . . . ." 16 *Hist. Outlook* 251–257 (1925).

Seitz, Don C., *Lincoln the Politician: How the Rail-Splitter and Flatboatman Played the Great American Game*. New York: Coward-McCann, 1931. 487 pp.

Selby, Paul, "The Editorial Convention, February 22, 1856." 3 *Trans. McLean Co. Hist. Soc.* 30–43 (1900).

———, "The Lincoln-Conkling Letter; Read Before a Union Mass-Meeting at Springfield, Ill., Sept. 3, 1863 . . . ." 9 *Trans. Ill. S. H. S., 1908*, 240–250.

Sellers, James L., "James R. Doolittle." 17 *Wis. Mag. Hist.* 168–178, 277–306, 393–401 (1933); 18 *ibid.* 20–41, 178–187 (1934).

———, "The Make-Up of the Early Republican Party." 37 *Trans. Ill. S. H. S., 1930*, 39–51.

Seward, Frederick W., *Reminiscences of a War-Time Statesman and Diplomat, 1830–1915*. New York: Putnam, 1916. 489 pp.

Seymour, Glenn H., " 'Conservative'—Another Lincoln Pseudonym?" 29 *Jour. Ill. S. H. S.* 135–150 (1936). Newspaper letters signed "Conservative" are identified as Lincoln's.

Shannon, Fred A., "The Federal Government and the Negro Soldier, 1861–1865." 11 *Jour. of Negro Hist.* 563–583 (1926).

———, *The Organization and Administration of the Union Army, 1861–1865*. Cleveland: Arthur H. Clark Co., 1928. 2 vols.

Shaw, Albert, *Abraham Lincoln: His Path to the Presidency*. New York: Review of Reviews Corp., 1929. 263 pp. *Abraham Lincoln: The Year of His Election*. New York: Review of Reviews Corp., 1929. 277 pp. These two profusely illustrated companion volumes constitute "A Cartoon History" as indicated on binding. Rich in contemporary cartoons and prints, often unidentified.

Shaw, Carey, Jr., "Invitation to Garibaldi." *N. Y. Times Mag.*, Jan. 11, 1942.

Sherman, John. *John Sherman's Recollections of Forty Years in the House, Senate and Cabinet: An Autobiography*. Chicago: Werner Co., 1895. 2 vols.

Sherman, William T. *Memoirs of General William T. Sherman*. New York: Appleton, 1875. 2 vols.

———, and Sherman, John. *The Sherman Letters . . .* , ed. by Rachel S. Thorndike. New York: Scribners, 1894. 398 pp.

Shortridge, Wilson P., "Kentucky Neutrality in 1861." 9 *M. V. H. R.* 283–301 (1923).

Shutes, Milton H., "Abraham Lincoln and the New Almaden Mine." 15 *Calif. Hist. Soc. Quar.* 3–20 (1936). See also Ascher, Leonard.

——, "Colonel E. D. Baker." 17 *Calif. Hist. Soc. Quar.* 303–324 (1938).

——, *Lincoln and California.* Stanford University, Calif.: Stanford Univ. Press, 1943. 269 pp.

——, *Lincoln and the Doctors: A Medical Narrative of the Life of Abraham Lincoln.* New York: Pioneer Press, 1933. 152 pp.

Smith, Donnal V., *Chase and Civil War Politics (Ohio Hist. Coll.,* II). Columbus: F. J. Heer Ptg. Co., 1931. 181 pp.

——, "The Influence of the Foreign-Born of the Northwest in the Election of 1860." 19 *M. V. H. R.* 192–204 (1932).

——, "Salmon P. Chase and the Election of 1860." 39 *Ohio Arch. and Hist. Quar.* 515–607 (1930).

Smith, Edward C., *The Borderland in the Civil War.* New York: Macmillan, 1927. 412 pp.

Smith, Elmer A., *Abraham Lincoln: An Illinois Central Lawyer* (paper read before Western Conference of Railway Counsel, Feb. 13, 1945). 23 pp.

Smith, George Winston, "Generative Forces of Union Propaganda . . . ." Doctoral dissertation (MS.), Univ. of Wis., 1939. Pressure groups treated.

Smith, Goldwin. "Goldwin Smith's Reminiscences: The American Civil War." 35 *McClure's* 545–558 (1910). Describes interview with Lincoln.

——, "President Lincoln." 84 *Littell's Living Age* 426–430 (1865).

Smith, Joseph P., *History of the Republican Party in Ohio.* Chicago: Lewis Publishing Co., 1898. 2 vols.

Smith, Theodore Clarke, *Parties and Slavery, 1850–1859 (American Nation Series,* XVIII). New York: Harpers, 1906. 341 pp.

Smith, T. V., *Lincoln: Living Legend.* Chicago: Univ. of Chicago Press, 1940. 83 pp.

Smith, Willard H., "The Colfax-Turpie Congressional Campaigns 1862–1866." 38 *Ind. Mag. Hist.* 123–142 (1942).

Smith, William E., *The Francis Preston Blair Family in Politics.* New York: Macmillan, 1933. 2 vols.

Smith, William H., "Old-Time Campaigning and the Story of a Lincoln Campaign Song." 13 *Jour. Ill. S. H. S.* 23–32 (1920).

Smith, William R., *The Royal Ape: a Dramatic Poem.* Richmond: West & Johnson, 1863. 85 pp. Scurrilous satire illustrative of the war mind. Viciously anti-Lincoln.

Sparks, Edwin E., ed., *The Lincoln-Douglas Debates of 1858* (Ill. State Hist. Lib. *Collections,* III). Springfield: Illinois State Historical Library, 1908. 627 pp. Best edition of the debates.

Speed, James, *James Speed, a Personality.* Louisville: J. P. Morton & Co., 1914. 136 pp.

Speed, Joshua Fry, *Reminiscences of Abraham Lincoln and Notes of a Visit to California*. Louisville: John P. Morton & Co., 1884. 67 pp. Memories of an early intimate friend of Lincoln.

Stanwood, Edward, *A History of the Presidency* . . . . Boston: Houghton Mifflin, 1916. 2 vols.

Starr, John W., Jr., *A Bibliography of Lincolniana, not Included in the Compilations of Daniel Fish and Joseph Benjamin Oakleaf*. Harrisburg, Pa., 1926. 69 pp.

———, *Lincoln and the Railroads: A Biographical Study*. New York: Dodd, Mead, 1927. 325 pp.

———, *Lincoln's Last Day*. New York: Frederick A. Stokes Co., 1922. 100 pp.

———, "Lincoln's Last Official Act." 23 *Mo. Hist. Rev.* 628–630 (1929).

———, "What Was Abraham Lincoln's Religion?" 15 *Mag. of Hist.* 18–37 (1912).

Starr, Thomas I., ed., *Lincoln's Kalamazoo Address Against Extending Slavery* . . . . Detroit: Fine Book Circle, 1941. 63 pp. Hitherto undiscovered text of speech at Kalamazoo, Aug. 27, 1856. Foreword by editor. Includes life of Lincoln by Joseph J. Lewis, in Chester County *Times,* West Chester, Pa., Feb. 11, 1860. 250 copies distributed as Bull. No. 34, William L. Clements Libr., Univ. of Mich. Based on rare copy in Burton Hist. Coll., Detroit Pub. Libr.

Stearns, F. P., "Vanderbilt and Lincoln, an Anecdote of the Civil War." 40 *New Eng. Mag* (new ser.) 58–59 (1909).

Steiner, Bernard C., *Life of Roger Brooke Taney* . . . . Baltimore: Williams & Wilkins Co., 1922. 553 pp.

Stephens, Alexander H., *Carpenter's Picture, Lincoln and Emancipation*. Washington: Darby & Duvall, 1878. 4 pp. Speech of Stephens in House of Representatives, Feb. 12, 1878.

———, *A Constitutional View of the Late War between the States*. Philadelphia: National Publishing Co., 1868–1870. 2 vols.

———. *Recollections of Alexander H. Stephens* . . . , ed. by Myrta Lockett Avary. New York: Doubleday, Page, 1910. 572 pp.

Stephenson, Nathaniel W., *Abraham Lincoln and the Union: A Chronicle of the Embattled North (Chronicles of America, XXIX)*. New Haven: Yale Univ. Press, 1918. 272 pp.

———, ed., *An Autobiography of Abraham Lincoln* . . . . Indianapolis: Bobbs-Merrill, 1926. 501 pp. Lincoln's own words arranged in chronological order to constitute an "autobiography." Sometimes faulty as to verification of Lincoln's indirectly quoted statements.

———, *Lincoln: An Account of His Personal Life, Especially of its Springs of Action as Revealed and Deepened by the Ordeal of War*. Indianapolis: Bobbs-Merrill, 1922. 474 pp.

———, "Lincoln and the Progress of Nationality in the North." *Ann. Rep. A. H. A.* 1919, I, 353–363.

Stern, Philip Van Doren, *The Life and Writings of Abraham Lincoln.* New York: Random House, 1940. 863 pp. Full selection of Lincoln's writings and speeches preceded by popular, uncritical sketch of his life. Foreword by Allan Nevins.

———, *The Man Who Killed Lincoln* . . . . New York: Random House, 1939. 376 pp. Life of Booth presented as a novel.

Stevens, Frank E., *The Black Hawk War, Including a Review of Black Hawk's Life.* Chicago: Frank E. Stevens, 1903. 323 pp.

———, "Life of Stephen A. Douglas." 16 *Jour. Ill. S. H. S.* 247–673 (1923–24).

Stevens, Walter B., "Lincoln and Missouri." 10 *Mo. Hist. Rev.* 63–119 (1916).

Stimmel, Smith, "Experiences as a Member of President Lincoln's Bodyguard, 1863–1865." 1 *N. Dak. Hist. Quar.* 7–33 (Jan., 1927).

Stoddard, William O., *Abraham Lincoln: The True Story of a Great Life* . . . . New York: Fords, Howard & Hulbert, 1896. 508 pp. The author, a journalist and popular writer, was an assistant private secretary of the President.

———, *The Boy Lincoln.* New York: Appleton, 1905. 248 pp.

———, *Inside the White House in War Times.* New York: Charles L. Webster & Co., 1890. 244 pp.

———, *Lincoln at Work: Sketches from Life.* Boston: United Society of Christian Endeavor, 1900. 173 pp.

———, *The Table Talk of Abraham Lincoln.* New York: Frederick A. Stokes, 1894. 154 pp.

Storey, Moorfield, "Dickens, Stanton, Sumner, and Storey." 145 *Atl. Mo.* 463–465 (1930). From Storey's diary, giving Stanton's and Sumner's 1868 recollections of the night of Lincoln's assassination.

Streeter, Floyd B., *Political Parties in Michigan, 1837–1860* (*Mich. Hist. Pubs.,* University series, IV). Lansing, Mich.: Mich. Historical Commission, 1918. 401 pp.

Strevey, Tracy Elmer, "Joseph Medill and the *Chicago Tribune* during the Civil War Period." Doctor's dissertation (MS.), Univ. of Chicago, 1930. 205 pp.

———, "Joseph Medill and the *Chicago Tribune* in the Nomination and Election of Lincoln." *Papers in Ill. Hist., 1938,* 39–63.

Summers, George W. See Sumter.

Sumner, Charles. *The Works of Charles Sumner.* Boston: Lee and Shephard, 1870–1883. 15 vols.

Sumter. "The Proposed Evacuation of Fort Sumter." 29 *Nation* 383–384 (1879). Contemporary correspondence between George W. Summers and J. C. Welling pertaining to the Sumter crisis.

Swisher, Carl B., *Roger B. Taney.* New York: Macmillan, 1935. 608 pp.

Taft, Charles Sabin. *Abraham Lincoln's Last Hours; from the Note-book of Charles Sabin Taft, M.D., an Army Surgeon Present at the Assassi-*

nation, Death, and Autopsy. Chicago, 1934. 16 pp. Previously printed in *Century,* Feb. 1893.

Tanner, James, "The Assassination of President Lincoln, 1865." 29 *A. H. R.* 514–517 (1924). "Copy of a letter written . . . April 17, 1865, by James Tanner . . . ."

———. See Peckham, Howard H.

Tansill, Charles C., "A Secret Chapter in Civil War History." 15 *Thought* (Fordham Univ. Quar.) 215–224 (1940). Treats the offer of the "highest Army Commission which it is in the power of the President to confer" to the Italian patriot Garibaldi in 1861. Based upon state department archives. Seward gave the instruction that Garibaldi be offered a U. S. commission as major general. The matter was bungled; it was misunderstood; Garibaldi set up impossible conditions; and it came to nothing.

Tarbell, Ida M., *In the Footsteps of the Lincolns.* New York: Harpers, 1924. 418 pp. Deals with ancestry.

———, *The Life of Abraham Lincoln Drawn from Original Sources and Containing Many Speeches, Letters and Telegrams Hitherto Unpublished* . . . . New York: Doubleday, Page, 1909. 2 vols. Copyright 1895 by S. S. McClure Co. Various other editions issued. Much of the material appeared originally in *McClure's.* (Vol. II includes numerous letters, documents, etc., by Lincoln.)

———, *A Reporter for Lincoln: Story of Henry E. Wing, Soldier and Newspaperman.* New York: Macmillan, 1927. 78 pp.

Tasher, Lucy L., "The *Missouri Democrat* and the Civil War." 31 *Mo. Hist. Rev.* 402–419 (1937).

Taussig, F. W., "The Lincoln Tariff Myth Finally Disposed Of." 35 *Quar. Jour. of Econ.* 500 (1921). Indicates how Lincoln was falsely quoted on the tariff, esp. as to steel rails.

Taylor, Florence Walton, "Culture in Illinois in Lincoln's Day." 42 *Trans. Ill. S. H. S., 1935,* 125–137.

Teillard, Dorothy Lamon, "Lincoln in Myth and in Fact." 21 *World's Work* 14040–14044 (1911). By the daughter of Ward Hill Lamon.

Thatcher, George H., "Lincoln and Meade after Gettysburg." 32 *A. H. R.* 282–283 (1927).

[Thayer and Eldridge.] *The Life and Public Services of Hon. Abraham Lincoln, of Illinois, and Hon. Hannibal Hamlin, of Maine.* Boston: Thayer & Eldridge, 1860. 128 pp. Registered for copyright May 28, 1860, but judged by Ernest J. Wessen to have been published in early June. In expanded form (1860) it was called the "Wide-Awake Edition" (q. v.).

Thayer, William R., *Life and Letters of John Hay.* Boston: Houghton Mifflin, 1915. 2 vols.

Thomas, Benjamin P., "The Eighth Judicial Circuit." *A. L. A. Bull.,* no. 40, 1–9 (Sep. 1935).

———, "The Individuality of Lincoln as Revealed in His Writings." *A. L. A. Bull.*, no. 32, 3–10 (1933).

———, *Lincoln, 1847–1853: Being the Day-by-Day Activities of Abraham Lincoln from January 1, 1847 to December 31, 1853.* Springfield, Ill.: Abr. Lincoln Assoc., 1936. 388 pp.

———, "Lincoln the Postmaster." *A. L. A. Bull.*, no. 31, 3–9 (1933).

———, "Lincoln's Earlier Practice in the Federal Courts, 1839–1854." *A. L. A. Bull.*, no. 39, 1–9 (1935).

———, *Lincoln's New Salem.* Springfield, Ill.: Abr. Lincoln Assoc., 1934. 128 pp.

———, "A Russian Estimate of Lincoln." *A. L. A. Bull.*, no. 23, 3–6 (1931).

———, *Russo-American Relations, 1815–1867* (J. H. U. Stud., ser. XLVIII, no. 2). Baltimore: Johns Hopkins Press, 1930. 185 pp.

Thompson, Charles M., *The Lincoln Way. Report of the Board of Trustees of the Illinois State Historical Library* . . . . Springfield, Ill.: Illinois State Journal Co., 1913. 22 pp. Concerned with determining the route of the Lincoln migration from Indiana to Macon Co., Ill., 1830.

Thompson, Richard W., *Recollections of Sixteen Presidents from Washington to Lincoln.* Indianapolis: Bowen-Merrill, 1894. 2 vols.

Tilley, John Shipley, *Lincoln Takes Command.* Chapel Hill: Univ. of N. C. Press, 1941. 334 pp. Severely anti-Lincoln. Deals with Sumter episode.

Tilton, Clint Clay, "Lincoln and Lamon: Partners and Friends." 38 *Trans. Ill. S. H. S., 1931,* 175–228.

Townsend, George Alfred, *Abraham Lincoln: A Talk with Mr. Herndon, His Late Law Partner.* New York: Bible House, 1867. 15 pp. By the colorful, well known journalist, "Gath."

———, *Campaigns of a Non-Combatant* . . . . New York: Blelock & Co., 1866. 368 pp.

———, *Washington, Outside and Inside* . . . . Hartford, Conn.: James Betts & Co., 1873. 751 pp.

Townsend, William H., *Lincoln and His Wife's Home Town.* Indianapolis: Bobbs-Merrill, 1929. 402 pp. Valuable on Mrs. Lincoln and on Lincoln's Lexington contacts.

———, *Lincoln and Liquor.* New York: Press of the Pioneers, 1934. 152 pp.

———, "Lincoln on the Circuit." 12 *Am. Bar Assoc. Jour.* 91–95 (1926).

———, *Lincoln the Litigant.* Boston: Houghton Mifflin, 1925. 116 pp.

———, "Lincoln's Defense of Duff Armstrong." 11 *Am. Bar Assoc. Jour.* 81–84 (1925).

———, "Lincoln's Law Books." 15 *Am. Bar Assoc. Jour.* 125–126 (1929).

Tracy, Gilbert A., ed., *Uncollected Letters of Abraham Lincoln.* Boston: Houghton Mifflin, 1917. 264 pp. Presents a number of Lincoln letters previously unassembled in published form.

The Tribune Almanac and Political Register . . . . Published yearly by Tribune Assoc., New York. Each issue carries its date on the title page

—e. g., *The Tribune Almanac and Political Register for 1860,* the same for 1861, etc.

Truesdell, Winfred Porter, *Engraved and Lithographed Portraits of Abraham Lincoln.* Champlain: Troutsdale Press, 1933. 241 pp.

Usher, John Palmer, *President Lincoln's Cabinet.* Omaha, 1925. 34 pp. Lincoln's secretary of the interior, 1863–65, gives brief reminiscences. Foreword and sketch of Usher by Nelson H. Loomis.

Vallandigham, James L., *A Life of Clement L. Vallandigham.* Baltimore: Turnbull Brothers, 1872. 573 pp.

Van Hoesen, H. B., "The Humor of Lincoln and the Seriousness of His Biographers." 7 *Books at Brown* 2–10 (1944–45).

Villard, Henry, *Lincoln on the Eve of '61: A Journalist's Story,* ed. by Harold G. and Oswald Garrison Villard. New York: Knopf, 1941. 105 pp.

——. *Memoirs of Henry Villard, Journalist and Financier, 1835–1900.* Boston: Houghton Mifflin, 1904. 2 vols.

Villard, Oswald Garrison, *John Brown, 1800–1859: A Biography Fifty Years After.* Boston: Houghton Mifflin, 1910. 738 pp.

Volk, Leonard W., "The Lincoln Life-Mask and How It was Made." 8 *Jour. Ill. S. H. S.* 238–248 (1915).

Vose, Reuben, *The Life and Speeches of Abraham Lincoln, and Hannibal Hamlin.* New York: Hilton, Gallaher & Co., 1860. 118 pp. This 32mo volume, rare as an original, was reproduced in its tiny format in 1938 by the Lincoln Nat. Life Found. of Ft. Wayne, Ind. One of the early campaign lives.

Wakefield, Sherman D., *How Lincoln Became President* . . . . New York: Wilson-Erickson, Inc., 1936. 184 pp. Emphasizes Bloomington, Ill., in the development of Lincoln's career.

Wall, Alexander J., *A Sketch of the Life of Horatio Seymour, 1810–1886* . . . . New York, 1929. 111 pp.

Wallace, Mrs. Frances. *Lincoln's Marriage: Newspaper Interview with Mrs. Frances Wallace, Springfield, Illinois. September 2, 1895.* Privately printed, 1917.

Wallace, Isabel, *Life & Letters of General W. H. L. Wallace.* Chicago: R. R. Donnelley & Sons Co., 1909. 231 pp.

Walsh, William S., ed., *Abraham Lincoln and the London Punch: Cartoons, Comments and Poems Published in the London Charivari, during the American Civil War (1861–1865).* New York: Moffat, Yard and Co., 1909. 113 pp.

The War of the Rebellion: . . . *Official Records of the Union and Confederate Armies.* Washington: Govt. Ptg. Off., 1880–1901. 4 series; 70 "volumes"; 128 books. Enormous collection of records for both sides of the conflict. (A similar set for the Union and Confederate Navies appeared in 26 vols., 1894–1922.)

Ward, William H. *Abraham Lincoln: Tributes from his Associates,*

Reminiscences of Soldiers, Statesmen and Citizens, with Introduction by the Rev. William Hayes Ward, D.D. New York: Thomas Y. Crowell & Co., 1895. 295 pp.

Warden, Robert B., *Account of the Private Life and Public Services of Salmon Portland Chase.* Cincinnati: Wilstach, Baldwin & Co., 1874. 838 pp.

Warren, Louis A., "The Early Portraits of Lincoln." 30 *Ky. Hist. Soc. Reg.* 211–220 (1932).

———, ed., *The Lincoln Kinsman.* Published monthly (since 1938) at Ft. Wayne, Ind.

———, ed., *Lincoln Lore* (April 15, 1929–date). Published periodically (as leaflet) by the Lincoln National Life Insurance Co., Ft. Wayne, Ind.

———, "Lincoln's Early Political Background." 23 *Jour. Ill. S. H. S.* 618–629 (1931).

———, "Lincoln's Hoosier Schoolmasters." 27 *Ind. Mag. Hist.* 104–118 (1931).

———, *Lincoln's Parentage and Childhood.* New York: Century, 1926. 392 pp. Complete on the Kentucky phase. Full of detail on Thomas Lincoln. Gives elaborate material from court records.

———, "The Romance of Thomas Lincoln and Nancy Hanks." 30 *Ind. Mag. Hist.* 213–222 (1934).

———, *The Slavery Atmosphere of Lincoln's Youth.* Fort Wayne, Ind: Lincolniana Publishers, 1922. 16 pp.

Washburne, Elihu B., *Abraham Lincoln, His Personal History and Public Record.* Speech in U. S. House of Representatives, May 29, 1860. Definitely included by Ernest J. Wessen among the early campaign lives.

Washington, John E., *They Knew Lincoln.* New York: Dutton, 1942. 244 pp. This Negro author deals sympathetically with William de Fleurville ("Billy the Barber"), William Slade (messenger), Elizabeth Keckley (modiste for the First Lady), and other colored friends of the Lincolns. Intro. by Carl Sandburg.

Watterson, Henry, "Abraham Lincoln." 46 *Cosmopolitan* 363–375 (1909).

Weaver, William Cartter, "David Kellogg Cartter." *The Historian,* Spring 1941, 165–180.

Weed, Thurlow. *Life of Thurlow Weed, Including his Autobiography and a Memoir* . . . , ed. by Harriet A. Weed. Boston: Houghton Mifflin, 1883–1884. 2 vols.

———, "President Lincoln as a Cabinet Maker." 3 *Appleton's Jour.* 437–438 (1870).

Weeden, William B., *War Government, Federal and State, in Massachusetts, New York, Pennsylvania, and Indiana, 1861–1865.* Boston: Houghton Mifflin, 1906. 389 pp.

Weik, Jesse W., "A Law Student's Recollection of Abraham Lincoln." 97 *Outlook* 311–314 (1911).

———, "Lincoln's Vote for Vice-President in the Philadelphia Convention of 1856." 54 *Century* (new ser.) 186–189 (1908).

———, *The Real Lincoln: A Portrait*. Boston: Houghton Mifflin, 1922. 323 pp. For this new treatment of Lincoln's early life and personal qualities the author again taps the elaborate resources of the Herndon-Weik MSS.

———. See also under Herndon.

Welles, Edgar, "Gideon Welles and Lincoln." 20 *Mag. of Hist.* 34–40 (1915).

Welles, Gideon, "Administration of Abraham Lincoln." 23 *Galaxy* 5–23, 149–159; 24 *ibid.* 437–450, 608–624, 733–745 (1877).

———, "Fort Sumter." 10 *Galaxy* 613–637 (1870).

———, "Lincoln and Johnson." 13 *Galaxy* 521–532, 663–673 (1872).

———, *Lincoln and Seward. Remarks upon the Memorial Address of Chas. Francis Adams, on the Late Wm. H. Seward . . . .* New York: Sheldon & Co., 1874. 215 pp. Answer to "misrepresentations" in address on Seward delivered by Charles Francis Adams in 1873. Objects to Adams's over-praising of Seward and underrating of Lincoln.

———, "Lincoln's Triumph in 1864." 41 *Atl. Mo.* 454–468 (1878).

———, "Nomination and Election of Abraham Lincoln." 22 *Galaxy* 300–308, 437–446 (1876).

———, "The Opposition to Lincoln in 1864." 41 *Atl. Mo.* 366–376 (1878).

———. For the diary of Gideon Welles see Morse, John T. For critique see Beale, Howard K.

Wesley, Charles H., "Lincoln's Plans for Colonizing the Emancipated Negroes." 4 *Jour. of Negro Hist.* 7–21 (1919).

Wessen, Ernest J., "Campaign Lives of Abraham Lincoln, 1860." *Papers in Ill. Hist., 1937*, 188–220. Full and authoritative. Supersedes Barton, "The Lincoln of the Biographers." Gives 1860 lives, their order of appearance, preparation, date of issue, etc. Assigns priority to Wigwam Edition.

———, and Monaghan, James, "Lincoln Bibliography." 1 *A. L. Q.* 192–206 (1940). This is the first of two articles under the same title; the second, by Paul M. Angle, appears in *ibid.*, 314–321 (1941). These articles treat the mooted question as to what belongs within Lincoln bibliography.

West, Richard S., Jr., *Gideon Welles: Lincoln's Navy Department*. Indianapolis: Bobbs-Merrill, 1943. 379 pp.

West, W. Reed, *Contemporary French Opinion on the American Civil War (J. H. U. Stud.*, ser. XLII, no. 1). Baltimore: Johns Hopkins Press, 1924. 159 pp.

Wetherbee, S. Ambrose, "Lincoln Collection: Illinois State Archives." 25 *Ill. Libraries* 114–125 (1943).

White, Andrew D. *Autobiography of Andrew Dickson White*. New York: Century, 1905. 2 vols.

White, Horace, "Abraham Lincoln in 1854." 5 *Putnam's Mo.* 723–729 (1909).

——, *Abraham Lincoln in 1854*. Springfield, Ill., 1908. 24 pp. Delivered before Ill. State Hist. Soc.

——, *The Life of Lyman Trumbull*. Boston: Houghton Mifflin, 1913. 458 pp.

——, *The Lincoln and Douglas Debates: An Address before the Chicago Historical Society, February 17, 1914*. Chicago: Univ. of Chicago Press, 1914. 32 pp.

White, Laura A., *Robert Barnwell Rhett: Father of Secession*. New York: Century, 1931. 264 pp.

Whiting, William, *War Powers under the Constitution of the United States* . . . . Boston: Lee and Shepard, 1871. 695 pp. The 43d ed. of this work. The author—Boston lawyer and solicitor of the war department—gives elaborate legal support for far-reaching war powers.

Whitney, Henry C., *Life on the Circuit with Lincoln*. Boston: Estes and Lauriat, 1892. 601 pp. Pub. also in 1940 by Caxton Printers, Caldwell, Idaho, with intro. and notes by Paul M. Angle.

——, "Lincoln's Lost Speech now First Published from the Unique Report." 7 *McClure's* 319–331 (1896). Lincoln's speech before Illinois Republican convention of 1856. Whitney's reconstruction of this speech, here given, has been discredited.

Wide-awake Edition. *The Life and Public Services of Hon. Abraham Lincoln, of Illinois, and Hon. Hannibal Hamlin, of Maine*. Boston: Thayer and Eldridge, 1860. 320 pp. See above, Thayer and Eldridge.

Wigwam Edition. *The Life, Speeches, and Public Services of Abram Lincoln, Together with a Sketch of the Life of Hannibal Hamlin* . . . . New York: Rudd & Carleton, 1860. 117 pp. Published June 2, 1860; 12,000 copies sold within a week. Pronounced by Ernest J. Wessen "The first campaign life of Lincoln."

Wiley, Bell I., *Southern Negroes, 1861–1865*. New Haven: Yale Univ. Press, 1938. 366 pp.

Wiley, Earl W., "Lincoln in the Campaign of 1856." 22 *Jour. Ill. S. H. S.* 582–592 (1930).

Williams, Samuel C., *The Lincolns and Tennessee*. Harrogate, Tenn.: Lincoln Memorial Univ., 1942. 33 pp. First appeared in *Lincoln Herald*.

Williams, T. Harry, "Benjamin F. Wade and the Atrocity Propaganda of the Civil War." 48 *Ohio Arch. and Hist. Quar.* 33–43 (1939).

——, "The Navy and the Committee on the Conduct of the War." 65 *U. S. Naval Institute Proc.* 1751–1755 (1939).

——, *Lincoln and the Radicals*. Madison: Univ. of Wis. Press, 1941. 413 pp.

Wilson, Charles R., "New Light on the Lincoln-Blair-Frémont 'Bargain' of 1864." 42 *A. H. R.* 71–78 (1936).

——, "The Original Chase Organization Meeting and *The Next Presidential Election.*" 23 *M. V. H. R.* 61–79 (1936). Pertains to presidential campaign of 1864.

Wilson, Francis, *John Wilkes Booth: Fact and Fiction of Lincoln's Assassination.* Boston: Houghton Mifflin, 1929. 321 pp.

Wilson, Henry, *History of the Rise and Fall of the Slave Power in America.* Boston: J. R. Osgood and Co., 1875–1877. 3 vols.

Wilson, James G., "Reminiscences of Abraham Lincoln." 74 *Independent* 395–397 (1913).

Wilson, James H., *Life of Charles A. Dana.* New York: Harpers, 1907. 544 pp.

——, *The Life of John A. Rawlins, Lawyer, Assistant Adjutant-General, Chief of Staff, Major General of Volunteers, and Secretary of War.* New York: Neale Publishing Co., 1916. 514 pp.

Wilson, Rufus Rockwell, ed., *Intimate Memories of Lincoln.* Elmira, N. Y.: Primavera Press, 1945. 629 pp.

——, *Lincoln Among His Friends* . . . . Caldwell, Idaho: Caxton Printers, Ltd., 1942. 506 pp.

——, *Lincoln in Caricature.* Privately printed, 1903. 17 pp. New and greatly enlarged ed., Elmira, N. Y., Primavera Press, 1945, limited to 600 copies.

——, *Lincoln in Portraiture.* New York: Press of the Pioneers, Inc., 1935. 317 pp.

——, *What Lincoln Read.* Washington: Pioneer Publishing Co., 1932. 95 pp.

Wilson, Woodrow, "The Genius of Lincoln." Speech at the official acceptance of the Lincoln Memorial, Hodgenville, Ky., Sep. 4, 1916. Arthur B. Tourtellot, ed., *Woodrow Wilson: Selections for Today* (1945), 14–18. One of the finest and most eloquent of all appreciations of Lincoln.

Winther, Oscar O., "The Soldier Vote in the Election of 1864." 25 *N. Y. History* 440–458 (1944).

Woldman, Albert A., *Lawyer Lincoln.* Boston: Houghton Mifflin, 1936. 347 pp.

Woodburn, James A., *The Life of Thaddeus Stevens: A Study in American Political History* . . . . Indianapolis: Bobbs-Merrill, 1913. 620 pp.

——, "Party Politics in Indiana during the Civil War." *Ann. Rep. A. H. A.,* 1902, I, 225–251.

Woodley, Thomas F., *Thaddeus Stevens.* Harrisburg, Pa.: Telegraph Press, 1934. 664 pp.

Woodward, Walter C., *The Rise and Early History of Political Parties in Oregon, 1843–1868.* Portland, Ore.: J. K. Gill Co., 1913. 276 pp.

Woollcott, Alexander, " 'Get Down, You Fool!' " 161 *Atl. Mo.* 169–173 (1938). Young Oliver Wendell Holmes is said thus to have addressed the President when he exposed himself to enemy fire.

Works. See Nicolay and Hay, *Complete Works* . . . [etc.].

Yates, Richard. *Speech of Hon. Richard Yates, delivered at the Republican Ratification Meeting, of the Citizens of Sangamon County, in the Hall of the House of Representatives, Springfield, June 7th, 1860.* No date. 9 pp. Interesting reminiscence of Lincoln in New Salem.

Young, J. Harvey, "Anna Elizabeth Dickinson and the Civil War: For and Against Lincoln." 31 *M. V. H. R.* 59–80 (1944). Based on doctoral dissertation (MS.), Univ. of Ill., 1941.

Young, Jesse Bowman, *The Battle of Gettysburg* . . . . New York: Harpers, 1913. 463 pp.

Young, John R., "Lincoln at Gettysburg." 62 *Frank Leslie's Illustrated Newspaper* 119 (April 10, 1886).

Zane, John Maxcy, "Lincoln the Constitutional Lawyer." *Abr. Lincoln Assoc. Papers, 1932,* 27–108.

Zimmerman, Charles, "The Origin and Rise of the Republican Party in Indiana from 1854 to 1860." 13 *Ind. Mag. Hist.* 211–269, 349–412 (1917).

INDEX

Abell, Elizabeth (Mrs. Bennett Abell), quoted, **II,** 335.

Abolition, summary and characterization of the movement in the North, **I,** 86 ff.; and the churches, 88-89; degrees and shades, position of Lincoln, 89-91; Lincoln's 1861 attitude, 296.

Abolitionists, slight influence in North, **I,** 91; encounter opposition in Boston, 133; praise John Brown, 134; would consent to withdrawal from Sumter, 328; and Negro colonization, **II,** 139; and Lincoln's emancipation plan, 144; impatient for action by Lincoln, 151-153, 158-159; reaction to emancipation proclamation, 169 ff. *See also* radicals, Garrison, Weld, Higginson, Gerrit Smith.

Abraham Lincoln Association, **I,** acknowledgments (xv), 176.

Adams, Charles Francis (1807–1886), **I,** 276; **II,** 244; free soil policies, **I,** 91; on committee of thirty-three, 224; possible cabinet member, 261; appointed minister to Britain, 272, 372; and Civil War diplomacy, **II,** 31 ff.; and *Trent* affair, 37 ff.; on British reaction to emancipation proclamation, 179-180 and n.

Adams, Charles Francis (1835–1915), quoted, **I,** 292.

Adams, H. A., Union naval officer, prevents reënforcement of Fort Pickens, **I,** 332.

Adams, Henry, **II,** 346; on Sumner's speech concerning *Trent* affair, **II,** 50 and n.

Adams, John Quincy, on Jackson's nullification policy, **I,** 221; and slavery, **II,** 126; on martial law and emancipation, 182.

Adrian resolution, recommending repeal of personal liberty laws, supported by Republicans, **I,** 228.

Aiken, William, opposes secession, **I,** 219.

Alabama, Democratic delegation at Charleston, **I,** 140; vote in 1860, 192; secedes, 211, 212; Buell in, 261.

Alabama, The, case of, **II,** 52 f.; preys on Union commerce, 265.

Albany, N. Y., visited by Lincoln, **I,** 283; response to Lincoln's call to arms, 355.

Albany (N. Y.) *Atlas and Argus,* on Lincoln as President Elect, **I,** 292; on Lincoln's inaugural, 305.

Albany (N. Y.) *Evening Journal,* **I,** 146.

Albert, Prince, and *Trent* affair, **II,** 43-44.

Alexander, E. P., Confederate artillery commander, on Pickett's charge at Gettysburg, **II,** 283.

Alexandra, The, case of, **II,** 52 f.

Aliens. *See* Canisius, Knownothing party, nativism, *Deutsches Haus.*

Allen, W. J., **II,** 214, 234.

Alton, Ill., scene of final Lincoln-Douglas debate, **I,** 110; Lincoln's speech at, 117.

Altoona, Pa., conference of governors at, **II,** 229.

Amboy, Ill., Lincoln speaks at, **I,** 118.

America. *See* United States.

American Anti-Slavery Society, **I,** 87.

American party. *See* Knownothing party.

Anderson, Robert, Union army officer, commands forts in Charleston harbor, **I,** 316; and Sumter crisis of April 1861, 328-342.

Andrew, John A., governor of Massachusetts, possible cabinet member, **I,** 261; offers Scott help, 276-277; on colonization, **II,** 140-141; and Negro troops, 184, 185-186; differs from Banks, 222.

Angle, Paul M., **I,** 99; on Lincoln as lawyer, **I,** 34; on wedding default, 54-55; on Ann Rutledge, **II,** 323; bibl., 343.

Antelope, The, case of, **II,** 133 and n.

Antietam, battle of, **II,** 114 ff.; 229, 230, 258; importance, 285.

Antislavery. *See* abolition.

Anti-Slavery Society, **I,** 90.

Archives, **II,** 352.

Arkansas, in 1860, **I,** 192; votes against secession, 251; secedes, 357; response to

Other titles of interest